GAMES AND SPORTS

BEING VOLUME III OF

**CHAMPLIN'S YOUNG FOLKS' CYCLOPÆDIAS, edited
by John D. Champlin, Jr., and Arthur Bostwick, 12mo,
831 pp., $2.50.**

The Nation: "Certainly no such collection has ever appeared before. . . A careful examination has failed to reveal any inaccuracies. . . The records of athletic contests are brought down to the present year. . . The illustrations are numerous, and, besides elucidating the text, add not a little to the attractiveness of the volume."

Outing: "A perfect mine. . . From the game of A B C to the making of a zoetrope nothing seems omitted which can amuse and instruct in the parlor or the playground."

N. Y. Tribune: "A mine of joy. . . A positive treasure to the game-loving boy and girl. One of the best features of the book is the careful presentation, for reference, of official rules and records."

Chicago Inter-Ocean: "A game to be interesting must be played according to fixed rules. These are often in dispute and it is well to have authority for their correct interpretation. . . The instructions are so clear and concise as to be easily understood. . . Mothers and fathers will find much of value and interest in the pages."

Congregationalist: "Although we have owned two or three such books, and have examined several others, we consider this as the most satisfactory of which we are aware."

The Epoch: "Mr. Champlin unites with elaborate training and wide experience a natural ability for his work which amounts to genius, and a sympathy with boys which has given him peculiar success in his efforts in their behalf. . . Many who understand games and sports can explain them only by appealing to the eye. The capacity to make them clear in writing is rare; and for this reason many so-called books of sports are failures. . . It is a purely American book, even the English games, as the editor announces in the preface, being described as played in this country. Adults will find it as valuable as the young people, since it includes, word for word, the official rules of athletic sports and standard games and the official records of athletic meets and events. To insure accuracy, such articles as the editors deemed necessary have been submitted to the revision of competent experts. The illustrations are numerous and illuminative. For mothers taking their children into the country, where the absence of their regular school duties is soon painfully shown, especially on rainy days, by their cry of 'What shall we do?' and for those desiring to give children's parties, as well as for the needs of every day among a family of growing children, this book is simply invaluable. The young people themselves will appreciate it fully. A boy of fourteen, who received many valuable presents on Christmas Day, has been overheard to tell several people, 'The very nicest thing I had was Mr. Champlin's Cyclopædia of Games and Sports.'"

Toronto Week: "Would prove a useful book of reference in the libraries of adults as well as of juveniles."

The Art Amateur: "An Encyclopædia Britannica for youngsters, a book to last not one season alone but through all the periods of childhood to adolescence. . . So comprehensive that any sport not found herein is probably a game not worth the candle."

Pittsburg Chronicle-Telegraph: "Of equal value to many adults. . . Includes the official rules of all athletic sports . . and official records of meets and events, . . all verified by special experts."

Richmond Dispatch: "Deeply interesting to young people, and old people too, for that matter."

Boston Journal: "A family possessing it . . will never be at loss for amusement."

Providence Journal: "Perfect treasure."

Literary World: "Admirable. . . Destined to a wide sale. . . Would be a treasure in every household that believes in games or sports of any sort."

Philadelphia Ledger: "Admirable."

The Book Buyer: "The book swarms with illustrations of every grade that render clear descriptions of things and processes that would else remain somewhat vague."

The Independent: "Should form a part of every juvenile library, whether public or private."

Boston Post: "No better book can be found as a gift for a healthy boy."

Chicago Advance: "A bonanza to wide-awake boys and girls."

Boston Transcript: "Should find a welcome in every household where there are growing children. . . We most heartily commend it."

Vol. I. COMMON THINGS. 690 pp. $2.50.
Vol. II. PERSONS AND PLACES. 956 pp. $2.50.

By JOHN D. CHAMPLIN, Jr.,
Late Associate Editor of the American Cyclopædia.

From a Report of the Connecticut Board of Education: "'The Young Folks' Cyclopædia' should be in every juvenile library."

The Independent: "The book will be as valuable as a small library to any young person."

Cincinnati Commercial: "Families and students who cannot afford the expensive set of encyclopædias will find in this a most excellent substitute in many things."

The Nation: "We know copies of the work to which their young owners turn instantly for inform-ation upon every theme about which they have questions to ask. More than this, we know that some of these copies are read daily as well as consulted, that their owners turn the leaves as they might those of a fairy-book."

St. Nicholas: "All our boys and girls who like to ask questions will be glad to hear of 'The Young Folks' Cyclopædia.' How many questions you young folks ask of older ones every day! Now, if you have one of these cyclopædias, instead of asking questions, you look in your book, and there is your answer."

HENRY HOLT & CO., Publishers, New York.

THE

YOUNG FOLKS' CYCLOPÆDIA

OF

PERSONS AND PLACES

BY

JOHN D. CHAMPLIN, JR.

LATE ASSOCIATE EDITOR OF THE AMERICAN CYCLOPÆDIA

WITH NUMEROUS ILLUSTRATIONS

SECOND EDITION, REVISED

NEW YORK
HENRY HOLT & COMPANY
1896

PREFACE.

THE YOUNG FOLKS' CYCLOPÆDIA OF PERSONS AND PLACES has been prepared by the writer as a companion volume to his "Young Folks' Cyclopædia of Common Things." The first publication included in its scope only things in Nature, Science, and the Arts; the present volume is devoted to accounts of noted Persons and Places, both real and fabulous, thus supplementing the first volume and with it covering the usual range of cyclopædic knowledge.

In its method the work is conceived in the same general spirit which marked the former one. The language is simple, within the comprehension of children, and technical terms, where admitted, are fully explained. A few abbreviations have been found necessary to save space, but they are only such as are in every-day use. As in the first volume, most of the etymologies have been put at the ends of the articles, so as not to destroy the continuity of the narrative; but in general the ordinary cyclopædic method has been followed, in order to accustom children to the forms in use in larger works, to which these volumes are intended to be but stepping-stones.

In selecting illustrations, care has been taken to avoid those common to the ordinary school geographies and histories; and especial prominence has been given to some notable restorations of classic scenes and famous buildings, which are new in books for young folks.

Another feature in this work, seldom found in the larger cyclopædias, is the introduction of the orthoepy of proper names. To bring this within easy comprehension of young folks, all diacritical marks have been avoided, and an attempt has been made to give the pronunciation as plainly as can be done with the simple letters of the alphabet. While recognizing the impossibility of attaining in this way the exact pronunciation of many foreign names, the writer has thought it better to give in a few cases an approximation only to the proper pronunciation than to load the book with reference tables which are often themselves more apt to mislead than to instruct.

Another novel feature is the comparative estimates of the areas and populations of countries and cities, to enable the reader to form an idea of the size of distant places by giving him some well-known standard of comparison at home. For instance, Spain is described as a little more than two thirds as large as Texas, while its population is about two sevenths that of the whole United States. In a similar way the city of Barcelona is compared with Baltimore; and in general, foreign cities are compared with cities of the United States, and those in the Northern and Eastern United States with those in the Southern and Western States.

The populations of foreign places have been carefully gathered from the best and latest European sources, while those of the United States have been taken as far as possible from the new census (1880), so that in this respect the work is in advance of all other cyclopædias, and will be useful as a book of reference even to grown-up people.

Although this volume has far exceeded the size of the first one, it has been found necessary to make a selection from the great number of titles treated in larger works. In doing this, regard has been had to their general importance, to their general interest, to their special interest to Americans, and last, but not least, to their interest to Young Folks. Taking it for granted that every family has its Bible and Bible Dictionary, no Bible titles have been admitted excepting such as have a connection with general history. Other omissions may seem to some to be less defensible than these, but it is not likely that any two persons would make precisely the same selections from so great a number of subjects, as no two would view the question from exactly the same standpoint.

The very flattering reception given to the "Cyclopædia of Common Things" by both the press and the public, induces the hope that the "Cyclopædia of Persons and Places" may meet with a similar greeting ; and if the latter shall be found worthy of a place beside that already accorded to the former in the school library and the home circle, the writer will be abundantly rewarded.

J. D. C., JR.

New York, Dec. 1, 1880.

PREFACE TO THE SECOND EDITION.

IN this edition official figures of the United States Census of 1890 have been used. Foreign populations have been corrected from the latest returns, and dates of biographical and other articles have also been revised.

New York, Sept. 5, 1891.

1. Gymnasium.   2. Theatre.   3. Temple of Juno.

SITE OF THE OLYMPIC GAMES, WITH

4. Temple of Jupiter Olympius.   5. Race Course.

THE BUILDINGS RESTORED (PAGE 605).

☞ Words printed in LETTERS LIKE THESE are explained in their alphabetical places.

☞ The references in parentheses, beginning C. C. T.,—for example (C. C. T., 150, II. u.),—are to the " Young Folks' Cyclopædia of Common Things," a companion volume to this, which explains a great deal not coming within the plan of this book. The Arabic figures refer to pages, the Roman figures to columns, and the letters u. or l. to the upper or lower half of columns.

A

AACHEN (*ah'khen*), a city of Germany, called by the French Aix-la-Chapelle, in Prussia, 43 miles W.S.W. of COLOGNE; population 96,000, or about as large as Albany, N. Y. Several important railways meet there, and it has large manufactures of railroad iron, pins and needles, buttons, tobacco, and woollen and silk goods. Aachen is

Aachen Cathedral.

a very old place, having been noted in the times of the Romans for its hot sulphur springs, which are still used. It was one of the capitals and the favorite city of CHARLES THE GREAT, who is called by the French Charlemagne. He built there a splendid palace where the

Town Hall now stands, and a chapel, on the site of the present cathedral, made on the same plan with the Church of the Holy Sepulchre at Jerusalem. He beautified this chapel with splendid columns brought from old palaces at Ravenna. The French carried some of these columns to Paris, but they have been put back again. Charles built a tomb for himself under the floor of the chapel, and his body was placed in it on his death in 814.

Nearly two hundred years afterward (A.D. 1001) the Emperor Otto III. had the vault opened. It is said that the body of the great Emperor was found in a wonderful state of preservation, seated on a marble throne, dressed in his imperial robes, with his crown on his head, his sword by his side, the Gospels lying open on his lap, and his sceptre in his hand. A large picture representing Otto and his nobles gazing on the dead Emperor, is painted on the walls of the great room in the Town Hall. In 1165 the Emperor Frederick Barbarossa again opened the vault and placed the remains of Charles in a splendid sculptured sarcophagus made of Parian marble, said to have been the one in which the Roman Emperor Augustus was buried. The bones lay in this till 1215, when the Emperor Frederick II. had them put into a casket of gold and silver, in which they are yet kept in the treasury of the cathedral. The marble throne on which the dead Emperor had sat for three hundred and fifty years, is also still to be seen in the cathedral. It was used as a throne in the coronation of the German emperors until 1558, after which the emperors were crowned at Frankfort. The crown and some of the other things found with the body are now preserved in Vienna.

The cathedral is very different now from what it used to be. The oldest portion is the eight-sided part with the dome, seen in the middle of the picture. In the centre of the floor of this part, right under the dome, which is held up by the ancient columns brought by Charles from Ravenna, is a large stone slab, marked CAROLO MAGNO (Latin, To Charles the Great), showing where the vault was. The other parts of the cathedral have been added in later times, and it forms now one of the most picturesque buildings in Europe.

A short distance from Aachen is Frankenburg, a large building which stands on the site of a hunting lodge of Charles the Great, where he and his beautiful wife Fastrada lived. History tells us that Fastrada had not a very lovely character, and that she made the Emperor much trouble; but according to a legend still told in Aachen, she kept her husband's love by means of a magic ring which she wore. The counsellors of the Emperor, finding that Fastrada's advice was heeded instead of theirs, got possession of the ring and threw it into a lake surrounding the hunting lodge. After that she lost her influence over him, and paled and died. When she was dead, Charles's love returned, and he used to spend hours gazing sadly into the lake where lay the magic ring. In the growth of the city most of the lake has been filled up, and it is now little more than a slimy pool.

Near Aachen also is the Emmaburg, where are a few remains of another hunting lodge of the great Emperor. Across the courtyard of this castle (now a very dirty barnyard), Emma, the Emperor's daughter, is said to have carried her lover, Eginhard, her father's secretary, on her back, for fear lest his footsteps in the new-fallen snow should betray that he had been to see her. When the Emperor found it out, he rewarded her devotion, it is said, by making the two man and wife. But this story is not true, for Eginhard did not marry the Emperor's daughter.

The Romans named the springs

at Aachen Aquis-Granum (Waters of Granus, from the Latin *aquæ*, waters, and *Grani*, of Granus), it is supposed from Granus, a Roman general. The old Germans called it Aachen (Waters, from *aquæ*), and the old French made this into Aigues. In time this became changed to Aix, and the place was finally called by the French Aix-la-Chapelle (The Chapel Waters), on account of the chapel built there by Charles, and to distinguish it from other places named Aix.

AB·BAS' THE GREAT, or **Shah Abbas,** that is, King Abbas, a noted king of Persia, born in 1557. He succeeded to the throne in 1587, and showed so much wisdom and energy that he gained the respect even of his enemies. He won many victories over the Turks, drove them out of his country, and conquered much territory. His fame became so great that ambassadors were sent to him from many of the countries of Europe. He died in 1628. Like many other Eastern rulers, Shah Abbas was cruel : he killed his eldest son, and left his throne to his grandson.

ABBASIDES (*ab-bas'sidz*), descendants of Abbas, Mohammed's uncle, who ruled as caliphs of the East from 749 to 1258, when the last one, Mostasem, was driven from the throne. HAROUN AL RASHID was one of the most noted of these caliphs. After leaving Bagdad, one of the family fled to Egypt, and his descendants ruled there under the MAMELUKES till the country was conquered by the Turks in 1517.

AB'BOTS-FORD, the home of Sir Walter SCOTT, on the south bank of the river Tweed, about three miles from the town of Melrose, Scotland. When Sir Walter Scott bought it, in 1811, it was a small farm called Clarty Hole. He at first built a small villa (now the western end of the house) and named it Abbotsford, making the name from a ford near by, where, in old times, the abbots of Melrose Abbey used to cross the river. Sir Walter afterward built additions to the house and made it a splendid mansion, building into the walls many sculptured stones from the ruined cas-

Abbotsford.

tles and abbeys of Scotland. In it he gathered a large library, and a most interesting collection of ancient furniture, arms and armor, and other relics and curiosities, especially connected with Scottish history, all of which are still to be seen there.

AB'BOTT, Jacob, author of the "Rollo Books," "Lucy Books," "Jonas Books," "Franconia Stories," "Harpers' Story Books," "Marco Paul" series, "Gay Family," series, and "Juno Books," was born at Hallowell, Maine, November 14, 1803, and was graduated at Bowdoin College in 1820. He stud.

ied divinity at Andover, Massachusetts, was for several years a professor of mathematics in Amherst College, then taught a girls' school in Boston, and afterward was a Congregational minister in Roxbury, Massachusetts. In 1838 he gave up his church there, and settled in Farmington, Maine, where he died when seventy-six years old (October 31, 1879). He wrote there most of his books, which number in all more than two hundred.

ABBOTT, John Stephens Cabot, a younger brother of Jacob Abbott, and author of many historical works, was born in Brunswick, Maine, September 18, 1805, and was graduated at Bowdoin College in 1825. He studied at Andover, became a Congregational minister, and was settled at different times at Worcester, Roxbury, and Nantucket, Massachusetts, and New Haven, Connecticut. He died in New Haven when seventy-two years old (June 17, 1877).

Among his works are : " History of Napoleon Bonaparte," " Napoleon at St. Helena," " Life of Napoleon III.," " History of the Civil War in America," and " History of Frederick the Great."

ABD-EL-KADER (*ahbd-el-kah'-der*), a famous Arab chieftain of Algeria, born about 1806. His father was a marabout, or religious noble, of great influence, and he gave his son the best education in his power. When only fourteen the boy knew the Koran by heart, and he soon became skilled in all warlike exercises, becoming the best rider among his people. He was celebrated too for his great and noble beauty. When the French drove the Turks out of Algeria, the Arab tribes of the interior, who had obeyed the Mohammedan Turks, rose against the French because they were Christians, and chose Abd-el-Kader as their emir (prince). From that time (1831) until 1847, when he was captured, he fought the French with so much skill, energy, and bravery that

he won even their admiration and praise. He finally gave himself up on condition that he might live either in ALEXANDRIA or ACRE, but he was sent to France and kept as a captive until 1852, when Napoleon III. gave him his liberty, and a pension of $20,000. He went first to Broussa, in Asia Minor, to live, but finally settled in DAMASCUS. When the Christians in Syria were attacked by the Mohammedans in 1860, Abd-el-Kader protected thousands of them, at the risk of his own life. He died when seventy-three years old (November 1, 1879).

ABELARD (*ah-ba-lar*), a very learned man of France, born near Nantes in 1079. His love of knowledge caused him to give up his rights to the family property to his younger brothers, and to devote himself wholly to study. He soon became a teacher himself, and when he was only twenty-two years old, he had become so famous that people used to flock to hear his lectures in such numbers that the other teachers in Paris were left almost alone ; and in time he came to be considered the most learned man of the age. Among his pupils was a beautiful young lady, named Heloise, whose uncle, Fulbert, was a canon or officer of the church. Abelard and Heloise fell in love with each other, and Fulbert tried to separate them, because Abelard being a priest could not marry ; but the lovers fled to the country and were privately married. Not long after, Heloise went back to her uncle's house and denied the marriage, in order that she might not stand in the way of Abelard's rise in the church ; for if it had become known that he was married, he could no longer have been a priest. Fulbert, very angry at this, attacked Abelard one night with a band of ruffians, and so wounded him that he was unfitted for service in the church ; for it is a rule that no maimed man can serve as a priest. Abelard then became a monk and Heloise a nun,

Abelard built a hermitage called Paraclete, in a desert place, and gave it to Heloise and her nuns for a dwelling, and when he died, at the age of sixty-three, after a sad and unhappy life (April 21, 1142), Heloise had him buried there. She died in 1164, and was buried by his side. In 1800 the remains of both were removed to Paris, and they now rest in the cemetery of Père-la-Chaise, in a beautiful chapel built of stones brought from the ruins of Paraclete. Within the chapel is the old tomb in which Abelard was first buried. His figure, sculptured in marble, lies upon it, and beside it is a statue of Heloise.

ABENCERRAGES (*ah-ben'ser-rah-ges*), the name of a noble Moorish family of Granada, Spain, who had a deadly quarrel with another noble family, the Zegris. The story is told that one of the Abencerrages, having fallen in love with a lady of the royal family, was caught in the act of climbing up to her window. The king, enraged, shut up the whole family in one of the halls of the Alhambra, and ordered the Zegris to kill them all. The apartment where this tragedy is said to have taken place is one of the most beautiful courts of the Alhambra, and is still called the Hall of the Abencerrages. Many poems and plays, and one opera (*Les Abencerrages*, by Cherubini) have been written on this subject, but the whole story is very doubtful, for the best historians do not mention it.

ABERCROMBIE (*ab'er-krum-be*), **James**, a British general, born in Scotland in 1706. He was commander-in-chief of the British forces in America in 1758. In the summer of that year he crossed Lake George with 15,000 men, and on July 8 tried to take Fort TICONDEROGA by storm, but was defeated with the loss of 2000 men. Sir Jeffery AMHERST then received command of the army, and Gen. Abercrombie went back to England the next year, and died

there, when seventy-five years old (April 28, 1781).

ABERCROMBY (*ab'er-krum-be*), **Sir Ralph**, a British general, born in Scotland in 1734. He served with much ability in Holland and in the West Indies, and in 1800 was chosen to command the forces to be sent against the French in Egypt. On March 8, 1801, he landed his army at Aboukir bay, near Alexandria, though strongly opposed by the French, and on the 21st fought the battle of Alexandria, in which he was victorious. He was struck by a musket ball in the thigh early in the action, but remained on the field giving his orders until the battle was over. He was then carried off in a hammock, cheered by the soldiers as he passed, and taken on board a ship in the bay, where he died, when sixty-seven years old (March 28, 1801).

ABERDEEN (*ab-er-deen'*), the principal city in the north of Scotland, situated at the mouth of the river Dee; pop. 120,000, or as large as Detroit, Mich. It is a very old place, having been made a city in the 12th century by King William the Lion, of Scotland. In 1336 it was burned by the English. It is now a manufacturing place, and many persons are employed in building ships, and in making cotton, linen, and woollen cloths. A great deal of granite is quarried near by and shipped from there. The University of Aberdeen has more than 800 students.

The word Aberdeen means "at the mouth of the Dee," it being made of the Gaelic *abyr*, at the mouth of, and *dyn*, the Dee.

ABERNETHY (*ab'er-ne-thy*), **John**, a celebrated English surgeon, born in London in 1764. He was famous as a lecturer, and made many improvements in surgery. He was also noted for his shrewdness and wit. A rich man who had the gout once asked him what he should do for it. "Live on sixpence a day, and

earn it," was the answer. Dr. Abernethy died in 1831.

ABOUKIR (*ah-boo-keer'*). See
NELSON.

ABRANTÈS (*ah-brahn-tes'*). See
JUNOT.

ABU-BEKR (*ah-boo-bek'er*), the father of Ayesha, wife of MOHAMMED,
born in MECCA about the year 573.
His real name was Abd-el-Kaaba,
but he was called Abu-Bekr (Arabic
for "Father of the Virgin") when
Mohammed married his daughter.
When Mohammed died, Abubekr
became the first *khalif* or caliph
(successor), a title taken by those
who succeeded the prophet. He
reigned only two years and three
months, but he carried on successful
wars to spread his religion against
the Persians and the Romans. He
was so strict and temperate in his
habits that, although he was a great
ruler, he left when he died (634) only
the one dress which he wore, one
camel, and one slave. His followers
called him the Just. The writings
and sayings of Mohammed were collected by him and formed into the
Koran, or Mohammedan Bible.

ABYDOS (*a-by'dos*), an ancient
city of Asia Minor, situated at the
narrowest part of the HELLESPONT.
It was here that XERXES built his
famous bridge of boats (B.C. 480),
and here too that ALEXANDER THE
GREAT crossed when he marched
into Asia (B.C. 334). The bridge of
Xerxes was built across to a place
called Sestos, on the European side,
where the strait is a little less than a
mile wide. As soon as it was built,
a storm arose and broke it into
pieces. When Xerxes heard of this
he was very angry, and ordered that
the sea should be given three hundred stripes with whips, and that
chains should be thrown into it. He
also ordered that the architects'
heads should be struck off, and appointed other architects to build two
new bridges, one for the army and
one for beasts of burden. These
were made by stretching across, side

by side, two rows of boats securely
fastened together ; they were then
boarded over and covered with earth,
and fences were built up on each
side so that the horses and cattle
might not be frightened by the sight
of the sea.

When all was done, Xerxes came
from SARDIS to Abydos, where the
people of the city had built a high
throne for him at a place where he
could see both his army and his
navy. When he saw the sea covered
with his ships and the plains of Abydos with his troops, he is said to
have burst into tears at the thought
that in a hundred years not one of
all that great number of men would
be alive.

At sunrise of the day set for the
passing over of the army, perfumes
were burned on the bridges, and the
way was strewed with myrtle. Xerxes, standing at the edge of the water, poured a libation—that is, an
offering of wine—into the sea out of
a golden cup, and turning toward
the sun, which the Persians worshipped as a god, prayed that his arms
might meet with success in Europe.
He then threw the cup, with a golden
bowl and a Persian sword, into the
Hellespont, and the great army
began its march, the horsemen and
footmen passing over the right hand
bridge and the wagons and beasts
of burden the left or lower one.
They marched day and night as fast
as they could, but it took them a
whole week to cross, for it was the
largest army the world has ever
seen.

Abydos too was the scene of the
story of Hero and Leander. Hero
was a priestess in the temple of
Venus in Sestos. Leander, her lover,
who lived in Abydos, used to swim
across at night to see her, guided by
the light of a torch which she held
on the top of a high tower beside
the water. One stormy night, while
trying to swim over, he was drowned,
and in the morning Hero found his
dead body on the shore. Overcome

with grief, she threw herself from her tower into the sea. In 1810 Lord Byron swam across from Sestos to Abydos to see if Leander could have done it. He got over safely, but he had to swim two or three miles in all, on account of the tide, which is very strong there.

ABYSSINIA (*ab-is-sin'e-ah*), a country in the eastern part of Africa, south of Nubia. It is mountainous, with high table-lands, from a mile to nearly two miles above the sea, and deep valleys made by the rivers. Some of the mountains are three miles high, and many of them are flat, as if their tops had been cut off. On the summit of one of these flat mountains, at a height of nearly two miles above the sea, was Magdala, a celebrated fortress. The principal rivers flow into the Nile.

The population is about four millions. Gondar, the largest city, has about 50,000 inhabitants, and Ankobar about 12,000. The people are of very dark color, and much like Arabs. Most of them call themselves Christians, but they are very superstitious and cruel. There are also many Mohammedans and Jews. The country is ruled by King Menelek II. The principal seaport, Massowah, is occupied by Italy, which power exercises considerable influence over the affairs of the country.

The most interesting thing in the late history of Abyssinia is the British capture of Magdala. In 1867, King Theodorus having imprisoned the British consul and some missionaries, an army of 12,000 men was sent from Bombay to Abyssinia, under command of Sir Robert Napier. The Abyssinians were defeated, and the British stormed the fortress, April 13, 1868. When King Theodorus heard that the gate had fallen, he fired a pistol into his mouth and killed himself. His little son was taken to England to be educated, but he died there in 1879, at the age of seventeen. Sir Robert Napier was raised to the peerage, and given the title of Lord Napier of Magdala.

Abyssinia is named, some think, from the Abai, one of its principal rivers ; but according to others, it is from the Arabic word *habish*, mixed, meaning that it is the country of the mixed races.

ACADIA (*a-ka'de-ah*). See NOVA SCOTIA.

ACHENBACH (*ah'ken-bahk*), Andreas, a famous German landscape painter, born in Cassel, September 29, 1815. He loves to paint grand mountain scenery, like that among the Alps and the mountains of Norway, and also picturesque Italian scenes. There are many of his pictures in the United States.

ACHENBACH, Oswald, brother of Andreas, a famous German landscape painter, born in Düsseldorf, February 2, 1827. He has painted mostly scenes in Italy, and some fine historical pictures. He is a professor in the painting school at DÜSSELDORF.

ACHILLES (*a-kil'leez*), the bravest of all the Greeks in the war against TROY, as told by HOMER in his poem called the Iliad. He is said to have been the sun of Peleus, King of Thessaly, and of Thetis, one of the NEREIDS. One of the many fabulous stories told about him is that when he was an infant his mother plunged him into the river STYX, which made his body invulnerable—that is, impossible to be wounded—in all parts excepting the heel, by which she held him. He was brought up by the centaur CHIRON, who fed him on the marrow of wild beasts, so that he grew up strong in mind and in body, and was taught the art of war by Phœnix, the son of the King of Argos. Thetis, having heard from an oracle that Achilles would be killed in the war against Troy, dressed him in girls' clothes and put him among the daughters of King Lycomedes of Scyros, where she thought he would be safely hidden. But it having also been foretold that Troy could not be taken without the help of Achilles, ULYSSES disguised himself as a pedler, went to the court of King Lycomedes, and offered jewels and arms for sale. The daughters of the king chose the jewels, but Achilles seized upon the arms. Thus found out, Achilles went to the war with fifty ships, accompanied by Phœnix and his friend Patroclus. He helped the Greeks very much, but after a while got angry at AGAMEMNON, because Agamemnon had taken away from him a beautiful female slave named Briseïs, and refused to fight any longer. The Greeks suffered greatly on account of this, for with Achilles away the Trojans easily defeated them. At last Patroclus, grieved at their troubles, put on the armor of Achilles, and went out with them, thinking that the Trojans would take him for Achilles. They were deceived for a while, and fled before him toward their city, but Patroclus, following them too far, was killed by Hector, son of King Priam, and leader of the Trojans. Upon this, Achilles forgot his anger, and again joined the Greeks. In the next battle he slew many Trojans, and after pursuing Hector three times around the city, killed him and dragged his body behind his chariot to the ships. When Priam went with gifts to the Greek camp to beg for the body of Hector, Achilles treated him kindly, gave him the body of his son, and promised to stop the war for ten days to give time to bury him. The Iliad does not tell any more about Achilles, but there are other accounts of him. One says that he fell in love with Polyxena, Priam's daughter, that when he was about to be married to her in the temple of Apollo, Paris shot him in his vulnerable heel with an arrow, and that he died of the wound. After this Troy was taken by the Greeks.

ACLAND (*ak'land*), **Lady Harriet**, wife of Major John Dyke Acland, commander of the British gren-

adiers in the battle of Stillwater in the Revolution. After the battle she heard that her husband, who had been taken prisoner, was mortally wounded, and though nearly worn out with want of food and rest, went to the American camp to look for him. She was treated there with great kindness, and her husband, who had been shot through both legs, soon got well under her careful nursing. The next year they went back to England, where Major Acland soon after died (Oct. 31, 1778). Lady Harriet died when sixty-six years old, at Tetton, near Taunton (July 21, 1815).

ACRE (*a'ker*), an ancient seaport town on the coast of Syria ; pop. about 10,000. Its harbor is not very good, but it is the best on that coast, and this has made it so important that many nations have struggled to possess it. It was one of the chief landing places of the Christians during the CRUSADES, but in 1187 it fell into the hands of the Saracens. When RICHARD I. went to the Holy Land in 1191, the Christians had been trying in vain for two years to recapture it, and more than 150,000 men had fallen before its walls. King Richard tried to storm the place, but his soldiers were driven from the battlements, and great numbers killed. The Christians failed to take the town, but its brave defenders were at last forced to surrender from starvation. Richard let most of them go free, but kept a large number as hostages until SALADIN should pay their ransom, which he agreed to do within a month. He failed to do this, and Richard had 2700 of his prisoners hanged before the walls. The Christian Knights of ST. JOHN of Jerusalem held Acre until 1291, when it was taken by the Egyptians, and in 1517 it was captured by the Turks. In 1799 Napoleon besieged it in vain for sixty days.

Acre is called Acca by the Turks. In the Bible it is called Accho, which is from an Arabic word meaning sandy shore. Acre is sometimes called St. Jean d'Acre (St. John of Acre), because it was the fortress of the knights of that name.

A-CROP'O-LIS. See ATHENS.

ACTIUM (*ak'she-um*), a promontory on the west coast of Greece, at the mouth of the Gulf of Patras, off which took place (31 B.C.) one of the most important naval battles ever fought, which made Octavius, afterward AUGUSTUS, ruler of the world. Octavius had 260 galleys or ships, and Mark ANTONY 220, besides 60 which CLEOPATRA had brought to his aid. Each had also a large army, but the two armies were on opposite sides of the bay and so took no part in the fight. Cleopatra became frightened and fled with her ships, and Antony soon followed, and his fleet and army surrendered to Octavius. (C. C. T., 240, II. 1.)

AD'AMS, Charles Francis, an American statesman, son of President John Quincy Adams, born in Boston, August 18, 1807. When only two years old he was taken by his father to St. Petersburg, and in 1815 travelled with his mother from there to Paris in a carriage. When his father was minister to England he was placed in a boarding school, where he had to fight the English boys who slandered his country. He afterward studied at Harvard College, where he was graduated in 1825, and then studied law with Daniel Webster. He was twice elected to Congress (1858 and 1860), and was minister to England from 1861 to 1868, when he resigned. His duties in England were very hard, on account of the trouble growing out of our Civil War, but he performed them all so well that he got the respect of everybody, both at home and abroad. In 1871 he was again sent to Europe with others to settle the claims of those who lost through the capture of ships by the Alabama and other Confederate vessels. He has published the "Life and Works of John Adams," and "Memoirs of John Quincy Adams." He died when seventy-nine years old (November 21, 1886).

Charles Francis, Jr., son of Charles Francis, born in Boston, May 27, 1835 (Harvard College, 1856), is also a lawyer. He served through the civil war, became Colonel of the Fifth Massachusetts Cavalry, and left the service with the rank of brigadier-general. He has written much about railway matters.

Henry Brooks, son of Charles Francis, born in Boston, February 16, 1838 (Harvard College, 1858), was the private secretary of his father when he was minister to England. He has been assistant professor of history in Harvard College and editor of the *North American Review*, and has published the "Writings of Albert Gallatin," "Life of Albert Gallatin," etc.

John Quincy, son of Charles Francis, born in Boston, Sept. 22, 1833, was graduated at Harvard College in 1853, and is a lawyer in Quincy. He has been a member of the legislature, and many times candidate for governor of Massachusetts.

John Adams.

ADAMS, John, second President of the United States, born in Braintree, Mass., October 19, 1735. His father was a poor farmer, but was able to send him to Harvard College, where he was graduated in 1755. He became a lawyer in Boston, and when the troubles with England began took part with his countrymen in favor of independence. When a member of the Continental Congress in 1775, he was the first to propose that Washington should be made commander of the American army. He was one of the committee appointed to write the Declaration of Independence, and was one of its signers. During the war he was sent to France and to Holland to secure the friendship of those countries, and after the war to Great Britain as minister. He was Vice-President from 1789 to 1797, while Washington was President, and President from 1797 to 1801. He then retired to his farm at Quincy, Massachusetts, where he died, when ninety years old (July 4, 1826), his son being then President.

ADAMS, John Quincy, son of John Adams, and sixth President of the United States, born in Braintree,

John Quincy Adams.

Mass., July 11, 1767. When a boy he went to France, Holland, and England with his father, and to St. Petersburg as private secretary to

our minister. On his return home he went to Harvard College, and was graduated in 1788. He studied law, became a Senator of the United States, minister to Holland, Prussia, Russia, and Great Britain, and in 1817 Secretary of State under President Monroe. While Secretary he brought about a treaty with Spain by which Florida was added to the United States. He was President of the United States from 1825 to 1829. In 1830 he was elected a member of Congress, and held that position until his death. While sitting in his seat in the Capitol at Washington, he was seized with paralysis or palsy, a disease which stops the use of the limbs, and died two days after, when eighty years old (February 23, 1848).

ADAMS, Samuel, an American patriot, born in Boston, September 27, 1722. He was second cousin of President John Adams. He was graduated at Harvard College in 1740, and became collector of taxes in Boston. Before the Revolution he strongly opposed the acts of England, and both spoke and wrote in favor of independence. The English tried to quiet him with offers of money and office, but though he was poor he refused all their bribes. He was a member of Congress for eight years, and one of the signers of the Declaration of Independence; and was Governor of Massachusetts from 1794 to 1797, when he retired to private life. He died in Boston, October 2, 1803.

AD'DI-SON, Joseph, an English author, born at Milston, Wiltshire, May 1, 1672. He was graduated at Oxford, where he was noted as a scholar, and his father, who was a clergyman, wished him to be one also, but he chose a political life. When twenty-seven years old he received, through the friendship of Lord Somers, to whom he had dedicated a poem, a pension of £300, and travelled in France, Germany, and Italy. When King William

III. died, three years after, his pension was taken from him, and after teaching a while he returned to England so poor that he had to live in a garret. Soon afterward he wrote a poem, called "The Campaign," about the battle of BLENHEIM, which so pleased the chief minister of the kingdom that he gave him an office, and after that he was almost always in office. In 1708 he was elected a member of Parliament. He arose once to speak, but he was so bashful that he could not say what he wanted to, and he never tried it again. But though he failed

Addison.

as a speaker, he became more famous as a writer than any other person of his time. He is chiefly celebrated for his essays in a paper called the *Spectator*, which are noted for their wit and the choice and beautiful arrangement of the words. In 1713 he published a tragedy called "Cato," which gave him great celebrity at the time, but is not much thought of now. When forty-four years old he married the Countess of Warwick, thinking that her rank would add to his fame, but she was proud and high-tempered, and made his life so uncom-

fortable that he is said to have spent much of his time after that in taverns, and to have drunk too much. He died three years after, when forty-seven years old (June 17, 1719), and was buried in Westminster Abbey.

A'DEN. See ARABIA.

AD·I·RON'DACKS. See NEW YORK (State).

AD·ME'TUS. See ALCESTIS.

A·DO'NIS, according to the ancient poets, was a youth so beautiful that even the goddess VENUS fell in love with him and left OLYMPUS for his sake. But he cared more for hunting than he did for her, and though Venus begged him to give it up he continued the sport until he was killed by a wild boar. Some accounts say that the boar was MARS, who also loved the goddess, and who changed himself into this savage animal in order to kill Adonis, of whom he was jealous. When Venus heard the cries of her favorite she flew to his aid, but too late. On the way she ran a thorn into her foot, and the blood from the wound fell on the rose and made it red, though it had always been white before. Venus bewailed the loss of Adonis, and changed his blood shed on the ground into the flower called anemone. Jupiter at last took pity on her grief and permitted him to live six months of the year with her on earth and the other six with PROSERPINE, who also loved him.

Adonis is a Syrian or Hebrew word meaning lord. In this fable he is supposed to stand for the sun or lord of day, and his living half the year on earth and the other half in HADES to mean the coming of summer and of winter. To speak of a very handsome man as "beautiful as Adonis" is therefore the same as saying that he is as beautiful as the sun or the day.

ADRIAN (*a'dre-an*), the name of six popes of Rome.

Adrian I. (772 to 795) gave

CHARLES THE GREAT the title of King and Patrician of Rome for driving the LOMBARDS out of Italy.

Adrian IV. (1154 to 1159) was the only Englishman who ever became pope. His real name was Nicholas Breakspear. He is said to have left England as a beggar, and to have first become a servant in a monastery near Avignon in France. He became a monk and then abbot of a monastery in Rome, where he was made a cardinal and finally elected pope.

ADRIANOPLE (*a-dr e-an-o'-ple*), a famous city of the Turkish empire, about 130 miles N.W. of Constantinople; pop. 71,000, or about as large as Cambridge, Mass. It is beautifully situated, but dirty and ruinous. It has a considerable trade in attar of roses, opium, and woolen, silk, and cotton goods.

Adrianople was founded by the Emperor HADRIAN, who named it Hadrianopolis (from Hadrian and the Greek *polis*, city), which in modern times has been changed to its present spelling. Like other cities near the line where Europeans and Asiatics meet, it has been the scene of many battles and sieges. The Turks took it from the Christians in 1361, and it was the capital of their empire until they captured Constantinople in 1453. In 1829 the Russians took it from the Turks, and again in 1878.

ÆNEAS (*e-ne'as*), the hero of the Æneid, a poem by VIRGIL. He is said to have been the son of Anchises, a prince of TROY, and the goddess VENUS. He married Creüsa, a daughter of King PRIAM, and had by her a son named Ascanius. Having fought for Troy until it was taken by the Greeks, he left the burning city, leading his son by the hand and carrying his aged father on his back, from which he was given the name of pious (Latin *pius*), which formerly meant dutiful to one's parent. He set sail with twenty ships, and after visiting many places and losing his father, who died in Sicily, he was shipwrecked near Carthage, where he was the guest of Queen DIDO. The Æneid begins with the storm which causes this shipwreck, and the earlier part of his story is told by Æneas to Dido. Dido wanted to marry him, but the gods warned him away, and he sailed to Sicily, and thence up the Tiber and landed in the country of Latinus, King of Latium. Latinus received him kindly, and promised him his daughter Lavinia in marriage, who had been before betrothed by her mother Amata to Turnus, King of the Rutuli. To prevent this marriage, Turnus made war against Æneas, but after many battles Æneas overcame him and killed him in a single combat, with which the Æneid ends. Æneas then married Lavinia, founded a city in her honor called Lavinium, and when Latinus died succeeded him as king. After a short reign he was killed in a battle against the Etruscans. He was succeeded by his son Ascanius, who is also called Iulus, from whom the Julian family of Rome (to which Julius Cæsar belonged) claimed descent. Ascanius founded the city of Alba Longa, and one of his descendants, King Numitor, was the grandfather of ROMULUS, who built Rome. Thus the Romans claimed that Æneas was the founder of their empire.

ÆOLIS (*e'o-lis*). See ASIA MINOR.

ÆOLUS (*e'o-lus*), in Greek fable, the god or ruler of the winds. He is said to have reigned over the Æolian Islands, now called the Lipari Islands, between Italy and Sicily, and to have been a great astronomer and the inventor of sails for ships. According to VIRGIL (Æneid, Book I.) he kept the winds shut up in caverns in the mountains, which they could leave only with his permission.

ÆSCHINES (*es'ke-neez*), a Greek orator and the rival of DEMOSTHENES, born in Athens, 389 B. C. When PHILIP of Macedon was trying to get possession of the states of Greece, and Demosthenes was doing his best to get the Athenians to go to the aid of some of the cities which Philip had attacked, Æschines was the head of the peace party and favored an alliance with Philip. When it was proposed by Ctesiphon to give Demosthenes a golden crown for his patriotic defense of his country, Æschines accused Ctesiphon of

Æschines.

doing what was not legal, and made a great speech against him; but Demosthenes replied in a still greater speech and overcame him, and Æschines had to leave Athens. He afterward set up a school of eloquence in Rhodes, which became celebrated. He once read to his pupils his speech against Ctesiphon, and when some of them said that they were astonished that he should have been defeated after such a display of eloquence, he replied: "You would cease to be astonished if you had heard Demosthenes." Æschines died in Samos in the seventy-sixth year of his age (314 B.C.).

ÆSCHYLUS (*es'ke-lus*), a Greek poet, born at Eleusis, 525 B.C. Little is known of his life, but one of the old writers (Pausanias) relates that when he was a boy he was set to watch grapes in the country, and fell asleep. In his slumber Bacchus came to him and told him to write tragedy. When he awoke, he tried to do so, and found that he could write verses with the greatest ease. He fought in the battle of MARATHON, and received great honors for his bravery, and six years after, when forty-one years old, he won his first prize for a tragedy. He gained in all thirteen prizes for tragedies, but was at last defeated by Sophocles (468). Soon after this he left Athens and went to live in Sicily. For many years he was esteemed the greatest of tragic poets. He is said to have written seventy plays in all, but only seven have been preserved, named "The Seven against Thebes," "The Suppliants," "The Persians," "Prometheus Bound," "Agamemnon," "The Choephori," and "The Eumenides."

Æschylus died at Gela, in Sicily, in the sixty-ninth year of his age (456 B.C.). It is said that while sitting in deep thought in the fields, his bald head was mistaken for a stone by an eagle which was flying over him with a tortoise in its bill. The bird dropped the tortoise to break the shell, and the poet was killed by the blow.

ÆSCULAPIUS (*es-ku-la'pe-us*), in Greek fable, the god of physicians. He is said to have been the son of APOLLO. He went around curing the sick, and brought so many of the dead to life again that PLUTO, the king of HADES, complained to Jupiter that his kingdom was fast losing its population, and at length Jupiter killed him with a thunderbolt. After death, Æsculapius was worshiped as a god at Epidaurus, in Greece, where he was born. In his temple was kept a peculiar breed of snakes, into whose bodies the god was supposed to pass. When a city was afflicted with sickness, it was customary to send to Epidaurus for one of these snakes, and the priests made a good deal of money out of their sale. In ancient times these priests, who were called Asclepiades, or sons of Æsculapius, were the only physicians.

Æsculapius is pictured as an old man with a long beard, holding in one hand a staff, with a snake coiled round it, and resting the other hand on the head of another snake. Hygeia, the goddess of health, was his daughter.

ÆSOP (*e'sop*), a Greek writer of fables, born about 620 B.C. it is supposed in Phrygia. When young he was brought to Athens and sold as a slave, but was freed by his master, and won so much fame as a writer that CRŒSUS, King of Lydia, invited him to live at his court. Crœsus sent him to DELPHI to consult the oracle there, and the Delphians, angry at his making fun of them, accused him of having hidden one of the sacred vessels of Apollo's temple, and put him to death by throwing him from a high rock. We do not know certainly that any of the fables called Æsop's were written by him, but they are thought to be only imitations of his real works, which are lost. The stories about his being very ugly and humpbacked are not now believed.

AFGHANISTAN (*ahf-gahn-is-tahn'*), a country of Asia, lying between British India and the Russian part of Turkistan; area 250,000 square miles, or not quite as large as the State of Texas; pop. about 4,900,000, or 2¼ times that of Texas; capital, CABOOL. It is a very rough country, with high mountains, on the tops of some of which snow lies all the year round, and with deep and very hot valleys.

Many of the mountains are covered with dense forests, the home of lions, tigers, and other wild beasts. The people, who are Mohammedans, are a strong and brave race, divided into tribes, which are often at war with each other.

Afghanistan, in case of war between Great Britain and Russia, would become very important on account of its position. It is governed by a ruler called the Ameer (Arabic *Emir*, prince), but in 1879 the British invaded it, because the people of Cabul had killed the British minister (Major Cavagnari), and took the capital, and the country is still largely under British influence.

Afghanistan means the country of the Afghans, the name given to this people by the Persians. The inhabitants sometimes call their country Caboolistan, and sometimes Vilayet, or the "mother country."

AFRICA (*af're-kah*), the second largest of the continents of the Old World (Asia being the largest); area about 11,400,000 square miles, or about 3¼ times as large as the United States; pop. about 200,000,000. If all Africa could be seen at once from a high place, it would look something like a long triangle, with the narrowest point toward the south; the surface would be seen to be mostly low and flat, partly fertile and partly desert (see SAHARA), and bordered along the edges with mountains, the longest and highest of which are on the eastern coast. Near the east side would be seen some freshwater lakes (see N'YANZA), out of one of which flows the NILE, the only large river on the north coast; one large river, the ZAMBESI (as long as the RIO GRANDE), would be seen on the east coast, and four, the Senegal (as long as the Columbia), the NIGER, the Congo, and the Orange (as long as the RHINE), on the west.

More than half of all the land in

the torrid zone is in Africa, and its climate is therefore hotter and dryer than that of any other of the continents. The trees and plants are of course mostly those which grow in very hot countries, but in the north parts many European plants are found, and many have been planted in other parts. Among the wild animals found only in Africa are the African or large-eared elephant, two-horned rhinoceros, hippopotamus, giraffe, baboon, gorilla, chimpanzee, zebra, and several kinds of antelopes. There are plenty of lions, leopards, and panthers, but no tigers, and very few common cats. Birds, reptiles, and insects abound.

Many ignorant persons think that the people of Africa are all negroes, but this is a great mistake. Almost

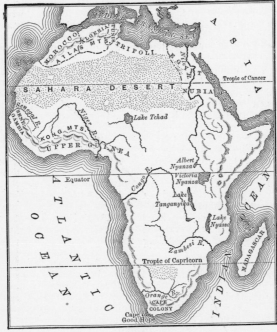

Africa.

all those who live on the north and east of the great desert are of the Caucasian race, being descendants of people who have gone there from Europe and Asia. The negro races live mostly in the middle and southern parts of Africa.

The ancients called the greater part of Africa Libya, the name Africa being given at first only to the parts around CARTHAGE. The Phœnicians are said to have sailed all round Africa about 600 B.C., and a Carthaginian named Hanno is believed to have gone down the west coast as far as Liberia (about 570 B.C.); but little was known of the shape of the continent until after the discovery of America, when Vasco da GAMA sailed round the Cape of Good Hope to the East Indies (1498). Since that time many travelers have explored it, especially during the present century, and nearly all parts of it are now pretty well known.

AG·A·MEM′NON, king of Mycenæ and one of the principal characters in the poem of HOMER called the Iliad. He married Clytemnestra and his brother Menelaus married HELEN, both daughters of Tyndarus, King of Sparta. When Helen was stolen by PARIS, Agamemnon was chosen leader of the Greek forces sent against TROY. He was very brave, but quarreled with ACHILLES, which caused the Greeks much trouble. On his return home, after the destruction of Troy, he was murdered by Clytemnestra and her lover Ægisthus, who had usurped his kingdom during his absence. It is said that his wife gave him, as he came out of his bath, a tunic with the sleeves sewed up, and while he was trying to put it on, struck him down with a hatchet. His death was avenged by his son ORESTES. Agamemnon was the father also of ELECTRA and IPHIGENIA. He and his brother Menelaus were sometimes called the Atridæ, because they were the sons or grandsons of Atreus, King of Mycenæ.

AGASSIZ (ag′as-se), Louis John Rudolph, a noted teacher of natural history, born in Motiers, Switzerland, May 28, 1807. He was educated at the universities of ZÜRICH, HEIDELBERG, and MUNICH, and when about forty years old came to the United States, and was made professor of zoology and geology in Harvard College (1847). In 1865 he explored the lower part of the AMAZONS and the rivers leading into it, and made a very large collection of natural-history curiosities, which are preserved in the Harvard College Museum. In 1872 he made another expedition around Cape Horn, and gathered many more curiosities by means of dredges from the bottom of the sea. Prof. Agas-siz published many works on natural history. He died in Cambridge, Mass., nearly sixty-seven years old (Dec. 14, 1873).

AGINCOURT (ah-zhan-koor′), now Azincourt (ah-zan-koor′), a village in the north of France, about 25 miles from Boulogne, near which King Henry V. of England, with only 14,000 men, defeated the French army of 50,000 men, Oct. 25, 1415. The English began the battle, and the French cavalry, who charged upon them, became entangled in a swamp between the two armies, where great numbers of them were shot by the English archers with their long arrows (C. C. T., 84, II., l.). The cavalry, taking to flight, threw the French foot soldiers into confusion, and the English, then charging with both foot and horse, soon won a complete victory. More than 10,000 French were killed, the greater part of them nobles and knights, and 1500 taken prisoners. Of the English only about 600 fell.

AGLAIA (ag-lah′yah). See GRACES.

AGRA (ah′grah), a city of India, on the river Jumna; pop. about 160,000, or about as large as Louisville, Ky. It is a very old place, but was most celebrated when it was the capital of the MOGUL sovereigns (1526 to 1658). Many splendid buildings of that time are still to be seen there, among them the fortress built by AKBAR, within the walls of which are the palace of Shah Jehan and the famous Pearl Mosque, so called on account of its wondrous beauty. Still more noted is the Taj Mahal, built by Shah Jehan as a tomb for himself and his wife, on which, it is said, 20,000 men worked for twenty-two years. It is of pure white marble, and both the outside and the inside are adorned with mosaics made up of twelve kinds of costly stones, lapis-lazuli, a beautiful blue stone, being used most. The whole of the Koran is said to be written in letters of these stones on the inside walls.

AGRICOLA (*a-grik'o-lah*), **Cneius Julius,** a Roman general, born at Forum Julii, now Fréjus in S. France, A.D. 37. After serving bravely in both Asia and Europe, he became consul when forty years old, and the next year was made governor of Britain. He conquered the whole of the island, and persuaded the savage Britons to wear the Roman dress, live in the Roman way, and teach their children the Latin language. His fleet was the first to sail around Britain and prove it to be an island. He died when fifty-six years old (A.D. 93). Agricola's daughter, Domitia, married TACITUS, the historian, who wrote a very interesting life of his father-in-law.

AGRIPPA (*a-grip'pah*), **Marcus Vipsanius,** a Roman general, born 63 B.C. He was of a common family, but went to school with Octavius, afterward the Emperor AUGUSTUS, and became one of his best friends. He commanded his fleet at the battle of ACTIUM, and afterward held many important offices, once having the care of the empire for two years during Augustus's absence in Asia. Rome was greatly beautified by him, and he built many splendid buildings, among them the Pantheon. He married the Emperor's daughter Julia, and his two sons, Caius and Julius, were adopted as his heirs by Augustus, but they both died young. Agrippa died in his fifty-first year (12 B.C.).

AGRIPPINA (*ag-rip-pi'nah*), daughter of AGRIPPA and Julia, was the wife of GERMANICUS, nephew of the Emperor TIBERIUS, and the mother of his nine children, one of whom was the Emperor CALIGULA. She was beautiful and good, but Tiberius hated her and banished her to a little island off the coast of Italy, where she died A.D. 33.

Agrippina, her daughter, was also beautiful, but was one of the worst women that ever lived. She was the mother of the Emperor Nero. Her brother Caligula banished her, but when he died and her uncle CLAUDIUS became Emperor she returned and married him. She then poisoned him, and her son Nero was made Emperor. She was so much trouble to him that he had her put to death, A.D. 59.

AIX-LA-CHAPELLE (*aiks-lah-shah-pel'*). See AACHEN.

AJACCIO (*ah-yaht'cho*), capital of the island of Corsica ; pop. 17,000, or about as large as Concord, N. H. Many sick and weak people go there in winter on account of its pleasant climate ; but it is chiefly noted as being the birthplace of Napoleon BONAPARTE. The house in which he was born is still standing.

A'JAX, son of Telamon, King of Salamis, was, next to ACHILLES, the bravest of the Greeks in the war against TROY. On the death of Achilles, Ajax strove with ULYSSES for the arms of the hero, and when they were given to his rival, he went mad and killed himself. This is the subject of the tragedy of "Ajax," written by SOPHOCLES. The blood of Ajax is said to have been turned into the hyacinth.

Ajax, son of Oïleus, King of the Locrians, also fought in the war against Troy. Next to Achilles, he was the swiftest of foot of all the Greeks. According to the poets, he made the gods angry, and they destroyed his fleet when on its way home from Troy. He escaped to a rock and defied the gods, when NEPTUNE split the rock with his trident, and threw him into the sea.

AK'BAR, the greatest of the MOGUL emperors of India, born Oct. 14, 1542. When he began to reign, when only twelve years old, he had only three provinces, but he extended his empire over nearly all India. He showed great wisdom in ruling, tried to educate his people and to improve his country, and gave such equal justice to all that he was called the "guardian of mankind." His court at AGRA was very magnificent, and he is said to have kept five thousand elephants, twelve thousand stable horses, and one thousand hunting leopards. Akbar died when sixty-three years old (1605).

The real name of Akbar was Jelal-ed-Deen (glory of the faith) Mohammed, and he was called Akbar, which in Arabic means very great or greatest, when he became very powerful. *Allah akbar*, the Mohammedan battle-cry, means God is greatest, not God is great, as is generally said.

ALABAMA (*al-a-bah'mah*), one of the Southern States of the United States; area 50,722 square miles, or about five sixths that of New England; pop. 1,513,000; capital, MONTGOMERY. The northern part is uneven, though there are no very high mountains, and the southern part is generally flat. Most of the great river valleys are very fertile. Cotton is the principal thing raised, but much corn and wheat are also grown. Among the minerals of the State are marble, granite, coal, iron, and black lead or plumbago. Its chief city is MOBILE.

Alabama, in the language of the Creek Indians, whose home it formerly was, means "here we rest." The country was first a part of Georgia, then a part of the territory of Mississippi, and in 1819 became a State of the Union. It seceded from the Union Jan. 11, 1861, and in the same year joined the Confederate States, but became a State of the Union again in 1868.

ALAMO (*ah'lah-mo*), a fort near San Antonio, on the banks of the river San Antonio, Texas, where 188 Texans fought 2500 Mexicans,

Feb. 23 to March 6, 1836, when it was taken and all alive massacred. Among the Texans, who were fighting for independence, were Col. James Bowie, from whom the bowie-knife was named (C. C. T., 339, II., u.), and Col. David Crockett, both of whom were killed. When the fort was taken by the Mexicans, who lost 1600 men, only six of the Texans were alive. These, including Crockett, were carried before SANTA ANNA, the Mexican leader, who ordered them killed at once. Only three, a woman, a child, and a servant, were spared. After that when the Texans fought the Mexicans, they used to go into battle with the cry, "Remember the Alamo!"

Alamo is Spanish for poplar-tree.

ALAND (*oh'lahnd*) **ISLANDS,** a group of about two hundred rocky islands in the Gulf of Bothnia, between Sweden and Finland; pop. about 16,000. They belong to Russia, but the people are mostly Swedes, and are noted as good sailors. The fortress of Bomarsund, formerly on the largest island, was captured by the French and English fleets in 1854 and blown up.

AL'AR-IC, King of the VISIGOTHS and a famous conqueror, born about 376. He served at first in the army of the Emperor THEODOSIUS, but when Theodosius died and divided his empire between his two sons, Alaric became the enemy of the Romans, and invaded Greece and Italy. Though defeated several times, he at last (408) reached the gates of Rome, then the largest and most splendid city in the world, but the citizens bought him off for 5000 pounds of gold and 30,000 pounds of silver. He besieged the city again the next year and made the Romans promise to make peace; but after he had left, they attacked him again, and he went to Rome a third time (410) and took it. His soldiers were allowed to plunder it for three days, but were commanded to spare the women and all churches and public buildings. He then set off to conquer Sicily, but died soon after (410).

It is said that his soldiers buried him in the bed of the river Busento, in S. Italy. They first turned the water into another channel, and after they had buried their chief and his treasures in the old bed, let the water flow back again. The digging was done by prisoners, all of whom were killed after the work was finished, so that the Romans might never find the place.

ALASKA (*a-las'kah*), a territory of the United States, in the N. W. part of North America; area 580,-000 square miles, or about one

Co-Yukon Winter House.

seventh of the whole United States; pop. about 30,000, of whom all but about 1000 are Indians; capital, Sitka. The territory includes the Aleutian Islands, a chain of islands stretching nearly across to KAMT-CHATKA, which, taken all together, are about three fourths as large as the State of Massachusetts. Alaska is a mountainous country, full of vol-canoes, ten of which are now burn-ing. The climate is very cold except on the west coast, where it is mild and very rainy. Sitka is the rainiest place in the world outside of the tropics, or countries near the equator, and good ice seldom forms there. Alaska has great forests of pine and spruce, and mines of coal, marble, and iron, and is rich in fisheries of cod, herring, and halibut. Many fur-seals are killed every year, on the islands along the coast, for their skins. The largest river of Alaska is the Yukon, which is more than 1800 miles long. On its banks live a fierce tribe of Indians called the Co-Yukons, who live in winter in curious underground houses.

Alaska was discovered in 1741 by the Russian explorer Vitus BEHRING. It was ruled for a long time by the Russian-American Fur Company (1799 to 1862), who had the sole right to hunt and fish there; but in 1867 it was sold by Russia to the United States for $7,200,000.

ALBA LONGA (*al'bah lon'gah*). See ÆNEAS and HORATII.

ALBANIA (*al-ba'ne-ah*), a mountainous country N. of Greece, belonging to European Turkey; pop. about 2,000,000. The people are a nation of warriors, and make the best soldiers in the Turkish army. The Turks call them Arnauts, and their country Arnautlik.

The word Albania means mountainous country, it being made from the Celtic *alp* or *alb*, a rock or cliff.

ALBANY (*awl'ba-ny*), the capital of the State of NEW YORK, on the HUDSON, 145 miles from New York City; pop. 95,000, or a third as large as Cincinnati. The Erie Canal ends there, and the Hudson River Railroad crosses the river there on a bridge. The new capitol, now building, will be, excepting the capitol at Washington, the most splendid building in America. Albany has a very large lumber, cattle, and grain trade.

Albany, next after JAMESTOWN, was the first settlement in the old thirteen colonies. The Dutch, who built a fort there in 1614, called the place New Orange after the Prince of Orange; but when the country was taken by the English (1664), the name was changed to Albany, in honor of the Duke of York and

Albany, who afterward became King JAMES II. It was made the State capital in 1797.

AL'BERT, Prince, husband of Queen VICTORIA, born at Coburg, capital of the duchy of Saxe-Coburg-Gotha, Germany, of which his father was duke, Aug. 26, 1819. He visited England when nineteen years old, and two years after (1840) was married to the Queen. He took great interest in the fine arts, in manufactures, and in agriculture, and was noted for his charities and for the purity of his life. He died in Windsor Castle, in his forty-third year (Dec. 14, 1861).

AL'BERT ED'WARD, Prince of Wales, son of Prince Albert and Queen Victoria, born in Buckingham Palace, London, Nov. 9, 1841. If living at the Queen's death, he will become King of Great Britain and Ireland and Emperor of India. In 1860 he visited the United States and Canada. When twenty-one years old (1863) he was married to Alexandra, daughter of King Christian IX. of Denmark.

AL'BOIN, King of the Lombards (about 560). He defeated and killed Cunimond, King of the Gepidæ, a German tribe, and made his daughter Rosamond become his wife. He had had a wine-cup made out of the skull of Cunimond, and once, after drinking much at a feast in VERONA, he ordered her to drink out of it. In revenge, she persuaded her lover, Helmichis, to kill the King in his afternoon sleep (574). She and Helmichis then fled to RAVENNA, where the Exarch Longinus wished to marry her. To get rid of Helmichis, she gave him poison, but he, finding out her treachery, made her drink half the cup, and the two died together,

ALBUQUERQUE (*ahl-boo-ker'ka*), **Alfonso de,** a famous Portuguese commander, born in 1453. He sailed round the Cape of Good Hope to India in 1503, and made the first Portuguese settlement there. Three years after he went again and attacked the island of Ormuz, in the Persian Gulf, then the great trading place between India and Persia, but was driven off. Having been made governor and commander-in-chief, he captured Goa (1510) and Malacca (1511), where he took a great deal of booty. In 1513 he entered the RED SEA with the first European fleet ever seen in its waters, and two years after took Ormuz. Enemies in Portugal, jealous of his fame, induced the King to send some one to take his place, and he felt the disgrace so much that he died at Goa in his sixty-third year (1515).

AL-CES'TIS, in Greek fable, daughter of Pelias and wife of Admetus, King of Pheræ in Thessaly. When Admetus wished to marry her, Pelias promised her to him if he would come for her in a chariot drawn by a lion and a wild boar. With the help of APOLLO, Admetus did this and so got Alcestis. On the day of his marriage he forgot to sacrifice to DIANA; this made that goddess angry, but she promised that when the hour of his death came he should be spared if his father, mother, or wife would die for him. Alcestis offered herself, and was taken to Hades; but some say that Hercules rescued her from death and brought her back again. The story of her devotion is told by EURIPIDES in his tragedy called "Alcestis."

ALCIBIADES (*al-se-bī'a-deez*), an Athenian general, born in Athens, 450 B.C. He belonged to a noble and very rich family, was brought up by PERICLES, and was the favorite pupil of SOCRATES. When a youth he excelled all his companions in studies and in bodily exercises. He was, too, very handsome, and grew up vain and very wild and dissipated. He was, however, so able that he was chosen one of the generals of an expedition against Sicily. One night, before he had

sailed, all the statues of Mercury in Athens were injured, and his enemies laid it to him, though there was no proof that he had had anything to do with it; he demanded a trial, but it was refused, and he set sail for Sicily, where he won victories and became the favorite of the soldiers. But his enemies had him recalled, and he, knowing that they were determined to destroy him, fled to SPARTA, the enemy of Athens, and stirred up the Spartans to make war against his country. After a while the Spartans got jealous of him, and tried

Alcibiades.

to have him killed, and he fled to the Persians and persuaded them, who were allies of the Spartans, to become friendly to the Athenians. For this he was recalled by the Athenians (411), and given the command of their fleet. He defeated the Spartans in several battles, but at last met with disaster, and fled again to the Persians, who were persuaded by the Spartans to murder him. His house was surrounded one night by armed men and set on fire, and when he rushed out, sword in hand, he was shot dead with arrows, in his forty-sixth year (404 B.C.).

ALCOTT (*awl'kot*), **Amos Bronson,** an American teacher, born in Wolcott, Conn., Nov. 29, 1799. He was the son of a farmer, and when still a boy went to Virginia as a peddler. While visiting different plantations he read many books which were lent him, and thus got a taste for study. On his return home he taught school, first in Connecticut and afterward in Boston and Philadelphia. He lived at Concord, Mass., which he has written about in a book called "Concord Days." Died March 4, 1888.

Louisa May, his daughter, born in Germantown, Pa., Nov. 29, 1832, has

Miss Alcott.

published many books for young folks. Among them are "Flower Fables," "Little Women," "An Old-Fashioned Girl," and "Little Men." Her stories are very popular and have made her name famous both in this country and in Europe, for many hundred thousand volumes of them have been sold. Most of them were written in Concord, where she lived with her parents in a picturesque old house. She died when fifty-six years old (March 6, 1888).

ALCOTT, William Alexander, author of the "Young Man's Guide," "Young Woman's Guide," "Young Housekeeper," "House I Live In," and many other books, was a cousin of Amos Bronson Alcott. He was born in Wolcott, Conn., Aug. 6, 1798, and died in Auburndale, Mass., March 29, 1859.

ALDEN (*awl'den*), **John,** one of the Pilgrims who came over in the Mayflower to PLYMOUTH in 1620. Miles STANDISH once sent him to ask a lady to marry him (Miles), but the lady liked John the best, and said: "Prithee, John, why do you not speak for yourself?" John afterward married the lady, and was for fifty years a magistrate of Plymouth colony. He died in 1687, at the age of eighty-nine.

ALDERNY (*awl'der-ne*). See CHANNEL ISLANDS.

ALDRICH (*awld'ritch*), **Thomas Bailey,** born in Portsmouth, N. H., Nov. 11, 1836, is the author of "The Bells," "The Ballad of Babie Bell," "Daisy's Necklace," "The Course of True Love Never did Run Smooth," "The Story of a Bad Boy," "Marjorie Daw," "Prudence Palfrey," "The Queen of Sheba," and other poems and prose works. He has written much also for magazines. He lives now in Cambridge, Mass.

ALEMBERT (*ah - long - bair'*), **Jean le Rond d',** a famous French writer and mathematician, born in Paris, Nov. 16, 1717. His mother, who was a court lady noted for her wit and beauty, but not married to his father, left him when an infant on the steps of the church of St. Jean le Rond, where he was found by the police and given to a glazier's wife. His father settled on him a pension of 1200 francs (about $240), which paid for his education. When only twenty-four years old he had become so famous that he was elected a member of the Academy of Sciences in Paris. His mother then made herself known to him, but he said: 'I know but one mother—the glazier's wife." He continued to live with his foster-mother for many years, and always treated her as his real parent. He was the author of many books and a member of all the learned societies of Europe. He died in Paris when sixty-six years old (Oct. 29, 1783).

ALENÇON (*ah-len'sun*), a town of Normandy, in N. France; pop. 18,000, or about as large as Norwich, Conn. It is chiefly noted for the famous lace called *point d'Alençon* (C. C. T.,341,II.,l.), which was made there more than two hundred years ago, and is still made to some extent.

A-LEP'PO, a city of SYRIA, in TURKEY in Asia; pop. about 125,-000, or twice as large as Wilmington, Del. The city, which is surrounded by a wall, has many bazaars and mosques. As it is on the only safe road from Syria to eastern Asia, all the Damascus and Bagdad caravans pass that way, so that it has a considerable trade. The people are mostly Mohammedans, but there are about 15,000 Christians and 4000 Jews. In 1822 thousands of its inhabitants were swallowed up by an earthquake, and it has often suffered much from the plague and the cholera.

ALESSANDRIA (*ahl-es-sahn'dre-ah*), a city of N.W. Italy, 58 miles E.S.E. of TURIN; pop. 30,000, or about as large as Altoona, Pa. Next after VERONA, it is the strongest fortified city in Italy. It is an important meeting-place of railways and has a large trade.

Alessandria is the Italian way of spelling Alexandria. The city was first built in 1168, and called Cæsarea, but the name was changed in honor of Pope Alexander III., because he made it the seat of a bishop.

ALEUTIAN (*a-lu'she-an*) **ISLANDS.** See ALASKA.

AL-EX-AN'DER,the name of eight popes of Rome. Of these **Alexander III.** (1159 to 1181) had a long quarrel with the Emperor FREDERICK BARBAROSSA. The Emperor finally submitted (1177), and knelt before the Pope in St. Mark's Church, Venice, where three slabs of red marble still mark the place. It is said that the Pope put his foot on the Emperor's neck, and a picture in the great hall of the ducal palace in Venice represents him doing this, but this story is probably not true.

Alexander VI. (1492 to 1503) was the worst of all the popes. He was born in Spain (1431), and was first a lawyer and then a soldier, but his uncle Pope Calixtus III. made him a cardinal, and in 1492 he was elected Pope. He had five children by a woman who was not his wife, one of whom was Cæsar and the other Lucretia BORGIA. He sold for money all the offices in the Church, and is said by historians to have committed many murders. Some say that his own death was caused by poison which he had prepared for some cardinals whom he had invited to dine with him, but this is not certain.

ALEXANDER I., Emperor of Russia, born in St. Petersburg, Dec. 23, 1777. His grandmother, the Empress CATHERINE II., who intended him to succeed her instead of his father, had him educated very carefully, and even wrote stories for him with her own hand. He had to work so hard at his studies that he is said to have thought of running away with one of his friends and going to America to live. When he was only fifteen years old he was married to Louisa, Princess of Baden, who was still younger. His father, PAUL, who became Emperor on the death of Catherine (1796), was assassinated in 1801. Alexander knew of the conspiracy against his father, who was half insane, but is said to have thought that it was only meant to dethrone him. As soon as he was on the throne he showed himself to be a good ruler, and did much to civilize and enlighten his people, encouraging the arts, trades, and commerce, and founding many universities and schools.

Alexander was at first friendly to Napoleon, but when Napoleon became Emperor and began to seize upon different parts of Europe, Alexander joined with other sovereigns against him. When Napoleon defeated all the armies sent against him, Alexander made peace and became his ally (1807); but in a few years more trouble broke out between them, and in 1812 Napoleon invaded Russia. Alexander then joined Prussia and England against Napoleon, defeated him and entered Paris with his allies (March 31, 1814), and by his firmness saved the city from the fury of the Russian soldiers, who, remembering MOSCOW, wished to destroy it. After the battle of WATERLOO, he again entered Paris as a conqueror, July 11, 1815. In the same year he made with the Emperor of Austria and the King of Prussia a treaty called the "Holy Alliance," to advance the cause of religion, truth, and justice, but it proved to be really a league against the liberty of the people. In his later years Alexander became very gloomy and distrustful of everybody, thought much upon the murder of his father, and became half insane. He died when forty-eight years old (Dec. 1, 1825), and, as he had no children, was succeeded by his brother NICHOLAS, the grandfather of the present Emperor of Russia.

ALEXANDER II., Emperor of Russia, born April 29, 1818. His father, the Emperor NICHOLAS, had him educated very carefully, and watched his studies daily. He was declared of age when eighteen years old, and after that helped his father rule until 1855, when his father died and he became Emperor. This was during the Cri-

mean war, when Russia alone was fighting England, France, Sardinia, and Turkey. Alexander kept up the war even after the capture of SEBASTOPOL, and the allies gained nothing more, and finally made peace with him (1856).

He made many reforms in Russia, freed all the serfs or slaves in his empire, built roads and railroads, and did much for education. In 1867 he sold ALASKA to the United States. He carried on a successful war against Turkey in 1877 and 1878, and would have taken Constantinople if Great Britain had not prevented it. After the close of the war he had great trouble with members of secret societies in Russia calling themselves Nihilists, who demanded more liberty for the people. Assassinated Mar. 13, 1881.

ALEXANDER III., Emperor of Russia, born March 10, 1845. In 1866 he married the Princess Dagmar, daughter of Christian IX. of Denmark, and succeeded to the throne March 13, 1881. Stringent laws directed against the Jews, and great activity in military and naval organization, were features of his reign. He died when forty-nine years old (Nov. 1, 1894).

ALEXANDER THE GREAT, one of the greatest soldiers that ever lived, son of PHILIP King of MACEDONIA, born in 356 B.C. On the side of his mother, Olympias, daughter of the King of Epirus, he claimed descent from ACHILLES. The first thing he learned was the Iliad of HOMER, and it is said that he always put a copy of that poem with his sword under his pillow at night. When he was thirteen years old his father sent for ARISTOTLE, who taught him for three years all kinds of knowledge, and so improved his body by manly exercises that he excelled everybody at his father's court, especially in riding. One day a splendid white horse named Bucephalus, because he had a black mark like an ox's head on his forehead (Greek *Boukephalos*, ox-headed), was offered for sale to the King, but none of the grooms or nobles could mount him, and Philip, displeased, ordered the horse taken away. Alexander, who had been looking on, asked his father to let him try. "What forfeit will you pay if you fail?" asked his father. "The price of the horse," said Alexander. This, according to an ancient writer (Pliny), was sixteen talents (about $20,000). "I will buy the horse if you will ride him," replied Philip. Alexander had noticed that Bucephalus was afraid of his own shadow; he therefore turned his head toward the sun, and soothed him until he was quiet, when he mounted and rode him. After that he always rode him with ease, and he was the favorite charger of Alexander in his wars, but no one else could ride him.

Alexander is said to have been sad when his father won a victory, because he feared that he would leave nothing for him to conquer. When only sixteen years old Philip made him governor of Macedonia during his absence, and two years after he fought at Chæronea, and by his bravery won that great battle, which made Philip master of Greece. Philip wept with joy at his success, and said, as he embraced him: "My son, seek for thyself another kingdom, for that which I have is too small for thee."

Philip, chosen general of all the Greeks, was getting ready to make war on Persia, when he was assassinated, and Alexander, not yet twenty years old, became King. He punished his father's murderers, and after conquering some of the Greek states, which had rebelled, and destroying the city of THEBES, set out to conquer Persia. In the spring of 334 B.C. he crossed the Hellespont at ABYDUS with only 35,000 men. and defeated the Per-

sians at the river Granicus, which they tried to prevent him from crossing. Mounted upon Bucephalus, he was the first to enter the river and charge the enemy, and though the magnificence of his armor and the superb beauty of his horse made him a mark for the arrows and spears of the Persians, he

Alexander the Great.

escaped unhurt and overthrew the son-in-law of King Darius with his lance. On the march toward Persia he came to Gordium, where was the celebrated Gordian Knot, tied by King GORDIUS. An oracle had foretold that whoever should untie this knot would become master of the world. Alexander, after trying in vain to undo it with his fingers, cut it with his sword, saying that was the proper way to untie it.

At Tarsus he came near dying of a fever, brought on, it is said, by his bathing in the waters of the river Cydnus, which are very cold. While Philip, his physician, was mixing him some medicine, Alexander received a letter from Parmenio, one of his generals, saying that Philip had been bribed by Darius to poison him. He handed the letter to Philip, and at the same time drank the medicine, thus showing that he believed in his honesty.

Darius having collected an army of more than half a million men, Alexander marched against him as soon as he had received reinforcements from home. The two armies met at Issus, near the coast of the Mediterranean, and the Persians were completely defeated. Darius escaped, but his treasures and his mother, wife, and two daughters were taken by Alexander, who treated the ladies with the greatest kindness. Darius now asked for peace, but Alexander replied that he could have it only by owning him to be the ruler of Asia. Darius then offered him all Asia as far as the Euphrates river. Parmenio advised him to accept, saying: "I would do it, if I were Alexander." "So would I," replied Alexander, "if I were Parmenio."

Alexander now turned southward and conquered Syria, Phœnicia, and Egypt, and founded a city, which he named after himself, ALEXANDRIA (332 B.C.). While in Egypt he visited the temple of Jupiter Ammon, in the Libyan desert, to consult the oracle there, and is said to have been saluted by the priests as a son of the god. In the spring he marched once more against Darius, who met him near Arbela, in Assyria, with 1,000,000 foot soldiers, 40,000 cavalry, 200 chariots armed with scythes on their axles, and 15 elephants, which

were then used for the first time in war out of their native country. Though Alexander had but 40,000 foot soldiers and 7000 horse, he soon put the great Persian army to flight (331). He charged them at the head of his own cavalry and tried to capture the Persian monarch, who, mounted on a chariot of great height and surrounded by splendid guards, was seen in the thickest of the battle. But his guards fled before the Macedonians, and Darius saved himself only by leaving his chariot and riding a swift horse from the field. All the Persian cities now fell into the conqueror's hands, and thus was this great empire destroyed.

These wonderful successes turned Alexander's brain, and he began to lead a life of riot and dissipation. He affected to believe himself the son of Jupiter, as the priests had told him, and thought that he could do anything. One night, when drunk, he set fire to Persepolis, the capital of Persia and one of the most beautiful cities in the world, and burned it to ashes. When he became sober he was ashamed of this, and he set out once more with his cavalry after Darius. He pursued him into Parthia, where the King was murdered by Bessus, one of his own officers. Alexander came up just in time to see the dying King, covered with wounds, lying on a chariot, and he is said to have shed tears at the sight. He ordered the body to be carried to Persepolis, and had it buried in the most magnificent manner in the tomb of the Persian kings. Bessus, his murderer, was punished by having his legs fastened to two trees which had been bent toward each other, and which, when they sprung back again, tore his body asunder.

Alexander, now become very intemperate, began to suspect his generals of conspiring against him. He condemned to death Philotas one of his best officers and son of Parmenio, and soon after had Parmenio himself murdered. While in Samarcand he killed with his own hand his friend Clitus, who had once saved his life in battle, because he ventured to rebuke him for his pride and for believing himself the son of a god. When Alexander became sober he was so grieved at this act that he touched neither food nor drink for three days and nights.

Alexander next (327) went southward into India, crossed the Indus, and defeated a king named Porus on the banks of the Hydaspes (now the Jhylum). When Porus, who was taken prisoner, was brought into the presence of Alexander, Alexander asked him how he would like to be treated. "Like a king," replied Porus. Alexander was so pleased with this answer that he gave him his kingdom, and Porus became his ally and friend. Bucephalus was wounded so badly in this battle that he died soon after. Alexander gave his noble horse a splendid burial, and founded a town at the place, which he named in his honor Bucephala.

After conquering many Indian nations and princes, Alexander went as far as the river Hyphasis (now the Sutlej), when his soldiers refused to go any further east into unknown countries, and he was obliged to turn back. He sailed down the Hydaspes to the Indus, and down that river to the Indian Ocean. From there his fleet, under command of Nearchus, sailed round to the Tigris, while he marched by land to Susa. He afterward went to Babylon, and while preparing for more conquests was taken sick and died (323 B.C.) when only thirty-two years old, after a reign of twelve years and eight months. In this short time he had made himself master of most of the world then known.

Alexander's body was carried to Alexandria, and buried with great pomp by PTOLEMY. The Egyptians and other nations worshiped him as a god after death. He had appointed no one to succeed him, but when asked on his death-bed who should inherit his throne, he replied: "The worthiest." His great empire was divided among his generals, who after a while took the title of kings.

ALEXANDER NEVSKOI, a Russian prince, born in 1219, who gained a great victory (1240) over the Swedes on the banks of the river Neva, near where St. Petersburg now stands. From this he was called Nevskoi, which means of the Neva. He is now a saint in the Russian Church, and a great monastery, built by Peter the Great, stands on the site of the battle. He died when forty-four years old (1263).

ALEXANDER SEVERUS, a Roman Emperor, born about A.D. 205. He was adopted by his cousin, the Emperor ELAGABALUS, who became jealous of him and tried to kill him; but Alexander escaped and became Emperor on the death of Elagabalus (222), taking the name of Severus. He ruled for nine years in peace; but in 231 he had war with the Persians, whom he defeated, and in 235 he started to fight the Germans, but was killed by his mutinous troops. He was a good and wise ruler, and did much for the empire.

ALEXANDER, William, an American major-general, born in New York in 1726. In American history he is generally called Lord Stirling, because he claimed that he was the rightful heir to the earldom of Stirling, in Scotland; but, although he spent a great deal of money in trying to prove it, he was unsuccessful. He was a strong patriot in the war of the Revolution, and fought in many of the most important battles. He died in Albany when fifty-seven years old (Jan. 15, 1783).

ALEXANDRIA (*al-ex-an'dre-ah*), a city of Egypt, founded by Alexander the Great, 332 B.C. It was laid out in squares, with two wide main streets crossing each other, beautified with colonnades and splendid buildings. In the centre, where these streets met, was the mausoleum of Alexander the Great, in which his embalmed body was first placed in a coffin of pure gold, and afterward, when that had been stolen, in one of alabaster. About a mile from the city, in the Mediterranean, was the island of Pharos, on which was built by PTOLEMY PHILADELPHUS the famous light-house, called one of the wonders of the world. It was a large square tower of white marble, so high that the fire which was kept always burning on its top by night could be seen many miles at sea. The King ordered the architect to engrave upon its top this inscription: "King Ptolemy, to the Gods the Saviors, for the Benefit of Sailors." But the architect, who wanted all the glory to himself, secretly cut in the marble another inscription, which he filled up with mortar, and cut the King's inscription on that. In course of time the mortar fell off, and then every one could read. "Sostratus the Cnidian, the Son of Dexiphanes, to the Gods the Saviors, for the Benefit of Sailors." This tower is now gone, but a light-house still stands on its site.

Dexiphanes, the father of the architect, built a great mole or pier from the city out to the Pharos, thus forming two harbors. Near the eastern harbor was the finest part of the city, containing the royal palaces, the great theatre, and the Museum, which had in it a library of 400,000 volumes. Among the other great buildings was the Serapeum, or Temple of Serapis, said to have been the most magnificent building in the world, with the exception of the Capitol at Rome. Within it was another great library of 300,000 volumes. When Julius CÆSAR besieged Alexandria, the library of the Museum was burned, but that in the Serapeum was saved. Queen CLEOPATRA afterward added to this the great library of the Kings of Pergamus, which Mark Antony gave to her, and in time this grew to be the greatest library in the world, containing, it is said, 700,000 volumes. But this would not amount to nearly as much as a modern library of the same number of printed books, because in those times, when all books were in writing, it was customary to call each part of a work a volume; for instance, the Iliad, which we call one volume, was then in twenty-four rolls (C. C. T. 81, I. l.), each of which was called a volume. In this great library was stored up all the learning of the world, and students and learned men came there from distant countries to study. For four hundred years it made Alexandria the centre of literature and the arts; but about A.D. 390 the Emperor THEODOSIUS THE GREAT, having given orders to have all the heathen temples in the Roman Empire destroyed, the Serapeum was torn down by the Christians of Alexandria, and with it fell the library. Some writers say that the Caliph OMAR ordered the library to be burned when the Arabs took Alexandria (640), but this is not very probable.

Alexandria fell into the power of the Romans 30 B.C., but its greatness continued until CONSTANTINOPLE was made the capital of the Empire, when it became chiefly a place for trade. When Vasco da GAMA found out that he could get to India by sailing round the CAPE OF GOOD HOPE, Alexandria lost all the East Indian trade, which used to go that way, and after that it went to decay. But the opening of the SUEZ Canal brought back a large part of the travel to the East, and the city is now growing very fast, having a population of 227,000, or about as many as Washington, D. C. Next to MARSEILLES, it is the most important port in the Mediterranean, and it has the best harbor in the eastern part of that sea. The new city is built on the mole between the old city and the island of Pharos, which now forms a broad neck of land.

In 1882 the affairs of Egypt were in such a condition that Great Britain was forced to interfere in order to protect her interests. Arabi Pasha was the leader of an insurrection, and he defied the British power. A fleet was sent to Alexandria, and resistance being made, the British bombarded the city July 11, and restored order.

Among the remains of the old city is the tall column commonly called Pompey's Pillar, but which ought to be called Diocletian's Pillar, because it was set up in honor of the Emperor DIOCLETIAN when he took Alexandria in A.D. 296. It is a Corinthian column (C. C. T., 146, I., 147, II.) of red granite, 99 feet high with the base and capital. Several years ago a party of eight English sailors, ashore on a frolic, flew a kite over the Pillar and let it come down on the other side so as to let the string fall over the top. They then pulled up a strong rope, and all climbed to the top, where they sat down and drank some punch, to the great astonishment of the Arabs.

The two obelisks called Cleopatra's Needles, which were brought by Julius Cæsar from HELIOPOLIS, where they had stood for more than twelve hundred years in front of the Temple of the Sun, and set up to adorn his own temple, called the Cæsarium. One of these was given by MEHEMET ALI to the British Government and taken to London in 1877 ; the other was given to the United States by ISMAIL PASHA and taken to New York in 1880.

ALEXANDRIA, a city of Virginia, on the Potomac River, 7 miles below Washington ; pop. 14,000, or about as large as Austin, Tex. It has a good harbor, with water deep enough for the largest ships. In the beginning of the civil war Alexandria was entered by Union troops under Colonel Ellsworth (May 24, 1861), who was shot dead by the landlord of a hotel for hauling down a Confederate flag.

AL-EX'IS, Czar of Russia, born March 10, 1629, came to the throne when sixteen years old (1645). He was one of the best of the Russian rulers, and did much to prepare his people for the reforms made by his son PETER THE GREAT. Peter's mother was a beautiful woman, but not of very high rank, named Natalia Narishkin. Alexis chose her for his wife after seeing her shoe, which made him think that she had a very small foot. He died when forty-seven years old (Jan. 29, 1676).

ALEXIS COM-NE'NUS, Emperor of Constantinople, born in 1048, came to the throne when thirty-three years old (1081). He was a very able ruler and valiant soldier, but he had a hard reign, his empire being in revolt and attacked by the Turks on the east and the Normans on the west. Alexis sent ambassadors to the Christian princes of the west of Europe for aid, and this was partly the cause of the first CRUSADE; but when the great armies of the Crusaders began to arrive, he was more frightened at them than at the Turks, and he was glad enough to see them go into Asia. He carried on wars against the Turks much of the time, until his death in his seventy-first year (1118).

ALFIERI (*ahl-fe-a're*), **Vittorio,** Count, the most celebrated Italian poet of his time, born in Piedmont, of a noble and wealthy family, Jan. 17, 1749. He had a poor education and was very dissipated in his youth, but when about twenty-five years old he wrote a play called

"Cleopatra," which was so successful when played on the stage that he made up his mind to lead a different life. He spent several years in hard study, and afterward wrote many tragedies (21 in all), several comedies, and other poems, and translated into Italian some of the works of ÆSCHYLUS, SOPHOCLES, and EURIPIDES. Among his poems are five odes on the American Revolution. He died when fifty-four years old (Oct. 8, 1803). His splendid monument, sculptured by CANOVA, is in Santa Croce, FLORENCE, between the tombs of MICHAEL ANGELO and MACHIAVELLI.

ALFONSO, the name of six kings of Portugal, and seventeen of different parts of Spain when that country was divided into several kingdoms.

Alfonso I. (1139 to 1185), the first king of Portugal, was called by the Portuguese the Conqueror, because he conquered that country from the Moors.

Alfonso V., King of Portugal (1438 to 1481), was called the African, because he made great conquests in Africa, and colonized Guinea.

Alfonso VI., King of Leon and Castile (1065 to 1109), in Spain, called the Valiant, had many wars with the Moors, in which the famous CID took part.

Alfonso X., King of Leon and Castile (1252 to 1284), was called the Wise, on account of his learning. He had the Bible translated into Spanish, wrote a book of laws for the kingdom which is still in use in Spain, and also a chronicle or history of Spain, astronomical works, and poems.

Alfonso V., King of Aragon, in Spain (1416 to 1458), conquered southern Italy, and became king also of Naples and Sicily.

ALFONSO XIII., infant king of Spain, born May 17, 1886. His mother, Maria Christina, acts as regent during the king's minority.

AL'FRED THE GREAT, King of the West Saxons, in England, born at Wantage, Berkshire, in 849. His mother, Osburga, taught him the Saxon ballads which related the deeds of the heroes of the past, and one day showed her children a book of poetry with painted letters, and said : " The one who can first say this book by heart shall have it." Alfred, then four years old, said · " Will you really give it to the one who learns it the quickest ?" His mother replied : " Yes, to him will I give it." Alfred got his teacher to read it to him until he had learned it by heart, when he repeated it to his mother and won the book. Soon after this (853) his father sent him to Rome, a long and difficult journey in those days, which had to be made on horseback. Alfred went, accompanied by a great number of nobles and other persons, and was anointed king by the Pope, who adopted him as his spiritual son. Two years after, Alfred made the same journey again with his father.

Alfred was twelve years old before he knew his letters, but in those times even kings were seldom able to read and write. After that he studied all he could, and improved his mind as he grew up ; and at the same time became strong and skilful in all manly exercises, and famous as a hunter.

When he was twenty-two years old (871) the Danes invaded England,and in a great battle with them King Ethelred, Alfred's brother, was killed, and Alfred became king. Though the Danes had been defeated in this battle, many more came from Denmark, and ravaged all parts of England, and unable longer to fight them, King Alfred, with a few followers, took refuge in the woods. He came one day alone to the hut of a cow-herd, in the middle of a swamp, while the man was absent at his work, and sitting down in the chimney-corner, began to mend his bow and arrow. The cowherd's wife, supposing from his shabby dress that he was one of her husband's companions, bade him watch some cakes which she had set to bake on the hearth, while she went to see after the cattle. Alfred, forgetting everything but his troubles, let them burn, and got a good scolding from the woman, who told him that though he could eat them fast enough, he was too lazy and good ιor nothing to help bake them.

After a while some of Alfred's friends ιound out his hiding-place and joining him there built a fort, from which they often sallied out to fight the Danes. It is said that Alfred, wishing to find out about the number and strength of the enemy, disguised himself as a harper, and went into their camp. He wandered round, singing and playing to the soldiers, watching everything he saw, and at last was ordered to go into the commander's tent. Godrun, or Guthrun, as he was called, received him kindly, and, much pleased with his songs, let him go without suspecting who he was. Alfred, having thus found out all about the Danish army, attacked it and defeated it with great slaughter (878). Godrun, who was taken prisoner, was given his liberty on condition that he and his followers should become Christians, and was allowed to live in the east part of England, where he continued to be Alfred's friend all the rest of his life.

Alfred was now really the ruler of all England, although he was never called so, and he began to do what he could to build up his country again. He rebuilt cities and castles, and erected many new ones; strengthened his army and built a navy; made good laws, set up schools, and did all he could to educate his people. It is said that he founded the University of Oxford and was the first to establish trial by jury, but neither of these is certain.

When thirty-nine years old he studied Latin, and afterward translated into Saxon many works which he thought his countrymen needed. In 894 the Northmen, under a leader named HASTING, invaded England, but after a struggle of three years they were driven out. Four years after (901), King Alfred died, aged fifty-two years, and was succeeded by his son Edward.

ALGER (*al'jer*), **Horatio, Jr.,** author of the "Ragged Dick," "Tattered Tom," "Luck and Pluck," "Brave and Bold," and "Campaign" series of books, and other books for young folks, was born at Revere, Mass., Jan. 13, 1834. He was graduated at Harvard College in 1852, and has been a teacher, editor of newspapers, and writer for magazines. He lives now in Boston.

ALGERIA (*al-je're-ah*), a French colony in N. Africa, on the Mediterranean, between Morocco and Tunis; area 250,000 square miles, or as large as California and Oregon together; pop. about 3,800,-000, or nearly the same as that of Illinois. It is mountainous in the N. and flat and sandy in the S., nearly half being desert, but there is also much fertile land, and the country is rich ιn grains and fruits, and abounds with minerals. The inhabitants are Arabs, Moors, Turks, and Kabyles, excepting about 250,000 Europeans and their descendants. The principal towns are ALGIERS, capital of the colony, (pop. 75,000), Constantine (pop. 45,000), and Oran (pop. 67,000).

Algeria was the ancient Numidia When CARTHAGE fell (146 B.C.) the Romans took Numidia, and held it until the Vandals conquered it (5th century). They ruled it about a hundred years, when it became a part of the EASTERN EMPIRE. At this time it was Christian, but the Arabs conquered it about 700, and most of the people have since been Mohammedans. The Moors who were driven from Spain (1492) settled in Algeria and became pirates, and for more than three hundred years the Algerians were the terror of the Mediterranean. They captured the merchant-ships of all Christian nations, and kept thousands of Christian slaves at work in Algiers. At last the French took the city of Algiers (1830), and after defeating Abd-el-Kader got possession of the whole country, which they still hold.

Algeria gets its name from AL-GIERS.

ALGIERS (*al-jeerz'*), a city of N. Africa, capital of ALGERIA; pop. 75,000, or about as large as Fall River, Mass. It is built on the side of a mountain, and looks very beautiful from the sea, the white houses rising in terraces one above the other. On the top of the mountain is the casbah, or castle, The city has a strong wall all around it, and the harbor is defended with forts. Algiers is nearly a thousand years old, having been founded in 935 by an Arab chief.

Algiers is named from an island near the city, the name having been changed from the Arabic Al-Jezirah (*Al*, the, *Jezirah*, island).

AL-GON'KINS. See AMERICAN INDIANS.

ALI (*ah'lee*), cousin of MOHAMMED and husband of Fatima the Prophet's daughter, born about A.D. 600. He is said to have been Mohammed's first disciple, and hoped to succeed him, but the power was obtained by ABU-BEKR. After that the Mohammedans were divided into two sects, the Sunnis, who did not believe in him, and the Shiahs, who were his followers. He at last became caliph, and ruled from 655 to 661, when he was killed by his enemies.

AL'I-SON, Sir Archibald, an English historian, born at Kenley, Shropshire, Dec. 29, 1792. His principal work is the "History of Europe," which was once very popular and was translated into many languages, even into Arabic and Hindostanee, but it is not much read now. He died near Glasgow, when seventy-four years old (May 23, 1867).

AL'LEN, Ethan, an American officer in the war of the Revolution, born in Litchfield, Ct., Jan. 10, 1738. When a boy his parents removed to Salisbury, where most of his youth was spent, and in 1765 he emigrated to what was then called the "New Hampshire Grants," now the State of Vermont. This was then claimed by both New Hampshire and New York, and the settlers there formed themselves into a company, called "Green Mountain Boys," to protect their interests, and chose Allen for their leader. Soon after the fight at Lexington (1775), he marched against Forts Ticonderoga and Crown Point. Landing with eighty-three men just before the break of day near Ticonderoga, he surprised the fort, getting inside and forming his men on the parade-ground, where they awoke the sleeping garrison with a shout of victory. Captain Delaplace, the British commander, rushed out in his night-dress, and asked : " What does this mean?" Allen, holding his sword over his head, ordered him to surrender. " In whose name ?" asked Delaplace. " In the name of the Great Jehovah and the Continental Congress," replied Allen. Delaplace, seeing that it was useless to resist, surrendered the fort with 120 cannon, many small-arms, and a large amount of ammunition and stores. On the next day Crown Point was taken by Col. Warner, and thus the Americans got command of Lake Champlain.

In September of the same year Allen was captured by the British while on an expedition against Montreal, and carried to England in irons. When he was landed at Falmouth, so great was the curiosity to see the man who had taken Ticonderoga, that the officers who had him in charge had to force their way through the crowds with drawn swords. After being kept a prisoner for two and a half years he was exchanged for a British colonel. The English, who admired his courage, tried to bribe him to take their side. Once, in New York, an officer told him that his faithfulness had won Gen. Howe's good opinion, and that if he would join the King's army he would be given a good position, and would be rewarded after the war with large estates in Vermont or Connecticut. Allen told him that he was so much obliged to Gen. Howe for his good opinion that he would not lose it by turning traitor. " As to the offer of lands," said he, " that is much like a similar offer once made by Satan to Christ of all the kingdoms of the earth, when in fact the old devil didn't own an acre."

Allen afterward became general of the Vermont State Militia. He wrote an account of his captivity, and some other works. He died on his estate near Colchester, Vt., when fifty-one years old (Feb. 13, 1789).

ALLSTON (*awl'ston*), **Washington,** a noted American painter, born in Waccamaw, S. C., Nov. 5, 1779. He was graduated at Harvard College in 1800, and the next year went to London to study art in the Royal Academy, of which Benjamin WEST was then president. He afterward studied in Rome, and finally settled in London, where he won much fame and many prizes for his pictures. When thirty-nine years old (1818) he returned to America, and lived afterward mostly in Cambridge, Mass., where he died in his sixty-fourth year (July 9, 1843). His large picture called "Belshazzar's Feast," on which he was working at the time of his death, is now in the Boston Athenæum.

ALMA-TADEMA (*al'mah tah-de'-mah*), a famous Dutch artist, born at Dronryn, Netherlands, Jan. 8, 1836. He studied in Antwerp and became noted as a painter of classical subjects,chiefly scenes in ancient Greek and Roman life. In 1870 he married an English woman and removed to London, where he now lives.

ALMADEN (*ahl-mah-dthen'*) a town of Spain, about 60 miles N. of Cordova; pop. about 9000. It is noted for its quicksilver-mines, which are the oldest and probably the largest in the world. They were worked by the Romans, who had a town there, and in later times by the Spanish government. The principal mine is directly under the town, and is about a fifth of a mile in depth. Convict labor was long employed, but now hired men are used. The mines are worked day and night in winter, but are closed during the summer, when the heat makes the fumes rising from the quicksilver too poisonous to breathe.

ALMAGRO (*ahl-mah'gro*), **Diego de,** one of the Spanish conquerors of Peru, born about 1464. He was a foundling, having been picked up when a baby in the town of Almagro, from which he got his name. Though he could neither read nor write, he came to America and won fame and wealth. He aided PIZARRO in the conquest of Peru (1533), and afterward attempted to conquer Chili, but was called back by a rising of the Peruvians, whom he defeated and took CUZCO. A civil war now took place between him and Pizarro, with whom he had always quarreled, and he was finally defeated and taken prisoner by Pizarro, who caused him to be put to death (1538).

ALPS, the highest chain of mountains in Europe, mostly on the borders of Italy, France, Switzerland, Germany, and Austria. They are divided into many parts, and are connected by smaller ranges with most of the other mountain chains of Europe. The average height of the different parts is about one mile and a half (7700 feet), from which more than four hundred peaks rise so high that their tops are always covered with snow. The highest peak of all is Mont Blanc (White Mountain), on the borders of France and Italy, which is about three miles (15,732 feet) high. On the north side is the beautiful valley of Chamouni, and the great glacier called Mer de Glace (Sea of Ice), which is fifteen miles long, five miles wide, and a hundred feet thick. There are also glaciers on almost all the snow-capped peaks, from which masses of partly melted snow and broken ice move into the valleys, bearing along trees and rocks, and destroying everything in their way. Avalanches too often slide down the precipices, burying forests and villages and filling up rivers; and whirlwinds frequently sweep through the mountains, driving before them the blinding snow and burying travelers who are unfortunate enough to be caught in them.

There are many roads over the Alps, most of which are passable for carriages. Some of these were known to the ancients, but it was thought a great feat to cross these mountains, and HANNIBAL'S passage of the Little St. Bernard with his army was long considered a very wonderful thing. In modern times they have been crossed several times with armies: in 1567 the Duke of Alva led 10,000 men over Mont Cenis, and in 1800 Napoleon crossed with 30,000 men from Switzerland into Italy over the Great St. Bernard. Napoleon's passage was a very difficult undertaking, for the wild and barren mountain was covered in great part with snow and ice. The cannon were dismounted and laid in logs hollowed like troughs, which were dragged by men; the wheels were carried on poles, and the ammunition and other things were loaded on to mules. The long march of forty miles began at midnight, and did not end until about nine o'clock the following evening, when the soldiers, though they had scarcely had time to eat anything since they started, gave themselves up to sleep without thinking of supper. The worst part of the march was going down the mountain, both men and horses often falling on the slippery ice, some even going over the precipices and being dashed to pieces on the rocks below.

Napoleon, who was dressed in his gray coat and cocked hat, in which he is so often shown in pictures, went a large part of the way with only a peasant for his guide. Talking with this man, he found out that his chief wish in life was to become the owner of a certain little farm. Napoleon, to reward him, afterward gave him the farm, to the poor man's great delight and surprise.

Napoleon made some fine military roads over the Alps in different places, and in later times railways have been built over two of the mountains, but they now go through tunnels, one, the Saint Gothard tunnel, from Italy to Switzerland, being the longest railroad tunnel in the world (9½ miles), and the other, the Mont Cenis tunnel, being next to it in length (nearly 8 miles).

The word Alps is from the Celtic *alp* or *alb*, a rock or cliff, and from this these mountains get their name.

ALSACE-LORRAINE (*ahl-sahs'-lor-rayn'*). See GERMANY.

ALTAI (*ahl-ti'*), the name of the great range of mountains separating China and Siberia. They are not very high at their western end, but their average height is nearly a mile, and in some places peaks rise nearly two miles high, where they are always covered with snow. These mountains are rich in minerals, especially gold, and in fur-bearing animals. The great trade route between St. Petersburg and Peking crosses the Altai near Lake Baikal. Altai means golden, the word being from the Tartar *altun,* gold.

ALTONA (*ahl'to-nah*), a city of Germany, on the river Elbe, just below and joining HAMBURG; pop. 143,000, or about as large as Omaha, Neb. It was built by Denmark as a rival to Hamburg, but Prussia took it in 1867, and now Altona and Hamburg are really one city, though they have different governments. Altona has a very large trade by railways and steamboats. Its principal manufacture is tobacco.

ALTOONA (*al-too'nah*), a city of Pennsylvania, at the E. base of the ALLEGHANY Mountains, 117 miles E. of Pittsburgh; pop. about 30,-000. At this place the Pennsylvania Railroad begins to go up the mountains by a grade so steep that double power is needed to move the trains going west, but in coming down they run the whole distance to Altoona (11 miles) without any steam at all. The scenery is very beautiful, and the engineering work quite wonderful.

ALTORF (*ahl'torf*). See TELL, WILLIAM.

ALVA (*ahl'vah*), **Fernando Alvarez de Toledo,** Duke of, a noted Spanish general, born of a noble Castilian family in 1508. He was trained as a soldier from his youth, and when only sixteen fought in a battle. He was with the Emperor Charles V. in most of his campaigns, and afterward (1555–56) when commander-in-chief under Philip II. defeated the French and Papal forces in Italy. In 1567 he was sent to the Netherlands, which then belonged to Spain, to put down a rebellion of the Protestants. He

showed himself to be a good general, but he failed to conquer the people, and he was recalled in 1573. During this time he acted with the utmost cruelty, and he boasted that he had put to death eighteen thousand persons, besides those who fell in battle. In 1580 he conquered Portugal and annexed it to Spain. He died when seventy-four years old, (Jan. 12, 1582).

ALVARADO (*ahl-vah-rah'do*), Pedro de, a Spanish soldier, born at Badajos near the end of the 15th century. He came to Cuba in 1518, and the next year went with CORTEZ to conquer Mexico, where he was noted for both gallantry and cruelty. He conquered Guatemala (1523) and was made its governor by CHARLES V. While on an expedition against the Indians his horse fell with him down a steep bank at a river crossing, and killed him (1541).

AMATI (*ah-mah'te*), the name of an Italian family of Cremona, noted as makers of violins, in the 16th and 17th centuries. Their instruments are among the best ever made, and are still highly prized.

AM'A-ZONS, a tribe of female warriors, who lived on the banks of the river Thermodon in Pontus, Asia Minor, who suffered no men to live among them. They are said to have been so called from their habit of cutting off the right breast (the word Amazon being from two Greek words, meaning without a breast), to give them greater freedom in using the bow. During the war against TROY they fought under their Queen, Penthesilea, against the Greeks. The Amazons are often mentioned by Greek writers, and the Greek artists loved to paint pictures of their battles, but it is doubtful if such a people ever lived.

AMAZON (*am'ah-zon*) **RIVER** of South America, flowing from the Andes in Peru to the Atlantic, into which it empties on the N. coast of Brazil. It is the largest river on the globe, but not the longest, the NILE being about the same length, and the Missouri and MISSISSIPPI together much longer. Its length is not exactly known, but is thought to be about 3000 miles; at its mouth it is 60 miles wide, and it is four miles wide 1000 miles from the sea, and more than a mile wide 2000 miles from the sea. Many other large rivers flow into it, and the waters of all are so deep that large vessels can sail from the sea over more than 10,000 miles. The valley of the Amazon is covered with thick forests, the home of many kinds of wild beasts, and the waters contain great numbers of fish. During the rainy season the river overflows its banks and floods a large extent of country. The upper part of the Amazon is called in Peru the Marañon, and the middle part is sometimes called the Solimoens.

The Amazon was discovered by Yañez PINZON in 1500, but it was first sailed upon by Orellana, one of Pizarro's officers, in 1541. He had a fight with what he called a nation of female warriors, or Amazons, and from this the river is supposed to have got its name; but they are thought to have been a tribe of Indians, who looked like women because they parted their hair in the middle and wore long tunics.

AM′BROSE, Saint, Bishop of Milan, born at Treves, in Gaul, in 340. His father was governor of Gaul, and he himself was made governor of Liguria, a province of which Milan was the capital, when only twenty-nine years old. When the Bishop of Milan died, though he had never been even baptized, he was so much beloved that he was chosen to succeed him. Though he did not want the office, he accepted it, and held it until his death, which took place at Milan, in his fifty-eighth year (397). He showed much piety and wisdom, and at the same time great courage. When

the Emperor THEODOSIUS was about to enter the cathedral of Milan, after the massacre of the people of Thessalonica, which had been done by his orders, Ambrose sternly forbade him, and afterward made him do public penance for the crime. Ambrose's fame spread far and wide, and he was known even among the barbarians. A Frankish chief once asked a Roman general who had conquered him, if he was a friend of Ambrose; and when he said that he was, the chief replied : " No wonder that you have beaten us, since you have the favor of a man whom the sun itself would obey if he should command it to stand still." St. Ambrose wrote many books ; he also did much to improve church music, and wrote some hymns, which are still sung. He is the patron saint of Milan, and the Ambrosian Library there was named after him.

AMERICA (*a-mer′e-kah*), one of the five continents of the earth ; area about 15,000,000 square miles, which is four times as large as Europe, as large as Europe and Africa put together, and about seven eighths as large as Asia ; pop. about 100,000,000, or nearly one fifteenth that of the whole earth. It nearly touches Asia on the N. W. and Greenland on the N. E., and stretches N. and S. about 9000 miles, thus being the longest body of land on the globe. It is the only one of the continents whose shores are washed by the four great oceans— the Atlantic, the Pacific, the Arctic or Northern, and the Antarctic or Southern ; and within it are the largest rivers and lakes, the largest valleys, the highest mountains (excepting the Himalayas), the greatest forests, and more than two thirds of all the volcanoes in the world. This great continent is divided into two nearly equal parts joined by the isthmus of Panama, which at its narrowest part is less than thirty miles wide. All north of this is called North America, and all south of it South America, while the part on the isthmus itself is known as Central America.

  North America is very irregular in shape, as will easily be seen on the map, its coasts being much broken into by seas. It has also several very large inland seas or lakes, of fresh water, which contain about a third of all the fresh water on the earth.

The surface of N. America is broken by two principal chains of mountains. The Rocky Mountains, which skirt the W. coast, extending from the Arctic Ocean southward until they join the Andes. These mountains really form two ranges, between which lies the valley of the Great Salt Lake. On the E. coast of N. America are the Appalachian Mountains, which also are

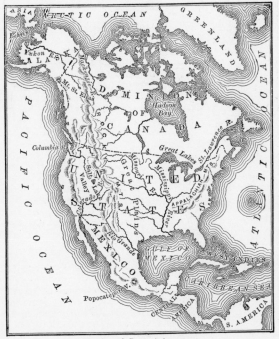

North and Central America.

divided into two ranges : the easternmost one forms the Green Mountains, the Highlands of New York, the South Mountains of Pennsylvania, and the Blue Ridge ; the other is made up of the Adirondack, Catskill, Alleghany, and Cumberland ranges. Between these lies a long valley, and between the Appalachian and the Rocky Mountain ranges is a great plain or series of plains. The highest mountain in N. America is Mt. Saint Elias, in Alaska, which is nearly three and three fourths miles (19,500 feet) high ; next to it is Popocatepetl in Mexico, more than three and a quarter miles (17,540 feet) high.

  The rivers of N. America empty into the Arctic, the Pacific, and the Atlantic Oceans, and the Gulf of Mexico. The principal Arctic river is the Mackenzie; the largest ones on the Pacific side are the Yukon, Columbia, and Colorado; the most important one on the Atlantic side is the St. Lawrence; and the largest ones emptying into the Gulf of Mexico are the Mississippi and the Rio Grande. Of these the Mississippi and its many branches are the most important, the country which they drain being larger than any drained by any other river in the world excepting the AMAZONS.

North America has almost all kinds of climate, and produces nearly all kinds of grains, fruits, and

South America.

vegetables. It is rich in every valuable mineral, especially the metals, all the important ones, excepting zinc and tin, being more plentiful than in any other part of the world; and it has more than seven eighths of all the coal known to exist.

Central America, or the part of the extensive isthmus lying between MEXICO and COLOMBIA, really belongs to N. America, though it is generally treated separately. The mountain range which extends through it, joining the Rocky Mountains and the Andes, is 300 to 1000 feet high, with several peaks 10,000 to 12,000 feet high. As Central America is wholly in the tropics, it has a wet and a dry season, and produces all the vegetables and fruits of the tropics. Its people are mostly Indians and mixed breeds, with a few whites and negroes.

South America is shaped much like AFRICA, and its coast is but little broken. Its W. coast is skirted by the ANDES, which extend from Central America to Cape Horn. With the exception of the Himalayas, these mountains are the highest in the world. Other important chains are in Venezuela and Brazil. Almost all the interior of S. America is occupied with immense level plains, some of which are covered with thick woods, and others with rich grass which supports vast herds of wild cattle. The most southern part (Patagonia) is a barren, treeless plain.

All the great rivers of South America empty into the Atlantic, the most important ones being the ORINOCO, the AMAZONS, and the PLATA. Other rivers, all of which are larger than the RHINE, are the Xingu, the Tocantins, the San Francisco, and the Colorado.

South America lies mostly within the tropics, and its climate is generally hot, moist, and sickly, but the highlands of the Andes are healthful. All the vegetables and fruits of warm climates grow there to perfection. It is rich in gold, silver, and copper, and in precious stones, but is not so well off as North America in iron and coal.

The population of South America is largely made up of Indians and mixed races.

America was first visited by NORTHMEN from Greenland about 986, and they afterward sailed down the coast as far as New England. It is supposed that they came on the coast at different times down to about a hundred years before COLUMBUS re-discov-

ered it (1492). Columbus saw only the West India Islands in his first and second voyages, and did not see the mainland until his third voyage (1498), when he sailed down the coast of South America. The year before (1497), the mainland of North America had been visited by John CABOT, who sailed from Labrador down to Florida.

America gets its name from Amerigo VESPUCCI, who sailed on the coast of South America about a year after Columbus visited it. He wrote an account of the voyage, but did not give his name to the continent himself; that was done by a German geographer in 1507.

AMERICAN INDIANS. The red people whom Columbus found living in the New World were called by him Indians, because he believed that the land which he had discovered was the west part of India ; and though it was soon proved that America had nothing to do with India, but was separated from Asia on the W. by the great Pacific Ocean, the name thus wrongly given has never been changed, and the islands which he first visited are still called the West Indies.

The Indians of North America, with a few exceptions, were all savages when they became known to Europeans, but they were not quite so low as many of them appear since they have learned the vices of the white man. They lived chiefly by hunting, though they tilled the soil in a rude way and raised corn and a few vegetables, the work being done by the women, for the men considered labor a disgrace. Their houses were mostly wigwams made of poles and skins, but some tribes built huts of wood, covered with bark or daubed with mud. They knew little of the arts, yet they made good boats and canoes, and showed much skill in forming their stone axes and hatchets, in making spears, bows and arrows, shields, and pipes, and in dressing sk.ns for clothes. According to all accounts, they were a happy and cheerful people, and fond of amusements and games, but in war they were cruel, sparing neither women nor children, and often torturing their prisoners before putting them to death. They did not fear to die, because they believed that man would live again after death, and would be happy or miserable according as he had behaved well or ill in this world.

They were divided into a great number of tribes, some containing as many as twenty or thirty thousand persons, but most of them being much smaller, each having its own country to live in, and each governed by chiefs called sachems. The tribes were generally divided into villages, each under the rule of a lower chief. The sachems were the rulers in time of peace, but in war the warriors were led by chiefs noted for skill and bravery. The names now commonly given to the different tribes are generally not their right ones, but names given them either by the whites or by other tribes of Indians as nicknames or to mark the places where they lived.

Though the Indians were divided into many tribes, each independent of the other, a large number of these tribes were alike in speaking the same, or nearly the same, language, so that they may all be classed in a few families or divisions. At least four fifths of all North America E. of the Rocky Mountains and N. of Mexico was peopled by four great families; namely, the Eskimos, the Athabascans, the Algonkins, and the Dakotas or Sioux.

The **Eskimos** lived along the shores of the Arctic or Northern Ocean, and down the Atlantic coast as far as the Gulf of St. Lawrence. They call themselves Innuits, which in their language means men; the name Eskimo (raw-flesh eaters) was given to them by the Algonkins, because they eat their food without cooking it.

The **Athabascans** lived south of the Eskimos, occupying a broad band of country from Hudson Bay to the Pacific, and almost to the great lakes below. On the W. side of the Rocky Mountains, some of them, under the names of Apaches, Navajos, and Lipans, have gone as far down as Mexico and Texas. Their name comes from Lake Athabasca, in British America.

The **Algonkins** occupied the Atlantic coast from the Eskimo country to North Carolina, and as far W. as the Mississippi River; but within their territory and surrounded by them was another family of Indians called Iroquois, told about below. To the Algonkin family belonged the New England tribes (including the Massachusetts Indians, the Narragansetts, Pequods, and Mohegans); the Delawares, and the Virginia and North Carolina Indians; the Ojibwas, Potawattamies, Chippewas, Otawas, and Crees, who lived along the great lakes; the Miamis, Shawnees, Sauks and Foxes, Menominees, and Kickapoos, of the country along the Mississippi; and the Blackfeet and Cheyennes, who lived first N.W. of the great lakes. All these Algonkin tribes spoke a language so nearly alike that they could easily understand each other. Most of the great men known to us in Indian history, such as King PHILIP, Canonchet, UNCAS, POWHATAN, BLACK HAWK, PONTIAC, and TECUMSEH, belonged to Algonkin tribes.

The name Algonkin, which was given to these tribes by the French, is supposed by some to be a changed form of an Indian word (*agomeegwin*) meaning people of the other shore.

The **Dakotas** lived between the Mississippi River and the Rocky Mountains, and between the Athabascans on the N. and the Arkansas River on the S. Among their tribes are the Dakotas or Sioux, Assiniboins, Iowas, Omahas, Poncas, Osages, Missouris, Kansas, Mandans, Ottoes, Arkansas, Minnetarees, Crows, and Winnebagoes. All the Dakotas were wandering tribes who did not till the ground much; they were tall and strong, and made daring hunters and bold warriors. The word Dakota is Indian, and means friends or allies.

The **Iroquois** were a fifth family living chiefly in what is now central and western New York, where, as said before, they were surrounded by Algonkin tribes. They were a brave and cruel race of warriors, who were often at war with their neighbors. When first known to the whites they were a nation made up of five tribes, the Mohawks, Oneidas, Onondagas, Cayugas, and Senecas; afterward the Tuscaroras were added to these, and then the whole were called by the English the Six Nations. The Hurons or Wyandots, the Eries, and some other tribes near the great lakes, also belonged to their family and spoke their language. RED JACKET and BRANDT were Iroquois.

The name Iroquois, which was given to them by the French, is a changed form of two Indian words (*hiro kouè*), much used in their councils or public meetings, the first meaning *I have said*, and the second being a word used by them for assent or applause, much like our *good*, which we cry out at public meetings when we like anything a speaker has said.

The **Cherokees** were a sixth family who lived along the Tennessee River and in the highlands of Tennessee, North Carolina, and Georgia. They spoke a language thought by some to be nearly like that of the Iroquois. In 1826 one of them named George GUESS made an alphabet of the language, having eighty-five letters in it, and they now print newspapers and books by means of it in their new home in the Indian Territory. It is not known what their name means.

The **Chahta-Muskokee,** another family, lived still further south in the present States of Georgia, Alabama, Florida, Mississippi, and part of Louisiana. Among their tribes were the Chahtas or Choctaws, Muskokees or Creeks, Chickasaws, Apalaches, Seminoles, and Natches.

These seven families occupied nearly all of North America E. of the Rocky Mountains when the whites came. West of the mountains the most important family is the Shoshones, which includes the Comanches and Utes; but there are also many others. Besides these savage Indians there were others in Mexico, Central, and South America who were more advanced toward civilization. Among these were those called Pueblo Indians, and the Aztecs, the Mayas, the Muyscas, and the Quichuas.

The **Pueblo Indians** were tribes living in New Mexico and Arizona, who were so called by the Spaniards because they lived in *pueblos* (Spanish for villages). They built large houses, sometimes of stone and sometimes of sun-dried bricks, usually several stories high, in which many families lived together. Some of these houses are standing now, and are still occupied by Indians. The lower story never has any doors or windows, and there are no stairs, those living in the houses getting in by ladders, which are afterward drawn up. Some of these houses have a great many rooms in them, and are often large enough to hold more than five hundred persons.

The **Aztecs** were the principal Indian nation of Mexico. They were still more advanced than the Pueblo Indians, though they were not what we call civilized. They built towns with large houses and temples of stone, worked most of the metals, wove cotton cloth, and made good earthenware; but they were ignorant of iron, and did not know the use of money, doing all their trading by barter; that is, by exchanging one kind of goods for another.

The **Mayas,** who lived in Yucatan and Central America, were perhaps more nearly civilized than even the Aztecs. They built the great stone temples whose ruins are still to be seen at Palenque, Uxmal, and other places. They had manufactures of many kinds, built sailing vessels, and carried on trade, and even had an alphabet and wrote books on paper made of the inner bark of trees. They had drums, too, and wind instruments, and used shells, cacao-beans, and pieces of copper for money.

The **Muyscas,** or Chibchas, who lived in what is now the United States of Colombia, in South America, built towns and great temples, carved in wood, bone, and stone, wove cotton cloth and dyed it of different colors, brewed a spirituous liquor out of maize, and made ornaments of gold.

The **Quichuas,** or Peruvians, were still more advanced. They paid great attention to farming, and made even deserts fertile by carrying water to them in aqueducts, built suspension-bridges, and made roads of stone many hundred miles long between their cities. Their houses were built of sun-dried bricks or of stone, with gables and arches; they worked mines of gold, silver, and copper, and made statues; wore clothes made of the wool of the llama and the alpaca; and wrote poetry, songs, and plays. They were governed by rulers called incas, whom they believed were descended from the sun, and they wor-

shiped the sun as a god and built great temples to it.

Besides these two nearly civilized nations, there were many more tribes in South America, some of which will be told about under the titles of the different countries where they lived; but they were most of them in a savage state, like the greater part of the North American Indians.

AMES (*aimz*), **Fisher,** an American statesman, born in Dedham, Mass., April 9, 1758. His father died when Fisher was six years old, but his mother took care of his education and sent him to Harvard College, where he was graduated when sixteen years old. He became a lawyer in Dedham, but when thirty-one years old (1789) he was elected to Congress, where he served eight years and showed himself to be one of the best debaters and speakers of his time. His writings have been published by his son. He died in Dedham in his fifty-first year (July 4, 1808).

AMHERST (*am'urst*), a town of Massachusetts, about eighty miles W. of Boston; pop. about 5000. It is chiefly noted for Amherst College (founded in 1821), which has fine museums and a library, and about 350 students. The Massachusetts Agricultural College (founded in 1866), about a mile north of the town, is the best school of the kind in the United States. The students work on the farm (300 acres) a certain number of hours every week, and are also drilled in military exercises.

AMHERST, Jeffery, usually called Lord Amherst, an English general, born in Kent, Jan. 29, 1717. He entered the army when fourteen years old, became a colonel when thirty-nine (1756), and came to America two years after as major-general. In 1759 he took TICONDEROGA from the French, then helped Gen. WOLFE conquer Canada, and finally succeeded Gen.

James ABERCROMBIE as commander-in-chief of the British armies in America. In 1763 he became governor of Virginia, and in 1776 was made a peer, with the title of Baron Amherst. He was afterward commander-in-chief of the British army (1772 to 1782 and 1793 to 1795), and was made a field-marshal (1796). He died the next year, when eighty years old (Aug. 3, 1797).

AMIENS (*am'e-enz*), a city of France, on the river Somme, 70 miles N. of Paris; pop. 80,000, or a little larger than Patterson, N. J. It has large wool and cotton factories; much cotton velvet is made there. The cathedral is one of the finest and largest in Europe. In one of the squares is a statue of PETER THE HERMIT, who was born there.

Amiens was called by the Romans *Samarobriva*, which means on the bank of the Samara or Somme. It was called by its present name because it was the capital of a Gallic tribe called the Ambiani, which means dwellers on the water.

AM'MON, a heathen god worshiped in ancient times in many countries. The Egyptians called him Amen-Ra (Ammon the Sun), the Greeks Zeus Ammon, and the Romans JUPITER Ammon. Ammon had a famous temple in Thebes, Egypt, and in the oasis of Ammonium in the Libyan desert. ALEXANDER THE GREAT visited the temple of Ammon in the desert, and afterward called himself the son of Ammon. The statues of the god were generally in the form of a ram, or of a man with a ram's head.

AMOOR, (*ah-moor*)', a river of N. E. Asia, forming part of the boundary between Siberia and China, and flowing into the Okhotsk Sea. It is about 2500 miles long, or more than the Volga, the longest river in Europe. It is navigable in the summer, but is frozen from November to March, when it is made a road for sledges.

The name Amoor is a changed form of the Mongol word *Mauran*, which means simply the river.

AM'STER-DAM, the largest city and the capital of the kingdom of the NETHERLANDS, situated at the mouth of the river Amstel; pop. 406,000, or nearly as large as Baltimore. It stands on low, flat, and marshy ground, and the houses are built on piles, or long sharpened beams, which are driven down forty or fifty feet into the hard earth below. Almost all the streets have a canal through the middle, by which the city is cut up into about 90 small islands, reached by nearly 300 bridges. Along the canals are neatly paved quays planted with trees. The waters of the ocean, which at high tide are higher than the city, are kept out by great dams fitted with gates; and these are so arranged that all the flat country around the city can be flooded to keep out an enemy.

In the beginning of the 13th century Amsterdam was a small fishing village, but between 1640 and 1750 it was the first city in Europe for trade. It is now one of the richest cities in the world, and has many fine public buildings. The most splendid one is the palace, built in 1655, which has in it a very large hall (111 feet long), lined with white Italian marble.

Amsterdam was formerly called Amsteldamme, which means the dam of the Amstel, and it was so named because a dam or dike was built there to keep out the water of the sea.

AMURATH (*ah'moo-rahth*) I., Sultan of the Ottoman Turks, born in 1326. He succeeded his father, Sultan Orchan, when thirty-three years old (1359), and soon invaded Europe, defeated the Christians everywhere, took ADRIANOPLE (1361), and made it his capital. His success was largely owing to his Janissaries (Turkish for New Soldiers). These were Christian boys, taken from the countries which he had conquered, and brought up as Mohammedans and trained as soldiers, and who, when they grew up, formed a very strong body of infantry.

While Amurath was absent in Asia, the Servians, whom he had conquered, rebelled. He hastened back, accompanied by his son BA-JAZET, and met the Servian army on the plains of Kossovo. His army was much smaller than that of the rebels, and as he had dream-ed the night before that he had been killed by an assassin, he did not like to fight them. But Baja-zet insisted, and after a bloody bat-tle the troops of Amurath gained a great victory. As the Sultan was walking over the field after the bat-tle, he was stabbed by a wounded Servian, and died in his sixty-fourth year (June 15, 1389).

AMURATH II., Sultan of the Ot-toman Turks, born about 1404. He succeeded his father, Mohammed I., when seventeen years old (1421), and two years after besieged Con-stantinople, but did not take it. He made war against Hungary, and was defeated several times by HUNYADY; but was at last victo-rious over him in a great battle on the plains of Kossovo (1448). Amurath died not long after, when forty-seven years old (Feb. 9, 1451). His son, Mohammed II., was the conqueror of Constantinople.

AMURATH IV., Sultan of the Ot-toman Turks, born in 1611. He suc-ceeded his uncle Mustapha when only twelve years old (1623). The principal event in his reign was the capture of BAGDAD (1638) from the Persians. Amurath finally gave himself up to drunkenness, and would sometimes rush out of his palace, sword in hand, and kill all he met in the streets; and at other times would sit in the window and shoot passers-by with his bow.

Happily for his people, he died when twenty-nine years old (Feb. 8, 1640).

A-NAC'RE-ON, a celebrated Greek poet, born at Teos in IONIA about 561 B.C. He lived some time in Samos and afterward in Athens, but not much is known about him. His poems were mostly odes and songs on love and wine, and he was so successful in this kind of writing that such poetry has ever since been called Anacreontic poetry. He is said to have died in his eighty-fifth year from being choked with a grape-stone.

ANAM (*ah-nahm'*), a kingdom of S. Asia, S. of China and E. of SIAM; area 107,000 square miles, or about as large as Colorado; pop. about 6,000,000, or about the same as that of New York State; under the pro-tection of France; capital, Hué. A range of mountains runs through the country from north to south. The principal river is the CAMBO-DIA or Mekong. The soil is fertile and produces much rice, cotton, sugar, and spices. The people are lazy and fond of gayety. Their lan-guage and customs are much like those of the Chinese, and in reli-gion they are mostly Buddhists.

The word Anam is said to mean the peace of the South.

AN-AX-AG'O-RAS, a celebrated Greek philosopher, born at Clazo-menæ, near Smyrna, in IONIA, about 500 B.C. He lived in Athens for thirty years, and had among his pupils PERICLES, SOCRATES, and EURIPIDES. He was among the first to teach that the sun is a mass of fiery matter and not a god, and that the moon does not shine by its own light (C. C. T., 405, I., u.). He also explained eclipses. For teaching these and other things which were then strange, he was banished for impiety, and died at Lampsacus, in Asia Minor, when seventy-two years old (428 B.C.). When on his death-bed, the magis-trates of the town sent to ask what

funeral honors he wished. "Give all
the boys a play-day," he answered ;
and for several centuries the day of
his death was kept as a holiday in
all the schools of Lampsacus.

A·NAX·I·MAN'DER, a noted Greek
philosopher, born at Miletus, Asia
Minor, 610 B.C. He is said to have
invented the sun-dial (C. C. T.,
134, II.), and to have been the first
to write a geography and to make
maps. He died when sixty-three
years old (547 B.C.).

A·NAX·IM'E·NES, a Greek historian, who lived in Lampsacus, Asia
Minor, about 350 B.C. He wrote a
history of Philip of Macedon and
of Alexander the Great, both of
which are lost. When Alexander
was about to destroy Lampsacus,
because its citizens sided with the
Persians against him, Anaximenes
saved the city by his ready wit.
When he came to beg that the city
might be spared, Alexander, knowing what he had come for, exclaimed : "I swear I will not grant
your request." "I implore you
then," said Anaximenes,"to destroy
Lampsacus, and make slaves of its
citizens." Alexander kept his word
and spared the city.

ANCÆUS (*an-see'us*), a fabled son
of NEPTUNE, and pilot of the ship
Argo in the expedition of the Argonauts. He was once told by one
of his servants, whom he pressed
with hard labor in his vineyard,
that he would never drink any wine
of his own making. He made
some, and called to his servant to
see him drink. The servant replied : "There is many a slip between the cup and the lip." Just
then Ancæus was told that a wild
boar had broken into the vineyard.
He set down his cup untasted, and
ran to drive out the boar, by which
he was killed.

ANCHISES (*an-ki'seez*). See
ÆNEAS.

ANCONA (*ahn-ko'nah*), a city of
Italy, on the Adriatic Sea, N. E. of
Rome ; pop. 48,000, or about as

large as Oakland, Cal. It is finely
situated, and has a good harbor and
a large trade. It is a very old city
and was an important port even in
the time of the Emperor TRAJAN,
who built there a mole 2000 feet
long, with a triumphal arch on it.
This arch, which is still standing, is
thought to be the finest in the
world. Ancona was so named because it is built in a bend of the
coast, the name being made from
the Greek word *angkon*, the bend
of the arm.

AN'CUS MARTIUS (*mar'she-us*),
the fourth king of Rome, said to
have been the grandson of NUMA.
He succeeded TULLUS Hostilius,
and reigned, it is said, from 640 to
616 B.C. He enlarged the walls
of Rome, built the first prison in
the city, and made a port named
Ostia at the mouth of the Tiber.

ANDALUSIA (*ahn-dah-loo'she-ah*).
See SPAIN.

ANDERSEN (*ahn'der-sen*), **Hans
Christian,** a famous Danish writer

Andersen.

for young folks, born at Odense, in
the island of Fünen, April 2, 1805.
His father was a poor shoemaker,
who lived with his wife and Hans
in one small room. He died when
Hans was nine years old, and his

mother, who had to do washing for their support, wanted Hans to be a tailor, but he had higher notions. He was first put to work in a factory and then sent to school, but he ran away from both because the boys laughed at his ugliness and awkwardness, and thinking it best to let him do as he pleased, she gave him some money to go to Copenhagen. There he was for some time employed in the theatre, and for a while lived on charity, but at last became acquainted with the Councillor Collin, who, noticing his brightness, got the King to have him educated at the expense of the State.

Hans then studied at the preparatory school, and finally went through the University of Copenhagen. He had written when quite young a few poems which had been liked by some but laughed at by others; but when about finishing his studies (1829) he published a book called "A Journey on Foot to Amak," in which he made fun of everything, and which had a large sale. With the money which he got from this he made a journey through several parts of Denmark, during which he fell in love with a beautiful young girl; but, unfortunately, she was engaged to another man, and as Andersen never met with any other woman whom he liked as well, he never married.

The King of Denmark now gave him money to travel, and he visited Germany, France, and Italy. He wrote some poems in France, and in Italy began his great novel, "The Improvisatore," which is a fine picture of scenery and manners in the south of Europe. He then wrote two more novels, "Only a Fiddler" and "O. T." These letters stand for *Odense Tugthus* (Odense Penitentiary), where the hero of the story is born. Like other criminals, he has the two letters burned into his arm, and in after years they lead to many strange adventures.

These stories made Andersen a great reputation, and the government gave him an annual salary, which was continued until his death. Among his other books are "Fairy Tales," "Wonder Stories," "Picture Book without Pictures," "A Poet's Bazaar," "The Story of My Life," and "New Fairy Tales." His books have been translated into all the languages of Europe, and even Chinese, Japanese, and Hindostanee boys and girls read his stories.

Hans Christian Andersen was very tall and thin, and stooped much when he walked. He wore clothes, too, which were old-fashioned and too large for him, and his picture shows that he was not handsome; but he never walked the streets of Copenhagen without attracting crowds of children. The boys took off their hats to him and the girls courtesied as he passed, and he had a kind word for all. Everybody mourned when he died in Copenhagen at the age of seventy years (Aug. 4, 1875), and flowers were sent for his funeral from many parts of Denmark, and even from Norway, Sweden, and Germany; and when subscriptions were taken up to erect a monument to him, everybody was anxious to give something to help honor the poor shoemaker's son who had done so much for the children of all the world.

ANDES (*an'deez*), the range of mountains along the northern and western coasts of South America. It is the greatest chain in the world, for the Himalayas, though higher in parts, do not have so great an average height for so long a distance. The Andes are about 4500 miles long, and have an average height of nearly two and a half miles (12,000 feet), while their bases spread over a breadth of country 50 to 350 miles wide. Along this range rise numerous peaks three to four miles high, whose tops are always covered with snow, and many of which are burning volcanoes. Even on the equator, in the hottest parts of the country, snow lies all the year round on peaks which are about three miles high, and in the southern parts, where the climate is much colder, it is always seen on parts less than a mile high. The highest peak of the Andes, and the highest mountain in the New World, is believed to be Aconcagua in Chili, which is about four and a quarter miles (22,422 feet) high, though some books make Sorata in Bolivia much higher; but the latest measurements make Sorata only 21,288 feet. The volcano of Sahama in Bolivia (22,350 feet) is probably, next after Aconcagua, the highest mountain in America. Aconcagua is not a volcano, though it is called so in many books. Chimborazo · in Ecuador (21,422 feet) was long thought to be the highest mountain in the world, but it is now known to be only the sixth among the Andes. Cotopaxi in Ecuador (19,500 feet) is the highest active volcano in the world, and

Cotapaxi.

one of the most terrible. Both Chimborazo and Cotopaxi were visited in 1880 by Edward Whymper, who climbed up to their tops. The showers of ashes and clouds of smoke which pour from the summit of Cotopaxi often shut out the light of the sun so as to make the country around it almost as dark as night.

The Andes are much steeper on the west side toward the Pacific Ocean than on the east, where they slope away little by little into the great plains. In some places they spread out into several chains with high plains between. In one of these great plains in Bolivia is Lake TITICACA, the largest lake in South America, and in the south part of the same plain, which is called the table-land of Desaguadero, is the city of POTOSI, the highest city on the earth, it being more than two and a half miles (13,330 feet) above the sea.

This great chain of mountains is much like an immense wall built through the whole length of South America, and almost cutting off trade between the Pacific coast and the east part. No rivers run through it, as in the case of most other mountain ranges, and there are no breaks in it; the only way of crossing is by wild rugged passes, most of which are very high, some being so blocked with snow in winter as to be impassable. Over these steep, narrow paths, which often wind along the edge of precipices, where a misstep might cause one to fall and be dashed to pieces on the rocks below, long trains of mules carry goods from the sea-coast inland and return laden with silver ore and other products of the mountains.

The Andes are rich in all kinds of minerals, especially in silver and copper, and most of the emeralds now sold come from the mines of Tunca, near Bogota. As they have all kinds of climate, so they have a great variety of plants and trees, from those which grow in the hottest places to those which are found in places near everlasting snow. In the highest parts of the Andes are found the alpaca and the llama, (C.C.T., 363, II, l.), the latter being much used by the Indians as a beast of burden, and the condor is seen flying even over the snowy peaks. The inhabitants, mostly Indians and Spanish-Americans, live principally in the high table-lands.

Andes means copper mountains, the word being made from the Peruvian *anta*, copper.

ANDORRA (*ahn-dor'rah*), a small republic in the Pyrenees Mountains, between France and Spain; area 190 square miles, or about three times as large as the District of Columbia; pop. about 12,000. It is a valley surrounded by high mountains, and the people are mostly farmers and cattle-raisers. This little republic has been free ever since the time of CHARLES THE GREAT, who gave the people the right to govern themselves because they helped him against the Moors.

AN'DO-VER, a town of Massachusetts, on the Merrimack river, 21 miles N. of Boston; pop. about 6000. It is chiefly noted as being the seat of Phillips Academy, a fine school for preparing boys for college; Abbot Female Academy, for the education of female teachers; and Andover Theological Seminary, for educating Congregational ministers.

Andover was settled in 1641, and was named from Andover, Hampshire, England, from which many of its first people came.

ANDRE (*an'dra*), **John,** a British officer hanged as a spy in the war of the Revolution, born of Swiss parents in London in 1751. He came to America when twenty-three years old (1774) as a lieutenant, and was a great favorite in society, both in Philadelphia and New York, where he was stationed, for he had lively and pleasant manners and could draw and paint and cut silhouette pictures, and sing and write verses. Some of the pictures which he drew and verses which he made in those happy days are still greatly prized by those who own them.

When twenty-eight years old (1779) he became adjutant-general of the British army with the rank of major, and soon after (1780) began to plot with Gen. Benedict ARNOLD, who wanted to betray his country. Arnold, who commanded at West Point, then the strongest and most important fort belonging to the Americans, agreed to give it into the power of the British, and to finish his plans for this desired to have a talk with André. André went up the Hudson, and one dark night was rowed ashore in a boat from the sloop-of-war Vulture and met Arnold in the woods below Stony Point. Morning came before they had done talking, and some Americans beginning to fire on the Vulture, she was obliged to go down the river. André, thus left within the American lines, was liable to capture at any moment. and had to hasten across the river and travel on horseback to New York. He changed his uniform for common clothes, and took the name of John Anderson. Arnold gave him a passport and six papers in his own handwriting, showing the British how the fort could be taken, which André hid in his stocking.

André rode on in safety until he came near Tarrytown, where three men with guns stopped him. "Gentlemen," said André, who thought they were Tories, "I hope you belong to our party?" "What party?" asked one of the men. "The lower party," replied André, meaning the British. "We do," was the answer. André then told them he was a British officer who must not be detained a minute, when, to his surprise, they said they were Americans, and that he was their prisoner. He then told them that he was

Andre. Drawn by himself.

an American officer, and showed them Gen. Arnold's passport. But the suspicions of his captors were now aroused, and they searched him and found Arnold's papers in his stocking André offered them his horse and watch, or any reward they might name. if they would let him go, but they were not to be bribed.

The prisoner was taken to Tappan, the headquarters of the American army, tried as a spy and condemned to be hanged. Sir Henry Clinton, the British commander in New York, did all he could to save him, and Washington gave him every fair chance, but by the rules of war he had to die and he was hanged at Tappan on the morning of Oct. 2, 1780, when only twenty-nine years old. While a prisoner he made himself so dear to all by the sweetness of his character and the charm of his conversation that his sad fate was as much lamented by the American officers as by the English. The day before his death he drew, with pen and ink, a likeness of himself, which is now owned by Yale College. The copy given of this is much smaller than the original. In 1821 his remains, which had been buried under the gallows were removed to England and placed in Westminster Abbey under a beautiful marble monument and in 1879 a monument to his memory was erected on the place of his execution at Tappan.

The names of André's captors were John Paulding, David Williams, and Isaac Van Wart. Congress gave each of them a pension of $200 a year and a silver medal, and in 1853 a monument was erected to their memory on the place where they captured André. John Paulding was the father of Rear-Admiral Hiram Paulding who died in 1878.

AN-DROM'E-DA, in Greek fable, a princess of Ethiopia, daughter of King Cepheus and Cassiopea. Her mother boasted that her daughter was more beautiful than the NERE-IDS, upon which NEPTUNE sent a sea-monster to ravage the country. An oracle said that the monster would go away if Andromeda were given to it, so she was chained to a rock by the shore; but PERSEUS killed the monster, rescued her, and made her his wife. After her death, Andromeda was made a constellation in the sky.

AN'DROS, Sir **Edmund,** an English gentleman, born in London, Dec. 6, 1637. When thirty-five years old (1672) he was a major in Prince Rupert's regiment of dragoons, and two years after was sent to this country as Governor of New York. In 1681 he went back to England, and was made a knight. Five years afterward (1686) he was sent out again as Governor of New England, and treated the colonists so harshly that he became very hateful to them. The people of Connecticut having held out against him, he went to Hartford with some soldiers, and bade them give up their charter—that is, the written paper, signed by King Charles II., which gave them the right to govern themselves. The General Assembly of the colony, which was then in session, received Sir Edmund in their hall, and kept him talking until night. Candles were then lighted, and the charter was brought in a box and laid upon the table. The room was filled with people, who did not look with very friendly eyes on the soldiers brought by Sir Edmund to force them to give up their rights. All at once the lights were blown out and the room was left in darkness and in silence, for no one spoke a word. When the candles were lighted again, the charter was nowhere to be seen, and all efforts to find it were vain.

Andros's tyranny lasted only till 1689, when King WILLIAM III., who had just come to the throne, ordered him back to England. The charter was then found again, and the story of its hiding was made known. When the lights were put out it was secretly carried out of the hall and put in the hollow of an oak tree. This tree was very old, and the story is told of it that when some one of the early settlers of Hartford was about to cut it down, the Indians begged that it might be spared, for it has been the guide of our people for centuries, they said, "as to the time of planting our corn. When the leaves are of the size of a mouse's ears, then is the time to put the seed in the ground." So the tree was permitted to stand, and after it had become famous as the hiding-place of the charter, it was known as the Charter Oak and reverenced by all the people of Connecticut as sacred to liberty. A few years ago the old tree was blown down, and nothing remains of it now but the stump on which it stood, and the pieces of its wood which were saved as relics.

Sir Edmund Andros was made Governor of Virginia in 1692, and returned six years after to England, where he died at the age of seventy-seven (Feb. 24, 1714).

ANGELICO (*ahn-jel'-e-ko*), **Fra,** an Italian painter, born at Mugello, Tuscany, in 1387. His real name is said to have been Giovanni Guido, but when twenty years old he became a monk in a monastery near Fiesole, and changed it to Giovanni da Fiesole. The rest of his life was spent in religious duties and in painting. He painted only sacred subjects, and his angels and saints were so beautiful that his countrymen called him *Angelico* (Italian, the angelic). He died in Rome when sixty-eight years old (1455).

ANGELO. See MICHAEL ANGELO

ANGERS (*an'jerz*), a city of France, on the Mayenne River near the Loire, 161 miles S. W. of Paris; pop. 73,000, or nearly as large as Fall River, Mass. It has manufactures of linen, cotton, woolen, and silk, and there are large slate quarries near by. Its university, once famous, was destroyed in the Revolution. Angers was a Roman city called Juliomagus. It gets its present name from the Andegavi, a people who lived near its site.

AN'GLES. See ANGLO-SAXONS.

AN'GLO SAX'ONS, the common name of several German tribes who conquered Britain after the Romans left it. They were mostly from three tribes, called Angles, Saxons, and Jutes. The Angles lived in the part of Schleswig still called Angeln, the Saxons in the country between the rivers Elbe and Eider, and the Jutes in what is now South Jutland. As soon as the Romans withdrew their troops from Britain (about 410) and left the Britons to take care of themselves, the German tribes began to invade the island. They were fierce heathen, who slew or made slaves of those whom they overcame, and drove the rest into the western part of the island. The Germans everywhere called the people of the Roman provinces Welsh (German *wälsch*, foreign) or foreigners, and the Anglo-Saxons in Britain gave the same name to the Britons, and their descendants are still known as Welsh, while the west part of the island to which they were driven is called Wales to this day.

The German tribes in Britain grew into one people under the name of Anglo-Saxons, though it would be better to call them Angles or English, for it was the Angles who finally gave their name to the country and changed Britain into England (Engla-land). The Anglo-Saxons cared nothing for the language, laws, or arts of the Romans, but kept their own language and religion. They did not become Christians until about the sixth century, and the language which we speak, though changed much, is still in its main substance the same as that of our heathen ancestors.

AN-NAP'O-LIS, a city, capital of Maryland, 28 miles S. of Baltimore

and 40 E. of Washington; pop. about 8000. It is chiefly noted as the seat of the United States Naval Academy, founded there in 1845, where officers of the navy are educated. There are usually about 370 students in the Academy who, after four years' study there and two years' service at sea, are examined for admission to the navy as midshipmen. While students, they are called cadet midshipmen, excepting those studying to be engineers, who are called cadet engineers.

Annapolis was settled in 1649, and was first called Providence; but it was finally given its present name in honor of Queen ANNE, it being made from Anna and *polis*, the Greek word for city.

ANN AR'BOR, a city of Michigan, 38 miles W. of Detroit; pop. about 9000. It is chiefly noted as the seat of Michigan University, founded in 1837, which has usually about 2500 students. Belonging to it are fine libraries, museums, and an astronomical observatory.

AN'NE, Queen of Great Britain and Ireland, daughter of JAMES II., born at Twickenham, near London, Feb. 6, 1664. She was married to Prince George of Denmark, and became Queen on the death of her brother-in-law, WILLIAM III. (1702), who left no children. In her reign took place the war with France called the war of the Spanish Succession, in which the Duke of MARLBOROUGH won great victories, and during which GIBRALTAR and NOVA SCOTIA were gained by England. In her reign also (1707) was brought about the union of England and Scotland into one kingdom by the name of Great Britain, so that she was the first sovereign styled of Great Britain. Queen Anne, who was the last of the family of Stuart who sat on the throne of England, died when fifty years old (Aug. 1, 1714). Her reign has been called the Augustan age of English literature, because it was noted for its great writers, among whom were ADDISON, POPE, SWIFT, STEELE, and DEFOE.

ANNE OF AUSTRIA, Queen of France, daughter of PHILIP III., King of Spain, born Sept. 22, 1601. When fourteen years old she was married to LOUIS XIII., King of France, and twenty-three years afterward (1638) she became the mother of Louis XIV. During the reign of her husband she suffered greatly from neglect and lived much of the time in exile and poverty, but on his death (1643), when Louis XIV. was only five years old, she became regent of the Kingdom. Cardinal MAZARIN, her minister, ruled France in her name, and is even supposed by some to have been married to her. She died when sixty-five years old (Jan. 20, 1666). She was called Anne of Austria from her mother, who was daughter of the German Emperor Maximilian II. Queen Anne is said to have been very fond of perfumes and of flowers, but to have hated roses so that she could not look at even a picture of one.

ANNE BOLEYN (*bul'len*), Queen of England, daughter of Sir Thomas Boleyn, born about 1507. She passed some years at the court of France, and when about twenty years old became maid of honor to Queen Catharine, wife of Henry VIII., of England. She was beautiful and lively, and soon attracted the attention of the King, who asked the Pope to divorce him from Catharine in order that he might marry Anne; but as the Pope was unwilling to do this, for fear of offending the Emperor CHARLES V., who was the nephew of Queen Catharine, Henry married Anne privately (Jan. 25, 1533). In the following May, Archbishop Cranmer pronounced Henry's marriage with Catharine void, and declared that Anne was his true wife. Catharine died in the beginning of 1536, and soon after Queen Anne lost the favor of the King, and was tried, found guilty, and beheaded (May 19, 1536) on a charge of unfaithfulness. Anne was the mother of Queen ELIZABETH.

AN'SELM, Saint, Archbishop of Canterbury, born in Piedmont about 1033. He was wild in his youth, but when twenty-seven years ol1 entered the monastery of Bec in Normandy, of which he became abbot in 1078. King WILLIAM RUFUS invited him to England and made him Archbishop of Canterbury in 1093. He had much trouble with King William and with HENRY I., and was obliged for several years to leave England. He was a very pious and scholarly man, and wrote some very learned books. He died when seventy-six years old (April 21, 1109).

AN'SON, George, Lord, a noted English admiral, born in Staffordshire, April 23, 1697. He entered the navy when a boy, and became a captain when twenty-seven years old (1724). In 1740 he was sent to the South Pacific to do what harm he could to the shipping and settlements of Spain, with which England was then at war. He lost most of his ships, and many of his crew died of scurvy, but he captured some rich prizes, and sailed round the world, exploring on the way many of the islands of the Pacific, and returning home after a voyage of three years and nine months (June, 1744). His account of his cruise, called "Voyage Round the World," was very popular and was translated into many languages. He was made an admiral, and in 1747 captured the French East India fleet, off Cape Finisterre, for which he was made a peer, with the title of Lord Anson, Baron of Soberton. He was First Lord of the Admiralty when he died, at the age of sixty-five (June 6, 1762).

AN-TÆ'US, in Greek fable, a giant of Lybia, son of Neptune and Terra. He obliged all who came to Lybia to wrestle with him, and he was so strong that he boasted that he would build a temple to Neptune out of the skulls of those whom he overthrew. Hercules, learning that he got all his strength from the earth, lifted him in his arms and strangled him.

ANT-ARC'TIC O'CEAN, or Southern Ocean, that part of the ocean which lies between the South Pole and the Antarctic Circle. It has not been explored as much as the Arctic Ocean, because there is more ice in it.

It gets its name from the Greek words *anti,* opposite, and *arktos,* a bear, and it is so called because it is opposite the constellation called the Great Bear.

AN'THON, Charles, author of a "Dictionary of Greek and Roman Antiquities" and of many Greek and Latin school books, was born in New York, Nov. 19, 1797. His father, a German by birth, was a surgeon in the British army, and settled in New York after the war of the Revolution. Charles was graduated at Columbia College when eighteen years old (1815), and became a lawyer, but was soon elected assistant professor of ancient languages in Columbia College, and in 1835 full professor. He wrote about fifty works, all of which were republished in England. He died in New York when seventy years old (July 29, 1867).

ANTHONY (*an'to-ny*), **Saint,** a Christian hermit, born in Egypt in 251. He was rich and well educated, but gave all he had to the poor and went to live in the desert, where he spent many years clothed simply in a hair shirt and never washing himself. Having become noted as a holy man, many flocked to him, and he became the head of a society of hermits near Memphis. These are said to have been the first monks, and Saint Anthony is called therefore the founder of monasteries. He is also said to have cured a skin disease now called erysipelas, but which was long known as Saint Anthony's fire. He died when one hundred and five years old (356).

ANTIETAM (*an-te'tam*), the name of a small but deep river in Maryland, emptying into the Potomac about six miles above HARPER'S FERRY, between which and the town of Sharpsburg was fought the battle of Antietam, Sept. 16 and 17, 1862. In this battle the Union army of about 87,000 men was commanded by Gen. McCLELLAN, and the Confederate army of about 70,000 men by Gen. Robert E. LEE. After fighting for two days, the Confederates asked on the morning of the 18th for time to bury their dead, which was given them, and the following night they retreated across the Potomac. The Union loss in killed, wounded, and missing was about 12,500, while the Confederates, who fought much of the time under cover of the woods, lost only about 9,000.

AN-TIG'O-NE, in Greek fable, a daughter of ŒDIPUS, King of Thebes. When Œdipus, on finding out that he had killed his father and married his own mother, put out his eyes in despair, she guided him to Attica and took care of him until his death. Her brothers, Polynices and Eteocles, having both been killed in quarreling for the throne of Thebes, she buried Polynices, though Creon, who after their death had become ruler of Thebes, had commanded that no one should do so. For this he ordered her to be buried alive, and her lover Hæmon, son of Creon, killed himself by her side. Her story is told by SOPHOCLES, in his tragedy called "Antigone."

AN-TIG'O-NUS, one of the most famous generals of Alexander the Great, born about 382 B.C. When the empire was divided on the death of Alexander, he got as his share Lycia, Pamphylia, and Greater Phrygia, in ASIA MINOR. He tried to enlarge his dominions, and having made himself master of a large part of Asia, took the title of King of Asia. PTOLEMY, LYSIMACHUS, SELEUCUS, and Cassander, other generals of Alexander made a league against him, and Antigonus was finally defeated and killed at the age of eighty-one in a great battle at Ipsus in Phrygia (301 B.C.). His son Demetrius Poliorcetes (Besieger, because he besieged many cities) became King of Macedonia (294), and his grandson Antigonus Gonatas (so called from his native town, Gona, in Thessaly) succeeded him (277), and his descendants held the throne until the country was conquered by the Romans.

ANTIGUA (*ahn-ti'gah*). See WEST INDIES.

ANTILLES (*ahn-teel'*). See WEST INDIES.

AN·TIN'O·US, a beautiful youth, page of the Emperor HADRIAN, drowned in the Nile A.D. 132. He was much loved by Hadrian, and is said to have drowned himself because an oracle had foretold that a great danger to the Emperor could be turned aside only by the death of the person whom he loved best. A city called Antinoöpolis (Greek for City of Antinous) was built near where he perished, a star was named after him, he was made a god, and many statues of him were erected. Several of these statues are still preserved, and are very beautiful, especially two now in Rome.

ANTIOCH (*an'te-ok*), an ancient city of Syria, on the river Orontes, built by SELEUCUS NICATOR about 300 B.C. Seleucus built sixteen cities of this name in memory of his father Antiochus, one of the generals of PHILIP of Macedon, but this one was the most magnifi-

cent of all. The ancients called it "Antioch the Beautiful," and it was for a long time the most famous city of the East. Its people were noted for luxury, intelligence, and wit, and they are said to have first given the followers of Jesus Christ the nickname of Christians as a jest. Antioch has been nearly destroyed several times by earthquakes, in one of which (526) 250,000 people were killed. It has also suffered much from sieges, and has been several times taken and nearly destroyed. It is now called by the Turks Antakieh, and has only about 12,000 inhabitants.

ANTIOCHUS (*an-ti'o-kus*), the name of several Kings of Syria, of the family called the Seleucidæ, because they were descendants of SELEUCUS NICATOR.

Antiochus I., Soter, son of Seleucus Nicator, born about 325 B.C., succeeded his father in 280. He gained a great victory over the Gauls (275) by means of his elephants, and took from it the name of Soter (Greek for Saviour). He was killed near Ephesus in battle with the Gauls (261 B.C.).

Antiochus II., Theos, son of Antiochus I., succeeded his father in 261. He was given the title Theos (Greek for God) by the people of Miletus because he put to death their tyrant Timarchus. To please PTOLEMY III. (Euergetes), King of Egypt, he put away his wife Laodice and married Berenice, Ptolemy's daughter. When Ptolemy died he took Laodice back, but she revenged herself by poisoning him (246), and killed Berenice and her son to make her own son, Seleucus Callinicus, King.

Antiochus III., the Great, son of Seleucus Callinicus, born about 238 B.C. He became King when only fifteen years old (223). His kingdom, of which ANTIOCH was the capital, included, besides Syria, Babylonia, Media, and part of Asia Minor. He even carried his arms into India, and crossed over into Europe and attacked Thrace (196). This brought him into trouble with the Romans, and HANNIBAL, who had taken refuge with him after being driven from Carthage, advised him to march at once into Italy. But he did not move till 192, and the next year he was defeated by the Romans at Thermopylæ. Two years afterward (189), the Romans crossed over into Asia, and Antiochus was totally defeated at Magnesia by Lucius SCIPIO, and had to give up all his dominions, except Syria. He was also obliged to pay the expenses of the war, and to give up to the Romans all his elephants and ships. While attempting to plunder the temple of Jupiter at Elymais, to raise money for the Romans, he was killed by the people (187 B.C.).

Antiochus IV., Epiphanes (Illustrious), a younger son of Antiochus III., was given up by his father as a hostage to the Romans (188), by whom he was kept twelve years. He succeeded his brother, Seleucus Philopater, as King in 175. He recovered Palestine, sacked Jerusalem and plundered the Temple, and conquered nearly all of Egypt, but left that country when ordered away by the Romans (168). His cruel persecution of the Jews caused a great insurrection, during which his armies were often defeated. He died in 164 B.C.

AN·TI'PA·ROS, a small island of the Grecian Archipelago, S. W. of PAROS, noted for a wonderful cave called the grotto of Antiparos. Its entrance is on the side of a mountain, about two miles from the coast, and the descent into the grotto is long, slippery, and dangerous; but when the bottom is reached the visitor enters into a very large cavern, the roof of which, higher than a four-story house, and the walls are of pure white marble. When this is lighted up with torches, the sight is mag-

nificent: the glistening marble takes the shape of columns, screens, trees, flowers, and other beautiful forms, and long pendants reach from the roof in many places and join crystallized pillars rising from the floor, so that the arch above appears to be upheld by them.

AN·TIP'A·TER, a Macedonian general, made ruler of Macedonia when ALEXANDER THE GREAT marched into Asia, born about 390 B.C. When the empire was divided after the death of Alexander, Antipater received Macedonia and Greece. The Athenians and some others of the Greeks having revolted, he defeated them at Crannon (322), and demanded that DEMOSTHENES should be given up to him, but the great orator escaped him by taking poison. Antipater died when seventy-one years old (319).

AN·TO·NI'NUS, Marcus Aurelius, a Roman Emperor, son-in-law of Antoninus Pius, born in Rome, A.D. 121. He became Emperor on the death of Antoninus Pius (161), and was as renowned as that good ruler for virtue and wisdom. He carried on several successful wars, during which he was absent from Rome for years at a time, and he won the love and esteem of his soldiers by his simple habits, and by sharing their hardships and dangers. The only blot on his character is that he permitted the Christians to be persecuted; and it is thought very strange that he did this because he wrote a famous book called "Meditations," in which the thoughts differ but little from the teachings of Christ. Marcus Aurelius died at Vindobona, now Vienna, when fifty-nine years old (Mar. 17, 180).

AN·TO·NI'NUS PI'US, Titus Aurelius Fulvius, a Roman Emperor, born at Lanuvium, near Rome, Sept. 19, A.D. 86. He was adopted by the Emperor HADRIAN, and became his successor (138). His reign was happy and prosperous, and he was so much loved that he was given the title of *Pater Patriæ* (Father of his Country), and was also called *Pius* (Pious). He did not carry on any wars for conquest, but took good care of all parts of the Empire. When told of conquering heroes, he replied: "I prefer the life and safety of a citizen to the death of a hundred enemies." He died when seventy-four years old (Mar. 7, 161), and was succeeded by Marcus Aurelius AN-TONINUS.

AN'TO-NY, Mark (in Latin, Marcus Antonius), a noted Roman general, born in Rome, 83 B.C. He spent his youth in pleasure, and got so deeply in debt that he had to run away to Greece, where he finished his studies. Soon after, he joined the army and fought bravely in Syria and in Egypt, and in Gaul under Cæsar, who helped him to get into office in Rome. While there, he talked so strongly in favor of Cæsar that he was forced to run away disguised as a slave and seek refuge in Cæsar's camp (49 B.C.). He helped Cæsar to get into power and was made his commander of cavalry when he became dictator; and he and Cæsar became consuls together in 44 B.C.

When Cæsar was killed, most of the assassins wanted to kill Antony also, but Brutus saved him. At the funeral of Cæsar, Antony made an artful speech, which excited the people so much that the conspirators were forced to flee from the city, leaving him in full power; and he would probably have succeeded Cæsar as dictator, if Cicero had not got the senate to take the side of Octavius (AUGUSTUS) against him. Antony fled, but afterward made friends with Octavius, and the two formed with LEPIDUS, a government called the Second Triumvirate (43), in which the three ruled equally. They put great numbers of their enemies to death,

among them Cicero, whom Antony caused to be murdered.

After defeating BRUTUS and CASSIUS at Philippi (42), Antony was given the government of Macedonia, Greece, and the provinces in Asia. He now gave himself up to luxury and vice, and having fallen in love with CLEOPATRA, Queen of Egypt, he deserted his wife, Octavia, sister of Octavius, for her sake. This made Octavius very angry and he sent an army and a fleet against him. Antony and Cleopatra were defeated at the battle of ACTIUM, and fled to Egypt, where Octavius followed them. Hearing a false report that Cleopatra had killed herself, he stabbed himself with his sword. When he heard that she was still living, he ordered himself to be carried to her, and died in her presence in his fifty-fourth year (30 B.C.). Antony is a principal character in two of Shakespeare's plays, "Julius Cæsar" and "Antony and Cleopatra."

ANT'WERP, the principal seaport of Belgium, on the river Scheldt, 45 miles from the sea; pop. 210,000, or a little larger than Detroit, Mich. As it is the most important place for trade in Belgium, it is very strongly fortified, and in time of war much of the flat country around it can be flooded with water. The cathedral of Antwerp, one of the finest in Europe, has a steeple so beautifully carved that it is said to look like Mechlin lace. Some of the best pictures of RUBENS and of other great artists are in it.

Antwerp was a city a thousand years ago. In the 15th and 16th centuries it was the centre of the trade of Europe, and had a much larger population than now. Its velvets, silks, and satins, were famous, and its merchants sent ships all over the world. The city has suffered many sieges, among the most noted of which was that of 1585, when it was taken by the Duke of Parma, the commander of the King of Spain, after a siege of thirteen months ; and that of 1832, when it was taken by the French.

Antwerp is called by the French Anvers, and by the Dutch Antwerpen. The name means the town "at the wharf."

APACHES (*ah-pah'chayz*). See AMERICAN INDIANS.

APELLES (*a-pel'leez*), the most famous of the Greek painters. It is not known where he was born, nor where he died ; but he lived in the time of ALEXANDER THE GREAT, whose friend he was, and whom he is said to have accompanied on his march into Asia. It is said, too, that Alexander would let no other artist paint his portrait, and one of Apelles' most famous pictures was Alexander holding lightning in his hand. But his most celebrated picture was " VENUS Rising from the Sea," painted for a temple in Cos. The Emperor Augustus carried it from there to Rome and put it in the temple of Julius Cæsar, where it was kept until age destroyed it.

Apelles is said to have painted another picture of Alexander with a horse, but the King did not like the horse much. Just then a horse passing by neighed at the one in the picture, upon which the painter said : " One would think that the horse is a better judge of painting than your majesty."

He used sometimes to hide behind his pictures to see what the people would say about them. One day he heard a cobbler find fault with the shoes on one of his figures. The artist, seeing that he was right, changed it. The next day the same man began to find fault with a leg, when Apelles put out his head and told him he had better keep to what he knew about. From this is said to have come the saying : " Let not the cobbler go beyond his last."

AP'EN-NINES, a chain of mountains in Europe extending from a branch of the Alps called the Maritime Alps, near Genoa, through the whole of Italy to the Strait of Messina on the south. They are generally about three-fourths of a mile high, but have many higher peaks, the highest, Monte Corno, near Aguila, being about one mile and three-quarters (9540 feet). The lower parts of the Apennines are covered with woods, but the upper parts are bare and rocky.

The word Apennines is made from the Celtic *pen*, meaning the top of a hill.

A'PIS, a bull worshipped by the ancient Egyptians, who thought the soul of OSIRIS lived in it. It was kept in Memphis, where it had a temple and priests to take care of it. When Apis got to be twenty-five years old, he was secretly killed by the priests, and his body embalmed and placed in a tomb. Many of these have been found in Egypt, and one is to be seen in almost any large museum. After his death all Egypt went into mourning until the priests found a new calf Apis, which had to be black with a white square or three-cornered spot on the forehead, and with various other marks on the body.

A-POL'LO, one of the principal gods of the Greeks, son of JUPITER and LATONA, and the twin brother of DIANA. He was called the god of light, and was therefore named also Phœbus and Phœbus Apollo, Phœbus being at first a name for the sun. He was said to have been born in Delos, from which he was sometimes called Delius. He was also the god of music and the protector of the MUSES, and is said to have made the first harp. Being the father of ÆSCULAPIUS, he was called the patron or protector of the art of medicine. He could fore-tell the future, and he had a very celebrated temple at DELPHI where people used to go to consult him

Apollo,

before beginning any important business. The Romans learned to worship Apollo from the Greeks, and built for him a temple at Rome.

Apollo's statues were made in the form of a beautiful youth with long hair, carrying a lyre or a bow and arrows in his hand. The most celebrated one now known is the Apollo Belvedere, so called because it is in the gallery of the Belvedere, in the Vatican, Rome. It was found (1503) in the ruins of ancient Antium.

AP'PI-AN WAY. See ROME.

AP-PO-MAT'TOX COURT HOUSE, a village in Virginia, 20 miles E. of Lynchburg, noted as being the place where Gen. R. E. LEE surrendered to Gen. Grant what was left of his army after the battles around Richmond. This, which took place April 9, 1865, ended the Civil War.

ARABIA (*a-ra'be-ah*), a country in the S. W. part of Asia, E. of the Red Sea: area more than 1,000,000 square miles, or about five times as large as France. A large part of it is desert, roamed over by Arab tribes called Bedouins; but in the interior are highlands in which are

many towns. There are no large rivers, and most of the streams are lost in the desert sands. The prin-cipal countries in Arabia are Hed-jaz, on the Red Sea, in which are the holy cities of MECCA and MEDINA; Yemen, also on the Red Sea, the most fertile part, where Mocha coffee grows; Oman, some-times called Muscat, in the south-east part; Nedjed, in the interior, where the best Arab horses are raised; and Shomer, north of Ned-jed. In the south-west part, on the Indian Ocean. is Aden, a strongly fortified place owned by Great Britain. The climate of Arabia is very hot and dry. The people, who are supposed to number about 15,000,000, are mostly Arabs, and they are nearly all Mohammedans.

Arabia was not of much conse-quence before the time of MO-HAMMED, under whose successors, the CALIPHS, the different tribes were joined together and became a strong power. They spread over the neighboring countries, conquer-ing western Asia and all north Africa, and even went into Europe and founded a strong kingdom in Spain. In the East the Arab con-querors were commonly called Saracens, but in the West they were known as Moors or Moriscos.

ARAGO (*ah-rah-go*), **Dominque Francois,** a noted French astrono-mer, born at Estagel, near Perpig-nan, Feb. 26. 1786. He was educa-ted at the Polytechnic School in Paris. and when only nineteen years old became secretary in the Obser-vatory. The next year (1806) he was sent by the Emperor Napoleon to Spain to finish measuring an arc of the meridian—that is, a part of a great circle round the earth—so as to get an accurate measure to be used instead of the common measure in feet and inches. From this work, which had been begun by others, was made what is called the metric system, in which a measure of length called the metre is used instead of the foot, and which is divided decimally—that is, into tenths and hundredths instead of into inches or twelfths.

Arago was helped in this work by another French astronomer named Biot. The two lived for many months in a hut on the top of one of the highest peaks of the PYRENEES, where they made signals to a party of Spanish astronomers on a little island in the Mediterranean. They had a hard time, for several times furious storms beat down their little hut and destroyed their papers. At last Biot went back to France and left Arago all alone. He was in the island of Majorca when war broke out between France and Spain. The Spaniards took him for a spy, and he was shut up several months in a fort to save him from the mob. He escaped to Algiers, but was captured by a Spanish vessel while going from there in an Algerine vessel to France and again sent to prison. He was released after a while, and sailed once more for France, but the ship was driven by a storm across to Algiers again, where he was made a slave. The French consul finally got him his liberty, and he arrived in France in 1809. Though he was only twenty-three years old, he was at once elected a member of the Academy of Sciences, of which he became secretary in 1830. At the same time he was made Director of the Observatory, a place which he held until his death. He became very famous for his discoveries, and wrote many books on science. He also wrote a book called "History of My Youth," in which he tells about his strange adventures. He was always a strong republican, and took much interest in public affairs, but when Louis Napoleon became Emperor, he gave up politics. He died in Paris, after being blind for three years, when sixty-seven years old (Oct. 2, 1853).

ARAGON (*ah'rah-gon*).   See SPAIN.

AR'AL, an inland sea in Asiatic Russia, about 200 miles W. of the Caspian Sea ; area about 24,000 square miles, or a little larger than Lake Michigan. Next to the Caspian, it is the largest inland sea in the Eastern Hemisphere. It is shallow, with many islands, and has no outlet, but several rivers flow into it. Its water is brackish, but horses will drink it and it is used for cooking.

ARBLAY (*ar'bla*), **Madame d,**' an English novelist, born in Lynn in 1752. Her maiden name was Frances Burney, and she was the daughter of Charles Burney, a music-teacher. As a child she was shy and dull, and did not know her letters until she was eight years old, at which time her father went to London to live. All the noted people of the time used to visit at her father's house there, and she learned much from hearing the talk of Dr. JOHNSON, BURKE, GARRICK, and others. When she was twenty-six years old (1778) she published secretly a story called "Evelina," which had a wonderful success, and people were much surprised when they found out that it was the work of a timid young woman who knew little of the world. Four years afterward she published a novel named "Cecilia," which was as successful as the first one. When thirty-three years old she was appointed Keeper of the Robes to Queen Charlotte, an office which she did not like, but which she kept for five years to please her father. In 1793 she married Alexandre Richard d'Arblay, a French officer then living in England, and afterward lived part of the time in Paris and part in England. She wrote other books, but they did not add to her fame, and died when nearly eighty-eight years old (Jan. 6, 1840).

ARCADIA (*ar-kay'de-ah*).   See PELOPONNESUS.

ARCHIMEDES (*ar-ki-me'deez*), a famous mathematician, born in Syracuse, Sicily, about 287 B.C. When quite young he is said to have visited Egypt, and to have made there machines for drawing water, among them one named after him the Archimedean screw. Hiero, King of Syracuse, having suspected a goldsmith of putting some other metal than gold in his crown, gave it to Archimedes to find out the cheat. Archimedes, while thinking over the matter one day, got into his bath, which chanced to be full, and he saw at once that as much water must run over the edge of the tub as was equal to the bulk or size of his body. He then saw that if he put the crown into a vessel full of water and weighed the water which overflowed, and then tried a piece of pure gold equal in weight to the crown in the same way, the water overflowed by the pure gold ought to equal in weight that of the crown, if it also were pure gold. But he found that it did not equal it, and he therefore knew that the crown was not pure gold. He had thus found out what is called the law of specific gravity, or the truth that any body held under water weighs just as much less as the weight of the water which it crowds out of its place. He was so overjoyed at this discovery that he ran home without waiting to put on his clothes, crying through the streets, "*Eureka! Eureka!*" (Greek for "I have found it! I have found it!")

When the Romans under MARCELLUS besieged Syracuse, Archimedes made machines which lifted their ships out of the water and let them drop with so much force that they sunk. He is also said to have set them on fire by means of burning glasses. Marcellus gave strict orders to his soldiers not to hurt Archimedes, and even offered a reward to him who should bring him safe to him. When the city was taken, a Roman soldier entered his house and found him so busily at work at a problem that he did not even know that the enemy had entered the gates. The soldier ordered him to come along with him, but Archimedes refusing to do so, he killed him, to the grief of Marcellus, who built a monument over his grave. He was about seventy-five years old when he died (212 B.C.)

ARC'TIC O'CEAN, or **Northern Ocean,** that part of the ocean between the North Pole and the Arctic Circle. Much of it is frozen during the greater part of the year, and its navigation is made dangerous by floating icebergs, fogs, storms, and almost endless night. Some think that there is an open sea around the Pole, and many expeditions have been made to find it and a way through its waters around America and Asia. It is visited every year by many ships after whales, which abound in it.

The Arctic Ocean is so named from the Greek *arktos*, a bear, because it lies under the constellation called the Great Bear.

AR·E·THU'SA, a fountain near Syracuse, Sicily, the waters of which the ancients believed were united with those of the river Alpheus in the PELOPONNESUS. According to the poets, Arethusa was a nymph of Diana who was pursued by the river-god Alpheus. She prayed to Diana for help, and was changed into a fountain which ran underground into Sicily. Alpheus, taking the form of a river, followed her under the earth until the two waters became one.

ARGENTINE (*ar'jen-teen*) **REPUBLIC,** a country in the S. part of South America, between Chili and the Atlantic Ocean; area, including PATAGONIA, about 1,100,-000 square miles, or less than a third that of the United States; pop. about 3,200,000; capital, BUENOS AYRES. It has many large fertile plains, called pampas, where millions of cattle, sheep, and horses find pasture; and the chief trade is in wool, hides, and tallow. The horsemen called Gauchos, who take care of cattle on the plains, are descendants of the early Spanish colonists. They live in huts built of mud, and catch wild horses, cattle, and other animals with lassos or the bolas (C. C. T., 308, I.). The other people of the country are

Gauchos Lassoing Wild Horses.

mostly Italians, Spaniards, French, and other Europeans; and there are also many Indians. The government is a republic, much like that of the United States. The religion is Roman Catholic.

The first settlement was made in this part of South America by the Spaniards at Buenos Ayres about 1535; and the country was held by them until 1813, when they were driven out, and the people made a government of their own. It has suffered much from civil wars and from wars with its neighbors.

The Argentine Republic (Spanish, *La República Argentina*) was named from the Rio de la PLATA (Spanish for " River of Silver"), the word Argentine being made from *argentum*, the Latin for silver.

AR'GO-NAUTS, in Greek fable, the heroes who went with Jason, before the war of TROY, in the ship Argo to Colchis after the Golden Fleece. The word, which is made up of two Greek words (*Argo* and *nautai*), means the " sailors of the Argo." The ship was named after its builder, Argus, son of Phrixus. Pelias, King of Iolcus in Thessaly, had been warned to be on his guard against a man with one shoe, and seeing his nephew Jason one day with only one sandal (the other having been lost in crossing a stream), he bade him go and fetch the Golden Fleece, hoping that he would be killed in the attempt.

The Golden Fleece was the hide of a ram which had been given to Phrixus, son of Athamas, by his mother Nephele. On the death of Nephele, Athamas married Ino, and Phrixus and his sister Helle lived very unhappily with their stepmother. Fearing that she might kill them they got on the ram and fled. As the ram soared through the air Helle got giddy and fell into that part of the sea ever since called after her the Hellespont (Greek for "Helle's Sea"). Phrixus went on to the palace of Æëtes, King of Colchis, where he sacrificed the ram to Jupiter, and hung up its Golden Fleece in a grove, where it was guarded by fire-breathing bulls and by an ever-watchful dragon.

Jason, accompanied by some of the principal heroes of Greece, set sail in the Argo, among them being HERCULES, CASTOR and Pollux, MELEAGER, and ORPHEUS. They passed safely through the Symplegades, rocks which opened and closed together all the time so quickly that a bird had scarcely time to fly through the passage between them ; and having gone through the land of the AMAZONS, at last reached Colchis, where Jason demanded the Fleece of King Æëtes. The king refused to give it up until Jason had ploughed land with the fire-breathing bulls and sowed it with the teeth of the dragon. Jason did these things with the aid of MEDEA, the King's daughter, who had fallen in love with him. She was an enchantress, and she anointed his body with an ointment which saved him from the fiery breath of the bulls, and showed him how by throwing a stone among the armed men who sprang from the dragon's teeth they would fight and kill each other. Jason then seized the fleece and fled by night, taking with him Medea and her brother Absyrtus.

King Æëtes pursued the Argo, but Medea cut up Absyrtus and threw his limbs one by one into the sea. Æëtes stopped to pick them up, and so the Argonauts got away; but on account of the crime against Absyrtus they had to pass through many dangers on their homeward voyage. They at last reached Iolcus, where Medea told the daughters of King Pelias to cut up their father and put him in a caldron, promising them that she would

bring him to life and make him young again. When they did so, she neglected to use her spells at the right moment, and the body was burned, and thus the warning to Pelias was fulfilled.

AR'GOS, a very ancient city of Greece, capital of Argolis in the PELOPONNESUS, near the head of the Argolic gulf, now called the gulf of Nauplia. The inhabitants of Argos were called Argivi (Argives), a name sometimes given to all the Greeks. Agamemnon was King of Argos at the time of the war of TROY.

AR'GUS, in Greek fable, a wonderful being with a hundred eyes, of which only two slept at a time. Juno set him to watch IO, who had been turned into a cow by Jupiter. Io complained to Jupiter, and he sent Mercury to free her. Mercury, disguised as a shepherd, lulled Argus to sleep with the music of his pipe, and cut off his head. Juno, grieved at his loss, turned Argus into a peacock and scattered his eyes over the tail of the bird.

A-RI-AD'NE. See THESEUS.

A-RI'ON, a musician of Lesbos, supposed to have lived about 600 B.C. He went to Sicily and Italy and made a great deal of money by playing on the cithara or lute, an instrument which he played better than any one else. While going from Italy to Corinth in a ship, the sailors agreed among themselves to throw him overboard and seize his money. He begged to be allowed to play one tune before dying, and when he had finished it jumped into the sea. It is said that many dolphins, drawn by his sweet music, had gathered round the ship, and that one, taking him on his back, carried him safely to land. Arion went to Corinth and told his story to his friend Periander, the ruler of Corinth, and when the ship arrived there the sailors were put to death.

ARIOSTO (*ah-re-os'to*), **Ludovico,** a famous Italian poet, born at Reggio, Sept. 8, 1474. His father wanted him to study law, but he liked better to write poetry. When twenty-four years old his father died, leaving him nine younger brothers and sisters to take care of, and he had to work hard to support them. His poems soon brought him to the notice of Cardinal d'Este, and of his brother Alfonso, Duke of Ferrara, by whom he was employed in several places of trust. When he was about thirty-one years old (1505) he began to write his great poem called "Orlando Furioso" (Orlando Furious or Mad), a story of the fabled knights of the time of CHARLES THE GREAT and of the wars carried on by that sovereign against the Saracens. In another poem called "Orlando Innamorato" (Orlando in Love), published (1495) by a poet named Boiardo, Orlando (who is the same as ROLAND) is made to fall in love with a princess named Angelica, who had been sent by the Saracens to stir up discord among the Christians. The story being left unfinished by Boiardo, Ariosto continues it, and makes Angelica fall in love with a young and humble squire, upon which Orlando gets furious and is crazy for a long time. This poem, which made the author very famous, has been translated into most of the languages of Europe. Ariosto died in Ferrara when fifty-nine years old (June 6, 1533).

ARISTIDES (*ar-is-ti'deez*), a celebrated Athenian, called on account of his wisdom the "Just." He was one of the ten generals at the battle of MARATHON (490 B.C.), each of whom held the command for one day, but he got the others to give up their day with him to MILTIADES, who was the most skilful of all. The next year he was made archon, or chief magistrate of Athens. Through the efforts of THEMISTOCLES, his rival, he was ostracized or banished by *ostrakon* (Greek for "shell"), so

called, because each person who wanted any one banished wrote his name on a shell and voted with it. It is said that when the voting was going on, an ignorant person who did not know Aristides asked him to write his (Aristides') name on a shell for him. "Has Aristides done you any injury?" asked he. "No," said the man, "but I am tired of hearing him always called the Just."

When XERXES invaded Greece, Aristides was recalled, and helped to win the battles of Salamis (480) and Platæa (479). After this he regained the people's favor. He died so poor that he had to be buried at the public cost; but his memory was so respected that the state gave dowries to his daughters when they were married. He died about 468 B.C.

ARISTOPHANES (*ar-is-tof'a-neez*), the most famous comic poet of Greece, born at Athens between 444 and 450 B.C. He began to write when very young and took several prizes for comedies under a false name, before he was old enough to try for them in his own name. It is not easy for us to enjoy his wit because it is all about the ways and habits of Athenian life at that time. He laughed at all new ideas and made fun of all the noted people of his time. In "The Clouds" he speaks with contempt of SOCRATES, whom he did not understand at all.

We have only eleven of the fifty-four comedies which he wrote, among them "The Wasps," "The Birds," "The Frogs," "The Knights," and "The Clouds." He had a clever way of introducing animals into his choruses and made frogs croak and pigs grunt in verse. He died about 380 B.C.

ARISTOTLE (*ar'is-tot'l*), one of the most famous of ancient philosophers, and one of the greatest men that ever lived, born in Stagira, Macedonia, in 384 B.C. From his birthplace he was sometimes called the "Stagirite." His father, Nico-machus, was physician to Amyntas, King of Macedon. When seventeen years old Aristotle went to Athens, where he lived for twenty years, being much of the time a pupil of Plato's; but he did not agree with all the teachings of Plato, though he was always a great favorite of his. When he was forty-one years old (343) Philip, King of Macedon, sent for him to come and teach his son Alexander, then thirteen years old. Aristotle is said to have lived sev_

Aristotle.

eral years at the court of Philip, who rebuilt Stagira, which had been destroyed, and set up a school for him there.

Alexander always loved his teacher, and after he had conquered Persia sent him eight hundred talents (nearly $1,000,000) to enable him to write a history of animals; and

he also employed a great many men in catching animals of all kinds for him. About 335 B.C. Aristotle removed to Athens, and set up a new school in a building named the Lyceum because it was near the Temple of Apollo Lyceius. His school is said to have been called the Peripatetic School, from a Greek word meaning to walk about, because he used to walk up and down while giving his lectures. He wrote numerous books which after his death were put into the great library of ALEXANDRIA, and many of them are still preserved. They are on almost every subject of science and art, but among the most important are his works on natural history, in which animals were first described rightly and first divided into classes.

After the death of Alexander, Aristotle, who was looked upon with distrust by many of the Athenians as being the friend of Macedon, had to flee. He went to Chalcis, in the island of Euboea, and died there when sixty-two years old (322 B..C).

ARIZONA (ar-e-zo'nah), a territory of the United States, lying between UTAH and MEXICO; area 114,000 square miles, or about the same size as Italy and nearly as large as all the Middle States put together; pop. about 60,000, of whom more than 30,000 are Indians; capital, TUCSON. The surface is mostly high table-lands, crossed by ranges of lofty mountains, with peaks here and there more than two miles high. They are also cut through by many rivers which have worn for themselves deep channels called cañons (kan'-yons), a Spanish word meaning "hollows." These cañons are sometimes very long and have straight high walls from half a mile to more than a mile high. The most noted one is the Grand Cañon of the Colorado.

Arizona is very rich in gold, silver, copper, iron, and many other minerals, and precious stones of several kinds are found. Though some of its land is desert, the greater part is fertile and its plains are excellent for feeding cattle. In many places are found the ruins of ancient cities and of aqueducts for carrying water for the land, which show that the country was very thickly peopled in old times.

The Spaniards went to Arizona as early as 1526, and they had missions there in 1600. It was formerly a part of NEW MEXICO, which the United States got from Mexico in 1848. It was cut off from New Mexico and made into a territory in 1863.

AR·KAN'SAS (formerly pronounced *ar'kan-saw*), one of the South-western States of the United States, lying on the W. side of the Mississippi River between Missouri and Louisiana; area 52,000 square miles, or a little larger than New York State; pop. 1,125,000, or about a fifth that of New York; capital, LITTLE ROCK. The eastern part is low and swampy, but the western part is made up of high prairies broken by hills and mountains, and watered by many navigable rivers. Much of the soil is good for farming, and there is plenty of coal and wood, and mines of iron, zinc, and lead. Mineral springs abound, the hot springs being noted for curing diseases of the lungs and liver. Near the hot springs are got the best whetstones in the world.

The first settlement of whites was made by the French in 1670. The country was a part of the territory of Louisiana, bought from France by the United States in 1803, and when Louisiana was made into a State (1812), it became a part of Missouri territory. When Missouri became a State (1819) it was called Arkansas territory, Arkansas being the name of an Indian tribe living there, and in 1836 it became a State of the Union. It seceded in 1861, and joined the Confederate States, but became a State of the Union again in 1868.

ARKWRIGHT (*ark'rite*), **Sir Richard,** inventor of the cotton-spinning machine, born at Preston, England, Dec. 23, 1732. He was a poor boy without education, and worked as a barber until he was twenty-eight years old, when he became a dealer in hair, and made money by discovering a hair-dye. When thirty-six years old (1768) he made a cotton-spinning frame, by which, for the first time, cotton thread could be made by machinery fine and strong enough for the warp, or long threads of cloth, which before his time were of linen, only the weft or cross threads being of cotton. The next year he set up a mill worked by a horse, but before long was able to use water-power. At first many workmen and manufacturers tried to ruin him, because they fancied his machinery would cut off their work, for by using his frame one man can do as much work as a hundred and thirty men could do before; but in spite of all he succeeded so well that he made a large fortune. He taught himself the simple branches of education after he was fifty years old. The King knighted him in 1786. He died when nearly sixty years old (Aug. 3, 1792).

ARMENIA (*ar-me'ne-ah*), an ancient country of western Asia, lying between ASIA MINOR and the CASPIAN Sea, now divided between Turkey, Russia, and Persia. It is a high, table-land, partly surrounded and covered by mountains, the highest of which, Mt. Ararat, on which Noah's ark is said to have rested after the Deluge, is more than three miles high, and is covered with everlasting ice and snow.

Many hundred years B.C. Armenia was a powerful kingdom. Alexander the Great conquered it (325 B.C.), and since that time it has been the scene of many wars, and has been ruled by many different nations. The Armenians became Christians about A.D. 300, and still remain so.

ARMINIUS (*ar-min'e-us*), a German prince, called by the Germans Hermann, born about 16 B.C. When quite young he served in the Roman army, and was made a Roman citizen and a knight; but when he returned home and saw how his people were oppressed by the Romans, he made up his mind to win back their freedom. He got up an insurrection, destroyed the Roman army under Varus (A.D. 9), who killed himself after almost all his troops had fallen, and six years afterward forced a large army under Germanicus to retreat. The next year (16), Germanicus marched against him with 100,000 men, but Arminius, though defeated in a great battle, began the fight again the next day, and forced him to leave Germany again. After this the Romans did not again try to conquer Germany, and so Arminius is called the liberator of his country. He saved Germany a second time by defeating the Marcomanni, who had invaded it. After this he ruled in peace, but he governed so strictly that he was murdered when only thirty-seven years old (A.D. 21). The Germans have many songs about him, and a large statue of him was erected in 1846 in the city of Detmold, near which the fight with Varus took place. The statue, which is made of copper, is 90 feet high to the point of the uplifted sword, and stands on a stone pedestal 93 feet high, so that the whole is as high as a common steeple.

ARM'STRONG, Sir William George, inventor of the Armstrong gun, born at Newcastle-upon-Tyne, England, Nov. 26, 1810. At his father's wish he studied law, but he gave all his spare time to machines.

In 1854, during the Crimean war, he began to try experiments with cannon, and soon after he found out how to make the kind of gun now named after him. These guns are made of bars of wrought iron two inches wide, heated white-hot, twisted round a round steel bar or core, and welded or hammered together into one piece. Another set of bars are then twisted round, but in the opposite way, and all are welded together very strong. The core is then taken out, and the inside rifled (C. C. T., 512, II. l.). These guns, which are made to load at the breech—that is, behind—will shoot a ball a great distance and through very thick armor-plates. For this invention Armstrong was knighted (1859) by Queen Victoria.

AR'NOLD, Benedict, an American general and traitor, born in Norwich, Conn., Jan. 3, 1740. When a boy he was noted for his wildness and love of mischief. He was apprenticed to an apothecary, but ran away and enlisted as a soldier, then deserted and became a merchant in New Haven, where he failed in business. When the war of the Revolution broke out he went to Cambridge, Mass., as captain of a company, and was soon made a colonel. He helped Ethan ALLEN to take Ticonderoga and commanded part of the force which, under Gen. MONTGOMERY, attacked Quebec (Dec. 31, 1775). For his services there he was made a brigadier-general, and he afterward fought gallantly in several battles. In 1777 he was made a major-general, but he was very angry because others had received this honor before him.

When thirty-eight years old (1778) he was sent to take command in Philadelphia, but he ran deeply in debt and behaved so badly that he was tried by court-martial in 1780 and sentenced to receive a reprimand from Washington. This made him still more angry, and when, shortly after, he became commander of West Point, he entered into a plot to give up the fort to the British. Major ANDRE, who had been sent by Sir Henry CLINTON to make the plan, was captured by the Americans, and Arnold, hearing of it, escaped on board the British ship Vulture, which lay in the Hudson, and got safely to New York. Arnold was made a major-general in the British army, and after the war he went to England and received a large sum of money as pay for his treason; but his life was very unhappy, for he was despised and shunned by all men of honor. He died in London when sixty-one years old (June 14, 1801).

ARNOLD, Matthew, an English poet, son of Dr. Thomas ARNOLD, born at Laleham, Dec. 24, 1822. He was educated at Winchester and Rugby, and graduated at Oxford, where he was made professor of poetry in 1857. He was made Government Inspector of Schools in 1851. He wrote several volumes of poems which have been much admired, but most of his later books were in prose. His writings have given him very high rank as a scholar and thinker. He died when sixty-six years old (April 15, 1888).

ARNOLD, Thomas, a famous English teacher of boys, born at West Cowes, Isle of Wight, June 13, 1795. When a boy he was indolent and shy, but when he went to Oxford University he studied very hard and gained the prize for Latin and English essays. After teaching privately for some years he became at the age of thirty-three (1828) head-master of Rugby School, which he made the best school for boys that has ever been in England. His idea was to train Christian gentlemen as well as scholars, and he trusted so entirely to the word of honor of the older boys that it grew to be a saying that " it was a shame to tell a lie to Dr. Arnold—he always believed one." Among his works the best is his " History of Rome," which goes only to the end of the Second Punic War. In 1841 he became professor of modern history at Oxford, but he held it only a year and died suddenly of heart disease at Rugby at the age of forty-seven (June 12, 1842).

ARRIAN (*ar're-an*), or **Flavius Arrianus,** a Greek historian, born in Nicomedia, Bithynia, about A.D. 100. He is best known by his history of the campaigns of Alexander the Great, which, in imitation of XENOPHON, he called the " Anabasis of Alexander." The Emperor Hadrian made him a Roman citizen and governor of Cappadocia (136). When fifty years old he settled in his native city for the rest of his life. Besides the Anabasis he wrote an account of a voyage in the Black Sea, an account of India, and other works.

ARTAXERXES (*ar-tax-erx'ees*), the name of three kings of Ancient Persia.

Artaxerxes II., called Mnemon (Greek for "memory") on account of his good memory, began to reign about 405 B. C. He is chiefly known from the revolt of his brother CYRUS the Younger, who was defeated by him in the battle of Cunaxa (401), and whose story is so well told by the historian XENOPHON. He died about 359 B.C.

ARTEVELDE (*ar'teh-vel-deh*), the name of two famous leaders of the people of Ghent against their oppressors, the Counts of Flanders, in the 14th century.

Jacob van, born about 1300. He was of noble family, but joined the guild or society of the brewers to get the favor of the people. He took the part of Edward III. of England, in his war with France; drove Count Louis I. of Flanders into France, and for many years was ruler of Flanders. At last he tried to make EDWARD the Black

Prince governor of the country, when the people turned against him, and he was killed by the mob, July 17, 1345.

Philip van, his son, born about 1340. When Count Louis II. besieged Ghent the people chose him governor (1381). He defeated the Count near Bruges and captured that city, but the French King, Charles VI., sent an army to the help of Louis, and Artevelde was defeated and slain (Nov. 27, 1382).

Philip van Artevelde is the hero of a play by Sir Henry Taylor, an English writer.

AR'THUR, the hero of the Round Table, supposed to have been a British Prince who lived in the 6th century. He is said to have fought many battles with the Saxons, and to have been killed finally by his nephew Mordred, who had rebelled against him. His exploits are told about in many old poems and romances, but they are so mixed up with fable that many think that there never was such a person as Arthur.

According to the story, Arthur was the son of Uther Pendragon, King of Cornwall. His birth was hidden, and when he was born he was given to a good knight to be brought up. When Uther died, many strove to be King, but the Bishop of Canterbury called all up to London, where in the churchyard was seen a great stone with a steel anvil sunk in it, and in the anvil a sword, about which was written in letters of gold : " Whoso pulleth this sword out of this stone and anvil is rightwise born King of all England." Only Arthur could do this, and he was crowned, and married Guenevere, the fairest woman in the land. With her he got the enchanted Round Table, which King Uther had once given to her father, King Leodegrance, and a hundred knights who sat about it. King Arthur added fifty

more knights to the number, and thus made a band whose adventures afterward became very famous. When Arthur was killed, the fairies are said to have borne him away to be cured in the valley of Avalon, from which, according to the legend, he will return some time to lead the Britons again against the Saxons.

ARTHUR, Chester A., twenty-first President of the United States, born in Franklin County, Vermont, October 5, 1830. He was graduated at Union College in 1849, and be-

Chester A. Arthur.

came a lawyer in the City of New York, where he held several political offices. He was collector of the port of New York from 1871 to 1878, was elected Vice-President of the United States in 1880, and on the death of President Garfield (September 19, 1881) became President of the United States. He died when fifty-six years old (Nov. 18, 1886).

AR'YANS. In very ancient times, so far back that history has no record of it, the forefathers of all the principal races of Europe and of some of those of Asia lived together in the high lands at the upper end of the River OXUS in Central Asia. Then they formed one people who spoke one language and who lived by farming and by raising cattle and sheep. They were not savages, but knew how to build houses, to plough the ground, to grind grain in mills, and to weave cloth, and were divided into families and had some ideas of government. The word *arya*, which is Sanscrit (the ancient language of the people of India), is supposed to have meant the same as our word farmer, and as farming was at first the most respectable business it came to mean "respectable," or "honorable."

In time many of the Aryans left their homes and went, some into what is now Persia, some across the mountains into India, and some into Europe. The language spoken by these different branches changed little by little after their separation, until finally each grew into a new language, but still keeping in it most of the common words used when all lived together. In this way grew up the languages of the principal nations of Europe, which, though seeming to differ greatly from each other, can easily be shown, by studying their simple words, to have come from the same source.

The Aryan nations of Asia are the ancient Persians and the high-caste Hindoos—that is, the better classes of the people of India. The Aryan races of Europe are the Celts, Greeks, Latins, Teutons (Germans and Scandinavians), Letts, and Slavs. The Aryan nations are sometimes called the Japhetic nations, from Japhet, son of Noah, from whom some think they are descended. They are also sometimes called the Indo-European races, to show the relation between the peoples of India and of Europe, and sometimes, especially by German scholars, the Indo-Germanic races.

ASHANTEE (*ash-an'te*), a savage negro kingdom on the W. coast of Africa; pop. supposed to be about 3,000,000, or less than that of Ohio; capital, Coomassie. The country is fertile, and rich in gold-dust and ivory. The king, who is a despot, lives in Coomassie, and has more than three thousand wives, who work on his farms. If any of his male subjects looks upon one of them, he is put to death. Many hundreds of people are sacrificed to the gods every year, and their bodies thrown into a grove near the town. Coomassie was taken by the British in 1874, and burned, but it has since been rebuilt.

ASHBUR-TON, Alexander Baring, Lord, an English statesman, born Oct. 27, 1774. He was the son of Sir Francis Baring, a merchant of London, and succeeded him in the business. He was in Parliament for many years, and was finally raised to the peerage with the title of Baron Ashburton (1835). Seven years later (1842) he was sent to the United States to settle the boundary between Maine and Canada and arrange other disputes which it was feared would lead to war. By the "Ashburton Treaty" (signed Aug. 9, 1842), the Canada boundary was fixed as it now is, and Great Britain and the United States agreed to keep ships on the coast of Africa to stop the slave trade, and to give up to each other all criminals. Lord Ashburton died when seventy-four years old (May 13, 1848).

ASHTOR-ETH, the goddess of the Moon, worshiped together with BAAL by the Phœnicians and Carthaginians. Her principal temples were in Tyre and Sidon. Her image was at first only a round white stone, but afterward a human figure with a cow's head, and finally a woman sitting on a lion with lightning in one hand and a sceptre in the other. The Greeks called her Astarte, and got their idea of Venus from her.

ASIA (*a'she-ah*), the largest of all the continents; area 17,400,000 square miles, which is more than four times that of Europe, an eighth more than that of America, and about a third of all the solid land on the earth; pop. 834,000,000, or nearly two thirds that of the whole earth. In Asia are the highest mountains, the largest and highest plateaus or table-lands, the largest peninsulas, the largest inland seas, the largest number of kinds of animals and of plants, and the largest number of races of people and of languages in the world.

The map shows that Asia is cut off from America on the northeast, by the narrow BEHRING Strait, and that it is joined to Europe on the northwest and to Africa on the southwest. Its surface is mostly made up of table-lands divided by great chains of mountains, the principal of which are the ALTAI, the HIMALAYA, and the HINDOO KOOSH ranges. There is much desert land in Asia, and great grassy plains called steppes. In this continent are some of the largest rivers in the world : on the north side the Obi, Yenisei, and Lena ; on the west the Amoor, Hoang - ho, and Yang - tse - kiang,

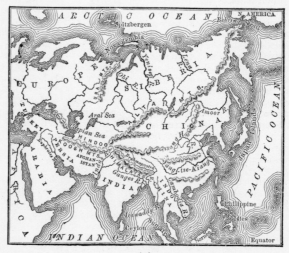

Asia.

and on the south the Cambodia, Irawaddy, Brahmapootra, Ganges, Indus, and Euphrates. South of Asia are the richest and most important groups of islands on the earth.

As Asia extends from the equator to the polar circle, it has of course all kinds of climate, from the hottest to the coldest ; and it has, too, all kinds of plants and trees. All of the grains, excepting Indian corn, and many of the best fruits and vegetables first grew there, and all the domestic animals, such as the horse, ass, ox, sheep, goat, hog, and common fowls, were brought from there. Asia is rich in almost all the metals, and nowhere else in the world are so many kinds of precious stones found.

The people of Asia belong mostly to two great races : nearly all of those north of the Himalaya and Hindoo Koosh mountains are Mongols, and most of those south of those mountains are Caucasians

(C. C. T., 381, I. l.). In the extreme south part and in the islands are many Malays. At least half of all the inhabitants of the earth live in China and India. More than a third of the continent is ruled by Russia and Great Britain, and small parts by other European powers.

The meaning of the word Asia is not known. The name was first given by the Greeks to a small part of Lydia, then to all ASIA MINOR, and finally to the whole continent. The human race is supposed to have first come from Asia; there grew up the earliest civilization, and the first great empires of the world; there began all science and literature, and from there came all the great religions.

A'SIA MI'NOR, the ancient name of the peninsula at the west end of Asia, between the Euxine or BLACK SEA and the Mediterranean; area about 212,000 square miles, or nearly the same as that of the Empire of Germany. In ancient times this country was divided up among many different tribes, whose names were afterward given to most of the parts where they lived. On the north coast the countries were called Bithynia, Paphlagonia, and Pontus; on the west, Mysia, Lydia, and Caria; on the south, Lycia, Pamphylia, Pisidia, and Cilicia; and in the interior Phrygia, Galatia, Cappadocia, Isauria, and Lycaonia. The Greeks had many colonies in Asia Minor, among which were Æolis, Ionia, and Doris, and built many important cites there. Asia Minor now forms a part of Turkey in Asia.

Asia Minor (Lesser Asia) was so called by the Greeks after the name of Asia had been given to the whole continent.

ASPASIA (*as-pa'she-ah*), a famous Greek woman, noted for her beauty and talents, who lived in Athens in the 5th century B.C. She was born in Miletus, and being a foreigner could not legally marry a Greek, but PERICLES thought so much of her that he took her as

Aspasia.

his wife and she lived with him until his death. She is said to have had great skill both in writing and in the art of speaking, and she was visited by all the most learned and famous people of Athens, even SOCRATES calling himself her pupil. Madame de Staël says, that "Aspasia was the loveliest of women, just as Alexander was the greatest of heroes."

AS-PIN'WALL, a town of the United States of COLOMBIA, on the Atlantic coast of the Isthmus of PANAMA, 48 miles from the city of Panama, on the Pacific coast; pop. about 6500. The railroad which runs from there to Panama was opened in 1855, and after that time until the opening of the Union Pacific Railroad (1869) nearly all travelers going to California passed through Aspinwall; and a great deal of freight, both from the United States and from South America, still goes through there to the Pacific coast. The town, which is built on an island owned by the railroad company, was named after Mr. Aspinwall, of New York. The people of Colombia call it Colon.

AS'SUMP'TION or **Asuncion** (*ah-soon-the-own'*), a city of South America, capital of PARAGUAY, on the river Paraguay; pop. from 20,-000 to 40,000. It is a very old town, having been founded by the Spaniards in 1536. It was the capital for nearly a hundred years of all the Spanish possessions on the Rio de la PLATA.

Its real name is Nuestra Señora de la Asuncion, (Spanish for Our Lady of the Assumption,) and it was named after the assumption (taking up into Heaven) of the Virgin Mary.

ASSYRIA (*as-syr'e-ah*), an ancient country of Asia, on the river Tigris. It had different capitals at different times, but when its power was greatest its capital was NINEVEH. The country is said to have got its name from Asshur, son of Shem. About 1250 B.C. Assyria had grown to be a strong kingdom, and it was at the height of its glory when Greece and Rome were just beginning. Among the greatest of the Assyrian kings were SENNACHERIB and Asshur-bani-pal, called by the Greeks SARDANAPALUS. About 600 B.C. Assyria was conquered by the Medes and ceased to be a kingdom.

AS'TAR'TE. See ASHTORETH.

ASTRAKHAN (*ahs-trah-kahn'*), a city of Russia, on an island in the river VOLGA, about 20 miles from its mouth in the Caspian Sea ; pop. about 57,000, or nearly as large as Reading, Pa. The population is made up from almost all the peoples of Asia and of Europe, and among its buildings are Christian churches, Mohammedan mosques, and Hindoo temples. Nearly all the eastern trade of Russia passes through this place, and great quantities of fish (mostly sturgeon) are sent from there.

ASTYAGES (*as-ty'a-geez*), the last King of ancient MEDIA, grandfather of CYRUS THE ELDER. He reigned thirty-five years, when he was dethroned by Cyrus (559 B.C.).

ASUNCION (*ah-soon-the-own'*). See ASSUMPTION.

ATAHUALLPA (*ah-tah-hwall'pah*), the last Inca of PERU. When his father, the Inca Huayna Capac, died, he left his throne to his eldest son Huascar, and gave Atahuallpa the government of the country of Quito, of which his mother had been a princess. This dividing of the empire led to civil war, and after a long and bloody struggle Huascar was taken prisoner and shut up in a strong fortress, and Atahuallpa became Inca. About this time PIZARRO came to Peru, and Atahuallpa ordered that he should be treated kindly and gave him quarters in one of his cities. A meeting between the two having been arranged, Atahuallpa went with unarmed followers and was treacherously seized by Pizarro, and thrown into prison.

To get his freedom, Atahuallpa promised Pizarro to fill the room in which he was as high as he could reach with gold. Pizarro agreed to free him if he would do so, but while the Peruvians were bringing in the gold from all parts, ALMAGRO came with more men, and Pizarro then made up his mind to kill the Inca and seize upon all his treasures. While in prison, Atahuallpa had given orders to have Huascar put to death, and it had been done. The Spaniards made this one of the charges against him at his trial, and he was found guilty and sentenced to be burned alive ; but they changed the manner of his death to strangling on his permitting a priest to baptise him. He was put to death Aug. 29, 1533.

ATALANTA (*at-a-lan'-tah*), in

Greek fable, the swiftest of mortals, daughter of Jasus. Her father, who had prayed for a son, was so angry when she was born that he exposed her on a mountain, where she was nursed by a she bear and learned to run very fast. She had many lovers, but refused to marry any one who could not outstrip her in running, the agreement being that all who were defeated should suffer death. At last one of them named Milanion beat her by dropping three golden apples, given him by Venus, which Atalanta stopped to pick up.

ATH'EL·STAN, the first King of all England, born about 895. He was a grandson of ALFRED THE GREAT, and he succeeded his father Edward the elder. He defeated the Danes, Irish, Scotch, and Welsh in a great battle (937), and extended his rule over the whole of England. He was a good king, and did much to build up trade and learning.

ATHENA (*a-the'nah*). See MINERVA.

ATHENÆUS (*ath-en-e'us*), a famous Greek writer, born in Egypt, who lived about the beginning of

View of Athens and the Acropolis, as it is now.

the 3d century A.D. He wrote a book called Deipnosophistæ (Banquet of the Learned), which describes a banquet at which the guests talk about many interesting things. It contains many anecdotes, and extracts from the writings of noted writers, and tells much about the private life of the people of that time.

ATH'ENS, a city, capital of the Kingdom of Greece; pop. about 107,000, about as large as Denver, Colorado. It is the residence of the king and his court, and is noted

for its university, which has more than fifty professors and teachers and a large library.

Athens is a very old city, and was very famous in ancient times. It was built around a rocky hill called the Acropolis, near which were several smaller hills, one of which was named Areopagus. The Acropolis (Greek for upper city), which was the citadel or fortress, had on it several splendid buildings, among the most magnificent of which was the Parthenon (Temple of Minerva, so called from Parthenos, virgin, one of the titles of that goddess), built of Pentelic marble (C. C. T., 386, II., u.), and containing the ivory and gold statue of Minerva, made by Phidias, and said to have been as high as seven men. The ruins of this great temple, which are still standing, are viewed with wonder by all who see them. The Areopagus (Greek for hill of Ares or Mars) was the place where the celebrated court of the Areopagus was held, and it is also noted as the place where St. Paul preached when in Athens. South-west of the Areopagus was another hill called the Pnyx, where was the stone pulpit from which orators spoke.

When Athens was most powerful all these hills and the city around them were surrounded by high walls, and two other long straight walls connected the city with its harbor called the Piræus, about four and a half miles distant. Athens must then have had a population of about 200,000, or nearly as much as Milwaukee, Wis.

The Parthenon, as it was in the time of Pericles.

According to the old Greek legends, Athens was founded by CECROPS, who built a fort on the rock afterward called the Acropolis and named it after himself Cecropia. One of the kings who ruled after him built there a temple of the goddess MINERVA, who was called by the Greeks Athena, and from her the city was called Athens (in Greek *Athenai*). In time the people of Athens extended their rule over the country around, which was called Attica, and of which Athens became the capital. Athens took part with the rest of Greece in fighting the Persians under her generals, MILTIADES, THEMISTOCLES, and ARISTIDES, and at the close of the war became the leader of the Greek states. The city was at the height of its splendor in the time of PERICLES (469 to 429 B.C.). It was then that the Parthenon and many of the other splendid buildings were erected, and Athens became the most magnificent city of Greece. This was the time, too, when the great poets ÆSCHYLUS, EURIPIDES, SOPHOCLES, and ARISTOPHANES

wrote, when the philosophers AN-
AXAGORAS and SOCRATES taught,
and when the great sculptor PHID-
IAS lived.

In 431, B.C., a great war called the
Peloponnesian war broke out between Athens and SPARTA, and it
finally ended (404 B.C.) with the capture of the city by the Spartans.
After this Athens got back her
freedom, but never again got back
her power. She fell under the rule
of the Macedonians and then under
that of the Romans, and in modern
times, with the rest of Greece, came
into the power of the Turks, who
held it till 1832. Three years afterward it became the capital of
Greece.

A'THOS, a mountainous peninsula
of Turkey in Europe, in the north-
west part of the Ægean Sea, about
30 miles long and 5 to 7 broad. At
its north end, where it joins the
mainland, it is low and only a little
more than a mile wide. Across this
part XERXES cut a canal for his
ships when he invaded Greece, so as
to escape the danger of sailing
around Mt. Athos at the south end.
It is said that part of this canal can
still be seen.

Mt. Athos is a tree-covered peak
more than a mile high (6,350 feet).
It is said that a sculptor once offered
to carve it into a statue of ALEX-
ANDER THE GREAT, holding a town
in its left hand and in the right a
basin to hold the waters which
flowed from it. Alexander liked the
plan, but said that the country
around was not fruitful enough to
feed the people who were to live in
the city.

Mt. Athos is now called the Holy
Mountain, and is famous for its
monasteries. Twenty of these dot
its sides, some of which are said to
date from the time of CONSTAN-
TINE THE GREAT. About six thousand monks live in them, and no
woman is permitted on the peninsula.

AT-LAN'TA, a city in the N. W.
quarter of Georgia, capital of the
State, and the largest and most
important city in the State; pop.
about 65,000, or about as large as
Memphis, Tenn. Many railroads
meet there, and it has a large trade
and is growing very fast. As it is on
high ground, its climate is mild
dry, and healthful. It is the site,
of Oglethorpe College, Atlanta
Medical College, and of several
other colleges.

Atlanta was first called Marthas-
ville, but in 1847, when it became
a city, the name was changed.
During the Civil War the Confederate Government had many factories there for making things
needed by soldiers. It was then
strongly fortified, and had a large
army to defend it. It was taken
by Gen. Sherman (Sept. 2, 1864),
who, when he left for CHATTA-
NOOGA (Nov. 15), made all the inhabitants leave, and burned the
machine shops, factories, and a
large part of the city. After the
war it was rebuilt, and in 1868 it
became the capital of the State.

AT-LAN'TIC OCEAN, that part
of the ocean which separates
America from Europe and Africa,
and which lies between the Arctic
Circle on the north and the Antarctic Circle on the south. The
part north of the equator is called
the North Atlantic, and the part
south of the equator the South
Atlantic. It is only about half as
large as the Pacific Ocean, but it
is much more important, for across
it are all the great highways between the Old and the New World.
In some places it is more than five
miles deep. The Gulf Stream is a
kind of river flowing through it
from the Gulf of Mexico, where it
starts, up the coast of America to
about New York, where it begins
to turn eastward, and then crossing
to the AZORES, where one part
flows past the British islands, and
the other turns back to the Gulf of
Mexico. This forms in the middle

of the North Atlantic near the Azores, a kind of eddy or whirlpool, called the Sargasso Sea, in which great quantities of sea-weed collect (C. C. T., 542, II., u). The water of the Gulf Stream is much warmer than that of the ocean, and it flows so swiftly that sailing-vessels from this country to Europe save a week in the voyage by keeping in it.

The Atlantic Ocean was called by the ancients simply the Ocean. It gets its name from Mount Atlas, which rises in Africa near its shores.

AT-LAN'TIS, a large island, said by some of the Greek geographers to have once been somewhere in the Atlantic Ocean, west of the coast of Africa. It was rich and powerful, and its kings conquered the west parts of Europe and of Africa. In time the people became very wicked, and the island was swallowed up by an earthquake. Some writers think that there never was such an island, but others think there may be some truth in the story.

AT'LAS, in Greek fable, one of the Titans, son of JAPETUS, and brother of PROMETHEUS. He was the leader of the TITANS in the war against Jupiter, and was condemned in punishment to bear up the heavens on his head and hands. Some writers says that Atlas was King of Mauritania in Africa. An oracle had foretold that he would be ruined by a son of Jupiter, and so he made up his mind that he would not see any stranger who called on him. When PERSEUS, who was a son of Jupiter, stopped to visit him, Atlas refused to entertain him, whereupon Perseus, angry at his want of hospitality, put his shield, which had on it the head of MEDUSA, before the eyes of Atlas, and turned him into a great mountain. This mountain, which is still called by his name, is so high that it was thought in old times to touch the heavens. The name Atlas was first given to a book of maps, because it had on its title-page a picture of Atlas holding up the heavens on his shoulders.

ATREUS (*a'tre-us* or *a'troos*), an ancient King of MYCENÆ in Greece, father of AGAMEMNON and MENELAUS, who from him were called the Atridæ, that is, descendants of Atreus. There is much about the crimes of Atreus and his family in Greek poetry and fable.

AT'TI-CA. See ATHENS and GREECE.

ATTILA (*at'te-lah*), a famous King of the HUNS, who called himself the Scourge of God. He began to rule, about A.D. 434, over the wandering tribes who lived in the north-west parts of Europe, and in a few years had made himself master of all Scythia and Germany. He told his people that he had found the sword of the Scythian god of war, with which he would conquer the world, and they believed that he could do anything. He attacked the EASTERN EMPIRE with an army of 500,000 men, mostly horsemen, destroyed a great many cities, and made the Emperor Theodosius pay him tribute. He then marched west with a still larger force through Germany into Gaul, and it looked as if he would conquer the whole Christian world; but, fortunately, he was met at Chalons by a great army of Romans under AËTIUS, and of Goths and Franks under their King Theodoric, and defeated in one of the greatest and most important battles ever fought (451).

Attila now went back across the Rhine, but the next year he led another great army into Italy, destroyed many cities, and would have taken Rome but for Pope Leo I., who visited him in his camp and begged him to spare the city. Soon after this, Attila was found dead in his bed (453 or 454) in Hungary. His body was put into three coffins, one of iron, one of silver, and an outer one of gold, and buried secretly at night with many of his treasures, and the prisoners who dug the grave were all killed lest some of them should tell where the place was. Attila is looked on by the Hungarians, who are descended from the Huns, as one of their great heroes, and his deeds are celebrated in many songs and romances. In the old German poem called the "Nibelungenlied," he is called King Etzel.

AUBER (*o-bair*), **Daniel Francois Esprit,** a noted French writer of operas, born in Caen, Jan. 29, 1782. His father, a print-seller, wanted him to follow the same business, but he liked music better. When thirty-one years old, he wrote an opera which failed, and almost discouraged him, but seven years later (1820) he brought out a comic opera which was successful, and after that his works were very popular. Among the best of his operas are "Masaniello," "Fra Diavolo," "L'elixir d'amour" (The Elixir of Love), "Le domino noir, (The Black Domino), and "Les diamants de la couronne" (The Crown Diamonds). Auber wrote his last opera when he was eighty-six years old. His music is very lively and graceful, and has in it many sweet airs. He died in Paris when eighty-nine years old (May 13, 1871).

AUBURN (*aw'burn*), a city of New York, about 175 miles W. of Albany; pop. 25,000, or about as large as Allentown, Pa. It has many cotton and woolen mills, machine shops, and tool factories. Auburn state prison, which is one of the largest in the country, has generally more than a thousand prisoners in it, none of whom are ever allowed to speak or to make signs to each other. They are all made to work at different trades, such as shoemaking, tailoring, weaving, furniture making, stone-

cutting, and blacksmithing, and the sale of the things they make pays the yearly cost of the prison. The buildings, shops, and yards, which cover twelve acres, are surrounded by a high wall on which guards walk night and day.

AUDUBON (*aw'doo-bon*), **John James,** a celebrated American writer on birds, born in Louisiana, May 4, 1780. When a boy he loved to keep birds as pets and often tried to make pictures of them. His father, who had been an officer in the French navy, seeing his talent, sent him when fourteen years old to Paris to study drawing and painting with the artist DAVID. When he came back (1798) he settled on a farm in Pennsylvania, and while living there drew many birds from nature, but was so unfortunate as to have them all destroyed by mice. About ten years later he removed to Henderson, Kentucky, and after that he spent many years in the woods of the West and South, catching all kinds of birds and painting pictures of them. In 1826 he went to England and published a work called "the Birds of America," which contained pictures of more than a thousand birds, all of life size and of their natural colors. This was followed by another great work on the habits of the birds of the United States, and after that he began a book on the "Quadrupeds of America," but he died before it was done and it was finished by his sons. Audubon died in New York when seventy-one years old (Jan. 27, 1851). His works made him very famous, and he was honored everywhere.

AUERBACH (*ow'er-bahk*), **Berthold,** a German novel writer, born in Nordstetten in Würtemberg, Feb. 28, 1812. He was of Jewish parentage, and his first book was Jewish stories; but he is most noted for his stories of German village life. Among these are those called in English "Black Forest

Village Stories," "Little Barefoot," "On the Heights," "The Villa on the Rhine," etc. His stories are quite popular and have been translated into several languages. He has also written some plays. He died when seventy years old (Feb. 8, 1882).

AU'GE-AS. See HERCULES.

AUGEREAU (*owzh-ro*), **Pierre François Charles,** Duke of Castiglione, a noted French general, born in Paris, Oct. 21, 1757. He was the son of a mechanic and had no education. When seventeen years old he joined the army and served as a private until he was thirty, when he became a fencing master in Naples. In 1792 he enlisted again in the army, and in less than two years became a general. He helped much to win the battles of LODI, Castiglione, and Arcola, and at EYLAU, though too sick to sit up, he made his servants tie him in his saddle and thus led his men into the fight. When Napoleon became Emperor he made him a marshal and gave him the title of Duke of Castiglione. Augereau afterward deserted Napoleon for LOUIS XVIII. He died when nearly fifty-eight years old (June 12, 1815).

AUGS'BURG (German *owgz'-boorg*), a city of Germany, in BAVARIA, on the river Lech, 33 miles N. W. of Munich; pop. about 65,-000, or nearly the same as that of Memphis, Tenn. Before America was discovered, Augsburg was a great centre of trade and its merchants became very rich and had ships on all known seas. Among the most noted of them were the Fugger family, descended from a poor weaver, who became at one time the richest family in Europe and were made counts and princes of the Empire. They did much for the city, and enriched it with libraries, galleries of paintings, and public gardens. Augsburg, though not as important as it used to be, still has a large trade and banking-business. Many books are printed there, and its great newspaper the *Allgemeine Zeitung* (Universal Journal), is one of the best in Germany.

Augsburg means the town of Augustus. It gets its name from a colony founded there (12 B.C.) by the Roman Emperor AUGUSTUS, and called Augusta Vindelicorum (Augusta of the Vindelicians), after a German tribe that he had conquered.

AUGUSTA (*aw'gus-tah*), a city, capital of the State of Maine, on the Kennebec River, 43 miles from the sea; pop. about 10,500. It is built on both sides the river, and has a bridge. The State House is one of the handsomest in New England.

AUGUSTA, a city of Georgia, on the Savannah River, 231 miles from the sea; pop. about 33,000, or about the same as Duluth, Minn. It has a good trade, especially in cotton, and has cotton and flour mills and machine shops.

Augusta was laid out in 1735 and named after an English princess. It became a city in 1817.

AUGUSTINE (*aw'gus-teen*), **Saint,** a famous scholar and preacher, born at Tagaste, near Carthage, in Africa, Nov. 13, 354. His father was a pagan nobleman, but his mother was a Christian. Augustine was educated in the best schools, and after teaching in both Carthage and Rome, went to Milan, where AMBROSE was then bishop. He had led an immoral life, but through the efforts of his mother and the preaching of Ambrose, he became a Christian (387), and soon after went back to Africa. He was made a priest, and when forty-two years old became Bishop of Hippo, in Africa, an office which he held until his death at the age of seventy-six (Aug. 28, 430). Augustine was one of the purest and wisest men that ever lived, and he was noted as one of the greatest preachers of his time. He wrote many books, among which his

"Confessions," in which he tells the story of his life, and his "City of God," which he wrote partly to prove that the miseries which had come to Rome in those days were not caused by the giving up of the heathen gods, as the pagans claimed, were very famous and are still much read.

AU-GUS'TUS, Caius Julius Cæsar Octavianus, first Emperor of Rome, born at Velitra, near Rome, Sept. 23, 63 B.C. He was the son of Caius Octavius, and of Atia, daughter of Julia, the youngest sister of Julius Cæsar, who was, therefore, his great-uncle. Julius Cæsar treated him as his own son, and made him his heir in his will. Octavius, as he was then called, was at school in Greece when his uncle was killed (44). He at once went to Rome, changed his name to Octavianus, and began to strive with ANTONY for the power. He defeated Antony in a battle near Mutina (Modena), but afterward made peace with him and formed with him and Lepidus a league, by which the three agreed to divide the Empire between them. This league is commonly called the Second Triumvirate, a like one formed by Julius Cæsar, Pompey and Crassus being called the First Triumvirate (government of three men).

After defeating BRUTUS and CASSIUS at Philippi (42), the triumvirs cruelly put to death thousands of their enemies. Octavius finally quarrelled with Anthony, defeated him at ACTIUM (31), and thus became master of Rome. When he had been consul seven times he offered to give up the power, but the Senate begged him to keep it. After this he took into his own hands one office after another until finally he was sole ruler of the empire. In the year 27 B.C., the Senate gave him the title of Augustus (noble or venerated), and he was afterward known by it; and the name of the month of Sextilis was changed to Augustus (English August.)

The reign of Augustus was peaceful and prosperous. He did much for Rome, and boasted that he had found it a city of brick and made it a city of marble. He set up libraries and schools, encouraged the arts, and made good laws. His age has been called the "Augustan age of literature," because in it lived many of the most famous of the Latin writers, among whom were VIRGIL, HORACE, OVID, CICERO, Catullus and TIBULLUS. Augustus died at Nola, near Naples, when seventy-seven years old (Aug. 19, A.D. 14), and was succeeded by Tiberius, the husband of his daughter and only child, Julia.

AU-RE'LI-AN, Lucius Domitius Aurelianus, a Roman Emperor, born in Pannonia, on the Danube, about A.D. 212. His parents were very common people and very poor. When he was a youth he joined the Roman army as a common soldier, and became so famed for his bravery that his comrades called him "Aurelian Sword-in-hand." He was very large and had great strength, and it is said that he killed eight hundred men with his own hand in his many battles. He rose quickly in rank and got to be so popular that the soldiers made him Emperor when the Emperor CLAUDIUS died (270). The principal event of his reign was the capture of Palmyra, the magnificent capital of Queen ZENOBIA. He spared her life and treated the people kindly, but after he had gone, the Roman garrison left there was massacred, and he returned and put the inhabitants to the sword, and carried Zenobia to Rome. Aurelian was on his way to fight the Persians when he was killed by his own soldiers near BYZANTIUM (A.D. 275).

AURUNGZEBE (*o'rung-zeeb,*) a famous Emperor of the MOGULS in India, born Oct. 22, 1618. When his father, Shah Jehan, who had made him governor of some of his provinces, was taken ill. Aurungzebe stirred up strife among his brothers, and finally, by killing them and putting his father in prison, got all the power into his own hands. His reign was a very brilliant one, and his empire covered nearly all of Hindostan and many of the countries around it. His real name was Mohammed, but he was called Aurungzebe (Ornament of the Throne) by his grandfather. When he became great he called himself Alum-Geer (Conqueror of the World). He died when eighty-eight years old and in the fiftieth year of his reign (Feb. 21. 1707).

AUS'TEN, Jane, an English novel writer, born at Steventon, Hampshire, Dec. 16, 1775. She was the daughter of a clergyman and was much better educated than most young ladies of her time, and beautiful and very interesting ; but she was disappointed in love when young and so never married. She published several novels, which became very popular, without putting her name to them. Among the best of her stories are " Sense and Sensibility" and " Pride and Prejudice." Sir Walter Scott said that she could describe commonplace things and people in a far pleasanter way than he could. She died in Winchester when forty-two years old (July 24 1817).

AUS'TER-LITZ (German *ows'ter-litz*), a town of Moravia, in Austria, 12 miles east of Brünn, population about 3,500. It is noted for the great victory won there by Napoleon over the Austrians and Russians, led by their Emperors, Francis and Alexander (Dec. 2, 1805). Napoleon managed so that his enemies should not find out the size of his army, which was nearly as large as their two, so he soon got the better of them. Toward the close of the battle, some of the allied soldiers tried to save themselves by crossing a frozen lake, but Napoleon ordered his guns to play on the ice, which was broken up, so that 2000 men were drowned. After this battle Napoleon had everything his own way.

AUSTRALIA (*aws-tra'le-ah*), the largest island in the world, called by some geographers a continent, lying S. E. of Asia ; area, about 2,550,000 square miles, or less than three-fourths that of the United States ; pop. about 3,323,000, or less than that of Ohio. Its surface is mostly an immense plain or table-land, much of which is barren, except in the rainy season. The principal mountain chain is on the east coast. Its highest peaks are only about a mile and a quarter high, not lofty enough for snow to lie on all the year. As there are few mountains, there are of course few rivers, the Murray, with its branch the Darling, being the largest.

Australia is very rich in minerals, especially in gold, copper, and tin. Silver, lead, coal, and precious stones also are found. The climate is very hot, especially in the north part, which is nearest the equator, but it is generally healthful. A large part of the country is good pasture land, where millions of sheep are kept, and more wool is sent from Australia than from anywhere else in the world. Many very singular plants grow there. Some of the trees shed their bark every year instead of their leaves, which stay green all the time, and in many the leaves grow with their edges turned toward the ground instead of their flat sides, so as to give but little shade, while others have no leaves at all. There are ferns which grow three or four times as high as a man, and have branches like trees, and trees, called gum-trees, which grow nearly a tenth of a mile (500 feet) high, or higher than the great trees of California, or the pyramids. Many of the plains are covered with kangaroo grass, which grows high enough to hide a horse and its rider. Very beautiful flowers bloom there, but few of them have any sweet smell, though the leaves of several kinds of trees are fragrant.

The animals of Australia differ too from those of other countries. The only bad beast of prey is the dingo, an animal looking like a dog, and about half way between a wolf and a fox in size, which roams about in packs, killing sheep. There are many pouched animals (C. C. T., 379, II., u.), one, the kangaroo,

Australia.

as large as a man, and others no larger than a rat. The duck-bill is a water animal like a beaver, but with a bill like that of a duck. Among the birds, is a kind of king-fisher, which has such a hoarse, screaming voice, that the people call it the "laughing jackass."

The natives of Australia are different from the races of the islands around them. They are nearly black, and have black, curly hair, but not crisp like that of the negro. Some have no fixed homes, but wander around naked, and live on raw flesh. They do not use bow and arrows, but have spears and

clubs, and a strange weapon called a "boomerang," a sharp-edged piece of bent wood, which they throw with great skill, so that it strikes the ground a good way off, and bounds back again toward the thrower. There are but few of these people left, and they will soon be all gone.

Australia, which belongs to Great Britain, is divided into five colonies, Victoria, New South Wales, Queensland, South Australia, and Western Australia. Of these, Victoria, the smallest but most important, is about as large as New England, New Jersey, Delaware, and Maryland put together. Each colony has a governor sent from England, but most of the other officers are elected by the people.

Australia was first seen probably by the Dutch in 1606, and was named New Holland. The first English settlement was made in 1788, when a shipload of convicts was sent to New South Wales. Many other prisoners were afterward sent there, but the free people who went there to live not liking this, the English government finally stopped sending them (1834). Since then the colonies have grown quite fast.

The name Australia, given to the country by the English, is made from the Latin word *australis*, southern.

AUSTRIA (*aws'tre-ah*), See Austro-Hungarian Monarchy.

AUSTRO-HUNGARIAN MONARCHY, an empire of Europe, lying between Germany and Turkey; area, about 265,000 square miles, or a little less than that of Texas; pop. about 38,500,000, or the same as that of the United States in 1870; capital, Vienna. It is almost entirely shut in by other countries, only a small part lying on the Adriatic sea. Next to Switzerland, it is the most mountainous country in Europe, the principal chains being the Alps and the

CARPATHIANS. Its chief river, the DANUBE, is, next after the VOLGA, the largest river of Europe.

The climate is mild and very healthful. The country is rich in all metals, except platinum, and in many kinds of precious stones, and more kinds of fruits and plants are raised there than in any other part of Europe. It has also great forests. Most of the people are farmers, but about three-tenths of all are engaged in trade and manufactures. The chief things sent to other countries are grain, salt, wool, timber, wine, beer, and goods made of woollen, linen, cotton, leather, iron, and glass. The wines of Austria are among the best in the world.

The Austro-Hungarian Monarchy is made up of two countries, the Empire of Austria and the Kingdom of Hungary, the Emperor of Austria being also King of Hungary. Each country has a government of its own, and there is a general government for the whole Empire. In 1878 the Turkish province of Bosnia was added to the Empire. The people of Austro-Hungary are of many different nations, and speak about twenty different languages. One fourth of all are Germans, and about one sixth are Magyars or Hungarians. The rest are Poles, Croats, Wallachians, Greeks, Jews, &c.

Austria gets its name from *Oestreich* (German for " Eastern Kingdom"), by which it was first called nearly nine hundred years ago. In 1273, Rudolph, Count of HAPSBURG, was elected Emperor of Germany, and since that time kings of that family have ruled in Austria. Francis II. was the first to take the title of Emperor of Austria (1804).

AU-TOL'Y-CUS, in Greek fable, a son of Mercury, noted for his cunning as a robber and a liar. He used to steal sheep, change their marks, and mix them with his own, so that no one would know them.

But Sisyphus, whose sheep he had taken, had marked his under their feet, and so found them, and made Autolycus give them up.

AVA (*ah'vah*). See BURMAH.

A-VER'NUS, a small lake about 8 miles W. of Naples, Italy, supposed by the ancients to be the entrance to HADES. It lies in the crater of an old volcano, and it is thought that its name (made up of two Greek words, meaning " no bird") was given to it, because the vapors which rose from it killed the birds that tried to fly across it. It is now called Averno.

AVIGNON (*ah-veen'yong*), a city of S. E. France, on the River Rhone; pop. about 41,000, or about as large as Peoria, Ill. It is surrounded by a wall with towers and battlements, and has many very old buildings. Silk is manufactured there, and it has a large trade in wine, brandy, and grain.

Avignon was the capital of a Gallic tribe before the time of JULIUS CÆSAR. Its name has been changed from Avenio, by which it was called by the Romans. From 1309 to 1377 the Popes lived there, and their palace is still standing and is used as a prison. It was then a great city, and had a large population. In 1791 it became a part of France.

AX'MIN-STER, a town of Devonshire, England, on the river Axe; pop. about 2,500. It was once famous for the manufacture of carpets, which were much like those brought from Turkey and Persia, but none are now made there.

AY'E-SHAH. See MOHAMMED.

AYTOUN (*a'ton*), **William Edmondstoune,** a Scottish poet, born in Edinburgh in 1813. He was educated at the University of Edinburgh, where he became a professor in 1845. He wrote a great deal for Blackwood's Magazine, in which was first printed his " Lays of the Scottish Cavaliers." Among his other books are " Bothwell," a story in verse about the Earl of

Bothwell, who was one of the husbands of Mary Queen of Scots. Aytoun died in Edinburgh when fifty-two years old (Aug. 4, 1865.)

AZ′ORES or **Western Islands,** a group of islands belonging to Port-

Azores' Wagon.

ugal, in the Atlantic about 800 miles W. of Portugal; area 1,000 square miles, or less than the State of Rhode Island; pop. 270,000. They are mountainous, with high, steep shores, and look very beautiful from the sea. They are all volcanic, earthquakes are frequent, and fresh volcanoes sometimes rise among them. In 1811 one rose out of the sea near San Miguel, the largest island, vomited ashes and stones, and then disappeared again. The climate is pleasant and healthful. The best harbor is in the island of Fayal of which the chief town, Horta, is commonly but wrongly called Fayal. Most of the trade is from this port. Azores means the islands of hawks. They were so called by the Portuguese, who first went there in 1432, on account of the great number of hawks there (Port. *açor*, hawk.)

AZ′OV, Sea of. See BLACK SEA.

B

BA′AL, the chief god of the Phœnicians, the same as Bel or Belus of the Chaldeans, and Jupiter of the Greeks and Romans, and supposed to be the sun. His image in his temples had the head of an ox and held a child in its arms. Baal is an Eastern word meaning Lord or Commander.

BAALBEC (*ba′al′bek*), an ancient city of Syria, 36 miles N. of DAMASCUS. Its age is not known, but it was rich and flourishing under the Romans. The Emperor ANTONINUS PIUS built there a splendid temple to Jupiter, one of the wonders of the world, which in after times was turned into a Christian Church. The city suffered from many sieges by the Moslem Caliphs, the Christian Crusaders, and the Turks, and was at last quite destroyed by an earthquake (1759) which left only a few columns and walls of the great temple standing. The ruins show that it was a very magnificent building.

Baalbec means the city of BAAL or the sun.

BABEL, the Hebrew or Chaldee name of Babylon and of the tower near it, the building of which is said in the Bible to have been stopped by the confusion of tongues. The vast mound of Birs Nimrod (Citadel of Nimrod) at Borsippa, near ancient Babylon, is thought to be the tower of Babel. It is built of bricks, and seems to have been seven stories high, each story painted a different color in honor of some god. It was used both as a temple and an observatory for astronomers. Babel is said to mean "confusion," but in

Chaldee it was probably Bab-Il—
"the gate of the highest God."

BABER (*bah'ber*), **Zaher ed-Din Mohammed,** the founder of the Tartar or Mogul Empire in India, born in 1483. He was descended from TIMOUR, and when about eleven years old succeeded his father as Sultan of Khokan, a Tartar kingdom. He spent his life in conquest, and finally planted his empire firmly in India, where he vanquished the ruler of DELHI in 1526, and made that city his capital. He died at the age of forty-seven (1530), and was succeeded by his son Humayun, who was the father of the great AKBAR.

BAB'Y-LON, one of the most famous of ancient cities, capital of Babylonia, on the river Euphrates. Babylonia included also the country called Chaldea, near the head of the Persian Gulf. Babylon was built on both sides of the river, in the form of a square, and its wall is said to have been fifty-six miles round and wide enough on top for a four-horse chariot to turn between the buildings which lined its edges. It had a hundred brazen gates, and was surrounded by a deep moat full of water; and within, besides its splendid buildings, palaces, and temples, were beautiful gardens and pleasure grounds. The famous hanging gardens were among the wonders of the world. They were built by NEBUCHADNEZZAR to please his Queen, who wanted something in this flat country to remind her of her native mountains of Media. Great terraces were made one above another, and covered with flat stones on which was put earth deep enough for the largest trees to grow in; and the whole was covered with grass, trees, shrubs, plants, and flowers, and laid out in walks, so as to make a beautiful mountain within the city.

Babylon was a very old place, but did not become of much importance till after the fall of NINEVEH. It then grew very fast, and

in the sixth century B. C. it was a great centre for trade and had a very large population. When in the height of its glory it was taken by Cyrus, King of Persia (538 B. C). Cyrus drew off the water of the river into a new channel which he had dug, and got into the city through its dry bed in the night time, taking by surprise the inhabitants, who thought they were safe behind their strong walls. After this, Babylon fell into decay little by little, and when ALEXANDER THE GREAT took it, it was almost a ruin. Alexander meant to rebuild it and make it the capital of his empire, but died there before he had finished his plans.

Babylon is the Greek form of BABEL, which was the real name of this city.

BACCHUS (*bak'kus*), in Greek fable, the God of the vine and its fruits, son of Jupiter and of Semele, daughter of CADMUS, King of Thebes. He taught men how to cultivate the vine and how to make wine, and did so much good to

Bacchus.

mankind that he was made a god. He went about the world in a chariot drawn by panthers or leopards, followed by bands of worshippers, mostly women, who were called Bacchantes. His worship in Greece and Rome consisted chiefly of feasts and noisy revels called Bacchanalia, which at last became so disgraceful that the Roman senate had to forbid them. The Greeks, who called Bacchus Dionysus, made his statue like a beautiful boy crowned with grape leaves and ivy. By the Romans he was sometimes called Liber.

BACH, the name of a noted musical family of Germany, founded by a Hungarian baker named Veit Bach, who was forced to leave his home in Presburg because he was a Protestant, and settled in Thuringia in central Germany about 1600. For more than two hundred years his descendants were celebrated for their musical genius. His great-great-grandson, John Sebastian Bach, born at EISENACH, March 21, 1685, was one of the greatest musicians that ever lived. He wrote beautiful church music and wonderful fugues, or compositions in which the different parts follow each other, each part repeating the subject or principal air at regular intervals. He wrote music for every instrument then used, and was the greatest master of keyed instruments in his time. He died at Leipsic when sixty-five years old (July 30, 1750), leaving ten sons, all fine musicians.

BA'CON, Francis, Viscount St. Albans and Baron Verulam, an English philosopher and statesman, born in London, Jan. 22, 1561. He was the youngest son of Sir Nicholas Bacon, Lord Keeper of the Seals, and as he was a bright and thoughtful child, Queen Elizabeth delighted to talk with him and ask him questions on deep subjects, often calling him her "little lord keeper;" but as he grew older she loved him less and would not give him the high offices which he desired. He studied at the University of Cambridge, and became a lawyer, and when twenty-eight years old was made counsel extraordinary to the Queen. Two years later he went to Parliament, where his speeches were so fine that Ben

JONSON said "The fear of every man that heard him was, that he should make an end." The Earl of Essex had always been his devoted friend, and gave him a large estate when he was poor, yet when he was disgraced, Bacon was base enough to turn against him, and use his skill as a lawyer to have him condemned, in hope of pleasing the Queen. But Bacon grew great and powerful only after James I. became King, when he rose from one post of honor and fortune to another, until he was made Lord Keeper at the age of fifty-six (1617), and Lord Chancellor the next year. He was also given the titles of Baron of Verulam and Viscount St. Albans (1621).

During all this time he had been writing books on philosophy and science, and at fifty-nine he completed his greatest work, the *Novum Organum* (Latin for New Instrument), in which he tries to show how false the old way of studying science was, and teaches what he considers a better method, called the "inductive," which means that we are to study facts and objects in order to find out the cause of them, and not to guess at the cause first and then try to make the fact fit into it. But in spite of his great intellect, he had not a noble character, and the year after the Novum Organum appeared (1621), he was accused by Parliament of the crime of accepting bribes as Lord Chancellor, that is, he allowed persons to give him money to decide cases in their favor, and his great offices were taken away from him, though the King said he should not pay a fine as was at first decided.

He spent the rest of his life in scientific studies, and died at Highgate, aged sixty-five (April 9, 1626). Thousands have admired and reverenced Bacon as a great teacher and philosopher, but as a man few so little deserve our admiration. Pope, the poet, calls him " The wisest, brightest, meanest of mankind."

BACON, Roger, an English scholar, born about 1214. When twenty-eight years old, he became a Franciscan monk at Oxford, and wrote many works in Latin on scientific subjects. He also lectured and tried experiments in physics and chemistry, with instruments made by himself. He is said to have found out how to make gun-powder and to have had some idea of the telescope; but in that ignorant age he was accused of magic. The Franciscans in Paris would not allow his books to be read, and ordered him to be shut up in his cell, when he was quite an old man (1278). He was released, however, after ten years, and died at the age of about seventy-eight (1292 or 1294).

BADAJOZ (*bad-ah-hoce'*), a town of Spain, on the river Guadiana, near the boundary of Portugal; pop. about 27,000, or nearly the same as that of Williamsport, Pa. It is built on a hill three hundred feet high, on the top of which are the ruins of a Moorish castle, and is strongly fortified. Its situation on the border of the two countries made it an important place formerly, and it has suffered many sieges. It was taken by the French in the wars of Napoleon (1811), and in the following year WELLINGTON took it by storm, after losing 5,000 men in besieging it, and let his soldiers plunder it for two days and nights.

The Romans called this place Pax Augusta. The Moors, who long held it, made this into Paxagousa, and this became changed in time into Badajoz.

BADEN (*bah'den*), a grand duchy, belonging to the German Empire, north of Switzerland, with the Rhine on the west and south, area about 5,910 square miles, or a fourth larger than Connecticut; pop. 1,-600,000, or about the same as North Carolina; capital, CARLSRUHE. The principal mountains are the Schwarzwald (Black Forest) and the Odenwald, often mentioned in stories of the Middle Ages. The country is full of mineral springs, the most famous being at Baden-Baden, where people flock from all parts of the world. There is a celebrated University at HEIDELBERG. About 1150 the Margraves of Baden first took their name. The ruler was made Grand Duke by Napoleon (1806), and the present Grand Duke, Frederic, married the daughter of the Emperor of Germany (1856).

Baden comes from the old German word *bad*, a bath.

BAFFIN, William, an English sailor, born in 1584. He spent several years exploring the coast of Greenland, and discovered the bay now called after him, when thirty-two years old (1616). After that he made voyages to the East and was killed by the Portuguese at Ormuz, an island at the entrance of the Persian Gulf (1622). He wrote accounts of his voyages.

BAG'DAD, a city of Turkey in Asia, on the river Tigris, pop. 90,-000, or about as large as Albany, N. Y. It is on both sides of the river, and the two parts are joined by two bridges of boats. The streets are narrow and unpaved, but there are fine bazaars and mosques, and many of the houses are surrounded by date groves and orange gardens. Bagdad was built (about 765) by the Caliph Al-Mansour for his capital, partly out of the ruins of BABYLON, and was called by him Medinet el-Salem (Arabic for City of Peace). While the Caliphs lived there, it was the great city of the East, and the chief seat of Arabian learning; and it is said to have had in 873 2,000,000 inhabitants, or twice as many as Chicago has now. It has frequently been taken by the Turks and Persians, and lastly by the Turks in 1638.

Bagdad means the Garden of Dad, a monk who had his cell near the city; the word *bag* or *bagh* being the Turkish for garden.

BAHAMAS (*bah-ha'mas*), a chain of islands belonging to Great Britain, lying between Florida and Hayti; pop. about 50,000; capital NASSAU. There are about six hundred islands in all, but only fifteen are inhabited. Many fruits and valuable woods grow there, and the principal trade is in oranges, pineapples, salt, and sponges. The largest island is called Grand Bahama. San Sal-

Blackbeard.

vador, or Cat Island, one of the group, is supposed by many to be the one called by the Indians Guanahani, which was the first land seen by COLUMBUS in the New World (Oct. 12, 1492). At one time the BUCCANEERS ruled these islands. One of their most noted leaders was called Blackbeard, probably from the color of his beard. The picture of him is taken from an old woodcut.

BAHIA (*bah-e'ah*), a city of Brazil, on the coast about 800 miles N. E. of Rio de Janeiro; pop. near-

ly 200,000, or nearly as large as Detroit, Mich. The older part has crooked and narrow streets, where loaded horses and donkeys often jostle the passer-by. The newer town is on a high bluff, and people go up to it from the lower town by means of a steam elevator. From the top there is a beautiful view over the bay, which is one of the finest harbors in the world. Bahia has a large trade in sugar, coffee, cotton, tobacco, and hides. It is one of the oldest cities in Brazil, having been founded about 1510. For a long time it was the capital of the country.

BAIRD, Spencer Fullerton, an American writer on natural history, born in Reading, Penn., Feb. 3, 1823. He was educated at Dickinson College, Penn. In 1850 he became Assistant Secretary of the Smithsonian Institution, Washington, and when the Secretary, Prof. Henry, died (1878), Prof. Baird was chosen to take his place. In 1871, he was made U. S. Commissioner of Fish and Fisheries, his duties being to study the fishes and other water animals of the coast. He published many papers on mammals, birds, reptiles, and fishes, and a fine work on the "Birds of North America." He died when sixty-four years old (August 19, 1887).

BA-JA'ZET I., a Sultan of the Ottoman Turks, called Ilderim (the lightning) on account of his rapid movements, born in 1347. He succeeded his father AMURATH I.,when forty-two years old (1389) and at once had his younger brother strangled for fear that he would make him trouble. He made all Asia Minor part of his dominions, conquered much of what is now Turkey in Europe, and overran Greece, Hungary and Wallachia. The nations of Europe became uneasy at his success, and Sigismund, King of Hungary, tried to stop his progress, but Bajazet utterly defeated him at Nicopolis (1396). At last

Tamerlane or TIMOUR invaded Asia Minor and defeated him in a great battle at Angora (1402), and is said to have carried him around with him in an iron cage until his death (1403), but this story is not now believed.

BALAKLAVA (*bah-lah-klah'vah*), a small town of S. Russia, on the Black Sea about eight miles from SEBASTOPOL. It is noted as the site of the battle of Balaklava, fought by the allied armies of England, France, Sardinia, and Turkey against the Russians (Oct. 25, 1854), during which took place the famous cavalry charge, celebrated by Tennyson in his poem, "The Charge of the Light Brigade." The English light cavalry, commanded by the Earl of Cardigan, charged on the Russian batteries, cut down their gunners, and rode back through a storm of shot and shell, losing all but 150 out of 600 men. It was a very brave deed, but a useless waste of life.

BALBOA (*bal-bo'ah*), **Vasco Nunez de,** a Spanish discoverer, the first European to see the Pacific Ocean, born at Xeres de-los-Caballeros, in 1475. He was of noble birth, but poor, and when twenty-six years old went to seek his fortune in the New World. While exploring the Isthmus of Panama, he climbed a high mountain and from its top (Sept. 26, 1513) got a view of the great Pacific Ocean. He set up a cross on the spot, and three days later, when he reached the sea shore he stepped into the water and took possession of the sea and the countries near it in the name of the King of Spain. This discovery was welcomed in Europe with much joy and the King made Balboa Admiral, so that he had means of making further explorations. But before the news was received a new governor named Davila had been sent out to Darien, a narrow-minded, cruel man who was meanly jealous of Balboa, although he allowed him to marry

his daughter. Just as Balboa had succeeded in building two ships for an expedition to Peru, Davila falsely accused him of intending to rebel and had him executed, at the age of forty-two (1517), to the grief of all the inhabitants.

BALDWIN (*bauld'win*), the name of several Counts of FLANDERS, whose descendants became Kings of Jerusalem and Emperors of Constantinople,

Baldwin I., called Bras de Fer (French for Iron Arm), married Judith, daughter of CHARLES THE BALD, King of France, who made him Count of Flanders. He died in 879.

Baldwin I., King of Jerusalem, born in 1058, was a descendant of the fifth Count of Flanders. He went with his brother Godfrey de BOUILLON on the first CRUSADE to the Holy Land (1096), and when Godfrey died (1100) succeeded him as King of Jerusalem. He was a very brave man and gained many victories over the Saracens. He died when sixty years old (1118). TASSO, in his poem of "Jerusalem Delivered," tells much about him and Godfrey.

Baldwin II., King of Jerusalem, cousin of Baldwin I., succeeded him in 1118. He was one of the bravest and best knights of his time. He died in 1131.

Baldwin III., King of Jerusalem, grandson of Baldwin II., born about 1130, was one of the bravest and most honorable of the Crusaders. He fought much against the celebrated NOUREDDIN, Sultan of Aleppo. When Baldwin died (Feb. 23, 1162), Noureddin was advised to attack the Christians during the funeral of their leader, but he replied: "No, let us respect their grief, for they have lost a King whose like is rarely to be met with."

Baldwin I., Emperor of Constantinople, born in 1171, was Baldwin IX., Count of Flanders. When the Crusaders took Constantinople from the Greek Emperor, they made him Emperor (1204), but he was taken by the Greeks the next year and put to death.

Baldwin II., Emperor of Constantinople (1228 to 1261) was his nephew.

BAL·E·AR'IC ISLANDS, a group of islands in the Mediterranean Sea, E. of Spain ; area, 1935 square miles, or about one and a half times as large as Rhode Island ; pop. 307,000, or a little more than San Francisco, Cal. The principal islands are called Majorca and Minorca. All are high and rocky, and noted for fine scenery. The climate is warm and pleasant.

Coal is found in Majorca and quarries of fine marble are worked in all the islands. There are many vineyards and a great deal of wine is made. Among the other products are olives and olive-oil, oranges, figs, and saffron. The islands belong to Spain and the people are much like Spaniards.

It is said that the name comes from the Greek word *ballein*, meaning to throw, because the people were very skilful in using the sling. The islands have belonged to the Phœnicians, Romans, Vandals, Visigoths, Moors, and French.

BALFE (*balf*), **Michael William,** a noted musician and writer of operas, born in Dublin, May 15, 1808. When eight years old he played the violin in concerts, and the next year wrote a song which was sung in the theatre. He became a singer himself when seventeen years old (1825), and won much praise in Europe and in this country, where he came in 1834. He wrote many operas, among which are the "Siege of Rochelle," "Joan of Arc," "The Rose of Castile," "The Enchantress," and "The Bohemian Girl," the last being the most popular of all his works. He died in London when sixty-two years old (Oct. 20, 1870).

BALIZE (*ba-leez'*). See HONDURAS, BRITISH.

BALKAN (*bahl-kahn'*) a long range of mountains in Turkey in Europe, south of the river Danube, running nearly east and west from the Black Sea to the Adriatic. The highest peaks are 8,000 feet high. There are several passes, the chief one called Shumla Pass. There are copper, lead, and iron mines and abundance of marble. In the last war between the Russians and Turks there was much fighting done in these mountains (1878).

BAL'LI·OL, the name of a noble family who came into England with WILLIAM THE CONQUEROR, and who got their name from the Manor of Baileul, in Normandy, France. In the reign of Henry III. of England, John de Balliol married a Scottish princess, descended from King David I. of Scotland. Their son John (born about 1259) claimed the throne after the death of the Princess Margaret of Norway (1290), but was opposed by Robert BRUCE and John Hastings, whose mothers were younger sisters of the princess who married Balliol. The three left the question to King Edward I. of England, who gave the crown to Balliol, and he was crowned in 1292. Being called upon to aid King Edward in a war against France, Balliol joined with the French king against England. King Edward marched against him, made him give up his crown, and kept him a prisoner in London until 1299. He finally went to his estate of Bailleul, and died there in 1315. Edward Balliol, his son, went to Scotland in 1332, and tried to win the kingdom from King David II., the son of Robert Bruce. With the aid of Edward III. of England, he defeated the Scotch, and was crowned King (Sept. 24, 1332. But most of the people did not want him, and after a reign of only three months, he fled to England, and died there in 1363.

BALTIC (*bawl'tik*) **SEA,** an inland sea of N. Europe, between Russia,

Sweden, Germany, and Denmark; area, 154,000 square miles, or not quite a fourth as large as the Gulf of Mexico. It is the shallowest of all the seas, and as it has many sand-banks and islands and is often swept by storms, its navigation is dangerous. Its water is not very salt, and it therefore freezes earlier than the ocean. The Baltic connects with the Cattegat and the North Sea by three channels, called the Sound, the Great Belt, and the Little Belt; and it is supposed to get its name on this account from the Latin word *balteus*, a belt.

BALTIMORE (*bawl'te-more*), a city of Maryland, and the seventh in size in the United States, on the Patapsco river, 14 miles from Chesapeake Bay and 38 miles from Washington; pop. 434,500 or not quite as large as Boston, Mass. It has much shipping and a large trade, and receives, next after New York and Philadelphia, more foreign goods than any other port in the United States, but there are six other ports which send more goods away to foreign countries. The port is defended by Fort McHenry, on a point between the river and the harbor. This fort was successfully defended in 1814 against a British fleet; and it was during this fight that our song of the "Star Spangled Banner" was written by Francis S. Key, who was then a prisoner on one of the British ships.

Baltimore is sometimes called the "Monumental City," on account of its handsome monuments. It has many schools and colleges, among them the Johns Hopkins University, and several libraries, of which the Peabody Library is the largest. Near the city is Druid Hill, a very beautiful park.

Baltimore was laid out as a town in 1730, and was named in honor of Lord Baltimore, who was Baron of Baltimore in Ireland. When the war of the Revolution began, it had only about 6,000 inhabitants. Congress sat there for a while in 1776, when the British threatened to attack Philadelphia.

BALZAC (*bahl-zahk*) **Honoré de,** a noted French writer of novels, born at Tours, May 16, 1799. When he left school, he became a clerk in a notary's office; but soon tired of this and began to write stories under different false names. He wrote many volumes before he was twenty-five years old, but they were all unsuccessful, and he came to great poverty. When thirty years old (1829), he published, under his own name, a novel called "The Last Chouan," after which his books, of which he wrote about a hundred, were successful, and he won great fame. His novels have been translated into many languages. He died in Paris when fifty-one years old (Aug. 20, 1850).

Laure de Balzac (**Mme. Surville**), his sister, born in 1800, wrote many fairy tales and stories for young folks. She died in 1876.

BAN'CROFT, George, an American statesman and author of a "History of the United States," born in Worcester, Mass., Oct. 3, 1800. He was educated at Harvard College and at the University of Göttingen in Germany. On his return to the United States in 1822, he became a tutor of Greek in Harvard for a year, and afterward taught school at Northampton, Mass., at the same time collecting materials for his history, the first volume of which was published when he was thirty-four years old (1834). Ten years afterward he became Secretary of the Navy under President Polk, and founded the Naval Academy at ANNAPOLIS (1845). In 1846 he was made Minister to Great Britain, in 1867 Minister to Prussia, and in 1871 Minister to the German Empire. The concluding volume of his history was published in 1882. He died when ninety years old (January 17, 1891).

BANG-KOK', a city, capital of SIAM, on the river Menam, 20 miles from the sea; pop. about 350,-000, or a little larger than Rhode Island. One-half the people are Chinese, who do most of the business, and the remainder are made up mostly of Siamese, Malays, and Hindoos. The river, which is about a quarter of a mile wide and deep enough for large vessels, is lined with rows of wooden houses built on bamboo rafts and fastened by chains to piles or large posts driven into its bed. Most of the common people live in these floating houses, each of which has a canoe belonging to it. Only the palaces of the two kings, the temples, and the houses of the nobles and great men are allowed to be built on the banks. Some of the temples are very beautiful, and are decorated with gold, silver, and precious stones. There are said to be 20,-000 priests belonging to the temples, all of which are supported by the gifts of the people, who are mostly Buddhists in religion. The royal palace is a splendid building surrounded by three walls and strongly fortified. Near it is the palace of the white elephant, an animal which is sacred in Siam.

BAN'GOR, a city of Maine, on the Penobscot River, 55 miles from the sea; pop. about 19,000, or about as large as Bayonne, N. J. The Penobscot runs through great forests of pine, spruce, and hemlock, and a great many men are employed in cutting down the trees, sawing it into lumber, bringing it down the river in rafts, and loading it on vessels in Bangor, to be sent to all parts of the world. More lumber is sent from there every year than from any other place in America exepting Chicago.

Bangor is said to have been named after the tune Bangor, and not from the city of Bangor (Bang'-ger) in Wales.

BAN'NOCK-BURN, a small vil-lage of Scotland, three miles from Stirling Castle, where a great battle was fought between the English and Scotch, June 24, 1314. The English, commanded by King Edward II., numbered nearly 100,000 men, and the Scots, under Robert BRUCE, only about 30,000. The Scots, knowing that the liberty of their country depended on the battle, spent the night before it in fasting, but the English, sure of victory, gave up their time to feasting and revelry. But on the next day the English lost 30,000 men, and King Edward had to fly on horseback. This battle made Scotland independent and gave Robert Bruce his throne.

Bannockburn means the brook (burn) of the bannocks, a kind of oaten cakes common in that country.

BAR-BA'DOES, a British island in the West Indies, the most easterly of the Caribbee group; area, 166 square miles; pop. about 170,-000, of whom only about one tenth are white. It is more thickly peopled than any other country in the world excepting MALTA. The climate is hot, and the island is often swept by hurricanes, in which sometimes many hundreds of people lose their lives. Sugar, cotton, aloes, and arrowroot, are sent from there.

Barbadoes was discovered in the 16th century by the Portuguese, who gave it its name, which means the "island of pines." The English first settled there in 1625.

BAR'BA-RY STATES, a name given to all the countries of Africa, N. of the desert of Sahara, and between Egypt and the Atlantic, thus including TRIPOLI, TUNIS, ALGERIA, and MOROCCO.

The name comes from the Berbers, the ancient people of the country.

BAR'BAULD, Anna Letitia, an English writer, born in Leicestershire, June 20, 1743. She was the daughter of the Rev. John Aikin, by whom she was educated. She was very bright when a child, and wrote poems at an early age. When thirty years old she collected and published them, and they at once gave her fame. The next year she married the Rev. Mr. Barbauld, and afterward helped him for many years in teaching school. She wrote many books, of which those for young folks are among the most useful and best of their kind.

She died near London when eighty-two years old (March 9, 1825).

BARCELONA (*bar-sa-lo'nah*), a city of N. E. Spain, on the Mediterranean; pop. about 430,000, or not quite as large as Baltimore, Md Next after Madrid, it is the largest and most flourishing city of Spain, and it is the most important seaport and manufacturing place in the kingdom. It is surrounded by a wall, and defended by strong forts and a citadel. Silk, woollen, and cotton goods, laces, paper, soap, and steel, are sent from there.

Barcelona is said to have been founded by Hamilcar Barca, the father of HANNIBAL, who called it Barcina, and from this its present name has come. It has suffered many sieges.

BARCLAY DE TOLLY (*bar-kla'-deh to-le'*), **Michael**, Prince, a famous Russian general, of Scotch descent, born in Livonia in 1759. He fought bravely in the wars against Turkey, Sweden, and Poland, and served in the campaigns against Napoleon, often holding the chief command. When fifty-two years old (1814), he was made marshal and a prince of the Empire. He died four years afterward in Prussia (May 25, 1818).

BARENTZ (*bah'rents*), **Willem,** a Dutch sailor, pilot of one of two ships which sailed from Amsterdam in 1596 to find a way to China and India around the north of Asia. The ships went to SPITZ-

BERGEN and then lost each other. Barentz sailed round NOVA ZEMBLA, when his ship got caught in the ice, and was frozen up in a little bay which Barentz named Ice Haven. There he and his crew had to spend the winter in a cabin which they built on the shore, suffering greatly from cold and want, and seeing no sun from the beginning of November to nearly the end of January. The next June (1597) they started in two small boats to sail homeward round Nova Zembla, but Barentz died a few days afterward (June 20). After a voyage of two and a half months, most of the rest of them reached Lapland, from whence they got back safe to Holland.

The place where they passed the winter was not visited again by man until more than three hundred years afterward (1871), when a Norwegian captain sailed round there and found Barentz's house still standing, and in it many things left there by him. Among them were guns, swords, axes, copper kettles, and a clock, all of which are now in the museum at the HAGUE.

BARI (*bah're*), a city of S.E. Italy, on the Adriatic Sea; pop. 58,000, or about as large as Camden, N. J. It is defended by strong walls, and by an ancient castle which is nearly a mile in circuit. The city has a good harbor and carries on a large trade in grain, olives, oil, and wine.

In ancient times Bari was called Barium. It has belonged at different times to the Saracens, Greeks, and Normans.

BARLOW (*bar'lo*), **Joel,** an American poet, born in Reading, Conn., March 24, 1754. He was graduated at Yale College when twenty-three years old, and soon after became a chaplain in the army of the Revolution. After the war, he studied law and went to Hartford to live. When thirty-two years old he published a poem called "The Vision of

Columbus," which was very popular. In 1788 he went to Europe, made a fortune in France, and wrote there a humorous poem called "Hasty Pudding," which was much admired. He came back to the United States in 1805, and three years afterward published "The Columbiad," which did not become so popular as the others. In 1811 he was sent as Minister to France, and while on his way to meet Napoleon, died near Cracow in Poland, when fifty-seven years old (Dec. 22, 1812).

BAR'MEN, a town of W. Germany, in Prussia, close to Elberfeld; pop. 103,000, or about as large as Allegheny, Pa. It is noted for its manufactures. More ribbons are made there than in any other town of Europe; and there are important manufactories of cotton cloth, velvet, silk, plated-ware, and chemicals. Barmen is formed of many little villages, which still keep their old names, though they have grown into each other. They extend for nine miles along the valley of the River Wupper, and form three groups, which are called Upper, Middle, and Lower Barmen.

BASEL (*bah'zel*), a city of Switzerland, on the Rhine; pop. 74,000, or about as large as Nashville, Tenn. It is the most important manufacturing and trading town in Switzerland, and is especially noted for its ribbons, in the making of which several thousand people are employed.

Basel is a very old place, and was first called Basileia, which means the "queenly city." It is said to have been founded by the Romans.

BASTILE (*bas-teel'*), the state prison and citadel of Paris, built by Charles V. about 1370. It had eight strong towers joined together by high walls, and was defended by a deep ditch, around which was an outer wall. In it were solitary cells for fifty prisoners, and dungeons nineteen feet below the court-

yard. Persons were often seized and shut up there without being told their offence, and treated with great cruelty. When the Revolution broke out the people stormed the Bastile, and destroyed it (July 14, 1789). In its place now stands the Column of July. The key of the Bastile was sent by Lafayette to Washington, and it is still kept at Mount Vernon.

BATAVIA (*ba-ta've-ah*), a city of JAVA, capital of the Dutch East Indies; pop. about 100,000, or nearly the same as that of Allegheny, Pa. Only about six thousand are Europeans, the rest being mostly natives and Chinese. It has a good harbor and the largest trade of any place in the Malay Archipelago. Rice, spices, coffee, sugar, indigo, tin, and rattans, are sent from there.

Batavia means the "good land." The city was founded by the Dutch in 1619.

BATH, a city of England, in Somersetshire, on the river Avon; pop. about 55,000, or as large as Charleston, S. C. It is built in a valley and on the sides of hills in terraces, and has a finer appearance than any other city in England. It gets its name from its hot springs, which bring many sick people there, but it is not as fashionable as it used to be.

The Romans, who found a town at this place when they came to Britain, called it Aqua Solis (Latin for "Waters of the Sun"). The ruins of their baths and temples are still to be seen there.

BATON ROUGE (*bat-un roozh'*), a city, capital of the State of Louisiana, on the Mississippi, 129 miles above New Orleans; pop. about 10,000. It was made the capital of the State in 1847. During the Civil War it was taken by the Union forces, and the State House was burned. When Louisiana came back into the Union (1868) New Orleans was made the capital of the State, but when the new constitution of the State was made (1879) it was decided that Baton Rouge should be the capital again after 1880.

BAVARIA (*ba-va're-ah*), a kingdom of Europe, forming part of the German Empire; area 29,292 square miles, or not quite as large as Indiana; pop. 5,420,000, or rather less than that of New York State; capital, MUNICH. It is a hilly country, with some high mountains, and has large forests. The principal river is the DANUBE. The climate is healthful but very cold in winter, and much snow falls in the highlands. Coal and iron are found everywhere. Bavaria is noted for its manufactures of beer, coarse linen, glass, and toys. Many cattle and sheep are raised.

Bavaria is called by the Germans Baiern, which means the "dwelling of the Boii," the ancient tribe who lived there. The rulers were called in modern times electors until after the battle of Austerlitz, when Napoleon made the elector a king to reward him for helping him against the Austrians. In 1871 Bavaria became a part of the German Empire.

BAYARD, (French, *bah-yar'*) **Pierre du Terrail,** Chevalier de, a French knight, born at the Château Bayard near Grenoble, France, in 1475. His ancestors were soldiers: his great-great-grandfather was killed at POITIERS, his great-grandfather at CRÉCY, and his grandfather at Montlhéry; and his father, though not killed, was often wounded in battle. When a boy he was page to the Duke of Savoy, with whom he learned horsemanship and the use of arms. Charles VIII., took him into his service when he was eighteen years old; and the young soldier showed so much valor at the battle of Fornovo in Italy (1494), where he captured a flag, that he was made a knight. He soon proved himself one of the most skillful soldiers of his time, and performed many brave deeds

in the Italian wars. So great was his renown as a soldier that the young King Francis I. asked to be knighted by his hand at the battle of Marignano in Italy (1515), and in 1522 he held with 1000 men the unfortified frontier town of Mezières for six weeks against 35,000 men under the Count of Nassau, who was thus prevented from marching into France. For this great deed he was given command of a hundred men in his own name, an honor till then kept for princes of the royal family. While fighting in Italy two years later he was mortally wounded, near the banks of the river Sesia, by a stone from an arquebuse. He caused himself to be placed against a tree so that he might die facing the enemy, and expired, after repeating the Miserere, at the age of forty-nine (April 30, 1524). He was the truest knight of his age, as good as he was brave, and perhaps the only hero of the time who deserved all the praise given him. His loyalty, purity, and honor gained for him the name of *Chevalier sans peur et sans reproche* (French for "fearless and blameless knight").

BAY CITY, a city of Michigan, on the Saginaw River, 4 miles from its mouth in Saginaw Bay; pop. 28,000, or as large as Williamsport, Pa. It contains many large saw-mills, and a great deal of salt is made there from the water of salt springs and wells. White-fish, trout, and other fish are caught in the bay and river, and salted, thousands of barrels of them being sold every year. Bay City was settled in 1836.

BAYEUX (*bah-yuh'*), a town of Normandy, France, 15 miles N.W. of Caen; pop. about 9000. In the Cathedral was long kept the famous Bayeux Tapestry, said to have been made by Matilda, wife of William the Conqueror. It is a strip of coarse linen 214 feet long and 20 inches wide, on which is worked with colored woolen threads seventy-two scenes in the Conquest of England. It is very valuable, as it gives a good picture of the manners and customs of that time and of the Norman dress. When Napoleon thought of invading England, he had this tapestry carried all over France and exhibited in the theatres to excite the people to a second conquest. It is now kept in the Town Hall of Bayeux, preserved under a glass case.

BAYONNE (*bah-yon'*), a city of S.W. France, on the river Adour, about 3 miles from the sea and 18 miles from the borders of Spain; pop. about 28,000, or about the same as that of Bay City, Mich. It is strongly fortified, and has one of the best arsenals in France. Though often besieged, it has never been taken, and for this reason the inhabitants call it the " virgin city." Timber, corks, tar, chocolate, and liqueurs are sent from there.

Bayonne means the "good bay." The town was long held by the English, but was given up by them to the French in 1451.

BEARD (*beerd*), **William H.,** an American painter, born in Painesville O., April 13, 1825. He has painted some portraits, but is best known by his amusing pictures of animals. His "Bears on a Bender" and " Raining Cats and Dogs" are good examples of his style. He has a studio in New York. His brother, James H. Beard, born in Buffalo, N. Y., in 1815 (died November 19, 1889), also painted animals.

BEAUHARNAIS, (*bo-ar-na'*), **Alexandre,** Viscount de, a French general, born in MARTINIQUE in 1760. When a major in the army he married Josephine Tascher de la Pagerie, who after his death married Napoleon Bonaparte and became the Empress JOSEPHINE. He served in the American Revolution under ROCHAMBEAU, and afterward in Europe. While on the Rhine he was accused of treason for suffering

the city of Mentz to be taken, and was guillotined in Paris when only thirty-four years old (July 23, 1794). He left two children, Eugène and Hortense, who became the mother of NAPOLEON III.

BEAUHARNAIS, Eugène de, son of Alexandre de Beauharnais and JOSEPHINE, and stepson of the Emperor Napoleon, born in Paris, Sept. 3, 1781. When only fourteen years old he called on Gen. Bonaparte to ask him for his father's sword, which had been taken away during the troubles in Paris. Bonaparte gave him the sword, and Eugène's mother having come soon after to thank him for his kindness to her son, he liked her so much that he married her the next year (1796). Bonaparte was very friendly to Eugène, and when he became Emperor made him a Prince of France and Viceroy of Italy. When twenty-four years old he married the Princess Amalie, daughter of the King of Bavaria, and Napoleon made him Prince of Venice and declared him his " adopted son and heir to the crown of Italy." He showed himself to be a wise and good ruler, and did much for Italy. He was also a good soldier, and he showed great skill in the wars against Austria and in the retreat from Moscow. After the fall of Napoleon he went to Bavaria, and became Duke of Leuchtenberg and Prince of Eichstädt. He died in Munich when forty-three years old (Feb. 21, 1824).

BEAUHARNAIS, Hortense Eugènie de, daughter of Alexandre de Beauharnais and JOSEPHINE, born in Paris, April 10, 1783. When nineteen years old (1802) she married Louis, brother of Napoleon BONAPARTE, and became Queen of Holland when he was made King. She had two sons, Napoleon Louis, who died young, and Louis Napoleon, who became the Emperor NAPOLEON III. She spent the last years of her life in

Switzerland, and died there at Arenenberg when fifty-four years old (Oct. 5, 1837).

BEAUMARCHAIS, (*bo-mar-sha'*), **Pierre Augustin Caron de,** a noted French writer and speculator, born in Paris, January 24, 1732. He was the son of a watchmaker named Caron, and when twenty-three years old became watchmaker to the court. Having great skill in playing the harp and being employed to teach the daughters of LOUIS XV., he became a favorite with them, and soon got an office which gave him noble rank. He then took the name of de Beaumarchais, got rich, and when the American Revolution broke out he made a bargain to send arms and ammunition to the Americans. The French Government helped him in this, and he furnished the colonists with a great many cannon and muskets and much powder and other ammunition. He also sent out to them Baron STEUBEN, PULASKI, and other officers.

When the French Revolution broke out Beaumarchais had to flee, and his property was taken by the government. He was finally allowed to go back to France, but could not get back his great wealth. One morning he was found dead in his bed in Paris (May 19, 1799), he being then sixty-seven years old.

During all his great business affairs Beaumarchais found time to write much, and was noted for his wit and powers of satire. He wrote several plays, the most successful of which were the "Barber of Seville" and the "Marriage of Figaro."

BEAUMONT AND FLETCHER, two English poets who wrote many plays together. Francis Beaumont, son of a judge, was born in Leicestershire, about 1585, and was educated at Oxford. He died before he was thirty years old (1615), it is said from too much literary labor. John Fletcher, son of a bishop, was born in 1576, and was educated at Cambridge. He died when forty-nine years old (1625). The two wrote more than fifty plays, which were very popular in their time, but are coarse and immoral. After Beaumont's death Fletcher is said to have been helped in writing his plays by Philip MASSINGER.

BEAUREGARD (*bo're-gard*), **Pierre Gustave Toutant,** an American general, born near New Orleans in 1818. He was graduated at West Point, and after serving in the Mexican war had charge of government works in New Orleans. When the Civil War broke out he joined the Confederate army, and commanded the forts which bombarded Fort Sumter in Charleston harbor. The first battle of Bull Run was planned by him, though Gen. J. E. Johnston commanded there. At the battle of Shiloh he was second in command until Gen. A. S. Johnston was killed, when he took full command. Being forced to retreat to Corinth, Miss., he defended that place for nearly two months. Afterward he defended Charleston for nearly a year, and in 1864 he aided in the defense of Richmond. He now lives in New Orleans.

BECKET, Thomas à, Archbishop of Canterbury, born in London, about 1117. His father, a Norman merchant and Sheriff of London, had him well educated at Oxford and Paris. Thomas became a priest, and when forty-one years old was made High Chancellor of England, and lived in great splendor and pomp. He was then very friendly with the King, HENRY II., who in 1162 had him made Archbishop of Canterbury. Becket then gave up all his pomp, led a very strict life, and opposed the King in many things. This made Henry very angry and led to a bitter quarrel, and Becket fled to foreign parts. At last he was allowed to come back to England, but he at once began to defy the King again, and one day Henry cried out in a rage: "What cowards have I brought up in my court! Not one will deliver me from this low-born priest!" Four knights, hearing this, went at once to Canterbury and killed the Archbishop with their swords in his own cathedral (Dec. 29, 1170). Two years afterward Becket was made a saint by the Pope, and his splendid shrine at Canterbury used to be visited by thousands of pilgrims every year. One of these pilgrimages is told about by CHAUCER in his "Canterbury Tales." When King HENRY VIII. broke up the monasteries, he declared that Becket was no saint but a rebel and a traitor, and he had his rich shrine destroyed.

BEDE (*beed*), a Saxon monk, commonly called "Venerable Bede," the first writer of a history of England, born in 672. He was one of the greatest scholars of his time, and besides his history, which was written in Latin and translated into Saxon by ALFRED THE GREAT, he wrote many other works. He also translated parts °of the Bible into Saxon. It is said that on the night of his death he was busy translating the Gospel of Saint John, which a scribe was writing for him. "How many chapters are left?" he asked the scribe. "Only one," he replied, "but you are too weak to finish it." "No," said Bede, "take your paper and write quickly." After some time, the scribe said: "Master, it is finished." "You say truly," answered Bede, "it is finished," and after saying a short prayer he died. He was then sixty-three years old (May 26, 735).

BEDOUINS (*bed'oo-inz*), the wandering tribes of the desert in Arabia, Syria, and North Africa. They have no houses but tents, and no settled homes, but move from place to place wherever they can find food for their sheep, goats, and camels, which are tended by the boys and girls. The men are fierce and warlike, and are much given to robbery and fighting. They are very fond of horses, and are among the best riders in the world. All the work is done by women and slaves. The Bedouins are divided into tribes, each of which is ruled by a sheik. They call themselves Mohammedans, but are not very strict in their religion.

The word Bedouin comes from the Arabic *Bedawi* (plural *Bedwan*), which means a dweller in the desert.

BEETHOVEN (*ba'to-ven*), Ludwig van, a famous musician, born in BONN, Dec. 17, 1770. He was of Dutch descent, and his father and grandfather had been musi-

Beethoven.

cians. Before he was four years old his father made him practise on the harpsichord, as the piano of that time was called, several hours every day, and when he was eleven he could play very hard music and even composed some that was good enough to publish. At the age of fourteen he became assistant organist to the court. Three years afterward he went to Vienna, where he studied under MOZART and HAYDN, and he lived there nearly all the rest of his life.

He loved the piano better than any other instrument, and soon excelled everybody in playing it. He became so famous that everybody wanted to know him, and he was honored by the rich and noble. But when about thirty years old he began to grow deaf, and after this he went but little into society and shut himself up among his books and his music. This did not keep him from writing, however, for some of his finest works were composed after this. He wrote almost every kind of music; some of his works, called symphonies, are thought to be the best ever written. He died in Vienna when fifty-six years old (March 26, 1827). A fine bronze statue of him was erected in Bonn in 1845.

BEHRING (*beer'ing*), **Vitus**, the discoverer of Behring Strait, born in Denmark in 1680. He became an officer in the Russian Navy, and was sent by the government to explore the Arctic Seas. He found out (1728) that Asia is not joined to Europe, as many thought, but is divided from it by a strait, about forty miles wide, which connects the Pacific and the Arctic oceans. The sea south of Behring Strait is called after him the Behring Sea. In 1741 he was wrecked on an island in this sea and died there when sixty-one years old (Dec. 8, 1741). The island also is named after him.

BEL-FAST', a N.E. city of Ireland, at the mouth of the river Lagan, 88 miles N. of Dublin; pop. 230,000, or nearly as large as Pittsburg, Pa. Next after Dublin, it is the largest and most important city in Ireland. It is the chief place for the linen trade of the north of Ireland, and it manufactures more linen than any other city in the world.

Belfast is a changed form of Bel-

feirsde, meaning the "ford of the sandbank." The linen trade began there in 1637.

BELGIUM (*bel'je-um*), a country of Europe, between Holland and France; area 11,372 square miles, or about the same as that of Maryland; pop. 6,094,000, or more than that of New York State; capital, BRUSSELS. Excepting the island of Malta, Belgium has more people for its size than any other country in Europe. The surface is mostly level, much of the soil is fertile, and the climate temperate. Next after England, the coal-mines of Belgium give more fuel than those of any other country in Europe, and it is rich in iron. It is also noted for fine horses and cattle, for its flax, and for its manufactures of silk, linen, cotton, woolen, leather, and iron. More than half of the people speak the Flemish language, but French is the language of the court. A great many of the people are poor and wretched. The government is a monarchy.

Belgium means the "country of the Belgæ," a German tribe living there when the Romans conquered it. In modern times the country has formed at different times part of Spain, Austria, France, and Holland, but in 1831 it became independent of Holland.

BEL-GRADE', a city, capital of SERVIA, on the Danube; pop. about 40,000, or nearly the same as that of New Bedford, Mass. It is the chief place of trade between Turkey and Austria, and was once strongly fortified, but its forts are now ruinous. As it stands in an important place, it has been the scene of many famous sieges and battles.

Belgrade means "white fortress."

BEL-I-SA'RI-US, a famous general in the time of the Emperor JUSTINIAN, born in Illyria about 505. When only twenty-four years old he was made general-in-chief by the Emperor, and the next year (530) he defeated the Persians, who had twice as many men as he had. Four years afterward he put an end to the VANDAL kingdom in Africa, and then went to Italy, and, after a long war, won back that country from the Goths, who had conquered it. But he had enemies at court who made the Emperor think that he was disloyal, and he was recalled and all his property was taken from him. He was afterward pardoned, and defeated the Bulgarians (559), but four years after he was again accused and thrown into prison in Constantinople, where he died when sixty years old (March 13, 565). Belisarius was one of the greatest generals that ever lived, for he did the greatest things with the smallest means.

BEL-LER'O-PHON, in Greek fable, son of Glaucus, King of Corinth. Having slain Bellerus (from which he got his name, which means "slayer of Bellerus"), he fled to the King of Argos, who sent him to Iobates, King of Lydia, with a letter asking Iobates to put the bearer to death. Iobates sent him to fight the Chimæra, a firebreathing monster which had the head of a lion, the body of a goat, and the tail of a dragon. Bellerophon caught the winged horse PEGASUS, and soaring into the air upon him, killed the monster. He then defeated the AMAZONS, and Iobates gave him his daughter in marriage and made him his heir. Bellerophon afterward tried to soar to heaven on Pegasus, but Jupiter sent a gadfly which stung the winged steed so that he threw his rider to the earth, and he was made blind by the fall.

BELLEVILLE (*bel'vil*), a city of Illinois, 14 miles S.E. of St. Louis, Mo.; pop. 15,000, or about as large as Columbia, S. C. It is surrounded by a populous and fertile country, with many coal-mines.

The city has a large trade, important manufactories, and one of the largest iron rolling-mills in the Western States.

BELLINI (*bel-le'ne*), an Italian writer of operas, born in CATANIA, Sicily, Nov. 3, 1802. He is chiefly known for his operas " La Sonnambula," " Norma," and " I Puritani," the last being his best work. His melodies or airs are very sweet and pleasing, but in other ways he was not a great musician. He died near Paris when only thirty-three years old (Sept. 24, 1835).

BELOOCHISTAN (*bel-oo-kis-tahn'*), a S. country of Asia, between AFGHANISTAN and the Indian Ocean; area about 106,000 square miles, or a little more than that of California; pop. about 400,000, or a little larger than that of Florida; capital, Kelat. It is a mountainous country, and the people are mostly wandering tribes, much like the BEDOUINS, who live by raising sheep, goats, and camels. They are all Mohammedans, and are ruled by a despot called the Khan.

The name comes from the Belooches, one of the tribes living there.

BEL-SHAZ'ZAR, son of Nabonadius and grandson of Nebuchadnezzar, kings of Babylon. At the time of the taking of BABYLON by CYRUS (538 B.C.) Belshazzar, who then shared the throne with his father, was killed, and his father, who was at Borsippa, was taken prisoner.

BE'LUS, the Greek name of the Chaldean or Babylonian god Bel, supposed to be the same as the Phœnician and Hebrew BAAL, the name under which the sun was worshiped. Belus had a great temple in Babylon.

BENARES (*ben-ar'ez*), a city of British India, on the Ganges, 100 miles above Calcutta; pop. 200,000, or nearly as large as Milwaukee, Wis. It is the holy city of the Hindoos, and contains a thousand temples, some very handsome, and more than three hundred mosques. Formerly its wealth and splendor were very great, and it is said that half a million people lived there, and swarms of pilgrims from every part of India filled its narrow streets, rich with carved shrines, and the steps leading down to the sacred river. It has a large trade, and cotton, woolen, and silk goods are made there.

BEN'E-DICT, the name of fourteen popes, none of whom were very famous.

Benedict XIV., born in Bologna in 1675, became Pope in 1740, and died when sixty-five years old (May 3, 1758). He did much for learning and the fine arts, and wrote many books.

BEN'E-DICT, Saint, founder of the order of monks called after him Benedictines, born at Nursa in Italy, in 480. He lived for some time all alone in a desert, and became noted for piety and good works. Finally he built a monastery on Monte Casino, near Naples, of which he was abbot for many years, and from which sprung many other monasteries throughout western Europe. He died when sixty-three years old (March 21, 543).

BENGAL (*ben-gawl'*). See INDIA.

BEN-NING'TON, a village of Vermont, 55 miles S. of Rutland, near which was fought a battle of the Revolution. The British General BURGOYNE, while on his way from Canada to invade the Northern States, sent Colonel Baum with part of his army to seize the stores at Bennington; but Gen. STARK met him with some "Green Mountain Boys," and in a furious fight killed or captured nearly all his force (August 16, 1777).

BEN'TON, Thomas Hart, an American statesman, born near Hillsborough, North Carolina, March 14, 1782. His father died when he was eight years old, and his mother removed to Tennessee, where Thomas became a lawyer. In the war of 1812 he was a colonel in Gen. Jackson's army. After the war he went to St. Louis, where he practiced law and edited a newspaper. When thirty-eight years old (1820) he was chosen United States Senator, and held that office for thirty years. He wrote a history of this time, called "Thirty Years' View." Mr. Benton was always in favor of a gold and silver currency instead of paper money, and on this account he was sometimes called "Old Bullion." He opposed Mr. CALHOUN'S scheme of nullification, and became his enemy through life. He died in Washington when seventy-six years old (April 10, 1858).

BERANGER (*barong-zha*), **Pierre Jean de,** a French poet, born in Paris, Aug. 19, 1780. He was of very humble birth, and lived with his grandfather, a tailor, until he was nine years old, when he was sent to school near the BASTILE; and from the roof of the house he saw the people attack and destroy that famous prison. He never forgot it, and when he grew up wrote a song about it. When about sixteen years old he began to write poetry, and in 1815 he published a book. His songs became popular, and were sung everywhere by the people, but the government thought they were too free and bold, and he was told that he had better not print any more. He went on, however, writing new songs, for which he was twice imprisoned and fined. His songs had a very large sale, and were sung all over France. He became famous, and when his friends succeeded in putting Louis Philippe on the throne of France he was offered fine positions, but refused them all. When it was known that he was very sick, the street where he lived was crowded with people who came to ask about him. He died in Paris when seventy-seven years old (July 16, 1857).

BER'LIN, a city, capital of Prussia and of the Empire of Germany, on the river Spree, a branch of the ELBE; pop. about 1,315,000, or about an eighth smaller than New York City. It is the largest German city, and, excepting LONDON and PARIS, the largest city in Europe. It stands on a sandy plain, and is built on both sides of the river, which is crossed by more than forty bridges. The walls which once surrounded it are now partly torn down. The new part of the city has many fine squares, streets, and buildings. Unter den Linden (Under the Lindens), the principal street, has four rows of linden or lime trees in it, and is lined with palaces and beautiful houses. The University of Berlin is one of the best in the world, and has about forty-eight hundred students. Berlin is noted for its libraries, museums, picture-galleries, and many fine public buildings and gardens. It is also famous for its manufactures, in which more than half of the people are engaged, and its trade is very large.

About the beginning of the 13th century two villages, called Kölln and Berlin, stood where the city now is. As they grew larger the name Berlin was given to both, because the other name was too much like that of Cologne (German, Köln). It first became a large city under FREDERICK THE GREAT.

BER-MU'DAS, a group of small islands in the Atlantic Ocean, about 600 miles E.S.E. of Cape Hatteras; area 24 square miles; pop. about 15,700; capital, Hamilton. There are more than three hundred, but most of them are mere rocks, and only a few are inhabited. The climate is so mild that the islands are green all the year round. Many vegetables are raised, and the earliest potatoes in our markets are brought from there.

The Bermudas were named after Juan Bermudez, a Spaniard, who discovered them in 1522. Shakespeare calls them, in his play of the "Tempest," the "still vexed Bermoothes."

BERN or **BERNE,** a city, capital of Switzerland, on the river Aar; pop. about 46,000, or the same as that of Saginaw, Mich. It is one of the finest cities in Switzerland, and is built on a rocky bluff, around three sides of which the river flows. The capitol, finished in 1857, is a splendid building. In the middle of the city is a high clock-tower which is very old. When the time comes for the clock to strike, the works set in motion a procession of bears, and an old man with an hour-glass, who strikes the hour on a bell. Bern has a university, fine museums, and an arsenal full of ancient weapons.

Bern is said to get its name from the German word Bären, "bears," and to have been so called by Duke Berthold V., who founded it in 1191, because he killed a bear there. A statue of him, with a bear by his side, stands in the city park, and in the city bears are always kept in two pits walled round with stones. In 1798, when the French took Bern, they carried the bears to Paris, and put them in the Garden of Plants, where one very large one, named Martin, became a great favorite with visitors.

BERNADOTTE (*ber-na-dot'*), **Jean Baptiste Jules,** a French general who became King of Sweden and Norway, born at Pau, France, Jan. 26, 1764. He was the son of a lawyer, and studied to be one himself, but when sixteen years old enlisted as a private in the Royal Marines. He rose in rank very fast, and was a general under Bonaparte in 1797. The next year he married the sister of the wife of Joseph Bonaparte, and he soon became Marshal of France and Prince of Ponte-Corvo, a place near Naples. In 1810 the Diet or Congress of Sweden elected him Crown Prince, and the King, Charles XIII., who had no child, adopted him as his son, under the name of Charles John. Napoleon did not like this much, but he finally gave his consent, and Bernadotte went to Sweden and took part with the King in the government. In 1813 he led the Swedish troops against Napoleon, and in 1814 he made the King of Denmark give up his claims to Norway, which then became part of Sweden. Four years afterward (1818) Charles XIII. died, and Bernadotte became King under the title of Charles XIV. John. He had a peaceful and prosperous reign of twenty-six years, and did much for education, trade, and agriculture. He died in Stockholm when eighty years old (March 8, 1844). He was succeeded by his only son, Oscar I., whose son, Oscar II., is the present King of Sweden and Norway.

BER'NARD, GREAT SAINT, a famous mountain pass over the Alps between Switzerland and Italy. Near the top of the pass, which is more than a mile and a half above the sea, is the monastery of St. Bernard, the highest dwelling in Europe, said to have been first built about nine hundred years ago. There is snow there nearly all the year round, and sometimes terrible storms take place which make traveling very dangerous. The monks and their dogs are very celebrated (C. C. T., 179, I., l, and 573, I., u.). The armies of Charlemagne, of Frederick Barbarossa, and of Napoleon crossed the ALPS by this pass.

Bernard, Little Saint, a pass of the ALPS S. of Mont Blanc. It is not quite as high as the Great Saint Bernard. Hannibal is thought to have crossed into Italy by this pass.

BER'NARD, Saint, Abbot of Clairvaux, born at Fontaines, BURGUNDY, in 1091. His father was a

knight, and his mother was a daughter of Count Bernard. On his mother's death he and his five brothers became monks, and he afterward set up a new monastery in a wild place which he named Clairvaux (French for "beautiful valley"). He was a very learned and pious man, and was so noted for his eloquence that he was selected by the Pope to arouse the people to go on a second CRUSADE to the Holy Land. He went through France and Germany preaching with so much effect that towns and castles were deserted, and everybody wished to join in the fight against the infidels. He died at Clairvaux when sixty-two years old (Aug. 20, 1153).

BERTHIER (*ber-te-a'*), **Louis Alexandre,** a French general who became Prince of Wagram, born in Versailles, Nov. 20, 1753. He was captain of dragoons under La Fayette in the American Revolution. In 1796 he became a general and chief of staff to Bonaparte, whose favor he gained, and he was made a Marshal of France and Prince of Neufchâtel (1806). After the battle of Wagram, in which he distinguished himself, Napoleon gave him the title of Prince of Wagram. Notwithstanding all these favors from the Emperor, Berthier was among the first to welcome LOUIS XVIII., who made him a peer. He was killed, when sixty-two years old, by falling from a window in Bamberg, Bavaria (June 1, 1815).

BERWICK (*ber'rik*), an English town at the mouth of the river Tweed, on the borders of Scotland; pop. about 15,000, or nearly as large as Pottsville, Pa. Berwick Castle, famous in the wars between England and Scotland, is now in ruins. The river is crossed there by a splendid railroad bridge built by Robert STEPHENSON.

Berwick is shortened from Aberwick, which means the "town at the mouth," that is, at the mouth of the river Tweed. In the 13th century it was the richest town in Scotland, and is said to have been equal to London. It is now commonly called Berwick-on-Tweed, because there is another Berwick in Scotland.

BESANÇON (*beh-zong-song'*), a town of E. France, on the river Doubs; pop. 57,000, or a little smaller than Trenton, N. J. It is noted for its manufactures of watches, in which it surpasses every other city in Europe except GENEVA. A great deal of Seltzer water is made there, and there are other important manufactures. The town is strongly fortified, and contains many hospitals and an artillery school. Besançon is a very old town, having been the chief city of the Sequani nation before the Romans conquered Gaul. Many remains of Roman buildings have been found there.

BES'SE·MER, Henry, an English engineer, born in Hertfordshire in 1813. He made many improvements in machines, but is best known as having first found out a new way of making steel, which is called after him Bessemer steel (C. C. T., 591, I., u.). His discovery has made him very rich.

BETH'LE·HEM, a town of Palestine, 6 miles S. of Jerusalem, noted as the birth-place of our Saviour. A church, called the " Church of the Nativity," said to have been built by Helena, mother of CONSTANTINE THE GREAT, stands on the supposed place. About three thousand people, mostly Greek and Roman Catholic Christians, live in the town and support themselves by selling crosses, beads, and other things which they make.

Bethlehem in Hebrew means the " House of Bread;" it was so named on account of its rich soil.

BEYROUT or **Beirout** (*ba'root* or *bi'root*), a town of SYRIA, on the Mediterranean, 85 miles from DAMASCUS; pop. about 80,000, or a little smaller than Toledo, O. It is the principal seaport of Syria, and has a large trade, carried on mostly by Europeans living there. Madder, olive-oil, grain, tobacco, figs, raisins, wool, and raw silk are sent from there. American Protestants have there a college and a medical school.

Beyrout in Hebrew means the "City of Wells." It is supposed to have been first built by the Phœnicians.

BID'DE·FORD, a city of S.W. Maine, on the Saco River, 9 miles from its mouth; pop. 14,400, or nearly as large as Keokuk, Iowa. The river there falls 42 feet, and the water-power is used for many cotton and woolen factories and saw-mills. There is a large trade in lumber.

Biddeford was settled about 1630, and was named after Biddeford in England. Saco, on the opposite side of the river, has about 6000 inhabitants and also contains many cotton-mills and other manufactories. It was separated from Biddeford in 1762.

BID'DLE, James, a United States naval officer, born in Philadelphia, Feb. 28, 1783. He entered the navy when seventeen years old, and became a captain when thirty-two (1815). When in command of the sloop-of-war Hornet he captured (March 23, 1815) the British sloop-of-war Penguin, for which Congress gave him a gold medal. He died in Philadelphia when sixty-five years old (Oct. 1, 1848).

BIERSTADT (*beer'stat*,) **Albert,** an American artist, born in Düsseldorf, Germany, in 1829. He was brought by his parents to the United States when two years old, but when he grew up he went back to Düsseldorf and studied painting. He came back to this country in 1857, and the next year he went with an expedition across the Rocky Mountains to the Pacific coast. On this and other visits there he made many drawings from which he painted large pictures of the YO SEMITE Valley and other scenes. He is now living in New York.

BILBAO (*bil-bah'o*), a city and seaport of N. Spain, on the river Nervion, near the Bay of Biscay; pop. 33,000, or about the same as that of Duluth, Minn. It is the principal seaport of N. Spain. Behind the town are high mountains, from which it gets its name, Bilbao in the Basque language meaning "Under the Hill." It was first built in 1300.

BINGEN, a town of Germany, on the Rhine, 17 miles below Mentz; pop. about 7000. It is a pretty place, and has an old bridge said to have been built by the Romans. Near Bingen is the Mäusethurm (Mice Tower), on a rock in the river, said to have been built many hundred years ago by Bishop Hatto of Mentz, who made all vessels passing by it pay toll. Bishop Hatto was a hard-hearted man, who oppressed the poor and made the people pay high taxes in order that he might build beautiful churches and palaces in Mentz. During a dreadful famine he bought up all the grain, and sold it only to those who could pay the highest prices for it. For this he is said to have suffered a terrible death, being eaten alive by mice in his tower, which thus got its name. The poet Southey has told this story well in verse.

Another story of the Mice Tower is that during the THIRTY YEARS WAR, when the Swedes took almost all the castles on the Rhine, some knights held this against them. The Swedes wanted to get it very much, but the brave knights would not give it up. At last all of them were killed but one, and the Swedes, admiring his bravery, called on him to surrender, offering to spare his life if he would do so; but he cried out, "Mercy neither for you nor for me. Knights can die, but they

cannot surrender." Then with the flag in one hand and his sword in the other, he cut his way through his enemies, plunged into the river, and was never seen again.

Bingen is a very old place. The Romans called it Vincum or Bingium, and this has been changed to its present name.

BIRMINGHAM (*bir'ming-am*), one of the greatest manufacturing cities in England, in Warwickshire, about 100 miles N.W. of London; pop. 400,700, or somewhat smaller than Boston. Being near the middle of England and also near great iron and coal mines, it has grown to be the most important place in Great Britain for the making of all kinds of hardware, and it has more than a thousand smelting furnaces at work. Among the things made there out of iron are steam-engines and other machines, tools, firearms, swords and bayonets, locks, and steel pens. Almost everything, too, which can be made out of gold, silver, brass, copper, and other metals are made there, and many thousands of men and boys are employed in the factories and shops. Moulds for making spear, arrow, and axe heads have been found near Birmingham, and it is supposed that the Britons made there the weapons with which they fought the Romans. But it was long only a little village, and it was not until after WATT found out how to make steam-engines that it grew very fast. At one time its name was pronounced "Brummagem," and from that all kinds of false jewelry and ornaments, which are largely made there, came to be called "Brummagem ware."

BISCAY, Bay of, a large bay of the Atlantic, between France and Spain. It is very stormy, because the west winds drive into it the waves of the Atlantic, which are rolled back again from the rocky Spanish coast.

Biscay is named from the Basques,

a people who have lived along its shores from the most ancient times.

BISMARCK-SCHÖNHAUSEN (*biz'mark-shaen'how-zen*), **Otto Eduard Leopold**, Prince, a famous German statesman, born at Schönhausen, near Magdeburg, April 1, 1815. Schönhausen is a large three-story building, shaded by linden and chestnut trees, in which his ancestors had lived since the middle of the 16th century. When six years old he was sent to school in Berlin, where he showed himself to be a quiet, home-loving boy, and made few friends; but when he became a student at the University of Göttingen (1832), he was wild and full of fun. The next year he went to the University of Berlin, and when twenty years old became a lawyer.

When Otto was thirty years old his father died, and he went to live in the old home at Schönhausen. Two years after he married, and in the same year he first took an interest in politics. At this time

Schönhausen.

Germany was divided up into several independent states joined together in a kind of union, in which Austria was the principal state. The country was divided into two parties, one of which wanted Prussia put at the head of the union and Austria left out, while the other wanted Austria to stay in the union. Bismarck took sides against Austria and did all he could to make Prussia the head of Germany. In 1859 he was sent as Ambassador to St. Petersburg, and in 1862, after serving a few months as Ambassador at Paris, he became Prime Minister of Prussia. In 1864 Prussia and Austria together conquered from Denmark the provinces of Schleswig-Holstein. Bismarck wished to join this to Prussia, but Austria would not agree to it. Bismarck made this the reason for war with Austria, though it was not the real cause. The war was to settle the question whether Prussia or Austria should rule in Germany. Bismarck got Italy to help him, and in a few weeks Austria was crushed at the great battle of

SADOWA (July 3, 1866), and Prussia became the head of the union called the North German Confederation.

But Bismarck was not yet satisfied, for Würtemberg, Bavaria, Saxony, and some other states, which together were called the South German States, would not join the Confederation. But in 1870, when France made war against Prussia, the South German States took the side of Prussia; and after the defeat of the French the South German States, proud of the German name, agreed to a union. The North German Confederation was changed

Prince Bismarck.

into a German Confederation, and the King of Prussia was made President of the Confederation with the title of German Emperor (1871). Thus Bismarck had brought about all that he had been striving for so long. By the war with Austria he had made Prussia the strongest power in Germany, and by the war with France he had raised Germany to the first place in Europe. The Emperor gave him the title of Prince, and made him Imperial Chancellor, by which office he was the head of the council of ministers and really carried on the whole business of the Empire.

While in office he several times suggested the relinquishment of it, but three successive emperors insisted on his retaining it; finally in 1890 he resigned, and was shortly afterwards elected a member of the Reichstag.

BITHYNIA (*bi-thin'e-ah*). See ASIA MINOR.

BLACK'BURN, a town of England, 22 miles N.N.W. of Manchester; pop. 104,000, or nearly as large as Allegheny, Pa. The country around it is barren, but contains a number of fine coal-mines, which give the city an important trade. Large quantities of cotton goods are manufactured there.

BLACK'FEET. See AMERICAN INDIANS.

BLACK FOREST, a range of mountains in the S.W. part of Germany, E. of the Rhine. Their tops are bare, and are covered with snow during eight months of the year, but their sides are covered with thick forests, from which the range gets its name. The Black Forest is rich in mines of silver, copper, iron, lead, and cobalt. The people live mostly by making wooden clocks and toys.

BLACK HAWK, an American Indian, chief of the Sacs and Foxes, a tribe living along the Mississippi River, born about 1768. He became chief when about twenty years old. In 1831 some of the Indians sold their lands in Illinois, but Black Hawk refused to give them up; but the whites went to live upon them, and the next year Black Hawk began a war, which has since been commonly called the Black Hawk War. Many were killed on both sides, but at last the Indians were defeated and Black Hawk captured. He was shut up in Fortress Monroe for awhile, but was permitted in 1833 to go back to his people, who had removed to Iowa. He died there when about seventy years old (Oct. 3, 1838).

BLACK SEA, an inland sea between Europe and Asia; area

180,000 square miles, or about twice as large as Lakes Superior, Michigan, Huron, Erie, and Ontario put together. On the north it connects with the Sea of Azov, which is nearly half as large as Lake Superior, and at the southwest end its waters flow into the Mediterranean through the Bosporus, the Sea of Marmora, and the Dardanelles. Its shores are owned partly by Russia and partly by Turkey. but for a long time the Turks kept the ships of all other nations out of it. In 1774 the Russians got the right to navigate it, and since the end of the Crimean War (1856) it has been open to the ships of all nations.

The Black Sea was called by the ancients the Euxine. It gets its name of Black not from the color of its water, but from its many storms.

BLACK'STONE, Sir William, author of a famous law-book called "Commentaries on the Laws of England," born in London, July 10, 1723. His father, a silk merchant, died before he was born, but William was well educated by his uncle, who sent him to OXFORD. He became a lawyer, but did not succeed very well at first, and thought of giving up the business; but in 1753 he gave a course of lectures at Oxford on English law, and five years afterward (1758) was made a professor of law in that university and after that he became famous and held many high offices. His Commentaries is the first book which law-students study. Blackstone died in London when fifty-seven years old (Feb. 14, 1780).

BLA'DENS-BURG, a town in Maryland, on the Potomac, 6 miles N.E. of Washington; pop. about 500. It is noted for the defeat of the Americans by the British (Aug. 24, 1814), who then marched into Washington and burned the capitol and other public buildings.

BLAKE, Robert, a famous Eng-lish admiral, born at Bridgewater in 1599. He was the son of a rich merchant, and was educated at OXFORD, where he hoped to spend his life in study; but when the civil war broke out between CHARLES I. and his Parliament he took part against the royalists, and bravely defended the city of Taunton against them. After King Charles had been beheaded (1649) the navy, under the command of Prince Rupert, the king's cousin, still kept up the fight and did great damage to English ships. Blake was given command of a fleet against him, and in a battle off MALAGA (1651) he defeated Prince Rupert and destroyed most of his ships.

Blake wished then to retire to private life, but in 1652 a war broke out between England and Holland, and he was made sole admiral. At that time the Dutch navy was very strong, and was under the command of Admiral VAN TROMP. For several years Blake and Van Tromp fought each other for the control of the seas, but Blake was generally the victor, and finally the Dutch gave up all hope of success and made peace with England.

War broke out between England and Spain in 1656, and Blake sailed with a fleet to try to catch the ships which every year brought silver from Mexico and Peru. The Peruvian fleet, afraid of him, took refuge in the harbor of Santa Cruz in the island of Teneriffe, where they were defended by many ships and by forts on shore. They thought they were safe there, but Blake attacked and defeated them and burned all the fleet. When the news reached London, bells were rung and bonfires lighted, and every one sang the great admiral's praise; but unfortunately he did not live to reach home, but died off Plymouth, at the age of fifty-eight (Aug. 17, 1657).

BLAR'NEY, a village and castle in Ireland, 4 miles N.W. of CORK.

Many songs have been made about the castle and the beautiful groves of Blarney. The castle stands on a steep rock overlooking the valley. On its top is the famous "Blarney Stone," which is said by the people living around there to give to those who kiss it great skill in making complimentary or pleasing remarks. The word blarney, meaning flattering or deceitful talk, comes from this.

BLENHEIM (*blen'im*), a village of Germany, in Bavaria, on the Danube. The English have named from it the great victory won near there (Aug. 13, 1704) by the English and Austrians, under the Duke of MARLBOROUGH and Prince Eugene, over the French and Bavarians, under Marshal Tallard, who was taken prisoner with many thousand of his men. The French and Germans call it the battle of Hochstädt, because it was really fought at a village of that name. For this splendid victory Queen ANNE gave Marlborough a large tract of land near Oxford, called Woodstock, on which was afterward built the Palace of Blenheim, one of the most magnificent houses in Europe. This place is still owned by the descendants of Marlborough, and every year the Duke sends to Windsor Castle, as a kind of rent, a little flag worked with the French fleur-de-lis, which is hung up in one of the great halls.

BLOOM'ING·TON, a city of central Illinois, 60 miles N.N.E. of Springfield; pop. 20,000, or about as large as Wilmington, N.C. Many railroads meet there, giving the city a large trade, and there are numerous mills and factories besides very large railroad machine-shops. There is a coal-mine near the city. Bloomington is the site of the Illinois Wesleyan University with 500 students.

BLÜCHER, (*fon bloo'ker*), **Geb-hard Leberecht von,** a famous Prussian general, born in Rostock, Dec.

16, 1742. He became noted as a cavalry officer in the wars against Napoleon, and finally rose to the command of the Prussian army (1813). Though he was defeated many times, he was finally victorious, and the next year (1814) he led the Prussian army into Paris, for which the King of Prussia made him Prince of Wahlstadt. In 1815 he got to Waterloo just in time to help Wellington defeat Napoleon, and he pursued the flying French all night and again went with an army to Paris. He was noted principally for his great courage and for the swiftness with which he moved his troops, and he was called by his soldiers Marshal Vorwärts (German for "Forward"). He died when seventy-seven years old (Sept. 12, 1819). Statues have been erected to him in Berlin and in Breslau.

BOADICEA (*bo-ad-i-se'ah*) queen of the Iceni, a tribe of BRITAIN. The Roman commander of one of the cities, whom she had made angry, had her publicly whipped. Burning for revenge, she gathered together her own and the neighboring tribes, stirred them up by a fiery speech, and herself led them against the Romans. She burned Londinium (London) and other Roman towns, and put to the sword at least 70,000 Roman people. The Roman governor, who was away in the Isle of Man, hastened back, and a great battle took place near St. Albans. Boadicea had the larger army, but the Roman soldiers were better drilled and armed, and after a fierce struggle the Britons were defeated and Boadicea poisoned herself in despair (A.D. 62).

BOCCACCIO (*bok-kaht'cho*), **Gio-vanni,** the most famous of Italian novelists, born in Paris in 1313. His father was a rich Italian merchant and his mother was French. His father wanted him to be a merchant, but he was more fond of study, and he became in time a very learned man. After living several years in Naples, he went to Florence, where, when forty years old (1353), he published a work called the *Decamerone*, or "Ten Days' Entertainment." This famous work is a collection of one hundred stories in prose, supposed to be told by a party of ladies and gentlemen stopping at a country house near Florence while the plague is raging in that city. It has been translated into all the European languages, and many other writers have used the stories to make poems and plays. Though this work made Boccaccio very famous, when he grew old he found himself poor and deserted by all his friends except PETRARCH, who wanted him to come and live with him; but Boccaccio declined and made his home in a little cottage in Certaldo. In 1373 he was made a professor in Florence, to lecture on DANTE; and he held this place until his death, which took place at Certaldo when he was sixty-two years old (Dec. 21, 1375).

BOGOTÁ (*bo-go-tah'*), a city, capital of the United States of Colombia; pop. 95,800, or nearly as large as Albany, N. Y. It is situated among the ANDES, on a table-land more than a mile and three quarters high, and has a fine climate. The city looks fine from a distance, but the streets are narrow (only mules and no carriages being used in them), and most of the houses are built low, on account of earthquakes, and without chimneys, because fires are mostly made in stoves. In the museum are kept PIZARRO'S flag and the robe of ATAHUALLPA'S wife. A few miles below the city is the cataract of Tequendama, where the river Funza leaps down a precipice 650 feet high.

Bogotá was founded in 1538 by the Spaniards, who named it Santa Fé (*san'tah fa*, Holy Faith),and its whole name is now Santa Fé de Bogotá.

BOHEMIA (*bo-he'me-ah*), a country of N.W. Austria; area 20,000 square miles, or a little smaller than West Virginia; pop. 5,820,000, or a trifle less than that of New York State; capital, PRAGUE. It is a high table-land shut in by mountains, and is rich in metals and precious stones. Its manufactures are the most important in Austria: linen, cotton, woollen, leather, and paper goods, and a great deal of fine glass-ware are made. Bohemian glass is famous all over the world, and much of it is sent to the United States.

Bohemia means the "Home of the Boii," a Celtic tribe who lived there in very early times. It was long an independent kingdom, and at one time its king ruled over also Poland and Hungary; but since 1526 it has belonged to Austria.

BOKHARA (*bo-kah'rah*), a walled city of central Asia, capital of a country of the same name; pop. about 70,000, or about the same as that of Cambridge, Mass. It is one of the most important places for trade in that part of Asia, and has large bazaars where all kinds of goods are sold. It has long been famous among Mohammedans for its colleges, where many thousand students are taught the Koran and a few other books. The country of Bokhara has a ruler called a Khan, who lives in the city, but the Russians really rule it.

Bokhara is said to mean "Treasury of Science." The city was burned by GENGHIS KHAN, and was long ruled by the successors of Tamerlane or TIMOUR.

BOLEYN (*bul'len*), **Anne.** See ANNE BOLEYN.

BOLIVAR (*bo-le'var*), **Simon,** a South American patriot, called the "Liberator," born in CARÁCAS, July 24, 1783. He belonged to a good and rich family, and was educated in Madrid. On his return to Venezuela (1811) he joined the party then trying to drive the Spaniards from the country, and soon made himself famous as a soldier. He was sometimes defeated, but in the end he overcame the Spaniards and won the freedom of the north-western parts of South America.

Bolivar became the most powerful man in South America, and when thirty-six years old (1819) he was chosen the first President of the republic of Colombia, which was made up of the countries now called COLOMBIA and VENEZUELA. In 1822 he drove the Spaniards out of Peru, and the next year was made dictator of that country. In 1825 he gave up this office, but the district of Upper Peru became a separate State, took the name of Bolivia in honor of him, and made him President for life (1826). The same year he was again chosen President of Colombia, but troubles broke out there and his enemies tried to kill him in his sleep. He escaped by jumping out of the window, but this and other things made him at length give up his authority. In his farewell address he told his people that they had been very ungrateful to him, who had given to them his life and his fortune. He died at San Pedro when forty-seven years old (Dec. 13, 1830). Twelve years afterward his body was removed to Carácas and a monument erected to him, and in 1858 the city of Lima erected in one of its squares a splendid bronze statue of him on horseback.

BOLIVIA (*bo-liv'e-ah*), a country of South America, between Peru and Brazil ; area about 530,000 square miles, or nearly twice that of Texas ; pop. about 2,300,000, or a little more than that of Massachusetts ; capital, La Paz. The western part, through which the ANDES pass, is the highest and most mountainous region of America. The mountains divide there into two great chains, between which lies the valley of the Desaguadero, the highest table-land in the world, excepting THIBET,

being more than two and a half miles above the sea. In this valley is Lake TITICACA, the largest lake in South America, and POTOSÍ, the highest city in the world. Eastern Bolivia is a lower plain, with tropical forests in the northern parts, where wild beasts roam, and grassy plains in the southern part, where great herds of cattle feed.

Bolivia is very rich in metals and useful minerals. Silver and gold abound, as well as tin, copper, and lead; and salt, nitre, sulphur, and coal are found in great quantities; but these riches are of little use because everything taken out of the country has to be carried over the Andes on the backs of mules and llamas. As the country has many climates, almost all kinds of fruits and vegetables grow in the different parts. Most of the people are Indians, only about one fourth being white. The civilized people speak Spanish, but the savage Indians have their own languages. The government is a republic, much like that of the United States.

The Spaniards first went into Bolivia in 1538, and soon after conquered it from the Indians. They named it first Charcas and then Upper Peru. In 1825 the people made themselves independent of Spain and called the country Bolivia in honor of Gen. BOLIVAR. In 1880 Bolivia and PERU had a war with Chili.

BOLOGNA (*bo-lone'yah*), a city of Italy, at the base of the Apennines, 80 miles N. of Florence ; pop. 138,-000, or nearly the same as that of Rochester, N. Y. It is a handsome city, and is surrounded by a wall with twelve gates. There are many beautiful palaces, adorned with paintings by the old masters, and the best streets are lined with arcades or covered porticoes, where people can walk sheltered from the rain or sun. The University of Bologna is the oldest and one of the most famous in Italy. It has now about 600 students, but in the 13th century it is said to have had many thousand. The city has a large trade in silk goods, liquors, scented soaps, macaroni, and sausages. The poodle-dogs of Bologna were once famous, but the pure breed is said to be almost gone.

Bologna is a very old town. It was first called Felsina, but when the Romans got it (189 B.C.) they changed its name to Bononia, and this has been changed in time to Bologna.

BOL'TON, or **Bolton-le-Moors,** a town of England, on a branch of the river Irwell, 11 miles N.W. of Manchester; pop. 105,000, or nearly as large as Denver, Col. It is noted for its great cotton-mills, bleaching and dyeing works, and print-works. Some of the most important improvements in cotton manufacture were first found out there. The town has also large foundries, and manufactories of steam-engines, machinery, and paper. Near it are many coal-mines.

BOM-BAY', a city of British INDIA, on the island of Bombay off the W. coast of Hindustan; pop. 773,000, or about half as much as that of New York. This island, which was the first land the British ever got in India, is about eight miles long and three miles wide. The city is built on the south end of it, and has a very fine harbor where the largest ships can go. Next after Calcutta and Canton, Bombay has the most trade of any place in Asia. The chief things sent from there are cotton, opium, wool, cashmere shawls, silk goods, coffee, spices, and sugar. Many ships are built there out of a very strong wood called teak, which grows chiefly in the East Indies. The people of Bombay are mostly Hindoos and Mohammedans, and there are only about 10,000 Europeans there. There are also about 30,000 Parsees, or descendants of

Persian fire-worshipers, who are among the richest and best of the population. On a high hill in the city is their walled cemetery, in which are five round towers about as high as a four-story house. When a Parsee dies, his body is placed on an iron grating on the top of one of these towers, and left there until the vultures have eaten all the flesh off, when the bones fall through the grating into the tower. A row of vultures may always be seen sitting round the edges of these towers waiting for their feast.

Bombay was named by the Hindoos after Bombé, an Indian goddess; but the Portuguese, who got the island in 1530, made it into Bom-bahia, which in their language means "good bay." It has belonged to England since 1662.

BONAPARTE (*bo'nah-part*, in Italian *bo-nah-par'ta*), sometimes spelled **Buonaparte,** the name of the imperial family of France. The Bonapartes were an Italian family living in the island of CORSICA, which had for a long time belonged to GENOA, but had won its independence by fighting, and in 1769 had been conquered by the French. Napoleon Bonaparte is said to have been born in that year after the island belonged to France, but his enemies said that he was born the year before and so was not a Frenchman by birth. The father of Napoleon was Carlo Maria Bonaparte (born 1746), a lawyer of Ajaccio, who married (1767) Maria Letizia Ramolino (born 1750). He had fought with PAOLI to free the island from the Genoese, but when the French conquered it he made friends with them, and afterward succeeded in getting Napoleon and two of his other children educated in the French government schools. Carlo Bonaparte died in Montpelier, France, when thirty-nine years old (Feb. 24, 1785), when Napoleon was only sixteen years old; but his wife, whom the French called Madame Lætitia, lived to see her children's wonderful rise and fall. She died in Rome when eighty-five years old (Feb. 2, 1836). Carlo and Letizia Bonaparte had five sons, Joseph, Napoleon, Lucien, Louis, and Jérôme, and three daughters, Elisa, Pauline, and Caroline. Of the daughters, Elisa, after Napoleon became Emperor, was made Grand Duchess of Tuscany; Pauline was made Duchess of Guastalla, and afterward became Princess Borghese; and Caroline, who married MURAT, became Queen of Naples.

BONAPARTE, Jérôme, King of Westphalia, youngest brother of the Emperor Napoleon I., born in Ajaccio, Corsica, Nov. 15, 1784. He joined the French army as a private soldier in 1800, but soon after went into the navy. In 1803, when he was a lieutenant on a ship which came to the United States, he married Miss Elizabeth Patterson, daughter of a rich merchant in Baltimore. After staying more than a year in the United States he went to Europe with his wife, but Napoleon, who was then Emperor, would not let them come into France because he did not like the marriage. Napoleon made him give up his wife, and afterward made him a French prince and heir to his throne. In 1807 he made him King of Westphalia and caused him to marry Catharine, daughter of the King of Würtemberg. Jérôme's son, Napoleon, commonly called Prince Napoleon (born Sept. 9, 1822), is now the heir to the imperial throne of France. He married (1859) the Princess Clotilde, daughter of Victor Emanuel, King of Italy. Jérôme Bonaparte and his first wife also had a son, Jérôme Napoleon (born 1805), who died in Baltimore (1870), leaving a son also called Jérôme Napoleon (born 1832), who has been an officer in the French army; but these are not owned as members of the im-

perial family. King Jérôme lost his throne when Napoleon fell. He died near Paris when seventy-five years old (June 24, 1860).

BONAPARTE, Joseph, King of Naples and King of Spain, eldest brother of the Emperor Napoleon I., born in Corte, Corsica, Jan. 7, 1768. His father wanted him to be a priest, but Napoleon wanted him to be a soldier. When twenty-six years old he married Marie Julie Clary, daughter of a rich merchant, whose younger sister married BERNADOTTE and became Queen of Sweden. In 1806 Napoleon made him king of Naples, and two years after made him give up that throne for that of Spain. But the Spaniards, who did not like to have a foreign king thus thrust upon them, made war upon him, and though Napoleon sent troops to help him, he was at last driven from his kingdom (1813). After the fall of Napoleon (1815) he came to the United States, and lived many years in Philadelphia and in a beautiful summer residence near Bordentown, New Jersey. He went to Europe in 1839, and died in FLORENCE when seventy-six years old (July 28, 1844).

BONAPARTE, Louis, King of Holland, a younger brother of the Emperor Napoleon I., born in Ajaccio, Corsica, Sept. 2, 1778. He married (1802) Hortense de BEAUHARNAIS, daughter of the Empress Josephine, and was made King of Holland by Napoleon in 1808. But he gave up the throne after two years, and afterward lived in Italy. He was the father of the Emperor Napoleon III. He died in Leghorn when sixty-eight years old (July 25, 1846).

BONAPARTE, Lucien, Prince of Canino, a younger brother of Napoleon, born in Ajaccio, Corsica, March 21, 1775. He helped Napoleon much, but did not marry to suit him, and finally quarreled with him, and went to live in Italy, where the Pope made him Prince of Canino. Napoleon offered to make him a king if he would give up his wife, but he refused. He died in Viterbo, Italy, when sixty-five years old (June 29, 1840).

BONAPARTE, Napoleon, Emperor of France, born in Ajaccio, Corsica, Aug. 15, 1769. When a baby, he is said to have been very beautiful, and very gentle and easy to take care of until he was two years old, when he became obstinate and would have his own way in everything. His mother, who was very firm with him, was almost the only one who could make him mind. He grew up to love and respect her, and he said when he grew up, " It is to my mother that I owe my fortune and all the good that I have ever done." When a boy he delighted in playing soldier, and he used to drill all the children at school with sticks for guns. Before he was ten years old he went to the military school at Brienne, France, where he was studious and well behaved, and good in mathematics, history, and geography, but behind in Latin and other studies. He finished his studies in the Military School in Paris, and when sixteen years old became a lieutenant of artillery. When twenty he became a captain, and at the siege of Toulon (1793), then held by the English and Spanish, he had the command of the artillery, and acted so skillfully that the place was soon taken. This made him well known, and the next year he was made a general; but not getting the place in the army which he thought he ought to have, he went to Paris and complained that he was not well treated. He was told that he was too young to command the artillery of an army. He replied: "One grows old very quickly on the field of battle."

At last an insurrection broke out in Paris, and though the government had plenty of men and cannon, there was no one to command them. " I have the man," cried Barras, the Minister of War, "a little Corsican officer, who will not stand on ceremony." This little Corsican was Napoleon. He placed his cannon so as to sweep the principal streets, and the insurgents, who had more than five times as many men as he had, were mowed down like grass. Napoleon at this time was very thin and slim. One day a very fat old woman was urging on the rabble to attack the soldiers. "There," cried she, "are the wretches that fatten in idleness while we starve!" "Look at her

Napoleon.

and look at me," said Napoleon, "and tell us which is the fatter." This raised a laugh, and the people went away.

Napoleon was now only twenty-five years old, yet he had made himself so famous that he was made Commander-in-chief of the army then fighting the Austrians and Sardinians in Italy. Seven days afterward he married JOSEPHINE Beauharnais, and in a few days more he was on his way to Italy. Austria had got a large army ready to march into France, and Napoleon found the French army poorly fed and clothed; but in four weeks he made the Sardinians ask for peace, and in less than two years he defeated the Austrians in eighteen battles and conquered Italy. When Napoleon went back to Paris he had the name of being the greatest soldier in Europe. He was greeted everywhere as a hero, and the government thought it best to get rid of a man who might prove dangerous. He was therefore given the command of the army to be sent to Egypt (1798). He took Alexandria and overran Egypt and Syria, being victorious everywhere except at ACRE. But in the mean time NELSON had destroyed his fleet at Aboukir, and Napoleon, hearing that the French armies had been defeated in Italy, returned to France, leaving KLEBER in command of the army in Egypt. He found Paris in confusion, and the people tired of a government which had brought shame on the country. Everybody looked to Napoleon as the strong man who could lead the country safely out of trouble. The government was changed, and Napoleon, now thirty years old, was chosen ruler of France for ten years, with the title of First Consul. There were two other consuls, but he had all the real power, and he and Josephine went to live in the Tuileries, the palace of the kings of France.

Napoleon now (1800) set out to reconquer what had been lost. He crossed the ALPS with his army, won back Italy from the Austrians, and made them ask for peace. In 1802 he was made First Consul for life, and two years afterward (May, 1804) he was chosen Emperor of the French, and crowned, with Josephine as Empress, in Paris, Dec. 2, 1804. He then made all his principal generals marshals, and gave them titles of nobility, and set up an imperial court.

Italy, which had been a republic, was made into the Kingdom of Italy, and on May 26, 1805, Na-poleon was crowned at Milan as King of Italy, and his stepson, Eugene BEAUHARNAIS, was made Viceroy.

Napoleon had taken so much territory from the other governments of Europe that he was greatly feared, and a league was formed against him by Austria, Russia, England, and Sweden. But Napoleon at once marched into Germany, defeated the Austrians at Ulm, took Vienna, and defeated the Austrians and Russians in the great battle of AUSTERLITZ (Dec. 2, 1805. He now made Kings of the Electors of Würtemberg and Bavaria, who had helped him, and made his brother Joseph King of Naples, and his brother Louis King of Holland. The King of Prussia now joined Russia in making war against Napoleon; but Napoleon overthrew him at the battle of JENA, took Berlin, and made out of some of his territory and some other German ground a Kingdom of Westphalia for his brother Jérôme. In the mean time the Russians had been defeated in several battles, and the Emperor ALEXANDER I. and Napoleon for a time became friends.

In 1807 Napoleon sent an army against Portugal, which was an ally of England, and the Portuguese royal family left their country and went to Brazil, which then was a colony of Portugal. The next year he made his brother Joseph King of Spain, making his brother-in-law MURAT King of Naples in his stead. But the Spaniards rose in arms, and the English sent an army to help them and to guard Portugal, and finally drove the French out. In 1809 Napoleon had another war with the Austrians, but he again defeated them and took Vienna, and made the Emperor Francis give up more territory. In the same year he divorced the Empress Josephine, and on April 2, 1810, he married the Archduchess

Maria Louisa, daughter of the Emperor of Austria. The next year his son, afterward called Napoleon II., was born.

At last the friendship between Napoleon and the Emperor Alexander of Russia began to give way, and in 1812 Napoleon marched with more than half a million men to conquer Russia. After a bloody battle at BORODINO the French marched into Moscow, but they found the city deserted, and they had scarcely got settled when fires broke out everywhere. The city was burned, and the French, though worn out and suffering, had to retreat. Winter came on early, and the poor soldiers had to plod through deep snows and sleep at night in the open air. Their food gave out, and they had to live mostly on the flesh of their horses. The Cossacks followed them closely, cutting off all who fell behind, and of the great army which had marched so proudly into Russia more than three fourths perished or were made prisoners.

The next year nearly all Europe joined against Napoleon. He won some great battles, but was defeated in others; France was worn out, and in 1814 the armies of the Russians, Prussians, and Austrians. entered France and, though defeated in several battles, took Paris (March 31). The allies declared that Napoleon, the disturber of Europe, should rule France no longer, and on April 5, 1814, he gave up the throne. He was allowed to keep the title of Emperor, and was given the island of ELBA to live in. All that Napoleon had won was taken from France, and LOUIS XVIII. took the throne. Napoleon went to Elba, but after living there nine or ten months he left one night and landed on the coast of France (March 1, 1815). His old soldiers received him joyfully, Louis XVIII. fled, and Napoleon again took his place in the

Tuileries, and began to raise another army to fight Europe with.

But every sovereign in Europe was resolved that he should not build up his power again, and every country raised its army once more. Napoleon tried to defeat them one by one before they could join their armies; but on June 18, 1815, he was totally defeated at WATERLOO, and the allies again marched into Paris (July 7) and put Louis XVIII. again on the throne. Napoleon, unable to escape, went on board of the British man-of-war Bellerophon, at Rochefort (July 15), and surrendered. He asked to be allowed to spend the rest of his days in England, but it was resolved to send him to the island of ST. HELENA. There he spent six years under the care of Sir Hudson Lowe, who watched him so carefully that he could not escape. He died there when fifty-one years old (May 5, 1821).

In his last moments Napoleon was out of his head, and his last words, *tête d'armée* (head of the army), prove that he thought himself at the head of his troops. He was buried under some weeping willows in a little valley on the island, and his grave was marked with a simple slab surrounded by an iron railing. In his will Napoleon said: "I desire that my ashes may rest on the banks of the Seine, amongst that French people whom I have so dearly loved." Twenty years after his sad death King LOUIS PHILIPPE had his remains taken with great pomp to France, where they were placed in a magnificent monument in the Hôtel des Invalides (Dec. 15, 1840).

BONAPARTE, Napoleon II., son of Napoleon I. and MARIA LOUISA, born in Paris, March 20, 1811. He was given the title of King of Rome at his birth. On the fall of the Empire, he went to Austria, where the Emperor made him an Austrian Prince, with the title of

Duke of Reichstadt. As he grew up he was carefully educated, and when twenty years old he was a lieutenant-colonel, and had command of a regiment of foot-soldiers in Vienna. He died in Schönbrunn when twenty-one years old (July 22, 1832).

BONAPARTE, Napoleon III., (Charles Louis Napoleon, commonly called Louis Napoleon), Emperor of France, born in Paris, April 20, 1808. He was the son of Louis Bonaparte, brother of the Emperor Napoleon, and of Hortense Beauharnais. After the death of Napoleon II. (1832) he became heir to the imperial throne, and in 1836 he made a foolish attempt to overthrow the government of LOUIS PHILIPPE, but he was arrested and sent to Brazil. The next year he came to New York and lived for several months in much want of money. He next went to live in London, and in 1840 again tried to get the throne of France, but was arrested, tried, and sentenced to imprisonment for life in the Fortress of Ham, an old castle sixty-seven miles from Paris.

After being there six years he escaped in the disguise of a working man, and went to England. When the republic was set up in France he was elected President for four years (1848). He was next (1852) made President for ten years, and in the same year he got the people to vote to restore the Empire, and took the title of Napoleon III. The next year he married a Spanish lady, Eugénie Marie de Montijo, Countess of Teba, who made his court a place of display and the centre of fashion.

In 1854 he joined Great Britain, Sardinia, and Turkey in a war against Russia. This war, commonly called the Crimean War, because it was fought mostly in the CRIMEA, ended in 1856 with the defeat of Russia. Three years afterward he made war with Austria to free Italy, but after the victories of MAGENTA and SOLFERINO he made peace with Austria, freeing only Lombardy from Austria instead of all Italy. In 1862 England, France, and Spain joined in an expedition against Mexico; but England and Spain soon withdrew, and Napoleon went on alone to conquer that country, and in 1864 set up MAXIMILIAN on the throne as Emperor. In 1870 came on the war with Prussia. Spain, being then without a King, had invited Prince Leopold of Hohenzollern, a kinsman of the Prussian royal family, to take the throne. Napoleon would not consent to this, and the Prince declined; but Napoleon insisted that the King of Prussia should give his word that no Prince of his family should be a candidate for the Spanish throne. This the King of Prussia would not do, and so France declared war and sent an army into Germany. But the French got only a little way on to German ground; they were speedily driven back and defeated everywhere, and at last, at SEDAN, Napoleon and the whole army surrendered (Sept. 2, 1870). Two days afterward the Empress Eugénie fled to England, and Napoleon, after being kept in Germany about six months, was allowed to join her. He died at Chiselhurst, England, when sixty-four years old (Jan. 9, 1873).

BONAPARTE, Napoleon IV. (Napoleon Eugène Louis Jean Joseph), Prince Imperial of France, born in Paris, March 16, 1856. He was the son of the Emperor Napoleon III. and of the Empress Eugénie. When the Prussian war broke out he was only fourteen years old; but his father took him with him in the army, and he is said to have fired the first cannon in the first battle. After the French had been defeated, the Emperor sent him for safety to Belgium, and he afterward joined his mother in

England. After his father's death he studied in the English military school at Woolwich, and when twenty-three years old he joined the English army in South Africa in the war against the Zulus. One day he rode out with a few men into the country, and was surprised and killed by some Zulus (June 1, 1879).

BONHEUR (*bo-nur'*), **Rosa**, a famous French painter of animals, born at Bordeaux, March 22, 1822. One of her most noted pictures, the "Horse Fair," of which many copies have been made, was shown at the World's Fairs in Paris in 1853 and in London in 1855. Many of her pictures are in England, where great prices have been paid for them. There is no one who can paint animals better than Rosa Bonheur. Her studio is a few miles from Paris.

BON'I-FACE, the name of nine Popes of Rome.

Boniface VIII., born about 1228, was Pope from 1294 to 1303, when he died in Rome. He claimed to be Emperor as well as Pope, and said that all other rulers were subject to him, King Philip the Fair of France, who would not own this, had a quarrel with him and even seized him and held him a prisoner for a time.

BONIFACE, Joseph Xavier. See SAINTINE.

BONN, a city of Germany, on the Rhine, 15 miles above COLOGNE; pop. 36,000, or about as large as Holyoke, Mass. It is beautifully situated amid fine scenery, and is visited by many travelers. It is most noted for its university, which has a very large library and fine museums.

Bonn is a very old town, and was called by the Romans Bonna, from which its present name has come.

BOONE, Daniel, an American hunter and pioneer, born in Bucks County, Penn., Feb. 11, 1735. His father, a farmer, moved to North Carolina when Daniel was eighteen years old. The boy had but little schooling, but he knew all about the woods and about hunting and Indian life, and it was his delight to wander off into the wilderness for weeks at a time. When thirty-four years old he went with five others into the wilds of Kentucky, where were then only Indians and wild beasts. He had many adventures and fights with the savages, and was captured by them, but escaped, and in 1773 moved his own and five other families there from North Carolina. To guard against the Indians he built a fort on the Kentucky River which he named Boonesborough. The Indians attacked the fort several times, but were driven off. In 1778 they caught Boone while away, and carried him to DETROIT, where one of them adopted him as a son. Hearing of a plan to attack Boonesborough he ran away, and reaching his fort, he made ready and defended it with about fifty men against a large force of Canadians and Indians. He continued to live there until 1792, when Kentucky had become so thickly settled that it became a State of the Union. He then went to live in Missouri, where he died when eighty-five years old (Sept. 26, 1820). In 1845 his remains were carried to Kentucky and buried at Frankfort.

BORDEAUX (*bor-do'*), a city of France, on the river Garonne, 58 miles from its mouth in the Bay of Biscay; pop. 240.500. or about as large as New Orleans. Next after Paris and Marseilles it has the largest trade with foreign countries of any city in France. Its harbor, which is very large, is always full of ships from the United States, Great Britain, and other parts of the world. The country around Bordeaux is famous for its vineyards, and the principal merchants in the city are engaged in the wine trade. Most of the claret, or red wine, and brandy sent from France are shipped at Bordeaux.

Bordeaux means "on the edge of the waters" (French *bord*, border or edge, and *eaux*, waters). There was a city there called Burdigala long before the time of Christ.

BORGIA, (*bor'jah*), **Cesare**, a noted Italian cardinal and soldier, born about 1457. He was a son of Pope ALEXANDER VI. and of a bad woman named Rosa Vanozza, and grew up with all the vices of his parents. His father made him a cardinal (1493), and King Louis XII. of France made him Duke of Valentinois (1498), from which the Italians commonly called him Duke Valentino. With the help of the Pope, who wanted to make a kingdom for his son, Cesare carried on war against the small states into which Italy was then divided and took many cities, but he behaved so cruelly that everybody hated and feared him. He was successful while his father lived, but after Julius II. became Pope he was thrown into prison (1504). Two years afterward he escaped, and he was killed in battle when about fifty years old (March 12, 1507). He is said to have been a very able and brave man, but he was bad in every way, and was believed to have helped his father poison many people.

BORGIA, Lucrezia, sister of Cesare Borgia, was famous for her beauty and talents. After having had two husbands (the second one of whom was murdered, it is said, by order of her brother) she married Alfonso d'Este, who became Duke of Ferrara. She had a splendid court and did much for men of letters, who praised her in their books, but she is said to have committed many crimes and to have been very wicked. Many books have been written about her, and some late writers say that she was not so bad as she has been thought. There is

also an opera called "Lucrezia Borgia," written by DONIZETTI.

BOR'NE·O, an island of the Indian Archipelago, S. of Asia; area, 290,000 square miles, or a little larger than Texas; pop. 2,000,000 to 3,000,000. Excepting Australia and perhaps Papua, Borneo is the largest island in the world. The line of the equator runs nearly through its middle, and of course its climate is very hot. Its shores are low and marshy, but inland are high mountains. Much of the island is covered with thick forests, in which are found most of the trees belonging to hot climates. Among the things which grow there are camphor, cinnamon, cloves, nutmegs, cocoanuts, and the breadfruit. The durion, said to be the most delicious fruit in the world. grows on a tree much like the elm. The fruit, a cream-colored pulp, has a hard outer shell covered with sharp spikes. It sometimes falls on people passing under the trees and wounds or even kills them. A singular plant called the pitcher plant, from its shape, grows large enough to hold two quarts of water. Among the wild animals is the orang-outang (C. C. T., 24, II., n.). Borneo is rich in minerals. Most of the antimony used is got there, and much gold, and many diamonds are sent from there. The largest diamond in the world was found there (C. C. T., 173, II., l.).

Most of the people are a dark-skinned race called Dayaks, with coarse black hair, who live by hunting and fishing. There are many tribes of these, who are all the time carrying on war with each other. When they kill a man they cut off his head, smoke it over a fire to preserve it, and keep it as a mark of victory and of bravery, just as the North American Indians keep the scalps of their enemies. They wear armor made of the skin of the wild bear, and helmets of bamboo, and carry a shield. Their arms are spears, a sword, called *mandow*. with which they can cut through a gun-barrel, and a blow-gun, called *sumpit*, through which they blow with the mouth small darts or arrows. In war-time they poison their arrows. Besides the Dayaks, there are many Malays and Chinese. Most of the southern part of Borneo belongs to the NETHERLANDS. In the north-west is a state called Sarawak, ruled by an Englishman, and the rest is under native chiefs.

BORODINO (*bor-o-dee'no*), a village of Russia, 70 miles W.S.W., of Moscow. It is on a little river called the Kolotcha, about two miles from where it joins the Moskva River. Near the river, opposite Borodino, took place a great battle between Napoleon and the Russians, Sept. 7, 1812. The French, who claimed it as a victory, called it the battle of the Moskva, and from it Marshal NEY got his title of Prince of Moskva; but the Russians, who said they were not defeated (though they gave up the field and let the French take Moscow a few days after), called it the battle of Borodino.

BOSNIA (*boz'ne-ah*), an E. province of Austro - Hungary; area 24,200 square miles, or not quite as large as New Hampshire, Massachusetts, and Vermont; pop. 1,335,000, or a little more than twice as much as that of Maine. This includes the country called Herzegovina. These were formerly provinces of European Turkey, but they were given to Austro-Hungary by the treaty of Berlin (1878), after the war between Turkey and Russia. Great quantities of dried prunes are sent from Bosnia, as well as timber, wool, honey, and wax. The Turks first took the country in 1528.

BOS'PO-RUS, the ancient name of the strait between the BLACK SEA and the Sea of Marmora, now often called the Strait of Constan-tinople. It is about sixteen miles long and one half to two miles wide. The city of Constantinople is at its south end, and opposite, on the Asiatic side, is Scutari. The ancients sometimes called this the Thracian Bosporus, and the strait leading from the Black Sea to the Sea of Azov the Cimmerian Bosporus.

Bosporus means in Greek the " ox ford," and the strait was probably so called because cattle could swim across it.

BOSSUET (*bos-swa'*), **Jacques Benigne,** a famous French preacher, born at Dijon, Sept. 27, 1627. He first came into notice by the sermons he preached while belonging to the Cathedral at Metz. These were so much admired that he was sometimes sent for by the king to preach to the court. In his day he had many arguments on religion with the Protestant ministers, and he is regarded by the Roman Catholics as the great defender of their religion. He had a great talent for making funeral orations, several of which have come down to us, among others one on the death of Henrietta Maria, the wife of King Charles I. of England. In 1681 he was made Bishop of Meaux. From this he is often spoken of as the "Eagle of Meaux." He died in Paris when seventy-seven years old (April 12, 1704).

BOSTON (*bos'tun*), a city, capital of Massachusetts, on Massachusetts Bay; pop. 450,000, or a little larger than Baltimore. Boston is the largest city of New England and the sixth city of the United States in population, and has a larger foreign trade than any other city of the United States, excepting New York and New Orleans. It has a fine harbor defended by forts, with anchorage for the largest ships, and has many great docks and wharves. The State House stands on Beacon Hill, fronting the park called the Common. From its top there is a very beautiful view of the bay and the country round the city. Boston has the best Public Library in the United States, a fine Music Hall with the largest organ in the United States, and many interesting galleries and collections. In the part called Charlestown is the Navy Yard, one of the largest in the country, and BUNKER HILL, where a very tall monument has been erected in memory of the battle.

Boston was first built in 1630 by people who came from England with John Winthrop. It was named Boston from Boston in Lincolnshire, from which many of the principal families came. Several years before the war of the Revolution there were frequent troubles between the English soldiers and the people, and on March 5, 1770, took place the "Boston Massacre," when the soldiers fired on and killed some of the citizens. This made the people very angry, and helped much to bring about the war. Some time before this the English Government had passed a law taxing tea and many things which the Americans wanted, and the people of Boston declared that they would not buy anything of England and forbade any ships to bring tea there. But in 1773 three ships laden with tea arrived, and lay at one of the wharves ready to land their cargoes. The people ordered them away, but they would not go, and one night (Dec. 16) a band of men dressed like Indians went on board the ships, smashed the chests with their tomahawks, and emptied the tea into the water. The English Parliament then closed the port of Boston to all trade, and made Salem the capital of the colony. But the brave people of Boston were not to be thus put down ; the other towns helped them, and two years afterward the first blood of the Revolution was shed at LEXINGTON. Boston was soon

after besieged by the Americans, and on March 17, 1776, the British were driven out.

BOS'WORTH, a market town of Leicestershire, England, 12 miles W. of Leicester. Near it was fought the battle of Bosworth (Aug. 22, 1485), in which King RICHARD III. was defeated by the Earl of Richmond, afterward HENRY VII., and killed. Richard had twice as many men as Richmond, but some of his officers had been gained over by his enemy and deserted him in the fight. Among these was Lord Stanley, Richmond's step-father, who, after the battle, took the crown from Richard's head and set it on the head of Richmond, who was hailed King. Richard's dead body was thrown on a horse and carried to Leicester, where it was buried in the Gray Friars' Church. This battle ended the civil war of the ROSES.

BOT'A-NY BAY, a bay of New South Wales, on the E. coast of AUSTRALIA. It is the place where Captain COOK first stopped when he sailed along the east coast of Australia (1770). There were so many beautiful flowers there that Capt. Cook's botanist called it Botany Bay. The English Government sent a ship-load of convicts there (1788), intending to make a convict station of it, but it was unhealthy and they were removed to Port Jackson.

BOUGHTON (*bow'tun*), George H., an English painter, born in Norfolk in 1834. He was brought to the United States when a child, and painted his first pictures in Albany, N. Y. He had a studio in New York for two years, but went abroad to study art in 1859, and has since lived chiefly in London. He paints landscapes and figure pictures of great merit. Many of them are owned in the United States.

BOUGUEREAU, (*boo-gwer-o'*), William Adolphe, a French painter, born in La Rochelle, Nov. 30, 1825. He has painted some fine religious pictures, but is best known by his pictures of domestic scenes or home-life, especially of mothers and children. Many of his paintings have been brought to the United States.

BOUILLON (*boo-yon'*). See GODFREY DE BOUILLON.

BOULOGNE (*boo-lone'*), a town of France, on the English Channel, 19 miles from Dover; pop. 46,-000, or a little larger than Utica, N. Y. From the upper part of the town, which is on a hill, the coast of England can be seen. Many English people live there, and as it is on one of the routes between London and Paris it has many visitors. Many vessels belonging there go to Newfoundland every year to fish for cod.

Boulogne gets its name from its old Roman name, Bolonia. It was there that Napoleon got together a great army and fleet for the invasion of England (1803), and it was there also that Louis Napoleon landed (Aug. 6, 1840) in his second attempt to make himself Emperor of France.

BOURBON (*boor-bon'*), the name of a famous French family, who became kings of France, of Spain, and of Naples. The Bourbons get their name from the Castle of Bourbon, which was a few miles from Moulins, near the centre of France. Only a tower of the old castle is now standing. In the year 1272 Beatrix, the heiress of this, married Robert, sixth son of King LOUIS IX., and their son Louis was made Duke of Bourbon (1327). In 1589, when Henry III., the last king of the family of Valois, died, the crown of France came to the Bourbon family, and HENRY IV. became King. After him reigned six of his descendants: LOUIS XIII., LOUIS XIV., LOUIS XV., LOUIS XVI., LOUIS XVIII., and CHARLES X. The death of the Count of Chambord, in 1883, extinguished this line.

The **House of Orleans,** a younger branch of the Bourbon family, is descended from Philip Duke of Orleans, who was a son of Louis XIII. and brother of Louis XIV. King Louis Philippe was of this family. This king had five sons: the Duke of Orleans, the Duke of Nemours, the Prince of Joinville, the Duke of Aumale, and the Duke of Montpensier. The Duke of Orleans, the eldest son, was accidentally killed in 1842, and his son, the Count of Paris, is now the heir of the Orleans family for the throne.

The **Bourbon Kings of Spain** are descended from Philip Duke of Anjou, grandson of Louis XIV. of France, who became king as Philip V., on the death of Charles II., the last of the Austrian House of Spain. Philip's successors have been Ferdinand VI., Charles III., Charles IV., Ferdinand VII., Isabella II., Alfonso XII., and Alfonso XIII.

The **Bourbon Kings of Naples** were descended from Don Carlos, second son of Philip V. of Spain. Francis II., whose throne was taken from him (1860) by King Victor Emanuel of Italy, was the last sovereign of this line.

BOYNE (*boin*), a river of Ireland, which flows into the Irish Channel near Drogheda, on the E. coast. On its banks, about three miles from Drogheda, was fought the battle of the Boyne (July 1, 1690), in which WILLIAM III. of England defeated James II. William, with his sword in his left hand—for his right arm was wounded—bravely led his troops through the river, and was foremost in the fight, while James looked on from a safe distance until he saw that the day was lost, when he galloped to the coast and sailed away to France. A tall obelisk (150 feet high) stands on the place where William was wounded.

BOZZARIS or **BOTZARIS** (*bot'-zah-ris*), **Marco,** a Greek patriot, born about 1790. His father, Kitzos Bozzaris, and all his male relatives were brave soldiers and patriots, and took an active part in the struggle against Turkey for Greek independence. At the age of twenty-three he joined a secret society having for its object the freedom of Greece, and a cruel war was carried on for years in which he fought with great bravery and little success. On a night in the summer of 1823 he attacked with 350 Greeks the camp of a large Turkish force near Missolonghi. The Turks were panic-stricken and badly defeated, but in the moment of victory Bozzaris received a mortal wound and was carried from the field. His last words were, "Could a Suliote leader die a nobler death?" He was then only thirty-three years old (Aug. 20, 1823). Fitz-Greene HALLECK wrote a fine poem about this battle.

BRAD'DOCK, Edward, a British general, born in Perthshire, Scotland, about 1715. He was a brave officer who had distinguished himself in many battles, and when war broke out (1755) between the French and English in America, he was sent from England to be commander-in-chief of the army. He started with a large force to attack Fort Duquesne, near where Pittsburgh now is, and when within a few miles of the fort was surprised by a party of French and Indians who were lying in wait for them, and defeated with a terrible loss. Washington, who was one of his aids, and who understood the Indian way of fighting, had wished the General to send out scouts, or men to go ahead of the army and find out if any danger was in the way. But Braddock was too proud to take advice, and so they fell into the hands of the enemy. The red coats of the British soldiers made them a mark for the shots of the French and Indians, who, hidden behind trees, could fire upon them without being seen. Braddock had

five horses shot under him, and was shot himself as he was mounting the sixth. Washington had two horses killed and four bullets shot through his coat, but was unhurt. The army was nearly destroyed, and a great quantity of arms and supplies were captured by the French. Braddock died two days afterward (July 13, 1755), and was buried secretly by the wayside, lest his body should be found by the Indians.

BRAD'FORD, a city of N. England, on a branch of the river Aire; pop. 225,000, or nearly as large as Washington, D. C. It is noted for its manufactures, especially of worsteds, in which it surpasses every other place in England. It also contains large cotton-mills, foundries, and manufactories of machinery and combs. Near the city are large iron-works.

BRAD'FORD, William, an American painter, born in New Bedford, Mass., in 1827. He paints seaviews, and has made many pictures of various parts of the north-eastern coast of America. For some years he has had a studio in New York.

BRAD'STREET, Anne, author of the first book of poetry written in America, born in Northampton, England, about 1613. She was the daughter of Gov. Thomas Dudley, and wife of Gov. Simon Bradstreet, and came to Massachusetts when seventeen years old. Her book of poems was printed in London (1650) under the title, " The Tenth Muse lately sprung up in America."

BRA·GAN'ZA, a small town in N.E. Portugal, from which the House of Braganza, which now rules Portugal, gets its name. The ancient castle there of the Dukes of Braganza is now in ruins. The first one of this family who became King of Portugal was the eighth Duke, who began to reign in 1640 as John IV. Since that time all the kings of Portugal have been of this family, The emperors of Brazil were also of the House of Braganza.

BRAGG, Braxton, an American general, born in North Carolina in 1817. He was graduated at West Point, and served with honor in the Florida and Mexican wars. In 1856 he resigned and became a sugar-planter, but when the Civil War broke out he joined the Confederates. He took part in the battle of Shiloh, and commanded an army which invaded Kentucky and drove back Gen. Buell, but was at length forced to retreat (Oct. 1862). Gen. Rosecrans defeated him at Murfreesborough, but Gen. Bragg won the battle of Chickamauga, and he was again defeated by Gen. Grant at Chattanooga (Sept. 19 and 20, 1863). After that he took little active part in the war. He died in Galveston, Texas, when fifty-nine years old (Sept. 27, 1876).

BRAHE (*brah'eh*), **Tycho,** a Danish astronomer, born at Knudstorp, Sweden, which town then belonged to Denmark, Dec. 14, 1546. He belonged to a noble family, and his father wanted him to study law and be a statesman; but he became interested in astronomy through watching an eclipse of the sun when he was a school-boy at Copenhagen, and when he was sent to Leipsic to study law he used to study astronomy when his tutor was asleep. When about twenty-five (1571) he returned to Denmark, and gave himself up entirely to the study of the heavenly bodies. The King of Denmark gave him a pension, and built an observatory for him on the island of Huen, not far from Copenhagen. This was the most splendid observatory that had ever been built in Europe, and was named Uranienborg ("City of the Heavens"). Tycho lived there twenty years, and made many important discoveries, but when the king died he lost his pension, and not being able to keep up his ob-

servatory, he went to live at Prague, where the Emperor Rudolph gave him a house and a pension for his support. But he died there soon after, when fifty-five years old (Oct. 13, 1601). Tycho Brahe did not believe that COPERNICUS was right, but thought that the earth is the centre of the universe, and that the sun and stars move around it.

BRAHMA (*brah'mah*), the name of one of the principal Hindoo gods. Brahma, VISHNU, and SIVA make up the Hindoo Trinity, Brahma

Brahma, Vishnu, and Siva.

being called the creator or maker of all things, Vishnu the preserver, and Siva the destroyer. The worship of these gods is called Brahmanism, which is the religion of a large part of the people of India; and the priests, or Brahmans, form the highest caste or class in that country.

BRAN'DY-WINE CREEK, a stream of Chester Co., Penn., which flows into the Delaware River near Wilmington, Del. On its banks, in Chester County, was fought the battle of Brandywine (Sept. 11, 1777), in which the Americans under Gen. Washington were defeated by the British under Gen. Howe. The result was the loss of Philadelphia, which the British entered on Sept. 26.

BRA-ZIL', the largest country of South America; area 3,200,000 square miles, or about as large as the United States, leaving out Alaska; pop. about 14,000,000, or only one quarter as much as the United States; capital, RIO DE JANEIRO. The northern part, through which the Amazons flows, is flat and covered with a great forest, the largest in the world; in the western part of it a circle a thousand miles wide could be made without touching the edges. This region is very wild, and many portions are still unexplored, being given up to roving Indians and savage beasts; there are no roads, and people pass from one village to another by the river. From the forest come India-rubber, Brazil-nuts, and many drugs, which are gathered by the Indians, and many kinds of palm-trees grow there. Central and Eastern Brazil are a great table-land, in some places covered with forest, and in others with open, grassy lands, and thinly settled, except near the coast, where there are large cities and villages. The people have great herds of cattle and plantations of sugar-cane, tobacco, and cotton. South-eastern Brazil is mountainous; one peak, called Ita-táia (hog-stone), is the highest in Brazil, its summit being about 10,000 feet above the sea. Among the mountains and hills are many fine coffee plantations, some of which have more than a million coffee-trees. This is the most thickly settled part of the empire, but a large portion of the people are negro slaves.

Brazil is rich in minerals, especially in gold, silver, copper, iron, and in diamonds and other precious stones. Some very large diamonds have been found there, as well as very beautiful sapphires, emeralds, rubies, and topazes. The soil is very fertile and produces almost every kind of vegetable and fruit, and the forests give many kinds of cabinet and dye woods. The climate is pleasant, much like that of the United States in summer. In the southern part frosts are sometimes felt in July, when it is winter there, but in other portions there is no cold weather. The people are about one third Portuguese whites, and the rest are made up of negroes, Indians, and mixed races. Brazil, up to November 1889, was the only monarchy in America; it then became a republic. The former government was much better than that of other South American countries, and the people were therefore peaceable and prosperous.

Brazil gets its name from the dyewood called Brazil-wood, which abounds there (C. C. T., 87, I., n.). The country was first seen in 1500 by the Portuguese, who called it Vera Cruz (True Cross). The English, the Dutch, and the French made some trouble at first, but after 1660 the Portuguese had the country all to themselves. In 1807, when Napoleon made war on Portugal, King John VI. went with his family to Brazil, and called himself king of Brazil and Portugal. In 1821 he went back to Portugal, leaving his son Prince Pedro to rule Brazil, and the next year the people declared themselves independent and Pedro I. was crowned Emperor.

BREMEN (*bra'men*), a free city or state of Germany, on the river Weser, near its mouth in the North Sea; pop. 165,000, or the same as that of Minneapolis, Minn. Bremen is called a free city, but is really a small state with a republican government, and makes its own laws. It has about 99 square miles of territory, in which is the city of Bremen (40 miles from the sea), a port called Bremerhaven (at the mouth of the river), and some other small places. Bremerhaven is where all large ships stop, and where the ocean steamers which go to Bremen have their wharves. Most of the German emigrants who come to the United States sail from there,

The city of Bremen has a very large trade and many kinds of manufactures. A large number of ships are built there. Most of the tobacco which goes to Germany is sent there, and many people are employed in making cigars.

Bremen was first built by the Emperor CHARLES THE GREAT in 788.

BREN'NUS, a famous leader of the Gauls who invaded Italy in 390 B.C. He defeated the Romans at the river Allia, eleven miles from Rome, and then marched on the city. Most of the citizens fled to the country, but the senators put on their robes and sat down before their houses to await the enemy. The Gauls entered the streets and gazed with wonder on these old men sitting there so quietly in their ivory chairs. At last a soldier stroked the long white beard of one of the senators, who, angry at the insult, struck him with his wand. This enraged the Gauls and they at once killed them all. Some of the Romans had taken refuge in the Capitol, which was on a steep hill called the Tarpeian Rock. One night the Gauls tried to take it by climbing up in the steepest place. The Roman sentinels were asleep, and the Gauls had nearly got to the top, when some geese kept there began to cackle. This awakened Marcus MANLIUS, who rushed to the spot just in time to throw down the Gauls and save the Capitol. At length the Gauls agreed to leave the city for a thousand pounds of gold, but while this was being weighed CAMILLUS is said to have come with an army and defeated them.

BRESLAU (*bres'-low*), a city of W. Germany, in Prussia, on the river Oder; pop. 300,000, or about as large as San Francisco, Cal. It is the largest city in Prussia except Berlin, and is very important for its manufactures of cotton, linen, woolen, and metals, Great

fairs are held at Breslau every year, and more wool is sold there than at any other place in Germany. The University of Breslau has nearly 1500 students and fine libraries and museums.

Breslau was once a town of Poland, and was first built about the 10th century. The Poles called it Wraclau, from their King Wratislau, and this name has become changed to its present form.

BREST, a city of N.W. France, on a bay of the Atlantic; pop. 71,000, or about as large as Cambridge, Mass. Brest is the most important naval station of France, and one of the strongest and best fortified ports in Europe. Foreign men-of-war would find it hard to get into its harbor, for the entrance is very narrow, and all ships going in have to pass under the guns of many forts and batteries. There is room in its harbor for more than five hundred men-of-war, and near by are great drydocks and places for ship-building, barracks for soldiers, and arsenals, magazines, and storehouses. Most of the ships of the French navy are fitted out there. A telegraph cable is laid from Brest to Duxbury, Massachusetts.

BRETON (*breh-ton'*), **Jules Adolphe,** a French painter, born at Courrières, 1827. He paints pictures of farm-life, women at work in the fields or resting after their labors. They are much admired, and many of them have brought high prices in England and the United States.

BREWS'TER, Sir **David,** a famous British philosopher and scholar, born at Jedburgh, Scotland, Dec. 11, 1781. He made many important discoveries in light, improved the microscope (C. C. T., 394, I., l.) and the telescope (C. C. T., 612, II., n.), and brought the stereoscope (C. C. T., 592, I., n.) into use. He also made the first kaleidoscope (C. C. T., 335, I., n.), whose brilliant colors and wonderful changing shapes have delighted so many children. Sir David became very famous, and did more than any other man of his time to make people interested in science. He died when eighty-six years old (Feb. 10, 1868).

BRICHER (*brish'er*), **Albert Thompson**, an American painter, born in Portsmouth, N. H., April 10, 1839. He paints landscapes both in oil and in water color. Many of his pictures are pretty sea-shore views, with women and children on the beach. His studio is in New York.

BRIDGE'PORT, a city of Connecticut, on Long Island Sound, 59 miles from New York; pop. 49,-000, or nearly the same as that of Los Angeles, Cal. It is the third city of Connecticut in population, and is noted for its manufactures. The "Wheeler and Wilson" and the "Howe" sewing-machines are made there, and there are also large factories for making firearms, carriages, locks, and many other things.

Bridgeport gets its name from bridges which connect it with East Bridgeport, on the east side of Pequonnock Creek. Most of the large factories are in East Bridgeport.

BRIGHT, John, a noted English statesman, born at Rochdale, Lancashire, Nov. 16, 1811. His father, Jacob Bright, a member of the Society of Friends or Quakers, was a poor boy who was brought up a weaver, but who by his energy and industry became one of the largest cotton-spinners in England and died very rich. John, the eldest of ten children, became the head of the firm. He, too, was a Friend and like his father did much good by setting up schools for his workmen, providing them with libraries, and making their labor pleasant for them. During more than fifty years that the business was carried on under their management, there was never a strike or any kind of trouble among the workmen.

Mr. Bright did much to extend the right of voting to the people. He sat for a long time in Parliament, and was for two years (1868-70) a member of the Cabinet, being the first Quaker who ever held this office in England. In 1880 he again became a member of the Cabinet, but retired in 1882, and died when seventy-eight years old (March 27, 1889).

BRIGHTON (*bri'tun*), a town of S.E. England, on the English Channel; pop. 118,000, or about twice as large as Camden, N. J. It is built partly on a low beach and partly on high chalk cliffs overlooking the sea. The trade and manufactures are small, and Brighton is chiefly noted as a watering-place In the summer it is visited by thousands of people who go there to bathe in the sea. Besides the many fine hotels there is a beautiful pavilion built by George IV., who lived in Brighton when he was Prince of Wales. A magnificent salt-water aquarium was opened in 1872, and hundreds of fishes and other marine animals can be seen in its tanks.

Brighton was originally called Brighthelmstone. It was plundered and burned by the French in 1513. Its fame as a watering-place began in the middle of the 18th century, when Dr. Richard Russell wrote a work recommending sea-bathing.

BRINDISI (*brin'de-se*), a seaport town of S.E. Italy, on a bay of the Adriatic Sea; pop. 15,000, or about the same as that of Columbia, S. C. In ancient times this was a very important town. It was the principal place where the Romans kept their war galleys, and from its ports sailed most of their fleets. The Appian Way, as the great paved road from Rome was called, ended there. In the time of the CRUSADES, many of the troops for Palestine set sail there. Its harbor finally became blocked up with sand,

and the place went to ruin; but since the opening of the SUEZ Canal it has again become important, because it is on the shortest route to the East, and its harbor has been cleared out. Passengers can now go by railroad to Brindisi and thence by steamer to Alexandria in Egypt, and thus save several days.

Brindisi gets its name from its Roman name, Brundusium or Brundisium.

BRIS'TOL, a city of S.W. England, on the river Avon, 8 miles from its mouth in Bristol Channel; pop. 224,000, or a little less than that of Washington, D. C. As large ships can go up the river to it, Bristol is a great place for foreign trade. At one time all the West India trade of England was carried on at Bristol and it was the second city in the kingdom, but LIVERPOOL got away much of its trade, and its business is now chiefly with

The Spectre of the Brocken. (See page 128).

Ireland. It has large basins for ships, and docks and ship-yards. The ship in which John CABOT discovered North America sailed from Bristol, as did also many other ships which brought people to help settle America; and the first line of steam vessels between the United States and Great Britain ran from there.

Bristol was a town before the Romans went to Britain. The Saxons called it Briegstow, which means the "Place at the Breach" (or chasm through which the Avon flows,)

BRI-TAN'NI-CUS, a Roman prince, son of the Emperor Claudius, born in A.D. 42. He was the lawful heir to the throne, but his stepmother, Agrippina, persuaded his father to make her own son his successor, and on the death of Claudius Nero became emperor. Being afraid that his young stepbrother would give him trouble,

Nero poisoned him. It is said that at his funeral his face was painted, but that a rain-storm washed off the paint and showed by the swollen and discolored features what a crime had been committed. Britannicus was not yet fourteen when he was murdered (A.D. 55).

BRIT′TA-NY. See GAUL.

BROCK′EN, the highest peak of the Hartz Mountains, a range in W. Germany between the rivers Weser and Elbe. The Brocken is a round mountain, about three fourths of a mile high, and has cultivated fields almost to its top, which overlooks all the country round. It is an old belief in Germany that the witches hold a great dance there every year on Walpurgis Night, or the night before the first of May. Sometimes people standing on the top of the Brocken at sunrise can see their own shadows greatly magnified on the clouds opposite; and this, which is called the "Spectre of the Brocken," is probably what gave rise to the story.

BRON′TE, Charlotte, an English writer of novels, born at Thornton, Yorkshire, April 21, 1816. She was the third daughter in a family of six remarkable children, five girls and a boy. Their father was a poor clergyman; their mother died when they were very young, and the children grew up in a lonely country parsonage without other playmates and few pleasures. Their father, the Rev. Patrick Bronte, taught them to take an interest in grave and solid matters, and at an age when other children would have been playing with dolls or reading fairy tales they talked about politics and religion and fine arts, and had their own opinion about the public people and public affairs of the day. When Charlotte was eight years old, she and three of her sisters went to a boarding-school where they were harshly treated, and suffered from hunger and cold.

The elder girls, Maria and Elizabeth, grew ill and had to be sent home, where they died soon after. Charlotte never forgot the misery of that year, and in her novel "Jane Eyre" she tells the story of the school in a very life-like way. When she grew up she became a school-teacher herself and then a governess. In 1846 the three sisters published a little book called "Poems by Currer, Ellis, and Acton Bell," but it was not very successful. Each of the girls then wrote a novel. Charlotte's, which was called "The Professor," brought her another disappointment, for she could not get it printed, though her sisters' books were accepted. Still she would not be discouraged, but went to work again, and wrote "Jane Eyre," which proved to be one of the most popular novels ever published. It was read everywhere, translated into numerous languages, and even made into a play. But Charlotte's enjoyment in her success was soon spoiled by a great sorrow. In December, 1848, her sister Emily died, and in less than six months afterward (May 28, 1849) Anne was buried beside her. She was not idle in her sorrow, however, but wrote two other books, "Shirley" and "Villette," and found time to do many kind things for others. She died at Haworth, where her father preached, when thirty-nine years old (March 31, 1855).

BROOK′LYN, a city of New York, at the E. end of Long Island, and separated from New York City by a strait called the East River; pop. 806,000, or about half as large as New York City. Most of the streets are broad and handsome, and shaded with trees. Some of the finest houses are on Brooklyn Heights, a line of bluffs which overlook New York City and Bay. Brooklyn has nearly three hundred churches, from which it is sometimes called the "City of Churches."

It has a beautiful park called Prospect Park, and in the outskirts are several large cemeteries, among them those called Greenwood, Cypress Hills, and Evergreens, where most of the people who die in New York are buried.

Many people who live in Brooklyn are New York business men, so that it has been called the "sleeping-room of New York;" but it has also many stores and business houses of its own. There are large manufactories of carpets, clothing, pianos and organs, iron-ware, chemicals, and soap, and more sugar is refined there than in any other city in the United States. The shores are lined with wharves, which are always crowded with ships, and there are immense elevators where more grain is stored than in any other city in the world. The Atlantic Dock is a great artificial bay which has two miles of piers and will hold five hundred ships. The Brooklyn Navy Yard, which belongs to the United States Government, contains one hundred and forty-four acres of ground and many large buildings where ships of war are built and repaired. Brooklyn is connected with New York by many lines of steam ferry-boats, and by the largest suspension bridge in the world.

Brooklyn was first settled in 1636 by Hollanders, who named it after Breuckelen, a village of Holland. Breuckelen, in Dutch, means marshy ground. The battle of Long Island was fought there in 1776. While the British army was in New York, American prisoners were kept in old ships anchored near Brooklyn, and the prisoners were so badly treated that more than 11,000 died.

BROOKS, Noah, an American writer, born in Castine, Me., in 1830. He was left an orphan when only eight years old, and had only a common-school education. When twenty-four years old he went to Illinois, and soon after he and four companions went across the plains to California. In 1871 he came to New York, where he was first one of the editors of the "Tribune" and later of the "Times." He has written ten stories for "Scribner's Magazine," and one long story for "St. Nicholas," called "The Boy Emigrants," which is said to be a true account of his adventures while crossing the plains, and of life in California at that time.

BROWN, George L., an American painter, born in Boston in 1814. He spent several years in Italy, studying landscape painting, but since 1860 has lived in Boston. Among his best-known works are "The Crown of New England," and "New York Harbor."

BROWN, John G., a well-known painter, born in England in 1831. His first art-studies were made in his own country, but he has painted in New York for the last twenty-five years. His pictures represent scenes from every-day life—ragged urchins in the streets, boys with the first cigar, and sometimes more ambitious subjects, with much success.

BRUCE, Robert, King of Scotland, born March 21, 1274. He was descended from King DAVID I., being the grandson of the Robert Bruce who had claimed the throne at the same time with John BALLIOL. After Balliol had lost his throne and King Edward I. of England had put down the revolt of William WALLACE, young Bruce made up his mind to free Scotland from the English and to get his throne. He called on the Scots to join him, and was crowned at Scone (March 27, 1306) as King Robert I. But the English defeated his little army, and for several years he was an outlaw with but a few followers. At one time he had to leave Scotland and hide in an island off the coast of Ireland. It is said that while lying in bed one day in a wretched hut, he saw a spider trying to spin its web from beam to beam over his head. The insect tried and failed six times, just as many times as Bruce had been beaten by the English. "If the spider tries again," thought he, "so will I." Once more the spider tried, and this time with success. Bruce took it as a happy omen, went back to Scotland, and from that time the tide turned in his favor. He won back all the cities and castles one by one until at last only Stirling was left to the English, and it was so closely besieged that it was almost ready to give up. King Edward II., for Edward I. was then dead, marched with 100,000 men to try to save it; but he was terribly defeated at the great battle of BANNOCKBURN, and so Bruce freed Scotland and won his throne. But as the English still refused to own Robert as king, the Scots carried the war into England and for many years laid waste the counties on the border. In these expeditions they carried no provisions except a small bag of oatmeal, which each man bore at his saddle, with a thin iron plate on which he baked his cakes. They burned and destroyed everything, and killed all the cattle they could not drive away. At last the English got tired of it and made peace with Scotland (1328). The next year King Robert died (June 7, 1329) at Cardross, leaving a son eight years old, who was crowned king as David II. King Robert asked that his heart should be carried to Palestine and buried in Jerusalem. James DOUGLAS tried to do this, but he was killed by the Moors in Spain and the heart was taken back to Scotland and buried in Melrose Abbey.

BRUGES (*broo'jiz*), a city of Belgium, about 8 miles from the North Sea; pop. 47,000, or about the same as that of Portland, Ore. It is divided by many canals crossed by more than fifty bridges, and several canals run from it to the ocean. It is now principally a manufacturing town, where linen, cotton, and woolen goods are made. Several thousand women and girls are employed in making lace. In the 15th century it was a very important place for trade, and had more than 200,-000 inhabitants. It was famous for its tapestries and woolen cloths, and its wool trade was of so much importance that PHILIP THE GOOD set up in honor of it the Order of the Golden Fleece, which became, next after the Order of the Garter, the most illustrious order of knighthood in Europe. Many fine old buildings of that time are still standing, among which is the celebrated belltower, with its chime of forty-eight bells.

Bruges is in Dutch Brugge, which means bridges.

BRUNEL, Isambard Kingdom, a famous English engineer, born at Portsmouth, April 9, 1806. He was the son of Sir Mark Brunel, and helped his father in building the Thames tunnel. He was the builder of several fine bridges, and also of the steamship Great Western, which was the first to cross the Atlantic Ocean on regular trips; the Great Britain, which was the first ocean screw steamer; and the Great Eastern, which is the largest steamer ever built. He died when fifty-three years old (Sept. 14, 1859).

BRU-NEL, Sir Mark Isambard, a noted engineer, born near Rouen, France, April 25, 1769. He was the son of a farmer, and went to school in Rouen. During the Revolution (1793) he left France and came to New York, where he worked as an engineer and architect. He drew a plan for the Capitol at Washington, but it was refused because it would cost too much to build. In 1799 he went to England, where he made many useful machines; but his most famous work was the tunnel under the river Thames, which took eighteen years to build. He was made a knight by the Queen in

1841. He died in London when eighty years old (Dec. 12, 1849.)

BRUNS'WICK, a duchy of the German Empire, in Central Germany; area 1425 square miles, or a little larger than Rhode Island; pop. 373,000, or a little less than that of New Hampshire; capital, Brunswick (pop. 85,000). Brunswick is a monarchy, and its ruler is called Duke of Brunswick. The first Duke was Otto, who began to rule in 1235. The present royal family of England is a branch of the House of Brunswick.

BRUSSA (*broo'sah*), a city of Turkey in Asia, about 60 miles S.E. of Constantinople; pop. 65,000, or the same as that of Atlanta, Ga. It stands in a beautiful plain near the foot of Mount OLYMPUS, and having a great many mosques with minarets, it makes a fine appearance. Near it are famous hot springs, which have been used since ancient times. Brussa is a place of large trade, and has fine bazaars and manufactures of silks, satins, and carpets.

Brussa was anciently the capital of Bithynia, and was named Prusa, from King Prusias of Bithynia. The Turks took it (1326) from the Greek emperors, and it was their capital until they captured ADRIANOPLE. Othman, their first Sultan, was buried there.

BRUSSELS, a city, capital of Belgium, on the river Senne, 27 miles S. of Antwerp; pop. (with suburbs) 450,000, or about as large as Boston, Mass. It is the most important city of Belgium, and one of the finest in Europe. It was once surrounded by walls, but they have been made into broad boulevards, lined with double rows of shade-trees. Brussels is noted for splendid public buildings, palaces, and churches, and its libraries, museums, galleries, botanic gardens, and observatory. It is also famous for the manufacture of Brussels lace, and for fine linens, dam-

asks, jewelry, porcelain, and glass. The old name of Brussels was Bruoch-Sella, the "site on the marsh," and out of this has grown its present name. It was first built about the 8th century.

BRU'TUS, Lucius Junius, a noted Roman patriot who lived about 500 B.C. His father, who was the husband of Tarquinia, sister of King TARQUIN THE PROUD, had been put to death, together with his eldest son, by the king, and Lucius, to save himself from a like fate, pretended to be insane. He acted so silly that he was called Brutus (Latin for brutish or stupid) by his uncle the king, who had taken all his property for himself. But he soon showed that he was not as stupid as he seemed. Lucretia, a noble and beautiful lady, was treated so badly by Sextus, the king's son, while her husband, Collatinus, was absent with the army, that she killed herself. Brutus snatched the dagger from the wound, and showing the bloody blade to the people, stirred up an insurrection which drove the king from the city and changed Rome into a republic. Brutus and Collatinus were chosen the first consuls. The two sons of Brutus, Titus and Tiberius, soon after joined in a plot to bring back the Tarquins, and the father ordered them to be scourged and beheaded. Brutus himself was killed in a battle with Tarquin, who tried in vain to get back his throne.

BRU'TUS, Marcus Junius, one of the murderers of Julius CAESAR, born 85 B.C. He was a descendant of Lucius Junius Brutus, and his mother was a sister of CATO the younger, whose daughter Portia, his cousin, he married. When the civil war broke out between Pompey and Cæsar, Marcus Brutus joined the party of POMPEY and fought bravely against Cæsar; but after the battle of Pharsalia (48 B.C.) Brutus made his peace with Cæsar, and accepted a great many honors and favors at his hands. He did not trust him, however, or serve him willingly; for he believed that Cæsar wished to make himself a king. He joined with CASSIUS in the plot against Cæsar's life, and was one of those who stabbed him,

When Brutus struck him, Cæsar is said to have cried out in wonder and grief, *Et tu, Brute!* (And thou, too, Brutus!) for he had not thought that one who had received

Marcus Junius Brutus.

so much kindness from him could raise his hand against him.

After the murder Brutus became unpopular in Rome, and he and Cassius fled to Macedonia, where they raised a large army to oppose ANTONY and Octavius (AUGUSTUS). The armies met at PHILIPPI, where two battles were fought. Cassius stabbed himself after the first battle, and Brutus died in the same way after the second one, twenty days later. When his wife Portia heard of his death, she also killed herself. Brutus was forty-three years old when he died (42 B. C.). Brutus is one of the prin-

cipal characters in Shakespeare's play of "Julius Cæsar."

BRY'ANT, William Cullen, an American poet, born in Cummington, Mass., November 3, 1794. He was a very bright boy, and when only ten years old wrote poetry that was thought worth printing. At fourteen he published two long poems, called "The Embargo" and "The Spanish Revolution," which were so good that it was doubted whether a mere boy could have written them. When sixteen years old he went to Williams College, but left at the end of two years to study law, and was admitted to the bar at the age of twenty-one (1815).

Bryant.

He soon gave up the law for a literary life, which better suited his tastes.

His remarkable poem "Thanatopsis," which is still considered one of the finest in the language, was written when he was but nineteen. In 1821 he published a volume which at once gave him high rank as a poet. In 1825 he came to New York City to live, and a year later became an editor of the *Evening Post*, a newspaper with which he was connected all the rest of his life. He traveled much both at home and abroad, and made himself acquainted with the language and literature of all the principal nations of Europe. His writings show his love of nature and of all things noble and pure, and are marked by strength of thought and delicacy of fancy and feeling. He died in New York beloved and honored, at the age of eighty-four (June 12, 1878).

BUCCANEERS (*buk-ka-neers'*), a name given to the bands of adventurers or freebooters who in the 17th century preyed on Spanish trade in the West Indies. About 1630 some Frenchmen, who were driven away from the island of St. Christopher, went to Hispaniola or Hayti, where they lived by hunting the wild cattle and selling their hides to Dutch traders. They used to dry the flesh for food, and hence were called in French *boucanier*, which means one who dries the flesh of animals. The Spaniards tried to drive them out, but they were joined by many other French and English, who liked their wild life, and finally became so strong that they attacked Spanish ships and even sailed over to the coast of America and took towns. Among the leaders of the Buccaneers was a Frenchman named Montbar, who destroyed so many ships and killed so many Spaniards that he was called the "Exterminator." But the most noted one was Henry Morgan, a Welshman, who formed a fleet of ships and showed so much military skill that he took strong fortresses and towns, winning an immense amount of booty from the Spaniards. He became rich and went back to England, where he was made a knight by CHARLES II. The Buccaneers were finally put down by the French and English governments.

BUCHANAN (*buk-an'an*), **James,** fifteenth President of the United States, born at Stony Batter, Franklin Co., Penn., April 22, 1791. His father came from Ireland to this country in 1783, and his mother was the daughter of a farmer in Pennsylvania. He was graduated at Dickinson College in 1809, and became a very successful lawyer, but retired from practice at the age of forty; after which he never tried but one case. This was in behalf of a poor widow who was in danger of losing her small property; and in spite of many difficulties in the way, Mr. Buchanan succeeded in getting for her her just claims. He became a member of the Pennsylvania legislature when only

James Buchanan.

twenty-three years old, and six years latter (1821) entered Congress, where he served for ten years, when he withdrew. Soon after he was sent by President Jackson as minister to St. Petersburg, and on his return (1833) was elected to the United States Senate. Under President Polk he was Secretary of State (1845 to 1849), and under President Pierce he was minister to England (1853 to 1856). He was President of the United States from 1857 to 1861, when he was succeeded by Abraham Lincoln. The remainder of his life was passed on his farm called Wheatlands, at Lancaster, Penn., where he died when seventy-seven years old (June 1, 1868).

BUCHAREST (*boo-kah-rest'*), a city, capital of ROUMANIA, on the river Dimbovitza, about 30 miles N. of the Danube; pop. 221,000, or not quite half as many as Boston. It is a dirty place and not very well built, but it has a large trade in grain, wool, cattle, hides, honey, and wax. It is said to be one of the gayest cities in Europe. Bucharest (Bukuresht) means the "City of Pleasure." The town was first built in the 13th century.

BUCKINGHAM (*buk'ing-am*), **George Villiers,** Duke of, an English statesman, born Aug. 20, 1592. He was handsome and witty, and became the favorite of JAMES I., who gave him one after another the titles of baron, viscount, earl, marquis, and duke. James used to call him "Steenie" and allowed Buckingham to treat him as his equal. When CHARLES I. became king he also made Buckingham his favorite and principal minister. and this was one of the causes of trouble between the King and Parliament, for Buckingham was a bad man and very unpopular. At last a man named Felton, thinking that he was doing his country a service, stabbed Buckingham at Portsmouth, and he died there when thirty-six years old (Aug. 23, 1628).

BUDA-PESTH (*bu'dah-pest*), a city, capital of Hungary, on the Danube, 130 miles S.E. of Vienna; pop. 439,000, or a little larger than Baltimore, Md. It is made up of the city of Buda, on the south bank of the river, and the city of Pesth, on the north bank, the two being joined by a splendid suspension-bridge. Buda is on high ground, and is built round a great rock called the Schlossberg (Castle Hill), on which is the citadel, the royal palace, and a cathedral where the Emperors of Austria are crowned as kings of Hungary. In

a chapel near by are kept the crown, sceptre, sword, and mantle of St. Stephen, the first Christian king of Hungary. This crown is said to have been sent to Stephen by Pope Sylvester II. in the year 1000. The Hungarians call it the "holy and apostolical crown of Hungary," and guard it with the greatest care.

Pesth is on a sandy plain, so low that it has to have embankments along the river to keep the water out; but it is the most splendid and largest city of Hungary, and about four fifths of the people of Buda-Pesth live in it. It has many fine buildings, among them the hall where the Hungarian diet or congress meets. The university of Pesth is, next after that of Vienna, the largest in Austro-Hungary, and has more than 2000 students, and splendid museums and libraries. Pesth has a larger trade in grain than any other place in the empire, and a very large trade in cattle, wool, leather, wine, and timber.

Buda was named after Buda the brother of ATTILA, who lived in the 5th century. Pesth is thought to have got its name from an old word (*pisch*) meaning sand, on account of the sandy plain around it. It also is a very old place, the Romans having had a town there. Both Buda and Pesth were taken by the Turks in 1526, and held by them for 160 years (1686).

BU'ELL, Don Carlos, an American general, born near Marietta, Ohio, March 23, 1818. He was graduated at West Point (1841), and served in the Florida and Mexican wars. During the Civil War he had at one time the command of Kentucky and Tennessee. At the battle of Shiloh he reinforced Gen. Grant, helping him to defeat the Confederates (April 6, 1862). In July and August, 1862, the Confederates, under Gen. Bragg, forced Gen. Buell to abandon part of Kentucky, and though Bragg retreated in October, Gen. Buell did not follow him. On this account his command was taken from him. He left the army in 1864, and now lives in Kentucky.

BUENA VISTA (*bwa'nah vees'-tah*), a village in Mexico, 7 miles S. of Saltillo, near which a battle was fought between the Americans under Gen. TAYLOR and the Mexicans under SANTA ANNA, Feb. 22 and 23, 1847. The Mexicans had 20,000 men and the Americans only 5000, but after two days' fighting Santa Anna retreated and left Gen. Taylor in possession of the field.

Buena Vista is Spanish, and means " pleasant view."

BUENOS AYRES (*bwa'noss i'rez*), a city of South America, capital of the ARGENTINE REPUBLIC; on the S. bank of the Rio de la Plata, 180 miles from the sea; pop. 561,000, or a fifth larger than Boston, Mass. Next after RIO DE JANEIRO, Buenos Ayres is the largest and most important city in South America; but its harbor is poor. Though the river is so wide there that one cannot see across it, it is so shallow that large ships have to anchor six or seven miles from the shore. Two wharves, each more than a quarter of a mile long, have been built out from the city, and passengers and goods are taken from the ships to these wharves in small vessels called lighters. But sometimes the water is so low that even the lighters cannot get up to the wharves, and then carts with large wheels go out to meet the lighters. Buenos Ayres has a very large trade in wool, ox and horse hides, tallow, and beef. There is a university there, and a fine museum which is said to have the best collection in the world of fossil animals (C. C. T., 516, I., l.) that lived before the deluge.

Buenos Ayres in Spanish means good airs, or pleasant breezes. The city was founded by the Spaniards in 1580.

BUF'FA-LO, a city of New York State, on the Niagara River, at the E. end of Lake Erie; pop. 256,000, or about as large as Cleveland, O. Its harbor is one of the best on the lakes, and it has a large trade in grain and in cattle, sheep, and hogs. It has also large iron manufactures, and many iron ships and steamers are built there.

Buffalo was first built in 1801.

BUF-FON', Georges Louis Leclerc, Count de, a famous French writer on natural history, born at Montbard, Burgundy, Sept. 7, 1707. He was educated to be a lawyer, but when about twenty years old he joined a young English nobleman in a tour through France, Switzerland, and Italy; and was so much struck by what he saw that he made up his mind to devote himself to the study of science. When thirty-seven years old (1739) he was made superintendent of the great botanical and zoölogical gardens in Paris, now called the *Jardin des Plantes* (Garden of Plants). This drew his attention to the study of nature, and he resolved to write a work describing all the forms of nature on the earth. After ten years of hard labor the first three volumes of his " Natural History" were published (1749), and many more volumes appeared between that and the time of his death. In these he tells chiefly about quadrupeds, birds, and minerals, and how the earth grew. His books were very popular because they differed from all which had been written before, giving not only the scientific accounts of things in natural history, but interesting facts concerning them. His books have been reprinted many times and translated into many other languages; and they are still much read, though some of his opinions are not now held by scientific men. He was made a count in 1776 by the King of France. Buffon died in Paris at the age of eighty-one (April 16, 1788).

BULGARIA (*bool-ga're-ah*), a country of Turkey in Europe, on the W. coast of the Black Sea, S. of Roumania; area 24,699 square miles, or about half as large as New York State; pop. (with Eastern Roumelia (area, 13,861), now incorporated with Bulgaria) 3,154,000, or a little less than that of Ohio; capital, Sofia (pop. 42,000). The people are mostly Christians and principally farmers, and the chief trade is in wheat and wool. Bulgaria was once a Christian kingdom, but was conquered by the Turks about 1392. After the war between Russia and Turkey it was made into a principality by the Treaty of Berlin (1878), and it is now ruled by a Christian prince, who pays a certain amount of money as tribute every year to Turkey.

BULL, Ole Borneman, a noted Norwegian violinist, born at Bergen, Feb. 5, 1810. His father wished him to be a minister, but he liked a musical life better. When four or five years old he could play on the violin all the songs he heard his mother sing, and when eight he played the first violin in the Bergen Theatre. At eighteen he was sent to the University of Christiania, but failed in his examinations. After living for a while in Germany, where he pretended to study law, he went to Paris, and fared hardly for a year or two; but finally was successful in giving concerts, became famous, and made a fortune.

He visited the United States several times, and played with great success. In 1852 he bought a large tract of land in Pennsylvania, and founded a colony which was called Oleana in his honor; but it was soon given up, and he went back to his concerts. He died in Norway when seventy years old (Aug. 17, 1880).

BULL RUN, a small stream in N.E. Virginia, on the banks of which two battles were fought in the Civil War. In the first battle (July 21, 1861) the Union army, under Gen. McDowell, was defeated by the Confederate army, under Gens. Beauregard and J. E. Johnston. Such a victory at the beginning of the war gave the South great hopes, and taught the North, whose people had thought that secession would be put down in a few months, that a great war was begun in which success could be bought only at a heavy cost.

In the second battle (Aug. 29 and 30, 1862) the Union army, under Gen. Pope, was defeated by the Confederate army, under Gen. Lee. After this battle the command of the Union army was taken from Gen. Pope and given to Gen. McClellan. The Confederates called these two battles the first and second battles of Manassas, because they were both fought near the railroad junction at Manassas.

BULWER-LYT'TON, Edward George Earl Lytton, Baron Lytton, a famous English writer, born in Norfolk, May, 1805. His father, General Bulwer, died when he was young, and he was brought up by his mother and by private tutors. At the University of Cambridge, where he was graduated in 1826, he took a prize for a poem on "Sculpture." The next year he published a novel called "Falkland," and after that he wrote many novels and became famous. He also became noted as a writer of plays, and his "Lady of Lyons," his "Richelieu," and his "Money" are still very popular. Among his first novels are "The Last Days of Pompeii," and "Rienzi, the Last of the Tribunes," and among his later ones are "Harold, the Last of the Saxon Kings," "The Caxtons,' "My Novel," and "What will He Do with It?" His stories are very popular, and have been translated into many languages. In 1838 Bulwer was made a baronet, and when his mother died he added her name of Lytton to his own. In 1866 he was made a peer, with the title of Baron Lytton. He died in London when sixty-seven years old (Jan. 18, 1873).

BULWER·LYTTON, Edward Robert, Earl of Lytton, an English statesman and poet, born Nov. 8, 1831. He was educated at HARROW School and at the University of BONN. When eighteen years old he came to the United States as private secretary of his uncle, Sir Henry Bulwer, who was Minister at Washington; and afterward was secretary at different courts in Europe and Minister to Portugal and France. From 1876 to 1880 he was Governor-General of India. He was made Earl of Lytton in 1880. In 1856 he published a volume of poems under the name of Owen Meredith, and since then he has published several others. The most popular one is "Lucile," a story in verse. He died when sixty years old (Nov. 24, 1891).

BUNKER (*bung'ker*) **HILL**, a hill in Charlestown, Mass., where the battle of Bunker Hill was fought between the British and the Americans, June 17, 1775. The British troops in Boston were shut in by the Americans, but being strengthened by the arrival of more troops, Gen. Gage, their commander, made up his mind to take possession of Bunker Hill. The Americans found out his plan, and to get ahead of him sent a thousand men there in the night and built an earth fort. The next day the British troops went over in boats and tried to drive them out, but the Americans drove them back twice with great loss. On the third attack the Americans got out of powder, and as they had no bayonets they had to retreat. The British lost more than a thousand in killed and wounded, and the Americans not half so many.

This was the first great battle of the Revolution, and though the Americans had to retreat, it was as good to them as a victory, for it taught them that British troops could be beaten. The British had laughed at the rebels, and thought they were going to defeat them easily, but after this battle Gen. Gage wrote home that they were not so despicable as many had thought them, and that their conquest would be no easy task.

BUN'YAN, John, author of the "Pilgrim's Progress," one of the most celebrated books ever written, was born at Elstow, near Bedford, England, in 1628. His father, who was a tinker, brought him up to the same business, and he traveled about the country for many years as a mender of old

Bunyan.

tin-ware. During this time he describes himself as a great sinner, much given to swearing and delighting in worldly amusements. On one occasion as he stood cursing at a shop-window, the mistress of the place rebuked him for it; and said that his example was enough to spoil all the youth of the town. Whereupon Bunyan was smitten with shame, and from that time dropped his oaths.

When seventeen years old he joined the army of the Parliament, but after about a year returned home. He was married at the age of nineteen (1647), and he soon began to lead a better life, and to preach to the poor people of Bedford. About 1655 he became a Baptist minister, and he preached with great success until the Cavaliers got into power again on the restoration of CHARLES II., when he was arrested for holding unlawful meetings, and shut up in Bedford jail, where he was kept a prisoner for twelve and a half years. He employed himself while there in making tagged laces for the support of his family, and in writing books. He was offered liberty if he would give up preaching; but he replied, "If you set me free to-day I will preach again to-morrow."

He was released in 1671, and began at once to preach again. In course of time a meeting-house was put up in Bedford, and he preached in it to large congregations for the rest of his life. Besides the "Pilgrim's Progress," which has been translated into more languages than any other book excepting the Bible, he wrote "The Holy War" and other less important works. He died in London, where he was wont to go to preach once a year, in the sixty-first year of his age (Aug. 31, 1688).

BURCKHARDT (*boork'hart*), **Johann Ludwig,** a Swiss traveler, born in Lausanne, Nov. 24, 1784. He went to England when twenty-two years old, and was chosen by a society there to explore Africa, which was then little known. After studying Arabic for several years he went to Malta (1809), dressed himself like an Arab merchant, took the name of Sheik Ibrahim ibn Abdallah, and went to Syria, where he gained such a knowledge of Eastern manners and customs, and learned to speak the language so well, that he passed for a learned Mohammedan. He visited PALMYRA, DAMASCUS, and the Dead Sea, and then went to Egypt, where he visited the principal ruins on the Nile. He also went to MECCA and MEDINA, the sacred cities of the Mohammedans, where no Christians were then allowed, and visited Mount Ararat and Mount Sinai. He was about to go down into Africa when he died in Cairo, when only thirty-three years old (Oct. 17, 1817). The Mohammedans, who thought he was a real sheik, buried him in their burying ground, which they would not have done if they had known him to be a Christian.

BURGOS (*boor'goce*), a city of Spain, 140 miles N. of Madrid ; pop. 31,000, or nearly as much as that of Quincy, Ill. It was formerly a very important place, and had a large trade, but it lost its greatness when Madrid was made the capital of Spain. Its cathedral of white marble is one of the most noted specimens of Gothic architecture in Europe.

Burgos means a fortified house or fort, and is the same as our word burg, which now means town or city. The name was first given to a castle built there in the 9th century.

BUR-GOYNE', **John**, a British general, born about 1730. During the war of the American Revolution he was given command of the British army in Canada, and led an army of British and Indians into New York. He took TICONDEROGA (July 6, 1777), but was defeated by the Americans in the two battles of Saratoga (Sept. 19 and Oct. 7), and was forced to surrender with his whole army (Oct. 17) to Gen. GATES. On his return to England he was much blamed for his conduct and he resigned from the army, but was restored to his rank (1782) and made commander-in-chief in Ireland. He wrote a comic opera and several plays, besides many poems. He died in London when about sixty-two years old (Aug. 4, 1792).

BUR'GUN-DY, a former country of

Europe, now a part of S.E. France. The Burgundians were a German tribe who went into GAUL about A.D. 407 and founded the Kingdom of Burgundy. The Franks conquered this (534) and ruled it about 300 years, when a second Kingdom was formed. It afterward had many changes, and at last the Duchy of Burgundy, of which the rulers had been very famous, was joined to France (1477).

BURKE, Edmund, a famous statesman and writer, born in Dublin, Jan. 1, 1730. He was the son of Richard Burke, an attorney, and was educated at Trinity College, where he was a fellow-student of Oliver GOLDSMITH. He studied very hard while there, and used to read three hours every day in the public library. One day his brother Richard, after hearing Edmund make a fine speech in Parliament, said : " I have wondered how Ned managed to get all the talents of the family ; but then I remember when we were at play he was always at work." Edmund studied law, but soon gave it up to become a writer, and wrote so well on politics, history, and other subjects that he won the friendship of many great men and became the best known of the critics of his day. He was so very honest that he gave up an office and a pension which had been given him when he found that they were a sort of bribe. When thirty-five years old (1765) he became private secretary to the new Prime Minister, and the next year was sent to Parliament. There he at once gained attention by taking sides with the American colonists, showing great knowledge of their affairs and boldly defending their rights. He urged kind and just measures, wrote papers on the subject, and made such earnest speeches against unjust taxation that he became unpopular with his own party. He then took up the wrongs of the people of the East Indies, and caused

the trial of Warren HASTINGS, the Governor of India for his injustice to them. His speech against Hastings is celebrated as one of the greatest ever made by any orator ; and, though Hastings was acquitted, it called the attention of the British people to the bad government in India and led the way to great reforms. Burke has been praised by the writers of almost all countries, and some have thought that he was the greatest orator that ever lived. He died at Beaconsfield when sixty-seven years old (July 9, 1797), and was buried in Westminster Abbey.

BUR'LING-TON, a city of S. E. Iowa, on the Mississipi River ; pop. 22,000, or nearly the same as that of Macon, Ga. It is built on a high bluff along the river, amongst orchards and vineyards, for which reason it is sometimes called the "Orchard City." Near by are large coal-mines, from which fuel is easily got for its many foundries and mills. Burlington was built in 1834, and was the capital of the State from 1837 to 1840.

BUR'LING-TON, the largest city of Vermont, on Lake Champlain, 40 miles N.W. of Montpelier ; pop. 15,000, or nearly the same as that of Rome, N. Y. It has a large trade in lumber and many manufactures. The University of Vermont (founded in 1791) stands on a hill overlooking the lake. In the cemetery is a splendid monument to Ethan Allen, who is buried there. Burlington was first settled in 1783.

BURN'LEY, a town of England, on the river Burn, 22 miles N. of Manchester ; pop. 59,000, or about as large as Camden, N. J. The surrounding region is rich in coal-mines, and the city has many manufactories, especially of cheap cotton cloths. There are several iron foundries, machine-works, breweries, tanneries, and mills.

BUR'MAH, a region of S. Asia, between India and China ; area, about 200,000 square miles, or nearly the same as that of France; pop. 5,000,000, or less than one-eighth that of France; capital, MANDELAY. It was once an independent kingdom, but Great Britain has taken possession of the whole country. Burmah is rich in metals, and has the best ruby-mines in the world. The people live mostly on rice. The tea plant is raised, but instead of making a drink of the leaves, the people eat them with oil and garlic. They also eat ants, of which they lay up great stores for food. The country was formerly ruled by a despot who called himself emperor, and who put any of his people to death whom he chose.

BURNS, Robert, a famous Scottish poet, born near Ayr, Jan. 25, 1759. His parents were poor peasants, but were very fond of reading; one day, when Robert was a little boy, a stranger, going into the cottage at dinner-time, found each one of the family seated at the table with a spoon in one hand and a book in the other. Robert wrote his first verses when sixteen years old about a "bonnie lassie" whom he fell in love with, and who used to work with him in the harvest-field. After his father died he and his brother were obliged to work harder than ever, and at night, when the day's work was done, Robert used to sit by the fire and write verses. It was at this time that he wrote one of his loveliest poems, "The Cotter's Saturday Night;" and some time after, when a little boy told Burns that he could never read that poem aloud because it made him "greet" (cry) so, Burns said: "Well, my lad, it made me greet, too, when I wrote it by my father's fireside."

Though he worked hard on the farm, he did not get along very well, and at last he made up his mind to go to the West Indies, and

to get money enough to pay his way he got a friend to have all his poems published. Just as he was about to start, and had written

Burns.

some verses bidding farewell to Scotland, a letter came from his friend telling him how everybody in Edinburgh, even the great lords and ladies, were praising his verses and buying his book, and that they all wanted to see the poet who could write such beautiful things. He felt as if he were dreaming, but he soon joined his friend and spent a year in the city, where everybody liked him, and gave him dinner-parties, and flattered him so that he began to love feasting and drinking too; and so, when he went back to the country, he took with him not only the five hundred pounds made by his poems, but these new tastes which were to him just like the Old Man of the Sea to Sindbad the sailor. His money left him pretty soon, but the love of drink never did, although he used to try to get rid of it. He wrote a great many beautiful poems, some of them brimful of fun and others just as full of tears. He died at Dumfries when only thirty-seven years old (July 21,

1796). There is a beautiful monument to his memory at Dumfries, and in 1880 a bronze statue of him was erected in Central Park, New York.

BURN'SIDE, Ambrose Everett, an American general, born at Liberty, Ind., May 23, 1824. He was a graduate of West Point, and when the Civil War broke out joined the army. In January, 1862, he captured Roanoke Island and Beaufort, N. C., and afterward won the battle of South Mountain (Sept. 14, 1862) and took part in the battle of ANTIETAM. He became commander of the army of the Potomac (Nov. 7, 1862), but, being defeated at the battle of Fredericksburg (Dec. 12), resigned his command. In 1863 he drove the Confederates from East Tennessee. In the autumn of that year he was besieged at Knoxville, Tenn., but the Confederates were at length forced to retreat. In 1864 he assisted Gen. Grant in the siege of Petersburg. He died at Bristol, R. I., when fifty-seven years old (September 13, 1881).

BURR, Aaron, a noted American politician, born in Newark, N. J., Feb. 6, 1756. He was graduated at Princeton College, of which his father was President, in 1772. When the war of the Revolution broke out he entered the army as a private soldier, and rose to be a lieutenant-colonel, but resigned in 1779 on account of poor health. He then became a lawyer in New York, and in 1789 was chosen attorney-general of the State, and two years after United States Senator. In 1800 Burr and Thomas Jefferson each had the same number of votes for President of the United States, so the House of Representatives had to choose between them. After voting for a long time, Jefferson was at last chosen President and Burr Vice-President.

In 1804 Burr was nominated for Governor of New York State, but was defeated. This led to a quarrel with Alexander HAMILTON, whom he shot in a duel and killed (July 11, 1804). The next year he was suspected of having formed a plan to conquer Mexico and to form a new government out of that country and a part of the territory of the United States in the south-west, and was tried for treason at Richmond (1807), but nothing was proved against him. After living for several years in poverty in Europe, he came to New York to practice law again. He died on Staten Island, N. Y., when eighty years old (Sept. 14, 1836.

BUT'LER, Benjamin Franklin, an American general, born in Deerfield, N. H., Nov. 5, 1818. He became a lawyer in Lowell, Mass., but when the Civil War broke out he joined the Union army, and commanded in Maryland and afterward at Fortress Monroe. Many slaves came into the Union lines, and when their masters demanded them Gen. Butler refused, saying that if slaves belonged to Confederates they were contraband of war. In this way escaped slaves got the name of "contrabands." In 1861 he captured Forts Hatteras and Clark, in North Carolina. In 1862 Gen. Butler and Admiral Farragut captured New Orleans, and Gen. Butler governed the city until November. In 1864 and 1865 he participated in the sieges of Petersburg and Richmond. Since 1866 he has been several times a member of Congress, and in 1882 he was elected governor of Massachusetts.

BY'RON, George Gordon, Lord, a famous English poet, born in London, Jan. 22, 1788. His father died when George was three years old, and his mother, who had gone to ABERDEEN to live, was left with very little for their support. She had a bad temper, and sometimes she would scold her son, who had a deformed foot, and call him a lame brat, and sometimes pet him and tell him he had the prettiest eyes in the world; and so he grew up a spoiled, overbearing boy. When George was ten years old, his great-uncle, Lord Byron of Newstead Abbey, died, and the poor lame boy, being the next heir, became Lord Byron. Newstead Abbey had been a very beautiful place, but his uncle had cut down many of the trees and let the place

Byron.

go to ruin, so that George got but little money from it to keep up his title.

Byron went to Harrow School and then to Cambridge, where, though lame, he became a fine swimmer and boxer and a good cricket-player. He spent some of his vacations at Newstead, where his favorite pet and playfellow was a noble Newfoundland dog, named Boatswain. This poor dog went mad and died, and Byron erected

over his grave a beautiful marble monument, which is still to be seen at Newstead. While at college he published a volume of poems, but they were not very good, and were much abused by the critics. When he became of age he went to take his seat in the House of Lords, but he had lived so wild a life that nobody wanted to know him, and he could not get any one to introduce him. Soon after, disgusted with England, he went traveling in the East, and did not come back for two years. He then published a part of a great poem called "Childe Harold," and at once became so famous that everybody wanted to know him. He had then grown very handsome, and was petted and praised by all the ladies.

When twenty-seven years old Byron married, but he behaved so badly that his wife could not live with him, and the next year she left him and went home with her infant daughter, and he never saw either of them again. Everybody now blamed him as much as they had praised him before, and Byron left England never to return. After this he led a wild life, mostly in Italy, but found time to write much beautiful poetry. In 1823 he went to Greece to help the people in their struggle with the Turks for freedom; but he never had a chance to fight for them. He was taken sick at Missolonghi of a fever, and died when only thirty-six years old (April 19, 1824). His body was carried to England and buried in Hucknall Church, near Newstead, where a small marble tablet marks the place.

BYZANTIUM (*by-zan'she-um*). See CONSTANTINOPLE.

C

CABANEL (*kah-bah-nel'*), **Alex-andre,** a French painter, born in Montpellier, Sept. 28, 1823. He painted historical, classical, and religious subjects, and was also well known as a portrait painter. He died in Paris when sixty-six years old (July 23, 1889).

CAB'OT, John, a famous navigator, who first found the continent of North America. He was an Italian by birth, but was living as a merchant in Bristol, England, when he got leave from King Henry VII. to search for new lands. He set sail (1497) with his son Sebastian, and after many weeks came in sight of the coast of NOVA SCOTIA. He landed, but saw no person, and soon returned to England. It is not known when he died.

CABOT, Sebastian, son of John, born probably in Venice about 1477. He was with his father when he found North America, and afterward made voyages himself. He sailed (1498) down the coast of North America as far south as the Gulf of Mexico, and afterward (1526) went down the coast of South America as far as the river PLATA. It is not known exactly when he died.

CABUL (*kah-bool'*), a city, capital of AFGHANISTAN; pop. about 70,-000, or nearly as large as Fall River, Mass. The city is on the Cabul River, in a valley among mountains, and it has a citadel or large fort, called Bala Hissar, on a high round hill. Many caravans from Persia and India pass through it, and it has a good trade. The country around it is noted for fine fruits. The people are very treacherous and cruel: they have twice murdered English officers who have been sent there, and to punish them the town has been taken by English armies and partly destroyed. It

was evacuated by the British in 1880, when Amir Abdur Rahman was placed on the throne.

CADIZ (*kay'diz*), a S. W. city of Spain, on the Atlantic coast; pop. about 63,000, or nearly the same as that of Memphis, Tenn. It is built on a long narrow neck of land, between which and the mainland is the Bay of Cadiz, which forms its harbor. The city is surrounded by walls and is strongly fortified. Cadiz is one of the principal seaports of Spain, though its trade is not as large as it was when Spain had many colonies in America. The principal thing sent from there now is sherry wine.

Cadiz is one of the oldest cities of Europe, it having been first built by the Phœnicians more than a thousand years before Christ. They called it Gadr, which means "city;" the Romans changed this to Gadez, and the name finally grew into Cadiz.

CAD'MUS, in Greek fable, a king of Bœotia, son of Agenor, king of PHŒNICIA. His father sent him in search of his sister EUROPA, who had been carried off by Jupiter, and told him not to come back without her. Having failed to find her, he was told by the oracle at DELPHI to follow a heifer until she stopped. She stopped at a place in Bœotia, and he built there a fort which he called after himself Cadmea, and which became in time the citadel of THEBES. Some of his companions having been killed by a dragon at a fountain where they went for water, Cadmus slew the monster, and sowed his teeth in the ground. From them sprang up many armed men, who killed each other as fast as they came up, excepting five only, who helped Cadmus build the city and became the ancestors of the Thebans. Cadmus is said to have taught the Greeks the use of sixteen letters of the alphabet, and also the art of writing in prose.

CAEN (*kon*), a town of Normandy, France, 120 miles W.N.W. of Paris; pop. 44,000, or about as large as Manchester, N. H. Nearly half the people are employed in lace-making. Much fine yellow building stone is quarried near the city, and sent from there all over the world. The cathedrals of Canterbury and Winchester and many other public buildings in England are built of it ; and among the churches of Caen that of St. Etienne (St. Stephen), built by WILLIAM THE CONQUEROR and in which he was buried. When his body was about to be put into the grave, a man stepped forward and forbade it. "The land on which this church stands belonged to my father, and now it is mine. I have never sold it nor given it away. In the name of God, I forbid you to put the body of the spoiler there, or to cover him with my ground." The matter was looked into, and it was found that William had really taken the land to build the church on, and had never paid for it. So the man was paid sixty shillings, which he set as the price of the grave, and he then consented to let the funeral go on. William's monument, erected in the church by his son William Rufus, was broken in pieces by the Huguenots in 1562.

CAERNARVON (*ker-nar'von*), or Carnarvon, a town of N.W. Wales, on Menai Strait; pop. 10,000, or not quite as large as Adams, Mass. Many people go there in the summer for sea-bathing. Near it is Caernarvon Castle, in which ED-WARD II., the first English Prince of Wales, was born. Its walls are more than a mile around, and have within them a covered gallery with loopholes made for shooting arrows through at an enemy. The castle is one of the finest ruins in Great Britain, and is visited by many travelers. In 1880 a tablet with the names of all the Princes of Wales on it was set up in the wall.

CÆSAR (*se'zar*), **Caius Julius,** a famous Roman soldier and statesman, born July 12, 100 B.C. From the earliest age he studied hard, and not only learned quickly but remembered what he learned. When quite young he got the enmity of SULLA, and had to flee for his life to Bithynia in Asia Minor

Julius Cæsar.

but on the death of Sulla he returned to Rome. When only twenty-three years old he won fame by a speech which he made, and wishing to study oratory more, he set out for Rhodes to practice with his old teacher, Apollonius Molo. On the way he was taken by pirates, who asked for him a ransom of thirty talents (more than $30,000). He agreed to pay it, but told them that if they knew who he was they would ask fifty talents, and added that if he ever caught them he would crucify them all. In time the money which he had sent for came, and he was set free by the pirates on the island of Delos. He at once got some ships, pursued and captured them, and executed them all as he had promised to do.

Cæsar had many friends in Rome, and he made more by his splendid style of living and by the free use of money. After holding several smaller offices, he was sent to govern the province of Spain, and won success both as a soldier and a ruler. In 59 B.C. he was chosen consul, and he formed a secret league with POMPEY, who had married his daughter Julia, and CRASSUS, which is called in history the First Triumvirate—that is, government of three. With these two great leaders on his side, Cæsar could get whatever he wanted. The next year he was sent to rule GAUL, where he spent about seven years in conquering the whole country. In the year 55 he went into Germany, and in the same year crossed over into Britain. He fought many victorious battles and extended the boundaries of Gaul to the river Rhine, but he did not make any lasting conquest either in Britain or beyond the Rhine.

While Cæsar was winning fame in Gaul, things were getting into confusion in Rome. Crassus had been killed in Parthia, and a coolness had sprung up between Cæsar and Pompey, whose wife was now dead. Pompey, who was jealous of Cæsar's fame, was the leader of the aristocratic party, while Cæsar took the side of the people. At last Pompey and his friends got the Senate to vote that, as the war was now ended, Cæsar should give up his army by a certain day or be treated as a public enemy. But instead of doing this, Cæsar made a speech to his troops and told them how badly he was treated, and they agreed to stand by him. He marched to the little river Rubicon, which was then the boundary between Gaul and Italy, and after thinking over the matter very earnestly, he made up his mind that he had got to go to Rome; and crying out, "The die is cast!" he led his troops through the river and invaded Italy (49). Pompey fled when he heard of his coming, and Cæsar, marching to Rome, was made by the people first Dictator and then Consul (48).

Cæsar now followed Pompey, defeated him at PHARSALUS, and in about three years overcame all who opposed him. After conquering Pharnaces, King of Pontus, in a single day, he wrote to the Senate a letter in which he said only " *Veni, vidi, vici!* " (I came, I saw, I conquered!). He then went into Africa, defeated SCIPIO, took Utica, where CATO killed himself, and returned to Rome master of the world. The people now almost worshiped him. His person was declared sacred and even divine; he was given a body-guard of knights and senators; his statue was placed in the temples with those of the gods; his portrait was put on the coins; the month Quintilis was called Julius (July) in his honor; and he was permitted to wear on all occasions a triumphal robe and a crown of laurel. He was made Dictator for life, and was given the title of *Imperator*, which means chief of the army, but which was given to Cæsar in a special way, and which we in English call Emperor. As this title did not give him the right to leave his power to a successor, he wanted also that of king. He had no son of his own, but he had adopted his grand-nephew Octavius, who afterward became the Emperor AUGUSTUS, and he wanted him to succeed him. But the title of King was hateful to the Roman people, and some young men led by Caius CAS-

SIUS and Marcus Junius BRUTUS made a conspiracy to kill him on the ides of March. Cæsar had had many warnings, but he paid no attention to them, saying that it was better to suffer death at once than to be always fearing it. On the day chosen to kill him, a paper giving a full account of the conspiracy was handed to him as he was entering the Senate House, but he thrust it unopened into his bosom. It was agreed that one of of the assassins, named Cimber, should offer a petition to him, and that while he was reading the paper all should crowd around and attack him together. All happened as they had planned. Cæsar defended himself at first, but when he saw Brutus, for whom he had done many kind acts, with a dagger in his hand, he said *Et tu, Brute!* ("Thou too, Brutus!") and wrapping his toga around him, gave up without any further struggle. He fell, pierced with twenty-three wounds, at the foot of the statue of Pompey (44 B.C.), when fifty-five years old.

Julius Cæsar was probably the greatest man that has ever lived. It is said that he conquered three hundred nations, took eight hundred cities, killed a million of men in his battles, and took prisoner another million. He was great not only as a soldier, but equally as a statesman and a scholar, and he was the greatest orator of his age except Cicero, and the greatest of Roman historians except Tacitus. He wrote books on grammar and on rhetoric, and tragedies and poems; but his best works are his histories of the Gallic War and of the Civil War, both of which are very valuable to us because they were written soon after the events took place, and are therefore believed to be trustworthy.

Cæsar is said to have been tall, and to have had a good figure. He was a fine horseman and well skilled in the use of weapons. In his youth he had been delicate, but by frequent exercise and exposure he became so strong that he could stand the privations and hardships of military life as well as any of his soldiers. He would often head his army on the march, sometimes on horseback and sometimes on foot, with his head uncovered in sunshine or in rain. His courage was very great, and he often rallied troops that had turned to fly by rushing among them, catching them by the throat, and forcing them back into the ranks. He was very strict with his men when the enemy was near, and often tried them by suddenly giving the signal to march in the night or on holidays; but when there was no danger to be feared he gave them great liberty. In speaking to them he called them comrades instead of soldiers, and by this and by other means he so attached them to him that they were willing to suffer anything and to brave all dangers for his sake.

CAGLIOSTRO (*kahl-yos'tro*), **Alessandro di,** an Italian impostor, born in PALERMO, June 2, 1743. He was of low birth, and his real name was Joseph Balsamo. When a boy he was a great rogue, and he had to run away from Palermo when sixteen years old for getting money by cheating. He called himself a count, and traveled in many countries under many different names and characters, pretending sometimes to be a nobleman, sometimes a physician, and sometimes a juggler. With the aid of his handsome wife, he cheated many people and made much money, especially by selling an elixir which would make people live forever and keep their beauty. He himself claimed to be very old, sometimes putting his age even at two hundred years. He also pretended that he knew how to make gold out of other metals, and many noble and rich people believed that he could do it. But at last his frauds were found out, and he was arrested in Rome, and the last eight years of his life were spent in prison. He died when fifty-two years old (1795).

CAIRO (*ki'ro*), a city, capital of Egypt, on a sandy plain on the E. side of the river Nile; pop. about 371,000, or a fifth larger than Cincinnati. It is surrounded by a wall, and is divided into several parts, the Mohammedans, the Jews, and the Christians each having a part, by other walls separated by gates, which are closed at night. The city looks handsome from the outside, but within most of the streets are crooked and dirty, and so narrow that loaded donkeys and camels going through them leave hardly any room for people to pass; and the houses of the poor are wretched mud-hovels. Some of the new streets, however, are wide enough for carriages and have fine houses where the rich live.

The citadel, which is built on a hill overlooking the city, has within its walls the palace of the Khedive, the mint, a gun-factory, barracks for soldiers, and a splendid mosque. There are nearly four hundred other mosques in the city, a large college, several theatres and libraries, and a museum with the best collection of Egyptian curiosities in the world. On an island in the Nile, near the city, is an old stone column, divided into parts by marks cut in it, used to tell the height of the waters of the river when they rise each year. This, which is many hundred years old, is called the Nilometer (Nile Measurer). About ten miles from Cairo are the Pyramids and the Sphinx. Cairo has a large trade with foreign countries, and many Greek, Italian, and French merchants live there. Every year a great caravan of pilgrims goes from there to MECCA.

Cairo was first built about 970 by the Arabs, who called it Al-Kahirah ("The Victorious"), in memory of their having conquered Egypt; and from this the name has changed to its present form.

CALAIS (*kah-lay'*), a seaport town of France, 19 miles N.N.E. of BOULOGNE; pop. 59,000, or nearly as large as Grand Rapids, Mich. As it is situated near the narrowest part of the Strait of Dover, being only twenty-six miles from Dover, in England, much of the travel between that country and France passes through it. It is strongly fortified, and was often fought for by the French and English. In 1347 it was taken by EDWARD III., after a siege of eleven months. King Edward was very angry because the people had held out so long, and wanted to put them all to the sword; but he agreed to spare them on condition that six of the principal citizens should come to him, bareheaded and barefooted and with ropes round their necks, and give themselves up to die. When they came, he ordered that their heads should be at once struck off, but he pardoned them when his queen, Philippa, fell in tears at his feet and begged of him their lives. He drove out most of the French, however, and settled the town with people from England, so that he might always have a door into France. It was held as an English town until Queen Mary's time (1558), when it was taken back by the French. It was no real loss to the English, though it had been called the "brightest jewel in the English crown," and over one of its gates had been put the boastful lines:

"Then shall the Frenchmen Calais win
When iron and lead like cork shall swim."

But Queen Mary thought it was a dreadful misfortune, for she said, when she heard the news : "When

I die, Calais will be found written on my heart."

CALCUTTA (*kal-kut'tah*), a city of Hindostan, capital of British India, situated on the Hoogly River, a branch of the GANGES, about 100 miles from the sea; pop., with the suburbs, about 800,000, or nearly as large as Brooklyn, N. Y. The city is built along the river-bank for more than six miles and extends back into the country about two miles. It is very strongly fortified; the citadel, called Fort William, has 619 cannon, and is large enough to hold 15,000 soldiers. It is the largest fort in India, and cost $10,-000,000. Calcutta has so many fine buildings that it is sometimes called the City of Palaces, and it has the largest trade of any city of Asia. The climate is hot and in the summer is very unhealthful.

The name Calcutta is Kali Ghatta in the Hindostanee language, and means the landing-place of the goddess Kali, wife of Siva, whose temple stood on the river-bank. There was only a village on the site when the English put up some trading houses there in 1698. In 1756 the place was taken by Surajah Dowlah, the Indian ruler of Bengal, and the British garrison of 146 men were shut up overnight in a small dungeon, eighteen feet square (or about as long as three men), with only two small barred windows on one side. In the morning only 23 were found alive, all the rest having been suffocated for want of air. This dungeon, which is still shown in Fort William, is called the Black Hole. A monument, 50 feet high, built in memory of this dreadful event, stands in front of the door. The English retook Calcutta the next year, and have held it ever since.

CALDERON DE LA BARCA (*kahl-da-rone' da lah bar'kah*), **Pedro,** a famous Spanish writer of plays, born in Madrid, Jan. 17, 1600. He is said to have written finer plays than any other writer of modern times, excepting Shakespeare. Calderon wrote his first play when he was fourteen years old, and his last one when eighty. When twenty-eight years old he became a priest, and after that he wrote both for the theatre and the church, making many religious plays founded on Bible stories, which were acted on church holidays when the regular theatres were shut. Calderon was a great worker, and wrote about 200 plays. He died in Madrid when eighty-one years old (May 28, 1681).

CALEDONIA (*kal-e-do'ne-ah*). See SCOTLAND.

CALHOUN (*kal-hoon'*), **John Caldwell,** an American statesman, born in the district of Abbeville, S. C., March 18, 1782. He was taught at home during his boyhood, and after his father's death helped his mother

John C. Calhoun.

on the farm until he was eighteen years old. After studying in a private academy two years he joined the junior class of Yale College, where he was graduated with honor in 1804, and after studying law in the Litchfield (Conn.) Law School, then the only one in the country, he was admitted to the bar. He served two sessions in the legislature and then went to Congress, where he had a great deal to do in urging on the war with Eng-gland (1812) and was very active in other plans for the public good. He was six years in the House of Representatives, became Secretary of War under President Monroe (1817), and was elected Vice-President with John Quincy Adams (1824). When Gen. Jackson became President (1828) Mr. Calhoun was again Vice-President. At this time he became the leader of those who believed in the doctrine of nullification; that is, that any State had the right to nullify or make null and void any act of Congress which seemed to the people of that State to be contrary to the Constitution of the United States. It was this doctrine which grew into secession in 1860. Mr. Calhoun resigned before his term ended, and took a seat in the Senate, which he kept from 1832 to 1843. He was Secretary of State for a short time under President Tyler, but went back to the Senate in 1845. His last speech was read for him (March 4, 1849) by another Senator, as he was too ill to speak it himself. He died in Washington, at the age of sixty-eight (March 31, 1850).

CALIFORNIA (*kal-i-for'ne-ah*), a State of the United States, on the coast of the Pacific Ocean, between Oregon and Mexico; area 189,000 square miles, or larger than New England, New York, Pennsylvania, and New Jersey together; pop. about 1,208,000, or about one-fifth that of New York State; capital, SACRAMENTO. With the exception of Texas, it is the largest of all the States. In the western part are the Coast Range mountains, close to the sea-shore and not very high; and in the eastern part is the Sierra Nevada (Snowy Ridge), some parts of which are more than two miles high and always covered with snow. On the west side of the Sierra is the famous YO SEMITE VALLEY. Between these ranges is the great valley of the Sacramento River. California is rich in gold, silver, mercury, and copper. Its gold-mines are among the richest in the world; but its manufactures are worth more than its minerals, and its grains, vegetables, and fruits are worth more than its minerals and manufactures together. The wheat of California is famous, and more barley is raised there than in any other State of the Union. The fruits are larger than those of the Eastern States. There are a great many vineyards, where excellent wine is made; and excepting Australia, it is the best country in the world for raising sheep. California has also the largest cone-bearing trees in the world. One kind called the mammoth tree, found only in the Sierra Nevada three fourths of a mile above the sea, grows sometimes more than four hundred feet high, or seven times as high as a common tree, and forty feet thick, or more than the length of six men. The redwood, another kind of these trees, so named from the color of its wood, grows almost as large. It is found mostly in the Coast Range.

California has other curiosities such as hot springs which boil up close by others in which the water is cold, and springs of boiling mud. There are also a petrified forest, where are many trees turned to stone, and several wonderful caves, lakes, and natural bridges. Most of the people of California are whites, but there are a good many Chinese and a few Indians.

It is not known from what California got its name. The country was first visited by the Spaniards, and it belonged to them until 1822, when Mexico got her independence. In 1847 the United States bought it of Mexico for $15,000,000. When gold was found, so many people went there that in 1850 it was made a State of the Union.

CA-LIG'U-LA, Caius Cæsar Au-

gustus Germanicus, third emperor of Rome, born A.D. 12. His real name was Caius Cæsar, but he was called Caligula, from the *caliga*, or half-boot of the Roman soldiers, worn by him in his youth, which was passed in camp with his father Germanicus. When twenty-five years old he succeeded his uncle TIBERIUS, and he was an excellent ruler for eight months, when he was attacked with a fever which seemed to unsettle his mind, for after that he became a monster of cruelty and committed so many crimes that he was assassinated in the twenty-ninth year of his age (Jan. 24, 41).

   CALIPHS (*ka'lifs*), the successors of Mohammed in his office of head of the Mohammedan religion. They had both spiritual and temporal power ; that is, the caliph in his one person held the two offices which correspond with those of pope and emperor among Christians. The four who immediately followed Mohammed (632 to 661) were called the "perfect caliphs." Then followed fourteen caliphs of the family of the Ommiyades (from Ommiyah, their ancestor), who ruled from 661 to 750. Their capital was Damascus. All but one of the Ommiyades having been slain, a new race called the Abbassides (from Abbas, their ancestor) succeeded, and removed the caliphate to Bagdad. There were thirty-seven of these, among them HAROUN AL RASHID, and their reign was from 750 to 1258. Abderrahman, the single member of the Ommiyades who escaped slaughter, went over into Spain and founded the caliphate of Cordova, which lasted from 756 to 1031. By the regular Mohammedans the Turkish sultans are regarded as successors of the caliphs.

   CALLAO (*kahl-yah'o*). See LIMA.
   CAL-LI'O-PE. See MUSES.
   CAL'VIN, John, a famous leader of the Reformation, born in Noyon, France, July 10, 1509. He was educated to be a priest and began to preach when only eighteen years old, but continued to study both law and theology until he became one of the most learned men of his time. He soon began to have doubt about the Roman Catholic faith, and finally became the leader of the French Reformers, commonly called Huguenots. His teachings were really further from those of the Roman Catholic Church than Luther's, and he was soon obliged to leave France. He settled in Geneva, where he became the real ruler of the city, and made it a very moral town and a place of learning, and the centre for people of all lands who became his followers and who were called after him Calvinists. Calvin wrote many religious books, the most important of which is the "Institutes of the Christian Religion," in which he gathered into one body the beliefs of the Reformers. His teachings have had great influence in the world, and the religious belief of most of the Protestant countries has been largely founded upon them. Though a very good and sincere man, he has been much blamed for having been the cause of the death of SERVETUS. Calvin died in Geneva when nearly fifty five years old (May 27, 1564).

   CALYPSO (*kal-ip'so*). See ULYSSES.

   CAMBODIA (*kam-bo'de-ah*), a country of INDO-CHINA, between Cochin China and Siam ; area 35,-000 square miles, or about as large as Maine; pop. 1,500,000, or about the same as that of New Jersey ; capital, Pnom-Penh (pop. 35,000). The greater part of it is in the valley of the river Cambodia or Mekong, and its soil is so rich that rice and other grains will grow with little care.

   Cambodia is called Cambodge by the French, who conquered COCHIN CHINA from it (1861), and took Cambodia under their protection.

   CAMBRIDGE (*kame'brij*), a city of England, on the river Cam, 49 miles N. of London; pop. 35,000.

or about as large as Denver, Col.
It is principally noted as the seat of
the University of Cambridge, which
is more than six hundred years old.
It is supposed that students used
to go to Cambridge to study more
than a thousand years ago, but the
schools there were not made into a
university until the time of Henry
III. (1231). The university is made
up of seventeen different colleges,
each ruled by its own laws, but all
governed by the general laws of
the university. There are many
fine buildings, splendid libraries,
museums, picture-galleries, botanical gardens, and an astronomical
observatory. There are about 3300
students at Cambridge, in addition to many graduates who live
there.

Cambridge means the "Bridge of
the Cam."

CAMBRIDGE, a city of Massachusetts, about a mile W. of Boston, from which it is separated by
the Charles River; pop. 70,000, or
nearly as large as that of Nashville, Tenn. It is a pretty place,
with many fine avenues shaded
with elms. One of the elms is
called the "Washington Elm," because under it Washington first
took command of the American
army (July 3, 1775), which was stationed in Cambridge when the
British held Boston. The house
in which Washington lived while
there was formerly the home of the
poet Longfellow. The first printing-office in the United States was
set up in Cambridge (1639).

Cambridge is principally noted
as the seat of Harvard University,
the oldest college in the United
States, having been begun in 1638.
Harvard is also the richest university in the United States, and has
many fine buildings, a large library, museums, a botanical garden,
and an astronomical observatory.
Harvard has generally about 2500
students.

Cambridge was first settled in
1630, and was called Newtown, but
when the college was put there the
name was changed to Cambridge
in honor of Cambridge in England,
because many of the chief men of
the colony had been educated
there. It became a city in 1846.

CAMBYSES (*kam-by'sees*), second
king of Persia, succeeded his father,
CYRUS THE GREAT, in 529 B.C. He
conquered Egypt, but was unsuccessful in wars with the Ethiopians,
losing many men by hunger and
disease. This made him crazy, and
he afterward acted like a madman.
He murdered his brother Smerdis
and his sister, and abused his subjects. During his absence from
Persia an impostor made believe
that he was Smerdis, and was declared king by the people.

Cambyses was hastening home
to subdue him, when he accidentally wounded himself with his
sword and died (522 B.C.).

CAM'DEN, a city of New Jersey,
on the Delaware River, opposite
Philadelphia; pop. 58,000, or the
same as Reading, Pa. It has large
iron foundries, glass-works, and
chemical works, but most of the
people who live there do business in Philadelphia, which is connected with Camden by ferries.
Many steel pens are made in Camden.

CA-MIL'LUS, Marcus Furius, a
noted Roman who, for his services
to his country, was called the
"Second ROMULUS." He captured
Veii after a siege of ten years, and
made a triumphal entry into Rome
in a chariot drawn by four white
horses. He was afterward accused of taking more than his just
share of the spoil, and went into
exile at Ardea. When the Gauls
under BRENNUS took and destroyed Rome he was recalled, and
arrived, it is said, at the city with
an army when the gold which was
to purchase peace from them was
being weighed out. "Rome buys
her freedom with iron," he cried,

and attacking the Gauls, utterly overthrew them. But this story is thought by the best historians to be very doubtful.

Another story told about Camillus is that when he was besieging Falerii, a schoolmaster of the city led all his scholars out to his camp and gave them up to him. As the boys were the sons of the principal citizens of the place, the schoolmaster hoped to get a large reward for his treachery, but Camillus, disgusted at his act, had his hands tied behind his back, and giving each of the boys a switch, bade them whip him back into the city.

CAMOENS (*kam'o-enz*), **Luiz de,** the most noted poet of Portugal, born in Lisbon in 1524. When very young he fell in love with a lady of the court, and the king, who also liked her, sent Camoëns into exile. The lady died of a broken heart, and the poet thought so much of her that he never married. After her death he went to fight the Moors in Morocco, and in battle an arrow put out one of his eyes. He hoped to get some office when he returned to court, but none being given him, he sailed for Goa in the East Indies; saying as he left Portugal, "Ungrateful country, thou shalt not possess my bones." There he made the Portuguese officers angry by a satirical poem and was banished to MACAO, where he was given an office with salary enough for his support. While living there he wrote most of his great poem "The Lusiads" (Lusitanians), named from the fabled hero Lusus, who is said to have come with Ulysses to the country now called Portugal and called it Lusitania. The poem tells about Vasco da GAMA and the other Portuguese heroes who sailed around the CAPE OF GOOD HOPE and opened a new route to the Indies. It is very popular in Portugal, and even the common people sing its verses with delight.

At last Camoëns was recalled from exile and allowed to go to Lisbon (1569). For a time the king gave him a small pension, but when the king died this was stopped, and Camoëns lived in poverty, cared for by a servant who had followed him from India, and who begged in the streets by night to get enough for them to eat. He finally died in a hospital in Lisbon when fifty-six years old (June 10, 1580).

CAMPBELL (*kam'el*), **Thomas,** a famous British poet, born in Glasgow, July 27, 1777. He was graduated at the University of Glasgow, where he was noted for making the best translations from the Greek tragedies. When twenty-two years old he published a poem called "The Pleasures of Hope," which at once made him famous. Among his other well-known poems are Hohenlinden, The Exile of Erin, Lochiel's Warning, Ye Mariners of England, and Gertrude of Wyoming. He died in Boulogne, France, when nearly sixty-seven years old (June 15, 1844).

CANADA, (*kan'a-dah*), **Dominion of,** a country of North America, belonging to Great Britain, including almost all of America north of the United States; area 3,500,000 square miles, or a little less than that of the United States; pop. about 5,000,000, or about one twelfth that of the United States; capital, OTTAWA. In the western part are the Rocky Mountains; in the eastern part are some lower mountains, near the St. Lawrence River, but nearly all the rest of the country is a great plain. In the southern part of this plain there are prairies; the northern region is a cold desolate wilderness, with great forests and swamps and much barren land, and here and there large lakes and rivers, and a few forts and settlements, sometimes hundreds of miles apart. In the Arctic Ocean are many large islands that belong to Canada.

In the forests of the north, bears, wolves, and deer are very common, as well as beavers, muskrats, otters, minks, and other animals, which are hunted for their fur. The climate of Canada is like that of the United States, but the winters are colder and longer, especially in the northern part. Most of the cities and villages are in the south-eastern part, where the people are English and French or their descendants. British Columbia, in the south-western, and Manitoba, in the southern, part have also many people; in the northern part the only people are a few Indians and trappers, who catch beavers and other animals and sell their furs. Canada is ruled by a governor-general, appointed by the Queen of England, and a parliament or congress chosen by the people.

Canada was discovered by Jacques CARTIER in 1534, and the first white people who went there were Frenchmen. In 1713 Newfoundland, Nova Scotia, and the region around Hudson's Bay were given to the English; after that there was a war between France and England, and the English conquered the whole country (1759). In 1867 all these provinces except Newfoundland were united to make the Dominion of Canada.

CANARIS (*kah'nah-ris*), **Constantine,** a noted Greek naval officer, born in the island of Ipsara about 1790. When the Greeks rose in rebellion against the Turks (1821), Canaris was captain of a merchant vessel. He at once took part in the war, and after the Turks had laid waste the island of Scio he took two fire-ships, or ships loaded with things which will burn easily, into the Turkish fleet and fastened them to two of their principal men-of-war, one of which was blown up with many hundred men and the other made a wreck. He afterward did other brave deeds and became the terror of the Turks.

He became a captain and finally admiral in the Greek navy, and when Greece became independent held many public offices in the government. He died when eighty-seven years old (1877).

CA·NA'RY ISLANDS, a group of mountainous islands belonging to Spain, off the N.W. coast of Africa; area 2800 square miles, or a little more than twice as large as Rhode Island; pop. 285,000, or about five-sixths that of Rhode Island.

Dragon Tree.

The best known is Teneriffe, on which is the famous volcano called the Peak of Teneriffe, more than two miles high. The top of this mountain is very steep and hard to climb. There are several craters or springs in it from which hot steam rises, and the rocks around them are always warm. There are but few animals and no snakes in these islands. Canary-birds first came from there (C. C. T., 101, I., l.). Among the trees are many singular ones called dragon trees. The people are mostly Spaniards, and Spanish is the language spoken. The principal thing sent to other countries is cochineal.

CANDAHAR (*kahn-dah-har'*), a city of Afghanistan, 275 miles S.W. of CABUL; pop. 40,000, or about the same as that of Hoboken, N. J. It is a fortified town and of considerable importance, having been once the capital of Afghanistan. It was taken by the British in 1839, and again in 1880.

CANDIA (*kan'de-ah*). See CRETE.

CAN'NÆ, a town of ancient Italy, on the river Aufidus (now Ofanto), about 6 miles from its mouth in the Adriatic. On its banks the Romans were terribly defeated by HANNIBAL (216 B.C.). The Romans had about 90,000 men, many more than Hannibal, but they could not stand against the Numidian cavalry, and lost 45,000 foot soldiers and 3000 horsemen. It is said that Hannibal sent to Carthage three bushels of gold rings, taken from the fingers of the dead Roman knights.

CA-NON'I-CUS, a chief of the Narragansett tribe of AMERICAN INDIANS, born about 1565. He was a firm friend of the whites, and during his life his tribe was always at peace with them. It was he who gave to Roger Williams the first land in Rhode Island (1638). He was succeeded by his nephew, MIANTONOMOH.

CANOVA (*kah-no'vah*), **Antonio,** a famous Italian sculptor, born at Possagno, Nov. 1, 1757. His family had for generations been stone-cutters, and he learned to cut marble at a very early age. When only twelve years old he modelled a lion in butter, which was so much liked by Signor Falieri that he sent him to be taught by Torretti, the most noted sculptor of the time. At sixteen he made a statue which won much praise, and his fame grew until he had orders for more work than he could do. He studied ancient art, and made many statues of classical subjects, as well as many monuments, busts, and statues of living people, among them Napoleon and Washington. The large fortune which he made was mostly spent in helping the poor, or in assisting other artists. He traveled much in Europe, where his works are to be seen in nearly all of the large cities, had many friends among great people, and was made a nobleman and received many honors. He died in Venice when sixty-five years old (Oct 13, 1822), and was buried in the town where he was born.

CANTERBURY (*kan'ter-ber-ry*), a city of England, 56 miles E.S.E. of London; pop. 18,000, or nearly the same as that of Newburgh, N. Y. It is principally noted for its grand cathedral, which is one of the finest in England. It was first built more than a thousand years ago, and has been added to at different times until it got its present form. In 1170 the Archbishop Thomas à BECKET was murdered in the cathedral, and his body was buried in a splendid shrine. So many pilgrims used to visit this in former times that the marble steps leading up to it were worn down by their knees. The shrine was broken in pieces (1538) by King Henry VIII. and the bones of Becket burned. The tombs of HENRY IV. and of EDWARD the Black Prince, and many other interesting monuments, are still to be seen in the cathedral. The Archbishop of Canterbury is the head of the English Church, and outranks everybody in England excepting the royal family. He always crowns the sovereign.

Canterbury means the "City of Kent," of which it was the capital in Saxon times.

CAN-TON', a city of China, on the Canton River, 70 miles from its mouth in the China Sea; pop. 1,600,000, or about a twelfth larger than New York. It is surrounded by a wall, and is defended by forts on the hills around it and on islands in the river. The city is divided into two parts, the old town, where the Tartars live, and the new town, inhabited by the Chinese. The foreign merchants live in a suburb facing the river, and separated from the Chinese part by a canal. About four miles from the city is the boat-town, where many thousand people live in boats and on rafts anchored near the banks.

Canton is supposed to be the oldest city in China. It has the largest trade of any city in the empire, and most of the tea and silk sent to foreign countries is shipped there. Its name in Chinese is Kwang Chou (the metropolis), which has been changed by Europeans into Canton.

CANUTE, (*ka-noot'*) or **Knut** (*knoot*), called The Great, the first Danish king of England, born in Denmark about 995. He was the son of Sweyn, King of Denmark, who conquered England in 1013. Sweyn called himself King of England, but he died the next year, leaving his throne to Canute. The Saxon King Ethelred, who had gone to Normandy, now came back, but died soon after, and the kingdom, after several battles, was divided between Canute and Edmund Ironside, son of Ethelred. Edmund then died (1016), and Canute was left with the sole power.

Canute, who had for some time been a Christian, proved to be a good ruler and tried to make his people happy. Besides being king of England and Denmark, he won Norway and part of Sweden, but he spent most of his time in England. A story is told about how he rebuked some of his courtiers, who had tried to flatter him by saying that all things were possible to him. He ordered his chair to be set on the sea-shore while the tide was rising, and when the water rolled near him he commanded it to go back and not dare to wet him, who was lord of the ocean. But the sea soon wet his feet, and he turned to his courtiers and said: " Let all men know how empty and worthless is the power of kings; for there is none worthy of the name but He whom heaven, earth, and sea obey."

Canute died when forty years old (1035). He left three sons: Sweyn, who became King of Norway; Harold, of England; and Hardicanute, first of Denmark, and lastly of Denmark and England.

CAPE COLONY, or **Cape of Good Hope,** a British colony at the S. end of Africa; area 232,000 square miles, or about as large as Texas; pop. 1,500,000, or a sixteenth less than that of Wisconsin; capital, CAPE TOWN. The surface is made up of mountains and high table-lands. Only about half the land is fit to live on, much of it being dry and barren. In the northern parts are famous diamond-mines, covering as much country as Massachusetts and New Hampshire put together. Many valuable diamonds have been found there, and great numbers of people are employed in digging them. The climate is healthful. There used to be great numbers of wild animals in this part of Africa, including the elephant, rhinoceros, hippopotamus, lion, giraffe, buffalo, zebra, antelope, and ostrich, but they have been hunted so much that they are scarcer than formerly. Great numbers of cattle and sheep are raised in the colony. The people are native Africans, called Caffres or Kaffirs and Hottentots; whites called Boers, or descendants of Dutch settlers; mixed races; and a few British. The colony, which is ruled by a governor sent out from Great Britain, is important because it guards one of the routes to the Indian Ocean, and soldiers kept there can easily be sent to India.

The Dutch first settled this region in 1652, but it has belonged to Great Britain since 1815. The British have had many wars with the Caffres, and lately one with the Zulus or Zooloos, a branch of the Caffres and a very brave and war-like people. They lived mostly in Natal, another British colony north of Cape Colony, which has been separate from Cape Colony since 1856. The Zulus were finally beat-en, and their king, Cetewayo, taken prisoner (1878).

CAPE OF GOOD HOPE, a point commonly called the southernmost point of Africa, though it is not so far south as Cape Agulhas; but it is more important than that because it is the point where ships going to India turn from south to east. It is a barren rocky promontory rising about a thousand feet above the sea, which washes its base. The first to sail round it was Bartolomeo Diaz, a Portuguese knight, who sailed with two ships down the coast of Africa in 1486 in search of a new way to India. His crew would not let him go any farther, and he was obliged to turn back. The weather was so stormy at the time that he named it the Cape of Storms, but when the King of Por-tugal heard that he had found the end of Africa, he called it the Cape of Good Hope, because he hoped that the way to India was at last found. CAMOENS, in his great poem of the "Lusiads," tells the story thus:

"At Lisbon's Court they told their dread escape,
  And from her raging tempests named the cape.
'Thou southmost point!' the joyful king exclaimed,
'Cape of Good Hope be thou forever named.'"

CAPE HORN, the southernmost point of South America, on one of the islands of TIERRA DEL FUEGO. It is a steep, black, craggy rock, rising like a precipice out of the sea which washes its foot. It was once thought very dangerous, but now most steamers go through the Strait of Ma-gellan and tug-boats are kept there to tow sailing vessels through, so there is no need of going round it at all. The first to sail round Cape Horn was the Dutch naviga-tor Schouten (1616), who named it after his native town, Hoorn in Holland.

CAPE TOWN, a seaport of S. Africa, capital of Cape Colony; pop. 60,000, or about as large as Wilmington, Del. It is built between Table Bay and Table Mountain, which rises up almost perpendicularly behind it. This mountain is so called because its top is flat like a table. Cape Town, which is defended by a strong fort, is visited by many ships going to and coming from India. It gets its name from the CAPE OF GOOD HOPE.

CAPE VERD ISLANDS, a group of ten islands in the Atlantic Ocean, two hundred miles W. of Cape Verd in Africa, from which they are named; area, 1600 square miles, or not quite as much as that of the State of Rhode Island; pop. about 110,000, or less than that of the city of Providence. The islands are mountainous, and on one of them is an active volcano, more than a mile and a half high. The climate is hot, and sometimes no rain falls for several years. In 1832, after a three years drought, 30,000 persons died of hunger. The people are mostly negroes and mu-lattoes, with a few whites. The islands were discovered about 1450 by the Portuguese, to whom they still belong. Cape Verd (Portu-guese, Cabo Verde) means "Green Cape."

CA'PET, a name given to Hugues or Hugh, the first king of the third line of French kings, some think on account of the size of his head (Latin *caput*), others on account of the monk's hood (Latin *cappetus*) which he wore, for he was an abbot as well as Duke of France. On the death of Louis V., the last Carlovingian king (987), he was crowned king by the consent of the nobles, and his descendants reigned in France for eight hundred years without change. When the French Revolution broke out all titles were done away with, and the king, Louis XVI., was brought to trial under the name of "Louis Capet," the nickname of the founder of the family being mistaken for a sur-name. But the direct line of Hugh Capet, commonly called the Capetian line, ended with Charles IV., who died in 1328. After him came the Valois line of kings, who were a collateral or side branch of the Capetian kings.

CAPPADOCIA (*kap-pa-do'she-ah*). See ASIA MINOR.

CAPRI (*kah'pre*), a small island belonging to Italy, in the Mediterraenean, near the Bay of Naples; pop. 5000. It is surrounded by steep cliffs, in which are many

Cape Town and Table Mountain. (Page 156.)

caves and grottoes. The most wonderful one, called the Blue grotto, is a large room as high as a four-story house, and can be entered only by a boat through an arch about a yard high. Inside the water is very deep and like the walls and roof, is of a beautiful blue.

CAPUA (*kap'yu-ah*), a city of Italy, 15 miles N. of Naples; pop. 12,000, or about the same as that of Moline, Ill. It is very strongly fortified and is the chief defence of Naples on that side. Ancient Capua, whose ruins are still to be seen about two miles south of the city, was a much more important place, and was only excelled by Rome in wealth and population. It was noted for its great school of gladiators, from which SPARTACUS escaped. After the battle of CANNÆ, it threw open its gates to HANNIBAL, and his soldiers became so weakened by living there a winter amongst its pleasures that it led to his final defeat. When the Romans again took the city (211) they punished the people severely for letting Hannibal in.

CARACALLA (*kar-ah-kal'lah*), **Marcus Aurelius Antonius**, a Roman

Emperor, born at Lyons A.D. 188. He was at first called Bassianus, but was nicknamed Caracalla from a new style of tunic which he brought from Gaul and made the fashion in Rome. When his father the Emperor Septimius Severus died the throne was left to him and his brother Geta, but he killed Geta so that he might reign alone. He also caused the murder of 20,000 people who took the part of Geta, and when some one in Alexandria wrote some witty poems about his crimes he went there with an army and slew nearly all the in-

Blue Grotto of Capri.   (Page 157,)

habitants. At last people got tired of his follies and crimes, and he was killed (211) by one of his guards named Macrinus, who was made his successor by the army.

CARÁCAS (*kah-rah'kahs*), a city, capital of VENEZUELA; pop. about 56,000, or about as large as Lynn, Mass. It is a handsome city, situated among mountains more than half a mile (3100 feet) above the sea, and is joined by a railroad seven miles long with its port, called La Guayra, on the Caribbean sea. The little river which runs through it is crossed by eight bridges, and there are many fountains in the streets and squares. The city has suffered much from earthquakes.

Carácas was founded more than three hundred years ago (1567), and named after the tribe of Indians which then lived near there.

CA-RAC'TA-CUS, the Roman name of Caradoc (*kah-rah'dok*), chief of a tribe of ancient Britons living on the river Severn in Wales. He fought the Romans for nine years, but was at last taken prisoner and sent to Rome (A.D. 51). When he saw the grand streets and stately buildings, he said: "How can a people who have such magnificence at home envy me my poor cottage in Britain!" The Emperor Claudius, struck with his noble bearing, pardoned him and sent him home with presents.

CARIA (*ka're-ah*). See ASIA MINOR.

CAR'IBS, the name of a race of Indians who, when Columbus came, lived in some of the West India islands and in parts of the coast of South America along the Caribbean Sea. They were very fierce and cruel, and used to eat the prisoners which they took in war. Columbus called them Caribales, and out of this has grown our English word Cannibal, meaning a man-eater.

CARLISLE (*kar-lile'*), a city of England, 50 miles W.S.W. of Newcastle; pop. 35,000, or nearly as large as Holyoke, Mass. It is a handsome city, and has an old castle built by the Normans (1092). In the wars between England and Scotland it was an important place, on account of its nearness to the border of the two countries. It is one of the oldest cities in England.

CAR·LO·VIN'GI·ANS. See FRANCE.

CARLSBAD (*karls'bahd*), a watering-place in BOHEMIA, noted for its hot mineral springs; pop. about 8000. It is much visited by those suffering from liver and kidney diseases.

Carlsbad, which in German is spelled Karlsbad, means Charles's Bath. The place was named after the Emperor Charles IV., who used to visit the baths in the 14th century.

CARLSRUHE (*karls'roo*), a city of Germany, capital of the Grand Duchy of BADEN, 39 miles from Stuttgart and about 5 miles from the Rhine; pop. about 61,000, or nearly the same as Troy, N. Y. It is built in the form of an open fan, the streets stretching out like the sticks of a fan from the palace of the Grand Duke in the middle. The city is noted for its schools, libraries, and museums.

Carlsruhe, which is spelled Karlsruhe in German, means Charles's Rest. The town was built around a hunting seat built by the Margrave Charles of Baden (1715) and named after him.

CARLYLE (*kar-lile'*), **Thomas,** an English author, born in Ecclefechan, Scotland, Dec. 4, 1795. His father was a small farmer, but he gave his son a good education at the University of Edinburgh, intending to make him a minister. Thomas taught school for two years

Thomas Carlyle.

after leaving college, and then made up his mind to be an author instead of a preacher. He began by translating books from the French and the German into English and writing for magazines. When thirty-one years old (1826) he married and went to live on a small farm belonging to his wife in a very wild part of Scotland, fifteen miles from any town. Here he worked hard and wrote several books, among them one called "Sartor Resartus" (Latin for "The

Stitcher Restitched"), a very singular work which he made believe was a translation from the German. He took it with him to London in 1832. For a long time he could get no one to print his book, for though full of curious and beautiful ideas, it was so unlike anything ever written before that the publishers were afraid it would be a failure. But it was finally printed in *Fraser's Magazine* (1834), and helped much to make him known.

Three years after (1837) he published a "History of the French Revolution," which, though much criticised, added to his fame.

He afterwards wrote many other books, one of the most important of which is his "History of Frederick the Great." All his writings have been much criticised for their strange style and peculiar ideas, but he has a great many friends and admirers who are glad to read his books and to do him honor. He died in Chelsea when eighty-six years old (February 5, 1881).

CARNARVON (*ker-nar'von*). See CAERNARVON.

CARNOT (*car-no'*), **Marie François Sadi**, grandson of the war-minister of the first republic, was born at Limoges, France, Aug. 11, 1837. He was educated as an engineer, and introduced several improvements in railroad and bridge building. He was elected a member of the Assembly in 1871, was twice a cabinet officer, and upon the resignation of President GRÉVY was chosen (Dec. 3, 1887) President of the French Republic. He was stabbed by an assassin, at Lyons, and died when fifty-seven years old (June 25, 1894).

CAROLINE AMELIA AUGUSTA, Queen, wife of King George IV. of Great Britain, and daughter of the Duke of Brunswick, born May 17, 1768. She was the cousin of George, and was chosen for him by his father, George III., as the richest and most suitable princess to be found for the heir to the British throne. She was a lively, romping girl, with blue eyes and fair hair, and she went joyfully to England to meet her bridegroom. When presented to him she tried to kneel; the Prince raised her and embraced her, and then turning to some one near, said with a horrid oath : "Pray get me a glass of brandy!" and left his poor, trembling young bride alone with strangers. This was only the beginning of what she had to suffer all her life long. After her little daughter Charlotte was born her husband left her, and although he told a great many stories about her, and tried to make people believe that she was a very wicked woman, very few believed him, and almost everybody felt sorry for his kindly, thoughtless wife. But her selfish, wicked husband accused her of being unfaithful to him, and had her tried before the House of Lords. She was not found guilty, but the King said that she should not be crowned with him, and when she went to Westminster Hall on Coronation-day, (July 19, 1821) she was refused admission, and this hurt her so much that she grew ill and died the next month, when fifty-three years old (Aug. 7, 1821).

CAR'O-LINE ISLANDS, or New Philippines, a group of many small islands, forming a chain 1500 miles long in the Pacific Ocean, N.E. of Papua; area, 1000 square miles, or nearly as large as the State of Rhode Island; pop. 36,000, or about twice as much as that of Newport. Most of them are low, flat, coral reefs, but some are mountainous. The climate is mild and pleasant. The people, who are mostly Malays, make excellent sailors.

The Carolines were first found by the Spaniards in 1543, and named after the Emperor CHARLES V. of

Spain (in Latin Carolus). They are still claimed by Spain, as part of the Philippines, but there are no Spanish settlements on them.

CARPATHIAN (*kar-pa'the-an*) **MOUNTAINS,** a range of mountains in Europe, mostly between Hungary and Austria proper. Some of them rise more than a mile and a half above the sea, but not high enough to have snow on them all the year round. There are many passes through them, which in old times used to be strongly fortified to keep the Turks out. The Carpathians are very rich in metals of almost all kinds.

CARRACCI (*kah-raht'che*), **Ludovico,** a famous Italian painter, born in Bologna, April 21, 1555. He was so dull and slow when young that his first painting teacher advised him to try some other business, and his schoolmates used to call him the ox. But when he grew up he became a great painter, and surpassed those who used to make fun of him. He set up a painting school in Bologna, which soon became so celebrated that all the other schools had to close for want of pupils. In this he was assisted by his cousins Agostino (born 1558, died 1601) and Annibale Carracci (**born 1560, died 1609**), both of whom were also famous artists. Ludovico died in Bologna when sixty-four years old (1619).

CARRARA (*kah-rah'rah*), a town of N. Italy, about 30 miles N.W. of Lucca; pop. about 12,000. It is situated near the mountains, where the celebrated Carrara marble is quarried, and on account of this many artists live in the town. The mountains, which are a part of the Apennines, are four miles from the sea-coast and are very high and rugged. The marble quarries are about half way up; there are nearly four hundred in all, but only thirty or forty are worked, and of these only a few give the beautiful white marble from which almost all

statues are now made (C. C. T., 386, II.). The other quarries are worked for building-marble, some of which is blue and some streaked.

CAR'ROLL, Charles, of Carrollton, an American patriot, born at Annapolis, Md., Sept. 20, 1737. When the war of the Revolution began he was the richest man in the English colonies; but though he had so much to lose, he made the most daring speeches and helped the patriot cause in every way. He was elected a member of Congress (1776), and was among the first signers of the Declaration of Independence. When he wrote his name "Charles Carroll," some one said: "There are many Charles Carrolls, and the British will not know which one it is." He at once added to his name "of Carrollton," and was ever afterward known by that title. He outlived all the other signers of the Declaration of Independence, and died when ninety-five years old (Nov. 4, 1832).

CAR'SON CITY, capital of Nevada, in the W. part of the State, near the Carson River; pop. about 5000. Near it are high mountains with many rich silver-mines, from which a great deal of ore is carried to the crushing-mills on the Carson River. There is a branch mint of the United States at Carson City, where much silver money is coined (C. C. T., 145. II., u.).

Carson City is named after Kit Carson, the famous trapper, who was Gen. Fremont's guide in the Rocky Mountains.

CARTAGENA (*kar-tah-je'nah*), a seaport of S.E. Spain, on the Mediterranean; pop. 76,000, or about as large as Lowell, Mass. It is a walled town and has a fine harbor defended by forts, but has little trade. In the time of PHILIP II., this was the great naval port of Spain. The people are mostly employed in mining lead and silver.

Cartagena means New Carthage.

It was first built by the Carthaginian general HASDRUBAL about 230 B.C., and when it was taken by Scipio (210 B.C.) it was said to be one of the richest cities in the world. Hannibal got silver from the mines there to carry on the war against Rome.

CAR'THAGE, a famous ancient city and state in N. Africa, on the Mediterranean Sea. The city, which stood near where TUNIS now is, is said to have been built by DIDO about 850 B.C.; but all we really know about it is that it was founded by people from PHŒNICIA.

It soon became very populous and strong, and ruled much territory both around it in Africa and beyond the sea, the Carthaginians being famous sailors and having many ships and war galleys. Carthage had large possessions in SICILY, and was constantly at war with the Greek cities there. When Rome had conquered all Italy it took the part of the Greek cities in Sicily against the Carthaginians, and this brought on the first war between Rome and Carthage, commonly called the First Punic War, Punic being the Latin form of the

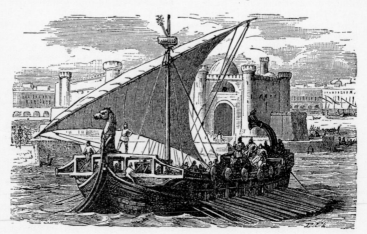

Carthaginian War Galley.

word Phœnician. This war began 264 B.C., and lasted twenty-four years (241 B.C.), and ended in the giving up by Carthage of Sicily, a large part of which became a Roman province. This was the beginning of the Roman dominion outside of Italy.

Twenty-three years afterward (218 B.C.) the Second Punic War broke out, and lasted seventeen years. The Carthaginians had built cities in Spain and conquered nearly the whole country under their generals HAMILCAR Barka, his

son-in-law HASDRUBAL, and his son HANNIBAL. These conquests made the Romans again hostile, and Hannibal crossed from Spain into Italy, where he fought for about fifteen years. But the Romans sent an army under SCIPIO into Spain, and conquered the Carthaginian colonies there, and then into Africa, so that Hannibal had to hasten to defend Carthage. He was defeated at Zama (202 B.C.), and Carthage got peace only by giving up all her possessions out of Africa, and by promising not to make war without the consent of Rome.

The Third Punic War began about fifty years later (149 B.C.), and ended in the fall of Carthage (146 B.C.). The Carthaginians had made war on Masinissa, King of Numidia, without asking leave of Rome, and when they sent ambassadors to Rome to ask forgiveness they were told that they could have peace only by giving up all their ships, arms, and military stores. When they did this, the Romans then said that they must leave their city and build another city inland at least ten miles from the sea. The people of Carthage heard this cruel order with horror, and determined to die rather than submit. They at once began to make new arms and to prepare their city for a siege. The Romans blocked up their harbor and surrounded the city, but the brave people held out for nearly three years; and even when the Romans had got within the walls, they fought from street to street, setting the houses on fire as they went. The city burned for seventeen days, most of the people perishing in the flames, and was wholly destroyed.

Long afterward the Emperor Augustus built a new Carthage on the site. This was conquered by the VANDALS and became the capital of their kingdom, and was finally destroyed by the Arabs (A.D. 698).

Carthage was called by the Phœnicians Kartha-Hadtha, the "New City," because it was built after Utica, which was near it. The Romans made this into Carthago, and from this has come the modern name.

CARTIER (*kar-te-a'*), **Jacques,** a French sailor, born at St. Malo, Dec. 31, 1494. King Francis I. sent him to explore in America, and on his first voyage (1534) he discovered and named the St. Lawrence river and gulf. The next year he sailed up the river to the Indian village of Hochelaga, built at the foot of a lofty hill. Cartier climbed this, and struck by the lovely view, he called it Mont Réal ("Royal Mount"), which afterward became Montreal. He died in France when sixty-one years old (1555).

CAR'VER, John, the first governor of PLYMOUTH Colony, born in England, He was one of the Pilgrims who came over in the Mayflower, and was chosen governor soon after landing. He helped to settle his people in their new homes, but died within four months (April, 1621).

CA'RY, Alice, an American poet, born near Cincinnati, Ohio, April 26, 1820. Her parents lived on a farm at a distance from good schools, and could not afford to give their large family of nine children a very good education. But Alice and her sister Phœbe were fond of reading and studied all they could. When Alice was seventeen and Phœbe thirteen years old they began to write verses, which were printed in newspapers, and in 1849 they published a book called "Poems of Alice and Phœbe Cary." This made them well known, and the next year they came to New York, where they gave themselves up to writing, and won much fame and many friends. Alice wrote, besides poetry, several stories in prose, among which were "The Clovernook Children" and "Snow Berries, a Book for Young Folks." She died in New York when fifty-one years old (Feb. 12, 1871).

CARY, Phœbe, an American poet, sister of Alice Cary, born near Cincinnati, Sept. 4, 1824. She wrote about a third of the "Poems of Alice and Phœbe Cary," and other poems. She loved her sister very dearly, and was nearly brokenhearted when she died, and lived only a few months afterward, dying in Newport, July 31, 1871, when nearly forty-seven years old. The sisters are buried at Greenwood, where a beautiful monument has been erected to them.

CASABIANCA (*kah-sah-bi-an'-kah*), **Louis,** a French naval officer, born at Bastia about 1755. He was captain of the L'Orient, the principal ship of the fleet which carried Bonaparte and his army to Egypt. At the battle of the Nile (Aug. 1, 1798), when NELSON attacked the French fleet in the Bay of Aboukir, Casabianca fought his ship bravely until he was killed. During the battle he had ordered his little boy, ten years old, to a certain part of the ship, and told him to stay there until he called him. Not knowing of his father's death, the little fellow stood manfully at his post, though the ship was on fire, and refused to leave with the others, because he had no orders to go. The fire soon reached the powder magazine, and the boy was blown up with the ship. Mrs. HEMANS wrote a beautiful poem about it called " Casabianca," which has made the son more famous than the father.

CASCA (*kas'kah*), **Publius Servilius,** one of the assassins of Julius CÆSAR. He is said to have been the first to strike Cæsar. When the signal was given, he rushed upon him and plunged a dagger into his neck behind, but was so nervous that he did not wound him very badly. Cæsar turned round quickly and caught him by the arm, crying in Latin : " Villain Casca, what do you do?" Casca, frightened, called to his brother in Greek, "Help, brother!" and the other conspirators then rushed upon Cæsar and finished the bloody deed.

CASHMERE (*kash-meer'*), a country of N.W. India; area 75,000 square miles, or about as large as Nebraska ; pop. about 3,500,000, or nearly the same as that of Ohio ; capital, Serinagur. The vale of Cashmere, where most of the people live, is a great plain shut in by mountains, some of which have their tops always covered with snow. The valley is one of the most beautiful places in the world, being like a park full of flowers and groves and green fields ; and it is famous for its fine fruits. There are also great gardens of roses, and attar of roses is sent from there to all parts of the world. A large number of the people are engaged in making Cashmere shawls (C. C. T., 116, I., l.). The climate is hot in summer and very cold in winter, and sometimes the snow falls so deep as to bury up houses and trees. Most of the people of Cashmere are Mohammedans. The country is a kingdom, but the ruler, called a rajah, is subject to Great Britain.

CASPIAN (*kas'pe-an*) **SEA,** an inland sea forming part of the boundary between Europe and Asia ; area 156,000 square miles, or one and two third times as large as Lakes Superior, Michigan, Huron, Erie, and Ontario together. The rivers Ural, Volga, and others empty into it, but none flow out of it ; the waters are therefore salt, but not so much so as those of the ocean. The coasts are mostly low, and the country between it and the Sea of ARAL is so low that it is thought that the two seas were once connected. The north part is very shallow, but the south part is deep. Sturgeon, salmon, and seals are taken in it in great numbers. The Russians have all of the trade of the Caspian Sea, and keep a fleet in it.

CASSANDRA (*kas-san'drah*), a noted prophetess, daughter of Priam, king of Troy. It is said, in Greek fable, that Apollo gave her the gift of prophecy, or the power to tell what would happen in the future, but afterward became angry with her and, being unable to take the gift from her, declared that no one should believe what she foretold. She foretold that the carrying away of HELEN would cause the fall of Troy, and warned the Trojans of all their troubles to come, but they treated her as a crazy person and shut her up in a tower. When Troy was taken Cassandra fled to the temple of Minerva and clung to the statue of the goddess for safety, but Ajax tore her away, and she was carried as a slave to Greece, where she remained in the household of Agamemnon until killed by his wife, CLYTEMNESTRA.

CAS'SEL, a city of Germany, in Prussia, on the river Fulda, 28 miles S.W. of Göttingen; pop. 64,-000, or nearly as large as Atlanta, Ga. It has a fine museum, library, and art collections. In its museum is one of the largest collections in the world of watches and clocks, from the first made to the present time. Near Cassel is the palace of Wilhelmshöhe, where NAPOLEON III. was sent a prisoner after the battle of SEDAN.

Cassel was anciently Castellum Cattorum, the castle of the Catti, a German tribe, and out of this has grown its present name.

CASSIUS (*kash'e-us*), **Longinus Caius,** the leader of the conspirators against Julius Cæsar. He was a noted soldier and one of the followers of POMPEY, but after Pompey's defeat surrendered to Cæsar, who gave him his life and showed him much favor. He married the sister of BRUTUS, and at the very time when Cæsar was most friendly to him was plotting with Brutus to kill him, because he thought that Cæsar had too much ambition. The day after Cæsar's murder he dined with Mark ANTONY, who asked him whether he had not then a dagger hidden in his bosom. "Yes," he replied, "to kill you if you aspire to tyranny."

After the death of Cæsar he was sent to govern Syria, where he raised an army to fight Antony and Octavius, but was defeated with Brutus in the first battle of Philippi. When he saw that all hope was lost, he ordered his servant to kill him (B.C. 42) with the same dagger, it is said, with which he had struck Cæsar. Brutus, who gave him a magnificent funeral, called him "the last of the Romans." Cassius is one of the chief characters in Shakespeare's play of "Julius Cæsar."

CASTILE (*kas-teel'*), an old kingdom of Spain, in the middle of what is now Spain, and covering about one fourth of the present kingdom. The northern part was called Old Castile, because it was the first to become independent of the Moors, and the southern part New Castile, because it was got later. The kingdom was begun about 1035 by Ferdinand I., who added Leon to it; and in 1479 Isabella, Queen of Castile and Leon, married Ferdinand II., King of Aragon. Thus the three kingdoms of Castile, Leon, and Aragon were united, and out of this grew the kingdom of Spain. The Castilians are a proud and brave race, and speak a purer language than any other of the Spanish peoples.

Castile is in Spanish Castilla (Land of Castles), and was so called from the large number of its castles.

CAS'TOR and **POL'LUX,** in Greek fable, two famous heroes, commonly called sons of Jupiter and of Leda, Queen of Sparta, and brothers of HELEN and CLYTEMNESTRA. Castor was noted as a tamer of horses, and Pollux as a boxer. They went with the ARGONAUTS in search of the golden fleece, and showed great courage on the expedition. During a storm which threatened the Argonauts with destruction two flames were seen hovering about the heads of Castor and Pollux, and the sea soon after became calm. They were therefore called the friends of sailors, and the twin balls of fire sometimes seen round the tops of the masts of ships at sea were named after them, and were thought to bring fair weather. The Romans believed that they owed to them the victory at Lake REGILLUS, where Tarquin the Proud was overthrown, and where they are said to have charged at the head of the Roman cavalry, clad in armor and mounted on splendid white horses. On account of this service a beautiful temple was erected to them in the Forum at Rome.

It is said that Castor was finally killed in a quarrel, and Pollux, who was himself immortal, begged Jupiter either to bring back Castor to life or to take away his own immortality, so that he might die. Jupiter would not grant this, but gave him permission to share his immortality with him; so afterward they took turns in living, the one staying in Hades while the other was on earth. At last both were taken to heaven and made a constellation called Gemini (twins), which never appear together, for when one rises the other sets.

CAS'TRO, Ines de, a beautiful maid of honor at the court of Portugal in the 14th century. Prince Pedro, heir to the throne, made her his wife, but kept the marriage secret for several years. When it was discovered King Alfonso IV., his father, was very angry, as he feared that her children might take the place of Pedro's other children as heirs to the throne. When Pedro was away on a hunting expedition the king went to her home to kill her, but she looked so beautiful as she begged for her life that he had not the heart to hurt her. After he had returned, however, he sent men who murdered her. When Pedro came home and found her bleeding body he was nearly wild with grief, and his mother had hard work to keep him from killing his father. After his father's death (1357) his rage broke out again, and he killed the assassins with terrible

tortures and had their bodies burnt and their ashes scattered to the winds. He also had the corpse of Ines taken from the grave and placed on the throne dressed in rich clothing, and made all the nobles and great men of the kingdom kiss the hem of her robe. The remains were then given a grand funeral, in which the procession traveled over sixty miles of road, the entire way being lined with people bearing torches. The story of Ines de Castro is told by many poets, but nowhere so well as in the "Lusiads" of CAMÖENS.

CAT-A-LO'NI-A. See SPAIN.

CATANIA (kah-tah'ne-ah), a city of E. Sicily, on the Gulf of Catania, near Mount Etna; population, 96,-000, or a little larger than Albany, N. Y. It is a very handsome city, with wide, regular streets, and many splendid buildings. Catania is one of the principal ports of Sicily and carries on a very large trade, especially in silk. It has large manufactories of silk and cotton cloth. Lava, procured from Mt. Etna, is used for building and for paving the streets, and chimmey-pieces, tables, toys, and many other things are made of it.

Catania is supposed to be about 2600 years old. Under the Romans it was a large and important city, and many remains of Roman buildings can be seen there. It has been destroyed several times by earthquakes and by eruptions from Mt. Etna.

CATHARINE (kath'er-in) I., Empress of Russia, wife of PETER THE GREAT, born about 1685. She was the daughter of a peasant, and when a little child was taken into his family by a Lutheran minister, named Glück, who brought her up. When about sixteen years old she married a Swedish dragoon; but when the war came on she was taken prisoner, with Glück and his family, by the Russian general and never saw her Swedish dragoon again. After this she had a great many lovers, among whom was Prince Menshikoff. At last the Czar Peter saw her, and was so struck with her great beauty that he fell in love with her too. Her real name was Martha, but in order to please Peter she changed both her name and religion, joining the Greek Church and taking the name of Catharine. She used to go with Peter to the wars, and once saved him from starving by bribing the Turkish Grand Vizier with her jewels to let him have food. This pleased Peter so much that she was declared Empress (1718). She was a very beautiful but a very bad woman: she had first one favorite and then another, and used to spend whole days and nights in dancing, feasting, and drinking with them. Many thought that she poisoned Peter. After his death she was sole empress for two years. She died in St. Petersburg when about forty-two years old (May 17, 1727).

CATHARINE II., Empress of Russia, born in Stettin, May 2, 1729. She was chosen by the Empress ELIZABETH to be the wife of her nephew Peter, afterward Peter III., who was to succeed her on the throne. She was a thoughtful girl, very fond of reading and study; and though a mere child when she married Peter, she at once set to work to study the Russian language and to learn the ways of the Russian people, so that she might know how to please them. Her boy husband was almost an idiot: fond of drinking, and of all sorts of boyish sports. He spent most of his time in drilling dogs and rats; he kept his dogs in a kennel next to his wife's bed-room, and flew into a passion if she ever laughed at his silly fancies. Of course they were both wretched, and after a while she grew wicked too. When the Empress Elizabeth died and Peter became Emperor of Russia, his wife thought

that she could govern the empire through him. But he was too bent on having his own way to let her have hers; so she headed a body of troops against Peter, and was proclaimed Empress in her own right. Peter was afraid to fight, was taken captive, and strangled in prison. Catharine was crowned with great show at Moscow, and made ever so

Catharine II.

many splendid promises of all the good things she meant to do for the people. But although she did make conquests, and many improvements in the industry, education, and commerce of the country, none of them seemed to last; and most of her works came to nothing before she died. She died in St. Petersburg at the age of sixty-seven (Nov. 17, 1796).

CATHARINE DE' MEDICI (*da med'e-che*), Queen of France, born in Florence in 1519. She was daughter of Lorenzo de'MEDICI, and when fourteen years old was married to the Duke of Orleans, afterward Henry II., and became the mother of Kings Francis II., Charles IX., and Henry III. She had an old head on young shoulders; and she began at once to try to gain the love of everybody whether she liked them or not. Through the reign of her husband she had little power, for he was ruled by a beautiful woman, named Diana of Poitiers. When her son Francis became king Catharine still led a quiet life, as he was under the spell of his wife, MARY STUART. After his death Catharine became Regent until her second son, Charles IX., then only ten years old, should be of age. At that time France was divided into two parties, one Protestant, the other Catholic; and as Catharine had no religion at all she wanted to be friends with both parties, so as to make use of them for her own ends. She was sometimes on one side and sometimes on the other, and was really the one to blame for the thirty years' civil war which burdened France. She persuaded the king to give the order for the Massacre of St. Bartholomew, and is said to have poisoned her sons Francis and Charles. She died in Blois when seventy years old (Jan. 5, 1589).

CAT'I-LINE, Lucius Sergius, a noted Roman conspirator. He was of an old and noble family, but was guilty in his youth of many crimes and vices. When he had spent his fortune and been refused the office of consul, which he wanted very much, he formed a plan to kill all the officers of the government, set Rome on fire, and share the public money with his friends. Many bad men joined him, but the plot was found out by CICERO, who was consul at the time, and who was one of those meant to be killed. Cicero called the Senate together and told them about the plot in a great speech which is known to every school-boy. Cataline tried to reply, but the Senators would not listen to him. The next night he fled from the city and went to Gaul, where his friends had raised an army. In a battle near Fæsulæ his army was defeated, and Catiline, finding all was lost, threw himself into the midst of his enemies and was killed (62 B.C.). The history of this conspiracy was written by SALLUST, who lived at the same time.

CA'TO, Marcus Porcius, a noted Roman patriot and statesman, born at Tusculum, about 234 B.C. He was of a plebeian family, and was at first called simply Marcus Porcius, but after holding the office of censor, he was known as Cato the censor, Cato meaning the Wise, and his descendants afterward took Cato for a surname. His father died when he was very young and left him a small farm, where he spent most of his youth in working. When seventeen years old he fought in the army against Hannibal (217), and afterward served in several campaigns with great courage, going home now and then to work on his farm. A rich neighbor, named Valerius Flaccus, became interested in him and got him to go to Rome, where he soon became noted as an orator. After holding other offices he at last became consul (195) with his patron Flaccus, and showed great military skill in putting down a rebellion in Spain, for which he was honored with a triumph on his return (194). Ten years later he and Flaccus became censors. While holding this office Cato opposed corruption, luxury, and immorality, and tried to bring back the Romans to the simple manners of their fathers, always setting them an example in his own mode of life. This made him numerous enemies among the rich patricians, who brought many accusations against him, but he was successful in defending himself against all. At the close of his censorship he was so much beloved by the people that they erected a statue to him. In his old age he urged the Senate to declare war against Carthage, and his hatred of that country became so great that he never made a speech, no matter on what subject, without adding : "I vote, moreover, that Carthage, must be destroyed." Cato wrote several books, but the only one now left is a work on agriculture, which gives rules for a farmer's life. He died in Rome when eighty-five years old (149 B. C.). He was sometimes called Cato the Elder, to distinguish him from his great grandson, who was called Cato the Younger.

CATO, Marcus Porcius, called Cato the Younger, a Roman patriot and statesman, great grandson of Cato the Elder, born in Rome 95 B. C. He lost his parents when young, and was brought up by his uncle. He took his great grandfather as his model in life, and as a youth was marked for his modesty and strength of character. When only fourteen years old he went with his tutor one day to call upon SULLA, and seeing the heads of several famous men who had been put to death by the tyrant carried away from the house, he asked why some one did not kill him. His tutor replying that no one dared to do so, he exclaimed that he himself would do it if he would give him a sword.

Though he was rich Cato lived in the most simple manner, always went on foot and often barefoot, and was careless about his dress. When twenty-three years old (72) he served in the army against SPARTACUS, and afterward in Macedonia. He held several offices in Rome, but failed to be elected consul because he was too honest to buy votes. He helped Cicero to defeat Catiline's conspiracy, and opposed Julius Cæsar. When the civil war broke out and Cæsar was marching towards Rome, he left the city and joined POMPEY, and after Pompey's death went to

UTICA, in Africa, which he wished to defend against Cæsar. On the approach of the conqueror the inhabitants refused to fight, and Cato made up his mind to die rather then fall into his hands. He talked pleasantly with his friends till night, then went to his room and after reading Plato's work on the immortality of the soul, stabbed himself with his sword. His friends, hearing him fall, ran in and bound up his wound, but he tore the bandages away and died at the age of forty-nine (46 B. C.), When Cæsar heard of it, he said : "Cato, I envy thee thy death, since thou hast deprived me of the glory of saving thy life." Cato was sometimes called Uticensis (Latin, of Utica), from the place of his death.

CATS'KILL MOUNTAINS. See NEW YORK (State).

CA-TUL'LUS, Caius Valerius, a noted Roman poet, born in Verona in 87 B.C. He went to Rome when young and soon became famous. Some of his poems are lyrical or fitted to be sung with the lyre, some elegiac or mournful, and some epigrammatic or pointed and witty. He is supposed to have died about **47 B.C.**

CAUCASUS (*kaw'ka-sus*), a range of mountains between the BLACK SEA and CASPIAN SEA, forming part of the boundary between Europe and Asia. The tops of some of them, which are more than three miles high, are always covered with snow, but the valleys are rich and yield rice, tobacco, cotton, indigo, and other plants of warm climates. Mt. Elbruz, one of the peaks of the Caucasus, is the highest mountain in Europe (18,500 ft). The people of the Caucasus, who form different tribes and speak different languages, are subject to Russia.

CAVOUR (*kah-voor'*), **Camillo Benso,** Count, a famous Italian statesman, born in Turin, Aug. 10, 1810. He was educated a soldier, and became an officer of engineers when only sixteen years old. But he did not like army life, and soon became interested in politics and was elected a member of the Sardinian Parliament. After holding several other offices he finally (1852) became chief minister of the kingdom, and from that time he carried on the affairs of Italy until it was nearly all free and united under one government. He showed great skill and ability in this office, and won the name of being one of the greatest statesmen of his time. He died in Turin when forty-nine years old (June 6, 1861).

CAWN-PORE', a city of British India, on the Ganges, about 96 miles S.W. of LUCKNOW; pop. 1,200,000, or a fifth larger than Chicago, Ill. It is an important British station for troops, and has barracks for 7000 soldiers. In the great mutiny of 1857, nine hundred Europeans, about two thirds of whom were women and children, were besieged in the fortifications for twenty-two days by the rebels under NANA SAHIB. They surrendered on a promise that they should be allowed to go in safety to Allahabad, but as soon as they got into boats to go down the river they were fired upon by cannon. Many were killed and the rest brought back to the shore. All the men left were then killed, and the women and children soon after, when the rebels heard that an English army was coming to their rescue, and their bodies thrown into a deep well. Three days afterward (July 18, 1857) the English under Gen. HAVELOCK entered the city, the rebels flying before them. A beautiful tomb has since been built over the well, and around it a splendid eight-sided building, in memory of the great massacre.

CAX'TON, William, the first English printer, born in Kent, about 1412. He was taught by his mother until fifteen years old, and was then apprenticed to a London mercer. In a few years he became agent for the Mercers' Company in the Netherlands, where he lived for twenty-three years. He translated a French "History of Troy" into English for the English Princess Margaret; and parts of this work show that he knew something about printing, which he must have learned in the Netherlands. The first three works which he printed were the French history, a speech of John Russell, and his translation of the same history. Caxton died in London when about eighty years old (1491 or 1492).

CAYENNE (*ki-en'*). See GUIANA.

CECROPS, in Greek fable, the first king of Attica and founder of Athens, said to have reigned about 1550 B. C. He taught his people good manners, marriage, agriculture, navigation, ship-building, and the worship of the Gods. The citadal or Acropolis of Athens was first called after him Cecropia, and the people of Attica were also sometimes called Cecropidæ.

CELLINI (*chel-le'ne*), **Benvenuto,** a famous Italian artist, born in Florence in 1500. He was especially noted as a worker in metals, and as an engraver or chaser on gold and silver. He decorated many beautiful shields, vases, cups, salvers, and sword and dagger handles, and engraved many medals. His works are very highly prized, and are preserved in museums and the cabinets of the rich. He died in Florence when seventy years old (Feb. 25, 1570).

CELSIUS (*sel'she-us*), **Anders,** a noted Swedish astronomer, born at Upsal, Nov. 27, 1701. He became professor of astronomy in the University of Upsal when twenty-nine years old, and built the observatory there. The centigrade thermometer (C. C. T., 615, I., l.) was first used by him, and is therefore sometimes called the Celsius thermometer. He died in Upsal when forty-two years old (April 25, 1744).

CELTS, or **Kelts,** the first of the ARYAN peoples who came from Asia into Europe. They drove out or killed the peoples whom they found, and were themselves driven in the same way by other Aryans from Asia until they were forced into western Europe to the ocean. Thus in very early times they were found in Gaul, Spain, and the British Islands. Of their languages, the British or Welsh, the Breton, spoken in parts of Brittany, the Irish, and the Gælic, spoken in the highlands of Scotland, are the only ones left.

C E N C I (*chen'che*), **Beatrice,** a beautiful Roman girl noted for her sad fate. The common story about her is that her father, who was a bad man but so rich that he escaped punishment for his crimes, sent her when she was only fourteen years old to a lonely castle among the hills. There she was treated with great cruelty and with all sorts of insults, and at last, to save herself, she, her stepmother, and her brothers hired men to kill her father. Beatrice, her stepmother, and one of her brothers were executed for the murder (1599), Beatrice being then only sixteen years old. There is a portrait of her in the Barberini Palace in Rome, said to have been painted by Guido Reni just before her execution, which represents her as a young and very beautiful girl, and several plays have been written about her. Beatrice's story is a very sad one, but it has lately been proved to be not altogether true. It is shown that she was neither so young nor so innocent as people have believed, and that her father was not quite so bad as history has made him. It is not even certain that the picture is a portrait of her, and it is certain that Guido Reni did not paint it, as he was never in Rome until nine years after her death.

CENIS (*suh-ne'*). See ALPS.

CENTAURS (*sen'tors*), in Greek fable, a race of beings with the head and arms like a man and the rest of the body like a horse. Some of the old writers really believed in such monsters, and PLINY says that he saw the body of one, embalmed in honey, which was brought to Rome from Egypt in the time of the Emperor Claudius. But others think that the story grew out of the riding of horses by the ancient Scythians, who were among the first to use this animal. The Greeks thought that the man and the horse were one being, just as the Mexicans did when they first saw the Spaniards riding (C. C. T., 307, I.). One of the most noted of the Centaurs was CHIRON. The Centaurs had a great battle with the LAPITHÆ, which was often painted by ancient artists.

CEN'TRAL A·MER'I·CA. See AMERICA.

CER'BER-US, in Greek fable, the dog which guarded the entrance to HADES. He had three heads and a tail like a snake, though some writers say that he had fifty heads. PLUTO placed him at the entrance to his kingdom to keep the living from going down and the dead from coming back to earth. See HERCULES.

CERES (*se'reez*), in Greek and Roman fable, the goddess of agri-culture. She is said to have been the daughter of SATURN and of Rhea, and the mother of Proserpine. Before her time the earth was rough and uncultivated, and all parts of it were common to everybody; but she taught men how to plow, to sow and to reap grain, called from her the cereals (C. C. T., 153, I.), to make bread, and also to grow fruits. When men learned these things they began to divide up and to own pieces of land, from which disputes arose about boundaries and limits of fields, and this made laws necessary. For this reason Ceres was called also the founder of laws.

Ceres lived on OLYMPUS with the other gods and goddesses until Jupiter let Pluto carry off PROSERPINE, when she came down to earth and wandered round disguised as an old woman, doing good to those who treated her well and punishing those who ill-used her. She came at length to Eleusis, where she became nurse to the infant son of King Celeus. She tried to make him immortal by bathing him in fire; but his mother, becoming curious to know what the nurse did to make her child grow so fast, peeped through a hole and, thinking

that Ceres was killing her son, screamed and ran into the room to save him. The goddess, to punish her, dropped the child into the fire, where it perished. To make up for the loss, she gave great favors to TRIPTOLEMUS, another son of the king. After this Ceres threw off her disguise, bade the people of Eleusis

Ceres.

to build her a temple, and taught them how to worship her; and she was afterward worshiped there with many secret and mystical ceremonies, which were called the Eleusinian Mysteries. The Greeks called Ceres Demeter.

CER'RO GOR'DO, a mountain pass in Mexico, 40 miles N.W. of Vera Cruz, where the Mexicans under Santa Anna were defeated by the Americans under Gen. Scott, April 18, 1847. Gen. Scott was on the march from Vera Cruz to the city of Mexico with 8500 men, when he was met by the Mexican army of more than 12,000 men. Santa Anna was badly defeated,

with the loss of 4000 men and 43 cannon.

CERVANTES (*ser-van'teez*) **SAAVEDRA, Miguel de,** a noted Spanish writer, author of "Don Quixote," born at Alcalá de Henares, Oct. 9, 1547. He came of a good family, was well educated, and wrote poetry when quite young; but having a taste for adventures, he became a soldier, and fought against the Turks under Don John of Austria. He was wounded in the battle of Lepanto (1571), so that he lost the use of his left arm and hand; but he kept in the army in

Cervantes.

spite of it until 1575, when he was taken prisoner by the Moors, who held him in slavery for five years. In the story called "The Captive" in the first part of Don Quixote he tells how cruelly he was treated during this time. His friends at last bought his freedom, and he returned to Madrid, where he soon married a beautiful young lady, and had to work very hard to support his family. He wrote many plays, but they were not very successful, and he became so poor that his family had to live in a garret. At last, when he was about fifty years old, he wrote his great novel of

"Don Quixote," and grew famous at once. At that time it was the fashion to read absurd stories of knights who went round the world seeking adventures, though there had been no such thing as knighthood for more than a hundred years. Cervantes meant to make fun of these silly stories in Don Quixote, and he succeeded so well that everybody was delighted with the old knight and his horse Rosinante and his servant Sancho Panza, and laughed over their ridiculous adventures. It is said that the king, Philip III., looking out of a window one day, saw a student laughing very loud over a book. "He is either crazy," said he, "or he is reading 'Don Quixote.'" So many copies of the book were sold that its author was relieved from want, and it was soon translated into many languages and read all over Europe; and it is still read and admired, though its writer has been dead nearly three hundred years. Cervantes died when sixty-nine years old, on the same day with Shakespeare (April 23, 1616).

CEYLON (*see'lon*), an island of Asia, in the Indian Ocean, S. of India; area 25,000 square miles, or three times as large as New Jersey; pop. 3,000,000, or about twice that of South Carolina; capital, COLOMBO. It is a very beautiful island, with high mountains, and with rich valleys and plains covered with palms and other trees of hot climates. In many places are thick woods and jungles, where many wild elephants live. Among the mountains is Adam's Peak, which is more than a mile high. It is shaped like a cone, and is so steep that it has to be climbed with the aid of a chain fastened to the top, yet it is much visited every year by pilgrims who go there to see what looks like a great footprint in the rock on its top. The Buddhists say it is a track left by Buddha when he stepped from Ceylon to Siam; but the Mohammedans think it was made by Adam when he was driven out of the Garden of Eden, and from this the mountain is called Adam's Peak.

Ceylon is rich in metals and in many kinds of precious stones, and off the west coast are great pearl-oyster beds from which are taken some of the best pearls in the world (C. C. T., 449, II. l.). Many kinds of fine woods are cut in the forest, and coffee, cotton, rice, tobacco, and spices are grown. The chief things sent to other countries are coffee, cinnamon, cocoanuts, hides, pearls, and plumbago or black lead. The people of Ceylon are mostly Buddhists, though there are many Mohammedans. The island belongs to Great Britain, and is ruled by a governor chosen by the crown.

Ceylon gets its name from its ancient name (Sanhala-Dwipa), which means the island of lions. It was settled in very early times, and there are many temples and ruins of ancient buildings still standing which show that the people were rich and powerful. The Portuguese went there in 1505, and held part of the island for 150 years. The Dutch drove them out (1656), and the British drove out the Dutch (1796.)

CHÆRONEA (*ke-ro-ne'ah*), a town of Greece, in Bœotia, famous for the victory of PHILIP of Macedon over the Athenians and Thebans (338 B.C.), which made Philip master of Greeee. A victory was also won there (86 B.C.) by SULLA over Mithridates, King of Pontus. PLU-TARCH was born at Chæronea.

CHALDÆA (*kal-de'ah*). See BABYLON.

CHAMOUNI (*shah-moo-ne'*). See ALPS.

CHAMPLAIN (*sham-plane'*), **Samuel de**, a noted French navigator, born at Brouage in 1567. His father, who was a captain in the navy, had him carefully educated as a navigator. After having made a voyage to Mexico, he was sent (1603) by King Henry IV. of France to found a colony in the New World. He went up the St. Lawrence above where Montreal now is, and afterward sailed up and down the coast, making surveys and maps as he went. In 1608 he again went up the St. Lawrence, founded QUEBEC, and planted a colony there. The next year he went with some Indians to fight

Samuel de Champlain.

the Iroquois, a nation of Indians living in what is now New York State, and found Lake Champlain, which was named after himself. While sailing down the lake with his Indians he met a large body of Iroquois coming up the lake in canoes. Both parties landed and began a fight in the woods, but Champlain killed two of the Iroquois chiefs at one shot with his gun, and the rest were so astonished that they fled.

Champlain lived many years in Canada—or New France, as it was called—of which he became governor, and did much to build up the colony. He was a brave and honest man, and tried hard to civilize and to Christianize the Indians. His accounts of his voyages and of his travels in Canada are very interesting. Champlain died in Que-

bec when sixty-eight years old (Dec. 25, 1635).

CHAMPOLLION (*sham-po'le-on*), **Jean Francois,** a French scholar, the first to read the Egyptian hieroglyphics, born at Figeac, Dec. 23, 1791. When other boys of his age were at play he was studying Hebrew, Arabic, Chaldee, and other ancient languages; and before he was seventeen years old he had planned, and partly written, a history of Egypt under the Pharaohs. When only eighteen years old (1809) he became professor of history in the University of Grenoble, where he was educated, and in 1814 published his "Egypt under the Pharaohs." He studied the Egyptian hieroglyphics or letters, and found out the secret of their alphabet, so that he was able to read the inscriptions on their monuments and their books written on papyrus (C. C. T., 81, I., l., and 440, II., l.). Champollion received many honors and won great fame, but he worked so hard that he injured his health, and died in Paris, in the midst of his labors, when only forty-one years old (March 4, 1832).

CHAN'CEL-LORS-VILLE, a village of Virginia, 65 miles N. by W. of Richmond. It is noted for the battle fought near it between the Union army under Gen. HOOKER and the Confederate army under Gen. LEE, May 2–4, 1863. After a terrible struggle of three days Gen. Hooker had to retreat, with a loss of about 18,000 men. The Confederates lost about 13,000

CHAN'NEL ISLANDS, a group of islands in the English Channel, off the N.W. coast of France; area 73 square miles, or about a third larger than the island of Rhode Island; pop. 90,000. The principal islands of the group are Jersey, Guernsey, Alderney, and Sark. The famous Alderney or Jersey cattle are brought from there. The Channel Islands were once part of the

Duchy of Normandy, of which WILLIAM THE CONQUEROR was Duke when he conquered England, and they have belonged to England ever since. The people still speak the old Norman-French language.

CHAPULTEPEC (*chah-pool-ta-pek'*), a Mexican fort or castle, on a high rock 2 miles S.W. of the city of Mexico, taken by the Americans under Gen. Scott, Sept. 13, 1847. It guarded the principal road into the city, and was the seat of the Mexican military school, and was therefore strongly defended. Its capture really ended the Mexican war, for Gen. Scott and his army marched into Mexico the next day.

CHARLEMAGNE (*sharl-mahn'*). See CHARLES THE GREAT.

CHARLES I., King of Great Britain, son of JAMES I., born at DUN-FERMLINE, Scotland, Nov. 19, 1600. He became king in 1625, and in the same year married Henrietta Maria, daughter of HENRY IV. of France. Believing that he had a divine right to rule, he did many illegal things and soon got into a quarrel with Parliament. He refused to dismiss his Prime Minister, the Duke of BUCKINGHAM, and when Parliament would not vote him money to carry on public affairs he laid illegal taxes on the people. He dismissed several Parliaments, and finally tried to rule without any. After the death of Buckingham (1628) he made Sir Thomas Wentworth, afterward Earl of STRAFFORD, and William LAUD, afterward Archbishop of Canterbury, his chief counsellors. Wentworth advised the king to do things which he had no legal right to do, and Laud persecuted the PURITANS severely.

Charles now tried (1634) to raise money by laying a tax called " ship-money," because it was pretended that it was for the support of a fleet. John HAMPDEN and many others refused to pay this, and the king became still more unpopular.

The Scots soon after rose in rebellion, because Charles tried to force them to use a prayer-book like that of England in their churches. In 1640 they invaded England and defeated the royal army, and Charles, finding that he could do nothing without money, called a new Parliament, since famed as the Long Parliament because it lasted so long. Parliament at once had Strafford tried for treason, and he was executed (1641), and Laud was put into prison. The next year Charles went with armed men to the House of Commons to arrest Hampden, PYM, and other leaders, but they had been warned and

Charles I.

were not to be found. Six days afterward Charles fled from London, and the Civil War between the king and Parliament began.

The two parties in the war were called Royalists and Parliamentarians, but were more commonly known as Cavaliers and Roundheads. The Roundheads are said to have been so named because some of the stricter Puritans cut their hair short, instead of wearing it long as the Cavaliers did. The Cavaliers were commanded by the king and by Prince RUPERT, and the Roundheads by the Earl of ESSEX, and afterward by Sir Thomas FAIRFAX aided by Oliver CROMWELL.

The three principal battles of the war were fought at Edgehill (1642), MARSTON MOOR (1644), and NASEBY (1645). Charles, though badly defeated in the last two, struggled till the next spring, and then surrendered himself to the Scots, who gave him up to the Parliament (1647). He was kept for some time in Carisbrooke Castle, Isle of WIGHT, and at last was tried and condemned for making war against his people, and beheaded in London, when forty-nine years old (Jan. 30, 1649). Of the children of Charles, Charles Prince of Wales became King CHARLES II., and James Duke of York became King James II. of England. Mary, his daughter, married William Prince of Orange, and her son became King WILLIAM III. of England.

CHARLES II., King of Great Britain, born May 29, 1630. Though a mere boy, he fought in the civil war with his father, CHARLES I., but left England after the battle of Naseby. He was at the HAGUE when he got news of his father's death (1649), and at once took the title of king. The Scots also proclaimed him king, and he went to Scotland and was crowned (1651). After his defeat by CROMWELL at the battle of Worcester he fled to France, which he reached in safety after many narrow escapes. A reward of £1000 ($5000) was offered for his arrest, but though he trusted himself to more than forty persons, none ever betrayed him. At one time, hidden among the leaves of a great oak-tree, which afterward was called the Royal Oak, he watched the soldiers of Cromwell hunting for him; at another time he lay many days in a wood, dressed as a peasant and with his hair cropped short. One day, after walking until he was tired, he borrowed the horse of a miller. Charles complained that the beast jolted him badly. "You must re-

member," said the miller, who knew him, "that it is carrying the weight of three kingdoms." Finally he disguised himself as servant to a gentlewoman, who rode behind him on a pillion, as ladies then used to travel, and reached Brighton, whence he sailed on a coal vessel to France.

After the death of Cromwell, Charles was called back to England and became king (1660). The first year of his reign was called the twelfth, because his reign was reckoned to begin at his father's death. At first Edward Hyde, Earl of CLARENDON, was his principal adviser, but he was forced to flee to France; after that Charles's leading ministers were called the Cabal, a word used in much the same sense as Cabinet, but given to them because it made the initials of their names or titles—the members being *Clifford*, Lord *Arlington*, the Duke of *Buckingham*, Lord *Ashley*, and the Duke of *Lauderdale*. The great plague, in which more than 100,000 died in six months (1665), and the great fire, which burned three days and destroyed a large part of London (1666), occurred in this reign. Charles II. was a good-natured gentleman of some talent, but had little in him worthy of love or admiration. His court was very corrupt, and his reign one of the worst in English history. He died when fifty-four years old (Feb. 6, 1685), and was succeeded by his brother JAMES II.

CHARLES II., called the Bald, the fourth Carlovingian king of France, born at Frankfort-on-the Main in 823. When his father, Louis I., died (840), he got as his share of the kingdom all of France west of the Rhone. In his reign the Northmen invaded France and plundered and burned many cities, even attacking Paris and forcing Charles to pay them tribute. On the death of his nephew, the Emperor Louis II. (875), Charles seized upon his crown, so that he is called Charles II. among the emperors of Germany as well as among the kings of France. He died in 877.

CHARLES III., called the Simple, the eighth Carlovingian king of France, born Sept. 17, 879. While a boy he was kept from his throne, but when he became of age he claimed his rights and was crowned. He was a weak prince, and being unable to keep out the NORTHMEN, he made peace with their chief Rollo by giving him his sister in marriage and the north-west part of his dominions, which has ever since been called Normandy. Charles's nobles at last rebelled against him, and he was kept a prisoner until his death (Oct. 7, 929).

CHARLES IV., called the Fair, the last of the Capetian kings of France, born in 1294. He helped his sister Isabella, wife of EDWARD II. of England, in her revolt against him. He died at Vincennes (Jan. 31, 1328), and was succeeded by Philip VI., the first king of the House of Valois.

CHARLES V., called the Wise, the third Valois king of France, born Jan. 21, 1337. He was the son of King John, who was taken prisoner by the English at the battle of POITIERS. He ruled while his father was a captive, and became king on his death (1364). Though he knew little of the art of war, by the help of his general, the brave DU GUESCLIN, he got back almost all those parts of France which the English had been holding. He was fond of learning, and founded the Royal Library in Paris. The Bastile was built in his reign. He died at Vincennes when forty-three years old (Sept. 16, 1380), and was succeeded by Charles VI.

CHARLES VI., called the Beloved, the fourth Valois king of France, born in Paris, Dec. 3, 1368. He

was the son of Charles V., and the first prince that was called dauphin. He had not reigned long when he became insane. His uncle the Duke of Burgundy and his brother Louis Duke of Orleans had a dispute as to which of them should rule in the king's place. Everybody in France took sides in this quarrel, so that there were two parties called Burgundians and Armagnacs. Henry V. King of England, thinking that this would be a good time to get back what the English had lost, invaded France, and the Burgundian party said that he might be king of France after the death of Charles; but Henry died about two month before Charles ended his sad life (Oct. 21, 1422). Charles VI. was succeeded by Charles VII.

CHARLES VII., called the Victorious, the fifth Valois king of France, born in Paris, Feb. 22, 1403. On the death of his father, Charles VI., the English held nearly all France, and many even of the French considered Henry the infant son of Henry V. of England as their king. But with the help of a brave peasant girl, called JOAN OF ARC, who put herself at the head of the French armies, the English were driven out of every place except Calais, and thus ended the war which had been going on for a hundred years between England and France. Charles died when fifty-eight years old (July 22, 1461), and was succeeded by Louis XI.

CHARLES VIII., called the Affable, the seventh Valois king of France, born at Amboise, June 30, 1470. He was the son of Louis XI., and came to the throne when only thirteen years old. His sister ruled for him until he was old enough to reign. When very young he liked to read of the great deeds of Alexander and Cæsar, and when he grew up he wished to do as they had done. So he tried to conquer Italy. He took Naples, but the other powers formed a league against him, and he had to give it up. He died from a blow on the head, when only twenty-seven years old (April 7, 1498), and was succeeded by Louis XII.

CHARLES IX., the twelfth Valois king of France, born at St. Germain-en-Laye, June 27, 1550. He was the son of Henry II., and came to the throne when only ten years old on the death of his brother Francis II. During his youth his mother, Catharine de' Medici, ruled in his name. His whole reign was disturbed by wars between the followers of the reformed religion, called Huguenots, and those of the old faith or Catholics. The court generally took part with the Catholics. Charles and his mother hated the Huguenots so much that they planned and carried out a fearful massacre in which thousands of those people were slain. This is always called the Massacre of St. Bartholomew, because it began on St. Bartholomew's Day, Aug. 24, 1572. He was afterwards very sorry for this, and suffered much on account of it. Charles died when twenty-four years old (May 30, 1574), and was succeeded by Henry III.

CHARLES X., the seventh and last Bourbon king of France, born at Versailles, Oct. 9, 1757. He was the grandson of Louis XV. and younger brother of Louis XVI. Before he became king he was known as the Count of Artois. During the French Revolution he was an exile, but when the other nations of Europe decided that it would be better for the Bourbons to rule once more in France he came back to his own country. He began to reign on the death of his brother Louis XVIII., but he did not please the people because they thought he did not give them enough liberty. So they rose against him, as they had done years before against LOUIS XVI., and

made him give up the throne and leave the country. He died at Görz, Austria, when seventy-nine years old (Nov. 6, 1836).

CHARLES I., THE GREAT, called by the French Charlemagne, Emperor of the West and King of the Franks, said to have been born at AACHEN, April 2, 742. He was the son of Pepin and grandson of CHARLES MARTEL, and became sole sovereign of the Frankish

Charles the Great.

kingdom on the death of his brother Carloman, who had shared it with him. Thirty years of his reign were spent in wars against the Lombards, the Saxons, and the Moors. He defeated Desiderius, the Lombard king, joined his kingdom to his own, and had himself crowned with the ancient iron crown of the Lombard kings. At the same time the Pope declared him king of Italy. At a later period Pope Leo III. gave him the gold crown of the emperors and pronounced him Emperor of the West, the successor of the Cæsars.

The Saxons were Christianized as well as conquered by Charles, but he was not so successful in Spain, his army being defeated at RONCESVALLES. The empire of Charlemagne reached from the North Sea to the Mediterranean, and from the Atlantic Ocean to the mouth of the Oder River. But Charlemagne was not only a great soldier, he was also a wise ruler, and he loved learning so much that he founded many schools and invited to his court wise men from all parts of Europe. Other nations thought so much of him that their kings sought his friendship and sent to his court messengers with costly gifts. Among these was the Caliph HAROUN AL RASCHID. Charlemagne died when seventy-two years old (Jan. 28, 814). He left his vast empire to his son Louis the Debonair. Guizot says of Charlemagne: "No sovereign, no human being, perhaps, ever rendered greater services to the civilization of the world."

CHARLES II., Emperor. See CHARLES II. of France.

CHARLES III., called the Fat, Emperor, and King of the Franks, born about 832. He was the grandson of CHARLES THE GREAT. After the death of his brothers he ruled over France, Germany, and Italy, and bore the title of emperor, but he had little power. The city of Paris was attacked during his reign by the NORTHMEN. Instead of fighting them he offered them money to go away. For this cowardly act his nobles said he should no longer be their king. He died the next year (888), poor and without friends, in a monastery near Constance.

CHARLES IV., Emperor of Germany, born in Prague, May 13, 1316. He was the son of King John of Bohemia, and was elected emperor in 1346, to succeed Louis V., whom the Pope forbade to be emperor any longer. The only thing of importance which he did for the empire was to make a decree, called the "Golden Bull," which for four hundred years was the law regulating the election of German emperors. By gifts of money to the electors, he got them to choose his son Wenceslas emperor after him. He died in Prague when sixty-two years old (Nov. 29, 1378).

CHARLES V., Emperor of Germany, born in Ghent, Feb. 24, 1500. He was the son of the Archduke Philip of Austria, and was elected emperor in 1519, to succeed his grandfather Maximilian I. He had already become King Charles I. of Spain, on the death of his other grandfather, Ferdinand, in 1516. Besides Spain, he had inherited Austria, Burgundy, the Netherlands, Naples, and large tracts of land in America, so that he was the richest and most powerful ruler of his time. His reign is one of the most important in modern history, and full of great events with all of which Charles had much to do. Francis I., the French king, had hoped to be chosen emperor, and he never got over his grudge against Charles for having been elected instead of him. From that time the two rivals became bitter enemies, and were almost always at war for twenty-three years. These wars were about Milan, Naples, and Burgundy, which were claimed by both kings. When Charles became emperor, Germany was much disturbed about the new ideas of Martin LUTHER, who found fault with some of the things taught by the Church, and got many people to think with him that it was best to leave the Church altogether,

Charles did not like these notions and he tried to put them down, making strict laws against the Protestants, as Luther's disciples were called. Then there was war between the emperor and these people, and Charles finally had to make a treaty allowing them to think as they pleased. At last he grew tired of so many wars, so he gave Austria to his brother Ferdinand, and his other dominions to his son Philip, and went to spend the rest of his days at the monastery of St. Yuste, in Spain. He died when fifty-eight years old (Sept. 21, 1558).

CHARLES VI., Emperor of Germany, born Oct. 1, 1685. He was the son of the Emperor Leopold I., and was elected emperor in 1711, to succeed his brother, Joseph I. He was brought up in the hope of being king of Spain, to succeed the childless Charles II., but Louis XIV. of France wanted his grandson Philip, Duke of Anjou, to have that throne, so there was a war about it called the "War of the Spanish succession." England, Austria, and a part of Spain were for Charles against France and the rest of Spain, who were for Philip. The war ended by all parties consenting that Philip should be king. Having no son, Charles wished to alter the law which did not allow any woman to rule, so that his daughter MARIA THERESA could inherit his estates. So he got the other sovereigns to consent to the "Pragmatic Sanction," a new law making her his heir. He died when sixty-five years old (Oct. 20, 1740), and was succeeded as emperor by Charles Elector of Bavaria, who became Charles VII.

CHARLES VII., Emperor of Germany, born at Brussels, Aug. 6, 1697. He was the son of Maximilian Emmanuel, Elector of Bavaria, and was elected emperor in 1742, to succeed Charles VI. Although Bavaria had agreed to the "Pragmatic Sanction,' the law which secured Austria to MARIA THERESA, Charles the Elector claimed a part of it, and was helped in the war that he waged to enforce his claim by France, Spain, Saxony, and Russia. England and Holland fought for Maria Theresa, and with their help she kept her inheritance. He died, when forty-eight years old, at Munich (Jan. 20, 1745), and was succeeded as emperor by Francis I., the husband of Maria Theresa.

CHARLES ALBERT, King of Sardinia, born Oct. 2, 1798. He was the son of Charles Emmanuel of Savoy-Carignan, a younger branch of the royal family, and he became king on the death of Charles Felix, the last of the elder branch, in 1831. He made several good laws, granting to the people more liberty than they had had. In his reign a large part of Italy was under the rule of Austria, but in 1848 several of the Italian states resolved to free themselves, and Charles Albert helped them. He was, however, badly defeated at Novara, and was forced to give up his crown to his son VICTOR EMMANUEL. He died, when fifty-one years old, at Oporto (July 28, 1840).

CHARLES I., King of Spain. See CHARLES V., Emperor of Germany.

CHARLES II., King of Spain, born Nov. 6, 1661. He was the son of Philip IV., and succeeded him in 1665. He was under the guardianship of his mother, Anne of Austria, until he was fourteen years old, when he began to rule alone. He proved a very poor king, feeble in mind and body. He had no children, so he made a will leaving his crown to his great-nephew Philip of Anjou, who succeeded him as PHILIP V. He died when thirty-nine years old (Nov. 1, 1700).

CHARLES III., King of Spain, born Jan. 20, 1716. He was the son of Philip V., and succeeded his elder brother Ferdinand VI. in

1759. When he was quite young he had been made king of Naples and Sicily; but he gave up this kingdom to his son Ferdinand when he came to the throne of Spain. He governed with great wisdom, and made many improvements. He died when seventy-two years old (Dec. 13, 1788), and was succeeded by his son Charles IV.

CHARLES IV., King of Spain, born in Naples, Nov. 12, 1748. He was the son of Charles III., and succeeded him in 1788. In the early part of his reign he declared war against the French Republic because of the execution of LOUIS XVI., who was his cousin. He was soon forced to make peace, and ever after this he was entirely under French rule. His prime minister, Godoy who had great power over him, was hated by the people, and they made him give up the throne to his son Ferdinand. But Napoleon Bonaparte would let neither father nor son be king, and gave the throne to his own brother, Joseph Bonaparte. Ferdinand, however, afterward got his crown again. Charles died, when seventy-one years old, in Rome (Jan. 19, 1819).

CHARLES X., King of Sweden, born at Myköping, Nov. 8, 1622. He was the son of John Casimir, Prince Palatine of Deux-Ponts, and nephew of GUSTAVUS ADOLPHUS, and succeeded his cousin Christina when she left the throne (1654). He was a ruler of great ability, and also a great soldier. His reign of six years was spent in successful wars with Poland and Denmark. John Casimir, the King of Poland, had claimed the Swedish throne, but Charles beat him so badly as to make him glad to give up his claim. The trouble with Denmark was that she and Holland had made a treaty keeping to themselves the navigation of the Baltic. Charles is sometimes called the "Pyrrhus of the North." He died,

when thirty-seven years old, at Gothenburg (Feb. 13, 1660), and was succeeded by his son Charles XI.

CHARLES XI., King of Sweden, born in 1655. He was the son of Charles X., and succeeded him in 1660. He took the rule of his kingdom when he was only seventeen years old, and at once made a bargain with Louis XIV. of France that each should stand by the other in all his quarrels. This often led him into wars that he would have done better to keep out of. The first part of his reign was full of disturbances, but the last half was peaceful, and he made good use of the great power which his people gave him. He died when forty-two years old (1697), and was succeeded by his son Charles XII.

CHARLES XII., King of Sweden, born in Stockholm, June 27, 1682. He was the son of Charles XI., and succeeded him when only fifteen years old (1697). His youth led

Charles XII.

Russia, Denmark, and Poland to unite against him, each wishing to get a part of his territory. But Charles subdued Denmark, won the battle of Narva against Russia, and then turned against Poland, whose king, Augustus II., he drove from his throne, giving it to Stanislaus in his place. Had he stopped then it would have been well, but Charles loved war for its own sake. The whistling of bullets, he used to say, was the sweetest of music to his ears. He renewed the war against the Czar of Russia, Peter the Great, and, being badly beaten by him at PULTOWA, fled for shelter to Turkey, where he spent several years. While there, he sometimes behaved himself in such a violent way that he had to be kept shut up like a prisoner. As soon as he went home he began an attack on Norway. In besieging Frederickshald he was killed by a cannon-shot, when only thirty-six years old (Dec. 11, 1718). A hundred years afterward Charles XIV. caused a monument to be erected on the spot where he fell. His tomb is in the Riddarholms Church, Stockholm, near that of Gustavus Adolphus; and the clothes and sword worn at the time of his death, and many flags and other trophies taken by him in his battles, are preserved there. Charles XII. had a great genius for war, but his conduct in many respects was so strange that he has been called the " Madman of the North." He was succeeded by his sister Ulrica Eleonora.

CHARLES XIII., King of Sweden, born Oct. 7, 1748. He was the son of King Adolphus Frederick, and a nephew of FREDERICK THE GREAT of Prussia. Before he was king he was an admiral in the navy, and won great credit. When King Gustavus III. was murdered, he was chosen to rule until his nephew Gustavus IV. should be grown. Gustavus, however, after having reigned a few years, was so much disliked by the nobles that they set him aside in 1809, and chose Charles, who proved to be a good ruler and kept Sweden in peace at a time when the rest of Europe was at war. He died when sixty-nine years old (Feb. 5, 1818), and was

succeeded by the French general BERNADOTTE, whom he had adopted as his heir, and who succeeded him as Charles XIV.

CHARLES XIV., King of Sweden. See BERNADOTTE.

CHARLES XV., King of Sweden and Norway, born May 3, 1826. He was the son of OSCAR I., whom he succeeded July 8, 1859. Many changes for the better were made in Sweden during his reign, and everybody liked him, not because he ruled well only, but because he was a good man. He was very fond of literature and art, and got together during his reign many beautiful pictures, leaving them to the State on his death, which took place at Malmö when he was forty-six years old (Sept. 18, 1872). He was succeeded by his brother, OSCAR II.

CHARLES THE BOLD, fourth and last Duke of Burgundy, born at Dijon, Nov. 10, 1433. He was the son of Philip the Good, and succeeded to the dukedom in 1467. He was one of the most powerful sovereigns of his time, but, great as he was, he was not satisfied with being a duke, and tried to get for himself a kingdom by uniting to his states Lorraine and Switzerland. In former times there had been a kingdom of BURGUNDY, and he wished to restore it. He was a great enemy of his neighbor LOUIS XI. of France, and was often at war with him. In his war against the Swiss they twice beat him very badly, first at Granson and then at Morat. In trying to take Lorraine, he was defeated and killed at the siege of Nancy (Jan. 5, 1477). His body was found lying in a ditch. As he left no son, Burgundy was joined to France.

CHARLES MAR-TEL', a famous leader of the Franks, born about 690. The King of France at that time was Chilperic, but he was king only in name, all the real power being in the hands of Charles

Martel, who had the title of Mayor of the Palace. The Moors had come into Spain from the north of Africa, and they were trying to get into France. Charles met them in 732, in a battle between Tours and Poictiers, and completely defeated them. From this victory he was called Martel, or the Hammer, from the strong blows he gave in the fight. This is one of the most important battles in history, and Charles got great renown from it. He died in 741, when about fifty-nine years old, and was succeeded by his son Pepin, who took the the name of king and was the first of the Carlovingian family to sit on the throne of France.

CHARLESTON (*charlz'tun*), a seaport city of S.E. South Carolina, on a peninsula between the Ashley and Cooper rivers, where they meet in Charleston Bay; pop. 55,000, or about as large as Lincoln, Neb. It is the principal city in the State, and its harbor is one of the best in the United States. A large trade is carried on, especially in cotton, rice, and lumber, and there are important manufactories, where phosphate and sulphuric acid are prepared from a kind of marl (C. C. T., 517, I., l.) found near the city. Most of the houses are surrounded by fine, shady gardens, which give the city a very beautiful appearance.

Charleston was settled by the English in 1679. During the Revolutionary war Col. William Moultrie built a fort of palmetto logs on Sullivan's Island at the mouth of the harbor. This was attacked by a British fleet, but the soft palmetto logs proved a good bulwark, and the fort was so bravely defended that the British were obliged to withdraw (June 28, 1776). They made another unsuccessful attempt to capture the city in 1779, and finally they took it in 1780, after a siege of six weeks. In later times a fort, called Fort Moultrie, was built on the site of the palmetto fort. There were other strong forts defending the harbor, and in 1861 the United States Government had nearly finished Fort Sumter, on an artificial island in the harbor mouth. Major Robert Anderson was in command of these forts, and he had a garrison of sixty-three soldiers in Fort Moultrie. On Dec. 20, 1860, the State convention, which had met in Charleston, declared that South Carolina had seceded from the Union. But the United States Government would not give up the forts in Charleston Harbor. Major Anderson heard that the State soldiers were going to seize Fort Moultrie, so he removed his garrison in the night (Dec. 26) to Fort Sumter, which was much stronger and more easily defended. General Beauregard, who commanded the State soldiers, demanded the surrender of Fort Sumter, but Anderson refused, and on April 12, 1861, Beauregard began a bombardment, which lasted three days. The barracks in Fort Sumter were set on fire, and at length, when he had no more food and ammunition, Major Anderson had to give up the fort. He was allowed to march out with flying colors, firing a salute to the United States flag before he left. Strange to say, nobody had been injured by the bombardment. This was the beginning of the Civil War, which lasted for four years. The Confederates repaired Fort Sumter and kept a large garrison there, and though the Unionists bombarded it many times, they could never take it. They succeeded, however, in mounting a very large cannon, which the soldiers called the "Swamp Angel," in the swamp about four miles from Charleston, from which bombshells were thrown into the city. Charleston was formally taken in February, 1865, just four years after Sumter was given up. Anderson, with a large party, went back to the fort, and raised again the same flag which he had pulled down when he surrendered the fort (April 14, 1865).

CHARLEVOIX (*sharl-vwaw'*), **Pierre François Zavier de,** a noted French traveler and historian, born at St. Quentin, Oct. 29, 1682. He became a member of the society of Jesuits when only sixteen years old. In 1720 he came to Canada, went up the St. Lawrence River and through the great lakes, and reaching the Mississippi through the Illinois River, sailed down it to New Orleans. He went from there to Santo Domingo, and then back to France, which he reached after an absence of two years. He afterward published a "History of New France" (Canada). He died when seventy-eight years old (Feb. 1, 1761).

CHAR'LOTTES-VILLE, a town of Virginia, 65 miles N.W. of Richmond; pop. about 5,600. It is principally noted as the seat of the University of Virginia, founded by Jefferson (1819). Monticello, Jefferson's home, is near Charlottesville, and he is buried there.

CHARON (*ka'ron*), in Greek fable, the ferryman of HADES, said to have been the son of Erebus and Night. It was his business to ferry the souls of the dead across the rivers of the lower world, and his charge for each person was a small copper coin called an obolus. If the poor mortal had not been buried, and so been provided with the fee for Charon, which was always put in the coffin, his spirit had to wander on the shore for a hundred years before he could cross over to the other world.

CHARYBDIS (*ka-rib'dis*), a whirlpool in the strait of Messina off the coast of Sicily, opposite the rock called Scylla, on the coast of Italy. It is caused by the meeting of currents and is seldom dangerous; but in ancient times it was much dreaded by sailors and gave rise to the

fable that Charybdis was a monster that swallowed the waters and threw them up three times a day, and Scylla was another monster with six long necks and mouths, each of which took a sailor from every vessel passing through the strait.

CHASE, Salmon Portland, an American statesman, born at Cornish, N. H., Jan. 13, 1808. He was graduated at Dartmouth College in 1826, and supported himself by teaching school while studying law with William WIRT. He became a lawyer in Cincinnati, was United States Senator from Ohio from 1849 to 1855, and was twice governor of Ohio (1855 to 1858). In 1861 he was again chosen United States Senator, but resigned when President Lincoln made him Secretary of the Treasury. He held this office during the greater part of the Civil War, during which he had to furnish money to carry on the struggle. The plan of issuing the national paper money, commonly called "greenbacks," was one of his measures, and he was also the author of the national banking system, under which the notes issued by any bank are good in any part of the United States. In 1864 Mr. Chase was appointed Chief Justice of the United States, and held that office until his death. He died in New York when sixty-five years old (May 7, 1873).

CHASE, William M., an American painter, born in Franklin Township, Ind., in 1849. He paints portraits and ideal or fancy pictures of the human figure. His studio is in New York.

CHATEAUBRIAND (*shah-to-bre-ong'*),**François Auguste,** Viscount de, a famous French author and statesman, born at St. Malo, Sept. 14, 1768. He came of an old and noble family, and was brought up in luxury. When nineteen years old he was a captain in the French army; at twenty-three, on account of the Revolution, he came to the United States, where he traveled for a year, spending much time with the Indians. When he returned to France, intending to fight for his king, LOUIS XVI., he found that he could do nothing to help the cause; and after a year or two of misfortune and disappointment, he went to London. There he was so poor that he had to live in a garret, and was often in want of food, and to support himself he gave French lessons.

He went back to France after some years of this life, and published a book called "Génie du Christianisme" (Genius of Christianity), which made him famous and did a great deal of good. On account of it Bonaparte made him Secretary of Legation at Rome in 1803, and the next year gave him a higher office which Chateaubriand, who sympathized with the royal family, soon afterward resigned. When the Bourbons came into power again, Chateaubriand was very active in public affairs, and held a great many high positions, until the revolution of 1830; after which he gave up politics, and spent the rest of his life in writing. He wrote many admirable books which have been translated into several languages; and, several years before he died, prepared a history of his own life to be published after death. He died in Paris, in the eightieth year of his age (July 4, 1848).

CHATHAM (*chat'am*), a city of S.E. England, on the river Medway, near its junction with the Thames; pop. 48,000, or nearly as large as Los Angeles, Cal. The town itself is dirty and ill-built, but is important on account of the great government dock-yard there, which contains large wet and dry docks, many shops, a rope-house nearly a quarter of a mile long, and an arsenal and barracks. Connected with the yard is a military and a naval school, and several large ships which are moored there are used as barracks for sailors. The yard and harbor are guarded by strong forts.

The Chatham dock-yard was begun by Queen Elizabeth, and improved by later sovereigns, until it is one of the finest in England. In 1667 a Dutch fleet, under DE RUYTER, sailed up the Medway, and burned several ships at Chatham. The English fired at them from one of their forts, but De Ruyter and his men sailed off triumphantly, carrying a ship of war with them.

CHATHAM (*chat'am*), **Earl of,** See PITT.

CHATTANOOGA (*chat-tah-noo'-gah*), a city of S.E. Tennessee, on the Tennessee River, at the base of Lookout Mountain; pop. 29,000. Several railroads meet there, and the city has a good trade. During the Civil War it was an important stronghold of the Confederates, until Sept. 8, 1863, when it was taken by a Union army under Gen. ROSECRANS. After the battle of CHICKAMAUGA Gen. Thomas was put in command of the city, where he was besieged by the Confederates under Gen. Bragg. The Union army was reinforced by Gen. Grant, and it was resolved to attack the Confederates, who were intrenched on Lookout Mountain high above the city. Gen. Hooker with 10,000 soldiers climbed the mountain in a dense fog, surprised the Confederates, captured 2000 of them, and forced the rest to retreat (Nov. 24, 1863). This was called the Battle of Lookout Mountain and sometimes the "Battle above the Clouds." The Unionists encamped on the mountain, and on the next day fought another great battle at Missionary Ridge, in which the Confederates were completely beaten and forced to give up Tennessee and retreat into Georgia.

CHAT'TER-TON, Thomas, a noted English poet, born in Bristol,

Nov. 20, 1752. He was sent to school when five years old, but did not learn, and was called a dunce, but after he had learned to read he soon proved that he was much brighter than other boys of his age. He studied and read much, and took especial interest in poetry, in curious old books, and in the old English language that had gone out of use. He took so great a fancy to old-fashioned writing and spelling that it led him to try to cheat people in a curious way. He wrote a number of poems, parts of sermons, and descriptions of old churches

Thomas Chatterton.

and castles, in the style of three hundred years back, and sent them to magazines and newspapers, pretending that he had found them in an old chest. There really was an old chest called "Canynge's Coffre," which had once belonged to a rich merchant of Bristol, and was kept in a room of the church of St. Mary Redcliffe, of which his father had been sexton. The boy, who was then only sixteen years old, had written these things on parchment which he had stained to look old, and many people, among whom were some learned men and authors, were at first completely

deceived; but after a while the writings were found out to be forgeries.

When Chatterton was seventeen years old he went to London, where he wrote for the newspapers and made some friends, but his writings brought him but little money, and he soon grew poor, discouraged, and heart-broken. He went without food whole days together, but was too proud to make his wants known. Finally in his despair he shut himself up in his room, tore all his writings to pieces, and took a dose of arsenic, from which he died (Aug. 24, 1770), before he was quite eighteen years old. He was buried in a work-house burial-ground, but the people of Bristol afterward put up a monument in the church to his memory.

CHAU'CER, Geoffrey, a famous English poet, born in London in 1328. Not much is known of his early life, but he had many friends among the great and became a page to King Edward III., who gave him

Geoffrey Chaucer.

a pension. He was the first great writer in the English language, and is therefore sometimes called the "father of English poetry." In the latter part of his life he wrote his most celebrated poem, the "Canterbury Tales," which has given him a place among the great poets of the world. In this he describes a company of pilgrims on their way to the shrine of Thomas à BECKET at Canterbury. They stop at an inn and agree that the one who tells the best story shall be treated by the others to a supper. This work, which Chaucer did not finish, is now hard to read, on account of the use of many words which have since been dropped from the English language. Chaucer died in London when seventy-two years old (Oct. 25, 1400).

CHEL'SEA, a city of E. Massachusetts, on the Mystic River, opposite Charlestown, and very near Boston; pop. 28,000, or about as large as Houston, Texas. Most of the people do business in Boston, which is connected with Chelsea by the oldest ferry in the United States, it having been begun in 1631. Chelsea has a woollen mill and other manufactories. It was settled in 1630, but was a part of Boston until 1738.

CHELTENHAM (*chelt'nam*), a town of W. England, on the river Chelt; pop. 51,000, or about as large as Evansville, Ind. It is noted for its mineral springs, which are used by invalids both for drinking and bathing. The springs and the beautiful scenery and the city attract thousands of visitors, so that Cheltenham has become one of the chief English watering-places. Many fine hotels, club-houses, and villas have been built there. Cheltenham College has more than 700 students and a very handsome building. The city has a large manufactory of railroad cars and wagons.

Cheltenham first became a fashionable place in 1788, when King George III. visited it for his health. Since then it has grown rapidly.

CHE'OPS, the name given by Herodotus to the Egyptian king who built the great PYRAMID. He is called Suphis by some, but his right name was Khufu or Khuphu. According to most writers he lived between two and three thousand years before Christ, but according to some more than four thousand. He was a warrior and made Egypt great and rich, but Herodotus calls him a bad king. He was buried in the great Pyramid.

CHERBOURG (*sher'burg*), a city and seaport of France, on the shores of the English Channel; pop. 37,000, or nearly the same as that of Covington, Ky. The French keep many of their ships of war there, and to guard them they have made twenty-four strong forts, mounting 3000 cannons, around the harbor and city. To protect the harbor from the winds and waves an immense breakwater or wall of stone has been built in the sea in front of it. This wall is more than two miles long, and a hundred feet broad on top; in the middle is a large fort, and at each end are smaller ones; it cost more than $12,000,000 to build it. There is a great navy-yard there, where ships of war are made, and three stone docks for ships have been cut out of the solid rock. The sea-wall and forts were begun by Louis XIV., and finished by Napoleon III. Altogether they have cost $100,000,000. When the great docks were opened in 1858, the Queen of England went to see them. It was off Cherbourg that the Confederate ship Alabama was sunk by the Kearsarge (June 19, 1864). Cherbourg was an important port in the time of WILLIAM THE CONQUEROR, and was several times taken by the English in their wars with France.

CHER-O-KEES'. See AMERICAN INDIANS.

CHES'TER, a city and port of W. England, on the river Dee, 17 miles S.S.E. of Liverpool; pop. 38,000, or about as large as Dallas, Tex. It is built on a high rock almost surrounded by the river. The city was a camp (Latin *castrum*) or military post of the

Romans when they were in Britain, and from this it gets its name. It is defended by walls and towers, built, as was the custom with the Romans, in the form of a square, with a gate in the middle of each side, and two main streets leading from them and crossing in the centre. The walls are still used for a promenade, and from the top there is a beautiful view. On one of the towers is an inscription which says that King Charles, looking down from it, saw his army defeated at the battle of Rowton Moor. The streets are sunk far below the houses, and instead of sidewalks there are long galleries in the houses, formed by the front part of their lower stories. Chester has many ancient buildings, some of which are very interesting. An old castle, first built in the time of William the Conqueror, has been rebuilt, and is now used for a jail, armory, and barracks for soldiers. Chester carries on a large trade along the coast, and fairs for the sale of cheese are held there every month. The Prince of Wales is Earl of Chester.

CHES'TER-FIELD, Philip Dormer Stanhope, Earl of, born in London, Sept. 22, 1694. He was a very able English statesman, and also a clever and polished writer. He is best known by a volume of "Letters to his Son," which were written for private use and not intended for publication. His son's widow caused them to be printed after his death, and they have been very widely read. There is a great deal of good advice in them, and a good deal more that is bad. Dr. Johnson said that every gentleman ought to study them ; but Lord Chesterfield's best friends were very sorry that these letters were ever given to the world. He died when seventy-nine years old (March 24, 1773).

CHICAGO (*she-kaw'go*) the largest city of Illinois, and the second city of the United States in population, on the Chicago River at the S. end of Lake Michigan ; pop. 1,100,000, or about the same as Philadelphia. It is built on low flat ground along the shores of the lake and on both sides of the river, and has a prairie stretching hundreds of miles behind it. Chicago is one of the busiest places in the world. Ships are all the time coming and going on the lake, and hundreds of trains of cars arrive every day on many railroads. Ships go from there through the great lakes and the St. Lawrence River directly to Europe. More corn and wheat are sold in Chicago than in any other city in the world excepting New York. The grain is drawn up from railway cars into great elevators, some of which will hold more than a million bushels; and from the elevators ships are loaded in half an hour. There is also a very great trade in lumber, salted meats, and many other things. More hogs are killed and packed there than in any other city in the world. The people of Chicago get their water from Lake Michigan, and, as that near the shore is dirty and unfit for drinking, a tunnel two miles long has been made under the lake to the clear water outside ; from this tunnel the water is pumped up and carried in pipes to all parts of the city.

The name Chicago is supposed to come from Cheecaqua, an Indian word meaning "strong." Though one of the largest, this city is one of the newest in the United States. There was an old French fort there in 1683, and in 1804 the United States built a fort in the same place. At that time almost the only people there were Indians, and even fifty years ago (1830) there were only a few families there, besides the soldiers in the fort. In 1837 Chicago became a city, and it has been growing ever since. In 1871 the finest part of it was destroyed by one of the most terrible fires ever seen in the world. More than 17,000 houses and stores were burned, and many thousand people were left without homes. But money, food, and clothes were sent from all parts of the United States and even from Europe, and in a year or two the city was built up again, better than before.

CHICK·A·HOM'I·NY, a river of S.E. Virginia, near which several battles of the Civil War were fought in 1862 and 1864. It rises about 20 miles N.W. of Richmond and flows S.E. and S.to the James River. At one place it is only six miles from Richmond. It is bordered in many places by swampy forests, which during heavy rains are so covered with water as to be almost impassable. After General McClellan had taken Yorktown, his army followed the retreating Confederates, and gained another victory over them at Williamsburg, on the York River, about ten miles below the mouth of the Chickahominy (May 5, 1862). The Confederates then retreated across the Chickahominy, and a part of the Union army followed them. Soon after a heavy rain came on, and the river and swamps were so flooded that they became impassable. The Union army was thus completely cut in two ; for though the two divisions were only a short distance apart, their only means of reaching each other was by a bridge many miles away.

General Johnston, who commanded the Confederates, resolved to attack the division that had crossed the river and destroy it before the rest of the army could come to its aid. The attack was made in two places, at the railroad station of Fair Oaks and at Seven Pines, about a mile from Fair Oaks. At first the Unionists were driven back and almost beaten ; but meanwhile the soldiers on the other side of the Chickahominy had succeed-ed in building a bridge, and several thousand men hurried over to help their friends, and the Confederates were driven back in their turn, General· Johnston being severely wounded (May 31, 1862). On the next day the attack was renewed at Fair Oaks, but the Confederates were again defeated and they retreated in disorder to Richmond.

If General McClellan had followed them, he would probably have taken the city ; but though the Confederate army was smaller than his, he supposed that it was much larger. He therefore advanced very slowly and cautiously, thus giving the Confederates time to build forts and to receive reinforcements. In a few weeks they had nearly as many men as the Unionists, their army now being commanded by General Lee. General McClellan up to this time had received his provisions and supplies by way of the York River, and his base (that is, the place where his provisions were landed) was at West Point, on that river.

General Lee's army now recrossed the Chickahominy, trying to get between the Union army and West Point and so leave the Unionists without provisions. Instead of trying to prevent this, General McClellan resolved to change his base to City Point, on the James River. To do this he had to unite his army on the west side of the Chickahominy and march toward City Point. The Confederates had already attacked the Unionists at Mechanicsville on the east side of the river, but after a bloody battle they were driven back (June 26, 1862). A still more bloody battle was fought on the next day at Cold Harbor, a settlement five miles from Mechanicsville. There General McClellan had left a rear-guard under General Porter, while the rest of the army crossed the river ; but the rear-guard was attacked so fiercely that many thousand soldiers recrossed the river to help it, and even then it was hardly saved from a terrible defeat. At night the rear-guard crossed the river, and the whole army was united on the west side; that is, the side nearest to Richmond. They might easily have taken the city, for General Lee and most of his army were still on the east side of the Chickahominy, and farther away from Richmond than McClellan was. But the Unionists still supposed that a large army was defending the city, and they began to retreat towards City Point, fighting as they went. At Savage's Station, near Fair Oaks, they had large hospitals and many military stores, which they could not take with them. The stores were burned and a train of cars loaded with bombshells was set on fire; at the same time the engine was started, and as the train rushed off the shells exploded, until the cars reached a broken bridge, where they plunged into the river. Soon after the Confederates attacked the Unionists at the station and drove them away, capturing the hospitals with 2500 wounded soldiers (June 29).

On the next day they made another fierce attack at Frazier's Farm where a bloody battle was fought without much advantage being gained on either side. Finally (July 1) almost the whole Confederate army attacked the Unionists at Malvern Hill, but they were beaten back with terrible slaughter and the Union army reached City Point in safety. The battles from Mechanicsville to Malvern Hill are often called the Seven Days' Battle, though they were really fought in six days. The Union loss during this time was 15,200; the Confederate loss, 19,400.

On June 3, 1864, a second battle was fought at Cold Harbor, between the Union army under General Grant and the Confederates under General Lee. The Confederates had much the smaller army, but they were in strong intrenchments, where the Unionists attacked them. After one of the bloodiest battles of the war, the Unionists were driven back, leaving the ground covered with dead and wounded.

CHICKAMAUGA (*chik-a-maw'-gah*), a creek in S.E. Tennessee, flowing into the Tennessee River about twelve miles S.W. of Chattanooga. It is noted for a great battle fought there during the Civil War between a Union army under Gen. Rosecrans and the Confederates under Gen. Bragg. Bragg had retreated from Chattanooga and Rosecrans was pursuing, but, unknown to him, Gen. Longstreet was marching to aid Bragg with a large reinforcement. The Confederates made a stand at Chickamauga, and a battle ensued which lasted two days (Sept. 19 and 20, 1863). On the first day neither party gained any advantage, but in the night Longstreet and his army arrived, and on the next day they attacked the Unionists so fiercely that part of them were routed; but the brave Gen. Thomas, who commanded one of the Union divisions, stood his ground until night, when he retreated in good order to Chattanooga, and so, though the battle was lost, the city and army were saved.

CHICOPEE (*chik-o-pe'*), a town of Massachusetts, on the Connecticut River, near Springfield; pop. 14,000, or about as large as Keokuk, Iowa. It is noted for its cotton and woolen mills and brass and iron foundries. The Ames Manufacturing Company makes many machines and bronze cannon, and more swords than any other manufactory in the United States. Among other things which have been cast in their foundries are some beautiful bronze doors in the Capitol at Washington and a statue of General Washington on horse-back, now in the public garden at Boston. Chicopee was settled in 1640, but was a part of Springfield until 1848.

CHILI (*chil'le*), a country of South America, on the Pacific Ocean, S. of Bolivia; area 130,000 square miles, or not quite so large as California; pop. 2,715,000, or a little more than that of Missouri; capital, SANTIAGO. Chili also claims PATAGONIA and TIERRA DEL FUEGO, which, if given to it, would double its size. The surface is mountainous, being mostly made up of the western side of the Andes, which are here very high. Some of the peaks are more than four miles high, and there are more than twenty volcanoes. The highest peak is Aconcagua, which is commonly called the most lofty of the ANDES. Earthquakes are frequent, and much damage has been done by them.

Chili is very rich in minerals, especially in silver and copper, and new mines are opened every year. One of the richest of the silver mines was found by an Indian, who built a fire against a rock one night, and found in the morning that the whole face of the rock was covered with silver which had melted out. Not much of the soil is good for farming, yet it is so rich that Chili sends to other countries considerable wheat. As the country is south of the equator, the hottest months are January and February. The people, who are largely of Spanish or of Spanish and Indian descent, are more enterprising than most other South Americans. In the southern part are many wild Indians called Araucanians, a brave people who have never been conquered. Chili is a republic much like that of the United States.

Chili was a part of the dominions of the Inca of Peru when Pizarro conquered that country. The Spaniards tried to conquer Chili also, and built some cities in the northern part, but could not get the southern part where the Araucanians lived. The country belonged to the Spaniards until 1818, when it became independent. In 1879 a war broke out between Chili and Bolivia and Peru, in which Peru was defeated.

CHIMÆRA (*ki-me'rah*). See BELLEROPHON.

CHIM·BO·RA'ZO. See ANDES.

CHINA (*chi'-nah*), a country of E. Asia, on the Pacific Ocean; area 4,000,000 square miles, or an eighth more than that of the United States; pop. said to be 400,000,000, or six and a half times as many as that of the United States; capital, PEKING. China has thus about one twelfth of all the land on the globe, and about one third of all the population of the world. What is called China Proper is only about one third of all its territory, and lies in the southeast part; the rest is made up of Mongolia, Thibet, Mantchooria, Corea, and some islands, which are ruled by China.

The surface is mostly made up of the valleys of the great rivers Yang-Tse Kiang, Hoang-Ho, and some others. Several of these valleys are divided by high mountains, and in the north and east are great sandy deserts. Besides the great rivers, China has many canals, one of which, called the Grand Canal, is the longest in the world, and many thousand miles of roads; and by means of boats on the rivers and canals, and wagons and caravans of camels on the roads, a very great trade is carried on with all parts. There are no railroads, and the people will not let any be built, because they are afraid that the graves of their ancestors (whom they worship) will be disturbed, the dead not being generally buried in cemeteries, as in other countries, but anywhere along the roads or in the fields. In 1876 a railroad about twenty miles long was opened at Shanghai, but the people disliked it so much that the government bought it and destroyed it. The country is rich in coal, salt, metals, kaolin or porcelain clay, and precious stones, but mines are not much worked.

Most of the people are farmers, tilling the soil being thought the most honorable business. Every year the emperor goes with his nobles to a place called the Sacred Field, and plows a furrow as an example for the people. Great quantities of rice and other grains are raised, but not enough to feed the vast population, and much has to be brought from Siam and other countries. Most of the tea and silk used in the world come from China, and great quantities of porcelain and lacquered ware, straw hats, rattans, palm-leaf fans, pictures, and

Chinese One-wheel Wagon with Sail.

firecrackers and fireworks (C. C. T., 236, I., l.) are brought from there. In the interior of China may often be seen curious one-wheeled wagons, something like a large wheelbarrow, moved partly by means of a sail spread to catch the wind and partly by a donkey in front aided by a man behind who keeps the whole steady by means of a strap across his shoulders.

The people of China are called Mongols. They are tawny yellow, with coarse black hair, commonly braided behind in a long queue, and eyes pointing downward toward the nose. They are peaceable and industrious, and though the poor can earn but a few cents apiece a day, they generally save money. Nearly all the men can read and write, but girls are not taught much. They are proud of their country, and though they wander all over the world to make money, they almost always go back to live, and if they die their bodies are sent back to be buried. They are skilful workmen, and can make almost anything if they have a pattern to copy, yet they seldom improve on things or make things which have not been made before. They must have been different in old times, for they are thought to have been the first to find out the mariner's compass, gunpowder.

printing, and the way of making porcelain, silk, and paper. China is ruled by an emperor, and the principal officers are called mandarins, who are chosen by examination from among the best-educated people. The religion of the educated people is that of CONFUCIUS, but most of the common people worship BUDDHA.

China is the most ancient nation in the world, and had a government long before Greece was civilized, but not much is known about it. In Europe in old times it was called Cathay, and it was Cathay which Columbus was in search of when he found America. The Chinese themselves call China Proper Chungkwoh, " Middle Kingdom," not because they think it to be the centre of the world, as some say, but be-

The Great Wall of China.

cause in the time of Confucius it was divided into several kingdoms, of which the middle one gave the name to the whole. More than two hundred years ago China was conquered by the Tartars, who still rule it. Before that there had been many wars with them, and the great wall was built more than two hundred years before Christ to keep them out. This wall, which is built along the north side of China Proper, is more than 1200 miles long, and in some places is six times as high as a man, and wide enough for six horsemen to ride abreast on it. The Chinese have always been very jealous of foreigners, and until within a few years have kept their country shut up; but now they have ministers in the principal foreign countries, and have opened several of their ports for foreign trade.

CHIRON (*ki'ron*), in Greek fable, the most celebrated of the CENTAURS. He was not only a great hunter, but also very wise and learned. He taught astronomy to

Hercules, and physic to Esculapius, and had many other pupils who came to his cave at the foot of Mt. Pelion to learn of him. He was killed by Hercules, who in a fight with some other centaurs shot him by accident. Chiron afterward became the constellation Sagittarius.

CHOC'TAWS. See AMERICAN INDIANS.

CHOSROES (*koz'ro-ez*), or **KHOSRU I.,** King of Persia from A.D. 531 to 579. His reign was marked by great victories in war and wise conduct in peace. His wars were chiefly against the Greek Empire, from which he took Antioch and other cities of Syria, and forced its emperors to pay him tribute. He enlarged his kingdom, and made his subjects love him by ruling justly and kindly. He lived to be eighty years old, and the forty-eight years of his reign have been called the golden age of Persia.

CHOSROES II., a king of Persia, grandson of Chosroes I., came to the throne in 591. He also was a great conqueror, but cared more for his own glory than for the good of the people. He sent out large armies to fight the Greeks, while he enjoyed at home the greatest splendor and luxury. His palaces, of which he built a new one every year, were wonders of the world. He had fifty thousand horses and twelve thousand wives; and his thrones were built of gold, inlaid with precious jewels. About A.D. 627 the Roman emperor HERAC-LIUS entered Persia with a strong army, destroyed the palaces and captured the treasures of Chosroes, and in less than six years reconquered all the territories that the Persian king had taken. At last his subjects, led by his own son, rebelled against him, and put him to death (628), after he had been king for thirty-seven years. It was during this king's reign that Mohammed began to preach. He wrote to Chosroes and commanded him to

recognize him as the prophet of God, but the king tore the letter to pieces. When Mohammed heard of it, he said, "Thus will God tear his kingdom and reject his prayers."

CHRISTIANIA (*kris-te-ah'ne-ah*), a city, capital of Norway, at the head of Christiania Fiord, about 55 miles from the sea; pop. 130,000. In the castle of Aggerhuus, which commands the harbor, are kept the records and regalia of the kingdom. The city has a university, a fine library, museums, and an observatory. It was founded in 1624 by King Christian IV.

CHURCH, Frederick Edwin, an American painter, born in Hartford, Conn., May 4, 1826. He paints landscapes, and his views of South American scenery, his "Niagara," and his pictures of the Labrador coast, are perhaps more widely known than the works of any other American painter. He has a studio in New York and one near Hudson, N. Y.

CHURUBUSCO (*choo-roo-bus'ko*), a small village of Mexico, 6 miles S. of the city of Mexico, on the Churubusco River. One of the principal roads to Mexico crosses the river there by a stone bridge, and in the village is the stone convent of San Pablo. During the war between Mexico and the United States the Mexicans under SANTA ANNA had a strongly fortified camp at Contreras near Churubusco. General Scott and his army drove them out of this camp, after a hard battle (Aug. 20, 1847). On the same day Santa Anna made a stand at the bridge and in the convent of Churubusco, and another bloody battle ensued, in which the Mexicans were completely routed. In the two battles they lost 4000 soldiers killed and wounded, and 3000 were captured besides many cannons. The American loss was less than a thousand in killed and wounded.

CIC'E-RO, Marcus Tullius, a

famous Roman orator and statesman, born at Arpinum, about 70 miles from Rome, Jan. 3, 106 B.C. His father, who was a rich knight, had him finely educated. When quite young he wrote poems which were much admired, but none have been preserved. He studied law, and when twenty-five years old began to speak in the Forum, and in a few years rose to be one of the greatest orators of his time. After

Cicero.

holding several other offices, he became consul (63 B.C.). Catiline, who was a defeated candidate for this office, had formed a plot to burn Rome and kill the senators; but Cicero found out the plot, and made in the Senate four speeches against CATILINE, which are among the most celebrated specimens of ancient oratory.

In 59 B.C. Cicero's enemies got into power and he was banished, but he was recalled two years after-

ward. In the civil war he took the part of Pompey against Cæsar, but after the battle of Pharsalia he submitted to Cæsar, who pardoned him. He thought the killing of Cæsar to be right, and he made several fierce speeches, called Philippics, against Mark Antony, who became his enemy. When Antony got into power, he ordered him to be killed. Cicero fled, but the soldiers overtook him and killed him in his litter (Dec. 7, 43 B.C.), when sixty-three years old. Cicero wrote many books, but only a few of them have been preserved.

CID (*sid*), the name given by the Moors to a famous Christian warrior who fought against them in Spain. His real name was Ruy or Rodrigo Diaz, but he became such a terror to the Moors and seemed to them to be so superior to all others that they called him *El Seid* (Arabic for "The Lord"), which the Spaniards made into Cid. They also called him *El Campeador* (Spanish for "The Champion"), and he was finally almost always called Cid Campeador (Lord Champion). The deeds of the Cid are so mixed with fable in the books about him that it is almost impossible to tell what he really did. One of the oldest poems in the Spanish language, called the "Poem of the Cid," gives a long account of him and his battles. From it SOUTHEY wrote his "Chronicle of the Cid;" the French poet CORNEILLE also wrote a play called the "Cid," and a great many other plays, poems, and romances have been written about him. He is supposed to have been born about 1040, and to have died in Valencia in 1099.

CILICIA (*si-lish'e-ah*). See ASIA MINOR.

CIMON (*si''mon*), a famous Greek statesman and general, son of MILTIADES, born about 510 B.C. His father, getting into debt, was put in prison and died there, and it is said that Cimon allowed himself to be imprisoned in his place until the debt was paid. Afterward he distinguished himself at Salamis (480 B.C.). He and ARISTIDES commanded the Athenian ships sent with other Greek ships against the Persians, and when PAUSANIAS was disgraced, they were given the command of the fleet. Cimon won many victories, and finally utterly defeated the Persian fleet at the mouth of the Eurymedon (466 B.C.). These victories gave him great fame and wealth, and he became the most popular statesman of Athens, and the rival of PERICLES. But after a time the Athenians accused him of taking bribes, and though acquitted at the time, he was finally banished (459 B.C.). Eight years afterward, when a Spartan army was marching against Athens, Cimon begged to be allowed to return. When this was refused, he asked his friends to fight and prove by their bravery that he was sincere. At the battle of Tanagra they carried his armor as a standard, and when the Athenians were defeated they fought around his armor until they were all killed. Three years afterward Cimon was recalled to Athens at the request of Pericles, and he was finally put in command of a fleet which was sent against the Persians. While besieging Citium, a city of Cyprus, he died, at the age of about sixty-one years (449 B.C.).

CINCINNATI (*sin-sin-nat'te*), the largest city in Ohio, and the ninth in the United States in population, on the Ohio River; pop. 297,000, or a little smaller than San Francisco, Cal. It is surrounded by beautiful hills, from which a splendid view is had of the city, the villages around it, and the winding river. Though the banks of the Ohio are high, its waters rise every spring from fifty to fifty-five feet, and sometimes even overflow the banks, and enter the streets in some places. There are two fine bridges across it to Covington and to Newport, in Kentucky; one, a suspension bridge, cost nearly two million dollars. One of the principal ornaments of Cincinnati is its great fountain, which is one of the most beautiful in the United States. It is made of bronze, and has many bronze statues on it, while at the top is the statue of a woman with arms outspread, and the water pouring like rain from her open hands. This fountain, which cost nearly $200,000, was made in MUNICH.

Cincinnati is a very busy place, and has a large trade and many factories and beer breweries. Most of the breweries are in a part of the city called "Over the Rhine," because it is inhabited almost entirely by Germans, who form about a quarter of the whole population. The most important business of Cincinnati is the killing and packing of hogs, of which nearly a million are killed every year—more than in any other city except Chicago. On this account it is a common joke to call Cincinnati "Porkopolis" ("City of Pork").

Cincinnati was named after the "Society of the Cincinnati," an association formed by the officers of the American army at the close of the Revolution. The society itself was named after the Roman CINCINNATUS. The city was first settled in 1788 by emigrants from New Jersey, and it became a city in 1814.

CIN·CIN·NA'TUS, Lucius Quintius, a famous Roman patriot, born about 519 B.C. On account of the constant quarrels between the two classes of the people, the patricians and the plebeians, in one of which his son had been killed, he grew disgusted with public affairs, and went to live on a small farm outside of the city. He was plowing in a field one day when messengers were sent by the senate to bring him back to Rome, where his advice was needed in a difficult matter. An army sent out to fight the Æqui, with whom the Romans were then at war, had fallen into great danger, the enemy having caught them in a narrow pass-way between the mountains, and blockaded them so that they could not get out. Nobody knew how to help them, until it was proposed to send for Cincinnatus and make him dictator. When he came, he ordered all the shops and places of business to be closed, called all the men in the city together, and marching by night silently surrounded the Æqui as they had surrounded the Roman army. The enemy, being thus shut in between two armies, were forced to lay down their arms.

After this great victory Cincinnatus returned to his farm, but many years after (439) he was again made dictator, to settle a tumult in the city. He held the office for twenty-one days, until the disturbance ended in the death of the plebeian Spurius Mælius, who had tried to make himself king; he then returned again to his farm, to leave it no more during his life.

CINNA (*cin'nah*), **Lucius Cornelius,** a noted Roman, who, though a patrician by birth, took the part of MARIUS in the civil war. In the year 88 B.C. he was elected consul, but for some illegal acts was driven from Rome, and his office and citizenship taken from him. In the year 86 B.C. he went back to Rome with Marius and an army, and put to death many of the patricians. After Marius died he raised an army to fight against SULLA in Greece, but was killed by his soldiers when about to set sail (84 B.C.)

CINQUE (*sink*) **PORTS,** the name given to the English seaport towns of Dover, Sandwich, Hastings, Romney, and Hythe, which had certain rights given them by William the Conqueror. They in turn were obliged to furnish a certain number of ships for the public service when the king wanted them.

CIRCASSIA (*sir-kash'yah*), a country in the Caucasus Mountains, N.E. of the Black Sea, belonging to Russia; area 25,000 square miles, or a little larger than West Virginia; pop. about 300,000, or not half that of West Virginia. It is a very wild region, almost covered with mountains, the roads through which are in very narrow passes, where often only one man can walk at a time. The name Circassia means country of the robbers, and was given by the Tartars, who hated the Circassians. They were, however, a brave and fine race. In 1829 the Sultan of Turkey gave Circassia to Russia, though he had no right to do so, because it did not belong to him. The Russians tried to keep the country, but the Circassians fought bravely against them; finally, rather than submit, nearly all of them left their mountain land and settled in Turkey; since then Circassia has formed a part of Russia.

CIR'CE (Greek *Kirke*), in Greek fable, a sorceress noted for her magic arts, who lived in the island of Ææa, near the coast of Italy. ULYSSES stopped at her island, and sent some of his sailors to ask for food. She gave them meat and wine, and while they were eating turned all of them, excepting Eurylochus, into pigs. He went back to the ship and told Ulysses what had happened; and Ulysses, aided by Mercury, who had given him a magic herb that saved him from Circe's enchantments, went to her palace and made her turn the pigs into men again. She afterward fell in love with Ulysses, and he and his companions stayed there a year.

CIVITA VECCHIA (*che've-tah vek'ke-ah*), a city of Italy, in the Mediterranean Sea, 37 miles N.W. of Rome; pop. 12,000, or about as large as Portsmouth, Ohio. It is the principal port for travelers going to Rome. The harbor, one of the best in Italy, is formed by two long marble piers, stretching out from the city, with a breakwater in front of them to keep out the waves. The city is defended by a strong fortress, designed by Michael Angelo. Water is brought to it through a stone aqueduct, the foundations of which, as well as those of the piers and breakwater, were made by the Emperor TRA-JAN, who founded the city. In old times it was called the Port of Trajan. Civita Vecchia means old city.

CLAR'EN·DON, Edward Hyde, Earl of, a British statesman and historian, born at Dinton, Feb. 18, 1608. He was first of the party against King Charles I.; but when he found to what lengths Parliament was going, he went over to the side of the king, who made him one of his privy councillors. When the royal cause failed,he went to France with the young Prince of Wales, afterward Charles II., and spent with him in France and Holland the long years of his exile. On the Restoration in 1660, he returned to England with Charles, who rewarded his faithfulness by making him Earl of Clarendon and Lord Chancellor. The reign of Charles II. was altogether unfortunate, and Clarendon was blamed for things that were not his fault. He wanted justice done to all parties, and would stand blindly by none. In this way he offended every party, and his enemies finally had him banished. King Charles was mean enough to let his faithful servant go a second time into exile. During his banishment Lord Clarendon wrote his great work, the "History of the Rebellion." He sent a touching letter to Charles, asking to be allowed to come home to die, but the heartless monarch took no notice of it, and Clarendon died at Rouen, when sixty-five years old (Dec. 9, 1674).

CLAUDE LORRAIN (*klaud lor-rane'*), a famous French painter, born in Lorraine in 1600. His real name was Claude Gelée, but when he became famous he was called Claude Lorrain, which means "Claude the Lorrainer." When a boy he worked with a pastry-cook, but when twelve or thirteen years old his parents died and he went to Rome with some young artists as a valet. There he found employment with a good painter, for whom he ground colors and at the same time learned to paint. After many struggles and much hardship he became one of the best painters of his time, and was called the prince and poet of landscape painters. During his life his pictures were so much admired that other artists tried to imitate him, and to sell their works for his. To prevent this, he kept a book of drawings of his own pictures, with dates and some notes, so that his works could be known from others. This book which he called his "Book of Truth," is owned by the Duke of Devonshire in England. Very large prices are now paid for Claude's pictures whenever any of them are sold. He died in Rome when eighty-two years old (Nov. 23, 1682).

CLAUDIUS (*claw'de-us*), **Marcus Aurelius Claudius Gothicus,** a Roman emperor, born in Illyria in A.D., 214. He was of a poor family, but won fame as a soldier, and when the Emperor Gallienus was murdered the soldiers made him emperor. The next year he gained a great victory over the GOTHS in Macedonia, from which he took the name of Gothicus. He died soon after (270), when fifty-six years old, of a disease which broke out in the camp of the Goths and spread to his own army.

CLAUDIUS, Tiberius Drusus Nero Germanicus, a Roman emperor, born at Lugdunum (Lyons), Aug. 1, 10 B.C. He was weak and timid in his youth, and was treated with neglect even by his mother; for which Augustus left him a fortune when he died, to which Tiberius largely added on his death. He was looked upon as so contemptible by Caligula that he escaped the cruelties of that tyrant, and when Caligula was killed (A.D. 41,), he was made emperor by the soldiers. This was the first time that an emperor was chosen by the army. He was disposed to be a kind and just ruler, but was led to do some cruel things by his wives and favorites. The conquest of Britain was begun by him, and it would probably have become a Roman state had not Claudius been recalled to Rome; and from his conquests in Germany he took the title of Germanicus. He did much good to his people and greatly improved Rome, building the harbor of Ostia and the Claudian Aqueduct, which supplied the city with water. He was poisoned by his wife Agrippina, who wanted the empire for her son NERO, in A.D. 54.

CLAUDIUS CRASSUS, Appius, a Roman decemvir, or one of the ten judges chosen to make laws and to rule the state. As Appius sat in the Forum he saw a beautiful girl, named Virginia, go by every day with her nurse to school. He fell in love with her, and got one of his friends, named Marcus Claudius, to claim that she was the daughter of one of his slaves. Virginia was seized and brought before the decemvir, but the excitement was so great that Appius did not dare to decide the case until the next day. Her father, Lucius Virginius, an officer in the army, hurried home when he heard of this and claimed his daughter. But notwithstanding his oath that Virginia was his own child, Appius ordered her to be given to Marcus Claudius, thinking thus to get her himself. Virginius then seized a knife from a butcher and killed her before the judgment-

seat, and, hurrying back to camp with the bloody knife in his hands, aroused the soldiers, who marched with him to Rome and overthrew the decemvirs. Appius was put into prison, where he killed himself (449 B.C.).

CLAUDIUS NERO, a Roman general, famous for his victory over HASDRUBAL in 207 B.C. He was in the south of Italy fighting against HANNIBAL, when he heard that Hasdrubal, Hannibal's brother, had crossed the Alps with an army. Before Hannibal knew of his brother's coming, Claudius joined his army with another Roman army under Livius, and defeated Hasdrubal in a great battle on the banks of the river Metaurus. It is said that Hannibal first heard of this disaster from seeing the head of his brother, which, by order of Claudius, was thrown into his camp. This was one of the most important battles ever fought; for if Hasdrubal had joined Hannibal with his fresh troops, it is probable that Rome would have fallen.

CLAY, Henry, an American statesman, born near Richmond, Virginia, April 12, 1777. He had little education, and before he was fifteen he was sent to Richmond to earn his

Henry Clay.

living in a store. He soon left this to become a clerk in a lawyer's office; and by the time he was twenty-one had fitted himself to practice law. He set up an office of his own in Lexington, Kentucky. His winning manners and pleasant disposition made him many friends, and being an eloquent speaker, he had great success in his profession.

When about twenty-six years old he was sent to the legislature for the first time, and four years afterward (1806) was elected to Congress. From this time till the time of his death he was almost always in some important public position. He was sent to England to make arrangements for peace after the war of 1812; was speaker in the House of Representatives for many years; was Secretary of State while John Quincy Adams was President; and twice ran for President himself, getting a great many votes, though he was both times defeated.

He said of himself that he would rather be right than be President; and very few men have been more generally beloved and respected than Henry Clay, both in his public and private life. He died at the age of seventy-five (June 29, 1852).

CLEARCHUS (*kle-ar'kus*), a Spartan general who commanded about 13,000 Greeks in the army of CYRUS THE YOUNGER when he tried to conquer the throne of Persia from his brother Artaxerxes II. When Cyrus was defeated at Cunaxa (401 B.C.), Clearchus and his chief officers were seized by treachery and put to death.

CLI'O. See MUSES.

CLEM'ENT, the name of fourteen popes of Rome.

Clement II., elected in 1046, was the first German pope. Died in 1047.

Clement III., elected in 1187, got up the third Crusade. Died in 1191.

Clement V., a Frenchman, elected in 1305, made Avignon his capital instead of Rome to please Philip the Fair of France. He put down the order of the Templars. Died in 1314.

Clement VII., who became pope in 1523, joined Francis I. of France against the Emperor Charles V., and when Rome was taken by the emperor's troops he was kept a prisoner for several months. It was he who refused to divorce Henry VIII. of England from Queen Catherine. He died in 1534.

Clement XIV., who became pope in 1769, was a very good and learned man. He put down the order of the Jesuits, but it was afterward set up again. He died in 1774.

CLEOPATRA (*kle-o-pa'trah* or *kle-op'a-trah*), Queen of Egypt, born 69 B.C. Her father, King Ptolemy Auletes, died when she was seventeen years old, and left his throne to her and her younger brother Ptolemy. Cleopatra is said to have been a wonder of beauty and grace; she knew ten different languages, her voice was like soft music, and she had such charming ways that nobody could resist her, and she knew well that they could not. So when Ptolemy tried to take all the power away from her, she made up her mind to ask Julius Cæsar, who was then in Alexandria, to help her. She could not go to him openly, because she was wached by her brother's friends; so she got a servant to carry her on his back in a roll of carpeting into the room of Cæsar, and when the carpet was unrolled the beautiful girl sprang out, threw herself at the feet of the Roman general, and begged him to take her part. Cæsar not only promised that he would, but swore that he would be her lover and slave too; and he did not leave Egypt until Ptolemy had been killed and Cleopatra had got back her throne.

Some years after, Cæsar was murdered and Mark ANTONY became the greatest man in Rome; so Cleopatra thought she would try to make him her slave too. Antony was then at Tarsus, a city of Asia, on the river Cydnus. She had built a splendid ship ornamented with gold and silver; the sails were of purple silk, and the silver oars kept time to soft, sweet music. Under a canopy of cloth of gold,

Cleopatra lay on a couch, with a crown on her head, to represent the goddess Venus, while beautiful boys with wings were fanning her. Antony was so charmed that he followed her back to Egypt, where he lived with her for some time.

Cleopatra was with Antony at the battle of ACTIUM, and was the first to fly. Antony followed her back to Egypt; after he had killed himself, she was taken prisoner by Octavius (AUGUSTUS), who ordered her to be watched carefully, intending to take her to Rome to grace his triumph. But she got a man to bring her a poisonous serpent called an asp, in a basket of figs, and dressing herself in her royal robes, with her crown on her head, put the asp on her breast, and died in a few moments from its bite, when thirty-nine years old (Aug. 30, 30 B.C.).

CLEVELAND, a city of N. Ohio, on Lake Erie, laid out in 1796; pop. 261,000, or a little larger than Buffalo, N. Y. Next to Cincinnati, it is the largest city in the State, and it is one of the finest in the country. The streets are very wide and handsome, and have so many shade-trees that Cleveland is often called the "Forest City." The port is one of the best on Lake Erie, and many railroads meet in the city, giving it a large trade, especially in coal, iron ore, petroleum, and grain. Cleveland is noted for its great petroleum works, more petroleum being refined there than in any other city expect Pittsburgh. There are also large iron-works and manufactories of sulphuric acid, railroad cars, farmers' tools, etc.

CLEVELAND, Grover, twenty-second and twenty-fourth president of the United States, born in Caldwell, N. J., March 18, 1837. In 1841 his parents removed to Onondaga County, N. Y., where he received a common-school education. In 1855 he entered

a law office in Buffalo, and in 1859 he was admitted to the bar. As a young lawyer he became so favorably known that in 1863 he was appointed assistant district attorney for Erie County. In

Grover Cleveland.

1870 he was elected sheriff of Erie County; in 1881, mayor of Buffalo; in 1882, governor of New York; and in 1884, and again in 1892, president.

CLINTON, DeWitt, an American statesman, born at Little Britain, Orange County, N. Y., March 2, 1769. He was the son of General James Clinton of the Revolutionary war, was graduated at Columbia College in 1786, studied law, and became (1790) private secretary to his uncle, Gen. George Clinton, then governor of New York. He was a member of the legislature in 1797, and two years later was elected to the U. S. Senate. He was afterward mayor of New York, and governor of the State. The opening of the Erie Canal was due to his energy and perseverance. He died when 59 years old (Feb. 11, 1828).

CLINTON, Sir Henry, a noted English soldier, born in 1738. He was a major-general at the battle of Bunker Hill (1775), and became commander of the British army in North America in 1778. He was forced by Washington to leave Philadelphia in June of that year, but besieged and took Charleston in the following May. His command was given to Sir Guy Carleton in 1781, and Clinton returned to England. He was soon after made governor of Gibraltar, where he died when fifty-seven years old (Dec. 24, 1795).

CLIVE, Robert, Lord, Baron of Plassey, a British general, founder of the British Empire in India, born at Styche in Shropshire, Sept. 29, 1725. He was a troublesome boy with a fiery temper, whom his father found so hard to manage that he got a place for him, when he was about eighteen, in the employ of the British East India Company, and sent him to Madras. Being without friends, he grew discouraged and twice tried to shoot himself, but failed both times. Soon after he got the position of an ensign in the army, and the chance to show himself to be a brave soldier and able officer.

The French were then trying to drive the English out of India, and were helped by one native ruler, while the English were helped by another. The French had been successful almost everywhere, when Clive, who had risen rapidly through his bravery and skill, turned the tide in favor of the English. He took possession of the town of Arcot with a force of 500 men, and held it for fifty days against a besieging army of 10,000. The enemy drove elephants, with iron plates on their foreheads, against the gates to batter them down; but Clive's men sent a volley of musket-balls among them, and the elephants turned and rushed upon their drivers, killing great numbers as they went. The besiegers were driven off at last with the loss of hundreds, but of Clive's men only five or six were

killed. He followed up this victory with attacks upon their cities, until he conquered the French everywhere and established the English power.

In 1753 he went back to England and was received with great honor, and a splendid sword adorned with diamonds was presented to him by the East India Company; and the next year he returned to India. Soon afterward, Surajah Dowlah, the Indian Nabob of Bengal, took CALCUTTA, and killed his English prisoners by putting them in the Black Hole. Clive marched against the Nabob's troops, captured Calcutta and other places, and finally, in one great battle, at Plassey (June 23, 1757) defeated an army of 60,000 men with a force of 3000.

He was rewarded with high honors and great sums of money for these and other victories. In 1760 he went to England again, was made a Lord, with the title of Baron Clive of Plassey, and became a member of Parliament. In 1765 he went back to India as governor and commander-in-chief of the British possessions in Bengal; but returned to England again two years afterward. He committed suicide on account of ill-health, which affected his mind, at the age of forty-nine (Nov. 22, 1774).

CLO'THO. See FATES.

CLO'VIS, the founder of the French monarchy, born at Tournai, about 465. He was the son of Childeric, and succeeded him as king of the Franks in 481. France at that time was called GAUL, and most of it was in the hands of the Romans. Clovis defeated the Roman governor, and thus became the owner of the greater part of Gaul, which in time was called after the Franks, France. Clovis had a Christian wife, Clotilda, who was the cause of his becoming a Christian. In one of his battles he was near losing the victory, when he made a vow that he would be a Christian if the God of Clotilda would give him aid. When the battle was won, he was baptized with 3000 of his subjects. He died in Paris when about forty-six years old (511), dividing his empire among his four sons. Clovis, which the Germans call Chlodwig, is the same name as Louis or Lewis.

CLY·TEM·NES'·TRA. See ORESTES.

COBLENTZ (*ko'blenz*), a city of Germany, in Prussia, at the junction of the rivers Rhine and Moselle; pop. 32,000, or about the same as Yonkers, N. Y. It is very strongly fortified, and on the opposite side of the Rhine, and connected with it by a bridge of boats, is the fortress of EHRENBREITSTEIN.

Coblentz was anciently called Confluentes, because it was at the confluence (flowing together) of the two rivers, and from this has come the present name.

CO'CHIN CHI'NA, a French colony in S. INDO-CHINA; area 23,-000 square miles, or about the same as West Virginia; pop. 1,800,-000, or about the same as Georgia; capital, SAIGON. It has a rich soil and a warm climate, and produces all kinds of fruits and plants which grow in hot countries. Rice grows everywhere, and great quantities are sent to other countries. The people are much like those of CAMBODIA.

Cochin China was a part of Cambodia, but was conquered by the French in 1861.

COL'CHIS. See ARGONAUTS.

COLD HARBOR. See CHICKA-HOMINY.

COHOES (*ko-hoze'*), a city of E. New York, on the Mohawk River where it joins the Hudson, 8 miles N. of Albany; pop. 22,500, or about as large as Springfield, Mo. A mile from its mouth the Mohawk has a beautiful fall, seventy feet high. The water power from this has been increased by dams, and it is used in the city for large cotton-mills and for knitting-mills, which produce one third of all the stockings and knit goods made in the United States. Cohoes also contains a rolling-mill, foundries, and large manufactories of pins, knitting-needles, axes, and many other things.

The first manufactory was built at Cohoes in 1811, when the site was a wilderness. Since 1840 the place has grown rapidly.

COLE, Thomas, a famous American landscape-painter, born in Lancashire, England, Feb. 1, 1801. His father, a woolen manufacturer, came to America when Thomas was eighteen years old, and settled in Steubenville, Ohio. Thomas worked in his father's shop for two years, but the coming of a portrait-painter to the village made him wish to be an artist. After a few lessons he set to work to paint pictures, and traveled for a while painting portraits and landscapes, but often had to paint chairs and japanned ware for a living. At last he came to New York, and by hard work succeeded in making himself one of the best landscape-painters in this country. He then became famous and made so much money that he was able to go to Europe and study the works of the old painters. After he came back he painted some well-known pictures, among the best of which are five called "The Course of Empire," and four called "The Voyage of Life." The last, showing childhood, youth, manhood, and old age, are very popular, and are well known through engravings. Cole died at Catskill, New York, when forty-seven years old (Feb. 11, 1848).

COLE'RIDGE, Samuel Taylor, a noted English poet, born at Ottery Saint Mary, Devonshire, Oct. 21, 1772. He was left an orphan when nine years old, and was sent by a friend to school at Christ's Hospital, London. He used to translate

Latin and Greek so well, and talk so charmingly, even when a child, that visitors to the school would stop to listen to him, and he was called "the inspired charity boy." The happiest time of Coleridge's life was when he and Wordsworth lived near each other in Somersetshire; they used to wander over the hills together, and then he wrote some of his best poems, "Ye Ancient Mariner" and "Christabel." Coleridge, Southey, and Wordsworth were called "the Lake Poets,' because they lived near the lakes of Cumberland and Westmoreland. Coleridge died in London at the age of sixty-two (July 25, 1834).

Hartley Coleridge, his eldest son, born Sept. 19, 1796, was also a fine poet, and wrote some of the best sonnets in the English language. He died when fifty-two years old (Jan. 6, 1849).

COLIGNI (*ko-leen'ye*), **Gaspard de,** a noted French Huguenot leader, born at Châtillon-sur-Loing, Feb. 16, 1517. He was a brave and determined soldier, and people used to say that his enemies were most afraid of him after they had conquered him. Once when severely wounded, so that he could not ride on horseback, he led the retreat from a litter, in such good order that the enemy were afraid to encounter an army commanded by such a brave and skillful leader. Coligni was the first victim in the St. Bartholomew massacre, when thirty thousand Protestants were killed by the Catholics in one day. A band of murderers entered his room; for a few moments they were awed by the presence of the great soldier, but soon one of them rushed forward and stabbed him in the stomach with a spear; his body was thrown into the court-yard, then dragged through the streets, and at last placed on a gallows, where it is said that Charles IX. went, with some of his courtiers to look at it.

After night some of Coligni's faithful servants stole his body and buried it at Chantilly. He was murdered in Paris when fifty-five years old (Aug. 24, 1572).

COLMAN (*kole'man*), **Samuel,** an American painter, born at Portland, Me., in 1832. He made his art-studies in Europe, and has spent most of his art-life there. He is a landscape-painter of much merit.

COLOGNE (*ko-lone'*), a city of Germany, in Prussia, on the Rhine; pop. 240,000, or a little larger than Pittsburgh, Pa. It is surrounded by strong walls and protected by forts, and is connected with the other side of the river by an iron railway bridge and a bridge of boats. The city is chiefly noted for the manufacture of eau de Cologne, or Cologne water, of which hundreds of thousands of bottles are made every year; but it has also a very large trade in grain, wine, and oil. The great cathedral, begun more than 600 years ago (1250), was finished in 1880, the last stone being laid in September of that year. It is very beautiful, and is said to be the largest Gothic cathedral in Europe. It is built in the form of a cross, and its two towers are higher than the Pyramids. In the picture their height is compared with that of many other public buildings. In the church of St. Ursula are shown many bones, said to be those of St. Ursula and her troop of 11,000 virgins who were massacred at Cologne by the Huns.

Cologne was first built by the Romans (A.D. 51) and called Colonia Agrippina, after the mother of NERO, and from this comes its present name. It was once much more important than it is now.

COLOMBIA (*ko-lom'be-ah*), **United States of,** a N.W. country of South America; area 500,000 square miles, or not quite twice as large as Texas; pop. about 4,000,000, or nearly the

Comparative Heights of Famous Buildings.

1, 2, Cologne Cathedral; 3, Great Pyramid; 4, Strasburg Cathedral; 5, St. Stephen's Church, Vienna; 6, Antwerp Cathedral; 7, St. Peter's, Rome; 8, Salisbury Cathedral; 9, St. Paul's, London; 10, Tower of Asinelli, Bologna; 11, Santa Maria del Fiori, Florence; 12, Kuttub-Minar, Delhi; 13, Porcelain Tower, Nanking; 14, Notre Dame, Paris; 15, Trajan's Bridge, Alcantara; 16, York Cathedral; 17, St. Sophia, Constantinople; 18, Fire Monument in London; 19, Leaning Tower, Pisa; 20, Column Vendome, Paris; 21, Tower of Garisenda, Bologna; 24, Trajan's Column, Rome; 23, Aqueduct of Segovia; 24, Obelisk in Rome; 25, Obelisk in Paris; 26, Sphinx.

same as that of Illinois; capital, Bo-GOTA. The western part is covered with high mountains of the Andes chain, on whose tops snow lies all the year round, while at their base it is always summer, and oranges and cocoa-nuts grow about the houses. On the north is the Isthmus of PANAMA, most of which belongs to Colombia. In the central and eastern parts are great grassy plains, where vast herds of horses and cattle feed in the rainy season; but the south-eastern part is all covered with wild forests, where jaguars, monkeys, and other wild beasts roam, the only people being a few roving Indians. Hardly anything is known of this forest region; the great river, Içá (e-sah), which flows through it was explored for the first time a few years ago. Neither this nor the rivers that flow into the Orinoco are much used for travel; but the Magdalena, which flows north into the Caribbean sea, is navigated by steamboats. The chief trade is in cinchona bark, from which quinine is made, hides, indigo, and Panama hats. There are rich mines of gold, silver, and other metals, and many precious stones, among which are the finest emeralds in the world. The government is much like that of the United States of America, but the people are always quarreling and changing their rulers.

Colombia was first visited about 1500 by the Spaniards, who soon conquered the Indians and named the country New Granada. In 1811 the people declared themselves independent of Spain. For a long time the country was called the Republic of New Granada, but in 1861 the name was changed to the United States of Colombia.

CO-LOM'BO, the capital and principal sea-port of Ceylon, on the W. coast of the island; pop. 110,000, or a little larger than Denver, Col. Part of the town stands on a rocky promontory, and is defend-ed by walls and a ditch, over which are draw-bridges. The rest of the town is unwalled, but the harbor is defended by several forts. Colombo has a large trade. It was taken by the Portuguese in 1517, by the Dutch in 1603, and since 1796 it has belonged to the English.

COLORADO (*co-lo-rah'do*), one of the Western States of the United States, lying between Kansas and Utah; area 104,500 square miles, or not quite as large as Great Britain and Ireland; pop. about 412,000, or a fifth more than that of Rhode Island; capital, DENVER. The Rocky Mountains pass through the middle of the State, so that some of the rivers flow westward into the Pacific, and some eastward into the Mississippi. The mountain region is very rich in mines of gold, silver, iron, and coal. On each side of the mountains are plains, which are sometimes so dry as to be like deserts; but in other places the land is good, and some of the finest wheat-farms in the world are in this State. Most of the people are white settlers, but there are still a few Indian tribes which are sometimes hostile. The climate is very fine, and invalids often go there for their health. Colorado sends wheat and gold to the rest of the world; but she has also sent us a very hateful little pest, the Colorado potato-bug: this insect first came from the Rocky Mountains, but has spread all over the United States and even to Europe.

The name Colorado is the Spanish for colored or ruddy, and was first given to the Colorado River on account of the reddish tint of its waters. The country was visited by the Spaniards as early as 1540. It was made a Territory of the United States in 1861, out of parts of Kansas, Nebraska, New Mexico, and Utah, and in 1876 became a State of the Union.

COLT, Samuel, the inventor of Colt's revolver, born in Hartford,

Conn., July 19, 1814. When ten years old he began to work in a woolen factory belonging to his father. When fourteen he was sent to school at Amherst, Mass., but soon ran away and shipped as a sailor. While at sea he made a wooden model of a revolving pistol, and afterward this was improved by him and patented in the United States, England, and France. In 1835 a large manufactory of his pistols was set up at Paterson, New Jersey, but they were so little thought of that in a few years the company which owned the factory failed. When the United States made war with Mexico, General Taylor wished to arm his soldiers with the Colt revolvers, but not one could be found for a pattern, and Mr. Colt was obliged to make a new model. After that the pistols sold rapidly and Colt became very rich. In 1852 he built a very large factory and armory at Hartford, which, with the houses for the workmen, cost more than $2,000,-ooo (C. C. T., 469, II., u.) Mr. Colt died in Hartford when forty-seven years old (Jan. 10, 1862).

COLUMBIA. See DISTRICT OF COLUMBIA.

CO·LUM'BUS, Christopher, the discoverer of the New World, born in Genoa, Italy, about 1435. His father was a wool-comber; but from the time he was a little boy Christopher wanted to be a sailor, and used to study geography, astronomy, and navigation that he might be a good one. He went on his first voyage when he was fourteen years old; he showed how brave and persevering he was even then, for, the ship taking fire, Columbus jumped into the water, and with the help of an oar swam six miles to the land. He used to pore over maps and charts, have long talks with old seamen about their voyages, and for hours together he would think over the wonders that must be hidden away in that far-

off western sea; for at that time the Eastern Continent alone was known, all the rest was thought to be water.

At last Columbus made up his mind that he might be able to get to India by sailing westward, and at once set to work to see what could be done. First of all he asked his own country to help him, then he tried Portugal, England, France, but all in vain; some people listened to his talk as if they thought him a dreamer; others would not stop to hear anything he had to say. For fifteen years, with a sort of divine patience, he kept his heart and soul

Christopher Columbus.

on that one object. At last he managed to get an interview at the Court of Spain, and told the story of his great hopes to the King and Queen. But the King and courtiers frowned it down as a wild scheme which would cost too much money; so poor Columbus was sent off with a heavy heart; but before he got far Queen Isabella sent for him to come back, and offered to pledge her jewels to raise the needed money.

So it came about that three ships were fitted out. These were much smaller than ships of the present day. Only one of them, the Santa

Maria, which Columbus himself commanded, had a complete deck. The others, the Pinta and the Niña, commanded by the brothers PINZON, were small undecked vessels called caravels. Columbus had 120 men in all, and food enough for a year. The little fleet set sail from the port of Palos on Friday morning, Aug. 3, 1492, and went first to the CANARY ISLANDS, and on September 6 they left there and steered westward into the unknown sea. When they lost sight of land and night set in, the men got frightened and begged to turn back. Some of them wept, some threatened Columbus; he quieted them as best he could, but kept on. Every day the men grew more unmanageable; in the midst of the turmoil of prayers and threats, Columbus alone stood fixed, with ever the same watchword, "Onward!"

A large reward had been offered to the one who should first see land. After sailing for seventy days in vain, at last one night Columbus saw a light in the distance. All were so anxious that no one thought of sleeping, and early on the next morning (Oct. 12, 1492) a sailor on board the Pinta first saw the New World, but the reward was given to Columbus because he first saw the light. When morning fully dawned a wooded island was seen, with many people running along the beach. At sunrise Columbus took the royal standard of Castile and was rowed to the shore, he being the first to land. All knelt and kissed the ground, and then Columbus rising, with his drawn sword in one hand and the flag in the other, took possession of the island in the name of the crown of Castile, and named it San Salvador (Holy Saviour). It is now called Cat Island, and is one of the BAHAMAS. Columbus, supposing it to be off the coast of India, called the people Indians. After

visiting Hayti (Hispaniola) and Cuba, he sailed home again and arrived at Palos in March, 1493. He was received with the greatest joy in Spain, was honored by the King and Queen, and was given the titles of Admiral and Viceroy of the New World.

But his good fortune lasted only a little while. On his third voyage he discovered the ORINOCO River; but when he went to Hispaniola he found that King Ferdinand had sent some one else to be governor of the island in his place; but more cruel than all, Columbus himself was loaded with chains and carried back to Spain. Some of the officers wanted to take the chains off, but Columbus proudly said, "No, they were put on by an order from their majesties; I will wear them until they shall order them to be taken off; and then I will preserve them as rewards for my services." The Spanish people were so indignant about this treatment that Ferdinand pretended there was some mistake. Columbus was very poor before he died, and said that he had no home but an inn, and but little money to pay for his food. He died in Valladolid, Spain, when about seventy-six years old (May 20, 1506).

CO-MAN'CHES. See AMERICAN INDIANS.

COM'MO-DUS, Lucius Aurelius Antoninus, a Roman emperor, born A.D. 161. He was the son of the good Emperor Marcus Aurelius but he had a bad mother and he grew up with all her vices. He came to the throne when only nineteen years old, and soon showed himself to be one of the worst rulers that Rome ever had. His chief pleasure was to fight with gladiators and to kill wild beasts in the circus. It is said that he once slew a hundred lions, one after another, with javelins, without once missing his aim. He called himself Hercules, and wanted the people to worship him as a god. At last everybody became afraid of him, and he was put to death when thirty-one years old (Dec. 31, 192).

CO'MO, a city of N. Italy at the S. end of the Lake of Como; pop. 25,000, or as large as Auburn, N. Y. It has manufactures of silk, wool, and cotton, and is noted for its splendid marble cathedral, begun in 1396. Como is a very ancient town, and was the birth-place of PLINY, VOLTA, and other distinguished men.

Lake Como is more than thirty miles long and one to three miles wide. It is one of the most beautiful lakes in the world, the waters being wonderfully clear and reflecting the high mountains around it. Along the shores are many handsome villas.

CONCEPCION (*kon-sep-se-own'*), A city of Chili on the Biobio River, seven miles from its mouth in the Pacific Ocean; pop. 24,000, or about as large as Newton, Mass. It is better built than most South American cities, and carries on a considerable trade through its port, Talcahuana, on Concepcion Bay, one of the best harbors in Chili. When Concepcion was founded (1550), it was built on the shore of this bay, but having been destroyed by an earthquake in 1751, it was rebuilt on its present site.

CONCORD (*kong'kurd*), a town of E. Massachusetts, 18 miles N.W. of Boston; pop. about 4000. It was the first inland settlement in Massachusetts, having been founded in 1635, and its name was given to it on account of the unity and concord among the first settlers. During the early part of the Revolution the Americans had a large stock of arms and military stores at Concord. Gen. Gage, the British commander in Boston, hearing of this, sent a body of soldiers to destroy these stores, and on their way they fought the battle of LEXINGTON, the first of the war. When they reached Concord they destroyed what stores they could find, but were soon driven off by the Americans (April 19, 1775). Concord is celebrated as the home of many famous writers; among them EMERSON, HAWTHORNE, THOREAU, and Miss ALCOTT.

CONCORD, the capital of New Hampshire, on the Merrimack River; pop. 17,000, or about the same as that of Amsterdam, N. Y. The capitol, a handsome granite building, stands in a beautiful park among shade-trees. Concord has a large trade and important manufactures, especially of carriages, cotton and woolen goods, and leather. Concord wagons and coaches are noted. Near the city are large granite quarries. Concord is built on the site of an old Indian village. An island near the city is still shown as the place where Hannah Dustin, another woman, and a boy, who had been taken captive by Indians at Haverhill, Massachusetts, killed the ten Indians when asleep with hatchets and so escaped. Concord was settled by the whites in 1725, but until 1765 it was called Rumford. It became a city in 1853.

CONDÉ, Louis II. de Bourbon, Prince de, called "The Great," a famous French general, born at Vincennes, Sept. 8, 1621. He showed great quickness of wit even when a little child. The house in which he lived and went to school at Bourges can be seen now, and carved on the balustrade is this motto: "*À cour vaillant rien impossible*" (Nothing is impossible to the brave). The young hero must often have read these words which he afterwards carried out in his life. He used to excel in his studies and in all sorts of athletic sports. Once, when about nineteen, he went on a journey, and on entering a town he was met by the mayor, who wanted to welcome him in a set speech which he had prepared with great care. He made a very low bow before the young duke, who took one leap over the Mayor's head. The old man, lifting himself up to begin his speech, found, to his surprise, that the young fellow was directly behind him. Turning around, and bent on saying his fine welcome, he again bowed, though not so low as before, when the duke placed his hands on the Mayor's shoulders, again leaped over his head, ran off, and escaped the long speech.

Condé married Clémence, niece of Cardinal RICHELIEU, very much against his will, and never became reconciled to his amiable, loving little wife. She was only thirteen when married, and wanting to look taller on her wedding day she wore a pair of very high-heeled shoes, so that she could hardly walk; and when the dancing began the poor little bride had such an awkward fall that all the company laughed aloud, even the groom, who got very angry with her too.

Condé's ruling passion was war. It was said of him that he was born a captain. In one of his battles he had two horses killed under him, and three wounded; he received a severe wound in his thigh, a pistol-shot in the elbow, and more than twenty cuts and blows on his armor. Once the great General Turenne was asked if he saw the Prince of Condé at the battle of St. Antoine; he said: "I did not see *one* Prince of Condé, I saw more than twelve, so rapidly did he seem to rush from danger to danger." Condé's hot temper occasioned many of the misfortunes as well as many of the successes of his life. He died at Chantilly when sixty-five years old (Dec. 11, 1686).

CONFUCIUS (*kon-fu'she-us*), the Latin name of Kung-fu-tze, a famous Chinese philosopher, born June 19, 551 B.C. His mother was his only teacher, and he was always fond of study. When twenty-four years old, he gave up a good position to mourn the death of his mother three years. After this he prepared himself to be a teacher, and used to travel about teaching and preaching wherever he went. He was very much beloved, and was made prime minister of China. His teachings, written in books partly by himself and partly by his followers, are looked upon by the Chinese much as the Bible is by Christian nations, and are studied in all the schools; and in many school-rooms there is a tablet on the wall sacred to him, before which every pupil has to bow.

Confucius had one son, who died before him; but he left a son, and the descendants of this grandson are the only nobility in China. There are now several thousand of them, and in one city, Kiofoohien, where Confucius is buried, they form the greater part of the inhabitants. A splendid temple, the finest in China, stands on the site of the house of Confucius, and in it is his statue. Confucius died when seventy-two years old (479 B.C.).

CONNECTICUT (*kon-net'e-kut*), one of the New England States of the United States, on Long Island Sound, between New York and Rhode Island; area 4750 square miles, or about half as large as Vermont; pop. 746,000, or nearly the same as that of West Virginia; capital, HARTFORD. Most of the surface is hilly, with broad valleys, in which several rivers flow from north to south. The largest of these is the Connecticut, which has a valley about forty miles wide and noted for its beautiful scenery. The mouths of these rivers form good harbors.

Connecticut has mines of iron and fine quarries of limestone, marble, and brown sandstone, much used for building houses in New York and other cities. There are many good farms, especially in the Connecticut valley, the principal crops being tobacco, corn, oats, and hay. Although Connecticut is one of the smallest States in the Union it is one of the most important for its manufactures, and the people are noted for their many labor-saving machines. Nearly all the clocks made in the United States come from Connecticut, and they are sent to all parts of the world. More India-rubber goods are made there than in any other State, and more hardware than in all the other States together. There are also large factories of sewing-machines, fire-arms, carriages, woolen, cotton, and silk cloths, axes and other tools, in all of which Connecticut is excelled only by two or three other States. Connecticut has a good deal of trade with foreign countries, as well as with other States. The State is also noted for its many colleges and academies, and has some of the best schools in the world.

Connecticut was named from the Connecticut River, which was called by the Indians Quonectakut, meaning "Long River." The English settled on the river in 1636, and at New Haven in 1638, and the two colonies were not joined in one until 1665. Connecticut was one of the thirteen original States of the Union.

CONRAD I., King of Germany. He was chosen in 911, and was the first of the elected rulers of Germany. His short reign was spent in putting down his nobles, who were always rebelling against him, Duke Henry of Saxony being the one who gave him most trouble. Many contests took place with him, and Henry showed so much ability that even Conrad admired him; and when he was mortally wounded in a battle with the Huns, Conrad begged his nobles to elect the Duke of Saxony to succeed him, which they did. Conrad died Dec. 23, 918, and was succeeded by Henry I.

CONRAD II., King of Germany and Roman Emperor. He was the son of Henry Duke of Franconia, and succeeded Henry II., the last of the Saxon emperors, in 1024. Like several of the emperors who had gone before him, he had trouble with his rebellious nobles, the chief of whom was his son-in-law, Ernest Duke of Suabia, whom he put under the ban of the empire. To put a person under the ban of the empire was publicly to pronounce a curse against him, and to deprive him of his property and privileges, the words of the ban being, "We declare thy wife a widow, thy children orphans, and we send thee, in the name of the devil, to the four corners of the world." Duke Ernest was subdued after a long struggle, and much poetry has been written and many stories told about his adventures. Conrad died at Utrecht (June 4, 1039), and was succeeded by his son Henry III.

CONRAD III., King of Germany, born in 1093. He was the son of Frederick Duke of Suabia, and the first of the Hohenstaufen family, and he was elected emperor in 1138, on the death of the Emperor Lothaire. For many years there had been a quarrel between the family of Conrad, the Hohenstaufens, and the Dukes of Suabia, who, with all their friends, were called Guelphs, from the name of several of their line. The Hohenstaufens and their friends were called Waiblingers, from one of their castles. This word was changed by the Italians into Ghibelline. These two parties were constantly at war through the next two hundred years, the struggle finally becoming an affair of Church and State, the Guelphs being for the popes and the Ghibellines for the emperors.

During the course of the struggle the town of Weinsberg was taken by the emperor's soldiers, and the women belonging to the garrison asked and gained permission to leave the castle, taking with them as much as each could carry. The Ghibellines were much astonished when each woman came out with her husband on her back. Conrad would not let the brave women be hindered, and in their honor called the hill on which the castle was built Weibertreue, or Woman's Faithfulness. Conrad went, with several other sovereigns, on the third CRUSADE. He died at Bamberg when fifty-nine years old (Feb. 15, 1152), and was succeeded by his son Henry III.

CON'STANCE, a city of Germany, in Baden, on Lake Constance; pop. 15,000, or about as large as Biddeford, Me. It is surrounded by walls and contains many handsome buildings, among which is a fine cathedral, more than 800 years old. Cotton cloth, yarn, silk, musical instruments, and watches are made there, and there are important fisheries near the city.

Lake Constance, which is about forty miles long, is very deep and clear. The Rhine enters it at the S.E. end, and flows out again below, and many smaller streams empty into it. The shores are low, but very beautiful, with many fine villages and mansions and ruins of old castles. Lake Constance gets its name from a castle built on its banks by Constantine the Great.

The Council of Constance was a famous assembly of the Roman Catholic Church, held there from 1414 to 1418, during which John HUSS and his disciple, Jerome of Prague, were convicted of heresy and burned near the town.

CONSTANS (*kon'stanz*), **Flavius Julius,** Emperor of Rome, born about A.D. 320. He was the youngest son of CONSTANTINE THE GREAT, on whose death (337) he got, as his share of the empire, Western Illyricum, Italy, and Africa. Three years afterward (340) his brother Constantine II. invaded Italy, and was killed in battle near Aquileia, when Constans became master of the whole of the Western Empire. He was a weak and cruel

ruler, and at last Magnentius, his general in Gaul, sent some conspirators to kill him. Constans fled to Spain, but was overtaken by them and slain (A.D. 350).

CON'STAN-TINE I., called the Great, a Roman emperor, born at Nissa in February, 272. He was the son of Constantius Chlorus, a Cæsar or lieutenant-emperor of the western portion of the empire, which at that time was ruled by the two Augusti, or emperors, Maximian and Diocletian. These emperors, however, retired to private life, and the army chose Constantine as emperor. Maximian soon

Constantine the Great.

grew tired of being only a citizen and once more took the title of emperor. Constantine marched against him and took him prisoner, and afterward caused him to be strangled. This brought on a war between Constantine and Maxentius, the son of Maximian. During this war it is said that Constantine saw in the sky a cross of fire bearing the words " By this sign thou shalt conquer." Constantine was victorious, and from that time the sign of the cross was put on the Roman banners.

Constantine made many changes in the government of Rome, and he is considered one of the most famous of all the Roman emperors. In the first place, he made Christianity the religion of the empire, and in order that he might better make it so he removed the capital from Rome to Byzantium, now Constantinople, which was not so much given up to heathen customs as Rome was. In 325 he called together the first general council of the Church at Nice, to decide between the doctrines of Arius, a priest of Alexandria, and Athanasius, who was bishop of that diocese. Athanasius was decided to be in the right, and this council, usually called the Council of Nice, put their belief into the words known as the Nicene Creed. Constantine was not a very good Christian in his life, and, although called "The Great," he committed many cruel acts which have left deep stains upon his name. He delayed his baptism until a few days before his death, so as to give himself liberty to commit as much sin as possible before having it washed away. He died near Nicomedia when sixty-five years old (May 22, 337), after dividing his empire among his three sons, Constantine, Constantius, and Constans.

CONSTANTINE II., Emperor of Rome, born at Arles in Gaul, Aug. 7, A.D. 312. He was the eldest son of CONSTANTINE I. the Great, on whose death (337) he got, as his share of the empire, Constantinople, Gaul, Spain, Britain, and a small part of Africa. Not satisfied with the division, Constantine demanded of CONSTANS, his brother, the whole of Africa. On being refused he invaded Italy, and was drawn into an ambush and killed (A.D. 340).

CONSTANTINE VI., Emperor of the East, born in 771. He was the son of the Emperor Leo IV., whom he succeeded in 780, under the control of his mother, Irene. The Eastern Church had been for some years disturbed by the dispute between the Iconoclasts, those who thought it wrong to have images in churches, and the Iconoduli, who wanted them. A law had been made against having images in the Eastern Church, but Irene tried to restore them. When her son grew older, he and his mother were constantly plotting against each other, and the end of it all was that Irene had him arrested and caused his eyes to be put out. Some say he died the same day (797), others that he lived some years afterwards.

CONSTANTINE XIII., Palæologus, the last Emperor of the East, born in 1394. His father and his brother had been emperors before him, and he did not get the throne until he was fifty-four years old (1448). At that time the Turks had conquered almost all of the EASTERN EMPIRE, and but little was left besides Constantinople and a few other cities. The Turkish Sultan, MOHAMMED II., determined to have Constantinople also, laid siege to it with a great army (April 6, 1453). Constantine, who had only about 9000 soldiers, fought bravely for nearly two months, but at last the Turks battered down part of the walls and rushed in with wild shouts, and the emperor and his little band of nobles were all slain. Constantine's body, found under a heap of the dead, was known by the gold eagles on his shoes. It is said that Mohammed had his head cut off and sent round as a show to all the cities of Arabia and Persia. Constantine was fifty-nine years old at the time of his death (May 29, 1453).

CONSTANTINOPLE (*kon-stan-te-no'p'l*), a city, capital of Turkey, on the European side of the Bosporus; pop. 874,000, or a little larger than Brooklyn, N. Y. The old city, which is called by the Turks Stambool or Istambool, is on a peninsula between the harbor called the Golden Horn and the

Sea of Marmora on the south. Opposite, on the Asiatic side, is a city called Skutari, and on the other side of the Golden Horn, across which there is a bridge of boats, are suburbs called Pera, Galata, Tophana, and Kasim Pasha. The Golden Horn or harbor is a large bay forming one of the finest harbors in the world, and is always full of ships, for Constantinople has a very large trade.

Pera is the residence of most foreigners living in Constantinople, and the foreign ambassadors have their palaces there. Galata has many large stores and warehouses. Tophana has a foundry where cannon are made, and at Kasim Pasha is the great government arsenal and navy-yard. Skutari has a large trade in silk and cotton goods and leather. Hundreds of small boats called *kaiks*, ply between these suburbs and Stambool.

Seen from a distance, Constantinople is very beautiful with its background of hills, and the domes and needle-like towers of many mosques rising above the other build-

View of Constantinople from Skutari.

ings. But on landing, the streets are found to be narrow, crooked, and dirty, and full of vile smells. The old city, or Stambool, is shut in on the land side by three walls with twenty-seven gates. It is divided into different parts, inhabited by Turks, Greeks, Armenians, and Jews. The Seraglio, or residence of the Sultan, is a city by itself, inclosed with walls two miles long, and containing palaces, mosques, gardens, and various government buildings. The outer gate of the Seraglio is called the Sublime Porte or Sublime Gate, and this name is often given to the government of Turkey. None of the buildings of the Seraglio are as fine as many other palaces of Europe. Outside of it most of the houses are small and poor, mostly built of wood, and many are partly ruined. The bazaars are very large buildings, with covered streets lined with small shops open to the sidewalks; in these the shopkeepers sit cross-legged and generally smoking long pipes, except when they are waiting on customers.

The most interesting buildings are the mosques, of which there are five hundred in the city. The most splendid of all is the mosque of Saint Sophia, which was founded by the Emperor JUSTINIAN (525) and was a Christian church until the city was taken by the Turks. It is built of brick, lined with colored marbles, and has a very large and beautiful dome. A gallery around it is held up by sixty-seven columns, some of which, of green jasper, are said to have been brought from the great temple of Diana at Ephesus.

In ancient times a city called Byzantium stood on the site of Constantinople. Its fine situation gave it a large trade with Egypt and Greece, and so rich did it become that its harbor, which is shaped like a horn, was called the Golden Horn. This old city used to stamp a crescent on its coins, and when the Turks took Constantinople they took this crescent for their national symbol. CONSTANTINE I. the Great, who made Byzantium his capital, changed its name to New Rome, but it was general known as Constantinopolis (City of Constantine), which we call Constantinople. It was the capital of the Roman Empire until it was divided, and afterward the capital of the Eastern Empire. The Turks took it on May 29, 1453, and have held it ever since.

CONSTANTIUS I. (*kon-stan'she-us*), called Chlorus, a Roman emperor, father of Constantine the Great, born about A.D. 250. Constantius served in the army with distinction under the Emperor Diocletian, and in 292, when the two emperors Diocletian and Maximian each appointed a favorite general as assistant emperor, under the title of Cæsar, Constantius received the place of Cæsar to Diocletian. In this position he was a very good ruler, and protected the Christians. After he had been Cæsar thirteen years he was made chief emperor, or Augustus, when Diocletian gave up the throne. He died at York, England, when about fifty-six years old (July, 306).

CONSTANTIUS II., a Roman emperor, second son of Constantine the Great, born Aug. 6, 317. Constantine on his death divided his empire among his three sons, Constantine, Constans, and Constantius, but at last the whole was united under Constantius. There were many rival emperors in his time, many disputes in the church, and many unsuccessful wars against the Germans and Persians. He had a cousin named Julian who won so many victories that the army proclaimed him emperor, and Constantius had to march against him, but he died on the way when forty-four years old (Nov. 3, 361), and was succeeded by JULIAN.

CONTRERAS (*kon-tra'ras*). See CHURUBUSCO.

COOK, James, an English navigator, born at Marton, Yorkshire, Oct. 27, 1728. His father, who was a farm-laborer, sent him to a village school until he was twelve years old, when he apprenticed him to a haberdasher, or small storekeeper. On the death of his father, James got his master to free him, and went as cabin-boy on a coasting vessel. He served in this business until he became a mate (1755), when he entered the English navy. He was much liked for his good conduct and bravery, and four years later was made commander of the frigate Mercury, which was one of a squadron sent out to aid Gen. Wolfe in the siege of Quebec, where he did good service. While on his way from the South Pacific to Behring Strait (1778) he discovered the group which he named the Sandwich Islands. Not being able to reach Behring Strait, on account of the ice, he returned to the Sandwich Islands to wait for a better season, and spent the time in cruising about the islands.

He tried all the time to improve himself by studying mathematics and astronomy, and became so well known for his knowledge and skill that when a ship was sent to the Pacific Ocean to explore, he was chosen to command it. He was gone three years, sailed round the world, and made many discoveries; and was so successful that he was sent on other voyages to the Pacific.

One day one of his boats was stolen by the natives, and the next day Capt. Cook went ashore with some of his men to try to get it. He was attacked by the natives and, after a sharp fight, was killed. It is supposed that he was eaten by them, as only his bones were found seven days afterward. He died when fifty years old (Feb. 14, 1779). In 1874 a monument was erected on the place where he was murdered.

COO'PER, James Fenimore, a noted American novelist, born at Burlington, N. J., Sept. 15, 1789. His father, Judge William Cooper,

James Fenimore Cooper.

removed, when James was a baby, to Otsego Lake in New York State, where he owned much land, and founded there a town called Cooperstown. In this wild but beautiful place Cooper passed his early years. In the neighborhood were many Indians, trappers, and bold settlers, whose stories of their adventures and accounts of the legends of the vicinity were a constant delight to the boy. When thirteen years old he was sent to Yale College, and three years later he entered the navy, where he served six years, and gained the rank of lieutenant. In 1811 he left the navy and went to live at Mamaroneck, near New York City. When thirty years old he published a novel called "Precaution," which was a failure; but two years afterward he wrote a story called "The Spy," which had a great success and was republished in Europe. After that he became very popular, and no other American story-writer has won more fame. His novels are especially interesting for their stories of Indian life and adventures; but he also wrote some very fine stories of the sea. He was the first American novelist whose works were translated into foreign languages. Among the best of his stories is the series known as "The Leather-stocking Tales." Mr. Cooper was very fond of children, and was always very bright and merry with them. He died at Cooperstown on the eve of his sixty-second birthday (Sept. 14, 1851).

COPENHAGEN (*ko-pen-ha'-ghen*), a city, capital of Denmark, on the Baltic Sea; pop. 375,000, or a quarter larger than San Francisco, Cal. It is built partly on the island of Sieland, and partly on the island of Amager, the channel between the two forming the harbor, which is very fine and always full of ships. Copenhagen is noted for its palaces, museums, and libraries. The palace or castle of Christiansborg, on a little island, is used as a meeting-place for the Danish Parliament. It is ornamented by four splendid bronze statues, made by THORWALDSEN, representing Strength, Wisdom, Justice, and Health. Instead of

Health, it was intended to have one of the statues represent Truth; but the order sent for them to Thorwaldsen, who was then in Rome, was badly written, and instead of the Danish word *Sandhed*, Truth, he read it *Sundhed*, Health. The Thorwaldsen Museum contains either the originals or copies of all the sculptures made by him, and in one room is kept the furniture of his sitting, room as he left it when he died. In the courtyard of the museum is his tomb, under a bed of roses and evergreen. In the Ethnographic Museum are arranged figures of different races of people, all dressed in their proper costumes and with the weapons used by them. The Museum of Northern Antiquities is a collection of the things used by the northern nations from the earliest times. In it may be seen the stone axes and knives of the Stone Age, the bronze weapons and tools of the Bronze Age, and the great swords, battle-axes, shields, and suits of armor used by the vikings in the Iron Age. In Rosenborg Castle is a collection showing the history of the Danish kings from the earliest times. One or more rooms are given to the reign of each king, and in them are arranged the furniture, dresses, and arms of the time.

Another of the curiosities of Copenhagen is the Round Tower, which is so built that a spiral road winds round between its inner and outer wall from the bottom to the top. In 1719, when PETER THE GREAT and Catharine were in Copenhagen, she drove a four-horse coach to the top while Peter led the way on horseback.

The University of Copenhagen has about 1200 students; it has a botanical garden and a large library. Copenhagen is the greatest commercial city of Denmark, and has a very large trade. Among the manufactures are porcelain and some of the finest watches and

chronometers in the world. The city is defended by a strong castle.

The name, Copenhagen, in Danish Kjöbenhavn, means "Merchant's Port." The city was founded in the 11th century, and has been the capital of Denmark since 1443. In 1807 it was bombarded by an English fleet for three days; hundreds of houses were destroyed and 2000 persons were killed.

COPERNICUS (*ko-per'ne-kus*), **Nikolaus,** a famous astronomer, born in Thorn, Poland, Feb. 19, 1473. His father, a German merchant in Cracow, died when Nikolaus was quite young, and he was brought up by his uncle the Bishop of Ermeland. After studying medicine at the University of Cracow, he went to Italy, studied as-

Copernicus.

tronomy at BOLOGNA, and then taught mathematics in Rome, where he won much fame. When about thirty years old he became a priest and went to Frauenburg, in Prussia, of which his uncle had made him canon, and while attending to his duties in the church practiced medicine among the poor, and studied astronomy, in which he took great delight. The tower from which he used to watch the stars is still shown in Frauenburg.

Copernicus soon saw that the

way of explaining the movements of the heavenly bodies then taught in the schools was all wrong; that the sun does not move round the earth, as PTOLEMY and all astronomers after him believed, but that it stands still, and that the earth and the other planets revolve around it (C. C. T., 629, I. I.). He spent many years in proving this, and wrote a book about it (1530), but he was so afraid of being persecuted that he did not publish it for many years. It is said that the first copy of his book was put into his hands on the very day he died (May 24, 1543). Very few then believed that he had found out the truth, but now everybody honors him as one of the greatest men of the world, and monuments and statues have been erected to him.

COP′LEY, John Singleton, a noted American painter, born in Boston, July 3, 1737. His father was from England and his mother from Ireland. His father died when he was young, and his mother married a portrait-painter and engraver, who gave John his first lessons in art. John worked hard and got on so fast that when he was seventeen years old he became a painter himself. After painting portraits in Boston for several years, he went to Italy to study, and about 1775 settled in London, where he soon became famous for his portraits and historical pictures. The most celebrated of his works is the " Death of Lord Chatham" (PITT), which shows the great statesman falling in a fit after making his last speech in Parliament against acknowledging the independence of the United States. He also painted other noted works, and many portraits of the royal family and of distinguished people. Copley died in London, when seventy-eight years old (Sept. 9, 1815). His son, John Singleton Copley (born in Boston, May 21, 1772), became Lord Lyndhurst, Chancellor of England.

CORDOVA (*kor-do'vah*), a city of S. Spain, on the Guadalquiver River; pop. 56,000, or nearly the same as that of Lincoln, Neb. It is beautifully situated, and is surrounded by a high wall with round, square, and eight-sided towers, built by the Moors. Its great cathedral, one of the most splendid buildings in the world, was built by the Moors for a mosque in 786. The roof is supported by many arches, which were once held up by 1200 columns, but 400 of them have been taken out so as to make space for Christian services. The Moors used to light the building with 4000 silver lamps.

Cordova is called by the Spaniards Cor′du-ba, its Roman name. It was built by the Romans about 125 B.C., and was a flourishing city in the time of Julius Cæsar. But it was most famous under the Moors, who made it the capital of their empire in Spain. In the 10th century it is said to have had 1,000,000 inhabitants and 900 baths. It was also a great centre of learning, and had fine schools and libraries.

COREA (*ko-re'ah*), a country of E. Asia, W. of Japan; area, 90,000 square miles, or nearly as large as Oregon; pop., 10,000,000, or about one sixth that of the United States. It forms a peninsula joined to China, and the country is claimed by the Chinese, but the king pays tribute to both China and Japan. The people are much like the Japanese, but in their manners are like the Chinese. They dress in white cotton clothes,

Corean without Hat.

Corean with Hat.

and arrange their hair in a knot under a cotton covering, over which they wear a broad-brimmed hat of open horse hair work. The Coreans are Buddhists in religion.

COR'FU. See IONIAN ISLANDS.

COR'INTH, a city of ancient Greece, on the Isthmus of Corinth, 48 miles W. of Athens. It was one of the largest and most populous cities of Greece, being especially famous for its commerce, the splendor of its buildings, and its works of art. It stood in the middle of the isthmus, at the foot of a steep, rocky hill, called Acrocorinthus, on which was its citadel. Its walls were five miles around, and it was connected with its seaports by walled roads. When at the height of its glory it was taken by a Roman army under MUMMIUS (146 B.C.), and entirely destroyed. The Romans carried away a vast spoil, and all the people were sold as slaves. Afterward another city, hardly less splendid, was built in the same place (B.C. 46) by Julius CÆSAR, and ruins of its temples and palaces may still be seen. St. Paul preached there and founded a Christian church, to which he afterward wrote his Epistle to the Corinthians. The Corinthian order of architecture, noted for its beautiful columns, was first used

Veturia, Volumnia, and Coriolanus.   Ancient Picture in the Baths of Titus, Rome.

at Corinth, and the Corinthians claimed to have found out the art of painting. The famous Isthmian games, so called from the Isthmus of Corinth, were held near Corinth. They were much like the Olympic games held at OLYMPIA.

A small town called Gortho now stands on the site of ancient Corinth.

CO·RI·O·LA'NUS, a noble Roman whose real name was Cneius Marcius, but who was given this new one for conquering the Volscian town of Corioli (about 490 B.C.). During a famine at Rome he advised that corn should not be given free to the common people unless they gave up some of the offices which were held by their class. For this he was banished. He went to Antium, the capital of the Volsci, took command of their army and led it against Rome. When the city was at his mercy, ambassadors were sent to him begging him not to destroy his country. He would not listen to the senators nor to the priests, but at length his mother Veturia, and his wife Volumnia, took his children and went to his camp. They threw themselves at his feet, and with tears asked him to spare Rome. "Thou hast saved Rome," he said to his mother, "but lost thy son." He then retreated with his army, and died in exile.

CORK, a city of S. Ireland, near the mouth of the river Lee; pop. about 80,000, or nearly as large as New Haven, Conn. It is the third city of Ireland in population, only Dublin and Belfast being larger. It has a fine harbor, divided into an upper and a lower part. In the lower harbor, on an island, is Queenstown, formerly called the Cove of Cork, but the name of which was changed in honor of Queen Victoria when she visited it in 1849. Many ships and steamers go from there to all parts of the world, and most of the Irish emigrants for America embark there.

Cork gets its name from the Irish word *corcach*, a swamp, and the place was so called because the ground near it is marshy. It is supposed to have been first built in the 6th century.

CORNEILLE (*kor-nale'*), **Pierre,** a celebrated French writer of plays, born in Rouen, June 6, 1606. He was educated in his native place, and became a lawyer, but being unsuccessful in his business began to write plays for the theatre. When twenty-three years old he wrote a comedy which was played with success, and he soon wrote others which made him known in Paris. But he first became famous through his tragedy called "Le Cid" (The CID), which was better than any play ever before seen on the French stage, and which was soon transla-

Pierre Corneille.

ted into most of the other languages of Europe. In 1639 he brought out a tragedy called "Les Horaces" (The HORATII) and another called "CINNA," and in the next year appeared "Polyeucte," a play founded on the story of a Christian martyr, which most writers think to be his best work. Corneille wrote other plays full of beautiful thoughts and fine poetry, but few of them added to his fame, and scarcely any, excepting those told about, are now played. He died in Paris when seventy-eight years old (Oct. 1, 1684).

CORNELIA, (*cor-ne'le-ah*), a noble Roman lady, daughter of the first Scipio Africanus. Though of the highest birth, she married one of the Gracchi, a plebeian family famous for its honesty and sympathy with the people. She was good and clever as well as beautiful, and very fond and proud of her children. A lady who wore a great many jewels begged one day to see some of Cornelia's ornaments. Cornelia sent for her sons; "These are my jewels," she said, "and their virtues are my ornaments." Two of these sons became so famous that when she died a statue was erected to her with the inscription which she had desired, "Cornelia, the mother of the Gracchi."

CORNWALLIS (*korn-wol'lis*), **Charles**, a British general, commonly called Lord Cornwallis, born Dec. 31, 1738. He was the eldest son of Earl Cornwallis, and became earl himself on the death of his father in 1762. In the beginning of the war of the Revolution he was sent to America, and served as a major-general with success at first, winning the battles of Camden (1780) and Guilford (1781). Not being strong enough to hold the country, he marched to YORKTOWN, Virginia, intending to embark his troops there. But being shut in by the French fleet and by the American and French armies, he was forced to surrender with his whole army (Oct. 19, 1781).

In 1786 he was made governor of Bengal and commander of the forces in India, where he won several victories which saved the British power. He went back to England in 1793, and was made a marquis. In 1798 he was made Lord-Lieutenant of Ireland, and restored peace there. He went to India again in 1805 as Governor - General, and died at Ghazepore when sixty-seven years old (Oct. 5, 1805).

COROT (*ko-ro'*), **Jean Baptiste Camille,** a French landscape-painter, born in Paris in July, 1796. His fame was of slow growth, for he had painted nearly thirty years before his pictures drew much attention. Since then they have ranked among the best works of modern art. He died in Paris, Feb. 22. 1875.

CORREGGIO (*kor-red'jo*), **Anto-**nio Allegri, a famous Italian painter, born at Correggio, now called Reggia, in 1493 or 1494. Not much of his early life is known, except that he was well educated by his father, and that his uncle Lorenzo Allegri, an artist, first taught him to paint.

The principal works and masterpieces of Correggio are his large pictures of religious subjects in Italian churches and upon their domes. His smaller works are better known to the world; his celebrated picture called "Notte," the Italian for Night, is the Infant Saviour adored by the shepherds at night, which is remarkable for its beautiful effect of the light, which is painted as coming from the Saviour. This picture is in the Dresden Gallery, and also "The Magdalen Reading," which is said to be one of the most perfect women ever painted.

This great painter died at Correggio, in his forty-first year (March 5, 1534).

CORSICA (*kor'se-kah*), an island of France in the Mediterranean, west of Italy; area 3400 square miles, or about a third larger than Delaware; pop. 279,000, or about one and two thirds that of Delaware; capital, AJACCIO. The island is mountainous, some of the peaks rising a mile and a half above the sea. The hills are covered with forests, and there are many beautiful plains and valleys. The people, who are much like the Italians, are principally engaged in raising cattle and mules. Corsica means "woody," and the island was named from its forests. It has belonged to many different nations. Since 1814 it has been a part of France. It is celebrated as the birth-place of Napoleon Bonaparte.

CORTES (*kor'teez*), **Hernando,** the conqueror of Mexico, born in Medellin, Spain, in 1485. After the discovery of America by Columbus, numbers of young Spaniards, seeking adventure or eager for gold, settled in the West India Islands. Among these was Hernando Cortes, who became the owner of an estate in Cuba. The Spanish governor of the island, Velasquez, fitted out an expedition against Mexico, which had but just been discovered, and gave the command to Cortes. The events of that expedition are more like romance than reality. Reaching Vera Cruz, Cortes burned his fleet, thus compelling his followers to conquer or die, marched boldly into Mexico, seized MONTEZUMA, the king of the Aztecs, and obtained from him a quantity of gold. Velasquez, who

Hernando Cortes.

was jealous of Cortes, sent out a force under another Spaniard, Narvaez. Leaving some of his men in Mexico, Cortes went to meet Narvaez, and took him prisoner. On his return to Mexico he learned that Montezuma had been killed by his own subjects, and that the Spanish troops had been driven out of the city. The battle of Otumba was fought, the Aztecs defeated, and Mexico made a Spanish province. Cortes was very badly treated by some of his countrymen in Spain, and it is said that he boldly

charged the Emperor Charles V. with ingratitude because he did not protect him. He died near Seville when sixty-two years old (Dec. 2, 1547).

COSTA RICA (*kos'tah re'kah*), a country of Central AMERICA, between Colombia and Nicaragua; area 22,000 square miles, or about the same as that of West Virginia; pop. about 214,000, or a little more than that of Utah; capital, San José. Near the coasts the land is low, but all the central part forms a high table-land, from which rises a chain of mountains, among which are several volcanoes. Earthquakes are frequent.

There are rich gold-mines in Costa Rica, and the country is covered with splendid forests, in which mahogany and other fine woods abound. Nearly all the plantations grow coffee, which is the wealth of the country. The climate is hot near the coasts, but cool and pleasant in the highlands. The people are mostly whites, of Spanish descent, but there are many negroes, Indians, and mixed breeds. The government is a republic, much like the United States in form.

Costa Rica is the Spanish for rich coast, and the country is said to have been so called on account of its gold-mines. It was discovered by Columbus in 1502. It remained a colony of Spain until 1821, and was afterward one of the States of Central America. In 1840 it became an independent government.

CO-TO-PAX'I. See ANDES.

COVENTRY (*kuv'en-tre*), a city of England, on the Sherburne River, 10 miles N.N.E. of Warwick; pop. 42,000, or nearly as large as Peoria, Ill. The most ancient part of the town has narrow and crooked steets, lined with curious old buildings; but the modern streets are wide and handsome. Coventry is noted for its manufactures. More watches are made there than in any other city of England, and there are large manufactories of silks, ribbons, fringes, ruffles, and bicycles.

Coventry was first called Conventre or Convent Town, from a large convent which was built there (1044) by a nobleman named Leofric and his wife GODIVA.

COVINGTON (*kuv'ing-tun*), a city of Kentucky, on the Ohio River, opposite Cincinnati, with which it is connected by a splendid suspension-bridge; pop. 37,000, or as large as Elizabeth, N. J. Many of the people do business in Cincinnati, but Covington has a large trade of its own, and manufactories of tobacco, beer, glass, iron, and many other things. Covington was laid out in 1815, and became a city in 1834.

COW'PENS. See MORGAN.

COW'PER (English *koo'per*), William, a noted English poet, born in Hertfordshire, Nov. 26, 1731. His father was a clergyman and chaplain to George II. William's mother died when he was six years old, but he always remembered her and wrote a beautiful poem about her when he grew up. His health was never good, and when a child at school he suffered much from the cruelty of older boys. In time he became a lawyer, but he was too timid to succeed, and finally went crazy and was sent to an asylum. His reason came back in two years, but his health was so poor that he did nothing; and it was not until he was fifty years old (1782) that he published his first volume of poems. Shortly after he wrote his ballad of "John Gilpin," which at once gave him fame. His longest poem, "The Task," was written at the request of a lady, who set him the task of writing some verses about a sofa, and what might be seen from it. Cowper's writings are noted for their true pictures of nature, and their piety and good sense. He died at East Dereham, Norfolk,

when sixty-nine years old (April 25, 1800).

CRACOW (*kray'ko*), a city of Austria, in Galicia, on the river Vistula; pop. 75,000, or about the same as that of Scranton, Pa. It has a large trade in Hungarian wines, wax, and salt. Near it are the celebrated salt-mines of Wieliczka, where more than a thousand miners are employed (C. C. T., 528, I., l.). Cracow was once a large and important city, and was for a long time the capital of Poland. The royal castle, where the kings lived, is now a barrack for soldiers. Near it is a beautiful Gothic cathedral, in which are buried many of the kings, queens and great men of Poland, among them Casimir the Great, John SOBIESKI, COPERNICUS, and KOSCIUSZKO. The university was long famous in Europe.

Cracow is said to have been founded in the 7th century, by a Slavic chief called Krakus, from whom it got its name.

CRAIK (*krake*), **Dinah Maria Mulock,** an English writer of novels and stories, born in Stoke-upon-Trent in 1826. She is the daughter of a clergyman, and is better known to Americans as Miss Mulock. She has written several stories that young folks delight in, among them being "A Hero," "Bread upon the Waters," and "Little Lychetts." Her best-known novels are "John Halifax" and "A Life for a Life." She began to write in 1849, and in 1864 she was given a literary pension of $300 a year. In 1865 she was married to Mr. George Lillie Craik. She died October 13, 1887.

CRAN'MER, Thomas, the first Protestant archbishop of Canterbury, born at Aslaeton, July 2, 1489. He was educated at Cambridge, where he studied to be a priest. He became noted for his learning, and having aided King Henry VIII. to divorce his wife Catharine of Aragon, Henry gave him several high offices. Cranmer opposed the pope and helped Henry to establish the Reformation in England; he had the Bible translated into English (1540) and caused the Lord's Prayer, the Creed, and the Ten Commandments to be taught in English. When Henry died (1547) he left his son, Edward VI., who was then but nine years old, to Cranmer's care. Cranmer now rose to great power

Salt Mines of Wieliczka. (See Cracow, page 223.)

and treated the Catholics very cruelly. In 1553 Edward died and his sister MARY became queen. She hated Cranmer for having been unjust to her mother, Catharine of Aragon, and had him tried for changing his religion. At first he was firm, then he felt afraid of death and said he would become a Catholic again. But this did not save him, and he was burned opposite Balliol College, in Oxford, when sixty-seven years old (March 21, 1556).

CRÉCY (*kre'se* or *kra'se*), a village of N. France, on the river Maye, a branch of the Somme; pop. about 1800. It is celebrated for a battle fought there between the English under King Edward III. and the French under King Phillip VI. The French had three or four times as many men as the English, and they expected to win an easy victory; but they were soon driven back by the English bowmen. Part of the English army now made a charge, headed by the Prince of Wales (afterwards called the Black Prince), a youth only fifteen years old. The French fought bravely, and the English sent to the king for reinforcements. "No," said the king, "tell my son that he must win his spurs;" that is, prove himself worthy to be a knight. Upon this the Prince and his soldiers charged again and completely routed the French (Aug. 26, 1346). The blind king, John of Bohemia, who was fighting on the French side, was killed as he rode between two cavaliers, with his horse tied to theirs so that they could guide him. As the custom was, his crest of three ostrich-feathers and his motto, "Ich dien" ("I serve"), was given to the young prince who had conquered him, and ever since this has been the crest and motto of the Prince of Wales. It is said that cannon were first used at the battle of Crécy by the English.

CREFELD (*kra'felt*), a city of Germany, in Prussia, 12 miles N.W. of Düsseldorf; pop. 90,000, or a little larger than Columbus, Ohio. It is noted for its large manufactures of silk and velvets, which were first made there in the 17th century by a colony of French Huguenots, or Protestants, who had to leave their country on account of persecution. Several thousand persons are now employed in the factories.

CRE·MO'NA, a city of N. Italy, on the river Po; pop. about 30,000, or nearly the same as that of Salem, Mass. It has manufactures of silk, cotton, and porcelain. In former times it was famous for its violins, which were considered the best in the world. Some of them have been sold for more than a thousand dollars a piece.

Cremona was first built (219 B.C.) by the Romans, who called the place Cremonensis Ager (Field of the Cremonensians), after a tribe of people living there, and this has become changed in time to its present name.

CRETE, or **Candia** (*kan'de-ah*), an island in the Mediterranean Sea, S.E. of Greece; area 3300 square miles, or one and a third times as large as Delaware; pop. 280,000, or a little larger than that of Cleveland, O. It is long and narrow, and a chain of mountains runs from end to end. The mountains and valleys are very beautiful, and there are many caves and other natural curiosities. The ancients used to get much chalk from the hills, and therefore called it *Creta terra* (Cretan earth). Crete is a fertile island but the people are so idle that they have few good farms. Many fruits are raised, and there is an important trade in olives, raisins, almonds, oranges, and lemons. Large numbers of silk-worms are bred, and the silk, sent to France and Austria, is noted for its fineness. Large flocks of goats and sheep are raised among the hills. The people are much like the Greeks. About four fifths of them are Christians, and the rest Mohammedans.

In ancient times Crete, which got its name probably from the Curetes who lived there, was very populous and had many fine cities. One of its early kings was MI-NOS, who built the famous labyrinth. The Cretans were noted as archers, and used to serve as such in the Greek and other armies. In later times, after belonging to the Romans, Byzantines, and Saracens, it was sold to the Venetians (1204), and ruled by them until it was conquered by the Turks (1669), to whom it has since belonged. Of late years there have been many insurrections among the people, who hate their Turkish rulers.

CRICHTON (*kri'ton*), **James,** called the "admirable Crichton," born in Scotland, Aug. 19, 1560. His father was lord advocate of Scotland, and his mother a member of the Stuart royal family. He was educated at St. Andrews, where he was made master of arts when only fourteen years old, and when seventeen he had mastered all studies then taught. He went to Paris when twenty years old, and offered to meet learned persons and argue in public upon any subject they would name in any one of twelve languages. When the time came he spoke nine hours before 3000 listeners, showing such skill and learning that he was given a diamond ring and a purse of gold. He then went to Italy, traveling from city to city and disputing with learned men on questions of divinity, philosophy, and mathematics. At Mantua he fought with and killed the finest swordsman of the day. The Duke made him tutor to his son, a bad, passionate young man. During the carnival, Crichton was set upon in the street by three men in masks. He disarmed one who proved to be his pupil. Crichton fell on his knee and offered his sword to the prince, who pierced him through the heart. He died in Mantua at the age of twenty-three (July 3, 1583).

CRIMEA (*krim-e'ah*), a peninsula of S. Russia, formed by the BLACK SEA and the Sea of AZOV; area 7600 square miles, or about the same as that of Massachusetts; pop. about 250,000, or one ninth that of Massachusetts; capital, Simpheropol. It is joined to the mainland by an isthmus only about four miles broad. The northern part is a dreary plain, where the people, mostly TARTARS, live in tents and raise cattle; but in the southern part are wooded mountains and fertile valleys. In this part is the fortress of SEBASTOPOL.

The name Crimea is supposed to come from the Cimmerians, who were the ancient inhabitants. The Greeks called it the Tauric Chersonesus, from a tribe of Scythians called Tauri, who lived in the mountains, Chersonesus being the ancient name for peninsula. There were several rich cities there in ancient times. In the 13th century the Tartars conquered it and called it Krim Tartary. Afterward the Turks got it, and in 1784 the Russians took it from them. It is most noted in modern times for giving its name to the Crimean War, which was fought mostly in it (1854-'56). This war was carried on by Great Britain, France, Sardinia, and Turkey against Russia, in order to check her growing power and to prevent her from taking Turkey.

CRI'TO, a friend and follower of SOCRATES. He was rich, and is said to have supported his great master; he tried to get him to save his life by escaping from prison, but Socrates refused. Crito is a character is one of PLATO'S dialogues, which is named after him.

CRŒSUS (*kre'sus*), King of Lydia, Asia Minor, came to the throne about 562 B.C. He was the richest king mentioned in history, and was also a great conqueror, at one time ruling over thirteen nations. He used to invite great men to SARDIS, his capital, and entertain them in his palace. Among those who visited him were ÆSOP and SOLON. One day Crœsus showed his riches to Solon and asked him who he thought was the happiest man in the world, expecting to hear himself named. "The man whom Heaven smiles upon to the last," said Solon. This made Crœsus angry, but soon afterward his fortunes began to change. His son Atys was killed while hunting, and the Persians under Cyrus made war upon Lydia and took Sardis by storm (548 B.C.). Crœsus was taken prisoner and condemned to be burnt alive. When the pile was lighted, he cried out, "Solon! Solon! Solon!" Cyrus asked what this meant, and when he heard the story he set Crœsus at liberty, made him his friend, and let him keep his title of king.

CROMWELL (*krom'wel* or *krum'-wel*), **Oliver,** Lord Protector of England, born at Huntingdon, April 25, 1599. He is said to have been

Oliver Cromwell.

a wild boy, little given to study. When seventeen years old he went to Cambridge University, but left the next year on his father's death, and after living a while in London, he settled on his estate in Huntingdon. After his marriage (1620) he became serious, and was noted as a good PURITAN. He was sent several times to Parliament, and was a member of the Long Parlia-

ment which opposed CHARLES I. He was not a good speaker, yet he sometimes took part in debates. Once when he was making a speech, Lord Digby asked John Hampden who the sloven was. Hampden told him that if there should ever be a breach with the king, that sloven would be the greatest man in England.

As soon as the civil war broke out, he raised a company of men and entered the army of the Parliament as a captain of cavalry. He soon became a colonel, and his regiment became famous as the "Ironsides," who were never defeated. The battles of MARSTON MOOR and NASEBY were won chiefly by their gallant charge, and within ten months after Naseby all England was conquered. Parliament gave him great rewards, and he became at once the foremost man in the nation. In 1648 a Scottish army made up of Royalists and Presbyterians invaded England, but Cromwell routed them at the battle of Preston. After King Charles had fallen into the hands of Parliament, some of the members showed a desire to make peace with him and bring him back to the throne again; but the army did not like this, and Cromwell sent Colonel Pride with a regiment of foot-soldiers, who shut out all who favored the king. This was called "Pride's Purge," because Parliament was purged of those members.

Cromwell was a member of the court which tried and condemned King Charles to death, and his name stands third among those who signed his death-warrant. England was now declared to be a commonwealth, to be ruled without a king or House of Lords; the House of Commons became the ruling power, and a Council of State, of which Cromwell was one, was appointed to carry on the government. After the death of Charles, all the Royalists or Cavaliers regarded his son

Charles, then nineteen years old, as king. They made a rebellion in Ireland, but Cromwell, who was sent there as Lord-Lieutenant, defeated them in several battles and nearly subdued the whole island in nine months, when he returned to England, leaving his son-in-law IRETON to finish the work. In the meantime young Charles went to Scotland, where the people received him as their king and raised an army to aid him in getting his throne. Cromwell went to Scotland and defeated the Scots at the battle of Dunbar (1650). The next year, while Cromwell was still in Scotland, the Scots raised another army and marched with Charles into England, hoping that the English Royalists would join them; but Cromwell overtook them at Worcester and defeated them again on the same day (Sept. 3) that Dunbar was fought.

There was still great rivalry between the army and the Parliament (sometimes called in contempt the "Rump Parliament," because only a part of it was left), and Cromwell one day (April 20, 1653) entered the House and, after speaking very bitterly to the members, called in some soldiers, turned all the members out, and locked the doors. Cromwell was now master of England, but the Puritans were unwilling that he should become king, for the name was hateful to them. He therefore called a new Parliament, called by some the Little Parliament, but by the Cavaliers generally the Barebone's Parliament, from the name of one of its members, Praise-God Barebone. In a few months most of the members gave up their powers to Cromwell, who took the title of Lord Protector of the Commonwealth of England, Scotland, and Ireland (Dec. 16, 1653).

Cromwell governed only five years, but his reign was one of the brightest England has ever known.

His rule was strong, but he did much for the prosperity of the country by building up trade and commerce, and by giving the people justice and freedom of religion; and under him England became more powerful than she had ever been before, and one of the greatest nations of Europe. He was a great general and a great prince, and after his death the people of England often looked back with regret and pride to the days when the mighty Oliver ruled. Oliver Cromwell died when fifty-nine years old (Sept. 3, 1658), and was buried in Westminster Abbey.

CRONSTADT (*kron'staht*), a city of Russia, on an island in the Gulf of Finland, near the mouth of the river Neva; pop. about 48,000, or the same as that of Bridgeport, Conn. Cronstadt is the principal port of Russia for foreign trade, and also the chief place for its navy. It is only thirteen miles from St. Petersburg, and as all ships going there have to pass by it, it is guarded by very strong forts, mounted with many hundred cannons. But this great port is of no use from November to April each year, because it is blocked up with ice.

Cronstadt means "Crown City." The town was first built by PETER THE GREAT in 1710.

CROPSEY (*krop'sy*), **Jasper Frank,** an American landscape-painter, born in Westfield, N. Y., Feb. 18, 1823. He studied art in Europe, and has spent much of his life in England. At present he lives in the United States.

CROTONA (*kro-to'nah*), or **Croton,** an ancient city of Italy, on the Ionian sea. It was founded by the Greeks about 700 B.C., and soon became very populous and powerful. In the war between SYBARIS (510 B. C.) it is said that the city sent out an army of 100,000 men, and conquered a Sybarite army three times as large. Crotona soon lost its power, and in the second Punic war (about 205 B.C.) it had not soldiers enough to guard its own walls. The school of philosophy founded by PYTHAGORAS was at Crotona.

CROWN POINT. See GEORGE, LAKE.

CROY'DON, a town of England, ten miles S. of London; pop. 79,-000, or as large as Paterson, N. J. It is the home of many people who do business in London, and has many fine dwellings. In old times it was called Cruiedune: that is, Chalk Hill. It contained a royal palace which William the Conqueror gave to Lanfranc, Archbishop of Canterbury, and he and his successors resided there for a long time.

CRUSADES (*kroo'saidz*), wars waged by the Christian powers of Europe to take the Holy Land from the Mohammedans. They were called crusades from the Latin word *crux* (cross), a cross being worn on the right shoulder of all who took part in them as a sign of their mission. They are usually reckoned as eight in number, the first and greatest beginning in 1096, and the last in 1291. For years Christians had been in the habit of making journeys to the tomb of Our Lord at Jerusalem. When the Saracens took that city Christian pilgrims were so badly treated that Peter the Hermit, a monk, went about in 1096 from place to place begging Christians to arm themselves for the rescue of the Holy Sepulchre. Multitudes thronged at his bidding of all ranks and conditions, peasants and kings, monks and beggars, even women and children. The first crusade ended in the capture of Jerusalem and the setting up of a Christian kingdom, of which GODFREY OF BOUILLON was elected king. This kingdom lasted about fifty years, when it was taken by its infidel neighbors, and a second crusade for its redemption was preached by the famed St. Bernard.

Although the Crusaders were often successful, they were not able to do any lasting good, and at the end of the two hundred years during which these wars went on things were pretty much as they were in the beginning. Some of the sovereigns who took part in them were Louis VII., Philip II., and Louis IX. of France, Richard I. and Edward I. of England, and Conrad III. and Frederick Barbarossa of Germany. The chief result of the crusades was that the nations of Western Europe became better acquainted with the Greeks and Saracens, and learned many useful things from them.

CUBA (*ku'bah*), the largest and most westerly of the West Indian Islands; area 47,000 square miles, or about as large as New York State; pop. about 1,522,000, or about the same as that of New York; capital, HAVANA. Near the coast the land is generally low, but a chain of mountains runs through the centre of the island, some of the peaks of which are a mile and a half high. Gold, silver, copper, iron, marble, and jasper are found, but the mines and quarries are little worked. There are fine forests, full of valuable woods, such as rosewood, mahogany, and the cedar, from which cigar-boxes are made; and cocoanut, lime, and wild orange trees are so abundant that the whole island seems like a grove of them. The principal things sent to other countries are sugar, molasses, cigars, tobacco, and coffee. Cuban cigars, commonly called Havana cigars, are the best in the world. The climate of Cuba is warm, but not unpleasant. About half of the people are whites; the rest are mostly negro slaves and mulattoes. The island is a Spanish province, and is governed by a captain-general, chosen by the king of Spain.

Cuba was the Indian name of the island. It was discovered by Columbus in 1492, and was settled soon afterward by the Spanish. Of late years the Cubans have made many efforts to become independent, but thus far they have been unsuccessful.

CUL·LO'DEN MOOR, a plain in Scotland, 4 miles E.N.E. of Inverness, famous as the site of the battle of Culloden, fought April 16, 1746, in which Prince Charles Edward STUART, the Pretender, was defeated by the English, led by the Duke of Cumberland. The prince's army was made up of Highlanders, who fought very bravely, but they had hardly any cannon and were half starved, and after the loss of many men they broke and fled in every direction. The victors were very cruel and gave no quarter, killing all the wounded.

CURIATII (*ku-ri-a'she-i*). See HORATII.

CURTIUS (*kur'she-us*), **Marcus,** a fabled Roman hero of the 4th century B.C. According to the story, an earthquake had opened a great chasm in the Forum of Rome, and though the people had tried to fill it up, it was as deep and wide as ever. One day the augurs, or fortune-tellers, said: "The chasm will be filled up only when that which is most precious to Rome is thrown in." Men and women stood around wondering and fearing, when Marcus Curtius, in full battle array, galloped forward on his war-horse. In a loud voice he said: "There is nothing so precious to Rome as a brave soldier," and leaped into the yawning chasm. Then the earth closed over it, and the place where the gulf had been was ever after called Lacus Curtius.

CUSH'MAN, Charlotte Saunders, the most famous of American actresses, born in Boston, July 23, 1816. She went upon the stage when nineteen years old, and soon became well known as an actress

in both tragedy and comedy. In 1845 she went to England and played there with success several years. Among her best characters were Lady Macbeth and Meg Merrilies. She died in Boston when sixty years old (Feb. 18, 1876).

CUVIER (*kew-ve-a'*), **Georges Chretien Leopold Frederic Dagobert,** Baron, a French writer on natural history, born at Montbéliard, Aug. 23, 1769. His father was an officer in a Swiss regiment in the French army. His mother, who was his first teacher, taught him to draw and showed him how to paint animals, in which he took great delight. When ten years old he entered the high school, where he became much interested in the study of natural history and learned all about birds and quadrupeds. When fifteen years old he went to the academy of Stuttgart, and four years later became private tutor to the son of Count d'Héricy, in Normandy, where he stayed until 1794, giving all his leisure hours to his favorite science. In that year he went to live in Paris, where his talents soon caused him to be acknowledged one of the first naturalists of Europe, and his lectures were attended by the most learned men of the time. In 1799 he was made professor of natural history at the College of France, and from this time honors of all sorts were heaped upon him. The Emperor Napoleon gave him many important offices, and he was made a member of all the learned societies of the world, for all thought it a great honor to have his name on their lists.

Before the time of Cuvier the animal kingdom had been divided up into classes according to the looks of the different animals, but he showed that the proper way to divide them was according to their bones or the way their different parts were put together. In 1817 he published a book called the

"Animal Kingdom," in which he separated animals into the four great divisions of Vertebrates, Articulates, Mollusks, and Radiates (C.C.T., 15, II.), and since his time this classification has been the basis of all the study of animals. He found out, too, a great deal about fossil animals (C.C.T., 516, I., l.), and showed that a great many kinds of animals, different from those now on earth, had lived in the earlier ages; and he studied them so carefully that he could make a drawing of one of these animals if only a single bone were shown him. Cuvier's manners were kind and pleasant, and he was very fond of the society of young people. He had the greatest love for order, and was very regular in all his habits. In 1819 he was made a baron, and in 1831 a peer of France. He died in Paris when sixty-two years old (May 13, 1832).

CUZCO (*koos'ko*), a city of Peru, in a valley among the ANDES; pop. about 20,000, or about the same as that of Chester, Pa. It is one of the highest cities in the world, being more than two miles above the sea. Before the Spaniards conquered Peru, Cuzco had two or three hundred thousand inhabitants and contained a magnificent temple of the sun, which the Peruvians worshiped as a god. Inside of this temple the walls were covered with gold and silver, and at one end was a picture or image of the sun, with a man's face made of gold and ornamented with emeralds and other precious stones. The temple was so arranged that when the sun rose, its first rays fell on this figure, causing it to glow so that it lighted up the whole temple and dazzled the eyes of the pilgrims who had come to worship it; yet, strange to say, this splendid temple had no better roof than a thatch of straw. Cuzco was defended by a fortress so large and strong that 20,000 men are said to

have been employed for fifty years in building it. When the Spaniards conquered the city they took away all the gold from the sun-temple, and built a convent in its place, but remains of the walls can still be seen.

CYB'E·LE, in Greek fable, the daughter of Ge, Earth, and Uranus, Heaven. She was the wife of Kronos or Saturn, Time, and the mother of all the other gods and goddesses. She is represented seated on a throne, wearing a crown, and with lions crouching beside her; but sometimes she is riding in a chariot drawn by lions. The Romans worshiped her under the name of Rhea.

CYCLADES (*sik'la-deez*), the name of a group of small islands in the Ægean Sea, belonging to Greece. The principal ones are called Syra, Delos, Andros, Tenos, Mykonos, Naxos, PAROS, ANTIPAROS, Siphnos, Seriphos, Kythnos, and Keos, but there are also many smaller ones. They were called Cyclades from the Greek word *kuklos*, a circle, because they form nearly a circle around the sacred island of Delos. Delos was one of the holiest places in ancient Greece, and was said to have been the birthplace of Apollo and Diana. Apollo had a famous temple and oracle there. Syra or Hermopolis (pop. 21,000), in the island of Syra, is the principal port of Greece and an important station for steamers. Naxos is very fertile, and produces fine wine, honey, wax and emery.

CY'CLOPS, in Greek fable, three sons of Uranus and Ge. Their names were Steropes, Lightning, Brontes, Thunder, and Arges, the heated bolt. They were giants, with only one round eye in the middle of the forehead. Their father threw them into TARTARUS, but Jupiter set them free. They helped Vulcan in making Jupiter's thunderbolts and the armor and weapons of gods and heroes.

The great walls found in Greece and some other countries, built of huge uncut stones without mortar, are called Cyclopean walls, because they are said to have been built by the Cyclops.

CYPRUS (*si'prus*), an island of Asia, in the E. end of the Mediterranean; area 3700 square miles, or nearly three times as large as the State of Rhode Island; pop. 186,000, or about half that of Rhode Island. It is mountainous, some peaks being more than a mile high. Copper, lead, and other metals are found among the hills, but no mines are now worked. The soil is fertile, but water is so scarce that there is sometimes not enough to drink, and all the crops dry up. The people, most of whom are Greeks, raise cotton, tobacco, silk, and grapes, and make wine. The grapes are the same as those grown in MADEIRA, and when the vines in that island died several years ago new ones were sent there from Cyprus.

The name of Cyprus is changed from its old Greek name Kupros, from which comes our word copper (C. C. T., 150, I. l.) The island was the principal place in ancient times of the worship of VENUS, who was said to have risen from the sea near it, and she had a splendid temple at a place there called Paphos. Cyprus has belonged to many nations, among whom were the Phœnicians, the Greeks, the Egyptians, the Persians, and the Romans. King RICHARD I. of England took it from the Saracens (1191), and it had kings of its own for nearly three hundred years, when it was taken (1489) by the Venetians, from whom the Turks conquered it in 1571. In 1878 Turkey gave it to Great Britain, and the English are now trying to make a strong place of it.

Many curiosities have been found in Cyprus. Gen. di Cesnola, who was for several years American consul there, dug up many old ruins and cemeteries, and found a great number of valuable things, which are now in the Metropolitan Museum in New York. At a place called Curium in ancient times, he found, under the ruins of a temple, three rooms full of gold and silver

Gold Earring from the Temple of Curium.

vases and ornaments, such as necklaces, brooches, earrings, and all sorts of valuable things. It is thought that the ancient people of the town, being threatened by enemies, hid all their valuables in these vaults under the temple, and were afterward either all killed or carried into slavery, so that the hiding-place was lost. The picture shows one of the gold earrings found there.

CY'RUS, The Elder, called the Great, founder of the Persian Empire. We do not know the date of his birth, but his reign was from 558 to 529 B.C. He was the son of Cambyses, a Persian nobleman, and grandson of Astyages, King of Media. Having rebelled against his grandfather and overcome him in battle, he took his throne and became the founder of an empire which soon comprised almost all the civilized parts of Asia. His first conquest was the kingdom of Lydia, whose king was CRŒSUS. Among his many exploits was the taking of BABYLON by turning the river Euphrates from its bed. When Babylon came into his hands he sent the Jews back to Jerusalem, and let them rebuild their temple, which had been destroyed by their Babylonish conqueror, NEBUCHAD-NEZZAR. According to Herodotus, he afterward marched against Tomyris, queen of a Scythian tribe, and was defeated and taken prisoner. Tomyris, angry because her son had been killed, is said to have cut off Cyrus's head and to have thrown it into a tub full of blood, saying: "Fill yourself with the blood which you crave!" But Xenophon, who wrote an account of his life, says he died a natural death in his own kingdom.

CYRUS, The Younger, son of Darius Nothus, King of Persia, and satrap or governor of Lydia and Phrygia. When his elder brother Artaxerxes II. ascended the throne, Cyrus formed a plan to dethrone him. Aided by some Greeks, one of whom was XENOPHON the historian, he made up a large army and met the king's forces at Cunaxa, where, too rashly exposing himself, he was killed (401 B.C.). Xenophon praises him highly, though for little reason that one can see from anything he tells us.

D

DAC'CA, a city, capital of the district of Dacca, in British India, 150 miles N.E. of CALCUTTA, on the river Buriganga ; pop. 80,000, or as large as New Haven, Conn. In 1610 it was chosen as the seat of the Mohammedan government of Bengal, which rank it retained for nearly a hundred years. Daeca was formerly celebrated for the manufacture of fine muslins, but, owing to English competition, almost its entire trade was diverted, and its once busy marts were deserted. The population fell from 200,000 to 69,000 in 1872. Of late its trade has revived somewhat, a railroad and waterworks have been constructed.

DÆ'DA-LUS, in Greek fable, a noted artist and inventor of Athens, who is said to have been the first to make many useful tools, among others the axe, the plummet, and the gimlet. He also invented glue, fitted ships with masts and sails, and carved statues so natural that they appeared to be alive. His nephew Perdix having made a saw, Dædalus became jealous and killed him. He was sentenced to death for this, but escaped and fled to Crete, where he built for King MINOS the labyrinth as a cage for the monster called the Minotaur, afterwards slain by THESEUS. Minos finally became angry with him and shut him up ; but Dædalus made wings for himself and his son Icarus, and flew out of Crete into Sicily. Icarus, however, flew higher than he ought, and, the wax with which his wings were fastened becoming melted by the sun, he fell into that part of the Ægean Sea which has been since called from him the Icarian Sea, and was drowned.

DAG'O-BERT, King of the Franks, born about 600. He was the son of Clothaire II., and became king of the whole Frankish dominion in 631. Dagobert caused the abbey of St. Denis to be built, decorating it with the workmanship of the goldsmith Eloi, whom he made one of his ministers. The oriflamme, or ancient royal standard of France, was given by him as a standard to this monastery, which he made his burial-place. He died at Epiny when thirty-eight years old (Jan. 19, 638).

DA'CON, an idol of the Philistines, whose temple at Gaza Samson destroyed while the Philistines were offering a great sacrifice to the idol for his capture. He was made with the upper part of his body like a man, and the lower part in the form of a fish.

DAGUERRE, (*da-gair'*), **Louis Jacques Mande,** the inventor of the daguerreotype, born in France, in 1789. He was a painter of scenery for theatres, and was the first to add to the effect of panoramas—that is, long pictures which, when unrolled little by little, give complete views of a city or country—by throwing colored lights and shadows upon the canvas so as to make the changes of day, night, etc. This invention he called the diorama. When about forty years old (1829) he began to experiment in making pictures by the action of light (C. C. T., 460, I.). About the same time a man named Niepce found out how to take such a picture, and the two then worked together until 1833, when Niepce died. Daguerre then worked by himself until 1839, when it was announced in the Academy of Sciences that he had succeeded in making sun-pictures and in fixing them so that they would not fade. The discovery was considered so important that the government gave him a pension of six thousand francs ($1,200), and made him an officer of the Legion of Honor. His pictures, called from him daguerreotypes, were taken on copper plates covered with a bright coating of silver. A few are still made for certain uses, but photographs have mostly taken their place. Daguerre died when sixty-two years old (July 12, 1851).

DAHL'GREN, John Adolf, an American admiral, born in Philadelphia in 1809. He became a midshipman when seventeen years old (1826), and a lieutenant when twenty-eight (1837). Ten years afterward he began to experiment in the casting of heavy cannon for naval warfare, and finally found out how to make the gun which is named after him. This is a solid cast-iron cannon, shaped much like a champaign-bottle, and is meant for firing only hollow shot or shells, though some have been used with solid balls. These guns, which are mostly made large enough for shot nine inches and eleven inches thick, are much used in our ships and sea-coast forts. In 1863 Dahlgren was made a rear-admiral. He died in Washington, when in command of the navy yard, in his sixty second year (July 12, 1870).

Ulric Dahlgren, his son, born in 1842, was a calvary officer in the Civil War, and became a colonel. In 1864, when in command of a force of cavalry, he made a raid into Virginia to try to rescue the Union prisoners in Libby Prison and at Belle Isle, Richmond, and was killed when only twenty-two years old (March 4, 1864).

DAHOMEY (*dah-ho'ma*), a country of W. Africa, E. of Ashantee; pop. about 200,000. The country has a large trade in palm oil, Indian corn, cattle, ivory, and India rubber. The people of Dahomey are negro savages, who live in huts and worship snakes and trees. They have priests who pretend to visit the world of spirits and bring back messages from the dead. The king has several thousand wives and a large body-guard of women, called Amazons, who are his best soldiers. When the king dies, several hundred persons are killed on his grave. Many are killed also every year to carry news to the dead. Rows of skulls from these victims adorn the walls of the temples, which are also partly built of them.

France has for many years had intimate trade relations with the country, but in 1889 trouble broke out between the king and the French merchants and officers, and in 1890 war resulted, in which the Dahomeyans fought desperately and with much success. Peace was finally restored and a new treaty made in September, 1890.

DAKOTA. See NORTH DAKOTA; SOUTH DAKOTA.

DAMASCUS (*dah-mas'kus*), a city of Asiatic Turkey, in Syria, about 45 miles E. of the Mediterranean; pop. about 150,000, or nearly as large as Louisville. It stands in a beautiful plain, which the Arabs call the fairest of the earthly paradises, and is surrounded by a wall, outside of which are well-cultivated fields and gardens. Damascus is the great centre of trade for Syria, and is also the meeting-place of pilgrims going to MECCA from the north. Sometimes large caravans of many thousands of merchants and pilgrims, with great numbers of camels, horses, and mules laden with goods, go from there to Bagdad, Cairo, and Mecca. The bazaars are said to be finer than those of Constantinople, and each business or trade has its own separate place. Damascus was once noted for the manufacture of swords which could be bent up double without breaking, and whose edges were so sharp as to cut through bars of iron or divide a gauze veil. The secret of their manufacture is not known, but the Russians have found out how to make just as good ones.

Damascus is one of the most ancient cities in the world and some think it is the oldest. It is often mentioned in the Bible in the time of Abraham. It has suffered a great many sieges, and has been at different times in the power of the Assyrians, Babylonians, Persians, Macedonians (333 B.C.), Romans (64 B.C.), and Saracens (A.D. 634), and was finally taken (1516) by the Turks, who still hold it. It is one of the sacred cities of the Mohammedans, and the Christians living there have suffered much from their persecutions.

DAMIETTA (*dam-e-et'tah*), a town of N. Egypt, on the E. branch of the Nile, 6 miles from its mouth; pop. 33000, or about as large as Lancaster, Pa. Most of the dwelling-houses are poorly built, but the mosques, bazaars, and marble baths are very large and fine. Formerly the town was noted for its manufacture of leather and striped cloth, and it is supposed that the name Damietta cloth was changed in time to the English word dimity.

In ancient times Damietta was close to the river mouth. During the Crusades it was attacked many times, and was once taken by Louis IX. of France (1249), but the king was soon afterward captured by the Arabs, and was obliged to give up the place as the price of his freedom. The old city was then destroyed, and a new one was built on the present site.

DAMOCLES (*dam'o-kleez*), a flatterer at the court of Dionysius, tyrant of Syracuse. He used to tell him how happy he ought to feel in being a rich and powerful king. Dionysius placed him at a splendid feast with a sword hung over his head by a single hair, meaning to show him by this that there is some danger as well as happiness in a king's life.

DA'MON and **PYTH'I·AS,** two young men of Syracuse, noted for their friendship. Pythias having been condemned to death by Dionysius, the ruler of Syracuse, begged to be allowed to go home to settle his affairs on condition that Damon should die in his stead if he did not return. Pythias came back just in time to save his friend from execution, and Dionysius, struck by so noble an affection, pardoned Pythias and begged that he might be admitted into their friendship.

DAM'PIER, William, a noted English sailor, born in Somersetshire. about 1652. He went to sea when still a boy, and when about twenty years old served in the war against

Holland. Soon after he came to America joined some buccaneers, and waged war against Spanish ships and trade along the western coast of South America. From thence he sailed to Australia and the East Indies, and finally came back to England (1691), where he published an account of his trip, called "A Voyage Round the World." He was afterward sent by the government on a voyage of discovery in the South Seas, and explored the coasts of Australia, Papua, and other islands. The Dampier Archipelago, off the northwest coast of Australia, and the strait between Papua and New Britain were named after him. He died about 1712.

DANA, (*da'nah*), **James Dwight,** an American writer on natural history, born in Utica, N. Y., Feb. 12, 1813. In 1836 he was appointed mineralogist and geologist of the United States exploring expedition, which cruised nearly five years in various parts of the world. On his return he spent many years in describing the marine animals and other curiosities he had collected. The descriptions were published by the government in three large volumes, each with a magnificent atlas of drawings made by him. He is the author also of a work on mineralogy which is used both in this country and in Europe, and his books on geology are widely known. Since 1850 he has been a professor in Yale College.

DANA, Richard Henry, an American poet, born at Cambridge, Mass., Nov. 15, 1787. He was educated at Harvard College, studied law in Boston, and practiced it in his native place. He was one of a club of gentlemen who began and carried on for a time *The North American Review*, and his earliest writings were published in it. Among his poems are the "Dying Raven" and "The Buccaneer." He died in Boston when ninety-one years old (Feb. 2, 1879).

DANA, Richard Henry, an American writer, son of the above, born in Cambridge, Mass., Aug. 1, 1815. He had to give up his studies in Harvard College for a time on account of weak eyes, and shipped as a common sailor on a voyage to California, of which he wrote a very interesting account in a book called "Two Years Before the Mast." He died when sixty-seven years old (January 7, 1882).

DAN'A-E, in Greek fable, the daughter of Acrisius, King of Argos, and mother of Perseus. Her father shut her up in a brazen tower where no one could get to her, because an oracle had said that he would be killed by her son. But Jupiter came to her in the form of a shower of gold and she became the mother of Perseus, and then Acrisius put her and the child in a chest and cast them into the sea. But Jupiter took care of them, and guided them to the island of Seriphus, where they were kindly treated by the king, Polydectes, and where PERSEUS grew to be a man.

DAN'A-US, in Greek fable, King of Argos, and twin brother of Ægyptus. He had fifty daughters, called the Danaïdes, who married the fifty sons of Ægyptus. Danaüs, having been warned by an oracle that one of his sons-in-law would take his throne from him, ordered his daughters to kill their husbands on the night they were married. They all obeyed except Hypermnestra, who spared the life of her husband, Lynceus, at the risk of her own. As a punishment the Danaïdes were condemned to the endless labor of pouring water into a vessel full of holes, knowing all the time that their labor was in vain. Danaüs was the fabled ancestor of the Danai, or Argives, one of the principal Greek tribes, whose name was sometimes given to all the Greeks.

D A N ' T E (Italian *dahn'ta*), a famous Italian poet, born in

Florence, May 14, 1265. His full name was Durante Alighieri (*doo-rahn'ta ah-le-ge-a're*), but it is commonly shortened into Dante. We know little of his boyhood except that he was a hard student; he took no holiday, but studied all the time; yet he was always joyous and bright, and full of fun. When he was nine years old he saw a beautiful girl named Beatrice, and although he never knew her well and probably never saw her more than three or four times, he used to write poems about her, and wor-

Dante.

shiped her memory long after her death; so that the names of Dante and Beatrice are often mentioned together.

In those days Florence was divided into two political parties, called the Neri and the Bianchi. Dante, who belonged to the last party and held a high office in the city, was sent to Rome on an embassy, and while he was away the Neri got into power and banished him, and ordered that if he came back he should be burned alive. After that he lived in many places, and died at last in Ravenna when fifty-six years old (Sept. 14, 1321).

Before Dante, the poets of northern Italy used to write in the Provençal language, which was spoken chiefly in the south of France, but Dante wrote in Italian, and from his time the Italian came to be a real language. His principal poem, called the *Divina Commedia* (Divine Comedy), describes himself as visiting Hell, Purgatory, and Heaven, and talking with those who had been best known for good or for evil on earth, especially in Florence. When Dante was dead the Italians found out that he was a great man, and all wanted to do him honor. Florence built him a monument and wanted his bones, but Ravenna would not give them up. The Italians now almost worship his memory, and call him divine, and in 1865 all Italy joined in celebrating the 600th year of his birth.

DAN'TON, Georges Jacques, a noted leader in the French Revolution, born at Arcis-sur-Aube, Oct. 28, 1759. He was a lawyer in Paris when the troubles between King LOUIS XVI. and the people began, and he at once took the side of the people and became one of their principal orators. He was tall and strong, bold and quick-tempered, and had a very powerful voice, which he loved to use in stirring up the people to violence. He led the mob to attack the palace of the Tuileries (Aug. 10, 1792), and took part himself in the fight, and the next month incited them to kill the royalists in the prisons. He also voted to put the king to death. Some of his friends having said that the people had no right to try the king, he replied: "You are right. So we will not try him, we will kill him."

The whole power was soon in the hands of Danton, MARAT, and ROBESPIERRE, and a committee, called the Committee of Public Safety, was appointed which had the power to judge and sentence to death any one it chose, and thousands of innocent people were tried and sent to the guillotine. Those days, so marked with blood, have ever since been called the Reign of Terror. At last Danton, having gained all he wished, was anxious to stop the bloodshed, but Robespierre would not listen to it. "We must not confound the innocent with the guilty," said Danton. "Who says that one innocent has suffered?" cried Robespierre. "Do you hear?" replied Danton, sneeringly; "Not one innocent has suffered!" From that time Robespierre, who was jealous of him, determined to get rid of him; and he was soon after arrested and tried by the committee which he had helped to set up. He treated his judges with contempt, and when they sentenced him to death, he exclaimed: "Robespierre follows me; I drag him after me." He was guillotined when only thirty-five years old (April 5, 1794).

DANT'ZIC, a city of Germany, in Prussia, on the river Vistula, 3 miles from the Baltic Sea; pop. 115,000, or a little less than that of Providence, R. I. It is surrounded by walls, and defended by a citadel and outer forts, so that it is one of the strongest places in Europe. On three sides the land is so low that it may be flooded with water in time of war. The principal trade of Dantzic is in grain, and on an island in the river, called Speicher (German for granary) Island, are great buildings for storing it in. No dwelling-houses, fires, or lights are allowed on this island.

Dantzic (German *Danzig*) means Danish fort, and the place was so called because a fort was built there by the Danes about the 10th century. It became in time a Polish city, and when POLAND was divided (1793) it was given to Prussia. In 1807 the French Marshal Lefebre took it after a bombardment of fifty-one days, and was made Duke of Dantzic for the skill with which he

carried on the siege over frozen land and water and with the trenches often filled with snow. Seven years later (1814) it was retaken by the Prussians after a twelve months' defense by the French General Rapp, who yielded only when the town was half battered down and the people nearly starved.

DAN'UBE, excepting the Volga, the largest river in Europe, it being about 1800 miles long, or nearly the same length as the RIO GRANDE. It rises in the Black Forest, in Germany, and after a winding course through beautiful and often grand scenery, empties into the Black Sea by seven mouths. It has always been of importance as the only great European river that flows east and west; and in early times its valley was the highway of the barbarians of the East in their expeditions into Europe. Great difficulties have been met in navigating it on acount of its reefs, shallows, and rapids, but efforts are now making to improve it. The worst part is the narrow place called the Iron Gate, where the river, shut in by high rocks on each side, is full of rapids and whirlpools; but this is now passed by steamers in a channel cut through the ledge. Steamboats go from Vienna down the Danube to Constantinople in about a week.

DAPH'NE, in Greek fable, a wood nymph loved by Apollo. Apollo pursued her, and when about to be caught she prayed her mother, Terra (earth), for aid. The earth opened and swallowed her, and on the place grew a laurel-tree, whose leaves were afterward sacred to Apollo.

DARDANELLES (*dar-da-nelz'*), the name of four castles or forts in Turkey, two on each side of the Hellespont, or Strait of Dardanelles. The castles were built to keep hostile ships from passing from the Mediterranean to the Sea of Marmora, and so to Constantinople. At one place the strait is less than half a mile wide, and chains can be stretched across. Two of the castles are built there. The other two castles are at the western end of the strait, where it is nearly two miles wide. All are mounted with many large cannon, but the castles themselves are not very strong, and they could easily be taken from the land side. Until 1870 the Turkish Government would not allow ships-of-war, even of friendly nations, to pass the Dardanelles. Dardanelles means little Dardanus, the castles having taken their name from an ancient city called Dardanus, which was on the Asiatic side of the strait. Near one of the old castles is the site of the ancient city of ABYDOS.

DAR'DA-NUS, in Greek fable, the founder of Troy. He came to Asia Minor from Samothrace, and founded a town at the foot of

Iron Gates of the Danube.   (See page 238.)

Mount Ida, which he called Dardania. Its name was changed to Troja, or TROY, by his grandson Tros.

DARE, Virginia, the first English child born in America, born at Roanoke, Aug. 18, 1587. She was the daughter of Ananias Dare and of Eleanor White, daughter of John White, governor of the colony sent out by Sir Walter Raleigh (1587). She was named after the district of Virginia.

DA-RI-EN'. See PANAMA.

DA-RI'US I., called Darius Hystaspis, or son of Hystaspes, King of Persia. Herodotus says that King CYRUS saw him in a dream with wings overshadowing Asia and Europe, and when Cyrus died without leaving a son to succeed him, Darius became king (521 B.C.).

He was a brave and skillful soldier and a wise ruler. He found Persia divided into bodies of people who were always quarreling with each other; and when he died he left it an empire firmly bound into one. He favored the Jews; and the temple of Jerusalem was rebuilt during his reign. Herodotus says he died when sixty-two years old (486 B.C.).

DAR'LING, Grace, an English heroine, born at Bamborough, Nov. 24, 1815. Her father was keeper of a lighthouse on one of the Farne islands, off the coast of Northumberland. One night in September, 1838, a steamer on its way to Scotland was wrecked near the lighthouse, and in the morning Grace saw some of the poor people clinging to the rocks or to fragments of the vessel. Her father was afraid to go to their rescue, but Grace at length persuaded him to help her launch a boat, and together they succeeded in saving nine persons. For this brave act a subscription of £700 ($3500) was raised for her, and she received many other valuable presents. She died at the age of twenty-seven (Oct. 20, 1842).

DARMSTADT (*darm'staht*), a town of Germany, capital of the grand duchy of Hesse, on the river Darm, 16 miles S. of Frankfort; pop. about 43,000, or nearly the same as Manchester, N. H. The old part of the town is dirty and crooked, but the new part is laid out in handsome streets and squares. The grand duke's palace is a beautiful building, and has a library of about 400,000 volumes and a fine gallery containing many paintings by the most noted artists.

Darmstadt means City on the Darm, *stadt* being the German word for city.

DARN'LEY. See MARY STUART.

DART'MOOR, a dreary barren tract of land in Devonshire, Eng-

land, noted for its great prison built in 1809 for French prisoners of war, 10,000 of whom were kept there at one time. The prison grounds occupy thirty acres, and are surrounded by two high walls. During the last war with the United States (1812-14) many American sailors, who refused to serve in the British navy against their country, were imprisoned there. The prison is now used for convicts.

DAR'WIN, Charles Robert, an English writer on natural history, born in Shrewsbury, Feb. 12, 1809. He spent five years (1831 to 1836) in an exploring voyage round the world in the ship Beagle, making many discoveries, especially about

Charles Robert Darwin.

coral islands and volcanoes. On his return, he wrote accounts of these discoveries and a narrative of the voyage, as well as descriptions of many animals. But he is best known for his work on the "Origin of Species," in which he attempts to show that the different kinds of animals and plants are descended from each other, or from other kinds which lived ages ago. He supposes, for instance, that reptiles are descended from fishes, birds from reptiles, mammals from birds, and higher mammals from lower ones. Mr. Darwin has written other books on the same subject, and in his "Descent of Man" he argues that men are descended from animals much like apes, and they in turn from lower animals. His views have been adopted by many learned men. He died when seventy-three years old (April 19, 1882).

DAUBIGNY (*do-been-ye'*), **Charles Francois,** a French landscape-painter, born in Paris, Feb. 15, 1817. His paintings have great merit, and his etchings and designs on wood have attracted much attention. He died in 1878.

DAUBIGNY, Karl Pierre, a son of C. F. Daubigny, was also favorably known as a painter of landscapes. He died when forty years old (May, 1886).

DAV'EN-PORT, a city of E. Iowa, on the Mississippi River, opposite Rock Island, Ill.; pop. 27,-000, or about as large as Brockton, Mass. Just above the city, the river forms rapids which furnish water-power for many manufactories. Among them are large flouring-mills, saw-mills, and manufactories of farming tools, carriages, wagons, and woolen goods. The surrounding region is very fertile, and abounds in coal, giving the city a large trade. Davenport was founded in 1836.

DAVID (*dah-vede'*), **Jacques Louis,** a noted French painter, born in Paris, Aug. 31, 1748. He was much thought of in the days of Napoleon, and was principal painter to that emperor. David was fond of imitating the old statues when painting, and it is said that he made the flesh in his figure-pieces look "as hard as marble." Among his best works are "The Coronation of Napoleon" and "The Death of Socrates." His picture of Napo-.eon on a rearing horse, on Mount

Saint Bernard, was a great favorite with the people in his day.

David died at Brussels in his seventy-eighth year (Dec. 29, 1825).

DAVID, Pierre Jean, a noted French sculptor, commonly called David of Angers, born in Angers, March 12, 1789. He showed great taste for sculpture when a boy, and went to study in Paris, where he was aided by the painter Jacques Louis David, though he was not related to him. When a student he visited London, and was asked to carve a monument in memory of the battle of Waterloo; but, though very poor, he was too patriotic to aid in commemorating the defeat of his countrymen. He afterward became famous in his art, and made a great number of statues, busts, medallions, and monuments. Being a strong republican, he preferred to sculpture subjects connected with freedom, and to make the statues and busts of men who had been useful to the world. Among his works are busts of Washington and Lafayette in the Capitol at Washington, a statue of Jefferson in New York, and the tomb of Marco BOZZARIS, at Missolonghi, Greece. He died in Paris when sixty-seven years old (Jan. 4, 1856).

DA'VIS, Jefferson, an American statesman, born in Kentucky, June 3, 1808. He was graduated at West Point in 1828, and served in several Indian wars. In 1835 he married the daughter of Zachary Taylor, and became a cotton-planter in Mississippi. In the Mexican war he distinguished himself in the battle of Monterey, where he was wounded, but remained in his saddle until the battle was ended. From 1847 to 1850 he was United States Senator, and from 1853 to 1857 Secretary of War. He again became Senator in 1857, but in 1861, when the Southern States seceded, he left the Senate, and the Southern Congress made him President of the Confederate States (Feb. 9, 1861). He was inaugurated at Montgomery, Alabama, on Feb. 18, and in April he ordered Gen. Beauregard to bombard Fort Sumter, thus opening the Civil War.

On May 20, 1861, the capital of the Confederacy was changed from Montgomery to Richmond, Va. At first the Confederates were successful, and Mr. Davis in his speeches prophesied that the war would soon be ended. In 1863 they met with many reverses, and to pay their soldiers they were

Jefferson Davis.

obliged to issue paper money, which soon became almost worthless. Mr. Davis was blamed by the Southern people for these misfortunes, though he was no more to blame than others. The Confederates were finally defeated at all points, and obliged to leave Richmond (April 2, 1865). Mr. Davis and his cabinet went to Danville, North Carolina, where they kept up the form of government for a week; but Lee and his army having surrendered, they were again compelled to fly.

A reward of $100,000 was offered for his capture, and he was at length taken by the Union cavalry at Irwinsville, Ga. (May 10, 1865), and

imprisoned in Fortress Monroe for two years. In May, 1867, he was brought before a court in Richmond on a charge of treason, but was released on bail, and in 1868 was pardoned by President Johnson. After his release Mr. Davis visited Europe. He died when eighty-one years old (December 6, 1889).

DAVOUST, or Davout (*dah-voo'*), Louis Nicolas, a French general, born at Annoux, May 10, 1770. He became a lieutenant in the army when only fifteen years old, and soon rose to be a general and went with Napoleon to Egypt (1799). In 1804 he was made a marshal, and he distinguished himself in many of Napoleon's battles. On the same day that Napoleon won the battle of JENA, Davoust gained an equally great victory at Auerstädt (Oct. 14, 1806), and he took so important a part in the battle of Eckmühl that he received the title of Prince of Eckmühl. After Napoleon's retreat from Russia, Davoust was besieged in Hamburg by the allied armies, but he defended the city successfully until Napoleon had been dethroned. When Napoleon returned from Elba, Davoust commanded the armies around Paris, finally surrendering the city to the allies on July 3, 1815. He died in Paris when fifty-three years old (June 1, 1823).

DAVY, Sir Humphry, a celebrated English chemist, born in Penzance, Cornwall, Dec. 17, 1778. He was the son of a wood carver, who educated him as well as he could, meaning to make him a physician; but Humphrey, while studying with an apothecary in Penzance, became so interested in chemistry that he gave himself up to that altogether. When only eighteen years old he found out that sea-plants take up carbonic acid and give out oxygen just as land-plants do (C. C. T., 4, II., and 5, I.), and soon after he made many experiments in breathing different kinds of gases, during which he nearly lost his life several times. He thus found out laughing-gas (nitrous oxide), which is now much used to dull pain in surgical operations and in pulling teeth. When only twenty-two years old his fame had become so great that he was appointed lecturer on chemistry in the Royal Institution of London, where his interesting experiments drew crowds of people.

When twenty-nine years old (1807) he found out that potash and soda are not simple substances, but are formed of the metals potassium and sodium united with oxygen. He afterward found out the new metals barium, strontium, calcium, and magnesium, and proved that chlorine, sulphur, phosphorus, and iodine are simple substances or elements (C. C. T., 213-14-15). In 1812 a great many men were killed by the explosion of gas in a coal-mine near Newcastle, and Davy was asked to try to find out some way of preventing such accidents. After some experiments with gas, he made the safety-lamp (C. C. T., 343, II., l.), which has saved thousands of lives. When some one asked him if he was not going to take out a patent for the invention, he answered: "No, my good friend, I never thought of such a thing; my sole object was to serve the cause of humanity." The owners of mines gave him for this a present of a service of silver plate, worth $10,000.

In the same year Davy was made a knight, and six years afterward a baronet. In 1827 he had to give up the presidency of the Royal Society, to which he had been elected seven times, and to travel for his health; but he did not get any better, and finally died in Geneva, Switzerland, when fifty-one years old (May 29, 1829). A statue has been erected to his memory at Penzance.

DAY'TON, a city of Ohio, at the junction of the Mad and Great Miami rivers, 46 miles N.N.E. of Cincinnati; pop. 61,000, or about as large as Wilmington, Del. It is noted for its manufactures of stoves, railroad-cars, and paper. Four miles from the city is the Central National Soldiers' Home, with forty large buildings in which disabled soldiers live at the cost of the government. A church, library, music-hall, billiard-room, and beautiful grounds are connected with it. Dayton was settled in 1796, and became a city in 1841.

DEAD SEA. See PALESTINE.

DE·CA'TUR, Stephen, a gallant American naval officer, born at Sinnepuxent, Md., Jan. 5, 1779. He entered the navy as a midshipman when nineteen years old, and became a lieutenant the next year (1799). On the night of Feb. 16, 1804, he sailed into the harbor of Tripoli and burned the frigate Philadelphia, which had been taken from the Americans by the Tripolitans, with whom the United States were then at war. A good many of the enemy were killed, but Decatur had only one man wounded, and he sailed safely out of the harbor again by the light of the blazing ship. For this gallant deed Congress gave him a splendid sword and made him a captain.

In the war of 1812-14 with England, when in command of the frigate United States, he captured the British frigate Macedonian after a hard-fought battle (Oct. 25, 1812), and for this Congress gave him a gold medal. In January, 1815, he sailed out of New York in the frigate President, but was pursued by four British ships, and, after losing many men in a running fight of eight hours, was forced to surrender. He was carried to Bermuda, but soon got his liberty, and in the summer of the same year (1815) he captured two Algerine ships off the coast of Spain, and then sailed to Algiers, where he forced the ruler of that country to make a treaty with the United States, in which he promised to do no more damage to

American commerce. After all this noble service, Commodore Decatur was killed, when fifty-seven years old (March 22, 1820), in a duel with Commodore Barron.

DECIUS (*de'she-us*), **Caius Messius Quintus,** a Roman emperor, born in Pannonia. He was chosen by the soldiers to succeed the Emperor Philip in 249. He began his reign by one of the most cruel and bloody persecutions the Christians ever suffered, which was interrupted by an invasion of the Goths. Decius and his son marched to oppose them, and were both killed (A.D. 251).

DEER'FIELD, a town of Massachusetts, on the Connecticut River; pop. 3500. It is one of the oldest towns in that part of the State, having been settled in 1670. At first it suffered much from the Indians. In 1675 a company of eighty-four men, under Captain Thomas Lathrop, fell into an ambush at Bloody Brook, about a mile from the village, and nearly all were killed. One night in the winter of 1704 the French and Indians attacked Deerfield, burning nearly all the houses, killing many of the people, and carrying more than a hundred away as captives. Among these was the minister Rev. John Williams and his family. On the second day's march his wife became so tired that she fell down and the Indians killed her. Mr. Williams and his children were taken to Canada, where they were well treated. After two years they were released. One of the daughters stayed with the Indians and afterward married one of them. Mr. Williams published a book giving an interesting account of his captivity. The door of the old block-house in which the people of Deerfield defended themselves against the Indians is still preserved. It bears many marks of bullets and tomahawks.

DEFOE (*de-fo'*), **Daniel,** a famous English writer, author of "Robinson Crusoe," born in London in 1661. He was the son of a butcher, and his real name was Daniel Foe, but he changed it to Defoe. He was educated for a minister among the Dissenters—that is, those who were opposed to the Church of England; but he became a tradesman, and afterward a writer. For making fun of the English High Church party in some of his writings he was arrested and imprisoned for two years, during which time he wrote several books. In the order for his arrest is this description of him: "He is a middle-sized, spare man, about forty years old; of a

Daniel Defoe.

brown complexion, dark brown colored hair, but wears a wig, a hooked nose, sharp chin, gray eyes, and a large mole near his mouth." He wrote more than two hundred books and pamphlets, but he is best known as the author of the "Life and Adventures of Robinson Crusoe," a book which is still read with delight by all young folks. Sir Walter Scott says of it: "Perhaps there exists no work in the English language which has been more generally read and universally admired than the Adventures of Robinson Crusoe." Though Defoe was so successful as a writer, he died quite poor. He tells his own story in these two lines :

" No man has tasted differing fortunes more;
And thirteen times I have been rich and poor."

He died in London when seventy years old (April 24, 1731).

DE HAAS(*deh hahs'*),**Maurice F.H.,** a marine painter, born at Rotterdam, Holland, in 1832. He came to New York when twenty-seven years old, and has since painted in that city. He paints coast scenes, sunsets and moonlights at sea, and shipwrecks.

DE KALB, John, Baron, a general in the American army of the Revolution, born in Bavaria, June 29, 1721. He first served in the French army, and in 1777 came to America with Lafayette and joined the forces of the colonies. Congress made him a major-general, and he served under Washington in Pennsylvania and New Jersey. He was the second in command in the army under Gen. Gates, and was so badly wounded at the battle of Camden that he died three days later (Aug. 19, 1780).

DELACROIX (*d'lah-krwah'*), **Ferdinand Victor Eugène,** a noted French painter, born at Charenton, April 26, 1799. His father had held high offices, and Eugène had the prospect of some fortune, but all was lost, and he was obliged to work hard for a living. When eighteen years old he went to study under a good painter, and exhibited his first work, called "Dante and Virgil," about five years afterward. His second picture, the "Massacre of Scio," won him much fame. When thirty-one years old he went to Algiers and Morocco, and on his return painted some fine pictures of scenes in those countries. After this he had plenty to do, and became very prosperous. He left many works; some of his large pictures may be seen at Versailles; others are in many of the churches in Paris. Delacroix died near Versailles when sixty-four years old (Aug. 13, 1863).

DELAROCHE (*d'lah-rosh'*), **Paul,** a French painter of historical scenes, born in Paris, July 17, 1797. His father was proud of Paul's talent for painting, and as he was rich was able to give him a good art education under the best teachers. Paul began at first to paint landscapes, but soon gave them up for scenes in history. He began to exhibit pictures when twenty years old, and after that showed fine works nearly every year, his subjects being mostly taken from French and English modern history. Among his most noted works are "Joan of Arc in Prison," "Execution of Lady Jane Grey," "Cromwell looking at the Dead Body of Charles I.," and "Napoleon at Mt. St. Bernard." He painted also many portraits, but he is most famous for his historical pictures, which were not surpassed by those of any other painter of his time. He died in Paris when fifty-nine years old (Nov. 4, 1856).

DEL'A·WARE, a State of the United States, on the Atlantic coast, between New Jersey and Maryland; area 2120 square miles, or about one fourth as large as New Jersey; pop. 168,000, or about an eighth that of New Jersey ; capital, Dover. Delaware is the smallest State in the Union except Rhode Island. In the northern part are low hills, but the southern part is flat and has many swamps. Delaware Bay, through which the Delaware River empties into the Atlantic, extends along most of its east side, but its shore is low and marshy and has scarcely any harbors. At Lewes, near where it opens into the Atlantic, a good harbor has been made by building out into the sea a great stone wall called the Delaware Breakwater.

There are a few iron-mines, and a kind of clay is found which is good for making porcelain. Many of the people are farmers, and many fine fruits, especially peaches, are raised for market. Some of the peach-orchards have thousands of trees. The only city is Wilmington. Delaware gets its name from the bay, which was named after Lord De la Warr, Governor of Virginia, who went into it in 1610; but Henry Hudson had been there the year before. The State was first settled by the Dutch, and then by the Swedes. In 1655 the Dutch drove away the Swedes, and in 1664 the English took it from the Dutch. Delaware was one of the thirteen original States, and was the first one to agree to the Union.

DELFT, a town of the Netherlands, between ROTTERDAM and the HAGUE; pop. 28,500, or about the same as that of Bay City, Mich. It is divided by many canals, which are crossed by more than seventy bridges. Delft was once noted for its glazed earthen-ware, which took from it the name of delft-ware, but little is now made there. The best is now made in England, where it is called "delf." On the roofs of many of the old houses in Delft may be seen boxes for storks, and

Nest of Storks.

it is considered a very fortunate thing for a family when one of these birds builds its nest and raises its young on the roof.

About six miles from Delft is Delft Haven, from which the Pilgrim Fathers sailed for Southampton (July 22, 1620) before coming to America.

Delft is from an old word, *delf*, meaning a canal.

DELHI (*del'le*), a city of India, on the river Jumna, a branch of the GANGES; pop. 185,000, or a little more than that of Newark, N. J. It is a walled city with eleven gates, four of which open on the river.

The seven on the land side are very large and are defended by strong towers. The walls and forts were built by Shah Jehan, when Delhi was the capital of the Mogul Empire, at which time it is said to have had 2,000,000 inhabitants. The palace of Shah Jehan was once the most magnificent one in India, but is now falling to ruin. In its great hall stood the famous Peacock Throne, made of gold and jewels, and which cost $30,000,000. The frame of the throne is in the museum there, but the jewels were all carried off by the Persians. The chief mosque, called the Jumma Musjid, built of white marble, is one of the most splendid buildings in the world. In the country around Delhi are many ruins which show it to have once been a magnificent city. The goldsmiths of Delhi are celebrated, and Cashmere shawls are embroidered there with gold and silver threads.

Delhi was a great city as early as the 10th century. In the time of Shah Jehan it was called Shah-jehanabad (City of the King of the World), and the Mohammedans still call it so. The British took it in 1803.

DE'LOS. See CYCLADES.

DEL'PHI, a city of ancient Greece, famous as the seat of the oracle of APOLLO. It was situated at the base of Mount Parnassus, amid wild peaks, huge rocks, and high cliffs, and was noted for the number, value, and splendor of its treasures, especially the temple of Apollo. Whoever wanted to consult this oracle

The Pythia on the Tripod.

had to bring rich presents and offerings, and to go through a great many ceremonies, before he could receive his answer, which was given by a priestess called the Pythia. The spot where the oracle was uttered was called the Pythium, and was believed to be the centre of the earth. There was a chasm in the earth there, from which a kind of vapor arose. The Pythia sat upon a tripod where she breathed this vapor, which threw her into spasms, and the words which she spoke when in this state were taken as the answer of Apollo.

DEMERARA (*dem-er-ah'rah*). See GUIANA.

DE-ME'TER. See CERES.

DEMETRIUS POLIORCETES (*de-me'tri-us pol-e-or-se'teez*), King of Macedon, born about 338 B.C. He was the son of Antigonus, one of the generals of Alexander the Great, who on the death of that monarch received a share of his dominions, and he was surnamed Poliorcetes (Besieger of Cities) on account of his success as a general. Most of the wars in which he took part were caused by the quarrels among Alexander's generals when they divided the spoils of that conqueror. Demetrius in 294 B.C. usurped the throne of Macedon, but he was driven out by Pyrrhus, king of Epirus, and he spent the remainder of his life in Syria, where he died when about fifty-five years old (283 B.C.).

DEMOSTHENES (*de-mos'the-neez*), the geatest orator of ancient times, born near Athens about 382 B.C. His father died when he was only seven years old, and left quite a large fortune to be divided between him and his sister. Their guardians robbed them of their

Demosthenes.

money, and when Demosthenes was eighteen years old he prosecuted them in the courts, pleaded his own cause, and won his case. He then made up his mind to be an orator, although there was much against him : his lungs were weak and he had a defect in his speech ; but he overcame these difficulties by hard work, and became the most eloquent orator of his time. When Philip of Macedon threatened the liberty of the Grecian states, Demosthenes spoke with great ability in their defence, and was so severe in his satire of Philip that abusive speeches are to this day called "philippics."

But Demosthenes had many enemies, and when his friend Ctesiphon asked the Senate to give Demosthenes a golden crown for his services, he was prosecuted by ÆSCHINES, his rival. On the trial of Ctesiphon, Demosthenes made his great speech on the crown, and far surpassed Æschines, who had to leave Athens.

About the year 325 B.C. Demosthenes, with several other patriots, was accused of having taken bribes from the Macedonians. There was no proof of his guilt ; but so great was the power of his enemies that he was thrown into prison. He escaped, however, and fled to Ægina, where he remained until the death of Alexander, when he was brought back in triumph by his countrymen. But before long his enemies attacked him again, and the Athenians were ordered by the Macedonians to give him up to be put to death. He tried to escape ; but, finding that he could not do so, he took poison, which he always carried in a quill, and died (322 B.C.).

DEN'IS, Saint, the patron saint of France, and the first bishop of Paris, in the 3d century. He suffered martyrdom during one of the persecutions of the Roman emperors, being beheaded in 272. His body was buried near the place of his execution, and over the spot was built a church which was afterward united by King Dagobert with the Abbey of St. Denis. This church contained the tombs of most of the kings of France, and of other great men. In 1793, when hatred of royalty was at its height in France, the tombs of the kings were opened and the bodies put into a common grave.

The Abbey of St. Denis had always the keeping of the crown, sceptre, and other ornaments used at the coronation of the kings of France. The oriflamme, a gold and red banner, which was originally that borne by its abbots, became the standard of the royal forces. The name of the Saint was long the war-cry of the French as they rushed into battle with the words "Montjoye, St. Denis!"

DEN'MARK a country of Europe, between the North Sea and the Baltic; area 14,700 square miles, or about the same as that of New Hampshire and Connecticut put together; pop. 2,172,000, or nearly the same as that of Indiana; capital, COPENHAGEN. Part of it is a peninsula, called Jutland, and the rest islands, of which the largest are called Seeland, Laaland, and Fünen. It is a low country, with no large rivers, but there are many fiords, or long bays, which reach far into the land. Some of them have very narrow entrances, but within they are long and crooked like lakes. The climate is much like that of New York or Pennsylvania, though Denmark is so far north that in the middle of the winter the days are only six and a half hours long. The people, most of whom live on the islands, are much like Germans, but their language is different. More than half of them are farmers; but there are also great dairy-farms, where cattle are kept and butter and cheese are made. Danish butter put up in cans is sent even to Asia and South America. Denmark is a kingdom; besides the king there is a Congress (called Rigsdag) much like that of the United States. Most of the people are Protestants, belonging to the Lutheran Church.

Denmark, called by the Danes Danmark, means the *mark* or land of the Danes. In early times, Denmark, Norway, and Sweden were inhabited by a people called Scandinavians or NORTHMEN. The Northmen of Denmark became noted sailors, and about a thousand years ago they conquered NORMANDY, in France, and invaded England and Scotland, and at last (1017) Canute, a Danish king, ruled over Denmark, Norway, England, and part of Sweden. About the same time Denmark, which had before been pagan, became a Christian country. In 1387 Queen Margaret of Denmark conquered all of Sweden, and Denmark, Norway, and Sweden were all united. But after that Denmark lost one country after another, until it became a very small kingdom. Besides the country properly called Denmark, the Danes own ICELAND, GREENLAND, the Faröe Islands, and the islands of Santa Cruz, St. Thomas, and St. John in the West Indies.

DEN-TA'TUS, Manius Curius, a famous Roman consul, lived in the 3d century B.C. His real name was Manius or Marcus Curius, but he is said to have been called Dentatus (from Latin *dens*, a tooth) because he had teeth when he was born. After being consul three times, during which he gained battles over Pyrrhus, the Samnites, and other enemies of Rome, he went to live on a little farm, which he worked with his own hands. One day, while he was boiling some vegetables in an earthen pot for his dinner, some of the chief men of the Samnites came and offered him costly presents. He refused their gifts, saying: "I prefer my earthen pots to all your vessels of gold and silver; I would rather rule over people who have money than to have it myself." He died about 270 B.C.

DE QUIN'CEY, Thomas, a noted English author, born near Manchester, Aug. 15, 1786. His youth was spent in the country, his playmates being his three little sisters. When he went to school he made such progress in Greek that at twelve years of age the master said that he could speak Greek as well as English. When fourteen, he wanted to go to the university, but his guardian refused, so he borrowed ten guineas and ran away from school. Soon all his money was spent; he was obliged to live on one meal a day; then on berries, or anything he chanced to get. At last he contrived to get to London, where for sixteen weeks he used to wander about without a roof to cover his head, and suffering the torments of starvation. He has written interesting accounts of this time of his life.

After a time he returned to his family, and was sent to the university, where he studied hard. He first began to take opium for rheumatism, by degrees grew fond of it, and kept on using it for many years; and it cost him a long and terrible struggle before he could give up the habit. Afterward he wrote a wonderful book about it, called the "Confessions of an English Opium-Eater;" and this and his other works soon made him famous. He died in Edinburgh when seventy-three years old (Dec. 8, 1859).

DER'BY (English *dar'by*), a town of England, about 30 miles N. of Birmingham; pop. 81,000, or about as large as New Haven, Conn. It has manufactories of silk, stockings, lace, iron and brass, porcelain, shot, and many other things. The first silk-mill in England was built there in 1718. Marble found near the city is used for making ornaments. Derby is noted for its many beautiful churches and public buildings.

DESAIX DE VEYGOUX (*deh-sa' deh va-goo'*), **Louis Charles Antoine,** a famous French general, born near Riom in Auvergne, Aug. 17, 1768. He is commonly called simply Desaix, and his name is often wrongly spelled Dessaix. He early won fame in the army, but, because he belonged to a noble family, nearly

lost his head in the French Revolution. He served bravely under Napoleon in Egypt, and conquered all Upper Egypt in eight months, for which Napoleon gave him a splendid sword. He followed Napoleon to Italy, and got to MARENGO just in time to save him from being defeated. When he arrived on the field he said to General Kellermann, "The battle is lost, but there is time to win another;" and he charged the Austrians so fiercely that they were soon put to rout. But he was shot through the heart and died on the field, when only thirty-two years old (June 14, 1800). Napoleon had a medal struck in his honor, and had him buried on the top of the Alps, near the monastery of Saint BERNARD.

DESCARTES (*da-kart'*), **René, a** famous French philosopher, born at La Haye, Touraine, March 31, 1596. He was a very inquisitive little boy; used to ask so many questions about different things, and think so long over the answers, that he was called the young philosopher. He left college when sixteen years old, and when twenty-one became an officer in the Dutch army, in which he served three years, when he joined the Bavarian army and fought in the battle of Prague (1620). But the dreadful things he saw sickened him of war, and he left military life and spent many years in traveling and in study, and finally settled in Holland and set himself to writing books.

Descartes was not a great reader, but he used to think over things, and make experiments, and find out for himself the truths, which he wrote out and published to the world. One time he was studying anatomy and chemistry together; a visitor came in the room, and asked where his books were. "Here they are!" said Descartes, pointing to the animals he had dissected. His writings made a greater change in philosophy than those of any other writer since his day. He became so famous that he was much interrupted in his studies by visitors, and he was therefore always changing his home. In Holland he lived at thirteen different places, and changed his dwelling-house twenty-four times. When nearly fifty-four years old, he received an invitation from Christina, Queen of Sweden, to visit her at Stockholm and give her lessons in philosophy. So at five o'clock every morning Descartes used to go to the palace in thin shoes and silk stockings, and stand on a marble floor, shivering in the cold, while he gravely taught his philosophy to the little Queen, who was snugly tucked up in bed while she listened to the wise lessons. He caught cold in this way, and died at Stockholm when fifty-four years old (Feb. 11, 1650).

DES MOINES (*de moin'*), a city, capital of Iowa, near the central part of the State, on the Des Moines River; pop. 50,000, or as large as Los Angeles, Cal. It contains a very fine capitol and other buildings, and has a woolen-factory, plow-factories, flouring-mills, and many other manufactories. Near the city are large coal-mines. Des Moines was founded in 1846, and became the State capital in 1857.

DESMOULINS (*da-moo-lan'*), **Benoît Camille,** a noted leader in the French Revolution, born at Guise, Picardy, in 1762. He was a bright boy, and was well educated at college. When the French Revolution broke out, Camille took the side of the people, and did all he could to stir them up both by his talk and his writings. One day he mounted a table, with a loaded pistol in each hand, and called on the people to fight for their liberty; he told them to wear green badges, and as there was not enough ribbon, he made them badges out of the green leaves of trees. The people shouted, almost embraced Camille, and marched in procession through the streets, calling out, "To arms!" This was really the opening of the revolution.

Camille could write better than he talked; and from that time he helped on the cause by publishing pamphlets in which he abused and made fun of the other side; and for this he became so noted that the greatest men and generals tried to make him their friend. But in time things changed, and people changed too, and some of his great friends turned against him. ROBESPIERRE ordered his writings to be burned. Camille flew into a passion, and shouted out: "Burning is not answering." This made his enemies angry, and he was arrested and sentenced to death. After the sentence was pronounced Camille had to be dragged from his seat to the prison, and on his way to the guillotine he tore his clothes into shreds, exposing his bare breast to the gazing crowd, and called on them to save him. His beautiful young wife tried to raise a riot in his favor, but she too was arrested, and suffered death a few days after her husband. He was beheaded in Paris when thirty-two years old (April 5, 1794).

DE SOTO (*da so'to*), **Fernando,** the discover of the Mississippi River, born in Estremadura, Spain, about 1496. He was of a noble but poor family, and was educated by Pedrarias Davila. When twenty-three years old he went with Davila to America, and soon became noted for his ability and independence of character. In 1532 he joined PIZARRO in the conquest of Peru, was the first to find the pass through the mountains, and aided greatly in the battle which led to the taking of CUZCO. He landed in America with nothing but his sword, but returned to Spain with a fortune, and was received with honor by the emperor, and married Davila's daughter. When forty-two years old (1538) he undertook at his own expense the conquest of Florida, a land said to be full of gold and jewels. He was joined by many Spanish and Portuguese cavaliers, in all more than 600 men, some of whom sold all their possessions in order to go with him. They sailed off gayly as if for a holiday. For four years they wandered about in search of the treas-

Fernando de Soto.

ures, deluded by the Indians, who always told them that there was gold farther on, because they wanted to get rid of them. At last, disappointed in his hopes, and having lost many men, De Soto died on the banks of the Mississippi, and his followers, wishing to conceal his death, wrapped his body in a mantle, and in the silence of midnight sunk it in the middle of the river. He died when about forty-six years old (1542), and his wife died of grief three days after hearing the news.

DESSAIX (*da-sa'*), **Joseph Marie,** a famous French general, born at Thonon, in Savoy, Sept. 24. 1764. He studied medicine, and practiced it in Paris until the Revolution began. He then joined the army and fought under Bonaparte, who gave him the surname of "The Intrepid," because he was such a brave and gallant soldier, and made him a count of the empire. The last years of his life were spent in a quiet way. He died when seventy years old (Oct. 26, 1834).

DETAILLE (*deh-tah-e*), **Édouard Jean Baptiste,** a French painter, born in Paris in 1848. His pictures represent soldiers and battle-scenes, and have already gained him much fame. A few of them are owned in the United States.

DETROIT', the chief commercial city of Michigan, on the W. side of the Detroit River; pop. 206,-000, or a little larger than that of Milwaukee, Wis. The Detroit River flows from Lake St. Clair to Lake Erie, and separates Michigan from Canada. It is very deep at Detroit, and makes the best harbor on the great lakes. Many steamboats and other vessels are always to be seen there, and Detroit has a very large trade, much of which is with Canada. It has also large manufactures, and is the meeting-place of many railroads. A little below the city is Fort Wayne, which when finished will be one of the strongest forts along the Canada boundary.

Detroit means the "Strait," and the town was so called by the French, who first settled there in 1701, the Detroit River being really a strait and not a river. The English got it in 1763, and held it until the end of the war of the Revolution, but the Americans did not go there until 1796. Detroit was the capital of the State of Michigan until 1847.

DEUCALION (*du-ka'le-on*), in Greek fable, King of Phthia in Thessaly, and son of PROMETHEUS. His story is much like that told in the Bible of Noah. Men on earth had got to be so wicked that Jupiter sent a flood to drown them. Deucalion, having been warned of this by Prometheus, built a boat, in which he and his wife Pyrrha were saved. After the flood was over the boat landed on Mount PARNASSUS. Deucalion then prayed that men might be put back on the earth, and Jupiter told him and Pyrrha to cast behind them the bones of their mother. They thought over this for a while, and then remembered that the earth was their mother; so they picked up stones from the hill side, and threw them as they were told, and from them sprang men and women.

DEV'ON-PORT. See PLYMOUTH.

DIANA (*di-an'nah*), in Roman fable, goddess of chastity, of hunting, and of the woods. She was

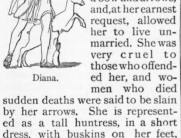

the daughter of Jupiter and Latona, and the twin sister of Apollo. She represented the moon, as Apollo did the sun. Jupiter gave her a bow and arrows, and, at her earnest request, allowed her to live unmarried. She was very cruel to those who offended her, and women who died

Diana.

men who died sudden deaths were said to be slain by her arrows. She is represented as a tall huntress, in a short dress, with buskins on her feet, and carrying a bow, quiver, and arrows. Sometimes she has a hound, or a stag, with her. The Greeks worshiped her under the name of Artemis.

DIAS (*de'ahs*), **Bartholomeu,** a noted Portuguese navigator, born about the middle of the fifteenth century. He sailed with several vessels down the west coast of Africa, and turned the southern point, which he called Cabo Tormentoso (Cape of Storms); but the king of Portugal changed it to CAPE OF GOOD HOPE. Dias sailed on several other voyages, and was commander of one of the vessels in the fleet under Cabral, when Brazil was discovered. On his way to India his vessel was lost at sea (May 29, 1500).

DICK'ENS, Charles, a famous English writer of novels, born at Landport, Feb. 7, 1812. He tells us that he was "a very small and not over-particularly-taken-care-of boy." Too sickly to join in boyish sports, he was greedy for books, and when other boys were playing,

Charles Dickens.

he was seated in his bed reading. He took to writing stories when a little child, and was often lifted up on the table that he might amuse his father's friends by telling them, and by singing comic songs. When about nine years old, his father lost money, and Charles was taken from school, where he was very happy, and moved, with his family, to mean lodgings in the poorest part of London suburbs. Everything about him was squalid and miserable; with no playmates, he wandered about alone, neglected and wretched, longing all the time to go to school somewhere, anywhere so that he could be taught something. He seemed to have been filled with a sort of amazement that nobody thought about him except to make him a mere household drudge; and so he went on cleaning boots, running poor little errands, and perhaps thinking out his beautiful stories all the time. Nobody took pity on the lonely little lad, whose heart, for this very reason, was afterward so full of love and sympathy for little children all his life long. A walk into real London town, he says, used to entrance him with delight, and the London night-sights were a constant joy and wonder to him.

His father grew poorer still, and at last was put into Marshalsea prison for debt, where his family were obliged, after a while, to join him. Charles, however, was sent to live with a cousin in the blacking business. The humiliation and misery of that time were terrible to the sensitive boy of ten; he says that his tears often mingled with the water in which he washed and rinsed the blacking bottles. Whenever he thought of those dreadful days, even after he grew to be a great man, he said he would turn faint, and seem to live it all over again. He stayed in the blacking warehouse two years; then his father, having a little money left to him, was able to leave the prison, and Charles was again sent to school for two years, after which he was put into an attorney's office to learn to be a lawyer. But he did not like this life, so he studied shorthand to report news for the newspapers, and soon began to write articles himself. He signed his writings "Boz," which was a nickname he had given to his younger brother, whom he called Moses for fun, pronouncing it through his nose like Boses, and then shortening it into Boz.

When he was about twenty-four years old he published the "Papers of the Pickwick Club," and soon Mr. Pickwick became known wherever the English language was spoken, and Dickens found himself all at once famous. After this whatever he wrote was eagerly read, and he was courted by everybody. He wrote a great many books and many beautiful Christmas stories and other stories, and became more celebrated than any other writer of his time; and when he died all the world mourned. He died at his home called Gadshill, near Rochester, when fifty-eight years old (June 9, 1870), and the poor little blacking boy was buried in Westminster Abbey by the side of kings and queens.

DIDEROT (*de-da-ro'*), **Denis**, a famous French writer and philosopher, born in Langres, Oct. 5, 1713. He was the son of a cutler, and was educated for the church; but that did not suit him; so he tried the law, and liked that as little. This vexed his father, who refused to give him any more money, and for a while Denis supported himself by teaching and finally by writing. He wrote many books, among them some novels and plays; his greatest work is his Encyclopædia, which, instead of writing only the truth about men and matters, he made the means of spreading his own views, and for this much fault was found with him. He labored over it like a slave for twenty years, and only got for his pains about £120 a year, the wage of a good cook. He was careless about spending money, and once had to offer his library for sale; Catherine II. of Russia bought it for 15,000 francs ($3000), and gave him a salary of 1000 francs ($200) a year to be the keeper of it; and, moreover, paid him fifty years' income in advance. He died in Paris when seventy years old (July 30, 1784).

DI'DO, a princess of Tyre, noted as the founder of CARTHAGE. After the death of her father, King Mutgo, her brother Pygmalion took the throne and murdered her husband, and she and many others set sail to find a new country. Landing on the coast of Africa, they bought as much land as might be covered with the hide of a bull, and by cutting it into very thin strips made it surround a large territory, on which Carthage was built.

When ÆNEAS came to Carthage Dido fell in love with him and wanted him to stay there and marry her, but he would not listen to her, and, as Virgil tells in the Æneid, when he sailed away she killed herself.

DIEPPE (*de-ep'*), a seaport town of France in Normandy, on the English Channel; pop. 22,500, or about the same as that of Cohoes, N. Y. It is celebrated for its fisheries, especially of oysters, for its ship-building, and for its manufactures of ivory and paper. In the summer Dieppe is one of the principal watering-places in France, and is visited by great numbers of people, who go there to bathe and enjoy the fine scenery and pure air. Dieppe was founded in the 10th century. It gets its name from a Norman word meaning deep water.

DIESKAU (*dees'kow*), **Ludwig August,** a German soldier who commanded the French army in Canada, born in Saxony in 1701. In 1755, with a body of Indians and Canadians, he attacked the British at Fort Edward, in New York. His men were frightened off, but Dieskau, although wounded three times, refused to go from the field. He quietly seated himself on the stump of a tree, and was taken and kept a prisoner for eight years, when he went back to France. He died near Paris when sixty-six years old (Sept. 8, 1767).

DIJON (*de-zhong'*), a city of France, 160 miles S.E. of Paris; pop. 60,000, or about as large as Grand Rapids, Mich. It is a handsome place, with many fine old buildings, and is the chief place where Burgundy wine is sold. It has also a large trade in grain, flour, and wool.

Dijon was called by the Romans Dibisdunum, or the fort on the two waters, meaning the rivers Ouche and Suzon, which meet there; and its present name has grown out of that. It was once the capital of Burgundy.

DIOCLETIAN (*di-o-cle'she-an*), **Valerius,** a Roman emperor, born near Salona in Dalmatia about A.D. 245. His parents had been slaves, and his name at first was Diocles, after the village where his mother was born; but when he became famous he changed it to Diocletian. He entered the army when young, and was so brave and popular that he soon got a high command. He was with the emperor Carus in an expedition against Persia when Carus died on the banks of the Tigris (284). Numerian, son of Carus, was soon assassinated, and the soldiers then made Diocletian emperor. Two years afterward (286) Diocletian made one of his fellow-soldiers named Maximian emperor with him, each taking the title of Augustus; and in 292 two more soldiers, Constantius, son of a nobleman, and Galerius, son of a shepherd, were made princes, each with the title of Cæsar. Diocletian lived in Nicomedia in great pomp. His robes were of silk and gold; and his shoes were studded with precious gems. When his subjects were admitted to his presence they fell prostrate on the ground, after the manner of Eastern nations. After a prosperous reign of twenty-one years he gave up the government, making Maximian give up also, and went to live at his birth-place, where he spent his time in building, planting, and gardening. Once, when his friends urged him to resume the power, he said, with a smile: "If you could see the cabbages which I have planted with my own hands, you would no longer ask me to exchange my quiet life for the crown." He died in A.D. 313.

DI-O-DO'RUS, a Greek historian, born in Sicily, lived in the first century B.C. He is commonly called Diodorus Sic'u-lus (the Sicilian). He wrote in Greek a history of the world in forty books, of which only fifteen are preserved. His work is not worth much, but he gives some important facts not noted by other historians.

DIOGENES (*di'oj'e-neez*), a famous Greek philosopher, born in Asia Minor about 412 B.C. When he first visited Athens, he went to Antisthenes, the founder of a society of philosophers called Cynics (from a Greek word meaning "like

Diogenes.

a dog"), because they were rude, snarling people who despised riches, the arts, and all the decent things of life. Antisthenes tried to drive him away, and even threatened to beat him. "Strike me," said Diogenes, "but you will never get so hard a stick as to keep me from you while you speak what I think worth hearing." He dressed in a coarse robe, which was his cloak by day, and his bed cover by night, and carried with him a wooden bowl and a bag to receive alms and food. One day he saw a boy drinking water from the hollow of his hand, and thinking that he could do likewise, he threw his bowl away as a useless luxury. He used to practice all sorts of hardships; and in order to endure both heat and cold, he rolled himself in the hot sand in summer, and in winter embraced statues covered with snow. His home was a large tub in the temple of Cybele. One day Alexander the Great saw Diogenes sitting in his tub in the sunshine. The king, surrounded by his courtiers, approached him, and said: "I am Alexander the Great !" The philosopher replied in a surly way: "I am Diogenes the Cynic !" Alexander asked him if he could do him any service: "Yes," said Diogenes, "don't stand between me and the sun !" Surprised at this reply, Alexander said: "If I were not Alexander, I would be Diogenes."

He used often to walk out in the daytime with a lighted lantern, peering around as if looking for something, and when questioned about it, he would say gravely: "I am searching for an honest man." Having heard PLATO say that man is a featherless biped (two-footed animal), Diogenes plucked a fowl and exclaimed, "Behold the man of Plato !" He was once taken by pirates and offered for sale as a slave in a market in Crete, and being asked by some one what he could do, replied, "I can govern men ; therefore sell me to some one who needs a master." He died when about eight-nine years old (323 B.C.).

DI-O-NYS'I-US, the Elder, tyrant of SYRACUSE, Sicily, born about 430 B.C. While young, and but a clerk in a public office, he began to form plans for making himself great, and finally succeeded in becoming sole ruler of the city. He soon showed himself to be a bad man, and went on from bad to worse as he grew in power, until he got the hateful title of tyrant. He was despised by his people, who tried several times to kill him, and at last he grew so suspicious that he always kept a body-guard of a thousand men. Nobody was allowed to come near him without being searched, and when he talked to his people it was from the top of a high tower. He was afraid to let a barber shave him, but taught his daughters to do it; and after they grew up he would no longer trust even them, but caused his beard and hair to be burned off. One day, when playing ball, he gave his sword to a youth whom he liked. A friend of the boy said jokingly: "He has now trusted his life to you." The lad smiled, and Dionysius ordered them both to be put to death; but when the deed was done, he is said to have grieved greatly over it.

One of his prisons was cut deep into a solid rock, and another was so built that he could hear every word spoken there; and he used to pass whole days in listening to what his victims said. Dionysius was generally successful in war, and is said to have been the first to make the catapult, or machine for throwing darts and stones, as well as a new kind of war-ship. He wrote several poems and plays; and when he chose to read them aloud at his table, everybody had to praise them. He died at the age of sixty-three, of too much eating (367 B.C.).

DIR'CE, in Greek fable, wife of Lycus, King of Thebes. She was jealous of Antiope, the first wife of Lycus, who had been put away by him, and caused her to be loaded with chains. In revenge Antiope's sons tied Dirce to a bull, and had her dragged about until she was dead. Two ancient sculptors of Rhodes carved out of a single block of marble a group showing the two sons tying Dirce to the bull, with Antiope standing by. This was in time sent to Rome, and in 1546 it was found in the ruins of the Baths of Caracalla. It is now preserved in the museum at Naples.

DISRAELI (*diz-rah'el-le*), **Benjamin,** Earl of Beaconsfield (*bek'ons-field*), a noted English writer and statesman, born in London, Dec. 21, 1805. He was the son of Isaac Disraeli, a rich gentleman of Jewish descent, who was noted as the writer of "Curiosities of Literature" and other works. Benjamin was educated by his father and by private tutors, and while still a boy was clerk in an attorney's office. After three years, growing tired of these duties, he was introduced into the best London society; and he was so handsome, and talked so well, that he soon became a great favorite. When twenty-one years old he published a novel called "Vivian Grey," which added to his fame. He was elected to Parliament when thirty-two years old, but his first speech was such a failure that the audience laughed and ridiculed it; yet he felt so sure that he would some day be a great man that he ended by saying: "I have begun several times many things, and I have often succeeded at last. I shall sit down now, but the time will come when you will hear me." He kept on making speeches, and in time became one of the best debaters in Parliament and the leader of his party. In 1868 he became Prime Minister of Great Britain, and the Queen offered to make him an earl; but he refused the honor, though he agreed that his wife might accept the title of Viscountess of Beaconsfield. But when he was made Prime Minister the second time (1874) he accepted the title, and he has since been called the Earl of Beaconsfield. He has written many novels; the last one called "Endymion," is thought to be partly a history of himself. He died at seventy-six (April 19, 1881).

DISTRICT OF COLUMBIA (*ko-lum'be-ah*), a Territory of the United States, on the N.E. side of the Potomac River, and surrounded on three sides by Maryland; area 64 square miles; pop. 230,000, or a little smaller than that of Pittsburg, Pa. It contains the cities of Washington and Georgetown, and was named in honor of COLUMBUS. It was chosen in 1790 as a seat for the capital of the United States. At first it was ten miles square, or 100 square miles in all, of which 64 square miles were in Maryland and 36 square miles in Virginia; but in 1846 the part in Virginia was given back to that State. Up to 1871 the District was governed by Congress; since then it has had a governor, and in 1878 it was placed in charge of three commissioners appointed by the President.

DODGE, Mary Mapes, a noted American writer for young folks, born

Mary Mapes Dodge.

in New York City. She first published "Irvington Stories" in 1864, and afterwards became well known as the auther of "Hans Brinker, or the Silver Skates," a story which has been published many times in this country and in England, and has been translated into many foreign languages. In France its translator was given a prize by the French Academy. Mrs. Dodge has also written "Rhymes and Jingles," and several books for grown-up people. Among her magazine articles is a very funny sketch called "Miss Maloney on the Chinese question." Mrs. Dodge was for several years one of the editors of "Hearth and Home," but when the "St. Nicholas Magazine" was started she became its editor, and she still holds that position.

DO-DO'NA, a city of Epirus, seat of the most ancient oracle of Greece. Although it was one of the three greatest oracles, no trace can be found of either the city or its noted temple of Jupiter. Before the temple was built, the oracles were given from a large oak-tree, whose branches were believed to have the power of speech.

DOLABELLA (*dol-ah-bel'ah*), **Publius Cornelius,** a Roman general, born about 70 B.C. In his youth he was guilty of so many crimes that he escaped death only through the aid of Cicero, whose daughter he married. He fought under Cæsar at Pharsalia and in Spain, but after the murder of Cæsar he joined his enemies and was made ruler of Syria. On his way to take his office he was guilty of such cruelties that he was declared to be a public enemy. Cassius was sent against him, and Dolabella, to avoid falling into his hands, ordered one of his own soldiers to kill him (43 B.C.).

DOMENICHINO (*do-ma-ne-ke'-no*), a celebrated Italian painter, whose true name was Domenico Zampieri, born at Bologna Oct. 21, 1581. He studied in Rome for several years under Annibal CARACCI, and though at first called slow and stupid by the other pupils, he became more famous than any of them. The most of his works are at Rome and at Naples. "The Communion of St. Jerome," in the Vatican is one of his masterpieces. Domenichino died in Naples when nearly sixty years old (April 5, 1641).

DOM'I-NIC, the founder of the order of monks called after him Dominicans, born in Castile, Spain, in 1170. The Dominicans are also called sometimes preaching monks, and Black Friars in England and Jacobins in France. The object of the order was to keep up a pure faith and to put down heresy. The conversion of the Albigenses was their first attempt, to accomplish which they practiced many cruelties. They had charge, too, of the Inquisition. The members of this order took a vow to remain poor always. In Bologna a rich citizen presented Dominic with a deed of all his estates. The enthusiastic monk tore it to pieces, saying that he wished to see his followers beg their bread rather than clog their usefulness by owning property. Dominic was a self-denying man and earnest in his efforts to benefit mankind. He cannot personally be charged with the faults for which the order after his time became noted. True to his principles, when dying, he lay on a sack of wool, refusing a bed. He died in Bologna when fifty-one years old (Aug. 4, 1221).

DOMIN'ICA (*do-min'i-kah*). See HAYTI.

DOMITIAN (*do-mish'e-an*), **Titus Flavius Domitianus Augustus,** a Roman Emperor, born Oct. 24, A.D. 51. He was the second son of VESPASIAN, and succeeded his brother TITUS (81). During his reign the conquest of Britain was finished by his general, AGRICOLA. At first he made many reforms and passed some good laws; but as he got to be older he became very cruel, and banished from Rome or murdered

almost all people noted for wealth or learning. At last, as Tacitus said, "Silent fear reigned at Rome." One of his favorite amusements was hunting and killing flies. A conspiracy was formed against him by some officers whom he had marked to be killed, and he was assassinated in his palace (Sept. 18, 96).

DONATI (*do-nah'te*), **Giovanni Battista,** an Italian astronomer, born at Pisa in 1826. His fame rests upon the discovery (June 2, 1858) of the comet which bears his name, and which it is supposed will not return for 1950 years. Donati was professor of astronomy in the Royal Observatory of Florence. He died there when fifty-seven years old (Sept. 20, 1873).

DONIZETTI (*don-e-zet'te*), **Gaetano,** a noted Italian writer of operas, born in Bergamo, Sept. 25, 1798. He studied law, but showed more talent for music. When twenty years old he composed short pieces, and soon began to write for the stage. He composed rapidly, and in his life wrote more than sixty operas. Some of them are lost; others are still very popular. Among his most famous operas are "La Favorita," "Lucia di Lammermoor," "La Fille du Régiment," "Lucrezia Borgia," and "Don Pasquale." He wrote his last opera, "Don Sebastian" in two months, and said at the time: "'Don Sebastian' will be the death of me." Soon after he had a stroke of paralysis, and ended his days in a lunatic asylum. He died in Bergamo when nearly fifty years old (April 8, 1848).

DORÉ (*do-ra'*), **Paul Gustave,** a French artist, born at Strasburg, Jan. 6, 1833. He has produced many striking religious paintings, but he is chiefly known for his drawings on wood, to be engraved. He illustrated the Bible, Dante's "Inferno," Milton's "Paradise Lost," and other famous works, besides making a great number of drawings for magazines and other periodicals. He died at Paris when fifty years old (Jan. 23, 1883).

DORIA (*do're-ah*), **Andrea,** a Genoese statesman and admiral, born Nov. 30, 1468. In the wars of Francis I. and Charles V., he rendered at first great service to the former, but not liking the way he was treated by Francis, he left him and went over to Charles. With his aid the French were soon driven from Genoa, and Doria was chosen ruler of the city with unlimited power. The senate called him "the father of peace," and ordered honors of every sort to be given to him. The last years of his rule were troubled by a revolution gotten up by the Fieschi family, who were jealous of his fame. He died in Genoa when ninety-two years old (1560).

DO'RIS. See ASIA MINOR.

DOUAI, or Douay (*dou-ay'*), a town of N. France, 18 miles S. of Lille; pop. 29,000, or about as large as Salem, Mass. It is defended by strong walls and forts, and has a large cannon-foundry and arsenal and a military school. Lace, embroidery, cotton, linen, delft-ware, and many other things are made there, and a large trade is carried on.

Douai was a Roman town called Duacum in the time of Cæsar. It has belonged at different times to France, Flanders, and Spain. In 1568 a Roman Catholic college and theological seminary was set up there for the education of young Englishmen, and the translation of the Bible called the Douai Bible was made by Englishmen connected with it.

DOUGLAS (*dug'lass*), the name of one of the oldest and most powerful families in Scotland, descendants, according to tradition, of a Fleming, Theobald by name, to whom in the twelfth century the abbot of Kelso gave lands on the Douglas, a word meaning "black water." The Douglases were pow-

erful, not only because they owned great estates, but because they were great soldiers. There is still a proverb in Scotland,

"So many, so good as of the Douglases have been,
Of one surname in Scotland never yet were seen."

Unfortunately the Douglases were haughty and ambitious, and they were often so unruly as to cause the kings of Scotland a great deal of trouble.

Sir James Douglas (Sir James the Good) is called the hero of seventy fights, all of which were in the cause of Robert BRUCE, whose greatest captain he was. He was killed in Spain by the Saracens in 1331, on his way to Palestine, whither he was carrying the heart of Bruce. The bloody heart was in this way added to the coat of arms of the Douglases.

Archibald Douglas, fifth Earl of Angus, called "Bell-the-Cat," got his title in a strange way. Several of the Scottish nobles had met to find out how they could best get rid of one of the king's favorites, who was much hated. Some one said that the meeting was much like that of the mice who thought that the best way to manage the cat was to put a bell around her neck. When some one asked who would do this, Douglas boldly answered, "I will bell the cat." His two sons having been killed at the battle of Flodden, he died shortly afterward, broken-hearted.

There have been two branches of the family, the elder styled the Black Douglases, which was overthrown in the time of King James II., and the younger, the Red Douglases. There have been three earldoms in the family, that of Mar, Angus, and Morton. For a long time Scottish mothers would soothe their children to sleep with the lullaby,

"Hush ye, hush ye, little pet ye,
The Black Douglas shall not get ye."

DOUGLAS, Stephen Arnold, an American statesman, born in Brandon, Vt., April 23, 1813. His father died when he was an infant, and his mother went to live on a farm, where Stephen worked until he was fifteen years old. He then became an apprentice to a cabinet-maker, but becoming ill he gave it up and went to Illinois, where he taught school during the day and studied law evenings. When twenty-one years old he began to practice law and soon became very successful; and before he was twenty-two years old was attorney-general of the State. The next year he was elected to the legislature, and in 1837 was a candidate for Congress, but was defeated. In 1841 he became judge of the Illinois Supreme Court. In 1843 he became a member of Congress, and in 1847 a United States Senator. In 1860 he was a candidate for President of the United States, but was defeated by Mr. Lincoln. He died in Chicago when forty-eight years old (June 3, 1861). Mr. Douglas was a fine orator, and had great power over the masses of the people. He was popularly called the "Little Giant."

DO'VER, a city of England, one of the CINQUE PORTS, on that part of the English Channel called the Strait of Dover; pop. 30,000, or a little larger than Altoona, Pa. It is the principal English sea-port for vessels crossing the channel, which is narrower there than at any other place; indeed, on a clear day it is possible to see across to the shores of France. On a high chalk hill near Dover is a very old castle, part of which was built by the Romans, not long after the time of Christ. Within the walls are a Roman lighthouse and the ruins of a church which is probably the oldest in England and one of the oldest in the world, having been built when many of the people of Britain were savages and idolaters. Dover Castle is still very strong and has a large magazine and barracks for soldiers. There is a long underground passage from the castle to the town, which goes down more than four hundred steps cut in the solid chalk.

The Romans had a fortified town there called Dubris, from which Dover gets its name.

DRA'CO, a noted Athenian, who lived in the 7th century B.C. When he became a ruler, he made laws so harsh that even the slightest offense was punished with death, and it was said of them that they seemed to be written with blood instead of with ink. Still the people thought much of him, for he was good and just; and it is said that he was killed by being smothered under a great number of cloaks and hats thrown upon him as he entered the theatre in Ægina, that being then a way of doing honor to a person.

DRAKE, Sir Francis, a celebrated English naval hero, born near Tavistock, Devonshire, about 1540. He was one of a large and poor family, and was apprenticed when a youth to the captain of a coasting vessel. He served so well in this position that when the captain died he gave Francis his ship, though he was then only eighteen years old. After making several voyages, he sold his vessel and joined Sir John Hawkins in his expedition to Mexico (1567), where all his property was taken by the Spaniards. Angry at this, he determined to revenge himself by attacking their ships, and when thirty years old sailed to America with several ships, plundered many Spanish towns, and made himself rich.

When he returned to England he found himself famous, and, aided by Queen Elizabeth, he soon set out (1577) with a fleet of five ships on a voyage to the Pacific, whose waters he had caught sight of several years before from the top of a tree in the Isthmus of Darien. He sailed through the Straits of Magellan and up the coast of South America, capturing Spanish ships and towns on the way, took possession of California in the name of his queen, and then, thinking that it would not be safe to go back the same way, went across the Pacific and around the Cape of Good Hope, and arrived safe at Plymouth (1580), being thus the first Englishman to sail round the world. For this he was made a knight by the queen, who dined on board his

Sir Francis Drake.

ship, named the "Golden Hind." She ordered the ship to be preserved at Deptford in memory of the great voyage. A hundred years afterward, when the timbers began to decay, the old ship was broken up, and out of the soundest parts was made a chair which was presented by Charles II. to the University of Oxford with these lines by the poet Cowley:

"Drake and his ship could not have wished
      from fate
 A happier station or more blest estate ;
 For lo! a seat of endless rest is given,
 To her in Oxford, and to him in heaven."

In 1587, when King Philip of Spain was known to be getting ready to attack England, Drake went into the harbor of Cadiz with a fleet, destroyed nearly a hundred ships, and brought away much spoil. This he called "singeing the king of Spain's beard." The next year he acted as vice-admiral of the fleet which defeated the Invincible Armada. In 1595 he went to the West Indies on another expedition, and died at sea when about fifty-five years old (Dec. 27, 1595).

DRES'DEN, a city of Germany, capital of Saxony, on the river Elbe, 100 miles S. of Berlin; pop. 246,000, or a little larger than New Orleans, La. It is divided into the old and the new town by the river, which is crossed by fine bridges. The city has many beautiful squares and places, and abounds in handsome buildings, among which are the royal palace and several other palaces. Dresden is noted for its picture-gallery, considered one of the finest in Europe. Among its celebrated paintings are the "Sistine Madonna" of Raphael, "The Night of the Birth of Christ" by Correggio, and pictures by Titian, Paul Veronese, Leonardo da Vinci, and other famous artists. In the royal palace is one of the finest collections of jewels, carvings, and other art treasures in the world. The royal library is one of the largest in Germany. Dresden has many celebrated schools and art academies. It is noted for its manufactures of machinery, farming tools, mathematical, philosophical, and musical instruments, china, gold and silver ware, and leather. The city has a very large trade.

Dresden gets its name from an old Slav word (drezany), meaning the haven. It was founded about 1206, and it has belonged to many different German nations. On Aug. 26, 1813, the Russian, Prussian, and Austrian armies attacked the French in Dresden, but Napoleon arrived with reinforcements, and on the next day won a great battle there. A garrison of 30,000 men which he left in Dresden was afterward surrounded by the Russians, and compelled to surrender (Nov. 11, 1813).

DRONTHEIM (*dront'hime*), a city on the W. coast of Norway; pop. 23,000, or about as large as Fort Worth, Tex. It is the third city of Norway in population, only Christiania and Bergen being larger. Its principal building is the beautiful Gothic cathedral of Saint Olaf, founded in the 11th century, in which the kings of Norway were consecrated and crowned for many hundred years; and the kings of Sweden are still crowned there as kings of Norway. The city is defended by a strong fortress built on a rock in the harbor. The principal trade is in ships' masts, copper, iron, goat-skins, and dried and salted fish.

Drontheim, or Throndhjem as it is called in Danish, means "throne dwelling." The place was first built in 997, and for a long time was the capital of Norway.

DRU'IDS, the name of the priests of the ancient Celtic tribes in Britain and Gaul. They lived in oak forests, where they attended to their religious duties, and taught young men, who went to them in great numbers. All knowledge and learning belonged to them; they were the priests, philosophers, teachers, physicians, and judges of the people, and if any one refused to submit to their sentence he was made an outlaw and cut off from all human sympathy. They were governed by an Arch-Druid, who held his office for life. They were never taxed, and were not required to serve as soldiers in time of war. Their worship was dark, cruel, and bloody, and they sacrificed human beings on their altars, as well as beasts. The oak and many plants, among them the mistletoe, were held sacred by them. The Druids were gradually driven out of all their strongholds by the Roman troops, their last resting-place being the island of Anglesea, where their traditions lingered longest. All over the central and western parts of France, and in some parts of England, are immense masses of stone, which are supposed to be the remains of the places of sacrifice and worship of the Druids. The most noted of these are at STONEHENGE in England, and at Carnac in France.

DRY'ADS, in Greek and Roman fable, nymphs of the woods. They had the care of all woods and trees, while the Hamadryads had each a particular tree, with which they came into being, lived, and died.

DRY'DEN, John, an English poet, born at Aldwinckle, Northamptonshire, Aug. 9, 1631. His father was a Puritan and a magistrate under Cromwell, and John was the eldest of fourteen children. He was educated at Westminster School and at Trinity College, Cambridge, where he was graduated in 1654. When twenty-two years old he went to live in London. He admired Cromwell, and on his death wrote a poem in his honor; but at the time of the restoration he took the side of the Royalists, and when Charles II. was crowned wrote a poem in his praise. From this time he remained true to the royal party. He soon became famous as a poet, and at the same time gained so much influence at court that he was made poet-laureate (1670). He afterward became noted for his plays, which were successful at that time but are not acted now. His prose essays are among the finest in the English language. He died when sixty-eight years old (May 1, 1700), and was buried in Westminster Abbey.

DRY TOR-TU'GAS, a group of ten coral islands in the Gulf of Mexico, S.W. of Florida; pop. about 250.

On Garden Key, one of the islands, is a lighthouse, and Fort Jefferson where during the Civil War Confederate prisoners were kept.

DUB'LIN, a city, capital of Ireland, on the E. coast, at the mouth of the river Liffey in Dublin Bay; pop. 353,000, or a third larger than New Orleans, La. Part of the city is well built and handsome, but other streets are filthy and the houses little better than huts. The river, which divides it into two nearly equal parts, is crossed by several fine bridges. Many of the public buildings and churches are very handsome, and there are many squares and gardens. Phœnix Park, which is more than twice as large as Central Park, N. Y., is one of the finest in Europe. Trinity College has 1300 students and a very fine library. Queens University and the Roman Catholic University are modern. The ruler of Ireland, called the Lord-Lieutenant, lives in Dublin Castle, on a hill in the city. Dublin has few manufactures, the most important being porter and silk-poplin. The harbor, though good, is not deep enough for very large ships, and most of the trade is with England.

Dublin (Irish *dubh-linn*) means black pool. The city is very old, having been known to the Romans not long after the time of Christ. It was first taken by the English in 1170.

DUBUFE (*du-bufe'*), Édouard, a French painter, born in Paris about 1818. For some years he painted religious and sentimental subjects, but at present devotes himself to portraits. Some of his pictures have been brought to the United States, among them a very large one called "The Prodigal Son."

DUBUQUE (*du-buke'*), the largest city of Iowa, on the Mississippi River, opposite the line which separates Illinois and Wisconsin; pop. 30,-500, or about as large as Salem, Mass. The country around it, on both sides of the Mississippi, is rich in lead mines, and some are in the city itself. Part of the ore is smelted in Dubuque, and the rest is sent to other cities. There are manufactories of carriages, wagons, and farming tools, and a large trade is carried on.

Dubuque is the oldest town in Iowa, having been settled in 1788 by Julian Dubuque, a French Canadian, after whom it was named.

DU CHAILLU (*du shah-yu'*), Paul Belloni, a noted traveler in Africa, born in Paris, July 31, 1835. When quite young he went to live on the west coast of Africa, where his father was a merchant, and soon became acquainted with the natives and fond of their wild life. He was probably the first white man who ever saw a gorilla, and the first who described the habits of that remarkable animal. When about twenty years old he made up his mind to explore the country on foot, and in four years he walked more than 8000 miles. In that time he stuffed more than 2000 birds and killed 1000 animals. His life seems one long hunting expedition, but he has rested long enough to write a number of books, intended chiefly for boys, which are very instructive and interesting to all who delight in tales of adventure.

DUDEVANT (*du-deh-vong'*), Amantine Lucille Aurore Dupin, a famous French writer of novels, born in Paris, July, 1804. Her father, Maurice Dupin, died when she was four years old, and she was left to the care of her grandmother, the Countess of Horn, with whom she spent her childhood at the family country estate of Nohant. When she was seventeen years old her grandmother died, and the estate fell to her; and the next year she married Casimir Dudevant, who had been an army officer. But their tastes being different and money being scarce, they were not happy together, and in 1831 she went to Paris to try to make her fortune as a writer. At first she was not successful; but a novel called "Rose and Blanche," which she wrote with her friend Jules Sandeau, was so well received that Madame Dudevant, under the assumed name of "George Sand," soon published one wholly written by herself, called "Indiana," which was a great success. After this she wrote and published many other novels and plays, and became very famous. Several of her novels have been translated and published in the United States. Her later books are especially charming, and so are the fairy stories which she wrote for her grandchildren in her last years. She died when nearly seventy-two years old (June 8, 1876).

DUD'LEY, a town of England, on a hill, 8 miles W.N.W. of Birmingham; pop. 46,000, or about as large as Portland, Ore. The surrounding country abounds in coal and iron, which are used in the city in large blast-furnaces, foundries, and iron-mills. Many articles of iron and steel, such as chains, anvils, edge-tools, files, nails, and many other things are made there. Limestone is quarried near the city, in mines and passages under the surface, one of which is two miles long and has a canal running through it. Near Dudley are the ruins of an old castle, built in the 8th century by a Saxon prince, called Dudo, from whose name the word Dudley has been made. In 1644 this castle was defended for three weeks by the royalists against the Parliamentary army.

DUD'LEY, Robert, Earl of Leicester, a courtier of the reign of Queen Elizabeth, born about 1531. He was the son of John Dudley, Duke of Northumberland, who was beheaded by Queen Mary for trying to make his daughter-in-law, the Lady Jane Grey, queen of England.

When Elizabeth became queen, the handsome and graceful Robert Dudley soon won a high place in her favor, which his tact enabled him to keep with but slight interruption all his life. His boldness went so far that it is said he wanted to marry the queen, having had his young wife, Amy Robsart, killed, to enable him to do so. He once gave Elizabeth a grand entertainment in his castle of Kenilworth, in which the festivities lasted seventeen days. This is told about by Sir Walter Scott in his novel of "Kenilworth." Although Elizabeth did not want to marry him, neither did she wish him to marry any one else, and she came very near having him put in the Tower when she heard that he had married Lady Essex. Leicester had several times important positions in the army, but he shone in the drawing-room much more than in the field. He died when fifty-seven years old (Sept. 4, 1588).

DU GUESCLIN (*du ga-klan'*), **Bertrand,** a famous French soldier, born near Rennes, Brittany, about 1314. When a boy he was dull at his studies, but, though of a clumsy figure, he excelled in all manly sports. When he grew up he became a famous knight, and often took prizes in tournaments. At that time the English held many places in France, and Du Guesclin won much fame in fighting against them. He gained a great victory over them in 1364, for which he was made a count, but soon after he was defeated by EDWARD the Black Prince, and taken prisoner. But he was soon ransomed, and the king made him constable of France, much the same as our commander-in-chief. The English now ceased to conquer, and Du Guesclin drove them little by little out of their possessions in France. He died of fever at the siege of a castle held by the English, in the south of France, when sixty-six years old (July 13, 1380), and the English captain, who said that he would not surrender to any meaner foe, laid the keys of the castle in his dead hand.

DUMAS (*du-mah*) **Alexandre Davy,** a noted French writer of novels and plays, born July 24, 1803. His father, a French general, was the son of the Marquis de la Pailleterie and a negress of Hayti. He died when Alexandre was three years old, and the family being poor the boy was not very well educated. When eighteen years old he began to write plays, but none of them were successful, and when twenty-one he set off for Paris to seek his fortune, where he made such good use of his time that he became famous in five years. At first he had the place of a clerk with a salary of $250 a year; and at the same time he wrote several plays, which, after some rebuffs, were brought on the stage. Then he began to write novels, and soon published many historical stories, among which "The Three Musketeers" and "The Count of Monte Cristo" are the most famous. His books were much liked, and there was such a demand for them that he wrote a greater number than any writer had ever done before in the same time; in one year alone writing forty volumes. In order to do this he was forced to employ assistants, whose work was guided by him; then he supplied a large number of young writers with plots for stories to which his name was attached. Meanwhile he became very rich, built a large theatre, where his dramas were to be played, and a beautiful castle at St. Germain, where he was to live and spend his money like a prince in a fairy-tale. But people began to find out the game he was practicing on them, and then came his downfall. His splendid theatre brought him in debt, until he was finally reduced to all sorts of schemes to make a little

money. With a weakened mind, with friends, health, self-respect all gone, Dumas ended his life far poorer than when he began it. He died at the age of sixty-seven (Dec. 5, 1870).

DUMAS, Alexandre, a noted French writer of novels and plays, son of Alexandre Davy Dumas, born in Paris, July 28, 1824. He wrote a volume of poems at sixteen, but they had little merit, and he then took to novel-writing. Unlike his father, he did his work slowly and carefully. He is best known by his romance "La Dame aux Camélias" (The Lady with the Camellias) which made him famous. It has been translated into many languages, and is made into a play which is played now upon the stage with great success. The plot of VERDI'S opera of "Traviata" is also from it. Dumas has since written many other novels and plays. He lives in Paris.

DUM-BAR'TON, a seaport of Scotland, on the Leven, 13 miles N.W. of Glasgow; pop. 14,000, or about the same as that of Pottsville, Pa. More than 3000 men are employed there in building ships, both of wood and iron. About a mile below the town is Dumbarton Castle, on a steep rock about twice as high as Trinity Church steeple, and which is almost an island at high water. This castle, which was a fortified place more than a thousand years ago, is very famous in Scottish history. Sir William WALLACE was imprisoned there before he was taken to London to be executed, and his great two-handed sword is still kept there.

Dumbarton means the "hill fort of the Britons," of whom it was the capital in ancient times.

DUMFRIES (*dum-freese'*), a town of S. Scotland, on the river Nith; pop. 18,000, or nearly the same as that of Norwalk, Conn. It is near the borders of England, and was often plundered and burned in the early wars. Robert BURNS lived there the last years of his life, and was buried there.

Dumfries means the "fort among the shrubs;" it was so named from a fort built there in very early times.

DU-MONT D'URVILLE (*du-mon' dur-vele'*), **Jules Sébastien César,** a noted French naval officer and explorer, born in Normandy, May 23, 1790. In 1822 he sailed on a voyage round the world under Captain Duperray, and brought home a very fine collection of animals and plants. In 1826 he was sent to the Pacific, surveyed the coasts of Papua, New Zealand, and other islands, and found out the probable place of the death of LA PEROUSE. He afterward explored the Antarctic or Southern Ocean, and made thousands of sketches of scenery and natural history, besides making very large collections. On his return (1840) he was made rear admiral, but soon afterward he and his wife and son were killed in a railway accident near Paris (May 8, 1842). The account of his voyages was published in twenty-four volumes, with six large volumes of illustrations.

DUN'CAN. See MACBETH.

DUN-DEE', a town of E. Scotland, at the mouth of the Tay River; pop. 163,000, or as large as Jersey City, N. J. It has fine docks and quays, which are always crowded with ships, and many ships are built there. More coarse linen cloth and more jute are made than in any other city of Great Britain, and there are important manufactures of leather and gloves.

Dundee was one of the residences of the old kings of Scotland.

DUNFERMLINE (*dun-ferm'lin*), a town of Scotland, 13 miles N.W. of Edinburgh; pop. 18,000, or the same as that of Cedar Rapids, Iowa. It was once a noted place, Dunfermline Abbey being long the place of burial of the Scottish kings. The body of Robert Bruce was found in 1818 in a lead coffin under the pul-

pit. King Charles I. of England was born in Dunfermline. The town is now principally noted for its manufactures of linen damask.

Dunfermline means the "fort of the winding pool." It is not known when it was first built, but it is an old place.

DUN'KIRK, the most northern city of France, on the Strait of Dover; pop. 38,000, or the same as that of Dallas, Texas. Being nearer to England than almost any other French town, Dunkirk was always an important place in the wars between England and France. It was taken several times by the English, and also by the Spaniards, who in the 16th century had possession of Belgium and were often at war with the French. In 1662 the English sold it to France, and though they afterward bombarded it twice, they could never get it back.

Dunkirk means the kirk or "church on the dunes." It got its name from a chapel built there in the 7th century on the dunes, or sand-hills.

DUPRÉ (*du-pra'*), **Jules,** a French landscape and animal painter, born at Nantes in 1811. As a boy he studied design with his father, who was a worker in porcelain, and exhibited his first oil-paintings when only nineteen years old. He painted mostly landscapes and sea pictures. He died at L'Isle Adam, France, aged seventy-eight (Oct. 6, 1889).

DUQUESNE (*du-kane'*), **FORT.** See PITTSBURGH.

DURAN (*du-rahn'*) **Carolus,** a French painter born at Lille in 1838. He has won great fame for his portraits of women and children.

DÜRER (*duh'rer*) **Albert,** a noted German painter and engraver, born in Nuremberg May 20, 1471. His father was a goldsmith and wanted Albert to learn the same trade, but as he wished to become a painter, he was placed at the age of fifteen, with the leading painter of Nuremberg, where he studied for four years. He then traveled for several years, studying art all the time; and when he returned home, being then twenty-three years old, he married the handsome daughter of a mechanic. His wife is said to have been an ill-tempered woman, who did not make him happy, but there is no good authority for the statement.

Dürer soon became more famous than any other German painter, and made many fine pictures, most of which are still preserved in the great collections in Europe. He was also very noted for his copperplate engravings and for his woodcuts, which have always been greatly prized. Dürer's character was so noble and good that he was loved by all his countrymen, from the emperor to the poorest artist in his garret. He was made court painter by two of the emperors, and all the cities of Germany were anxious to get his pictures.

Three hundred years after the birth of Albert Dürer the cornerstone of a monument to his memory was laid in his native city, and in 1840 a bronze statue of him was put upon it. The house where he was born is still kept with great care. Dürer died in Nuremberg when fifty-seven years old (April 6, 1528).

DUROC (*du-rok'*), **Gerard Chris-** tophe **Michel,** Duke of Friuli, a noted French general, born near Nancy, Oct. 25, 1772. He was a favorite officer of Napoleon, was with him in Egypt, and was afterward made lieutenant-general and governor of the Tuileries. He was employed in many public offices, and was much trusted by the emperor, who made him Duke of Friuli. Duroc was killed by a cannon-ball while going with Napoleon to a high piece of ground, adjoining the battle-field of Bautzen, and died in a farm-house near by. Napoleon afterward bought the house, and had a monument built there; but Duroc's body was taken to Paris in 1845, and now rests near that of the emperor in the Church of the Invalides. He was forty years old when he died (May 22, 1813).

DUS'SEL-DORF, a city of Germany, in Prussia, at the junction of the river Düssel with the Rhine, 20 miles from Cologne; pop. 115,000, or a tenth larger than that of Allegheny, Pa. It has a large trade by railroads and steamboats, and important manufactures, but is best known for its school of painting, which is one of the most famous in the world. Many great artists have been educated there. Düsseldorf means the town on the Düssel.

E

EADS (*eedz*), **James B.,** an American civil engineer, born in Lawrenceburg, Ind., May 28, 1820. He was at first a clerk on a steamboat on the Mississippi, but in 1842 went into the business of raising sunken vessels and made a fortune. In the Civil War he built iron-clad gunboats for the government. Afterward he became famous for building the great steel arch bridge over the Mississippi River at ST. LOUIS, which is one of the most wonderful bridges in the world. He next turned his attention to improving the South Pass of the MISSISSIPPI River, which was successfully completed in 1879; and the deepening of the channel as far as the Ohio River by means of jetties. He died when sixty-seven years old (March 8, 1887).

EAKINS (*a'kins*), **Thomas,** an American painter, born in Philadelphia in 1844. He is a figure and portrait painter of great power. His studio is in Philadelphia.

EAST INDIES (*in'diz*), a name

sometimes given to India, south-eastern Asia, and the large islands between Asia and Australia. In the 15th century this region was called simply India, or the Indies, and Columbus supposed that he had reached it when he discovered America. When it was found that America was really a separate continent, it was called the West Indies to distinguish it, and the name East Indies was given to the Asiatic India.

EAST RIVER. See NEW YORK City).

EAS'TERN EM'PIRE, called also the Byzantine or Greek Empire. A quarter of a century after the death of Constantine the Great, the Roman Empire was divided into two parts: the eastern portion, with CONSTANTINOPLE for its capital, taking the name of Eastern or Byzantine Empire, and the western, with Rome as its chief city, that of Western Empire. These two parts were united under the Emperor Theodosius the Great, but after him, A.D. 395, they were again separated, his son Arcadius taking the East, and a younger son, Honorius, the West. From this time the empire remained divided. The early Byzantine emperors were mostly either weak or vicious monarchs, and their court presented a sad picture of depravity. The first of these rulers worthy of being remembered was JUSTINIAN. Justinian's successors were very corrupt princes, and the people were sunk in wickedness, but Constantinople was through the middle ages the seat of learning and refinement. In 1057 Isaac Angelus, one of this family, having been deprived of the throne by his brother Alexius, presented himself in Venice before the leaders of the fourth Crusade and begged their aid. The Western knights went to Constantinople and took it, but when they demanded a great reward for this, the people excited an insurrection, during which the emperor and his son died. The Franks then made themselves masters of Constantinople and the neighboring country, parceling the land out among their chiefs, the imperial family making the seat of their empire at Nicæa. In 1260 one of these emperors, Michael Palæologus, succeeded in getting back Constantinople. He was an able prince, but he lost the favor of the people by attempting to bring the Greek Church under the rule of the pope. During the reign of his successors the Ottoman Turks took many parts of the empire, and pressed close up to Constantinople, which at last fell into their power in 1453. Thus ended the Eastern Empire, its ancient seat becoming the residence of the sultan.

EAST'LAKE, Sir Charles Lock, a noted English painter, born in Plymouth, Nov. 17, 1793. He studied first in the schools of the Royal Academy in London, and afterward in Paris and in Rome. He was in Paris when Napoleon came back from Elba, and had to run away. Soon afterward, when the English man-of-war Bellerophon lay off Plymouth, with Napoleon on board (1815), Mr. Eastlake made sketches of him as he walked the deck, and painted from them a full-length portrait, which was the last one of the fallen emperor painted in Europe. Mr. Eastlake became very famous, and when fifty-seven years old he was made a knight and chosen president of the Royal Academy. Among his most celebrated pictures is "Christ Weeping over Jerusalem" and "Christ Blessing Little Children." He died in Pisa, Italy, when seventy-two years old (Dec. 23, 1865).

EASTLAKE, Charles L., nephew of Sir Charles Eastlake, is the keeper of the National Gallery of Paintings in London, and the author of "Hints on Household Taste." From this book, in which he tells much about furnishing houses, his name has been given to a certain style of furniture, though much of that called Eastlake furniture is very different from what he recommends.

EAS'TON, a city of E. Pennsylvania, on the Delaware River; pop. 14,000, or as large as Stockton, Cal. Near it are many zinc and iron mines, and large blast-furnaces, rolling-mills, and other ironworks. The city has an oil-refinery, a rope-walk, and other manufactories, and a large trade is carried on. It is the site of Lafayette College, which has about 300 students. Easton was founded in 1738.

EATON (*e'ton*), **William,** an American soldier, born in Woodstock, Conn., Feb. 23, 1764. He was brought up on a farm, but, being fond of adventure, ran away at sixteen and joined the Revolutionary army, which he left three years later with the rank of sergeant. When twenty-six years old he was graduated at Dartmouth College, and two years after became a captain in the army. In 1799 he went to Tunis as American consul. At that time all the Barbary States were nests of pirates, who forced Christian nations to pay tribute, or else captured their merchantships and made slaves of their seamen. Mr. Eaton made the ruler of Tunis promise he would not attack United States vessels any more. In 1805 he was made navy agent, and set out for Tripoli, to rescue some American prisoners there. With the aid of Hamet Caramelli, rightful ruler of Tripoli, whose brother had usurped the throne, he raised in Egypt a force of about five hundred men, mostly Arabs, with a few Christians and nine Americans; after a march of 600 miles across the desert, he captured Derne, a city of Tripoli, defeated a large force of Tripolitans, and was about to march on the city of Tripoli when he heard that a treaty had been made, and the prisoners

ransomed for $60,000. When he returned to the United States he was received with great honor. He died in Brimfield, Mass., when forty-seven years old (June 1, 1811).

E'BRO, a river of N.E. Spain, flowing into the Mediterranean. The ancients called it the Iberus, and from it Spain was first called Iberia.

ECBATANA (*ek-bat'a-nah*), the ancient capital of Media, said to have been founded by Semiramis. It was built on a hill, and had seven walls, each inner one higher than the next outer one, and all of different colors: the inmost one, which surrounded the royal palace, being gilded, the next silvered, and the others in order painted orange, blue, purple, black, and white. Ecbatana was the favorite summer home of the kings of Persia.

ECHO (*e'ko*), in Greek fable, a wood-nymph, daughter of Earth and Air. Jupiter sent her to detain Juno with her chatter while he amused himself with the other nymphs, but Juno found it out and caused her to melt away into nothing but a voice. Soon after Echo fell in love with Narcissus, son of a river-god. He treated her with disdain, but she followed him everywhere, repeating his name, until she pined away and nothing but her plaintive voice was heard calling him in lonely places. Narcissus afterward fell in love with his own face which he saw in a fountain, and drowned himself in despair.

ECUADOR (*ek'wa-dore*), a republic of South America, on the Pacific Ocean, between the United States of Colombia and Peru; area about 103,-000 square miles, or about as large as Oregon; pop. 1,155,000, or nearly three quarters more than that of Oregon; capital, Quito. It is very mountainous, a large part of it being covered by the Andes, many of the peaks of which are volcanoes, and some are so high that they have snow on them all the year. Among the highest are Cotopaxi and Chimborazo. The climate is healthful, excepting on the sea-coast, where it is very hot. The people are made up of whites of Spanish descent, Indians, negroes, and mixed breeds. As Ecuador is close to the equator, the trees and plants are mostly those of hot countries, among them being the cocoa-nut and India-rubber trees and the cinchona tree, from which quinine is made.

Ecuador was conquered from the Indians by the Spaniards, and held by them from 1533 to 1822, when the people declared themselves independent. It was first a part of Colombia, but in 1831 was made into a republic named Ecuador, which in Spanish means equator.

EDGE'WORTH, Maria, author of "Harry and Lucy," "Rosamond," "Moral Tales," "Castle Rackrent," "Helen," and many other novels and stories, unlike any that had been written before, because they described every-day life, was born near Reading, England, Jan. 1, 1767. Her father, Richard Lovell Edgeworth, a clever writer and inventor, succeeded to the family estate at Edgeworthtown, Ireland, when Maria was fifteen, and this was her home until she died in her eighty-third year (May 21, 1849).

EDINBURGH (*ed'in-bur-ro*), a city of Scotland, near the Frith of Forth, 400 miles N. of London; pop. 267,000, or a little larger than Cleveland, Ohio. It is built on three ridges. On a high rock at the W. end of the middle ridge stands Edinburgh Castle, once a strong fortress, but not good for much in these days of large cannon. In one of its rooms are kept the ancient crown, sceptre, and sword of state of Scotland. At the other end of the same ridge is the palace of Holyrood (Holy Cross), where the Scottish kings once lived, and where Mary Queen of Scots' bed-chamber is, almost the same as when she used it. The old town is full of houses five to eleven stories high, built against the sides of the ridges, with steep lanes between them; but the new town, on lower ground, is finely laid out, and is noted for its splendid buildings and monuments to great men. The most beautiful monument is that to Sir Walter Scott, 200 feet high, with his marble statue in the centre. There are many schools and colleges, including the University of Edinburgh, and great numbers of books are printed there. The port of Edinburgh is LEITH.

The city, which was called in Gaelic Dunedin, was named Edwin's Burgh, from Edwin, King of Northumbria, who lived there in the 7th century. It was made a walled town and the capital of Scotland in the 15th century. People sometimes call it now the "Athens of the North."

ED'I-SON, Thomas Alva, an American inventor, born in Milan, Ohio, Feb. 11, 1847. He had little education, and when quite young became a newsboy on a railroad. Becoming interested in chemistry, he fitted up a small laboratory in one of the cars, where he tried experiments; but one day he came near setting fire to the train and the conductor kicked the whole out. He then got some old type and printed a little newspaper of his own, which he sold on the trains.

Becoming acquainted with the telegraph operators along the line, he determined to learn how to telegraph, and finally got a place in a telegraph office; but he tried so many experiments and attempted so many things thought to be impossible, that he soon got the name of "Looney" (for Lunatic) and lost his situation. But at last he became so skilful that he was asked to take the best place in the telegraph office in Boston. All the operators were afraid of this place, because the operator in New York who sent messages there worked so fast that no one could keep up with him. When the other operators saw Edison, who looked like a green country boy, sit down before the instrument, they all crowded round to see the fun. But Edison received every one of the messages without a mistake, and when done the New York man telegraphed, " Who the deuce *are* you, anyhow ?" Edison replied, "I'm Tom Edison—shake hands."

After experimenting a long time Mr. Edison found out how to send several telegraphic messages over the same wire. He has also made many improvements in the telephone (C. C. T., 612, I., l.), and in the electric light; but his greatest invention thus far is the phonograph (C. C. T., 459, II., u.). He lives at Llewellyn Park, West Orange, New Jersey, where he has erected large workshops and a laboratory for his experiments.

EDWARD I., fourth Plantagenet King of England, son of Henry III., born June 16, 1239. He was called Longshanks, because his legs were very long. He was away on a crusade to the Holy Land when Henry died, and he was not crowned until two years after. He first conquered the Welsh, and promised to give them, in place of their prince Llewellyn, who had been killed, another prince who should be a Welshman born, and who could not speak English. He did this by making his little son, born a few days before at Carnarvon Castle, Prince of Wales, and this title has been borne ever since by the eldest son of the king of England. In 1289 he made war on Scotland. He defeated William WALLACE, and was trying to subdue Robert BRUCE when he died, aged sixty-eight years (July 7, 1307). He made some good laws, but was very cruel to the Jews.

EDWARD II., fifth Plantagenet King of England, son of Edward I., born in Carnarvon Castle, Wales, April 25, 1284. He was weak and passionate, and had a miserable reign. He had trouble with his nobles, who were angry at the favor he showed Piers de Gaveston and Hugh le Despenser, for whom he neglected everybody else. He made war against Scotland, but was defeated by Robert BRUCE at BANNOCKBURN (1314). At last his subjects got out of patience with him, and his queen, Isabella, a corrupt woman, got up a rebellion against him with the aid of a bad man named Roger Mortimer. Edward was made prisoner, and, Parliament having resolved that he should reign no longer, he was shut up in Berkeley Castle, where he is generally said to have been murdered when forty-four years old (Sept. 21, 1327); but some think that he escaped from England and died a hermit in Italy.

EDWARD III., sixth Plantagenet King of England, son of Edward II., born at Windsor, Nov. 13, 1312. He was made king while his father was alive, but after his murder he punished Mortimer by death and shut his mother up in Castle Rising for the rest of her life. He was brave and determined, and made war with Scotland, and afterward with France, the throne of which he claimed because he was grandson of Charles IV. He gained the famous battles of CRÉCY (1346), and POITIERS (1356). At last the "great peace" was made (1360), and he gave up his claims, only keeping the French provinces that were his by inheritance. He founded the Order of the Garter. It is said that the Countess of Salisbury at a tournament at Windsor dropped her garter, much to the amusement of the people around. The king gallantly took it up and handed it to her, saying in French, *"Honi soit qui mal y pense"* (Evil to him who evil thinks), which is now the motto of the Order of the Garter and also on the Great Seal of England.

Edward III. died when sixty-five years old (June 21, 1377), and left his throne to his grandson RICHARD II.

EDWARD IV., King of England, first sovereign of the House of York, born in Rouen, April 29, 1441. He was the Duke of York and head of the House of York, which carried on a civil war against the Lancastrians, who fought for King Henry VI. Having won the battle of Mortimer's Cross, Edward marched to London and was proclaimed king on March 4, 1461. Soon after (March 29) he totally defeated the Lancastrians at Towton, and again at Hexham in 1464, and took Henry prisoner. In 1470 the Earl of WARWICK, who had become offended at him, drove him from his kingdom, but Edward came back the next year, defeated Warwick at Barnet, and got back his throne. On May 4, 1471, Edward gained the battle of Tewkesbury, which ended the War of the Roses. He died when forty-two years old (April 9, 1483), and was succeeded by Edward V.

EDWARD V., King of England, second sovereign of the House of York, son of Edward IV., born Nov. 4, 1470. He was a child of twelve when his father died, and his uncle Richard, Duke of Gloucester, took charge of the kingdom with the title of Protector. Instead of having the young king crowned, he put him and his brother, the Duke of York, in the Tower of London. They were never seen again, and were said to have been smothered to death (1483). Two hundred years afterward some children's bones, supposed to be theirs, were found buried at the foot of the Tower stairs, and were removed to Westminster Abbey.

EDWARD VI., King of England, third sovereign of the House of Tudor, son of HENRY VIII. and Jane Seymour, born Oct. 12, 1537. His father died when he was nine years old, and he lived to be only sixteen. He was brought up a Protestant, was carefully educated, good and clever, and while he lived the government and church were Protestant but his affairs were managed; first by his uncle the Duke of Somerset, whom the people hated, and who was beheaded (1552), and then by the Duke of Northumberland, who persuaded him to make Lady Jane GREY his heir instead of his sisters. Edward VI. died July 6, 1553, and was succeeded by Queen MARY I.

EDWARD THE CONFESSOR, King of England, born about 1004. He succeeded his step-brother, Hardicanute, the last of the Danish kings, when thirty-eight years old (1042). His early life was spent in Normandy, and he was no better than a foreigner and liked to have Normans about him; still his people loved him, and the laws of "Good King Edward" were long remembered. He had much trouble with his father-in-law, Earl Godwin, a Saxon noble whose daughter Editha he had married. Edward banished him and his sons, but they came back with a strong fleet and forced the king to give them their possessions again. After Edward's death, which took place in his sixty-third year (Jan. 5, 1066), HAROLD, son of Earl Godwin, seized the throne, though it was claimed by Edward's cousin, William of Normandy, afterward called the Conqueror. Edward who was the last of the Saxon kings of England, excepting Harold, was named the Confessor about a hundred years after his death, when he was made a saint.

EDWARD, Prince of Wales, son of Edward III., called the Black Prince from the color of his armor, born June 15, 1330. When fifteen years old he fought under his father in the battle of CRÉCY with great valor, and afterward took for his own the crest and motto of the blind king of Bohemia, who was slain there. This crest, which was three ostrich-feathers, and the motto *Ich dien* (German for I serve) have ever since been used by the Princes of Wales. Later he gained the victory at POITIERS, took the French King John prisoner, and brought him to England. He treated him with the greatest respect, and when they entered London rode a pony beside King John, who was in his royal robes on a splendid white war-horse. In 1361 King Edward made the Black Prince ruler of all his dominions in France, under the title of Prince of Aquitaine. The prince afterward helped Peter the Cruel win back his throne of Castile, in Spain, where his health became ruined. On his return to Aquitaine, the French again made war on him, and he captured and burned LIMOGES, and killed all the inhabitants, for which he has been much blamed. After this he went to England, and died when forty-six years old (June 8, 1376). His tomb is in Canterbury Cathedral, and above it still hang his helmet, shield, and gauntlets.

EG'MONT, Lamoral, Count of, a soldier of the NETHERLANDS, born in 1522. When a boy he was a page of the Emperor CHARLES V., and

Ancient Egyptian Soldiers on the March.   From Picture on a Monument.

he served in his army in Algiers and France. PHILIP II. made him stadtholder, or governor, of Flanders and Artois, where, though he was a Catholic, he showed favors to the Protestants, and tried to keep the Inquisition out of the Netherlands. This and his popularity made Philip jealous, and the king sent the Duke of ALVA, Egmont's enemy, to the Netherlands with an army. Egmont went to meet him with presents, but Alva had him arrested, tried, and beheaded at Brussels, with Count Horn, June 5, 1568.

EGYPT (*e'jipt*), a country of N.E. Africa, on the Mediterranean Sea; area 175,000 square miles, or about three times as large as the State of Georgia; pop. 6,800,000, or about five times that of Georgia; capital, CAIRO. Besides Egypt proper there is a very large country on the upper Nile and in Central Africa under the rule of Egypt, covering more than 1,000,000 square miles and having more than 11,000,000 people.

Most of Egypt proper is a desert, the only fertile portion being the plain of the river Nile, which flows through the country from south to north. Every year in June the Nile rises and overflows its banks for a long way on each side. As the waters go down grain and other seeds are scattered over the mud, and sheep and goats turned loose to trample them in. When the waters are lowest, cotton and sugar are raised; the plantations are then moistened by water brought from the river in canals, for it seldom rains in Egypt. Grapes, oranges, lemons, and other fruits abound near the cities; there are no forests, and almost the only trees seen are groves of date-palms about the villages. Camels, horses, asses, and oxen are used as beasts of burden, and cows and sheep are common. The prin-

cipal trade of the country is in cotton, wheat, and sugar.

Most of the Egyptians are a dark race, much like the Arabs. They are Mohammedans, and dress in long robes and turbans. Some of the city people are wealthy, but most of the country people, called *felláhs*, are very poor, and live in wretched huts. About one tenth of the people are Christians, chiefly Copts and foreigners. The Copts are said to be descendants of the ancient

An Egyptian Priest offering Sacrifice to an Idol.

Egyptians, and have a language of their own. They live mostly in the cities. In the desert are many Arabs called Bedouins, who live in tents and wander from place to place. Egypt is governed by a ruler called the Khedive.

Though not a very important country now, Egypt was once the most powerful kingdom in the world, and in many parts are still to be seen wonderful ruins of temples and other great buildings which show that it was very rich and

far advanced in the arts at a very early period. The people were idolators, and the ceremonies in their temples when sacrifices were offered to the gods were very splendid. The most ancient rulers of Egypt were called Pharaohs, a term which means much the same as King. The Pharaohs built the PYRAMIDS, the SPHINX, and many other of the oldest monuments, and dug a canal from the NILE to the RED SEA. It was during the reign of one of these Pharaohs, called Merneptah I. (1300

B.C.,), that the Israelites left Egypt. The Pharaohs ruled until about 525 B.C., when the Persians conquered Egypt. ALEXANDER THE GREAT took it from them (332), and made ALEXANDRIA the capital. After his death, PTOLEMY (Soter), one of his generals, became its ruler, and he and his successors, thirteen in all, are known in history as the Ptolemies. Egypt was very prosperous under them, especially under the first three, who did much for learning and founded schools and a great library and museum at Alexandria, making it the rival of Athens and of Rome.

Egypt became a Roman province in 30 B.C. The Arabs conquered it in A.D. 640, and after being held by them as a province for more than two centuries, it became an independent Mohammedan kingdom, of which SALADIN was at one time the ruler. He and his successors had a body of soldiers called MAMELUKES, made up of slaves brought from the countries near the Caspian Sea, who in time became so powerful that they chose the rulers

A Pharaoh in Battle.

of the country themselves. In 1517 the Turks conquered the country, and it still belongs to them in name, and its rulers pay them tribute.

EHRENBREITSTEIN (*er-ren-brite'stine*), a famous fortress of Germany, in Prussia, on the Rhine, opposite COBLENTZ, built on a rocky height, with a small town at its foot. The fortress will hold 100,000 men, but 5000 can defend it. It is said to have been built by the Roman Emperor JULIAN, and rebuilt in the 12th century. It has stood many sieges, but was starved out by the French in 1799 and blown up.

Ehrenbreitstein is a German word meaning "broad stone of honor."

EISENACH (*i'zen-ahkh*), a town of Saxe-Weimar, Germany; pop. 20,-000, or about as large as Lynchburg, Va. It is walled and has a castle. Outside the town on a lofty height is the famous castle of Wartburg, where in old times the minnesingers, or minstrels, used to contend for the prize of poetry. It was there, too, that Martin LUTHER was hidden after the Diet of Worms (1521), when he was carried to Wartburg for safety by the Elector of Saxony. He lived there many months, during which he translated the Bible into German. The chapel in which he preached and the chamber in which he lived are still shown there. On the wall of the chamber are some ink-stains, said to have been made by Luther throwing his inkstand at the devil, whom he thought he saw.

Eisenach means iron-water, being made from two German words (*eisen*, iron, and *ach*, water).

E-LA-GAB′A-LUS, a Roman emperor, cousin of CARACALLA, born in Emesa, Syria, about 205. His real name was Varius Avitus Bassianus, but when a child he was

Castle of Wartburg.

made priest of the Syrian sun-god Elagabalus, and called by his name. He became emperor when about thirteen years old (218), and then took the name of Marcus Aurelius Antoninus. His cruelty and vices soon disgusted the people, who had welcomed him at first, and at last the soldiers murdered him and his mother (222), and threw their bodies into the Tiber.

ELBA (*el′bah*), an island of Italy, in the Mediterranean Sea, between CORSICA and Italy; pop. about 24,000. It is mountainous, but fertile. It is famous as the place to which NAPOLEON I. was banished in 1814, with the title of King of Elba. The villa in which he lived is now a museum of his relics. The name Elba has been changed from Ilva, the Roman name of the island.

ELBE (*elb*, German *el′beh*), a river of Germany, rising in Bohemia, and flowing into the North Sea. It is about 700 miles long, and is important for navigation. There are many large cities on its banks.

ELBERFELD (*el′ber-felt*), a city of W. Germany, on the river Wupper, a branch of the Rhine, and close to BARMEN; pop. 106,500, or nearly as large as Denver, Col.

It is noted for its great cotton factories, but silks, ribbons, carpets, buttons, and other things are also manufactured there, and there are very large dyeing establishments. Two great fairs are held in Elberfeld every year, and it has a very large trade. The city was first settled in 1527, by people who fled from the Netherlands, but its growth is mostly modern.

ELEANOR (*el'a-nor*) **OF AQUITAINE,** Queen of France and of England, born about 1122. She was so called because she was daughter of the Duke of Aquitaine. She first married LOUIS VII. of France, who divorced her (1152), and she then married HENRY II. of England; and it was through her that the English kings claimed the duchy of Aquitaine. Henry's neglect of her turned her love to hatred, and she stirred up her sons to rebel against him, for which she was kept in prison about fifteen years. She afterward ruled England as regent when her son RICHARD I. went to the Holy Land, and when he was imprisoned in Germany she went there to carry his ransom. King JOHN was also her son.

ELECTRA (*e-lek'trah*), in Greek fable, daughter of AGAMEMNON and Clytemnestra. She persuaded her brother Orestes to kill Ægisthus and her mother for having murdered her father. Her life was very unhappy until Orestes returned from his wanderings, when she married his friend Pylades. Her story is the subject of the "Electra," one of the best plays of SOPHOCLES, and of many other poems.

ELEPHANTA (*el-e-fan'tah*), an island of British India, in Bombay Harbor, five miles from the mainland. It is about five miles around, and consists of two hills with a valley between them. It got its name from a great stone elephant which was found there. On the island are three temples cut out of the solid rock, like caves. One of these is very large, the two others being smaller. The rocky roofs are supported by long rows of stone columns, and all the temples are filled with stone figures of Hindoo gods. They have long since been abandoned by the priests, and they are only frequented by women, who go there to pray that they may have children. The temples are at least a thousand years old, and perhaps much older.

ELEUSIS (*e-lu'sis*), a town in Greece, famous for the religious festivals, or thanksgivings, in honor of the goddess Ceres, which were held there. They were called the Eleusinian mysteries, and consisted of games and religious exercises. They were celebrated in the latter part of September and the first of October, and lasted nine days.

EL'I-OT, George, the assumed name of Mary Ann Evans, a famous English writer of novels, born Nov. 22, 1819, at Arbury Farm, Derbyshire. She was the wife of George Henry LEWES, but after his death (1878) married (1880) John Walter Cross, a banker of London. Among her novels are "Adam Bede," "The Mill on the Floss," "Romola," "Middlemarch," and "Daniel Deronda." With few exceptions, her novels are mostly pictures of English village life. She died when sixty-one years old (Dec. 22, 1880).

ELIOT, John, called the "Apostle of the Indians," born in England, in 1604. He came to Massachusetts in 1631, and became the minister of the church in Roxbury. He thought the Indians were the descendants of the lost tribes of Israel, and learned their language so that he might preach to them. In 1646 he began his labors among them, made them his friends, and got great influence over them. He translated the Bible into their language and had it printed (1661-1663), and this was the first Bible printed in America. It is now very rare, a copy of it having been sold for more than $1000. Mr. Eliot died in Roxbury when eighty-six years old (May 20, 1690).

E·LIZ'A·BETH, a city of New Jersey, on Newark Bay, 11 miles W.S.W. of New York; pop. 28,000, or about as large as Salem, Mass. Elizabethport, the part on the bay, has many manufactories, among them the Singer sewing machine factory, one of the largest of its kind in the world. Elizabeth proper has fine streets and houses, and many of the people do business in New York. The city was settled in 1665, and at first was called Elizabethtown. From Feb. 24, 1755, to Sept. 13, 1757, it was the capital of the colony of New Jersey.

ELIZABETH, Queen of England, daughter of HENRY VIII. and Anne Boleyn, born Sept. 7, 1533. Until she was two years old she was considered the heir to the throne; after that she was very little thought of, though her father had her carefully educated. While her sister Mary was queen, she was treated with suspicion and kept in prison most of the time. She was twenty-five years old when she became queen, on the death of Mary (1558), and she made the country Protestant again as it had been in the time of EDWARD VI. All the Protestants in Scotland, France, and Flanders looked to her as their head. Mary's

husband, Philip II. of Spain, wanted to marry her, and when she refused he became her greatest enemy.

Elizabeth's cousin, MARY STUART, Queen of Scots, was generally looked upon as heir to her throne, she being the granddaughter of Margaret, sister of Henry VIII. When Mary had to flee from Scot-

Queen Elizabeth.

land (1568), she sought Elizabeth's protection; but Elizabeth, afraid that the Catholics would make her Queen of England, kept her a prisoner for nearly nineteen years, and finally had her beheaded (Feb. 18, 1587).

Mary had sent word to King Philip of Spain that she gave her rights to the crown of England to him because her son was a Protestant. Philip had all the time been trying to stir up trouble in England and Ireland, and Queen Elizabeth had aided the Protestants of the Netherlands against him. He now made up his mind to try to conquer England, and got together a fleet of a hundred and fifty ships, which he called the "Invincible Armada" (Spanish for fleet), and which was to be aided by an army.

Lord Howard commanded the English fleet, many ships of which were only merchant-vessels, and he had with him such brave men as Francis DRAKE, John HAWKINS, and Martin FROBISHER. The Armada went up the English Channel, and the English ships, coming out of Plymouth behind them, fought the Spaniards as they sailed along until they anchored off CALAIS. At midnight the English set eight ships on fire where they would drift among the Spanish ships, and the Spaniards, becoming frightened, put to sea in disorder. At daybreak they were attacked on all sides, and, being poorer sailors and gunners than the English, were soon put to flight with the loss of many ships. They tried to get home by sailing up the North Sea and around Scotland and Ireland, but were overtaken by a great storm, and only fifty-four vessels got back to Spain.

Queen Elizabeth had many royal and noble suitors, but she refused all of them, although her people wished her to marry, and she is sometimes called, therefore, the "Virgin Queen." One of her favorites was Robert DUDLEY, Earl of Leicester, and when she was quite an old woman she cared very much for the Earl of ESSEX. Though she was vain and had many private weaknesses, she was one of the best rulers England ever had. Cecil Lord Burleigh was her minister for forty years. Her reign, which is sometimes called the "Elizabethan Age," is famous for its statesmen, soldiers, and scholars, numbering among the last SPENSER, SHAKE-SPEARE, SIDNEY, BACON, and RALEIGH. The famous East India Company, out of which grew the British Empire in India, was begun in her reign (1600). Elizabeth died at sixty-nine years old, when she had been queen for forty-five years (March 24, 1603). She was the last of the Tudor family, and was succeeded by JAMES I., the son of Mary Stuart.

EL'LI-OTT, Charles Loring, an American portrait-painter, born in Scipio, N. Y., in 1812. He painted more than 700 portraits, many of which rank among the best in American art. He died in Albany, N. Y., Aug. 25, 1868.

ELMIRA (*el-mi'rah*), a city of S. New York, on the Chemung River; pop. 30,000, or about as large as Topeka, Kans. It is surrounded by a very beautiful and fertile country, and several railroads and canals meet there, giving it a large trade. There are many important manufactories, including large railroad car-shops, rolling-mills and other iron-works, breweries, tanneries, and large manufactories of boots and shoes. It is the site of Elmira Female College.

Elmira was settled in 1790, but it was called Newtown until 1828. During the Civil War it was used as a station for Union troops, and many thousand prisoners of war were kept there.

ELYSIUM (*e-lizh'e-um*), among the Greeks and Romans, the home of the blessed after death. It was supposed to be a beautiful plain, adorned with bright gardens and shady groves, on which the sun never set. It was a home of peace and joy, where care, toil, and suffering never came. Whoever had resisted a great temptation three times on earth entered there. It was ruled by Rhadamanthus, who had been the justest of men when on earth.

EM'ER-SON, Ralph Waldo, a noted American writer, born in Boston, May 25, 1803. In his eighth year he was sent to a public grammar-school and was soon able to enter the Latin school. His first attempts at composition were not the usual dull efforts of a schoolboy, but original poems which he read with real taste and feeling. He was graduated at Harvard when eighteen years old, and taught school afterward for five years. Then he became a clergyman; but in about six years he left his church and sailed for Europe, where he stayed a year. On his return to America he began his career as a lecturer and writer. His style of writing is very poetical and full of meaning, but is sometimes hard to understand because his ideas are not always clearly expressed; yet he is thought to be a brilliant writer, and is very famous both in America and in England. He has published several volumes of both prose and poetry. He died at Concord, Massachusetts, when seventy-seven years old (April 27, 1882).

EMPEDOCLES (*em-ped'o kleez*), a Greek philosopher, born in Sicily, about the middle of the 5th century B.C. He was a poet, a priest, a physician, and a philosopher. It is said that he restored dead people to life, that the winds stopped still and the waters flowed at his bidding. He was very vain, and used to move about among the people dressed in long purple robes with a golden girdle, his flowing hair bound with a garland, a branch of laurel in his hand, and sandals of brass on his feet, while a procession of slaves followed him. He told the people that he was a god, and they believed him. Strange stories are told of his death; some said that one night, after a feast, he was caught up in a blaze of glory;

others, that he had thrown himself into the crater of Etna, hoping that people would think he had been translated to heaven; but the volcano cheated him, and cast forth one of his brazen sandals, so that everybody might know what he had done.

EN'DI-COTT, John, Governor of Massachusetts, born in Dorchester, England, in 1589. He came to America when he was thirty-nine years old, and was several times chosen governor of Massachusetts. He was a very strict Puritan, and very severe in carrying out what he thought to be right. Endicott had such a dislike of anything like Popery that he cut out the cross from the military flag. He was opposed to long hair, ordered the women to wear veils over their faces in public meetings, and had four Quakers put to death while he was governor. He died in Boston when seventy-six years old (March 15, 1665).

ENDYMION (*en-dim'e-on*), in Greek fable, a shepherd of great beauty, who used to go to sleep every night in a cave of Mount Latmus, in Caria. While he slept the goddess Selene, or the moon, saw him, and fell in love with him. When the moon was eclipsed, she was thought to be in the Latmian cave with Endymion. They had fifty daughters; and Jupiter condemned Endymion to fifty years' sleep.

EN'FIELD, a town of Connecticut, on the Connecticut River; pop. about 7000. The religious society called Shakers have a farm there, noted for raising garden-seeds, of which great quantities are sold every year. In the town of Enfield are the villages of Thompsonville, famous for its carpet-factory, and Hazardville, where is one of the largest gunpowder mills in the world.

EN'FIELD, a town of England, 10 miles N.E. of London; pop.

19,000, or about the same as that of Leavenworth, Kans. It is noted for its great rifle-factory, where the rifles for the English army are made. The Enfield rifle took its name from Enfield, but the kind made there now is called the Martini-Henry rifle, from its inventors.

ENGHIEN (*ong-ghe-an'*), **Louis,** Duke d', a French prince, son of the Prince of Condé, born in Chantilly, Aug. 2, 1772. He was one of the nobility who had to leave France when the Revolution broke out (1789), and, though very young, he fought bravely against the republic. About 1801 he fell in love with a beautiful princess, Charlotte de Rohan, who lived in Ettenheim, Baden ; and he bought a château there, in order to be near her. Some people said that they were privately married ; and all might have gone well, but he was accused of visiting Paris secretly, and of plotting to take the life of Bonaparte, who was then First Consul. Bonaparte determined to frighten his enemies by seizing and executing the duke. He sent three hundred soldiers, who surrounded the château in the night, arrested the duke in his bed, and carried him off to the fortress of Vincennes. He asked to see the First Consul and to be allowed a confessor, but was refused. After a mock trial, he was shot by torchlight early in the morning in a ditch outside the walls. When one of the soldiers offered to bind his eyes, he said : "You are Frenchmen ; at least you will do me the service not to miss your aim." They threw the body of the brave young prince into a grave which had been dug the day before. No act of Napoleon's life made a darker blot upon his fame. The Duke d'Enghien was thirty-two years old when executed (March 21, 1804).

ENGLAND (*ing'gland*), a country of W. Europe, forming with Wales the southern part of the island of Great Britain ; area (without Wales), 51,000 square miles, or nearly as large as the State of Wisconsin ; pop. 27,500,000, or less than half of that of the whole United States ; capital, LONDON. It is more thickly peopled than any other country in Europe excepting Belgium. The surface is varied with hills and valleys, rolling lands, and plains, watered by many rivers, making it one of the most beautiful and fertile countries in the world.

England has very fine coal-beds, and many mines of iron, tin, copper, zinc, and lead. Some of the tin-mines in the south-western part have been dug out far beneath the bed of the sea. Much of the land belongs to noblemen or rich people, who have fine castles or mansions, and live in beautiful parks often covered with woods in which deer and pheasants are kept. The farmers generally hire their land of these rich men, and they cultivate it so well that some parts of England look like a garden. Among the principal crops are wheat, oats, barley, rye, potatoes, turnips, and flax. Where the land is not good for planting, it is used for pasture, and the finest horses, cattle, and sheep are reared. England is the greatest manufacturing country in the world, being especially celebrated for her great cotton and woolen mills and iron-works. More ships are built there than in any other country, and there are immense manufactories of cutlery, tools, paper, and many other things. More cotton cloth is made than in all other countries put together. Most of the cotton comes from the southern United States. During the Civil War in the United States, when the supply of cotton was stopped, many of the English mills were closed, and so many people were thrown out of employment that there was a terrible famine. England has also more ships and a larger trade than any other nation. There are many splendid cities and palaces, but England has also many poor people, who are often very ignorant and miserable. The country is governed by a king or queen, and by a Parliament, much like the Congress of the United States. It consists, like that, of two parts: one, called the House of Lords, made up of the principal noblemen, and the other, the House of Commons, chosen by the people.

The first known inhabitants of England, or Britain as it was then called, were savages who lived in huts and dressed in the skins of animals. They made boats called

Briton with his Coracle.

coracles out of wicker-work, which were so light that a man could easily carry one on his head (C. C. T., 47, I., 1.). They had chiefs, and priests called Druids who often killed men as sacrifices to their gods. Julius Cæsar invaded the island with a Roman army in 55 B.C., but the Romans did not fairly conquer it until a hundred years afterward. They kept it for nearly four hundred years, during which most of the people were converted to Christianity. In the 5th century the Romans were obliged to use all

their armies at home, and Britain was left to itself. About that time fierce tribes from Scotland invaded the country, and the Britains, who had forgotten how to fight, invited the Angles and Saxons from Denmark to come and defend them. Their defenders soon turned enemies, and killed or enslaved nearly all the Britons. The few who remained were driven into Wales, where their descendants still live; and so a new race was formed in Britain, which then took its name of England from the Angles. At first the country was divided into different kingdoms which were at war with each other, until Egbert, King of Wessex, conquered them all (827). A little later the country was invaded and partly conquered by the Danes, and it was for his fights against them that King Alfred the Great was most noted. Saxon and Danish kings ruled the country until William Duke of Normandy in France invaded it with a great army, beating the English king, Harold, at the battle of Hastings (Oct. 4, 1066). William made slaves of the Saxons, and he himself became king of England, while his followers were made nobles. England has since been governed by kings and queens mostly descended from him, who are told about under their own names.

ENNIUS (*en'ne-us*), **Quintus,** a Roman poet, the father of Roman literature, born in 239 B.C. Cato the Elder took him to Rome, where he taught Greek and Latin, and gained the friendship of the noblest Romans of his day. He was famous for his learning and his charming conversation. His writings were a poem on Roman history, plays for the theatre, many of them adapted from the finest Greek plays, and short poems, a few of which remain. He died in Rome when seventy years old (169 B.C.).

E-PAM-I-NON'DAS, a famous

Theban general, born in the 5th century B.C. He was of a noble but poor family, modest, strictly truthful, and a great soldier. Before the battle of LEUCTRA (371 B.C.), Sparta held the highest place in Greece, but after that battle, when the Thebans under Epaminondas gained such a splendid victory, Thebes became the greatest power. After this battle, when all around were praising him, he said that his chief pleasure was in thinking how happy it would make his father and mother. In one of his campaigns he saved the life of his friend Pelopidas by risking his own. In his last battle, fought at MANTINEA against the Spartans, he was pierced in the breast with a javelin, and was carried off the field to a little hill; his first question was if his shield was safe; and when it was shown to him he allowed his wound to be examined. He was then told that when the javelin was taken out he might bleed to death; his weeping friends refused to attempt it; but he waited quietly until he heard that the victory was gained, and then grasping the shaft drew it out with a firm hand, and died in a few moments (362 B.C.).

EPHESUS (*ef'e-sus*), an ancient city of Asia Minor, on the river Cayster, near its mouth. Nothing is known of its origin, though an old legend says it was founded by the AMAZONS. It was finally taken by the Ionian Greeks, under whom it became very rich and powerful. It was chiefly noted for its magnificent temple of Diana, which is said to have been rebuilt seven times. During the night in which Alexander the Great was born it was burned by a man named EROSTRATUS. Alexander offered to rebuild it if the people would name it after him, but they refused and rebuilt it themselves, the work occupying 220 years. It was the largest of all the Greek temples, and was called one

of the wonders of the world. It contained a splendid ivory and gold statue of Diana, and was ornamented with sculptures by PRAXITELES and a large painting by APELLES. In A.D. 54 St. Paul preached in Ephesus, and founded a Christian church there, to which he afterward wrote a letter called his epistle to the Ephesians. St. John also lived in the city, and in later times several Christian councils were held there. The Goths sacked Ephesus and destroyed the temple about A.D. 260, and after that the city fell to decay. At present there are a few small villages on the site, and remains of the temple and of an immense amphitheatre have been found.

On Mt. Prion, near the ancient city, is a cave called the Grotto of the Seven Sleepers. There is a story that seven Christians who were persecuted during the reign of DIOCLETIAN fled to this grotto, and fell asleep and only awoke after 200 years. Supposing that they had only taken a nap, they went down to the city again, and were astonished to find things so changed. The cave is visited by Christians and Mohammedan pilgrims, and the story of the seven sleepers was placed by Mohammed in the Koran.

EPICURUS (*ep-e-ku'rus*), a celebrated Greek philosopher, born in the island of Samos, 342 B.C. He began to study and teach philosophy when only eighteen years old. When he was thirty-five he bought a garden in the city of Athens, and there, surrounded by his pupils and friends, he spent the rest of his life. He made pleasure the highest good, but he taught that the way to be happy was to live simply and temperately, to be kind to other people and contented with one's own lot. Epicurus practiced what he preached; but some people who hated him said that he did not. And it is through his enemies that his name has come to us connected with high living, so that now when one is called an epicure he is supposed to be very fond of good eating and drinking. He died at the age of seventy-two (B.C. 270.)

E-PI'RUS, a country of ancient Greece, now the S. part of Albania. It is a wild and mountainous region, and was noted in ancient times for its fine horses and oxen. The most noted king of Epirus was PYRRHUS. The oracle of DODONA was in Epirus.

ERASMUS (*e-raz'mus*), **Desiderius,** a famous Dutch scholar and writer, born in Rotterdam, Oct. 28, 1467. When nine years old he was sent to school, and gave proofs of uncommon memory; he studied the Greek language diligently, and used to say that as soon as he could get any money he would buy Greek books first, and then clothes. When quite young, his tutors tried to get him to quit the world and become a monk; his reply was that he did not yet know what the world was, nor what a monastery was, nor what he himself was. After many persuasions, however, and some lapse of time, he took religious vows; yet he was always more scholar than priest, and became the most distinguished writer of his age. One day a monk, hearing Erasmus praised, looked dissatisfied, and on being asked the reason, said he could not bear to hear a man so flattered who was so fond of eating fowls. He loathed fish, and was very choice about his wines, and used to say that his stomach was Lutheran but his heart was Catholic. He lived at the time of the Reformation, when Roman Catholics and Protestants were quarreling with each other, but he did not give himself up wholly to either party; he saw the faults on both sides, and tried to preserve a middle course. The consequence was that the hot-tempered ones of each party abused him, but when he died both Catholics and Protestants mourned for

him. He left all his fortune to the old, the poor, and to fatherless children. The monument erected to his memory in the cathedral at Basel is still the chief object of interest there. He died at Basel when sixty-nine years old (July 12, 1536).

ERCKMANN-CHATRIAN (*erk-man-shat-re-an'*), the names of two French novelists, who wrote in partnership. They were born in Lorraine, Emile Erckmann on May 20, 1822, and Alexandre Chatrian on Dec. 18, 1826. Their works are faithful pictures of life among the peasants of Alsace and Lorraine, of the wars of the Revolution and first Empire. Both were strong republicans, and their writings did much to cure the French of their love of an empire. Among their works are "Stories of the Rhine Border," "Madame Thérèse," "History of a Conscript of 1813," and "Waterloo." Chatrian died when sixty-four years old (Sept. 4, 1890).

ER'E-BUS, in Greek fable, the abode of Night. It was supposed to be a gloomy place, situated at the end of the earth, through which the souls of the blessed had to pass on their way to ELYSIUM.

ERECHTHEUS (*e-rek'thuse*), a hero of Greek fable. He was a favorite of Minerva, who educated him secretly, and then made him king of Athens. He is said to have invented the covered four-wheeled carriage, for which he was set among the stars as Auriga (the Charioteer). The Erechtheum, a temple of Minerva on the Acropolis, Athens, is said to have been built by him.

ERFURT (*er'foort*), a city of Germany, in S. Prussia, on the river Gera; pop. 50,000, or about as large as Charleston, S. C. Erfurt is a strong fortress, and is important because it is on the principal road on which armies would march into Central Europe. In its cathedral is an immense bell, more than four hundred years old. It is named Santa Maria Gloriosa ("Glorious Saint Mary"), but the people call it Grosse Susanna (Big Susan), that having been the name of another bell melted by a fire that burned the town (1251). Martin Luther was a monk at Erfurt, in a monastery which is now used as an orphan asylum. In 1808 the two emperors, Napoleon and Alexander of Russia, and several kings met in Erfurt and made a treaty of peace.

The name of Erfurt has been changed from Erpisford, its ancient name, which means the "ford of Erpe" or Erpes, by whom it was first built in the 5th century,

ERICSSON (*er'iks-son*), **John,** a famous Swedish engineer and inventor, born in the province of Wermeland, Sweden, July 31, 1803. He studied military engineering,

John Ericsson.

and after serving for a while in the Swedish army he resigned and gave his time wholly to inventing machines. In England he gained a prize for the best locomotive engine, and soon afterward he invented a steam fire-engine. He also made a caloric engine, or one which was moved by heated air instead of by steam. In 1836 he made the first screw steamer, and this was so successful that nearly all steamers are now moved with screws instead of paddles. Three years afterward he came to the United States, and was employed by the government to build a war steamer, the first ever moved by a screw propeller. When the Civil War broke out, the United States government got him to make a new kind of iron-clad vessel made to float very low, so that the deck was only a few inches above the water. Instead of port-holes in the sides, there was a small tower, called the turret, on the deck, which could be turned by machinery so that the two great cannons in it could be pointed in any way. The first of these turret-ships, called the "Monitor," was finished and sent to Hampton Roads just in time to defeat the Confederate iron-clad ship Virginia, formerly the "Merrimack." The Virginia, which was many times larger than the Monitor, was finally obliged to retreat, and the "cheese-box on a raft," as the sailors called the Monitor, became famous all over the world. After that Ericsson made many more turret-ships, which were called Monitors, after the name of the first one. Some had two or three turrets, and very large cannon. He died in New York when eighty-five years old (March 8, 1889).

ERIE (*e're*), **Lake,** one of the five great lakes between Canada and the United States; area 9600 square miles, or about as large as the State of Vermont. By the Detroit River at its western end, it receives the waters of Lakes Superior, Huron, Michigan, and St. Clair, and its waters flow into Lake Ontario by the Niagara River. Lake Erie is generally shallow, few points being more than 120 feet deep. The shores are often high and picturesque, and there are many islands, especially at the western end. The principal harbors are Buffalo, Dunkirk, Erie, Cleveland, Sandusky, and Toledo. The lake is generally frozen from December to April.

ERIE (*e're*), a city of N.W. Pennsylvania, on Lake Erie ; pop. 40,634, or about as large as Peoria, Ill. It has a good harbor and a large trade is carried on, especially in lumber, coal, iron ore, and petroleum. There are many manufactories of iron and steel articles, such as stoves, steam-engines, carwheels, and many other things. Erie also has large petroleum refineries, breweries, a brass foundry, and manufactories of organs, pumps, leather, and bricks.

Erie was first settled by the French, who built there a fort called Fort de la Presque Isle, or Peninsula Fort (1749). The town was laid out in 1795. During the war of 1812 Com. PERRY equipped a fleet there, with which he soon afterward fought the battle of Lake Erie.

E-ROS'TRA-TUS, a man who set fire to the temple of Diana on the night in which Alexander the Great was born (356 B.C.). When put to the torture, and asked his reason for committing the deed, he replied: "To make my name immortal." The Ephesians passed a law that his name should be forgotten, but his base deed has preserved it forever.

ERZERUM (*er-zeh-room'*), a city of Asiatic Turkey, in Armenia, on the west branch of the river Euphrates ; pop. 60,000, or nearly as large as Troy, N. Y. It is defended by three walls with iron-covered gates, and by a brick citadel; but these are half ruined. The streets are narrow and dirty, and most of the houses are plastered with mud, and have flat roofs covered with earth and sod, on which donkeys are sometimes allowed to graze. Droves of half-starved dogs wander about, barking savagely at strangers. Many caravans stop at Erzerum. and there is a considerable trade in wheat, goat and sheep skins, mohair, and galls.

Erzerum was founded by a general of the Emperor Theodosius II. (415), and called Theodosiopolis, or "City of Theodosius." The people around used to call it Arz-er-Roum, or the "fortress of the Romans," and from that came its present name.

ESKIMOS (*es'ke-moze*). See AMERICAN INDIANS.

ES'SEX, Robert Devereux, second Earl of, born at Netherwood, Herefordshire, Nov. 10, 1567. He came to the court of Queen Elizabeth when only seventeen years old, and was so handsome and agreeable that the queen made him her chief favorite , and although she was nearly sixty years old at that time, some ill-natured folk said she was in love with him. She loaded him with honors, but they were heavy chains too, as he found out to his cost. The first thing he did to make her angry was to join Admiral DRAKE'S expedition to Portugal without asking her leave ; when she heard he had gone, she wrote a letter ordering him to come back at once, at his peril. Our headstrong young hero had to put his pride in his pocket and obey his queen, who, after a while, forgave him.

The next thing that made her angry with him was that he got married. Essex kept this a secret for some time, but when she found it out she swore great oaths, like her father Henry VIII., and only forgave him when he agreed to leave his young wife at home, while he spent his time at court. For some time after this everything went on smoothly ; but Essex began to grow tired of his slavery, and was sometimes even rude to the queen. This did not suit her hot temper ; so one day she boxed his ears, whereupon the young fellow swore that he would not put up with such an insult if it came from Henry VIII. himself. After a while they seemed to be friends again, but it was only a sort of patched-up peace; and in 1599 Essex was arrested for high treason. The queen signed his death-warrant, but it was said that she was never really happy afterward. He was executed when only thirty-three years old (Feb. 25, 1601.)

ESSEX, Robert Devereux, third Earl of, son of Elizabeth's favorite, born in London in 1592. When the war broke out between King CHARLES I. and the Parliament, he took the side of the Parliament and fought against the king at Edgehill. He afterward met with disaster and lost his army, but escaped himself and was honored by Parliament for his services. When he found out that Oliver Cromwell wanted to make a new government, he tried to have him arrested; but Cromwell took his revenge by getting passed a bill called the " Self - denying Ordinance," by which no member of the House could hold any office at all; so that Essex had to resign his commission. He died in London when fifty-four years old (Sept. 14, 1646).

ETHIOPIA (*e-the-o'pe-ah*), an ancient country of Africa, S. of Egypt. The Ethiopians were a powerful people and had many wars with the Egyptians. The Greeks called all the dark-skinned peoples of both Africa and Asia Ethiopians.

ETNA (*et'nah*), **MOUNT.** See SICILY.

E'TON, a town of England, on the river Thames, opposite Windsor, and 22 miles W. of London; pop. about 4000. It is celebrated for its public school or college, which was founded in 1440 by King Henry VI., and is now the greatest school in England. It generally has more than 900 boys, 70 of whom, called king's scholars, have their board and teaching at the cost of the English Government. The provost, or president, is appointed by the Queen. The head boy is called the " captain." Until 1844 the students of Eton had a curious custom, called the "montem." Once a year, headed by their captain, they marched to a mound called Salt Hill, and there spent the day in festivities, and in making the passers-by give them money which they called " salt." As many people went there on purpose to see them, the sum obtained was sometimes as much as $5000. After paying the expenses, what remained was given to the captain.

ETRURIA (*e-tru're-ah*), an ancient country of Italy, covering what is now called Tuscany and some other territory. The people, who were called Etruscans or Tyrrhenians, were great builders and very skillful in the arts. Many of their tombs have been opened, and found to contain great numbers of vases, urns, and ornaments, which show that they excelled in the making of pottery and articles of bronze.

EUBŒA (*u-be'ah*, modern Greek *ev've-ah*), the largest island of the Grecian Archipelago, on the E. side of the mainland of Greece; area 1400 square miles, or a little larger than the State of Rhode Island; pop. 95,000, or about a third that of Rhode Island. At one point it is only two hundred feet from the mainland, with which it is connected by a bridge. A range of mountains runs the whole length of the island, and the coasts, especially on the eastern side, are very steep and rocky. The scenery is very beautiful, and the soil is exceedingly fertile. Corn, olives, grapes, and many other fruits are raised in large quantities, and olive-oil and wine are among the principal things sent to other countries. In early times Eubœa was inhabited by Ionian Greeks, and among its important cities were

Chalcis and Eretria. After the Persian war, the island belonged to the Athenians, who valued it very highly because it furnished them with corn, wood, and pasturage for their cattle. It afterward belonged to the ..Iacedonians, Romans, Venetians, and Turks. It now forms a part of Greece.

EUCLID (*u'klid*), a famous Greek writer on mathematics, who taught in Alexandria, Egypt, in the 3d century B.C. We know but little of his life, though his fame was so great that, even for several hundred years after his death, almost everybody who wanted to study mathematics went to the school which he set up in Alexandria. Euclid is most celebrated for his book on geometry, which with some changes is still taught in schools and colleges. Many young folks find some of his problems pretty hard, but as they are necessary for the thorough understanding of mathematics they have to be mastered. It is probable that King Ptolemy, who ruled Egypt when Euclid lived there, had met with the same difficulty, for he one day asked Euclid if geometry could not be made easier. " There is no royal road to geometry," replied Euclid.

EUGÈNE (*uh-zhane'*), François, Prince of Savoy, born in Paris, Oct. 18, 1663. His family intended to make him a priest, but his taste was for a soldier's life, and as LOUIS XIV. refused to give him a regiment in the French army, he went as a volunteer in the army of Leopold, Emperor of Austria, to fight against the Turks (1683), saying that he would never again enter France except as an enemy. He soon became so famous as a soldier that Louis XIV. wanted him back again, and offered him a high position in the French army; bnt Eugène refused to leave the emperor, and was given the chief command of the Austrian army. He marched against the Turks, and

won a grand victory at Zenta, in Hungary (1697). In 1704 the allied armies of Germany and Austria, under Prince Eugène, joined the British army, under the Duke of MARLBOROUGH, in Bavaria, and together won the battle of BLENHEIM (1704) against the French. Prince Eugène was next sent against the French in Italy, and though at first defeated, finally drove them out. He then helped Marlborough to gain the battles of Oudenarde (1708) and MALPLAQUET (1709).

Prince Eugène next won famous victories over the Turks at Peterwardein (1716) and at Belgrade, where he was wounded (1717). This was the worst defeat the Turks ever suffered. In 1718 he retired from the army, and lived for many years at Vienna, honored by all for his noble nature as well as for his valiant deeds, and enjoying science, art, and literature. He died at Vienna when seventy-two years old (April 21, 1736). Eugène is one of the five greatest European generals of modern times, the other four being Napoleon, Wellington, Marlborough, and Frederick the Great.

EUGÉNIE (*uh-zha-ne'*), **EMPRESS.** See BONAPARTE, NAPOLEON III.

EURIPIDES (*u-rip'e-deez*), a famous Greek poet, born in the island of SALAMIS, 480 B.C. He was the last of the three great tragic poets of Greece (the other two were ÆSCHYLUS and SOPHOCLES). His father was an Athenian citizen who fled to Salamis when Xerxes and his Persians came to Athens. Euripides was a pupil of ANAXAGORAS, and afterward the pupil and friend of Socrates. His first play was written when he was only eighteen years old, but it was not played on the stage. The first one played was brought out when he was twenty-five years old (455). He took many prizes for his plays, sometimes over Sophocles. Some say that he wrote seventy-five and others that he wrote more than ninety tragedies but only nineteen have been saved. Among these are "Alcestis," "Hippolytus," "Hecuba," "Ion," "Andromache," "Iphigenia in Aulis," and "Orestes."

Euripides had many enemies in Athens, and about the year 408 he went to live at the court of Archelaus, king of Macedonia. He died when seventy-four years old (406

B.C.). Some say that he was torn to pieces by the hounds of the king, set upon him by two envious poets. Archelaus would not let his bones be taken to Athens, but built him a splendid monument in Pella on which he inscribed, "Never, O Euripides, will thy memory be forgotten." The Athenians built a magnificent tomb for him, on the road to

Europe.

the Piræus, on which they inscribed, "All Greece is the monument of Euripides : Macedonian earth covers but his bones."

EUROPE (*u'rup*), one of the five continents of the earth ; area 3,822,-350 square miles, or a little more than a fourth as large as America ; pop. 318,434,000, or about three and a fourth times that of America. It is

the smallest of the continents, excepting Australia. It is really only a great peninsula of Asia, with which it forms almost one unbroken mass, but from the oldest times it has been considered a continent by itself.

If Europe could be looked at all at once from a high place, it would be seen to be made up of a great central plain, with three peninsulas

(Spain, Italy, and Greece) on the south, and two peninsulas (Denmark, and Sweden and Norway) and some islands (Britain) on the north. In the southern part would be seen a mass of mountains, some so high that their tops are always covered with snow From these mountains the waters drain into the Adriatic through the river Po, into the Mediterranean through the Rhone, into the North Sea through the Rhine, and into the Black Sea through the Danube.

Though Europe is divided into many countries, whose inhabitants speak different languages, most of its peoples are descended from a common stock, ARYANS, who came from Asia. But the Turks, the Magyars of Hungary, and the Tartars of Russia were once TURANIAN tribes. Most of the people are Christians, but there are some Mohammedans and Jews. All the great countries of Europe are told about under their own titles.

The Greeks said that the name of Europe was taken from EUROPA.

EUROPA (*u-ro'pah*), in Greek fable, the daughter of Agenor, king of Phœnicia, and sister of CADMUS. Jupiter fell in love with her, and, changing himself into a white bull, came up to her as she was gathering flowers. She admired him, and at last mounted on his back, when he ran off with her, and carried her over the sea to CRETE. She was the mother of Minos, Sarpedon, and Rhadamanthus.

EURYDICE (*u-rid'i-se*). See ORPHEUS.

EU·SE'BI-US, called Pamphili, a writer of the early church, born in Palestine about 265. He taught a school at Cæsarea, and afterward became bishop there. He was a man of great learning and talents, and has been called the father of church history. Among his works, which were written in Greek, are an "Ecclesiastical (church) History," a "Universal History," and a "Life of Constantine the Great." He died when about seventy-five years old (340).

EUTAW (*u'taw*) **SPRINGS,** a small branch of the Santee River in South Carolina, where, during the Revolutionary War, a battle was fought between the Americans, under General Green, and the British, under Colonel Stuart. The British, had more soldiers, but the Americans attacked them so bravely that they were driven from their camp. The Americans then began to plunder the tents and drink the liquors which they found; but just then the British renewed the fight, and the Americans, in turn, were driven back (Sept. 8, 1781). When night came on, the British retreated towards Charleston.

EUTER'PE. See MUSES.

EUXINE (*u'xin*). See BLACK SEA.

EV'ANS, Marian. See ELIOT, GEORGE.

EV'ANS-VILLE, a city of S. Indiana, on the Ohio River; pop. 50,756, or about as large as Paterson, N. J. It has many flouring-mills and manufactories of machinery, stoves, saddlery, clothing, and cotton goods. A large trade is carried on, especially in grain, flour, pork, cement, cotton, tobacco, and iron. There are mines of coal and iron near the city. Evansville was founded in 1817.

EV'ER-EST, MOUNT. See HIMALAYA MOUNTAINS.

EYLAU (*i'low*), a town of Germany, in N.E. Prussia; pop. 3500. It is celebrated for the bloody battle fought there (Feb. 7-8, 1807) between Napoleon and the Russians and Prussians. About 160,000 soldiers were engaged in this battle, and more than a fourth of them were killed or wounded. The victory was claimed by both sides. A heavy snow-storm raged all the time, so that often the two armies could not see each other.

F

FA'BI-US MAX'I-MUS, Quintus, a celebrated Roman general. When a boy he had the name of Verrucosus, the Latin word for a wart, because he had a small wart on his upper lip; and as he had a mild, amiable disposition he was called Ovicula, which means a little sheep. When he became a general he got the name of Cunctator (the delayer), because he would not attack the Carthaginian army under Hannibal, but kept his own forces close by, watching the enemy, hindering them from getting food, and tiring them out in a useless sort of hide-and-seek, until they were brought to great straits. Hannibal at last made up his mind to outwit Fabius. He took two thousand oxen, and caused torches and dry sticks to be tied to their horns. When night came these were lighted, and the oxen were driven near the pass where the Romans lay. The Romans thought it was a great body of men, and fearing that they should soon be surrounded, quitted the pass and fled to their camp, and Hannibal's troops then marched safely through. Still Fabius nearly always got the better of Hannibal, and might have conquered him, but some of his own men thought it would be finer and braver to fight, and abused Fabius, calling him a coward and a weak-minded fool. At last they succeeded in dividing the command between him and Minucius, who was one of the rash sort, and rushed headlong into the fight, and would have lost everything had not the prudent Fabius come to help him. After that the people knew how wise he was. He died at a very old age (B.C. 203), and every citizen gave some money toward his funeral expenses, not that he died poor, but because they wished to bury him as the father of his people.

FAHRENHEIT (*fah'ren-hite*), **Gabriel Daniel,** a noted German instrument-maker, born in Dantzic about 1690. He made his home in AMSTERDAM, and made there the thermometer which is named after him, and which is the one commonly used in the United States, Great Britain, and Holland. He is said to have been the first to use mercury in thermometers instead of spirits of wine. He died at Amsterdam when forty-six years old (Sept. 16, 1736).

FAIR'FAX, Thomas, Baron, one of the generals of the Parliament in the war with Charles I., born in Yorkshire in January, 1611. He was of noble birth, and was educated at Cambridge. His father disliked the king, Charles I., and his wife was a Presbyterian, so when the war broke out he joined the Puritan side and fought with Cromwell. He soon rose in the army, and at last was made commander-in-chief. He was a very brave soldier, was always seen in the thickest of the fight, and at the battle of NASEBY, after his helmet was beaten to pieces, he rode bare-headed and bleeding at the head of his army, urging on his men to victory. But when the king's son, Charles II., claimed his own, Fairfax was one of the first to welcome him. He was a good scholar and lover of books, and wrote a short account of his own life. He died at the age of sixty (Nov. 12, 1671).

FAIR'FAX, Thomas, Baron, a British nobleman, born about 1690. He was educated at Oxford, and had a good position in society, but having fallen deeply in love with a young lady, who jilted him on the eve of their marriage, he left England and came to America, where he owned much land in Virginia. He liked the country so well that he spent the rest of his life there. He took a fancy for Washington, then a youth in his seventeenth year, and employed him to look after his lands. Fairfax was of great size and strength, and was fond of fox-hunting and all sorts of field-sports. He was very generous when in the humor, sometimes giving away whole farms to his tenants, and often taking for a year's rent only a turkey for a Christmas dinner. There is a tradition in Virginia that when he first built his house, called "Greenway Court," he made it all in one room, and marked out the different rooms on the floor with chalk, a parlor in one place, a dining-room in another, etc., and using them as they were marked out, without having any partition at all to separate them. He died at Greenway Court when about ninety-two years old (1782).

FAIR OAKS. See CHICKAHOMINY.

FALIERI (*fah-le-a're*), **Marino,** Doge of Venice, born about 1275. The doge was the chief officer of the Republic of Venice. He was elected to his office, and his doings were very strictly inquired into by two councils made up of nobles. Although Venice was called a republic, the government was very strict, and all who did not obey were very severely punished. Marino Falieri was elected doge in 1354, when he was nearly eighty years old. Not long afterward, at a carnival ball, his wife was grossly insulted by Michele Steno, a young noble; and as the senate refused to punish the offender, Falieri made a plot to destroy all the nobility. The conspiracy was found out the

evening before the deed was to have been done, and the doge, after a full confession, was beheaded. The visitor to the council-hall of the Doges' Palace in Venice will see in the long line of portraits of the doges a vacant space draped in black, with the words—"Space for Marino Falieri, decapitated." He died when eighty years old (April 17, 1355).

FALKLAND (*fawk'land*) **ISLANDS,** a group of about two hundred rocky islands in the South Atlantic Ocean, 350 miles E. of Patagonia; area about 7600 square miles, or about the same as that of Massachusetts; pop. less than one thousand. There are no trees on them, but large tracts are covered with tall grass, on which great numbers of wild cattle feed. These cattle are the descendants of tame ones left there by Europeans. The islands belong to Great Britain, and there is an English colony called Stanley on one of them, much visited by whale-ships to get water and fresh provisions. The islands were discovered in 1592.

FALL RIVER, a seaport city of S.E. Massachusetts, at the mouth of Taunton River; pop. 74,398, or nearly as large as Scranton, Pa. It is noted for its great factories, where more cotton cloth is made than in any other city in the United States. It also has a woolen factory, two mills where calico is printed, and several other mills and machine-shops. The harbor is very fine, and is visited by many vessels.

Fall River took its name from a small river which flows through the town, and has several falls. Formerly these falls were used for running the mills, but most of them are now run by steam-engines.

FANEUIL (*fun'il*), **Peter,** founder of Faneuil Hall, Boston, born in New Rochelle, N. Y., in 1700. He was a rich merchant in Boston, and built and gave to the city a building for a market and town-hall. The building, which was finished just before his death in 1743, was burned down in 1761, and the present one was built two years after by the town. So many important patriotic meetings were held in Faneuil Hall during the Revolution that it has been called the "Cradle of American Liberty."

FAR'A-DAY, Michael, a famous English chemist, born at Newington, Surrey, Sept. 22, 1791. He was the son of a poor blacksmith, and had little teaching when a boy. He was apprenticed to a bookbinder, but never liked his trade, and used to steal off by himself, making all sorts of experiments, and trying to find out all about different machines. One day, when he was eighteen, he heard Sir Humphry Davy, the great chemist, lecture. He took notes and sent them to the lecturer with a few lines, begging him to help him escape from his trade. Sir Humphry did help him, and after a time made him his assistant. Faraday tried to find out all about electricity (C. C. T., 208, I., l.), and he used to lecture to large crowds of people in London, and make the most beautiful experiments to illustrate what he was talking about. When Sir Humphry was once asked what was the greatest discovery he had ever made, he replied: "Mike Faraday." Faraday died at the age of seventy-six, at Hampton Court (Aug. 25. 1867).

FAR'RAGUT, David Glascoe, an American admiral, born near Knoxville, Tenn., July 5, 1801. He entered the navy when eleven years old, and in the war of 1812 was with Captain David Porter on his famous cruise in the Essex. During the Civil War he commanded the fleet which captured New Orleans (April, 1862). He then sailed up the Mississippi and tried to capture Vicksburg, but was unsuccessful. In the autumn he was made a rear-admiral, and commander of the whole navy. In March, 1863, he again ascended the Mississippi, but the Confederate forts at Port Hudson drove back most of his ships, destroying one, and only the flag-ship and one other succeeded in passing. With these Farragut aided the Unionists in the siege of Vicksburg and Port Hudson until both places surrendered. Farragut also commanded the Union fleet in the terrible battle of Mobile Bay (Aug. 5, 1864). He received many honors, and the ranks of vice-admiral and finally of full admiral were made especially for him. He died at Portsmouth, N. H., when sixty-nine years old (Aug. 14, 1870).

FATES or **Parcæ,** in Greek and Roman fable, goddesses who ruled over human life. According to HESIOD there were three of them: Clotho, who spun the thread of life; Lachesis, who turned the spindle and drew off the thread of life; and Atropos, who cut the thread of life when it had become long enough.

FAUNS, in Roman fable, the gods of the woods. They lived in the forests and groves, and the peasants sacrificed lambs and kids to them. They are represented in human form, but with erect, pointed ears, horns, and the figure of a goat below the waist. They are much like the satyrs, but not so hideous.

FAUST (*fowst*), **Johann,** Dr., a celebrated German magician and conjuror, born about 1480. He performed so many wonderful tricks that ignorant people used to say he was taught by the devil, and had given his soul to the fiend in payment; that this bargain was written out and signed with Faust's own blood, and that from that time the devil followed him about in the shape of an ugly, fierce-looking servant man, called Mephistopheles. On the night that Faust died the neighbors said that his house was shaken from top to bottom, and terrible shrieks and peals of laughter were heard, as the devil flew off with his soul. The next morning his room was empty, there was a strong smell of sulphur, and the floor was bespattered with blood and brains. The story of Faust, or Faustus as he is sometimes called, has been made the subject of many dramas, poems, and romances. Among them the poem by Goethe is the most famous.

FAWKES (*fauks*), **Guy** or **Guido,** one of the conspirators in the Gunpowder Plot, born in Yorkshire, England. This plot was got up by a few Roman Catholics, who, angry at the severe laws which had been passed against their religion, determined to blow up the Parliament House, with the king (James I.) and all the members of Parliament. They hired a cellar under the House of Lords, put barrels of gunpowder in it by night, and chose Guy Fawkes, who had been a soldier in the Spanish army fighting against the Netherlands, to fire it. The day selected for the blowing up was the 5th of November, 1605, when the king was expected to open the Parliament in person; but on account of some suspicions the cellar was examined on the night of November 4, and Guy Fawkes found there with things in his pocket to fire the mine with. He was tried and executed with seven others, (Jan. 30, 1606).

For more than two hundred years afterward the 5th of November was kept as a holiday in all parts of England, and it is still kept in many places. On these occasions a stuffed figure of Guy Fawkes is carried through the streets in procession, all the boys singing a song which has been handed down from the early days; and in the evening the body is burned on a bonfire, while fireworks are set off. In 1879 Guy Fawkes's day was celebrated in Southampton, England, and the song as then sung by the boys is as given here:

" Please to remember
The 5th of November.
Is gunpowder treason forgot ?
I see no reason
Why gunpowder treason
Should ever be forgot.
Guy Fawkes—Guy,
Poke him in the eye ;
Shut him in the chimney
And there let him die.
Penny loaf to feed him,
A gallon of beer to wash it down,
Good old fagots to burn him,
Burn his body from his head
And then cry, Pokey day, pokey day.
Hooray ! hooray ! hooray !
God save the Queen !"

FAYAL (*fi'ahl*). See AZORES.
FEE'JEE ISLANDS. See FIJI ISLANDS.

FENELON (*fen'eh-lon*), **François de Salignac de la Mothe,** a famous French writer, born at the Château of Fénelon, in Périgord, Aug. 6, 1651. He was educated at home until twelve years old ; he was always pious even when a little child, and his parents wanted him to be a priest when he grew up. He preached a sermon when he was fifteen before a large number of people, who flattered him so that his uncle, being afraid he would get vain, sent him off to a seminary. When he grew to be a man he became a priest, and was made tutor to the grandsons of King LOUIS XIV. He was a born teacher, patient, gentle, and sweet-tempered, yet firm and determined ; and he needed all these qualities in training one of his pupils, the young Duke of Burgundy, who was so passionate that he was known to break the clock for striking the hour which summoned him to an unpleasant duty. But Fenelon managed him so wisely and well that he learned to conquer himself, and if he had lived he might have been a blessing to France. The beautiful letters which Fenelon wrote to the young princes have been doing people good ever since. He wrote his " Aventures de Télémaque " (Adventures of

Telemachus) in three months, and it was so neatly and carefully written that it is said there were only ten erasures in the whole manuscript. We are told that he did not mean to publish it, but a dishonest servant sold a copy to a bookseller, without telling who wrote it, and in this way it was given to the world. He died in Cambrai, of which he was archbishop, when sixty-three years old (Jan. 7, 1715).

FER'DI-NAND I., Emperor of Germany, born at Alcalá, Spain, in 1503. He was the son of Philip I. of Spain and brother of the Emperor Charles V., whom he succeeded (1556). Ferdinand was a good ruler, mild, humane, and tolerant, faithfully keeping the Peace of Religion granted by his illustrious brother. He was a sincere believer in the Roman Catholic Church, and longed if possible to heal the split caused by the Reformation. The famous Council of Trent came to an end in his time. He wished Protestants to send deputies to it, but they would not. The decrees of this famous council are considered as giving the true belief of the Roman Church. Ferdinand died in Vienna when sixty-one years old, (July 25, 1564), and was succeeded by his son Maximilian II.

FERDINAND II., Emperor of Germany and King of Hungary and Bohemia, born July 9, 1578. He was the son of Charles, Duke of Styria, and grandson of Ferdinand I., and succeeded his cousin Matthias in 1619. His entire reign was spent in the great struggle of the THIRTY YEARS' WAR, which broke out in Bohemia. The people of that state were Protestants, and they rebelled against their Roman Catholic rulers and chose Frederick, the Elector Palatine, king. It took Germany many long years to get over the terrible effects of this long war. The imperial armies had brave soldiers and skillful generals, but so had the other side. Foreign

powers, too, who had long been jealous of the House of Hapsburg, stepped in and kept up the strife. Ferdinand was very devout and lovable in his family, and exceedingly good to the poor. His life is without reproach, but he did not understand the times, and he made many mistakes. He was much under the influence of priests, his own confessor once saying of him that if an angel and a monk gave him contrary advice, he would follow the monk. He died in Vienna when fifty-eight years old (Feb. 15, 1637), and was succeeded by his son Ferdinand III.

FERDINAND III., Emperor of Germany and King of Hungary and Bohemia, born at Gratz, in Styria, July 20, 1608. He was the son of Ferdinand II., and succeeded him in 1637. The THIRTY YEARS' WAR went on during his reign, becoming at last entirely a political instead of a religious war, as it was at first. France coming into the conflict with her great armies to help the enemies of the emperor, Ferdinand was obliged to sign the Peace of Westphalia, which gave him very bad terms. This was in 1648. Ferdinand died at Vienna when forty-nine years old (April 2, 1657), and was succeeded by his son Leopold I.

FERDINAND V., King of Castile; II. of Aragon, III. of Naples, and II. of Sicily; called the Catholic, born at Sos, Aragon, March 10, 1452. He was the son of John II. of Navarre and Aragon, and succeeded him in those kingdoms in 1479. He had married ISABELLA, heiress of King Henry IV. of Castile, on whose death the royal pair were proclaimed joint sovereigns of Castile, and they are generally spoken of as Ferdinand and Isabella. Before their marriage Spain was divided into four separate kingdoms: Castile, Aragon, Navarre, and Granada. The last was held by the Moors, but they were conquered in 1492, and Spain became one kingdom. The same year saw the discovery of the new world by Columbus. Thus Spain became rich and powerful, Sicily and Naples being soon added to her possessions. Ferdinand was a shrewd monarch, bent on getting territory by every means in his power. This surname of the Catholic, which the kings of Spain have kept ever since, was given him because of his conquest of the Moors. The power of the crown was made very strong by him, and the court of the Inquisition was set up to put down heresy. Ferdinand died at Madrigalejo when sixty-four years old (Jan. 23, 1516), and was succeeded by his grandson Charles I. of Spain and V. of Germany.

FERDINAND VII., King of Spain, born in San Ildefonso, Oct. 13, 1784. He was the son of Charles IV., whom he succeeded March 19, 1808. Napoleon Bonaparte had fixed his eye on the Spanish crown for his brother Joseph, so he came to Spain with an army and, declaring that the house of Bourbon had ceased to reign in Spain, made Joseph king. Ferdinand and his brother were sent to Valençay, where they were kept for six years under strict watch. At length they were freed, and Ferdinand got his crown again. He did not get along at all peaceably, his whole reign being a time of insurrections against his rule. He died in Madrid when forty-nine years old (Sept. 29, 1833), and was succeeded by his daughter Isabella, mother of Alphonso XII., the present king.

FERRARA (*fer-rah'rah*), a city of N.E. Italy, on the Volano, a branch of the river Po; pop. 75,-000, or nearly as large as Allegheny, Penn. It contains many interesting old palaces and churches, and a castle which was once the residence of the dukes of Ferrara. The church of San Francesco is noted for its echoes, a sound being repeated there sixteen times. The city is inclosed by walls and defended by a citadel. The country around is swampy and unhealthy.

Ferrara was called in ancient times Forum Alieni, the market-place of the strangers, and its present name has grown out of this. In the 15th and 16th centuries it was the capital of a duchy of the same name, and was celebrated for its wealth and splendor. Among the famous persons who lived there were, TASSO, ARIOSTO, and CALVIN.

FEUILLET (*fuhl-ya'*), **Octave,** a French writer of novels and plays, born in St. Lô, Aug. 11, 1812. He wrote many comedies and dramas which are very popular; but he is best known by his story called "The Romance of a Poor Young Man," which has been translated into English. He died when seventy-eight years old (Dec. 29, 1890).

FEZ. See MOROCCO.

FIELD, Cyrus W., an American merchant, famous for laying the telegraph-cable between Europe and America, born in Stockbridge, Mass., Nov. 30, 1819. He became a clerk in New York when fifteen years old, and in a few years was at the head of a large mercantile house. When he got rich he gave up his business, and became interested in a plan for laying a telegraphic cable under the ocean between Europe and America. He went to England several times to get some rich Englishmen to join him in carrying out his project; he had his heart so set on it that he gave one fourth of the money himself, and sailed with the ships when they started off with the cable. The first two attempts were disappointments; the third time was successful, and several messages were flashed across; everybody all over the world rejoiced; but in a little while the messages stopped, the cable no longer worked, and people began to say that it was all a humbug—that it never could be done. Field alone kept up a brave heart; seven years passed by; again he urged another trial; some improvements were made, and the "Great Eastern" steamed off with the new cable. People again began to listen eagerly for the good news; but soon the ill tidings came that by a sudden lurch of the ship the cable was broken in mid-ocean, and although they tried their best to fish it up, they were unsuccessful. After this, people lost all patience with Field's plans, but with the resolved will of a hero, he succeeded in 1866 in uniting the two hemispheres, amid the rejoicings and congratulations of the world. The Englishmen who took part in the undertaking were made knights by the queen, but as Field was an American he was obliged to be contented with a gold medal instead. He died when seventy-three years old (July 11, 1892).

FIELD'ING, Henry, a noted English writer of novels, born in Somersetshire, April 22, 1707. He was one of a noble but large and not wealthy family. He was never fond of study, had high spirits, and lived mostly by his wits. When he began to write he used to scribble off newspaper articles and plays just to get money enough to live on for a week or two, and when he squandered that he would earn a little more in the same way, or beg or borrow it from somebody, he cared little from whom, or indeed how the money came, so that he got it and could spend it. When he was twenty-seven years old he married a beautiful young lady, and for a while behaved better, but he soon spent all of her money, and went on again in the old way. He wrote a great many novels, and the most famous one, "Tom Jones," is said to be the story of his own harum-scarum life. He died in Lisbon when forty-seven years old (Oct. 8, 1754).

FIGUIER (*fe-ge-a'*), **Guillaume Louis,** a noted French writer, born in Montpellier, Feb. 15, 1819. He became a physician when twenty-three years old, and afterward was made a professor of pharmacy. He is principally noted for his books on natural history, geology, and other scientific subjects, which are very interesting and beautifully illustrated. English translations of most of them have been printed in England and the United States, where they are much read. Among the best known are "The Insect World," "The Vegetable World," "The Ocean World," and "The World before the Deluge."

FIJI (*fee'jee*) or **Viti** (*vee'tee*) **Islands,** a group of 225 islands in the S. Pacific Ocean, nearly N. of New Zealand; area 8000 square miles, or nearly the same as that of Massachusetts; pop. 125,000, or about one third that of New Hampshire. Two of the islands, called Viti Levu and Vanua Levu, contain nearly all the land; many of the others are very small, and only about 80 are inhabited. Nearly all are high and rocky, and full of grand scenery, some of the peaks being a mile above the sea.

The forests contain many fine timbers, and cocoa-nuts, bread-fruits, bananas and other fruits of warm countries. Yam and taro roots are the principal food, the natives making bread from them. Most of the natives are a dark-skinned race, and until within a few years were cruel savages, who were almost always at war with each other, and who ate their captives. When a man died his wife was strangled, and his friends cut off their little fingers in sign of mourning, but chiefs sometimes cut off their servants' fingers instead of their own. Yet missionaries ventured to go and preach to these savages, and now nearly all of them have become Christians and have given up their cruel customs.

The Fiji Islands were first found by TASMAN in 1643. Since 1874 they have belonged to Great Britain.

FILL'MORE, Millard, thirteenth President of the United States, born in Cayuga Co., N. Y., Jan. 7, 1800. That part of the State was then a wilderness, and the nearest house to his father's was four miles away. He had but little schooling, and was apprenticed, when fourteen years old, to a fuller; but when nineteen he bought his time, and two years afterward went on foot to Buffalo, where he taught school while studying law. After

Millard Fillmore.

practicing law in Aurora for several years, he removed to Buffalo. In 1828 he became a member of the legislature, and in 1832 was elected to Congress, where he served several terms. He was nominated in 1844 for Vice-president of the United States, and for governor of New York, but was defeated. In 1848, when Gen. Zachary Taylor was nominated for President, Mr. Fillmore was nominated for Vice-president, and was elected; and he became President on the death of Gen. Taylor (July 9, 1850). In 1856 he was again nominated for President, but was defeated by Mr. Buchanan. He died in Buffalo, when seventy-four years old (March 8, 1874).

FIN'GAL'S CAVE. See HE-BRIDES.

FIN'LAND, a country of N.W. Russia, between the Baltic Sea and the Arctic Ocean; area 134,000 square miles, or about half as large as Texas; pop. 2,000,000, or nearly a fourth more than that of Texas; capital, HELSINGFORS. The country is mostly a plain, full of swamps and lakes, and with forests covering nearly all the southern part. In the northern part there are no forests, and it is so cold that snow lies on the ground nearly all the year. In the south parts winter lasts seven months; in the north the sun goes down in December, and does not rise again until the middle of January, and the summer is very short.

Finland has iron-mines and quarries of granite, marble, and porphyry, but the most important trade is in pine, fir, and oak timber. The soil is not very good, but much rye, barley, and oats are raised in the southern part. In the northern part people keep many reindeer to draw their carts and sledges, and also to milk. Bears, wolves, and other wild animals are common. The people are called Finns. They are governed by the Czar of Russia, who is called Grand Duke of Finland, but they have a Congress of their own.

Finland is a Swedish word meaning "Marshland." Until 1809 the country belonged to SWEDEN.

FIRDUSI, or **Ferdousi** (*fer-dow'se*), **Abul Kasim Mansour,** a famous Persian poet, born near Thus in Khorasan, about A.D. 940. Sultan Mahmoud invited him to his court and employed him to write the "Shah Nameh," a poem telling the history of the great deeds of the Persian kings from the beginning of the world. Fir-

dusi spent thirty-five years writing
this famous poem, which contains
60,000 verses. The most interesting part is the story (half fable) of
the hero, Rustum. Mahmoud had
promised Firdusi a piece of gold
for every verse; but he sent, instead, 60,000 pieces of the smallest
silver coin. The poet was very
angry, and it is said that he divided
the sum among his servants and
the slave who brought the money.
He wrote in revenge a severe satire
upon the sultan, and then fled to
Bagdad. He afterward returned to
Thus, where he died when eighty
years old (1020).

FITCH, John, an American inventor, one of the first to try to
make boats go by steam, born in
Windsor, Conn., Jan. 21, 1743. He
worked on his father's farm until
he was seventeen, with small
chances for education. When
about twenty-two years old the
idea came to him of making a carriage go along an ordinary road by
means of steam; but this he soon
gave up, and devoted his attention
to steamboats. After many trials
and failures he at last succeeded
(1786) in moving a small skiff on
the Delaware by steam. The next
year he tried a larger boat on the
Delaware, but the machinery was
not large enough to be of any real
use. Rich men could not be found
who would furnish money for
more attempts, and for months
Fitch wandered about the streets
of Philadelphia, a ruined man.
Some people felt sorry for him,
others thought him crazy, but none
had faith in his enterprise. He
made one more effort and went to
France, hoping to succeed better
there, but again failed, and had to
work his way back to America as
a common sailor. At last, morti-
fied and disappointed, he killed
himself with opium, in Bardstown,
Ky., when fifty-five years old (1798).

FITCH'BURG, a city of Massachusetts, on a branch of the Nashua
River, 40 miles N.W. of Boston;
pop. 12,000, or about as large as
Keokuk, Iowa. It is formed of
several villages called Crockers-
ville, Rockville, South Fitchburg,
West Fitchburg, and Traskville.
Fitchburg is noted for its large
machine-shops and manufactories
of paper, chairs, edge-tools, and
cotton and woolen cloth. It once
formed a part of Lunenburg, from
which it was separated in 1764.

FLAN'DERS, a former country
of Europe, now forming a part of
the Netherlands, Belgium, and
France. In old times it was a
very rich country, and had many
fine cities, such as GHENT and
BRUGES, which were famous for
their manufactures. The people
were called Flemings. In 1384
Flanders became a part of BUR-
GUNDY. Afterward it belonged to
Austria, Spain, and France, and on
the fall of the French Empire was
divided.

FLAT'HEADS. See AMERICAN
INDIANS.

FLAX'MAN, John, a famous English sculptor, born in York, July 6,
1755. His father was a moulder of
plaster casts. John had a sickly
childhood; his figure was high-
shouldered and weakly, with a
head too large for his body. He
had very little schooling, but picked
up most of his learning for himself
at home; he used to delight in
drawing models and in moulding
the plaster in his father's shop, and
most of the customers took a fancy
to the puny little fellow, praised
his efforts, and after a while gave
him orders. When eleven years
old, and again at thirteen, he won
prizes from the Society of Arts; and
at fifteen won the silver medal from
the Royal Academy. He made
many statues, but is best known for
his beautiful outline pictures illustrating the poems of Homer,
Æschylus, and Dante. Whenever
one sees on the cover of a book
that the designs are by Flaxman,

it is just like having a keener edge given to the appetite; the book is at once eagerly opened because of the good and beautiful pictures sure to be found within. He died in London at the age of seventy-one (Dec. 9, 1826).

FLETCH'ER, John. See BEAU-MONT.

FLOD'DEN, one of the Cheviot Hills in N. England, which gave its name to the battle of Flodden Field, fought Sept. 9, 1513, between the Scots under King James IV. and the English under the Earl of Surrey. King James would not take the advice of his nobles, but came down from the hills and met the English on the plain. The English were at first driven back, but in a few minutes they rallied and drove back the Scots in their turn. King James, with his best soldiers, made a final charge, but he himself was killed, and of those who charged with him not one was left alive. Nearly every noble family in Scotland lost some of its members in this battle.

FLORA (*flo'rah*), in Greek fable, the goddess of flowers. She was the wife of Zephyrus (west wind), and is represented as a beautiful woman with a wreath of flowers, either on her head or in her left hand, and a cornucopia of flowers in her right hand.

FLOR'ENCE, a city of Italy, on the river Arno, 140 miles N.N.W. of Rome; pop. 180,000, or about the same as Newark, N. J. It lies in a charming valley, with the Apennine Mountains around it, and is one of the most beautiful cities of Italy. The Italians call it La Bella ("The Beautiful"). Florence is noted for its many old palaces, which look more like prisons than houses, having been built for fortresses in times of civil war, when every great man had to defend his home from enemies. The most famous is the Pitti Palace, in which is one of the most celebrated galleries of pictures

in the world. In another gallery joined to it, called the Uffizi, is another collection of pictures, many ancient statues and busts, among which are the Venus de Medici, Niobe and her Children, and busts of almost all the Roman emperors, and great numbers of bronzes, medals, and gems. Besides these, Florence has other galleries and splendid museums and libraries, making it one of the most interesting cities in Europe.

The Duomo (Cathedral) of Florence is almost equal in size and beauty to St. Peter's at Rome. Its dome is one of the largest in the world (C. C. T., 187, I., u.). Near it is the famous *campanile* (belfry) of GIOTTO, a square tower built in four stories. In the church of Santa Croce (Holy Cross) are the tombs of MICHAEL ANGELO, MACHIAVELLI, GALILEO, ALFIERI, and many other noted men.

Florence was founded by the Romans (about 80 B.C.), and was named by them Florentia ("The Flourishing"). In the 13th century it had become the richest city in Europe, and its merchants carried on a very large trade with foreign countries. It was for a long time a republic, but in the 16th century it came under the rule of the MEDICI family. In 1860 it became a part of the kingdom of Italy, of which it was the capital from 1864 to 1871.

FLORIDA (*flor'e-dah*), the most southerly State of the United States; area 59,200 square miles, or a little larger than Michigan; pop. about 391,000, or less than one fifth that of Michigan; capital, TALLAHAS-SEE. Florida is mostly a long peninsula lying between the Atlantic and the Gulf of Mexico. It is very flat, and the southern part is mostly a great swamp called the Everglades, full of alligators and wild animals. In the rainy season, from June to October, this looks much like a lake filled with islands. One great lake, called Okeechobee, is forty miles long and thirty wide. Off the southern coast of Forida are many small islands, called the Florida Keys, one of which, Key West, formerly the home of pirates and smugglers, is now an important naval station for United States ships-of-war. It has a fine harbor, and is very strongly fortified. Among the people living there are many wreckers; that is, men who save the crews and cargoes of wrecked vessels. Outside of the Keys is a coral reef, called the Florida Reef.

From Florida we get cotton, sweet potatoes, and oranges, lemons, and other fruits. Much yellow-pine lumber is also sent from there, and cedar wood for making lead-pencils (C. C. T., 453, I., u.). The forests in the Everglades and on the banks of the St. Johns River are very grand and beautiful, with great vines hanging from the trees. The climate is one of the finest in the world, and many people go there for their health. The people are about half whites and half negroes, most of whom were formerly slaves.

Florida is a Spanish word meaning flowery. It was given to this region by the Spaniards, some think, because it appeared so beautiful, but others think because it was first seen by them on Easter Sunday, which they call Pascua Florida (" Flowery Easter").

It was first visited in 1512 by PONCE DE LEON, who went there to look for the fabled fountain of youth, which was said to make old people young again. There were many attempts to settle the country. In 1565 the Spaniards built a fort at ST. AUGUSTINE, and most of the country was held by them until 1763 when Spain gave it to Great Britain for Cuba, which the English had taken. The British kept Florida until 1781, when the Spaniards drove them out again. After the war of the Revolution, the country belonged to Spain until 1821, when it

was sold to the United States. In 1835 a war broke out between the Seminole Indians and the whites living there, which lasted seven years, when most of the Indians were removed to the Indian Territory, but five or six hundred of them still live in the Everglades. In 1845 Florida became a State of the Union; in 1861 it seceded and joined the Confederate States; but in 1868 it again came into the Union.

FLOTOW (*flo'to*), **Friedrich von,** a German writer of operas, born in Tentendorf, April 27, 1812. He was so fond of music that he gave up all his other studies for it. He went to live in Paris, and wrote several operas before he was nineteen years old; but none of the theatres would bring them out until they had won success when played privately. After that his works were in demand and he became famous. " Stradella" and " Martha," are the best liked. The opera of " Martha" is full of sparkle and fun, and always attracts crowds. He died when seventy-one years old (Jan. 24, 1883).

FOND DU LAC, a city of E. Wisconsin, at the S. end of Lake Winnebago; pop. 12,000, or about as large as Brookline, Mass. It is surrounded by a rich farming country, and a large trade is carried on in horses, cattle, hogs, and other farm products. The city contains many saw-mills and manufactories of farming tools, wagons, and railroad cars. Excellent water is got from artesian wells (C. C. T., 644, II., l.), of which there are many.

FONTAINE (*fon-tan'*). See LA FONTAINE.

FONTAINEBLEAU (*fon-tane-blo'*), a town of France, thirty-five miles S.S.E. of Paris; pop. 13,000, or about as large as Lansing, Mich. It is celebrated for its palace, which was first built in the 10th century, but was rebuilt in the 12th century by Louis VII. Since then it has been greatly enlarged and ornamented by various kings, and by

Napoleon, with whom it was a favorite residence. It is now one of the most beautiful palaces in France, and besides its ornaments, pictures, and statues, it contains a very fine library. Several French kings have lived at Fontainebleau, and it has been the scene of many great events. Philip IV., Henry III., and Louis XIII. were born there, and it was there that LOUIS XIV. signed the revocation of the edict of Nantes. Napoleon imprisoned Pope Pius VII. in the palace for more than a year and a half, and he himself signed his abdication there in 1814, and again after the battle of Waterloo, in 1815. The courtyard where he took leave of the Old Guard is still shown. The town has a college, hospital, barracks for soldiers, and manufactories of porcelain and earthenware. The forest of Fontainebleau, in which the palace stands, is kept as a park and hunting ground, and is adorned with statues, lakes, and many fountains.

FON-TE-NOY' (French, *font-nwah'*), a village of Belgium, 5 miles S.E. of Tournay, noted for a great victory won there by the French over an English, Dutch, and Austrian army (May 11, 1745). The French were besieging Tournay, and the allies with 50,000 men came to help it. The French went to meet them at Fontenoy with a still larger army, commanded by Marshal Saxe. The French king, Louis XV., and his son were also present. A large body of English soldiers, led by the Duke of Cumberland, made a bayonet charge against the French. At first they were successful, and Saxe urged King Louis to fly from the field, but the English, being outnumbered, were at length obliged to retreat after many thousands had fallen. Soon after Tournay was taken by the French.

FOO-CHOW', a city and port of China, 420 miles N.E. of Canton; pop. 630,000, or less than half as large as New York. It is a walled, well-built town, and the streets are paved with granite, but they are very filthy and full of beggars. Screens, blue cloth, and combs are manufactured, and there are several hundred furnaces for making porcelain. Foochow is near a great tea-growing region, and being one of the places open to foreign ships, the trade in tea is very important. It is also a great centre of Chinese learning, and has a great hall with ten thousand little rooms, in which students are examined.

FORMOSA (*for-mo'sah*), an island, 90 miles from the E. coast of China; area 15,000 square miles, or nearly twice as large as Massachusetts; pop. 2,000,000, or about seven eighths that of Massachusetts. The western part is a plain, but in the eastern part there are mountains, some of which are more than two miles high, and are always covered with snow. Most of the people are Chinese, who live in the plain; the mountains are inhabited by copper-colored, long-haired savages, much like Malays, and with whom the Chinese are most of the time at war. They live in bamboo houses, and their arms are spears and bows and arrows.

Formosa is a Portuguese word meaning "beautiful." The island was first found by Spaniards who were shipwrecked there in 1582. It now belongs to China.

FORT DON'EL-SON, a fort in N.W. Tennessee, on the Cumberland River, famous for a victory won there by Gen. Grant during the Civil War. The fort was built by the Confederates, and they had another one called Fort Henry on the Tennessee River, ten miles distant. Fort Henry was captured by Admiral Foote with a Union fleet (Feb. 6, 1862), but the garrison escaped to Fort Donelson, which was defended by about 15,000 Confederates under Gen. Floyd. Gen.

Grant, who had twice as many soldiers, succeeded in surrounding the fort, except on the river side, where it was attacked by Admiral Foote's gunboats (Feb. 14, 1862). The gunboats were finally driven away, and on the next day the Confederates attacked the Union army. Though at first successful, they were at length driven back to the fort (Feb. 15). During the night Generals Floyd and Pillow with about 2000 men escaped across the river, and on the next day (Feb. 16) Gen. Buckner, who was then in command, surrendered to Gen. Grant.

FORT WAYNE, a city of N.E. Indiana, at the junction of the St. Mary's and St. Joseph's rivers; pop. 35,000, or nearly as large as Holyoke, Mass. Several railroads meet there, and the city contains large railroad machine-shops and car-shops, besides many other manufactories. Fort Wayne was named after General Wayne, who built a fort there in 1794. The French and English had already had forts in the same place.

FOSTER (*faws'ter*), **Stephen Collins,** a noted American writer of songs, born in Pittsburgh, Pa., July 4, 1826. He had a good voice, was fond of music, and liked to sing his own songs set to his own music. He wrote some negro melodies, "Old Uncle Ned" and "Oh, Susanna," which were so popular that he made up his mind that music should be the business of his life. On the song "Old Folks at Home" he made $15,000. "Nelly Bly," "My Old Kentucky Home," and "O Boys, Carry Me 'Long," were just as popular. He wrote more than one hundred songs in all, and most of them have been translated into other languages. He died in New York when thirty-seven years old (Jan. 13, 1864).

FOTH'ER-IN-GAY, a village of England, 27 miles N.E. of Northampton. It was once noted for its castle, first built in the time of William the Conqueror, in which King Richard III. was born and Mary Queen of Scots was tried and beheaded. When King James I., son of Queen Mary, came to the throne of England, he ordered this castle, in which his mother had suffered so much, to be pulled down.

FOUQUÉ (*foo-ka'*), **Friedrich Heinrich Karl de la Motte,** a famous German novelist and poet, born in Brandenburg, Feb. 12, 1777. When young he was a soldier and fought against Napoleon, but his health was not good and he was obliged to leave the army. He then gave himself up to study, and wrote many charming stories. "Undine" and "Sintram" are the best; they are read and loved by everybody, both young and old. He died in Berlin at the age of sixty-six (Jan. 23, 1843).

FOX, Charles James, a famous English statesman and orator, born in London, Jan. 24, 1749. He went to Eton when nine years old, and although not naturally studious, whenever he chose to learn he did so with ease. His father's affection for him was great. Once Charles heard him say to his mother: "Charles is dreadfully passionate; what shall we do with him?" and his mother's reply: "Oh, never mind, he is a very sensible little fellow, and he will learn to cure himself." From that time Charles set to work to conquer his temper, and succeeded in making himself a pattern of gentleness and amiability.

He afterward studied at Oxford, but left there when he was seventeen years old, and spent two years in traveling on the continent of Europe, during which time he was elected a member of Parliament. He made his first speech when twenty years old, and was at once pronounced a brilliant orator. His appearance when speaking was very fine: his black hair hung carelessly over his forehead, his eyes were dark and piercing, and his voice and manner when excited in debate were very forcible. When he grew older he became careless in his dress, but as a young man he was what was then called a "macaroni"— the swell of our own day. He was very particular in the choice of his satin waistcoats, and used to walk about the streets in a little French hat and high-heeled red shoes. His opponent in Parliament was the great orator PITT, who was on the side of the king (George III.). Fox became so powerful that the country was divided into two parties, the party of Fox and the party of the king, and Dr. Johnson said that it was a doubt whether the nation should be ruled by the sceptre of George III. or by the tongue of Fox. Fox was opposed to the Revolutionary War in America, and to the manner of carrying on the war against Napoleon; he was also opposed to the cruel measures toward the natives in India, and he helped BURKE in the trial of Warren HASTINGS. He died at the age of fifty-seven (Sept. 13, 1806).

FOX, George, founder of the Society of Friends, or Quakers, born in Leicestershire, England, July, 1624. He had but little education, and was brought up a shoemaker. When about twenty-one years old he went to a fair on business for his father, and was so deeply shocked to see the young people frolicking and drinking that he quickly left them. That night he dreamed that an angel came to him, warning him to forsake all and follow the Lord. After this, for four years he devoted himself entirely to religion, sometimes sitting in a hollow tree for days, fasting and praying; and he said that he was often so happy as to think himself in heaven. After this he went about preaching as the spirit

moved him; he was told in a vision not to take off his hat to anybody, high or low; not to bid people "good morning" or "good evening," and not "to bow or scrape his leg to anybody." He usually met with kindness from people, because they knew him to be meek and upright, and really pious. The name "Quaker" is said to have been first given to him and his followers at Derby, where he told a justice before whom he had been brought to "quake at the word of the Lord." In 1671 he came to America, and preached in many places. He died in London when sixty-six years old (Jan. 13, 1691).

FRANCE, a country of W. Europe, between the Mediterranean Sea and the Atlantic Ocean; area, including CORSICA, 204,000 square miles, or a little less than that of New England, New York, New Jersey, Pennsylvania, and Ohio put together; pop. 37,000,000, or about three fifths that of the United States; capital, PARIS. It is separated from Spain by the Pyrenees Mountains, and from Italy by the Alps. Lower mountains and hills divide the rivers which flow into the Mediterranean Sea from those which flow into the Atlantic Ocean and the English Channel. Most of the western and northern parts are low, but in the north-western corner is the peninsula of Brittany, which is hilly and rugged, and noted for its beautiful scenery. The four largest rivers are the Rhone, which flows into the Mediterranean, the Seine, which flows into the English Channel, and the Garonne and Loire, which flow into the Bay of Biscay. All these and many smaller rivers can be navigated. The most important seaports are MARSEILLES, on the Mediterranean, and CHERBOURG, HAVRE, and DIEPPE, on the English Channel. The climate is mild and pleasant, and the winters are never very cold.

France has fine mines of coal and iron, and many quarries of granite, marble, and other building stones. The soil is very fertile, and almost every part of it is cultivated, though most of the farms are small. About half the people are farmers. Wheat, corn, and other grain are raised, principally in the northern part. In the central part are many vineyards, and more wine is made than in any other country. In southern France are numerous olive-orchards, and large quantities of olive-oil and canned olives are sold. In many places beets are grown for making sugar.

France is rich in cattle, sheep, and goats, and in fine poultry, and many fowls and eggs are sent to other countries. Silk-worms are reared in many places, but of late years a disease has killed so many that less silk is now made than formerly. Raw silk is now brought from China and other countries, for the great silk factories, where more silk and velvet cloths are made than in all the rest of the world. France is generally ahead of other countries in those manufactures which need great taste and skill, such as laces and embroideries, gloves, fans, and finely ornamented things. More jewelry and bronze-works are made than in any other country. There are also large factories of iron-ware, cutlery, leather, linen, woolen and cotton cloth, and fine porcelain and pottery. More leather is sold than in any other country in Europe. The French have many ships and a large trade.

The people are noted for their intelligence and enterprise. The government is republican, much like that of the United States; to protect the country, it keeps a fine navy and nearly half a million soldiers. The principal colonies are ALGERIA and Senegal in Africa, French GUIANA in South America,

and the islands of MARTINIQUE and Guadaloupe in the West Indies; these, with some smaller colonies, contain altogether twice as many square miles as France itself.

France is shortened from the old name Frankreich, the "kingdom of the Franks." What is now France was a part of the Roman Gallia Transalpina (GAUL beyond the Alps). It was conquered by the FRANKS and made into a kingdom under CLOVIS, who became a Christian. Clovis and his successors, who ruled until 753, are called the Merovingians, from Meroveus, grandfather of Clovis, who had ruled over the Franks. In the last years of their rule the Merovingian kings had but little power, the real ruler being an officer of the court called the Mayor of the Palace. At last one of these mayors, Pepin, called the Short, son of CHARLES MARTEL, was himself elected king of the Franks (753). He was the first of the Carlovingians, or sons of Charles (Martel), who ruled until 987, when Hugh CAPET became the first of the Capetian kings.

The greatest of the Carlovingian kings was CHARLES THE GREAT, who became not only king of the Franks but also emperor of the Romans. His kingdom, like that of the Merovingians, was a German kingdom, and German was his language. After the death of his son Louis, his dominions were divided, and finally the Frankish Empire was broken up (887), and from this time the eastern and western Franks were never again united. The eastern Franks went on speaking German, and the western Franks spoke a language called Romance, a mixture of Latin with German languages, out of which has grown the French language.

The real beginning of the kingdom of France was when Hugh Capet became king (987). Paris then became the capital, and the name of France became spread over almost all of Gaul. Some time before this the NORTHMEN had invaded Gaul many times, and had even sailed up the Seine and laid siege to Paris. One of their chiefs, named Rolf, called in Latin Rollo, settled at ROUEN (911), and was given lands at the mouth of the Seine. He and his followers became Christians and learned to speak French; their name was softened into Normans, their land was called Normandy, and their prince was called Duke of the Normans. They became the most powerful princes in France, and finally, under WILLIAM THE CONQUEROR, conquered England. The Capetian kings of France ruled more than eight hundred years, though their direct line really ended with Charles IV. (1328), who was succeeded by his cousin Philip Count of Valois, who became king as Philip VI., and founded what is commonly called the House of Valois.

EDWARD III. of England now claimed the throne of France, because through the female line he was the nearest relative to Charles IV., and this led to long and terrible wars which lasted more than a hundred years. Finally, under JOAN OF ARC, the English were defeated, and in 1453 were driven from the country.

The House of Valois held the throne until 1589, when the crown fell to HENRY IV., called Henry of Navarre, who became the first king of the House of BOURBON. For some years before this, religious wars had been raging in France between the Catholics and Protestants. The French Protestants were followers of John CALVIN; they called themselves the Reformed, and were commonly known as Huguenots. The principal event of these times was the massacre of Saint Bartholomew (1572), in which thousands of Huguenots were slain in Paris. Henry

IV. belonged to the Reformed party, but when he came to the throne he found that the greater part of the kingdom would not own him, so he turned Catholic (1593). The greatest king of the House of Bourbon was LOUIS XIV., under whom France became more powerful than ever before. He carried on many wars, and won much territory. But under him and his successor grew up great abuses which men could no longer bear. The king, the nobles, and the clergy had all the power, and the people were heavily taxed while the country was all the time getting into debt. This brought on the Revolution; the monarchy was abolished, the king (LOUIS XVI.) beheaded, and France became a republic (1792). Then came on the long wars of the Revolution, which saw the rise of Napoleon BONAPARTE, who became master of France and almost master of Europe.

After the fall of Bonaparte's empire, Louis XVIII., of the House of Bourbon, came to the throne. He was a brother of Louis XVI., and he was succeeded by another brother, Charles X. Charles X. tried to bring back the old order of things, and the people of Paris soon got tired of him and drove him out (1830). His cousin Louis Philippe, Duke of Orleans, was then made king, but he also was driven out (1848) and a republic set up, of which Louis Napoleon Bonaparte was elected president. He made himself emperor (1852), and after his fall (1870) France again became a republic.

FRANCIS I., the ninth Valois king of France, born at Cognac, Sept. 12, 1494. He was the son of Charles Count of Angoulême, and succeeded his cousin and father-in-law, LOUIS XII., Jan. 1, 1515. This king had many noble traits of character, and his reign might have been a blessing to his country had he not been ambitious of being the greatest prince in Europe. This wish led him into many wars. First he conquered Milan, winning the great battle of Marignano (1515). To get the help of HENRY VIII. of England, in a war that he was about to begin with Charles V., he had a celebrated meeting with him (1520) on the " Field of the Cloth of Gold," so called because of the splendor shown by both French and English. Henry, however, took the side of Charles, who was his wife's nephew. Francis had wars with Charles for more than twenty years about Naples, Milan, and Burgundy. On the whole, the French had the worst of it in these wars. Francis is called the " Father of Letters," because he did so much for learning and the fine arts, which took a great start in his time. He died, when fifty-two years old, at Rambouillet (March 31, 1547), and was succeeded by his son Henry II.

FRANCIS II., the eleventh Valois king of France, born in Fontainebleau, Jan. 19, 1543. He was the son of Henry II., and succeeded his father when only sixteen years old (1559). He was married to MARY STUART, the beautiful Queen of Scots, and, in consequence, her uncles the Duke of Guise and Cardinal Lorraine had a great deal to do with public affairs. The princes of the blood—that is, the young king's nearest relations—did not like the Guises to have so much power, so they made a plot to kill them and seize the king. Just as they were about to carry out their plan it was told to some one belonging to the court, and many who were concerned in it were executed. Francis died in Orleans, when only seventeen years old, Dec. 5, 1560, and was succeeded by his brother Charles IX.

FRANCIS I., Emperor of Germany, born Dec. 8, 1708. He was the son of Leopold Duke of Lorraine, whom he succeeded in that duchy in 1729. In 1735 he gave up Lorraine to Stanislaus, father-in-law of Louis XV., agreeing to take in exchange for it the duchy of Tuscany on the death of its duke. This took place in 1737. He married MARIA THERESA, daughter of the Emperor Charles VI. On the death of the Emperor Charles VII. (1745), Francis was chosen to succeed him. He cared much more for Tuscany than Germany, leaving that country in charge of his wife, the noble Maria Theresa, called the Empress Queen. He died, when fifty-seven years old, at Innspruck (August 18, 1765). He was succeeded in Germany by Joseph II., his oldest son, and in Tuscany by his younger son Leopold, who was afterward also emperor of Germany.

FRANCIS II., Emperor of Germany, born in Florence, Feb. 12, 1768. He was the son of the Emperor Leopold II., whom he succeeded in 1792. This was the year of the French Revolution, and Marie Antoinette, wife of Louis XVI., was the aunt of Francis. His connection with the French royal family led to a war with France which lasted almost all the time until 1815. Again and again Francis rose against the power of Napoleon Bonaparte, but each time he was defeated and he always had to make a treaty in which he got very bad terms. In 1806, after his great defeat at AUSTERLITZ, he was forced to give up the title of Emperor of Germany, and to call himself Emperor of Austria. This was the end of the Holy Roman Empire, which had lasted nearly a thousand years. In spite of his hatred of Bonaparte, he gave him in marriage his daughter MARIA LOUISA, but kept on being his enemy all the same, and helped the other European powers to put an end to the course of that great conqueror at WATERLOO (1815). Francis had seen so much harm come from the people's having their own way that, during the rest of his life, he went to the other extreme, and ruled with great severity. Whenever he heard of any uprising against rulers, he was sure to send his soldiers to put it down, no matter how reasonable the poor people might be. He died in Vienna when sixty-seven years old (March 2, 1835), and was succeeded as emperor of Austria by his son Ferdinand IV.

FRANCIS JOSEPH, Emperor of Austria and King of Hungary, born Aug. 18, 1830. He is the son of the Archduke Francis Charles and nephew of the Emperor Ferdinand IV., who gave up to him his throne in 1848. Austria was quite willing that Ferdinand should do this, but the Hungarians did not want Francis Joseph for their king and had to be put down by force of arms. Now they are quite pleased with his rule. Besides this war with Hungary, he has had two others, one in 1859 with France, who made Austria give up Lombardy to Sardinia, and one in 1866 with Prussia, which still further reduced the Austrian dominions. Francis Joseph is a kind ruler and is much liked by his people, who comprise many nations, speaking a variety of languages. All of these Francis Joseph has learned, so that he can speak with any of his subjects. He will be succeeded by his brother, the Archduke Charles Louis, born in 1833.

FRANCIS OF ASSISI, Saint, the founder of the order of friars called Franciscans, born at Assisi, Italy, in 1182. When young he gave up all he had, and determined to live on charity. So he went around preaching, depending on alms for his daily bread. Large numbers soon followed his example, and about 1209 they were formed into a society, which was named after him. The Franciscans were also sometimes called Minor Friars and sometimes Cordeliers, because they wore a cord around their waists. Francis died in 1226.

FRAN'CIS, Sir **Philip,** a British statesman, born in Dublin, Oct. 22, 1740. He wrote very cleverly, but was never able to speak well in public. He was brave and manly, but of fierce temper and never forgot an injury. When he was about twenty-nine years old a series of letters were published in the principal newspaper of that day, which created the greatest excitement throughout the kingdom. They were signed "Junius," and were addressed to the greatest men of the nation, including one letter to the king himself. They were remarkable for their bitterness, fierce satire, and ability; court secrets were made known, the houses of Parliament were freely spoken of, and no person was too high, no cause too sacred, to escape the keen wit and fury of the writer. The secret was faithfully kept, although every effort was made to find it out. More than one hundred books and pamphlets have been written on the subject; and only in late years it has been proven that Sir Philip Francis was the author.

Sir Francis held many high offices, and in 1774 was sent to India as a member of the council. There he had a quarrel with the Governor-General, Warren HASTINGS, which ended in a duel. Francis was shot through the body, but got well and went back to England. But he never forgave Hastings, and long after, when the Governor was tried before the House of Lords for cruelty to the natives in India, Francis pursued him with bitter hate. The trial lasted years, and most of Hastings' enemies grew tired, but Francis never did. He seemed to "nurse his wrath to keep it warm," and went on trying to embitter the life of Hastings as long as his own life lasted. He died in London at the age of seventy-eight (Dec. 22, 1818).

FRANCONIA (*fran-ko'ne-ah*). See GAUL.

FRANK'FORT, the capital of Kentucky, on the Kentucky River; pop. about 7000. Besides the State-house, it contains the State penitentiary and other large public buildings. There is a considerable trade, especially in lumber. The cemetery of Frankfort contains the grave of Daniel BOONE. Frankfort was founded in 1787, and became the capital of Kentucky in 1792.

FRANK'FORT-ON-THE-MAIN, a city of Germany, in Prussia, on the river Main, 20 miles from its mouth in the Rhine; pop. 155,000, or twice as large as Paterson, N. J. It is one of the richest and handsomest cities in Germany. All around it, in the suburbs, are elegant promenades and pleasure-grounds, and the city itself contains many fine streets and squares. Frankfort is noted for its great banking houses. The founder of the rich Rothschild family was born there, and some of his descendants now own the largest bank in the city. Many of the principal German publishing houses and book-stores are located at Frankfort. There are also important manufactories of carpets, jewelry, sewing-machines, and tobacco; and the city has a very large trade. Great fairs for the sale of horses and farm produce are held there every year. Frankfort, or Franconenford as it was then called, was a city in the time of CHARLES THE GREAT. It was formerly a free German city, and the German emperors used to be elected and crowned there.

FRANKFORT-ON-THE-ODER, a city of Germany, in Prussia, on the River Oder, 45 miles E.S.E. of Berlin; pop. 54,000, or about as large as Charleston, S. C. It is a prosperous town with a large trade, and has three annual fairs, where large quantities of cotton, woollen, silk, and other goods are sold.

FRANK'LIN, Benjamin, a famous American philosopher and statesman, born in Boston, Mass., Jan. 17, 1706. His father was a tallow-chandler, and when Benjamin was ten years old he was taken from school and employed in tending the shop and cutting wicks. This work was so disagreeable to him that he was apprenticed to his brother James, a printer. He now had a chance for reading, and began to write ballads, but his father thought it a waste of time; so "in this way," Franklin says, "I escaped being a poet." But he wrote some letters for his brother's

Benjamin Franklin.

newspaper which made much talk, and caused his brother to grow jealous of him; and in time things became so unpleasant between them that Benjamin sold his books and went to Philadelphia.

He arrived there on a Sunday morning with one dollar and a shilling in his pocket. He bought three rolls of bread, and ate one as he walked up the street, with the others under his arm. His pockets were stuffed full of stockings and shirts, and as he walked along munching his roll, he passed by the house of his future father-in-law, Mr. Read. Miss Read, who in time became his wife, then a pretty girl of eighteen, was standing at the door, and laughingly jested about his awkwardness. Franklin at once got work with a printer, and when he had leisure wrote letters for the newspapers. The governor of Pennsylvania, Sir William Keith, saw one of Franklin's letters, and thought it so good that he went to see him, and asked him to set up printing for himself, promising to help him if he would do so. Franklin went to England to buy types, but found that he had been deceived by Sir William and was alone and penniless in a strange land. But he got work with a printer in London, with whom he worked for a year. In 1726 he came back to America, and soon after began in Philadelphia the *Pennsylvania Gazette* and an almanac which was called "Poor Richard's Almanac;" this was full of wise and witty sayings, which everybody liked and laughed over. While busy with his pen, Franklin made a great many experiments in electricity. He proved that electricity and lightning are the same by sending up a kite in a thunder-storm. (C.C.T., 337, II.1.), and found out how to make houses safe from lightning by putting lightning-rods on them.

Throughout his long life Franklin was ever doing something for the public good; and he received many honors both at home and abroad. He assisted in writing the "Declaration of Independence" and was one of those who signed it. His countrymen then sent him to France, that he might get the French nation to recognize their independence. He secured all that they wanted, and was himself an object of respect and admiration. A great Frenchman said that it was "impossible to refuse fleets and armies to the countrymen of Franklin." He was beloved and honored through a long life, and 20,000 persons assembled at his

funeral to show their respect to his memory. He used to say: "My rule in life is to go straight forward in doing what appears to be right, leaving the consequences to Providence." He died in Philadelphia when eighty-four years old (April 17, 1790).

FRANK'LIN, Sir **John,** an English naval officer and arctic explorer, born at Spilsby, Lincolnshire, April 16, 1786. His father wanted him to be a clergyman, but he had a fancy for the sea; once he spent a holiday in walking twelve miles to look at the ocean, which he had before only heard of, and was so delighted that he was more anxious than ever to be a sailor. When fourteen he was admitted into the navy as a midshipman, and served in NELSON's hardest-fought battle of Copenhagen when only fifteen years old. In 1805 he fought at Trafalgar, and in 1815 he was made a lieutenant for services in the war with the United States.

He afterward made several expeditions to the arctic seas to try to find a way to India around the north coast of America. The day of his departure on his second expedition, his wife, although dying, insisted on his going, and gave him a silk flag which she wanted him to hoist when he reached the Polar Sea. She died the day after he left England; and on his return he married the second Lady Franklin. He was made a knight when forty-three years old; and after serving as governor of TASMANIA for several years, he was sent (1845) on a new arctic expedition. He sailed with two fine ships manned with the best men that could be found, and reach Baffin's Bay, where he was seen by a whaler on July 26, 1845. After that no further news could be got of him, and though several expeditions were sent out by his wife and by the British Government to look for him, nothing was heard of his fate until 1859, when Captain McClintock found in the arctic regions a record which showed that Sir John died on June 11, 1847, and that his men perished one by one in trying to find their way southward.

FRANKS, the name of several German tribes, who first appear in history about the middle of the 3d century. They were dangerous enemies of the Roman Empire, and gave a great deal of trouble to the emperors Constantine and Julian. After Julian's time they were divided into two branches, the Salians and the Ripuarians. The Salian Franks under Clovis in the fifth century attacked the Roman Empire in GAUL, and founded a monarchy in that province, which afterward became France. The Ripuarians spread eastward from the Rhine, and gave the name of their tribe to the part of Germany called Franconia. During the Crusades, the Saracens were in the habit of giving the name Franks to all Europeans, because most of those who went on the first Crusade were French-speaking people.

FREDERICK I., called Barbarossa (Redbeard), Emperor of Germany, born in 1121. He was the son of Duke Frederick II. of Suabia, and succeeded his uncle Conrad III. as emperor in 1152. Frederick was great as a statesman and as a soldier; was well educated and tried to make his people so. He had much trouble with his Italian towns, which rebelled against him and tried to make themselves into little republics. The pope encouraged them in this because he did not like Frederick, and it was not until he had made friends with the pope that these towns let him be their

master. One of his vassals, Henry the Lion, also rebelled against him, and Frederick had no peace until he had taken away from him his lands and sent him out of the country. The name of Henry's family was Welf; the Hohenstaufens, Frederick's family, were some times called Waibling. The Italians called these names Guelph and Ghibelline. The famous quarrel that lasted for years between the

Barbarossa Sleeping in the Cave.

GUELPHS and Ghibellines began in this way.

In 1189, when Frederick was quite an old man, he set out, at the head of a large army, on the third CRUSADE to the Holy Land. But he did not live to reach it, for while his army was crossing a river in Asia Minor, he became impatient because the bridge got blocked up, and dashed into the water on horseback. The stream swept him away, and before help could reach him he was drowned (June 10, 1190). He was buried in ANTIOCH, but in after-times a story arose that he was not dead, but was asleep with his knights in a cave in a mountain in Germany, and that when the ravens should cease to fly round the mountain he would awake and restore Germany to its ancient greatness. According to the story his red beard has become so long that it has grown through the table beside which he sits. His eyes are half closed in sleep, but now and then he raises his hand and sends a boy out to see if the ravens have yet stopped flying. Frederick was succeeded by his son Henry VI.

FREDERICK II., Emperor of Germany, born near Ancona, Dec. 26, 1194. He was the son of the Emperor Henry VI., and was crowned at Aachen in 1215, and in Rome in 1220. He had promised the pope to go on a Crusade to the Holy Land, but he was not prompt to keep his promise, and when he did go he did not succeed very well. The pope said that this was his fault, and that as a punishment he should no longer have any of the privileges of the Church Although Frederick at last took Jerusalem, the pope would not forgive him, and while he was away stirred up a general war against him, in the midst of which he died. Frederick II. was the greatest sovereign of the 13th century. He founded the universities of Vienna and Naples, and helped several artists to become famous. He died at Fiorentino when fifty-six years old (Dec. 13, 1250), and was succeeded by his son Conrad IV.

FREDERICK III., Emperor of Germany, born in Innspruck, Dec. 21, 1415. He was the son of Duke Ernest of Styria, and was elected emperor after the death of Albert II. in 1440. Although Frederick loved peace, his long reign of fifty-three years was taken up in wars,

in which he was nearly always unsuccessful. Although he had many virtues, he was not strong enough to rule Germany in such unquiet times. He liked study better than ruling, so he finally gave up to his son Maximilian his state business, and retired to Linz to follow his favorite pursuits of astrology, alchemy, and botany. There he died when seventy-eight years old (Aug. 19, 1493), and was succeeded by his son Maximilian I.

FREDERICK WILLIAM, eleventh Elector of Brandenburg, generally called the Great Elector, and the founder of the Prussian monarchy, born Feb. 6, 1620. He was the son of George William, tenth Elector of Brandenburg. His forefathers had ruled so badly that when he succeeded to his father's dominions, he found them in a sad state of ruin. He, however, was wise and energetic, and soon put things to rights. He freed his country from subjection to Poland, and made several conquests. He did all he could to make his people happy and prosperous ; favored trade, had good roads made, and had his subjects taught how to manufacture various useful things. A great many French Protestants, who had been driven from their own country, helped him in this. He died, when sixty-eight years old, at Potsdam (April 29, 1688), and was succeeded by his son Frederick I. There is a splendid bronze statue of the Great Elector on the Elector's Bridge in Berlin, showing him on horseback.

FREDERICK I., first King of Prussia, born in Königsberg, July 22, 1657. He was the son of Frederick, Elector of Brandenburg, whom he succeeded in 1688. He did not receive the title of king till 1701, at the close of the War of the Spanish Succession. In return for the privilege of wearing a crown, he was obliged to promise to do a great many things for the emperor.

He made a great deal of money by lending his soldiers to other kings to fight their battles. He was fond of show and very extravagant. The taxes he laid on the people were very heavy. He died when fifty-five years old (Feb. 25, 1713), and was succeeded by his son Frederick William I.

FREDERICK WILLIAM I., second King of Prussia, born in Berlin, Aug. 15, 1688. He was the son of

(Statue of the Great Elector, Berlin.   (See page 313.)

Frederick I., and succeeded him in 1713. This king was as saving as his father had been lavish. He was altogether a very strange man. Sometimes he seemed to be very just, and then again terribly cruel. He was very harsh to his children, and sometimes gave them blows. He particularly disliked his oldest son, Frederick, afterward FREDERICK THE GREAT. In spite of these unlovely traits, he seemed to wish to do good to his country. He thought the chief thing needed to make her great was a good army, and he was very anxious that none but tall men should be-

long to it. He died when fifty-two years old (May 31, 1740), and was succeeded by his son Frederick II.

FREDERICK II., called Frederick the Great, third King of Prussia, born in Berlin, Jan. 24, 1712. He was the son of Frederick William I., and came to the throne in 1740. Before he became king he had seemed to care for nothing but music and poetry, but when he found himself really king he soon showed that this would not be an empty title. His first undertaking was to make war on MARIA THERESA for the possession of Silesia, a province which his family had for some time claimed. He gained two decided victories, and Austria made a treaty giving him what he wanted. He also fought the greater part of Europe in the SEVEN YEARS' WAR, in which he won many great victories and suffered some severe defeats. In this war his great genius won the admiration of the world, and raised his country from the position of a petty kingdom to rank with the five great powers of Europe. But he did one very wrong thing. When Catherine, the Em-

Frederick the Great.

press of Russia, proposed to him that Prussia, Austria, and Russia should divide Poland among them he consented, and took a large part of that poor country, the other two powers doing the same. Frederick is considered as the great man of his time. He gave himself but very little trouble as to the justice of his undertakings, so, although we must admire him for many things, we cannot do so altogether. Although a German, he despised the German language and customs, and wanted everything done in the French way. Yet the Germans have an enthusiastic regard for his memory, because he made Prussia a great nation. He

died when seventy-four years old at the château of Sans Souci near Potsdam (Aug. 17, 1786), and, leaving no children, was succeeded by his nephew Frederick William II.

FREDERICK WILLIAM II., fourth King of Prussia, born Sept. 25, 1744. He was the son of Augustus William, brother of Frederick the Great, and succeeded his uncle in 1786. His father having died when he was quite young, he was adopted by his uncle, and looked upon as his heir. He was brought up very strictly and not allowed to spend much money; but when he became king he lived a life of self-indulgence. Of course he was not a good ruler. After a war with France in 1793, he was obliged to give up his lands beyond the Rhine; but he took another slice of Poland, and later still another, until there was no Poland left. He was not liked by his people because he ruled them harshly. The best thing that he did was to put in force some laws which had been made by Frederick the Great. He died when fifty-three years old (Nov. 16, 1797), and was succeeded by his son Frederick William III.

FREDERICK WILLIAM III., fifth King of Prussia, born Aug. 3, 1770. He was the son of Frederick William II., whom he succeeded in 1797. Frederick tried at first not to take sides in the wars that Napoleon was carrying on with all his neighbors, but he soon found that this was impossible. So in 1806 he joined the party against Napoleon, but in less than a year his defeats at JENA and FRIEDLAND made him beg for peace. Napoleon stripped Prussia of half her territory and treated the other half as a conquered province. He even forced the Prussians into his armies. In 1813, however, after Napoleon's defeat in Russia, Prussia again joined his enemies and helped win the great battle of Waterloo, which gave peace to Europe. The last half of Frederick's reign was very peaceful and prosperous. He died when seventy years old (June 7, 1840), and was succeeded by his son Frederick William IV.

FREDERICK WILLIAM IV., sixth King of Prussia; born Oct. 15, 1795. He was the son of Frederick William III., and succeeded him in 1840. Almost his entire reign was a struggle between himself and his people as to the exact degree of power belonging to each. In 1848 the people took up arms, and would not be quieted until the king had given them some of the things they wanted. In 1849 several of the German States thought it would be better for them all to unite and form one great empire, and invited Frederick William to be their emperor. This invitation, however, he refused. In 1858 he became insane. His brother William, the first emperor of modern Germany, was chosen to rule over Prussia in his place, and succeeded him on his death (Jan. 2, 1861).

FREDERICK III., eighth King of Prussia and Emperor of Germany, son of WILLIAM I., was born near Potsdam, October 18, 1831. He commanded an army of 125,000 in the Austro-Prussian war of 1866, and one of 200,000 in the Franco-Prussian war of 1870. He won the victories of Weissenburg and Wörth and bore a distinguished part in the succeeding events of the war. After arousing the world's best expectations by his goodness and wisdom no less than by his bravery, he ascended the throne on March 9, 1888, during his last illness, in which he suffered as heroically as he had fought. He died when fifty-seven years old (June 15, 1888). He was succeeded by his son WILLIAM II.

FRED'ER-ICKS-BURG, a city of E. Virginia, on the W. side of the Rappahannock River; pop. about 5000. A great battle was fought near there (Dec. 13, 1862). A Confederate army of 80,000 men under Gen. Lee was drawn up along a line of bluffs about a mile behind the city, and a still larger Union army under Gen. Burnside was on the other side of the river. Burnside made bridges of boats, and sent nearly all of his army across, took Fredericksburg, and on the next day attacked Lee. The battle was one of the most terrible of the war. Along the foot of the bluffs was a sunken road like a wide ditch. In this were many Confederates who could not be seen by the Unionists; and, as often as the Unionists advanced, kept up a terrible fire, while cannon-balls and shells were rained down from the bluffs. The Union army lost heavily and was obliged to recross the river.

FREE'MAN, Edward Augustus, an English writer of history, born in Harborne, Staffordshire, in 1823. He was educated at Oxford University, and was examiner there for several years in law and modern history. He has written many books, but is chiefly noted for his "History of the Norman Conquest." He was also the editor of "Freeman's Historical Course for Schools." He died when sixty-nine years old (March 16, 1892).

FREIBERG or **FREYBERG** (*fri'-ba-erg*), a city of Germany, in Saxony, at the foot of the Erzgebirge, 19 miles S.W. of Dresden; pop. 27,000, or nearly the same as that of Williamsport, Pa. The Erzgebirge (ore-mountain range) is a range of hills full of mines of silver, lead, copper, and cobalt, of which more than 150 are worked. Freiberg has a famous mining-school, to which students go from all parts of the world. Freiberg means "free mountain;" that is, the mountain free from wood.

FREIBURG (*fri'boorg*), a city of Germany, in Baden, 72 miles S.S.W. of Carlsruhe; pop. 41,000, or about the same as that of

Peoria, Ill. It has a good university, founded in 1454. Its Gothic cathedral is one of the finest in Germany. Freiburg means "free city."

FRE-MONT', John Charles, a noted American explorer and general, born in Savannah, Georgia, Jan. 21, 1813. His father, who was a Frenchman, died when John was five years old. For some years after he left college, John supported himself and his mother by teaching mathematics. He then joined a corps of engineers, and was ordered to survey the frontier of the State of Missouri and the South Pass of the Rocky Mountains. With four men Fremont ascended the highest peak of the Wind River Mountains, now named after him "Fremont's Peak." The next year (1843) he went to the Great Salt Lake, about which but little was then known, and afterward visited the Columbia and the Sacramento rivers. During this trip he was troubled by deep snows in the mountains, and by hostile savages, and his party suffered greatly from cold and hunger. In 1845 he went on a third expedition, and visited California, and the next year helped to drive out the Mexicans. He was governor of the Territory, and when it became a State he was chosen United States Senator (1850). In 1853 he went across the plains again to find a safe route to California, and in 1856 he was nominated for President of the United States, but failed to be elected. He was made a Major-General in the Civil War, but did not serve long. In 1878 he was made governor of Arizona Territory. He died when seventy-six years old (July 13, 1890).

FRÈRE (*frare*), **Pierre Édouard,** a French painter, born in Paris, Jan. 10, 1819. He painted domestic scenes and children extremely well, and many of his pictures are widely known through engravings and photographs. He died when sixty-seven years old (May 23, 1886).

FRIBOURG (*fri'boorg*), a city of Switzerland, on the river Sarine, 18 miles S.W. of Bern; pop. 12,000, or about the same as that of Brookline, Mass. The river runs through a narrow valley, and part of the town is along its banks, and part on the high hills. The valley is crossed by a suspension bridge a little more than half as long as the BROOKLYN bridge, but about forty feet higher, the roadway being 174 feet above the river, or about two thirds as high as the steeple of Trinity Church, New York. Fribourg means "free city."

FRIEDLAND (*freet'lahnt*), a town of N.E. Germany, in Prussia, on the river Alle, noted for a bloody battle fought there between the French under Napoleon and the Russians under Benningsen (June 14, 1807). Napoleon, who had the larger army, won a complete victory, capturing and killing 17,000 Russians and taking 80 cannon. The French lost about 8000 men. Benningsen retreated with the rest of his army to Tilsit, where soon after a treaty was signed between Napoleon and the Russian emperor.

FROB'ISH-ER, Sir **Martin,** a noted English sailor, born near Doncaster, but in what year is not known. He was the first Englishman who ever tried to find the north-west passage; that is, a way by sea around the north of America to China and the East Indies. He visited Labrador and Greenland and found the bay named after him, which was long thought to be a strait, and is still wrongly called so in many maps. He did not find the north-west passage, but found what he thought was gold, and made two other voyages to those parts in search of it, but without success. Frobisher afterward commanded a ship in the great fight against the Spanish Armada, and was made a knight by Queen ELIZABETH for his bravery. In 1594 he was sent with four ships of war to help HENRY

IV. of France, and while attacking a fort at Brest was wounded so badly that he died on his return to Plymouth (Nov. 7, 1594).

FROISSART (*frwah-sar'*), **Jehan** or **Jean,** a French historian, born in Valenciennes in 1337. He was brought up to be a priest, but when about twenty years old he was asked by Count Robert of Namur to write a history of the wars of those times. The young man was delighted with the notion, but instead of poring over books to find out what to write about, as people do nowadays, he used to get on his horse and, with his greyhound following, gallop down the French country roads; and whenever he met knights or esquires, he would politely introduce himself, and ask questions of the battles they had fought themselves, and also of those they had heard about. The knights were always glad to tell the lively young fellow all that he wanted to know; and when they stopped at an inn or castle for the night, Froissart would jot down in his note-book all he had heard through the day. In this way he made his history, or chronicles as they are called, so interesting that although they were written five hundred years ago, everybody likes to read them still. Froissart used to be much with great people: once he was attached to the household of Edward III. of England, and once to that of King John of France. He knew how to please his grand friends too; when he went to see the Count of Foix, who loved dogs and had sixteen hundred of them about him, he carried him four beautiful greyhounds as a present. Froissart lived a bright, happy, useful life, and died when about seventy-three years old (1410).

FROUDE (*frood*), **James Anthony,** a noted English historian, born at Totness, Devonshire, April 23, 1818. He was graduated at Oxford when twenty-two years old, and studied to be a clergyman, but gave up that and devoted himself to literature. He has written many articles for different reviews, but is best known for his "History of England from the Fall of Wolsey to the Defeat of the English Armada," in which he pictures Henry VIII. as being better than, and Elizabeth not quite so good as, people have general thought. Froude holds a high rank among English scholars.

FUL'TON, Robert, a famous American inventor, born at Little Britain, Lancaster Co., Penn., in 1765. He had a common-school education, and when seventeen years old became a miniature-painter. Before he was twenty-one he had saved

Robert Fulton.

money enough to buy a little farm, where he placed his mother. Soon afterward he went to London, where he studied painting under Benjamin WEST, but finally gave it up and became a civil engineer. He was fond of machinery, and soon began to improve some of those which were already in use. Then he invented some himself, among them one for spinning flax, one for making ropes, and a boat for running under water. This boat would sail on the water like any other boat; but was so made that her mast and sail could be taken in, and the boat shut up and sunk at any time under water, where she was made to go by an engine turned by men. Fulton found out a way of getting plenty of fresh air while under water, and one time he and several other men sailed under water in the harbor of Brest, France, for more than four hours. It is supposed that Jules VERNE got his idea of his wonderful submarine ship, told about in his story of "Twenty Thousand Miles under the Sea," from Fulton's boat.

While in France Fulton tried also to make a steamboat, and though he built one which would go, it did not sail as fast as he expected. In this he was helped by Robert R. Livingston, then United States Minister to France, who also got the Legislature of New York to give him and Fulton the sole right for several years to move vessels by steam in all the waters of that State. Fulton then came to New York and built a steamboat, which he named the "Clermont," after Mr. Livingston's place on the Hudson River. Everybody laughed at him while his boat was building, and more than one rich man thanked his stars that he knew too much to throw away money on such idle schemes. But when the Clermont was seen moving along on the Hudson against both wind and tide, the shores rung with shouts of delight, and those who had jeered were silent with wonder. The boat created great surprise on her first trip from New York to Albany (1807). Pine-wood was used for fuel, and when the fires were stirred the

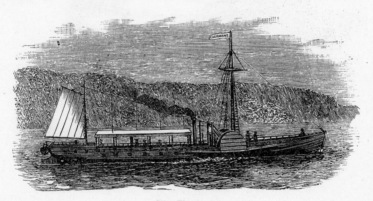

The Clermont.

flames shot up above the top of the flue or chimney and gave off a shower of sparks, which looked very beautiful in the night. Many people, who had never even heard of a steam-engine, thought that the Clermont was some terrible monster moving along on the waters and vomiting fire to light its way; and it is said that the crews of vessels passed on the river shrunk beneath their decks or hastened ashore in fear.

Fulton now built other steamboats to run on the Hudson, the Ohio, the Mississippi, and Long Island Sound, and the first ferryboats between New York and New Jersey and New York and Brooklyn. In 1814 he built for the United States the first steam war-vessel ever made. He died in

New York when fifty years old (Feb. 24, 1815).

FUNCHAL (*foon-shahl'*). See MADEIRA.

FU'RIES, called also Erinnyes (*e-rin'ni-eez*) and Eumenides (*u-men'i-deez*), in Greek fable, the daughters of Night. They punished crime by pursuing the criminal from place to place, giving him no peace day or night. They are de-scribed as having snakes instead of hair and hideous faces with bloody eyes, and carrying torches or dag-gers. They are generally said to be three in number, Tisiphone, Alecto, and Megæra.

FUSIYAMA (*fu-se-yah'mah*) or **Fujinoyama** (*fu-je-no-yah'-mah*), a famous volcanic mountain in Japan, on the island of Nippon, 70 miles S. W. of Tokio. It is the highest moun-

Fusiyama, from a Japanese Sketch.

tain in Japan, its top being nearly three miles above the sea (14,170 feet). It is shaped like a beautiful cone, and its top is almost always covered with snow. The Japanese hold it sacred, and thousands of pilgrims climb its sides every year. Japanese artists love to paint it, and pictures of it are often to be seen on Japanese china and lacquer ware, and even on common fans and screens. The picture of it given here is from a sketch by a native artist. Although a vol-cano, Fusiyama has not been in eruption since 1707, when a terrible one took place. Japan-ese writers say that this moun-tain was thrown up by an earth-quake in a single night in the year 283 B.C., and that the hollow of the great lake near it, which was formed at the same time, is about equal in size to the mass of the mountain. Fusiyama means Rich Scholar Peak.

G

GAGE, Thomas, the last royal governor of Massachusetts, son of Viscount Gage, born in England in 1720. He was so weak and changeable that the people did not trust him, neither were they afraid of him. He began his rule in Boston just at the time when the people were getting ready for rebellion. Instead of punishing the leaders at once, as he was told to do, he did not dare even to have them arrested. This gave them time to make all their plans, and carry them out. After the battle of Bunker Hill, Gen. Howe was sent to take his place. He died in England, when sixty-seven years old (1787).

GALAPAGOS (*gahl-lah'pah-gose*) **ISLANDS,** a group of 13 small islands in the Pacific Ocean, 600 miles W. of Ecuador. They are the tops of volcanoes and are very mountainous. Nearly all have craters, some of which are still burning. The animals are very interesting, because most of them are different from those of other countries. Tortoises, called by the Spaniards *galapagos*, are very abundant, and the islands were named from them. There are several kinds of lizards, one of which is the only kind known that lives in salt water. The Galapagos had no inhabitants until 1832, when a party of exiles from Ecuador went there.

GALATEA (*gal-a-te'ah*), in Greek fable, one of the Nereïdes, or seanymphs. She was beloved by Polyphemus, a Cyclop; but she loved Acis, a handsome shepherd. Polyphemus one day saw them together on the sea-shore, and hurled a huge rock upon them. Galatea escaped into the sea; but the rock fell on Acis, who was changed into a brook, whose waters flowed from beneath it.

GALATIA (*ga-la'she-ah*). See ASIA MINOR.

GALATZ (*gah'lahts*), a city of Rumania, on the river DANUBE; pop. 80,000, or about the same as New Haven, Conn. It is one of the most important ports on the Danube, and has a large trade in wheat, corn, flour, and timber. Only small vessels can go up to the city, and larger ships anchor below, near the mouth of the river. The people of Galatz are of almost all nations, including many Greeks, Armenians, Jews, Italians, and English.

GALBA (*gal'bah*), **Servius Sulpicius,** a Roman Emperor, born Dec. 24, B.C. 3. He was of a noble and very rich family, and showed so much talent when a boy, that the Emperors AUGUSTUS and TIBERIUS both said that he would one day be at the head of the Roman world. This really came to pass; for he was commander of the army in Spain when the Emperor NERO died (68), and was so popular with the soldiers that they made him emperor when seventy-one years old. But he soon became severe to his soldiers, made promises to his friends which he did not keep, and hoarded up his money like a miser. He was murdered, after a reign of only seven months, at the age of seventy-one (Jan. 15, 69).

GA'LEN, Claudius, a noted ancient physician, born in PERGAMUS, A.D. 130. He was the wisest and most skilful doctor of his time, and knew a great many other things besides; but he was very vain of his learning, and used to speak with contempt of other medical men. When thirty-four years old he went to Rome to live, and won great fame for his wonderful cures, but when old he went back to Pergamus. He wrote many books on medicine, and for more than one thousand years his opinion was thought the very best, and was followed by physicians all over Europe. He died when about seventy years old (A.D. 200 or 201)..

GALES'BURG, a city of W. Illinois, 160 miles W. S. W. of Chicago, pop., 15,264, or about as large as Stamford, Conn. It is surrounded by a rich farming country, and has a large trade in farm products. Railroad machine-shops, founderies, and other manufactories have been built there. Galesburg is the seat of Lombard University and of Knox College.

GAL·I·LE'O, GAL·I·LE'I (Italian, *gah-le-la'o gah-le-la'e*), an Italian philosopher and mathematician, born at Pisa, Feb. 15, 1564. His father was too poor to give his sons much education, but Galileo was fond of study, and learned Latin and Greek, as well as music, drawing, and painting. When he was about twenty years old, he watched a swinging lamp in the Cathedral of Pisa, and noticed that the same space of time was taken up in the movement from one side to the other, whether the distance passed through was great or small, and from this fact discovered what is called the law of the pendulum (C. C. T., 135, I., u.). When twenty-seven years old, Galileo was elected professor in the University of PADUA, and the crowds who went to hear him were so great that he often had to lecture in the open air. While there he made a new kind of thermometer, and made a telescope through which he saw for the first time that the surface of the moon is made up of hills and valleys, and discovered the moons of Jupiter. Indeed, he was the first man who ever saw the wonders of the heavens.

In those days, if anybody was known to own a curious astronomical or mathematical instrument, he was tortured, and sometimes burned to death, because he was thought to deal in witchcraft. People thought that the sun moved around the earth, and it was as much as a man's life was worth to say that it did not. And so when Galileo began to talk and write about his great discoveries, he got a storm of abuse for his pains. Some said it was very wicked to scoop out valleys from the fair face of the moon; a great professor at Padua said that as there were only seven metals, seven days of the week, and seven openings in a man's head, so, of course, there could be only seven planets; and when he was obliged to own that Jupiter's moons could be seen through the telescope, he said that if a man could not see them with his naked eye, they were of no use, and if they were of no use, they could not really be there. After a while the preachers

Galileo.

began to abuse him from the pulpit, and at last Galileo was brought before the Inquisition, a sort of court where the judges were priests, and he was made to promise never again to teach, either by speech or writing, that the earth moves around the sun. Sixteen years passed by; Galileo forgot his promise, or thought other people had forgotten it, and wrote a long paper about the earth's motion, which again got him into trouble. He was brought before the Inquisition, and this time he was condemned to be imprisoned, and to recite once a week, for three years, seven Psalms. Dressed in sackcloth, he was made to kneel down on the Gospels and swear never again to say that the earth moves around the sun. Some said that when he arose from his knees, he said in a low whisper, "It does move though." After a short confinement, he was allowed to return to his own house; but he was always watched by spies for the rest of his life. He became both blind and deaf before his death, but he used to say that none of the sons of Adam had ever seen as much as he had. His pupils loved him very much; one of them wrote to him: "I learnt more from you in three months than in as many years from other men." Another said, "I thank God for having given me for a master the greatest man the world has ever seen." He died when seventy-eight years old (Jan. 8, 1642).

GAL'VES·TON, a city of Texas, on the N. E. end of Galveston Island, at the mouth of Galveston Bay; pop. 29,000, or about as large as Dubuque, Ia. The harbor is the best in Texas, and the city has good wharves and storehouses, and a large trade. A great deal of cotton is shipped there for Europe. There is also a considerable business in preserving beef to be sent to foreign countries. In 1817 Galveston Island was occupied by pirates. They were driven away four years afterward, but Galveston did not begin to grow until about 1840.

GAMA (*gah'mah*), **Vasco da,** a famous Portuguese navigator, born at Lines, about 1460. When a young

Ship of the Time of Vasco da Gama.

man he fought in the wars, and was afterwards known as a brave sailor; so that his King Emanuel gave him command of an expedition to discover a passage to the Indies by sea. He sailed around the CAPE OF GOOD

Hope, and reached Calcutta (1498), being the first who ever sailed there from Europe. This was very important, for it changed the course of trade between Europe and the East. Before this it had gone by the way of the Mediterranean and the Red Seas, but after this it went by the longer but easier way around the Cape of Good Hope. When Da Gama returned to Portugal, the King welcomed him with honor, made him a noble, and gave him the high-sounding title of "Lord of the conquests of Ethiopia, Arabia, Persia, and India." The next time that Gama went to India he was very cruel to the natives, because they had murdered some of the Portuguese. Once he seized a large ship

Pilgrims Washing in the Ganges at Benares. (Page 325.)

with three hundred pilgrims on their way to Mecca, and murdered all except twenty children, whom he spared, so that he could make them good Christians like himself. When he got back after this voyage the King did him still greater honor, and gave him the title of "Admiral of the Indian Ocean," and the poet Camoens made him the hero of his poem, the "Lusiads." In 1524 he was made viceroy of the Indies, but died before the end of the year (Dec. 25, 1524).

GAMBETTA (*gam-bet'tah*), **Leon,** a noted French statesman, of Geno-ese Jewish descent, born in Cahors, Oct. 30, 1838. He was the son of a grocer, and, until the year 1868, was an obscure lawyer. A single speech brought him into notice, and was the stepping-stone to his present position. His speech was against the empire of Napoleon III., and in praise of Bandin, a representative of the people who had been killed before one of the barricades. At once Paris rang with his name. Frenchmen have called him a "*Champignon de Cimetière*" ("Grave-Yard Mushroom"), because a funeral oration caused him **to**

spring up in a day. He was one of the first to propose to abolish the empire, and to set up a republic. At first he was a violent Republican or Communist, but later on he abandoned his early friends. His power over the people was very great. He had but one eye. He died at Paris when forty-four years old (December 31, 1882).

GAMBIA (*gam'be-ah*), an English colony in W. Africa, consisting of two islands and part of the mainland along the River Gambia; area, 21 square miles; pop., about 15,000. The soil is rich, but the climate is hot and unhealthy. Beeswax, pea-nuts, and hides are sent from there. Only about 60 of the people are whites, the rest being negroes. The River Gambia is 600 miles long, and can be navigated for 90 miles.

GANGES (*gan'jeez*), a great river of India, rising in the Himalaya Mountains, and flowing to the Bay of Bengal, into which it empties by many mouths; length, 1,540 miles. Its source is nearly 2 miles above the sea, the water flowing out of a cave of ice at the bottom of a glacier (C. C. T., 202, II. and 319, II.) in one of the valleys. Many other rivers join it, and it finally becomes more than a mile wide and very rapid. Between the different mouths of the Ganges are swampy islands, called the Sunderbunds, which are covered with forests haunted by crocodiles and tigers. The air is so unhealthy that no one can live there. To the Hindoos the Ganges is sacred, and the city of BENARES on its banks is to them the holiest place on earth. Hundreds of thousands of pilgrims go there every year to bathe in the water and so, as they think, wash away their sins. The river-banks are steep there, and the people go down from the temples to the water by broad flights of steps, called ghauts. Large quantities of Ganges water are carried by the pilgrims who visit there to all parts of India.

GANYMEDE(*gan'i-meed*), a prince of Troy, said in fable to have been the most beautiful of mortals, and to have been stolen and carried to heaven to pour wine for Jupiter. Other stories say that Jupiter him-self took the shape of an eagle, car-ried Ganymede to heaven, and gave him Hebe's place of cup-bearer. As-tronomers give the beautiful boy a place among the constellations of stars as Aquarius, or the water-bearer.

GARCILASO DE LA VEGA (*gar-the-lah' so da lah va'gah*), a noted Span-ish soldier and poet, born in Toledo in 1503. When seventeen years old he was made guardsman to Charles V., showed great bravery in battle, and became a favorite with the Emperor. Garcilaso did not write many poems, but he has been more praised and studied than any other Spanish poet. He is some-times called the Spanish Petrarch. He died in Nice when thirty-three years old (1536).

GAR'FIELD, James Abram, an American general and statesman, born in Orange, O., Nov. 19, 1831.

James A. Garfield.

He was the son of a poor farmer, and when a boy drove horses on the tow-path of a canal. By hard study at odd moments he fitted himself for Williams College, Massachusetts, where he was graduated in 1856. He then studied law, practised in Ohio, and was a member of the Ohio Senate in 1859 and 1860. When the Civil War broke out, he entered the army as colonel of an Ohio volunteer regiment. He became a brigadier-general in 1862, and the following year served under Gen. Rosecrans as chief of staff, and was made a major-general for gallantry at the battle of CHICKAMAUGA. He resigned from the army on Dec. 5, 1863, to take his seat in Congress, to which he had been elected, and he was elected to each Congress after that until 1880, when he was elected President of the United States. He was shot by an assassin in Washington, July 2, 1881, and died at Long Branch, N. J., when fifty years old (Sept. 19, 1881).

GARIBALDI (*gar-e-bal'de*), Giuseppe, an Italian patriot, born at Nice, July 4, 1807. His father was a sailor, and brought up his son for the same life. When very young Garibaldi made several voyages to Rome, and these visits to that famous city influenced the rest of his life. He says that he used to dream nd pray about Rome, which had once been the capital of the world, and was then in ruins; and just as soon as he knew that the Italians were thinking of fighting for their country, he made up his mind to give his life to that object. He was, however, always fond of adventure. At one time we find him fighting in Egypt; again, in South America, where, with his devoted wife Anita, who always followed him, he lead a stirring life. Once he lived on Staten Island, N.Y., where he made soap and candles; now we see him at the head of a body of troops in Italy; again, as poor as ever, living as a farmer on a desolate island. But Italy was really on his heart all the time; and, whenever he thought he could do her any good, he never failed to be ready and eager to do it. And 1859, when the war broke out

between Sardinia and Austria, he became the leader of a body of troops called the " Hunters of the Alps," which did good service to Italy. He conquered Sicily, and aided in conquering Naples, the result being that the Kingdom of the Two Sicilies was united to Italy. He now set his heart on the capture

Garibaldi.

of Rome, and got up several expeditions against it, but was stopped either by his own government or by the French. At last, when NAPOLEON III. lost his throne (1870), Garibaldi was rejoiced to see Rome become once more the capital of Italy. In the war between France and Germany, he served for a while as a general in the French army. Since then he has lived most of the time on the little island of Caprera. When seventy years old, he was elected a member of the Italian Parliament. He died in Caprera, when seventy-five years old (June 2, 1882).

GARRICK, David, an English actor, born in Hereford, Feb. 20, 1716. He was of a French Protestant family, who took refuge in England on the revocation of the Edict of Nantes. His love for the stage was shown at a very early age by his gifts of mimicry and a love for theatre-going. With the famous Dr.

Johnson, his teacher, he went to London; Johnson to try his fortune in literature, and "little Davy," as his master called him, to study law. But Garrick soon gave up the law for the stage, and became one of the most famous actors that ever lived. He played both tragedy and comedy equally well. In Richard III. he was said to excel all actors before his time. Garrick had among his friends some of the most noted men and women of his day. He died in London, when sixty-three years old (Jan. 20, 1779), and was buried with great pomp in Westminster Abbey, beneath Shakspeare's monument.

GASTON DE FOIX (*gas′ton′ deh fwah*), a famous French general, born in 1489. When twenty-three years old he was made commander of the French army in Italy. He defeated the army of Venice, near Brescia, and took the city by storm on the same day. A few weeks afterward he won a victory at Ravenna over the enemy's forces, in one of the hottest battles ever fought; 20,000 men being killed on each side. The victory was so splendid that the hot-blooded young hero got impatient when he saw some of the enemy's infantry leave the field slowly and in good order; so he madly rushed after them in person, followed by BAYARD and about twenty knights. He broke the enemy's line, but his horse was wounded and fell; and when Gaston's friends reached him he was dead. He was killed when only twenty-three years old (April 11, 1512).

GATES (*gaitz*), **Horatio**, a noted American general, born in England, in 1728. He was educated for the army, and came to America when about twenty-seven years of age, with the British general BRADDOCK, at whose defeat he was badly wounded. At the close of the war, he bought a farm in Virginia, and settled there; but when the Revolutionary War began, he joined Washington, and was made adjutant-general. At first he was unpopular in the army, but after he had won a great victory over the British at SARATOGA, everybody made a hero

Horatio Gates.

of him, some even wanting to place him above Washington. In 1780 he lost the battle of Camden, and his place was given to Gen. GREENE. After the war was over, he went back to his Virginia farm to live, but he removed to New York in 1790, and died there when seventy-eight years old (April 10, 1806).

GATLING, **Richard Jordan**, the inventor of the Gatling gun, born in Hertford Co., N. C., Sept. 12, 1818. When a boy, he helped his father to make machines for sowing cotton-seed, and thinning out cotton plants. Afterwards he became a physician in Indianapolis. Soon after the Civil War began he invented a cannon, called the Gatling gun, which, by the aid of machinery, could be made to fire 400 shots in a minute. A few of these guns were used by the Union army towards the end of the war, and they have since been adopted in the armies of the United States, and of several European nations. Dr. Gatling now lives in Hartford, Conn.

GAUL (*gawl*), called by the Romans Gallia, at first meant the northern country on both sides of the Alps, from which came the swarms of CELTS, or Gauls as the Romans called them, that threatened Rome. Afterward it meant the northern part of Italy, and a part of the country beyond the Alps along the Mediterranean, where a few Greek cities had been built. The Romans called the first part Gallia Cisalpina, Cisalpine Gaul (Gaul on this side the Alps — that is, nearest to Rome), and the other Gallia Transalpina, Transalpine Gaul (Gaul beyond the Alps). The Romans first made a province in Transalpine Gaul in 125 B. C., and it is still called Provence. Julius CÆSAR conquered the whole of it (58-51 B.C.). Under the Emperor AUGUSTUS, Cisalpine Gaul was added to Italy, and from that time Gaul meant only Transalpine Gaul. This covered not only what is now France, but also Belgium, and parts of Holland, Switzerland, and Germany. Besides the first province, the Romans divided Gaul into Aquitaine, in the southwest; Celtic Gaul, in the middle; and Belgic Gaul, in the north-east.

The Romans built great cities in Gaul; and the Latin language was spoken everywhere excepting in the peninsula in the north-west, which was called Britannia Minor, Lesser Britain or Brittany, because the Celts there were joined by many others who came across from Britain. In time the German tribes, or TEUTONS, began to press on the Gauls and Romans in Gaul from the east, and in the course of the 4th and 5th centuries they had overrun the whole country, the Goths in the south, the Burgundians in the east, and the Franks in the north. The Franks, under their King Chlodwig (481-511), commonly called CLOVIS, which is the same as Louis in modern French, conquered all Gaul. They ruled also part of their old country in Germany, and gave their name to part of both countries, calling their kingdom Frankreich (Kingdom of the Franks). This was made into Francia in Latin, and from it a part of Germany is still called Franconia, and part of Gaul is still called FRANCE.

GAY, John, an English poet, born in Devonshire in 1688. He was of humble parentage, and began life as an apprentice to a silk mercer, but soon gave up trade for literature. He wrote several plays and made quite a fortune, which he lost in the South Sea Company, and in his last days he was supported by the charity of the Duke of Queensbury. He wrote a book of "Fables," some plays, the best known of which is the "Beggar's Opera," and several beautiful ballads, among them "Black-Eyed Susan." He died in London when forty-four years old (Dec. 4, 1732).

GENEVA (*jen-e'vah*), a city of Switzerland at the lower end of the lake of Geneva; pop., with suburbs, 72,000, or a little larger than Cambridge, Mass. The River Rhone flows out of the lake, and through the city, where it is crossed by six fine bridges. Geneva has many beautiful buildings, and it is noted for its watch stores and factories, more than a hundred thousand watches being made there every year. A great many clocks and music-boxes are also made, and there are manufactories of velvet, silks, musical, surgical, and mathematical instruments, and cutlery. Some of the largest banks and commission houses in Europe are in Geneva. John CALVIN lived and preached in Geneva, and ROUSSEAU and many other distinguished men were born there. Geneva University was founded in 1568.

GENGHIS KHAN (*jen'gis kahn*), a famous Tartar conqueror, born about A.D. 1160. He was the son of a chief who ruled over thirty or forty thousand families. When his father died he was only fourteen years old; and the princes who lived near, thinking that they could easily frighten such a young boy, marched into his country in order to take it for their own. But Genghis marched at the head of his army, and, after some defeats, made himself master of the neighboring tribes. It would be well if he had been content with this; but it is said that he had 70 of the chiefs thrown into kettles of boiling water. His name was really Temudjin, but a fortune-teller told him that he would conquer the whole world, and so he changed it to "Genghis," which means *Greatest*, and called his people Mongols, "the bold." He gained a great many victories, and conquered most of Tartary, Persia, and China; destroying PEKING, SAMARCAND, and many other great cities, and killing, it is said, five million men. He was planning more victories when Death, which conquers everybody, came to Genghis Khan, and conquered him too. He died when about sixty-seven years old (A.D. 1227).

GENII (*je'ne-i*), in Greek and Roman fable, a class of beings who were the protectors, or guardians, of the people. They were thought to be always near the persons under their care, to direct their conduct, and, in some degree, to control their fate, a power which was given them by Jupiter. Every living thing and every place had its genius. Some believed that each person and place had two—an evil and a good genius.

GENOA (*jen'o-ah*), a city of Northern Italy, on the Mediterranean Sea; pop. 210,000, or a little larger than Detroit, Mich. It is sometimes called Genoa the Superb, on account of its beautiful situation and many splendid palaces. The land on which it is built is very high and rocky; and, from the sea, palaces and churches are seen rising one above the other on the hills, while back of all are the snowy mountains of the Alps. The city is surrounded by walls, and is one of the strongest places in Europe. It has a fine harbor, and the people carry on a large trade.

Genoa is older even than Rome, and it has a very interesting history. For a long time it was an independent city, and was very rich and powerful. Its merchants sent ships to all parts of Europe, and the sailors were noted for their daring enterprises. The most celebrated of all was Columbus, who was born and lived there in his youth. In 1861 Genoa was united to the kingdom of Italy.

GEORGE I., first Hanoverian king of Great Britain, born at Osnabrück, May 28, 1660. He was the son of Ernest Augustus, Elector of Hanover, and great grandson of James I. of England, and succeeded to the English throne on the death of Queen Anne in 1714. He was not the nearest heir to the throne; but he became king in consequence of a law passed some years before, settling the crown on the descendants of the Electress of Hanover, the English Parliament having determined to shut out the Roman Catholic Stuarts. One of these, called the Pretender, the son of James II., joined in an attempt to get back his father's throne, but failed, and those who had helped him were punished. It was in the reign of this king that so many people lost their money by giving it into the hands of a number of men called the "South Sea Company." They thought that they would grow rich; but, instead of that, they were ruined. George was a bad husband and father. He was very unkind to his son, afterwards George II., and kept his own wife in prison for thirty-three years, until her death. He never liked the English, nor did the English like him. He could not even speak their language. He died on a visit to Hanover, near Osnabrück, his birthplace, when sixty-seven years old (June 10,

1727), and was succeeded by his son George II.

GEORGE II., second Hanoverian king of Great Britain, born in Hanover, Oct. 30, 1683. He was the son of George I., and succeeded him in 1727. From childhood he had been hated by his father, who took no pains with his education. But he had a wife, Queen Caroline, who had great good sense, and made up in some degree for his wants. His reign was made glorious by many great artists, authors, soldiers, and statesmen. Several wars occurred while he was king; first the War of the Austrian Succession, in which England aided MARIA THERESA to keep her estates, and then the SEVEN YEARS' WAR, when she was the ally of Prussia against France, and which resulted in the conquest of Canada from the French. Then Lord Clive made many conquests in India, which led to England's owning a great empire in that country; and a rebellion headed by Charles Edward, the Young Pretender, grandson of James II., was put down by the victory of Culloden. In 1752, the new method of reckoning time, introduced by Pope Gregory XIII., was adopted in England. The year was made to begin on Jan. 1, instead of March 25, and eleven days were dropped from the month of September. George II. died in Kensington Palace, when seventy-seven years old (Oct. 25, 1760), and was succeeded by George III., his grandson.

GEORGE III., third Hanoverian king of Great Britain; born in London June 4, 1738. He was the son of Frederick, Prince of Wales, and grandson of George II., whom he succeeded in 1760. His reign, which covers sixty years, the longest in the history of England, is full of great events. In this reign began the American Revolution which ended in the independence of the colonies, acknowledged by England in 1783. The French Revolution broke out

in 1792, and King George, who was a great enemy of that movement, joined (1793) most of the other European powers to make France bring back the Bourbons. England never rested until she had gained her end, for which she spent a great deal of blood and treasure. Sometimes she

George III.

fought Napoleon almost single-handed, but she was victorious in the end, and it was her Wellington to whom was due the great victory of the Allies at Waterloo. Another war broke out in 1812 with the United States, and lasted two years. In 1810 the king lost his reason, and never recovered it. His son, afterwards George IV., was appointed to rule for him during the remainder of his life, which was ten years. George III. was by far the best of the Hanoverian sovereigns of England. He was a man of pure life and high moral character. His troubles were chiefly owing to narrowness of mind and an obstinate disposition. He died at Windsor when eighty-one years old (Jan. 29, 1820), and was succeeded by his son, George IV.

GEORGE IV., fourth Hanoverian king of Great Britain, born Aug. 12,

1762. He was the son of George III., and succeeded him in 1820. He was noted, as Prince of Wales, for his bad morals, and he never mended them after he became king. His daughter, the lovely Princess Charlotte, who was married to Prince Leopold of Saxe Coburg, had died three years before he came to the throne, to the great distress of all England, who hoped that she would one day be their queen. George was very unkind to his wife, the Princess CAROLINE of Brunswick, bringing her to trial on charges of which she was declared not guilty by the British Parliament. A great many reforms were made in his reign, for which, however, the country owes no thanks to him. Up to this time there were some very strict laws against the Roman Catholics, but these were done away with by a law called the Catholic Emancipation Act. George IV. died when sixty-eight years old (June 26, 1830), and was succeeded by his brother, the Duke of Clarence, as William IV.

GEORGE, Lake, a lake of E. New York, having its outlet in Lake Champlain; length 36 miles, width from three-quarters of a mile to 4 miles. It is noted for the beauty of its scenery. The water is very clear, reflecting hundreds of little islands, which are scattered over the surface, and the hills and mountains along the shore. During the summer this lake is visited by many travellers. Near the outlet is the best mine of graphite, or blacklead (C. C. T., 72, II., l.), in the world.

Lake George was discovered by the French from Canada in the early part of the 17th century. They called it Lake of the Holy Sacrament, but the English named it Lake George after King George II. of England. For a long time Lake Champlain and Lake George were the channels by which people passed from the settlements in Canada to those on the Hudson. The English had a fort called Fort William Henry, near the south end of Lake George. During the French and Indian War, this fort was attacked by a French army under Gen. Montcalm. After a severe struggle, the garrison surrendered, when they were all murdered by the Indian allies of the French (1757). During the next year an English army under Gen. Abercrombie sailed across the lake in 1,000 boats, and attacked the French fort at Ticonderoga, on the outlet. They failed to take it, but in July, 1759, Gen. Amherst, with another large army, took both Ticonderoga and another French fort at Crown Point on Lake Champlain. The two forts were then enlarged and strengthened, and English garrisons were placed in them.

Soon after the Revolutionary War began, Colonel Ethan ALLEN surprised and captured Fort Ticonderoga, and at the same time, another party under Seth Warner took Crown Point (May 10, 1775). The forts were recaptured by the British under Burgoyne, in July, 1777. The ruins of these two forts can still be seen.

GEORGE, Saint, the patron saint of England. His true history is not clearly known. A story is told about him that he slew a dragon, which had been sent by a magician to devour an Egyptian princess, and he is generally shown in pictures as in the act of killing the monster. Some say the real Saint George was a soldier in the army of Diocletian (A.D. 300), and that he suffered death for the Christian faith. English crusaders brought home his fame from the East, and Edward III. made him patron of his new Order of the Garter. His name became the English battle-cry, and since then he has been considered the especial saint of chivalry, and the protector of England. He is also the patron saint of Russia, and the Russians have an order of Saint George.

GEORGE'TOWN, a city of the District of Columbia, on the Potomac River, and separated from Washington by Rock Creek; pop., 14,000, or about as large as Newburyport, Mass. Steamboats and ships ascend the Potomac as far as this place, which is the only port of the District of Columbia. It is the residence of many congressmen, and of merchants doing business in Washington. Georgetown University, founded by the Jesuits in 1789, has about 300 students. Georgetown was laid out in 1751, and became a city in 1789.

GEORGIA (*jor'je-ah*), one of the Southern Atlantic States of the United States, between South Carolina and Alabama; area, 58,000 square miles, or about six-sevenths that of the New-England States together; pop., 1,837,000, or about two-fifths that of the New-England States; capital, ATLANTA. The southern part is low and flat, with great swamps covered with thick forests, and full of alligators and snakes; the Okefinokee swamp is 180 miles around. Farther north the land is higher, with great pine forests, where much lumber is cut and sent to other States.

Georgia has mines of gold, iron, and copper, but few of them are worked. Among the trees is the live-oak, which gives the best wood for ship-building. In southern Georgia the climate is warm, so that oranges, lemons, and bananas grow very well, but in the northern parts it is cool and pleasant. The chief crop is cotton, of which more is raised than in any other State except Mississippi; sea-island cotton grows on islands near the coast, and rice, sweet potatoes, corn, tobacco, and many other things are largely raised. Nearly half the people of Georgia are negroes who were once slaves, or the descendants of slaves.

Georgia, which was named after King GEORGE II. of England, was first settled in 1733, by Gen. James Oglethorpe, who founded the city of Savannah. It was one of the thirteen original States of the Union. In 1861 it seceded and joined the Confederate States, but in 1868 it came into the Union again.

GERMANY, (*jer'ma-ne*), a country of Europe, on the North and Baltic Seas, between France and Russia. Area, 212,000 square miles, or a little larger than Oregon and Nevada together; pop. 47,000,000, or about three fourths that of the United States; capital, BERLIN. The southern part, near the Alps, is very mountainous, the central part is varied with hills and tablelands, and the northern part is flat. The coasts have but few good harbors, and most of the German ports are on rivers, near their mouths. The Rhine, Weser, Elbe, Oder, and Vistula flow across the country to the northern seas, and the Danube rises in southern Germany. Most of these rivers can be navigated, and their shores abound in wild and beautiful scenery, with old castles and forts crowning the hills. Most of the country is thickly settled, with many large cities.

Germany has rich mines of coal, iron, tin, lead, zinc, antimony, silver, and some gold. Amber is found on the shores of the Baltic, and salt, porcelain-clay, and fine building-stones are abundant. There are many mineral springs, some of which are celebrated for curing diseases, and their waters are bottled and sent to all parts of the world. Much of the land is very fertile, and as the Germans are excellent farmers, even the poorer parts are made to yield good crops. Large quantities of wheat, maize, and other grains are raised, besides flax, hemp, tobacco, potatoes, and many other things.

In southern Germany are many vineyards, and a great deal of wine is made, while in other places hundreds of fields are planted with beets used to make beet sugar. Most of the forests which once covered the country have been destroyed, but some still remain, and the Germans have planted many new ones; these are considered so valuable that even the owners of forests are not allowed to cut more than a few trees each year. In many places the farmers have fine cattle and sheep, and a great deal of wool is sent to other countries. Germany is one of the greatest manufacturing countries in the world. Among the most important things made are linen, cotton, woollen, and silk cloths, iron and steel ware, jewelry, silver-ware, philosophical instruments, and furniture. Many of the wooden toys sold in the United States come from Germany, more being made there than in any other country in the world. There are many immense breweries; and besides drinking a great deal of beer themselves, the Germans send thousands of barrels of it to other countries. Germany carries on a very large trade, and has many fine ships. The people are noted for their enterprise, intelligence, and military skill, which have made them one of the greatest nations in the world. Every child is obliged to attend school, and there are many splendid universities and academies, called gymnasiums.

Germany is an empire formed by the union of twenty-six states, of which four, PRUSSIA, BAVARIA, SAXONY, and WÜRTEMBERG, are kingdoms, and the rest grand-duchies, duchies, principalities, and free cities. Some of these are very small; the largest is Prussia, the king of which is Emperor of all Germany, and commander-in-chief of the army and navy. He is assisted by a council of fifty-nine statesmen, chosen by the different States, and there is also a kind of Congress called the Diet, which is chosen by votes of the people. The army is the largest and strongest in the world. Every young man, when he is twenty years old, must be a soldier for seven years, three of which are spent in active service, and the other four in the reserve army, which can be used in time of war. After that he must still serve five years in the *Landwehr,* a kind of home army, which is only called out in time of great danger. Finally, if the country is invaded, every German between the ages of seventeen and forty-two, who is not already in the army, can be enrolled in what is called the *Landsturm,* or "land rampart." So the whole German nation is really one grand army. There are many fine fortresses, and a fine navy.

The early Germans were a tall, strong, light-haired, blue-eyed people, divided into many tribes, among which were the Teutons, Longobards or Lombards, Suevi, Goths, Saxons, Frisians, Burgundians, Vandals, Franks, and Alemanni. All the Germans belong to the great ARYAN family. They call themselves Deutschen (Dutch), which means people, and are divided into two groups, High Dutch, who live in the inland or high parts of Germany, and the Low Dutch, who live by the mouths of the rivers flowing into the North Sea. The ancient Germans lived mostly in small villages, and their chief business was hunting, and taking care of cattle. They were brave, warlike, and fond of liberty, and fought hard against the Romans. Julius Cæsar and other generals partly conquered them, but the Romans were finally driven out by ARMINIUS (A.D. 9). And though they made many attempts afterward to overcome them, they met with little success.

In time the FRANKS became the most powerful tribe, and formed a great empire under Clovis, who conquered Gaul. CHARLES THE GREAT, or Charlemagne, conquered the Saxons, and under him all the Germans became united. His great empire was divided among his grandsons, Lothaire getting Italy; Charles the Bald, France; and Louis, Germany. From this time is commonly dated the beginning of

Germany as a separate kingdom. The Carlovingian rulers of Germany ended in 911, and were succeeded by the Saxon emperors, so called from Henry, Duke of Saxony, who became Henry I., called the Fowler. Otho I., of this family, became also King of Lombardy, and Roman Emperor, and from his time the German kings claimed as their right both of these crowns. They were still German kings, but they were usually spoken of only as emperors. The Saxon line was succeeded by the Franconian emperors, named from Count Conrad of Franconia, who was crowned as Conrad II. in 1027. The Hohenstaufen family succeeded, with five rulers. Frederick I., Barbarossa, of this line, called the empire the Holy Roman Empire, but for what reason is not exactly known, and after him it generally bore this name. After the Hohenstaufens there were several rival kings, until 1273, when Rudolph of Hapsburg was elected. Rulers of different families succeeded Rudolph until 1438, when Albert, Duke of Austria, was chosen as Albert II. After him the house of Austria or Hapsburg ruled until the THIRTY YEARS WAR (1618 to 1648), which left Germany cut up into many small States.

Prussia became a kingdom in 1701, and, jealous of the power of Austria in Germany, tried to keep these States from forming a great empire again, but the ruler of Austria continued to bear the title of emperor of Germany. In 1806 the Kingdom of Germany and the Holy Roman Empire came to an end, and Francis II., who had been called emperor of Germany and Austria, became simply emperor of Austria. After the downfall of Napoleon the jealousy of Austria and Prussia would not permit the forming of a new empire, so the States joined in a confederation. But the German people wanted a closer union than a mere collection of States, and this was finally brought about by BISMARCK, who united

Germany again in an empire, leaving Austria out. After the war with France (1870) Alsace-Lorraine, which belonged to France, was united to Germany, and made a part of the empire.

GEROME (*zha-rome*), **Jean Leon,** a French painter, born at Vesoul, May 11, 1824. He has travelled in Egypt and Turkey, and the subjects of some of his most famous pictures are drawn from Eastern life.

GE·RO′NA (Spanish *hay-ro′nah*), a city of N. E. Spain, about 20 miles from the coast of the Mediterranean; pop. 15,000, or about as large as Stamford, Conn. It is a very old town, having been the city of the Ausitani, a barbarous people who lived in Spain two thousand years ago. In later times it was one of the strongest fortresses in Europe, and is famous for having been besieged twenty-five times, and taken only four times. It has one of the finest cathedrals in Spain.

GE′RY·ON, in Greek fable, a savage monster with three bodies and three heads. He lived in the island of Gades, where he had immense flocks and herds, which were guarded by a herdsman, Eurythion, and a two-headed dog, called Orthos. One of the twelve labors of Hercules was to kill Geryon, and get possession of his flocks.

GET′TYS·BURG, a town of Pennsylvania, 36 miles S. W. of Harrisburg; pop., about 2800. It is noted as the scene of one of the bloodiest and most important battles in the civil war. The Confederates, under Gen. Lee, had resolved to invade the Northern States, and for this purpose a splendid army of nearly 100,000 soldiers was gathered in Northern Virginia. This force crossed the Potomac River (June 24 and 25, 1863), and marched rapidly across Maryland into Pennsylvania, intending to take Harrisburg and Philadelphia. They were pursued by the Union army, under Gen. Meade; and at length Lee saw that if he went further, Meade would get behind him, and cut him off from his friends in the South. He therefore turned back to fight the Unionists, who were near Gettysburg. The battle began on July 1, 1863, and lasted three days. On the first day the Confederates were successful, driving the Union army out of Gettysburg and taking 5,000 prisoners, besides killing and wounding as many more. The Unionists retreated to Cemetery Ridge, a line of hills about a mile south of Gettysburg, while Lee drew up his men on Seminary Ridge, which is separated from Cemetery Ridge by a valley. Each army had about eighty thousand men, and for two more days they fought with varying success. On the last day Lee ordered a grand charge across the valley and up Cemetery Ridge. The charge was made gallantly; but, after a desperate hand-to-hand struggle, the Confederates were driven back with terrible loss. During the three days they had lost more than a third of their army in killed, wounded, and prisoners, and the Union loss was hardly less severe. The Confederates kept their position for a day longer; but on the night of July 4 they retreated to the Potomac, which they finally crossed, thus ending the great invasion of the Northern States. If Lee had won this battle, the whole result of the war might have been changed. The Union soldiers killed at Gettysburg were buried on Cemetery Ridge, where they fought so bravely. The National Cemetery, where they lie, was dedicated on Nov. 19, 1863, with grand ceremonies. The custom of decorating soldiers' graves once a year was first begun in this country at Gettysburg.

GHENT (*gent*), a city of Belgium, at the junction of the Rivers Scheldt and Lys; pop. 152,000, or twice as large as Nashville, Tenn. It is a very picturesque city, many of the houses being old and quaint, and orna-mented with curious carvings. The Cathedral of St. Bavon is one of the finest in Belgium, and is ornamented with paintings by the old Flemish artists. The University of Ghent has 400 students. The city is noted for its great cotton factories and sugar refineries, and for its extensive trade.

Ghent is at least 1200 years old. In the 12th century it became the capital of Flanders, and in the 15th century it was the most powerful and cultured city in Europe. The Emperor Charles V. oppressed the people so heavily that they twice revolted, and in 1576 they captured and destroyed a citadel where Charles kept his soldiers. In 1584 the city was again given up to Charles, but a third of the inhabitants preferred to leave it rather than submit to Spanish cruelty. In 1814, a treaty was signed there between Great Britain and the United States, closing the second war between those countries.

GHIBELLINES (*gib'el-lins*). See GUELPHS.

GI'ANT'S CAUSE'WAY, a curious rock formation, on the N. W. coast of Ireland. The rock is basalt, formed into six-sided columns, from one to two feet thick, and set upright, close together, like the cells of a honeycomb. The Causeway is divided into three parts, called the little, middle, and great causeways. The largest one is from twenty to thirty feet wide and three hundred feet long, and the tops of the columns are broken off so evenly that they form a kind of roadway. The little and middle causeways are separated from this by rocky walls. High cliffs, formed of similar columns, extend for eight miles along the coast, and some of them look like ruins of walls and castles.

GIB'BON, Edward, a famous English historian, born at Putney, near London, April 27, 1737. He was a very delicate child, but had a kind aunt, who took such good care of him that he often said she saved his life. Gibbon lived in the days when boys were flogged by their teachers, and he says that his Latin lessons cost him many tears and some blood. When he was too ill to go to school he tells us how he used to look over the books on the shelf; and when he fancied a title, how he would snatch the book down and steal off by himself to read it; and how he often had to be dragged from his precious book, even when dinner time came. When Gibbon was sent to Oxford he says that he had "a stock of learning which might puzzle a doctor; but of which a schoolboy might be ashamed."

He staid there only fourteen months, became a Roman Catholic, and was obliged to leave the college, as it was under the Church of England. His father then sent him to a French Protestant tutor in Lausanne, and in eighteen months Gibbon left the Roman Catholic Church and turned Protestant again, but the end of it all was, that, after a while, he had no religion at all.

His tutor describes him as a thin, short, little figure, with a large head and turned-in feet, and with a mouth like a round hole cut nearly in the centre of his face. This odd-looking youth fell in love about this time with a young French girl, but his

Giant's Causeway.   (Page 335.)

father objected; so Gibbon tells us that "he sighed as a lover, but obeyed as a son," and gave her up. Indeed he could not well have done any thing else, for he had no money, and his love was not warm enough to "light a fire in the kitchen," and very soon we find Gibbon having a good time in London. In those days, when there were no telegraphs or telephones, people used to write

long letters to each other, telling how every body dressed, and what they all said; and so we read in one of these letters of Gibbon at a dinner-party, dressed in a suit of flowered velvet, with a bag and sword; that while he talked he tapped his snuff-box, smirked and smiled with his funny little mouth, and said very pleasant things in a very courtly way.

In 1768, when thirty-one years old, he began his great history called "The Decline and Fall of the Roman Empire." He says that the first chapter was composed three times, and the second and third chapters twice, before he was satisfied. When it was published, the success was greater than he ever hoped for, and it is still regarded as one of the greatest histories ever written.

He died in London at the age of fifty-seven (Jan. 16, 1794).

GIBRALTAR (*je-brawl'tar*), a fortified rock and town in S. Spain, belonging to Great Britain, on the Strait of Gibraltar; they are on a peninsula, separated from the Spanish possessions by a low, narrow isthmus. English and Spanish soldiers constantly stand sentinel on this isthmus, and keep people from passing across without leave. The fortress of Gibraltar is probably the strongest in the world, and is very important, because by keeping a fleet there ships can be kept from entering the Mediterranean Sea. It is on a rock, more than a quarter of a mile high, and seven miles around. Besides the walls and batteries on top and along the sides, there are long tunnels, or galleries, in the rock

Gibraltar.

itself, with port-holes and cannon every twelve yards. Several of these galleries have been made, one above the other, and together they are nearly three miles long. Immense sums of money have been spent on these works. They now have more than a thousand great cannon, and several thousand soldiers are kept in barracks on top of the rock. The bay of Gibraltar, on the W. side of the rock, is used as a harbor for ships of war and merchant men. The town on the shore has a mixed population of English, Spaniards, Moors, and Jews. A small trade is carried on with the states of northern Africa, and many tourists visit the town and fortress. Besides the artificial galleries, there are curious natural caves in the rock. Gibraltar is the only place in Europe where wild monkeys are found. They live among the rocks, and are sometimes hunted by the soldiers.

The name Gibraltar was made from the Arabic name Jebel ıl-Tarik, that is, the Mount of Tarik. Tarik was a Saracen, or Moor, who built a fort on the rock in the year 712. It was captured by the Spaniards in 1309, recaptured by the Moors in 1333, and finally taken by the Spaniards in 1462. The Spaniards fortified it until they thought it never could be conquered; but it was taken by an English and Dutch fleet in 1704, and since then it has always belonged to the English. It was attacked by the Spaniards in 1727, and afterward was besieged for nearly four years by a French and Spanish army of 40,000 men and a large fleet (1779-1783). This was one of the greatest sieges that ever occurred. At one time, more than a thousand cannon were bombarding the fortress, while forty-seven great ships, with many smaller vessels, attacked it from the sea. Afterwards, ten great batteries on rafts were sent against the fort, and a tremendous bombardment ensued. The little English garrison defended itself bravely, set the batteries on fire with red-hot cannon-balls, and finally the allies were obliged to give up the siege.

GIBRALTAR, Strait of, the channel joining the Mediterranean Sea with the Atlantic Ocean. It lies between Spain and Morocco, and at one point is only nine miles wide, but at the Rock of Gibraltar is about fifteen miles wide. Opposite Gibraltar, on the African coast, is a hill called by the English Ape's Hill, on account of the monkeys there, but which was called by the ancients Mount Abyla. This and the Rock of Gibraltar, which was called Calpe by the Greeks, form what the ancients called the Pillars of Hercules, not named after the Greek Hercules, but after the Phœnician god of the same name. In old times the Strait of Gibraltar was looked upon as the western boundary of the world.

GIFFORD, Robert Swain, an American painter, born at Gosnold, Mass., Dec. 23, 1840. He paints landscapes in oil and in water-color, and has made some fine etchings. He has a studio in New York.

GIFFORD, Sandford Robinson, an American painter, born at Greenfield, Saratoga Co., New York, July 10, 1823. He sketched in many parts of his own country, as well as in Europe and the East, and was among the best and most successful of American landscape painters. He died in New-York city, when fifty-seven years old (Aug. 29, 1880).

GIORGIONE (*jor-jo'na*), a noted Italian artist, born at Castelfranco in 1477. His real name was Giorgio Barbarelli; but he was commonly called, from his great size and noble look, Giorgione, which means George the big or great. He studied in Venice, in the same school with TITIAN, who afterward became his rival, and who only excelled him in the use of colors. Not much is known of his life; but it is said that he loved a young woman very dearly, who finally left him to run off with another painter, who had once been his friend. This was such a blow to his happiness that Giorgione could never recover from it. He played the lute, and sometimes made songs which he sung; but he was fond of painting, and would not long neglect his art. He worked in Venice, painting frescoes, at the same time with Titian; but the damp climate, fires, and time have destroyed most of his pictures. His works are rare now; but there are a few in the church at Castelfranco, in the National Gallery, England, and in the Pitti Palace, Florence. Giorgione's portrait, painted by himself, is in the Munich Gallery. He died of the plague at Venice when only thirty-four years old (1511).

GIOTTO (*jot'to*), a noted Italian painter, born at Vespignano in 1276.

He was the son of a poor shepherd, and, when a boy, tended sheep in his native valley. It is said that Cimabue, the artist, once found him drawing a picture of one of his sheep on a smooth piece of slate, and was so struck with his skill that he took him to Florence and taught him to paint. Art was then in a very rude state, and Cimabue had done much to improve it; but Giotto soon beat his master, and became a better painter than any of the Italian artists before him. He was the first of modern artists to make pictures real copies of nature, and the first to paint good portraits. He was also a good sculptor and architect. He died in Florence when sixty-one years old (1337).

GIRARD (*ge-rard*), **Stephen,** a noted American merchant and banker, born near Bordeaux, France, May, 24, 1750. He was the son of a seaman, and when ten years old, sailed as a cabin-boy to the West Indies and New York. He was so good and industrious, that after a while he had a vessel of his own; and in a few years made enough money to go into business for himself in Philadelphia. When the yellow fever broke out there, he spent his time in taking care of the sick, and in burying the dead. Afterwards he took charge of two hundred children whose parents had died of the fever. When Girard died he left $9,000,000 to different institutions. Girard College, in Philadelphia, was founded by him for the education and support of the white orphan children of that city. He died in Philadelphia when eighty-one years old (Dec. 26, 1831).

GIULIO ROMANO (*joo'le-o ro-mah'no*), an Italian painter, born at Rome in 1492. His real name was Giulio Pippi, but he was commonly called Romano (the Roman) from his birth-place. He was a favorite of Raphael's, and his most distinguished pupil; he assisted his master in many of his paintings, and Raphael chose him to complete his unfinished works. After Raphael's death he painted some fine pictures, among the best of which are the "Stoning of St. Stephen," in Genoa, and the "Defeat of the Titans," in Mantua. He was also an architect, and was chosen to take charge of St. Peter's in Rome, but died the same year (1546) in Mantua, when fifty-four years old.

GLADSTONE, William Ewart, a famous English statesman, born in Liverpool, Dec. 29, 1809. His father, who removed from Glasgow to Liverpool in 1785, made a fortune as a merchant, and was created a baronet in 1846. William went to Eton and to Oxford, where he was graduated in 1831 with the highest honors. The next year he entered Parliament; in 1853 he became president of the Board of Trade, and since then has been almost continuously in office. From 1868 to 1874 he was Premier of England, and from 1880 to 1886 he held the same position. Mr. Gladstone has written much for reviews, and has published several books. He is one of the greatest men of the century.

GLASGOW (*glas'go*), a city of Scotland, on the River Clyde, 21 miles from its mouth in the Firth of Clyde; pop. 674,000, or about half as large again as St. Louis, Mo. It has a larger trade and more manufactures than any other city in Scotland, being especially noted for its great iron-foundries, machine-shops, and ship-yards. The iron ships made there are used in all parts of the world. Rich coal and iron mines near the city furnish material for the iron-works, and employ thousands of workmen. Glasgow is also famous for its manufacture of chemicals; the St. Rollox chemical works being the largest in the world, and having a chimney 450 feet high, or as high as the great pyramid of Egypt. There are many large cotton-mills, glass-works, paper-mills, dye-works, and manufactories of fertilizers. Among the fine buildings is Glasgow Cathedral. built in the 12th century, and said to be the finest Gothic church in Scotland. Glasgow University, founded in 1443, has 2,200 students.

The Romans had a military station on the site of Glasgow; but the city itself is said to have been founded about A.D. 560.

GLAU'CUS, in Greek fable, son of Sisyphus and Merope, and father of Bellerophon. He was said to have fed his horses on human flesh, that they might be more spirited, and swifter in the race. This made the gods angry, and they caused his horses to upset his chariot and kill him.

GLAUCUS, in Greek fable, a fisherman who became immortal. When he pulled fishes out of his nets and threw them on the shore, he saw that they got their strength again by touching a certain herb. He wondered at this; and, tasting the herb himself, leaped into the water, and became a god of the sea.

GLENCOE (*glen-ko'*), a wild, rocky valley in W.Scotland, where a Highland chief, named MacDonald of Glencoe, once lived with his people. After King James had been dethroned in 1688, MacDonald, with many other highland chiefs, still remained in arms, refusing to own the authority of King William. At length the English Government offered to pardon them, if they would take the oath of allegiance to the king before the year 1692. By a mistake, MacDonald did not take this oath till six days after the given time. Some enemies who heard of this determined to ruin him; so they told King William that MacDonald had not submitted at all, and that he was in command of a band of robbers. The king then ordered that he and his clan should be destroyed. A company of soldiers was sent to Glencoe; and, as they pretended to be friendly, MacDonald received them hospitably, and they were entertained in his village for two weeks. On the night of Feb. 12,

1692, after the officers had supped with MacDonald, they and the soldiers fell on the people, killed Mac-Donald and many others, burned the houses and drove off the cattle, and left the rest to die of cold and hunger in the mountains.

GLOUCESTER (*glos'ter*), a city of England, on the River Severn; pop., 20,000, or nearly as large as Chelsea, Mass. It has large manufactories of pins, hardware, gloves, and other things, and carries on a considerable trade. Several important colleges and schools are located there. Gloucester Cathedral is one of the finest Gothic buildings in the world.

Gloucester was a Roman military station, named Claudia Castra. The Saxons mispronounced this Gleauceaster, and from this the modern name has come.

GLOUCESTER, a city of E. Massachusetts, on the peninsula of Cape Ann, 30 miles N.N.E. of Boston; pop. 25,000, or about as large as Springfield, Ill. It is noted for its great fisheries, more cod and mackerel being caught by Gloucester vessels than by those of any other port in the country. The fishermen go to various parts of the coast, and to the Newfoundland banks, and often suffer great hardships. The business is also very dangerous, about 250 of the vessels having been lost since 1830. The city has manufactories of articles required by fishing-vessels, and in the surrounding country are large granite quarries. Gloucester was first settled in 1642. The first schooner ever made was built there in 1713.

GOBELINS (*gob'linz*), the name of a manufactory in Paris, where the famous tapestry of that name is made. It was begun in the 15th century by two brothers, Jehan and Gilles Gobelin, supposed to have come from Holland, who found out a scarlet dye which became famous. Louis XIV. bought the factory, and since then it has belonged to the French Government. Splendid tapestries and carpets are made there, and are used either in the royal palaces or given as presents to foreign princes, none having been sold in a long time. Some of the carpets made there cost $30,000 to $40,000 and take many years to weave.

GOD'FREY DE BOUILLON (*deh boo-yon'*), the hero of the first CRU-SADE, born in South Brabant about 1060. He was said to be so strong that with one blow of his sword he could cut a horseman in two from head to saddle, and that with one back stroke he could cut off an ox's or a camel's head. When twenty years old he took the side of Henry IV. of Germany in a quarrel which he had with the Pope; and he was the first to scale the walls of Rome, and plant Henry's banner there. For this Henry made him Duke de Bouillon. Godfrey got sorry for this as he grew older, because Rome was St. Peter's city; so, after thinking it all over, he made up his mind to ease his conscience by going on a crusade to the Holy Land. He took Nice, Antioch, and Jerusalem, and the Christians made him King of Jeru-salem; but he said he would not wear a crown of gold where his Lord had worn one of thorns; and he would never let them call him by any other title than the simple one of Duke. He died in Jerusalem when forty years old (July 18, 1100). Godfrey is the hero of TASSO's great poem of "Jerusalem Delivered."

GO-DI'VA, Lady, wife of Leofric, Earl of Mercia, and master of Coventry, in England. He was so cruel, and laid such heavy taxes upon the people of the town, that they suffered greatly. Lady Godiva, who was very good, begged him to be kinder to them, and to lighten their burthens. He said he would do so if she would ride naked, through the streets of the town. He did not think she would consent, for she was very modest; but she did, and he had to keep his word.

All the people were ordered to stay in their houses, and not to look out of door or window, as she passed. It is said that one man who did peep out of a window became blind, and also that the earl had him hung soon afterward. Tennyson has written a poem about her.

GOD'WIN, Earl of Wessex, a Saxon nobleman, father of HAROLD, King of England, born about the end of the 10th century. He was originally a cowherd, but, having married a relative of King CANUTE, he became in time the greatest nobleman in England. It is sup-posed that he murdered Prince Alfred, the brother of Edward the Confessor; but Edward pardoned him, and Godwin did much to place Edward on the throne. Afterwards he rebelled against him, and was obliged to flee from England; but he returned with an army, and forced Edward to give him back his estates and offices. It is related that, at a banquet given by the king, Godwin stood up to declare that he was innocent of Alfred's death; but at that moment he fell down speech-less and soon died, at the age of about sixty years (1053).

GOETHE (*guh'teh*), **Johann Wolf-gang Von,** a famous German novel-writer and poet, born in Frankfort-on-the-Main, Aug. 28, 1749. His father was cold and stern; his mother bright, gay, and affectionate. He says, "I get my frame and my mind from my father, and, from my dear little mother, my happy disposi-tion and love of story-telling." He was a very forward child, and was brought up mostly at home with his only sister Cornelia, whom he loved very much. Before he was ten years old, he wrote in several languages and made up beautiful fairy stories which he used to recite to his mother's friends. When he was twenty-five years old, he wrote his first great novel, called "The Sor-rows of Werther." It is a sad story; Werther, the hero, goes through all sorts of sorrows, gets tired of this world, and thinks he will try the next; so he shoots himself like the veriest coward. But this suited the people of Goethe's day, and it was read and liked by everybody; it was translated into every language, even the Chinese; young women used to cry over it, and young men shot themselves, with a volume of Werther in their hands. At last the Werther fever became so bad that in some countries booksellers were forbidden by law to sell it.

Goethe.

Goethe always wrote from his heart, and so he found the way to other people's hearts. After he first read Shakspeare, he said he felt like a blind man who suddenly sees. A German writer, Knebel, says of Goethe: "He rose like a star in the heavens; everybody worshipped him, and especially the women." Goethe always fancied himself in love with somebody, and often with two or three at a time. He wrote a number of novels and poems; his last and greatest work, his drama of "Faust," is founded on the story of Dr. John Faust; when he finished it he said that the work of his life was done. Goethe is not only the greatest poet of Germany, but one of the greatest of all ages and countries. His last words were: "Open the shutters,

and let in more light." He died in Weimar when eighty-three years old (March 22, 1832).

GOFFE (*gof*), **William**, an officer of Cromwell's army, and one of the judges who condemned King Charles I. of England to death, born about 1605. When Cromwell died, and the royal family was restored to the throne, the judges were obliged to fly for their lives. Goffe, with his father-in-law, Edward Whalley, came to Boston, Mass., where they were at first received kindly by the English governor. Soon after, warrants came for their arrest, and a price was set on their heads. They fled from place to place, pursued by white men and Indians, and living in deserted houses, mills, and caves. At length they found refuge in the house of a clergyman at Hadley, Mass., where they lived unknown for years. At one time, when the people of Hadley were at church, they were attacked by the Indians under King Philip. They would have been defeated and killed, had not a white-bearded old man appeared and rallied them, so that they drove the savages off. The old man disappeared as soon as the victory was won; and the people thought he had been sent from heaven to lead them, but he was really William Goffe, who had come out from his hiding-place. Goffe finally died in his retreat when seventy-four years old (1679). Before his death he was visited by John Dixwell, another of the judges, who had been living in New Haven under the name of John Davids. There he had married and had two children; and there he finally died, a very old man, in 1689.

GOLCONDA (*gol-kon'dah*), a city and fortress in southern India. It was once the capital of a great kingdom, and beautiful tombs of the old kings are still seen there, but the city is in ruins. Golconda was once famous for its diamonds; but they were only cut and polished there, the mines being many miles away.

GOLD'SMITH, Oliver, a famous English author, born in Pallasmore, Ireland, Nov. 10, 1728. He had the small-pox when eight years old, which scarred his already homely little face. In his letters he pities himself for his ugliness, and it gave him trouble all his life long. An old woman in the village where he lived taught him his letters, and declared him to be a dunce. In those days, when a boy was sent to school, he was said to be placed under the master's cane; and poor little Oliver was whipped more than most boys, for he was very idle, playing ball instead of studying, and making all his pocket-money fly as if it had wings. He used to cry over his floggings, but

Oliver Goldsmith.

the next minute he would be singing and dancing. One night, when he was capering about in his father's kitchen, the old fiddler laughed at him for his ugliness, calling him Æsop; and Oliver said: "See Æsop dancing, and his monkey playing."

He entered Trinity College as a sizar, or poor scholar; this class of students wore black gowns, and the servant's badge of a scarlet cap; they were made to sweep the courts, carry up the dishes from the kitchen to the fellows' table, and wait in the hall until they had dined. Goldsmith hated this life, but said that he could blow off his rage through his flute. He used to write songs for the street-singers, who paid him a crown for a poem, and then he would steal off at night to hear his verses sung; and, it is said, he rarely got back to the college with the crown in his pocket. He never was so poor that he could not find somebody poorer, whom he could help; he often stripped off part of his own clothing to give to some shivering wretch; once he gave away his blankets to a starving woman, and crept himself into the ticking for shelter from the cold. When he was a teacher, he spent his earnings in treats for the boys; and the landlady used to say that she ought to keep Mr. Goldsmith's money for him, as well as the boys'.

After leaving college (1749), he spent two years in preparing for the church; but as he went before the bishop, to be ordained, in a pair of scarlet breeches, he was rejected. He then tried to be a doctor, but, getting into debt, ran away from Edinburgh, and travelled on foot for two years in different parts of Europe, supporting himself as he went along by playing his flute and singing. When he came back to England he lived in a garret, and made a poor living for a time by writing for magazines. After a while, his writings began to be read by everybody, and in time he became very famous. But although he got very large prices, they were never large enough for his wants. He wrote the "Vicar of Wakefield," a sweet story, which everybody has read, or ought to read, to keep himself out of prison. His best known poems are "The Traveller," and "The Deserted Village;" and his comedy "She Stoops to Conquer" is still played on the stage. Goldsmith's generous, cheerful temper made him a favorite with his friends ; but he was always idle and reckless, and kept on getting into trouble up to the day of his death, which took place in London when he was only forty-five years old (April 4, 1774).

GOOD'RICH, Samuel Griswold, better known as "Peter Parley," a famous writer for young folks, born in Ridgefield, Conn., Aug. 19, 1793. He was a book-publisher, first in Hartford, Conn., and afterward in Boston, Mass. Soon after he went to live in Boston, he began to write, under the name of "Peter Parley," books for young folks, of which he published more than a hundred. He was also the editor, for many years, of "Merry's Museum" and "Parley's Magazine." His "Peter Parley" books comprised geographies, histories, travels, stories, and works on the arts and sciences, and won him much fame. He died in New York when nearly sixty-seven years old (May 9, 1860).

GOOD'WIN SANDS, dangerous sand-banks in the Strait of Dover, separated from the coast of England by a roadstead five and a half miles wide, called the Downs. At high tide they are covered with water, but at low tide many parts are dry. They are very dangerous to ships, especially at night and in foggy weather, and many wrecks have occurred there. It is said that these sands were once high and dry, and formed a part of the coast of the mainland, and that they got their name from the Saxon Earl Godwin, to whom they belonged. They sank into the sea about A.D. 1200.

GOOD'YEAR, Charles, a famous American inventor, born in New Haven, Conn., Dec. 29, 1800. He was educated at a public school, and when he grew to be a man, became his father's partner in the manufacture of hardware. In 1830 he began to make experiments with India rubber. He succeeded in making it useful, especially for shoes; but he was not yet satisfied, and kept

on trying. At last (1839) a piece of rubber with which sulphur, among other things, was mixed, was by accident placed near a red-hot stove. Instead of melting, it became hardened and yet was elastic or springy. Then he knew that he had found the secret of vulcanizing India rubber, which has made it one of the most useful things in the world (C. C. T., 322, II, u.). Mr. Goodyear died in New York when nearly sixty years old (July 1, 1860).

GORDIANUS (*gor-de-a'nus*), **Marcus Antonius,** called Africanus, a Roman emperor, born in Rome A.D. 158. He was descended on his father's side from the Gracchi, and on his mother's from the emperor Trajan, and was a good and learned man. After being governor of Africa for many years, he was elected joint emperor with his son at Carthage. His son was killed in battle six weeks after, and the old man in his grief, killed himself, having been emperor less than two months. He died at Carthage, when eighty years old (238).

GORDIANUS, Marcus Antonius, a Roman emperor, grandson of the above, born about 223. He was made emperor at Rome, on the death of his father and grandfather in Africa. He became a noted warrior, and defeated the Persians several times in Syria (242). While he was marching with his troops into Persia, his general, an Arabian named Phillippus, had him murdered (244), and became emperor in his stead.

GORDIUS (*gor'de-us*), a fabled king of ancient Phrygia, the father of Midas. The legend says he was a peasant ; that one day, when ploughing, an eagle lighted on the yoke of his oxen and staid till evening, and that a prophetess told him this was the sign of his future greatness. Gordius afterwards married the prophetess ; and, when their son, Midas, had grown to be a man, they drove one day in a car to a place where the people had gathered to elect a new king. Just before they arrived an oracle had declared that the new king would come in a car. Accordingly the people made Gordius their king. The yoke on which the eagle had alighted was consecrated to Jupiter, and Gordius hung it up in the temple of Gordium, tying it with a very hard knot. An oracle declared that whoever should untie this knot would become king of Asia, but it is related that ALEXANDER THE GREAT cut it with his sword.

GORGES (*gor'jes*), Sir **Ferdinando,** one of the first owners of Maine, born in Somersetshire, England. He sent several ships to explore the coast of New England and to make settlements there, and in 1620 got a right for the "governing of New England." He made a colony in Maine, of which he was made lord proprietor, but it did not succeed. He was a very old man when he died, in 1623.

GOR'GONS, in Greek fable, three sisters named Stheno, Euryale, and Medusa. They were frightful to behold, having snakes for hair, brass hands, bodies covered with hard scales, huge gold-colored wings, and teeth as long as the tusks of a wild boar, and they could turn to stone all on whom they looked. At last PERSEUS cut off Medusa's head while she was asleep, and, after doing many wonderful things with it, gave it to MINERVA, who wore it ever after on her shield.

GORTCHAKOFF (*gor'chah-kof*), **Alexander,** Prince Chancellor of the Russian Empire, a famous statesman, born July 16, 1798. He is descended from a Russian princely family of the royal House of RURIK, several members of which have been famous. He has taken part in a great many affairs of state, in which he has always shown himself a very able manager, his first feat in state craft being his success in keeping Austria from joining the enemies of Russia during the Crimean War, in 1854. Whenever Russia has had to make treaties with other powers, he has been the one to take care of her interests. He died at Baden-Baden, when 85 years old (March 11, 1883).

GOTHA (*go'tah*), a town of Germany, capital of the duchy of Saxe-Coburg-Gotha ; pop. 28,000, or about as large as Chelsea, Mass. Its manufactures and trade are very important; and it contains a celebrated gymnasium, or college, an observatory, and many fine schools. The palace of Friedenstein near the town has a very large library of books and manuscripts, a gallery of fine arts, and one of the largest collections of coins in Europe. The Gotha Almanac has been published there for 117 years (1880). It is filled with facts about all the countries of the world and their rulers.

GOTHS, a tribe of Germans first mentioned as living on the shores of the Baltic Sea during the 4th century B.C., and disappearing in the 8th century A.D. In the third century A.D., these barbarians invaded Dacia, and fought so successfully with the Romans, as to force them to give them that province. Here they became a quiet, civilized people, many of them being Christianized through the efforts of their bishop, Ulfilas, who translated the Bible into their language. During this period the Goths were divided into East and West Goths, or Ostrogoths and Visigoths. The Visigoths were a restless people, and, on the death of Theodosius the Great, conquered and sacked Rome under their famous King ALARIC. Under Athaulf, the successor of Alaric, they went into Gaul, crossed the Pyrenees, and founded an empire comprising the southern part of France and the northern part of Spain. In the beginning of the 6th century they lost the northern part of their kingdom, being obliged to give it up to the king of the Franks ; but they prospered in Spain until they were routed by the Saracens at Xeres de la Frontera

(711), their empire broken up, and their name destroyed. The Ostrogoths, under their King THEODORIC, overthrew ODOACER, the first barbarian king of Rome, and for eighteen years ruled Italy to the Alps. After Theodoric's death, Belisarius and Narses, the generals of Justinian, Emperor of the East, broke down the Ostrogothic empire in Italy, and their name too vanished from history.

GÖTTINGEN (*get'ting-en*), a city of Germany in Prussia; pop. 22,000, or about as large as Springfield, Mo. It is noted for its university, which was founded in 1734 by King George II. of England, who was also Elector of Hanover. At the end of the last century it was the most celebrated university in Europe, having many thousand students. When the University of Berlin was founded in 1810 it drew many students from Göttingen, and many more left in 1837, because the government expelled seven of the best professors who had opposed its laws. There are still more than a hundred professors and nearly a thousand students there. The University contains one of the finest libraries in Germany, and a very rich museum, including an immense collection of skulls from nearly every nation of the world. Several seminaries and schools are attached to Göttingen University.

GOUNOD (*goo-no'*) **Charles François,** a French writer of music, born in Paris June 17, 1818. He at first wrote sacred music; but he has had much success in operas. The work on which his fame chiefly rests is the opera of "Faust" (1859). He has written many masses, and has set to beautiful music the 137th Psalm, beginning, "By the waters of Babylon." He died when seventy-five years old (Oct. 18, 1893).

GRACCHUS (*grak'kus*), **Caius Sempronius,** brother of Tiberius Sempronius Gracchus, born 159 B.C. At the death of Tiberius he went into retirement until 126, when he was sent to Sardinia as quæstor. Two years later he went back to Rome, and was chosen tribune, in which office he made many wise regulations, called the Sempronian laws, to benefit the people. He proposed to give the allies of Rome the power to vote; but the Romans did not like this, and would not make him tribune a second time. At last the senate met, and took back one of his laws. This led to bloodshed between the friends of each side. A combat took place, from which Gracchus fled, and reached a suburb on the right bank of the Tiber, where he was slain by his slave, at his own command. He was a man of great eloquence. He died when thirty-eight years old (121 B.C.).

GRACCHUS, Tiberius Sempronius, a Roman statesman, born about 168 B.C. His father, Tiberius Gracchus, had held many high offices; and his mother, Cornelia, was the daughter of Scipio Africanus, the conqueror of Carthage. In 134 he was elected tribune, and the following year he brought back an old law called the Licinian law, by which it was forbidden to any one to own more than five hundred acres of land. This was in order to keep some people from being so rich, and others so poor. The great landholders hated the tribune for depriving them of their land, and made a party against him. They pretended that he was trying to be king, and a mob set upon him and his followers, and murdered him. He died when thirty-five years old (133 B.C.).

GRACES, in Greek fable, three sisters, named Euphrosyne, Aglaia, and Thalia, noted for their great beauty and gracefulness. They usually attended upon VENUS, though sometimes upon Apollo. The Graces are represented as three very beautiful women, standing with their arms intwined about each other.

GRANADA (*grah-nah'dah*), a city of S. Spain, built partly on the sides of the Sierra Nevada Mountains, and partly on the plain below them; pop. 73,000, or nearly as large as Fall River, Mass. It was founded by the Moors in the 10th century, and was the capital of the Moorish Kingdom of Granada, which was conquered by Ferdinand and Isabella, after a war of ten years (1482 to 1492). The city itself was taken in 1492 after a long siege, in which the Moors defended themselves with desperate valor. Granada is still celebrated for its beautiful Moorish palace of the Alhambra, and for other Moorish and Spanish buildings.

GRAND RAP'IDS, a city of W. Michigan, on the Grand River, 30 miles E. of Lake Michigan; pop., 60,000, or very nearly as large as Troy, N. Y. The river forms there a long rapid, which furnishes water-power for manufactories of carriages and wagons, farming-tools, barrels, tubs, and many other things. Gypsum is obtained near the city, and corn-colored bricks, called Milwaukee bricks, are manufactured there. There is also a large trade in pine lumber. Grand Rapids was settled in 1833, and became a city in 1850.

GRANT, Ulysses S., eighteenth President of the United States, born at Point Pleasant, O., April 27, 1822. His real name was Hiram Ulysses Grant, but by mistake he was appointed to West Point as Ulysses S., and ever since has kept that name. After graduation at West Point (1843), he served bravely in the Mexican war, and became a captain. In 1854 he resigned and went to live in St. Louis, and afterward at Galena, Ill., where he assisted his father in the tanning business. When the Civil War began, he was made captain of a company of volunteers, and soon after was promoted to be a colonel. In August, 1861, he became a brigadier-general, and in December of the

same year was made commander of the department of Cairo, which included parts of Illinois, Kentucky, and Missouri. Aided by Commodore Foote, he soon captured Fort Henry on the Tennessee, and Fort Donaldson on the Cumberland, River. Gen. Grant was made major-general, and, by the death of Gen. C. F. Smith, was left in command of the army stationed at Pittsburg Landing, where he fought the great battle of Shiloh (April 7, 1862). After winning the battle of Iuka, Miss. (Sept. 19, 1862), he besieged and captured Vicksburg with 27,000 prisoners (July 4, 1863). Soon after, he was placed in command of the whole region near the Mississippi, and on Nov. 24 and 25, 1863, he won a victory at Chattanooga, over Gen. Bragg.

Ulysses S. Grant.

Congress voted Gen. Grant a gold medal for his services; and on March 1, 1864, he was made lieutenant-general, and commander of all the armies of the United States. He immediately directed Gen. Sherman to march against Atlanta, Ga., while he himself, with Gen. Meade and the army of the Potomac, moved toward Richmond. He tried to get between Gen. Lee and Richmond, and in doing so fought the great

battles of the Wilderness, Spottsylvania, the North Anna River, and
Cold Harbor. Not being able to
get behind Gen. Lee, he besieged
Petersburg, which was one of the
principal defences of Richmond.
Meanwhile, Gen. Sherman captured
Atlanta, and, marching across Georgia, took Savannah; thence, he
marched north, to join Gen. Grant
in Virginia; but before the two
armies met, Petersburg and Richmond were taken, and Gen. Grant
finally captured Lee and his whole
army at Appomattox Court-House
(April 9, 1865). On July 25, 1866,
the rank of full general in the
United States army was created by
Congress for Gen. Grant.

In 1868 he was elected President
of the United States, and in 1872 he
was again elected to the same office.
After giving up his office (March 4,
1877), he spent several years in a
voyage around the world. He died
at Mt. McGregor, N. Y., when sixty-
three years old (July 23, 1885).

GRATIAN (*gra'she-an*), **Augustus
Gratianus,** a Roman Emperor, born
in Pannonia in 359. He was the
son of the Emperor VALENTINIAN
I., and succeeded to the throne on
the death of his father, in 375.
Being a Christian, he helped greatly
by destroying the Pagan temples, in
putting down the ancient religion.
He was a just and good man,
although at first very severe. During his reign there were several
wars with the tribes on the Rhine
and Danube, in which he was successful. He was murdered at Lyons,
during a revolt in Gaul (Aug. 23,
383).

GRAVELOTTE (*grah-vel-lot'*), a
village of W. Germany, on the River
Moselle, 8 miles W. of Metz; pop.,
700. It is noted for a great victory
won there by the Germans, under
King William, over the French,
under Marshal Bazaine (Aug. 18,
1870). It was one of the hardest-
fought battles of the war, and more
than 30,000 men were killed on both

sides. The French went to METZ,
but were besieged there, and had to
surrender.

GRAVESEND (*graivz-end'*), a
town of England, on the River
Thames, 21 miles below London;
pop., 31,000, or nearly as large as
Quincy, Ill. Vessels going to London are obliged to stop at Gravesend, to be examined by the Custom-
House officers. A large business is
carried on in stores and provisions
for vessels, and many ships are built
there. POCAHONTAS was buried at
Gravesend, in the parish church.

GRAY, Asa, an American botanist,
born in Paris, Oneida Co., New York,
Nov. 18, 1810. He studied to be a
physician; but soon gave up that
profession for botany. In 1842, he
became professor of botany in Harvard College. Besides many articles in scientific journals, and
government reports, he published
several books about the plants of
the United States. He wrote,
with Dr. Torrey, a great work on
the "Flora of North America."
Dr. Gray is best known for his text-
books of botany, among which are
"How Plants grow," and "Lessons
in Botany." He died when seventy-seven years old (Jan. 30, 1888).

GRAY, Thomas, an English poet,
born in Cornhill, London, Dec. 26,
1716. He was finely educated, being
learned in botany, natural history,
architecture, art, the Greek classics,
history, and philosophy. Yet, with all
his learning, he has left the world only
a few beautiful poems and some fine
letters. His most noted poems are
the odes, "The Progress of Poesy,"
"The Bard," "On a Distant Prospect of Eton College," and the exquisite "Elegy written in a Country
Churchyard." Gray died in London when fifty-four years old (July
24, 1771).

GREAT BRITAIN (*brit'an*), the
name of the largest island of Europe,
containing England, Wales, and
Scotland. Britain was its ancient
name, and this was made by the

Romans into Britannia. It was first called Great Britain to distinguish it from Bretagne, Brittany, or Little Britain in France. When England and Scotland were united (1707), Great Britain became the name of the kingdom, and it is now often used for the whole British Empire. Scotland is sometimes called North Britain.

GREAT SALT LAKE. See UTAH.

GREECE, a country of S. E. Europe; area, 20,000 square miles, or about half as large as Kentucky; pop. 1,980,000, or somewhat less than that of that State; capital, ATHENS. The southern part, called the PELOPONNESUS, is almost cut off from the rest by the deep gulf of Corinth, the connecting isthmus of Corinth being only five miles wide. A large number of islands near the peninsula belong to Greece: of these the most important are, EUBŒA and the CYCLADES on the east, and the IONIAN ISLANDS on the west. Both the mainland and the islands are very mountainous, some of the peaks being more than a mile and a half high. The mountain-chains are very steep, and some of them can only be passed by narrow gorges. The mountain sides are covered with forests, and the many fertile valleys and glens make Greece one of the most beautiful countries in the world. The climate is mild and pleasant.

Greece has mines of lead and emery, and the finest marble quarries in the world. The soil is good; but the people are poor farmers, and only a small part of the land is planted. The most important crops are olives and Zante currants (C. C. T., 506, I., l.). Grapes are also cultivated, and a poor kind of wine is made. There are hardly any manufactures, and but few railroads or telegraph wires. The people are intelligent, frugal, and brave, and very proud of their country, though it is now so poor. The city people dress like Americans; but most of the country people wear a Turkish cap, a richly-embroidered silk jacket and sash, and a short skirt like that of the Highlanders in Scotland.

Greece is governed by a king, and by a congress chosen by the people every four years. Nearly all the Greeks belong to the Greek Church, which is something like the Roman Catholic Church.

Though Greece is not very important now, it has the most glorious history of any country in the world, and the ruins of its ancient cities have more interest than many great modern towns. The Greeks were among the first of the ARYAN peoples to come into Europe, and they were the first Aryan nation whose deeds were written in history. They called their country Hellas, and its people Hellenes, from their fabled ancestor, Hellen, son of DEUCALION; but the early people of Italy called them Græci, from one of their tribes, and from that the country was named Greece. Many small states were founded by them, both on the mainland and on the islands off their coasts, which soon became noted for civilization and love of freedom. They early began to navigate the seas and to send out colonies, and settled the coasts of Macedonia and Thrace, and many parts of the Mediterranean coast, even as far west as Gaul, where they built the city of Massilia, now Marseilles. Miletus in Asia, Sybaris in Italy, and Syracuse in Sicily were also famous Greek cities.

In Greece itself, each city, when strong enough, formed an independent state, which ruled its own little territory around it. Of this kind were Sparta, Argos, and Mycenæ in the Peloponnesus; Corinth, on the isthmus; and Megara, Athens, and Thebes beyond the isthmus. Sometimes several towns joined together in a league, each ruling itself, but all making war as a single state.

The Greek colonies in Asia were

in time conquered by the Persians, and from this disputes arose with the Persian kings. At last King Darius made up his mind to bring all the Greeks under his power. The first Persian expedition into Greece was defeated by the Greeks at MARATHON (490 B.C.). Ten years afterwards, XERXES, son of Darius, invaded Greece with an immense army and fleet; but was defeated at Thermopylæ and Salamis (480), and afterwards at Platæa and Mycale; and the Persians never again dared to invade Greece.

In the beginning of the Persian wars, Sparta was the chief state of Greece; but ATHENS soon took the lead, and rose to a wonderful power and splendor. This made many of the other Greek cities jealous; and at last a war broke out between Athens and her allies, and Sparta and her allies, among whom were most of the cities of the Peloponnesus; and from this it was called the Peloponnesian War. It began in 431 B.C., and lasted twenty-nine years, and ended in Athens losing her power, and becoming a member of the Spartan alliance.

Sparta now held the power for a

Fleet of Ancient Greek War Ships.

while; but in 379 the Thebans rose against them, and, under Pelopidas and Epaminondas, became for a short time the chief power of Greece. Soon after, Macedonia began to grow strong; and King Philip got himself elected captain-general of the Greeks, to make war on Persia. But he was murdered (336), and his son ALEXANDER THE GREAT became the head of the Greeks. Alexander's conquests made a great and lasting change in a large part of the world. Many cities, such as Alexandria and Antioch, were built and settled by Greeks, who made changes among all the peoples around them. The

Greek language became the common speech of the civilized world, much as French has been in modern times, and Greek learning and science were spread everywhere. Thus Greece had a wonderful influence on the world, and aided greatly in its civilization. The Greeks first showed mankind what freedom and civilization were, and they did more for art and science than any other people.

At last the Romans began to meddle in the affairs of Greece; and, in the 2d century B.C., Greece and Macedonia became Roman provinces. When the Roman Empire of the East fell, the Turks conquered most of Greece, and held it until the Greek revolution (1821–1829), by which the people won their freedom. In 1830 it was made a kingdom.

GREELEY, Horace, a noted American writer, born at Amherst, N.H., Feb. 3, 1811. His father had a small farm; and Horace as a child used to help in the farm-work, at the same time reading every book he could get. He learned to read when two years old, and before he was ten had borrowed all the books for miles around. His father moved to Vermont in 1821, and Horace worked with him, clearing wild land, for five years. After that he was a printer's apprentice for four years; and then, tired of hard work and poor pay, tied up his little bundle of clothes, and went to New York with ten dollars in his pocket, to seek his fortune. He worked as a journeyman printer in newspaper offices until 1833; when he began a daily newspaper called "The Morning Post." This soon failed; and next year he began a weekly paper called "The New Yorker," which did not succeed much better; but it was finally made with another paper into "The New York Tribune" (1841), which became one of the most successful newspapers in the country. Mr. Greeley was a member of Congress in 1849. In 1851 he went to Europe, and was one of the judges of the World's Fair in London. He took an active part in politics, especially during and after the Civil War; and was a candidate for the presidency in 1872, but was defeated by Gen. Grant. His health was broken down by his hard work during the election, and he died when sixty-one years old (Nov. 29, 1872). Besides newspaper articles, lectures, and public speeches, Mr. Greeley wrote several books, among them a history of the Civil War called "The American Conflict," and a volume called "Recollections of a Busy Life."

GREENE, Nathanael, a noted American general, born at Potow-

hommet, R.I., May 27, 1742. His father, a Quaker preacher, worked a farm and an anchor forge, and Nathanael had to work hard from his childhood; but he was fond of study, and, by reading whenever he could, he picked up a very fair education. He took great delight in studying about the art of war, and was turned out of the Society of Friends or Quakers for joining a military company. In 1775 he was made brigadier-general, and given the command of the Rhode-Island troops in the army before Boston; and from this time, until 1783, he was in active service, and won the name of being the best general of the Revolution next after Washington.

Nathanael Greene.

In September, 1775, he was made major-general, and was given command of the troops in New Jersey. He took part in the battles of TRENTON and PRINCETON; and at those of GERMANTOWN and the BRANDYWINE, distinguished himself by his bravery. He soon won the esteem and favor of Gen. Washington, who gave him many important commands. In 1780 he was sent to take command of the Southern army, and remained until the close of the war, doing so much good work that Congress presented him with a gold medal for his conduct at the battle of Eutaw Springs. He was also given much valuable land in North Carolina, South Carolina, and Georgia. He died near Savannah, when forty-four years old (June 19, 1786).

GREEN'LAND, a region of unknown size, N.E. of North America, from which it is separated by Davis Strait, Baffin Bay, and Smith Sound.

It is mountainous, and the greater part of it is covered all the year round with snow and ice. The shores are mostly high and rocky, divided by long narrow bays called fiords. From the mountains glaciers or ice rivers (C.C.T., 202, II, l.), are all the time moving downward to the sea. As the ice reaches the water it breaks off in great masses, which form icebergs sometimes two or three miles long, and higher than most church steeples. Some of

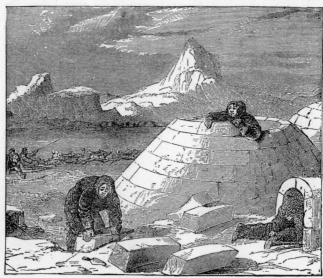

Esquimaux building Snow-Huts.

these float down into the Atlantic, and often make navigation dangerous.

During the two summer months, June and July, when the sun is always above the horizon, it becomes quite warm along the fiords of the west coast, so that potatoes and a few other vegetables may be grown. No tall trees are ever seen; a few stunted shrubs grow in the south parts, while in the north there are little more than mosses and lichens. Though the climate is very cold, it is healthful, and there are several settlements along the west coast. The people, who are mostly Esquimaux (only about 300 being Danes), live by hunting and fishing. There are plenty of bears, reindeer, and foxes, and the seas abound with whales, porpoises, walruses, narwhals, and seals (C.C.T., 540, II, l.), while the coasts are filled with seafowl. The Greenlanders keep a few sheep and cattle and many dogs, which they train to draw sleds. Sometimes these dogs go wild, and wander round the country in packs hunting reindeer. Good coal and several kinds of metals are found in Greenland, but the only mineral sent to other countries is cryolite, from which soda is made.

Esquimau Boy.

Greenland belongs to Denmark. The country was first seen in the 9th century (876) by the Northman Gunnbjörn, but it was not visited until 983, when Eric the Red sailed there from Iceland. It is thought that its climate was then milder than now; for he named it Greenland from the color of its shores, and made a colony there. The Northmen lived in Greenland until the middle of the 15th century, when they gave it up, and nothing more was heard of it until 1576, when Martin FROBISHER found it again.

GREEN'OCK, a town of Scotland, at the mouth of the river Clyde, 18 miles W. N. W. of Glasgow; pop., 78,000, or as large as Paterson, N. J. It is noted for its large iron founderies and sugar refineries, and for the ship-yards in which many iron ships are made. Greenock carries on a large trade. Steamers going to Glasgow touch first at this port, where there are fine docks and wharves. Until the end of the 17th century, Greenock was a little fishing village, but since then it has grown rapidly. James WATT, the inventor of the steam-engine, was born there.

GREENWICH (*grin'ij*), a town of England, on the river Thames, just below London; pop. 47,000, or about as large as Saginaw, Mich. It is celebrated for its observatory, which was founded by King Charles II. English and American sailors generally reckon their longitude from this observatory, which, on their charts, is at longitude 0°. Public clocks in all parts of England are regulated by telegraph from the observatory. Greenwich is also noted for its Royal Naval College, built on the site of an old royal palace, in which King Henry VIII., Queen Mary, and Queen Elizabeth were born. Until 1873 this was a hospital for seamen.

GREG'O·RY, the name of sixteen popes.

Gregory I., called the Great, born in Rome about 540, was a man of much learning and ability. He sent missionaries to England and other countries, and did much to strengthen the Church.

Gregory VII., born in Tuscany about 1018, was the greatest of all the popes. His name was Hildebrand, and he was the son of a carpenter, but was educated by his uncle and became a monk. He was elected pope in 1073, and at once began to reform the Church. He said that no sovereign should have the power to appoint any person to any Church office, and this led to a long quarrel between him and the Emperor HENRY IV. of Germany, which plunged Italy and Germany into terrible civil wars. Gregory died at Salerno, when sixty-seven years old (May 25, 1085).

Gregory XIII., born in Bologna Feb. 7, 1502, was a learned and able man. He changed the calendar, so as to make time right. The year fixed by Julius Cæsar was $365\frac{1}{4}$ days long, but this was nearly 14 seconds too much. To change this so as to make the year come right, Gregory ordered ten days to be dropped from the calendar (1582), but the change was not made in England until 1752, and in Russia and Greece the old style is still kept. Gregory died when eighty-three years old (April 10, 1585).

Gregory XVI., born in Belluno Sept. 18, 1765, was pope before Pius IX. He died when eighty-one years old (June 1, 1846).

GRENOBLE (*greh-no'b'l*), a city of S. E. France, on the river Isère, 58 miles S. E. of Lyons; pop., 52,000, or about as large as Hartford, Conn. Grenoble is noted for its great factories of kid gloves, in which many thousand persons are employed. There are also manufactories of leather and liquors; and a large trade is carried on in hemp, marble, and iron.

In the 4th century, the town was named Gratianopolis, or Gratian City, in honor of the Roman emperor GRATIAN. In course of time this has been changed to Grenoble.

GRÉVY (*gra-ve'*), **François Jules Paul,** was born at Mont-sous-Vaudrey, France, Aug. 15, 1813. He was a member of the Constituent Assembly of 1848, was President of the Chamber of Deputies 1871-73 and again 1876-79. In 1879 he was elected President of the French Republic, and re-elected in 1885. He resigned his office in 1887, and died September 9, 1891.

GREY, Lady Jane, great granddaughter of Henry VII., King of

England, born in Leicestershire in 1537. From her childhood she showed a great love of study, and, when fifteen years old, understood Latin, Greek, French, Italian, and other languages. In 1553 she was married to Lord Guilford Dudley, son of the Duke of Northumberland. The Duke knew that King EDWARD VI., then on the throne, intended to make Lady Jane his successor, and he hoped by this marriage to get his son on the throne. Lady Jane did not know of this; and when the king died (July 6, 1553), she did not wish to be made queen; but at last she yielded and was crowned. But the people thought that Mary, Edward's sister, was the true heir, and when she claimed the crown, Lady Jane gave it up, after being a queen for only nine days. She and her husband were thrown into prison, and both were executed (Feb. 12, 1554).

GUATEMALA (*gwah-ta-mah'lah*), a country of Central AMERICA, between Honduras and Mexico; area, about 46,000 square miles, or about as large as Tennessee; pop., about 1,400,000, or four-fifths that of Tennessee; capital, Guatemala. Most of the country is a high table-land, diversified by mountain-peaks, some of them volcanoes, and by beautiful valleys. Earthquakes are frequent.

Guatemala is rich in gold, silver, copper, and iron. Coffee is cultivated on large plantations, and is the principal article of trade. Sugar, vanilla, tobacco, and cochineal also are raised. The climate is hot on the coasts, but cool and pleasant on the high lands. The people are mostly Indians and mixed races: only one person in a hundred is white. Guatemala is a republic much like the United States. It was discovered by Columbus in 1502; it was a colony of Spain until 1821; later it formed one of the states of Central America; but since 1847 it has been independent.

GUATEMOZIN (*gwah-te-mo'zin*), the last Aztec ruler of Mexico,

nephew and son-in-law of MONTE-
ZUMA, born about 1495. The Spanish army, led by CORTEZ, attacked
the city of Mexico; but Guatemozin
would not give up until his army
was so weakened by want of food
and illness that he could not do any
thing else. Cortez took him prisoner; and, in order to make him tell
where his treasures were hidden,
had his feet burned at a slow fire.
When somebody spoke of his calmness in bearing the torture, he said,
"Do you think, then, that I am
taking my pleasure in a bath?" All
that he would say about the treasures
was, that "much treasure had been
thrown into the water;" but the
lakes and canals were dragged, and
nothing was found. After this he
was accused of forming a plot to
murder Cortez, and was executed
when thirty years old (Feb. 15, 1525).

GUELPHS and GHIBELLINES
(*gwelfs and gib'el-ins*), the names of
two great parties which divided Italy
and Germany during the Middle
Ages. These names in their German form, Welfen and Waiblingen,
were first known at the siege of
Weinsberg, when Conrad, Duke of
Franconia, and Henry the Lion,
Duke of Saxony, fought for the imperial crown, Waiblingen being the
seat of the Franconian family, and
Welf the family name of the House
of Saxony. As time went on, the
name Ghibelline was given to all
those who supported the emperors,
and that of Guelph to all who
opposed them; and, as the Popes
became the great enemies of the
emperors, they finally became leaders
of the Guelphic party. In Germany
these parties soon died out; but they
were kept up in Italy nearly four
centuries, and met in many a bloody
struggle. As a rule the nobility
were Ghibellines and in favor of a
strict rule, and the people, Guelphs
and in favor of a liberal government;
but these distinctions did not always
hold good. Sometimes the two parties were strangely mixed up, and

quarrelled about things that had
nothing to do with the original question. In Florence there are two
streets bearing these names, Via
Guelfa and Via Ghibellina. The
struggle there was so bitter that private gentlemen built their houses
like forts to stand a siege. This
accounts for the peculiar way these
houses are built. In the fifteenth century these names ceased to be heard,
the bitter enmities which gave them
birth having worn themselves out.

GUERNSEY (*gern'sy*). See CHAN-
NEL ISLANDS.

GUESCLIN (*ga-klan'*). See DU
GUESCLIN.

GUESS (*gess*), **George, or Sequo-
yah**, a half-breed Cherokee Indian,
born about 1770. He was a farmer
and also a silversmith. In 1826 he
invented an alphabet of the Cherokee language, which could be used
in writing and printing, and which
was very easy to learn. When his
tribe moved west of the Mississippi,
he went with them. He died at San
Fernando, in Mexico, where he had
gone with some other Indians, in
1843.

GUIANA (*ge-ah'nah*), a country in
the N. E. part of South America,
between Brazil and the Caribbean
Sea; area, 195,000 square miles, or
about as large as France. It is
divided into three parts, called from
the countries they belong to, and the
languages spoken in them, English;
Dutch, and French Guiana. English Guiana is farthest west, and is
larger than the others. Guiana is
mountainous in the southern part,
where it is inhabited only by Indians,
but the parts near the coast are flat,
and contain cities and villages, with
many fine sugar-plantations. The
climate is hot, and often unhealthy.
The principal trade is in sugar.
English Guiana is sometimes called
Demerara, Dutch Guiana Surinam,
and French Guiana Cayenne.

English and Dutch Guiana were
first settled by the Dutch, about 1580.
The English conquered their portion

in 1796. French Guiana was settled by the French in 1604. It was taken by the English in 1809, but restored in 1814.

GUIDO (*gwe'do*) or **Guido Reni,** a famous Italian painter, born near Bologna in 1575. He studied with the CARACCI, and afterward lived many years in Rome, where he painted many fine pictures. Among the most noted of his works are the " Massacre of the Innocents," the " Martyrdom of St. Peter," and " Aurora." He died in Bologna when sixty-seven years old (1642).

GUILLOTIN (*ge-yo-tan'*), **Joseph Ignace,** a French physician, born May 28, 1738. He was a member of the assembly in Paris, in 1789, and proposed that persons condemned to death should be beheaded instead of hanged. When the guillotine was made, it was named after him, although he did not invent it nor help make it. Dr. Guillotin died in Paris when seventy-six years old (May 26, 1814).

GUINEA (*gin'ne*), a name given to part of West Africa, extending along the coast about 3,500 miles. It is divided into Upper Guinea, including Sierra Leone, Liberia, Ashantee, Dahomey, Benin, and other countries; and Lower Guinea, made up of Loango, Congo, Angola, and Benguela. The whole is a wild, hot, and unhealthy region, covered with forests, swamps, or grassy plains, in which lions, gorillas, and other wild animals abound. Most of the people are savage negroes, and formerly many slaves were brought from there.

GUISCARD (*gees-kar'*), **Robert,** a famous Norman soldier, founder of the kingdom of Naples, born about 1015. Robert was the sixth of twelve sons; the three eldest went to Italy to seek their fortunes, and had such good luck that the younger brothers were fired with a wish to do likewise. Robert became Duke of Apulia in Italy, and was so wise and cautious that he was surnamed Guis-

card, which means prudent or adroit. The poets praised him for being more cunning than ULYSSES, and more eloquent than CICERO. In battle he wielded his sword in his right hand, and his lance in the left. In one battle he was unhorsed three times, and at the close of the day was thought worthy to bear away the prize of valor from the warriors of two armies. His conquests in Italy were united by him in what was afterward the kingdom of Naples, now a part of the kingdom of Italy. He died when seventy years old (July 17, 1085).

GUISE (*gweez*) **House of,** a branch of the ducal family of Lorraine. This family was very noted during the religious wars in France in the 16th century. Many of them were cardinals, and they were all firm supporters of the Roman Catholic religion. Its most noted members were François and Henry, second and third Duke of Guise.

François de Lorraine, second duke of Guise, born Feb. 17, 1519, a great soldier who lived in the reigns of the French kings, Henry II. and Francis II. It was through his influence that Mary Stuart, his niece, the beautiful Queen of Scots, was married to Francis, the heir to the throne of France. He died when forty-four years old (Feb. 24, 1563).

Henry de Lorraine, third duke of Guise, son of the preceding, was born Dec. 31, 1550, and killed by order of King Henry III. Dec. 23, 1588. This prince bore the surname of " The Scarred." He was the great spirit of the St. Bartholomew massacre, and the head of the League.

GUIZOT (*ge-zo'*), **François Pierre Guillaume,** a famous French statesman and historian, born at Nîmes Oct. 4, 1787. When he was seven years old his father was beheaded, and his mother took her little son to Geneva, where he was educated. He began writing for the public when he was twenty-two years old. He filled many public offices, and was at one time ambassador to England. He was always in favor of having peace with the other European states, and may be called one of the great and good men of France. He is best known as a historian. All of his histories are translated into English. His "History of Civilization" is studied in many schools and colleges, and his "History of France — for my grandchildren" is one of the most interesting histories of that country ever written. He spent some years before his death in writing a history of Spain; and, in order to do it well, he studied Spanish when he was seventy-two years old. He died at his villa, in Valricher, near Paris, when eighty-seven years old (Sept. 13, 1874).

GUSTA′VUS I., known as **Gusta-vus Vasa** (*vah′sah*), King of Sweden, born at the castle of Lindholm, May 12, 1496. Gustavus belonged to the royal house of Sweden; but when he grew to be a man, Christian II., king of Denmark, had conquered Sweden. He was indignant to think that his countrymen were willing to be ruled by such a tyrant, so he made up his mind to free them, or die in trying to do it. The new king set a large price upon his head; but Gustavus heard of it, disguised himself in rags, and worked in the country as a miner and wood-cutter. The peasants hated Christian from the first; and when Gustavus went among them from house to house, talking to them about their wrongs, he found ready listeners. At last, he collected an army of about six hundred men who took up arms, and declared him to be "lord and chieftain of the realm." The feeling spread quickly over the coast; town after town yielded to Gustavus; and the blood-thirsty Christian had to go back in disgrace to Denmark. Gustavus refused the crown several times; and, before he took it, he openly gave up the Roman Catholic faith, and declared himself a Lu-

theran. In 1528 he was crowned by a Lutheran archbishop, and made Lutheranism the State religion. He reigned for thirty-two years with great success; and he holds the same place in the hearts of the Swedes, that ALFRED THE GREAT does in that of every Englishman. He died in Stockholm when sixty-four years old (Sept. 29, 1560).

GUSTAVUS II., Adol′phus, King of Sweden, grandson of Gustavus Vasa, born in Stockholm, Dec. 9, 1594. He was only seventeen years old when he began to reign, but even then showed great military talent. He defeated the attempts of his relative, Sigismund of Poland, to deprive him of his crown, and made a very wise treaty of peace with the czar of Russia. The Protestants of Germany were then suffering from the persecutions of the Austrian emperor, Ferdinand II., which brought about what is called the THIRTY YEARS' WAR. Gustavus went to their aid, and for two years was the head of the Protestants in Germany, carrying on the war with wonderful success and defeating the best generals of the age. He never had a single defeat of any importance. His name is one of the most faultless in the great roll of kings, and as long as he lived Sweden was the best governed kingdom in Europe. Although a firm Protestant, he never steeled his heart against those who chose to serve God in other ways; he was never puffed-up with pride by his victories, and was never known to commit a cruel or ungenerous act. In 1832, on the two hundredth anniversary of his death, the Protestants in Germany founded a society to support new and poor Protestant congregations, and called it the Gustavus Adolphus Union. He was killed at the battle of Lützen, when thirty-eight years old (Nov. 16, 1632).

GUSTAVUS III., King of Sweden, born in Stockholm Jan. 24, 1746. The most remarkable thing in this reign was, that he turned the government upside down in a single day, without the loss of one life. He talked to the people very eloquently and affectionately about what he wanted them to do, and about what he meant to do for them, and ended with these words : " I am obliged to defend my liberty and that of the kingdom against the aristocracy, which reigns. Will you be faithful to me, as your forefathers were to Gustavus Vasa and Gustavus Adolphus ? I will then risk my life for you and my country." The people consented with loud shouts of "Long live Gustavus!" This odd scene was closed by Gustavus taking a small psalm-book from his pocket, and all joined in praising God for his goodness. This was all; from that time Gustavus had every thing his own way, and became one of the most despotic monarchs in Europe. He had great talent, but was changeable and deceitful, so that, after a while, the people found him out, and nobody trusted him. At last some of his nobles conspired against him, and he was killed at a masked ball in Stockholm when forty-six years old (March 29, 1792).

GUSTAVUS IV., King of Sweden, only son of Gustavus III., born Nov. 1, 1778. He was declared to be of age, and was crowned when only eighteen years old; he was very vain and boyish, and unfit to be a king. He used to try to imitate CHARLES XII., and Napoleon said that he was the heir of that king only in " jack-boots and audacity of tongue." He used to give an order on one day, and countermand it on the next ; people began to think him insane, and at last he was obliged to give up his kingdom. After this the Swedish government gave him a pension of $26,000 a year, but he proudly refused it, and used to wander about Europe in thread-bare clothes, seeming to glory in his poverty. He died in a humble dwelling at St. Gall, Switzerland,

when fifty-eight years old (Feb. 7. 1837).

GUTENBERG (*goo'ten-ba-erg*), **Johann,** the inventor of printing, born at Mentz, Germany, about 1400. He was of noble birth, and held a good position in his native city until, on account of political troubles, he was obliged to go away in 1420. He went to Strasburg, and is supposed to have worked at printing, though we know of no books printed by him there. In 1448 he returned to Mentz, and two years after he set up a printing-office in partnership with Johann Faust, a rich goldsmith who furnished the money. They printed a book with letters cut out of wood; but soon after they made letters out of copper or tin and printed a Latin Bible. He and Faust separated after working together for five years, and Faust carried on the business at the same place with his son-in-law, Peter Shaeffer. Gutenberg set up another printing-office and worked there until 1465, when he gave it up and entered the service of the Elector Adolphus of Nassau. He died in Mentz when about sixty-seven years old (Feb. 24, 1468).

GUY (*gi*), **Seymour Joseph,** an American artist, born in England in 1824. He came to the United States when thirty years old, and has since had a studio in New York. He paints family groups, portraits, and ideal or fancy pictures.

GYP'SIES, a wandering people, now found in most parts of the world. The name is supposed to come from the word Egyptians. They are called Zingari in Italy, Gitanos in Spain, Zigeuner in Germany, and Bohemians in France. Where these people came from is uncertain, and there are many opinions on the subject. They first appeared in Europe in the fifteenth century. They have no settled home, and follow no trade, making their living by thieving, and telling fortunes. In many countries severe laws have been passed against them.

H

HAARLEM (*har'lem*), a city of the Netherlands, in N. Holland, on the river Spaarne, 3 miles from the sea; pop. 51,000, or about as large as Evansville, Ind. Its streets, which are kept very clean, are divided by many canals. The city has manufactures of cotton, silk, linen, and velvets, and in the outskirts are great nursery gardens, noted for their tulips and hyacinths, in which there is an important trade. St. Bavon's Church, built in the 15th century, is the largest church in Holland, and has one of the largest organs in the world. In the square in front of it is a marble statue of Coster, whom the Dutch say was the inventor of printing. Haarlem is famous for its heroic defence against the Spaniards under the Duke of Alva, who besieged it for seven months (1572-3). The citizens fought hard for their liberty, even the women forming a company of three hundred soldiers. After the Spaniards had lost 10,000 men they gave up trying to take the city by fighting, and tried to starve the garrison by keeping food from coming into the city. After the last mouthful was eaten the people were obliged to surrender; but instead of saving their lives as they had agreed, the Spaniards killed them all.

Haarlem Lake, near the city, was fourteen miles long and ten broad. It was formed in the 16th century by an inundation from the sea, which washed away several villages. In 1839 the people began to drain it with steam pumps, and after twelve years nearly all the water was pumped out, and the lake bottom was made into fine farms, on which about 10,000 people live.

HADES (*ha'deez*), in Greek fable, the place to which the souls of the dead went, over which Pluto was king. It included both ELYSIUM, the place of reward, and TARTARUS, the place of punishment. Its gates were kept closed, that no soul might return to earth, and were guarded by the three-headed dog CERBERUS.

HA'DRI-AN, or **A'dri-an** (Publius Ælius Hadrianus), a Roman emperor, born in Rome, Jan. 24, A.D. 76. He was the son of a senator and a relative of Trajan, afterward emperor, who was his guardian. He was with Trajan in most of his conquests, and won rank and fame as a soldier, and when Trajan died he was proclaimed emperor by his soldiers at ANTIOCH (117). On taking the throne he made peace with the Parthians, with whom Trajan had been at war, and forgave the debts of the Roman people. Two years afterward he began to make a tour of his empire, and visited Gaul, Germany, Britain, Asia, Africa, and Greece. During these journeys he did much to improve the condition of the people, built cities and great public works, and raised the character of the Roman army. In A.D. 132 a revolt of the Jews broke out, which he put down with great bloodshed, the barbarities continuing until most of the Jews in Palestine were killed or driven away. In his reign the Christians too were cruelly persecuted, but generally he was a wise and able ruler. He aided writers and artists, and wrote in both prose and verse, but none of his books have been saved. Among the great buildings erected by him was a magnificent villa at Tibur, now TIVOLI, and his mausoleum, now the Castle of St. Angelo in ROME. He died when sixty-two years old (July 10, 138).

HADRIAN (popes). See ADRIAN.

HAGUE (*haig*) **The,** a city of the Netherlands, near the west coast, about 2 miles from the sea; pop.

153,000, or about twice as large as Nashville, Tenn. Though Amsterdam is the capital, the king and his family and the principal officers reside at the Hague, and the Netherlands Parliament meets there. The Hague is one of the finest cities in Europe, and is noted for its grand palaces and houses, and its parks and wide, shady streets. It has also fine libraries, picture galleries, and a museum. Hague (Dutch *hage*) means a "hedge," and the city gets its name from a hedge around a hunting seat built there in the 13th century by the Count of Holland.

HAKLUYT (*hak'loot*), **Richard,** a noted English writer, born about 1553. He studied at Oxford, where he was afterward a lecturer on geography, and was the first to teach the use of globes. He wrote a number of books ; his largest work, in three volumes, contains accounts of two hundred and twenty voyages made by English navigators. He died when sixty-three years old (Oct. 23, 1616).

HALE, Sir Matthew, a famous English judge, born in Alderley, Nov. 1, 1609. He was educated at Oxford, and became a lawyer a few years before the civil war broke out between King Charles and the Parliament. He was employed on the royal side in the trials of Archbishop Laud and other royalists. When Cromwell became Lord Protector of England, Hale was made judge of the court of common pleas, and performed his duties with great ability and honor. In 1660 he was one of the Parliament which recalled CHARLES II. to the throne, and he was soon made a knight and given a high office ; and in 1671 he became Lord Chief Justice of England. The only blot upon his record as judge is that he allowed two women to be put to death as witches. He died when sixty-seven years old (Dec. 25, 1676).

HALE, Nathan, an American soldier and patriot, born in Coventry

Conn., June 6, 1755. He was graduated at Yale College in 1773, and intended to be a minister, but when the Revolution broke out he joined the army as a lieutenant, and soon became a captain. After the defeat on Long Island, Washington wished to get information about the strength and plans of the British, and Hale volunteered to go. He went in disguise to the enemy's camp, and found out all he wanted, but on returning was captured, and executed as a spy by order of Sir William Howe. He was hanged in New York, when only twenty-one years old (Sept. 22, 1776). His last words were, "I only regret that I have but one life to lose for my country." A fine monument has been erected to his memory at Coventry.

HAL·I·CAR·NAS'SUS, an ancient city of Caria in Asia Minor. Its site is now occupied by a dirty Turkish town called Boodroom, 96 miles south of Smyrna. Halicarnassus was a Greek city, but was under Persian rule. Its most famous prince was Mausolus. On his death (352 B.C.) his wife Artemisia built for him one of the most splendid tombs ever known, and named it after him the Mausoleum, from which has come our word mausoleum. HERODOTUS was born in Halicarnassus.

HAL'I-FAX, a city, capital of Nova Scotia, on a bay of the Atlantic Ocean ; pop. 42,000, or a little less than Savannah, Ga. The harbor is one of the best in the world, being sixteen miles long and deep enough for the largest ships. Halifax is the principal station for English ships of war in North America, and also for English soldiers in Canada. A great many ships go from there to catch fish on the Newfoundland Banks, and the principal trade of the city is in codfish. Halifax was founded in 1749 by the Earl of Halifax, after whom it was named.

HALLE (*hahl'leh*), a city of Germany, in Prussia, 20 miles N. W. of Leipsic; pop. 82,000, or about as large as New Haven, Conn. It is noted for its university, founded in 1694, which has had many famous men among its professors. It now has about 1500 students, and a large library and museums. There are very large salt-works in and around Halle, and the city has many factories and a good trade.

HALLECK, Fitz Greene, a noted American poet, born in Guilford, Conn., July 8, 1795. He began life as a clerk in a store in Guilford, but when twenty-one years old he was employed in a banking-house in New York, where he remained many years. At last he became a clerk for John Jacob Astor, who left him in his will $200 a year for the rest of his life. Halleck then retired from active life, and passed the rest of his days at Guilford. His earliest poem, "Twilight," was printed in 1818. Five years after he visited Europe, and in 1827 a volume of his poetry, including "Marco Bozzaris," appeared. He died in Guilford when seventy-two years old (Nov. 17, 1867). A bronze statue of him has been erected in Central Park, New York.

HALLECK, Henry Wager, an American general, born at Waterville, N. Y., Jan. 15, 1815. He was graduated at West Point in 1839, and in 1845 the government sent him to examine the armies and forts of Europe. He afterward served in California, and in 1854 resigned and became a lawyer, and president of a railroad in San Francisco. When the Civil War began he was made a major-general and commander of the Union armies in the Mississippi Valley. From July, 1862, to March, 1864, he was commander-in-chief of all the armies of the United States. When General Grant became commander, Halleck was made chief of the staff. After the war he commanded at Richmond, on the Pa-

cific, and finally in the Southern States. He died at Louisville, Ky., when about fifty-seven years old (Jan. 9, 1872).

HAMBURG, a city of Germany, on the River Elbe at the mouth of the River Alster; pop. 306,000, or a little larger than San Francisco, Cal. Close to it, and really forming a part of it, though having a different government, is the city of ALTONA. Hamburg is the most important seaport of Germany, and many steamers go from there to the United States and South America. As very large ships cannot ascend to the city, they anchor some miles below at Cuxhaven. Hamburg is noted for its many canals and beautiful bridges and promenades. It has a large museum and fine libraries.

Hamburg is a very old place. Since 1770 it has been a free city; that is, it has been allowed to make its own laws, and is subject only to the Emperor of Germany. In 1813 the French Marshal Davoust defended Hamburg in a terrible siege. Fearing that the people would eat the provisions which he wanted for his soldiers, he drove out 30,000 of them, in the middle of the winter, and more than a thousand died of cold and hunger.

HAMELN, a town of Germany, in Prussia, 24 miles S. W. of Hanover, on the rivers Hamel and Weser; pop. 12,000, or about as large as Appleton, Wis. It is a quaint old town, with houses ornamented with wood carvings. Hameln is the scene of the story of the pied piper, who offered to clear the town of rats and mice, with which it was overrun, for a certain price. He played his pipe through the streets, and all the vermin came out of the houses and followed him to the bank of the Weser, where they were drowned. The people, freed from the pest, refused to pay the sum agreed upon, and the piper went off swearing to be revenged. On the feast of Saints Iohn and Paul (June 26), in the year

1284, he came back and again played his pipe through the streets. This time all the children in the town flocked from their houses and followed him, charmed by his sweet music, into a cavern in the mountains, and were never seen again. This story has been made into a pretty poem by Robert Browning.

HA·MIL'CAR BARKA (*bar'kah*), a noted Carthaginian general, born shortly before the First Punic War. He was still very young when he was sent to take the command of the Carthaginian army in Sicily. The Romans had nearly driven the Carthaginians from the island; but Hamilcar soon won back the greater part of it, when he was called back to defend Carthage itself. Peace was made soon after, and three years later (238) he went to Spain, taking his young son, HANNIBAL, with him. In Spain he was successful, and had conquered the whole southern and eastern parts when he was killed in battle (229 B.C.)

HAM'IL·TON, a city of S. Canada, at the W. end of Lake Ontario; pop. 43,000, or about as large as Savannah, Ga. It is noted for its manufactures, especially of iron-ware, machinery, agricultural implements, sewing-machines, cotton and woollen cloths, and glassware. The surrounding country contains many fine farms.

HAMILTON, a city of S. W. Ohio on the Miami River; pop. 18,000, or about as large as Columbus, Ga. It is noted for its manufactures, especially of iron-ware, paper, woollen goods, flour, beer, ploughs, and railroad supplies. The surrounding country is very fertile, and a large trade is carried on in farm products.

HAMILTON, Alexander, a famous American statesman, born in the island of Nevis, West Indies, Jan. 11, 1757. His father, a merchant, failed in business and became very poor, and young Hamilton was cared for by his relations who sent him to New York, where he entered King's College (now Columbia). While studying there the Revolutionary War broke out, and Hamilton immediately sided with the Americans. He made speeches and wrote against the English, and though only seventeen years old became quite famous in the city. He joined a company of soldiers, and in 1776, when nineteen years old, was made a captain of artillery. He took part in several battles, and soon attracted the attention of Washington, who made him his aide-de-camp (1777). Washington em-

Alexander Hamilton.

ployed him in writing important letters, and though he was so young, Hamilton conducted the most delicate business with great skill and wisdom. In 1780 he resigned his position, because Washington had given him a reproof, which he thought undeserved. Washington afterward apologized for this, and Hamilton remained his close friend, but would not take his old position again, though he remained in the army.

When the war closed he became a lawyer in New York City, and soon became very successful. He took great interest in politics, and held several offices, and was one of the convention which met in Philadelphia (1787) to form a constitution for the United States. When Washington became President he chose Hamilton to be the first Secretary of the Treasury. He resigned in 1795 and returned to New York. At that time the two great political parties were called Federalists and Republicans. For a long time Hamilton was one of the most noted men of the Federalist party, and he was bitterly opposed by Jefferson, Aaron BURR, and others of the Republican side. Burr became angry at Hamilton because he thought he had defeated him in the election for governor, and challenged him to fight a duel. The duel took place at Weehawken, New Jersey, opposite New York, and Hamilton received a wound of which he died the next day, aged forty-seven years (July 12, 1804).

HAM'LET, a prince of Denmark, well known as the hero of one of Shakespeare's greatest plays. The time when he lived is not known ; some people say about 500 B.C., others A.D. 700. His grave is shown at Elsinore, the scene of Shakespeare's play, and there is a garden near by which is called Hamlet's Garden. Some historians say that he was king of Denmark for several years ; but others think that he never lived at all.

HAMMERFEST (*hahm'er-fest*), a seaport of N. Norway ; pop. about 2000. It is noted as being the most northern town in Europe. The climate, especially in winter, is very cold, and for two months the sun does not rise at all ; but one of the days in summer is two months long. Most of the people are engaged in cod fishing, and the principal trade is in cod-fish, cod-liver oil, furs, and walrus teeth. Hammerfest means the "rock fortress."

HAMP'DEN, John, a noted English statesman, born in London in 1594. He belonged to an old and rich family in Buckinghamshire, and was cousin to Oliver Cromwell. When twenty - seven years old he was elected to Parliament, and soon showed himself to be a strong lover of liberty. When King Charles I. tried to raise money by laying a tax on the people without consent of Parliament, Hampden refused to pay his share, and was thrown into prison. But he was soon freed and was elected to the new Parliament, where he continued to oppose the acts of the king. Hampden became the most popular man in England, and in the famous Long Parliament (1640) he was the leader of the people's party. In 1642 King Charles tried to arrest Hampden and four other members of Parliament on a charge of treason, but they escaped, and this act roused the people, who loved Hampden, to arms. When the civil war broke out (1642) he raised a regiment in his own county and marched against the king, and in several battles showed great bravery. In a fierce skirmish at Chalgrove he received a severe wound, of which he died six days later, when forty-nine years old (June 24, 1643).

HAN'COCK, John, a noted American statesman, born in Quincy, Mass., Jan. 12, 1737. He was graduated at Harvard College in 1754, and became a merchant and heir to a large fortune. He had strong common sense, and when the troubles began before the Revolution, took sides with the people. He was president of the body of men called the Provincial Congress, which met at Concord, Mass., in 1774, to prepare to fight if necessary for the rights of the colonies. The British called him an "arch rebel," and made many unsuccessful efforts to take him prisoner. In 1775 he was made president of the Continental Congress, which met in Philadelphia, and by which Washington was elected commander-in-chief of the American army. Hancock was the first signer of the Declaration of Independence, July 4,

John Hancock.

1776 In 1780 he was elected first governor of Massachusetts, and he was re-elected almost every year afterward until his death. He died at Quincy when fifty-six years old (Oct. 8, 1793).

HANCOCK, Winfield Scott, an American general, born in Montgomery Co., Penn., Feb. 14, 1824. He was graduated at West Point in 1844. He served first in the Indian territory, and then in the war with Mexico, taking part in the battles of San Antonio, Churubusco, Molino del Rey, and in the capture of the City of Mexico. He was in California when the Civil War broke out, but was recalled to Washington and made a brigadier-general (Sept. 23, 1861). He aided Gen. McClellan in his campaign in the Peninsula, and took part in the siege of Yorktown and the battles of Williamsburg, Frazer's Farm, and other engagements. In the Maryland campaign he fought at South Mountain and Antietam, and having been made a major-general of volunteers (Nov. 29, 1862), commanded a division at Fredericksburg, Marye's Heights, and Chancellorsville. On the first

day of the battle of Gettysburg (July 1, 1863), Gen. Meade sent Hancock to decide whether the battle should be fought there or the army should fall back to another place. Hancock decided that Gettysburg was the place for the fight, and on the two following days he commanded the principal point of attack, repulsed the grand last assault of Lee's army, and fell badly wounded in the moment of victory. For his gallantry there he was given the thanks of Congress.

In the campaign of 1864, though suffering from his wound, he bore a prominent part in the battles of the Wilderness, Spottsylvania Court House, North Anna, Cold Harbor, and in the assault on Petersburg. After the war he was in command of several departments at different times, and finally (1872) of the Department of the East. He received many votes for the Presidential nom-

Winfield Scott Hancock.

ination in 1868, and in 1880 was nominated for President, but was defeated by James A. GARFIELD. He died at Governor's Island, N. Y., aged sixty-two years (Feb. 9, 1886).

HÄNDEL, Georg Friedrich, born in Halle, Germany, Feb. 23, 1685. His father wanted him to be a doctor, and forbade him to play any instrument; but the boy secretly taught himself to play on an old spinet in the garret. When eight years old he was heard playing on the chapel organ, and his father was so delighted with his skill that he permitted him to study music. In 1710 he became chapel-master to the Elector of Hanover, afterwards George I. of England, and this took him to London, where most of his after life was spent. He became one of the greatest musicians that ever lived, and wrote a large number of works, among them more than fifty operas ; but he is best known for his grand oratorios, the most famous of which are *The Messiah*, *Israel in Egypt*, *Judas Maccabæus*, and *Samson*. He died in London when seventy-four years old (April 14, 1759), and was buried in Westminster Abbey.

HAN'NI·BAL, a famous Carthaginian general, born in 247 B.C. When his father, HAMILCAR BARKA, set out to conquer Spain, he took Hannibal with him, then a boy only nine years old. Before starting the old warrior made his son swear on the altar to always hate the Romans. After Hamilcar and his son-in-law HASDRUBAL had both been killed in Spain, Hannibal became leader there, and after a few other victories captured the city of Saguntum, a Greek city but an ally of Rome. Rome demanded that the young general should be given up to them for this act, and when this was refused they declared war against CARTHAGE, and thus began the Second Punic War. Hannibal did not wait for the Romans to attack him, but went to meet them. The ALPS were between him and his enemies, but he climbed them with his heavily armed soldiers and his horses and elephants, and in a short time was in northern Italy. The Romans were so taken by surprise that they were badly beaten in several small engagements, and finally in two great battles, at THRASYMENUS and CANNÆ. It is thought that if the Carthaginians had then gone on to Rome the city would have fallen, but they stayed at

CAPUA and enjoyed so much the gayeties of that place that it proved fatal to them. The Romans recovered from their fear, and gave Hannibal some hard hits, but they could not get him out of their country. They then determined to carry the war into Africa, and Scipio, who had already won back Spain, was sent with an army against Carthage. When Hannibal heard of this he had to leave Italy, where he had been fifteen years, and take his soldiers home to defend it. He met Scipio at the battle of Zama (202),

Hannibal.

and was badly beaten. The Romans then made peace with Carthage, but were very hard in their terms.

Hannibal then became the chief man in Carthage, and tried to bring about many reforms, but he had enemies who complained of him to the Romans, and even sought his life. He fled to the court of ANTIOCHUS the Great, of Syria, and stirred him up to make war on the Romans. When Antiochus was defeated the Romans asked him to give up Hannibal, who fled to the court of Prusias, King of Bithynia (187). The Romans told Prusias he must surrender him, and he was about to do so when Hannibal, determined not to become a slave of his old enemies, took poison, and died in Nicomedia, when sixty-four years old (183 B.C.).

HAN'NI-BAL, a city of N. E. Missouri, on the Mississippi River ; pop. 13,000, or about as large as Dover, N. H. A fine railroad and wagon bridge crosses the river there, and several railroads meet in the city. There is an important trade, especially in lumber, tobacco, pork, and flour. Near the city are many coal-mines and lime-kilns. Hannibal College has about 100 students.

HAN'NO, a famous Carthaginian navigator, supposed to have lived about 500 B.C. He was sent on a voyage of discovery along the western coast of Africa, with sixty vessels of fifty oars each. On his return to Carthage he caused an account of the voyage to be written on a tablet, called a *Periplus*. From this, of which a Greek translation has been preserved, we know that he built a city near the Strait of Gibraltar, and others on the coast reaching to Cape Bojador. He tells, too, of human beings, like animals, covered with hair, which are thought by some to have been gorillas (C. C.T., 24, I., l.).

HAN'O-VER, a city of N.W. Germany, in Prussia, 64 miles S.E. of Bremen; pop. 140,000, or a little smaller than Omaha, Neb. It was formerly the capital of the kingdom of Hanover, which was ruled by the kings of England, from George I. to William IV. Victoria could not become Queen of Hanover, because by the laws of that country no woman could inherit the throne; so the brother of William IV., being next heir, was made king of Hanover. His son, George V., sided with Austria in the war against Prussia, in 1866 ; and when the Austrians were conquered the city was taken by the Prussians, and the kingdom of Hanover became a prov-

ince of Prussia (1866). The old royal palace is still standing, and there is a fine royal library. The city has many manufactories.

HAN'O-VER, House of, one of the oldest families in Germany, a branch of which holds the throne of Great Britain. The province of Hanover belonged from ancient times to the family of Brunswick-Lüneburg, and for this reason this line of English sovereigns is sometimes called the House of Brunswick. Their right to the throne of England comes from Sophia, the granddaughter of James I., who married the elector of Hanover, and whose son became king of England (1712) under the title of George I. There were many others to claim the throne nearer than George I., but they were all Roman Catholics, and Parliament, to shut them out, passed a law called the Act of Settlement, giving the crown to the descendants of Sophia, electress of Hanover. England has had six sovereigns of this line, the four Georges, William IV., and Victoria. The Hanoverian rulers of England have had less talent than any of the lines before them, and most of them have been immoral in their lives. An English writer has written these lines on the four Georges:

" George the First was very vile,
   George the Second viler,
   And no mortal ever heard
   Any good of George the Third.
   When George the Fourth the throne descended,
   Heaven be praised, the Georges ended."

England and Hanover had one ruler until the time of Victoria, when the crown of Hanover went to Ernest Augustus, a son of George III. In 1866 it was conquered by Prussia, and made a province of that country.

HAPS'BURG, or **Habs'burg, House of,** named from a ruined castle of Switzerland called Habichtsburg, or Hawk's Castle, on the right bank of the River Aar. Two square towers of this castle are all that remain standing, on a steep hill now belonging to a farmer, the family of Hapsburg having lost their Swiss possessions in the fourteenth century, when the Swiss Confederation was formed. The first Count of Hapsburg was Werner, who died in 1096, the year of the First Crusade, but RUDOLPH I. is considered the founder of the family. After his election to the imperial crown he waged a war with his rival, Ottocar, King of Bohemia, and took possession of his provinces of Austria, Styria, and Carniola, for his sons. In this way the family was transplanted from Switzerland to Austria. The most distinguished of this house were CHARLES V., and the Empress Queen MARIA THERESA. From 1438 to 1806 the imperial crown was held by members of this family, branches of which have ruled in Spain and in other countries. The Hapsburgs have always been firm upholders of the Roman Catholic Church. The present Emperor of Austria is a Hapsburg.

HAR-DEE', William J., an American soldier, born in Savannah, Ga., in 1818. After serving in the Florida and Mexican wars, and in the West, he became a teacher of military tactics—that is, of the drilling of soldiers—at West Point, where he had been graduated. He also wrote a book of tactics, called "Hardee's Tactics," which was long used in our army. When the Civil War broke out he became a general in the Confederate army. He died when fifty-five years old (Nov. 6, 1873).

HARFLEUR (*har-flur'*), a town of N. W. France, on the little River Légarde, 2 miles W. of the Seine; pop. 2000. It was formerly one of the principal seaports of France, and was defended by strong walls. In 1415 it was captured by the English King Henry V.; the English were driven out in 1433, but they recaptured the town and kept it until 1450. The town is chiefly noted for its fine old Gothic church.

HAR'OLD I., called Harefoot from his swiftness in running, King of the Anglo-Saxons. He was the second son of CANUTE. When Canute died the Danes wanted Harold to be king, while the Saxons preferred his younger brother, Hardicanute, because he was the son of a Saxon princess. But Harold seized the crown and got possession of all England. He died at Oxford (March 17, 1040), and was succeeded by Hardicanute.

HAROLD II., the last of the Anglo-Saxon kings, son of Godwin, Earl of Wessex. He was a leader in the armies of EDWARD THE CONFESSOR, and did good service in Scotland and Wales. About 1065 he was shipwrecked on the French coast, taken prisoner, and sent to William, Duke of Normandy, who would not let him go until he had sworn to help him get the throne of England when Edward should die. But as soon as Edward died Harold had himself crowned, Jan. 10, 1066. Duke William sent and asked him to give up the crown, but Harold refused, and William and his barons then prepared to invade England. Harold's brother, Tostig, aided by the King of Norway, Harold Hardrada, also invaded England. Harold marched against them and defeated them in a battle near York, in which both Tostig and the King of Norway were killed, Sept. 25, 1066. A few days later the Duke of Normandy landed in England. Harold went to meet him, and a bloody battle was fought near Hastings, in which Harold was killed (Oct. 14, 1066).

HAROUN AL RASHID (*hah'-roon ahl rahsh'id*), a famous Caliph of Bagdad, the fifth of the ABBASSIDES, born about 765. His name means Aaron the Just. During his father's reign he invaded the Eastern Empire, ruled by Irene, and encamped opposite Constantinople, and at last forced the empress to agree to pay a large sum in gold every year. Whenever after this the tribute was not paid he would attack and lay waste her territory. In 786 he succeeded his elder brother Hadi, and under him the caliphate became noted for its splendor. He had two ministers, Yahia and his son Giaffar, who helped him greatly in his government, in his wars, and in making his court the centre of learning and civilization. But in 803 he suddenly turned against them, deprived them and all their family of their rank and fortune, and had them either imprisoned or put to death. He is the hero of many of the stories in the "Arabian Nights." He died in 809.

HAR'PER'S FER'RY, a town in the N. E. part of West Virginia, on the Potomac River, at the mouth of the Shenandoah; pop. 2500. The river at this place passes through the Blue Ridge, between high, rocky banks, which are noted for the grandeur of their scenery. Before the Civil War the United States had a large armory and arsenal at Harper's Ferry, which was taken and held for nearly a day by John Brown and his companions (Oct. 16, 1859). At the beginning of the war the armory was partly burned by the Confederates. In 1862 a Union army of 12,000 men was stationed at Harper's Ferry, under the command of Colonel Miles. A much larger Confederate army surrounded it, firing into the town from the heights above it, until Col. Miles and his army were obliged to surrender (Sept. 15, 1862). Col. Miles was mortally wounded almost at the moment of surrender.

HAR'RIS BURG, a city, capital of Pennsylvania, on the Susquehanna River; pop. 39,000, or about as large as Kansas City, Kans. It has wide, shady streets, and many fine houses. The surrounding country is very fertile, and is noted for its beautiful scenery. It abounds in coal and iron, which are used in the city for large iron-foundries, rolling-mills, and other factories. Harrisburg was founded about 1726 by an Eng-

lishman, John Harris. It became the State capital in 1812.

HAR'RI SON, Benjamin, elected Nov. 6, 1888, twenty-third President of the United States. Born Aug. 20, 1833, at North Bend, Ohio, the home of WILLIAM HENRY HARRISON, his grandfather. Graduated at Miami University, Oxford,

Benjamin Harrison.

Ohio, 1852. Studied law in Cincinnati, and began practice in Indianapolis, 1854. Entered the Union Army as lieutenant in 1862. Led brigades in the Atlanta campaign and in the fighting around Nashville, then was with SHERMAN till the close of the war. Went home brevet brigadier-general, and resumed the practice of law. Defeated as candidate for governor of Indiana in 1876; elected to the United States Senate in 1881.

HARRISON, William Henry, ninth President of the United States, born in Berkeley, Va., Feb. 9, 1773. He joined the army when nineteen years old, and fought against the Indians under General Wayne. In 1801 he became governor of the new Territory of Indiana, which belonged almost entirely to the Indians. He made treaties with them by which a great deal of land was gained for the government. Harrison was a general in the war of 1812, and won so great a reputation that it led to his being elected President in 1840. He died just one month

William Henry Harrison.

after taking the oath of office, when sixty-eight years old (April 4, 1841).

HART, James McDougal, an American landscape-painter, born at Kilmarnock, Scotland, in 1828. Like his brother, he learned the trade of a coachmaker, but soon gave it up to practise art. His studio is in New York.

HART, William, an American landscape-painter, brother of James McD. Hart, born at Paisley, Scotland, in 1823. He came to this country in his boyhood, and his first pictures were painted on coaches and window-shades. For many years he has had a studio in New York.

HARTE (*hart*), **Francis Bret,** a noted American writer, born in Albany, New York, Aug. 25, 1839. When fifteen years old he went to California, where he dug gold, taught school, was express agent, set types in a printing-office, and became editor of a newspaper. He then started a magazine, called the "Overland Monthly," and wrote two stories, called "The Luck of Roaring Camp" and "The Outcasts of Poker Flat," which were much talked about and liked. In 1870 he wrote a poem called "Plain Language from Truthful James,"

but which is commonly known as "The Heathen Chinee," which made him known everywhere. It was published over and over again, and Bret Harte found himself famous. He has since published many other poems and stories. In 1878 he was sent as United States Consul to Crefeld, Germany, and in 1880 to Glasgow, Scotland, where he remained until 1885. He now resides in London.

HART'FORD, a city, capital of Connecticut, near the middle of the State, on the Connecticut River, 50 miles from its mouth; pop. 53,000, or a little larger than St. Joseph, Mo. Hartford is noted for its manufactures, especially of steam-engines, carriages, sewing-machines, silk, hardware, screws, gold pens, spectacles, pistols, and rifles. The works of the Colt Firearms Company cover one hundred and twenty-three acres of ground. The city is also celebrated for its fine libraries and schools, and for its great insurance companies, which have agents all over the United States. It is the seat of Trinity College.

Hartford was founded in 1635, and named after Hartford in England. It has been a city since 1784.

HAS'DRU-BAL, a Carthaginian general, son-in-law of Hamilcar, and his successor (229 B.C.) in command of the Carthaginian army in Spain. With the aid of his young brother-in-law, Hannibal, he continued the conquests of Hamilcar, and founded the city of New Carthage, now called Carthagena. He governed in Spain for eight years, when he was assassinated (221 B.C.).

HASDRUBAL, a Carthaginian general, brother of Hannibal. He commanded in Spain when Hannibal crossed the Alps into Italy. He fought against the Romans in Spain with various success until 211, when he defeated Publius and Cneius Cornelius Scipio in a battle in which both the Roman commanders were killed. Several years afterward he crossed the Pyrenees to carry reinforcements to Hannibal, but was defeated and killed on the banks of the Metaurus by the Romans under CLAUDIUS NERO.

HASDRUBAL, a Carthaginian general, who fought against the Romans in Africa in the Third Punic War, and defeated them twice. When Scipio Africanus the Younger had taken Carthage and was destroying it (147 B.C.), Hasdrubal went into Scipio's camp to beg for mercy. The conqueror spared his life, but forced him to show himself to the defenders of the city which he had deserted, and he saw his wife throw herself and her children into the flames of the burning temple of Æsculapius. He was taken captive to Italy, where he died.

HAS'TINGS, a famous viking or sea rover of the NORTHMEN, born about 812. He was the leader of a band of pirates, dreaded on land and sea, who attacked chiefly France, Spain, and the islands in the Mediterranean. Once he planned to go to Rome, and sailed along till he came to the Gulf of Spezia. In the distance he saw a city, and thinking it was Rome he landed and sent to ask permission to enter its gates that he might refit his ships. He also sent word that he wished to become a Christian and quit his roving life. The count and bishop of the city came out and baptized him, but they would not let him or his men enter the city. He then pretended to be dead, and his men made a long funeral procession and bore him on a bier to the city gates. They were admitted ; but as soon as the bier was placed before the altar of the cathedral, the chief sprang up and knocked the bishop over, and his men drew their swords and rushing to the gates let in the rest of his followers. They won the town, and then learned that it was not Rome, but a place called Luna. He afterward went to England and sailed up the Thames as far as Gravesend ; but he was driven back by ALFRED

THE GREAT. The last that we know of him is that he went back to Denmark when he was about seventy years old.

HAVANA (*hav-an'nah*), a city, capital of Cuba, on a beautiful bay of the N.W. coast of the island ; pop. 199,000, or not quite as large as Milwaukee, Wis. Next to New York it is the most important port of the Western Continent, being especially noted for its trade in sugar and tobacco. The tobacco is the finest in the world, and it is said that nearly three million cigarettes are made in the city every day. The harbor of Havana is defended by six forts, one of which is called Moro Castle. The houses are built of stone, painted with bright colors, and there are many beautiful public parks and promenades, adorned with rich tropical plants. The climate is warm but pleasant during the winter. In the summer it is hot, and Havana is then the chief centre of yellow fever. The people are Spanish whites, negroes, and mulattoes.

Havana, or, in Spanish, Habana, means a harbor. The city was founded by the Spaniards in 1519. The body of Columbus, which was first buried in Santo Domingo, was removed in 1796 to the Cathedral of Havana.

HAV'E-LOCK, Sir Henry, an English general, born in Durham, April 5, 1795. He entered the army in 1815, was engaged in several wars, and wrote histories of the wars in Burmah and Afghanistan. When the Sepoy rebellion broke out in India, Havelock was sent with an army to help the English garrison at Cawnpore, which was besieged by the rebels under Nana Sahib (July, 1857). Before he arrived the English had been massacred, but he defeated the Nana several times. He was joined in September by Gen. Outram, who, though his rank was higher than Havelock's, consented to fight under him. They marched to Lucknow, fighting their way through thousands of rebels who had surrounded the brave little garrison there. As they approached the fort where the garrison was shut in, the bagpipers of the Scotch regiments played " The Campbells are Coming," and the garrison heard them, and hastened to let their friends in (Sept. 25, 1857). The English had still to withstand a long siege, but on November 22 they escaped toward Cawnpore. Gen. Havelock's health had been broken by fatigue and exposure, and he died on the march, when sixty-two years old (Nov. 25, 1857). Before the news reached England he had been made a baronet, on the day after his death ; the title was given to his son, with nearly $5000 a year for his life.

HAVERHILL (*hav'er-ill*), a city of Massachusetts, on the Merrimack River, 27 miles N. of Boston ; pop. 27,000, or about as large as Houston, Tex. It is noted for its manufacture of boots and shoes, in which it surpasses every other place in the country except LYNN. About 8000 persons are employed in the shoe factories. Haverhill was settled about 1640, and became a city in 1870.

HAVRE (*hahv'r*), a city of France, on the English Channel ; pop. 112,-000, or about twice as large as Lynn, Mass. It is the most important seaport in France except Marseilles, many steamers and ships sailing from there to the United States and other parts of the world. The finest vessels made in France are built in the ship yards of Havre. In the summer many people go there to bathe in the sea. Havre, in French, means a harbor. The city was founded in the beginning of the 16th century by King Louis XII. The English took it in 1562.

HAWAI'AN (*hah-wi'e-an*) or **Sandwich Islands,** a group of twelve islands in the Pacific Ocean, between Mexico and China ; area, 6100 square miles, or about three fourths as large as New Jersey ; pop. 81,000, or about half that of Jersey City ; capital, HONOLULU. The largest island is Hawaii, it being about two thirds the size of all the islands together. All are mountainous and volcanic, and are more or less covered with forests, with many beautiful valleys near the seashore. On Hawaii is an active volcano, called Mauna Loa, which is about two and a half miles high, and is noted for its terrible eruptions. The crater at its top is not always active, but it has another, on its side, called Kilauea, which is always burning. It is the largest burning crater in the world, being eight miles around and a fifth of a mile deep, or about seven times as deep as Niagara Falls are high. To reach it the traveller has to ride over many miles of rough lava-beds, and all of a sudden, without going up hill much, he comes to the edge of this great abyss, which looks large enough to put a whole city in. Far down on the bottom the lava floor shines like black satin, and three miles away rise a few slender columns of smoke. But in the night these columns of smoke look like pillars of fire, and the heavens above are so ablaze with their glow that it is seen on ships a hundred miles at sea. All these rise from a pit of boiling lava, near the middle of the crater, called by the people *hale-mau-mau*, or House of Everlasting Fire. It is a great lake of bubbling, hissing lava, which is all the time groaning and heaving and spouting up fiery red jets. Occasionally the edges crack and fall in, and are at once devoured by the angry flood. All around are cracks from which steam is ever rising, and in which food may be quickly cooked. Sometimes the lake boils over, and then one can dip up the melted lava and mould it into any shape ; and sometimes the lava overflows the great crater and runs across many miles of country into the ocean.

The climate of the Hawaiian Islands is warm and pleasant. The principal things raised are sugar, rice, coffee, cotton, tobacco, maize, and arrowroot ; and almost all fruits grow well. A kind of root called taro, from which bread is made, is the principal food of the inhabitants. The natives are a brown race, very good natured and intelligent, but rather lazy. Nearly all can read and write their language, which is so simple that it is written with twelve letters. They are skilled in swimming and in the use of canoes, and make good sailors. Many white people now live among them, and the native race is dying out. The islands are governed by a king and a parliament chosen by the people. The principal trade is in sugar.

The Hawaiian Islands were discovered by the Spaniards two hundred years ago, and rediscovered by Captain Cook in 1778. At that time the natives were savages and idolaters, and they killed COOK. Since 1820 most of the natives have been Christian, and they have now many schools and churches.

HAW'KINS, Sir John, a noted English navigator, born in Plymouth about 1520. He was one of the first Englishmen to carry on the slave trade, in which so little shame was seen in those days that Queen Elizabeth allowed him to use as the crest of his coat-of-arms a Moor bound. He afterward became noted in fighting the Spaniards, was a rear-admiral in the great struggle with the Spanish Armada, and commanded expeditions with FROBISHER and DRAKE. He died at sea in the West Indies, when seventy-five years old (Nov. 21, 1595).

HAW'THORNE, Julian, a noted American writer of novels, son of Nathaniel Hawthorne, born in Boston, June 22, 1846. He studied in Harvard College and in the scientific school of that university, and became a civil engineer. In 1871

he began to write stories, and in 1873 published a novel called "Bressant." He has since written many others.

HAWTHORNE, Nathaniel, a famous American author, born in Salem, Mass., July 4, 1804. His father, a shipmaster, died when Nathaniel was four years old ; and his mother took his loss so much to heart that for the rest of her life (thirty years) she took all her meals alone in her own room. Her little boy thus led a very lonely life ; he grew up by himself, and perhaps this is the reason that he always loved to be alone. He was graduated at

Nathaniel Hawthorne.

Bowdoin College when twenty-one years old, and afterward, for many years, lived in Salem, apart from everybody, even his own household ; he used to walk out by night, and passed days in his own room writing wild tales, some of which he burned, and others were published without his name. He was very shy and afraid of company.

In 1837 he collected many of his stories, and published them under the title of "Twice-Told Tales," so named because they had been published before in magazines and newspapers. After living in Boston a few years he went to CONCORD, and made his home in an old parsonage, from the windows of which the minister of the town is said to have looked out on the battle fought by his people with the British in the first days of the Revolution. He tells about his life in this house, called the "Old Manse," in his book entitled "Mosses from an Old Manse."

Mr. Hawthorne next lived in Salem, which he tells about in his stories of "The Scarlet Letter" and the "House of the Seven Gables." About the same time he published "The Wonder Book for Boys and Girls" and "The Tanglewood Tales," both of which are very interesting. In after days, when he had travelled in Europe, he wrote his longest story, called "The Marble Faun," which gives a true and good idea of the city of Rome. Hawthorne died in Plymouth, New Hampshire, when nearly sixty years old (May 19, 1864).

HAY'DEN, Ferdinand Vandeveer, an American geologist, born in Westfield, Mass., Sept. 7, 1829. He studied to be a physician, but soon began to make geological explorations in the Western Territories, first at his own expense, and afterward for the Smithsonian Institution. During the Civil War he was a medical officer in the army. In 1867 he was made chief of the United States geological survey of the Territories, an office which he held for many years. Dr. Hayden visited many wild regions near the Rocky Mountains, and was the first to make a careful exploration of northwestern Wyoming, and to propose that it should be made a national park. He published many reports of explorations and articles for scientific journals. He died when fifty-eight years old (Dec. 22, 1887).

HAYDN (*hayd'n*), **Joseph,** a famous German writer of music, born at Rohran, Lower Austria, March 31, 1732. His father was a wheelwright, his mother a cook in a nobleman's family ; both were musical, and when only five years old little Joseph used to stand by his parents and join in the family concerts, with a piece of wood in each hand, one serving for a violin, the other for a bow. A cousin of the family named Frank, who was a music teacher, noticed the boy's talent and undertook to teach him all that he knew. It was at his house that Haydn saw Reuter, the chapel-master of the cathedral in Vienna ; he was looking out for choir-boys, and gave the lad a chant to sing at sight ; he was surprised at the beauty of his voice, but only said, "It is a pity you don't know how to shake." The boy replied quickly, "How could you expect me to shake when my cousin does not know how to do it himself?" "Come here," said Reuter, "and I will teach you." In one lesson the child made a good shake, and Reuter was so pleased that he filled his pockets with fine cherries. When Haydn grew to be a great man he loved to tell this story, and said that he always fancied he had the beautiful cherries in his mouth whenever he happened to shake.

Haydn was one of the greatest musical authors. In fifty years he wrote 527 pieces of music. The last time he appeared in public was to hear the performance of his great work, "The Creation." In the midst of storms of applause he was seized with faintness, and had to be taken out in a large chair ; as he was leaving he turned to the orchestra, and with tears streaming down his cheeks, he stretched out his hands as if to bless them. This was his farewell to the world. He died in Vienna when seventy-seven years old (May 31, 1809).

HAYES (*haze*), **Isaac Israel,** a noted American Arctic explorer, born in Chester Co., Penn., March 5, 1832. He became a physician, and was surgeon in the second Grinnell expedition to the Arctic regions under Doctor KANE. He started from Boston, in 1860, in command of the schooner United States, in search of the polar sea, sailed as far as he could, and then went on in sledges and open boats. Soon he had to send the boats back, and he and three companions, with two dog-sledges, pushed on till their food gave out, when they had to turn back, although they could see open water beyond. In 1869 he explored the shores of Greenland. He wrote several interesting books about his adventures. He died when forty nine years old (Dec. 17, 1881).

HAYES, Rutherford Birchard, nineteenth President of the United States, born in Delaware, Ohio, Oct. 4, 1822. He was graduated at Kenyon College in 1842, and became a lawyer. He served in the Civil War, became a general of volunteers, and resigned in 1865, when he was elected to Congress. In 1867, 1869, and 1875, he was elected Governor of Ohio. In 1876 he was nominated by the Republican Party for President of the United States, and Samuel J. Tilden was nominated by the Democratic Party. In the election 184 Democratic and 173 Republican electors were unquestionably chosen, but the 4 votes of Florida and the 8 votes of Louisiana were claimed by both parties. In each of those States the votes were required by law to be counted by officers called a Returning Board ; and the Returning Boards, which were made up of Republicans, declared that the Republican electors had been elected. The Democrats claimed that the Returning Boards had fraudulently refused to count a large number of Democratic votes, and asked Congress to refuse to accept their decision. To avoid a possible civil war, an act called the Electoral Commission Act was passed by Congress, which created a body called an Electoral Commission, made up of five Senators, five Rep-

resentatives, and five Justices of the Supreme Court. This commission, which was made up of eight Republicans and seven Democrats, decided that the votes must be counted as they came from the officers of the States, and that it had

Rutherford B. Hayes.

no power to examine them, the eight Republicans voting in favor of it and the seven Democrats against it. So Mr. Hayes was declared to have received 185 votes, and to have been elected President by one vote over Mr. Tilden.

HAYTI (*hay'te*), an island of the West Indies, S. E. of Cuba ; area, 28,000 square miles, or about a third as large as Minnesota; pop. about 960,000, or about as large as Maine and Vermont together. Excepting Cuba, it is the largest and most beautiful of the West India Islands. It is crossed from west to east by three chains of mountains, with rich valleys and plains between them. The forests, with which much of the country is covered, furnish cabinet and dye woods, gums, and medicines ; and oranges, bananas, and other fruits, and many flowers grow around most of the houses. The climate, though hot on the coast, is cool and pleasant among the mountains ; but hurricanes are frequent on the south coast, and often blow down trees and houses.

The Indians called the island Haïti (*hah'e-te*), or "mountainous country." When Columbus landed (Dec. 6, 1492) he called it Espagñola (Little Spain), which in Latin is Hispaniola. The first European settlements in the New World were made on it. The Spaniards held the whole island until 1697, when the French got the west part, and called it Saint Domingue. In 1795 France got the rest of the island, and the name Saint Domingue was then given to the whole of it. Under TOUSSAINT and other leaders the negroes finally drove the French out, made the island independent (1804), and gave it again its old name of Hayti. The Spaniards finally got back the east end, and called it Santo Domingo; but in 1844 this part became independent. The island is now divided into two republics— Hayti, where the people speak the French language, and Dominica, where Spanish is spoken.

Hayti is at the west end of the island; area, 10,000 square miles, or a little larger than Vermont; pop. 550,000, of whom nine tenths are negroes, and the rest mostly mulattoes; capital, PORT AU PRINCE. The chief things sent from there are coffee and cotton.

Dominica (*do-min'e-kah*) is at the east end of the island; area, 18,000 square miles, or about as large as New Hampshire, Massachusetts, and Rhode Island put together; pop. about 350,000, mostly mixed Spaniards, Indians, and negroes; capital, SANTO DOMINGO.

The chief things sent from there are tobacco and sugar.

HEBRIDES (*heb'ri-deez*), or **Western Islands,** the name given to the large group of islands off the W. coast of Scotland; total area, about 3000 square miles, or about a third as large as New Hampshire; pop. about 100,000, or about two sevenths that of New Hampshire. There are several hundred of these islands, but some are very small,

Fingal's Cave.

and only about one hundred and twenty have people on them. The largest are Lewis, Skye, Mull, and Islay; all are rugged and rocky. The people are like the Scotch, but many speak only Gaelic. They raise curious little black cattle, and catch fish on the coasts. Many travellers go to the Hebrides to visit Fingal's Cave, on the little island of Staffa. The sides and roof of this cave are formed of natural stone columns, and some parts look like a Gothic church. The sea covers the floor, so that people can enter only in boats, the water being twenty feet deep even at low tide.

HECATE (*hek'a-te*), in Greek fable, a goddess who had power on earth, in the sea, and in the heavens. She could give victory, wealth, and renown, as she wished, and was the guardian of families and children. She was generally represented with three heads.

HECLA (*hek'lah*). See ICELAND.

HEC'TOR. See ACHILLES.

HECUBA (*hek'u-bah*), second wife of Priam, King of Troy, and mother of HECTOR, PARIS, CASSANDRA, Creüsa, and other children. She was carried as a slave by the Greeks to Chersonesus, where, in one day, she saw her daughter, Polyxena, offered as a sacrifice, and the body of her murdered son, Polydorus, cast on the shore. In revenge she killed the two sons of Polymestor, his murderer, and tore out the eyes of their father.

HEIDELBERG (*hi'del-ba·erg*), a city of Germany, in Baden ; pop. 27,000, or about as large as Pawtucket, R. I. It is famous for its great university, which is 500 years old, and has 108 professors and more than 800 students. The library is one of the largest in Germany, and has many old manuscripts. In 1622, when the Bavarians captured Heidelberg, all the books were taken away and given to the Pope, who put them into the Vatican library at Rome. In 1797 thirty-eight of the best manuscripts were taken from Rome by Napoleon and given to the library of Paris, and those left in Rome were given back to the Heidelberg library, from which they had been taken almost 200 years before. The country around Heidelberg is very beautiful. Near the city is an old ruined castle, in the cellar of which is a great beer-barrel, once the largest in the world. To this day the people of Heidelberg make a great deal of beer.

HEINE (*hi'neh*), **Heinrich,** a famous German poet, born at Düsseldorf, Dec. 12, 1799. In his youth he was an excellent scholar, but disliked business. His uncle therefore sent him to study law, but his own wish was to be a writer. His first verses were published in 1822, and were not noticed much, but his after-writings, which ridiculed everything and slandered everybody, became so displeasing to the Prussian Government that he had to fly to Paris (1831), and he lived there most of the rest of his life. One of his most noted works is his " Buch der Lieder" (Book of Songs), which made him more widely known than any other German writer of his time. He wrote many other books in Paris, and died there when fifty-six years old (Feb. 17. 1856.)

HEL'EN, wife of MENELAUS, and the most beautiful woman among the Greeks. According to the poets, she was the daughter of Jupiter and Leda, and sister of CASTOR and POLLUX. She had suitors from all parts of Greece, but accepted Menelaus. Three years afterward she ran away with Paris to TROY. All the Greek princes then took up arms to help Menelaus get back his wife, and the consequence was the Trojan war. After the war Helen returned to Greece and was forgiven by her husband.

HELENA (*hel'e-nah*), **Saint,** wife of the Emperor Constantius Chlorus, and mother of CONSTANTINE THE GREAT, born at Drepanum, Bithynia, in A.D. 247. When Constantine became emperor, he wanted to have a high-born lady for his wife, so he put Helena away and married Theodora, the stepdaughter of the Emperor MAXIMIAN. But when her son Constantine became emperor (306) he gave his mother the title of Augusta—that is, noble—and made her live in his palace at Treves. When seventy-nine years old she went on a pilgrimage to Jerusalem, and built there the Church of the

Holy Sepulchre and that of the Nativity. There is a story that she found in Jerusalem, and brought to Europe, the true cross on which Christ was crucified. She died about 327, and her body was carried to Rome, where a splendid tomb was erected to her memory. She was afterward declared to be a saint.

HEL'I-CON, a range of mountains in Bœotia, Greece, N. of the Gulf of Corinth. The MUSES loved to live there in a beautiful grove sacred to them. Near it was the famous fountain of Aganippe, which inspired those who drank of its waters. Higher up was the well called Hippocrene, made by PEGASUS striking the ground with his hoof.

HELIGOLAND (*hel'e go-lahnd*), or **Helgoland,** an island in the North Sea, about forty miles from the coast of Germany ; pop. 2000. It is only about a mile long and a third of a mile wide. Part of it is low, and the rest is a table-land, with cliffs nearly all around it. Most of the people are descendants of the Frisians, an ancient tribe of Germany, and they still speak the Frisian language. The men are fishermen and sailors, and leave the care of their little farms to their wives and daughters. Heligoland formerly belonged to England, but was ceded to Germany in 1890. Heligoland means Holy Land. The name was given it, it is supposed, because in ancient times the Frisians had a temple of one of their gods on the island.

HELIOPOLIS (*he-le-op'o-lis*), a city of ancient Egypt, on the E. side of the delta of the River Nile. Its Egyptian name was On, or An, and in the Bible it is called Bethshemesh, but the Greeks called it Heliopolis, or City of the Sun, because the sun was worshipped there. Its priests were noted for their learning, and people went from Greece and other countries to study with them, as they would now go to a university. SOLON, THALES, and PLATO stud-

ied there. Heliopolis fell to decay. several hundred years before Christ Some of the ruins, which can still be seen there, are among the most ancient in Egypt. The obelisk now in Central Park, New York, once stood before the temple of the sun in Heliopolis.

HE'LI-OS, in Greek fable. the god of the sun, who gave light to gods and men. He had two beautiful palaces, one in the east and another in the west. No secrets could be hidden from him, for he saw and heard all things. He is represented riding in a chariot drawn by four horses, and surrounded by the hours and the seasons.

HEL'LE. See ARGONAUTS.

HEL'LES-PONT. See DARDANELLES.

HEL'SING-FORS, a city of Russia, capital of FINLAND ; pop. 58,000, or about as large as Camden, N. J. It has a fine harbor, guarded by the strong fortress of SVEABORG. The Alexander University, which has its seat there, is one of the best in Russia. There is also a military school, fine museums, and a botanical garden and observatory. The town has a large trade in grain, iron, timber, and fish.

Helsingfors was founded by King Gustavus I. of Sweden, in the 16th century, and it became the capital of Finland in 1819.

HEM'ANS, Felicia Dorothea, an English poet, born in Liverpool, Sept. 25, 1794. Her father, a merchant named Browne, met with losses in business when she was about seven years old, and went to live in a country place in Wales, where the rest of her childhood was passed. Before she was fifteen years old she published a volume of poems called '' Early Blossoms,'' which was not a success ; but in 1812 she published another, which won her some fame. The same year she married Captain Hemans. But they were not happy together, and in 1818 he left her, and she went with her five sons to live with her mother in Wales. There she wrote many sweet and tender poems, and became one of the most popular writers of her time. She died near Dublin, Ireland, when forty-one years old (May 12, 1835).

HENGIST (*heng'gist*) and **HORSA** (*hor'sah*), two Saxon chiefs, who, at the request of Vortigern, a British prince, came to aid the Britons against the Picts and Scots, who had overrun Britain. They drove away the Picts and Scots, and then turned upon the Britons themselves, and soon made themselves masters of a great part of the island. Hengist sent home for his daughter Rowena, who was young and beautiful, and at a feast which he gave for Vortigern, she acted as cupbearer. Vortigern fell in love with her and married her. The Britons tried to get rid of the Saxons, and in one battle between them Horsa was killed. But Hengist held his ground, and founded the kingdom of Kent, with CANTERBURY for his chief city. He died there about 488.

HENRY I., called Beauclerc (good scholar), third Norman King of England, born at Selby, Yorkshire, in 1068. He was the son of William I., the Conqueror, and succeeded his brother, William II., in 1100. His older brother, Robert, who was in the Holy Land, was the lawful heir to the throne, but Henry seized the crown and held on to it against all the attempts of Robert, and, after his death, of his son William, to regain it. He was a very shrewd monarch, and knew how to manage men and win them to his side. By his marriage with Matilda, daughter of the King of Scotland and niece of the Saxon Edgar Atheling, he secured the good-will of the Scots and Saxons, who helped him keep the throne he had so unlawfully won. His only son William having been drowned while crossing from France to England, he left his daughter Matilda as his heir. He

died at Rouen when sixty-seven years old (Dec. 1, 1135), and was succeeded by his nephew, Stephen, Count of Blois, who took Matilda's throne.

HENRY II., the first Plantagenet King of England, born in Le Mans, France, in March, 1113. He was the son of Geoffrey Plantagenet, Count of Anjou, and Matilda, daughter and heiress of Henry I. On the death of Stephen, Count of Blois, (1154), who had taken the throne rightfully belonging to Matilda, he became king of England. By his marriage with Eleanor, the divorced wife of the king of France, he became master of a third of France. His reign was eventful. He had troubles with the clergy, who did not want to be tried by the same courts of justice as other people, and which led to the murder of Thomas à BECKET, archbishop of Canterbury. Ireland was conquered in 1172, and has ever since been subject to England. The last years of Henry's life were made very sad by the undutiful conduct of his sons, whom their mother encouraged to rebel against him. He died at Chinon when fifty-six years old (July 16, 1189), and was succeeded by his son Richard I.

HENRY III., fourth Plantagenet King of England, born at Winchester, Oct. 1, 1207. He was the son of King John, and succeeded him in 1216. He reigned fifty-six years, longer than any other British monarch except George III. A great part of this time was spent in contests between the king and his barons, headed by Simon de Montfort, Earl of Leicester, who carried on this struggle to regain some of the privileges they had lost under Henry II. In one of these encounters the barons took the king prisoner, and he had to make with them such a treaty as suited them. The House of Commons may be said to date from this reign, as the Parliament called together by De Montfort was the first that admitted any besides nobles. Henry died at Westminster, when sixty-five years old (Nov. 16, 1272), and was succeeded by his son Edward I.

HENRY IV., first Lancastrian King of England, born at Bolingbroke, Apr. 4, 1366. He was the son of JOHN OF GAUNT, Duke of Lancaster, the fourth son of Edward III. He was banished from the kingdom by his cousin, King Richard II., who seized upon his immense estate ; but when Richard was absent in Ireland Henry determined to return to England and gain not only his own property but the English crown. The people had been disgusted by Richard's crimes and follies, and all classes joined him. When Richard came home he found himself without a crown and Henry's prisoner. He shortly afterward died, having been killed by Henry's order, it was said. Henry's entire reign was spent in putting down rebellions. so that he did not have much pleasure in wearing the crown, to win which he had done so much that was wrong. He died in Westminster when forty-seven years old (March 20, 1413), and was succeeded by Henry V., his son.

HENRY V., second Lancastrian King of England, born at Monmouth, Aug. 9, 1388. He was the son of Henry IV., and succeeded him in 1413. As Prince of Wales he was a favorite with the English people, and his coming to the throne was hailed with joy. The English have always been very proud of Henry V., and his bravery and gallant conduct have been admired by everybody. Seeing that France was in a disturbed state, he thought the time favorable for renewing the claim of his great grandfather, Edward III., to the French crown ; so he crossed the Channel and won the great victory of AGINCOURT in 1415. One of the two parties into which France was divided took his side, and a treaty was made saying that he

should be king on the death of the insane Charles VI., if he would marry the Princess Catherine, his daughter. This Henry did, but he did not live to be king of France. He died at Vincennes when thirty-four years old (Aug. 31, 1422), and was succeeded by his infant son, Henry VI.

HENRY VI., third and last Lancastrian King of England, born at Windsor, Dec. 6, 1421. He was the son of Henry V., and succeeded him when but nine months old, Sept. 1, 1422. The next month he was likewise proclaimed king of France, on the death of his grandfather, Charles VI. The poor babe soon lost his French possessions through the efforts of those who favored Charles VII., son of the late king, and his English crown caused him only sorrow his whole life long. Though son of the warlike Henry V., he was more fit to be a monk than a king, and those who remembered that his grandfather had stolen the crown, and thought his family had no right to it, now came out in defence of the Duke of York, who was descended from both the second and third sons of Edward III., Henry being descended from the fourth son. Still England had loved King Henry V., and many brave men gave up all they had in support of the cause of his son. The wars that went on about this lasted thirty years, and killed off almost all the old nobility. They are called the Wars of the Roses, because the badge of the House of Lancaster was a red rose and that of the House of York a white rose. At last, in 1461, Edward, Duke of York, was victorious, and was made king in place of Henry ; and ten years afterward (1471) Henry VI. was found dead in the Tower, where he had been imprisoned by his foes.

HENRY VII., first Tudor King of England, born in Wales, Jan. 21, 1450. He was the son of Edmund Tudor, Earl of Richmond, and Margaret Beaufort, great-granddaughter of John of Gaunt. After the death of Henry VI. the Lancastrians regarded him as the heir to the throne. During the reigns of Edward IV. and Richard III. he was in France. He came to England in 1485, and won the battle of BOSWORTH Field, depriving Richard of crown and life. He was a wise, prudent monarch, with a great talent for making money, but not always by lawful means. He married Elizabeth, heiress of the Yorkist claims to the throne, and united his two daughters to the kings of France and Scotland, and his son to the daughter of the King of Spain. He died at Richmond when fifty-three years old (April 22, 1509), and was succeeded by his son, Henry VIII.

HENRY VIII., second Tudor King of England, born at Greenwich, June 28, 1491. He was the son of Henry VII. and Elizabeth of York, and was the first English king since Richard II. whose claim no one disputed. He succeeded his father April 22, 1509. The reign of this king is one of the most important in English history, on account of the great questions that had to be decided. Wishing to marry Anne BOLEYN, a young lady of his court, Henry asked the Pope to have him separated from his wife, Catharine of Aragon, to whom he had been married nineteen years, on the ground that she had been the wife of his brother. The Pope would not do this, so he took the matter into his own hands, sent off Catharine and married Anne Boleyn. Having done this, he said that the Church of England should no longer be under the Pope, and passed a law called the Act of Supremacy, making himself the Head of the Church. For refusing to agree to this law, Sir Thomas MORE, one of England's best and greatest men, lost his life. Henry then went on making a great many changes in church matters, and obliged everybody to agree to them under penalty of death. One of the things that he did was to de-

stroy all the monasteries and give their lands to his noblemen. Many beautiful ruins of these buildings can still be seen. Henry was married six times. His wives were Catharine of Aragon, Anne Boleyn, Jane Seymour, Anne of Cleves, Catharine Howard, and Catharine Parr. The first and fourth he divorced, the second and fifth he beheaded, the third died a natural death, and the sixth outlived him. Henry VIII. has always been regarded as a monster of cruelty, but of late years some historians have made excuses for him, and shown that a great deal of good grew out of his reign. He died when fifty-five years old (Jan. 28, 1547), and was succeeded by his son, Edward VI.

HENRY I., third Capetian King of France, born about 1011. He was the son of Robert II., and succeeded him in 1031. He was a weak king, and his reign was much disturbed by civil wars and public calamities. One of his wars was with the Duke of Normandy, who had been his ally. This quarrel went down to their descendants. There was a terrible famine in France in his time. He died at Vitre when forty-nine years old (Aug. 4, 1060), and was succeeded by his son, Philip I.

HENRY II., tenth Valois King of France, born March 31, 1519. He was the son of Francis I., and succeeded him in 1547. He inherited not only his father's crown, but also his grudge against the House of Austria, so the old war still went on, at first with Charles V., and then with his son, Philip II. In these wars France gained little territory or credit. Finally he made with Philip the shameful treaty of Cateau-Cambrèsis, giving back all the places he had taken in Italy and the Netherlands. His wife was the famous Catharine de' Medici. On July 10, 1559, he was mortally wounded while tilting with one of his officers, and died in Paris when forty years old (July 10, 1559). He was succeeded by his son, Francis II., the husband of Mary Queen of Scots.

HENRY III., thirteenth and last Valois King of France, born in Fontainebleau, Sept. 19, 1551. He was the son of Henry II., and succeeded his brother, Charles IX., in 1575. He was elected King of Poland in 1573, but he and his Polish subjects did not like each other, and he was glad enough to go back to France, when his brother's death made him king of that country. A party was at once formed, called the League, under the Duke of Guise, to protect the Church, which the Roman Catholics thought not safe in this king's hands. Henry was fickle, and sometimes was with the League, and sometimes against it. He hated the Duke of Guise, and at last had him murdered, for which he was detested by all parties. He was at last himself stabbed in the back by a monk, Jacques Clément, who was put up to this act by the Guises. He died when thirty-eight years old (Aug. 2, 1589), and was succeeded by Henry IV., the first of the House of Bourbon.

HENRY IV., first BOURBON King of France, born at Pau, Dec. 14, 1553. He was the son of Antoine de Bourbon, a descendant of LOUIS IX. He became King of Navarre in 1572, and was crowned king of France in 1594, succeeding Henry III., the last Valois king, who was murdered in 1589. For five years after this event there was really no king in France. Henry of Navarre was the lawful heir to the throne, but most of the French people were Roman Catholics, and would not have a Protestant king. He took up arms to win his throne, and gained many victories over his enemies, who had put themselves under control of the League, a party headed

Statue of Henry IV., Paris.

by the family of Guise. These years were full of horror and bloodshed, and no one could see any way out of the troubles, when Henry went over to the Roman Catholic faith, thinking that if he did this no one would any longer object to his being king of France, and there would be peace. He was right: those who had fought against him laid down their arms, and he was crowned without opposition. France enjoyed great prosperity under him. He did much for trade and agriculture, and his chief adviser, SULLY, helped him make many wise arrangements. His people all loved him, and his Protestant subjects were most grateful to him for making the Edict of Nantes, a law giving them many privileges. He was stabbed by a half-crazy man named Ravaillac, and died in Paris when fifty-seven years old (May 14, 1610) He was succeeded by his son, Louis XIII.

HENRY I., called the Fowler, King of Germany, born in 876. He was the first of the Saxon line, and was the son of Otho, Duke of Saxony. When Conrad I., King of Germany, died (919), he made Henry his successor. The messengers who went for him found him in the mountains hunting with his falcons, and from that he was called the Fowler. He was terrible in war, and just and wise in peace. He conquered Lorraine, and gained a great victory over the Huns, the most dangerous of the enemies of Germany. He has sometimes been called the " Founder of Cities," from his having built a great many fortresses which were the beginnings of towns. He died at Mansleben (July 2, 936), and was succeeded by his son, Otho I. the Great.

HENRY II., called the Lame, Emperor of Germany, born May 6, 972. He was the son of Otho III., and succeeded him in 1002, being the last of the five Saxon emperors. He was called the Lame from an accident which hurt him, and his love for the clergy and the Church, which he showed by founding the Cathedral of Bamberg, caused him to be called also the " Saint." He and the pope were great friends, and when Henry went to Rome he promised that the German emperors would always defend the popes against their enemies. This promise afterward led to trouble. Henry

died at Grone when fifty-two years old (July 13, 1024), and was succeeded by Conrad II., of the House of Franconia.

HENRY III., Emperor of Germany, born at Osterbeck, Oct. 28, 1017. He was the son of Conrad II., and succeeded him in 1039. He was of the Franconian line. Nature had given him the mind and character fitting him for an able ruler, and he was also well educated. In everything he showed great energy, and he was probably the strongest ruler since Charles the Great. He made the nobles and clergy obey him, and to keep his people from fighting so much he established the " Truce of God," a law requiring everybody to keep the peace between Wednesday evening and Monday morning, as well as during the whole seasons of Lent and Advent. He died at Botfeld when thirty-nine years old (Oct. 5, 1056), and was succeeded by his son, Henry IV.

HENRY IV., Emperor of Germany, born Nov. 11, 1050. He was the son of Henry III., whom he succeeded in 1056, under the control of his mother Agnes. When he grew up he made many enemies among his subjects, and had a quarrel with Pope Gregory VII. The pope had made a law forbidding kings to give places in the Church, but Henry would not mind this law, and said that Gregory should cease to be pope. Gregory in turn refused to regard Henry any longer as a member of the Church. This made still more enemies for him among his subjects, and Henry saw that they would all desert him unless he begged the pope's pardon, and was forgiven by him. He did this, going to meet Gregory at Canossa, where he was kept three days waiting in the courtyard. The quarrel soon began again, and Henry's own children sided with his enemies. His youngest son took him prisoner, but he escaped to

Liége, where he died, when fifty-six years old (Aug. 7, 1106). He was succeeded by his son, Henry V.

HENRY V., Emperor of Germany, born Aug. 11, 1081. He was the son of Henry IV., and succeeded him in 1106. He was the last of the Franconian line. The old dispute about the way to elect bishops, which had vexed his father's reign, still went on. Four times he was turned out of the Church by the pope, and four times taken back again. At last the dispute was settled in this way : the pope said that the election of the bishops might be made in presence of the emperor, but without his interference, and the emperor gave up the right which he had insisted on of giving to the newly elected bishop the signs of his office, the ring and crosier. He died at Utrecht when forty-four years old (May 23, 1125), and as he had no children the Germans elected Lothaire of Saxony to succeed him.

HENRY VI., called the Cruel, Emperor of Germany, born in 1165. He was the son of Frederick I., Barbarossa, and succeeded him in 1190. He had married Constance, heiress of the kingdom of Naples and Sicily, and on the death of the king he wanted to get the kingdom for his wife. But the Sicilians did not want him for their ruler, and they chose another king. A short time before this Richard the Lion-hearted, King of England, had been taken while going through Germany and put into prison. With the money which Henry received for this king's ransom he got up an army, went to Naples, and took it. The revenge that he took on his enemies was frightful. He was so much hated by the Sicilians that, when he died at Messina at the age of thirty-two (Sept. 28, 1197), it was thought that he had been poisoned. He was succeeded by his son Frederick, a child two years old, who became Frederick II.

HENRY VII., Emperor of Germany, born in 1262. He was the first of the House of Luxemburg, and was elected emperor four years after the death of Albert I. During these four years Germany had no emperor. He added Bohemia to the estates of his family by marrying his son John to the sister of the last king, who was childless. Then he went to Italy, where there were two parties at war with each other, the GUELPHS and the Ghibellines. He took the side of the Ghibellines, made himself master of northern Italy, and went on to Rome, where he was crowned. While marching against the Guelphic city of Florence, he died near Siena, when fifty one years old (Aug. 24, 1313), and was succeeded by the Duke of Bavaria, as Louis IV.

HENRY, Joseph, an American scholar, born in Albany, N. Y., Dec. 17, 1797. He studied in the Albany Academy, and became professor of mathematics there in 1826. He soon began to experiment with electricity and magnetism, and made several important discoveries. Before Morse made his first telegraph, Prof. Henry had shown that the electro-magnet (C. C. T., 375, I. l.) could be used for ringing bells and for making other motions at a distance, and this made the telegraph possible. In 1832 he became a professor in the College of New Jersey, and when the Smithsonian Institution was opened (1846), he was appointed secretary and principal director. He held this office until he died in Washington, when eighty years old (May 13, 1878).

HENRY THE LION, Duke of Saxony and Bavaria, born in 1129. He was the son of Henry the Proud, a rebellious noble who had been deprived of his estates by Conrad III. On his death these dukedoms were restored to his son Henry the Lion, who became the greatest of all the German princes. Great improvements were made by him in his dominions, and he became so powerful as to determine to be no longer a subject even to the emperor. At the battle of Legnano he caused the emperor Frederick Barbarossa to be defeated by withdrawing his troops from the field. Frederick for this took away his estates, and banished him for three years to England, He is one of the ancestors of the present royal family of England. Henry died when sixty-six years old (1195).

HENRY THE NAVIGATOR, a noted Portuguese prince, son of King John I., born March 4, 1394. When twenty-one years old he was knighted for his bravery in war. He had great learning, and founded a school at Sagres, where young men were taught navigation ; he was the first European to use a compass in sailing the seas. It was then thought that Cape Nun, on the coast of Africa, was the end of the world ; but Prince Henry thought not, and sent vessel after vessel to go farther south ; many failed, but Henry persevered ; and when, at last, one of his vessels went as far as Cape Bojador, everybody rejoiced. Just before his death one of his vessels reached what is now Sierra Leone. He was much beloved by all. He died at Sagres, when sixty-six years old (Nov. 13, 1460).

HENRY, Patrick, a famous American orator and statesman, born in Hanover Co., Va., May 29, 1736. He was taught chiefly by his father, but was much fonder of hunting and fishing than of studying. When he grew to be a man he went into business, but failed twice ; he then became a lawyer, but for three years got very little practice, when by some lucky chance he was chosen as lawyer in a case called the " Parsons' Cause," because it was a quarrel between the parsons and the planters. To the surprise of everybody, Henry made a wonderful speech, and though he lost his case, from that time he was famous. He soon became the leader of the people's party, and when a member of the legislature (1765) he

took a strong stand against the Stamp Act ; and in his speech against it used these celebrated words : " Cæsar had his Brutus, Charles I. his Cromwell, and George III." (here people cried out ' Treason !') " may profit by their example. If this be treason, make the most of it." In 1774 he was the first speaker of the General Congress which met in Phil-

Patrick Henry.

adelphia. The next year he made his famous speech in Virginia in favor of putting the colony in a state of defense, in which he concluded : " I know not what course others may take, but as for me, give me liberty or give me death !" Patrick Henry was twice governor of Virginia, and refused many high offices. He died at Red Hill, Va., when sixty-three years old (June 6, 1799).

HEPHÆSTION (*he fest'i-on*), a Macedonian general, who went with Alexander the Great to Persia and India. He was the great friend of Alexander, with whom he is said to have been brought up. Alexander trusted several important commands to him, and rewarded him with a golden crown for his services. He died of a fever at Ecbatana (324 B.C.), and Alexander is said to have so mourned his loss that he tasted no food for three days.

HER·A·CLI'US, a Roman Emperor of the East, born about 575. He was the son of Heraclius, Governor of Africa, and he succeeded the Emperor Phocas in 610. This Phocas was a usurper, having murdered the preceding Emperor Maurice and taken his throne. Heraclius went against the tyrant, drove him from his throne, and was himself chosen to fill it. He had a war against CHOSROES, King of Persia, and in this war he showed himself a great general, defeating his enemy and concluding an honorable peace with his successor, Siroes. He would have ended his reign with the most splendid renown, but for the appearance on the world's stage of the Saracens, the victorious followers of the Prophet Mohammed, who overran the East and deprived Heraclius of several provinces. Heraclius died when about sixty-six years old (641).

HERAT (*her-aht'*), a town of N. W. Afghanistan; pop. about 30,000, or nearly as large as Terre Haute, Ind. It is surrounded by walls, and has a strong citadel. Herat has a very large trade, goods from Afghanistan and India being exchanged there for other articles from China, Russia, Turkey, and Persia. It is one of the principal markets for saffron and assafœtida, and carpets and many other things are made there.

Herat is a very important military post. The Persians captured it in 1856, but the English made war on Persia and compelled the Shah to give it up, and it was afterward united to Afghanistan.

HER·CU·LA'NE·UM. See POMPEII.

HERCULES (*her'ku-leez*), in Greek fable, a famous hero, son of Jupiter and of Alcmena, granddaughter of Perseus. Jupiter meant that he should have the throne of Perseus, but Juno contrived that Eurystheus, grandson of Perseus, should have it. Jupiter then made Juno

promise that Hercules should become immortal when he had finished twelve great labors for Eurystheus. Hercules was very strong from his birth, and even when a baby in his cradle had strangled two serpents which Juno had sent to destroy him. The labors, which are generally called the twelve labors of Hercules, are commonly stated as follows :

1. He strangled an enormous lion, called the Nemean lion because it lived in the woods of Nemea.

2. He killed the Lernæan hydra, a nine-headed serpent living in Lernæ.

3. He caught the swift Arcadian stag, which had golden horns and brazen feet, and carried it alive to Eurystheus.

4. He caught alive the Erymanthean boar, which

Hercules.

lived on Mt. Erymanthus, by chasing it in the deep snow until it was tired.

5. He cleansed the Augean stables, where King Augeas of Elis had kept 3000 oxen for thirty years, by turning the rivers Alpheus and Peneus so that they flowed through them.

6. He killed with his arrows the Stymphalian birds, which lived in a lake near Stymphalus and fed on human flesh.

7. He caught the Cretan bull, which Neptune had caused to go mad and ravage the Island of Crete.

8. He overcame Diomedes, a cruel tyrant of Thrace, and gave his body to his mares, which had always been fed on human flesh, to eat. The mares became tame after eating their master.

9. He defeated the Amazons, and took from Hyppolite her girdle, which Mars had given to her.

10. He killed Geryon, a monster who lived in the Island of Erythia,

and brought his red oxen to Eurystheus.

11. He killed the dragon that watched the golden apples in the garden of the Hesperides, and brought the apples away with him.

12. He seized Cerberus, the watchdog of Hades, brought him to the upper world, and then carried him back again.

Hercules is said to have performed many other wonderful deeds, which are told about by the poets. At last he fell in love with Omphale, Queen of Lydia, and Dejanira, his wife, sent him a poisoned shirt, which Nessus the Centaur had told her would win him back to her. When Hercules put it on it poisoned him so that he tore his flesh in agony. Unable to bear the pain any longer, he heaped up a pile of wood, and seating himself on it set fire to it. But when the flames began to reach him, a cloud from the sky covered him, and he was taken up to heaven.

HERMANN (*her'mahn*). See ARMINIUS.

HERMES (*her'meez*). See MERCURY.

HE'RO. See ABYDOS.

HE-ROD'O-TUS, a famous Greek historian, born in Halicarnassus, Asia Minor, about 484 B.C. Little is known of his life, but he is said to have belonged to a noble and rich family. He is best known by his history of the war between the Greeks and the Persians, and as he is the first of the Greek historians whose works have been preserved entire, he is often called the " Father of History." His history gives most interesting accounts of Egypt, Babylon, Asia Minor, Greece, and Italy, and tells in a most pleasing and simple way about the manners and customs of the people. People used to think that Herodotus was not truthful, but the more that is known of the countries he visited, the more accurate he is shown to be. He is supposed to have died in Italy about 420 B.C.

HERSCHEL (*her'shel*), **Sir William,** a noted English astronomer, born in Hanover, Prussia, Nov. 15, 1738. His father, who was a musician, made him one too, and when only fourteen years old William was a player in a military band. When twenty-eight, while he was organist at Bath, in England, he began to study astronomy, and became so interested in it that every spare moment was passed in studying the heavens. Before his time astronomers could not make much use of a very large telescope, because if it magnified a great deal the light would become dim ; but Herschel made one in which the object could be magnified in a very strong light. The news soon spread abroad, and great men came from London to take a peep through this wonderful tube ; then they carried reports of all they had seen to the palace of St. James, where the king and queen lived ; and so the musician became famous, and was made the king's astronomer, with a pension of about two thousand dollars a year. Among his first discoveries was a planet which he called after the king, Georgium Sidus (Georgian Star) ; but which is now commonly known as Uranus. He afterward made many more wonderful discoveries, mostly with a very large telescope which he set up at his home, and which up to that time was the largest telescope ever made (C. C. T., 613, II., l.). King George III. made Herschel a knight, and he became known all over Europe as the greatest astronomer of the time. He was aided much in his work by his sister, Caroline Herschel, who also became noted as an astronomer. Sir William Herschel died at his home at Slough, near Windsor, when eighty-three years old (Aug. 23, 1822). His son, Sir John Frederick William Herschel (born 1792, died 1871), was also a famous astronomer.

HESIOD (*he'she-od*), one of the

earliest Greek poets, of whose life nothing is known. The ancient writers say that he lived near Mt. Helicon, before or about the time of Homer. He wrote a poem called "Works and Days," in which he tells about home life and the duty of labor. In another he relates all the stories about the gods and goddesses, the heroes of fable, and the wars between the gods and the TITANS. He is said by some to have given the names to the gods.

HESPERIDES (*hes-per'e-deez*), in Greek fable, three or four nymphs who guarded the golden apples growing in the enchanted gardens in the western part of the world, so near the setting sun that no man could reach it. They were assisted by a dragon that never slept ; but Hercules killed the dragon and carried off the fruit.

HI'E-RO, a tyrant or ruler of Syracuse who succeeded his brother Gelon about 478 B.C. He was successful in war both in Sicily and Italy, and gained a great victory over the Etruscan fleet near Cumæ (474). He did all he could to encourage learning and to help poets and authors. He died at Catania in Sicily (467).

HIERO, King of Syracuse, born about 307 B.C. He was a good soldier, and became commander of the armies of Syracuse, and in 270 was raised to the throne. In the First Punic War he at first sided with the Carthaginians, but being defeated by the Romans he made peace with them and became their ally. He was a good ruler, and had a splendid and prosperous reign. He died about 216 B.C.

HIG'GIN-SON, Thomas Wentworth, an American author, born in Cambridge, Mass., Dec. 22, 1823. He began life in the ministry, from which he retired in 1858 to devote himself to literature. He lives in Cambridge, Mass. Most of his writings have appeared in the columns of the "Atlantic Monthly"

before their publication in book form, nearly all of them being essays. He is the author of "Young Folks' History of the United States ;" also of "Young Folks' Book of American Explorers."

HIL'DE-BRAND. See GREGORY VII.

HIMALAYA (*him-ahl'ah-yah*) **MOUNTAINS,** a mountain chain in Asia, separating Hindostan or India from Thibet. It is the highest mountain range in the world, and its highest peak, Mt. Everest, in the central part of the chain, is about five miles and a half above the sea (29,000 feet), or higher than any other single peak on the globe. Its top is always covered with snow, and no one has ever climbed to it. Mount Kintchinjunga, farther east, is almost as high. Another noted peak is Manda Devi, which is 25,750 feet high. It is looked upon as sacred, and every twelfth year the natives of India make a pilgrimage to it. The few who succeed in climbing it hold a religious festival at a point below the summit, which no one has reached. Nearly all the principal rivers of southern Asia take their rise in the Himalayas. The name comes from two Sanscrit words meaning "the abode of snow."

HIN'DOO KOOSH, a range of mountains in Afghanistan, N. of Cabul. The range extends 300 miles east and west, and some of the peaks are nearly four miles above the sea. The highest parts are covered with ice and snow, and the mountain-sides are so sterile that hardly any plants grow on them. Several passes lead through the range, but all of them are over two miles above the sea. Hindoo Koosh, or Hindu Kuh, in Persian, means Indian Mountain. The ancients called this range the Indian Caucasus.

HIPPOCRATES (*hip-pok'ra-reez*), the most famous of Greek physicians, born in the island of Cos 460 B.C. He is called "the father of medicine," because he first made it a science. He made many discov-ries in medicine, and wrote many

Hippocrates.

books, some of which still exist. He died at Larissa, in Thessaly, about 360 B.C.

HO·BO′KEN, a city of N. E. New Jersey, on the Hudson River, oppo-site New York and just N. of Jersey City ; pop. 44,000, or a little larger than Seattle, Wash. Most of the peo-ple, about half of whom are Germans and other foreigners, do business in New York. Hoboken has large iron-works, railroad machine-shops, and manufactories of steam-engines, and lead pencils. Several lines of ocean steamships have their wharves there. The Stevens Institute of Technology, founded there by Edwin Augustus Stevens, is one of the best scientific schools in the country. Hoboken was settled by the Dutch in the early part of the 17th century, and was named after a village in the Nether-lands.

HOCHE (*hosh*), **Lazare,** a noted French soldier, born near Versailles, June 25, 1768. He was son of a working-man, and enlisted in the army when only sixteen years old. By working at spare moments he got enough money to buy books and to give himself an education. When the Revolution began he rose rapidly, though ROBESPIERRE and his party did not like him. He was made a general, and gained splendid victories over the Austrians. Soon after he was thrown into prison, but the downfall of Robespierre saved his life. He was let out of prison, and sent to put down the Royalists in La Vendée. He did so com-pletely, but with less cruelty than suited those who sent him. Hoche afterward commanded another army on the Rhine, and greatly distin-guished himself. He died suddenly, supposed to have been poisoned, in his twenty-eighth year (Sept. 18, 1797). A noble bronze statue is erected to him at Versailles, near which is his native village.

HO′FER, Andreas, a patriot of the TYROL, born in a tavern in the val-ley of Passeyr, Nov. 22, 1767. He was a wine-merchant and horse-drover, but in 1796 he led a company of riflemen against the French invad-ers of his country. In 1809 he headed a rising against Napoleon, and in a week the Tyrol was free and the French driven out. In spite of an agreement between France and Austria that Napoleon should keep the Tyrol, Hofer continued to fight the French with success, but after the Peace of Vienna his own sover-eign commanded him to yield to the French emperor. Hofer sent in his submission to Eugene BEAUHAR-NAIS, but, repenting, took up arms again. This time he was defeated. He was betrayed, and was shot at Mantua when forty-two years old (Feb. 20, 1810). The Austrian em-peror ennobled his family, turned the inn where he was born into an asylum for old soldiers, and placed a marble monument over his grave.

HO'GARTH, William, a famous English painter, born in London, Nov. 20, 1697. His father was poor, so William had little instruction, but he early showed his taste for art by ornamenting his school-books with drawings. When fifteen years old he was apprenticed to a silversmith, and at odd times he learned to draw from nature. When about twenty-one he was occupied in engraving for the booksellers, but soon afterward attended the lectures of the court painter, Sir James Thornhill, whose daughter he mar-

William Hogarth.

ried some years after, without his consent. Sir James was not much pleased at this marriage, but when Hogarth began to win fame he was very glad to own him for a son-in-law. Hogarth soon showed great skill in painting portraits, but he became most famous for making drawings of scenes in the life of the people of that time, which he engraved himself. He made several series of these pictures, some of which are very laughable, and at the same time teach a lesson by showing the follies of society. He died when sixty-seven years old (Oct. 26, 1764)

HOGG, James, a Scottish poet, commonly called the "Ettrick Shepherd," born in the parish of Ettrick, Selkirkshire, Jan. 25, 1772. He belonged to a family of shepherds, and he was brought up a shepherd himself. He had very little schooling ; but he was fond of study, and read as much as he could. His mother used to sing old Scottish ballads to him, and from her he learned to love poetry. He began to write songs when he was twenty-four years old, and soon became known to the shepherds and farmers as "Jamie the poeter.' In 1801 he went to Edinburgh to sell some sheep, and while there published a volume of his poems ; and not long after Sir Walter Scott, who was a kind friend to him, persuaded him to publish another. In 1810 he went to Edinburgh to live, and three years afterward published a fine poem called "The Queen's Wake," which met with great success. After this he published many poems and stories, and became famous both in Scotland and in England. He died when sixty-three years old (Nov. 21, 1835).

HOHENLINDEN (*ho-en-lin'den*), a village of Germany in Bavaria, 20 miles E. of Munich, noted as the scene of a great battle between the French under General MOREAU and the Austrians under the Archduke John, Dec. 3, 1800. Part of the battle was fought at night, and in a heavy snow-storm. The Austrians were compelled to retreat after they had lost 18,000 men in killed, wounded, and prisoners. The poet CAMPBELL saw this fight from a place near by, and wrote about it one of his finest poems, beginning,

"On Linden when the sun was low,
All bloodless lay the untrodden snow."

HOHENZOLLERN (*ho-en-zol'-lern*), a princely family in Germany which takes its name from the castle of Hohenzollern in Sigmaringen. It first appears in history about the 11th century. To it belongs the royal family of Prussia, whose ancestor Frederick, burgrave of Nuremburg, bought the March of Brandenburg from the Emperor SIGISMUND, and was created Elector of Brandenburg. In 1701, when Prussia was added to Brandenburg, the two were made into a kingdom. The greatest name in this royal line so far is that of Frederick II., the Great. The Emperor William of Germany is of this family.

HOLBEIN (*hol'bine*), **Hans,** a German painter, born about 1497. He was the son of a painter of the same name, and after painting for a while in Basel, Switzerland, removed to England, where he lived the rest of his life. Henry VIII. made him his court painter, and he painted the portraits of the king and all the principal persons of his court. Hans Holbein was also a fine engraver, and is noted for his series of 53 woodcuts called "The Dance of Death," in which Death is represented in different costumes dancing with people of all ranks and leading them to the grave. Holbein died in London, of the plague, in 1543 or 1554.

HOL'LAND. See NETHERLANDS.

HOLLAND, Josiah Gilbert, a noted American writer, born in Belchertown, Mass., July 24, 1819. Dr. Holland was educated a physician, and practised medicine a few years, but gave it up for a literary life. He was for many years one of the editors of the "Springfield Republican" newspaper, and from 1870 till his death editor of "Scribner's Magazine." He wrote many books, some under his own name and some under that of "Timothy Titcomb." Among his books for young folks are "Letters to the Young" and "Lessons in Life." He also wrote many popular novels and poems. Of his novels, one of the best is "Seven Oaks," and among the best of his poems are "Bitter-Sweet" and "Kathrina." He died in New York when sixty-two years old (October 12, 1881).

HOLMES (*homes*), **Oliver Wendell,**

a noted American author, born in Cambridge, Mass., Aug. 29, 1809. When twenty years old he was graduated at Harvard College, and studied both law and medicine; and in 1847 was appointed professor in the Harvard Medical College. He was called " the poet " in college, and wrote many short poems for " The Collegian," a magazine published by the students. He became famous for his songs and humorous poems, which have been published both in this country and in England. He is equally noted for his prose writings, of which the best known are his books called "The Autocrat of the Breakfast Table," "The Professor at the Breakfast Table," and "The Poet at the Breakfast Table." Even in old age his writings retained the boyish, cheerful, loving freshness of youth. Many wise and witty sayings from his books are household words in American homes. He died when 85 years old (October 7, 1894).

HOLYHEAD (*hol'e-hed*), a seaport town of Wales, in a small island 67 miles W. of Liverpool; pop. 9000. Holyhead Island, which is a barren rock, is joined to the island of Anglesea by a bridge. Its coast is exposed to storms and surf, which have washed out great caverns in the rocky shores; and to protect ships a harbor of refuge has been built. It was only completed in 1873, after twenty-five years of labor and very great expense. Holyhead is now the end of the railway route between London and Dublin, passengers taking the steamer there.

HOL'YOKE, a city of Massachusetts, on the Connecticut River, 7 miles N. of Springfield; pop. 36,000, or about as large as Fort Wayne, Ind. The Connecticut forms there several rapids and falls, and a great dam has been built across the river, furnishing a fine water-power used for many large paper-mills, cotton and woollen mills, and other factories. Holyoke was separated from

Springfield in 1850, and became a city in 1873.

HO'MER, the supposed writer of the Greek poems called the "Iliad" and the "Odyssey." Where he was born is not known, nor even the date of his birth. Many cities are said to have striven for the honor of having been his birthplace, among them Smyrna, Colophon, and Miletus, as well as the islands of Chios, Ios, Cyprus, and Crete;

Homer.

and the date of his birth is given at different times from the 11th to the 7th century B.C. It is said that he was a blind harper, who went about from place to place singing his own poems. Though nothing is certain as to his life, the Iliad and the Odyssey will live forever, for they are the noblest of all poems. The Iliad sings of the battles that took place before TROY in the last year of its siege by the Greeks, and the Odys-

sey of the fate and adventures of ULYSSES on the homeward voyage after the taking of Troy. Most scholars now think that these poems were not written by any one man, but are collections of songs which had been handed down by minstrels from ancient times; and that they were first written down and connected so as to make one poem by PISISTRATUS about 600 B.C. The picture is from an ideal bust of Homer in the Capitoline Museum, Rome.

HOMER, Winslow, an American painter, born in Boston, Feb. 24, 1836. He began to draw and paint in early boyhood, and during the Civil War made many war pictures for "Harper's Weekly." The first of his oil paintings which attracted notice was "Prisoners from the Front," an actual scene, in which all the figures were portraits. He is one of the best and most original of American artists. His studio is in New York.

HONDURAS (*hon-dvo'rahs*), a country of Central AMERICA, between Nicaragua and Guatemala; area, 50,000 square miles, or two thirds as large as Nebraska; pop. about 432,000, or a little more than two fifths that of Nebraska; capital, Comayagua. The surface is mostly hilly or mountainous, and covered with thick tropical forests, or with rich grass-lands, on which cattle are pastured. The country is rich in gold, silver, copper, and many other minerals, but the mines are little worked. The forests are among the finest in the world, and yield mahogany, dyewoods, gums, and drugs. The climate is hot, and in the rainy season there are many violent hurricanes and thunder-storms. Most of the people are Indians or mixed races, only one inhabitant out of eighty being white. Honduras is a republic, much like the United States, but the government is very weak, and there are frequent civil wars.

Honduras is the Spanish for "deep water," and the country is said to have been named from the Bay of Honduras, which was so called by the Spaniards on account of its great depth. Honduras was discovered by Columbus in 1502, and conquered by Cortez in 1526. It was a Spanish colony until 1821, and has been an independent republic since 1839.

HONDURAS, BRITISH, or Balize (*ba-leez'*), a British colony of Central America; area, 13,500 square miles, or a little larger than Maryland; pop. 27,500, or only about one thirty-seventh that of Maryland; capital, Balize. The country is mostly covered with magnificent forests. The people are negroes and Indians, with a few whites; the principal business is cutting mahogany in the forest, and dragging the logs to the shore. Conch-shells, found on coral reefs along the coast, are sent to Paris to be made into jewelry and ornaments. Balize was first settled by the English, and has always belonged to them, though the Spaniards made several attempts to drive them away.

HONFLEUR (*ong'flur*), a town of N. W. France at the mouth of the River Seine; pop. 10,000, or about as large as Portsmouth, N. H. It is an ill-built town, and is principally noted for its fisheries and its trade in eggs, fruits, and vegetables, which are sent to England. A few ships are built there. Honfleur was once important for its commerce, and during the wars between France and England it was long held by the English.

HONG KONG, an island belonging to Great Britain at the mouth of the Canton River, China, 75 miles from Canton; area, 29 square miles; pop, 216,000, or more than twice as large as Denver, Col. The island is rocky and bare, but on its north side has a fine harbor, where is built the city of Victoria, a place of great importance for trade. A great amount of tea is shipped from there to all parts of the world. There are only about 5000 Europeans there, most of the inhabitants being Chinese, several thousand of whom live in boats in the harbor. Hong Kong has belonged to Great Britain since 1842.

HONITON (*hun'e-tun*), a town of S. W. England on the River Otter; pop. 4000. Honiton lace got its name from this town, where it was first manufactured. It is now made in many other places. Honiton has a large trade in butter.

HONOLULU (*hon-o-loo'loo*), the capital of the HAWAIIAN ISLANDS, on the S. side of the island of Oahu; pop. 20,000, or about as large as Lincoln, R. I. It lies partly on a coral reef, and the king's palace and many other buildings are made of coral. In the museum are to be seen all the weapons formerly used by the islanders, such as bows and arrows, swords and spears, feather war cloaks made of thousands of yellow, red, and black feathers, and hideous war masks, some of which are shown in the picture. The climate is warm and pleasant, and the country around is full of beautiful scenery. Honolulu has a large trade with the United States, and many ships go there from California and Oregon.

HO-NO'RI-US, Flavius, a Roman emperor of the West, born in Constantinople in 384. He was the second son of Theodosius the Great, and obtained the West on the division of the empire in 395. He was a weak monarch, but he had a good adviser in STILICHO, whose daughter he married. After the death of Stilicho the empire suffered from the constant attacks of barbarians. In 410, ALARIC, King of the Visigoths, took Rome, and the empire then went to ruin. Honorius died in Ravenna, when thirty-nine years old (423).

HOOD, John Bell, an American general, born in Bath Co., Ky., June 29, 1831. He was a graduate of West Point, but when the Civil War

broke out became a general in the
Confederate army. He lost an arm
at Gettysburg and a leg at Chickamauga. In July, 1864, he succeeded
Gen. Joseph E. Johnston as commander of the Confederate army
which was fighting against Gen.
Sherman at Atlanta. He attacked
the Union army three times, but was
driven back, and at length was compelled to give up Atlanta (Sept. 1,
1864). He then marched northward,
through Tennessee, allowing Gen.
Sherman's army to move southward
unobstructed. After fighting a
bloody battle at Franklin, Tenn.

(Nov. 30), Gen. Hood was defeated
by Gen. Thomas near Nashville
(Dec. 15 and 16, 1864). Soon after
his command was taken from him.
He died in New Orleans when forty-
eight years old (Aug. 31, 1879).

HOOD, Robin, a famous outlaw,
supposed to have lived in England
about the thirteenth century. He is
said to have lived in the depths of
Sherwood Forest in Nottinghamshire, and Barnsdale Forest in Yorkshire, and to have been the leader of
a large band of outlaws like himself,
who made their living by poaching
and robbing. Among the most

Sandwich Islanders in War Masks. (See page 392.)

noted of his band were Little John,
Friar Tuck, and Maid Marian. In
the old ballads about him Robin
is represented as a jolly, good-natured fellow, who never robbed wom-
en nor poor people, and often gave
to the poor what he took from the
rich. He was very brave, and never
killed anybody excepting in self-de-
fence. He was a famous archer, and
seldom missed his aim. In "Ivanhoe" Sir Walter Scott represents him
as taking part in an archery contest
under the name of Locksley and
winning all the prizes. Friar Tuck
also is a character in the same story.

Robin used to go around in all
kinds of disguises, and when he got
into trouble or needed his merry
men, all he had to do was to blow
his bugle-horn, and a hundred stout
fellows were ready to obey his call.
It is said that he once changed
clothes with a beggar on the highway and went into Nottingham,
where three men were to be hanged
that day for stealing the king's deer.
He begged the hangman to spare
their lives, but he refused. "Then
I will save them!" cried Robin, and
he blew his horn with all his might.
His men rushed to his aid, killed the

hangman, and set free the prisoners, who at once joined his band. Robin was finally taken sick, and went to a nun who was skilled in medicine to be bled. She let him bleed to death, and buried him in Kirklees Park, Yorkshire.

HOOD, Thomas, an English poet and writer, born in London, May 23, 1798. Hood's "Up the Rhine," "Whims and Oddities," and other humorous works are very gay and amusing. His "Song of the Shirt," "Bridge of Sighs," and "Song of the Laborer" are among the most pathetic poems ever written, and were composed while Hood was on a sick bed from which he never rose. He died in London when nearly forty-seven years old (May 3, 1845.)

HOOKER, Joseph, an American general, born in Hadley, Mass.,Nov. 13, 1814. He was graduated at West Point in 1837, and fought in the Florida and Mexican Wars, being three times promoted for gallant conduct. In 1853 he resigned, and became a farmer in Oregon. When the Civil War began he entered the army again, and soon became a major-general. He fought under McClellan on the march to Richmond, and afterward in northern Virginia and Maryland, receiving a wound at the battle of Antietam. He was so brave that his soldiers nicknamed him "Fighting Joe Hooker." On Jan. 26, 1863, he was made commander of the Army of the Potomac, and in May he fought the bloody battle of Chancellorsville. Owing to a difference between him and the commander-in-chief, General Halleck, Hooker resigned his command (June 27, 1863), but he still served as a major-general, and fought under Gen. Grant at Chattanooga, and under Sherman at Atlanta. After the war he commanded in different departments, and in 1868 he retired from the army. He died at Garden City, N. Y., when sixty-five years old (Oct. 31, 1879).

HOOKER, Worthington, an Amer-

ican physician and writer, born in Springfield, Mass., March 2, 1806. He became a physician in Norwich, Conn., and in 1852 was appointed a professor in the medical school of Yale College, a position which he held until his death. He was the author of several medical works, and of many books on natural history, chemistry, and physiology for the young, among them the "Child's Book of Nature." He died at New Haven when sixty-one years old (Nov. 6, 1867).

HORACE (Quintus Horatius Flaccus), a famous Roman poet, born in Venusia, Apulia, Dec. 8, 65 B.C. His father was a freedman, but gave his son the best education that could be had. Horace was first a soldier, and fought under Brutus at Philippi. After the defeat he fled to Rome, where his offence was soon forgiven. Poverty, he says, made him write verses. His poems won the notice of Virgil and MÆCENAS, who gave him a farm and became his patron, and after that he was able to live at his ease. He wrote beautiful odes and satires, in which he gives pictures of the life and manners of the Romans of his time. Indeed, without them we should have but a faint idea of the refined and educated life of those days. He also wrote poetical epistles, which are the most perfect of his works. Horace has been more read and more often quoted than any other ancient writer, and his poems are still often published. He died when nearly fifty-seven years old (Nov. 27, 8 B. C.).

HORATII (*ho-ra'she-i*), in Roman legend, three brothers who fought with the Curiatii, three brothers, of Alba, to settle a quarrel between the cities of Rome and Alba. The two armies were drawn up in order of battle when the leaders agreed that three on each side should fight. The combat took place in the sight of both armies, and soon two of the Horatii were slain and all the Curiatii were wounded. Then the last

Horatius pretended to fly, and the Curiatii followed, each as he was able. But when Horatius saw that they were apart from each other, he turned and slew them one by one. So the Romans won the victory.

Horatius marched home at the head of the army in triumph, bearing the spoils he had won. As he drew near to the city his sister came out to meet him. Now one of the Curiatii had been her betrothed lover, and when she saw his cloak, which she had wrought with her own hands, on the shoulders of her brother, she knew it and wept aloud. At the sight of her tears Horatius drew his sword in anger and stabbed her to the heart, saying, "So perish the Roman maiden who shall weep for her country's enemy." For this dreadful deed he was condemned to death, but because he had conquered his country's enemies he was par-

The Horatii Receiving their Swords.

doned, and ever afterward sacrifices were offered to atone for the blood by the members of the family of the Horatii. In the picture, which is from a painting by Jacques Louis DAVID, the Horatii are shown receiving their swords before the fight.

HORN, Philip, Count , a Flemish soldier and statesman, born 1522. He was at first Philip de Montmorency-Nivelle, but took the name of Horn to please his step-father. He was a brilliant soldier, and at first much trusted by PHILIP II., whom he served well for many years ; but in 1561 he joined the Prince of Orange and Egmont in protesting against the cruel rule of Spain in the Netherlands. When the Duke of Alva was sent to the Netherlands to put down Protestantism, Horn and his cousin Egmont were arrested, and after half a year's imprisonment were beheaded in the great square of Brussels (June 5, 1568).

HORSA (*hor'sah*). See HENGIST.

HORTENSIUS (*hor-ten'she-us*), **Quintus**, a Roman orator, born in 114 B.C. After having served for some years in the army, he devoted his life to the practice of law, and he was considered the ablest advocate in Rome until Cicero rose to fame. Hortensius made a great deal of money by his practice, and had splendid villas at Tusculum and other places. He died when sixty-four years old (50 B.C.).

HO'RUS, the ancient Egyptian god of silence. He was the son of Isis, and is represented as a child seated on his mother's lap. The Romans honored him under the name of Harpocrates, and represented him holding his finger on his lips in token of secrecy.

HOS'MER, Harriet, an American sculptor, born in Watertown, Mass., Oct. 9, 1831. She began to model figures in clay while yet a child, and her taste for sculpture grew with her years. When she was twenty-one she went to Rome to study art, and has since then lived in that city. Among her works is a fine statue called "Zenobia."

HOS'PI-TAL-LERS, Knights, called also Knights of St. John of Jerusalem, Knights of Rhodes, and Knights of Malta, a religious and military order, founded in the middle of the eleventh century. The name "Hospitallers" comes from a hospital dedicated to St. John the Baptist, which was built at Jerusalem for the use of pilgrims going to the Holy Land. The order was divided into three classes, serving brothers who took care of sick pilgrims, priests who attended to religion, and knights who fought with infidels and escorted pilgrims. Its members wore a black habit with a white linen cross on the left breast. After the conquest of the Holy Land by the Saracens, the knights obtained the Island of Rhodes, and when this was taken from them by the Turk Solyman II., in 1552, Malta was given to them by the Emperor Charles V. Here they were again attacked by Solyman, who, repenting of having spared the order when he had driven it from Rhodes, now determined to destroy it. On May 24, 1565, the Turkish fleet began the attack on the little fort of St. Elmo, one of the defences of the island. The Grand Master was Jean de la Valette, and though seventy years old he was full of the fire of youth. This siege is noted for the heroic valor of the besieged, in their resistance to the mighty force which opposed them. St. Elmo fell, yet the knights did not lose courage, and when summoned to surrender gave for answer to the Turks, while pointing to a ditch, "That is the only place we intend for you."

Months went by, and finally aid came to the besieged, sent by Philip II. of Spain. Alva with six thousand men gave battle to the Turks, who suffered a total defeat and set sail the next day for Constantinople. Valetta, the capital of the Island of Malta, was called by the name of its heroic defender. In 1798 Napoleon drove the order from Malta, and the English, who took the island two years after, would not restore it. Hompesch, the last Grand Master, resigned his dignity to Paul, Emperor of Russia, but the Pope would not recognize as head of the order a man belonging to the Greek Church. At present the society is governed by a lieutenant and college residing at Rome, but it exists in little else than in name.

HOUDIN (*oo-dan'*), **Robert,** a French conjurer, or juggler, born in Blois, Dec. 6, 1805. He was a watchmaker, and made many mechanical toys and machines. From an early age he had been interested in juggling and sleight of hand, and in 1845 he began to exhibit his skill, and soon became famous for his wonderful tricks. The Arabs of Algeria were often excited to rebellion by the pretended miracles of their priests, and in 1856 the French Government sent Houdin there, hoping that he might excel them in tricks, and thus make the Arabs lose faith in them. Houdin aroused their wonder and succeeded in breaking up the influence of the priests among the Arabs, who became very much afraid of him. At one time he allowed an Arab to shoot at him with a marked ball, but instead of killing him the ball was found between his teeth. After that they believed that he could do anything. Houdin died in Blois when sixty-five years old (June, 1871).

HOUDON (*oo-don'*), **Jean Antoine,** a noted French sculptor, born in Versailles, March 20, 1741. He studied in Paris and Rome, and made many fine busts of celebrated men. In 1785 he came with Franklin to America, to make a model of a statue of Washington which the State of Virginia had ordered, and spent two weeks at Mount Vernon for the purpose. This statue is in the capitol at Richmond, and is said to be the best likeness of Washington ever made. He died in Paris when eighty-seven years old (July 15, 1828)

HOUGHTON (*ho'ton*), **Richard Monckton Milnes,** Lord, an English author, born in Yorkshire, June 19, 1809. He was graduated at Trinity College when twenty-two, and was elected to Parliament five years later. In the House of Commons he was the friend of the poor, wanted all religions to be equally free, was in favor of education for the rich and poor alike, and was on the side of Italy in her struggles for freedom. He has travelled much in Europe and in the East, and has published several volumes telling about the countries and the people he saw, besides many poems. He was made a peer in 1863, with the title of Baron Houghton. He died Aug. 11, 1885.

HOUSTON (*hu'stun*), **Sam,** an American soldier, born near Lexington, Va., March 2, 1793. When quite young he ran away and went to live with the Cherokee Indians

one of whose chiefs adopted him for his son. He afterward became noted as an Indian fighter, and fought bravely under Gen. Jackson at the battle of Tallapoosa (Mar. 24, 1814). In 1827 he was chosen Governor of Tennessee, but for some reason resigned his office and went back to the Indians. In 1834 he went to Texas, which was then a part of Mexico. In 1835 the Texans began a war of independence, and Houston was appointed commander-in-chief of the army. He met the Mexican army, under Santa Anna, the Mexican President, at the San Jacinto River, and though he had only half as many men Houston gained a splendid victory (April 21, 1836). The next day Santa Anna himself was captured, and forced to sign a treaty by which Texas was made independent. Twice afterward Houston was elected President of Texas, and ruled the country well and wisely. He made treaties with warlike Indian tribes, brought back trade and peace with Mexico, and finally succeeded in having Texas admitted to the Union (1845). After that he was a United States Senator and Governor of Texas. He died at Huntersville, Texas, at the age of seventy (July 25, 1863).

HOWARD, John, a noted English philanthropist, or one who loves to do good, born in Enfield, Sept. 2, 1726. He spent his fortune and his life in bettering the condition of the poor and suffering. He began by building schools and model cottages on his estate at Cardington, Bedfordshire. While on his way to Lisbon in 1756 he was taken prisoner by a French privateer, and this drew his attention to the necessity of having prisons cleaner, and the treatment of prisoners less cruel. He afterward travelled all over Europe examining prisons and hospitals, and publishing what he saw in each, thus bringing about many reforms. In 1789 he started for the East to study the hospitals there, but died at Kherson, Russia, when sixty-three years old (Jan. 20, 1790).

HOWARD, John Eger, an American soldier and statesman, born in Maryland, June 4, 1752. He was one of the bravest patriots of the Revolution, and fought in many battles. Congress gave him a gold medal for his bravery at the battle of the Cowpens, the bayonet charge of his troops having won the victory for the Americans. In 1788 he became Governor of Maryland, and was afterward United States Senator. He died when sixty-five years old (Oct. 12, 1827).

Gen. Greene said of Howard that he deserved "a statue of gold no less than Roman and Grecian heroes."

HOWE, Elias, a noted American inventor, born in Spencer, Mass., July 9, 1819. When a boy he helped his father, who was a farmer and miller, during the summer, and went to a district school in winter, until he was sixteen years old, when he began to study to be a machinist. He has been called the inventor of the sewing-machine ; but he only invented the needle which is now used, and improved on a machine which had been known for some time, so as to make it the useful thing it now is (C. C. T., 545, l., l.). A great many attempts were made to rob him of his rights ; but in 1854 the matter was settled in his favor, and afterward he became very rich. He died in Brooklyn, N. Y., when forty-eight years old (Oct. 3, 1867).

HOWE, William, Viscount, a British general who commanded the British army in America from 1775 to 1778, born Aug. 10, 1729. He commanded in the attack on Bunker Hill, defeated the American troops on Long Island (Aug. 27, 1776), took New York (Sept. 15), and won the battles of White Plains, Fort Washington, Brandywine, and Germantown. He was succeeded by Sir Henry Clinton (1778). Howe

died in England when eighty-five years old (July 12, 1814).

HOWELLS, William Dean, an American author, born in Martinsville, Ohio, March 1, 1837. He worked in a printing-office for twelve years, and then became assistant editor of a newspaper. President Lincoln made him consul at Venice, where he lived several years. He afterwards published two books about Italy, and some very pretty poems and stories. From 1871 to 1884 he was editor of the "Atlantic Monthly Magazine," in Boston, and is now on the staff of "Harper's Magazine."

HOWITT, William, an English author, born at Heanor, Derbyshire, in 1795. His family were of the Society of Friends, or Quakers, and when twenty-eight he married Mary Botham, a member of the same society. They made a tour on foot through Great Britain, and afterward wrote many books together. Among their works are the "Boys' Country Book," "Student Life of Germany," "Stories of English Life," and "Birds and their Nests." Mary Howitt has also herself written several books for the young, and made many translations from Hans Andersen and other foreign writers. We are so used to seeing the names of William and Mary Howitt together that it is hard to know them apart. William Howitt died in Rome, when eighty-four years old (March 3, 1879), and his wife died in Rome, when ninety-one years old (January 30, 1888).

HUD'DERS-FIELD, a town of N. England, on the River Colne, 35 miles S.W. of York ; pop. 82,000, or nearly as large as Worcester, Mass. It is one of the most noted places in England for the manufacture of all kinds of woolen goods. Every week a fair is held for the sale of woolen cloths, which is attended by as many as 600 manufacturers.

HUD'SON BAY, a great inland sea of British N. America, joined to the Atlantic Ocean by Hudson Strait ;

area, 300,000 square miles, or twice as large as the Baltic Sea. On the northern side are several large islands, but these and the neighboring mainland are cold, dreary wastes, which have never been fully explored. On the southern and western shores are a few settlements and English forts. Ships can only sail in the bay two months of the year; all the rest of the time it is frozen over or full of floating ice. Hudson Bay was discovered in 1610 by Henry Hudson, after whom it is named.

HUDSON, Henry, an English navigator, of whose early life nothing is known. In 1607 he sailed in

Henry Hudson.

search of a short way to China and India by way of the Northern Ocean, but was stopped by the ice off the coast of Greenland and forced to return. In 1609, while in the service of the Dutch East India Company, he discovered the Hudson River, which is named after him, and sailed up it to where Albany now stands. While on a fourth voyage (1610) he discovered Hudson Strait and Bay, which also are named after him. Being stopped by the ice, he determined to spend the winter on the shores of the bay. But he and his men suffered terribly from want

of food and started (1611) to return home. But the men mutinied, and, getting possession of the ship, put Hudson, his son John, and seven sailors, into an open boat and turned them adrift. Nothing was ever known of their fate. He was called by the Dutch Hendrik Hudson.

HUDSON, Jeffery, a favorite dwarf of Charles I. of England, born in Oakham, in 1619. He was so small that he was once hidden in a pie-crust and served up at a royal banquet. At a given signal, out he jumped, dressed like a knight in full armor. At one time, a young courtier having teased him, Jeffery challenged him to fight a duel. The young man came armed only with a squirt. Jeffery was so angry at this that a real duel was fought, with pistols on horseback, in which the young courtier was killed. Jeffery was afterward taken prisoner by the Turks, and was for a while a slave in Barbary. During the civil wars he was a captain in the royal army. Later he was imprisoned on a suspicion of conspiracy, and died in prison, when sixty-three years old (1682).

HUDSON RIVER, a river of E. New York, rising in the Adirondack Mountains and flowing south to New York Bay. It has its sources in many small lakes, and in its upper part has many rapids and falls, some of which are used for waterpower; but at Troy, 151 miles from the mouth, the river begins to be navigable, and even the tides are felt there. Splendid steamboats run from Troy and Albany to New York, passing some of the finest scenery in the world. At first there is a hilly country, covered with beautiful farms and groves, and with many cities and villages along the banks. Farther south the Catskill Mountains are seen on the western side, and below Newburgh the river enters the Highlands, flowing between wild precipices and forest-clad hills, many of which are a quarter of a mile high. Below the Highlands on the western side are the Palisades, high precipices lining the river bank for fifteen miles. Part of these are opposite New York City, where the Hudson is often called the North River, a name formerly given to it to distinguish it from the Delaware, or South River. The Hudson was first found in 1524 by VERRAZZANI, an Italian in the service of France. It was again visited in 1609 by Henry HUDSON, after whom it was named.

HUGH CAPET. See CAPET.

HUGHES (*huze*), **Thomas,** an English author, born in Uffington, Berkshire, Oct. 20, 1823. He was educated at Rugby and Oxford, became a lawyer, and was a member of Parliament from 1865 to 1874. He is the writer of "Tom Brown's School Days at Rugby," in which he describes the school life at Rugby under Dr. ARNOLD; "Tom Brown at Oxford," and several other works. He did much for the laboring classes, and was principal of the college for working men and women in London. He visited the United States several times. He died when seventy-three years old (March 22, 1896).

HU'GO, Victor Marie, a famous French poet and novel writer, born in Besançon, Feb. 26, 1802. When seven years old he began the study of Greek and Latin under the care of his mother and an old priest. Before he was fifteen he wrote three poems and sent them to the judges who were appointed by the French Academy to give prizes; these old gentlemen thought that young Hugo mocked them in sending them his boyish verses, and so they denied him the prize. Hugo was very angry, and sent his three poems to another academy at Toulouse, and there won with them three different prizes. When twenty years old he married a bride of fifteen, Mlle. Foucher, who had been the playmate of his boyhood.

In 1851 he opposed the plans of

the Emperor Napoleon III., and was exiled from France. He tried to live in Belgium and in London, but the fogs and bad weather annoyed him, so that he could not be content in either place. So he took up his abode in the Isle of Jersey, where from his windows he could see the shores of France. "The good God who has deprived us of country will surely leave us the sun," he said. In a little while he was again banished from Jersey because he wrote a disrespectful letter to the empress about a criminal who was to be hanged; he then went to live in the Isle of Guernsey, but when Napoleon lost his throne Hugo returned to Paris. Everybody liked Victor Hugo's poems and novels from the very first. He has written a great many novels, which have been translated into different languages. The one called "Les Misérables" is one of the best liked in America. In all his stories he shows his pity for the poor and the unhappy; and his descriptions of children make the most beautiful chapters in his books. He died when 83 years old (May 22, 1885).

HUGUENOTS (*hu'ge-nots*, French *hu-ge-no'*), a name given to the Protestants of France in the 16th and 17th centuries. It is supposed to have been made from Eidgenossen (German for confederates or allies), the name of the Swiss confederates or leaguers, Geneva, in Switzerland, being then the headquarters of Protestantism. The Huguenots were a strong party in France in the reigns of CHARLES IX., HENRY III., and HENRY IV.

HULL, or **Kingston-upon-Hull,** a seaport city of N. E. England, on the River Hull, at its mouth in the Humber; pop. 154,000, or about twice as large as Lowell, Mass. It is built on a low plain, which is protected from the river floods by walls and embankments. The streets are very crooked, but they are lined with handsome buildings, some of which are very ancient. Hull has a fine harbor and docks, and a larger trade than any other port in England, except Liverpool and London.

Kingston-upon-Hull means the King's Town on the River Hull.

HULL, Isaac, an American naval commander, born at Derby, Conn., March 9, 1775. In July, 1812, he commanded the frigate Constitution, which was chased by a British squadron for three days, but escaped by skilful sailing. While cruising in the Atlantic Ocean he met the British frigate Guerriere, which, after a bloody fight of half an hour, surrendered (Aug. 19, 1812). The Guerriere was so injured in the battle that she soon sunk. This was the first naval battle of the war of 1812, and Congress gave Capt. Hull a gold medal for his services. He died in Philadelphia when nearly sixty-eight years old (Feb. 3, 1843).

HUMBERT I., King of Italy, is the oldest son of VICTOR EMANUEL, and was born March 14, 1844. He was married in 1868 to the Princess Maria Margaretha of Savoy, and ascended the throne, upon the death of his father, Jan. 9, 1878.

HUMBOLDT (*hum'bolt*), **Friedrich Heinrich Alexander Von,** Baron, a famous German traveller and scholar, born in Berlin, Sept. 14, 1769. His father took great care in selecting his tutors. His first tutor, when Alexander was only six years old, was Joachim Campe, who had written many books of voyages for boys, and was also the editor of "Robinson Crusoe." Alexander was very fond of his tutor, and there is little doubt that this good man told the boy many stories of foreign lands, which made him eager to go and see for himself. Then there was an old friend of the family, a botanist, one who loved plants and grasses, and who studied all about them ; this old man lived near the Humboldts, and every day he used to ride over to see them just about dinner

time. After he had eaten a hearty dinner he would take Alexander and his brother out for a walk, and talk to them about the wonderful life of flowers and trees ; and this was called their lesson in botany.

When Alexander grew up to be a man he travelled in many parts of the world, especially in South America, where he visited the head waters of the Amazons River, and ascended many peaks of the Andes. He took with him a young French botanist named Bonpland, and they found out things that nobody knew before about flowers and plants, and the earth we live upon. Humboldt lived in Paris from 1808 to 1827, and published there an account of his travels,

Humboldt.

and many large works on the natural history, geology, and history of the countries he visited. In 1829 the Emperor of Russia sent Humboldt, Ehrenberg, and Rose to explore the Caspian Sea and Northern Asia to the frontiers of China. They were accompanied by a band of soldiers, and though they were gone only nine months they travelled 10,000 miles, and made many discoveries. In his later life Humboldt was sometimes employed as a statesman and ambassador, and after 1848 he lived in Prussia, often with the king at Berlin. One of his greatest works is called "Cosmos, a View of the

Universe," which he finished just before his death. He also wrote a great work on the geography of America, an account of his discoveries in Asia, and many other books. He died in Berlin when nearly ninety years old (May 6, 1859).

Baron **Karl Wilhelm von Humboldt,** his brother, was born in Potsdam, June 22, 1767. He was a celebrated statesman, and in 1809 was placed in charge of the schools and colleges of Prussia. The University of Berlin was founded by him. He also wrote many important works on various languages, and the science of language. He died at Tegel, when nearly sixty-eight years old (April 8, 1835).

HUME, David, a famous Scottish historian, born in Edinburgh, April 26, 1711. His father died when he was an infant, and David, who grew up a very studious boy, was educated for a lawyer; but he liked literature better, and gave himself up to writing. His first book was a failure, and he thought himself an ill-used man, and never forgot what he considered the injustice done to his work. When forty-one years old he was made a librarian in Edinburgh, and soon after began to write a " History of England." Very few copies of the first volume were sold, but Hume, although very angry and disappointed, kept at work. After a while, as the other volumes came out, the sales grew larger, and at last Hume made a little fortune on his history; but he never quite forgave the public for not seeing its merits at once.

When Hume was about fifty years old he went to Paris as secretary to the Marquis of Hertford, the English minister. Though very shy, and speaking wretched French, he was overwhelmed with attentions from the youth and beauty of Paris, and at the opera his broad face and figure were always to be seen between two pretty belles. The part he played there must have been very droll. But he was the fashion, and

the pretty women thought his mistakes and awkwardness very charming. A great gossip of that day, Horace Walpole, wrote about him : " The French believe in Mr. Hume ; the only thing in the world they do believe in implicitly, for I defy them to understand any language he speaks." He died in Edinburgh when sixty-five years old (Aug. 25, 1776).

HUN'GA·RY, a country of Europe, forming part of the AUSTRO-HUN-GARIAN MONARCHY; area, 125,000 square miles, or a little larger than New England, New York, and New Jersey together; pop. 17,000,000, or about a third more than that of those States; capital, BUDA-PESTH. This includes Hungary proper, which is only about two thirds of this size, Transylvania, Croatia, and Slavonia. Hungary is mostly shut in by the Carpathian Mountains on the north and east, and by offshoots of the Alps on the west. Its principal river is the Danube. Its soil is very fertile, and it is rich in minerals. The chief things sent to other countries are wheat, rapeseed, galls, wax and honey, tobacco, wine and brandy, copper, cattle and hides, sheep and wool, and wood. The people are made up of many different nations, who speak different languages, but the Magyars (*madj'yars*) are the chief race.

In ancient times Hungary formed the Roman provinces of Pannonia and Dacia. In the 9th century the Magyars or Hungarians, a Turanian people from Asia, supposed by some to have been a branch of the Huns, invaded Central Europe, spreading as much terror by their deeds on land as the NORTHMEN did on the sea. They were heathens, but before the end of the 10th century they became Christians, and had formed a strong kingdom. In the 14th century, when the Turks became dangerous to Europe, Hungary and Poland were the bulwarks of the Christian countries, and the great Hungarian leader, Hunyady, defeated the Turks in many battles. His son, Matthias Corvinus, who was king from 1458 to 1490, won great victories over the Austrians, who were trying to get Hungary for themselves. In the 16th century a great part of Hungary was conquered by the Turks, and soon after the crown of Hungary passed to the archdukes of Austria, who have ever since held it. In the end of the 17th century the Turks were finally driven out. The Hungarians have tried several times, under KOSSUTH and other leaders, to get their freedom from Austria, but have always failed ; and in 1867 Austria and Hungary were made two distinct states under one ruler.

HUNS, a people of northern Asia, who, in the fifth century, invaded and conquered a great part of Europe. In 376 they crossed the Dnieper, defeated the Goths, and drove them into the Roman provinces. In 434 A.D., under their leader ATTILA, they crossed the Danube, and the Roman Emperor Theodosius II. could not stop them except by paying them tribute. When the tribute was withheld, after the death of Theodosius, Attila pushed on into Gaul, when he was defeated at the battle of Chalons, after which he retreated. On the death of Attila the Huns disbanded, and mingled with other tribes.

HUNT, James Henry Leigh, a noted English writer, born in Southgate, Middlesex, Oct. 19, 1784. He was educated at Christ's Hospital, left when fourteen years old, and studied law. He began to write verses when between twelve and sixteen. When twenty-four years old he edited a journal with his brother, and they were both imprisoned for using disrespectful language about the prince regent. When a fashionable paper spoke of him as " an Adonis," the Hunts added, " a fat Adonis of fifty." Hunt had an easy way of living off his friends ; he borrowed money and never paid it back

again. He was bright and witty, and began life with plenty of friends, but after a while people lost their respect for him, and when he died nobody cared. Most of his works are forgotten now. He died when seventy-four years old (Aug. 28, 1859).

HUNT, William Holman, an English painter, born in London in 1827. He paints figure pictures of which the subjects are sometimes taken from the Bible, but more often from the English poets. His " Light of the World" and " Shadow of Death" are well known through photographs. He sold the " Shadow of Death," which cost him four years' labor, for $50,000. It was exhibited in the United States in 1880.

HUNT, William Morris, an American artist, born in Brattleboro, Vt., March 31, 1824. He was a portrait, figure, and landscape painter. In 1878 he painted his last pictures on the walls of the Assembly Chamber of the State Capitol, at Albany, N. Y. They represent " The Flight of Night" and " The Discoverer." He died at the Isle of Shoals, N. H., in his fifty-sixth year (Sept. 8, 1879).

HUN'TING-TON, Daniel, an American painter, born in New York, Oct. 14, 1816. He has painted landscapes, but is best known by his portraits and ideal heads, some of which have been engraved. His studio is in New York.

HUNYADY (*hoon'yad-dy*), **Janos,** called Corvinus, a Hungarian general, born near the end of the 14th century. He was the hero of his country, and of Christendom in his day, against its enemies, the Turks. He was so brave and victorious that the Turks named him " the Devil." He defeated them several times, and at last drove them from Belgrade, which they had besieged. He died in 1456. His son, Matthias Corvinus, became King of Hungary.

HU'RON, a lake of North America, between Michigan and Canada, and connecting Lakes Michigan and Superior with the Detroit River, its outlet ; area, 21,000 square miles, or nearly twice as large as Maryland. It is 578 feet above the sea, and is very deep. Georgian Bay is a great bay on the north-eastern side, almost separated from the rest of the lake by islands and a peninsula. The best harbors of Lake Huron are on Saginaw Bay on the western side. The waters abound in fine fish.

HU'RONS. See AMERICAN INDIANS.

HUSS, John, a famous Bohemian reformer, born about 1373. He was a professor in the University of Prague, and early began to teach the doctrines of WYCLIFFE. His party having become powerful, he was made rector of the university, and he preached very strongly against the abuses of the Church. This made the clergy hate him, and at last the pope turned him out of the Church and forbade any one to shelter him. He was ordered to appear before a great council of the Church at CONSTANCE, and as the king promised that he should not be harmed he went. But the council told the king that he ought not to keep his word with a heretic, and Huss was seized, thrown into prison, and finally burned alive (July 6, 1415). Jerome of Prague, one of Huss's followers, was burned the next year. These acts caused a very bitter feeling in Bohemia, and led to the Hussite war, which lasted for fifteen years, and in which the followers of Huss were led by John ZISKA, one of the greatest generals that ever lived.

HUX'LEY, Thomas Henry, an English writer on natural history, born in Middlesex, May 4, 1825. He became a physician in the English navy, and from 1846 to 1850 accompanied the ship Rattlesnake on a voyage of exploration to Australia, Papua, and around the world. During this voyage he made many discoveries in natural history, accounts of which were written by him for scientific journals. Since 1854 he has been professor of natural history in the Royal School of Mines, and a professor in other colleges. In 1872 he was made Lord Rector of the University of Aberdeen. He has given many popular lectures, both in England and the United States, which he visited in 1876. He has written many books.

HUYGENS (*hi'gens*), **Christian,** a famous Dutch astronomer, born at the Hague, April 14, 1629. When sixteen years old he began to study law ; when twenty-two he published his first book on mathematics, and four years afterward was made doctor of laws ; but his name is known chiefly for his discoveries in astronomy. He found the first satellite of Saturn, and three years afterward discovered the ring of that planet. He made many improvements in the telescope ; is known as the inventor of the pendulum clock ; and the first watch with a hair-spring was made under his direction and sent to England. He died at the Hague when sixty-six years old (July 8, 1695).

HY-A-CIN'THUS, in Greek fable, a beautiful boy, son of Amyclas, King of Sparta. He was a favorite with both Apollo and Zephyrus, but Zephyrus became jealous, and one day, when Apollo and Hyacinthus were playing quoits together, he blew the quoit which Apollo had pitched so that it struck Hyacinthus and killed him. Apollo turned his blood into the flower called Hyacinth.

HY'DER ALI (*ah'le*), Sultan of Mysore, born about 1718. He was of mean birth and without education, but having entered the service of the Rajah of Mysore (1749) he proved to be so good a soldier that in ten years he rose to the command of his troops. He then set aside the rajah and took the government himself. The English, alarmed at his power,

made war on him, but he fought
them with success for several years.
At one time even MADRAS was in
danger from him, and he forced the
British to make peace under the
walls of the city. In 1780 he got
angry because the British did not
keep this treaty, and invaded their
part of India with a large army.
For a time he was successful everywhere, and destroyed many cities,
and the English had a hard struggle
to keep India ; but in the midst of
the war Hyder died (Dec. 7, 1782),
and was succeeded by his son, Tippoo Saib.

HYGEIA (*hy-ge'e-ah*), in Greek
fable, the goddess of health, daughter of ÆSCULAPIUS. The Romans
called her Salus, which means
" health." She is usually represented as a young girl with a serpent
twined about her right arm, which
she is feeding from a cup held in
her left hand.

HY'MEN, in Greek fable, the god
of marriage. Songs, called hyme-
neal songs, were sung in his praise
at marriage feasts. He is represented as a handsome youth, bearing
a bridal torch in his right hand.

I

ICARUS (*ik'a-rus*). See DÆDA-
LUS.

ICE'LAND, an island in the North
Atlantic Ocean, 160 miles E. of
Greenland , area, nearly 40,000
square miles, or about as large as
Ohio ; pop. 69,000, or a little
less than Cambridge, Mass.; capital, Reykiavik (pop. 1500). It
is a very wild and rocky country, with many mountains, several of which are volcanoes. The
largest, Mt. Hecla, is noted for its
terrible eruptions. One, in 1766,
threw out an immense river of lava,
and the clouds of ashes and smoke
were so thick that daylight was
turned into night by their shadows.
In 1845 the ashes from Hecla were
blown by the wind to the Shetland
Islands, about 500 miles. Not far
from Mt. Hecla are the famous boiling springs or Geysers, nearly fifty
of which are gathered within a few
acres of ground. Once or twice a day
the water bursts out in a fountain,
sixty or seventy feet high, forming
clouds of steam. Along the coasts
are many long, narrow bays, called
fiords, which have high, rocky sides,
and are noted for their wild scenery.
    The soil of Iceland is poor, so
that most plants will not grow.
The trees are very small, and some

as high as a two-story house are

The Great Geyser.

shown to strangers as curiosities.

A few oats, potatoes, and other things are grown, but the best land is pasture, on which sheep, cattle, and ponies are fed. Large herds of wild reindeer are found, but no tame ones are kept. Though Iceland is so far north, the climate is not much colder than that of Canada. The people came originally from Norway, and they speak the Norse language. Most of them are very poor, and live in damp, miserable huts, where, even in winter, no fires are made, except small ones for cooking. Their principal food is fish, and coarse cakes made of a kind of wild corn. They have no roads, no wagons, and hardly any tools or furniture; yet they think that their dreary country is the finest land in the world. Nearly all of them can read and write, and they are very good and honest people.

The island was discovered in the year 860 by the Norwegians, who first called it Snowland, and then Iceland. Since 1387 it has belonged to Denmark.

IDA (*i'dah*), **MOUNT,** a mountain in Asia Minor, near the site of ancient Troy. The rivers Simois, Scamander, and Granicus, famous in fable and history, flow from it. PARIS gave the golden apple to Venus on Mount Ida, and from its top the gods witnessed the battles between the Greeks and Trojans.

Another Mount Ida, in the island of Crete, is where Jupiter is said to have been born and brought up.

I'DA-HO, a N.W. State of the United States, E. of Oregon and Washington; area, 86,000 square miles, or nearly as much as that of New England, New Jersey, Maryland, and Delaware together; pop. about 84,000; capital, Boisé City. The surface is mostly a table-land, with hills and low mountains in different parts. In the southern and central parts are great barren regions covered with lava from old volcanoes, but there are no living volcanoes there now.

There are rich mines of gold and silver, and many of the people are miners. Wheat is the principal grain raised on the farms. The climate is very pleasant, and the winters are not so cold as in the Eastern States. There are still many Indians, who sometimes make war on the whites; and there are also some Chinese. Idaho was made a Territory in 1863, from parts of Dakota, Nebraska, and Washington territories. It then included Wyoming and Montana. In 1890 it became a State of the Union.

ILLINOIS (*il-lin-oyz'*), one of the States of the United States, between Indiana and Missouri and Iowa; area, 55,400 square miles, or about the same as that of New York and New Jersey together; pop. 3,826,000, or somewhat more than five eighths that of New York; capital, Springfield. It is one of the most level States in the Union, most of its surface being prairie. More than half of it has coal mines under it, and more than 400 mines have been opened. Much lead and some copper and zinc are mined. But Illinois is richest in its farms, its soil being so rich that it gives immense harvests. More wheat, corn, and oats, and more horses and swine are raised than in any other State, besides a great many cattle and sheep.

Illinois gets its name from the Illinois tribe of Indians. The Indian word is said to have been *Illini*, meaning "real men," or "great men," which the French changed to the present form. The country was discovered by the French in 1679, and was given up in 1763 to the English, who had conquered Canada. After the war of the Revolution it became a part of the United States. It was made a Territory in 1809, and in 1818 became a State of the Union.

INDIA (*in'de-ah*), or **Hindustan** (*hin-doos-tahn'*), a country of Southern Asia; area, 1,500,000 square miles, or about half as large as Brazil; pop. 273,533,000, or nearly twenty times that of Brazil. The great Himalaya Mountains form the northern boundary, and south of them are low plains, in which the rivers GANGES and INDUS flow. All the southern part is a table-land, with ranges of hills or mountains crossing it. Most of the country is very fertile and beautiful, but in the northwestern part is a great sandy desert where hardly any trees grow. The climate is warm, and often unhealthy.

India has mines of coal, iron, copper, lead, and antimony, and some of the largest diamonds in the world have been found there. Among the strange trees is the banian, the branches of which take root and grow into new trees, until they cover four or five acres of ground. The teak and saul trees of India are the best in the world for making ships, and its sandal wood is made into boxes, fans, and ornaments. The principal grain grown is rice, which is the food of all the poor people. There are also large plantations of cotton, sugar-cane, indigo, jute, and opium, and tea and coffee are raised. Among the wild animals are lions, tigers, elephants, rhinoceroses, deer, and many kinds of monkeys. The tigers kill many people and cattle every year. They are often hunted with tame elephants, on which the hunters ride. There are many beautiful birds, and more than 150 kinds of snakes, many of which are poisonous. The rivers swarm with crocodiles.

The people are of many different races, who speak different languages. A large part of them are Brahmans in religion, but there are also many Mohammedans and Christians. The Hindoos are divided into castes or classes, and those belonging to each caste can do only certain kinds of work, and eat certain foods, and they cannot live with people of other castes. The Brahman priests form the highest caste, and even the shadow of a low-caste man falling on a Brahman is held to be unclean. Formerly, a Brahman could kill a low-caste man who touched him. Another strange custom, now forbidden, was the suttee, a funeral ceremony in which widows were burned with their dead husbands.

India is a very old country, and has always been famed for its riches. The Hindoos, or the present people, are the descendants of ARYANS, who came into the country from the northwest and conquered it. In the 6th century B.C. Darius, King of Persia, overran much of India; and after him Alexander the Great conquered parts of it. About the year 1000 the Mohammedans attacked India, and in time founded several kingdoms. In the 16th century the MOGULS took Delhi, and set up an empire which finally ruled nearly all of Hindostan, until the English took it.

For a long time the rich goods of India were carried to Europe by camels across the deserts. At length, in 1498, Vasco de Gama sailed for the first time around the southern point of Africa, and thus found a new road to India. The Portuguese made settlements there, and soon carried nearly all the trade in their ships; but in 1603 the English East India Company, a society of merchants in London, began to trade with India. After that, the English conquered one state after another until the whole country belonged to them. They hired native soldiers, called Sepoys, and in 1857 these Sepoys rebelled and murdered many of the English, but they were subdued after a terrible war. In 1877 Queen Victoria was made Empress of India, but many of the native kings still rule their own countries as her governors.

Hindustan means the land of the River INDUS, *stan* being a Persian word meaning land or country. India is made from the same word.

Hindustan is sometimes called Hither India to distinguish it from INDO-CHINA, which is called Further India.

INDIANA (*in-de-an'ah*), a State of the United States, between Ohio and Illinois; area, 34,000 square miles, or a little less than that of Maine; pop. 2,192,000, or more than three times that of Maine; capital, INDIANAPOLIS. The surface is mostly level, in some places forming broad grassy prairies, and in others covered with forests or groves where fine timber is cut. Nearly all the land is very fertile, and some of the finest farms in the world are in this State. More wheat is raised than in any other States except Illinois and Iowa, and great quantities of corn and other crops.

There are very fine coal and iron mines in Indiana, and excellent building stones are quarried. The Wyandotte cave, near Leavenworth, is one of the most wonderful in the world. It is twenty-two miles long, and one of the rooms is large enough to set a church in, steeple and all. In it is a high hill, on top of which are three great stalagmites, or pillars made by the dripping of lime-water; one, called Lot's wife, is pure white, and looks like a statue with a cloth thrown over it. Above all is an immense dome, called Wallace's Grand Dome. There are, also, other beautiful rooms, one of which, called the White Cloud Room, has walls and ceilings covered with snow-white crystals.

Indiana was first settled by Frenchmen from Canada about the year 1700. In 1763 it was given up to England, and after the Revolution it became a territory of the United States. At that time it was much larger than it is now, including also Ohio, Illinois, and Michigan. In 1816 Indiana was admitted as a State of the Union.

IN-DI-AN-AP'O-LIS, the capital and principal city of Indiana, in the central part of the State, on the West Fork of White River; pop. 105,000, or about the same as Allegheny, Penn. Besides the State-house it contains the State asylums for the blind, deaf, and dumb, and lunatics, and a United States arsenal. Many railroads meet there, and the city has a large trade, especially in farm products. More than half a million hogs are slaughtered every year, and large quantities of lard, ham, and salt pork are prepared. Indianapolis has many iron foundries, rolling mills, and other important manufactories.

Indianapolis was settled in 1819. In 1821 it was chosen for the State capitol, and the name Indianapolis, or City of Indiana, was given to it.

INDIAN OCEAN, that part of the ocean lying between Africa, Asia, and Australia. It is the third in size of the great oceans, only the Pacific and the Atlantic being larger. Over the northern part of this ocean passes an immense number of ships engaged in the trade between Europe and America with India and China, but its southern part is not much navigated.

INDIANS. See AMERICAN INDIANS.

INDIAN TERRITORY, a tract of land lying between Kansas and Texas, set apart by the United States for the Indians; area, 69,000 square miles, or a little larger than Missouri; pop. about 75,000, most of whom are Indians. It is divided into parts called reservations, which are given for homes to such tribes as are willing to live there. Among the principal tribes now living there are the Cherokees, Creeks, Chickasaws, Choctaws, Seminoles, and Shawnees. Many of the Indians have become Christians, and have built villages with good houses, churches, and school houses. Several newspapers are printed in the territory. The Indian Territory was part of Louisiana, bought from France in 1803. The territory of

OKLAHOMA was set apart from Indian Territory in 1889.

IN'DO-CHINA, or **Further China,** a name sometimes given to the southeastern part of Asia, including Burmah, British Burmah, Siam, Anam, Cochin China, and the Malay Peninsula, with several islands near them. It is sometimes called also India beyond the Ganges.

IN'DUS, or **Sinde,** a river of S. Asia, rising in the Himalaya Mountains, more than three miles above the sea, and flowing to the Indian Ocean ; length, 2000 miles. Almost the whole of it is in India. The river is from half a mile to a mile wide, and boats can ascend for 930 miles. For a long distance the Indus flows through a very dry region, and canals have been dug to carry its waters over the country, so that plantations can be made. The mouths spread over 130 miles of coast. The name Indus is made from the Sanscrit word *sindhu,* meaning a river.

INGELOW (*in'je-lo*), **Jean,** a noted English writer, born at Boston, England, in 1830. She has written a number of charming stories for young folks, three volumes of poems, and several very bright novels. Of her poems, "The Songs of Seven" is the most widely known. Among her prose works are "Off the Skelligs," "Poor Matt," "A Sister's Bye-hours," "Stories Told to a Child," "Tales of Orris," and "Mopsa the Fairy."

INKERMAN (*ink-er-mahn'*), a village of S. Russia, on the peninsula of the Crimea, at the head of the harbor of Sebastopol. On a hillside near it there are many curious caves supposed to have been dug by Christians in early times when they were persecuted. Near by are the Heights of Inkerman, where, during the Crimean War, the French and English gained a victory over the Russians (Nov. 5, 1854).

IN'MAN, Henry, an American painter, born in Utica, N. Y., Oct.

20, 1801. . He was noted for his skill as a portrait painter, and besides making portraits of Chief Justice Marshall and many other distinguished Americans, he visited England and painted portraits of Wordsworth and Macaulay. In 1845 he began a series of historical paintings for the Capitol at Washington, but before they were completed he died in New York, at the age of forty-four years, Jan. 17, 1846.

IN'NESS, George, an American painter, born in Newburgh, N. Y., May 1, 1825. He is one of the best of American landscape painters. For some years he lived in Boston, but now has a studio in New York.

INNESS, George, Jr., son of George Inness, has his father's skill in landscape painting, and is also a fine animal painter. He occupies the same studio with his father.

INNSPRUCK (*ins'prook*), a city of W. Austria, on the river Inn ; pop. 23,000, or about as large as Malden, Mass. It is surrounded by high and steep mountains, which are noted for their grand scenery. Among the many interesting buildings of Innspruck is the Franciscan church, in which the Emperor Maximilian I. had a splendid monument built for himself. As it turned out, the emperor was not buried there at all ; but the monument is none the less worth seeing, for it is one of the finest in Europe. The sarcophagus which was to have held Maximilian's body is covered with beautiful sculptures representing scenes in the emperor's life ; and near it are twenty-eight large statues, mostly of distinguished members of his family. Innspruck has a Catholic university with 700 students and nearly 50 professors. Silks, ribbons, gloves, calico, and glass are manufactured in the city.

Innspruck, called by the Germans Innsbruck, means Bridge of the Inn. For a long time it was the residence of the archdukes or princes of Austria.

I'NO, in Greek fable, daughter of Cadmus and Harmonia. She married Athamas, who, seized with sudden madness, killed their eldest son, Learchus, and then pursued Ino, who, with her youngest boy, Melicertes, jumped into the sea, where Neptune made her a sea goddess, under the name of Leucothea, and Melicertes became a god called Palæmon.

IN-VER-NESS', a town of N. Scotland, on the river Ness; pop, 17,000, or about as large as Kalamazoo, Mich. It has a large trade in grain, wool, ropes, whiskey, and other things. Ships sail from it to foreign countries and towns on the Scottish coast, and to central Scotland by the Caledonian Canal, which begins there.

Inverness is a very old town, and it is supposed that King Duncan was murdered by Macbeth in a castle which once stood there.

IONIA (*i-o'ne-ah*). See ASIA MINOR.

IONIAN (*i-o'ne-an*) **Islands,** the name of seven islands, W. and S. of Greece; area, 1113 square miles, or not quite as large as the State of Rhode Island; pop. 250,000, or five sevenths of that of Rhode Island. Six of them—called Corfu, Santa Maura, Ithaca, Cephalonia, Zante, and Paxo—are in the Ionian Sea, a part of the Mediterranean between Greece and Italy; the other, named Cerigo, is at the south end of Greece. All the islands are mountainous, and they are noted for beautiful scenery. Some of them have mines of coal, iron, and manganese, and quarries of marble and chalcedony. The farmers raise grain, flax, and cotton, and many of them have vineyards and olive-orchards, and plantations of Zante currants (C. C. T., 506, I., l.) which are dried and sent to other countries. The people are much like Greeks, and speak the Greek language; but Italian is also spoken in the towns.

The Ionian Islands were conquered in the 12th century by the kings of Sicily, and in the 14th century by the Venetians, to whom they belonged until 1797. From 1814 to 1863 they formed a republic called the United States of the Ionian Islands, under the protection of England, but in the latter year they were joined to Greece.

IOWA (*i'o-wah*), an inland State of the United States, between the Mississippi and Missouri Rivers; area, 55,000 square miles, or as large as New York and New Jersey together; pop. 1,912,000, or more than a third that of New York; capital, Des Moines. The surface is mostly made up of beautiful grassy prairies, with here and there a forest or grove of trees. The soil is rich, and Iowa has some of the best and richest farms in the world. More wheat and corn are raised than in any other State, except Illinois. Sometimes whole miles of land are covered with a single wheat or corn field. The climate is very pleasant and healthful, though the winters are cold.

There are fine coal and lead mines; the lead ore is found in cracks and caves in the rocks, and sometimes many million pounds are taken from a single cave.

The name Iowa is an Indian word, meaning "beautiful land." Iowa was first settled in 1788 by the French, and was a part of Louisiana until 1803, when it was sold to the United States. In 1838 it was made a Territory, and in 1846 it became a State of the Union.

IPHIGENIA (*if-i-je-ni"ah*), daughter of AGAMEMNON and Clytemnestra. Her father, having offended the goddess Diana, had sworn to offer to her as a sacrifice whatever most beautiful was born to him during the year. Iphigenia was born, but Agamemnon put off the sacrifice until the Greeks were ready to sail against Troy. The winds being wrong, Chalcas the seer said that Diana was angry because

Agamemnon had not kept his vow. When Iphigenia was about to be sacrificed, Diana saved her and bore her away in a cloud to Tauris, where Iphigenia became her priestess. When her brother ORESTES came to carry off the image of Diana she helped him and fled with him. Her story is the subject of tragedies by Euripides, Racine, and Goethe.

IPSAMBUL (*ip-sam-bool'*), a ruined place in Nubia, on the banks of the Nile, famous for its wonderful temples, which are hewn out of the solid rock. There are two of these temples, the smaller one having six great statues in front, and the larger one four much larger ones, seated on thrones. These statues, the largest in Egypt, are as tall as

Festival at the Great Temple of Ipsambul.

the height of eleven men (65 feet), their faces alone being taller than the height of a man. Within the temple is a great chamber more than 200 feet long, cut out of the solid rock and ornamented with square columns adorned with statues. All of these are so well preserved that they look as if lately sculptured. The picture shows a festival at the great temple in ancient times when Egypt was in its glory.

IPS'WICH, a city of E. England, on the river Orwell, 10 miles from the sea; pop. 51,000, or about as large as Los Angeles, Cal. It has large iron foundries, breweries, and soap factories, and ship-yards. Among the fine buildings is a school called Queen Elizabeth's Grammar School, which was founded in the reign of Edward IV. and improved by Queen Elizabeth. The original name of the town was Gippeswich, and it is supposed to refer to the River Gipping, which empties into the Orwell near the city.

IRE´LAND, an island of Europe, W. of England, between the Irish Sea and the Atlantic Ocean; area, 32,500 square miles, or not quite as large as Indiana; pop. 5,175,000, or about two and a half times that of Indiana; capital, DUBLIN. Most of the surface is a plain, but there are hills near the coasts. Much of it is covered with swamps or bogs, from which the people get a kind of fuel called peat (C. C. T. 450, II., u.). There are many fine rivers and lakes, and the whole country is so green and beautiful that it is often called the "Emerald Isle." Along the coasts are deep bays, some of which form excellent harbors.

Ireland has mines of coal, copper, iron, and lead. Most of the farmers have no land of their own, but hire small farms for a yearly rent. The principal crops are oats and hay, and potatoes, which are the chief food of the poor. More than half the land is used for pasturing cattle, horses, and sheep, which form the chief wealth of the farmers. Flax is cultivated, and the most important manufacture is linen cloth. The climate is much like that of the Eastern United States, but the winters are not so cold. The upper classes are intelligent and well educated, but many of the poor people are so ignorant that they cannot even read. They have a language of their own, but nearly all of them speak English. About three fourths are Roman Catholics, and the rest Protestants. Ireland belongs to England, and is governed by a governor called the Lord-Lieutenant.

Ireland was known about 800 B.C to the Greeks, who called it Iernis or Ierne. The Romans called it Hibernia, and the Irish themselves gave it the name of Erin. In early times the Irish were divided into several tribes, each governed by a king or chief; but they finally became united under one king. About the middle of the 5th century A.D., Patrick (now called St. Patrick), a native of Gaul, went to Ireland and converted the people to Christianity, and from that time until the 12th century Ireland was noted for being more advanced in learning than any of the neighboring countries. In 1155 Pope Adrian IV. gave King Henry II. of England leave to conquer Ireland. He took possession of a part of it, but it was not for many ages that the English kings got all of it, and cruel wars long went on between them and the natives. The last rebellion was put down in 1800, and in that year Ireland became a part of the United Kingdom of Great Britain and Ireland. But there has always been much discontent, and especially a great deal of trouble between the farmers and the owners of the land.

I·RE´NE, an empress of Constantinople, born in Athens about 752. She was famous for her beauty, genius, and wickedness. Her husband, Leo IV., at his death in 780, left the empire in her charge until their son Constantine VI. should be grown up. When Constantine became a man he took the throne, but she liked to rule so well that she tried to have him murdered, and at last got a man to put out his eyes. The cruel woman then ruled in great splendor, and when her chariot of gold and precious stones passed through the streets it was drawn by four white horses led by four nobles on foot. In 802 her treasurer Nicephorus was secretly made emperor, and he banished Irene to the island of Lesbos, where she had to gain her bread by spinning. She died there the next year (803).

IRE'TON, Henry, a noted English soldier, born in Nottinghamshire in 1610. He was brought up to the law, but when the war broke out between Charles I. and his people he joined the army of the Parliament. He married Bridget, daughter of Oliver Cromwell, and soon got high rank in the army. At NASEBY he commanded the left wing of the Roundhead army, and was wounded and made prisoner, but escaped. When King Charles was tried he sat as one of the judges, and signed his death-warrant. He went with Cromwell to Ireland (1649), and was left there as Lord Deputy, but died two years afterward at Limerick in the forty-second year of his age (Nov. 26, 1651).

I'RIS, in Greek fable, the goddess of the rainbow, the constant attendant of Juno, and messenger of the gods.

IRKUTSK (*ir-kootsk'*), a city of S. Siberia, on the Angara River, 35 miles from Lake Baikal ; pop. 39,000, or about as large as Harrisburg, Pa. It is the capital of Eastern Siberia, and the chief station for trade between Russia and China. In the surrounding country are rich mines, and many farms. The city is surrounded by a wall, and is well built, though most of the houses are of wood. Among the public buildings are large workshops where convicts from Russia are employed. A great fair is held at Irkutsk every year in June. Irkutsk means the town on the Irkut, a branch of the River Angara.

IRON MASK, Man in the, a prisoner of state, in the reign of Louis XIV., who died in the Bastile, Nov. 19, 1703. No one knows who he was. He was brought to the Bastile in a close litter, and accompanied by a mounted guard, his face covered with a black velvet mask fastened with steel springs which he was forbidden to take off on pain of death.

He was permitted to speak to no one, and the greatest care was taken to keep him from having anything to do with any one outside his prison walls. After his death everything which had ever been used by him was burned. Although more than a century and a half have passed since then, no one has been able to find any clue to the strange mystery of this man. Who could he have been, and why so much secrecy about him, are questions which have never been satisfactorily answered. A few years ago a book was written on the subject, but it still remains a mystery.

IROQUOIS (*ir'o-kwoy*). See AMERICAN INDIANS.

IRRAWADDY (*ir-rah-wod'de*), a river of Asia, rising in the Himalaya Mountains, near the boundary of Burmah and Thibet, and flowing S. through Burmah and British Burmah, to the Bay of Bengal ; length, 1060 miles. In the lower part it is four or five miles wide during the yearly floods, which last from June to September. It can be navigated by small vessels for more than 800 miles. The Irrawaddy has many mouths, which enclose a large, swampy delta.

IRVING, Washington, a famous American author, born in New York City, April 3, 1783. He belonged to a family whose tastes were literary, and though he studied law, never practised it. His first writings were published when he was about nineteen years old, in a newspaper edited by his brother. His first book was a humorous history of New York, published under the name of Diedrich Knickerbocker. This was not intended for a real history, but it gave offence to some of the descendants of the old Dutch settlers, who thought their ancestors were ridiculed in it. " The Sketch-Book," which was published in England under the name of Geoffrey Crayon, was the first of his books that had a great success. This was highly praised in England, and gave him a wide reputation. He afterward wrote "Bracebridge Hall," "Tales of a Traveller," "History of Columbus," "The Conquest of Granada," "Tales of the Alhambra," and other books which were very popular, and brought him a great deal of money. These were all written in Europe, where he lived for seventeen years. He came back to America in 1832, travelled all over the West, and

Washington Irving.

wrote other books; then in 1842 went to Spain as American minister, and stayed there four years. On his return he wrote the "Life of Washington," which was his last and longest work. He was the most successful of American authors, and one of the most loved and honored. He died at Sunnyside, his beautiful home at Tarrytown, N. Y., when seventy-six years old (Nov. 28, 1859).

IS·A·BEL'LA I., called the Catholic, Queen of Castile and Leon, born in Madrigal, April 23, 1451. She was the daughter of King John II., and she succeeded her half-brother Henry IV. on the throne when twenty-three years old (1474). She had previously been married (1469) to Ferdinand, who soon after became

King of Aragon, and the crowns of Castile and Aragon were ever afterward joined together, except for a short time. In 1481 the Catholic kings, as Ferdinand and Isabella were called, began a war with the Moorish kingdom of GRANADA, and in 1492 they took the city of Granada and united the kingdom to Castile. This was the beginning of the kingdom of Spain, which soon grew to be the greatest power in Europe. Queen Isabella herself took part in this war, and the armor which she wore is still kept in Madrid. She is best known for the aid which she gave to COLUMBUS, the ships in which he sailed having been fitted out at her cost. She was beautiful and good, and ruled with such wisdom that her memory is still cherished in Spain. One of her daughters, Juana, was the mother of the Emperor CHARLES V., and another, Catharine, was the wife of HENRY VIII. of England. She died when fifty-three years old (Nov. 26, 1504).

I S A U R I A (*i-saw're-ah*). See ASIA MINOR.

I'SIS, the chief goddess of the Egyptians, the wife of OSIRIS and mother of HORUS. She was the mother of all things, and first taught the people how to raise wheat and corn. The cow was sacred to her. She was worshipped also in Greece and in Italy.

Isis and Horus.

ISLES OF SHOALS, a group of nine little islands, about ten miles from the coast of New Hampshire. Appledore, the largest island, contains only 400 acres, but a fine hotel has been built on it. This and the other islands are visited in summer by thousands of pleasure-seekers from Portsmouth. Star Island (150 acres) contained nearly 100 inhabitants, mostly fishermen, but in 1872 all their land was purchased and a large hotel was built there. The islands were discovered by CHAMPLAIN in 1605.

ISMAIL I. (*is-mah-eel'*), fifth khedive or viceroy of Egypt, born in Cairo, in 1830. He was the son of Ibrahim Pasha. In 1863 he became viceroy of Egypt, and in 1866 the sultan said that that office should descend in his line, in return for which favor Ismail agreed to pay more tribute. The next year his title was altered to khedive, which is that now used by the Egyptian viceroys. Originally they ruled Egypt under the sultan, but in 1873 they became almost independent. The khedive is the owner of all the land of Egypt, and his subjects are only his tenants. Ismail was obliged to give up his power, Aug. 8, 1879, and his son, Mohammed Tewfik (born Nov. 19, 1852) is now khedive.

ISOCRATES (*i-sok'ra-teez*), an Athenian orator, born in 436 B.C. The famous Socrates was his teacher, and his education was the best that could be had in Athens. He founded a school, and had for his pupils young men who became the greatest statesmen, orators, and philosophers of their day. After the battle of Chæronea, which gave Philip of Macedon the mastery over Greece, he killed himself by starvation, because he did not wish to live to see his country enslaved. He died when ninety-eight years old (338 B.C.).

ISPAHAN (*is-pah-hahn'*), a city of Central Persia, 210 miles S. of TEHERAN; pop. 90,000, or a little larger than Columbus, O. It was once the capital and grandest city of Persia, and though many of the palaces are falling to ruins, enough still remains to make it a very splendid place. The great square, called the Maidan Shah, is surrounded by magnificent mosques and by fine buildings once used for the court officers. The great bazaar is two miles long, and roofed to keep out the rain and sun,

but hundreds of the shops which line it are now deserted.

Formerly the cloths and ornamental work sold at Ispahan were among the finest in the East, but the trade in them has greatly fallen off. The people of Ispahan are better educated than most Persians, and many of them are very intelligent and shrewd. The country around is very fertile, and is covered with vineyards, orchards, and farms, with many palaces and villages among them.

Ispahan means in Persian the "place of horses." The city is about 1600 years old. It was captured by TIMOUR in 1387, and 70,-000 of the inhabitants were killed.

ITALY (*it'a-le*), a S. country of Europe, forming a long peninsula between the Mediterranean and Adriatic Seas, and including also the islands of SICILY and SARDINIA, and some smaller islands; area, 114,500 square miles, or about as large as the State of Nevada; pop. 31,000,000, or about one half that of the United States; capital, ROME. In the northern part is the beautiful plain of Lombardy, which is separated from Austria and Switzerland by the Alps, and from France and the Mediterranean by the Apennines. Through this plain runs the Po, the largest river of Italy. The Apennines extend quite to the end of the peninsula, and are bordered on each side by plains, which in some places are low and marshy. Next to the Po the principal rivers are the Tiber and the Arno on the western side. There are many beautiful lakes, most of which are in the craters of dead volcanoes. The only active volcano on the peninsula is Mt. Vesuvius at NAPLES; but there are two others on the islands—Mt. Etna, in Sicily, and Mt. Stromboli, on one of the Lipari Islands, north of Sicily. In many places are hot springs, some of which will coat with stone any things placed in them. Italy has important mines of iron, lead, and salt. The most beautiful marble in the world is quarried at CARRARA, and a great deal of it is sent to the United States and other countries for making statues. Among the other fine stones are alabaster, porphyry, lapis lazuli, jasper, agate, and chalcedony. There are many fine farms, where wheat, corn, and vegetables are raised. Chestnuts are very common, and many poor people eat them for bread. More olives are raised, and more olive-oil is made in Italy than in any other country. There are also large vineyards, and a great deal of wine is sold. Silk worms are reared in many places, and more silk is sold than in any other country except China. Some of it is made into velvet and silk cloth, and there are also large factories of woollen and cotton cloths. Among the other manufactures are straw hats, gloves, perfumery, and many fancy articles. The Italians are very skilful in making cameos, mosaics, and other kinds of jewellery, and the country is famous for its paintings and statuary. The climate in the summer is warm, and the sky is clear and deep blue. The winters are mild, snow falling only in the northern part, and among the mountains.

The people of Italy generally have dark skins and black hair and eyes. Most of the poor people are very ignorant and lazy, and hundreds of them spend their lives in begging; but the upper classes are very intelligent and refined. The cities are noted for their palaces and churches, and their priceless museums and libraries. The country is governed by a king and a congress, much like that of the United States, except that the senators are appointed for life. The principal religion is the Roman Catholic, but people of all other religions are allowed to worship as they please.

Some of the old writers say that Italy got its name from *italos*, a Greek word meaning an ox, because it was a good country for cattle; others that it was named from an ancient King Italus. The name first belonged only to the southern end, next to Sicily, but in the time of the Emperor AUGUSTUS it was given to the whole country. Sicily and the south part of Italy were first settled by Greeks, from whom this part got the name of Magna Græcia (Great Greece). In the northern parts lived the Etruscans, Umbrians, Oscans, Latins, Sabines, Samnites, Volsci, Æqui, and other tribes. All these people were made into one nation by the Romans, who conquered all Italy about 275 B.C.

Italy belonged to the Roman Empire until the end of the 8th century, when it passed into the hands of the Germans, and CHARLES THE GREAT became emperor (A.D. 800). In the 13th century Italy began to fall away from the German Empire. Soon after the popes began to get power in Rome and in other parts, and many small commonwealths, ruled over by different cities, grew up, some of which became powerful. Among these were MILAN, VENICE, GENOA, PISA, and FLORENCE; in the south was the Kingdom of Sicily, which ruled the island of Sicily and a good deal of the mainland. In the 13th century this kingdom was divided, and the part on the mainland was commonly called the Kingdom of Naples. But the kings in each called themselves kings of Sicily, so that when the two were joined again (1504) they were called the Kingdom of the Two Sicilies.

In the 16th century Italy was the battle-field where the princes of Europe fought out their quarrels, but in 1530 most of it came under the power of the king of Spain. In the 17th century the dukes of Savoy began to get power, and in the beginning of the 18th century they got Sicily, and the duke became king of Sicily. But soon after he exchanged Sicily for Sardinia, and after that took the title of king of Sardinia. When Bonaparte became emperor of France he made northern Italy into a kingdom, of which he made himself king ; and southern Italy into a Kingdom of Naples for his brother Joseph. Sicily and Sardinia were still held by their own kings, Bonaparte not being able to conquer them because they were islands and the British fleet could help them. When Bonaparte fell, the king of Sicily got back Naples and the rest of his territory on the mainland, the king of Sardinia got back Savoy and Piedmont, Austria took Venice and other territory along the Adriatic, the pope again got Rome and the rest of his territory, and several other smaller governments were set up. Napoleon III. helped the king of Sardinia to free part of Italy from Austria (1859) ; Garibaldi freed the Two Sicilies and added them to the Kingdom of Sardinia, and in 1861 the king of Sardinia became king of all Italy except a part held by Austria and the pope's dominions. At last Italy got Venice and Verona from Austria (1866), and Rome from the pope (1870), and it is now once more united under one king.

ITHACA (*ith'a kah*). See IONIAN ISLANDS.

I'VAN, the name of several rulers of Russia.

Ivan III., called the Great, reigned from 1462 to 1505. Before his time the Russians had paid tribute to the Mongols, but he refused to pay it longer, and when they invaded his country he drove them out. He also conquered several neighboring states and part of Siberia, and was the first to assume the title of "Autocrat of all the Russias." He married Sophia, an imperial princess of Constantinople, and took for his arms the double-headed eagle of the Eastern and Western Empires, which since his time has always been in the arms of Russia.

Ivan IV., his grandson, reigned from 1533 to 1584, and was called the Terrible on account of his cruelty in war. In 1570 he put more than 60,000 men to death in Novgorod, and his whole life was stained with crimes, though he made his country very powerful.

IVRY-LA-BATAILLE (*eve'ry lah bat-tah'e*), a village of France, on the River Eure, 40 miles W. of Paris; pop. about 1500. It contains some celebrated manufactories of wind musical instruments, and the ruins of an ancient castle. Ivry is chiefly noted for the great victory won by the Huguenots, under King HENRY IV., over the army of the League (March 14, 1590). Before the battle the Huguenots sang a psalm, and the king made a speech, saying, "Upon them ! God is for us. Behold His enemies and yours. If signals fail you, follow my white plume. It shall lead the way to honor and victory !" Macaulay has written a fine ballad about this battle.

Ivry-la-bataille means Battle-Ivry. It is so called to distinguish it from Ivry-sur-Seine, or Ivry-on-the-Seine, which is close to Paris, and has a strong fort.

IX'I-ON, in Greek fable, King of the Lapithæ, in Thessaly. He married Dia, the daughter of Deïoneus, promising to give her father valuable bridal gifts. When Deïoneus claimed them he invited him to a feast, and then had him thrown into a fiery pit. For this he was shunned by all, until Jupiter forgave him. But he again angered Jupiter, who had him chained to a wheel which was made to turn round forever.

J

JACK'SON, a city of Michigan, on the Grand River, near its source; pop. 21,000, or about as large as Lincoln, R. I. Several railroads meet there, and the city contains large railroad machine-shops, and the finest railroad depot in the State. There is a large rolling-mill and manufactories of chemicals, bricks, pottery, wagons, and iron-ware. The Michigan State penitentiary is at Jackson.

JACKSON, Andrew, seventh President of the United States, born at Waxhaw Settlement, N. C., March 15, 1767. His father, a very poor man, died before Andrew was born, and the boy had to make his own way in life at a very early age. But he was a plucky little fellow, quite ready to fight the British when only thirteen years old, and not to be conquered by them even when he was taken prisoner. A British officer one day ordered him to clean his boots; but Andrew refused, and

Andrew Jackson.

though the officer beat him cruelly with his sword, he could not make the boy obey him. After his mother's death, when he was about sixteen, he worked in a saddler's shop for a while, then taught school and studied law, and before he was twenty began to practise. He became by and by the District Attorney of Tennessee, and afterward, when Tennessee became a State, he was its first member of Congress. He fulfilled his duties there so well that he was soon elected to the Senate; and afterward was a judge of the Supreme Court, and a major-general of the State militia.

In 1813, when the Creek Indians began a war, he raised an army of volunteers, and conquered them so thoroughly that they were never a power in the country again. For this he was made a major-general in the United States army. Soon afterward he captured Pensacola, and won his famous victory over the British at NEW ORLEANS. He also conquered the Seminole Indians in 1817. After Spain ceded Florida to the United States he was governor of the territory for a short time; was chosen United States Senator from Tennessee in 1823, and in 1828 was elected President. He held the office for two terms, and was one of the most popular of all our presidents. He died at his farm called the Hermitage, near Nashville, Tenn., when seventy-seven years old (June 8, 1845).

JACKSON, Thomas Jonathan, commonly called "Stonewall Jackson," an American general, born in Clarksburg, Va., January 21, 1824. He was graduated at West Point, and served with distinction in the Mexican and Seminole wars, but in 1852 resigned and became a professor in a military academy at Lexington, Va. He was a deacon in the Presbyterian Church, and was noted for his piety and his bashfulness. When the Civil War broke out he entered the Confederate army, and soon became a general. At the battle of Bull Run, when it appeared that the Confederates were defeated, he made a brave stand with his soldiers, and some one cried, "There stands Jackson, like a stone wall"; and after that he was called Stonewall Jackson.

In the spring of 1862, Gen. Jackson commanded in the Shenandoah Valley, where he successfully fought armies much larger than his own. After fighting in the battles of Cold Harbor and Malvern Hill, he was again sent northward, and took part in the battles of Cedar Mountain, August 9, 1862, and the second battle of Bull Run, August 29 and 30, 1862. On September 15 he captured 11,000 Union soldiers at Harper's Ferry, and by quick marching joined Gen. Lee at the battle of Antietam, September 17. After the battle of Fredericksburg he was made lieutenant-general. At the battle of Chancellorville, May 2, 1863, he surprised the Union army, and drove part of it back. While riding with a few officers in the woods to reconnoitre, he and his men were mistaken for Unionists and fired upon by his own men. He was struck by three balls, and died near Fredericksburg, a few days after, aged thirty-nine years (May 10, 1863).

JACK'SON-VILLE, a city of Illinois, 30 miles W. by S. of Springfield; pop. 11,000, or about as large as Denison, Tex. It has a woollen mill and other manufactories, and contains several colleges and academies, and state institutions for the deaf and dumb, blind, insane, and for feeble-minded children.

JACQUARD (*zhahk-kar'*), **Joseph Marie,** the inventor of the Jacquard loom, born in Lyons, France, July 7, 1752. He was a weaver, but spent so much time in trying to make new looms that he became very poor, and was obliged to sell his shop. During the French Revolution he and his son fought as private soldiers. Returning to Lyons, he continued his inventions, and finally contrived several looms which could be used with half the labor needed by the old

ones. The weavers, fearing that they would no longer find employment, opposed him at first, and broke his looms; but when they found that their use added to the number of laborers, by giving more work, they favored him, and he became very rich and famous.

Joseph Marie Jacquard.

By means of his loom the finest and richest kinds of cloths, even those with all kinds of figures and patterns on them, can be woven almost as easily as plain cloths. Jacquard also made a machine for weaving nets. His machine was shown to Napoleon and Carnot, and Carnot asked him if he was the man who pretended to do the impossible—to tie a knot in a stretched string. But Jacquard showed him how it could be done by his machine, and he was given a gold medal for his discovery. He died when eighty-two years old (Aug. 7, 1834).

JAFFA (*jaf'fah*), or **Yafa,** a town of Palestine, on the Mediterranean Sea, 35 miles N.W. of Jerusalem; pop. about 8000, or about as large as Winston, N. C. It is surrounded by walls, and from a distance has a very picturesque appearance; but a closer view shows that the streets are very narrow and dirty, with hardly any good buildings. Jaffa has no harbor, except a small one for boats, but it is the only port of Palestine, and has an important trade. It is the landing-place for travellers going to Jerusalem.

Jaffa was anciently called Joppa, and it is often mentioned in the Bible. It was an important place during the CRUSADES, and was captured by Napoleon in 1799. In 1866 a colony of Americans went there to live, but most of them soon gave up and went home.

JAMAICA (*ja-ma'kah*), an island of the West Indies, south of Cuba; area, 4500 miles, or about as large as Connecticut; pop. about 617,000, or not quite five sixths that of Connecticut; capital, KINGSTON. The island is mountainous, and presents a grand sight from the sea, some of the peaks being more than a mile high.

There are great plantations of sugar-cane, and fruits, such as oranges, bananas, and cocoa-nuts, grow in abundance; mahogany and other fine timbers are found in the woods. The climate is hot and unhealthy near the sea-shore, but cool and pleasant among the mountains. There are frequent hurricanes, which sink ships, blow down houses, and often destroy many lives. Sometimes the island is visited by terrible earthquakes; one in 1692 shook the whole island, making great cracks in the ground and swallowing up many people. Many of the inhabitants are negroes and their descendants; but most of the planters and merchants are Englishmen. Jamaica belongs to Great Britain, and is ruled by a governor-general appointed by the Queen.

Jamaica was discovered by Columbus in 1494; it was settled by the Spaniards, captured by the English, and recaptured by the Spaniards; but finally (1655) was taken again by the English, and has ever since been held by them. For a long time the negroes were slaves, but they were freed in 1833.

JAMES I., third Stuart King of Scotland, born at Dunfermline, about 1394. He was the son of Robert III., and succeeded him in 1406. The year before his father's death he set sail for France to be educated, but his vessel was taken by the English, and he was kept a prisoner for nineteen years. He was well treated by the English kings, Henry IV. and Henry V., who gave him an excellent education, and he became an author, and wrote poems which are still admired. When he went back to Scotland (1425) he found everything in disorder. In restoring quiet he was so severe against the unruly nobles that some of them had him murdered at Perth when forty-three years old (Feb. 21, 1437). He was succeeded by his son, James II.

JAMES II., fourth Stuart King of Scotland, born in 1430. He was the son of James I., and succeeded him, when seven years old, in 1437. During his childhood there were constant quarrels between his tutors and the powerful family of DOUGLAS. When he grew up he continued these disputes, and slew one of the Earls of Douglas with his own hand. He took the side of Henry VI., the Lancastrian King of England, in the Wars of the Roses. In 1460, while besieging a fortress, he was killed by the bursting of a gun. He was succeeded by his son, James III.

JAMES III., fifth Stuart King of Scotland, born in 1453. He was the son of James II., and succeeded him in 1460. His reign was one of the most unfortunate in Scottish history. The nobles were rough and ignorant, and therefore hated their king, who was fond of peace and of learning. The whole of this reign was taken up with quarrels with these wild nobles, James' own brothers siding with them. Scotland had trouble, too, with England because of the aid that she gave to the Lancastrian party against the Yorkists. At last the Scotch nobles persuaded young Prince James, the king's son, then only fifteen years old, to join in a rebellion against his father; and a battle was fought in which the king was defeated and slain in 1488. He was succeeded by his son, James IV.

JAMES IV., sixth Stuart King of Scotland, born March 17, 1472. He was the son of James III., and succeeded him in 1488. He made friends with the nobles instead of making them his enemies, as the other kings had done, so that there was no more strife in Scotland, and this quiet was used for the good of the kingdom. He invaded England, however, in the cause of Perkin WARBECK, whom he and many others thought to be Richard, Duke of York, the young son of Edward IV., who was supposed before this to have perished in the Tower. He married Margaret, the daughter of the English king, Henry VII. Some years later troubles began with England, leading to a war during which he was killed at the battle of FLODDEN (Sep. 9, 1513). He was succeeded by his son, James V.

JAMES V., seventh Stuart King of Scotland, born at Linlithgow, April 10, 1512. He was the son of James IV., and succeeded him when only a year old (1513), under the guardianship of his mother. When he began to rule he found that the nobles had got the upper hand, and he had much trouble to bring them to order. He married first Madeleine, daughter of Francis I., of France, and, on her death, Mary of Guise. In this way he became very friendly to the Roman Catholic party in Europe, and consequently had a falling out with his cousin, Henry VIII., of England, who had rebelled against the Pope. War was the result. James was defeated at Solway Moss, and died broken-hearted a few days afterward (Dec. 13, 1542), leaving to succeed him his infant daughter, Mary, the celebrated Queen of Scots.

JAMES I., first Stuart King of England, born at Edinburgh, June

19, 1566. He was the son of Henry Stuart, Lord Darnley, and Mary, Queen of Scots. He was also James VI. of Scotland, and the ninth Stuart sovereign on the Scottish throne. He became King of Scotland in 1567, his mother having been dethroned, and he succeeded Elizabeth as sovereign of England in 1603. His title came from his great-grandmother, Margaret, daughter of Henry VII. His reign is marked by many events. It was he that found out the " Gunpowder Plot," when Guy FAWKES tried to blow up the Parliament House. In his time began the Thirty Years' War, but he took no part in it, though his daughter Elizabeth, Electress Palatine, had much to do with it. The most remarkable event of his reign is the translation of the Bible into English, by his order. James was a man of some learning, of which he was very vain. He was very weak, and was ruled by favorites. He died, when fifty-eight years old (March 27, 1625), and was succeeded by his son, Charles I.

JAMES II., fourth Stuart King of England, born Oct. 15, 1633. He was the son of Charles I., and succeeded his brother Charles II. in 1685. Before he became king he was called the Duke of York. He was a Roman Catholic, and many of the English wanted to keep him from the throne on this account. The first thing he had to do on becoming king was to put down a rebellion headed by the Duke of Monmouth, and great cruelties were shown to those who had taken part in it. In a very short time he showed how right were the fears of those who did not want him to be king. He paid no attention to the law, and tried his best to restore the Roman Catholic religion. The people rose against him and sent to Holland begging William, Prince of Orange, and his wife, Mary, James's daughter, to come over and take the throne, which they did. James fled to France, where he spent the rest of his life trying to get back his throne. In 1689 he went to Ireland and raised an army among his friends there, but was defeated at the battle of the BOYNE (1690), and returned to France. He died at St. Germain, when sixty-eight years old (Sept. 16, 1701).

JAMES, George Payne Rainsford, an English writer, born in London in 1801. While a boy he was in the habit of writing pieces for the magazines, the first book bearing his name being a "Life of Edward the Black Prince," written when he was twenty-one years old, and published by advice of Washington Irving. He held some positions under his government—that of historiographer of England, under William IV., and later was consul at Norfolk, Virginia, and at Venice. Among his best writings are "Richelieu," "Darnley," and "Life and Times of Louis XIV." He died in Venice, when fifty-nine years old (June 9, 1860).

JAMES, Henry, Jr., an American writer, born in New York, April 15, 1843. He is the son of Henry James, an author of some celebrity, and was educated partly in this country and partly in Europe. He has lived mostly in France and Italy, and has written stories, sketches of travels for reviews and magazines, and several books, among them "The American" and "The Europeans."

JA'ME·SON, Anna, a noted British writer, born in Dublin, May 19, 1797. She was the daughter of an artist, and many of her books are about pictures, and painters, and other art matters. In 1823 she married Mr. Robert Jameson, and went with him to Canada, where he had a government office. The marriage not being a happy one, she left her husband and gave herself up to writing, by means of which she educated her younger sisters, and did a great deal for her family. Among her books are the "Lives of

Celebrated Female Sovereigns," "Memoirs of Italian Painters," "The History of Sacred and Legendary Art," and "Legends of the Madonna." She died in London, when nearly sixty-three years old (March 17, 1860).

JAMES'TOWN, the first English settlement in what is now the United States, on the James River, Virginia, 32 miles from its mouth. In 1607 a party of 105 colonists arrived there from England, under the command of Christopher North. They named the river in honor of King James II., and began to build the town in May. During the first year they suffered much, and were only saved from death by Captain John SMITH. Jamestown was burned in 1676, and since then the river has partly changed its bed, so that the site is now an island. All that can now be seen of the settlement is a ruined church tower, with some old tombstones standing around it.

JAN'I-ZA-RIES. See AMURATH I.

JANES'VILLE, a city of S. Wisconsin, on Rock River; pop. 11,000, or about as large as Augusta, Me. Several railroads meet there, and there is a large trade. The city contains many flour and saw mills, machine-shops, founderies, woollen mills, breweries, and other manufactories. Janesville was founded about 1836, and became a city in 1853,

JA'NUS, a Roman god, who presided over the beginning of everything. He was also the keeper of the gates of heaven, and of all gates and doors on earth. The first day of the year was sacred to his worship, and the first month was called January after him. He went to aid the Romans in time of war; but stayed in his temple in time of peace. Therefore the doors of this temple were kept open when the Romans were at war and closed when they were at peace. He is represented sometimes with two and sometimes with four faces.

JA·PAN', a country made up of a group of islands off the E. coast of Asia; area, 150,000 square miles, or more than three times as large as New York State; pop. 39,000,000, or not quite seven times that of New York; capital, TOKIO. The principal islands are called Nippon, Kiushiu, Shikoku, and Yezo or Yesso; but Japan also owns some of the KURILE islands and the Riu Kiu or Liu Kiu Islands, commonly called Loo Choo, and many small islands. Nearly all the islands are mountainous, and many have burning volcanoes.

The most famous mountain is FUSIYAMA, on the island of Nippon, 70 miles from Tokio. Great damage has been done in Japan by volcanoes, and also by earthquakes, sometimes whole cities having been destroyed. Slight earthquakes are felt almost every month; ignorant people say they are caused by the flopping of a great catfish under one of the islands.

Japan is very fertile and well cultivated, though almost all farming is done by hand and with very rude tools. The climate is much like that of our Middle States, but floods of rain and high winds are common.

ships, houses, and lives. Japan is rich in gold, silver, mercury, copper,

Mutsu Hito, Mikado of Japan.

tin, lead, coal, salt, sulphur, and fine building stones. Iron is found, but it is not very good. Many timber and cabinet trees grow in the woods, and fruits and vegetables are plentiful. The principal crops are rice and tea. There are not many kinds of wild animals, but monkeys are so plentiful as to be often a pest. The people eat them. Horses are small, in some places no larger

Japanese Boats.

Cyclones or typhoons sometimes do immense damage, destroying many than Shetland ponies, and in one part they are woolly. Most of the cats have short stumpy tails. The waters are full of fish, and fish is the principal animal food of the people, many liking it raw.

The Japanese people are of middling size, and are strong and active. They are rather darker than the Chinese, and have straight, coarse, dark-brown hair. Men used to shave all of the head except a tuft on top, but most of them now dress their hair as we do. Each class has a peculiar kind of dress, but many have adopted the European costume, and all government officers are obliged to wear it. The picture of the Mikado shows him as he used to dress. The Japanese are also adopting European manners and customs, and are sending their children to Europe and the United States to be educated.

The people are bright and quick at understanding things, and are very industrious. They are, too, very lively, and fond of music, danc-

A Jinrikisha.

ing, and amusements. Japanese jugglers, conjurors, and tumblers are famous (C.C.T., 226, II.). Most of them are Buddhists in religion, though many believe in what is called Shinto, which is supposed to be the ancient religion. The Shintoists worship their ancestors and offer sacrifices to departed heroes. The Japanese are very skilful in working metals and in carving in wood, ivory, and stone. They are also noted for their manufactures of paper, cotton, and silk, for beautiful lacquered work, and for fine porcelain and earthenware. In the art of painting they show great taste, as may be seen in their pictures on porcelain, and on screens and fans.

The roads in Japan are very good, but there are few vehicles drawn by horses. People travel mostly on horseback, or in a kind of carriage called *jinrikisha*, which is drawn by men. Each of these holds one person, and they go very fast. Merchandise is mostly carried by water, and there are a vast number of boats used of many kinds. Their large vessels are much like Chinese junks, but many steamers and other European vessels are now used.

Japan is ruled by an emperor called the Mikado. The name Japan is made from a Chinese word meaning Sunrise Kingdom; the Japanese call their country Dai Nippon. Its history goes back more than two thousand years. In 1274 it was invaded by the Mongols, but they were soon driven away. The Portuguese made settlements in Japan in the 16th century, but they were afterward driven out, and for a long time the Japanese would not let foreigners come into their country. In 1854 the United States sent a fleet there under Commodore Perry, and the Mikado was forced to make a treaty with him. Since then they have made treaties with other nations, and everybody can now go there.

JA-PE'TUS. See TITANS.

JAS'PER, William, an American soldier in the Revolution, born in South Carolina about 1750. When the war began he joined the army and soon became a sergeant. During the attack on Fort Moultrie, in Charleston harbor, by a British fleet, the flag was shot away by a cannon ball and fell outside the fort on the beach. Jasper leaped down, amid a shower of balls, picked up the flag, and restored it to its place. For this brave act he was offered a lieutenancy; but he refused it, and instead accepted from his commander, Colonel Moultrie, a commission to go about the country with a few men, surprising and attacking the enemy's outposts. He and his men did many daring and wonderful deeds in this way, and had many narrow escapes. During the attack on Savannah by the Americans, Jasper was shot, while attempting to fasten the flag of South Carolina on one of the parapets. Although fatally wounded, he held his flag firmly, and had it placed where it would be safe, before he died (Oct. 9, 1779).

JAVA (*jah'vah*), an island of the East Indian Archipelago, S.E. of Sumatra, between the Java Sea and the Indian Ocean; area, 50,000 square miles, or about as large as North Carolina; pop. 22,000,000, or more than thirteen times that of North Carolina; capital, Batavia. The island is long and narrow, and a range of high mountains extends from one end to the other, through the centre. Some of the peaks are two miles high, and nearly forty of them are burning volcanoes, which have killed thousands of people during their eruptions. The Tenger volcano has the largest crater in the world, except that of Kilauea in the Hawaiian Islands. The plains and valleys of Java are very fertile, and are celebrated for their coffee plantations, which are the finest in the world. Rice, sugar, indigo, cotton, tea, and many other crops are also produced. The Javanese are a brown race much like the Malays. They have a peculiar language, and are noted for their intelligence and industry, and their skill in working in metals. Nearly all of them are Mohammedans. The Sundese, who live on the western end of the island, are similar to the Javanese, but much less intelligent. Java belongs to the Netherlands, and many of the merchants and planters are immigrants from that country.

In ancient times the Javanese were very rich and powerful, and the remains of their temples and palaces are among the most splendid ruins in the world. The Dutch first went to Java in 1595, and they gradually conquered the whole island.

JAY, John, the first chief justice of the United States, born in New York, Dec. 12, 1745. He was educated at King's (now Columbia) College, and in 1768 became a lawyer in New York. When the Revolution began, he first proposed that there should be a congress of the United Colonies, and he himself was a member of the Congress, and at one time its president. Being absent in July, 1776, he did not sign the

Declaration of Independence, but he heartily approved of it. He was one of a convention appointed to form a government for the State of New York, and nearly all of the Constitution was written by him. Afterward he was chief justice of the State. In 1779 he was appointed minister to Spain, and in 1782 he and Franklin were the principal members of the commission sent to Paris to arrange a treaty of peace with Great Britain.

Afterward Jay was secretary of foreign affairs and a member of the Congress which formed a Constitution for the United States in 1789. When Washington became President, he offered Jay his choice of any office he could give him, and Jay decided to be chief justice (1789). In 1794 he was made a special minister to England, where he arranged an important treaty. Many Americans were opposed to this treaty, and there was great excitement about it, some going so far as to burn an effigy of Jay in the streets of Boston ; but the treaty was finally approved by Washington and Congress. Mr. Jay was governor of New York State from 1794 to 1800. At the end of that time he was again chosen chief justice, but he declined the honor, and gave up public life altogether, going to live at Bedford, N. Y., where he died, when eighty-three years old (May 17, 1829).

JEDBURGH (*jed'bur-ruh*), a town of S. Scotland, on the River Jed, 42 miles S.E. of Edinburgh ; pop. 3400. It is noted for the ruins of a fine old abbey and for its castle, in which many of the Scottish kings lived, but which is now used for a prison. In old times Jedburgh was one of the chief Scottish strongholds, and many battles were fought there between the Scotch and English. Jedburgh means the town on the Jed.

JEF'FER-SON, Thomas, third President of the United States, born at Shadwell, Albemarle County, Va., April 2, 1743. He was the son of a wealthy planter, was educated at William and Mary's College, and afterward became a successful lawyer. When twenty-six years old he was a member of the House of Burgesses

Thomas Jefferson.

of Virginia, and began to take an active part against Great Britain. When the first Congress met, in 1776, he was one of the delegates, and was chosen to write the Declaration of Independence. During the war he was governor of Virginia, and in 1784 was sent as minister to France. In 1789 he was Secretary of State under General Washington, in 1797 Vice-President under President Adams, and from 1801 to 1809 was President himself. Jefferson believed in religious freedom ; that is, he held that every man had a right to his own religious opinions, and was not bound to support the church of England unless he chose to. He secured this liberty for the people of Virginia, and also abolished the law of entail, which required a man to leave all his landed property to his eldest son. He tried to put a stop to the slave-trade, and to keep slavery out of the territories. He died at his estate of Monticello, eighty-three years old, on the fiftieth anniversary of the Declaration of Independence (July 4, 1826).

JEMMAPES (*zhe-map'*), or **Ge-**

mappe, a village of Belgium, on the River Haine, 3 miles W. of Mons ; pop. 12,000, or about as large as Rutland, Vt. It is noted for a victory gained there by a French army, commanded by Dumouriez, over the Austrians (Nov. 6, 1792). This was the first great battle won by the Republicans after the French Revolution, and the results were very important.

JENA (*jen'ah*), a town of Central Germany, on the River Saale, 12 miles S.E. of Weimar ; pop. 12,000. It lies in a valley, partly surrounded by steep mountains, and noted for its beautiful scenery. Jena has a celebrated university, which was founded in 1547, and has had some of the greatest German scholars among its professors. During the last century it generally had from 2000 to 3000 students, but at present there are about 450. The university library is one of the best in Germany, and there are fine museums, a botanical garden, an observatory, and many large buildings.

Near Jena, Napoleon gained a great victory over the Austrians, commanded by Prince Hohenlohe (Oct. 14, 1806). On the same day Marshal Davoust won a still more glorious victory over another Prussian army at Auerstadt, a few miles north of Jena.

JEN'GHIS KHAN. See GENGHIS KHAN.

JEN'NER, Edward, a noted English physician, born in Berkeley, Gloucestershire, May 17, 1749. He is famous for his discovery that vaccinating people with cow-pox would save them from taking small-pox, a disease which had long been very common in Europe. He got his idea from hearing that peasants who had accidentally caught the cow-pox from milking cows diseased with it were free from danger of small-pox. He worked many years to find a sure way of vaccinating one person from another, as well as from the pock of

a cow ; and although he proved it a success, it took many years more to get the London physicians to believe in it. At last, about the year 1800, vaccination began to be widely practised, and soon spread all over the globe. Wealth and honors were bestowed upon Jenner, and he was called a benefactor of mankind Jenner was very fond of the natura history of birds, and wrote an admirable work on the English cuckoo. He was a man of fine tastes and intellect, and did much good among the poor in Gloucestershire. He died at Berkeley, when nearly seventy-four years old (Jan. 26, 1823).

JEREZ, or **Xeres de la Frontera** (*ha-res' da lah fron-ta'rah*), a town of S. Spain, 13 miles N.E. of Cadiz ; pop. 65,000, or a little larger than Memphis, Tenn. It contains many curious old buildings, the finest of which is the Alcazar, or old Moorish citadel, a kind of fortress and palace together. Jerez is in one of the most fertile regions in Spain, and from the grapes raised there large quantities of wine are made. The most celebrated of these wines is Sherry, which is only the English way of pronouncing Jerez.

Jerez is one of the oldest cities in Spain. Near it Roderic, the last king of the Visigoths, was defeated by the Moors, in a battle which is said to have lasted a week (A.D. 711).

JEROME (*jer-ome'* or *jer'om*), **Sophronius Eusebius Hieronymus,** Saint, one of the Fathers of the Church, born about 340. He is considered the most learned of the Latin Fathers, and ranks as one of the doctors of the early Church. For a time he resided in Rome, but finally went to Bethlehem with Paula, a rich and noble Roman lady, to be the head of the monastery which she there founded. It was here that he finished the work to which he owes his fame, the Latin translation of the Bible known as the Vulgate, which became to the Western

Church what the Greek Septuagint was to the East. St. Jerome died in Bethlehem, when about eighty years old (Sept. 30, 420).

JERROLD (*jer'uld*), **Douglas William,** a noted English comic writer, born in London, Jan. 3, 1803. His father was manager of a theatre in a small town, but Douglas did not like the stage, and began life as a midshipman. He soon got tired of that, and when his father moved to London went to work with a printer. When only fifteen years old he wrote a comedy, which was played with success in 1821 ; and soon afterward he wrote another one, founded on the ballad of "Black-Eyed Susan," which made him quite famous. After that he wrote many other plays, and became one of the chief writers for "Punch." His "Caudle Lectures" in "Punch" were read by almost everybody. He also wrote several novels, and was celebrated in social life for his witty sayings. He died in London, when fifty-four years old (June. 8, 1857).

JERROLD, William Blanchard, son of Douglas Jerrold, born in London in 1826. He has been a writer for many of the principal newspapers of London, and has written plays, novels, books of travel, and other works, including "Trips through the Vineyards of Spain," "The Story of Madge and the Fairy Content," "London," and "Life of Napoleon III." He died in London when fifty-eight years old (March 10, 1884).

JER'SEY. See CHANNEL ISLANDS.

JERSEY CITY, a city of N.E. New Jersey, on the Hudson River, opposite New York ; pop. 163,000 or about as large as Minneapolis, Minn. It has many large and important manufactories, especially of iron and steel, machinery, and locomotives, glass, soap, crucibles, lead pencils, and rubber goods. The great abattoirs, where cattle are killed for the New York markets, are in Jersey City. Several railroads have their stations in Jersey City, but a tunnel is now being dug under the Hudson River, so that the cars can come into New York instead of stopping there. In 1802 Jersey City was called Paulus Hook, and it then had only thirteen inhabitants. It became a city in 1838.

JE·RU'SA·LEM, a city of Palestine, formerly the capital and principal city of the Jews, on a high, rocky hill, 33 miles E. of the Mediterranean Sea, and 15 miles W. of the Dead Sea ; pop. 34,000, or a little larger than Augusta, Ga. It is surrounded by walls, and the streets are narrow, crooked, and very dirty. The finest building is the mosque called Kubbet es Sakhra (Dome of the Rock), and sometimes the mosque of OMAR, which is built on or near the site of Solomon's Temple. The Church of the Holy Sepulchre is said to be built over the spot where Christ was buried, and where St. HELENA found the cross on which he was crucified. A marble slab, which is supposed to cover the sepulchre, has been worn smooth by the kisses of many thousand pilgrims. A hill beside the church is pointed out as Mt. Calvary, and other places connected with the crucifixion and burial are shown, but it is by no means certain that they are the true places. In the same church are the tombs of GODFREY DE BOUILLON and BALDWIN I., King of Jerusalem, and the sword with which Godfrey fought. Other places in the city are called the tombs of David and of the Virgin Mary. Beads, crosses, and other ornaments, made mostly of olive wood, are largely manufactured in Jerusalem and sold to visitors.

Jerusalem, or in Hebrew Yerushalaim, means "possession of peace." The place was a fortress of the Canaanites, but was taken by David and made the capital of his kingdom. About 971 B.C. it was taken and plundered by Shishak, king of Egypt, and afterward it was several times captured by the Assyrians,

Babylonians, and Romans. In A.D. 66 the Jews revolted, and Jerusalem was retaken by Titus after one of the most terrible sieges ever known. Hundreds of thousands of Jews are said to have perished, many killing themselves, when all hope was lost, by throwing themselves from the walls or into the flames of the burn-

Statue of Joan of Arc, in Paris.

ing city. The beautiful Temple was destroyed, and all the houses and walls were thrown down. The Emperor Hadrian rebuilt it and named it Ælia, after his family name of Ælius. When Constantine the Great became emperor, it got its old name again, and was made a place of pilgrimage for all Christians. In the middle ages, when Jerusalem had been conquered by the Saracens, the

Christian kings of Europe made many expeditions called CRUSADES, to free it from them. The city is now of little importance except as a resort for travellers and pilgrims, it being a holy city both of the Christians and the Mohammedans, the Mohammedans putting it next to Mecca and Medina.

JID'DAH, or Jeddah, a town of Arabia, in the Red Sea; pop. 22,000, or about as large as Springfield, Mo. It is surrounded by walls, and many of the houses are built of coral. Jiddah has the best harbor on the Red Sea, and a large trade is carried on in coffee, gum arabic, spices, ivory, ostrich feathers, and other things. The natives are engaged in fishing, or diving for a kind of black coral of which they make mouthpieces for pipes and cigar-holders. Jiddah is one of the principal ports of Mecca and Medina, and during the months of pilgrimage more than 100,000 pilgrims pass through. Most of them stop to visit a rude stone structure near the city, believed by Mohammedans to be the tomb of Eve.

JOAN OF ARC, (French, Jeanne d'Arc, *zhahn dark*), called also the Maid of Orleans, born at Domremy, Lorraine, about 1411. She was the child of poor and ignorant people, and in her girlhood was a servant in a tavern. France was then at war with England, and the whole country was in great trouble. Joan used to listen to the talk of the travellers, and think a great deal about the misfortunes of her country.

She longed to do something to help the king, and by and by she fancied that she had visions from heaven, and heard voices telling her that she must save the nation. This idea took such hold of her that at last she made people believe that God had really sent her to do a great work. The king, Charles VII., consented to let her lead the soldiers in an attack upon the English at the siege of Orleans ; and she did it so well that the English were beaten and driven out of the town in a week's time.

After this, and after the king was crowned at Rheims, Joan wanted to go home, for she thought her work was ended. But there were more battles to fight, and everybody now believed that wherever she went she would bring victory for the French army. So they would not let her go ; and in the end poor Joan was taken prisoner by the enemy, after an unsuccessful battle, and burnt for a witch in the market-place of Rouen, May 31, 1431. The French king acted in a very mean and ungrateful way about it ; and the cruel death of a noble and innocent girl was a shameful thing to every one concerned in it. All the world has honored her since her death, and a statue has been put up to he her memory both in Rouen and in Paris.

JOHN, the name of twenty-three popes.

John XII., born in Rome about 937, became pope when only nineteen years old. His real name was Octavianus, but he changed it to John, he being the first pope who thus changed his name. He crowned OTHO I., but he was so bad that the emperor had him degraded, and Leo VIII. chosen in his place. He died in 964.

John XXII., born in Cahors, France, about 1244, became pope in 1316. In the strife between the GUELPHS and Ghibellines he took the side of the Guelphs while the emperor

sided with the Ghibellines ; and for a time the pope was deposed, but he finally got into power again. He died in 1334.

JOHN, the third Plantagenet King of England, born at Oxford, Dec. 24, 1166. He was called Lackland, on account of his small estate. He was the son of Henry II., and succeeded his brother, Richard I., in 1189. The rightful heir to the English throne was Arthur, a son of John's older brother, and the king of France went to war in his behalf. John kept his throne, but lost nearly all his French lands. Like the German emperors, he disputed with the popes about the election of bishops, but the dispute ended by John's becoming a sort of subject of the Pope. This made the English very angry. His barons could not stand his tyranny, so they got together in a plain called Runnymede and made John sign the Magna Charta, a paper giving them a great many privileges. He did not keep these promises, so the barons made war on him. In this war he died at Newark, when fifty years old (Oct. 19, 1216), and was succeeded by his son, Henry III.

JOHN II., called the Good, second Valois King of France, born April 26, 1319. He was the son of Philip VI., and succeeded him, being crowned at Rheims, Sept. 26, 1350. During his reign France was invaded by Edward III. of England, and in 1356 was fought the battle of POITIERS, in which John was defeated and made prisoner by Edward the Black Prince. He was taken to London, and he lived in captivity there for four years. At length a treaty was made, giving him liberty on condition that France gave to England some of her best land and a large sum of money. His son, the Duke of Anjou, was left in London, and he said he would stay there a prisoner if the French did not fulfill the treaty. They did not, but the Duke of Anjou broke his word and left England. When

John heard this he went back to England, and died there, when forty-five years old (April 8, 1364). He was succeeded by his son, Charles V.

JOHN II. CAS'I·MIR, King of, Poland, born March 21, 1609. He was the son of Sigismund III., and succeeded to the Polish throne on the death of his brother Ladislaus (Nov. 20, 1648). His reign was very unfortunate for Poland. Having begun wars against Charles X. of Sweden, and also against the Czar of Russia, he was defeated by both monarchs, and made to sign treaties by which Poland lost much of her territory. He had no control over the Polish nobles, and worn out with contending with them, he resigned the crown (Sept. 16, 1668), and spent the rest of his life in France. He died in Nevers, France, when sixty-three years old (Dec. 16, 1672).

JOHN II. SOBIESKI (*so-be-es'ke*), King of Poland, born June 2, 1624. He was the son of Jacob Sobieski, Castellan of Cracow, and was carefully educated. He was a great soldier, winning so much glory in various wars that, in 1667, he was made commander-in-chief of the Polish army. He was holding this position when he was chosen king (1674). In 1683 the Turks appeared in great force before Vienna. The Emperor fled, and not Austria only, but all Europe was in danger; but after a hard battle Sobieski defeated them, and drove them into Hungary. John Sobieski was a greater soldier than statesman. He died, when seventy-two years old (June 17, 1696), and was succeeded by Frederick Augustus, of Saxony.

JOHN OF AUSTRIA, generally called Don John, son of the Emperor Charles V., a famous Spanish general, born in Ratisbon, Feb. 2, 1547. He had great talents both as a soldier and a statesman, and won much glory in his military exploits against the Barbary pirates, the revolted Moors in Granada, and

particularly by his great naval victory over the Turks at LEPANTO (1571). He was, however, no match in state craft for the politic William the Silent, whom he opposed while commanding for his brother Philip II. of Spain, in the Netherlands. He had made a plan, which he soon gave up, for rescuing Mary, Queen of Scots, and making himself King of Scotland. He was in all respects a most brilliant man. He died at Namur, when thirty-one years old (Oct. 1, 1578).

JOHN OF GAUNT, or **Ghent,** Duke of Lancaster, born in Ghent, in 1340. He was the fourth son of Edward III. of England, and was made Duke of Lancaster in 1362. He was a brave soldier, and showed great valor in the wars of his brother, Edward the Black Prince. He was the friend and defender of John WYCLIFFE, the great English reformer, when he was tried on the charge of holding a false belief. The Lancastrian and Tudor kings of England were descended from him. He died, when fifty years old (Feb. 3, 1399).

JOHN OF LEYDEN, a noted Dutch fanatic, belonging to a religious sect called the Anabaptists, born in Leyden about 1510. His true name was Johann Bockelson, and he was a tailor by trade. Having met Matthias of Haarlem, another Anabaptist, he went with him to the town of Münster, where they were joined by others. They drove out of the city all who did not think with them, and set up their own government. Bockelson was crowned, taking the title " King of Zion," and calling his throne the " Chair of David." For more than a year Münster was under the senseless rule of these men. At last the city was besieged by the Bishop of Münster, and was taken after a brave defence. Bockelson and his chief associate were tortured to death, and their bodies hung up in iron cages as a warning. This happened in 1536. Myerbeer's opera of the "Prophet" is founded on the story of John of Leyden.

JOHNSON, Andrew, seventeenth President of the United States, born in Raleigh, N. C., Dec. 29, 1808. His parents were two poor to send him to school, and when only ten years old he became a tailor's apprentice. A gentleman used to come to the shop and read aloud to the workmen now and then. This made Andrew like books, and he taught himself to read, spelling out his lessons in the evening after his day's work was over. But he never learned to write or cipher until he was about twenty, when he married

Andrew Johnson.

a clever girl who taught him all she knew herself. Soon after this he began to interest himself in politics, and was elected alderman of the village of Greenville, in Tennessee. In a year or two he became mayor, then went to the Legislature and the State Senate, and in 1843 was sent to Congress, where he served ten years. In 1853 he became Governor of Tennessee, and in 1857 went to the United States Senate. When the Civil War broke out he took sides with the Union party, and during the war protected the Union refugees who were driven from their homes after Tennessee left the Union. He

was made military governor of the State in 1862; and in 1865, when Abraham Lincoln became President for a second term, Andrew Johnson was elected Vice-President. On the death of Mr. Lincoln, he took his place, and was President for four years. He died near Elizabethtown, Tenn., when sixty-six years old (July 31, 1875).

JOHNSON, Eastman, an American painter, born at Lovell, Me., July 29, 1824. His pictures represent American domestic scenes, and negro life. Many of them are well known through chromo-lithographs and engravings. His studio is in New York.

JOHNSON, Rossiter, an American writer, born in Rochester, N. Y., in 1840. He was educated at Rochester University, and was a newspaper editor for several years, and afterwards associate editor of the "American Cyclopædia." He was also editor of "Little Classics," of "Works of the British Poets," and other books, and has written stories for "St. Nicholas," "Wide Awake," "Youth's Companion," and other magazines. More recent works are "History of the War of 1812," and "A Short History of the War of Secession."

Helen Kendrick Johnson, wife of Rossiter Johnson, born in Hamilton, N. Y., in 1844, is the daughter of Prof. A. C. Kendrick, of Rochester University. She has written for most of the young folks' magazines, and for several weekly papers, and has published "Roddy's Romance," "Roddy's Reality," and "Roddy's Ideal," and has edited "Tears for the Little Ones" and "Our Familiar Songs."

JOHNSON, Samuel, a famous English writer, born in Lichfield, Sept. 18, 1709. His father died when he was a boy, and the family being poor, Samuel had to suffer many privations to obtain an education. He studied several years at Oxford, but was too poor to finish his course.

In 1737 he went with GARRICK to London, where he lived in great poverty, writing for magazines and and doing other literary work for very small pay. Later in life he became famous as a writer, though he was never rich. In 1755 he completed the first good dictionary of the English language ever written. Among his other works are several series of essays; "Rasselas, Prince of Abyssinia," a story, said to have been written in the evenings of a single week; and "Lives of the English Poets," written when he

Samuel Johnson.

was more than seventy years old. Dr. Johnson also wrote some fine poems. In his old age he was noted for his eccentricity and gruffness. He died in London, when seventy-five years old (Dec. 13, 1784).

JOHNSON, Sir William, a British general, born in Warrentown, Ireland, in 1715. In 1738 he came to America to take charge, for his uncle, of a large tract of land on the Mohawk River, New York. He became a friend of the Indians, learned to speak their language, and got such influence over them that they made him a chief and named him *Warraghiaghy* (He who has charge of affairs). For many years he was commissioner or agent of the government to the Indians, and he did

much to make them friendly to the whites. He also aided in settling and improving the country, and he held several important offices. During the French and Indian war he commanded a British army which defeated the French on Lake George (1755), and for this service he was made a baronet. He died at his home near Johnstown, N. Y., when fifty years old (July 11, 1774).

JOHN'STON, Albert Sidney, an American soldier, born in Mason County, Ky., in 1803. He was graduated at West Point, served in the Black Hawk War; left the army for some years, then enlisted as a private in the Texan army, and showed himself to be so brave and skilful a soldier that he was given chief command of the army of Texas. In 1846 he fought in the Mexican War, and won fame at the siege of Monterey. He led the expedition against the Mormons in 1857, and was for some time in command of the military district of Utah. During the Civil War he fought on the side of the Southern Confederacy, and was killed at the battle of Shiloh, when fifty-nine years old (April 6, 1862).

JOHN'STON, Alexander Keith, a Scotch geographer, born in Kirkhill, Mid-Lothian, Dec. 28, 1804. He was brought up an engraver, but gave up that business to study geography, and taught himself four or five foreign languages so that he might read the best books on the subject. He published a "Dictionary of Geography" and many fine atlases. He died, when sixty-six years old (July 9, 1871).

JOHNSTON, Joseph Eccleston, an American general, born in Prince Edward Co., Virginia, in 1807. He was graduated at West Point in 1829, fought the Florida Indians in 1842, and won rank for gallant conduct there, and for brave service in the Mexican War in 1847. In 1860 he had the rank of brigadier-general in the U. S. army; but on the out break of the Civil War he resigned and became a general in the Confederate army. He commanded in the first battle of Bull Run, and at Yorktown and Richmond. When Sherman marched into N. Carolina, Johnston commanded against him, and after Lee's surrender, surrendered (April 26, 1865). He published a book about the war. He died in Washington when eighty-four years old (March 21, 1891).

JOLIET (*zho-le-a'*), **Louis,** a French traveller, one of the first to explore the Mississippi River, born in Quebec, in 1645. He was the companion of MARQUETTE in his voyage down the Mississippi, and did much to make the country known. He afterward went to Hudson Bay, and finally was royal map-maker at Quebec. He died when about fifty-five years old (1700).

JOLIET (*jo'le-et*), a city of N.E. Illinois, on the Des Plaines River, 35 miles S.W. of Chicago; pop. 23,000, or about as large as Fort Worth, Tex. It is surrounded by a rich farming region, and a large trade is carried on, especially in grain. Near the city are fine quarries of building stone. The State penitentiary at Joliet is one of the finest prison buildings in the country.

JOMINI (*zho-me-ne'*), **Henri,** Baron, a noted French soldier and military writer, born at Payerne, Switzerland, March 6, 1779. When very young he entered the Swiss Guard of Louis XVI., but when it was disbanded returned to his own country, and before he was twenty years old was made head of the War Department. In 1803 he went to Paris and became aide-de-camp to NEY, who recommended him to the Emperor. In 1805 he quarrelled with Ney in Spain and went back to Switzerland; but in 1812 he was invited by Napoleon to make the campaign of Russia, and was appointed historian of the Grand Army. When the cause of Napoleon was almost lost he resented an af-

front he had received by going over to the Allies. Napoleon bore him no ill-will for this course, saying, "He was not a Frenchman, and there was no love of country to retain him." The Emperor of Russia made him his aid and lieutenant-general, and he served in the war against Turkey. He is known chiefly by his works on military history and the art of war. He died at Passy, near Paris, when ninety years old (March 24, 1869),

JONES, John Paul, a famous American naval officer, born at Arbigland, Scotland, July 6, 1747. His

John Paul Jones.

real name was John Paul, and he himself added the name Jones. He made several voyages to Virginia and the West Indies, and was engaged for a short time in the slave trade, but when the Revolution began he entered the American navy as a first lieutenant. It is said that he hoisted over his ship the first American flag ever displayed. He was soon made commander of the sloop Providence, with which he captured sixteen British vessels in six weeks. Afterward he commanded other ships, and made many captures. In 1777 and 1778 he sailed along the coast of Scotland, attacked Whitehaven, and captured the Drake, a sloop of war larger than his own. In 1779, being in France, he was given the command of an old merchant ship, which he repaired and named the "Bon Homme Richard" (Poor Richard), in honor of Dr. Franklin, who published an almanac under that name. Accompanied by five other vessels, he cruised along the coast of England, and in a month captured twenty-six vessels. On Sept. 23, 1779, the Bon Homme Richard had a terrible fight with a much stronger English ship, the Serapis, which was guarding a fleet of merchant vessels. Jones lashed his ship to the Serapis, and finally captured it, but the Bon Homme Richard was so much injured that it sunk soon afterward. At the same time, another of his ships, called the Pallas, captured the English ship Countess of Scarborough, which was sailing with the Serapis. For his services Jones received a gold medal from Congress, and King Louis XVI. of France presented him with a sword. He afterward entered the Russian navy, but falling into disfavor, resigned and went to Paris, where he died very poor, at the age of forty-five years (July 18, 1792).

JON'SON, Benjamin, generally called Ben, an English writer of plays, born in Westminster, about 1573. He became a soldier, and afterward an actor in London, and when but little more than twenty years old began to write plays, some of which became very popular, though they are not acted now. Among them are "The Alchemist," "Catiline," "Every Man in his Humor," and "Cynthia's Revels." In 1619 he was made poet laureate of England, with a pension ; but being careless of money, was often in debt. Jonson was a friend of Shakespeare, who is said to have acted in some of his plays. He died in London, when

seventy-four years old (Aug. 6, 1637), and was buried in Westminster Abbey. On his tombstone, which has since been removed, was inscribed only : "O rare Ben Jonson."

JOR'DAN, River. See PALESTINE.

JOSEPH I., Emperor of Germany, born July 26, 1678. He was the oldest son of the Emperor Leopold I., and succeeded him as Emperor in 1705, having been crowned King of Hungary in 1687. The whole of his reign was spent in waging two wars ; one, the War of the Spanish Succession, against Louis XIV., in behalf of Leopold's brother, the Archduke Charles, who wanted to be King of Spain, and one against the Hungarians, who had revolted under Francis Rákóczy. Leopold's allies in the War of the Spanish Succession won so many victories for him that he was able to send a great many troops to Hungary, and thus soon brought the rebels to terms. Joseph was very fond of hunting. The Academy of Arts at Vienna was founded by him. He died, when thirty-three years old (April 17, 1711) and was succeeded by his brother, Charles VI.

JOSEPH II., Emperor of Germany, born March 13, 1741. He was the son of the Emperor Francis I., and succeeded him as Emperor in 1765, having also been made by his mother, Maria Theresa, fellow-sovereign of her hereditary dominions. Joseph had great schemes of reform, and set about making everything perfect according to his own ideas without consulting any one else, and paying no regard to the old laws of his different kingdoms. In the end he did more harm than good, being obliged to undo all that he had done, except giving freedom in religious matters and doing away with serfdom, or slavery.

A great many interesting stories are told of Joseph. In order that he might better judge of the condition of things in his kingdom, he used to travel about disguised, under an assumed name, generally calling himself Count Falkenstein. Once he stopped, disguised as a courier, at an inn of a little village, and his pleasant manners so pleased the host and his wife that they invited him to be sponsor to their little child who was to be christened on that evening. To the astonishment of the good people he came at the time appointed, in his own proper person, and wearing the various orders by which they knew him at once to be the Emperor. He had a great admiration for Frederick the Great of Prussia. Frederick returned the feeling, and had his palace at Sans Souci hung around with Joseph's portraits, saying that he was a young man of whom he could not see too much. Joseph was so much under Frederick's influence that he allowed himself to be drawn into the plan for dividing Poland. Joseph once said of himself, "My tomb should be inscribed, 'Here lies a monarch who, with the best intentions, never carried a single design into execution.'" He died broken-hearted at the failure of his plans, when forty-nine years old (Feb. 20, 1790), and was succeeded by his brother, Leopold II.

JOSEPHINE (*jo'sef-een*), **Marie Joséphe Rose Tascher de la Pagerie,** Empress of France, first wife of Napoleon Bonaparte, born in the island of Martinique, June, 1763. Her family name was Tascher, the surname Pagerie being that of an estate near Blois, in France. When she was eighteen years old she married the Viscount de Beauharnais, son of the governor of the island, and went with him to live in Paris, but the marriage was not happy. In 1794, during the reign of terror in France, the Viscount de Beauharnais was guillotined, and his wife would have shared his fate but for Madame Tallien, a very influential lady, who rescued her from prison. After two years of widow-

hood she married Napoleon Bonaparte, and went with him to Italy, then the seat of war; but she could not bear the sight of the battle-field, and soon went back to France. For many years Napoleon and Josephine were very happy in each other. When Napoleon became emperor (1804) Josephine was at the same time crowned empress, and well did her beauty and grace adorn her husband's court. Her two children, Hortense and Eugene Beauharnais, were greatly loved by Napoleon, and everything was done by him to aid their fortunes. Although he loved

Empress Josephine.

his wife as much as it was his nature to love any one, he began after a while to find that she stood in the way of his ambition, so in 1809 he put her away and married MARIA LOUISA, Archduchess of Austria. Josephine retired to Malmaison, a beautiful country place, where she spent the remaining five years of her life, beloved by all who came near her. She never ceased to love Bonaparte, and on his banishment to Elba wished to go to him. She died at Malmaison, near Paris, when fifty-one years old (May 29, 1814). Her daughter Hortense married Louis Bonaparte, King of Holland, the brother of Napoleon, and became the mother of Napoleon III., the late emperor of France.

JO·SE'PHUS, Flavius, the most famous of Jewish historians, born at Jerusalem about A.D. 37. He was of a noble and rich family, and received a good education. When twenty-six years old he was sent to Rome to ask that some Jewish priests who were imprisoned there might be released. On his return he tried to prevent the Jews from rebelling against the Romans, but finding that they would not listen to him, he took command of the Jewish army in Galilee, and fought bravely against the Romans under Vespasian and Titus. He was defeated and taken prisoner, and carried to Rome, where Titus befriended him. He was with Titus at the siege of Jerusalem, and was sent with offers of peace to his countrymen, but they would not listen to him. He returned with Titus to Rome, where he was rewarded with so many favors by Vespasian and his son that, as a mark of gratitude, he took their family name of Flavius. His "History of the Jewish War" is his most famous book. He lived the rest of his days in Rome, and died about A.D. 100.

JOURDAN (*zhoor-dan'*), **Jean Baptiste,** Count, a famous French general, born in Limoges, April 29, 1762. He was the son of a poor surgeon, on whose death he was put in his uncle's silk store in Lyons. He did not like this, and when sixteen years old enlisted as a common soldier in the French army, and served five years in America in the war of the Revolution. After the war he went home, married, and opened a milliner's shop, but when the French Revolution broke out he became captain of the national guard of Limoges. After that he rose fast in rank, until, in 1793, he became the commander-in-chief of one of the French armies. He won several battles from the Austrians,

and was made a marshal of the Empire in 1804. Though he was a good soldier, Napoleon did not think much of him; but after the fall of the Empire Louis XVIII. made him a count (1815) and a peer of France (1819). He died in Paris, when seventy-one years old (Nov. 23, 1833).

JOVIAN (*jo've-an*), **Flavius Claudius,** a Roman emperor, born in Pannonia in 331. He was the son of Varronianus, a noted general, and became captain of the body guards of the Emperor JULIAN, on whose death he was chosen emperor by the soldiers. He declared himself to be a Christian, changed the laws which Julian had made against the Christians, and forbade their persecution, but would not let the Pagans be oppressed on account of their religion either. After reigning seven months, he was found dead in his bed one morning, suffocated, it is supposed, by a charcoal fire which had been used in his room to warm it, (A.D. 364).

JU'AN FER·NAN'DEZ (Spanish, *hwan' fer-nahn-deth*), a high, rocky island in the Pacific, 420 miles W. of Chili, to which it belongs. The surface is covered with grass or forest. It is celebrated as the island on which Alexander Selkirk was left in 1704. He was a sailor who, having quarrelled with his captain, asked to be put on shore. He stayed there alone for more than four years, living chiefly on wild goats, which he shot or caught. It is supposed by many that Daniel DEFOE made his story of "Robinson Crusoe" from this; but Crusoe's island was near the mouth of the Orinoco River. At present there are a few Chilian settlers in Juan Fernandez.

JUBA (*joo'bah*), King of Numidia, born in 62 B.C. He succeeded his father, Hiempsal, who, after being driven from his throne, was restored by Pompey. In the war between Cæsar and Pompey, Juba took sides with the latter, and defeated Cæsar's lieutenant, Curio. Three years later Cæsar's and Pompey's forces met again at Thapsus, and the battle going against Pompey, Juba fled from the field, and, after wandering a few days, killed himself.

JUDEA (*ju-de'ah*). See PALESTINE.

JUG-GER-NAUT', or **Jagannath,** a town of India, on the Bay of Bengal; pop. 22,000, or about as large as Springfield, Mo. It is a holy city of the Hindoos, celebrated for its great temple dedicated to Krishna, who is there called Juggernaut (Lord of the world). The temple stands within a great square, where also are smaller temples, dedicated to other Hindoo idols. The three principal idols have chariots. That belonging to Juggernaut is the largest, being nearly as high as a three-story house (45 feet), and mounted on sixteen wheels. Every year, in March, the idols are placed on their chariots and thousands of people drag them with ropes to their country house, near by. Many years ago some of the worshippers used to throw themselves beneath the heavy wheels to be crushed and killed, but the British authorities do not now allow this. Juggernaut is visited every year by a million pilgrims.

JUGURTHA (*ju-gur'thah*), a king of Numidia, born in the 2d century B.C. He was adopted by his uncle, King Micipsa, and carefully educated with the king's sons, Adherbal and Hiempsal, and when his uncle died Jugurtha was made joint heir with them and regent of the kingdom (118 B.C.). Soon afterward he had Hiempsal killed, and Adherbal fled to Rome and complained of him to the Senate. But Jugurtha bribed the senators, and got a larger and better share of the kingdom than Adherbal. He then besieged Adherbal's city of Cirta, captured him, and put him to death with all his followers. The Romans declared war and sent an army against Jugurtha, but he bribed the generals to make peace. At last METELLUS was sent to carry on the war. Jugurtha tried to bribe him, but Metellus made him fight, and defeated him. Jugurtha fled to Bocchus, King of Mauritiana, who raised an army to aid him. In the year 107 MARIUS, who had been elected consul and given the command of the war against Jugurtha in the place of Metellus, defeated both Jugurtha and Bocchus in a bloody battle, and Bocchus soon after deserted Jugurtha and gave him up to SULLA. Jugurtha was taken to Rome, and at the triumph of Marius he walked before his chariot in chains. He was then thrown into the Mamartine prison, and starved to death (104 B.C.). The story is told by SALLUST, in his history of the Jugurthine war.

JULIAN (*jool'yan*), **Flavius Claudius,** commonly called the Apostate, a Roman emperor, born in Constantinople, Nov. 17, 331. His cousin, the Emperor Constantius, exiled and imprisoned his brother Gallus and himself when they were mere children. But when they grew up they were set free, and in 355 Julian was proclaimed Cæsar and sent to Gaul, where he defeated the Germans and drove them beyond the Rhine. In 360 the emperor's troops revolted and declared Julian emperor, and the death of Constantius soon after gave him the entire control of the empire. He had been brought up a Christian ; but he now declared himself a pagan and tried to restore heathen worship, and to destroy Christianity. He shut up the Christian schools, and even forbade the use of the name Christian, but did not allow the Christians to be persecuted, as some of the other emperors had done. In other things, however, he was a good and wise emperor. In 363 he marched against the Persians, who had attacked some parts of his empire, and gained a great victory over them at their royal city of Ctesiphon. But shortly after he was shot in battle, and died from the wound (Jan. 26, 363.)

JULIUS (*jool'yus*), the name of three popes.

Julius II., born in 1441, became pope in 1503. In 1508 he joined Louis XII., of France, and the Emperor Maximilian of Germany, in a league, called the League of Cambray, to break up the commonwealth of Venice, each one pretending that a part of its territories belonged rightfully to himself. Venice was on the point of ruin, when Julius, having got what he wanted, and seeing that he had more to fear from the French than from the Venetians, made peace with the latter and got up what he named the Holy League to drive the barbarians, as he called the French, out of Italy. He began St. Peter's Church, and was the patron of Michael Angelo and of Raphael. He died Feb. 21, 1513.

JUNIUS (*joon'yus*). See FRANCIS, Sir PHILIP.

JU'NO, in ancient fable, the daughter of Saturn and Rhea, and the wife of Jupiter, called by the Greeks Hera. She was the queen of gods and men. All the other gods a n d goddesses were present at her marriage, and brought her beautiful gifts. She was very vain, proud, and obstinate, and often her jealousy roused the anger of Jupiter, who once, as a punishment, bound her with golden chains and hung her up in the air. She is represented as a stately woman, sitting in a chariot drawn by peacocks, or having a peacock at her side. Juno was the

Juno.

mother of Mars, Hebe, and Vulcan.

JUNOT (*zhu-no'*), **Andoche,** Duke of Abrantès, a famous French soldier, born at Bussy-le-Grand, Oct. 23, 1771. He was educated a lawyer, but joined the army and early became the comrade and friend of Napoleon, with whom he served in Italy and in Egypt. But though a good friend to Napoleon, Junot was not a very good general, and he was greatly disappointed that he was not made a marshal when Napoleon became emperor. In 1807 he was sent to Portugal, where with a small army he took the town of Abrantès, for which Napoleon made him Duke of Abrantès, and afterward seized Lisbon. But Wellington soon arrived, and Junot was defeated at Vimieiro and forced to leave Portugal. After this he served in Germany and in Russia, but he was too slow to please the emperor, who made him commander of Venice. This, which was a kind of banishment, made him insane, and he committed suicide by throwing himself from a window (July 29, 1813).

Laure Permon, Duchess of Abrantès, his wife, born in Montpellier, Nov. 6, 1784. She was one of the most brilliant ladies of Napoleon's court, but she had a very sharp tongue, and used to make such biting remarks that the Emperor called her *petite peste* (little pest). Toward the close of her life she became poor, and supported herself by writing, and she is best known for her "Memoirs of Napoleon," which are still read with interest. She died in a private hospital near Paris, when fifty-four years old (June 7, 1838.)

JU'PI-TER, the king and father of the gods, called by the Greeks Zeus. He was the son of Saturn and Rhea, and was born and brought up on Mount Ida in Crete. When he grew up he robbed his father of his kingdom, which he shared with his two brothers, giving to Neptune the sea, to Pluto the lower world and keeping the earth and heavens for himself. His first wife was Metis, whom he swallowed, because an oracle had said that a child of hers would take his throne from him. The goddess Minerva afterward sprang from his head. He had several other wives; but the most famous was JUNO. He lived on Mount Olympus, and ruled over gods and men. All good and evil came from him, and at his will people were happy or unhappy. He was armed with thunder and lightning, and he bore a shield, made for him by Vulcan, which sent forth terrible storms when he shook it. He is generally represented seated on a throne, grasping a thunderbolt in his right hand, and a sceptre in his left, with an eagle standing beside him.

Jupiter.

JUS-TIN′I-AN, or **Justinianus, Flavius Anicius,** called the Great, Emperor of the East, born near Sardica (now Sophia) in Bulgaria, in A.D. 483. He belonged to a poor Gothic family, but when his uncle, JUSTINUS I., was crowned emperor, he was given a share in the rule, and on his death he succeeded him on the throne. Among the chief events of his reign was the conquest of the Vandal Kingdom in Africa, of which CARTHAGE was the capital, by his great general, BELISARIUS. Italy too was won from the Goths by Belisarius and NARSES, and was governed by a ruler called the exarch, who lived at RAVENNA. Justinian also carried on a long war with CHOSROES, King of Persia. During his reign Constantinople and other cities of the Empire were adorned with splendid buildings, of which the great church of Saint Sophia, now the mosque of Sofia, in Constantinople, was the most famous. Silkworms were brought from the East, and manufactures and commerce were cared for. Justinian also put the laws of Rome into the form of a regular code, thus forming that complete system of law called the Civil Law, which is still the groundwork of the laws of almost all European countries. He died, when about eighty-two years old (Nov. 14, 565), and was succeeded by his nephew, Justin II.

JUSTINIAN II., called Rhinotmetus (Shorn Nose), Emperor of the East, born in A.D. 669. He succeeded his father, Constantine IV., in 685, and was one of the worst of the Eastern emperors. He made war against the Saracens, and won some splendid victories in Syria and Sicily; but on account of his great cruelty his general, Leontius, drove him from the throne, cut off his nose, and banished him to the CRIMEA. In 705 he got his throne back, and put Leontius and many others to death, when his shameful crimes started a new revolt, and he was killed by Philippicus Bardanes, who became Emperor in his stead (711).

JUS-TI′NUS I., or **Jus′tin the Elder,** Emperor of the East, born in Bulgaria, in A.D. 450. He was a Gothic shepherd, and when very young went with two other youths to Constantinople to seek his fortune; and on account of his great size was put into the imperial guards. His courage and ability gained him rank, and in time he rose to be commander of the guards. When the Emperor Anastasius died, Justin was made his successor (518). He was very ignorant, not being able to read or write, but his chief minister, Proclus, ruled for him, and his reign was prosperous. Soon after adopting JUSTINIAN, his nephew, as his successor, he died in Constantinople (Aug. 1, 527).

JUSTINUS II., or **Justin the Younger,** Emperor of the East, succeeded his uncle, Justinian I., in A.D. 565. His reign was very unfortunate. To please his wife he recalled his general, Narses, from Italy, when the barbarian Lombards overran that country, and it was forever lost to the Greek Empire. In a short time too the Persians invaded Syria. The emperor became crazy, and the Empress Sophia ruled in his place. As he had no sons, she got him to adopt as his successor Tiberius, one of his generals, who came to the throne on the death of the Emperor (Oct. 5, 578).

JU'VE-NAL, Decimus Junius, a famous Roman poet, born about the latter part of the 1st century. He was educated for a lawyer, but little of his life is known. Next to Horace, he was the greatest writer of satires—that is, severe witty poems —of all the Roman poets. When eighty years old he is said to have been sent to Egypt by the Emperor for writing a severe poem about an actor who was liked at court, and to have died there soon after of grief.

K

KABUL (*kah-bool'*). See CABUL.

KAMTCHATKA (*kamt-chat'kah*), a peninsula of E. Siberia, between the Kamtchatka Sea and the Sea of Ochotsk ; area, 100,000 square miles, or about as large as Colorado ; pop. about 7000, or one fifty-ninth that of Colorado. It is traversed by a chain of high mountains, which are always covered with snow, and among which are seventeen volcanoes. Earthquakes are frequent and violent. The climate is very severe, the winter lasting nine months, while frost is common even in the summer. The only fertile portion is in the southern part, where barley, oats, and vegetables are raised. Of the inhabitants the Kamtchatdales are very short and stout, with flat features and thin black hair. They dress in furs, and in summer live in huts built on a scaffolding of poles ; but in winter their houses are made in holes in the ground. The Koriaks, a wandering tribe, keep many reindeer, and live chiefly on them. A few live in the villages. Most of the people are engaged in fishing and hunting, both game and fish being very abundant. The principal trade is in furs and whale oil.

KANDAHAR (*kahn-dah-har'*). See CANDAHAR.

KANE, Elisha Kent, a noted American Arctic explorer, born in Philadelphia, Feb. 3, 1820. He was educated a physician, entered the navy, and sailed (1843) as physician to the embassy to China. On his

Elisha Kent Kane.

way home he travelled through part of Asia, Egypt, and Europe. He afterward travelled in Africa, and served in the war in Mexico, where he was severely wounded. In May, 1850, he sailed as surgeon to the expedition sent by Henry Grinnell, of

New York, in search of Sir John FRANKLIN. They did not succeed, and another expedition, under Dr. Kane's command, started May 30, 1853. After many adventures and much suffering the party had to leave their ship in the ice, and for eighty-four days travelled in sledges and boats until they reached the coasts of Greenland, where they found help. They had not found any traces of Sir John Franklin; but they had found what they thought was an open polar sea. Kane's health was seriously injured, and he went to Havana, hoping to get better, but died there, when thirty-seven years old (Feb. 16, 1857).

KAN'SAS, a N. W. State of the United States, between Missouri and Colorado; area, 81,000 square miles, or about twice as large as Louisiana; pop. 1,427,000, or more than one and a fourth times that of Louisiana; capital, TOPEKA. Most of the land is beautiful rolling prairie, with forests in the river valleys, which are low and flat, but often bordered by high bluffs. The western part of the State is highest, so that all the rivers flow toward the east.

Kansas has fine coal mines, and salt-springs, besides quarries of limestone and marble, and beds of sulphur, gypsum, and kaolin, or porcelain clay. It is one of the most important farming States, and it is said that no other State has so little poor land. A great deal of corn and wheat is raised, but in some years the fields are much injured by a kind of grasshopper which is found there. Cotton is grown in the southern part. The western part is excellent for grazing, and the farmers have very large herds of cattle. Buffaloes and other wild animals used to be very common, but the buffalo has been nearly exterminated for the sake of its hide and bones.

Kansas gets its name from the Kansas tribe of Indians. It was once a part of Louisiana, bought

from France in 1803. It was made into a territory in 1854, and became a State of the Union in 1861.

KANSAS CITY, a city of W. Missouri, on the Missouri River, just below the mouth of the Kansas River, and near the boundary of Kansas; pop. 133,000, or about as large as Rochester, N. Y. Next to St. Louis, it is the largest city in the State, and many railroads meet there, crossing the Missouri by a splendid railroad bridge. A very large trade is carried on, especially in cattle, horses, hogs, and grain. Kansas City was founded in 1830, and since the Civil War has grown very fast.

KANT, Immanuel, a German writer, born in Königsberg, April 22, 1724. His father was a Scotchman, and from him, no doubt, the son got his taste for metaphysics, or those studies that relate to the powers of the mind. Kant thought much about reason, and in his work he gives his idea of the things on which reason can properly act, and tries to explain the connection between the outer world of nature and the inner world of the human mind, very hard subjects which always have puzzled people, and which always will do so. At all events, wise men seem to think that Kant gave a better explanation of these things than those who have gone before him, and his system soon penetrated all the sciences, and excited the learned world. Kant was never out of his native city except to take a walk of a few miles into the country. He died when eighty years old (Feb. 12, 1804).

KARS, a city of Russia in Asia, on a high, rugged plain by the River Kars; pop. about 9000, or nearly as large as Watertown, Wis. It is defended by walls, and has a strong citadel. Kars has a considerable trade, and it has been an important military post in the wars between Turkey and Russia. The Russians captured it from the Turks in 1828, and kept it for two years. In 1855 they again captured it after a long and bloody siege, in which it was defended by the Turks under the English General Williams. In the last war between Russia and Turkey the Russians took it again, and it was given to Russia by the treaty of Berlin (1878).

KASAN (*kah-zahn'*). See KAZAN.

KASH-GAR', a city of Asia, capital of Eastern Turkestan; pop. 120,000, or nearly as large as Providence, R. I. It is surrounded by an earthen wall, and the houses are built of sun-dried bricks. The people are Mohammedans, and most of them Tartars. Marco Polo was the first European who passed through Kashgar, and only a few modern travellers have visited it.

KAUFMANN (*kowf'mahn*), **Maria Angelica**, a Swiss artist, born in Coire, Oct. 30, 1741. She studied painting and music in Milan, and in 1763 went to live in Rome, where she became celebrated as a portrait painter. In 1765 she went to England, and there became one of the thirty-six original members of the Royal Academy of Arts. An imposter, who called himself Count Horn, induced her to marry him, but she afterward got a divorce, and in 1781 married Antonio Zucchi, an Italian artist. The remainder of her life was spent in Rome, where she died, sixty-six years old (Nov. 5, 1807).

KAULBACH (*kowl'bahkh*), **Wilhelm von,** a German painter, born in Arolson, Oct. 15, 1805. His father was a poor engraver, and Wilhelm and his sister often sold engravings to the peasants for stale bread. As he grew older he showed so great a talent for painting that he was admitted to the Art Academy at Düsseldorf. In 1825 he went to live in Munich, when he became director of the Royal Academy of Arts, and painted many beautiful frescoes for the palace and art galleries. Among these are "Homer

and the Greeks." "The Destruction of Jerusalem by Titus," and "The Battle of the Huns," in which the spirits of dead Huns and Romans are seen fighting in the air. He died in Munich, when sixty-eight years old (April 7, 1874).

KAZAN (*kah-zahn'*), a city of E. Russia, on the Kazanska River, three miles from its junction with the Volga; pop. 141,000, or about the same as Omaha, Neb. Most of the Russian trade with Siberia is carried on from this place, and it has many important manufactories. In its university are taught many of the languages spoken by the different nations of Asia.

KEAN, Edmund, an English actor, born in London, March 17, 1787. His father was a carpenter who worked for the theatre, and his mother an actress. When he was a very little boy he was considered a good actor of children's parts. His first appearance on a London stage was as the Jew Shylock, in Shakespeare's "Merchant of Venice." He succeeded at once, and soon became famous. His chief parts were Hamlet, Richard III., and King Lear. He made three visits to the United States—in 1820, 1825, and 1833. His last appearance was in Richmond, Virginia, as Othello. During the performance his strength failed him and he fell into the arms of his son, Charles John Kean, who was acting Iago's part. Kean has been considered one of the greatest actors that ever trod the boards. He died in Richmond, when forty-three years old (May 15, 1833).

KEARNY (*kar'ny*), **Philip,** an American general, born in New York, June 2, 1815. In 1837 he entered the army as a lieutenant, and being sent to Europe on a government commission, studied at a French military academy, and served as a volunteer in the French army in Algeria. Returning to America, he distinguished himself in the Mexican War, losing an arm at the storming of the city of Mexico. In 1851 he again went to Europe to pursue military studies, and in 1859 he fought with the French army at the battles of Magenta and Solferino, receiving the Cross of the Legion of Honor for his bravery. When the Civil War broke out he was made a general in the Union army, and distinguished himself at the battles of Williamsburg, Seven Pines, and Frazier's Farm. During a battle at Chantilly, Virginia, he rode forward to reconnoitre, and was killed, when forty-seven years old (Sept. 1, 1862).

KEATS (*keets*), **John,** a noted English poet, born in London, in a livery stable, Oct. 29, 1795. His father valued education, and sent him to a good school, but John gave less time to his studies than to reading. He was next apprenticed to a surgeon, but he had made up his mind to be a poet, and he soon published a volume of poems which were greatly admired by many. But the book was severely reviewed in some of the magazines, and this hurt his feelings so that some of his friends thought his death was caused by it. He was, however, in consumption, and, going to Italy for a warmer climate, died at Rome, when twenty-five years old (Feb. 27, 1821). He grieved that he had not lived long enough to write some famous poems, and wished these words put upon his tomb : " Here lies one whose name was writ in water." That name now stands high among his brother poets.

KEBLE (*ke'b'l*), **John,** an English clergyman and poet, born near Fairford, Gloucestershire, April 25, 1792. He lived ten years at Oxford, and then became a clergyman, working as his father's curate at Fairford for twenty years. When thirty-five years old he published a book of poems, called "The Christian Year," which gives proper verses for all the Sundays and holidays throughout the year. It is very popular, and has been printed a great many times,

both in England and the United States. He was afterward made Vicar of Hursley, near Winchester (1835), and lived there a retired life with his wife and sister. Besides " The Christian Year," he wrote the " Lyra Innocentium" for children, and other books. He died, when seventy-four years old (March 29, 1866). Keble College, Oxford, was founded in his honor by his friends.

KELLERMANN (*kel-ler-mahn'*), **François Christophe,** Duke of Valmy, a famous French soldier, born in Strasburg, May 30, 1735. When seventeen he joined the army as a private soldier, and rose through every rank until he became a general. When the revolution broke out in France he was made general-in-chief, and won the battle of Valmy against the Prussians and their allies who were marching on Paris. In the wars of Napoleon Kellermann was a brilliant cavalry officer, and the Emperor made him Duke of Valmy and Marshal of France. Among other things he gave him the famous hill Johannisberg on the Rhine, celebrated for its grapes and wine. When Kellermann died he ordered that his heart should be buried at Valmy with this inscription : " On this field died the brave men who saved France, September 20, 1792. A soldier who had the honor to command them on that day, Marshal Kellermann, Duke of Valmy, twenty-eight years later directed with his last breath that his heart should repose among them." The remainder of his body is buried in Paris, where he died, when eighty-five years old (Sept. 12, 1820).

KEL'LOGG, Clara Louisa, an American singer, born in Sumter, S. C., of New England parents, in 1842. Except a few lessons which she took in London, her musical education has been mostly received in New York. As an opera singer she is a great favorite in Europe as well as in this country. One of her best parts is that of Marguerite in the opera of " Faust," but she prefers comic opera to any other style. The fortune that she has made she owes not only to her musical ability but to her talent for business. As a woman, she is respected for her blameless life and kind heart.

KEMBLE (*kem'b'l*), the name of a family of British actors, the founder of which was Roger Kemble, born in Hereford, March 1, 1721. He was himself an actor, and the father of twelve children, five of whom went on the stage, the two most distinguished being Sarah, who became Mrs. Siddons, and John Philip. Mrs. Siddons was the oldest member of the family, having been born July 5, 1755. After going on the stage she at once stood at the head. It is probable that Lady Macbeth will never be acted as well as by her. She died in London when seventy-six years old (June 8, 1831).

John Philip Kemble was born in Lancashire, Feb. 1, 1757. In his acting of Coriolanus, Macbeth, and King Lear he had no rival in his time. He died at Lausanne when sixty-six years old (Feb. 26, 1823).

Frances Anne Kemble (Mrs. Butler) was born in London in 1811. She was the granddaughter of Roger Kemble, being the daughter of Charles. She had no fancy for the stage, but made it her profession to aid her father, who was poor. She made her first appearance in " Romeo and Juliet," she taking the part of Juliet, her father that of Romeo, and her mother that of the nurse. She married Mr. Butler, an American living in Philadelphia ; but a separation took place at the end of a few years. She published three interesting books giving an account of her life, and a novel. She died when eighty-two years old (January 16, 1893).

KEM'PIS, Thomas à, a noted German writer, born near Cologne, about 1380. He was a monk in the monastery of Saint Agnes, near Zwolle, and spent his life in making copies of the Bible and other religious books, the art of printing not being then known. He is best known as the author of a famous book called " De Imitatione Christi" (Of the Imitation of Christ), but it is not certainly known whether he wrote it or only copied it. He died, when about ninety-one years old (July 26, 1471).

KEN'IL-WORTH (English, *kil'ling-urth*), a village of England, about five miles from Warwick, noted for the ruins of Kenilworth Castle, built there in the 11th century by Geoffrey de Clinton, the treasurer of King Henry I. It afterward belonged to John of Gaunt, who made large additions to it. Edward II. was once imprisoned there. Queen Elizabeth gave the castle to Dudley, Earl of Leicester, and she herself made three visits to it. Sir Walter Scott, in his novel of " Kenilworth," describes one of these visits.

KEN'NE-DY, John Pendleton, an American writer, born in Baltimore, Md., Oct. 25, 1795. He served as a volunteer in the second war with England, afterward studied law, and became noted in politics. He was elected to Congress three times, and under President Fillmore was Secretary of the Navy. He wrote several novels which were very popular in their day, among which " Swallow Barn," a story of plantation life in Virginia, and " Horseshoe Robinson," a story of the Tories in the Revolution, are the best known. Mr. Kennedy died, when nearly seventy-five years old (Aug. 18, 1870).

KEN'SETT, John Frederick, an American artist, born in Cheshire, Conn., March 22, 1818. In early life he was an engraver of banknotes, but a picture which he painted in England, where he went in 1840, met with such success that he was induced to become a landscape painter. After spending several years in England and Italy, he returned to New York, and during the rest of his life made many beautiful paintings of American scenery, especially of the White Mountains, Adirondacks, and Lake George. He died in New York, when fifty-four years old (Dec. 16, 1872).

KENT, James, an American lawyer, born in Philippi, N. Y., July 31, 1763. He was graduated at Yale College in 1781, became a lawyer when twenty-two years old, and soon became noted for his legal learning. He was several times elected to the State Legislature, and in 1796 became professor of law in Columbia College. Afterward he was chosen to many important offices, becoming Chief Justice of New York in 1804, and Chancellor (that is, judge of the Court of Chancery) in 1814. His wise decisions in hundreds of law cases are often appealed to by other lawyers who have similar cases to settle ; but he is best known for his "Commentaries on American Law," which were published from 1826 to 1830, and are now used by every American lawyer, as well as by many in other countries. Chancellor Kent died in New York, when eighty-four years old (Dec. 12, 1847).

KENTUCKY (*ken-tuk'e*), a Southern State of the United States, N. of Tennessee and S. of the Ohio River ; area, 37,700 square miles, or a little larger than Maine ; pop. 1,859,000, or more than two and three fourths times as much as that of Maine ; capital, FRANKFORT. The Cumberland Mountains, which pass through the eastern part, are noted for their grand and beautiful scenery. The rest of the State is a table-land, through which the rivers flow in deep valleys. Most of the rivers are navigable by steamboats, and Kentucky has therefore a large trade. Near the Green River, and in other places, are many caves, one of which, the Mammoth Cave, is supposed to be the largest in the world, having been explored for more than ten

miles. It contains many beautiful rooms, the walls and roofs of which are coated with stalactites. In one place is a stream in which the fish are blind ; and blind insects are found crawling under the stones.

Kentucky has fine mines of coal and iron, and a rich soil ; and it is one of the most important farming States. Nearly half the tobacco and more than half the hemp sold in the United States come from there, and great quantities of corn, oats, potatoes, and other things are raised. Kentucky is noted for its fine cattle and horses, and large numbers of sheep and swine are raised. Among the important manufactures are iron, flour, and leather. More whiskey is made than in any other State.

Kentucky was called by the Indians Kan-tuck-kee, the "dark and bloody ground," because the different tribes who used it as a hunting ground used to have bloody fights there. Among the early settlers was Daniel BOONE. Kentucky was first a part of Virginia, but was made a separate State of the Union in 1792.

KE'O-KUK, a city of Iowa, in the S.E. corner of the State, on the Mississippi River ; pop. 14,000, or about as large as Easton, Pa. The largest steamers can ascend the river to Keokuk, just above which are rapids, called the Des Moines Rapids, extending twelve miles. The government has constructed a ship canal around these rapids. Keokuk has a large trade, and it contains many flour-mills, foundries, and other manufactories.

KEP'LER, Johann, a famous German astronomer, born in Würtemberg, Dec. 27, 1571. His father, who had once held a high position, lost all his money and became an innkeeper ; and Johann, when young, helped him in his business. But he was enabled to go to school, and finally to the University of Tübingen, where he was graduated when twenty years old. Afterward he gave himself up to the study of astronomy, and became professor of mathematics in the University of Gratz. He had to leave there on account of religious troubles, and about 1600 went to visit Tycho BRAHE at Prague. Tycho died the next year, and Kepler succeeded him as mathematician to the emperor. He is famous for finding out the laws which rule the motions of the planets, by which we are enabled to

Johann Kepler.

tell the place of any one of them in its orbit (C.C.T., 631, I.) at any time, past or present. From these laws sprang the great discoveries of Newton. Kepler had much trouble all his life, and was very poor, being often unable to get his salary on account of the wars in the empire, but he never lost his love for science. He died in Ratisbon, when sixty-nine years old (Nov. 15, 1630).

KEY, Francis Scott, author of the song "The Star-Spangled Banner," born in Frederick County, Md., Aug. 1, 1779. He was a graduate of St. John's College, Annapolis, and for many years attorney of the District of Columbia. "The Star-Spangled Banner" was composed while he was a prisoner in the British fleet, at the time of the attack on Fort McHenry in 1814. He died in Baltimore, when nearly sixty-four years old (Jan. 11, 1843).

KEY WEST. See FLORIDA.

KHARKOV, or **Kharkow** (*kar-kov'*), a city of S. Russia, on the Kharkova River, a branch of the Donetz; pop. 171,000, or nearly as large as Newark, N. J. It has a university, but is chiefly noted for its fairs, to which traders go from all parts of Russia. The great wool fair in the spring is the most important.

KHERSON, or **Cherson** (*ker-son*), a city of S. Russia, on the River Dneiper, 50 miles from the Black Sea; pop. 64,000, or a little larger than Wilmington, Del. It was formerly a very important place, but the bad climate has injured it. John HOWARD died in Kharkov, and the Emperor Alexander I. built there a monument to him.

KIEL (*keel*), a seaport of Germany, in Prussia, on a bay of the Baltic Sea, 52 miles N. by E. of Hamburg; pop. 52,000, or nearly as large as Hartford, Conn. It is walled and is fortified by several strong forts. Kiel is important as the principal harbor of Germany, where its war ships are kept. It has great shipyards, wharves, iron foundries, and arsenals, and is the site of the naval academy, where officers are trained for the navy. Kiel was a town in the 11th century.

KIEV, Kiew, or **Kieff** (*ke-ev'*), a city of Russia, on the River Dnieper; pop. 170,000, or a little smaller than Newark, N. J. It is one of the oldest and finest cities of Russia, and has many splendid buildings. The Cathedral of St. Sophia, built in the 11th century, is a magnificent structure, and the Petcherskoi Monastery is one of the largest in Russia. The University of Kiev has 1700 students.

Kiev is said to have been founded in the 5th century. It was the principal place of the Russian heathen worship, and when Russia became Christianized it was the capital for a long time.

KINGS'LEY, Charles, a famous English clergyman and writer, born in Holne, Devonshire, June 12, 1819. He was educated at Cambridge University, studied law for a short time, but became a minister, and in 1844 was made rector of Eversley, in Hampshire, where he soon became widely known as a preacher and an author. He took great interest in the poor, and worked hard to get better wages and more comfortable homes for them, while he taught them how to be good and happy. In his first novel, "Alton Locke," he showed the wrongs the working classes of England had to suffer, and what might be done to help them. Among his other novels are "Yeast," "Hypatia," "Westward Ho," and "Two Years Ago." He also published two volumes of poems, and several works for young folks, among them "The Heroes : Greek Fairy Tales for My Children ;" "The Water Babies : a Fairy Tale for a Land Baby ;" and "Madame How and Lady Why." He died at Eversley, when nearly fifty-six years old (Jan. 23, 1875). The year before his death he visited the United States and lectured.

KINGSLEY, Henry, an English writer, brother of Charles Kingsley, born at Holne, in 1824. He passed a large part of his life in Australia, and the scene of one of his novels, "Geoffrey Hamlyn," is laid there. He wrote several other novels, which though not as finished in style as his brother's, are full of strong characters, and, like his brother's, have always a high moral tone. He died, when fifty-two years old (May 24, 1876).

KING'S MOUNTAIN, a mountain range on the borders of North Carolina and South Carolina, near the S. end of which, in South Carolina, was fought the battle of King's Mountain between the Americans and the British, Oct. 7, 1780. After the battle of Camden Lord CORNWALLIS sent Major Ferguson with a British force to make a raid in the western part of South Carolina. After committing all sorts of crimes on the people, he was at length met by the Americans at King's Mountain, and defeated, many being killed and wounded, and nearly all the rest taken prisoners. Ferguson himself was killed. This battle helped the American cause very much.

KINGS'TON, a city of Canada, on the St. Lawrence River, where it flows out of Lake Ontario ; pop. 16,000, or about as large as San Diego, Cal. It has a fine harbor, which is so well defended by forts that Kingston is one of the strongest places in Canada. It has a large trade, both by steamboats and by railroads. Many ships are built there, and there are manufactories of machinery, steam engines, locomotives, and pianos.

Kingston is one of the oldest cities in Canada, a fort having been built on its site by the French in 1672. This was called Fort Cataraqui, and afterward Fort Frontenac. The present name was given by the British, who captured the place in 1762.

KINGSTON, a city, capital of Jamaica, West Indies, on the S. coast of the island ; pop. 40,000, or about the same as Erie, Pa. It has a very fine harbor, but the city itself, though well built is hot and unhealthy. Many of the richer people have country houses on the mountains above the city, where the air is cool and pleasant, and the scenery very beautiful. Near the city are many sugar plantations, and a large trade is carried on in sugar, rum, coffee, tobacco, and dyewood.

Kingston was founded in 1693, after the old capital, Port Royal, had been destroyed by an earthquake.

KINGSTON, a city of New York, on the Hudson River, 90 miles N. of New York City ; pop. 21,000, or a little larger than Bloomington, Ill. It is built partly on a hill, and partly on the river bank at the mouth of Rondout Creek, which forms its harbor. The lower town was once a separate village, and is still known by its old name of Rondout. Near Kingston are many quarries of flagging stones, with which most of the sidewalks in New York City are paved. There are also large quarries of limestone, from which cement is made, and the largest cement manufactory in the United States is at this place.

Kingston was settled about 1665. During the Revolution the first State covention of New York met, first at Fishkill and afterward in Kingston, and there the first constitution of the State was framed (Feb., 1777). Soon after the village was captured by the English, who plundered it, and then burned every house but one (Oct. 17, 1777).

KIRCHHOFF (*keer'k'hof*), **Gustav Robert,** a German astronomer, born in Königsberg, March 12, 1824. His studies have been mostly about electricity, heat, and magnetism, things belonging to a branch of learning called physics, and he has made an instrument called the spectroscope (C.C.T., 602, I. u.), which has helped scientific men to discover some wonderful things. With it we can tell what a body is made of, no matter how far off it may be, by means of the light which comes from it. In this way we have learned the materials of which the sun and many of the planets are made.

KISH'EN-EV, a city of Russia, on the Byk, a branch of the River Dniester, 86 miles N.W. of Odessa ; pop. 120,000, or twice as large as Grand Rapids, Mich. It has a large trade in tallow, hides, wool, and wheat, and great quantities of plums and prunes are sent from there.

KISSINGEN (*kis'sing-en*), a town of Germany, in Bavaria, on the Salle River ; pop. 4000. It is noted for its mineral springs, which are visited every year by thousands of people. The water is used for drinking and bathing, and a great deal of it is bottled and sent to the United States and other countries. Near Kissingen are large salt-works, the salt water being got from an Ar-

tesian well (C.C.T., 644, II. l.) 2000 feet deep. Kissingen has been noted for its waters since the 16th century.

KLE'BER (French, *kla-bair'*), **Jean Baptiste,** a French general, born in Strasburg, about 1753. He first served as an officer in the Austrian army, but resigned in 1783. When the French Revolution broke out he enlisted as a private, but was rapidly promoted for bravery, and in 1794 became a general. In 1798 he went with Napoleon to Egypt and Syria, where he distinguished himself by his skill and bravery. On one occasion he was attacked near Mt. Tabor by a Turkish army much larger than his own ; but he formed his soldiers in a hollow square, and beat back the Turks until Napoleon came with reinforcements, when a great victory was won. When Napoleon went back to France he left the government of Egypt to Kléber, who ruled so well that the Arabs called him "Sultan the Just." Believing that he could not keep Egypt, he made a treaty of peace with the English general, Sir Sydney Smith. By this treaty he was to give up Egypt to the Turks, and he and his army were to be allowed to return to France. After Kléber had given up several cities and forts he was told that the English government had refused to allow the treaty, and that his army must become prisoners. Instead of submitting, Kléber immediately attacked his enemies, gained a great victory at Heliopolis (March 20, 1800), and was soon master of Egypt again. Not long after, while walking in his garden at Cairo, he was killed by an assassin, when forty-seven years old (June 14, 1800).

KLOP'STOCK, Friedrich Gottlieb, a famous German poet, born at Quedlinburg, July 2, 1724. His parents were well off, and he was brought up to study, and early made up his mind to be a poet. When twenty-four years old he published the first part of his great poem, the "Messiah," which at once made him famous. But poetry was not much thought of then in Germany, so he went to Denmark, where the king gave him a pension, and he lived twenty years in Copenhagen. After that he lived in Hamburg, where he finished his poem. Klopstock was the first of the great German poets. He died in Hamburg, when seventy-nine years old (March 14, 1803).

KNATCH BULL-HU GES-SEN, Edward Hugessen, an English statesman and writer, born in Kent, April 29, 1829. He was graduated at Oxford University in 1850, became a member of Parliament in 1857, and still holds that position. He has written many books for young folks, among them "Stories for my Children," "Tales at Tea Time," "Queer Folk," "Whispers from Fairy Land," "Higgledy-Piggledy," and "Uncle Joe's Stories."

KNAUS (*knows*), **Ludwig,** a German painter, born at Wiesbaden, Oct. 5, 1829. His pictures are well known in the United States, where many of them have been exhibited. One of them represents a woman playing with two cats ; another, a mother with her child looking at a mouse in a trap. He paints the human figure well, and his works bring high prices.

KNELLER, Sir **Godfrey,** a noted portrait painter, born at Lübeck, Aug. 8, 1646. He was intended for the army, but liked painting better. When thirty years old he went to London, where he painted the portraits of seven sovereigns, Charles II. being the first one. He also painted Louis XIV., Peter the Great, and Charles VI. of Spain. George I. of England made him a baronet when he was sixty-nine years old. He painted groups of children very well, and it is said he was very skilful in painting hair. There is a series of forty-three portraits by Kneller which were much

liked, and have been engraved. Sir Godfrey died in London, when seventy-seven years old (Oct. 27, 1723). There is a monument to his memory in Westminster Abbey.

KNOWLES (*noles*), **James Sheridan,** a noted British writer of plays, born in Cork, Ireland, in 1784. He wrote his first play when only twelve years old, and acted in it with some of his young companions in a private performance. At twenty-two he decided to become an actor, but he was unsuccessful for several years. He wrote at last, in 1815, a play called "Caius Gracchus," and soon after another, called "Virginius," which at once gave him fame, and he was considered for many years one of the best play-writers in England. He acted the chief characters in his own plays, and was much admired. In the latter part of his life he gave up the theatre and became a Baptist minister. He died at Torquay, in Devonshire, when seventy-eight years old (Nov. 30, 1862).

KNOX (*nox*), **Henry,** an American general, born in Boston, Mass., July 25, 1750. He had only a common

Henry Knox.

school education, and became a bookseller in Boston, his store being a favorite resort of cultivated people.

He was also an officer in a military company, and when the Revolution broke out, he escaped from the city with his wife, who hid his sword in the folds of her dress, and took part in the battle of Bunker Hill. He soon attracted the attention of Washington by his skill in planning fortifications and his knowledge of artillery, and all through the war he commanded the artillery in various battles. After the capture of York-town Congress made him a major-general, and from 1785 to 1795 he was Secretary of War. Afterward he lived in Maine, and died at Thomaston, in that State, when fifty-six years old (Oct. 25, 1806).

KNOX (*nox*), **John,** the leader of the Protestant Reformation in Scotland, born in Haddingtonshire, in 1505. He was educated at St. Andrews University, and became a priest, bnt soon gave up the Roman Catholic religion, and in 1542 declared himself a Protestant. At that time there were few Protestants in Scotland, and he suffered much persecution, being often threatened by assassins. In 1547 he was taken prisoner with many other Protestants by the Catholics and their French allies, and kept in the galleys in France for nineteen months. When released, he went to England and became one of the chaplains of Edward VI., but fled from England when Mary got the throne (1553), and finally settled at Geneva, Switzerland, where he had an English congregation.

Meanwhile the Protestants had increased in Scotland, and in 1559 he returned there to bear his share in the struggle that was going on with the Catholics. For thirteen years he labored for what he believed to be the truth, speaking it boldly even to the highest in power. His last public address was a bitter and eloquent sermon on the terrible massacre of St. Bartholomew. He died in Edinburgh, when sixty-seven years old (Nov. 24, 1572). At his funeral

the regent of Scotland, Morton, said of him : "Here lies him who never feared the face of man."

KNOXVILLE (*nox'vil*), a city of E. Tennessee, on the Holston River, an upper branch of the Tennessee River; pop. 23,000, or about as large as Malden, Mass. It is built on high ground, from which there is a beautiful view of the river and the surrounding country. Knoxville has important manufactures, and a larger trade than any other city of eastern Tennessee. It is the seat of the East Tennessee University and the State Agricultural College. Knoxville was settled in 1789, and was named after Gen. Henry KNOX. From 1794 to 1817 it was the capital of Tennessee. During the Civil War the city was at first held by the Confederates, but was afterward taken by the Unionists who built many strong forts around it. In the fall of 1863 Gen. Burnside and the Union soldiers were besieged there by Gen. Longstreet, with a much larger army. The Confederates tried to storm the forts, and were partly successful (Nov. 18, 1863), but the next day they were driven back, and a week afterward the siege was given up.

KNYPHAUSEN (*knip'how-zen*), **Henry,** Baron, a German soldier, born in Alsace about 1725. He served in the wars of Frederick the Great against Austria, and in 1776 came to America in command of the Hessian troops, sent here by Great Britain. He took part in the battles of Long Island, White Plains, and Brandywine. In 1780 he made an expedition into New Jersey, but did little besides burning a few villages. He died in Berlin, when about sixty-four years old (May 2, 1789).

KOEKKOEK (*kook'kook*), **Bernard Cornelis,** a Dutch landscape painter, born in Middelburg, Oct. 11, 1803. His father, Johannes Herman Koekkoek, was famous as a painter of sea scenes. Bernard lived in Cleves, Prussia, for many years, and had a painting school there. He died in Cleves, when fifty-eight years old (April 5, 1862). He had several brothers, who also were fine painters.

KÖNIGGRÄTZ (*kehn'ig-rates*). See SADOWA.

KÖNIGSBERG (*kehn'igz-ba-erg*), a city of Germany, in Prussia, on the River Pregel, about 20 miles from the Baltic Sea; pop. 151,000, or twice as large as Scranton, Pa. It is built partly on the river banks, and partly on an island, and is defended by walls and forts which make it one of the strongest cities in Germany. It is important for its trade and its manufactures of soap, leather, starch, and cloths. The Königsberg University has about 750 students, and contains a very fine library and collections. At one time it had 2000 students. Among its celebrated teachers was KANT, a native of Königsberg, who is buried in the porch of the cathedral. The name Königsberg means the "Mountain of Kings."

KÖNIGSTEIN (*kehn'igz-stine*), a town of Germany, in Saxony, on the River Elbe, 15 miles S.E. of Dresden; pop. about 3000. It is noted for its fortress, built opposite the town, on a high rocky hill which can be ascended only by one narrow passage. Rooms cut in the solid rock are used for storehouses, and water is got from a well 600 feet deep. In time of war the crown jewels and treasury of the Kingdom of Saxony are brought to this fortress for safe keeping. The name Königstein means "the Rock of Kings."

KÖRNER (*kur'ner*), **Karl Theodor,** a famous German poet, born in Dresden, Sept. 23, 1791. His parents loved books and authors, and SCHILLER was their dearest friend. Körner took part in what was called in Germany the War of Freedom, in opposition to the Emperor Napoleon, joined the army as one of a corps called the Black Huntsmen, and wrote stirring battle songs. His last one, called the "Schwertlied" (Sword Song), was written while waiting orders in a wood to attack the French at Rosenberg. In the fight which followed he fell mortally wounded, and died when only twenty-two years old (Aug. 26, 1813). A fine monument has been erected over his grave, near the battle-field, and is much visited by travellers.

KOSCIUSZKO (*kos-se-us'ko*), **Tadensz** (Thaddeus), a Polish patriot, born near Novogrudek, in Lithuania, Feb. 12, 1746. He belonged to a noble family, and was educated in the best military schools of Europe. He became a captain in the Polish army, but having fallen

Thaddeus Kosciuszko.

in love with a young lady who did not care for him, he left his country and came to the United States. In 1776 he was made an officer of engineers, and was the chief engineer in building the works at West Point. He was also aide-de-camp to General Washington, and served with honor until the end of the Revolution, when he went back to his native country. When the Poles rose in rebellion against the Russians (1794) he was one of their bravest leaders ; but though his countrymen fought well and did many fine deeds, they were not successful, and at the battle of Maciejowice he fell, covered with wounds, and was taken prisoner by the Russians. In 1797 he was set free, and returned to the United States, where he received a grant of land and a pension. The next year he went to France to live, and in 1816 settled at Solothurn, in Switzerland, where he was killed by a fall from his horse, when seventy-one years old (Oct. 15, 1817). His body was carried to Cracow and buried in the Cathedral, and the people brought earth from all the battle-fields of Poland and built near the city a mound as high as a common church steeple (150 feet) to his memory.

KOSSUTH (*kosh'oot*), **Lajos** (Louis), a Hungarian patriot, born at Monok, Hungary, Sept. 16, 1802. He was a member of the Hungarian diet or congress, and distinguished himself by opposing the despotism of the Austrians. At one time he was imprisoned for treason for several years, but this caused so much indignation that he was released (1840). At length the Hungarians declared themselves independent, and made Kossuth their governor ; but he was beaten by the Austrian and Russian armies, and forced to fly to Turkey (1849). There he was imprisoned, but at the request of the United States and England he was released, and Congress sent a war vessel to bring him to this country (1851). He made many speeches in the cities of England and America, where he was received with great enthusiasm, and was given many contributions of money in aid of Hungarian independence. Preparations were made for another revolution in that country, but this

and other attempts were unsuccessful. In 1862 Kossuth went to Turin, Italy, where he remained until his death. He died in his ninety-second year (Mar. 20, 1894).

KOTZEBUE (*kot'seh-boo*), **August Friedrich Ferdinand von,** a noted German writer of plays, born in Weimar, May 3, 1761. When a young man he became secretary to the governor-general of St. Petersburg, and through the rest of his life was much in the employ of the Russian government. Once he was banished to Siberia, on a charge of having written something against the Emperor Paul ; but afterward the emperor read one of Kotzebue's plays, and finding himself flattered in it, he recalled him, gave him an estate, and made him an imperial councillor. Among Kotzebue's best-known plays are "The Stranger" and "Pizarro." Though he was a good writer, his countrymen despised him as a mere tool of the Russian emperor ; and in revenge for some letters which he wrote to the emperor, ridiculing the secret societies of the German students, he was stabbed by one of them and killed at Mannheim, when fifty-seven years old (March 23, 1819).

KRUPP (*kroop*), **Alfred,** a German iron and steel manufacturer, born at Essen, in Prussia, April 26, 1812. He inherited from his father (Friedrich) large cast-steel works at Essen, and he enlarged them so much that they are now the greatest steel and iron works in the world. They cover more than a square mile of ground, and more than thirty miles of railroads connect the different parts. There are more than 1000 smelting furnaces, and 300 steam engines, besides forges, machine-shops, and many other establishments ; and 20,000 men are employed in making cannons, cannon-balls, rails, machinery, and a hundred other articles of steel and iron. Alfred Krupp was the first to find out how to cast steel in very large masses. The great steel siege guns used by the Germans in the five months' siege of the city of Paris in 1871 were made by him. He died when seventy-five years old (July 14, 1887). His son Alfred succeeded him in the control of the works.

KUBLAI KHAN (*koo'bli kahn*),the founder of the Mongol Empire of China, grandson of GENGHIS KHAN, born in the 13th century, A.D. At that time China was suffering much from the invasion of the Eastern Tartars, and in 1250 the Emperor asked Kublai Khan, who commanded the Western Tartars, to come and help him drive out the invaders. With this aid the Eastern Tartars were defeated, but instead of going away, Kublai Khan called himself Emperor of China (1260), and dethroned Li Sung, the real emperor. He governed the country wisely, and made it very powerful. Many learned men were invited to his court, among them the Venetian traveller, Marco POLO. Kublai conquered Cochin China and Tonquin, and finally ruled over the largest empire in the world. He died at Peking in 1294.

KURDISTAN (*koor-dis-tahn'*), a region of W. Asia, lying partly in Persia and partly in Turkey; area and population not known. In the northern parts are high mountain chains, but in the southern parts are fertile plains. The people, who are called Kurds, are mostly Mohammedans, and live sometimes in stone houses and at other times wander from place to place. They are fine horsemen, skilled in the use of arms, and very brave. The chiefs have forts among the mountains, to which they go with their tribes in time of war. Most of them are almost independent of Turkey and Persia. Kurdistan means the country of the Kurds.

KURILE (*koo'ril*) **ISLANDS,** a chain of twenty-six islands of E. Asia, extending from Yezo in Japan to Kamtchatka. They are very mountainous, and have several burning volcanoes. Most of them are covered with forests, in which wild animals are common. They are inhabited by only a few people, called Ainos, a dark race, so hairy that the Japanese say they are descended from bears. They are very dirty, and live in miserable huts.

The islands were discovered by the Russians in 1713. Part of them belong to Japan and part to Russia.

KUTUZOFF (*koo-too'zof*), **Mikhail,** Prince of Smolensk, a famous Russian soldier, born in 1745. He entered the army when sixteen years old, served in the wars against the Turks, and soon reached high rank. In the wars against Napoleon he did good service, and commanded the allied armies at Austerlitz, but was not to blame for the defeat. In August, 1812, he was given command of the Russian armies against Napoleon, who was then marching on Moscow, and although he lost the battle of Borodino, was made a marshal for his bravery. After the burning of Moscow he followed the French army, defeated Eugene Beauharnais at Smolensk (Nov. 16), and on the two following days defeated Marshals Davoust and Ney at Krasnoi, taking thousands of prisoners and more than 200 cannon. For his great services the emperor made him Prince of Smolensk, and gave him the surname of Smolenskoi. He followed the enemy as far as Buntzlau, Prussia, where, overcome by his labors, he fell ill and died, when sixty-eight years old (April 28, 1813).

L

LABRADOR (*lab-rah-dore'*),a country of E. North America on the Atlantic Ocean, N.E. of Canada; area, 450,000 square miles, or more than one and a half times as large as Texas. Most of it is a dreary table-land so cold and sterile that hardly any trees or plants grow on it. In winter the sea is commonly frozen from December to June, and it is almost impossible to travel on the land. Most of the people are engaged in fishing for cod-fish, herrings, and salmon, which abound along the coast. In the summer, hundreds of fishermen go there from Newfoundland and New England. Many seals are killed and, in the interior, the hunters find great numbers of reindeer, bears, wolves, and other wild animals. Labrador proper, or the eastern part, belongs to NEWFOUNDLAND. In the western part, which belongs to the Dominion of CANADA, about one third of the people are Indians, and most of the whites are French Canadians.

Labrador was first found by John CABOT in 1497. The Portuguese named it Terra Laborador, which means "cultivable land," and this has become changed to its present name.

LACEDÆMON (*las-e-de'mon*). See SPARTA.

LA CROSSE (*lah kross'*), a city of W. Wisconsin, on the Mississippi River, at the mouths of the Black and La Crosse Rivers; pop. 25,000, or about as large as Auburn, N. Y. Several railroads meet there, and the city has a large trade, especially in lumber. It contains large manufactories of saddlery and harnesses, ploughs, and many other things. La Crosse was founded in 1851, and became a city in 1856.

LADRONE (*lah-drone'* or *lah-dro'-na*) **ISLANDS.** A group of about twenty islands in the Pacific Ocean, W. of the Philippine Islands. They are mountainous and contain several volcanoes. Most of them are fertile, and bread-fruit, cocoa-nuts, and other tropical fruits are abundant. The islands belong to Spain, and most of the people now living on them are descended from Spanish emigrants who came from Mexico and the Philippine Islands.

These islands were first found by Magalhaens (1852), who named them Ladrone Islands (Islands of Thieves) because the people stole so much. They are sometimes called the Marianne Islands, after Queen Mariana of Spain, who sent missionaries there in the 17th century.

LA FARGE, John, an American artist, born in New York, March 31, 1835. He is especially noted for his pictures of flowers, but paints also landscapes and the human figure. Of late he has turned his attention to decorating the inside of buildings. The frescoes in Trinity Church, Boston, and St. Thomas's Church, New York, were done by him. He has a studio in New York.

LAFAYETTE (*lah-fa-et'*), a city of W. Indiana on the Wabash River; pop. 16,000, or about as large as Lockport, N. Y. Steamboats can ascend the Wabash as far as this place, and a large trade is carried on. The city contains many machine-shops and foundries, breweries, flouring-mills, and manufactories of woollen goods, ploughs, and reaping-machines. It is the site of Purdue University. Lafayette was founded in 1825. About seven miles north of it is the battle-ground of Tippecanoe, where General HARRISON defeated the Indians, Nov. 7, 1811.

LAFAYETTE (*lah-fa-et'*), **Marie Jean Paul Roch Yves Gilbert Motier,** Marquis de, born in Auvergne, September 6, 1757. He belonged to one of the oldest, noblest, and richest families of France, and became an officer in the army before he was nineteen years old. In 1776, hearing one day at a dinner party that the

Lafayette.

Americans had declared their independence of Great Britain, he made up his mind to cross the water, and help them fight for their liberty. His friends opposed it, and the French king, even after Lafayette had set sail, sent officers to bring him back. But he escaped from them, and landed safely in South Carolina, April 24, 1777. The Americans welcomed him gladly, and made him a major-general in the army, where he did the country great service, not only by his skill and courage, but by his successful efforts to get help from France in carrying on the war. He afterward took part in the French Revolution, and as commander-in-chief of the National Guards, tried to protect the rights both of the people and of the king. But his ideas did not suit men who had taken the law into their own hands, and Lafayette's arrest was ordered. In trying to escape, he fell into the hands of the Austrians, with whom the French were at war, and was kept a prisoner for five years, and most cruelly treated. Great efforts were made in the United States and in England to get his release, but the Austrian Government refused to give him up. He was at last set free

on the demand of Bonaparte (August 25, 1797).

In 1824 he visited the United States by special invitation, and was welcomed with all the honor and affection that he so well deserved from Americans. The whole country turned out to greet him, and Congress voted him a township of land and $200,000 in acknowledgment of his great services. He died in Paris in his seventy-seventh year (May 20, 1834).

LA FONTAINE (*lah fon-tane'*) **Jean de**, a famous French writer of fables, born in Château Thierry, July 8, 1621. He was educated to be a priest, but soon gave it up, and led such an idle, dissipated life that nobody thought he would be good for anything. But, in spite of this, he was fond of reading and showed a great talent for writing poetry. Like a good many other poets, he always seemed to be in a dream, or, as people say, "in a brown study," and did not know how to take care of himself; but he had a good many rich friends, who took care of him and gave him a home all his life. When about forty-four years old he began to write fables, of which he published several books that made him famous. They have been translated into many languages, and are being printed almost all the time. La Fontaine died in Paris when seventy-four years old (April 13, 1695).

LAHORE (*lah-hore'*), a city of N. India, on the Ravee River; pop. 149,000, or twice as large as Fall River, Mass. In the 12th century it was the capital of a great empire, and many ruins around it show its ancient grandeur. Near the city are magnificent tombs of the old emperors. The modern city is defended by a brick wall and a citadel, and has many fine mosques and Hindoo temples.

LAKE DWELLINGS. See SWITZERLAND.

LAMARCK (*lah-mark'*), **Jean Baptiste Pierre Antoine de Monet de**, a noted French writer on natural history, born in Picardy, August 1, 1744.

He was first a priest, and then a soldier, but when his health failed, he went to Paris, and gave himself up to scientific studies. In 1776 he wrote a book about the air, and in 1778 a work on plants, which was much praised. After some years, he was put in charge of a part of the museum of natural history in Paris, which made him give his whole attention to invertebrate animals (C. C. T., 15, II., 1.) or animals without a backbone. The rest of his life was given up to this, and his books upon the subject are among the most important that have been written. He died in Paris when eighty-five years old (Dec. 18, 1829).

LAMARTINE (*lah-mar-tine'*), **Alphonse Marie Louise de,** a famous French poet, born in Macon, Oct. 21, 1790. His early education was given him by his mother, and when twelve years old he was sent to college. He was always fond of reading, and when he left college he spent his time in studying the poets. When thirty years old he published a book called " Poetical Meditations," which was very successful. He married a very rich young English lady, and after some years made a grand tour in the East with his wife and daughter ; he travelled like a prince, making splendid presents, having houses built on the road to suit his fancy, and troops of men and horses in his service ; so that the Arabs called him the French Emir. He was in high favor with the French people as a statesman and orator, and for a short time was really the ruler of France. Lamartine wrote poems and histories, and was well paid for his work ; but his generosity was too great for the length of his purse, and he had to suffer for it. After his bills had been paid, very little money was left, and as Lamartine grew old he grew poor too. Two years before his death the French people voted him a certain sum of money to be paid him every year, as a " token of their gratitude to one of their greatest poets, historians, and most honest states-men." He died in Paris when seventy-nine years old (March 1, 1869).

LAMB (*lam*), **Charles,** a famous English writer, born in London, Feb. 18, 1775. His parents were poor, and he was sent to the charity school of Christ's Hospital, where he stayed until he was fifteen years old ; at this school he and the poet COLERIDGE met, and got to be fast friends. Charles was a small, delicate boy, and it seemed that he could never fight his way among hundreds of strong, hearty lads ; but his sweet, affectionate temper won him the good will of all. His life was saddened in the very outset by a great trouble ; his sister, Mary Lamb, had attacks of insanity, and once, in one of these fits, she seized a knife, and pierced her mother to the heart. Charles placed her in an asylum, where she stayed until she got well again ; and then her brother promised to take care of her for the rest of her life. His income was only £100 ($500) a year, but he took his sister to his own home, and although only twenty-two years old, he gave up all thoughts of marrying, and devoted himself to this duty. Mary's dreadful illness used to come on very often in her life, but she always knew when the fits were near ; and then Charles would get leave of absence from the office for a *day's pleasure*, and with his sister's hand clasped in his, they would go off together, both of them in tears, to the asylum near London, where Mary was left until she was well enough to go back to her brother's home. No sadder story, and no life more heroic can be found among men. The most famous authors of that day were Lamb's intimate friends ; he was very modest, and hesitated in his speech ; and at their evening parties, Lamb used to stammer out his puns and witty sayings, to the great delight of all around. His writings are an odd mixture of wisdom and fun. He is best known as the author of " The

Essays of Elia," which is thought to be one of the most exquisite works in the English language. All young folks should have a copy of it. Charles Lamb died in Edmonton, when fifty-nine years old (Dec. 27, 1834).

LAM'BERT, Daniel, an English giant, born in Leicester, March 13, 1769. When about nineteen years old, he succeeded his father as keeper of the prison at Leicester, and as his duties gave him little exercise he grew very fat. Finally, he began to show himself in London and other places, where many fashionable people went to visit him. He was nearly six feet high, and before he died weighed 739 pounds. He was a noted swimmer, and could float with two men on his back. He drank nothing but water, and was very healthy. Lambert died in Stamford when forty years old (June 21, 1809).

LAMOTTE - VALOIS (*lah-mot' val-wah'*), **Jeanne de Luz de St. Remy,** Countess de, a Frenchwoman known for her share in the story of the diamond necklace, born July 22, 1756. She was a wicked woman, who contrived to get acquainted with the French queen, MARIE ANTOINETTE, and also with the Cardinal de Rohan, one of the king's high officers, whom the queen disliked. She made the cardinal think that she could make the queen like him, and told him that if he would get from the court jewelers a certain very splendid and costly diamond necklace which the queen wished for, and give it to her to take to Marie Antoinette, the queen would give him her friendship in return. The cardinal got the necklace for her, but instead of giving it to the queen, who knew nothing of the whole affair, Madame Lamotte sold it in London. Finally, a bill for the payment of the necklace was sent by the jewellers to the queen ; and when she denied having had it, inquiries were made which ended in a public trial. The countess and the cardinal were put in prison, and there was a great excitement about it, many people believing that the queen had received the necklace, in spite of her denials. It was at last decided that the only guilty person was Madame Lamotte ; and while the cardinal was released, she was sentenced to be whipped, and imprisoned for life. She escaped from prison in about two years, and went to London, where she died (August 23, 1791).

LAN'CAS-TER, a city of E. Pennsylvania, on the Conestoga River ; pop. 32,000, or about as large as Kansas City, Mo. It contains large iron-foundries and blast-furnaces, locomotive works, and manufactories of rifles, axes, and carriages. A large trade is carried on, especially in coal and lumber. It is the site of Franklin and Marshall College. Lancaster was founded about 1718, and from 1799 to 1812 it was the capital of Pennsylvania. Until 1825 it was the largest inland town of the United States.

LAN'CAS-TER, House of, a family of kings of England, a branch of the Plantagenets, who occupied the throne from 1399 to 1461. They were descended from JOHN OF GAUNT, Duke of Lancaster, the fourth son of Edward III. In 1399, Henry of Bolingbroke, the son of John of Gaunt, raised an army, and obliged his cousin Richard II. to give up to him his crown, in this way becoming Henry IV., the first sovereign of the Lancastrian family. Two of his descendants in the male line, Henry V., and Henry VI., succeeded him on the throne, and Henry VII., the first Tudor, inherited its claims in the female line. Henry VI., the last of this house, was, after much fighting and bloodshed, driven from the throne by Edward IV., son of the Duke of York. The wars between these two lines are called the Wars of the Roses.

LAN'CAS-TER, Joseph, an English teacher, born in London in 1771. He taught upon a plan known as the Lancastrian system, by which the scholars assist the teacher, and help to educate each other, through the means of monitors chosen among themselves. He was very successful among the poor children of London, and opened a number of schools in different parts of the country. These being broken up by a rival teacher, he came to Canada and the United States, to introduce his system. He wrote several school-books, and a work on "Improvement in Education." He died in New York when sixty-seven years old (Oct. 24, 1838).

LAN'CE-LOT OF THE LAKE, a fabled British hero, one of the knights of King ARTHUR'S Round Table. He was Arthur's favorite and bravest knight, and was sent by him to bring his royal bride Guinevere to the court. But it came to pass that Lancelot and Guinevere fell in love with each other at first sight, which, of course, gave everybody no end of trouble. TENNYSON has made him the hero of two of his "Idyls of the King," called "Elaine" and "Guinevere."

LAN'DON, Letitia Elizabeth, an English author, born near London in 1802. She began to write poetry when only thirteen years old, always signing her initials, L. E. L., to her writings. Her works were very much liked, especially by sentimental young women ; and she wrote both prose and verse for the best papers and magazines of her day. She married George Maclean, Governor of Cape Coast Castle, Africa, and died soon after reaching there, when thirty-six years old (Oct. 15, 1838).

LAN'DOR, Walter Savage, a noted English author, born at Ipsley Court, Warwickshire, Jan. 30, 1775. His parents were rich, and he was educated at Rugby and Oxford. After his father's death, when he got possession of the property, he spent large sums in buying more land and in building a splendid house ; but one day, in a freak of ill-temper, he sold off everything, ordered his superb

house to be torn down, and left the country. He wrote many books, both poetry and prose ; his best work is called "Imaginary Conversations of Literary Men," in which many great men of past and present times are made to talk together. He died in Florence, Italy, when eighty-nine years old (Sept. 17, 1864).

LAND'SEER, Sir Edwin, a famous English artist, born in London in 1803. His father, John Landseer, an engraver, used to take him to the fields and teach him to draw animals, and when he grew up he became one of the most famous animal painters that ever lived. Among his best pictures are "Deer Stalking in the Highlands" and "Sir Walter Scott and his Dogs," of which engravings are often seen. He died in London, when seventy years old (Oct. 1, 1873).

LANNES (*lahn*), **Jean,** Duke of Montebello, a famous French soldier, born April 11, 1769. He began life as a dyer's apprentice, but went into the army when twenty-three years old. He was soon noticed as a brave soldier, and was rapidly promoted by Bonaparte to high rank. In 1804 he was made a marshal of the Empire, and went with Bonaparte through all the wars in Austria, Prussia, Spain, and Germany, until he was shot at the battle of Essling (May 22, 1809). He lived nine days after he was wounded, and died in Vienna when forty years old (May 31, 1809).

LAN'SING, the capital of Michigan, in the S. part of the State, on Grand River ; pop. 13,000, or about as large as Yonkers, N. Y. Besides the State House, it contains the State Reform School and other public institutions.

Lansing was settled and became the State capital in 1847. It was made a city in 1859.

LA-OC'O-ON, in Greek fable, a Trojan hero and priest of Neptune. He did not wish the Trojans to let the wooden horse of the Greeks enter TROY, and rushing forward, thrust his spear into its side. Two great serpents then rose from the sea and, twining themselves around him and his two sons, crushed them to death.

Laocoon.

There is a famous piece of statuary representing their death in the Vatican at Rome.

LA·O·DA'MI·A, a fabulous Greek princess, wife of Protesilaus, the first Greek slain in the war of TROY. Laodamia entreated the gods to permit her to converse with him once more, and her request was granted. But when he had to leave her to go back, she could not bear the separation, and died of grief. Wordsworth wrote a beautiful poem about it.

LAON (*lah-ong'*), a town of N. France, 74 miles N. E. of Paris, pop. 14,000, or about as large as Mansfield, Ohio. It is built on a steep hill, and is defended by a citadel and by ancient walls. It contains an old cathedral, a museum of Roman and Celtic antiquities, and many other interesting things.

Laon is a very ancient town, and was the residence of some of the early French kings. ANSELM and ABELARD were teachers in its school. It has been besieged many times. In the last war with Germany, the Germans took it (Sept. 9, 1870), and while they were marching in a French soldier blew up the powder magazine and killed and wounded a great many of them.

LA PEROUSE (*lah pa-rooz'*), **Jean François de Galaup,** Count of, a noted French navigator, born in Languedoc, Aug. 22, 1741. He went into the navy at fifteen, fought his country's battles when a young man, and afterward served in the American Revolution. In 1785 he took command of two French ships, fitted out by Louis XVI., to explore in the Pacific. He sailed along the American coast to California, and afterward along the Asiatic coast, making various discoveries, for two or three years. In February, 1788, he was heard from at Botany Bay; but after that no news of the expedition reached France. Ships were sent in search of him without success, and it was not until 1828 that any trace of him was discovered. It then appeared that his ships had been wrecked, and the crew most likely murdered by savages, in the Island of Vanikoro, one of the New Hebrides group, some time in 1789.

LAPITHÆ (*lap'i-the*), in Greek fable, a people who lived among the mountains of Thessaly. They are chiefly known for their wars with the CENTAURS, whom they at last defeated. They were supposed to have invented bits and bridles.

LA PLACE (*lah-plahss'*), **Pierre Simon,** Marquis de, a famous French astronomer, born at Beaumont-en-Auge, Lower Normandy, March 23, 1749. His parents were poor, but rich friends sent him to college; and when eighteen years old he went to Paris to seek his fortune. There, with the help of a friend, he was made professor of mathematics. When twenty-four years old, he read some papers before the Academy of Sciences, and got this praise from the society: "This society has never known so young a person to furnish in so short a time so many important papers on so many diffi-

spruce and fir, while other parts are too sterile for any plants except moss. Most of the people are Finns, but there are about 20,000 Lapps, from whom the country took its name. The Lapps are very small, and they have yellow skins and very black hair. They dress in furs, live in huts or tents, and subsist by fishing, or by keeping herds of reindeer. When a man wishes to marry, he buys a wife, paying from twenty to one hundred reindeer for her. The Lapps are now Christians, belonging to the Lutheran or the Greek Church.

LA ROCHEFOUCAULD (*lah rosh-foo-ko'*), **François,** Duke de, Prince of Marsillac, a famous French writer, born in Paris, Dec. 15, 1613. He left school when sixteen years old, and entered the army, but he was so timid that he soon found out for himself that he was not fit to be a soldier ; so he thought he would try the pleasures of court life, which he liked better. He then began to form plots against Cardinal RICHELIEU, who had great power in France ; but he was found out, and sent away from Paris.

Lapps with Reindeer Sledge.

After he was forty-seven years old he turned his mind to writing. His book called "Reflections, or Moral Maxims," made a great talk, and some of the sayings are often quoted ; but all of them teach that love of self is at the bottom of everything we do. It has been well called " a sad book." He died in Paris when sixty-six years old (March 17, 1680).

LA ROCHEJAQUELIN (*lah rosh-zhak-lan'*), **Henri du Verger,** Count de, a noted French Royalist, born in Vendée, Aug., 1772. When the French revolution began, he joined the king's side, and the people of VENDEE chose him as their leader when he was only twenty-one years old. He said to his soldiers : "I am young and without experience ; but I burn to show myself worthy to be your leader. Let us meet the enemy ; if I fall back, kill me ; if I go forward, follow me ; if I die, avenge me !" He took a brave part in all the battles, was twice chosen commander-in-chief of the whole Royalist army, and although so young, he was felt to be the mainstay of that party. He was killed at Nouaillé, when twenty-two years o'd (March 4, 1794).

LARREY (*lah-ra'*), **Dominique Jean,** Baron, a noted French surgeon, born at Baudéan in 1766 He went to Paris, and entered the navy as surgeon, and afterward became a surgeon in the army. He invented the *ambulance volante* (flying hospital), an easy wagon for carrying the wounded, and for this was made surgeon-in-chief. He served under Napoleon in the wars in Egypt, Germany, and Spain, and was much loved by the soldiers, because he was a brave man, a skilful surgeon, and a tender nurse. Once he killed his own horses to make soup for the wounded men under his care. Napoleon said of him : "If the army ever erect a monument of gratitude, it should be to Larrey ;" and in his will said : "I leave 100,000 francs to the Surgeon-in-chief Larrey, the most virtuous man I know." There is a bronze statue of Larrey in Paris, in which he is shown standing and holding Napoleon's will in his hand, open at these words. Baron Larrey died in Lyons when seventy-six years old (July 25, 1842).

LA SALLE (*lah sahl'*), **Robert**

Cavelier, Sieur de, a noted French navigator, born in Rouen in 1643. He came to America in 1667, and became a trader in furs, and the owner of a great tract of land in Canada. In 1682 he sailed down the Mississippi River to its mouth, being the first European who had ever done so. He took possession of the land around the Gulf of Mexico, called it Louisiana, after the French king, and went to France to get men and means to colonize it. He succeeded in bringing over four vessels. But quarrels arose between him and the commander of the fleet, which ended in the return of the ships, with fifty of the people, to France. With the others La Salle kept on his way, but failed to find the Mississippi again, and wandered from place to place, until his followers were nearly all dead. At last, giving up hope of reaching the land he was looking for, he started for Canada with sixteen men (1687). On the way two of the men, who hated La Salle, agreed to kill him ; and having first murdered his nephew, they shot him (March 19, 1687).

LAS CASAS (*lahs kahs'as*), **Bartolomé de,** a Spanish missionary to the American Indians, born at Seville, in 1474. He came to America in 1502, and taught the Christian religion to the natives of Hispaniola. Finding them cruelly treated, he tried to relieve their sufferings, and appealed to the Emperor Charles V. to right their wrongs. He made several journeys to Spain for this purpose, and bore many hardships and persecutions in his noble labors for the Indians. After fifty years of self-sacrifice in America, he returned to Spain, where he died (July, 1566).

LAT'I-MER, Hugh, a noted English bishop, born about 1490. He was educated at Cambridge, became one of the preachers there, was afterward a chaplain to King Henry VIII., and in 1535 was made Bishop of Worcester. At first a Catholic, he soon became a Protestant, and his sermons, declaring the right of the people to read the Bible for themselves, gave great offence. He was several times called to account for them, but it was not until the reign of Queen MARY I. that he was tried as a heretic, and sentenced to death. He was burned at the stake in Oxford when sixty-five years old (Oct. 16, 1555), at the same time with Ridley, Bishop of London. When they were about to be burned, Latimer called to Ridley to " play the man," and said : " We shall this day light such a candle, by God's grace, in England, as I trust shall never be put out."

LATIUM (*la'she-um*). See ÆNEAS.

LATONA (*la-to'nah*), in Greek fable, the wife of Jupiter before he made Juno his queen, and the mother of Apollo and Diana. Juno being jealous of her, she was driven from place to place by a great serpent, and found no rest until the sea-god Neptune gave her the floating island of DELOS for a home.

LATOUR D'AUVERGNE (*lah-toor' do-vern'*), **Théophile Malo Corret de,** a noted French soldier, born at Carhaix, Brittany, Nov. 23, 1743. He entered the French army when twenty-four years old. He was such a brave soldier that the people wanted to give him a high-sounding title, but although he commanded a body of 8000 men, he would have no other title than captain. His men fought so well that they were called the Infernal Column. Napoleon sent him a sword, with an inscription saying that he was the first grenadier of France ; but he sent the sword back, saying, " Among us soldiers there is neither first nor last." When peace came, Latour went to his home and lived quietly until war again broke out ; then he joined the army again in place of the only son of a friend. After his death his name was called at roll for many years, and the oldest sergeant used always to answer for him, " Died on the field of honor." He fell in battle at Oberhausen,

Bavaria, when fifty-seven years old (June 27, 1800).

LAUD, William, Archbishop of Canterbury, born in Reading, Berkshire, Oct. 7, 1573. He was the son of a clothier, but was educated at Oxford, and became one of the king's chaplains. Through the aid of the Duke of Buckingham, he rose to great rank and power in the kingdom, but he used his power in a cruel way to persecute people who did not agree with him in religion. His cruelty made him so hateful to the people that he was accused of treason, and after three years' imprisonment, was put to death on Tower Hill, London (Jan. 10, 1645).

LAU'RENS, Henry, an American statesman, born in Charleston, S. C., in 1724. He was educated for a merchant, and was a very successful one, making a large fortune. When the war of the Revolution broke out, he showed himself to be a true patriot. In 1776 he became a member of the Continental Congress from South Carolina, and was elected its president. In 1779 he was sent on important business to Holland, but was captured on the way by a British ship-of-war, and taken to London, where he was kept a prisoner in the Tower for fifteen months. When the war was ended, he was set free, and became one of the ministers to make arrangements for peace. He died in Charleston (Dec. 8, 1792), leaving directions in his will for his body to be burned, instead of being buried.

LAURENS, John, son of Henry Laurens, born about 1756, was an officer in the army of the Revolution, and one of Washington's favorite aids. He was a very brave and skilful officer, and distinguished himself in many battles. He was a great favorite, and his death was mourned all over the country. He was shot by the British while leading a night attack upon them, when only twenty-six years old (Aug. 27, 1782).

LAUSANNE (*lo-zahn'*), a city of

Switzerland, near the N. shore of Lake Geneva; pop. 33,000, or about as large as Duluth, Minn. It lies among grand and beautiful scenery, and is noted for its beautiful cathedral and other fine old buildings, and for its schools. Woollen cloth, leather, and jewelry are manufactured. In one of the streets is the house where GIBBON wrote his history of the "Decline and Fall of the Roman Empire."

Not far from Lausanne is the old castle of Chillon, built on a rock in the lake, and joined to the mainland by a wooden bridge. For a long time this castle was used as a prison by the Dukes of Savoy. Bonnivard, a brave priest of Geneva, had offended one of these dukes. One day while he was travelling near Lausanne, he was stopped by a band of highwaymen, who robbed him and carried him to the castle (1530). When the Duke of Savoy came to Chillon, instead of freeing Bonnivard, he commanded that he should be put into a dungeon beneath the castle. He was chained to a pillar and kept for four years, but was finally freed. The dungeon and the stone pillar to which he was chained, are still shown. Lord Byron visited the castle, and was so interested that when he returned to Lausanne he wrote "The Prisoner of Chillon," one of his finest poems.

LAVATER (*lah'vah-ter*), **Johann Kasper,** a noted Swiss minister and writer, born in Zurich, Nov. 15, 1741. He was a very sensitive, dreamy boy, fond of poetry, and noted for his love of truth. He was the first to teach the science of physiognomy, or that a man's character can be known by his features. He taught that a man's life, good or ill, may be read in his face, as in a book. This made a great talk, and when any of Lavater's pupils entered a drawing-room, many people were afraid of them, and left at once; so that Lavater himself became almost a bugbear to ill-doers. When Zurich was taken by the

French under MASSENA, Lavater was shot by a soldier in the streets (1799), and after suffering more than a year, died when sixty years old (Jan. 2, 1801).

LAW, John, a British banker, born in Edinburgh, April 21, 1671. He was an educated man, but gambled and led an immoral life. Having killed a man in a duel, he was obliged to leave Scotland; and went to Holland, where he studied the subject of banking in the great bank of Amsterdam. He made a fortune by gambling, went to Paris, and opened a bank by the king's authority. He also started a company called the Mississippi or West India Company, which was to have the sole right to trade with Canada, and to send settlers to Louisiana. Still another company, called the Company of the Indies, was begun, and Law made them both very successful for a while. But not being founded on sound business principles, they failed before long, and all the great fortunes that had been suddenly made by his system were as suddenly lost. He died poor, in Venice, when fifty-eight years old (May 21, 1729).

LAWRENCE, a city of E. Massachusetts, on the Merrimack River, 22 miles N. of Boston; pop. 45,000, or about the same as that of Utica N. Y. It is noted for its great cotton and woollen factories, in which about 12,000 people are employed. The water-power for the factories comes from a dam across the Merrimack, which cost $250,000.

Lawrence was named after the Lawrence family of Boston, rich merchants who helped to build the mills.

LAWRENCE, James, a noted American naval officer, born in Burlington, N. J., Oct. 1, 1781. When seventeen years old he entered the navy as midshipman, and when twenty-nine years old had command of the ship Hornet; on Feb. 24, 1813, he had a battle with the British sloop-of-war Peacock, and captured her in fifteen minutes, for which Congress gave him a gold medal for his bravery. After this, he was made commander of the Chesapeake. On June 1, 1813, he had a battle off Boston with the British frigate Shannon, and after a hard fight, in which he was mortally wounded, his ship was taken by the enemy. Lawrence showed great bravery in the battle, and as he was being carried below called out "Don't give up the ship!" He died when thirty-one years old (June 5, 1813). His tomb is in Trinity Churchyard, New York City.

LAYARD, Sir Austen Henry, a noted English traveller and antiquary, born in Paris, March 8, 1817. He spent some years in Florence, where he took lessons in drawing ; after this he studied law in England, but soon got tired, and started off on an exploring trip to the East. He went to see every sacred spot and ruin he had ever read or heard about, learned the languages of the countries, and used to dress himself like the natives, so that he was often mistaken for one of them. He took great interest in the history of ancient ASSYRIA, and in 1845 found the ruins of NINEVEH by digging into a great mound of earth on the banks of the Tigris. With the aid of Arab workmen he dug long trenches in the mound, and found many sculptured stones and statues, winged bulls and lions with human heads, specimens of glass and pottery, and many other curious things, which he sent to the British Museum. He published a book about them called "Nineveh and its Remains," and afterward another book called "Discoveries among the Ruins of Nineveh and Babylon," both of which are very interesting. Mr. Layard has held many important offices, and been minister to Spain and to Turkey.

LEAVENWORTH (*lev'en-worth*), the largest city of Kansas, in the N. E. part of the State, on the Missouri River; pop. 20,000, or a little larger than Bangor, Me. Several railroads meet there, and by these and steamboats a large trade is carried on. The city has large saw-mills, machine-shops, and other manufactories. Two miles farther up the river, is Fort Leavenworth, the headquarters for the United States army on the Missouri. It is not a real fort, but only a military post, with large barracks, store-houses, a hospital, and a parade-ground. Leavenworth was settled in 1854.

LEDYARD, John, a noted American traveller, born in Groton, Conn., in 1751. When about twenty-one years old, he was sent to Dartmouth College to fit himself for missionary work among the Indians ; but he soon grew tired of college life, and went to sea as a common sailor. After a trip to Gibraltar and back again, he went to England and joined Captain COOK in his last voyage round the world. Some years later he tried to get up an expedition to the N. W. coast of America ; but failing in that, he undertook a journey overland, through the north of Europe and Asia, and across Behring Strait to the western continent. Being driven out of Russia, he had to give up that plan and return to London, where he joined an exploring party just starting for Africa, got as far as Cairo in Egypt, and was there taken ill, and died (January 17, 1789).

LEDYARD, William, a soldier of the revolution, uncle of John Ledyard, born in Groton, Conn., about 1750. He commanded in Fort Griswold, Groton, when the British attacked it. He had only 157 men, but he fought bravely against 800 of the enemy, and killed nearly 200 of them, including their leader. When the British at last forced their way into the fort, their commander, Major Bromfield, a Tory, asked : "Who commands this fort?" "I did, sir," replied Ledyard, "but you do now," at the same time handing him his sword. Bromfield at once stabbed Ledyard with it, and his men killed most of the Americans who were left. A monument has been put up near the place in memory of the event. Ledyard was killed Sept. 7, 1781.

LEE, Ann, founder of the Shaker societies in America, born in Manchester, England, Feb. 29, 1736. She was a poor blacksmith's daughter, and worked in a cotton factory during her girlhood. She joined a society of Friends or Quakers in Manchester, and in time claimed to have revelations from Heaven, and came to be looked upon as a messenger from God to teach the people. They called her Mother Ann, and in 1774 a number of them followed her to America, where they set up Shaker societies at Watervliet, N. Y., and at New Lebanon. Ann Lee died in Watervliet when forty-seven years old (Sept. 8, 1784).

LEE, Arthur, an American statesman, born in Virginia, Dec. 20, 1740. He was sent to school at Eton, England, and afterward was educated as a doctor at the University of Edinburgh. Coming back to Virginia, he was successful as a doctor, but gave up his practice to study law and politics. In 1776 he went to London, and there became distinguished as a lawyer, and also as an active defender of American rights. In 1776 he became an agent of the American Congress at Paris, and from there went to Spain, and then to Prussia, to get those countries to acknowledge the new republic and lend it a helping hand. In these difficult matters he did the country great service, and won an honorable name for himself. When he returned to America he was chosen to fill other important offices, and in them all gained the respect of the best men of his times. He died in the fifty-second year of his age (Dec. 12, 1792).

LEE, Charles, a major-general in the American Revolution, born in England in 1731. He was a lieutenant in a British regiment, and after six years of service in America fighting the French, he went with the British army to Portugal, and distinguished himself by his brave conduct; but owing to his bad temper, he did not get the rank he expected.

After leading a wandering life for ten or more years, he finally came to the United States, and offered his services in the war of independence. The Americans made him a major-general in the Continental army, and believed that he would be of great use to them. But Lee was too vain to obey Washington's orders, and through his neglect of them was taken prisoner by the British (1776). While in their hands, in order to save himself from being punished as a deserter, he meanly offered to betray the plans of the Americans, and show their enemies how to conquer them. This was not discovered until some time afterward, and meanwhile he was exchanged for another prisoner, and put in command again. But he acted so shamefully at the battle of Monmouth that he was tried by court-martial; and after being deprived of his command for a year, was dismissed from the army altogether. He died in Philadelphia when fifty-one years old (Oct. 2, 1782).

LEE, Francis Lightfoot, an American statesman, younger brother of Richard Henry Lee, born Oct. 14, 1734. He was rich, well-educated, and a favorite in society, but did his part well in public affairs also, being a member of the General Congress, and one of the signers of the Declaration of Independence. He died in Richmond in 1797.

LEE, Henry, a noted American general, born in Virginia Jan. 29, 1756. He was related to Richard Henry and Arthur Lee, and distinguished himself in war as they did in politics. When twenty years old he became the captain of a cavalry company, which soon grew famous under the name of Lee's Legion. It was Washington's body-guard at the battle of Germantown, and when Greene retreated before Lord Cornwallis, it was the rear-guard of the American army. Through all the battles in the South "Light Horse Harry," as he was called, was one of the most daring and successful officers. After the war ended, he was in Congress for several years, and for three years was Governor of Virginia. When Washington died, Henry Lee was chosen by Congress to write a eulogy on him; in it occurs the famous words, "First in war, first in peace, and first in the hearts of his countrymen." Gen. Lee died at Cumberland Island, Georgia, when sixty-two years old (March 25, 1818). He was the father of Gen. Robert E. Lee.

LEE, Richard Henry, a famous American statesman, born at Stratford, Westmoreland County, Va., Jan. 20, 1732. He was sent to England to be educated. Coming home when he was about twenty, he kept up his studies, and became learned in matters of law and politics as well as in the classics. He held an important legal office before he was twenty-five; and when the colonies began to make a stand against British impositions, he took an active part in the cause of liberty. He was a delegate to the first Congress (1774), and was chosen to write many of the important state papers. If it had not been for the illness of his wife, which obliged him to go home suddenly, he would have had the honor of writing the Declaration of Independence. During the years that followed he was in Congress a number of times, and was one of the first two Senators from Virginia when the Constitution of the United States was adopted. He was a very eloquent speaker, a true patriot, and a noble-minded, generous man both in private and public life. He died in Westmoreland County when sixty-two years old (June 19, 1794).

LEE, Robert Edward, a famous American general, born in Virginia Jan. 19, 1807. He was a son of "Light Horse Harry" Lee, and was graduated at West Point in 1829. He fought bravely in the Mexican War, was afterward superintendent of the Military Academy at West Point, and gave up his commission as colonel of cavalry to join the Southern Confederacy when the Civil War began in

1861. For a time he held no important command, but on June 3, 1862, he became commander-in chief of the Confederate army of Northern Virginia, and he held the command from that time until the army surrendered

Robert Edward Lee.

to Gen. Grant at Appomattox (April 9, 1865). After the war he became President of Washington College, Lexington, Va., where he died when sixty-three years old (Oct. 12, 1870).

LEEDS, a city of N. England, on the River Aire; pop. 364,000, or twice as large as Newark, N. J. It is famous for its manufactures of woolen cloth and leather, in which it surpasses all other cities of England. There are also large manufactories of linen. Leeds has a large trade both by railroad and by the River Aire, which can be navigated to this point. Near it are many large coal mines. The city is noted for its great musical festivals, which are attended by thousands of people from all parts of England. The town-hall of Leeds is one of the finest buildings in that country.

LEGENDRE (*leh-zhondr'*), **Adrien Marie,** a famous French mathematician, born in Toulouse in 1752. When a boy he liked to study mathematics, and when a man was a very successful teacher in a military school. He was a hard worker, and wrote many books, the best known of which is his "Elements of Geometry," which has been translated into many languages and largely used as a school-book. He died near Paris when eighty-one years old (Jan. 10, 1833).

LEG'HORN, a city on the W. coast of Italy; pop. 98,000, or nearly the same as that of Albany, N. Y. Next to Genoa, it is the most important sea-port in Italy. The harbor is always crowded with ships, most of which trade along the coasts of the Mediterranean, but some go to distant countries. From this place we get straw hats and bonnets. In the summer Leghorn is visited by many fashionable people, who go there to bathe and to enjoy the see breezes.

Leghorn is called by the Italians Livorno. It was only a village in the 11th century.

LEIBNITZ (*libe'nitz*), **Gottfried Wilhelm,** a famous German philosopher, born in Leipsic, July 2, 1646. His father died when he was six years old ; his mother took great interest in his education, but he was almost entirely self-taught. Before he was twelve years old, he says he " understood the Latin authors very well, had begun to lisp in Greek, and wrote verses with singular success." When seventeen, he wrote an exercise which astonished the professors. As he grew older he used to study far into the night, often taking only a few hour's sleep in his chair. His memory was so good that when he was seventy he could recite long passages from Virgil without making a mistake. George I. used to call him a " living dictionary." He wrote many books on philosophy, politics, and religion ; some of them are said to be full of treasures of wisdom. He died in Hanover when seventy years old (Nov. 14, 1716).

LEICESTER (*les'ter*), a city of central England, on the River Soar, 87 miles N.N.W. of London; pop. 154,-000, or not quite as large as Louisville, Ky. It is the centre of a great farming and wool-raising district,

and is noted for its manufactories, more stockings been made there than in any other city of England, except Nottingham. Fairs for the sale of cattle, horses, and sheep are held there twelve times every year. Leicester probably gets its name from Leire, the old name of the River Soar, and the Latin *castrum* (camp or fort) ; it means therefore the " fort on the Leire." It was an important place both in Roman and Saxon times.

LEIPSIC (*lipe'sik*), a city of Germany, in Saxony, 92 miles S. S. W. of Berlin; pop. 287,000, or nearly as large as Cincinnati, Ohio. It is a dirty city, but is one of the most important places of trade in Germany, and is the centre of the German book trade and the seat of oneof the largest universities in the world. It has also a splendid opera-house and conservatory of music, and is famous for its concerts. The university, which is excelled only by that of Berlin, has 3000 students, among whom are many Americans who go there to finish their education. The city has fifty printing-houses, and more than two hundred book-stores, and a great book fair is held there every year.

More than eight hundred years ago tradespeople who came to Leipsic at Easter and Michaelmas used to offer goods for sale in the market-place after attending mass (German, *messe*) in the churches, and from this the fairs came to be called *messen* (masses). The Leipsic messen or fairs are held now three times a year, and people go to them from all parts of Europe to buy goods. The principal things sold are cloths, leather, furs, wool, porcelain, earthenware, and glass. Booths and shanties made of boards are put up in all the public squares, and goods and boxes are piled up everywhere. Earthenware lies in stacks on the ground, and bushels of little china dolls and playing marbles may be seen in heaps for sale. Many booths are filled with all kinds of toys, and the women who keep them shout to everybody to come and buy. Almost everything may be bought at these fairs, in which $50,000,000 worth of goods are sold in a year.

One of the famous places in Leipsic is Auerbach's beer-cellar, told about by GOETHE in his poem of "Faust." As the story goes, Dr. FAUST, who was there one night with the fiend, Mephistopheles, drinking with some students, complained that the wine was not good. So he bored a hole in the edge of the table, and at his command any kind of wine called for flowed out of it ; but when a little was spilled on the floor it turned to fire. The cellar is still used for a drinking house, and many students go there to drink beer and to look at two pictures on the wall, one of Faust drawing wine from the table, and the other showing him riding out of the door on a barrel. Goethe, who was a student at Leipsic, made this one of the scenes in his "Faust," only he makes Mephistopheles do these wonderful things instead of Faust.

Leipsic, which the Germans spell Leipzig, means the "place of the linden trees." The town was first built about A.D. 1000. Many battles have been fought in the plain around it, but the most famous one was that between Napoleon, with 160,000 men, and 300,000 Russians, Prussians, Austrians, and Swedes (Oct. 16-19, 1813). The French were at first successful, but finally had to retreat toward the Rhine. More than 100,000 men were killed and wounded in this battle.

LEITH (*leeth*), a city of Scotland, on the Water of Leith, where it joins the Frith of Forth, only two miles from EDINBURGH, of which it is the seaport; pop. 61,000, or a little smaller than Dayton, Ohio. It has an excellent harbor, which is always full of ships, both from other ports in Scotland and England and from foreign countries. Edinburgh and Leith form really one city, the ground between them being filled with houses. Leith gets its name from its river.

LE'LAND, Charles Godfrey, an American writer, born in Philadel-

phia, Aug. 15, 1824. After graduating at the College of New Jersey, Princeton (1846), he studied in Germany and in Paris, and became a lawyer, but gave up that business for literature. Among his books are "Meister Karl's Sketch Book." "Hans Breitmann's Ballads," "Pictures of Travel," and "Book of Songs," the two last being translations from HEINE. He lives most of the time in London.

LE'LY, Sir Peter, a noted English painter, born at Soest, in Westphalia, in 1617. The family name was Van der Faes, but Peter's father changed it to Lely. When twenty-three years old Peter Lely went to England, and became the most noted portrait painter of his time. He painted a portrait of Charles I.; and also one of Cromwell, who told him to paint him just as he was, with all his pimples and warts, or he would not pay him a farthing for the picture. He was appointed painter to Charles II., who made him a knight, and he painted the portraits of the beautiful ladies of the court which are still to be seen at Hampton Court, and are very celebrated. Sir Peter Lely died in England, when sixty-three years old (Nov. 30, 1680).

LEM'NOS, now **Limni,** an island belonging to Turkey, in the N.E. part of the Mediterranean Sea, 40 miles S.W. of the Dardanelles Strait ; area, 195 square miles ; pop. about 10,000 ; capital, Castro. Most of the land is hilly and rocky, and not very fertile. The people of Lemnos are Greeks and Turks, who live by farming or by fishing.

In ancient times Lemnos was sacred to the god Vulcan, and it was said that he had his workshop there. The island was also celebrated for a great labyrinth, with 150 stone columns ; a child could open the gates, but the passages within were so mixed up that any one who went in without a guide was almost sure to be lost. A kind of earth dug at Lemnos was used by the ancient Greeks for medicine.

LENA (*le'nah*), a river of Siberia,

rising near Lake Baikal, and flowing into the Arctic Ocean ; length, 2500 miles, or somewhat longer than the St. Lawrence. It is a very large and long river, being five or six miles wide 800 miles above its mouth. The Lena can be navigated for nearly its whole length, but it is of little use, because the country through which it flows is generally barren and deserted.

LE'O, the name of thirteen popes.

Leo I., called the Great, born in Rome about 390, became pope in 440. He was a very able man. When ATTILA invaded Italy, Leo visited him in his camp and persuaded him to spare Rome. He died in 461.

Leo II., who became pope in 795, crowned Charles the Great Emperor of the West. He died in 816.

Leo IV., born in Rome about 800, became pope in 847. He built a wall around the Vatican part of Rome, which was called after him the Leonine City. He died in 855.

Leo X., born in Florence, December 11, 1475, was the son of Lorenzo de' Medici, the Magnificent. He became pope in 1513. He was an able man, did much for learning and art, and made his court one of the most splendid of the time. He built up libraries and universities, and employed Michael Angelo and Raphael in some of their greatest works. To get money to build St. Peter's Church, he sold indulgences, enabling people to pay money instead of doing some other penance for sin. This aroused Martin LUTHER and led to the Reformation. Died in Rome, aged forty-six, Dec. 1, 1521.

Leo XIII., born at Carpineto, Italy, March 2, 1810, was elected on the death of Pius IX. (1878). His real name is Joachim Pecci.

LEO I., called the Thracian, an Emperor of the East ; born about A.D. 400. He succeeded the Emperor Marcian in 457. In his reign the Huns were defeated by his generals, but an expedition which he had fitted out against the Vandals in Northern Africa was unsuccessful. His time was marked by an earthquake which destroyed the city of Antioch, a great fire in Constantinople, and an eruption of Vesuvius, which was so violent as to send showers of ashes as far as Constantinople. Leo died, when about seventy-four years old (474).

LEO III., called the Isaurian, an Emperor of the East, born about 680. He was the son of a farmer, and after many wonderful changes of fortune became emperor. The Saracens made an attempt during his reign to take Constantinople, but their fleet was destroyed by Greek fire. It was in Leo's reign that the contest began between those who wanted to use images in churches and those who did not, Leo himself being an Iconoclast—that is, he was opposed to the use of images. There were bloody contests about this question, and in 732 the Iconoclasts were condemned by a council assembled at Rome. In the end this led to a separation between the Roman and Greek churches. Leo died, when sixty-one years old (June 18, 741).

LEO V., called the Armenian, an Emperor of the East. He reigned from 813 to 820, succeeding Michael I., who was dethroned. Leo was a strict ruler, and improved the government very much by making good laws and insisting that they should be kept. In the troubles about the use of images he sided with the Iconoclasts, and was very severe in his treatment of the other party. Having sentenced to death a powerful subject, he was killed by the friends of the doomed man, who came into the royal chapel disguised as priests, at the time of the morning service. Leo fell, vainly trying to defend himself with no other weapon than the large cross over the altar (820).

LEO AF·RI·CA'NUS, a Moorish traveller, born in Granada, Spain, about 1485. His name in his own language was Al-Hassan Ibn Mohammed. He made extensive journeys over various parts of Africa, some of which had hitherto never been explored by Europeans, and he also travelled in the East. While at sea he was captured by pirates and taken to Pope Leo X., who gave him his own name and had him instructed in Christianity ; but it is said that he went back to Mohammedanism. He wrote a book about his travels in Africa, which gave the best account of that country written up to his time. He died when about forty-one years old (1526).

LE·O·NAR'DO DA VINCI (*dah vin'che*). See VINCI.

LE·ON'I·DAS. See THERMOPYLÆ.

LE'O·POLD I, Emperor of Germany, born June 9, 1640. He was the son of the Emperor Ferdinand III., whom he succeeded in 1657. The Turks were then in Hungary, and on one occasion they advanced as far as the gates of Vienna. Leopold fled on their approach, leaving it to John Sobieski, King of Poland, to save his capital and throne. Wars with Louis XIV. went on during his reign and that of his son and successor, Joseph I. Leopold died in Vienna when sixty-five years old (May 5, 1705), and was succeeded by his son Joseph I.

LEOPOLD II., Emperor of Germany, born May 5, 1747. He was the son of the Emperor Francis I., and became emperor in 1790, on the death of his brother Joseph II. Before he was called to be Emperor of Germany, he ruled the Duchy of Tuscany with very great wisdom. The violent changes made by his brother Joseph had caused great dissatisfaction in various parts of his dominions, and he had to meet trouble at home and abroad. He was gathering up all his strength to go against the French revolutionists, when he died, at the age of forty-five (March 1, 1792). He was succeeded by his son Francis II.

LEP'I·DUS, Marcus Æmilius, a noted Roman soldier. In the war between Pompey and Cæsar, he sided with the latter, who gave him the government of Rome during his absence in Italy. After the death of Cæsar, he joined himself to the party of Mark ANTONY, and

was the least noted member of the second triumvirate, the other two members being Antony and Octavius Cæsar (AUGUSTUS). When, after the battle of Philippi, he was ordered by Octavius to aid him against Sextus Pompeius, he tried to throw off the authority of Octavius. But his soldiers deserted him at the last moment, and he had to throw himself on his knees and beg for mercy. His life was spared, but he was deprived of all share in the government. He died 13 B.C.

LE SAGE (*leh sahzh'*), **Alain René,** a noted French writer of novels and plays, born at Sarzeau, Brittany, May 8, 1668. He was left an orphan, when fourteen years old, to the care of his uncle, who spent all his money and sent him to the Jesuit college at Vannes to be educated. He studied law in Paris, but instead of practising his profession, he used to spend his time in writing, made several translations. and wrote plays and novels of his own. His best-known novel is "Gil Blas," a Spanish story, noted for its true pictures of life and of all kinds of people in Spain. It made him famous, and has been translated into all the languages of Europe. Le Sage died in Boulogne when seventy-nine years old (Nov. 17, 1747).

LES'BOS. See MYTILENE.

LESSEPS (*la-sep'*), **Ferdinand,** Viscount de, a French diplomatist, born at Versailles, Nov. 19, 1805. When twenty years old he began his public life as attaché at Lisbon ; and when twenty-six, went to Egypt, where he was afterward made consul-general three different times. In 1854 he asked the Viceroy of Egypt to allow him to cut a canal across the Isthmus of SUEZ, so as to join the waters of the Red and the Mediterranean Seas ; the viceroy gave his consent, and De Lesseps set about the work at once. Although hindered by all sorts of difficulties, he raised the money, began the canal in 1859, and finished it in ten years, and it was opened with great rejoicing on Nov. 17, 1869, many of the crowned heads of Europe being present at the ceremony.

This was a proud day for De Lesseps, but he took very little time to think of what he had already done ; we find him beginning at once to form other great plans, such as that of making a railroad through the centre of Asia, and of turning the Desert of Sahara into an inland sea by letting in water from the Mediterranean. In 1880 he began the work of cutting a canal through the Isthmus of Panama, so that ships can pass through from the Atlantic to the Pacific Ocean, and thus save the long voyage around Cape HORN.

LES'SING, Gotthold Ephraim, a noted German writer, born in Saxony, Jan. 22, 1729. At first he studied medicine and theology, but he soon gave up these studies for general literature. In 1760 he went to Breslau, and while there, in the midst of the Seven Years War, wrote the play " Minna von Barnheim," and soon afterward, "Emilia Galotti; the last, which is founded on the story of Virginia,is one of the best tragedies in the German language. His last and greatest work is "Nathan the Wise," in which the three principal characters are a Jew, a Christian, and a Mohammedan. Lessing did much to improve the style of his country's literature. He has sometimes been called the Luther of German literature, of the German drama, and of German art. He died in Brunswick, when fifty-two years old (Feb. 15, 1781).

LE'THE, in Greek fable, the name of a river in HADES, the waters of which the dead drank before entering the Elysian Fields. It had the power of making them forget all the pain and sorrow they had known on earth.

LEUCTRA (*luke'trah*), a village of ancient Greece, in Bœotia, celebrated for a battle fought there between the Thebans under Epaminondas and Pelopidas, and the Spartans under Cleombrutus, in which the Thebans won a comlpete victory. The site of Leuctra is marked by a pile of stones, where a thousand Spartans who fell in the battle are said to have been buried.

LE'VER, Charles James, a noted Irish novelist, born in Dublin, Aug. 31, 1806. He was educated for a physician, and was such a good doctor that when the cholera broke out in Ireland he was appointed medical superintendent in Londonderry. He wrote his first novel, " Harry Lorrequer," when twenty-nine years old. It was very much liked, and he afterward wrote many more, as well as many short stories, in all of which he gives droll pictures of Irish life. Among his best-known works are " Charles O'Malley," " Tom Burke of Ours," and " Maurice Tiernay." He died at TRIESTE when sixty-six years old (June 1, 1872).

LEVERRIER (*leh-va-re-a'*), Urbain Jean Joseph, a famous French astronomer, born at St. Lô, March 11, 1811. He first made improvements in chemistry, but finally gave himself up to the study of astronomy. In 1846 he astonished everybody by telling them that a new planet might be found at a certain place in the heavens, and shortly afterward a German astronomer discovered very near the place pointed out by Leverrier the planet now called Neptune. This made a great stir, and Leverrier received many honors from different nations. In 1853 he succeeded ARAGO as director of the Observatory. He was always studying and working, and did much to improve general education. He died when sixty-six years old (September, 23, 1877).

LEWES (*lu'is*), George Henry, a noted English author, born in London, April 18, 1817. In his youth he was clerk in a commission house, but afterward studied medicine, and later gave himself up entirely to studying and writing about philosophy and science. He is well known as the first husband of Marian Evans (George ELIOT). He died in London when sixty-seven years old (November 30, 1878).

LEW'IS·TON, a city of S. Maine, on the Androscoggin River ; pop. 22,000, or about as large as Council Bluffs, Iowa. The river there has a fall of more than fifty feet, and the water-power, increased by large dams, is one of the best in New England. It is used for many large cotton and woollen factories, and saw-mills. The town has also large manufactories of machinery, boots and shoes, twine, jute, and bricks. Bates College, at Lewiston, was named after Benjamin E. Bates, of Boston, who gave it $200,000. Lewiston was settled in 1770, and became a city in 1863.

LEX'ING·TON, a town of Massachusetts, 10 miles N.W. of Boston; pop. about 3000. It is noted as the scene of the first fight between the British and Americans in the war of the Revolution, April 19, 1775. On the evening of April 18, Gen. Gage, the British commander in Boston, sent 800 soldiers, under Major Pitcairn, to destroy the American supplies at Concord. Paul Revere, of Boston, escaping their sentinels, galloped out to Lexington and Concord with the news, so when the British reached Lexington at daybreak, they found about seventy Americans waiting for them on the village common. Captain John Parker, their commander, ordered them not to shoot until the English did. Major Pitcairn rode forward and called out : '' Disperse, ye rebels !'' but though the Americans were outnumbered ten to one, they stood firm. Then Pitcairn ordered his men to fire, and four Americans were killed and nine wounded. Some shots were fired in return, and three English soldiers were wounded ; but after that the Americans retreated, some being killed as they ran. The British marched on to CONCORD, but meanwhile the

whole country was aroused, and as they came back, hundreds of Americans attacked them from behind the houses and stone walls by the roadside. They were only saved from destruction by the arrival of reinforcements under Lord Percy. Though not a very great battle, this was one of the most important ones that ever was fought. As soon as the Americans found that the war had really begun, hundreds of men hurried to the army, and not long after the British were driven out of Boston.

A small monument at Lexington marks the spot where the war began.

LEXINGTON, a city of Kentucky, 20 miles S. E. of Frankfort ; pop. 22,000, or about as large as Lewiston, Me. It is surrounded by a beautiful country, and has an important trade. It is the seat of the University of Kentucky. Ashland, the former home of Henry Clay, is at Lexington.

Lexington was settled in 1775, and was named after Lexington, Mass., because the news of the first battle of the Revolution fought there was received when the town was being laid out.

LEXINGTON, a town of Virginia, 110 miles W. by N. of Richmond ; pop. 4500. It is chiefly noted as the seat of Washington and Lee University and of the Virginia Military Institute.

LEYDEN (*li'den*), a city of the Netherlands, on the old Rhine River, 6 miles from the sea ; pop. 46,000, or about as large as Saginaw, Mich. It is in a low, flat country, and is cut up by many canals, which are crossed by more than a hundred bridges. Around it are beautiful meadows and pleasure-gardens, with many wind-mills. The University of Leyden, founded by William of Orange, has about seven hundred students. It was once so celebrated that students went there from all parts of Europe, and on account of its learning the city was called the "Athens of the West." Leyden is now the principal place in the Netherlands for the sale of wool and woollen goods.

Leyden was called by the Romans *Lugdunum Batavorum*, which means the "marsh fort of the Batavians," a tribe of people who lived there, and the modern name has grown out of that. When the city was besieged by the Spaniards (1574), the people were almost starved. The Prince of Orange, who came to help them, cut the dikes, and the sea-water came in so rapidly that many of the Spaniards were drowned, and at the same time a great many vessels full of provisions were floated into the city ; so the place was saved. The Pilgrims lived in Leyden ten years before they came to America.

LIBERIA (*li-be're-ah*), a country on the W. coast of Africa ; area, 9700 square miles, or about the same as that of Vermont ; pop. 1,068,000, or thrice that of Vermont; capital, Monrovia (pop. about 3000). Most of the people are negroes born in Africa, but there are a few thousand from the United States, mostly former slaves or their descendants, who rule the country. The settlement was begun in 1822, by negroes sent there by a society in the United States, to show that the black race is able to govern itself. Twenty-five years afterward it was made into a republic, and it has ever since been ruled by black men ; but it has not succeeded very well. The principal thing raised is sugar. The name Liberia is made from the Latin word *liber* (free) and the country is so called because there are no slaves in it.

LIEBIG (*le'big*), **Justus von,** a famous German chemist, born in Darmstadt, May 12, 1803. When a boy he was for ten months a clerk in a druggist's shop ; when sixteen years old he entered the University of Bonn, and afterward became a doctor of medicine and

a professor of chemistry in the University of Giessen. He set up there the first laboratory in Germany where experiments were made to show how chemistry can be made of use in every-day life. The university became very famous through his labors, and students flocked there from all parts of Europe. His name is well known in connection with the essence of meat. He also claimed the honor of discovering chloroform (C.C.T., 129, II. u.). In 1852, he became professor of chemistry in the University of Munich. He died in Munich when seventy years old (April 18, 1873).

LIÉGE (*le-aizh'*), a city of Belgium, on the River Meuse ; pop. 146,000, or a little larger than Omaha, Neb. It is a very important place for manufactures, especially of iron, and hence it is sometimes called the "Birmingham of Belgium." The country around it is rich in iron and coal, and mines are worked even under the city and the river. The Royal Cannon Foundry of Belgium is there, and guns, pistols, and different kinds of machines are made in its factories. It is, therefore, a dingy, smoky city, but it has many fine buildings, a university, and academies of music and painting. The city is defended by a citadel, on a hill near by, and by several forts.

Liegé gets its name from an old town called Legia, or Leodium, which stood there more than a thousand years ago.

LILLE (*leel*), a city of N. France, on the River Deule, 7 miles from the boundary of Belgium; pop. 188,-000, or rather more than that of Newark, N. J. This is one of the most important places in France, and is very strongly fortified, many soldiers always being kept there. It has many great linen and cotton factories, and the fields near the city are always white with cloths spread out to bleach. Ribbons are also made there, and the French Government has a tobacco factory where several million pounds of tobacco are prepared every year.

Lille gets its name from an old castle which once stood there in the middle of a marsh, and was therefore called L'Isle, or " the Island." The city itself was founded in the 9th century.

LIMA (*le'mah*), the capital of Peru, on the Rimac River, seven miles from Callao, its port on the Pacific Ocean ; pop. 100,000, or a little less than that of Allegheny, Pa. A large part of it is surrounded by walls, through which there are twelve gates. The houses are generally built only two stories high, on account of the frequent earthquakes. Many of them are painted with gay colors, and have courts within, ornamented with fountains, statues, and trees. Several of the palaces and churches were built by PIZARRO, whose body is buried in the cathedral. The University of Lima, founded in 1551, is the oldest in America. Most of the people of Lima are of mixed race, descended from whites, Indians, and negroes ; but there are also many foreigners. Callao, the port of Lima, with which it is connected by railway, and the chief seaport of Peru, is defended by strong forts. Lima was founded in 1535 by Pizarro, who called it Ciudad de los Reyes, or " City of the Kings," because it was begun on the festival of Epiphany, when the worship of Christ by the wise men or kings of the East is celebrated.

LIMOGES (*le-mozhe*), a town of France, on the River Vienne ; pop. 68,000, or nearly the same as that of Cambridge, Mass. It is noted for its manufacture of porcelain, made from a fine kind of kaolin clay found near the city ; also for an excellent breed of horses, which are raised in the country near by, and are used for the French cavalry.

Limoges gets its name from the old Celtic tribe of the Lemovices, who lived there before the Romans conquered the country.

LINCOLN (*lin'kun*), **Abraham**, sixteenth President of the United States, born in Hardin County, Ky., Feb. 12, 1809. When he was seven years old his father moved to Indiana, and Abraham helped him to clear the land for a farm, on which he worked hard for the next ten years, getting only about a year's schooling in all the time. As a young man he did any kind of work that came in his way, split rails for fences, made log cabins, helped to

Abraham Lincoln.

build flat-boats and to work them, was a clerk in a country store, then joined a volunteer company and was made captain of it, when the Black Hawk war began in 1832 ; and finally got a situation as postmaster in New Salem, Illinois, and spent his evenings studying law from books that he borrowed at night, and had to return in the morning. In 1834 he went to the legislature, and two years afterward began to practice law with great success. In 1846 he was elected a member of Congress, and took an active part in public affairs, until the time of his election as President in 1860. He was inaugurated March 4, 1861, just before the beginning of the Civil War. In 1863 he issued the Emancipation Proclamation, by which the slaves in all the territory in arms against the United States were declared free. In 1865, he was elected for a second term, but lived only for a few weeks afterward, being shot, when fifty-six years old, by an assassin in a theatre in Washington (April 14, 1865). His body was embalmed, and carried in state through the principal Northern cities, receiving funeral honors everywhere, until buried at Springfield, Illinois.

LIND, Jenny, a famous Swedish singer, born in Stockholm, Oct. 6, 1821. She was left an orphan when very young, with one great gift, a fine voice, and was always singing, whether at work or at play. One day she was sitting by the window, stroking a pet cat and singing, when a lady, in passing, stopped to listen to her lovely voice. The next day she came again with a music master, and they paid the woman who had charge of her to give her up; and thus when nine years old Jenny's musical education began. She began to sing on the stage when ten years old, and when sixteen became the favorite in the Stockholm Opera House. She was received everywhere in Europe with wild delight, and men paid hundreds of dollars for choice seats when she sang. In 1850 she came to the United States and sang with great success in most of the large cities. While here she was married to Otto Goldschmidt, a young pianist, and returned to Europe with him in 1852. After that she sang but rarely on the stage. She was very good, giving large sums to the poor. She died when sixty-six years old (Nov. 2, 1887).

LINGARD (*ling'gard*), **John,** a noted English historian, born in Winchester, Feb. 5, 1771. His parents were Roman Catholics, and he became a priest when twenty-four years old. His greatest work is the "History of England" in ten volumes. It has been translated into several languages, and ranks among the best histories. After it was published Lingard was offered a cardinal's hat, which he refused. He died at Hornby, near Lancaster, when eighty years old (July 13, 1851).

LINNÆUS (*lin-ne'us*), the Latin name of Carl von Linné, a famous Swedish writer on botany, born May 24, 1707. His father was a minister, and intended his son to be one also; but Carl was more interested in botany and natural history than in theological studies, and his father was persuaded to let him have his choice. He had to bear a great deal of hardship, and often went cold and hungry on account of his poverty; but he persevered in his studies until he became the most famous botanist in the world. He wrote a great many important books about the growth and formation of plants, and received the highest honors and rewards for his valuable discoveries. He died in Upsal when seventy-one years old (January 10, 1778); and the people caused a medal to be made with his likeness, and a monument put up in his honor.

One day Linnæus was taking a walk with another botanist, who complained that there were no new things to be found out. Linnæus stooped down, and laying his hand on the ground said: " I will wager that you will find something new here." They then examined the plants growing there, and found several things which they had never seen before.

LINLITHGOW (*lin-lith'go*), a town of Scotland, on Linlithgow Lake, 17 miles W. by N. of Edinburgh; pop. 4000. It is noted for the ruins of a large and beautiful palace which was begun by King Edward I. of England, and burned in 1746. In this palace Mary Queen of Scots was born. Near it is a church founded by King David I., of Scotland, which is considered the finest Gothic church in that country.

LIPARI (*lip'ah-re*) **Islands,** a group of 17 volcanic islands in the Mediterranean Sea, between Sicily and Italy ; pop. about 17,500. They are very mountainous, and one of them, called Stromboli, has a burning volcano. Earthquakes are very common. Lipari, the largest of the group, is almost entirely covered with pumice-stone formed by an ancient volcano, and nearly all the pumice used in Europe is got there. On this island is the town of Lipari (pop. 5000).

LIP'PIN-COTT, Sara Jane, an American, born at Pompey, New York, Sept. 23, 1823. The name of this lady, before her marriage, was Clark, but her readers know her best as " Grace Greenwood," the title under which she writes. She has published several books for young folks, among others " Greenwood Leaves," " History of My Pets," " Merrie England," " Bonnie Scotland," " Stories from Famous Ballads," and " Stories and Legends." Besides writing books, she delivers lectures, and often writes for the newspapers.

LIS'BON, the capital and chief city of Portugal, on the River Tagus, about 9 miles from its mouth ; pop. 242,000, or nearly as large as New Orleans, La. The harbor is the best in Portugal. The city is built on several hills, and nearly all the houses and palaces are white, so that, seen from the river, it has a very fine appearance. Within, it is not nearly so handsome, for the older streets are narrow, crooked, and dirty. The people carry on a large trade in wine, olive-oil, canned fruits, and many other things. It is not certainly known when Lisbon was founded, but it is a very old city. The name Lisbon, or Lisbuna, was given to it by the Moors, who conquered the city in 711, and kept it until 1147. On Nov. 1, 1755, Lisbon was almost destroyed by one of the most terrible earthquakes that has ever been known. It came in the morning when many of the people were at church. The church was shaken down, with all the houses near it, and a moment after the lower part of the city was engulfed by a great wave fifty feet high, that came rolling up from the sea. In a few minutes 50,000 people were killed. Some of the buildings sank 600 feet deep into the river. Lisbon has never recovered from this great calamity, and some parts of the old town have not been rebuilt to this day.

LITTLE ROCK, the capital and chief city of Arkansas, situated on the Arkansas River, near the centre of the State ; pop. 26,000, or about as large as Auburn, N. Y. The principal public building is the State House, which is built of brick. The city was founded in 1820, and was named after the low cliffs along the river, called Little Rock, to distinguish them from the Big Rock or high cliffs near by.

LIV'ER-POOL, a city of W. England, at the mouth of the River Mersey ; pop. 613,000, or more than twice as large as San Francisco, Cal. It is the largest city in England, except London, and its trade with foreign countries is almost equal to that of all the other English ports put together, being greater than that of any other city in the world, except New York. More than 15,000 vessels enter the harbor every year. Unfortunately, the tides at Liverpool are very strong, and large vessels are likely to get aground at low water, or to be injured by the rapid flow. To remedy this, nearly forty great docks have been made, all joined together, and extending along the shore for five miles. They are surrounded by strong stone walls, and are always full of water, being opened only at high tide to let ships pass in and out. On the opposite side of the river, at Birkenhead, there are other docks extending for two miles. Altogether, the Liverpool and Birkenhead docks cost $51,000,000, but they well repay even this enormous expense. Birkenhead was a little fishing village until the docks were built there, but they have brought it so much trade that it has become a large and handsome city. Liverpool has a larger trade in cotton than any other city in the world, two-thirds of the cotton raised in the United States being sent there. There are immense buildings where sugar is refined, and others where soap is made. At Birkenhead there are large iron foundries and manufactories of pottery, varnish, boilers, guns, and many other things.

Americans who go to Europe generally land first at Liverpool, and they find much to interest them in the tall warehouses, the great docks crowded with ships, and the many fine streets and beautiful dwellings. Three railroads run through the city, two of them in tunnels under the houses, and the other on great arches above the roofs.

Liverpool is supposed to get its name from *Llyr pool,* which, in Welsh, means the sea-pool. It became a sea-port in 1173, but the city did not begin to be very important until about a hundred years ago.

LIV'ING-STON, Edward, an American statesman, born in Clermont, N. Y., May 26, 1764. He was a graduate of Princeton College, and while quite young became noted as a lawyer. He was a member of Congress several times, Mayor of the City of New York for two years, and later in life was United States Senator from Louisiana, to which he had removed in 1804. In 1831, he became Secretary of State of the United States, and afterward Minister to France. But he is best known as the author of the Code—a collection of laws concerning crimes and their punishments, which has been of great use both in Europe and America. He died at Rhine-

beck, N. Y., when seventy-two years old (May 23, 1836).

LIVINGSTON, Philip, an American statesman, born in Albany, N. Y., Jan. 15, 1716. He was a member of the first Continental Congress, a signer of the Declaration of Independence, and a member of the State Assembly and Senate afterward. In every position he was upright, honorable, and devoted to the good of his country. He died in York, Pennsylvania, when sixty-two years old (June 12, 1778).

LIVINGSTON, Robert, an American statesman, born in New York City, Nov. 27, 1746. He was graduated at King's College (now Columbia), studied law, and soon became noted. He was one of the committee chosen to draw up the Declaration of Independence; helped also to prepare the first Constitution of the State of New York, and became the first Chancellor of the State. In 1801, he was Minister to France, and bought Louisiana for the United States. He took an interest in the arts and sciences, and was the friend and helper of Robert Fulton in his invention of the steamboat. He died when sixty-seven years old (Feb. 26, 1813).

LIV'ING-STONE, David, a Scotch traveller and author, born near Glasgow, March 19, 1813. When ten years old, he began to work in the cotton mills, and spent his evenings in study. At nineteen he began to fit himself for a foreign missionary; and in 1840 went to South Africa, where he worked for nine years, studying the language and customs of the natives, preaching to them, and founding schools in different places. He then (1849) started on his first exploring expedition to the interior, and visited Lake Ngami, being the first European who had done so. He spent six years after this in exploring journeys, and then went to England (1856), where he published an interesting account of his discoveries.

In 1858 he returned to Africa, and went with a party of explorers on an expedition to the Zambezi River. During this journey, which lasted five years, his wife, who was with him, died at Shupanga, in 1862. He went again to England, in 1864 ; published a history of the Zambezi expedition, and then started on another journey, from which no account was heard in a long time, and an English company, under Mr. Young, was sent out to look

David Livingstone.

for him. They did not find him, but letters were received at last, which proved him to be alive. After another long silence, the New York *Herald* sent Mr. Henry STANLEY in search of him, and he was found at Ujiji in 1871. He continued his missionary journeys for two years after this, and died in Central Africa when sixty years old (May 1, 1873). His body was taken to England, and buried in Westminster Abbey.

LIV'Y, or **Titus Livius,** a famous Roman historian, born in Padua, 59 B.C. Very little is known of his life, but his History of Rome is one of the wonderful works of the world. It was written in one hundred and forty-two books, only thirty-five of which are now in existence. He died A.D. 17.

LOCKHART (*lok'art*), **John Gibson,** a noted Scottish author, born at Cambusnethan, Lanarkshire, in 1794. He was educated at the University of Glasgow, and studied law, but gave it up for literature. When twenty-six years old, he married the daughter of Sir Walter Scott. He wrote much for *Blackwood* and other magazines, and published several novels, and lives of Burns, Napoleon Bonaparte, and Sir Walter Scott. The last is the best life of Sir Walter Scott, and one of the most interesting biographies in the English language. His translations of "Ancient Spanish Ballads" was very much liked, and has been printed many times. Scott's "Tales of a Grandfather" were written for Lockhart's eldest son. Lockhart died at ABBOTSFORD when sixty years old (Nov. 25, 1854).

LOCK'PORT, a city of W. New York, 20 miles E. of Niagara Falls ; pop. 16,000, or about as large as Decatur, Ill. It gets its name from the great locks there of the Erie Canal. The waste water from the locks is used as a water-power for running many large flouring and saw mills, and cotton and woollen factories.

LODI (*lo'de*), a town of N. Italy, on the River Adda, 18 miles S.E. of Milan ; pop. 19,000, or a little larger than Winona, Minn. It has important manufactories of majolica and delft ware, and chemicals, and there is a very large trade in cheese, which is made in the surrounding villages from the milk of cows brought every year from Switzerland. The city is surrounded by walls.

Lodi is said to have been founded by the father of Pompey the Great. The old town was destroyed in 1158, and a fortress was built, about six miles from the ruins by Frederick

Barbarossa. Around this fortress the new town was gathered. During Napoleon's first invasion of Italy, an Austrian army was posted at Lodi to defend the town and the bridge which crossed the river. They thought it would be impossible for an army to pass this bridge, which was guarded by many soldiers and cannon, but the French, headed by Napoleon and Lannes, rushed across it, in the face of a terrible fire, and captured the town (May 10, 1796).

LO'GAN, a celebrated Indian chief, born about 1725. His real name was Tah-gah-jute, but he was called Logan after the Secretary of Pennsylvania, who was a great friend of the Indians. Logan was a good friend to the white people, until the spring of 1774, when his whole family was murdered without cause by a party of white men. In revenge for this Logan made war upon the Western settlers, and a great many innocent people were killed. When the Indians were at last conquered, and the other chiefs asked for peace, Logan refused to go with them, but sent by an interpreter his famous speech that has been printed in so many school-readers, and learned by heart by so many school-boys. He became very intemperate after this, and in consequence of one of his violent acts when drunk, was killed by a countryman of his own in the summer of 1780.

LO'GANS-PORT, a city of Indiana, on the Wabash River, pop. 13,000, or about as large as Woburn, Mass. It is surrounded by a rich and fertile country, and there is an important trade in farm products and lumber. The city has large foundries and railroad machine shops.

LONDON (*lun'dun*), a city of S. Canada, on the river Thames ; pop. 27,000, or about as large as Houston, Tex. It lies in the midst of a rich farming country, and there is a large trade in farm products. London contains large iron foundries, ma-

chine-shops, chemical works, petroleum refineries, and other manufactories.

LONDON, the capital of Great Britain, and the largest city in the world, situated on both sides of the river Thames, England, 60 miles from its mouth ; pop. 4,422,000, or four times as large as Chicago. As the city has grown, many villages have been united with it ; and some of them still keep their separate names, as Chelsea, Hampstead, Strand, Stepney, and Lambeth. London was first on the north side of the Thames, and that part is now the richest and finest of all, being called "the city." The Thames is crossed by many bridges, of which Waterloo bridge is the finest, but London bridge has the most travel over it. Besides these, there are several tunnels under the river. Both shores are bordered with handsome stone quays called embankments, built at a very great cost, along the tops of which are wide roads.

Among the most crowded streets of London are Cheapside, Bishopsgate Street, Gracechurch Street, Cornhill, and Leadenhall Street, which are lined with stores. Regent Street is the handsomest street, and contains the finest stores, while the most fashionable houses are in Belgravia, in the western part of the city. London has several fine parks. Regent's Park contains a botanical garden and the finest menagerie and zoological garden in the world. In Hyde Park is the Albert Memorial, erected in memory of Prince Albert. It is the most magnificent monument of modern times, being ornamented with many statues, and with 169 sculptured portraits of illustrious artists, poets, and musical composers, with a statue of Prince Albert in the centre under a splendid carved canopy. Buckingham, St. James, and Kensington Palaces are the London houses of the Queen, but she visits Buckingham Palace only on grand occasions. The Prince of Wales lives in Marlborough House, and the Mansion House is the residence of the Lord Mayor of London.

Parliament meets in Westminster Palace, or the Houses of Parliament, a magnificent building close to the river. It contains the House of Lords, the House of Commons, and more than a thousand other rooms. The House of Lords is splendidly ornamented, and contains, besides seats for the members and visitors, a throne for the Queen and a chair for the Prince of Wales. Ever since the gunpowder plot of 1605, the cellars under this room are examined before the Queen comes in to open Parliament. The finest museum in London, and in the world, is the British Museum, which contains thousands of ancient statues and sculptures, besides great collections of natural history specimens, and one of the largest libraries in the world. The South Kensington Museum has very fine galleries of paintings, sculptures, and antiquities, and adjoining it is the beautiful Royal Albert Hall, used for exhibitions and musical festivals. There are also many other museums and libraries.

London has more than 1500 churches, the finest being St. Paul's Cathedral and Westminster Abbey. St. Paul's has one of the largest domes in the world, and contains the tombs of Wellington, Nelson, and other famous persons. Westminster Abbey was begun in the

Westminster Abbey.

7th century. All the British Kings and Queens from the time of Edward the Confessor have been crowned there, and many of them are buried in the Abbey, or in the chapels which open into it, as well as many distinguished Englishmen. The Bank of England is the most important bank in the world, and besides having an immense business of its own, it manages the entire debt of the English Government, receiving a large sum for its services.

The Tower of London is an ancient fortress or castle, long used as a prison for persons accused of crime against the king or government. A gate which leads from it to the river is called Traitors' Gate, because prisoners were brought in through it. Many persons famous in English history have passed through this gate, and afterward been beheaded on Tower Hill. In the Bloody Tower, opposite the

Tower of London.

gate, the sons of Edward IV. were murdered. The sceptre, crown, and other royal ornaments are kept in the Jewel Room ; and in the Horse Armory is a fine collection of ancient arms and armor. The Tower is now used principally as an arsenal, but there are barracks for several thousand soldiers.

London is the richest city in the world, and it has an immense trade. Its great docks, having several miles of wharves, are always crowded with ships. Railroads connect it with all parts of England, and in the city are many miles of railways in tunnels. The air of London is always smoky, and thick fogs are very common, but the city is generally healthy. Summer is the most fashionable season, and at that time London is visited by thousands of strangers.

London was a city of the ancient Britons. Its name, which was made into Londinum by the Romans, who took it about A.D. 50, means the fort or city on the marsh. The first walls are supposed to have been built by CONSTANTINE THE GREAT. It has been the capital of England

for more than a thousand years. London was visited by the plague in 1349 and in 1604, and again in 1665, when more than 100,000 persons died. A year after (1666), almost the whole city was destroyed by a fire, which burned four days and nights. Most of the fine buildings and houses in London are modern.

LONG'FELLOW, Henry Wadsworth, a famous American poet, born in Portland, Me., Feb. 27, 1807. He was graduated at Bowdoin College when eighteen years old (1825), and began to study law in his father's office, but left it to become professor of modern languages in Bowdoin College. In 1835 he was appointed professor of modern languages and belles-lettres in Harvard University, which place he held until 1854, when he resigned. Since then he continued to live in Cambridge, in the house in which Gen. Washington lived when in command of the army there.

Longfellow wrote some of his best-known poems when a student in college. He published many books of poems, and is better known than any other American poet. His works are as much read in England as in his own country, and they have been translated into many languages. Among his longer poems are " Evangeline," " The Song of Hiawatha," " The Courtship of Miles Standish," " Tales of a Wayside Inn," and " The New England Tragedies." He also published prose works and translations. Among the latter is the " Divina Commedia," of Dante. Many of Longfellow's poems are household words. Even little children know them. Every school-boy can repeat " Excelsior," and every school-girl knows the "Psalm of Life" by heart.

Henry Wadsworth Longfellow.

He died in Cambridge when seventy-five years old (March 24, 1882).

LONGINUS (*lon-ji'nus*), **Dionysius Cassius,** a famous Greek writer, born about A.D. 213. In his youth he travelled and studied a great deal and then settled at Athens, where he had a school of rhetoric and philosophy. He was one of the ablest writers of his time, and was so learned that he was called "the living library." He went later to Palmyra, and became the chief adviser of Queen ZENOBIA. When the Roman Emperor Aurelian conquered Palmyra he put Longinus to death, because he had advised Zenobia to resist him. He was executed at Palmyra in A.D. 273.

LONG ISLAND. See NEW YORK (State).

LONG ISLAND CITY, a city of New York, at the W. end of Long Island, opposite New York City, and separated from Brooklyn on the S. by Newtown Creek; pop. 31,000, or about as large as Dubuque, Iowa. It was formed in 1870 by uniting Astoria, Ravenswood, and Long Island City or Hunter's Point.

The first two have many fine streets and residences belonging to New York merchants. At Hunter's Point are large oil refineries, lumber-yards, and manufactories of varnish, chemicals, steam-engines, and other things.

LOO CHOO ISLANDS. See JAPAN.

LOS'SING, Benson John, an American author, born at Beekman, N. Y., Feb. 12, 1813. He was a watchmaker at Poughkeepsie, N. Y., but in 1835 became editor of the Poughkeepsie *Telegraph*, and in 1838 of "The Family Magazine." He studied drawing and engraving, so as to make pictures for his magazine, and afterward travelled over the United States, making drawings of battle-fields and other noted places, and collecting facts, which he used in the "Pictorial Field-book of the Revolution," "Pictorial History of the United States," "Life of Washington," "Philip Schuyler," and many other historical works. He died when seventy-eight years old (June 3, 1891).

LOTHAIRE (*lo-thair'*) **I.,** Emperor of the West, born about 796. He was the son of Louis le Débonnaire, and grandson of Charles the Great. Lothaire excited his brothers Pepin and Louis to rebel against their father, and to dethrone him. On the death of his father, Lothaire became emperor. He soon had a war with his brothers, and suffered a defeat at Fontenay. Finally, the three brothers (843) made the Peace of Verdun, dividing Charlemagne's vast empire among them. By this Lothaire received Italy, Burgundy, and a district called after himself Lotharingia, now Lorraine. After some time he concluded to divide these dominions among his own sons and become a monk. He died six days after entering the convent, when fifty-nine years old, at Prum (Sept. 29, 855).

LOTHAIRE II., called the Saxon, Emperor of Germany, born near

Celle in 1075. He succeeded Henry V. in 1125. The Dukes of Suabia and Franconia would not own him as emperor, but with the help of Pope Innocent II., he defeated the Duke of Suabia, and had no further trouble. The events of his reign are few and of little importance. He died when sixty-two years old (Dec. 3, 1137), and was succeeded by Conrad III., of Suabia.

LOUIS (*loo'e*) **I.,** called le Débonnaire, King of the Franks, and Emperor of the West, born at Casseneuil, in 778. He was the son of Charles the Great and succeeded him as emperor. He was induced to divide his dominions among his three sons. When a fourth was born, and he wished to make another division, the three older sons rebelled. Peace was restored, but fresh rebellions kept breaking out between father and sons. At last, while marching against his son Louis, the father died of grief. His last words were, " I pardon my son Louis, but let him know that he is the cause of my death." He died when sixty-two years old (June 20, 840).

LOUIS IV., called Outre Mer, tenth Carlovingian King of France, born about 921. He was the son of Charles the Simple, who was dethroned in 922. During childhood he lived in England, and this is why he was called Outre Mer, which means "Beyond the Sea." His reign was a continual strife between him and Hugh of Paris, father of Hugh called CAPET, who wanted to be the King's master. At last they took up arms, and Louis was taken prisoner by the Count of Paris. He was released, giving the town of Laon in ransom. Louis died in 954, owing to a fall from his horse while hunting. He was succeeded by his son Lothaire.

LOUIS V., called le Fainéant (the Idle), twelfth and last Carlovingian King of France, born in 968. He was the son of Lothaire and

grandson of Louis IV. He succeeded his father in 986. His reign lasted but a year, and he died, poisoned by his wife, in 987. With him ended the Carlovingian line, which had occupied the throne for nearly two hundred and fifty years. Hugh CAPET, Count of Paris, became King on his death.

LOUIS VI., called the Fat, fifth Capetian King of France, born about 1078. He was the son of Philip I., and succeeded him in 1108. He was a brave and active prince, who tried to make his nobles obey the laws and to raise the throne from the low position it had held before him. When Henry I., of England, seized upon Normandy, the duchy of his nephew William, son of his brother Robert, Louis took up arms against him. In a battle at Brenneville, he came near being taken prisoner by an English soldier who seized his horse's bridle crying, " The king is taken." But Louis replied with great calmness, " The king cannot be taken, even in chess," and with a blow laid the soldier dead at his feet. Louis did not keep Normandy for his favorite, William, but he gave him the County of Flanders. He died Aug. 1, 1137, and was succeeded by his son, Louis VII.

LOUIS VII., called the Young, sixth Capetian King of France ; born in 1120. He succeeded his father Louis VI., when he was seventeen years old, in 1137, having the same year married Eleanor, heiress of Aquitaine, a very rich princess. Against the advice of his very able minister, the Abbé Suger, Louis went to the Holy Land to recover the tomb of the Saviour from the Turks. After spending three years in a vain attempt to take Damascus, he returned to France, which had been well governed during his absence by the wise Suger. His queen, Eleanor, had brought disgrace upon herself and him by her misconduct while in the East, and the first thing he did after his return was to divorce her. Her riches caused her hand to be immediately sought by Henry II., of England, who lived to be sorry enough for this marriage. Louis died when sixty years old, and was succeeded by his son Philip II.

LOUIS VIII., called the Lion, eighth Capetian King of France, born in 1187. He was the son of Philip Augustus, and succeeded him when thirty-six years old, in 1223. His short reign of three years was spent in wars with the English, who insisted upon his giving up Normandy to them, and with the Albigenses, the inhabitants of Albi, a town in the south of France, who were considered by him as heretics. After taking Avignon, the chief city of the Albigenses, he was attacked by a disease which had broken out in his army, and died at Montpensier, when thirty-nine years old (Nov. 8, 1226). He was succeeded by his son Louis IX.

LOUIS IX., called Saint Louis, ninth Capetian King of France, born at Poissy, April 25, 1215. He was the son of Louis VIII., succeeding him when only eleven years old (1226), under the guardianship of his mother, Blanche of Castile, whom Louis respected so much as to leave her in full charge of affairs until he was twenty-three years old. After a dangerous illness, during which he made a vow that he would march against the Turks if he got well, he set out on the seventh Crusade. The issue of this was unfortunate, the Christian army being routed in Egypt by the Saracens, and Louis taken prisoner. During his captivity his behavior was such as to win the admiration of the infidels, in proof of which the Sultan struck off a fifth part of the sum he had first asked for the ransom of his prisoners. On his return to France he set about caring for the affairs of his kingdom with great diligence and good sense. His justice won the

love of his subjects and the respect of his neighbors. For a great many years after his death the French delighted to show an oak-tree at Vincennes, beneath which he used to sit on the grass, giving justice to the poor as well as to the rich. Notwithstanding the ill-success of his expedition to the Holy Land, he could not give up the idea of relieving the Christians in that country, and he fitted out the eighth Crusade. While the French were engaged in besieging Tunis, a pestilence broke out in the army, and the King was one of its victims. In his last moments he asked to be laid on a bed of ashes, and there he breathed his last, with his hands crossed on his breast, and his lips murmuring, "O Jerusalem! Jerusalem!" He died when fifty-five years old, near Tunis (Aug. 25, 1270), and was succeeded by his son Philip III.

LOUIS X., twelfth Capetian King of France. The date of his birth is not known, but he was the son of Philip IV., and succeeded him in 1314. The curse which Pope Boniface VIII. had laid on Philip seems to have descended to his family. His three sons, who reigned successively after him, under the titles of Louis X., Philip V., and Charles IV., died young, without male heirs, and their three reigns lasted but fourteen years, a time of bloody executions and fierce persecution of the Jews, lepers, and sorcerers. Louis reigned but two years. All the serfs that were left in France were obliged by him to buy their freedom, Louis saying that the King of France should have only free men as subjects. He died when quite young, in 1316, and was succeeded by his brother Philip V.

LOUIS XI., the sixth Valois King of France; born in Bourges, July 3, 1423. He was the son of Charles VII., and came to the throne in 1461, when he was thirty-eight years old. This king, on account of his cruelties and his meannesses, has left behind him one of the most hated names in history. He gloried in being deceitful, one of his favorite sayings being, "He who knows not how to dissemble, knows not how to reign." His reign was, nevertheless, a memorable one, because many of the great estates, formerly held by powerful nobles, were joined to the crown-lands, so that the Kings of France became much more powerful than they had ever been before. Charles the Bold, of Burgundy, was his cousin and near neighbor, but they soon became open enemies, Louis stirring up Charles's subjects to revolt. On the death of Charles, Burgundy was taken by Louis, and added to the other territories he had won. It is said that he had a dungeon, where all who offended him in any way were imprisoned and tormented by being put into cages so small that the poor prisoners could neither lie down nor stand up. But of all his state prisoners no one was more a prisoner than he made himself, so afraid was he that some one would kill him. He died in his castle of Plessis les Tours, when sixty years old (Aug. 30, 1483), and was succeeded by his son, Charles VIII.

LOUIS XII., eighth Valois King of France, born in Blois, in 1462. He was the son of Duke Charles of Orleans, and great-grandson of Charles V., and succeeded Charles VIII. in 1498. He has been called the "Father of his People," a title which he seems to have deserved, from the love he bore his subjects and his efforts for their improvement. But he would have had a still better claim to this name if he had not wasted so much blood and treasure in wars. Louis conquered Milan, but he was unlucky in his attempts on Venice and Naples. When he became king, he set about reducing the expenses of the government with so much zeal that he was accused of being miserly. The king, hearing this charge, is

said to have answered, "I would rather that my courtiers should laugh at my avarice, than that my people should weep for my extravagance." Louis died when fifty-three years old (Jan. 1, 1515), and was succeeded by his cousin, Francis I.

LOUIS XIII., second Bourbon King of France ; born at Fontainebleau, Sept. 27, 1601. He was the son of Henry IV., the Great, and succeeded him, when he was only nine years old, under the guardianship of his mother, Maria de Medici. He was declared of age to reign when sixteen years old but he had naturally a weak mind, which had not been improved by education, and he soon became the tool of any one who happened to gain influence over him. Cardinal RICHELIEU was king in all but name for eighteen memorable years, and he made France the chief power in Europe. Louis did not like Richelieu, but he kept him in power on account of his great ability, and because he could not do without him. Louis died at St. Germain-en-Laye, when forty-two years old (May 14, 1643), and was succeeded by his son, Louis XIV.

LOUIS XIV., third Bourbon King of France ; born in St. Germain-en-Laye, Sept. 16, 1638. He was the son of Louis XIII., and succeeded him when only five years old (1643). The reign of this monarch was seventy-two years, the longest and the most glorious in French history. So many great men and events united to throw lustre on especially the first part that the world has given Louis the name of Great, and we speak of the age in which he reigned as "the age of Louis XIV." Until he was twenty-three years old, the government was carried on by Cardinal MAZARIN, the chief adviser of Anne of Austria, the Queen Mother. For many years he was hated by the people, and a party, which many nobles joined, was formed against him. Soon a contest began, called the War of the Fronde (sling), a name given by the other side in ridicule of the slings which were the only weapon of some of these men. This war lasted four years, and only died out because the people grew tired of fighting.

Louis XIV.

Cardinal Mazarin died when Louis was twenty-three years old. The young king had been brought up to love pleasure, and every one thought that he would, of course, find it necessary to choose another minister to bear the weight of the government. "To whom shall we address ourselves?" asked the President of the Council of Louis XIV, the morning following Mazarin's funeral. "To me," said the young monarch ; and ever afterward Louis XIV. was his own prime minister. Wise men aided him with their counsel, but to none would he give up the duties that he rightly thought his alone. One of his great merits was that he knew how to discern and value all those superior men who lived in his time and clustered around his throne, and to give each

his fitting place. It would be impossible even to name the distinguished men of the court of Louis XIV. Early in his reign he chose as his chief Minister of Finance the great Colbert, who encouraged trade and commerce, and set up many manufacturing establishments. At the same time the arts and sciences made a great advance, the king being their patron.

Well would it have been for France, had their king been content with those peaceful pursuits, but he also engaged in many wars which made him pay dearly for the new territory which he sometimes added to his dominions. These wars covered nearly a half century, with only here and there a few brief intervals of peace. At first the French arms were everywhere victorious, but at last the other nations raised up some great generals, who learned to beat the soldiers of Louis. When not occupied with war, this monarch devoted his attention to building superb palaces and surrounding them with magnificent gardens. One of the monuments of his reign is the beautiful palace of Versailles, the like of which can scarcely be found in the world, and which cost immense sums of money. The Hotel des Invalides, too, he built for his worn-out and disabled soldiers.

The court of Louis XIV. was the most brilliant and polished that the world has ever seen. Beautiful women, equally famed for wit and grace, were its chief ornament, and courtly gentlemen were seen displaying a splendor almost royal ; but it must be said that many of them led very immoral lives. Toward the close of his reign, Louis took back the Edict of Nantes, the law giving liberty of worship to the Protestants, and thousands of these people took refuge in other countries. This was a bad thing for France, as the Huguenots were skilful workmen, and they were a great loss to the country.

At last Louis got to be an old man, oppressed with many infirmities, and taking no pleasure in the splendor which had surrounded him all his life. Many of his children and grandchildren had gone before him to the grave, and his heir was a five-year-old child, his great-grandson. His last words to him were, " My child, you are about to become a great king. Do not imitate me, either in my taste for building or in my love of war." Louis died at Versailles when seventy-seven years old (Sept. 1, 1715), and was succeeded by his great-grandson, Louis XV.

LOUIS XV., fourth Bourbon King of France, born in Versailles, Feb. 15, 1710. He was the son of Louis Duke of Burgundy, and great-grandson of Louis XIV., whom he succeeded when only five years old, Sept. 1, 1715. The king was under the guardianship of his cousin, the Duke of Orleans, a corrupt man, who taught him nothing that was good, and his court soon became noted for the most shameless wickedness. Although the royal treasury was nearly empty, he indulged in all sorts of extravagance, to pay for which there was no other way than to make still heavier the taxes already pressing too heavily on the people. When Louis grew up, he was ignorant of all that a king should know, and cared for nothing but eating, drinking, and hunting. Under his rule things went on from bad to worse. Louis knew well enough that terrible times were to come, but he did not care so long as they did not come in his day. " *Après nous le déluge* " (After us the deluge), he said, and went on. To make matters worse, a host of infidel writers sprang up, whose works were scattered freely among the people, destroying not only their respect for religion, but their love for everything they had hitherto held sacred. In strange contrast with the wickedness of the king.

shone the pure Christian lives of his wife and children, who were as much beloved as he was detested. As may be supposed, he did not enjoy his home much, and he found all his pleasure in the society of wicked women whose lives were more like his own.

France took part in the three wars which went on during this time in Europe : the war to restore to the Polish throne Stanislaus Leczinski, the king's father-in-law ; the war of the Austrian succession ; and the SEVEN YEARS WAR, in whch she lost her American colonies in Canada. The small-pox at that time was making dreadful ravages all over Europe, the physicians then knowing nothing of vaccination. Louis was attacked with it and died. His body was buried in St. Denis, with no funeral rites, and unaccompanied except by the curses of the passers by. And yet this was the king, who, in the earlier part of his reign, had been surnamed the " Well-beloved." He died at Versailles when sixty-four years old (May 10, 1774), and was succeeded by his grandson Louis XVI.

LOUIS XVI., fifth Bourbon King of France, born in Versailles, Aug. 23, 1754. He was the son of Louis the Dauphin, and grandson of Louis XV., whom he succeeded when twenty years old, May 10, 1774. An empty treasury, a selfish nobility, a ruined people, whose misery had almost changed them to biutes, sullen murmurings, and an utter hatred of all rule, human or divine—such was the fearful inheritance left by Louis XV. to his young grandson. Nor is it strange that his first act on hearing that he was king, was to seize the hand of his young wife, Marie Antoinette, and throwing himself on his knees with her, to exclaim : " O God, guard and protect us, we are too young to reign." Louis was a good man, and loved his people, but his character did not fit him to meet the difficulties he was called to face, and he became the victim of the most terrible revolution recorded in history. His goodness was often weakness, his simplicity stupidity. He was obstinate when he should have yielded, and often gave way when he should have stood firm. So historians say, but while this may all be true, he would indeed have been an extraordinary man who could have guided the fearful storm let loose over France by the crimes and follies of centuries. The first difficulty of the new government was that of filling the empty treasury. Turgot, the

Louis XVI.

Minister of Finance, proposed as the only means strict economy and the sharing of the burden of taxation by the nobles and clergy, who had up to this time had no taxes to pay. A storm of wrath arose against him, raised by these two classes, and he was obliged to give up his place. His successors were no luckier than he, and the evils daily grew greater.

Four years after Louis came to the throne, France made a treaty with the United States, who were at that time fighting for their independence, and fought her old enemy, England, while aiding her rebellious provinces. The United States were at last free, and the French soldiers who had helped to make them so returned to their country filled with admiration for the young republic which they had assisted in setting up. This feeling soon spread among the lower classes and hastened the crisis. To settle some of the great difficulties to be met, the King called together the States General, a body something like our Congress. It was a stormy meeting, the different classes quarrelling about rights and privileges. The representatives of the people finally won over to their side some of the clergy, the discontented nobles refusing to take further part in their acts. This body, calling itself the National Assembly, proceeded to make a new constitution or set of laws. Meanwhile, the excited people stormed the Bastile, an old castle which had been used as a state prison, took it, and destroyed it (July 14, 1789), after a fight of five hours. The key of this celebrated building was afterward given by Lafayette to General Washington, and may still be seen at Mount Vernon. "What, a riot?" cried Louis XVI., on hearing the news that the Bastile had fallen. "Sire," said one of his nobles, more far-sighted than the king, "it is a revolution." Two weeks later (Aug. 4), the National Assembly made a number of changes which entirely put an end to the old order of things. The clergy and nobility lost all their privileges, titles were done away with, and all Frenchmen were to be called by no other name than "citizens." The king saw that royalty would soon be overthrown, and made an attempt to leave France with his family, all being disguised ; but they were recognized and brought back to Paris (June 21, 1791).

Change now followed change, and at last the National Assembly said they would act without the king, and decreed "to place the king and family under control, and to assemble a National Convention." The Temple, a strong fort, once occupied by the Knights Templars, soon became their prison. The National Convention was made up of violent men who thirsted for the king's blood. After declaring France a republic, they then proceeded to try the king on a charge of treason. The trial was only a form, and on Jan. 20, 1793, Louis was condemned to death. That night he took leave of his family, and the next morning he calmly went forth to die. His last words on the scaffold were: "Frenchmen, I die innocent of all the crimes laid to my charge. I pardon the authors of my death, and I pray to God that my blood may not be visited on France." He died when thirty-nine years old (Jan. 21, 1793).

LOUIS XVII., called King of France, born in Versailles, March 27, 1785. He was the son of Louis XVI., and on his father's death, in 1793, he succeeded to his claims, but not to his throne, France having been proclaimed a republic. When the Count of Provence, uncle of the little king, learned, in Westphalia, of his brother's sad fate, he took the title of regent, and notified the different courts of Europe of the accession of Louis XVII. While foreign powers recognized the young king, the poor child was trying to comfort his mother in the doleful prison of the Temple.

The Parisians were angry that foreign powers had not recognized the republic they had proclaimed, and they became more violent against the innocent victims that they held in their hands. It was ordered that the "Wolf Cub of the Temple," as they called the little king, should be parted from his mother, and given to the charge of a shoe-maker named Simon. "What shall I do with him?" said Simon.

"He is to be gotten rid of," was the reply. The hint was enough. The wretch shut him in a room which no one ever entered, except to thrust a little food and water in at the door. It was never cleaned, and though they gave him a bell, he never rang it, preferring everything to the presence of his tormentors. There he pined away his little life, while the mad crew who ruled Paris went on voting that there was no God, no hereafter, no anything that people had loved and honored, changing the names of the very months, and making the week ten days, so that Sunday might no longer be reverenced; and daily the soil of France was watered with the blood of her best and noblest. For three fearful years endured the Reign of Terror, whch may be said to close with the death of ROBESPIERRE. The more sensible members of the convention then said it was time for the prison doors to be opened. Those whom the guillotine had spared came forth, but it was too late to save the gentle little king. Neglect and ill-treatment had done their work. He lay on the bed, a mass of sores and dirt, and would notice no one, nor even eat. When asked why, he said, "Because I want to die." A year after this he lingered on, but at last his wish was granted. He died when only ten years old (June 8, 1795), and left as his heir his uncle, Louis XVIII.

LOUIS XVIII., seventh Bourbon King of France; born in Versailles, Nov. 17, 1755. He was the son of Louis the Dauphin, and the grandson of Louis XV., and he succeeded his brother, Louis XVI., in 1814. The Count of Provence, as Louis was called before he became king, fled from Paris on the breaking out of the French Revolution, to Coblentz, where he kept up a sort of court, being joined from time to time by such of the French nobles as made their escape from France after the execution of Louis XVI.

After the lapse of twenty-three years, during which time France went through many changes, he returned to fill the throne of his ancestors, the nations of Europe having decided that it was better for the Bourbons to be restored. Before a year had passed, he was again compelled to flee, the fickle Frenchmen thinking they would rather have for their ruler the Emperor Napoleon BONAPARTE, who had returned from Elba, to which place he had been banished, but whose reign of a hundred days was ended by the battle of Waterloo. Louis was once more called to the throne, which he succeeded in keeping until his death. He was a lazy, good-humored man, and wanted to do more for the people than his party would let him do. He died at Paris when sixty-nine years old (Sept. 16, 1824), and was succeeded by his brother, the Count of Artois, as Charles X.

LOUIS PHILIPPE (*loo'e fe-leep'*), King of the French, first of the Orleans branch of the Bourbons ; born in Paris, Oct. 6, 1773. He was the son of Philippe Egalité, Duke of Orleans, and was called to the throne to succeed Charles X. On account of their republican principles, he and his father were excepted from the decree by which the French revolutionists banished the Bourbon family in 1792. At a later period, however, he had to flee from France, and spent twenty years in exile and poverty, in different parts of Europe and in the United States, supporting himself sometimes by teaching and sometimes by the labor of his hands. When Bonaparte fell, he returned to Paris, where he soon made many friends, and after the July revolution of 1803, which in three days dethroned Charles X., Louis Philippe was called to the throne not as those before him had been, as King of France, but as "King of the French." This change in the title was to show that the King reigned, not by his own will, but by that of

the people. The Citizen King, as he was called, soon lost his popularity, both with the upper and lower classes. They missed the splendor to which they had been accustomed around the throne. There was nothing to feed their love of glory, and they could not bear the stingy ways which were the fashion of the court, from the king down to its lowest officers. The consequence was another revolution (1848), and Louis again fled, this time to England. He died at Clermont, near London, when seventy-seven years old (Aug. 26, 1850). France was immediately declared a republic, and there has never since been a King of France.

LOUIS IV., called the Bavarian, Emperor of Germany ; born about 1285. He was the son of Louis, Duke of Bavaria, and was chosen by most of the electors (1314) to succeed Henry VII., the other electors having chosen his cousin Frederick the Fair, of Austria. A long and bitter war began between the two emperors, but the battle of Mühldorf decided in favor of Louis, and Frederick was taken prisoner and kept a captive three years. At the end of that time he was released on condition that he would return to prison, if he should be unable to persuade his friends to give up his claims as Emperor. Failing in his attempt, Frederick kept his word and returned to captivity. Louis was so much touched by this noble conduct that he became his best friend and made him governor of his Bavarian possessions. Louis died suddenly during a boar-hunt, near Feirstenfeld, when about sixty-two years old (Oct. 11, 1347), and was succeeded as Emperor by Charles IV.

LOUISBURG (*loo'is-burg*), a town of Nova Scotia, on the S.E. side of the Island of Cape Breton. It was settled in the early part of the last century by the French, who named it after King Louis XIV. About

1715 they began to build walls and forts there, and Louisburg soon became one of the strongest places in America. The harbor, which is a very fine one, was used for French ships of war and for privateering ships, which often captured the English fishing-vessels. At length an army was raised in New England and sent under the command of William PEPPERELL against Louisburg. At the first approach the French abandoned one of their principal forts, spiking the cannon, but the English smiths succeeded in boring out the spikes, and these cannon were used in bombarding the town. A French ship with re-enforcements and provisions was taken by the English fleet, and at length the garrison of the town surrendered, after they had been besieged for seven weeks (June 17, 1745). Louisburg was given back to France in 1748, but was again taken by the English under General Amherst (July 26, 1758), after the garrison had made a brave resistance. During the last siege the town was almost ruined, and when it was taken the English destroyed the walls and forts, taking the people away to France. Louisburg has never been rebuilt, and now only a few fishermen live there.

The drums used by the New England soldiers when they marched into Louisburg, on June 17, 1745, were beaten by them, just thirty years afterward, at the battle of Bunker Hill.

LOUISIANA (*loo-e-ze-ah'nah*), one of the Southern Gulf States, of the United States, between Mississippi and Texas; area, 41,300 square miles, or a little larger than Ohio; pop. 1,119,000, or about three tenths that of Ohio; capital, BATON ROUGE. It is a very low and flat region, most of it having been formed by the overflow of the Mississippi River. Much of it is lower than the river, and has to be protected from the floods by banks called levees, which are built along the river banks. Generally these keep the river in its own channel, but sometimes, when the flood is great, the levee breaks, and the water rushes through with terrible force, destroying farms, carrying away houses, and often drowning people and cattle. Such breaks are called crevasses. Near the mouth of the Mississippi are many swamps and lakes, and hundreds of small channels, called bayous, run through the country like canals. In the northern part of the State are many prairies, good for pasturing cattle. Most of the large plantations are on lands near the rivers.

Nearly all the sugar made in the United States comes from Louisiana, and a great deal of cotton, corn, and rice. The climate is warm and not very healthful in summer; there is seldom snow. Many of the people speak only French. About half the people are negroes. Louisiana was named after the French King Louis XIV. It originally included Arkansas, Indian Territory, and all of the present United States north of the Arkansas River, and between the Mississippi and the Rocky Mountains. The country was discovered by DE SOTO in 1541, and settled by the French in 1699. In 1803 Napoleon sold it to the United States for $15,000,000, and in 1813 the present State was admitted to the Union. It seceded in 1861, but in 1868 was re-admitted.

LOUISVILLE (*loo'is-vil*), the largest city of Kentucky, on the Ohio River; pop. 161,000, or nearly as large as Jersey City, N. J. Opposite the city are the falls or rapids of the Ohio, over a ledge of rocks crossing the river. In some places are deeper passages called chutes, through which steamboats can pass when the river is high. During low water they go around through a canal. At the head of the falls is a beautiful iron bridge across the

Ohio, a mile long, over which railway trains pass to Indiana. More tobacco is sold in Louisville than in any other city in the world, and it has a very large trade in pork, beer, and whiskey. Louisville was begun in 1778, and was named in 1780, after King Louis XVI., of France, because his soldiers helped the Americans in the Revolutionary war. It became a city in 1828.

LOUVAIN (*loo-vayn'*), a town of Belgium, on the River Dyle, 15 miles E. of Brussels; pop. 39,000, or about as large as Harrisburg, Pa. It has a beautiful cathedral and town hall, and a university with 1300 students. The principal trade is in beer. In the 14th century, Louvain was one of the largest manufacturing cities in the world, and had more than 200,000 inhabitants.

LOUVOIS (*loo-vwah*), **François Michel Letellier,**. Marquis de, a noted French statesman; born in Paris, Jan. 18, 1641. When twenty-five years old, he became Secretary of War under Louis XIV. He married a rich heiress, and soon after gave up the pleasures of the court, and devoted himself to studying the condition of the army. He was so industrious, showed so much wisdom and skill, and flattered the King so cunningly that at last Louis thought nothing could be done without him, and he used to get him to plan campaigns and manage things for him generally. All this power was too much for him to bear; he grew haughty and overbearing to the King himself, so Louis got angry with his favorite, and one day, after a stormy talk with his master, Louvois died suddenly. Some people said he had been poisoned, but this is not known to be true. He died in Paris when fifty years old (July 16, 1691).

LOVER (*luv'er*), **Samuel,** a noted Irish author, born in Dublin, in 1797. He first became known to the people of Ireland by singing one of his own songs at a public dinner given to the great Irish poet, Thomas MOORE. He wrote a number of novels, and some very sweet songs and ballads. His chief novel is called "Handy Andy," and everybody knows his song, "Rory O'More." He was very much liked as a lecturer in England, Ireland, and America. He died when seventy-one years old (July 6, 1868).

LOWE (*lo*), **Sir Hudson,** a noted British soldier, born in Galway, Ireland, July 28, 1769. He was the son of a surgeon-general in the British army; served in several wars —in Egypt, the Peninsular War, in Naples and Sicily, and in the conquest of the Ionian Islands, of which he was the first governor, but is now chiefly known as the governor of the island of St. Helena, when Napoleon was imprisoned there. He was praised by some for his treatment of Napoleon, and blamed by others, so that he wrote a defence of his conduct. His manner was stern and severe, but his friends said that he had a warm heart. He died in London when seventy-five years old (July 10, 1844).

LOWELL (*lo'el*), a city of Massachusetts, on the Merrimac River, 25 miles N.W. of Boston; pop. about 78,000, or a little larger than Nashville, Tenn. It is the second city of Massachusetts in population, and is noted for its manufactures. More cotton-cloth is made there than in any other place in the United States, excepting, perhaps, Fall River. It has also large print works, where calicoes are printed (C.C.T., 98, I. l.), and factories where woollen cloths, shawls, carpets, and stockings are made. Many thousand persons, including boys and girls, are employed in the factories.

Lowell was first built in 1821, and was named after Francis C. Lowell, a merchant of Boston, who was one of the first to begin the making of cotton cloth in the United States.

LOWELL, James Russell, a famous

American poet, born in Cambridge, Mass., Feb. 22, 1819. He was graduated a* Harvard College when nineteen years old, and studied law, but gave up the profession for literature. He was made professor of modern languages and belles-lettres at Harvard after Longfellow resigned. His poems and essays are liked by all educated people, both in America and England. Besides several volumes of poems, he has published " The Vision of Sir Launfal" and the " Biglow Papers," the last a witty satire in rhyme in the " Yankee " dialect. Mr. Lowell became United States Minister to Spain in 1878, and still later was appointed Minister to England. He died in Cambridge, Mass.. in his seventy-third year (Aug. 12, 1891).

LOYOLA (*lo-yo'lah*), **Ignatius de,** founder of the Society of Jesus, or Jesuit Order ; born in Guipuzcoa, Spain, in 1491. His real name was Iñigo, but in later life he changed it to Ignatius. He was first a page at the court of Ferdinand and Isabella, and afterward a soldier until he was thirty years old. Having been badly wounded in the leg at the siege of Pamplona, he read religious books when in the hospital, and made up his mind to lead a better life. He wished to become a priest, but he found that he was too ignorant, so he went to school when thirty-three years old with little boys. Finally (1537) he became a priest, and founded the Order or Society of Jesuits. As he had been a soldier, the soldier's ideas are plainly to be seen in the rules which he made for the government of the order, and each member is obliged to obey his superior officer just as a soldier does in the army. Loyola died in Rome when sixty-four years old (July 31, 1556).

LUBECK (*loo'bek*), a city of N. Germany, on the River Trave, near the Baltic Sea; pop. 68,000, or nearly as large as Cambridge, Mass. It is one of the three free German cities,

which are allowed to make their own laws, and send representatives to the German Congress. Most of the houses are old and quaint. The cathedral is one of the finest in North Germany. A considerable trade is carried on in corn, cattle, wool, and iron, and there are manufactories of ironware, tobacco, linen and cotton goods, and paper.

Lübeck was founded in the 12th century, and was made a free city in 1226. Formerly it was one of the richest and most important seaports of Germany.

LU'CAN (Latin LUCANUS), **Marcus Annæus,** a noted Roman poet, born in CORDOVA, Spain, about A.D. 39. His father, who was a brother of Seneca, took his son to Rome to be educated, and he wrote his poems there. It was discovered that he was engaged in a conspiracy against the Emperor NERO, and to save his life he betrayed all his companions, even his own mother. But Lucan gained nothing by his treachery, for Nero condemned him to die. Finding that he could not escape, the poet caused his veins to be cut open, and bled to death while repeating some of his own poetry, when only twenty-six years old (A.D. 65). The only work of Lucan that has been preserved is a long poem called " Pharsalia," which describes the wars of Cæsar and Pompey, and the battle of Pharsalia.

LUCCA (*luk'kah*), a city of W. Italy, on the River Serchio, 10 miles N.E. of Pisa ; pop. 68,000, or a little larger than Atlanta, Ga. It is a least 2000 years old, and in the 6th century it became the capital of a State of the same name, which was sometimes independent and at other times was subject to Pisa, Germany, Austria, or France. In 1847, it was joined to Tuscany, and in 1860 to the Kingdom of Italy. Many of the old palaces are still standing, and their strong walls show that they were used for fortresses as well as houses. Cotton and woollen cloths are manufactured. The warm mineral springs of Lucca, about fourteen miles from the city, are visited by thousands of invalids, who use the water for bathing.

LUCERNE (*loo-sern'*), a city of Switzerland, at the N.W. end of Lake Lucerne; pop. 20,000, or about as large as Lincoln, R. I. It is walled in on the land side, and has many curious old watch-towers. The River Reuss, which flows through the city, is crossed by several ancient bridges, which are roofed over and ornamented inside with paintings. The scenery round the city is very grand and beautiful. The Lake of Lucerne is 25 miles long, and is partly surrounded by high mountains. William Tell is said to have lived on the banks, and many stories of his life are connected with the lake.

LUCIAN (*lu'she-an*), a famous Greek writer, born in Samosata, on the River Euphrates, about A.D. 120. His parents, too poor to give him a good education, set him to work with his uncle, a sculptor; but Lucian became angry with his master because he gave him a beating, and went home to study for himself. He became a lawyer in Antioch, but not being successful, he made a living by teaching rhetoric in the cities of Greece, Italy, and Gaul, and finally got rich, when he went home and wrote books. His most celebrated works are the "Dialogues," which are short pieces, generally written to show the follies of the Pagan gods and philosophers of that time. Lucian finally became a Roman officer in Egypt, where he died about A.D. 200.

LUCK'NOW, a city of India, on the River Goomtee, a branch of the Ganges; pop. 261,000, or about as large as Cleveland, Ohio. It contains many beautiful palaces, mosques, and Hindoo temples, but the older streets are narrow and dirty. Lucknow was formerly the capital of the native kingdom of Oude, but the king was dethroned in 1856, and his kingdom was added to the British possessions. In 1857, during the Sepoy rebellion, the British garrison of Lucknow was besieged by 10,000 Sepoys, or native soldiers. After three months, Generals Havelock and Outram, with a small army, came to help them, fighting their way through the besiegers. The siege lasted for a month longer, when the garrison was re-enforced by Sir Colin Campbell, and on Nov. 22, 1857, they retreated to Cawnpore. Lucknow was fortified by the Sepoys, who were besieged there in 1858, by Sir Colin Campbell and the city was finally recaptured (March 21).

LUCRETIUS (*lu-kre'she-us*), a famous Roman poet, born about 95 B.C. It is said that he was insane, and that he finally died by his own hand, when about forty-two years old (52 B.C.). His great poem "De Rerum Natura" (On the Nature of Things), is said to have been written in the time between his fits of insanity. It is a kind of treatise in verse on the teachings of EPICURUS, and treats of all things in nature, such as the origin of the world and all things that happen in it. It is one of the finest poems ever written.

LU-CUL'LUS, Lucius Lucinius, a noted Roman general, born about 109 B.C. During the first war with MITHRIDATES, he served under Sulla, in Greece and Asia, and commanded a fleet with which he conquered the fleet of Mithridates, near Tenedos. He was afterward in office at Rome (80 B.C.), and the splendid public games which he held there were the first in which fights between elephants and bulls took place. In 74 he was made Consul, and for eight years he commanded in a second war against Mithridates, and but for a revolt of his solders would have overthrown and captured him. In 66 B.C. his command was given to Pompey, and he went to live in a splendid villa near Rome. He delighted in entertaining his friends there, and is said to have once spent more than $8000 for a single supper. He was the first to bring cherry-trees to Europe from Asia. Lucullus died when about fifty-two years old (57 B.C.).

LUN'DY'S LANE, a place in Canada near Niagara Falls, where a battle was fought during the war of 1812, between the Americans and the British, July 25, 1814. The battle began near sunset, and at first the Americans were successful, capturing General Riall, the British commander, and his staff officers. Afterward they attacked and took a British battery of nine cannons, defeating three attempts to rescue it. Gen. Brown and Col. Scott, the American commanders, were both wounded, and finally the Americans retreated, leaving the cannons for which they had fought so hard because they had no horses to drag them away. This is sometimes called the battle of Bridgewater and sometimes the battle of Niagara.

LU'THER, Martin, the leader of the Reformation in Germany, born at Eisleben, Germany, Nov. 10, 1483. His father was a poor miner, and with difficulty saved money enough to send Martin to school. After studying a year at Magdeburg Martin went to the Latin school at Eisenach, where he had to sing in the streets for bread. One day, after singing in vain for money, he and some other boys who had formed a choir, came to the house of Conrad Cotta, where Madame Cotta gave them all that they could eat, and afterward gave Martin a home until he went to the University of Erfurt. He was very religious, and once when in danger of being struck by lightning, vowed that if his life were spared he would become a monk. So when twenty-two years old he joined the Augustinian Monastery at Erfurt, and three years afterward

he became a professor in the University of Wittenberg, where he soon won fame as a preacher. At this

Statue of Martin Luther at Wittenberg.

time Pope Leo X. was trying to raise money to rebuild Saint Peter's Church in Rome by the sale of indulgences by which he claimed to free men from the temporal or temporary punishment of their sins. A Dominican monk named Tetzel, who was intrusted with the giving out of these indulgences in Saxony, made the granting of them little better than an open sale. This shocked many good men, and Luther preached against Tetzel and fastened on the door of the church a paper called a thesis, in which, among other things, he denied that the Pope had the power to forgive sins. This caused fresh excitement, and a party was at once formed which demanded a reformation in religion. Luther wrote much in favor of this and grew very popular. At last (1520), the Pope issued a writing called a Bull against Luther, threatening to cut him off from the Church unless he took back what he said in sixty days ; but Luther burned the Bull publicly and preached the harder, and thousands of people became his followers. This frightened the Emperor CHARLES, who called a great meeting of his princes at Worms (1521), and called Luther before them for trial ; but Luther would not take back anything he had said, and left the council, which then condemned him. His friends, fearing that he might be killed, got the Elector of Saxony to shut him up in the old Castle of Wartburg, near EISENACH, where he stayed nearly a year. During this time he translated the New Testament, which before had always been printed in Latin and Greek, into the German language, so that the people could read it. When the emperor could not find Luther, he had all his books burned, which only made the people more eager to read them. The excitement now spread over a good portion of Germany, and so the emperor called another meeting at Spire (1529), to enforce the Edict of Worms, and commanded that there should be no change in the religion of the empire. Against this decree the princes who followed Luther protested, and from this the reformers got the name of Protestants. Luther and Melanchthon then wrote a statement of what they believed, which was called the Confession of Augsburg, and this afterward became the standard of belief for the Lutheran Church. Five years before Luther had married an escaped nun, Catherine Von Bora, and lived with his family for many years in Wittenberg, where he preached to thousands of people who came from

all Germany to hear him, and where he wrote a great many religious works. He lived to see his Church firmly founded in Germany. His reforms also spread into other countries, and were the means of reforms in Britain, Switzerland, and France. Luther died at Eisleben, when sixty-three years old (Feb. 18, 1546), famous the world over for his bravery, zeal, great abilities, and good life. He was buried in the church at Wittenberg, and in 1868 a magnificent monument was set up in that city to his memory.

LUX'EM-BURG, a country of Europe, lying between Germany, France, and Belgium ; area, 1592 square miles, or a little larger than Rhode Island; pop. 213,000, or about five eighths that of Rhode Island ; capital Luxemburg (pop. 18,000). It once belonged to the German Confederation, and the City of Luxemburg, which was the strongest fortress in Europe, except Gibraltar, was held by Prussian soldiers. In 1867 the fortress was destroyed, and the country is now a grand duchy, of which the King of the Netherlands is the grand duke ; but it is independent of the Netherlands and has a government of its own.

LY-CA'ON, in Greek fable, a king of Arcadia, who had many sons, all noted for wickedness. Jupiter, determined to punish them, visited their home disguised as a poor man. They gave him at dinner the flesh of a boy whom they had murdered. Jupiter would not eat it, and changed Lycaon and all his sons but one into wolves.

LYCAONIA (*ly-ka-o'ne-ah*). See ASIA MINOR.

LYCIA (*lis'e-ah*). See ASIA MINOR.

LY-CUR'GUS, a famous law-giver of Sparta. Nothing is known certainly about him ; but he is thought to have been the son of Eunomus, King of Sparta. His elder brother, Polydectes, became king after his father's death, but he soon died, and then Lycurgus became the guardian of his son, who was a baby. The first thing he did was to travel to other countries to study their laws and see which were the best, so that he could make wise and good laws for Sparta. When he got home he drew up a set of laws which he taught the people to obey. Then he went away, after making the Spartans promise that they would keep his laws unchanged until he returned, and he was never seen again. Sparta was governed by his laws for five centuries. He made no difference between the rich and poor. All were treated alike and fared alike —even eating at the same public tables. Children were not allowed to belong to their parents, but were the property of the State and were brought up by the State. His laws were very severe ; but under them the Spartans, who had been a weak and worthless people, became a nation of brave and hardy warriors.

LYDIA (*lyd'e-ah*). See ASIA MINOR.

LY'ELL, Sir Charles, a noted British writer on geology, born at Kinnordy, Scotland, Nov. 14, 1797. He was graduated at Oxford, and began to study law, but gave it up for things which pleased him better. Some works on geology having interested him greatly, he soon took to roaming over the country. hammer in hand, breaking off bits of rock to study the different layers, and collecting specimens and fossils. When thirty-three years old he published the results of his studies in a book called " Principles of Geology," which made him famous. A second work, " Elements of Geology," was published a second time with additions and alterations, as the "Student's Manual of Geology." In 1841 Lyell visited the United States to deliver a course of geological lectures in Boston. He spent a year in traveling through this country, Canada, and Nova Scotia, and on his return home published a book called " Travels in North America in 1841-2." This work contained the best geological map of the United States then published. In 1845 he visited the United States a second time, and stayed nearly a year. In 1848 he was made a knight by Queen Victoria, and in 1864 he was created a baronet. He died when seventy-eight years old (Feb. 22, 1875).

LYNDHURST (*lind-hurst'*). See COPLEY.

LYNN, a city of Massachusetts, on Massachusetts Bay, 10 miles N. E. of Boston ; pop. 56,000, or about as large as Lincoln, Neb. It is the greatest shoe manufacturing town in the United States, and nearly every family in it is connected in some way with the shoe business. About 10,000,000 pairs of shoes are made and sold every year. Lynn was settled by the Puritans in 1629.

LY'ONS, a city of S. France, at the junction of the River Saône with the Rhône ; pop. 402,000, or about half as large as Brooklyn, N.Y. It has more manufactures than any other city in France, being especially famous for its silk, in which it exceeds every other place in the world. About 140,000 people and 70,000 looms are employed in weaving silk cloths. Instead of having large mills, the manufacturers employ master-weavers, supplying them with patterns and raw silk. Each master-weaver has a number of looms in his own house, and the work is done by himself and his family and by hired laborers. In the city there is a school of art, where pupils are taught to make designs for silk cloths. Lyons is also noted for its manufactures of imitation jewelry, glass, carriages, ironware, machinery, drugs, leather, colored paper, felt hats, and shawls. The City Hall is one of the finest buildings in France, and there are many beautiful churches, some of which are very ancient. The quays which line the river-banks are said to be the finest in the world. Many forts surround the city, making it one of the strongest places in France.

Before the time of Christ, Lyons was a Roman colony, called Lugdunum, which means the fort on the marsh. During the French Revolution Lyons rebelled against the republican Convention or Congress, but it was taken after a siege of two months (1793), and several thousand persons were put to death.

LY-SAN'DER, a noted Spartan general. Nothing is known of him until the year 407 B.C., when he was made commander of the Spartan fleet and defeated the Athenians off the promontory of Notium. He afterward defeated and seized the Athenian fleet at Ægospotami, and in 404 B.C. took Athens. He then became the most powerful man in all Greece, but he was so proud that no one liked him, and he could not keep any office long. He was killed while fighting against the Thebans (395 B.C.)

LYSIMACHUS (*li-sim'a-kus*), a Greek general, King of Thrace, born in Macedonia, about 360 B.C. He was a general of Alexander the Great, on whose death he became ruler of Thrace. In 302 he invaded Asia Minor, and aided by Seleucus and others, conquered Antigonus at the great battle of Ipsus (301 B.C.). In 288 he conquered Macedonia and added it to his domains. His new wife, Arsinoë, induced him to kill his son Agathocles, but the widow of Agathocles fled to Seleucus, who to revenge her marched against Lysimachus with a large army. The two kings, who were the last living generals of Alexander, met on the plain of Corus, in Phrygia, and Lysimachus was defeated and killed, when nearly eighty years old (281 B.C.).

LY-SIP'PUS, a famous Greek sculptor, born at Sicyon, near the Gulf of Corinth ; lived in the 4th century, B.C. He was so skilful that Alexander the Great gave orders to have no one but Lysippus make statues of him. One of his most celebrated works was a statue of Jupiter, sixty feet high. Another beautiful statue, representing a bather, was kept in the palace of the Emperor Tiberius. There is a story that Lysippus made the famous horses of St. Mark, which are now in Venice.

M

MAC-AD'AM, John Loudon, inventor of the roads called after him "macadamized roads ;" born in Ayr, Scotland, September 21, 1756. He came to New York in 1770, and during the American Revolution was a British agent there for the sale of captured American ships. Returning to Scotland, in 1783, he became a trustee of roads, and afterward spent many years travelling through Great Britain, and making improvements for roads. In 1816, having been appointed to take charge of various roads, he began to macadamize them, that is, to put broken rock on them instead of earth, and before his death nearly every road in Great Britain had been macadamized. He died at Moffat, Scotland when eighty years old (Nov. 26, 1836).

MACAO (*mah-kow'*), a city on the coast of China, at the mouth of the Canton River ; pop. 59,000, or about as large as Reading, Pa. The city is built on a peninsula, which is joined to an island called Hang Shang by an isthmus, only a quarter of a mile wide. There used to be a wall guarded by Chinese soldiers across this isthmus, to keep foreigners from going on the rest of the island, but now they are allowed to go everywhere. About nine tenths of the people are Chinese, who live in miserable huts ; the rest are foreigners of almost every nation, but principally Portuguese and English. The chief trade is in tea, rice, opium, and silk.

Macao has belonged to Portugal since 1585, when it was given by China as a reward for aiding that country in driving away a Japanese pirate. CAMOENS lived in Macao several years, and a grotto where he wrote part of his poem called " The Lusiads" is still shown.

MA·CAU'LAY, Thomas Babington, Lord, a famous English historian, born in Leicestershire, Oct.

Lord Macaulay.

25, 1800. He began writing a history of the world when seven years old, and at eight had composed many verses. He was graduated at Cambridge University in 1822, and when twenty-five years old wrote for the " Edinburgh Review" an essay on Milton which at once made him famous. When thirty years old he became a member of Parliament. In 1834 he went to India as one of the Supreme Council for the East India Company, and stayed four years. On his return he again entered Parliament, and held many offices. But he is best known for his " History of England from the Accession of James II. (1685)." He

lived to complete four volumes of it which brought his account down to the Peace of Ryswick (1697). He wrote also "Lays of Ancient Rome," and his " Essays" and " Speeches" form several volumes. In 1857 he was made a peer, with the title of Baron Macaulay of Rothley. He died at Holly Lodge, Campden Hill, in his sixtieth year (Dec. 28, 1859).

MAC·BETH', a Scottish chieftain, who lived in the 11th century. Little is really known of him, but it is supposed that he was a powerful chief of northern Scotland. King Duncan invaded his territories, but was defeated and killed in a battle near Elgin (1039). Macbeth then became king of Scotland, but he was beaten by the English at Dunsinane (1054), and two or three years afterward, Malcolm, the son of Duncan, aided by Macduff, defeated and killed him at Lumphanan. Malcolm then became king. Macbeth is the hero of Shakespeare's play of " Macbeth," but the history given in the play is very different from the real one.

McCLEL'LAN, George Brinton, an American general, born in Philadelphia, Dec. 3, 1826. He was graduated at West Point, in 1842, and served bravely in the Mexican War. In 1855, he was sent with others to study European methods of war in the Crimea. In 1857, he resigned and became president of a railroad, but when the Civil War broke out he was made major-general in the Union army, commanding in Western Virginia, where he was very successful. Afterward, he became commander of the Army of the Potomac, and on Nov. 1, 1861, commander-in-chief of the United States armies ; but he held the latter position only a short time.

With the Army of the Potomac he marched toward Richmond, on the peninsula between the York and James Rivers (March, 1862). He captured Yorktown after a long siege, and fought many battles on the CHICKAHOMINY River, but after the battle of Malvern Hill fell back to Harrison's Landing. In Aug., 1862, the Confederates having invaded Maryland, he hurried to the Potomac to resist them, and fought the great battle of ANTIETAM (Sept. 16 and 17, 1862). After this battle McClellan followed the Confederates across the river, but on Nov. 7, 1862, his command was taken from him and given to Gen. Burnside. After that he took no part in the war. In 1864 he was nominated to be President of the U. S., but was defeated by ABRAHAM LINCOLN. McClellan resigned from the army Nov. 8, 1864. From 1878 to 1881 he was Governor of New Jersey. He died suddenly when fifty-nine years old (Oct. 29, 1885).

MAC-DON'ALD (French *mahk-do-nahl'*), **Etienne Jacques Joseph Alexandre,** Duke of Taranto, a famous French soldier, born at Sancerre, Nov. 17, 1765. He entered the army at nineteen, and fought so bravely in many battles that he was made a general of division. He helped Bonaparte to make himself Consul, and was rewarded by him with honors and office. At the battle of Wagram his splendid charge upon the Austrians won him his rank as marshal, and shortly after he was made Duke of Taranto. He served afterward in Spain, Russia, and Germany, and at the battle of Leipsic swam the Elster on horseback, after the bridge had been destroyed. He was true to Bonaparte until he gave up his throne, in 1814, but would not break the oath he then took to the Bourbons by serving under him on his return from Elba. He died near Guise, at the age of seventy-five (Sept. 24, 1840).

MAC-DON'ALD, Flora, a Scottish heroine who saved the life of the Pretender, Charles Edward STUART, born in South Uist, one of the HEBRIDES, in 1720. After the battle of Culloden, when Charles was hunted from place to place by the king's troops, a large reward being offered for his capture, Flora saved him, disguised as an Irishwoman, by taking him with her, as her maid, to the Isle of Skye. After the prince's escape she was arrested and kept for several months on ships and in prison, but was finally set free. About 1775 she and her family came to North Carolina to live, but in time returned to Skye, and she died there when seventy years old (March 4, 1790). She was buried in a sheet of the bed in which Prince Charles had slept at Skye, which she had always carried with her.

MAC-DON'ALD, George, a noted Scottish writer of novels, born at Huntly, in 1824. He was educated at the University of Aberdeen, and became a minister, but gave it up for the life of an author. Among his works are "Annals of a Quiet Neighborhood," "The Vicar's Daughter," and "Wilfrid Cumbermede." In 1873 he visited the United States and lectured. He now lives in London.

McDONOUGH (*mak-don'o*), **Thomas,** an American naval com-

Thomas McDonough.

mander, born in Newcastle Co.,

Del., Dec. 23, 1783. He entered the navy in 1800, and served in the war against Tripoli. In 1814 he commanded an American fleet on Lake Champlain, which was attacked at Plattsburg by a larger and stronger British fleet, under Commodore Downie, but after a bloody battle several of the British vessels surrendered and the rest retreated (Sept. 11, 1814). For this victory Congress gave McDonough a gold medal, and he received other honors. He died at sea when about forty-two years old (Nov. 16, 1825).

McDOW-ELL, Irvin, an American general, born in Franklin Co., Ohio, Oct. 15, 1818. He was graduated at West Point in 1838, served in the Mexican War, and soon after the Civil War began was made brigadier-general, and commanded at the first battle of Bull Run (July 21, 1861). Afterwards he had charge of the forts at Washington, and he served during 1862, in Northern Virginia, fighting also in the second battle of Bull Run. He died in San Francisco when sixty-seven years old (May 5, 1885).

MACEDONIA (*mas-se-do'ne-ah*), an ancient country of Europe, north of Greece. The people were much like Greeks, and the country was ruled mostly by Greek kings, but it was not considered a part of Greece until late times. King Philip, father of Alexander the Great, got Macedonia owned as a Greek state, and he finally became the head of all Greece. He was murdered just as he had got ready to lead the Greeks against the Persians to avenge the old invasions by DARIUS and XERXES, and Alexander took his place as captain-general of the Greeks and carried out his father's plans. Macedonia, in later times, had wars with Rome, and finally became a Roman province (148 B.C.). It is now a part of Turkey in Europe.

McEN'TEE, Jervis, an American painter, born at Rondout. N. Y

July 14, 1828. He is especially noted for his pictures of autumn scenes, but of late has given much attention to figure painting. His studio is in New York.

MACHIAVELLI (*mah-ke-ah-vel'le*) **Niccolo,** a famous Italian statesman, born in Florence, May 3, 1469. At twenty-nine he began public life as secretary of the Florentine Republic, held that office fourteen years, and carried on during that time all state correspondence of importance. His skill in the conduct of public affairs caused him to be often employed as minister at foreign courts. He tried at one time to form a body of Italian militia, as he thought that the custom of hiring soldiers from abroad weakened the republic. His book on "The Art of War" was written to defend his views on the subject. But he is best known by "The Prince," a work in which he seeks to teach rulers how to gain and keep despotic powers. He wrote also a "History of Florence," and several comedies and poems. He died at Florence in his fifty-ninth year (June 22, 1527).

MACMAHON (*mak-mah-own'*), **Marie Edme Patrice Maurice,** Duke of Magenta, President of France, born near Autun in 1808. His ancestors were Irish, who went to France after the downfall of the Stuarts in England. He served with the French army in Algeria, distinguished himself in the Crimean war, and was made Duke of Magenta after the battle of MAGENTA, which was won through his bravery and skill (June 4, 1859). Afterward, he was Governor-General of Algeria. During the Franco-German war, he commanded a part of the French army, but was several times defeated, and finally compelled to surrender with the Emperor at SEDAN. When the rebellion of the Commune broke out in Paris, he commanded the government army, which finally conquered. On May 24, 1873, he was made President of

France, and held that office until 1879, when he resigned. He died near Orleans when eighty-five years old (October 17, 1893).

MACON (*mah-kong'*), a city of France, on the Saone, 37 miles N. of Lyons; pop. 18,000, or about as large as Sandusky, Ohio. It has manufactures of clocks and watches, earthenware, and velvet, and a large trade in Burgundy wine.

MACON (*ma'kun*), a city of Georgia, on the Ocmulgee River; pop. 23,000, or nearly as large as Malden, Mass. It is at the head of steamboat navigation, and has an important trade. There are large railroad workshops there, besides iron-foundries, and cotton and flour mills. The city was founded in 1823.

MACREADY (*ma-kre'de*), **William Charles,** an English actor, born in London, March 3, 1793. His first appearance on the stage was when he was seventeen years old, in Shakespeare's play of "Romeo and Juliet." From that time he steadily improved until he was considered the best actor of English tragedy. Twice he came to the United States, and each time had a great success. Once, when he was playing in New York (May 7, 1848), there was a riot in front of the theatre, made by the friends of Edwin Forrest, with whom Macready was on bad terms. The rioters said that Macready should not play, and attacked the theatre with stones. The military had to be called out, and many rioters were killed and wounded before they were driven away. Macready died in England, when eighty years old (April 29, 1873).

MAD-A-GAS'CAR, an island in the S.W. part of the Indian Ocean, 250 miles E. of Africa, from which it is separated by the Mozambique Channel; area, 230,000 square miles, or about a ninth smaller than Texas; pop. 5,000,000, or more than twice that of Texas. It is a long island and with chains of mountains running through it, but near the coasts there are plains and swampy forests, in which wild animals abound. The principal things grown are rice, tobacco, sugar, and indigo. A kind of lichen (C.C.T., 352, I. u.) is gathered and sold in large quanti-

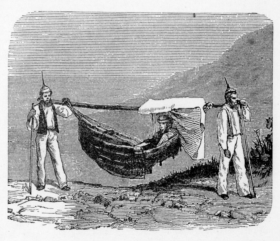

Hammock-riding in Madeira (page 504.)

ties for a dye, and india-rubber and ebony are found in the forests. Among the curious plants is the "travellers' tree," from which water can be obtained by gashing the stems. The climate is hot and unhealthy on the plains, but cool and pleasant among the mountains.

The people of Madagascar are divided into many tribes, those on the western side of the island being black, and much like the Austra-lians, while those on the eastern side are brown, like Malays. The most powerful tribe are the Hovas, who are ruled by a king or queen, and who call themselves Christians, though they still keep many of their savage customs. Many of them are slaves, and parents sometimes sell their children into slavery. France has had troubles with the Hovas, and considerable fighting has been done. The French now exercise a sort of protectorate over the country.

MADEIRA (*mah-da'e-rah*), an island in the Atlantic Ocean, 500 miles W. of Morocco, in Africa; area, including the small island of Porto Santo, near it, 317 square miles, or nearly a fourth as large as Rhode Island; pop. 134,000, or about two fifths that of Rhode Island; capital, Funchal (pop. 20,-000). It is very rocky and moun-tainous, and has many deep, narrow valleys, called *currales* or cattle-pens, which are celebrated for their wild scenery. The soil is very fer-tile, and every part that is not too rocky is cultivated. Formerly most of the ground was planted with grapevines, and the Madeira and Malmsey wines made there were cel-ebrated all over the world. In 1851, a disease killed nearly all of the vines, and since then sugar-cane and corn have been cultivated. But fresh vines have since been brought from CYPRUS, and a way has been found of curing the vine-disease, so that a good deal is now made again. The climate is very fine, and many con-sumptives go to Madeira for their health. The island belongs to Por-tugal, and most of the people are Portuguese. It was discovered in 1419 and called Madeira (Portuguese for " wood "), because it was cov-ered with forests.

MAD'I-SON, a city, capital of Wis-consin, in the S. part of the State, 75 miles W. of Milwaukee; pop. 13,-000, or about as large as Potts-town, Pa. It lies between two fine lakes, and the scenery around is very beautiful. The city has wide, regu-lar streets, and many fine buildings, among which are the State Capitol, Court House, Soldiers' Orphans' Home, and the State Insane Asy-lum. The University of Wisconsin has four buildings. Madison has several manufactories, and carries on a large trade with the surround-ing region. Madison was selected for the capital of Wisconsin in 1836, when the whole region was a wilder-ness. The capitol building was com-menced in 1837.

MAD'I-SON, James, fourth Presi-dent of the United States, born at King George, Va., March 16, 1751. He was the son of a wealthy plant-er, was graduated at Princeton College when about twenty, and then began to study law. He took a great interest also in theology, and became well known as a defender of the Baptists, and other religious societies, who were ill-treated because they would not join

James Madison.

the Established (Episcopal) Church. He thought every man had a right to his own religion, and did a great

deal to get freedom for the people
in these matters. In 1776 he became a member of the Virginia
Convention, and three years later
was a delegate to Congress. After
this he held a great many high
offices, doing his country good service in them all, until he was elected
President after Thomas Jefferson,
in 1809. He served for eight years,
and carried on the second war with
Great Britain till victory was won.
His goodness of heart and greatness
of mind made him everywhere loved
and respected. He died at his coun-
try-house, Montpelier, near Orange
Court House, Va., when eighty-four
years old (June 28, 1836).

MAD-RAS′, a city of S. India, on
the Bay of Bengal ; pop. 406,000, or
twice that of Milwaukee, Wis. It
was founded by the English in 1639,
and as the native kings have never
ruled there, it contains very few
Hindoo temples and palaces. In
their place are many fine buildings
like those of Europe, including three
cathedrals, several colleges, a museum, and an astronomical observatory. The principal streets are wide
and handsome, but those inhabited
by the natives are narrow and dirty.
Madras carries on a large trade,
though it has no harbor, and ships
are obliged to anchor two miles from
shore, the cargoes being landed
through the surf, in very light, flat-
bottomed boats, called *masulahs.*
Sometimes the surf is so high that
even these boats cannot be used, and
then fishermen go out on rafts made
of two or three light logs fastened
together.

Madras is the capital of a province
of the same name, which occupies
all the southern end of India.

MADRAZO (*mah-drah′zo*), **Federico de,** a Spanish painter, born in
Rome, Feb. 12, 1815. He paints
historical pictures and portraits, and
is the court painter at Madrid.

MADRAZO, Raimundo de, a Spanish painter, son of Federico de Madrazo, born in Madrid. He paints

landscapes and church interiors of
much merit. Some of them have
been brought to the United States.

MAD-RID′ (Spanish *mah-dreed′*),
the capital and chief city of Spain,
on the Manzanares River, nearly in
the centre of the kingdom ; pop.
472,000, or a little larger than St.
Louis, Mo. It stands in a sandy
plain or table-land, nearly half a mile
above the sea, with a beautiful background of snow-topped mountains
in the north ; and is surrounded by
a brick wall, outside of which is a
shady drive or boulevard, with many
beautiful gardens and parks. The
older streets are narrow, crooked,
and dirty, but the new ones are
wide, and straight, and bordered by
handsome houses and palaces. One
called the Alcalà is one of the widest
and finest streets in the world.
There are seventy public squares,
many of which are ornamented with
statues and fountains, and shaded
with trees. The most famous square
is the Puerto del Sol, or Gate of the
Sun, at one end of which is the
splendid Government Palace. The
Royal Palace is still more magnificent. It is built of granite and white
marble, and within it is splendidly
decorated with paintings. It contains a grand library, a large collection of coins, and a museum of armor in which are shown the armors
of Columbus, Cortes, and many
other noted persons. The National
Library is rich in valuable books,
and the National Museum has the
greatest collection in the world of
paintings by old masters. Madrid
is the centre of all the inland trade
of Spain, and the great fairs held
there every year draw thousands
of people from all parts.

Madrid gets its name from Ma-
gerit, the name given to it by the
Moors, who first built it, but its
meaning is not known. The Christians took it from the Moors in the
11th century, and it was made the
capital of Spain in 1560.

MÆCENAS (*me-se′nas*), **Caius**

Cilnius, a Roman statesman, born between 73 and 63 B.C. He was for many years the chief friend and adviser of the Emperor AUGUSTUS, but at last he lost favor with him and retired to his beautiful palace on one of the hills of Rome, where he spent the rest of his days. He was the friend of all poets and authors, and his house was the meeting-place of all the wits and literary men of the day. Both Horace and Virgil received kindnesses from him. He wrote a little himself; but his works have all been lost. He died in Rome in 8 B.C.

MAELSTROM (*mayl'strum*). See NORWAY.

MAESTRICHT (*mahs'trikt*), a city of the Netherlands on the River Maas; pop. 33,000, or a little larger than Yonkers, N. Y. It is one of the strongest fortresses in Europe, and the principal defence of the Netherlands. Parts of the country around it can be flooded with water. The city is built on a hill called Pietersberg, and underneath it are many thousand passages from which stone has been quarried. Some of these are as high as a house, and the ground pierced by them is thirteen miles long and six miles wide, and together they form such a tangled labyrinth that one who goes into them without a guide is very apt to be lost. Many curious fossils have been found in these passages, among them the bones of a great lizard called the monitor, which lived thousands of years ago.

Maestricht is called by the Dutch Maastricht, and means the pasture on the Maas. The people of Maestricht were among the first to drive out the Spanish soldiers of ALVA, but the Spaniards recaptured the city after a terrible siege, in which thousands of people were killed. In revenge for their losses, the Spaniards massacred 6000 of the inhabitants (1679).

MAGALHAENS (*mah-gahl-yah'-ens*), **Fernando,** commonly called in English Magellan, a Portuguese explorer, the first who crossed the Pacific Ocean, born in Oporto, about 1470. The pope having decided that all countries discovered west of the AZORES should belong to Spain, while all east of them should fall to the Portuguese, Magalhaens, who had already served in the Portuguese navy, went to Spain, and persuaded the Spanish rulers that he could reach the MOLUCCAS by sailing westward, and thus secure them for Spain. He set sail in 1519, with five vessels, went south, along the coast of South America, and passed through the strait called after him the Strait of Magellan. After sailing for three months over the Pacific, he discovered the LADRONE and PHILIPPINE Islands. Landing on the Island of Mactan, one of the Philippines, he was attacked by the natives and killed, when fifty-one years old (April 27, 1521). One of his ships, with eighteen men, finally reached Spain, it being the first ship that ever sailed round the world.

MAG'DE·BURG, a city of Germany, in Prussia, on the River Elbe, 76 miles S.W. of Berlin; pop. 160,000, or about as large as Louisville, Ky. It has a citadel on an island in the river, and many forts, so that it is one of the strongest places in Europe. The fortifications are so large that 100,000 men are needed to man them. Lafayette was imprisoned for a time in the citadel. Magdeburg has one of the finest Gothic cathedrals in Germany, built in the 13th century. It has many manufactures, and a very important trade. Magdeburg was a town in the time of CHARLES THE GREAT. During the THIRTY YEARS WAR it was taken by Tilly (1631), who burned most of the town and slaughtered 25,000 of the inhabitants.

MAGELLAN (*mah-jel'lan*). See MAGALHAENS.

MAGENTA (*ma-gen'tah*), a town of N. Italy, on the River Ticino, 15 miles W. of Milan, noted for a great battle fought there between the Austrians under Count Gyulai, and the united French and Sardinian armies under the Emperor Napoleon III., and King Victor Emanuel, June 4, 1859. A part of the Austrian army was in Magenta, and the French drove them out after a terrible fight in the streets and houses. In the night the Austrians retreated, and soon after they were driven out of Italy. The French General MAC-MAHON was made a marshal of France and Duke of Magenta after this battle.

MA·HOM'ET. See MOHAMMED.

MAINE (*mane*), one of the New England States of the United States, on the Atlantic Ocean ; area, 35,000 square miles, or about the same as that of South Carolina; pop. 661,000, or about four sevenths that of South Carolina ; capital, AUGUSTA. Most of the land is hilly, and in the northern part are mountains covered with forest, where bears, moose, and other wild animals are common ; but the southern part is well settled. Along the coast are many deep bays, and hundreds of rocky islands. All over the State are crooked little lakes, from which much ice is cut in winter and sent away.

There are fine quarries of granite, slate, and marble, and a great deal of lime is made from limestone rocks. In the southern part are many good farms, and all along the coast are fisheries, where more fish are caught than on the coast of any other State, except Massachusetts. The great forests give employment to hundreds of lumbermen, who go every winter to cut the trees and slip them over the snow to the river-banks ; there they are made into rafts, and floated down with the spring freshets to BANGOR and other places, where they are sawn into boards and sent to all parts of the United States. Owing to this fine supply of lumber and its many good harbors the coast of Maine is

a fine place for ship-yards, and more ships are made there than in any other State except New York. There are many other important manufactures, such as cotton and woollen goods, paper, and leather.

Maine belonged to MASSACHUSETTS until 1820, when it became a State of the Union.

MAINTENON (*mant-non'*), Françoise d'Aubigné, Marchioness de, born in the prison at Niort, where her father lay under a charge of treason, Nov. 27, 1635. She had great beauty, and at sixteen was married to the poet Scarron, who died eight years later, leaving her very poor. She came to court as governess, and soon won the favor of King Louis XIV., who gave her the title of marchioness and made her lady-in-waiting to the dauphin's wife. After the queen's death he secretly married her. When he died she entered the convent at St. Cyr, which she had founded, and died there at the age of eighty-four (April 15, 1719).

MAISTRE (*maitr*), Xavier, Count de, a noted writer, born in Chambéry, Savoy, in 1764. When he was quite young he entered the Sardinian army, but when that country was conquered by France he went to Russia, and gained his living as an artist. Afterward he joined the Russian army, and was made a major-general in a war against Persia. The latter part of his life he spent in St. Petersburg, writing books. His most popular works are "Voyage Around My Room" and "The Prisoners of the Caucasus." He died in St. Petersburg when eighty-eight years old (June 12, 1852).

MAJORCA (*mah-jor'kah*). See BALEARIC ISLANDS.

MAKART (*mah'kart*), Hans, a German painter, born at Salzburg, Austria, in 1840. The subjects of his pictures are often taken from history, or from the Greek and Latin poets. He has also painted portraits. A very large picture of his was shown at the Centennial Exhibition in 1876. He died when forty-four years old (October 3, 1884).

MALACCA (*ma-lak'kah*). See STRAITS SETTLEMENTS.

MALAGA (*mal'ah-gah*), a city of Spain, on the Mediterranean Sea; pop. 134,000, or about the same as that of Rochester, N. Y. It lies in a valley, with mountains on all sides, except toward the sea, and is surrounded by a wall with nine gates. On a high hill within is an old Moorish castle called Gibralfaro. Many streets are so narrow that wagons cannot pass through them. The houses are mostly large and well built, and there is a fine cathedral. Malaga has one of the best harbors on the Mediterranean Sea, and it is visited by hundreds of ships. The chief trade is in wine and raisins, many of the raisins being sent to the United States.

Malaga is a very ancient city, having been founded by the Phœnicians, who named it Malacca, from *malac*, salt, because it had a large trade in salt or salt fish. In the year 714 it was taken by the Moors, who kept it until 1487, when it was conquered by the Spaniards, under King Ferdinand, after a very long siege.

MALAY' PEN-IN'SULA, a peninsula S.W. of Siam, forming the S.E. end of Asia; area, 80,000 square miles, or about as large as Kansas; pop. supposed to be about 500,000. A range of high mountains runs through it, but on each side are plains covered with thick forests, in which the gutta-percha and other valuable trees are found. The most important mineral is tin. The people of the northern part are Siamese, but in the southern part live Malays, a dark-brown race, some of whom are civilized and settled, while others lead a wandering life, either on land or in boats on the water. The more civilized Malays are Mohammedans, but the wandering tribes are still pagans, and many of them are pirates. Most of the pen-

insula belongs to Siam, but the city of Malacca, and the islands of Penang and Singapore, near the southern end, belong to Great Britain.

MALDEN (*mawl'den*), a town of E. Massachusetts, on the Malden River, 5 miles N. of Boston; pop. 23,000, or about as large as Rockford, Ill.

It is noted for its manufactures, especially of india-rubber boots and shoes, enamelled leather, lasts, and trimmings for carriages. Malden is connected with Charlestown by a bridge nearly half a mile long.

MALIBRAN (*mah-le-brahn'*), Maria Felicita', a noted singer, born in Paris, Nov. 24, 1808. Her father, Señor Manuel Garcia, a Spaniard, was also a singer and a writer of music. Maria learned to sing and to speak Spanish and French at a very early age, and afterward studied Italian, German, and English. She practised singing so faithfully that she became *prima donna* (Italian for first lady or principal singer) of the Italian Opera in London when only seventeen years old (1825). The same year she came with her father to New York and sang in opera, this being the first time that Italian opera was ever performed in the United States. While in New York she married M. Malibran, a French merchant, but she soon left him and went back to Europe, where she won many triumphs in all the principal countries, and was looked upon as one of the greatest singers and actresses that ever lived. She died when only twenty-eight years old (Sept. 23, 1836), at Manchester, England.

MALPLAQUET (*mahl-plah-ka'*), a village of France, near the border of Belgium, noted for a battle which was fought there between the English and Germans, under the Duke of MARLBOROUGH and Prince EUGENE, and the French, commanded by Marshal Villars, Sept. 11, 1709. The Duke's soldiers began the attack, but were beaten back until Marshal Villars was wounded ; his generals could not resist the English charges, and the French at length retreated, after they had lost half of their soldiers. The loss of the English and Germans was also great, and this is said to have been the bloodiest of all Marlborough's victories.

MALTA (*mawl'tah*), an island in the Mediterranean Sea, 60 miles S. of Sicily ; area, 115 square miles, or about a twelfth as large as the State of Rhode Island ; pop. 164,000, or less than half that of Rhode Island ; capital, Valetta. There are several other islands near by which belong to Malta, and which have a few inhabitants. Malta is very rocky, and has no lakes, rivers, forests, nor shrubs. To make farms, the people have been obliged to bring earth from Sicily, yet by careful cultivation they raise fine crops, especially of cotton, in which Malta has a large trade. The chief manufactures are cotton cloth, furniture, and jewelry. The climate is very hot in summer, but delightful in winter, the air being so clear that at sunrise and sunset it is possible to see the top of Mt. Etna, 130 miles distant. The people are a dark race, most of them being descended from the Arabs. Their language is made up of Arabic, Italian, and many others, but the higher classes speak English. Malta belongs to Great Britain. The capital, Valetta, has 68,000 inhabitants, and is one of the strongest places in the world, many of the fortifications being cut out of solid rock. Malta gets its name from its ancient name Melita. From 1530 until 1798 it belonged to the Knights of St. John, who from this were also called Knights of Malta. Napoleon took it from them, and the English took it from the French in 1800.

MALTE-BRUN, (*mault-brun'*), a Danish geographer, born Aug. 12, 1775. His real name was Malthe Conrad Brun, but the French changed it. In 1800 he was banished, and went to live in Paris, where he published a great work on geography in sixteen volumes. He afterward wrote a still more important work, called "Universal Geography," which has been translated into English. In 1808, he began a French geographical magazine called *Annales des Voyages* (Annals of Voyages). Malte Brun died at Paris when fifty-one years old (Dec. 14, 1826).

Victor Adolphe Malte-Brun, his son, born in Paris in 1816, is now editor of the *Annales des Voyages*. He is also the author of many geographical works.

MAL'THUS, Thomas Robert, a noted English writer, born at Albany, Surrey, in 1766. The book by which he is best known is "An Essay on the Principles of Population," the leading idea of which is that most of the troubles in the world come from there being more people in it than can properly be supported. According to him war or any other scourge that tends to lessen the number of the world's inhabitants is a blessing. His views have been ably disputed by those acquainted with the subjects on which he writes. He died in Bath, when sixty-eight years old (December 29, 1834).

MAL'VERN HILL. See CHICKAHOMINY.

MAM'E-LUKES, a body of soldiers who ruled Egypt for several hundred years. The name Mameluke is taken from an Arab word meaning slave, and these men were so called because they were at first made up of young captives. In the middle of the thirteenth century they were introduced into Egypt. They formed the body guard of the Sultan until the accession of Turan Shah, who was so much hated by them that they murdered him and made one of themselves sultan. For nearly three hundred years they kept that office in their own body, and even when they were forced to give it up they still had a great deal of power. The Mamelukes were very fine cavalry soldiers. When Napoleon saw their manœuvres in a battle which he fought with them, called the battle of the Pyramids (1798) he said that he could have made himself master of the world, if he could have had in his army the Mameluke cavalry and the French infantry. In 1811, nearly all the Mamelukes were massacred by Mehemet Ali, Viceroy of Egypt. A few escaped to Nubia, but these were destroyed in 1820.

MAM'MOTH CAVE, a cavern of Kentucky, near Green River, about 75 miles S.S.W. of Louisville. It is the largest cave known in the world, being eleven miles long, and having more than one hundred and fifty miles of rooms and passages. Some of the rooms are as large as the largest buildings in the world. One, called Lucy's Dome, is higher than Trinity Church steeple in New York

View in Mammoth Cave.

(285 feet) and very wide. Another, called the Temple is nearly as high, and covers four or five acres. Cleveland's Cabinet is a passage two miles long, wider than any common street, and nearly as high as two men, and the walls and sides are covered with beautiful stalactites, which sparkle in the torch-light like diamonds. The Star Chamber is a very large and beautiful room ; its roof is covered with black gypsum, studded with numberless white points, which look like stars. In other places are stalactites like statues, celery plants, Corinthian columns, or cream candy. There are many pits ; one called the Maelstrom and another the Bottomless Pit are each as deep as the height of a common church steeple. The cave contains several streams and ponds, the waters of which rise and fall with those of Green River, showing that they are connected by underground channels. The River Styx, which is

quite deep, has over it a high natural bridge of rock. Echo River is three-quarters of a mile long, and in some places two hundred feet wide. Lake Lethe and the Dead Sea are two large ponds. Fish and crawfish without eyes are found in the streams, and there are blind insects in the cave. Mammoth Cave was discovered in 1809.

MAN, Isle of, an island of Great Britain, in the middle of the Irish Sea ; area 227 square miles, or nearly a sixth as large as Rhode Island ; pop. 54,000, or about a sixth that of Rhode Island. It is high and rocky, and is noted for fine scenery. Lead is largely mined, and zinc, copper, and iron are found. The soil is good, but farming is not well attended to. There is a peculiar breed of cats on the island, which have no tails. The people, who are much like the Irish, still speak in some parts a language called Manx, though English is generally understood.

MAN-AS'SAS. See BULL RUN.

MAN'CHES-TER, a town of S.W. England, on the River Irwell, 31 miles E. by N. of Liverpool ; pop. 379,000, or about one fourth that of New York. It is the greatest manufacturing town in England, having more than two thousand factories, in which over seventy thousand people are employed. The most important are the cotton factories, in which more cotton cloths are made than in any other place in the world. Besides these, there are silk and worsted factories, hundreds of clothing factories, glass works, chemical works, paper-mills, and immense iron works. The city has many handsome buildings and parks, and several colleges. Water is obtained from great water-works connected with ten artificial lakes.

Manchester was called by the Saxons Mamcestre, meaning the " camp of the place or district," and from this has come its present name. Cloth was manufactured there in the 14th century.

MANCHESTER, a city of S. New Hampshire, on the Merrimack River ; pop. 44,000, or about as large as Salt Lake City, Utah. It is the largest city in the State, and one of the greatest manufacturing towns of New England. Water-power is furnished by the Amoskeag Falls of the Merrimack, which are forty-seven feet high, with rapids above them. Manchester is especially noted for its great cotton and woollen mills, but there are also manufactories of linen, cloth, paper, boots and shoes, stockings, locomotives, and machinery. Manchester was settled about 1730, but until 1810 it was called Derryfield.

MANCHOORIA. See MANT-CHOORIA.

MAN'CO CA'PAC, the fabled founder of the Empire of Peru, and the first of its Incas. He is said to have appeared with Mama Oello, his sister, on an island in Lake TITICACA. He taught the Peruvians to worship the sun, of which he said that he and his sister were the children, and instructed them in civilization and the arts. He founded the city of CUZCO, and after a long and happy reign, left his throne to his descendants, who ruled as Incas when the Spaniards came.

MANCO CAPAC, Inca of Peru. He was placed on the throne of Peru by Pizarro, in 1534 ; but finding that Pizarro would not let him have any power, he escaped and rousing the people to arms laid siege to CUZCO. But after five months, he had to draw off his troops. Most of his followers left him, and he fled with a few to the Andes. They became the terror of the Spaniards, surprising and attacking them whenever they could ; but at last he was killed by a party of Spanish soldiers in 1544.

MANDELAY, (*mahn-da-li'*), a city, capital of Burmah, near the Irrawaddy River ; pop. 150,000, or twice as large as Scranton, Pa. The old capital, called Amarapura, is a little farther south, but in 1856, the king made up his mind to have a new capital, and by his order Mandelay was built in a single year. It is divided into three parts, one within the other, and separated by strong walls. The king's palace and gardens and the chief government buildings are in the centre. The second part contains the houses of chief officers and barracks for the soldiers, and outside of all are the houses and shops of the common people. Some of the palaces and temples are very fine, but the poorer houses are mere huts.

MAN'DE-VILLE, Sir John, a noted English traveller, born at St. Albans about 1300. In 1327 he travelled to the East, visited the Holy Land, Egypt, Armenia, Persia, India, and Tartary, and returned to England in 1355. He wrote his travels in Latin, French, and English, and dedicated his work to Edward III. His book is full of wonderful stories, many of which were taken from other books. It is the first book known to have been written in English prose. He died when about seventy at Liége (November 17, 1372).

MAN'E-THO, an Egyptian highpriest and historian, who lived in the 3d century B.C. He wrote in Greek a work on the religion and history of Egypt and a poem on the influence of the stars. The materials for the work on Egypt were taken from the sacred records in the temple at Heliopolis. Recent discoveries made by travellers in Egypt prove the correctness of many of his dates.

MAN'FRED, Prince of Tarentum, King of the Two Sicilies, born in Sicily about 1233. He was the son of the Emperor Frederick II., and on the death of his father became regent in Italy during the absence of his brother Conrad IV., who, dying shortly afterward, left him still in the place of regent for his infant son Conradin. Manfred and Conradin

were of the Hohenstaufen blood, a race hated by the Popes, and Urban IV. determined to deprive them of their inheritance. So he excommunicated Manfred, and offered Naples and Sicily to Charles of Anjou, brother of Louis IX., of France under condition that he should conquer that kingdom and pay a yearly tribute to the Popes. Charles invaded the kingdom at the head of a large force, and defeated Manfred, who was killed in a battle near Beneventum. He died when thirty-three years old (February 26, 1266).

MANILA (*mah-ne'lah*), the capital of the PHILIPPINE ISLANDS, on the Island of Luzon; pop. 182,000, or about as large as Newark, N. J. Manila is surrounded by walls. The streets are wide and straight, and the houses are very strongly built, to protect them against earthquakes and hurricanes, which are very frequent there. The city has been often damaged by earthquakes, and in 1880 (July 18) was almost entirely destroyed by one, all the large buildings being thrown down. Many of the native houses are built of bamboo. Manila has a large trade, especially in sugar, tobacco, cigars, coffee, copper, indigo, and Manila hemp. The tobacco and cigars are prepared in large government factories, which employ 20,-000 workers. About one-tenth of the people of Manila are Spanish whites, the rest being natives or Chinese.

Manila was founded by the Spaniards in 1571, on the site of a native town.

MANITOBA (*man-i-to'bah*). See CANADA.

MAN'LI-US CAP-I-TO-LI'NUS, Marcus, Consul of Rome in 392 B.C. He was given the name of Capitolinus for saving the capitol from the Gauls under BRENNUS, having been awakened by the cackling of the sacred geese just as the Gauls had nearly reached the top of the Tarpeian Rock, on which the capitol stood. He was afterward condemned for exciting the common people to revolt, and put to death by being thrown from the Tarpeian Rock, (381 B.C.)

MANNHEIM, or **Manheim** (*mahn' hime*), a city of Germany, in Baden, on the Rhine, where it joins the Neckar; pop. 61,000, or about as large as Dayton, Ohio. It is built on low ground, and has a dike to keep out the waters of the rivers when they are high, but it is a very neat place and was called by GOETHE " the pleasant, cleanly Mannheim." Its palace is one of the largest in Germany, and has a broad avenue leading from it to the suspension bridge across the Neckar. Schiller lived for a time in Mannheim, and his play of " The Robbers" was first performed there in the theatre. Mannheim was first built in 1606.

MANTCHOORIA (*mant-choo're-ah*), a country of Asia, forming part of the Empire of China, east of MONGOLIA. A large part of it is a wilderness, and most of it is drained by the Amoor River. It is inhabited by the Mantchoos, a branch of the Mongols, who belong to the Turanian class of mankind. In 1644 the Mantchoos conquered China, and since that time they have ruled it. The Chinese custom of wearing the hair in a tail was introduced by the Mantchoos.

MANTINEA (*man-ti-ne'ah*), a city of Ancient Greece, in Arcadia, near the borders of Argolis. It was a republic, like Sparta, and, at different times was an ally of that city; but the Spartans, growing jealous of Mantinea, attacked it, and broke down its walls and houses by turning the waters of the River Ophis against them. The city was rebuilt, and the people became allies of the Thebans, but soon left them to join the Spartans again. A Theban army, under EPAMINONDAS, was sent to subdue them, and in a battle fought at Mantinea, the Thebans were victorious over the Spartans

and Mantineans, but Epaminondas was killed (362 B.C.) The ruins of Mantinea can still be seen.

MANTUA (*man'tu-ah*), a city of N. Italy, on an island in the Mincio River; pop. 28,000, or about as large as Waterbury, Conn. It is defended by strong walls and forts, and until lately was surrounded by marshes, which made it almost impossible for an enemy to take it; but most of the marshes are now drained. The chief trade of Mantua is in silk.

Mantua is a very old city, having been founded 400 years before Rome was built. It is celebrated as the birth-place of Virgil. It belonged to Austria for a long time, but in 1866 became a city of the new Kingdom of Italy.

MAN'U-EL I., Comnenus, a Byzantine Emperor, born about 1120. He was the son of John II., who made him his heir rather than his older brother, on account of the valor shown by him in fighting the Turks. He was a brave soldier, and spent most of his life in war against the Dacians, Hungarians, and Turks. His most important wars, however, were against Roger, King of Sicily, and Raymond, Prince of Antioch. He died, when sixty years old, (September 24, 1180).

MANUEL II., Palæologus, a Byzantine emperor, born in 1348. He was the son of John V., and at the time of his father's death, he fled to Constantinople from the court of the Sultan Bajazet, where he had been left as a hostage by Sigismund, King of Hungary. Bajazet made war upon him, defeated him at Nicopolis, and laid siege to Constantinople, whose last hour seemed now to have come. But Bajazet was obliged to return to his own dominions, to defend them against TIMOUR, and thus Constantinople was saved for a while. Manuel died when seventy-seven years old (July 21, 1425).

MARACAYBO (*mah-rah-ki'bo*), a city of N.W. Venezuela, on the outlet of Lake Maracaybo; pop. 32,000, or about as large as Lancaster, Pa. It has a fine harbor, defended by three forts; but only small vessels can ascend to the city. A large trade is carried on in cacao, cotton, sugar, dye-woods, and coffee, and many ships are built at the city. Near Maracaybo immense herds of cattle are pastured. Maracaybo was named after an Indian chief, who once lived near the lake. It was founded in 1571.

Lake Maracaybo is 100 miles long and 75 wide and is connected with the sea by a channel 45 miles long. Hundreds of small streams empty into it, keeping the water fresh, except when the wind blows from the sea; then the salt water comes in, making the lake water brackish. On the N. E. shore is a bed of mineral pitch; the sailors call this the lighthouse of Maracaybo, because on hot nights it shines with a bright phosphorescent light, like lightning.

MARAT (*ma-rah'*) **Jean Paul,** a French revolutionist, born near Neufchatel, Switzerland, May 24, 1744. He studied medicine, did not succeed well as a doctor, and at the age of twenty-eight went to Edinburgh, where he earned his bread as a private tutor. In 1779 he went back to Paris, and for some years wrote works on science, intended to show that the theories of Newton were false. Meeting no greater success in this than he had in medicine, he became horse-doctor to the Count of Artois, afterward Charles X. When the Revolution broke out, he wrote articles and pamphlets which excited the fury of the people and caused an order for his arrest, but he escaped by hiding himself. With Robespierre and Danton he ruled France during the worst days of the Reign of Terror. He was stabbed, at Paris, in his fiftieth year, by Charlotte Corday, just as he was making out a long list of others whom he meant to put to death (July 13, ˜793).

MAR'A-THON, a town of ancient Greece, 18 miles N.E. of Athens. It is celebrated for the great battle fought there between the Greeks under MILTIADES, and the Persians under Datis and Artaphernes. Most of the Greeks were from Athens, and they had ten generals, each of whom had a right to command for one day; but they all gave up their places to Miltiades. The Persian army was ten times as large as his, but the Greeks attacked it so bravely that, after a short battle, the Persians fled in dismay to their ships. A pile of stones still marks the burial-place of 192 Greeks who were killed in the fight. Had the Persians won this battle, Greece would have become a Persian province, and probably the fate of Europe, and of the world, would have been changed.

MAR-CEL'LUS, Marcus Claudius, a noted Roman soldier, born about 268 B.C. He became a skilful soldier when quite young, and fought against both the Carthaginians and the Gauls. Having won much fame by killing the leader of the Gauls with his own hands, he was chosen, after the battle of CANNÆ, to lead the army against HANNIBAL in Italy, and gained three small victories over his troops. He was then sent to Sicily, where he laid siege to SYRACUSE by sea and land. This was one of the most famous sieges of ancient times. For nearly three years he was kept from taking the city by the skill of ARCHIMEDES, who destroyed his ships and the great machines which he built to batter down the walls; but at last he won it, and stripped the temples and other public buildings of all their paintings and statues and carried them to Rome. This is said to have been the first time that any Roman general ever carried off such things from a captured city. After his return to Italy Marcellus again fought against Hannibal, and was at last killed while away from his camp with a few soldiers (208 B.C.).

Hannibal gave his body a magnificent funeral, and sent his ashes in a silver urn to his son.

MAR'CO PO'LO. See POLO, MARCO.

MAR'CUS AU·RE'LI·US. See ANTONINUS.

MAR·DO'NI·US, a famous Persian general, son-in-law of King DARIUS. He commanded for Darius the first army and fleet that invaded Greece, and it was by his advice that XERXES, who was his cousin, invaded Greece with a still larger army and fleet. After the Persians had been defeated at SALAMIS, Mardonius was left in Greece in command of the army. He took Athens and kept it for several months, but was at length defeated and killed by the Greeks under PAUSANIAS at PLATÆA (479 B.C.)

MARENGO (*mah-ren'go*), a village of N. W. Italy, on a plain by the River Bormida, famous for a great victory won by Napoleon over an Austrian army under General Melas June 14, 1800. Napoleon had crossed the Alps, and a part of his soldiers under General Victor had taken Marengo, when Melas attacked them. At first the French were driven back, but as soon as Napoleon and the rest of his army arrived, the battle changed and the Austrians suffered a terrible defeat. The battle was a very bloody one. The French General Lannes said, " I could hear the bones crack like hailstones against a window." Among the killed was General DESAIX.

MAR'GA·RET, Queen and patron saint of Scotland, born in Hungary, in 1046. Her father was the son of Edmund Ironsides, but fled to Hungary from CANUTE, and married a daughter of the Emperor Henry II. His children, Margaret, Edgar Atheling, and Christina, were brought to England by Edward the Confessor, who wished Edgar to succeed him on the throne. But when William the Conqueror invaded England, they fled into Scotland, where Margaret married King Malcolm, the son of that Duncan who was murdered by Macbeth. She was the mother of nine children, three of whom were kings of Scotland and one a queen of England. She was a good wife, a good mother, and a good ruler. In 1093 her husband and one of her sons were slain in battle, and Margaret lived only four days after hearing the news. She died at Edinburgh in her forty-seventh year, (November 17, 1093).

MARIA THERESA (*ma·ri'ah te·re'sah*), Queen of Hungary and Bohemia and Empress of Germany, born in Vienna, May 13, 1717. She was the daughter of the Emperor Charles VI., and succeeded him in the dominions he had inherited in 1740. Her husband, Francis I., was elected Emperor of Germany, so that she is often called the Empress Queen. Few names in history shine with a brighter fame than that of this sovereign, who will always occupy a high place among the world's most illustrious women. No sooner had she ascended the throne, on her father's death, than her neighbors, Frederick the Great of Prussia, and Charles, Elector of Bavaria, formed a league to rob her of a great part of her territory, and sent large armies against her. The spirited young queen, then only twenty-three years old, bravely turned upon her foes, appealing to her brave Hungarians for support. She appeared in the Hungarian Diet with the crown on her head, the sword of state by her side, and holding her infant son in her arms. In a Latin speech she threw herself on the Hungarian nobility and roused them to such a pitch of enthusiasm that the vast assembly shouted, as their swords leaped from their scabbards, " Let us die for our king, Maria Theresa." They defended her so successfully that she kept all her territory except Silesia, which she had to give up to Frederick. This was called the War of the

Austrian Succession. She never ceased to grieve for the loss of Silesia, and she took part in the SEVEN YEARS WAR against Frederick in the hope of getting it back. When the war ended, however, Frederick still kept Silesia.

Maria Theresa.

When her husband Francis I., was elected Emperor of Germany, he left the control of everything to her. She did many wise things, and in everything the good of her subjects was her first care. Her court was a great contrast to the wicked courts which disgraced most other European rulers of her time. On the death of her husband, she admitted her eldest son, Joseph, to share her throne. It was during her life that the treaty was made dividing Poland. She was very unwilling to have anything to do with it, and at first refused to sign it until she was told that Poland would be divided even without her consent, and that her refusal would lead to

war. On the edge of the copy given her to sign, she wrote '' *Placet*,'' (I consent) '' because so many great and learned men will have it so, but after I am dead and gone people will see the consequences of thus breaking through all that has hitherto been held holy and just. M. Th.'' This noble woman died in Vienna, when sixty-three years old (November 29, 1780), and was succeeded by her son Joseph II.

MARIE ANTOINETTE (*mah-ré on-twah-net'*), Queen of France, wife of LOUIS XVI., born in Vienna, November 2, 1755. She was the daughter of Francis I., Emperor of Germany and Maria Theresa, and was married in her fifteenth year to Louis XVI. She had been brought up in the freedom which marked the family circle of her imperial parents, and there was little sympathy between her and the stately court dames in Paris ; and as years went on she was still more disliked, in spite of her great beauty and winning manners. The people called her spitefully '' The Austrian,'' gave wrong explanations to her most innocent actions, and blamed her for all their miseries. When it was shown that more money had been spent by the government than had been received, the ignorant charged this upon her, and called her '' Madame Deficit.''

After the Revolution began, Marie Antoinette was in favor of putting it down by force ; but she could not give her brave spirit to her husband. During the attacks made on the royal family she showed herself a true daughter of MARIA THERESA. Once when the mob stood without the palace at Versailles (October 5, 1789) clamoring for '' The Austrian,'' she came out on the balcony, leading her daughter by one hand and her son by the other. '' No children !'' was the cry. She sent back the children and calmly stood looking at the angry multitude before her, a mark for a thousand muskets. One only was raised.

Her courage, for a moment, sent a thrill of admiration over the vast throng, and instead of the shot of musketry was heard the cry of " *Vive la Reine* " (Long Live the Queen). The following June the royal family left Paris disguised, the queen as a governess, the king as a valet. The king was recognized by a postmaster's son from his likeness to his head on the coins, and the whole party, amid the jeers of the lowest of the people, were taken back to Paris. That night it is said changed Marie Antoinette's beautiful gold locks to the snow-white curls which she cut with her own hand the morning of her execution. Nine months after the king's death, she was brought to trial before the Convention, found guilty of being an enemy of France, and condemned

Marie Antoinette.

to death. She sewed her own white robe, and wrote a sweet letter of farewell to her children and sister. The next morning she was dragged to the place of execution on a hurdle amid cries of *Vive la République"* (Long live the Republic). She

showed no anger, but stepped with firmness on the scaffold and met her doom. She died, when forty-one years old (October 16, 1793). She left one son, the dauphin, called Louis XVII., who shortly followed her, and a daughter who became the Duchess of Angouléme, and whose face from the day of her mother's death never knew a smile.

MARIETTA (*ma-re-et'tah*), a city of S. Ohio, on the Ohio, at the mouth of the Muskingum River; pop. 8,000. It is built on the site of a group of ancient works built by the " mound-builders," the walls of which can still be seen in some places. The city contains several iron foundries and has a large trade in petroleum. It is the site of Marietta College.

Marietta is the oldest town in the State of Ohio, having been settled in 1788. It was named after Queen Marie Antoinette of France.

MAR'I-ON, Francis, a noted American general, born near Georgetown, S. C., in 1732. He was a daring and useful officer in the Revolution, sometimes fighting with the army, sometimes with bands of patriotic farmers and backwoodsmen on horseback, dashing through the country, surprising the enemy at two or more different points in the same day, suddenly appearing to storm a fort, waylay a troop of soldiers, set free the prisoners they had taken, cut off their supplies, seize their ammunition and arms, then vanishing as suddenly. The British were in constant dread of " the Swamp Fox," as they called him. Marion and his men lived in the swamps and forests, and had little food or clothing. A British officer, sent to ask an exchange of prisoners, was led blindfolded into Marion's camp at Snow Island. Marion invited him to dinner, and the officer was surprised to find that the meal consisted wholly of sweet potatoes roasted in the ashes, and a drink made of vinegar and water.

He was still more astonished to hear that this was a feast, as they had usually corn only. After the Revolution, Marion filled important positions in South Carolina. He died when sixty-three years old (February 28, 1795).

MA'RI-US, Caius, a famous Roman soldier, born near Arpinum, in 157 B.C. He was of humble birth, but won fame and rank as a soldier, and when about thirty-three years old married Julia, aunt of Julius CÆSAR, who belonged to one of the best families in Rome. In the war against JUGURTHA he was at first second in command under METELLUS, but had a quarrel with him, got himself elected Consul (107) and his successor, and defeated Jugurtha, who was taken prisoner the next year by SULLA. Sulla then claimed that he had ended the war, and this began a quarrel between him and Marius.

When Marius was Consul the fourth time Gaul was invaded by a host of barbarians called Cimbri and Teutons, but he defeated the Teutons in a great battle in Gaul (102) and the next year he overthrew the Cimbri, who had gone into Italy. For these great services he was ranked with ROMULUS and CAMILLUS and given the title of the third founder of Rome, and was again chosen Consul.

In the year 90 B.C. began a war called the Social War, because it was with the Socii or allies of Rome living in Italy. In this struggle, which ended by most of the allies becoming Roman citizens, Sulla won more fame than Marius, and when the war with MITHRIDATES broke out he was given command of the Roman army (88 B.C.) ; but while Sulla was away fighting Mithridates, Marius got a law passed taking it from Sulla and giving it to him. Sulla came back and with his friends drove Marius from Rome, and he set sail for Africa ; but being forced by bad weather to land in Italy, was taken by his pursuers and put into prison. A soldier was sent to cut off his head, but when the old man asked him if he dared to kill Caius Marius, the sword dropped from his hand. When the people of the town heard this, they rose in his favor and set him free. He went to Africa, landing near Carthage. The Roman governor sent him word to leave or he would treat him as an enemy. "Go tell him," said Marius to the messenger, "that you have seen Caius Marius sitting on the ruins of Carthage," meaning by this to compare his own fate with that of the unfortunate city.

Soon after this Marius heard that CINNA had taken his part in Rome. He went to Italy, marched with Cinna into Rome like a conqueror, and took a dreadful revenge on his enemies. Thousands of noble Romans were slaughtered, and the streets ran with blood. Marius and Cinna made themselves Consuls, this being the seventh time Marius had held this high office, but worn out with care and old age, Marius died a few days afterward, when sixty-nine years old (86 B.C.).

MARK ANTONY. See ANTONY, MARK.

MARLBOROUGH (*mawl'b'ro*), **John Churchill,** Duke of, a famous British general, born at Ashe, Devonshire, June 24, 1650. He was at first a page in the household of the Duke of York, afterward James II., but when William of Orange came to the throne, Churchill offered his sword to him. As a reward for this he was made Earl of Marlborough. But William never trusted him, and at one time put him into prison, on account of some papers which were found by which it seemed that he was trying to bring back King James. When Anne became queen, England joined Austria in a war against France called the War of the Spanish Succession. Marlborough was put at the head of the allied armies and from this time for ten years his life was one course of

victory. After his first great triumph at Blenheim, the queen made
him a duke, and gave him the manor
of Woodstock, and built for him a
palace, calling it BLENHEIM. He won
other great victories at Ramilies, Oudenarde, and Malplaquet. His wife
was the famous Sarah Jennings, a
beautiful but high-tempered woman,
who for several years had great power
over the queen. At last she became
so haughty that Anne could stand

Duke of Marlborough.

her no longer, so she sent her away
from court and at the same time removed Marlborough from the army.
When Anne died, Marlborough got
back his place and honors. He was
a soldier by nature and owed his victories to his genius, but his character was stained by avarice and
treachery. He died in London,
when seventy-two years old (June
16, 1722).

MAR'LITT, E., a German novelist, who writes under this name,
born in Thuringia, December 5,
1825. Her real name is Eugénie
Johns. Her fine voice caused her to
be adopted by a German princess
and educated for the stage. Becoming suddenly deaf, she was
obliged to leave the stage, and she
then began to write novels. Many
of her books have been translated
into English. Some of them are

"Gold Elsie," "Old Mamselle's
Secret," "Countess Gisela," and
"The Princess of the Moor."

MARLOWE (*mar'lo*), **Christopher,**
a famous English writer of plays,
born at Canterbury, in 1564. His
father was a shoemaker, but he sent
his son to a good school and afterward to the University of Cambridge. His principal plays are
"Tamburlaine," "Dr. Faustus,"
and "Edward II." Some think he
helped Shakespeare in writing parts
of "Henry VI." He was killed in
a street quarrel at Deptford, when
only twenty-nine years old (June 16,
1593).

MARMONT (*mar-mon'*), **Auguste
Frederic Louis Viesse de,** Duke of Ragusa, a noted French general, born
at Chatillon-sur-Seine, July 20, 1774.
He entered the army when only fifteen years old, and served bravely
under Bonaparte in Italy and in
Egypt. When Napoleon crossed
the Alps (1800), it was principally
through Marmont's aid that the artillery was got over the mountains.
Napoleon made him Duke of Ragusa
and Marshal of the Empire. For a
long time he was the most successful of Napoleon's generals, but was
defeated in Spain by Wellington.
When the allied armies took Paris
(1814), he agreed to give up Napoleon and obey the new government
which had been formed, and he afterward took service under the BOUR-
BONS, who loaded him with honors.
In 1830 he was recalled from his
country seat to put down a revolt of
the people against CHARLES X.; but
being unsuccessful, he was obliged
to go with the Bourbons into exile.
His name was struck from the rolls
of the army and he was banished
from the country. He died in Venice, the last of the Marshals of the
first French Empire, when seventy-
seven years old (February 28, 1852).

MARMORA (*mar'mo-rah*), **Sea
of,** a small sea between Europe and
Asia, connected with the Black Sea
by the Bosporus and with the

Archipelago by the DARDANELLES. The ancients called it the Propontis. It gets its modern name from the island of Marmora in it, which is famous for its marble (Latin, *marmor*).

MARQUESAS (*mar-ka'sahs*), **ISLANDS,** a group of 13 small islands in the Pacific Ocean, N.E. of the Society Islands ; area, 480 square miles, or a third as large as Rhode Island ; pop. about 5,000, or one fourth that of the city of Newport, R. I. They are very rocky, each island being a mountain ridge about half a mile high. Yams, cocoanuts, bread-fruits, and other plants and fruits of hot climates grow luxuriantly, almost without cultivation. Most of the people are savages, who worship idols and sometimes eat human flesh. Their only clothing is the bark of the mulberry tree, which is made into a kind of coarse paperlike cloth by beating between two stones. Both sexes tattoo themselves. The women are allowed to have several husbands. Wars between the tribes are very frequent.

The Marquesas were discovered in 1595 by the Spaniard Mendaña de Neyra, who named them Las Marquesas de Mendoza in honor of the Marquis of Mendoza, then Viceroy of Peru. They are sometimes called the Mendaña Archipelago, after their discoverer. Since 1842 the islands have belonged to France.

MARQUETTE (*mar-ket'*), **Jacques,** a noted French explorer, born at Laon in 1637. He was a Jesuit missionary and travelled and preached among the Indians several years in Canada. In 1673 he started from Mackinaw, on Lake Michigan, with Louis JOLIET and five other Frenchmen, in two canoes, went down Green Bay and Fox River, then carried their canoes across the land to the Wisconsin River, floated down that stream to the Mississippi, and down the Mississippi nearly to its mouth, voyaging 2,500 miles in open canoes and suffering greatly. These

were probably the first Europeans who saw the Mississippi after DE SOTO. While on a mission to some Indians Marquette died, when thirty-eight years old (May 18, 1675), on the banks of a river on the east side of Lake Michigan which now bears his name.

MAR'RY-AT, Frederick, a British naval officer and writer of novels, born in London, July 10, 1792. He became a midshipman when fourteen years old, and served for many years, fighting in more than fifty battles. When he became captain of a ship, he began to write novels, mostly sea-stories, in which many of his own adventures are told. Among these are "Frank Mildmay," "Midshipman Easy," "The Phantom Ship," "Masterman Ready," "Settlers in Canada," and "The Little Savage." They were once very popular, but are not now read much. Marryat died when fifty-six years old (August 2, 1848).

MARS, the Roman god of war, son of Jupiter and Juno. The Greeks called him Ares. He delighted in war and strife, and presided over wild, fierce warfare. He was of huge size and great strength, and it is said that he could roar as loud as nine or ten thousand men. The Romans looked upon him as the founder and protector of their nation. He is represented as a warrior in full armor, bearing a shield and spear.

Mars.

MARSEILLES (*mar-sailz'*), the principal seaport city of France, on a bay of the Mediterranean ; pop. 376,000, or about one fourth that of New York. It has several fine harbors, crowded with ships from all parts of the world, but especially from other cities on the

Mediterranean. The wharves are made lively and picturesque by ships loading and unloading, with sailors of twenty nations passing by. The country around is very beautiful, being planted with vineyards and olive-gardens, among which are hundreds of fine country houses.

Marseilles gets its name from its ancient name of Massilia, given it by the Greeks, who first built the city about 600 B.C It was at one time the rival of Carthage, with which it carried on war, and was afterward the ally of Rome.

MARSH, Othniel Charles, an American writer on natural history, born in Lockport, N. Y., October 29, 1831. In 1866 he became a professor in Yale College, and with his students he has made many excursions to the unexplored regions near the Rocky Mountains, and gathered large collections of the bones of strange animals which once lived in that region. Among them are birds with teeth, lizards with wings, horses with several toes, and animals with six horns. These collections are now in the museum of Yale College, and Prof. Marsh has published descriptions and drawings of many of them.

MAR'SHALL, John, Chief-Justice of the United States, born in Fauquier County, Va., September 24, 1755. He was in the American army during the Revolution, but at the close of the war became a lawyer, and was several times elected to the Legislature of Virginia. In 1788, he was a leading member of the Virginia Convention, which voted to accept the Constitution of the United States. In 1797, he was appointed Minister to France, where he did so well that on his return he was received with very high honors. In 1799 he was elected to the United States Congress, where he made many eloquent speeches. A year after, he was made Secretary of State, and on January 31, 1801, he was chosen Chief-Justice of the

United States. He died in Philadelphia, when nearly eighty years old (July 6, 1835).

MARS'TON MOOR, a plain of N. England, 8 miles N.W. of York, famous for a victory won by the army of the Parliament under Lord Fairfax and the Earl of Leven, over a Royalist army under Prince RUPERT, July 2, 1644. At first Prince Rupert was so successful that a large part of the Parliamentary army was routed ; and Fairfax and Leven, thinking that all was lost, fled as fast as they could. But while the Royalists were scattered over the field, searching for plunder, the Parliamentary generals gathered their remaining soldiers and attacked their enemies so fiercely that they won a great victory.

MAR-TEL',Charles. See CHARLES MARTEL.

MAR'THA'S VINEYARD (*vin' yard*), an island off the S. coast of Massachusetts, separated from the mainland by Vineyard Sound ; pop. about 4,000. It is mostly level and much of it is covered with low forests. Most of the people are fishermen and sailors. The principal town is Edgartown, at the east end. Near this is Wesleyan Grove, where the Methodists hold a great camp-meeting every August, which is visited by 20,000 people. The village of Oak Bluffs has been laid out near it, and has several hotels and many cottages for summer visitors.

Martha's Vineyard was settled in 1642 by the English, and became a part of Massachusetts in 1692.

MARTIN, the name of five popes, of which Martin V., born in 1365, was the most important. He did much for learning and art in Italy. He was pope from 1417 to 1431, when he died.

MAR'TIN, Homer Dodge, an American painter, born in Albany, N. Y., October 28, 1836. He began to draw and paint in his earliest childhood, and with the exception of two weeks spent in the studio of

James M. HART, he has been entirely self-taught. He confines all his endeavors to landscape painting.

MARTINEAU (*mar'te-no*), Harriet, a noted English author, born in Norwich, June 12, 1802. She was a shy, deaf little girl, and very apt to think that the people she met did not understand her. So she took to reading books and writing stories, at first only to amuse herself, but later because she found herself obliged to earn her living and that of others. Her first work, a prayer-book for young folks, was published when she was twenty-one. For many years she wrote a great deal, chiefly tales and tracts intended to teach people how to save money, how to spend it wisely, and how to keep themselves in health and comfort. She visited the United States when she was thirty-two years old, and spent two years, afterward writing two books about her travels. Among her works are also two about the Hóly Land, one written in her youth, and the other after she had been there, in 1847. She died at Ambleside, at the age of seventy-four (June 27, 1876).

MARTINIQUE (*mar-te-neek'*) or Martinico, one of the West India islands, 30 miles S.E. of Dominica; area, 381 square miles, or about a fourth as large as the State of Rhode Island; pop. 176,000, or more than half that of Rhode Island; capital, Port Royal. Most of the surface is mountainous, and there is a burning volcano nearly a mile high. The scenery is very beautiful. The western side called *Basse Terre* (Low Land), is less mountainous than the rest, and contains many fine plantations of sugar-cane, coffee, cotton, and indigo. The people are whites, negroes, and coolies or workmen from China. The island belongs to France, and French is the common language. St. Pierre is the largest town, and principal port.

Martinique was discovered by Columbus in 1502, and settled by the French in 1635. It is celebrated as the birthplace of the Empress JOSEPHINE.

MA'RY I., Queen of England, fourth of the Tudor line, born February 18, 1516. She was the daughter of Henry VIII., and succeeded her brother Edward VI., October 1, 1553. Her mother was Catharine of Aragon, who, when Mary was sixteen years old, was divorced by Henry, who then made Anne Boleyn his wife. Mary shared her mother's disgrace, and while Anne Boleyn lived was neglected by her father. When she became queen, one of her first acts was to behead her beautiful cousin, the Lady Jane GREY. She then set her heart on restoring England to the Church of Rome, and tried to undo all that her father and brother had done. The idea of those days was that error in religion should be put down by persecution, so Mary had many of the best and greatest men in England burned alive, Archbishop CRANMER among others. It is said that two hundred people perished in this way. Mary had married PHILIP II. of Spain, and he of course did all he could to bring about this state of things. Mary allowed Philip to get her into a war with France in which she lost CALAIS. She died at St. James's Palace, London, when forty-two years old (November 17, 1558), and was succeeded by her sister Elizabeth.

MARY II. See WILLIAM III.

MA'RY-LAND, an E. State of the United States, beween Virginia and Pennsylvania; area, 11,100 square miles, or nearly the same as that of Belgium; pop. 1,042,000, or more than one sixth that of Belgium; capital, ANNAPOLIS. In the western part are mountains, most of which are covered with forest, but the eastern part is low and is almost cut in two by Chesapeake Bay, an excellent harbor, where hundreds of ships can always be seen. Most of them go to BALTIMORE, the principal port, and the only large city in the State.

There are many coal and iron mines in Maryland, and more marble is quarried than in any other State. The best farms are in the eastern and central parts, where much tobacco, corn, and wheat are grown. Many of the farmers are engaged in raising peaches and strawberries, which are sent to New York and Philadelphia, or preserved in cans at Baltimore. In the winter thousands of people are employed in dredging for oysters in Chesapeake Bay, where most of the oysters sold in the United States are obtained. The bay is also celebrated for its wild ducks, especially canvas-backs (C. C. T., 192, II., u.), thousands of which are shot by the hunters and sent to New York and other markets. The climate of Maryland is mild and pleasant, and the winters are never very cold. About one-fourth of the people are negroes.

Maryland was first called Mary's Land, in honor of Henrietta Maria, Queen of CHARLES I. The first lasting settlement was made by the English at St. Mary's on the Potomac River. Maryland was one of the thirteen original States of the Union.

MARY STU'ART, Queen of Scots, born in Linlithgow Palace, in 1542. Her father, King James V., died when she was a baby, and she was crowned Queen of Scotland before she was a year old. When six years old (1548), she was promised in marriage to Francis, the dauphin or son of the king of France, and was sent to be educated at the French court. The marriage took place when she was sixteen years old (1558) and the next year, on the death of Francis's father, they were crowned king and queen of France. Francis died two years after (December 5, 1560), and Mary returned to Scotland (1561) and took her place there as queen. But the Scottish people were Protestants, while she was a

Roman Catholic, and much trouble arose on that account. Then, too, she was fond of gayety, while they were very strict and opposed to all her amusements. Still, her reign was quiet at first.

Mary Stuart.

In 1565 Mary married her cousin, Henry Stuart, Lord Darnley, and had one son, who was afterward James VI., of Scotland and JAMES I. of England. Mary soon tired of her husband, and he, finding that she would not give him an equal share in the government, plotted with the Protestant nobles to imprison her. She had a secretary and favorite named Rizzio, an Italian musician ; and one evening, while she was at supper with him in Holyrood Palace, Darnley and other armed men rushed into the room and killed Rizzio before her eyes (1566). About a year afterward the house in which Darnley was staying was blown up, and he was killed. The Earl of Bothwell was accused of this murder, and Mary was thought to have approved of it. But he was not punished, and three months after Darnley's death, the queen married him. This roused the anger of every one. Bothwell escaped to Denmark, and Mary was shut up in the castle of Loch Leven. But she escaped (May 9, 1568), and raised an army ; but was defeated at Langside, and, to avoid falling into her enemies' hands, fled to England.

Queen Elizabeth treated her like an enemy, and had her shut up in prison. She was kept a prisoner for eighteen years, during which time she was the cause of many plots against Elizabeth and the peace of England. At last a plot for killing Elizabeth was discovered, and Mary was accused of being concerned in it. She was tried, found guilty, and condemned to death; and finally was beheaded in Fotheringay Castle, where she had been a prisoner for a long time, when forty-four year old (February 8, 1587).

MASANIELLO (*mah-sah-ne-el'lo*), an Italian fisherman, whose real name was Tommaso Aniello, born in Amalfi, in 1620. When Philip IV., King of Spain, who then ruled Naples, laid a new tax on fruit and vegetables, which were the chief food of the common people of that city, they rose in revolt and chose Masaniello for their leader. At the head of 50,000 men he compelled the king's viceroy, the Duke of Arcos, to set aside the tax and to pardon all the rioters. But Masaniello then showed himself to be cruel and a tyrant, and the people turned against him, and nine days after making him their chief they killed him (July 16, 1647). The opera of Masaniello, by AUBER, is made from the story of his nine days' rule.

MAS·I·NIS'SA, King of Numidia, born about 240 B.C. He was the son of Gala, King of a Numidian tribe. HASDRUBAL, the Cathaginian general, having promised him his daughter Sophonisba in marriage if he would aid Carthage against Rome, he led his father's army against Syphax, king of another Numidian tribe and a friend of the Romans, and defeated him. He afterward fought against the Romans in Spain; but hearing that Hasdrubal had married Sophonisba to Syphax, he turned his arms

against Carthage. With the aid of SCIPIO, the Roman commander, he defeated Syphax, took Sophonisba captive, and made her his wife; but Scipio claimed her as his prisoner, and Masinissa sent her a cup of poison, which she drank. The Romans made him king of Numidia, and he reigned in peace for fifty years, until the third Punic War began, when he again fought against Carthage although more than ninety years old. He died in the second year of the war, (148 B.C.)

MASK, Iron. See IRON MASK.

MA'SON AND DIX'ON, the names of two noted English astronomers and surveyors, who surveyed the boundary line between Pennsylvania and Maryland (1763 to 1767). Before their time there had been much trouble about the boundary between these two States, and it often led to riot and bloodshed. They made the right boundary, and set up at every fifth mile a stone with the arms of the Penn family engraved on one side and those of Lord Baltimore on the other. Before the Civil War, the term "Mason and Dixon's line" was often used when speaking of the boundary between the slave and free States.

MA'SON, George, an American statesman, born in Virginia, in 1726. He took the part of the colonists in the Revolution, and, in 1776 drew up the Constitution of Virginia and its declaration of rights, by which it was separated from England. In 1777, he became a member of Congress, and afterward one of the convention which framed the Constitution of the United States (1789), but, being dissatisfied with the Constitution when it was adopted, he refused to sign it. He was elected the first United States Senator from Virginia, but declined the office, and soon after died, when sixty-six years old (1792).

MA'SON, John, Major, a Connecticut soldier who defeated the Pequot Indians; born in England in 1600.

The Pequots, a powerful tribe who lived near the Pequot River, now the Thames, had massacred a party of whites in 1637, and the colonists sent Mason with ninety men to attack them. Aided by the Narragansett tribe, he destroyed the Pequot forts, killing many hundred Indians and compelling the rest to join the friendly Mohegan and Narragansett tribes. Major Mason commanded the Connecticut soldiers more than thirty years, and from 1660 to 1670 he was deputy governor. He died in Norwich, Conn., when seventy-two years old (1672).

MA'SON, Lowell, an American writer of music, born in Medway, Mass., January 8, 1792. He was a music-teacher and leader of church choirs in Savannah, Ga., and afterward in Boston, where he published many music-books for churches, Sunday-schools, and schools. All the books contain pieces which he wrote. Mr. Mason died in Orange, N. J., when eighty years old (August 11, 1872).

MASSACHUSETTS (*mas-sa-choo' sets*), one of the New England States, on the Atlantic Ocean ; area 7800 square miles, or nearly a fourth larger than Connecticut and Rhode Island together ; pop. 2,239,000, or a little less than that of Denmark ; capital, BOSTON. The western part is mountainous, and covered in many places with thick forests. One of the ridges, called the Hoosac range, has been pierced by a tunnel, the longest railroad tunnel in the United States (C. C. T., 623, I., u.). East of the mountains lies the beautiful valley of the Connecticut River, the most fertile part of the State, where are many fine farms. The north-eastern part of the State is hilly, but the south-eastern part, including the long peninsula of Cape Cod, is low and sandy. Massachusetts owns several islands, of which Martha's Vineyard and Nantucket are the largest.

In the eastern part are fine quarries of granite, and iron is found among the western mountains. The soil is not very good in most places, though by hard work many good farms have been made. But Massachusetts is most noted for its manufactures, and more cotton and woollen cloth and more boots and shoes are made than in any other State ; and the cutlery and straw goods factories do as much work as those in all the rest of the United States put together. The coast cities have a very large trade, in which many ships are employed. Massachusetts is also celebrated for its fisheries. Most of the American whaling ships, and half the cod and mackerel fishing ships sail from New Bedford, Gloucester, and other towns of this State. Of course, with all their factories and ships, many of the people are very rich : but they are also generous and intelligent, and spend their money for good purposes. They have more and larger libraries than are found in any other State, and are noted for their fine schools and colleges.

Massachusetts is an Indian word meaning the "blue hills." The coast is supposed to have been visited by the NORTHMEN about the year 1000. The English made a settlement on some of the islands in 1602, but the first lasting one was made by the Pilgrims (1620), who founded the Plymouth Colony. In 1628 another colony settled on Massachusetts Bay, and each of these colonies had its own governor until 1692, when they united under one government. The whole of Maine belonged to Massachusetts until 1820. Massachusetts was one of the thirteen original States of the Union.

MAS-SA-SOIT', a sachem or chief of the Wampanoags, a tribe of Indians in S. Massachusetts and Rhode Island, born about 1541. The tribe once numbered 30,000, but in the early part of the 17th century all but about 300 had died of a fever. Soon after the Pilgrims landed at Plymouth, Massasoit came to the settlement with sixty warriors, made a treaty of peace with the whites, and kept it for fifty years. When any other tribe was about to make war on the Pilgrims, Massasoit generally heard of it and told them of it in time to save the settlements. He died at the age of eighty years (1661).

MAS-SE'NA (French *mahs-sa-nah'*), **André,** Prince of Essling, a famous French soldier, born at Nice, May 6, 1758. He was the son of poor parents, and served fourteen years in the Sardinian army as a private. But when he entered the French army, at the age of thirty-four, his bravery soon gained attention, and in two years he became a brigadier-general. In 1799 he saved France from invasion by defeating the allied Austrians and Russians at Zurich, and the next year held Genoa for three months against an Austrian army besieging it by land and an English fleet blockading it by sea. He took the chief command of the French forces in Spain in 1810, where he held Wellington in check for a time, but had to resign on account of ill health a year later. He was as mean and cruel as he was brave. His soldiers hated him, and Napoleon called him a robber. He died in Paris when fifty-eight years old (April 4, 1817).

MAT-A-MO'ROS, a city of Mexico, on the Rio Grande River, 40 miles from its mouth, opposite Brownsville, in Texas; pop. 14,000, or about as large as Beatrice, Neb. It has a considerable trade in gold and silver, wool, hides, and horses. Most of the people are of Spanish descent, but the town is more like a United States city than a Mexican one.

Matamoros was first built about the beginning of this century. It was captured by General Taylor during the war with Mexico (1846).

MATANZAS (*mah-tan'zahs*), a seaport of Cuba, on the N. coast, 53 miles E. of Havana; pop. 88,000,

or about as large as Syracuse, N. Y. It has a fine large harbor. The country around is covered with splendid sugar plantations, and the trade of the city in sugar and molasses is very great. The climate, though very hot, is more healthful than that of Havana.

MAT-THI'AS COR-VI'NUS, called the Great, King of Hungary, born in 1443. He was a son of John HUNYADY, governor of Hungary, and was elected in 1458 to succeed Ladislaus as King of Hungary. Many of the nobles elected a rival king, Frederick III., but he soon gave up his claim to Matthias. During his reign there were many wars against the Turks and Poles. Matthias was noted for his justice, so much so that after his death a proverb arose, "King Matthias gone, justice gone." Hungary was very prosperous under his rule. He was very fond of learned men and gathered a great many about him. A university was founded by him at Buda, and he also established a library, which was very famous in his time. He died in Vienna when forty-seven years old (1490), and was succeeded by Vladislas II.

MAURICE (*mau'ris*), Count of Nassau and Prince of Orange, Stadtholder of the United Dutch Provinces, born at Dillenburg, November 14, 1567. He was the son of William the Silent, and although but seventeen years old when his father was assassinated, was chosen Stadtholder. In the war with Spain he showed himself to be a great soldier, defeating the ablest generals of the age. But he put himself at the head of the party opposed to the patriot John Barneveldt, and had him brought to the scaffold on the charge "that he had troubled the state and religion." That one act has left upon the fame of Maurice a stain which disfigures his brilliant reputation as a soldier. He died at the Hague when fifty-eight years old (April 23, 1625).

MAURICE, Duke and Elector of Saxony, a German general, born in Freiberg, March 21, 1521. He was a son of Henry the Pious, and was by him brought up in the reformed religion. At that time the Protestant princes of Germany, headed by John Frederick of Saxony, cousin of Maurice, and Philip of Hesse, his father-in-law, were in arms against the Emperor Charles V., in defence of their religion. But Maurice took up the cause of the Emperor, and enabled him to gain over his enemies the victory of Muhlberg. As a reward for this, Charles took away from John Frederick the electorate and gave it to Maurice, whose descendants now occupy the throne of Saxony. As soon as Maurice had won the price of his treachery to his own party, he threw off the mask, and placed himself at the head of the Protestant league. Victory seemed to follow him, for no sooner had he left the Emperor's cause than it met with severe reverses, and at length Charles was obliged to sign a treaty called the Peace of Passau, giving the Protestants the liberty they wanted. Maurice died from a wound received in the battle of Sievershausen against Albert of Brandenburg, who would not submit to the Peace of Passau. In 1853 a monument to his honor was erected on the battle-field. He was only thirty-two years old at the time of his death (July 11, 1553).

MAURICIUS (*mau-rish'e-us*), **Flavius Tiberius,** an emperor of the East, born about 539. He was descended from an ancient Roman family, and so much distinguished himself in his wars against Persia that the Emperor Tiberius II., on his deathbed in 582, named him as his successor. At first he was very much liked, but he soon became unpopular, and his reign is marked only by a series of wars which he let his generals fight for him, he remaining quietly at home. At last a strong party was formed against him headed by Phocas, who got up a revolt. Mauricius fled, but was caught and beheaded, and Phocas was proclaimed emperor. Mauricius died when sixty-three years old (November 27, 602).

MAURITANIA (*maw-ri-ta'ne-ah*), the ancient name of a part of N.W. Africa, including what is now Morocco and a part of Algeria. The people were called Mauri, from which comes our name of Moors.

MAURITIUS (*maw-rish'e-us*), or **Isle of France,** an island in the Indian Ocean, about 500 miles E. of Madagascar ; area, 700 square miles, or one third as large as Delaware ; pop. 360,000, or more than twice that of Delaware ; capital, Port Louis. It is a very beautiful island, with high, forest-covered hills, and many fertile valleys. There are three chains of mountains, some of the peaks of which are of very singular shape. One, called the Peterbote, ends in a tall steeple of rock, on the point of which is balanced a rock much larger round than the steeple itself. Another is Le Pouce (the Thumb), because it looks much like a human thumb. There are also many singular caves. The island is surrounded by coral-reefs, but there are passages through which ships can pass to a safe harbor within. The climate is warm, and often unhealthy near the coast, but in the hills it is very fine. The chief product is sugar, but coffee, indigo, and cotton are also cultivated. In the woods are many beautiful timbers, including the finest ebony in the world.

In former times Mauritius was the home of a wonderful bird called the " dodo" and of a kind of water hen called the " giant," which was taller than a man. None are now living, but their bones are still sometimes found. The people of Mauritius are Europeans, negroes, Hindoos, and Chinese, besides many of mixed races. French is the language most spoken, though the island belongs to Great Britain. It is ruled by an English governor, who also has control over many neighboring islands, among which are Rodriguez, the Seychelles, and the Almirantes.

Mauritius was discovered in 1505 by the Portuguese, who called it Cerné. It was taken from them by

Peterbote Mountain.

the Dutch (1598), who changed the name to Mauritius, in honor of Prince Maurice of Nassau. The French took it in 1715 and called it the Isle of France, and the British took it from them in 1810.

More than a hundred years ago a young lady, returning from France to her family and her lover at Mauritius, was wrecked and drowned in sight of the land she was seeking. It was from her history that Bernardin de SAINT-PIERRE made his beautiful story of "Paul and Virginia."

MAU'RY, Matthew Fontaine, an American naval officer and geographer, born in Spottsylvania County, Va., January 14, 1806. He entered the navy in 1825, and became a lieutenant, but in 1839 he was made lame by an accident, so as to be unable to serve at sea, and was placed in charge of the naval charts and instruments at Washington. In 1856 he published his "Physical Geography of the Sea," for which he had gathered materials, not only from his own voyages, but from the observations of hundreds of naval officers in all parts of the world. He also published several school geographies and treatises on navigation. When the Civil War broke out he resigned his place at Washington and became a commodore in the Confederate navy. He died in Lexington, Va., when sixty-seven years old (February 1, 1873).

MAVROCORDATOS (*mahv-ro-kor-dah'tos*), **Alexander,** a statesman of modern Greece, born in Constantinople in 1791. He was in Italy when the Greek insurrection against the Turks broke out in 1821, and he hastened to Athens with many French and Italians who had volunteered to fight for Greece. He was president of the national assembly which formed a constitution for Greece and made a declaration of independence in 1822. Afterward he was commander-in-chief of the Greek armies, and, the war being ended, held various important offices, being a member of the cabinet of King Otho and ambassador to Bavaria, Prussia, England, and France. He died in Ægina, when seventy-four years old (August 18, 1865).

MAX·IM'I·'AN. See DIOCLE-TIAN.

MAXIMILIAN I. (*mak-se-me'le-an*), Emperor of Germany, born in Neustadt, near Vienna, March 22, 1459. He was the son of Frederick III., and was chosen to succeed him in 1493. Maximilian's reign is considered the link between the Middle Ages and modern times. His bold and dangerous huntings and his valiant deeds in battle and tournament are stamped with the character of the Middle Ages, while, on the other hand, the new discoveries and inventions of his day were the heralds of the modern period. He has been styled "The last of the Knights." He once appeared at a tournament as champion of the German name, and won a complete victory. By the marriage of his son Philip to the daughter of the king of Spain he brought that kingdom into the house of Hapsburg. Maximilian died at Wels, when sixty years old (January 12, 1519), and was succeeded as Emperor by his grandson Charles V.

MAXIMILIAN, Ferdinand Maximilian Joseph, Arch-Duke of Austria and Emperor of Mexico, born in Vienna, July 6, 1832. He was the brother of the present Emperor of Austria. In 1863 Napoleon III. had it in mind to conquer Mexico and set up an empire, and he offered the crown to Maximilian, who went to Mexico in 1864. The country had long been in a state of confusion, and at first the people seemed inclined to welcome him and look for peace under his rule. But he pleased no one, the people rose against him, and in 1867, when the French troops left the country, the empire fell to pieces. Maximilian tried to form a native army for his own defence, but he was captured by the

Republicans, and, after a trial, shot near Queretaro, in his thirty-fifth year (June 19, 1867).

MAX'I-MIN, Caius Julius Verus, a Roman Emperor, born in Thrace in the latter part of the second century. He was a common shepherd, but by leading his countrymen against robbers became used to a soldier's life. He joined the Roman army when young and in time rose to the highest rank. Having won the admiration of the soldiers by his bravery, he brought about the assassination of the Emperor ALEXANDER SEVERUS (235), and got himself proclaimed emperor. But he proved to be a monster of cruelty, and was killed by his soldiers after a reign of only three years (A.D. 238). Maximin is said to have been eight feet high, and so strong that he could draw a loaded wagon and break the teeth of a horse with a blow of his fist. His finger was so large that he could wear his wife's bracelet as a ring.

MAYAS (*mah'yas*). See AMERICAN INDIANS.

MAY'ER, Alfred Marshall, an American scholar, born in Baltimore, Nov. 13, 1836. He was graduated at St. Mary's College, Baltimore, studied at the University of Paris, and is now a professor in the Stevens Institute of Technology, Hoboken, New Jersey. He has made a study of acoustics, or the science of sound, and has made some curious and important discoveries, and written several books.

MAYER, Constant, a French arti, born in Besançon, Oct. 4, 1832. H came to the United States in 1857. and has painted many pictures here. He paints mostly figure pieces. Among his best works are those called "Good Words" and "Consolation," the latter a lady reading prayers to a wounded soldier. A picture painted by him in 1880, called "The Broken Violin," represents a pretty little girl looking very sad over the loss of her broken violin.

MAZARIN (*mah-zah-ran'*), **Jules,**

Cardinal, a famous French states-man, born near Naples, Italy, July 14, 1602. He was educated as a lawyer, and had won some fame in the service of the Pope when Cardinal RICHELIEU gave him an office in France. The Italian name of his family was Mazarini (*mahd-zah-re' ne*), but he changed it to its French form when he went to France. Richelieu had him made a cardinal (1641), and when he died (1642) recommended that he be made his successor as Prime Minister of France. LOUIS XIII. was then wasting away, and on his death (1643) he was succeeded by his son, a child only five years old, afterward famous as LOUIS XIV. His mother, the Queen, called ANNE OF AUSTRIA, became regent of the kingdom, but it was really ruled by Mazarin, to whom the queen trusted everything. Some historians even think that she was married to him privately. He had as much power as Richelieu had had, but he ruled more by craft and cunning than Richelieu did, and so people used to say, "After the lion comes the fox." But the people did not like him because he was a foreigner, and a civil war broke out (1648), called the war of the Fronde, in which friends of the cardinal were called Mazarins and his enemies Frondeurs. Mazarin was banished and lived in Germany for a time, but at the end of the war (1654) he got into power again, and ruled Louis XIV. as he had ruled the queen. He died in Paris when fifty-eight years old (March 9, 1661).

MAZZINI (*maht-se'ne*), Giuseppe (Joseph), a noted Italian patriot, born in Genoa, June 28,1805. When still a young man he devoted himself to the cause of freeing Italy, which was then oppressed by the Austrians. Having been banished for this, he went to Marseilles, France, and started a society called "Young Italy," for the purpose of uniting Italy in one free state and making it a republic. He hoped to arouse the

people and to drive out the Austrians by force, and he called on the King of Sardinia to aid him; but the king could not do this, for he did not wish to make Italy a republic. So Mazzini went on working in secret trying to get up a rebellion, and was even accused of assassination, but there is no reason to suppose that he was guilty of that. When Italy was finally united under one government, Mazzini worked to have it made into a republic, but as this would overthrow the government of King Victor Emmanuel, he was arrested and imprisoned. But he was soon set free, and lived in Italy until his death, which took place at Pisa when he was sixty-six years old (March 10, 1872). It is said that more than 80,000 people attended his funeral. There is a bronze bust of him in Central Park, New York.

MEAD (*meed*), **Larkin Goldsmith,** an American sculptor, born at Chesterfield, N. H., January 3, 1835. When a boy he one day made an angel in snow, which was greatly admired; and it won him friends who sent him to Italy to study art. He has since lived there most of the time. Among his statues are those on the Lincoln monument in Springfield, Ill., and that of Ethan ALLEN in the Capitol at Washington.

MEADE (*meed*) **George Gordon,** "the victor of Gettysburg," born in Cadiz, Spain, where his father at the time was United States Consul, December 30, 1815. He was graduated at West Point when twenty years old, but left the army and became a civil engineer. In 1840 he was re-appointed in the army, and served through the Mexican War. When the Civil War broke out (1861) he was made a brigadier-general of volunteers and attached to the Army of the Potomac, with which he remained until peace was restored. He did such good service at South Mountain and Antietam that he was made major-general of volunteers, and in 1863 received the chief command of the Army of the Potomac. After the great battle of Gettysburg, where he commanded, Congress promoted him to the rank of brigadier-general in the regular army, rewarding him still further by

George Gordon Meade.

the rank of major-general after Lee's surrender. At the close of the war he was given command of the military division of the Atlantic, with his headquarters at Philadelphia, where he died, in his fifty-seventh year (November 6, 1872).

MECCA (*mek′kah*), a city of W. Arabia, 65 miles from the Red Sea ; pop. 60,000, or about the same as Grand Rapids, Mich. It is celebrated as the birthplace of Mohammed, and on that account is the principal holy city of the Mohammedans, being visited every year by 100,-000 to 200,000 pilgrims. The most holy place is the great mosque called the Caaba, which the Mohammedans say was built by Abraham and Ishmael. It is a house of stone, about forty feet square and high, and with a flat roof. Built into the wall on the outside is a black stone which

is said to have been brought from heaven by angels. Near the Caaba are shown the supposed tombs of Ishmael and Hagar, and the well or spring which Hagar found in the wilderness when Ishmael was about to die of thirst. All these are enclosed, with the Caaba, in a great square, surrounded by a wall and a colonnade. Pilgrims who come to Mecca walk around the Caaba, and kiss the black stone, which has been worn smooth by their lips. They also go to the hill of Arafat, another holy place, twelve miles east of Mecca ; there they encamp and perform certain ceremonies, listening to a sermon, which is preached every year. None but Mohammedans are allowed to approach the Caaba, but a few travellers have gone to Mecca disguised as pilgrims and have seen all the sacred places. Had they been found out they would have been killed.

MECHLIN (*mek′lin*), a city of Belgium, on the River Dyle, 13 miles N. by E. of Brussels ; pop. 50,000, or about as large as Los Angeles, Cal. It has manufactures of woollen and linen cloth, and lace. Formerly the lace manufactures were celebrated, but they are now much less important, and the city has little business. The streets are very old-fashioned and picturesque, and there is a fine cathedral.

MEDEA (*me-de′ah*), in Greek fable, a daughter of Aetes, King of Colchis. She was famous as a sorceress, and by the skill helped Jason and the ARGONAUTS to carry off the Golden Fleece. Medea went with Jason to Greece and became his wife, but was deserted by him for Creüsa, daughter of Creon, King of Corinth. In revenge she killed Jason's children, and sent to Creüsa a poisoned dress which burned her to death. She then fled to Athens, where she married Ægæus, but she afterward went to Asia with her son Medus, who founded Media. EURI-BIDES, CORNEILLE, and other poets have written tragedies about the story of Medea.

MEDIA (*me'de-ah*), an ancient country of Asia, E. of Assyria and Armenia. Media belonged at first to Assyria, but got its independence, and under its King Cyaxares became one of the greatest nations of Asia. Cyrus the Persian finally conquered Media, and it then became a part of Persia.

MEDICI (*med'e-che*), a famous Florentine family that began to be known in the fifteenth century. The first Medici that we hear of, Cosmo, was a merchant, a man of lofty mind who governed Florence from 1428 to 1464, without taking any title, though history has given him that of "Father of his Country." His grandson Lorenzo, called the Magnificent, made Florence the seat of every art and sciene, and kept a court of which artists, poets, and writers were the chief ornaments. But he destroyed the liberty of his people, and after his death the Florentines were stirred up by SAVONAROLA to drive out the Medici, and to restore the republic. The Medici returned, and were again banished. This time Pope Clement VII., who was himself of that family, with the aid of Charles V., the Emperor, took Florence, and forced the cruel Alexander de' Medici upon the people as their ruler. Pope Leo X. was also a member of this family, and so was Catharine de' Medici, who planned the massacre of St. Bartholomew.

MEDINA (*med-e'nah*), a city of W. Arabia, about 250 miles N. of Mecca; pop. 16,000, or nearly the same as that of San Diego, Cal. Medina is the second most holy city of the Mohammedans, who say that one prayer in Medina is worth a thousand made anywhere else, except in Mecca. It is celebrated as the place to which Mohammed fled when driven from Mecca. Mohammed and his first two successors, ABUBEKR and OMAR, are buried in Medina, and a large mosque has

been built over their tombs. Thousands of pilgrims visit the mosque, but the tombs are concealed by a silk curtain, and the priests say that whoever looked at them would be blinded by light from heaven. The city is surrounded by a wall, and on one side there is a castle. The holy ground extends for five or six miles around.

Medina is the Arabic for "city." The Arabs call it Medinat-al-Nabi, which means "City of the Prophet."

MEDUSA (*me-du'sah*). See GORGONS.

MEHEMET ALI (*meh'heh-met ah'le*), pasha of Egypt, born in 1769. He went to Egypt in the year 1800, at the head of the Turkish troops sent there to fight Napoleon, and after the departure of the French was made viceroy (1806) by the Porte. In this position he conquered the MAMELUKES, and did much for Egypt, though his ways were despotic and often cruel. He conquered a great part of Arabia and invaded Syria. This brought on a war with Turkey, and the sultan sent an army against him; but he defeated the Turks, took all of Syria, and would have taken Constantinople and crushed the Turkish Empire if the powers of Europe had not stopped him. In the last years of his life he lost his mind. He died in Cairo when eighty years old (Aug. 2, 1849).

MEISSEN (*mice'sen*), a city of Germany, in Saxony, on the River Elbe, 12 miles N.W. of Dresden; pop. 15,000, or about as large as Galesburg, Ill. It is noted for its porcelain factories, in which the china or porcelain commonly called Dresden china is made (C. C. T., 487, 11., 1.).

MEISSONIER (*ma-so-ne-a'*), Jean Louis Ernest, a French painter, born at Lyons in 1811. His pictures are usually painted on very small canvases, and sometimes on wood. They represent soldiers, chess-players, men in different positions, but seldom women. They sell for very high prices, and many of them are owned in the United States. His large picture of Napoleon at Friedland is in the Metropolitan Museum of New York. He died when eighty years old (Jan.31,1891).

ME-KONG'. See CAMBODIA.

ME-LANCH'THON (German *malahnk'ton*), **Philipp,** one of the leaders of the Reformation in Germany, born at Brettin, Baden, February 16, 1497. His name was originally Schwarzerd (black earth), of which Melanchthon is a Greek translation. He was highly educated at the University of Heidelberg, and became professor of Greek at Wittenberg, where he met LUTHER and soon took his side. He was noted for his gentleness, his great learning, and strong mind. In 1530, when the Emperor Charles V. called together the princes of the empire at Augsburg in a great meeting called the Diet, the followers of Luther laid before the Diet a statement of their belief, which had been written by Melanchthon and approved by Luther. This statement was afterward called the Augsburg Confession, and it became the standard of faith in all the Lutheran churches. After the death of Luther, Melanchthon had many bitter quarrels with different theologians, and to one so gentle this gave great distress. He wrote a great many religious works, which gave him great fame. He died at WITTENBERG when sixty-three years old (April 19, 1560), and was buried in the church there beside Luther.

MELBOURNE (*mel'burn*), a city, capital of the colony of Victoria, in S.E. Australia, on the Yarra-Yarra River, near its mouth in the bay of Port Philip; pop. 438,000, or nearly as large as Boston, Mass. It has a larger trade than' any other port of the British colonies, the principal things sent to other countries being wool, tallow, hides, and gold. The harbor is at the mouth of the river, and is connected with the city by a railroad. It is always full of ships, and is defended by strong forts. Melbourne contains a university, and many fine public buildings. It was founded in 1835, and named after Lord Melbourne, who was then Prime Minister of England.

MELEAGER (*me-ie-a'jer*), in Greek fable, a famous hero, son of Œneus, King of Ætolia, and Althea. When he was born the Fates placed a piece of wood near the fire, and told his mother that he would live as long as that wood was not burned. She hid it away carefully. The boy grew to be a man, and became famous for his brave deeds. He was one of the ARGONAUTS, and he killed the Caledonian boar which Diana had sent to ravage the fields of Calydon, because the king had neglected to sacrifice to her. But he finally offended his mother by killing her two brothers, and she in her anger threw the wood into the fire. As it burned away his strength failed, and at last he died. Althea afterward killed herself in remorse.

MEL-POM'E-NE. See MUSES.

MEM'PHIS, a city of ancient Egypt, on the River Nile, 10 miles S. of the modern city of Cairo. It is said to have been founded by Menes, the first king of Egypt, and the later kings built many fine palaces. Near the city were the pyramids, which were built for tombs of the kings. Memphis had temples to Isis and Serapis, and a splendid one dedicated to the god Ptah. The city itself was called Ma-en-Ptah, or the abode of Ptah, and the modern name is supposed to have come from that. After Alexandria was founded Memphis fell to decay, and even its ruins became covered with sand, so that they have only recently been discovered.

MEM'PHIS, the second largest city of Tennessee, in the S.W. corner of the State, on a bluff of the Mississippi River; pop. 64,000, or a little larger than Wilmington, Del. It has a very large trade, especially in cotton, more being sold there than in any other city of the United States, except New Orleans. There are several large foundries and machine shops, and mills for making oil from cotton seed. Memphis was founded in 1820, and was named after ancient Memphis in Egypt. It became a city in 1831. During the Civil War it was held by the Confederates until their vessels on the Mississippi were destroyed by the Union gunboats, when the Unionists took the city (June 6, 1862). They kept it during the rest of the war, except for a short time in August, 1864, when the Confederate General Forest made a cavalry raid on Memphis and captured several hundred prisoners, leaving soon afterward. Memphis has been visited by yellow fever several times, and in the summers of 1878 and 1879 the disease became so terrible that nearly everybody left the city. Since then, by improving the drainage of the city, it has been made much more healthy.

ME·NAN'DER, a Greek comic poet, born at Athens, in 342 B.C. He wrote a great many comedies, which were celebrated for their freedom from coarse wit and for showing real life. They are all lost except a few fragments. The plays of TERENCE are mostly translations of Menander's. He was drowned, while swimming, in the harbor of Athens (291 B.C.).

MENDELSSOHN·BARTHOLDY (*men'dels-sone-bar-tol'de*), **Felix,** a famous German musician, born in Hamburg, Feb. 3, 1809. His father was a Jew named Abraham Mendelssohn, the name Bartholdy, which he added to his own, being that of his wife. The Mendelssohn-Bartholdys, though Jews, were converts to Christianity, and their son Felix was brought up in the Lutheran religion. When he was less than six years old he played with great

skill on the piano, and when eight he could read the most difficult music, and wrote pieces for the piano and violin. He had a sister Fanny who was also musical, and the two would often play together their own pieces in presence of the visitors who came to their house. The first of his works that were known to the public was his "Midsummer

Mendelssohn.

Night's Dream," his principal other compositions being his oratorios of "Elijah" and "St. Paul," and his charming "Songs without Words." He wrote beautiful letters to his friends, which have been published since his death. The last twelve years of his life were spent at Leipsic, where he died when thirty-eight years old (Nov. 4, 1847).

MENDOZA (*men-do'za*), a family of Spain, several of whose members were famous authors or statesmen.

Inigo Lopez de Mendoza, Marquis of Santillana, born in 1398, was noted both as a poet and as a general against the Moors. He was the first to write sonnets in Spanish. He died in 1458.

Pedro Gonzales de Mendoza, his son, born in Castile, in 1428, was archbishop of Seville, and afterward a cardinal. His influence with Ferdinand and Isabella was so great that he was called the "third king." He was also a general, distinguishing himself in several battles. He died, when sixty-six years old (January 11, 1495).

Diego Hurtado de Mendoza, grand-nephew of Inigo, was born in Granada about 1503. He wrote poems, and was employed by the Emperor Charles V. as an ambassador in Italy, but King Philip II. banished him from his court for many years. He died in Madrid when seventy-two years old (1575).

Antonio de Mendoza, his brother, born in Granada about 1495, was appointed (1535) viceroy of New Spain, or Mexico. He governed very wisely, founded the first college in Mexico, and set up the first printing-press there. In 1551 he was made viceroy of Peru. He died in Lima, when fifty-seven years old (July 21, 1552).

MEN-E-LA'US, King of Sparta, son of ATREUS and brother of AGAMEMNON. He married the beautiful HELEN, who afterward ran away with PARIS, and was the cause of the war with TROY. Menelaus was one of the Greek heroes at the siege of Troy, and was one of those who entered the city in the wooden horse. After the taking of Troy he got back Helen and returned to Sparta.

MEN'TOR, one of the most faithful friends of ULYSSES, in whose care Telemachus, his young son, was left when Ulysses went to the war of TROY. When Telemachus went on his travels in search of his father, the goddess Minerva took the form and voice of Mentor and accompanied him. In FENELON'S story of "Télémaque" Minerva as Mentor forms one of the principal characters.

MER'CU·RY, an ancient god of the Greeks and Romans, son of Jupiter and Maia, a daughter of Atlas. The Greeks called him Hermes. He was famous for his cunning, dexterity, and swiftness, and was the god of speech and eloquence, and the guardian of thieves. He was born in the morning, played on a lute of his own making at noon, and stole Apollo's oxen in the evening. He invented the lyre of Apollo, who in return gave him a wand, having wings at one end and two snakes twined about it, which had the power to calm passions and still quarrels. He was the messenger of the gods, especially of Jupiter, and had many duties to perform, one of which was to conduct the souls of the dead to HADES. He is usually represented as a slender youth, with winged sandals on his feet, and carrying his wand in his hand.

Mercury.

MER'I·DEN, a city of Connecticut, 18 miles N.E. of New Haven ; pop. 22,000, or about as large as Lexington, Ky. It has large manufactories of iron, steel, and brass, also machinery and cutlery. Britannia and plated silver ware are also made, the Meriden Britannia Company being the largest of its kind in the world.

Meriden was first built in 1806, and became a city in 1867.

MERLE (*merl*), **Hugues,** a French painter, born at Saint-Marcellin. His pictures of women and children are much admired, and are well known in the United States, where many of them have been sold.

MER'LIN, a Welsh seer and wizard, said to have lived about the fifth century A.D. According to the fable, his father was a demon and his mother was a Welsh princess. Even in his childhood he foretold many wonderful things, and when he grew up he became the counsellor of King ARTHUR, whom he aided against his enemies and saved from many perils. When Merlin grew old he fell in love with a beautiful lady called Niniame, and followed her everywhere ; but she soon grew weary of his love and made sport of him, and only let him stay with her because he showed her many wonders. One day, as they sat together in a wood, she begged Merlin to teach her a certain spell by which a man might be shut up forever in a small space, unseen by all for evermore. She begged this with tears, and promised to love him if he would show it to her ; and at last, won by her sweet words, he showed her all she asked. Then she lulled him to sleep, and rising softly, wrought the spell in the air and so shut up Merlin in a blackthorn tree in the wood that he never got free again. Tennyson tells this story in one of his " Idyls of the King," but he calls the lady " Vivien."

MERTHYR TYDFIL (*mer ther tid'vil*), a town of S. Wales, 21 miles N. by W. of Cardiff ; pop. 49,000, or about as large as Bridgeport, Conn. The surrounding country contains hundreds of iron and coal mines, and in the city there are more than fifty great iron works. Most of the people are workmen or miners, who live in small houses, so that the town is not a very handsome one. Before 1750 it was a small village, but the mines have caused it to grow very fast.

MERV, a city of S. Turkistan, about 300 miles S.E. of Khiva ; pop. about 3000. The Persian rulers of Turkistan formerly lived there, and the city had a large trade. Merv was sacked by the Tartars in the early part of the present century, and since then it has fallen to decay. But it was once a flourishing and beautiful town, and was the capital of many of the rulers of Persia.

MES'DAG, Hendrik Willem, born at Groningen, Netherlands. He had a picture at the Centennial Exhibition in 1876 which gained a medal. He paints landscapes and coast scenes, with boats and shipping.

MES·SA·LI'NA, Valeria, a Roman empress, who lived in the first century of the Christian era. She was the wife of the Emperor Claudius. She was very bad, and caused many noble Romans to be put to death. At last her husband had her beheaded (A.D. 48).

MESSINA (*mes-se'nah*), a city of N.E. Sicily, on the Strait of Messina ; pop. 140,000, or about the same as Omaha, Neb. It is very strongly fortified, and has one of the best harbors in the world. There are manufactories of satins and damasks, and the city has a large trade, especially in oranges, lemons, and olive-oil. Many of the hills around are planted with orange orchards.

Messina is said to have been founded about 800 B.C., by the Greeks, who named it after Messene in Greece. It has always been an important city.

ME·TEL'LUS, the name of a family of Roman plebeians or commoners, many of whom were noted from 250 to 60 B.C. Among the most famous was,

Quintus Cæcilius Metellus Numidicus, who got his last name for fighting against JUGURTHA in Numidia (109). He had a quarrel with MARIUS, who went to Rome and got his command away from him and had him banished to Rhodes, but he was recalled the next year.

Quintus Cæcilius Metellus Pius, his son, got his last name on account of his efforts to get his father recalled from exile, the Latin *pius* meaning dutiful to one's parent. He fought in the Social War. Quintus Cæcilius Metellus Pius SCIPIO was his adopted son.

METTERNICH (*met'ter-nik*), **Clemens Wenzel Nepomuk Lothar,** a famous Austrian statesman, born in Coblentz, May 15, 1773. He first appeared in public life at the coronation of the Emperor Leopold, when only seventeen years old

(1790), and for sixty years he was almost always in office. From the beginning to the end of his career he was a strong absolutist—that is, he thought a very strict rule best for the people ; but in 1848 the people of Vienna rose against him, and the hated prime minister barely escaped with his life. He went to England, then to Holland, and at the end of three years returned to Vienna, where he died, when eighty-six years old (June 11, 1859). In his long life he saw many people and things which he has told about in his recently-published memoirs.

METZ, a city of W. Germany, at the junction of the Seille and Moselle Rivers ; pop. 54,000, or nearly the same as that of Hartford, Conn. It is very strongly fortified, being surrounded by walls, and having nine gates defended by drawbridges. There are many fine public buildings and a beautiful cathedral. Among the manufactures are woollen goods, embroidery, and silk plush for making hats.

Metz was called by the Romans Divodurum, which means " on the two rivers." In the sixth century it was called Mettis, which means " in the midst of waters." It belonged to Germany for a long time, but was joined to France in 1648. In 1870 it was besieged for two months by the Germans, who finally captured it, together with a French army under Marshal Bazaine, who had defended it. The French gave up Metz to Germany the next year, but many of the French people who lived there have gone away.

MEXICO (*mex'e-ko*), **United States of,** a country of North America, between the United States and Central America ; area, 760,000 square miles, or about a fifth as large as the United States ; pop. 11,601,000, or less than a fifth that of the United States ; capital, MEXICO. Near the coasts the land is low and flat ; farther inland it rises by terraces to a great table-land about a mile and a quarter above the sea, which covers all the central part of the country. On this table-land are hills, valleys, and lakes, and across it is a line of great mountains the tops of some of which are more than three miles above the sea. Though some of these peaks are volcanoes, they are covered with snow and ice all the year round. The highest are Popocatepetl and Orizaba.

Mexico is rich in silver, gold, and other metals, and in many kinds of precious stones ; and its forests abound in many kinds of timber, and in cabinet and dye-woods. Every kind of fruit known in Europe or America grows there, and the grains and other plants of both hot and cool climates are cultivated. The climate differs according to the height : in going by railroad from VERA CRUZ to the City of Mexico one passes, in a few hours, from tropic heat, with sugar-cane and plantations, to cool hillsides, with pine and fir trees, maize, and temperate fruits. More than half of the people are Indians, and most of the rest are mixed races, only about one twentieth of the whole population being whites. The language spoken is Spanish, and the religion is Roman Catholic. The government is republican, much like that of the United States, only the president is elected for six years. But the country is often the scene of civil war, and it is seldom that a president holds his office during the whole of his time.

Before the whites came Mexico was occupied by Indian tribes, the chief of which were the Aztecs, who were much more civilized than the other AMERICAN INDIANS. They built great cities with rich temples for their idols, to which they made human sacrifices. The coast of Mexico was first visited by a Spaniard in 1517 ; two years later it was conquered by CORTES. From that time the country was a Spanish province until 1821, when it became independent. It then covered, besides the present territory, TEXAS, CALIFORNIA, and NEW MEXICO. In 1845 Texas, which had revolted from Mexico, was joined to the United States, and this brought on a war with this country, which ended in 1848, and gave us also California and New Mexico. In 1862 there was a war between Mexico and France; the French conquered the country, and forced it to become an empire, the Archduke Maximilian of Austria being made emperor. He arrived in the capital in 1864, but in 1867 the French troops who had defended him were taken away; and Maximilian, being unable to uphold his own power, was captured and shot by the Mexicans, who did not want an empire at all.

MEXICO, a city, capital of the republic of Mexico; pop. 330,000, or twice as large as Minneapolis, Minn. It is situated in the beautiful valley of Mexico, in the middle of the great table-land of the country, and has a grand and splendid appearance from all sides. The finest of its squares is the Plaza de Armas (Place of Arms), on one side of which is the president's house, built on the site of the palace of Cortes. and on another the cathedral, one of the largest churches in America, which stands on the site of the great Aztec pyramid, where human sacrifices were made. The national museum, next to the president's house, has in it the statue of the Aztec god of war, and many other curiosities of the ancient inhabitants.

The name of Mexico is made from Mexitli, one of the gods of the Aztecs. This city was their capital, and Cortez, who captured and destroyed it, says it was the "most beautiful thing in the world." It was built on an island in a lake named Tezcuco, and was entered on several sides by very long causeways or roads built of stone and earth with many open places crossed by wooden bridges. The shortest of these

roads was a mile and a half long and only thirty feet, or five times the length of a man, broad. Canals, crossed by bridges, ran through the city, many of the streets were wide and lined with shade trees, and a thousand men were kept all the time at work sweeping and watering them. The houses of the rich were built of stone, and were surrounded by beautiful gardens, cooled with fountains. In the middle of the city was a large public square, or market-place, on one side of which rose the great temple or pyramid, built in five stories, from the top of which one could look over the lake and all the country around. On this were altars where fires were kept forever burning, and on which living human beings had their hearts torn out and their blood offered to the gods, their shrieks being drowned by the beating of a great drum which could be heard for miles around. Many thousand persons were put to death in this way every year. The Spaniards say that Mexico had 500,000 inhabitants at this time. Cortes tore down nearly all the city when he took it, and afterward rebuilt it.

MEYERBEER (*mi'er-ba-er*), **Giacomo,** a famous German writer of operas, born in Berlin, Sept. 5, 1794. He belonged to a wealthy Jewish family by the name of Beer, Meyer being his middle name, but he put the two names together, making Meyerbeer. From his earliest childhood he showed great love for music, and when only five years old used to play little tunes on the piano. He and Von WEBER studied music together in the same school and were great friends all their lives. Meyerbeer's first opera, "Jephthah," brought out in 1812, was a failure, but he was not disheartened, and after visiting Italy to learn something of Italian music, he began to please the public. His operas of "Robert le Diable," the "Huguenots," and the "Prophet," are among the most

splendid ever written. Meyerbeer

Meyerbeer.

died in Paris when seventy years old (May 2, 1864).

MI·AN·TON'O·MOH, a sachem or chief of the Narragansett Indians, nephew of CANONICUS. He became chief in 1636, and was always a friend of the whites, aiding them in their wars against the other Indians. In 1642 one of his chiefs was attacked by the Mohegan sachem, UNCAS. To avenge this insult, Miantonomoh made war on Uncas with nearly a thousand warriors, but was defeated and taken prisoner. Uncas took him to Hartford and told the English officers there that he would do with his captive whatever they commanded. Though Miantonomoh had made war with their consent, they advised that he should be killed. He was therefore taken back to Norwich, where he had been defeated, and killed by Uncas with a tomahawk (1643). A monument was erected in 1841 on the place, which is still called Sachem's Plain.

MICHAEL ANGELO (*mi'ka-el an'je-lo*), a famous Italian painter, sculptor, and architect, born near Florence, March 6, 1474. His father, Lodovico Leonardo Buonarotti Simone, was at the time of his son's birth governor of a fortress near Florence. At a very early age Michael showed great fondness for drawing, and he attracted the notice of Lorenzo de' Medici, who helped him in every way with his art studies. When Lorenzo died and his family were overthrown by the Florentines, the artist went to Venice, but returned to Florence when the Medici came back. A statue of the Sleeping Cupid made by him gave him such fame that he was invited by some distinguished men in Rome to go there. The best of his works made at this time is the Piesta, the Mourning Mary with the dead Christ in her lap, which now stands in a chapel near the entrance of St. Peter's. In 1499 Michael Angelo returned to his native city, but he again went back to Rome on the invitation of Pope Julius II., who gave him an order to build a splendid tomb for himself in St. Peter's. Among the many wonder-

Michael Angelo.

ful things to-day to be seen in Rome are the frescoes painted by him on the ceiling of the Sistine Chapel, done in the short space of twenty months. Another celebrated painting is his " Last Judgment," on the wall of the Sistine Chapel. Owing to various causes, the great artist left many unfinished works. He was not only a sculptor and painter, but also an architect and a poet. The great dome of St. Peter's Cathedral was his design, and the sonnets that he wrote are among the best in the Italian language. He died in Rome when eighty-nine years old (February 17, 1563).

MICHELET (*meesh-la'*), **Jules,** a French historian, born in Paris, August 21, 1798. His father, who was a painter, gave him a fine education. When only twenty-three years old he was made professor of history and of ancient languages in the Collége Rollin, and in 1838 he became professor of history in the College of France. Many other offices and positions of honor were given to him, and he filled all well; but in 1851 he lost his places and titles because he would not take the oath to uphold the government of the Emperor Napoleon III. He then retired to his own home and gave himself up to writing, publishing many valuable books, most of which have been translated into English. His most important work is the " History of France." He died at Hyères, when seventy-five years old (February 9, 1874).

MICHIGAN (*mish'e-gan*), one of the W. States of the United States, N. of Ohio and Indiana, and E. of Wisconsin; area, 56,500 square miles, or larger than New York and New Jersey put together; pop. 2,094,000, or not quite a half more than that of New Jersey; capital, LANSING. It is formed of two great peninsulas, one between Lakes Huron and Michigan, and the other between Lakes Michigan and Superior, the two parts being separated by Mackinaw Straits. Thus, though not on the sea, Michigan has more miles of coast than any other State except Florida.

Along the northern peninsula the shores are often high and rocky, and many of the cliffs are remarkable for their bright colors, or for the curious caves and arches made by the waves; hence they are called " Pictured Rocks." The southern peninsula is low and flat.

The northern peninsula is very rich in mines, especially in copper and iron. The copper mines are the richest in the world, excepting those of Chili; and more iron ore is mined than in any other State excepting Pennsylvania. In the southern peninsula are coal mines and some of the finest salt-beds in the United States. But this region is much more important for its farms, and here most of the people live. In the northern part are great pine forests, where many lumbermen are employed in cutting the trees. More lumber is sold in Michigan than in any other State. The great lakes are celebrated for their fisheries, especially of whitefish.

The name Michigan is made from two Indian words —*Mitchi*, great, and *Sawgyegan*, lake. It was first given to both Lakes Michigan and Huron, but finally to Lake Michigan alone, and from that the State was named. Michigan was first settled by the French, from whom the English got it in 1763. It came to the United States after the war of the Revolution, was made a Territory in 1805, and became a State of the Union in 1837.

MICHIGAN, Lake, one of the great lakes of North America, lying entirely within the United States, and having its outlet by the Straits of Mackinaw, and Lake Huron; area, 22,400 square miles, or about as large as the State of West Virginia. In most places it is about 1000 feet deep. The shores are low, and there are but few good harbors, those of Chicago, Milwaukee, and Sheboygan having been artificially improved. Lake Michigan abounds in fine fish.

MI'DAS, the name of a fabled King of PHRYGIA. He showed favor to BACCHUS, and that god gave him the power of turning everything he touched to gold. But as his food, as well as all other things, was changed, he came near starving to death, and he begged Bacchus to take away the gift. By order of Bacchus he bathed in the River Pactolus, which ever after flowed over sands of gold. APOLLO became angry with Midas because in a musical contest he gave the prize to PAN instead of to him, and changed his ears to those of an ass. Midas wore a cap to hide them; but the slave who cut his hair could not keep the secret. He dug a hole, whispered into it : "King Midas has ass's ears," and filled it up with earth. But a reed sprang up there, and whenever it was moved by the winds repeated his words. So the secret was discovered.

MID'DLE-TOWN, a city of Connecticut, on the Connecticut River, 30 miles from its mouth; pop. 9000, or about as large as Piqua, Ohio. It has large cotton-mills, foundries, and manufactories of hardware, britannia, and silver-plated ware, sewing machines, tools, screws, and other things. A considerable trade is carried on, both by railroads and by vessels on the river. Middletown is the seat of the Berkeley Divinity School of the Episcopal Church, and of the Wesleyan University, which has nearly 200 students.

MILAN (*mil'an*), a city of N. Italy, in a plain S. of the Alps; pop. 420,000, or nearly as large as Baltimore, Md. The most thickly-settled part is surrounded by a canal, and outside of that, enclosing the suburbs and gardens, is a wall with twelve gates. Milan is one of the pleasantest cities in Europe, and is noted for its fine buildings and its many libraries and art galleries. Among its splendid churches is the cathedral, which is the largest church in Italy except St. Peter's in Rome, and is one of the finest buildings in the world. It is crowned by a great number of steeples, and is so richly ornamented that from a distance it looks like lace-work. It was begun in 1387, and is not yet finished. The great theatre of Milan, called La Scala, will seat nearly 4000 persons. The city has a larger inland trade than any other place in Italy.

Milan gets its name from its ancient name, Mediolanum, which means "in the midst of the marshy land." The Romans got possession of it about 222 B.C., and under them it became very important. During the present century it belonged to Austria most of the time until 1859, when it was again joined to Italy.

MILL, John Stuart, a famous English writer, born in London,

John Stuart Mill.

May 20, 1806. His father, James Mill, was a literary man, and he began his son's education so early that the son says of himself, " I have no remembrance of the time when I began to learn Greek, but I have been told it was when I was three years old." When eight years old he was reading the works of the principal

Latin and Greek authors. In spite of his learned education, he entered the office of the East India Company when seventeen as clerk, remaining in its service twenty-five years, and at the same time writing books. Most of his works are on political economy, a study which teaches nations how to use their wealth for the best good of their people. When the East India Company was disbanded, Mill gave himself up altogether to writing. In 1865 he was elected to Parliament, and his chief object while there was to get the laws of the country altered, so that women could vote. His great admiration and love for his wife seem to have given him a high opinion of all women. When she died, in 1859, he took up his residence near her grave at AVIGNON, and devoted all his thoughts to her memory. He died at Avignon when sixty-seven years old (May 9, 1873). Mill did not believe in the Christian religion, as he himself tells us in his autobiography, or life written by himself, published after his death.

MIL-LA IS', John Everett, an English painter, born in Southampton, June 8, 1829. He began drawing when very young, and received a medal from the Society of Arts when only nine years old. He paints historical and other figure pictures, many of which are well known through engravings and photographs. The "Huguenot Lovers" is one of the most famous of his works.

MILLET (*me-ya'*), **Jean François,** a French painter, born at Grouchy, Normandy, Oct. 4, 1814. He was famous for his pictures of the village and peasant life of France, which possess very great merits. He died at Barbison, near Paris, when sixty-one years old (Jan. 18, 1875).

MIL'MAN, Henry Hart, a famous English clergyman and author, born in London, February 10, 1791. He was the son of Sir Francis Milman, physician of George III., and was educated at Oxford. When twenty-

four years old he wrote a tragedy called "Fazio," which was played with success in London. In 1820 he published "The Fall of Jerusalem," a poem which made him famous, and the next year he was made professor of poetry at Oxford. He also wrote a "History of the Jews" and other histories, and published an edition of Gibbon's "Decline and Fall of the Roman Empire," with notes. He died in London, when Dean of St. Paul's, when seventy-seven years old (Sept. 24, 1868).

MI'LO, a Greek athlete, born in Crotona, in Italy, in the latter part of the sixth century B.C. He was famous for his great strength, and many wonderful stories are told of him. It is said that he once carried a bull on his shoulders to the sacrifice and killed it with a blow of his fist, and ate it all in one day. Once when he was listening to Pythagoras, with others of his scholars, the pillar which held up the roof gave way, but Milo held up the whole building until all had time to escape. When quite an old man, in trying to pull apart a tree which some wood-cutters had partly split, he got caught in such a way that he could not help himself, and was eaten by wild beasts.

MILTIADES (*mil-ti'a-deez*) a famous Athenian general who lived about 500 B.C. When the great Persian army was marching toward Athens he persuaded the Athenians to fight in the field and not wait to be attacked in the city ; and, with a much smaller force than that of the Persians, won the great battle of MARATHON (490). To reward him the Athenians gave him the principal place in a great painting of the battle. Afterward he sailed with seventy ships against the island of Paros, and besieged the town. While consulting a priestess there he was struck with sudden fright, and fell, injuring his thigh so badly that he gave up the siege. On his return to Athens he died soon after of his wound.

Miltiades.

MIL'TON, John, a famous English poet, born in London, Dec. 9, 1608. As a school-boy, Milton was far ahead of most of his companions, who took their revenge upon him by making fun of his pink and white complexion and calling him "the

John Milton.

lady of the College." He was graduated at Cambridge in 1632, and then went to his father's house in Buckinghamshire, where he spent five years in reading and study. There he wrote some of his most beautiful poems, including "L'Allegro," "Il Penseroso," and the masque or play called "Comus," which was performed by young folks at Ludlow Castle (1634).

On the death of his mother, in 1637, he set out on his travels over the continent of Europe, visiting chiefly France and Italy, and returning at the end of two years to find his country just entering on the great civil war between King Charles I. and his Parliament. Milton was a firm Puritan, and at once joined heart and soul in the cause of the people. When Cromwell became Protector, he appointed Milton his foreign secretary, to write his letters to the courts of other nations. This place he kept for eleven years, till he was deprived of it by the return of Charles II.

For six years blindness had been coming upon him, and the year of the Restoration (1660), saw him deprived of sight, and with no support for himself or family. Then he wrote his greatest work, the sublime poem of "Paradise Lost," which he sold to a bookseller for £5 cash, with a promise of like sums on the sale of the first, second, and third editions. Milton was three times married. His first wife, Mary Powell, belonged to a Royalist family, and the marriage was not a happy one. At one time a divorce was seriously thought of. He had three daughters who grew to womanhood, but they were not dutiful children, and they caused their father much sorrow. Milton's prose works, which are numerous, are mostly on political and religious subjects. He died when sixty-six years old (Nov. 8, 1674).

MILWAUKEE (*mil-waw'ke*), the chief city and port of Wisconsin, on the W. side of Lake Michigan, at the mouth of the Milwaukee River; pop. 204,000, or about as large as Detroit, Mich. It has one of the best harbors on the lake, and carries on a very large trade, especially in grain and flour. The city contains fine breweries, tanneries, iron mills, and other manufactories. The houses are mostly built of cream-colored brick, which gives them a very handsome appearance. Milwaukee was settled in 1835, and became a city in 1846.

MINERVA (*mi-ner'vah*), an ancient goddess of the Greeks and Romans, called by the Greeks Athena, Pallas, or Pallas Athene. She was the goddess of thought, wisdom, and of the arts and sciences, and was supposed to have sprung from the head of Jupiter clad in full armor. She was the patron of scientific warfare, and was therefore said to be superior to Mars, who was only the god of brute force. Among the things which she taught mankind the use of were the flute, every kind of work proper for women, the olive, and several instruments of war and of farming. She is usually represented clad in armor, with a helmet on her head, and carrying a shield and spear. Minerva or Athena was the principal goddess of Attica and of Athens, which was named from her. The poets said that Neptune and Minerva strove for the possession of Attica. Neptune, striking the earth with his trident, brought forth the war-horse ; but Minerva produced the olive (the symbol of peace), and won the victory. She had a magnificent temple in ATHENS called the Parthenon, in which was her great statue by Phidias.

MIN·NE·AP'O·LIS, a city of Minnesota on the Mississippi River, at the Falls of St. Anthony, 8 miles W.N.W. of St. Paul; pop. 165,000, or about as large as Jersey City, N. J. Vessels can pass from the Gulf of Mexico up the river to this place, and in the summer small steamboats run from Minneapolis to St. Cloud, on the upper Mississippi. The St. Anthony Falls, which here stop navigation, are about 18 feet high, and give water-power for many large flouring mills, saw-mills, and other manufactories. The University of

Minnesota at Minneapolis has 1000 students. The country around is noted for its beauty. Three miles from the city are Minnehaha Falls, a beautiful cascade, 45 feet high. Minneapolis was settled in 1849.

MINNESOTA (*min-ne-so'tah*), a N. State of the United States, between Wisconsin and Dakota, and almost exactly in the centre of North America ; area, 83,500 square miles, or larger than all New England and Maryland put together ; pop. about 1,302,000, or about a fourth more than that of Maryland; capital, ST. PAUL. Most of the surface is level, and scattered over the State are thousands of beautiful lakes, whose bright, clear waters are full of fish. These lakes are remarkable because three of the four largest rivers in North America rise in them : the MISSISSIPPI, the ST. LAWRENCE, and the RED RIVER of the North. The Mississippi in this region is noted for its beautiful scenery, and in some of the streams that flow into it there are fine falls, one of which, not far from St. Paul, is called Minnehaha, an Indian word meaning "laughing water." In the northern part of the State are great forests of pine and other trees, where thousands of logs are cut every year and floated down the rivers in rafts, on which the lumbermen build their shanties and live. But the principal wealth of Minnesota is in its fine farms, the soil being so rich that immense crops are raised ; only three or four States grow more wheat. The people are very proud of their beautiful country, and are doing everything that they can to improve it. The climate is pleasant and healthful, but the winters are so cold, especially in the northern part, that the mercury sometimes freezes in the thermometer.

Minnesota gets its name from the Minnesota River, and it is said to mean in the language of the Indians "sky-tinted waters." The greater part of the State was once a part of Louisiana, which was bought from France in 1803. It was made a territory in 1849, and a State of the Union in 1858.

MINORCA (*min-or'kah*). See BALEARIC ISLANDS.

MI'NOS, in Greek fable, a King of Crete, said to have been the son of Jupiter and EUROPA. He was the husband of Pasiphaë, who became the mother of the Minotaur, a creature with the body of a man and the head of a bull, which was shut up by him in the famous labyrinth built by DÆDALUS. Minos is said to have been a great law giver, and to have become after death one of the judges of HADES.

MIRABEAU (*me-rah-bo'*), Gabriel Honoré Riquetti, Count de, a famous French author and statesman, born near Nemours, March 9, 1749. At birth he was lame, tongue-tied, and had two back teeth, and his ugliness was made greater by an attack of smallpox, which left him badly scarred. His father seems to have had nothing but hate for this ugly but brilliant son, and he sent him to school in Paris, under a false name, because he was ashamed of him. At eighteen Mirabeau entered a cavalry regiment, gambled, fell into debt, and was sent as a prisoner to a fort on the isle of Ré. The next year he was released, and behaved so well as a soldier in Corsica that he won praise from officers and men; and on his return he was allowed for the first time to take his own name and title. He married, became poor, and was refused help by his father, who again threw him into prison; but he escaped and fled from France. In 1777 he was arrested, taken to Paris and put into prison at Vincennes, where he lay for more than three years, until his father let him out and became at last his friend. In 1789 he was elected a member of the Assembly of the States General. He led no party in the Assembly,

but took a course of his own, defending the cause of the people but working also for the just rights of Louis XVI. He wrote many works, chiefly on political matters, and died in Paris, after a severe illness, at the age of forty-two (April 2, 1791).

MISSISSIPPI (*mis-sis-sip'pe*), one of the Southern States of the United States, on the E. side of the Mississippi River; area, 47,000 square miles, or the same as that of New York State; pop. 1,290,000, or less than two ninths that of New York State; capital, JACKSON. Most of the surface is hilly or rolling, part of it being prairie and the rest covered with woods. Near the Mississippi the land is generally low and swampy, with great thickets of canes and other plants. In other places the swamps have been drained and protected from the river by levees, making the finest plantations in the State. At Vicksburg, Yazoo, and other places are high bluffs along the river. Mississippi has about ninety miles of sea-coast, but as none of the harbors are deep enough for large vessels, most of the trade goes through Mobile or New Orleans. Mississippi is noted for its great cotton plantations, more cotton being raised there than in any other State. Besides this, corn and wheat are raised in the northern, and sugar-cane and rice in the southern part. The climate is so warm that oranges and other tropical fruits grow very well. More than half of the people are negroes.

Mississippi was named from the River Mississippi. It was a part of Louisiana, bought from France in 1803. It became a territory in 1798, and a State of the Union in 1817. In 1861 it seceded and joined the Confederate States, but became a State of the Union again in 1870.

MISSISSIPPI RIVER, the principal river of North America, rising in Lake Itasca in N. Minnesota, and flowing into the Gulf of Mexico; length 2600 miles. With the Missouri, its principal branch, it is about 4200 miles long, and is probably the longest river in the world. Other large rivers flowing into it are the Ohio, the Arkansas, and the Red. Where it leaves the lake, the Mississippi is only ten or twelve feet wide and eighteen inches deep. In its upper course it has many rapids, and passes through several beautiful lakes. The channel, in many places, is filled with little islands, and along the sides are high, rocky cliffs, noted for their grand scenery. About four hundred miles from Itasca Lake the river flows over a precipice eighteen feet high, called the Falls of St. Anthony. Below this there are only two rapids, one near Rock Island, Illinois, and the other near the mouth of the Des Moines River; but both of these have been so improved that steamboats can go up as far as St. Anthony Falls; above that small steamboats can go almost to the source. Between the falls and the mouth of the Missouri River there are many sand-banks, which the river is constantly forming and washing away, so that they often hinder navigation. Sometimes trees, washed down by the river, get caught by their roots on the bottom and lie with their heads pointed down stream. These are called "sawyers," and in dark nights steamboats going up the river are apt to run against them and be sunk.

The lower Mississippi is about three fourths of a mile wide, and is bordered by wide, swampy plains, which are often overflowed when the river rises in the spring. As these lands are very fertile, many fine plantations have been made on them. To protect the fields, the people have made walls called levees along the river banks, but sometimes the levees break and the lands are flooded, destroying the crops and even drowning many people. Such breaks are called crevasses. Along the lower Mississippi are many lakes and side-channels, called bayous. Near its mouth the river breaks up into several channels, between which are the low, sandy, and swampy lands called the delta of the Mississippi. Sometimes one of the channels becomes covered with floating grass or rubbish, forming a bridge, or raft as it is called, entirely across it. Such a raft was formed on the Atchafalaya channel in 1778, and it remained for nearly sixty years until large trees grew in it. It was finally removed after many men had been engaged for four years in clearing it away.

At the mouth of the Mississippi are bars of sand and mud, which make it difficult for large ships to enter the river. As the mud was washed down, these banks constantly grew in size, until they threatened to block up the river. By command of the Government, Captain EADS, a noted engineer, constructed what are called jetties at one of the mouths. These consist of two walls, one on each side of the channel, which is thus narrowed so that the current washes out the mud and leaves it always clear and deep.

The Mississippi is said to have been called by the Indians Miche Sepe, which means the Great River. The river was discovered by DE SOTO in 1541, and it was first descended by the Frenchmen, MARQUETTE and Joliet, in 1673.

MISSOURI (*mis-soo're*), one of the W. States of the United States, on the W. side of the Mississippi River, and almost in the centre of the United States; area, 65,350 square miles, or nearly as large as all New England; pop. 2,679,000, or about five ninths that of New England; capital, Jefferson City. The Missouri River divides it into two parts. The northern part is nearly level, but the southern part is a fine, rolling country. Much of the land is prairie, but there are also large forests, and near the Mississippi are many swamps. Some of these swamps have been drained, and the farms made from them are among the richest in the world.

Missouri has fine coal mines, and some of the best iron and lead mines in the United States. It is one of the most important farming States in the Union. Besides great fields of corn, wheat, and tobacco, the farmers have large herds of cattle and swine, and cotton is cultivated in the southern part. In some places there are fine vineyards, and more wine is made than in any other State except California. Many of the streams have good water-power, and so many mills and factories have been built that Missouri is one of the greatest manufacturing States. The large rivers can be navigated with steamboats, so that grain and other things are easily carried from one place to another. Most of the produce is brought to St. Louis, the largest city, whence it is sent to the East by railroads, or down the Mississippi in steamboats and other vessels.

Missouri, which was named from the Missouri River, was a part of Louisiana, bought from France in 1803. It became a territory in 1812, and in 1821 a State of the Union.

MISSOURI RIVER, the principal branch of the Mississippi and the longest river of North America, rising in the Rocky Mountains, in Montana, and flowing into the Mississippi; length 2900 miles. Its sources are in many little streams rising among the mountains, amongst grand and beautiful scenery. About 400 miles from the source the river flows through a very deep and narrow valley called the "Gates of the Rocky Mountains." The rocks on each side of this rise straight up from the water to the height of a quarter of a mile. About 145 miles below are the Great Falls, consisting of four cataracts, one of which is eighty-seven feet high. These falls and the rapids between them show some of the grandest scenery in the world. Below the falls the

river flows generally among prairies and open lands, but near the mouth there are low forest-covered plains, which are sometimes overflowed, and are very fertile. Steamboats ascend to the mouth of the Yellowstone, and they can go much farther, but as yet the country along the upper Missouri is very thinly settled, almost the only people being Indians and miners. The river water is very muddy, and from this it gets its name, Missouri being an Indian word meaning Mud River. The principal branches are the Yellowstone and Platte.

MITCHELL (*mich'el*), **Donald Grant,** an American writer, born in Norwich, Conn., in 1822. As a writer he has taken the name of "Ik Marvell." For some time he was an editor of the *Hearth and Home*, and he has frequently appeared as a lecturer. For two years, from 1853 to 1855, he was Consul for the United States at Venice. His best known works are "Reveries of a Bachelor," "Dream Life," "My Farm of Edgewood," and "Doctor Johns." He lives at Edgewood near New Haven.

MITFORD, Mary Russell, a noted English writer, born in Alresford, Hampshire, December 16, 1786. Her father, a physician, having lost all his money, she began to aid him when quite young by writing. She published some volumes of poems when twenty years old, and from that time till 1854 wrote many novels, tales, and plays. Her most popular books are "Our Village," containing interesting sketches of country life in Berkshire, and "Recollections of a Literary Life." Her most popular play is "Rienzi." For more than forty years she lived near Reading in Berkshire, greatly loved and respected, and died there, when sixty-eight years old (January 10, 1855).

MITHRIDATES (*mith-ri-da'teez*) VI., King of Pontus, commonly called the Great, born about 132 B.C. He succeeded his father as

king when only eleven years old, but very soon began to show skill as a soldier. Pontus, his kingdom, was in Asia Minor, on the south coast of the Euxine Sea (now BLACK SEA), from which it got its name, Pontus in Greek meaning the sea, and especially the Euxine Sea. At this time the Romans had a province called Asia in the west part of Asia Minor, and Mithridates, having got into a quarrel with them, conquered this and massacred all the Romans living there. It is said that 80,000 were killed in one day. He then crossed over into Greece, where many of the Greeks took his side; but SULLA soon defeated him in two great battles, and Mithridates made a peace in which he agreed to give up all he had won (85 B.C.).

But as soon as he had a good opportunity, he began the war again (74), and it lasted this time ten years. The Romans sent against him first LUCULLUS and then POMPEY, and his kingdom was finally overthrown and the Roman power made firmer than ever. It is said that Mithridates was so afraid of being poisoned that he accustomed himself to take strong drugs, and when he took poison to save himself from falling into the hands of his enemies, it had no effect on him; so he ordered a soldier to kill him with his sword. He died when about sixty-nine years old (63 B.C.).

MNEMOSYNE (*ne-mos'i-ne*). See MUSES.

MOBILE, (*mo-beel'*), a city of S. Alabama, on Mobile River near its mouth in Mobile Bay, and 30 miles from the mouth of the bay in the Gulf of Mexico; pop. 31,000, or about as large as Salem, Mass. It is the largest city and only seaport of Alabama, and has an important trade, especially in cotton. Mobile Bay is a very fine one, and is defended at its mouth by two strong forts, named Gaines and Morgan. During the Civil War these forts were held by the Con-

federates, who also had several war ships in the bay. The Union fleet under Admiral Farragut, after a hard-fought battle of an hour, during which the leading Union ship, the Tecumseh, was sunk by a torpedo, at last passed the forts and got into the bay, where the Confederate ships were soon sunk or captured (Aug. 5, 1864). Forts Gaines and Morgan were taken soon after, but the city of Mobile, which is thirty miles above the forts, was not taken until 1865 (April 12).

MOCHA (*mo'kah*), a city of S.W. Arabia, in Yemen, on a bay of the Red Sea, near the Strait of Bab-el-Mandeb; pop. about 5,000. The harbor is not very good, but many small ships frequent it and there is a large trade, especially in the famous Mocha coffee.

MODENA (*mod'a-nah*), a city of N. Italy, in a plain near the River Secchia; pop. 58,000, or nearly the same as that of Camden, N. J. It has a citadel and is surrounded by walls or ramparts, which have been turned into beautiful walks. Modena has a university, a library rich in manuscripts, coins, and medals, and many fine churches and palaces, some of which are noted for their paintings and statuary. Modena is a very old city, having been a Roman colony in the year 183 B.C. Its ancient name was Mutina, which means the "fortified place." From 1452 it was the capital of the Duchy of Modena, which was united to the Kingdom of Italy in 1860.

MŒSIA (*me'she-ah*), an ancient country of eastern Europe, covering nearly the same territory as Bulgaria and Servia.

MO-GULS', a name changed from Mongols, given by the people of Hindostan or India to the Tartars who invaded their country. They took Delhi (1526), and put their leader, Baber, a descendant of TIMOUR, on the throne. His successors were called the Mogul emperors. Among the most famous of them were AKBAR and AURUNG-ZEBE. Europeans used to call the Mogul emperor the Great Mogul. The English finally conquered the empire, and in 1858 the last Mogul had his title taken from him because he took part in the great mutiny against the English.

MO·HAM′MED, or Mahomet, the founder of the Mohammedan religion, born in Mecca, A.D. 570 or 571. He was the son of Abdallah, a rich merchant of the priestly race of Koreish. During his youth he made frequent journeys with caravans into foreign lands, where he met many Jews and Christians, and became convinced that their religion must be better than the idol worship of his own people, the Arabs. The Jews were looking all the while for a coming Messiah, and in the Gospel he had read of Christ's promise to send a Comforter to those that loved him, and his imagination led him to the belief that he must be that person, the one of whom the world stood in need. After five years given up to lonely thought, much of which time he spent in a cave, where he said that he had visions of the Angel Gabriel, he appeared in his fortieth year, announcing himself as God's messenger and proclaiming his doctrine in the words, "There is but one God, and Mohammed is his prophet."

At first he had few followers, scarcely any besides his own relatives, and a tumult arose against him, in which he was obliged to fly from Mecca to Medina. The date of this event, called the Hegira (622), is important, because Mohammedan countries count their time from it. In Medina he composed some of the Koran, the book containing his religion, which, since his time, has been the Mohammedan Bible. Eight years later he returned to Mecca, which opened its gates and proclaimed him as prophet. Mohammed and his successor spread his religion by the sword, and it is

to-day the faith of many of the nations of Asia and Africa. There is no doubt that Mohammed believed in his own divine mission. He had many gifts which fitted him to be a leader of men. His grave in the mosque at MEDINA is visited by thousands of pilgrims every year. He died in Medina when sixty-one years old (June 8, 632).

MOHAMMED II., a Turkish sultan, called the Great, born in Adrianople, in 1430. He was the eldest son of Amurath II., and succeeded him in 1451. His fame rests on the capture of Constantinople, May 29, 1453, which ended the Greek Empire, and set up in its place that of the Ottoman Turks. Mohammed extended the power of the Ottomans over the neighboring country, conquering in all twelve independent empires, and two hundred cities. He carried on successful wars against the Venetians and the Persians, but he was badly defeated in his attack on Rhodes by the HOSPITALLERS, or Knights of St. John. Mohammed died near Scutari, when fifty-one years old (1481). He was one of the ablest of all the sultans.

MOHAMMED IV., a Turkish sultan, born in 1642. He was the son of Ibrahim I., whom he succeeded in 1648. He was a man of neither talent nor energy, but his armies made some conquests, through the skill of his grand vizier, Mohammed Kuprili. The last of his reign was disastrous, the Turkish arms meeting a repulse at Vienna by John SOBIESKI, and a defeat at Mohacz. At last the army mutinied at Belgrade, and marching to Constantinople, dethroned Mohammed, raising his brother Solyman III. to the throne. Mohammed spent the rest of his life in prison. He died when about fifty years old (1692).

MO′HAWKS. See AMERICAN INDIANS.

MO·HE′GANS. See AMERICAN INDIANS.

MOLDAVIA (*mol-da've-ah*). See ROUMANIA.

MOLIERE (*mo-le-air'*), a famous French writer of comic plays, born in Paris, January 15, 1622. His real name was Jean Baptiste Poquelin. His father and grandfather were valets to King Louis XIII., who early took notice of the boy, and was at one time served by him. When fourteen years old he persuaded his father to send him to be educated by

Molière.

the Jesuits, and afterward began to study law; but his taste for the stage was too strong, and he joined a company of actors and took the name of Molière. He was little known until he published his first comedy (1653), but after that he soon became very famous as a playwriter and actor. Louis XIV. was proud of having such a man of genius at his court and gave him many privileges, and nobles and great men were proud to know him. His last play was the "Malade Imaginaire" (The Imaginary Invalid). He was sick when it was about to be played and his friends thought him too ill to act in it. "Ah!" he exclaimed, "think of the poor actors who, if it is not played, will lose their bread! I must act for their sakes, if possible." During the play he was taken with convulsions and died an hour after, aged fifty-one (Feb. 17, 1673).

MOLOCH (*mo'lok*), a heathen god worshipped by the ancient Ammonites, a tribe living east of Judea, and by the Phœnicians and Carthaginians. The Israelites also worshipped this idol sometimes, and Solomon built a temple to him. The statues of Moloch were heated, and human beings, generally children, were thrown into the red-hot arms, as a sacrifice in his honor.

MOLTKE (*molt'keh*), **Helmuth Karl Bernhard Von,** Count, a famous German general, born in Mecklenburg, October 26, 1800. His father was a Danish general, and he was educated at the military academy of Copenhagen. He entered the Prussian army in 1822; wrote a book about the Turkish and Russian war in 1835; and in the same year went to Turkey, where he spent four years, and served several campaigns with the Turkish army. After his return he held many high military positions, and was at last (1858) made chief officer of the staff. In this position he has won splendid victories in wars with Denmark, Austria, and France; and has made his name famous as one of the greatest soldiers in the world. The title of count was given him after the victory of Metz; and a large sum of money, with other honors and rewards, at the close of the French War. He was a very learned man, and understood several languages, but talked very little; so it has been well said of him that he is silent in seven tongues. In 1880 he refused the title of prince. He died when ninety years old (Apr. 24, 1891).

MOLUCCAS (*mo-luk'kaz*), or **Spice Islands,** a group of several hundred islands in the Malay Archipelago, between Celebes and Papua;

area, 43,000 square miles, or nearly as large as New York State ; pop. 250,000, or about a sixth that of New York City ; capital, Amboyna. Many of them are small and uninhabited, but three, Ceram, Gilolo, and Booro are quite large. Nearly all are rocky and high, and there are several burning volcanoes, and earthquakes are frequent. The climate is mild and pleasant. The most important products of the islands are cloves and nutmegs, in which there is a large trade. Cotton, sugar-cane, coffee, and pepper are also cultivated. The sago-palm is very common ; from its pith is made a kind of bread which is the principal food of the poor people. Most of the inhabitants are Malays, but in the interior of the larger islands are dark-skinned savages like those of PAPUA.

The Moluccas were discovered and settled by the Portuguese in 1511. Sixty years later they were conquered by the Dutch, and since then they have twice belonged to the English. In 1814 they were given back to the Dutch, to whom they still belong.

MO'MUS, in Greek fable, a god who delighted in mocking and finding fault with both gods and men. When Neptune, Minerva, and Vulcan strove to see which was the most skilful, Momus was chosen judge to decide between them. Neptune made a bull, Minerva a house, and Vulcan a man. But Momus found fault with all three : he said that Neptune should have put the bull's horns more in front, for then he could fight better ; that Minerva should have made her house movable, so that it could be carried to another place in case it was built among bad neighbors ; and that Vulcan should have made a window in the man's breast, so that his thoughts could be seen. All were so disgusted with his fault-finding that they turned him out of heaven. Venus was the only one in whom Momus could find nothing to

blame, and he vexed himself to death in consequence.

MONACO (*mon-ah'ko*), a country of N.W. Italy, on the Mediterranean Sea, and bounded on the land side by France. It is the smallest independent country in the world, having an area of only about 6 square miles, and a population of 13,000. About one fourth the people live in the town of Monaco, which is noted as a watering-place. Monaco is governed by a prince, who rules his little country as he pleases, but there is a garrison of Italian soldiers.

The Principality of Monaco was founded in the 16th century. It was united to France in 1793, but again became independent in 1815.

MONGOLIA (*mon-go'le-ah*), a country of Asia, forming the north part of the Empire of China. It is mostly a great plain, almost wanting in water, and covered in parts with forests where many wild animals

Mongolian Prince.

live. The people, called Mongols, belong to the TURANIAN class of mankind. GENGHIS KHAN and TIMOUR were Mongols. The MOGULS came from Mongolia.

MONK (*munk*), **George,** Duke of Albemarle, a famous English general, born in Devonshire, December 6, 1608. When young he served in the army of the Netherlands, but when thirty years old he went back to England and took the side of King Charles I. in the civil war.

He was soon taken prisoner by the Roundheads, and shut up in the Tower of London for about two years. When he was let out he joined the Parliament against the king, and showed so much skill as a soldier in Ireland that Cromwell gave him a high command in the army in Scotland. After conquering Scotland, he took part in two naval battles against the Dutch, in one of which VAN TROMP was killed.

When Cromwell died and his son Richard was made to give up his power, Monk marched to London with the army from Scotland, and shortly afterward (1660) brought about the restoration of CHARLES II. Charles made him Duke of Albemarle and gave him other honors and high offices. He was governor of London when the plague broke out (1665), and when all other officers fled he stayed and did his duty, though he said he should have thought himself much safer in battle. He died in London when sixtyone years old (Jan. 3, 1670). Albemarle County in Virginia and Albemarle Sound in North Carolina were named after him.

MONMOUTH (*mon'muth*), a county of central New Jersey, which gave its name to the battle of Monmouth, fought at Freehold during the Revolutionary War, June 28, 1778. The British under Sir Henry Clinton were attacked by a part of the American army under Gen. Lee, who had orders to keep up the battle until Washington arrived with the rest of his army. When Washington rode up, he found Lee and his soldiers retreating ; this made him very angry and he rebuked Lee sharply. It is said that was the only time that an oath was ever heard to come from Washington's lips. The Americans were rallied, and the fighting continued all day. The weather was very hot and many on both sides died of sunstrokes. In the night the British retreated

Gen. Lee was court-martialed and suspended from command for one year.

MON'ROE, James, fifth President of the United States, born in Westmoreland County, Va., April 28, 1758. He was educated at William and Mary College, and entered the army in 1776. During the Revolution he distinguished himself in many battles ; but he finally studied law, and soon made himself known as a statesman. He was elected to the Assembly of Virginia, and became a member of the Executive Council when only twenty-three years old ;

James Monroe.

and after that time he filled many honorable public offices. He was sent as minister to France and to England ; was Governor of Virginia for several years ; Secretary of State, and also of War under President Madison ; and finally was chosen President twice (1817-1825). During his first term Mississippi, Illinois, and Maine became States of the Union, and Spain gave up her possessions in Florida to the United States. During his second term the famous Missouri Compromise, which permitted slavery in Missouri, but in none of the States north of it, was brought about. In one of his messages to Congress, President Monroe spoke of the war which Spain was then carrying on against some of her revolted colonies in America, and declared that the United States would not interfere in any European war, nor permit any European power to get too much influence in this hemisphere. This has ever since been called after him the Monroe Doctrine. Monroe was one of the best Presidents the country has ever had, and did more than any one who ruled before him to improve the army, the navy, and the business of the nation. He died in New York when seventy-three years old (July 4, 1831).

MON'TA-GU, Lady **Mary Wortley,** a noted English writer, daughter of the Duke of Kingston, born at Thoresby in Nottinghamshire, about 1690. She learned Greek, Latin, and French with her brothers, and wrote verses when very young. In 1712 she married Edward Wortley Montagu, a country gentleman of literary tastes. The marriage was not a happy one, but she went with him (1716) to Constantinople, whither he went as ambassador. Her letters home telling about the manners and customs of the East were charming and were published after her return. Separated from her husband, distressed by the bad conduct of her only son, and in poor health, she went to Venice (1739) where she lived twenty-two years. She at last returned to England, but the journey was too much for her, and she died in London when seventy-two years old (August 21, 1762).

MONTAIGNE (*mon-tane'*), **Michel de,** a famous French writer, born at the Castle of Montaigne, Périgord, February 28, 1533. His father brought up his boy to speak Latin, and taught him French as a foreign tongue. He studied law and soon became famous for his wisdom and

honesty. But he is now best known by his "Essays," in which a great number of subjects are talked about in a very pleasant and sensible way. The only book known to have belonged to Shakespeare was a copy of Montaigne's "Essays," which, with Shakespeare's name written in it, is in the British Museum. Montaigne died at Montaigne Castle when fifty-nine years old (Sept. 13, 1592).

MONTANA (*mon-tah'nah*), a north-western State of the United States, between Dakota and Idaho; area, 144,000 square miles, or more than twice as large as New England; pop. 132,000, or about one thirty-fifth that of New England; capital, Helena. The western part is mountainous, but the eastern part is a plain. Much of the land is so dry that farms cannot be made unless they are watered from the rivers; but most of it is good for pasture. Antelopes, deer, and other wild animals are very common.

Montana is rich in gold mines. Silver is also found. In the south-western part are many curious geysers, or spouting springs, like those of the National Park, a small part of which lies in Montana.

Montana in Spanish means a mountain. The territory was made from a part of Idaho in 1864, and in 1889 became a State of the Union.

MONT BLANC (*mong blong'*). See ALPS.

MONTCALM (*mont-kahm'*) **DE SAINT VÉRAN,** Louis Joseph, Marquis de, a noted French general, born near Nîmes, February 28, 1712. When only fourteen years old he entered the army and fought in Italy and Germany. In 1756 he was made commander of the French army in New France (Canada). Two years later while at Fort Carillon, (Ticonderoga), with only 3,600 soldiers, he gained a splendid victory over the British, who had more than four times as many men. When the English under Gen. WOLFE tried to

take Quebec, he defended it bravely, and at first drove them back ;
but when Wolfe and his men climbed the steep sides of the Heights
of Abraham (Sept. 13, 1759), and
attacked the French army in the
rear, he was defeated. Both he and
Wolfe were killed in the battle.
After Montcalm was wounded and
had been told that he could not live
long, he said, " So much the better ;
I shall not live to see the surrender
of Quebec." He died at the age of
forty-seven (Sept. 14, 1759).

MONTENEGRO (*mon-ta-na'gro*),
a country of Europe, between Austria and Turkey ; area, 3550 square
miles, or about three fourths as large
as Connecticut ; pop. 236,000, or
less than a third that of Connecticut. It is covered with mountains,
many of which are densely wooded.
The people are simple and rough,
and live by farming, fishing, and
hunting. They belong mostly to
the Greek Church. The attempts
of the Turks to conquer them have
always failed, for every man is
trained as a soldier. The country
is a monarchy, and is ruled by a
prince.

MONTEREY (*mon-ta-ray'*), a city
of N.E. Mexico, on the Monterey
River ; pop. 42,000, or about as
large as Peoria, Ill. It is one of
the principal manufacturing towns
in Mexico, and carries on a large
trade. During the war between the
United States and Mexico, Monterey
was strongly fortified and garrison-
ed by 11,000 Mexican soldiers under
Ampudia. General Taylor attacked
it with less than 7000 men (Sept.
19, 1846). The Mexicans were driv-
en from their ramparts, but they
fought through the streets, and from
house to house, for five days.
Finally, on September 24, the Mexicans surrendered.

MONTEVIDEO (*mon-ta-ve-da'o*)
a city, capital of URUGUAY, on the
Rio de la Plata ; pop. about 175,-
000, or nearly as large as Newark, N. J. It is situated on a
small horseshoe-shaped bay, which
forms its harbor ; but very large
ships cannot enter, as the water is
shallow. This is the cleanest and
healthiest city in South America, and
it is rapidly growing. It has a large
trade in salt beef, hides, hair, and
tallow, got from the great herds of
cattle which live on the plains of
Uruguay.

Montevideo means " beautiful
mountain," and the place is named
from a mountain behind it, on which
is an old Spanish castle. The city
was founded by the Spaniards in
1717. It became the capital of Uruguay in 1828.

MONTEZUMA (*mon-te-zu'mah*)
I., Emperor of ancient Mexico, born
about 1390. He began to reign in
1436. He was a good soldier and
very successful in his wars, and at
one time brought more than 6000
captives to Mexico, where they were
sacrificed to the god of war. He
died in 1464.

MONTEZUMA II., the last of
the Aztec Emperors of Mexico, born
about 1480. He was a priest in the
great temple of Mexico, and was
sweeping the temple stairs when
the news came that he had been
made emperor. He began his
reign by making war and taking a
great number of captives, who were
sacrificed at his coronation. He
had a splendid court, but his heavy
taxes and severe laws caused many
rebellions.

About the year 1519 comets and
other strange objects were seen,
and the seers told Montezuma that
these were signs of the end of the
empire. This discouraged him, so
that when CORTEZ and the Spaniards came he was afraid to resist them, and he finally invited them
to the City of Mexico. A week
after, Cortez made Montezuma
prisoner, pretending that he was to
blame for some wrongs that his people had done to the Spaniards
Cortez finally offered to free him,
but he was ashamed to go back to

his nobles, and remained a prisoner for several months, swearing to obey the King of Spain. His people finally attacked the Spaniards, and at Cortez's desire Montezuma made a speech to them from the wall of his prison. At first the people listened respectfully, but when he asked them to treat the white men kindly, they answered by throwing stones, one of which hit him on the temple, and stunned him. He tore off the bandages that were put on his wound, and would take no food, so that he died a few days after, when about forty years old (June 30, 1520).

MONTGOLFIER (*mon-gol-fe-a'*), **Stephen** and **Joseph,** two brothers who were paper manufacturers near Lyons, France. They are noted for making and sending up the first balloon. It was made of linen, lined with paper, and like our common paper balloons, was filled with heated air, from a small fire of straw under it. It went up nearly a mile, and then came down slowly (June 5, 1783). For some time balloons were called after the two brothers, " Montgolfières."

MONT-GOM'ER-Y, a city, capital of Alabama, near the central part of the State, on a high bluff by the Alabama River; pop. 22,000, or about as large as Oswego, N. Y. It carries on a large trade in cotton and other things, both by steam-boats on the river and by several railroads, which meet in the city. About half the people are negroes.

Montgomery was founded in 1817 and became the State capital in 1847. It was the capital of the Confederate States from February 4, 1861, to May of the same year, when the Confederate Government removed to Richmond.

MONTGOMERY (*mont-gum'e-re*), **James,** a famous British poet, born in Ayrshire, Scotland, Nov. 4, 1771. His father was a Moravian preacher and wanted him to be one, but

he ran away from school and became a shop-boy. He afterward edited a newspaper in Sheffield, and was imprisoned several times for publishing things which were then against the laws. But he soon became famous as a poet, and published many works which were very popular. In 1835 Queen Victoria gave him a pension of $750 a year. He died near Sheffield when eighty-two years old (April 30, 1854).

MONTGOMERY (*mont-gum'e-re*), **Richard,** a noted American general, born near Raphoe, Ireland, Dec. 2, 1736. When quite young he entered the British army, and took part in an expedition against Martinique and Havana. Afterward he came to New York and in 1775 was appointed a general in the Revolutionary army, and sent against the English in Canada. He took Montreal and several other important places, and on the night of December 30, 1775, tried to take Quebec ; but while climbing up to the upper town, he was killed by a cannon-ball, at the age of thirty-nine (Dec. 31, 1775). In 1818 his remains were taken to New York and placed under a monument in front of St. Paul's Church.

MONTHOLON (*mon-to-long'*), **Charles Tristan,** Marquis de, a French soldier, born in Paris, July 21, 1783. He first distinguished himself at the battle of Wagram, under Napoleon, who made him a count for his bravery. Through all Napoleon's fortunes Montholon served him faithfully, showing his devotion by following him to ST. HELENA. When Montholon returned to Europe, after Bonaparte's death, he published " Memoirs of France under Napoleon, Written at St. Helena, under his Dictation." He was much attached to the whole Bonaparte family, and when Louis Napoleon, in 1840, tried to overturn the government of Louis Philippe, he was on his side and was put into prison with him. Afterward, however, he was pardoned. He died in Paris, when seventy years old, (Aug. 21, 1853).

MONTPELIER (*mont-peel'yer*), the capital of Vermont, on the Onion River, near the centre of the State; pop. 4200. The State capital, a fine granite building in the form of a cross, has a high dome, with a statue of CERES on the top. The country around Montpelier is hilly, but finely cultivated.

MONTPELLIER (*mong-pel-le-a'*), a city of S. France, 27 miles S.W. of Nîmes; pop. 57,000, or a little larger than Lynn, Mass. It has large manufactories of cotton, woollen, linen and silk cloths, leather, bronze, and chemicals. Formerly the city contained a university, but in its place there are now three schools, of medicine, sciences, and literature. The medical school is one of the most celebrated in France. It has a very fine library, and a collection of portraits of the professors who have taught there since 1289.

MONTREAL (*mon-tre-all'*), a city of Canada, on an island in the St. Lawrence River, at the mouth of the Ottawa; pop. 200,000, or about as large as Milwaukee, Wis. It is a very handsome city, with many fine public buildings and residences. The new Roman Catholic cathedral is the largest and finest church in Canada, and the old church of Notre Dame is also very large. McGill University, at Montreal, is the most important in British America, and there are several Catholic colleges. The Victoria Bridge, which crosses the St. Lawrence there, is two miles long. It is a great square tube made of wrought iron plates fastened together and raised above the river on stone piers. Montreal has a larger trade than any other city in Canada, and fine piers and wharves for vessels. About two-thirds of the people are of French descent.

Montreal was settled by the French in 1642, and was named Mont-real, or Mount Royal, from a hill on the island. In 1761 it was taken by the British, and during the Revolution was captured by the Americans under Gen. MONTGOMERY (1775).

MONT-ROSE', a town of E. Scotland, at the mouth of the South Esk River; pop. 15,000, or about as large as Watertown, N.Y. It has one of the best harbors in eastern Scotland, and a considerable trade is carried on. Montrose is noted for its manufactories of linen, and for its ship-yards. The Montrose Pits are deep places in the sea, near Montrose, where great numbers of codfish are caught.

MONT'ROSE, James Graham, Marquis of, a Scottish nobleman, born at Montrose in 1612. When the civil war broke out between King Charles I. and his Parliament, Montrose at first took the side of the latter, but when he saw how far they were going, he went over to the king, and after his death fought for Charles II. While leading his army over from the Orkney Islands to the mainland (1650), his troops were routed, and he himself was some time after taken prisoner disguised as a Highland rustic. He was condemned to be hanged on a gibbet thirty feet high, his head to be fixed on the tolbooth or prison of Edinburgh, his body to be quartered, and his limbs to be placed over the gates of the principal towns of Scotland. When the sentence was read to him, he said he felt more honored in having his head set on the prison for the cause in which he died, than he would had they ordered a golden statue to be erected to him in the market-place. As to his limbs, he wished he had flesh enough to send some to each city of Europe, in memory of the cause in which he died. These thoughts he put into poetry on the last night of his life, and wrote these lines with a point of a diamond on his prison window:

" Let them bestow on every withe a limb,
Then open all my veins, that I may swim
To thee, my Maker, in that crimson lake:
Then place my parboiled head upon a stake,
Scatter my ashes, strew them on the air:
Lord, since thou know'st where all these atoms
    are,
I'm hopeful thou'lt recover once my dust,
And confident thou'lt raise me with the just."

Montrose was a scholar and a gallant soldier, and he went to his death with such courage that many of his bitterest enemies wept. He died at Edinburgh, when thirty-eight years old (May 21, 1650).

MOORE, Sir **John,** a noted British general, born in Glasgow, Scotland, Nov. 13, 1761. He was made an officer in the army in 1776, and at one time, served with the British troops in the American Revolution. During the wars with Napoleon, he served in Holland, Egypt, Sicily, and Sweden and was wounded several times. For his valor in Egypt, he was made a knight. In 1808 he was appointed to the command of the British army in Portugal. He at once marched to Salamanca, Spain, expecting to be reinforced there by Spanish armies, but the Spaniards were defeated, and Moore was forced to retreat. He reached the sea-coast at Corunna, where he was attacked by the French under Marshal Soult. The British repulsed the attack and got away in safety to their ships; but Moore was killed in the battle by a cannon-ball, when forty-seven years old (Jan. 16, 1809). He was buried in the citadel, where Marshal Soult ordered a monument to be erected to him. The English poet, Charles Wolfe, described his burial in the fine poem beginning,

" Not a drum was heard nor a funeral note,
    As his corse to the rampart we hurried ;
Not a soldier discharged his farewell shot
    O'er the grave where our hero we buried."

MOORE, Thomas, a famous Irish poet, born in Dublin, May 28, 1779. His father, who was a grocer, had him educated at Trinity College, Dublin, and he afterward studied law in London. When twenty-one years old he published a volume of poems called the " Anacreon," which met with success. He was given an office in the Bermudas in 1803 and went there and travelled through the West Indies and the United States during the next year. His most noted poems are " Irish Melodies," many of which have been set to music, and " Lalla Rookh." Moore also wrote a " Life of Byron" and a " History of Ireland." He was a good talker and a fine singer, and often sang his own songs in company. He died when seventy-two years old (Feb. 25, 1852).

MORAN, Edward, an English painter, born at Bolton, England, in 1829. He paints landscapes, sea views, and animals. He lives in New York.

MORAN, Thomas, an American painter, brother of Edward Moran, born at Bolton, England, Jan. 12, 1837. He came to America when a child. He paints landscapes and the human figure, in oils and water-color. He has painted some very large pictures of Western scenery, among them " The Grand Cañon of the Yellowstone" and " The Chasm of the Colorado." His studio is in New York.

MORE, Hannah, a noted English writer, born at Stapleton, Gloucestershire, Feb. 2, 1745. Her father, though educated for a clergyman, had become a village school-master, and she and her four sisters opened a young ladies' school at Clifton which became celebrated. When only sixteen years old she wrote a play called " The Search after Happiness," and this was soon followed by other plays and poems which made her famous. After a while she gave up writing for the theatre, and wrote moral tales and stories, among the most noted of which was " The Shepherd of Salisbury Plain " and "Cœlebs in Search of a Wife." Her life was spent in literary labors and in good works. She died at Clifton when eighty-eight years old (Sept. 7, 1833). She made much money by her writings, and left one-third of it to charity.

MORE, Sir **Thomas,** a famous English statesman, born in London in 1480. He was educated at Oxford, became a lawyer, won fame, and was elected a member of Parliament. When about thirty-five years old he wrote in Latin a book called "Utopia," in which he gives an account of an imaginary country of that name on an island in the Atlantic, the laws, manners, and customs of which he described as worthy of being imitated in England. It became very popular and was translated into all the principal languages of Europe. The word utopian, made from it, is often given to fanciful political schemes. More received many high offices and was made a knight in 1521. When Henry VIII. took the title of Head of the Church, More refused to take the oath to him under that title and was tried and condemned for treason. He was executed in the Tower of London when fifty-five years old (July 6, 1535). He was one of the best scholars and purest characters of his time.

MOREA (*mo-re'ah*). See PELOPONNESUS.

MOREAU (*mo-ro'*), **Jean Victor,** a famous French general, born at Morlaix, Aug. 11, 1763. In 1792 he joined the French republican army, and by 1794 had become a general. After serving in Holland, he was made commander of the French army fighting the Austrians on the Rhine. He won many victories, but at length being nearly surrounded by armies much larger than his own, he made one of the most famous retreats ever recorded, not only saving his own army, but taking many prisoners and cannon on his march (1796).

In 1799 Moreau helped Napoleon when he made himself First Consul, and Napoleon sent him with an army to invade Austria. He won a great victory at HOHENLINDEN, and was within two days' march of Vienna when the Austrians sued for peace. In 1804 Moreau was accused of conspiring with PICHEGRU and Georges Cadoudal, against Napoleon. Very little was proved against him, but he was exiled, and came to the United States, and lived for nine years on a farm at Morrisville, Pa. Finally the Emperor Alexander of Russia induced him to join him in the invasion of France. He became Alexander's close friend, and planned the movements of his army until the battle of Dresden, where, as he was riding with the Emperor, both of his legs were broken by a cannon-ball. The surgeons were obliged to cut them off, and Moreau smoked a cigar and talked with them as they worked. He was carried with the army as it retreated before Napoleon, but died five days after the battle, at Laun, Bohemia, when fifty years old (Sept. 2, 1813).

MOR'GAN, Daniel, a noted American general, born in New Jersey in 1736. In 1775 he went as a teamster with General BRADDOCK'S expedition against Fort Duquesne, and on account of some supposed rudeness to a British officer, was given five hundred lashes with a whip. When the war of the Revolution began, he headed a company of Virginia riflemen, and marched six hundred miles to Boston. He was made colonel of a regiment and sent to North Carolina, where in 1781 he defeated the British under General TARLETON at the Cowpens. For this victory Congress gave him a gold medal. He died at his home in Winchester, Virginia, at the age of sixty-six (July 6, 1802).

MOR-GAR'TEN, a narrow pass in Central Switzerland between Morgarten Hill and Lake Egeri, noted for a victory of the Swiss over the

Austrians, Nov. 16, 1315. The Swiss were fighting for freedom from Austrian rule. They had only 1400 ill-armed men, while the Austrians had 20,000 trained soldiers ; but they attacked their enemies as they were marching through the pass, hurling down great rocks from the hills and then charging so fiercely that nearly all the Austrians were killed. Services are held every year on the date of the battle in a little chapel at the foot of the hill.

MO-ROC'CO, a country of N.W. Africa, on the Atlantic Ocean, at the mouth of the Mediterranean Sea; area 220,000 square miles, or nearly five times as large as the State of New York ; pop. 5,000,000, or about five sixths that of New York ; capitals, Fez and MOROCCO. It is crossed from N.E. to S.W. by the Atlas Mountains, some of the peaks of which are more than two miles high and nearly always covered with snow. Their lowest parts are clothed with great forests, where lions and other wild beasts are found. Near the coast is a lower range called Er-Rif. South of the Atlas range, the country is a dry desert. On the northern side it is very fertile and beautiful, but only a small part is cultivated, and so poorly that the crops are hardly enough for the people. When the harvests are small, many people starve. The principal crop is barley ; dates, oranges, grapes, and other fruits are abundant. Many cattle, sheep, goats, and camels are raised, and some of the finest horses in the world. The sheep have very broad, flat tails, which sometimes weigh fifty pounds each, and are the most valuable part of the animal. The principal manufactures of Morocco are carpets and rugs, embroideries, the red woollen Turkish hats, called Fez hats, and Morocco leather, which was first made there. Most of the town people are Moors, who often have fine houses, but the country people are mostly wandering Arabs, who live in tents. There are also many negro slaves. A warlike people called Berbers live among the mountains. The people are mostly Mohammedans, and very ignorant. Morocco is governed by a despotic ruler called the sultan.

In ancient times, Morocco and part of Algiers was called Mauritania, or the country of the Moors. The Arabs conquered it about 1100 years ago and founded the kingdom of Fez. This was afterward united to Morocco, which became a kingdom in 1058.

MOROCCO, a city, one of the capitals of Morocco, in the W. part of the country, near the River Tensift ; pop. 50,000, or nearly as large as Los Angeles, Cal. It is surrounded by a wall with towers, but it is ruinous. Most of the houses open on an inner court, and have no windows or doors next to the street, the entrance being in a narrow lane at one side. About an eighth of the people are Jews, who have to live in a part of the town by themselves, and are not allowed to enter the main city unless they walk barefooted. The only manufacture is Morocco leather.

Morocco was founded in 1072. At one time it was noted for its riches and learning, and is said to have had half a million inhabitants.

MORPHEUS (*mor'phuse*), in Greek fable, the god of dreams, and son of Night. He could change his shape as he wished and cause sleepers to dream. There were two gates to his palace—one of ivory, through which false dreams passed, and the other of transparent horn, through which true dreams came. He is represented as an old man with two large wings on his shoulders and two smaller ones on his head. Sometimes he is lying down and crowned with poppies.

MOR'RIS, George P., a noted American song writer, born in Philadelphia, Oct. 10, 1802. Early in life he moved to New York, and began to write verses when fifteen years old. Among the most popular of his songs are "Woodman, Spare that Tree," "We Were Boys Together," "Long Time Ago," and "My Mother's Bible." Many of them have been set to music. He resided at Undercliff, near West Point, and died in New York when sixty-one years old (July 6, 1864).

MORRIS, Robert, an American statesman and a signer of the Declaration of Independence, born in Lancashire, England, Jan. 20, 1734. He came to America when thirteen years old, and was employed as a clerk by a merchant in Philadelphia. Afterward he entered into partnership with his employer's son, and became very rich. When the Revolution broke out, he was elected to the Continental Congress. He voted against the Declaration of Independence, but signed it with the rest when it was adopted. During the latter part of the Revolution he had almost the entire charge of the money affairs of the Americans, and when the government and army could get no money, Mr. Morris borrowed it for them. The Bank of North America, which was started by him, did much to aid the government. When Washington was made President, he chose Mr. Morris to be his Secretary of the Treasury, but he declined and recommended Alexander Hamilton for the place. In his old age, Mr. Morris lost all his money and was imprisoned for debt. He died in Philadelphia, when seventy-two years old (May 8, 1806).

MORSE, Edward Sylvester, an American writer on natural history, born in Portland, Me., June 18, 1838. He studied engineering, and was draughtsman in the Portland Locomotive Works until 1859, when he went to assist Prof. Agassiz, at the Museum of Zoology at Cambridge, Mass. Afterward he was professor of natural history at Bowdoin College, lecturer at Harvard College, and an officer of the Peabody Academy of Science, at Salem, Mass. Since 1874 he has been a professor in the Imperial University of Japan. He has written many important articles for scientific journals, with illustrations from his own drawings.

MORSE, Jedidiah, a noted American geographer, born in Woodstock, Conn., Aug. 23, 1761. He studied at Yale College, and in 1789 became pastor of a Congregational Church in Charlestown, Mass. In 1784 he wrote a small geography, which was the first one ever published in America. This was followed by larger works on geography and history, especially of the United States. His books were so highly valued that they were republished in England, and translated into French and German. Mr. Morse died in New Haven, Conn., when nearly sixty-five years old (June 9, 1826).

MORSE, Samuel Finley Breese, the inventor of the electric telegraph, son of Jedidiah Morse, born in Charlestown, Mass., April 27, 1791. He was graduated at Yale College in 1810, and afterward studied painting with Washington ALLSTON and Benjamin WEST, becoming a distinguished artist, and the first president of the National Academy of Design. He first got the idea of a telegraph when on his return from a trip in Europe in 1832. His apparatus was not completed until 1835, when he sent messages through a wire half a mile long. In 1837 he gave a public exhibition of the telegraph, got a patent for his invention, and tried to get Congress to help him build a telegraph line from Baltimore to Washington, but in vain. He then went to Europe and tried to get European governments to aid him, but was unsuccessful and could not even get a patent for his invention there. Returning to the United States, he continued his efforts for four years more, living meanwhile in poverty. Finally, when he had given up hope, the Congress of 1842–43 voted him

MORTIMER   561   MOSCOW

$30,000 to build his Baltimore and Washington line. It was finished in 1844, and proved so successful that others were made almost immediately.

Samuel F. B. Morse.

Mr. Morse also made the first submarine cable, in New York harbor, and he first suggested a telegraph across the ocean. He made the acquaintance of DAGUERRE in Paris, and instructed by him took the first sun pictures or daguerreotypes ever made in America. When the telegraph was fairly established he received a great many honors and marks of distinction both from Americans and Europeans. Nearly every king and queen in Europe sent him a medal or decoration, and the different governments together gave him about $80,000 for his services. A bronze statue of him has been erected in Central Park, New York, the money for it being given by people employed in telegraph offices. Mr. Morse died in New York when nearly eighty-one years old (April 2, 1872).

MOR'TI-MER, Roger, Earl of March, noted in history as the lover of Isabella, the faithless queen of Edward II. He plotted with Isabella against the king, had him put to death, and for some years governed in the name of the young prince Edward III. But the nobles were soon weary of the haughty earl, and Edward, when he grew up, determined to overthrow him. While he and the queen were lodged in Nottingham Castle, during the session of Parliament in that town, Edward and one of his lords entered by night, and carried off the earl, amid cries from Isabella of " Spare the gentle Mortimer." They were, however, unheeded, and he was condemned and executed as a traitor (Nov. 29, 1330).

MOSCOW (*mos'ko*), a city of Central Russia on the River Moskva, a branch of the Volga; pop. 753,000, or about half as large as New York. It is surrounded by an earthen wall twenty-three miles long, and is divided into five parts. Near the middle is the Kremlin or citadel, which contains the principal palaces, cathedrals, and monuments. It is enclosed by a high wall with strong towers, and five gates. The principal gate, called the Redeemer Gate, has a picture of Christ over it, and even the emperor must take off his hat when he passes through. Among the buildings of the Kremlin are the great Imperial Palace; the Cathedral of the Assumption, in which the Russian emperors have been crowned for three hundred years; the Cathedral of the Archangel Michael, in which they are buried; and that of the Annunciation, in which many of them were baptized and married. In front of the arsenal are long rows of cannon taken by the Russians from their enemies. The Ivan Veliki, or Great Tower, is higher than Trinity Church steeple in New York, and contains thirty-four bells. Near it is the Tzar Kolokol, or Great Bell (C. C. T., 61, II. l.).

The principal streets of Moscow lead from the Kremlin like the spokes of a wheel, and across them run two handsome boulevards forming circles, one a mile and the other a mile and a half from the Kremlin. East of the Kremlin, inside of the inner boulevard, is the Kitai Gorod, or "Chinese Town" which is also surrounded by a wall. In it are the principal stores, and the great bazaar which covers three squares and is divided into many small shops. The rest of the space between the Kremlin and the first boulevard is called the Beloi Gorod or "White Town." It has many public buildings, among others a great foundling asylum which sometimes has the care of 25,000 children; the riding school, with one room large enough for 2000 infantry soldiers or 1000 cavalry soldiers to drill in; and the great Temple of the Saviour, begun in 1812 to commemorate the victory of Russia over Napoleon. Its dome is so high (343 feet) that a high church steeple could stand under it. Between the inner and outer boulevards is the Zemlianoi Gorod or "Earthen Town," so called because of an old earthen rampart which once surrounded it; and outside of this are the slobodi or suburbs. Moscow has fine libraries and museums, and a famous university with many students. It is the principal manufacturing town in Russia; woollen, cotton, and silk cloths, jewelry, hardware, glass, porcelain, and many other things are made there. The city has a very large trade by railroads and canals in summer, and by sledges in winter.

Moscow is called by the Russians Moskva, and gets its name from the River Moskva, which means "mossy water." The city is said to have been first built about 1150. From the 14th to the 18th century it was the capital of Russia, and it is still the richest city. It has been captured and nearly destroyed several times. In 1812 it was captured by Napoleon, but it was set on fire by the Russians and nearly all burned.

This caused the retreat of Napoleon and the loss of nearly the whole of his army.

MO'SUL, a city of Asiatic Turkey, on the River Tigris, near the site of the ancient city of Nineveh; pop. 57,000, or nearly as large as Trenton, N. J. The streets are narrow and dirty, and most of the houses are mean and poor. They have flat roofs, surrounded by walls, and these are used as a kind of upper story, but the stairs are always on the outside of the house. The walls which surround the city are half ruined. In old times Mosul was much more important than it now is, and was noted for its manufacture of muslin, which took its name from the city.

MOTLEY, John Lothrop, an American writer of history, born in Dorchester, Mass., April 15, 1814. He became a lawyer in 1836, but soon began to write books, publishing "Morton's Hope," a novel, in 1839, and "Merry Mount," in 1849. He also began to write a history of Holland, but, not being able to find at home the books and manuscripts which he needed, he went to Europe, and spent many years there, studying in the great libraries and collecting facts for his history. This was finally divided into three parts, called "The Rise of the Dutch Republic," "History of the United Netherlands," and "The Life and Death of John of Barneveldt." He also wrote a "History of the Thirty Years War." These works were translated into several languages, and Mr. Motley received many honors both in Europe and America. At different times he was American Minister to Austria and England. He died in England when sixty-three years old (May 29, 1877).

MOUNT DES'ERT, an island on the coast of Maine, 30 miles S.E. of Bangor; area, 100 square miles; pop. about 4,000. There are three towns on the island, called Eden,

Mount Desert, and Tremont; the people are mostly engaged in fishing for cod and mackerel. The island is noted for its magnificent scenery, part of the coast being lined with high, rugged cliffs, while in the interior are green mountains and beautiful lakes. There are many hotels, and in summer the island is visited by hundreds of travellers.

The French, who discovered the island in the 17th century, called it Mount Desert, because they found no people on it.

MOUNT VER'NON, the home of Washington, in N.E. Virginia, on

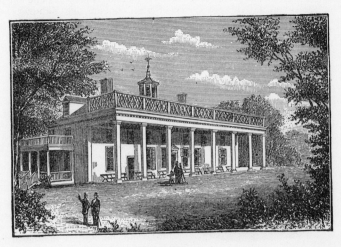

Mount Vernon.

the Potomac River, 15 miles below Washington City. The house is of wood, two stories high, and with a portico in front. The rooms are plainly furnished, but they are very interesting because some of them are kept just as they were when Washington died. Around the house are many fine old trees, and a beautiful lawn slopes down to the river's side. Not far away is the vault where the body of Washington was placed after his death, and the new vault where it has lain since 1830.

Mount Vernon was built by Washington's elder brother Lawrence, who named it in honor of Admiral VERNON. It was Washington's home from his boyhood to his death. In 1858 it was bought of his heirs by an association of ladies who keep it for the benefit of visitors.

MOZAMBIQUE (*mo-zam-beek'*), a region of E. Africa, on the Mozambique Channel; area, 293,000 square miles, or about one fourth as large as Nebraska; pop. about 1,500,000, or about one third more than that of Nebraska; capital, Mozambique. Most of the surface consists of great plains, often covered with forests, in which elephants, lions, and other wild animals abound. Most of the people are negroes, who are generally governed by their own chiefs, though the whole country is claimed by Portugal. Mozambique, the capital, is on a small coral island near the mainland. It was formerly one of the greatest slave markets in the world. Its principal trade is in ivory, gold dust, pearls, tortoise-shell, and ebony.

MOZART (*mote'sart*) **Wolfgang Amadeus,** a famous German writer of music, born in Salzburg, Jan. 27, 1756. When he was only four years old, he played the piano with great ease, and even made little pieces, which his father wrote down for him. When he was six years of age, his father took him and his sister, who was four years older, to exhibit their powers in Munich and Vienna.

Mozart.

Every one was amazed at their talent, especially at that of the boy. Two years later, the father and children again visited the chief cities of Europe, and again excited the wonder of all. It would be hard to believe the accounts of Mozart's wonderful musical feats, if they were not so well known to be true. When he was fourteen years old, he was appointed director of the Archbishop of Salzburg's concerts. Soon afterward he went to Italy, and when at Rome he wrote down from memory, after hearing it but once, the whole of the "Miserere," a very long and difficult piece of music.

When he was twenty-four years old he settled in Vienna, and gave music lessons for his support. The Emperor Joseph II. liked the Italian style of music, and he did not at first give Mozart any help, but after a while he gave him the place of composer to the court. As this office would not support him, he still gave lessons and concerts. He wrote some splendid operas, of which "Don Giovanni" (Don Juan), "Nozze di Figaro" (Marriage of Figaro), and "Die Zauberflöte" (The Magic Flute) are the best known. His most sublime work is his "Requiem," written on his death-bed, for a mysterious stranger who had come to him and ordered it, refusing to say for whom it was intended. All this was so strange that Mozart fancied there was something supernatural about it, and this same requiem was played at his own funeral. Mozart died in Vienna, when thirty-five years old (Dec. 5, 1791). He and Beethoven are considered Germany's two greatest musical geniuses.

MUM'MI-US, Lucius, a famous Roman general of the 2d century B.C. He was of common birth, but rose to high rank in the army. After conquering the Lusitanians in Portugal, he became Consul, and was sent to command the Roman army in Greece. He took the city of COR-INTH, plundered and burned it, and carried off as spoil many of the finest paintings and statues of Greece. It is said that he was so ignorant of their value that he told those charged with carrying them to Rome that if they lost any they must replace them with new ones. With this great victory the Romans finished their conquest of Greece, and for it Mummius was given the surname of Achaicus, after Achaia, the province he had conquered. Mummius, though an ignorant soldier, was an honest man and a good general, and was much respected by the Romans.

MÜN'CHAU-SEN (Ger., *moonkh-how'sen*), **Hieronymus Karl Friedrich,** Baron, a German soldier, born in Hanover in 1720. He served when young in the Russian army against the Turks, and in after life he was accustomed to tell wonderful tales of his deeds, from which he got the reputation of being the greatest liar in Germany. About 1785 a book, called " Baron Münchausen's Narrative of his Marvellous Travels and Campaigns in Russia," was published in London, but it is supposed to have been written by a German exile named Raspe. Many of the stories told in it are much older than the time of the real Baron Münchausen, and it is supposed that Raspe wrote it as a satire on some other travels.

MUNICH (*moo'nik*), a city of Germany, capital of Bavaria, on the River Isar ; pop. 262,000, or a little larger than Cleveland, Ohio. It is one of the handsomest of the German cities, and is noted for its many fine palaces and churches. The royal palace is one of the largest and most splendid in Europe. The Royal Polytechnic School has about 1500 students. The Ludwig-Maximilian University is 400 years old, and is one of the most celebrated in Europe, being attended by 3000 students. The University Library has 300,000 volumes, but it is less than a third as large as the Royal Library, which is one of the greatest in the world. Munich has fine museums of natural history and antiquities, a large botanic garden, and many other important institutions.

But Munich is most famous for its great art galleries and academy of fine arts. The Glyptothek, or sculpture gallery, contains twelve halls filled with ancient and modern sculptures. The Pinakothek, or picture gallery, is still larger, and contains 1300 paintings and 22,000 drawings, many of them by the old masters. One whole room is filled with paintings by Raphael, and there are nearly a hundred by Rubens. The new Pinakothek contains modern paintings. The Ruhmeshalle, or Hall of Fame, is a splendid marble palace, modelled after the Greek temples, and adorned with statues. In front

of it is a bronze statue, 100 feet high, representing Bavaria. Munich is noted for its great breweries, manufactories of optical instruments, glass and porcelain works, and bronze foundries. A large trade is carried on, especially in grain and cattle.

Munich was settled by monks in the 12th century, and the name came from the German word Mönche, meaning Monks. A settlement which sprang up around the monastery soon became a city and the capital of Bavaria, but most of the fine buildings and art galleries have been built during the present century.

MUN-KAC'SY, Mihaly, a Hungarian painter, born at Munkàcs. He paints figures and portraits. One of his best works represents a prisoner who, according to an old Hungarian custom, is exposed before his execution to the gaze of all who choose to stare at him.

MUNTHE (*moon'te*), **L.,** a Norwegian landscape painter. Some of his winter scenes which have been exhibited in Paris within the last two or three years, have been highly praised.

MURAT (*mu-rah'*), **Joachim,** a famous French soldier, afterward King of Naples, born near Cahors, March 25, 1771. He was the son of an inn-keeper and was educated to be a priest, but enlisted as a soldier. He rose rapidly in rank, became a favorite of Bonaparte, and when only twenty-eight years old was made a general. When Bonaparte became First Consul he gave Murat his sister Caroline in marriage, and when he became emperor made him a marshal of France and an imperial prince. He commanded the cavalry in many of Napoleon's great battles, and was much admired for his handsome figure, splendid dress, and great bravery. He was called *le beau sabreur* (the handsome dragoon), and Napoleon said he was the best cavalry officer in Europe. In 1808 Napoleon made him King of Naples, with the title of Joachim I.

Napoleon. But he differed from Napoleon about the way he should rule his kingdom, and after that he was sometimes on the emperor's side and sometimes against him. After the battle of Waterloo, he was forced to leave France, and went with a few followers to try to get back his kingdom ; but he was caught by the Austrians and shot (Oct. 13, 1815).

Napoleon Achille, son of Murat, born Jan. 21, 1801 ; came in 1821 to the United States, settled in Florida, and died near Tallahassee (April 15, 1847).

Napoleon Lucien, second son of Murat, born May 16, 1803, also came to the United States, but returned to France in 1848 and was made an imperial prince by Louis Napoleon in 1853. He died when seventy-five years old (April 10, 1878).

MU-RIL′LO (Spanish, *moo-reel′yo*), **Bartolomé Estéban,** the most famous of Spanish painters, born in Seville in 1617. As soon as he could read and write, he was placed in the academy of his uncle, Don Juan del

Murillo.

Castillo, the teacher of some of the greatest artists in Spain, where he improved so rapidly that he soon painted as well as Castillo himself. After leaving the academy he used to draw sketches of peasants and beggar-boys, which he painted re-

markably well. When twenty-six years old he went to Madrid, where he became a pupil of VELASQUEZ. He returned to Seville in 1645, and in a few years married a rich and noble wife, to whom he was much devoted ; but his beautiful art was not neglected, and he painted many valuable pictures, up to the date of his death. Murillo excelled in the painting of light clouds, flowers, water, and drapery, and in the use of beautiful colors. A story is told of him that when one day about to leave a convent where he had been at work, the cook begged him for some little sketch. He replied that there was no more canvas. "Never mind," said the cook, "take this napkin ;" and she held out the one which the artist had used at dinner. Murillo, much amused, took the napkin, and before evening it was worth its weight in gold. He had painted on it a Virgin and child, which is still known as the "Virgin of the Napkin."

Murillo died in Seville when sixty-four years old (April 3, 1682), from injuries received in falling from a staging in a church in Cadiz, where he was painting a picture on the wall.

MUR′RAY, Lindley, author of Murray's English grammar, born at Swatara, Penn., in 1745. He was first educated in a Quaker school in Philadelphia, and afterward in New York, where he became a very successful lawyer. He published several books, the most important being "A Grammar of the English Language," which for more than fifty years was used in nearly all our schools and was the great authority on English grammar. He died near York, England, when eighty-one years old (February 16, 1826).

MUS′CAT, a city of Oman, in S.E. Arabia, on an inlet of the Indian Ocean ; pop. 50,000, or about as large as Evansville, Ind. It is almost surrounded by steep cliffs, through which there is only one pass. The town and the forts which once defended it are half ruined, and there are no fine buildings. The people are of many nations, but the principal language is Hindostanee. Muscat has a large trade in dates, madder, hides, and horses. Muttra, four miles west of the main city, has 25,000 inhabitants, mostly fishermen and sailors, and there are docks there for making and repairing ships. From 1507 to 1648, Muscat belonged to the Portuguese, and it was a very important city.

MU'SES, in Greek and Roman fable, goddesses of music, poetry, and the arts. There were nine of them and they were the daughters of Jupiter and Mnemosyne. With Apollo for their leader, they used to play and sing at the banquets and marriages of the gods, and they were invoked or prayed to by poets to confer on them the gift of poetry. Their names were Clio, the muse of history ; Melpomene, of tragedy ; Thalia, of comedy ; Calliope, of heroic poetry ; Euterpe, of lyric poetry ; Polyhymnia, of oratory ; Erato, of love songs ; Terpsichore, of dancing ; and Urania, of astronomy.

MYCENÆ (*my-se'ne*), a city of ancient Greece, in the N.E. part of the peninsula of the Peloponnesus. It was one of the oldest Greek cities, and when the Persian war began it had declined in importance, though it was still independent. It was finally captured by the armies of other Greek cities and destroyed (about 468 B.C.). The ruins, which can still be seen, are among the grandest in Greece. Some of the stones which form them are larger than those of any modern building. Dr. Schliemann explored the ruins of Mycenæ,

making excavations among them, and was rewarded by finding many interesting antiquities.

MY'ER, Albert J., chief officer of the Signal Service of the United States, born in Newburg, N. Y., Sept. 20, 1828. He was graduated at Geneva College in 1847, and became a physician and assistant surgeon in the army (1854). In 1860 he was made chief signal officer, and as such served through the Civil War, his duties being to take charge of the army telegraphs and signal stations then in use. After the war he had the rank of brigadier-general, and the charge of all the weather stations in the United States, where the coming of storms was watched and telegraphed to all parts of the country. He was sometimes called in the newspapers "Old Probabilities," because the probabilities of the weather are always given from the chief signal office at Washington one day in advance. Gen. Myer died in Washington when fifty-two years old (Sept. 21, 1880).

MYSIA (*mi'she-ah*). See ASIA MINOR.

MYTILENE (*mit-i-le'ne*), an island of the Grecian Archipelago, near the coast of Asia Minor ; area, 276 square miles ; pop. 36,000. It has beautiful hills and plains, and the soil is very fertile ; olives, grapes and cotton are the principal crops. Most of the people are Greeks. The island was formerly called Lesbos, and it was settled by the Greeks in very early times. It contained many large cities, one of which, called Mytilene, is still the chief town. Sappho, Theophrastus, and other distinguished Greeks were born on the island.

N

NAGASAKI (*nah-gah-sah'ke*), a city of Japan, on a bay of the W. side of the island of Kiushiu ; pop. 44,000, or about as large as Spring-

field, Mass. It has one of the finest harbors in the world, and the scenery around it is very beautiful. It is visited by many ships, the chief trade being in tea, porcelain, camphor, isinglass, and drugs. It is also an important coaling station for steamers, as there are rich coal mines near the city. Nagasaki is partly built on the sides of the mountains, which are so steep that in many places the floor of one house is on a level with the roof of the one below it.

Nagasaki means "Long Cape." The place was a small village until 1568, when the Japanese invited Portuguese merchants and missionaries to come there ; but they made so many converts to Christianity that the Japanese became jealous and persecuted them. In 1643 the Christians took refuge in the rocky island of Pappenburg, near Nagasaki, and many thousands of them were driven into the sea and drowned. After the Portuguese were driven away, the Dutch were allowed to send one ship there each year, and this was all the foreign trade permitted ; but since 1854, Nagasaki has been open to ships of all nations.

NA·HANT′, a town of Massachusetts, on a peninsula in Massachusetts Bay, 10 miles N.E. of Boston ; pop. 900. It is a famous summer resort for the people of Boston, many of whom have cottages along the shore. The beach is often gay with horses and carriages, the sand there being so hard that the horses' feet hardly leave a trace. Among the rocks are many singular caves made by the waves.

NAIADS (*na′yads*), in Greek fable, nymphs who had charge of fresh waters. They could give the gift of poetry to those who drank of the streams and fountains, and could cure sick people. They are represented as young and beautiful maidens with long flowing hair.

NANA SAHIB (*nah′nah sah′ib*), the title of a Hindoo chief born in India about 1825, who became the leader of the great rebellion in India in 1857. When a little baby, he was brought to the town of Bithoor and adopted by the chief of the Mahratta tribe, to whom the English paid a large salary every year. When the chief died, Nana succeeded him, but the English refused to pay him the money, and he never forgave them. He was allowed, however, to rule the town of Bithoor, and seemed so friendly with the English that when the Sepoy mutiny broke out (1857) they sent to him for soldiers to guard their treasury at CAWNPORE. He sent the soldiers, but soon after besieged the English in Cawnpore, and when they surrendered killed them all, just one day before General Havelock came to their rescue. After being defeated several times by English generals, Nana escaped, was chosen chief of the Mahrattas, and for a long time fought the English in a small way in the north of India. His death has been reported several times, but whether truly or not is not known.

NANCY (*nan′se*), a city of E. France, on the Meurthe River ; pop. 79,000, or a little larger than Paterson, N. J. It is one of the most beautiful cities in France, having handsome buildings, with fine squares and shady promenades. The cathedral, a handsome building, has two very tall towers (250 feet). Nancy has a college, and manufactories of woollen, calico, and lace.

Nancy means "valley dwellings."

NANKING (*nahn-king′*), a city of E. China, near the Yangtse-Kiang River, 200 miles from its mouth ; pop. 450,000, or about as large as St. Louis, Mo. The city stands on marshy ground, and is unhealthy for foreigners. It is surrounded by a wall eighteen miles long, but only a small part of the space within is filled by houses. The town is divided by a wall into two parts, in one of which the Chinese live, and in the other the Mantchoo Tartars. Nanking was once a much larger city, but many of its best buildings were destroyed by the Taiping rebels. Among them was the famous porcelain tower, nine stories high, each surrounded by a gallery with a cornice above, from which were hung bells that rang when the wind blew. The Taiping rebels, who tried to overthrow the government of CHINA, captured Nanking in 1853 and made it their capital for eleven years; but in 1864 they were defeated by the army of the emperor which had besieged Nanking. The besiegers made a mine under the wall, blew it up with gunpowder, and entered the city through the breach. When they reached the palace of the rebel emperor they found that he had committed suicide, surrounded by vast treasures that he had gathered.

NANTES (*nantz*), a city of W. France, on the River Loire, near its mouth; pop. 127,000, or about twice as large as Memphis, Tenn. It has a fine harbor and large ship-yards, in which a fourth of all the French trading-ships are built. The city carries on an extensive trade, especially in wheat and flour, and it has large sugar refineries and cotton and woollen factories. Nantes has a fine old cathedral, and a castle in which many of the kings of France have lived at different times.

Nantes got its name from the Nannetes, a people who lived there in ancient times. During the wars between France and England it was often taken by different armies.

NAN-TUCK'ET, an island of Massachusetts, E. of Martha's Vineyard; area 48 square miles; pop. about 4500. It is level and sandy, and has hardly any trees. Many of the people are fishermen. The principal village, also called Nantucket, was formerly the greatest whaling port in the world, but since 1860 few whaling ships have been sent from there.

Nantucket was first settled in 1659. At that time there were trees on it, and many Indians lived there.

NAPIER (*na'pe-er*), Sir **Charles**

James, a noted British general, born in London, Aug. 10, 1782. He entered the army when very young, and at the battle of CORUNNA was left for dead on the field, having received five severe wounds. After distinguishing himself in other battles he was made governor of Cephalonia, one of the Ionian Islands (1824). In 1841 he took the command of the British Army in Bombay, and added greatly to his fame by the conquest of Sinde. Napier was made governor of the conquered country, and ruled wisely for several years. He died near Portsmouth, England, seventy-one years old (Aug. 29, 1853). A monument was erected to his memory in Trafalgar Square, London.

NAPIER OF MAGDALA. See ABYSSINIA.

NAPLES (*na'p'lz*), the largest city in Italy, on the bay of Naples, 118 miles S.E. of Rome; pop. 517,000, or about half as large as Philadelphia. The bay is one of the most beautiful in the world, and is famous for the burning volcano of Mt. Vesuvius near its shores. The city is on a hillside overlooking the bay. A few of the streets are wide and fine, but most of them are very narrow, and the balconies of houses almost meet overhead. The roads are paved with lava from Vesuvius, but there are hardly any sidewalks. The poor people live much out of doors, and one often sees children washing and dressing in the streets. Probably there are more beggars than in any other city in the world.

Naples has several ancient castles, many palaces, and more than 300 churches, the finest being the cathedral, in which Charles Martel, Pope Innocent IV., and other famous persons are buried. There are several colleges and libraries, and one of the finest aquariums in the world. The museum is very large, and contains thousands of curiosities from Pompeii and Herculaneum. The most important manufactures are macaroni and vermicelli, which are the principal food of the poor people, and are sent to all parts of the world. Silk cloth, carpets, glass, perfumery, porcelain, gloves, and many other things are also made.

It is supposed that Naples was founded by the Greeks. It was a favorite summer resort of the Romans, and Virgil lived there for many years. It has belonged to many different countries, but it was a separate kingdom from 1734 to 1860, when it became a part of the Kingdom of Italy.

NAR·CIS'SUS, in Greek fable, a youth so beautiful that many fell in love with him, though he never loved any one. The nymph Echo died of grief because he would not return her love. He used to idle along the banks of clear waters, and gaze at

Naples, the Bay of Naples, and Mount Vesuvius.

the image of his own face, until he pined away with love of it. After death he was changed into the flower which bears his name.

NARSES (*nar'seez*), a noted general of the Eastern Empire, born about A.D. 473. He was a slave of the Emperor JUSTINIAN, but for important services was given high offices. In 538 he commanded an army sent to Italy to aid BELISARIUS

against the Goths, but the two generals quarrelled with each other, and in the end the Goths took Milan. In 552 he commanded another army against the Goths in Italy, where he defeated and killed the Gothic king TOTILA and captured Rome. Teias, the successor of Totila, marched against him with an immense army, but after a battle of two days, near Naples, he was defeated and slain. Soon afterward Narses defeated the Franks and Alemanni at Casilinum, and the power of the barbarians in Italy was completely broken ; Narses was then made exarch, or governor, of Italy. After he had ruled for four-teen years at Ravenna. he was dismissed from office, and he invited the Lombards to invade Italy, hoping that he would be chosen to resist them ; but being disappointed in this, he is said to have died of grief at

Crater of Mount Vesuvius, after the Eruption of 1869.

the ruin caused by the Lombards (568).

NASEBY (*naze'be*). a village of England, 12 miles N.N.W. of Northampton, famous for a battle fought there between a Royalist army, commanded by King Charles I. and the Parliamentary soldiers under Fairfax, Cromwell, and Ireton, June 14, 1645. Part of the King's army was led by Prince Rupert, who made such a fierce charge that he drove some of the Parliamentary soldiers back ; but while he was pursuing them, the

King, with the rest of the army, was attacked on both sides, and before Rupert could return to aid him the royal forces were beaten. The king escaped with difficulty.

NASHUA (*nash'u-ah*), a city of S. New Hampshire, at the junction of the Merrimack and Nashua Rivers; pop. 19,000, or about as large as Aurora, Ill. It is noted for its great manufactories, among which are several cotton and woollen mills, and factories of carpets, furniture, card-board, tools, and many other things. The iron-works there have the largest steam hammer in the United States. The water-power for these manufactories comes from a fall on the Nashua River, from which a wide and deep canal has been made, three miles to the city. Many railroads meet there. Nashua owes its foundation to the Nashua Manufacturing Company, which built a mill there in 1823. It became a city in 1853.

NASH'VILLE, the capital of Tennessee, in the N. part of the State, on the Cumberland River; pop. 76,000, or about as large as Lowell, Mass. It has a cotton mill, and several other important manufactories, and carries on a large trade with the interior of the State by railroads and by steamboats. It is the seat of Vanderbilt University, and of several other colleges. The State House is one of the finest buildings in the United States. About twelve miles from Nashville is President Andrew Jackson's former home, called "The Hermitage."

Nashville was first built in 1779, and become a city in 1806. It became the capital of the State in 1843. In December, 1864, when in possession of the Union forces, it was attacked by the Confederates, but after several bloody battles they were finally driven off.

NASSAU (*nas'saw*), capital of the islands of New Providence, one of the BAHAMAS; pop. 5000. It has a fine harbor, which is visited by many ships. The principal trade is in cotton, pineapples, and sponges. The climate is very fine, and invalids often go there in the winter. During the Civil War in the United States Nassau was noted as a resort of blockade-runners, or vessels which carried on a trade with the ports in the Southern States, notwithstanding that they were watched closely by Union ships.

NAST, Thomas, an American artist, born at Landau, Bavaria, Sept. 27, 1840. He was brought to America when six years old, and began to make drawings for illustrated papers when only fifteen. Most of his pictures have been drawn for "Harper's Weekly."

NATCH'EZ, a city of S. W. Mississippi, on the Mississippi River; pop. 10,000, or about the same as that of Peabody, Mass. It is divided into two parts. The first, called Natchez-under-the-Hill, or Natchez Landing, is on the river shore, and contains most of the business houses and stores. The second, called Natchez-on-the-Hill, is built on the bluffs, about one hundred and fifty feet above the water. The principal trade is in cotton, which is brought in from the country around, and sent to New Orleans on steamers.

Natchez was founded in 1716 by the French, who named it after the Natchez Indians. From 1798 to 1820 it was the capital of the territory of Mississippi.

NA'TION-AL PARK. See YELLOWSTONE.

NAVARINO (*nah-vah-re'no*), a town of S. W. Greece, on the Bay of Navarino; pop. about 2000. It is fortified, and has a citadel on a high rock. The bay is about three miles long and two wide, and forms an excellent harbor. Navarino is celebrated for a great naval battle fought in the bay during the Greek war for independence, in which the Turkish fleet was completely destroyed by a fleet of British, French, and Russian ships, which had come to help the Greeks (Oct. 20, 1827). This victory enabled Greece to become independent.

NAVARRE (*na-var'*). See SPAIN.

NAV'I-GA-TORS ISLANDS. See SAMOAN ISLANDS.

NAX'OS. See CYCLADES.

NEARCHUS (*ne-ar'kus*), a noted Greek admiral, born in Crete in the 4th century B.C. When ALEXANDER THE GREAT was invading and conquering India, Nearchus had command of his fleet, which was sent down the river Indus. After a very dangerous voyage the ships reached the mouth of the Persian Gulf, and sailed up the river Pasitigris to Susa, which was one of Alexander's capitals and treasure cities. For this service Alexander gave him a crown of gold, and told him that he rejoiced more in the success of his voyage than in the conquest of Asia. After Alexander's death he was made governor of Lycia and other provinces. It is said that Nearchus wrote an account of his voyage, which was used by later historians.

NEBRASKA (*ne-bras'kah*), one of the Western States of the United States, on the W. side of the Missouri River, between Dakota and Kansas; area 76,000 square miles, or nearly as large as New England and Maryland put together; pop. 1,059,000, or somewhat larger than that of Maryland; capital, LINCOLN. Most of the State is a plain, covered in many places with prairies, where buffaloes and other wild animals once roamed in great numbers. The valley of the Platte River, which crosses the State from west to east, is one of the most fertile regions in the world, and in it are most of the great corn and wheat farms of Nebraska. In some other parts of the State there is excellent pasturage, and cattle are often driven from Texas and Kansas to fatten on the prairies before they are sent to market. Southern Nebraska has large salt springs, where some of the best salt in the world is made. In the northwest is a part called the Bad Lands, which is so poor that hardly anything will grow in it. Scattered over it are curious low hills which at a distance look like ruined towers and walls; and buried in those hills are thousands of bones of strange animals which lived on the plains in the early ages of the world.

Nebraska is an Indian name. The State was once a part of Louisiana, bought from France in 1803. It was made into a Territory in 1854, and in 1867 became a State of the Union.

NEBUCHADNEZZAR (*neb-u-kad-nez'zar*), a famous king of ancient Babylon, born about 645 B.C. He was son of Nabopolassar, and being sent by him against Necho, King of Egypt, he defeated Necho and conquered Palestine. In 604 B.C. he became king, took Jerusalem (606), and made Zedekiah king as his vassal. Zedekiah soon rebelled, and Nebuchadnezzar again took Jerusalem, after a terrible siege, destroyed the temple, threw down the walls of the city, and carried the people captives to Babylon. He took TYRE after a siege of thirteen years, overran Egypt, and became one of the most powerful sovereigns of his time. Among the captives whom he carried to Babylon was the Prophet Daniel, who tells much about him in the book of Daniel in the Bible. Nebuchadnezzar died when about eighty-four years old (561 B.C.)

NEL'SON, Horatio, Lord, a famous English naval commander, born at Burnham Thorpe, in E. England, Sept. 29, 1758. He entered the navy as midshipman when only twelve years old, and became a captain at twenty, being employed in important services in all parts of the world. In 1794 he commanded a small fleet against the French in Corsica, and captured the town of Bastia after a siege of seven weeks. At the siege of Calvi, not long after, he lost one eye. Nelson commanded a ship in the fleet with which Admiral Jervis fought the Spaniards at the battle of Cape St. Vincent, near the coast of Portugal. Disobeying the admiral's orders, he ran close to the Spanish ships, and captured two of them by boarding (Feb. 14, 1797). Before the news of this battle reached England, Nelson had been made a rear-admiral, and when his brave attack was known he was knighted.

Horatio Nelson.

During the same year, in an attack on Santa Cruz, on the Island of Teneriffe, Nelson lost his right arm. In 1798 he was sent to the Mediterranean to watch the fleet which Napoleon had collected at Toulon. The fleet passed him in a fog, and sailed for Egypt, with Napoleon and his army on board. Nelson followed, and on August 1, 1798, attacked the French fleet in the Bay of Aboukir, near Alexandria, Egypt. The battle lasted all day, and Nelson gained a great victory, the French flag-ship L'Orient being blown up, and all the rest, except four, either destroyed or taken. This is called the battle of Aboukir, or of the Nile, and Nelson received the title of Baron of the Nile,

with many splended presents, and a pension of $10,000 a year.

In 1799, the King of Naples having been driven from his kingdom, Nelson reconquered it, and restored the king to his throne. For this service he was made Duke of Bronte. In 1801 the English sent a fleet against the Danes, Sir Hyde Parker going as commander, and Nelson as second in command. Nelson led the attack in a great battle, which was fought with the Danish fleet in the Bay of Copenhagen. After three hours Sir Hyde Parker hoisted a signal flag, ordering the attack to cease, but Nelson putting his glass to his blind eye, said, "I don't see the signal ; keep up my signal for closer battle, and nail it to the mast." In two hours more he had taken, or destroyed, nearly every Danish ship. After various other important services, Nelson sailed against the French and Spanish fleets, which he found near Cape Trafalgar, Spain. While sailing toward the enemy, he hoisted the signal, "England expects every man to do his duty," and the sailors answered with loud cheers. Nelson wore a bright uniform, which made him a mark for sharpshooters, and during the battle he was struck by a musket-ball. He lived only long enough to learn that he had gained a great victory. "Thank God, I have done my duty," he said, and died without a groan (Oct. 21, 1805). His body was placed in a coffin which had been made long before of the mast of L'Orient, the French flag-ship at the battle of the Nile. The coffin had been given to Nelson after his victory there, and before he sailed for Trafalgar he had it put in order, saying that he would need it. He was buried with magnificent ceremonies in St. Paul's Cathedral, London, and large pensions were given to his brother and sisters.

NEMEA (*ne-me'ah*), an ancient city of Greece, near the Isthmus of

Corinth. It was celebrated for the festival in honor of Jupiter, which was held there once in two years. It consisted of various games, such as horse and chariot races, shooting with the bow, throwing the spear, wrestling, and musical contests. Those who proved most skilful in these were crowned with a wreath of olive or parsley, which was considered a great honor. King Philip of Macedon was once made president of the Nemean games.

NEM'E·SIS, in Greek fable, the goddess of punishment, daughter of Night. A figure of her was placed beside the bench of judges. She punished crime, took away luck from the unworthy, and tracked every wrong to the one who did it. No one could escape from her. She is represented as a thoughtful and beautiful figure wearing a crown, and holding a bridle, or branch of an ash tree, in one hand and a wheel with a sword or a whip in the other.

NE·OP·TOL'E·MUS, a famous Greek warrior, son of Achilles and Deidamia. He was sent for to aid the Greeks in the siege of TROY, because it had been predicted that the city could not be taken without his help. He was one of the warriors who were hidden in the wooden horse. When the Trojan women were divided among the Greek heroes as captives in war, Andromache was given to Neoptolemus.

NEP'TUNE, in Greek and Roman fable, the god of the sea. He was the brother of Jupiter, but had not so much power. His home was in the sea, and he was the especial ruler of the Mediterranean. He had power over clouds and storms, and could cause earthquakes. He watched over ships and sailors, and governed all the other gods and goddesses of the sea. He was said also to have made the horse, and to have been the first to teach horsemanship His wife was Amphitrite. He is represented as holding a three-

pointed sceptre, called a trident, in his hand, and riding in a chariot drawn by sea monsters, while others play in the waves around.

Neptune.

NE'RE·IDS, in Greek and Roman fable, nymphs of the sea, daughters of Nereus, a sea-god. There were about fifty of them. They were the especial nymphs of the Mediterranean, and were supposed to take the chief care of sailors. The most famous was Thetis, the mother of Achilles.

NEREUS (*ne'ruse*), in Greek fable, a sea-god, son of Oceanus (ocean) and Terra (earth). He married Doris, an ocean nymph, and their fifty daughters were called the Nereïds, or sea-nymphs. Nereus had the gift of prophecy, and could tell the fates of those who consulted him. He is represented as an old man with long beard and hair crowned with sea-weed.

NE'RO, a Roman Emperor, born at Antium, on the coast of Latium, in A.D. 37. He was the nephew of the Emperor CALIGULA, and was adopted by the Emperor Claudius, who married AGRIPPINA, Nero's mother. Agrippina murdered Claudius, and Nero then came to the throne in A.D. 54. He began his reign with pretended kindness, but soon plunged into extravagance and cruelty. He poisoned Britannicus, the son of Claudius, and put his own mother and his young wife Octavia to death. Shortly afterward a dreadful fire broke out in Rome, by which two thirds of the city was burned. It is said that Nero did it, and watched the fire from a high tower, singing to his lyre verses on the burning of Troy ; but he laid the

Nero.

blame of it on the Christians, whom he terribly persecuted, having some wrapped in the skins of wild beasts and torn to pieces by dogs, and others covered with pitch and burned in his gardens for torches. He then rebuilt the ruined portion of Rome with great magnificence, putting up a splendid palace for himself on the Palatine hill, which was called Nero's golden house. A plot to murder him, but which failed, gave him opportunity for more cruelty, and he killed with others his old teacher SENECA, and LUCAN the poet, and shortly after his wife Poppæa by a kick. He was guilty of the most foolish whims ; going to Greece to contest for prizes as a singer, he came back

as a conqueror, riding in the chariot of Augustus, and entering the city through a breach in the walls made for that purpose. But the people would not endure him any longer, and a revolt broke out in Gaul and Spain, Rome sharing in it. In great terror, Nero fled to the villa of a friend. The Senate condemned him to death, and sent soldiers to arrest him, when he killed himself with a dagger (June 11, 68).

NERVA (*ner'vah*), **Marcus Cocceius,** a Roman Emperor, born at Narvia, in Umbria, A.D. 32. He was chosen Emperor by the Senate on the murder of DOMITIAN (Sept. 18, 96). He showed great wisdom by reducing the taxes, and by forgiving all persons exiled or on trial for crimes against the empire. Having trouble with the Roman guards, who were insolent because he was so old, Nerva adopted as his successor M. Ulpius Trajanus (TRAJAN), who was at the head of the army in Germany ; they were afraid of this stern soldier and his legions, and they at once became orderly. Nerva died in Rome after a reign of less than two years (Jan. 23, 98), and was succeeded by Trajan.

NES'TOR, in Greek legend, son of Neleus, and King of Pylos. He went to the siege of TROY with sixty ships, and being the oldest of the Greeks and noted as a soldier his advice was sought by all the other leaders. It was he who settled the quarrel between Agamemnon and Achilles. He went back to Greece in safety after the war.

NETH'ER - LANDS, commonly called Holland, a country of W. Europe, on the North Sea ; area, 12,680 square miles, or a little larger than Maryland ; pop. 4,549,000, or more than four and a third times that of Maryland. It is a low, flat country, made mostly by the mud of the RHINE and other rivers which flow through it, and the sand thrown up by the sea. Some parts of it are even lower than the sea, and to keep the water out, great walls, called dykes, made of stones brought from Norway, timber, turf, and clay, have been built along the shores. In old times the land inside these dykes was swampy, with large lakes in many places ; but now the water is drawn out by hundreds of pumps, worked by great windmills, or sometimes by steam engines. The people have even begun to drain the great bay called the Zuyder Zee, which is almost as large as Rhode Island. The water from the lowlands is pumped into canals, of which there are so many that the people use them instead of roads, travelling about in little steamboats and canalboats drawn by horses, and sometimes even by dogs. In the winter, when the canals are frozen, people travel on skates (C. C. T., 564, I., I.). By care and hard work this once poor country has been made one of the richest in the world. Almost every foot of land is cultivated, and there are hardly any poor people. Besides grain - fields, the farmers have fine pasture lands and large herds of cattle, and their butter and cheese are sold all over the world. The Netherlands are also noted for manufactures, especially of linens, earthenware, and gin, for their fisheries, and for their ships.

The climate is much like that of New England. The people, who are commonly called Hollanders or Dutch, are very bright and active, and are to be found in all parts of the world. Besides their country at home, they have many colonies, especially in the East Indies, where they rule over 29,000,000 people, or more than six times as many as in the Netherlands. The most important of these colonies are in JAVA, SUMATRA, BORNEO, and other islands of the East Indian archipelago ; but they also own a part of GUIANA, and several islands in the West Indies.

Netherlands means the " Low Countries." Holland means the same, but the Dutch give this name only to two of their provinces, North and South Holland. This part of Europe was first brought under one government by CHARLES THE GREAT. In the 15th century the Low Countries, of which Belgium was then a part, were ruled by the Dukes of BURGUNDY, and were very rich and populous. About the middle of the 16th century (1555) they came under the rule of Spain. Most of the people were Protestants, and the Spaniards, who were Catholics, treated them so cruelly that they rebelled (1568). After a long war, all excepting what is now Belgium won their independence, and formed a republic called the " Seven United Provinces." This war was one of the most famous in history, and many great soldiers took part in it ; on the side of the Dutch the leaders were the Prince of Orange, called WILLIAM OF NASSAU, and, after his murder, (1584), his son MAURICE, and on that of the Spaniards, the Duke of ALVA, Don JOHN OF AUSTRIA, the Duke of Parma, and the Marquis of Spinola. After this the Dutch made their country one of the strongest in Europe. Their sailors were among the best in the world, and for a century their ships almost ruled the seas. They set up colonies in America and in the East Indies, and for a time even kept down the English. Afterward they fought bravely against Louis XIV., at one time driving the French out of their country by cutting the dykes and flooding it. In 1795 the country was conquered by France, and in 1806 Napoleon made it into the kingdom of Holland for his brother Louis. When Napoleon fell, Holland and Belgium were joined in one kingdom, but this lasted only until 1830, when Belgium became a kingdom by itself.

NEVADA (*ne-vah'dah*), a State of the United States, between California and Utah ; area, 112,000 square miles, or nearly two and a half times as large as New York State; pop. 46,-000, or about one one-hundred-and-thirtieth that of New York; capital, CARSON CITY. It is a high table-land, crossed by rocky, barren mountain ranges, the tops of some of which are more than two miles above the sea. Some of the valleys have good land for farming, and in some places are good pastures, but a large part of the land is barren. Some of the plains are muddy in the rainy season, but when dry are covered with soda, and are then called alkali deserts. Hardly any plants grow on these deserts, and it is very unpleasant to travel over them on account of the soda dust which, blown into the eyes and nostrils, makes them smart. Some of the springs also contain soda or borax, and in many places there are hot-water springs, from which the steam rises in clouds. To make up for its poor soil, the State is very rich in minerals, especially in gold, silver, and lead. More silver is mined in Nevada than in any other State in the Union, and more gold than in any other except California ; and the value of the gold and silver together is more than that of any other State. The Comstock lode, at Virginia City, is probably the richest silver bed in the world ; it is at least five miles long, and hundreds of deep mines have been made in it. Salt is found in many parts of the State.

Nevada is a Spanish word, meaning snowy, and was first given to the Sierra Nevada Mountains on the western side of the State, on account of their snowy peaks. This region was a part of the territory got from Mexico in 1848. It was made a territory in 1861, and in 1864 it became a State of the Union. In 1866 a part of Utah was added to it.

NEW ALBANY (awl'ba-ny), a city of S. Indiana, on the Ohio River, opposite Louisville in Kentucky ; pop. 21,000, or about as large as Oswego, N. Y. The falls of the Ohio, just above the city, give the finest water-power in the West, and this is used to run many large mills and factories. Among the principal things made there are cotton and woollen cloth, machinery, iron and brass ware, and glass. The buildings of the Star Glass Company cover fifteen acres, and are the largest glass works in the United States. There are also large pork packing houses.

New Albany was founded in 1813, and was named after Albany in New York. It became a city in 1839.

NEW'ARK, the chief city of New Jersey, in the N. E. part of the State, on the Passaic River, 9 miles W. of New York ; pop. 182,000, or about three times as large as Grand Rapids, Mich. It is noted for its great manufactories, of which it has more than a thousand, among the most important of which are jewellery, saddles and harnesses, hats, carriages, trunks, boots and shoes, tools, and machinery. There are also large, smelting works where gold, silver, and lead are prepared from the ores.

Newark was first settled in 1666, by people from Connecticut, and was named from Newark in England. It was made a city in 1836.

NEW BED'FORD, a city of S. Massachusetts, at the mouth of the Acushnet River in the Atlantic Ocean ; pop. 41,000, or about the same as that of Erie, Penn. The river is crossed by a bridge nearly a mile long, below which is a fine harbor. Nearly all the whaling vessels of the United States are sent from New Bedford, and there is a large trade in whale-oil and whale-bones. Formerly, before kerosene oil came much into use, the whaling business was much more important, and New Bedford was the richest city in the United States for its population.

New Bedford was at first a part of Dartmouth. It was made a town by itself in 1787.

NEW BRIT'AIN, a town of Connecticut, eight miles S.W. of Hartford; pop. 19,000, or about as large as Norristown, Penn. It is noted for its manufactures of hardware, cutlery, stockings, hooks and eyes, and many other things. New Britain was made from the town of Berlin in 1850.

NEW BRUNS'WICK, a province of the Dominion of Canada, between Maine and the Gulf of St. Lawrence; area, 27,300 square miles, or about three fourths as large as Kentucky; pop. 321,000, or about one sixth that of Kentucky; capital, Fredericton. Most of the surface is flat, and the coasts are rocky, but have many good harbors. The Bay of Fundy, between New Brunswick and Nova Scotia, is remarkable for having the highest tides in the world. In some places they rise from forty to sixty feet, and flow so rapidly that animals feeding along the shore are overtaken and drowned. The climate of New Brunswick is pleasant in the summer, but the winters are very cold. A large part is covered with forests of pine, spruce, cedar, and other trees, from which immense quantities of lumber are obtained. There are also many farms, the principal crops being wheat, corn, barley, oats, and potatoes. The cod and herring fisheries near the coast employ thousands of fishermen and many ships. The people of New Brunswick are mostly of English descent. They are ruled by a lieutenant-governor, appointed by the governor of Canada.

New Brunswick was settled in 1639 by the French, who named the country (including it and Nova Scotia) Acadia, or New France. Acadia became a colony of England in 1713, and in 1784 New Brunswick was separated from Nova Scotia. In 1867 it was made a province of the Dominion of Canada.

NEW'BURGH, a city of S.E. New York on the Hudson River; pop. 23,000, or about the same as that

of Rockford, Ill. It has a large trade in lumber and grain, and manufactories of engines, ironware, carpets, pianos, and other things. During the Revolutionary War Newburgh was a very important place. Washington lived there for a time, and had his headquarters in an old stone house, which is now owned by the State and kept as a museum of relics of the Revolution. Newburgh became a city in 1865.

NEWBURYPORT (*nu'ber-re-port*), a city of E. Massachusetts, on the Merrimack River, three miles above its mouth; pop. 14,000, or about the same as that of Rock Island, Ill. It is a very handsome town, has large cotton mills and other manufactories, and important ship-yards. The city is also noted for its schools, which are among the best in the United States.

Newburyport was first settled in 1635, but was until 1764 a port of the village of Newbury, from which it got its name. Before the Revolution, when the British Government put a tax on tea, the people of Newburyport burned a quantity of tea which was stored in their town. This was before the tea was thrown overboard in Boston harbor. Newburyport became a city in 1851.

NEW CALEDONIA (*kal-e-do'ne-ah*), an island in the Pacific Ocean, about 900 miles E. of Australia; area, 6700 square miles, or not quite three fourths as large as New Jersey; pop. 66,000, of which about 18,000 are Europeans, the rest natives; capital, Numea. It is rocky and mountainous, and generally barren, but there are a few fertile valleys near the coast, where cocoanuts, bananas, yams, and bread-fruits grow in abundance. These are the principal food of the people, who are a black race, with coarse frizzled hair. Most of them go without clothes, and they paint their faces in curious patterns. Their houses, which are shaped like pointed beehives, are built of reeds, covered with bark, and have doors so small that one has to crawl on the hands and knees to enter them. Formerly the New Caledonians were canni- bals, but they are now giving up their savage customs.

The island was discovered by Captain Cook in 1774, and was named after northern Scotland, which in ancient times was called Caledonia. In 1853 the French took possession of it, and it is now used as a station for their men-of-war, and a place to send convicts to.

NEW'CAS·TLE - UPON·TYNE, a city of England on the River Tyne, 8 miles from its mouth in the North Sea; pop. 159,000, or not quite as large as Louisville, Ky. It is a fine city, built on three hills, and has large manufactures, especially of glass, locomotives, and railway car- riages, iron-ware, paper, and glue. Armstrong cannon are made there, and many ships and iron vessels are built; and Newcastle has a much larger trade in coal than any other place in the world. The railway bridge across the Tyne is as high as a common steeple (118 feet). Among the public buildings is a castle built by William the Conqueror, which is one of the best preserved castles in England.

Newcastle was once called Monk- chester, on account of the monaster- ies there. Its present name was given it when the new castle was built there.

NEW ENGLAND, the name of that part of the United States in- cluded in the States of Maine, New Hampshire, Vermont, Massachu- setts, Connecticut, and Rhode Island. It was first called North Virginia, but Captain John Smith named it New England when he made a map of the coast (1614).

NEWFOUNDLAND (*nu'fund- land*), an island on the E. coast of N. America, opposite the mouth of the St. Lawrence River; area, 40,- 200 square miles, or about as large as Ohio; pop. 193,000, or about

one nineteenth that of Ohio; capital, St. Johns. The interior is a barren wilderness, with hun- dreds of marshes, and so many lakes and ponds that one third of the island is supposed to be cov- ered with water. In sheltered places are low forests, mostly of evergreens, but elsewhere the only plants are stunted bushes and herbs. Bears and other wild animals are common. Among the domestic an- imals are Newfoundland dogs, which were first raised in this island among the Indians. The climate is raw and sometimes very cold, and heavy fogs are common. There are hardly any farms, nearly all the people being engaged in fishing for cod-fish, seals, herrings, and salmon. The cod-fisheries of the "banks" or shoals near Newfoundland (C. C. T., 142, I., l.) are the finest in the world, and besides the Newfound- land fishing vessels, hundreds of vessels go there from France and the United States. Herrings are caught with nets in bays along the coast. Salmon are found in the rivers, and seals are speared or shot on the ice in the spring. The people of Newfoundland are mostly descended from English and Irish ancestors. The island is a province of England, separate from Canada, and is ruled by a governor appoint- ed by the Queen of England. The name Newfoundland was given on the discovery of the island by John or Sebastian Cabot, about the year 1498. The island has always be- longed to England, but the French often tried to make settlements on it, and they had many fights with the English. By a treaty made in 1713, the French were allowed to fish along a part of the coast, which is therefore called the French coast.

NEW GUINEA (*gin'ne*). See Papua.

NEW HAMP'SHIRE, a State of the United States, between Vermont and Maine; area, 9280 square miles, or about the same as that of Massachusetts and Rhode Island together ; pop. about 377,000, or about a twelfth more than that of Rhode Island ; capital, CONCORD. Much of the surface is covered by granite mountains, from which it is sometimes called the Granite State. The principal range, called the White Mountains, because its tops are covered with snow eight months of the year, runs through the whole State from north to south. It has many peaks, of which Mt. Washington is the highest point in New England. Some of the most beautiful scenery in the world is to be found in the White Mountains, and thousands of people visit them every year. New Hampshire has only eighteen miles of seacoast on the Atlantic, and Portsmouth is its only seaport where large ships can go in.

The soil is not very rich, but by hard work the people have made many good farms. The climate is very cold in winter, and the ground is generally covered with snow from November until spring. In the north part are large forests, where a great deal of lumber is got. Among the trees are many sugar-maples, from which much maple sugar and syrup are made. There are fine granite quarries near Concord and in other parts of the State. But New Hampshire is chiefly noted for its manufactures, especially of cotton and woollen goods, boots and shoes, and carriages and wagons. New Hampshire was named after Hampshire, a county of England, from which many of the early settlers came. The country was first visited by Europeans in 1614, and settlements were first made in 1623. In the early days it was a part of Massachusetts, but in 1741 it was made a province by itself, and remained so until after the Revolution, when it became one of the thirteen original States of the Union.

NEW HA'VEN, a city of S. Connecticut, on New Haven Bay ; pop. 81,000, or nearly the same as Rich-

mond, Va. It is a very beautiful place, many of the streets and squares being shaded with magnificent elm-trees, from which New Haven is often called the "City of Elms." The finest public buildings are those belonging to Yale College, one of the oldest American colleges, having been founded at Saybrook in 1701, and removed to New Haven in 1718. The name was given in honor of Elihu Yale, who made gifts of books and money to the college. Of late years far larger sums have been given, and now Yale College has many fine buildings, with large museums and a library, more than a hundred professors and teachers, and 1200 students. Many of the most distinguished men in the country have been educated there.

New Haven is noted for its manufactures of clocks, carriages, iron-ware, rubber goods, and many other things. A large trade is carried on by ships, steamboats, and by several railroads which meet in the city.

New Haven was first settled in 1638. Until 1662 it was a separate colony from Connecticut. From 1701 to 1875 it was one of the capitals of Connecticut, Hartford being the other.

NEW HEBRIDES (*heb'rid-eez*), a group of about twenty volcanic islands in the Pacific Ocean, 1200 miles N. E. of Australia ; area 5700 square miles, or nearly a fifth larger than Connecticut; pop. 70,000, or about one sixteenth that of Connecticut. They are very rocky and mountainous, and on one of them is a burning volcano. Most of them are covered with forest, in which sandal-wood, ebony, and other beautiful woods are found. The natives are a black race, much like those of PAPUA. The islands were visited in 1773 by Captain Cook, who named them after the HEBRIDES, near Scotland. In 1871 one of the finest islands, called Aurora, sunk into the ocean, and nothing has since been seen of it.

NEW HOL'LAND. See AUSTRALIA.

NEW JER'SEY, a Middle State of the United States, on the Atlantic Ocean, between New York and Delaware; area, 8300 square miles, or about one third as large as Indiana; pop. 1,445,000, or somewhat less than two thirds that of Indiana; capital, TRENTON. In the northern part are mountains, many of which are still covered with forest. The Delaware River, which separates New Jersey from Pennsylvania, flows through these mountains in the Delaware Water Gap, a very deep and narrow valley, noted for its beautiful scenery. The central and southern parts of the State are low, and contain many fine farms. Along the seashore, at Long Branch and other places, are beautiful white sand-beaches, where thousands of people go to bathe in the summer.

New Jersey has rich mines of iron and zinc, and there are great blast-furnaces and iron-works in many places. The manufactures are very important. Among them are flour, hats and caps, and rubber goods, and more silk goods are made than in any other State. Great quantities of vegetables and fruits are raised for the New York markets, so that this State is sometimes called the market-garden of New York. Where the land is too swampy for other crops, it is often planted with cranberries, and half the cranberries used in the United States come from these plantations. New Jersey was first settled at Bergen, near New York (about 1617) by the Dutch, who claimed it as a part of New Netherlands. After the English took New Amsterdam (NEW YORK), the Dutch gave up also their settlements in New Jersey, which the English named after Jersey, one of the CHANNEL ISLANDS, of which one of the English leaders had been governor. New Jersey was one of the original thirteen States of the Union.

NEW LONDON (*lun'dun*), a city and seaport of S. E. Connecticut, on the Thames River near its mouth in Long Island Sound; pop. 14,000, or about as large as Rock Island, Ill. The harbor is the best on Long Island Sound, and one of the best in the United States. It is defended by a strong fortress, called Fort Trumbull, and there is a United States navy-yard near the city. Many of the people of New London are engaged in whale-fishing, more whaling ships being sent out than from any other American city except New Bedford. Other vessels are sent out to hunt for seals, and to fish for mackerel and cod. New London is visited in the summer by hundreds of people from New York and Boston, and many of them have fine houses there.

New London was founded in 1644 by a son of Governor Winthrop of Massachusetts, and named after London in England. During the Revolution Benedict ARNOLD captured the town with an English army (Sept. 6, 1781), and burned the stores and ships and many of the houses. After that he attacked Fort Griswold at Groton, on the opposite side of the Thames, and though the garrison surrendered they were all murdered.

NEW MEXICO (*mex'e-ko*), a Territory of the United States, between Texas and Arizona; area, 121,000 square miles, or three times as large as New England; pop. about 154,000, or about a third that of Rhode Island; capital, SANTA FÉ. It is a high table-land, crossed from north to south by the Rocky Mountains, among which are pleasant valleys with good farm lands; but the soil is generally so dry that it has to be watered by canals from the rivers. There are also great prairies and desert plains, where nothing will grow. Many parts are good for pasture, and large flocks of sheep are raised. The most important mineral is gold. The climate in the north part is cold in winter, but in the south is so warm and pleasant that people can sleep out of doors all the year round. There are still some wild Indians in New Mexico, but the people are mostly of mixed races. The white people are Spanish Americans, like the Mexicans, and the language commonly spoken is Spanish.

New Mexico was visited by Spaniards a hundred years before the Pilgrims came to New England. It belonged to Mexico until the Mexican war, when it was conquered by the United States. It was made into a Territory in 1850; at that time it was very much larger than it is now, Arizona and parts of Colorado and Nevada having been cut off from it.

NEW ORLEANS (*or'le-unz*), the principal city of Louisiana, in the S.E. part of the State, between Lake Pontchartrain and the Mississippi River; pop. 242,000, or a little more than that of Pittsburg, Pa. It is about 100 miles from the mouth of the Mississippi. The older part was built around one of the river curves, forming a half circle like a new moon, and from this it is often called the Crescent City. But it now extends ten or twelve miles along the river and around another curve, so that it is really more like a letter S. The land on which it is built is lower than the Mississippi River during its yearly floods, and to keep it from being overflowed great walls called levees have been built along the river and lake shores, and the ground between is drained by ditches and canals.

New Orleans has a larger trade than any other city in the United States, except New York. More cotton is sold than in any other city in America, and there is a very large trade in sugar and rice. The wharves at the river levee are always crowded with cotton, brought from all parts of the Lower Mississippi Valley, where it is packed into bales by great presses, and loaded on vessels to be sent to Europe and the Northern States. Sugar is stored in immense sugar-sheds, where it is heaped up like coal in a coal-yard. About one fourth of the people of New Orleans are colored persons. Many of the whites are descended from French ancestors, and still speak the French language.

New Orleans is celebrated for its carnival sports, which take place between Christmas and Lent, and consist of parties, concerts, masked balls, and processions. The grand procession takes place on Mardi Gras, or Shrove Tuesday, when hundreds of people, dressed to represent animals, goblins, and all sorts of fantastic creatures, march through the streets with music and torches. They set off fireworks in all directions as they go, making one of the finest shows in the world.

New Orleans was founded by the French in 1718, and named after Orléans in France. In 1803 it was sold to the United States with the territory of LOUISIANA. In 1815 the battle of New Orleans was fought there, in which an American army under General JACKSON gained a victory over the English. During the Civil War the city belonged to the Confederates until 1862, when a Union fleet under Admiral Farragut passed the forts below it, and a Union army took the city (May 1, 1862). From 1868 to 1880 New Orleans was the capital of Louisiana.

NEWPORT, a city of Kentucky, on the Ohio River, opposite Cincinnati, and separated from Covington by the Licking River; pop. 25,000, or about as large as Gloucester, Mass. It contains large rolling-mills, foundries, saw-mills, and other manufactories. Many of the people do business in Cincinnati, which is connected with Newport by a fine iron bridge, and there is also a suspension bridge to Covington.

NEWPORT, one of the capitals of Rhode Island, on the W. side of the island of Rhode Island, in Narragansett Bay ; pop. 19,000, or about as large as Lynchburg, Va. It has an excellent harbor, defended by Fort Adams, one of the strongest forts in the United States ; but the trade is not very great, and the city is chiefly famous as a summer resort. Many splendid summer cottages have been built there, and the island has been laid out with beautiful drives and promenades. The shores are good for sea-bathing, and the scenery is very beautiful. Along the south shore is a road called the Ocean Drive, which on pleasant days is filled with fine carriages. Among the places much visited are Touro Park, the Old Mill, the Redwood Library, and on the beach, Purgatory Rocks, the Hanging Rocks, and the Spouting Cave. The Old Mill is a stone tower built on arches, and is supposed by some writers to have been built by the NORTHMEN, who visited the coast of Rhode Island nearly 500 years before Columbus came ; but it is now thought by most people to have been built by the early settlers for a mill. The Newport Mercury is the oldest newspaper in the United States, having been started in 1758 by James Franklin, nephew of Benjamin Franklin.

Newport was founded in 1738 by colonists from Roger WILLIAMS'S party at Providence.

NEW SOUTH WALES. See AUSTRALIA.

NEW'TON, a city of Massachusetts, on the Charles River, 8 miles W. of Boston; pop. 24,000, or nearly as large as Springfield, Ill. It was formed by the union of nine villages, called Auburndale, Chestnut Hill, Newton, Newton Centre, Newton Highlands, Newton Lower Falls, Newton Upper Falls, Newtonville, and West Newton. These still keep their separate names, and they look more like villages than a city. There are ten different railroad stations. Many of the houses

and grounds are very fine, and the country around is noted for its beautiful scenery. Most of the people of Newton do business in Boston, but there are manufactories of boots and shoes, print-cloths, paper, carriages, stockings, shirts, and many other things. Newton was settled in 1630, and became a city in 1873.

NEW'TON, Sir **Isaac,** a famous English philosopher and mathematician, born at Woolsthorpe, Lincolnshire, Dec. 25, 1642. This was the year that the civil war broke out in England, and the year that GALILEO died. His father, a farmer, died before Isaac was born, but his

Sir Isaac Newton.

mother had him well educated. At first he was rather dull at his lessons, but having been badly treated by the boy next above him in the class, he made up his mind to beat him, and soon got ahead not only of the bully, but of all the rest of the class. He is said also to have shown great skill in machines, and to have made, while at school, a windmill, a water-clock, and a sundial (C. C. T., 134, I., l.). When nineteen years old he was sent to Trinity College, Cambridge, where he became noted for finding out new ways of doing problems. After he was graduated (1665) he went home ; and one day, while sitting in his garden at Woolsthorpe, he saw an apple fall from a tree. This set him to thinking what made it fall, and he soon made up his mind that all things on the earth are drawn alike toward the centre of the earth. From that time on he set himself to studying whether things near the sun, the moon, and the planets are not also drawn toward them in the same way; and thus he finally worked out what is called the law of gravity or of gravitation, by which can be explained all the movements of the heavenly bodies. He wrote a book about this, called the " Principia" (1687), which made him very famous.

Long before this he had made experiments with light and telescopes, and he made the first reflecting telescope (C. C. T., 613, I., l.) that was ever pointed toward the heavens. He was the first, too, to show that light is a mixture of different colored rays, and to divide it into the parts of which it is made up (C. C. T., 355, I., l.). In 1669 he became professor of mathematics at Cambridge, and he was twice sent to Parliament as the member for the university. In 1699 he became master of the mint, where he had charge of coining all the money for the kingdom, and he held this office until his death. Queen Anne made him a knight in 1705. When he died at the age of eighty-four (March 20, 1727), he was buried with great pomp in Westminster Abbey, where a monument was afterward erected to his memory (1731). In Pope's epitaph on him are the following lines :

"Nature and all her works lay hid in night,"
God said, Let Newton be, and all was light."

The house in which Newton lived is still standing in St. Martin's Street, London, and is much visited by travellers. On its top is the observatory built by him, where he used to study the heavens.

NEW YORK, one of the Middle States of the United States, N. of Pennsylvania ; area, 47,000 square miles, or about the same as that of Mississippi; pop. 5,998,000, or more than five times that of Mississippi; capital, ALBANY. In the eastern part there are many mountains, mostly covered with forests. Different groups of these mountains are called the Adirondacks, Catskills, Shawangunk mountains, and Highlands. The Adirondacks, in the north-east part, are very wild and full of beautiful lakes and rivers, and abounding with wild animals. This region is much visited every summer by sportsmen and others, and hotels have been built in many places. Great numbers of people also go to the Catskills, where there is much fine scenery and many hotels and boarding - houses. West of the mountains, the southern part of the State is a table-land,and the northern part, near Lake Ontario, is low and flat. There are many small lakes, which are noted for their fine scenery and for the beautiful glens and cascades along their shores. Niagara Falls, between New York and Canada, are famous all over the world. Among other places of resort are many mineral springs, the most noted of which are those of SARATOGA. Most of the seacoast of New York is on Long Island, on the shores of which are many places where hundreds of people go to bathe in the summer. The only important seaport is New York City, but New York has many ports on Lakes Erie, Ontario, and Champlain, and on the Niagara and St. Lawrence Rivers. The Hudson River can be navigated by steamboats to Troy ; its scenery is among the finest in the world.

New York is not only the most populous State in the Union, but it is also the most important in almost every other way, having more railroads and canals, more steamboat lines, and more large cities than any other State.

In minerals it is not quite so important, yet there are many fine iron mines, besides quarries of limestone, sandstone, granite, and marble, and the finest salt springs in the United States. It is the most important farming State; for, though Illinois has more land in farms, those of New York are worth the most. Much corn and wheat is raised, and more hay, potatoes, vegetables, and fruits than in any other State. Besides these, New York has the most cattle and horses, and a great many sheep. More butter is made than in any other State, and more cheese than in all the other States put together. New York is also the most important manufacturing State, having about one sixth of all the manufactures in the Union. Among those in which it stands first are flour, clothing, leather, furniture, and ship-building. The people of New York are very intelligent and enterprising, and they have built many important public institutions, such as colleges, schools, and libraries.

New York was first settled near Albany by the Dutch (1623), who named the country New Netherlands. But the English claimed it as part of Virginia, and King CHARLES II. gave it to his brother, the Duke of York, in 1664. The same year the English took it from the Dutch, and named it New York. New York was one of the thirteen original States of the Union.

NEW YORK, the largest city of America, in the S. E. part of New York State, at the mouth of the Hudson River; pop. 1,515,000, or nearly two fifths as large as London, and about two thirds as large as Paris. Most of the city is on the long, narrow island of Manhattan, between the Hudson River and the East River, which separates it from Long Island. Besides this, it includes other small islands, and part of the mainland separated from Manhattan Island by the narrow channels called Harlem River and Spuyten Duyvel Creek. New York Bay is between Long Island, Staten Island, and New Jersey. It is one of the finest harbors in the world, and is always crowded with ships. The entrance, called the Narrows, is defended by

Statue of Liberty, erected in New York Harbor.

strong forts, and there are other forts on islands in the harbor. On Bedloe's island stands a colossal statue of Liberty, with a torch in her upraised arm, which gives light at night over all the bay around. The statue was presented to the United States by the people of France.

The oldest part of New York is at the S. end of Manhattan Island,

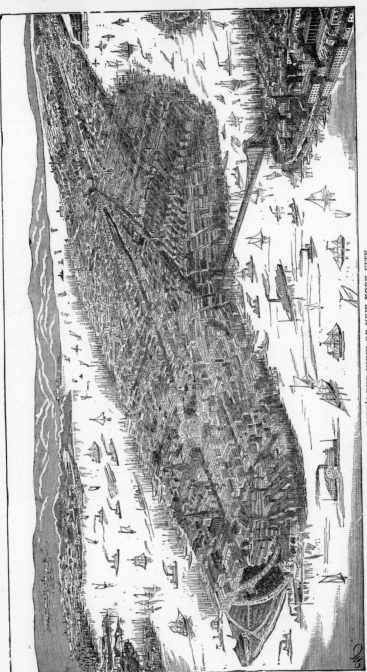

BIRD'S-EYE VIEW OF NEW YORK CITY.

The picture shows the Bridge across the East River to Brooklyn, and the Hudson River, Jersey City and Hoboken, in the background. At the left end is the Battery and Castle Garden. Leading from it is Broadway, near which comes the Bowery, or the street which appears to run from the end of the bridge. Above that is Fifth Avenue, running through the upper part of the island. Central Park begins near the upper end of the picture. At the right end of the picture, in the East River, is seen part of Blackwell's Island, and below that, Greenpoint in Brooklyn.

which is now covered with great stores and warehouses. At the southern point is the Battery, a small park, so called because there was once a fort there. From the Battery Broadway runs north more than three miles, and is lined everywhere with fine buildings, including the largest retail stores in the city. The sidewalks are crowded from morning to night, and there are so many wagons and omnibuses that it is often difficult to cross the street. Wall Street contains the great banks and brokers' offices, and Fifth Avenue and Madison Avenue have the finest residences, besides many theatres, hotels, and churches. Near the middle of the island is Central Park, which covers more than a square mile of ground, and has many beautiful drives and paths. It contains a menagerie and a fine art museum, and connected with it is one of the largest natural history museums in the country. The Lenox Library, near the Park, has in it a fine collection of old and rare books, besides paintings and other works of art. The Astor Library and the Mercantile Library are each among the largest in America. The finest churches of New York are St. Patrick's Roman Catholic Cathedral and Trinity Episcopal Church, but there are many others almost as handsome. Columbia College is one of the richest in America, and connected with it are schools of medicine, law, and mining. Besides it are the University of the City of New York, the College of the City of New York, the Normal College, and many other colleges and schools. New York is supplied with water from the Croton River by an aqueduct more than forty miles long. On Blackwell's Island, in the East River, are large jails, workhouses, and an insane asylum belonging to New York, and in the city itself are many hospitals and asylums. Horse railroads connect the different parts of the city, and there are several elevated railroads on which cars are drawn by locomotives high above the streets. Brooklyn and Long Island City, on Long Island, and Jersey City and Hoboken, in New Jersey, are really suburbs of New York, and are connected with it by many ferries. Between Brooklyn and New York is the largest suspension bridge in the world; and a tunnel, now being made under the Hudson, will connect New York with Jersey City. The bridge is three fifths of a mile long in all, and more than a fourth of a mile between the two towers which hold it up. The floor is 135 feet above the water, or nearly half as high as Trinity Church steeple. The manufactures of New York exceed those of every other American city, and they include nearly every kind of goods. Many ships are built, and there are immense buildings where sugar is refined. New York has a larger trade than any other city in the world, and more than half the commerce of the United States centres there. It is, too, the principal grain market of the world. Corn and wheat brought from the Western States are stored in immense elevators, from which they are loaded into ships and taken to Europe. Manufacturers in all parts of the country send their goods to New York to be sold, and most of the great railroads and banking companies have offices in the city.

New York was settled in 1623 by the Dutch, who called it New Amsterdam. In 1664 the English took it, and changed the name to New York, after the Duke of York. During the Revolution, the Americans, being beaten at the battle of Long Island, were obliged to give up the city (Sept. 15, 1776). The British finally evacuated it on Nov. 25, 1783. From 1784 to 1797 New York was the State capital, and from 1785 to 1790 the United States Congress met there, Washington having been inaugurated in the City Hall (April 30, 1789).

ELEVATED RAILROAD STATION AT TWENTY-THIRD STREET AND SIXTH AVENUE, NEW YORK.

NEW ZEALAND (*ze'land*), a group of three islands in the Pacific Ocean, about 1,000 miles S. E. of Australia; area, 105,000 square miles, or nearly as large as Nevada; pop. 662,000, or nearly fifteen times that of Colorado; capital, WELLINGTON (pop. 33,000). Stewart's Island is small; the other two—called North Island and South Island—are of about equal size. All are mountainous, some of the peaks being from two to two and a half miles high, and always covered with snow; and among them are several burning volcanoes. There are many wonderful hot springs and geysers, and some of them have the power of coating with stone everything that is put into them, even birds and fruits. Earthquakes are very frequent.

New Zealand has mines of silver and coal, and some of the richest gold mines in the world. Nearly all the trees are evergreens. There are no wild animals except rats, and no snakes, which is very remarkable on such large islands. The climate is very fine, and the winters, which come in June and July, are never very cold. Many of the farmers have immense herds of sheep, and the principal trade is in wool. Most of the people are Englishmen, but there are about 40,000 natives, called Maoris, who have brown skins and black hair, and many of them have their bodies tattooed all over with curious patterns. Before the whites went there the Maoris were savages and idolaters, going without clothes and always at war with each other. The prisoners that they took were kept as slaves, or were killed and eaten. Most of the Maoris are now Christians.

New Zealand is a colony of Great Britain. It was discovered in 1642 by the Dutch, who named it after Zeeland in Holland. Captain Cook visited it in 1769, and took possession of the islands in the name of England, to which they have since belonged.

NEY (*na*), **Michel,** Duke of Elchingen and Prince of the Moskva, a famous French general, born at Saar-Louis, Jan. 10, 1769. He entered the army as a private, when eighteen years old, but rapidly rose in rank, becoming a general in 1797 and a marshal in 1804. He fought at HOHENLINDEN, Jena, Eylau, Friedland, and many other battles. Napoleon often called him the "Bravest of the Brave," and for his valor at the battle of Elchingen gave him the title of Duke of Elchingen. In 1812 he accompanied Napoleon to

Statue of Ney in Paris.

Russia, and distinguished himself at Smolensk and Borodino. After Borodino Napoleon gave him the title of Prince of the Moskva. Ney commanded the rear-guard in the retreat, and once defended a bridge almost alone against thousands of Russians. When the allies invaded France, Ney did all he could to defend Napoleon, but as soon as the emperor had abdicated, Ney sought employment with his enemies, and King Louis XVIII. made him one of his principal generals. After Napoleon returned from Elba, Ney promised Louis to capture him, but the soldiers deserted to the emperor, and Ney went with them. At Waterloo he had five horses shot under him. When Napoleon was finally conquered, Ney was arrested, tried by a court-martial for desertion, and condemned to be shot. He was taken into the garden of the Luxembourg Palace at Paris, and as the soldiers aimed at him, he said, " Long live France ! My comrades, fire at me !" He fell, pierced by many balls, at the age of nearly forty-seven years (Dec. 7, 1815).

NIAGARA (*ni-ag'a-rah*) **RIVER,** a river between the United States and Canada, flowing from Lake Erie to Lake Ontario ; length, 33 miles. Near Lake Erie it contains a large island, called Grand Island. Some miles below this it is narrowed to less than a mile, and is divided into two parts by Goat Island. On either side of this island the water rushes down a long incline, called Niagara rapids, and at the foot of these it falls over a precipice, forming the Cataract of Niagara, the grandest in the world. Goat Island, which ends at the cataract, divides it into two parts. That on the American side is 164 feet high, while the fall nearest Canada is only 150 feet ; but the Canada fall is much broader, forming a curve like a horseshoe, with the hollow side turned down the stream. Great clouds of spray rise from the falls, and the roar of the water can be heard many miles away. From the American side there is a bridge above the falls to Goat Island ; and on the other side of the island a small ridge leads to a rock, almost on the edge of the Canada falls. On this is a tower, called the Terrapin Tower, from which there is a magnificent view of the falls. The rock which forms the top of the precipice is harder than that below, which has been worn away by the water, forming a hollow, called the Cave of the Winds. Visitors, clad in oil-skin suits to protect them from the spray, go into the cave behind the falls, but it is almost impossible to hear or see there, and few care to make a second trip. Below the falls the river flows through a long, narrow gorge, with rocky cliffs on each side. The water there is full of eddies and whirlpools, but

small boats can be rowed on it, almost to the foot of the falls. About one eighth of a mile below the cataract is a suspension bridge, nearly 200 feet above the water ; and two miles farther down is another suspension bridge, on which railroad trains cross. Still farther down is a very large and turbulent whirlpool. Many thousand people visit Niagara every year, and large hotels have been built there for their accommodation.

The name Niagara is changed from Oni-aw-ga'rah, an Indian word meaning " thunder of waters." The falls were first found by Father Hennepin, a French priest, who wrote about them in 1678.

NICARAGUA (*nik-ah-rah'gwah*), a country of Central AMERICA, between Costa Rica and Honduras ; area, 58,000 square miles, or the same as that of Georgia ; pop. about 313,000, or about a sixth that of Georgia ; capital, Managua. The surface is partly made up of mountains and high plains, where many cattle are raised, and partly of great forests, which yield fine cabinet and dye woods. In the eastern part is a wild region called the Mosquito Coast, inhabited by Mosquito Indians. A range of mountains near the west coast has many volcanoes, some of which are active, and the country is frequently shaken by earthquakes. East of these mountains are the beautiful lakes of Nicaragua and Managua. Lake Nicaragua lies very near the Pacific coast, but its waters flow into the Caribbean Sea by the San Juan River. Many think that this is a better place to make a ship canal across the isthmus than at Panama, the plan being to make the river navigable so that ships can go up it into the lake, and then to cut a canal from the lake into the Pacific.

Nicaragua has mines of gold, copper, quicksilver, and other metals. Coffee, cotton, oranges and other tropical fruits grow on the plantations. The climate is warm, except on the highest mountains. Most of the people are Indians or mixed races, only one twentieth part being white. Nicaragua is a republic, much like the United States in form, but it is very badly governed, and there have been many civil wars. There are few schools, and there is not a single library or newspaper in the country.

Nicaragua was discovered by Columbus in 1502. In 1523 an Indian chief, named Nicarao, lived by one of the great lakes ; so the Spaniards called the lake Nicarao-agua (Spanish for " Water of Nicarao"), and this has been shortened to Nicaragua. The country was a colony of Spain until 1821, when it became independent. In 1823 it became one of the States of Central America, but since 1839 it has had a separate government.

NICE (*nees*), a city of S. E. France, on the Mediterranean Sea ; pop. 77,000, or about the same as that of Lowell, Mass. It is built on a plain, between the Alps and the sea, and the country around is noted for its beautiful scenery. Nice is a famous watering-place, and is visited in the winter by thousands of invalids, especially English people, who are so numerous there that a part of the city where they live appears almost like an English town. There are also many French, German, Russian, and American visitors.

Nice is a very old place, and was first built by Greeks from Massilia (Marseilles), who named it Nicæa. The Italians call it Nizza. It was given to France in 1860 by Italy, to which it then belonged.

NICHOLAS (*nik'o-las*) I., Emperor of Russia, son of Paul I., born in St. Petersburg, July 6, 1796. In 1817 he married Charlotte of Prussia, the eldest daughter of King Frederick William III. Nicholas had two elder brothers, the Emperor ALEXANDER I. and Constantine, who

was the real heir to the throne after Alexander's death ; but by a secret agreement Constantine refused to reign, and so Nicholas became emperor (Dec. 1, 1825). Many of the Russians hated him, and a rebellion broke out ; but it was quickly put down, and the leaders were hung, and hundreds of others sent as exiles to Siberia.

All through his life Nicholas showed a pitiless spirit, persecuting Jews and Protestants, suppressing schools, and making himself hated by his despotism. Yet he was very temperate and frugal, and a good husband and father. In his wars he was generally successful, gaining many victories over the Turks and Persians from 1827 to 1829, putting down rebellions of the Poles in 1831 and 1846, and aiding the Austrians to crush a rebellion in Hungary in 1849. In 1853 his ambition led him into another war with Turkey. The English, French, and Sardinians aided the Turks, and won many battles on the Danube and in the CRIMEA. Nicholas was so troubled at this that he fell sick, and died in St. Petersburg when fifty-eight years old (March 2, 1855).

NICIAS (*nis'e-as*), a Greek general of Athens, who lived in the 5th century B.C. Nicias and PERICLES together commanded several armies, and afterward Nicias fought in the Peloponnesian war, gaining several victories, and finally making a treaty of peace, called the " Peace of Nicias." The Athenians honored him for his liberality and honesty, but they laughed at his superstition. He sacrificed to the gods every day, and kept a soothsayer in his house, who told him what to do. In an expedition against Syracuse (415) he was at first successful, but the Spartans having sent an army to help the Syracusans, Nicias suffered many reverses. As he was about to retreat he took an eclipse of the moon as a sign for him to stay until the next full moon. In consequence of the delay his ships and army were destroyed, and he himself was captured and killed (413 B.C.).

NIEBUHR (*ne'boor*), **Barthold Georg,** a noted German historian, born in Copenhagen, Denmark, Aug. 27, 1776. He held many important offices under the German and Danish governments, and in 1816 was sent as Prussian ambassador to Rome. Before that time he had been appointed historian to the king of Prussia, and lecturer in Berlin University. Returning from Rome he was chosen (1823) professor of history at Bonn University. He is best known for his great "History of Rome," but he also wrote other works, which were published during his life and after his death. He died in Bonn when fifty-four years old (Jan. 2, 1831).

NIEL (*ne-el'*), **Adolphe,** a noted French general, born at Muret in S. France, Oct. 4, 1802. He joined the army as second lieutenant, gained rank rapidly, and in 1837 became the chief of engineers for the French army in Algeria. He afterward distinguished himself in nearly all the French wars, becoming a general in 1853, and took part in the siege of Sebastopol in 1855. At the battle of Solferino (June 24, 1859), he commanded the artillery, and through his skill the French gained a great victory. For this he was made a marshal of France. In 1867 Marshal Niel was appointed Minister of War, which office he held until he died in Paris when nearly sixty-seven years old (Aug. 13, 1869).

NI'GER, a great river of W. Africa, rising in the Kong Mountains and flowing into the Gulf of Guinea. It is sometimes called in its upper part the Joliba, and its middle part the Quorra. It has not yet been thoroughly explored.

NIKOLAYEV (*ni-ko-lah'yev*), a city of S. Russia, on the River Bog, near its mouth in the Black Sea; pop. 67,000, or nearly as large as Cambridge, Mass. It is strongly

View on the Nile.

fortified, and has great dockyards for building and repairing ships. Since the fall of SEBASTOPOL it has been made one of the principal stations of the Russian navy.

NILE, the principal river of Africa, and one of the greatest rivers in the world. It is formed by the junction, at Khartoom, the capital of Nubia, of two rivers, called the Blue

Nile and the White Nile. The Blue Nile rises in the mountains of Abyssinia, and the White Nile in Central Africa, in the great lakes called N'yanza. The White Nile, which is the true Nile, is a strong stream in its upper part, with many rapids. Below Khartoom the river becomes sluggish and often widens into lakes. The lower Nile flows through sandy deserts, with only narrow strips of good land along its edges, which is kept fertile by the annual overflow of the river. Before reaching the sea the Nile divides into several branches, forming what is called the Delta, because it is shaped like the Greek letter delta (Δ). The valley of the Nile has been thickly peopled for thousands of years, and the ancient inhabitants, whose lives depended on the overflow of the river to water their crops, used to worship the stream as a god.

NIMES, or **NISMES** (*neem*), a city of S. France, 62 miles N. W. of Marseilles; pop. 70,000, or about as large as Cambridge, Mass. It is noted for its ancient Roman buildings, among which the great amphitheatre, or circus-building, is one of the most perfect in Europe. It had

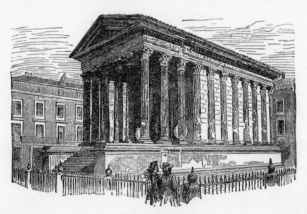

Maison Carrée.

seats for about 20,000 people, or enough to make a good-sized city. The Maison Carrée (square house) is an ancient Roman temple, which has been repaired and is now used for a museum. Ruins of walls, gates, and baths are also seen, and near the city is a magnificent Roman aqueduct, now called the Pont du Gard. Nimes also has a cathedral and many fine modern buildings. There are many manufactures there, and the people carry on a large trade in wines and silk.

Nimes gets its name from its Roman name of Nemansus, which means the "sacred grove." It was a very important city under the Romans.

NIN'E-VEH, the principal city of ancient Assyria and for a long time its capital, on the River Tigris, opposite the present city of MOSUL. Only great mounds of earth are to be seen on its site. These mounds were dug into by Mr. LAYARD (1845–47) and afterward by others, and many remains of palaces and other buildings were found. The doors of the palaces were guarded by great winged lions or bulls cut in white stone, and the walls were covered with slabs sculptured with battle scenes, sieges of cities, triumphs, and other scenes of Assyrian life. George Smith, who was one of the last to explore the ruins, read many of the inscriptions on the walls, and collected many tablets of baked clay covered with inscriptions which formed the royal library, and from which he afterward read the Assyrian account of the Deluge and much of the history of Assyria. These tablets and most of the things found at Nineveh are now in the British Museum. Nineveh, according to Greek writers, was founded and named by Ninus, the first king of Assyria, but his name is not found in the inscriptions. It was a great city 1900 years before Christ.

NI'OBE, in Greek fable the daughter of Tantalus, King of Lydia. She was the mother of six sons and six daughters. Apollo and Diana shot her children one by one because she had boasted herself superior to their mother Latona, who had but two children. When the last arrow struck, she was changed by her great grief into a stone, down which the silent tears constantly flowed. Her story was a favorite subject of the poets, and a beautiful group of statuary, now preserved in Florence, was made of her and her children.

NIP'HON. See JAPAN.

NIZHNI NOVGOROD (*nizh'ne nov-go-rod'*), a city of Central Russia, on the River Volga; pop. about 67,-000, or about as large as Atlanta, Ga. Most of the town is built on a promontory, four hundred feet high, lying between two rivers ; on this promontory is the citadel, surrounded by a high wall and many towers. The city has a very large trade. It is celebrated for its three great fairs. One in January, for the sale of timber, is held on the river, which is frozen at that time. The next is in July, when horses only are sold. The greatest of all, the Peter Paul fair, lasts from the first week in August to the end of September. People come to this fair from all parts of Russia, and sometimes there are 200,000 persons there, and $100,000,000 worth of goods are sold. The principal things sold are tea, grain, cotton, wool, horse and camels' hair, hides, iron, copper, jewels, and fur. The name Nizhni Novgorod means Lower NOVGOROD.

NORDENSKJÖLD (*nor'den-shuhlt*), **Nils Adolf Erik,** a noted Swedish explorer, born in Helsingfors, Finland, Nov. 18, 1832. His father was chief of the mines in Finland, and Adolf when a boy used to collect minerals and insects, and so

Adolf Nordenskjöld.

got a taste for natural history. After studying at the University of Helsingfors he went to Stockholm, where he became superintendent of the Mineralogical Museum. In 1858, 1861, and 1864 he went with expeditions to Spitzbergen, and in 1868 he went in a small vessel farther north than any vessel had ever been before in the Eastern Hemisphere. In 1870 he visited Greenland and in 1872 went again to Spitzbergen and stayed there all winter, being nearly starved to death. In 1875 he went to the Yenisei River, in Siberia, in a small vessel, which he sent back while he went up the river and returned home by land. In 1878 he sailed all round the north coast of Asia, returning home by the way of Behring Strait, being the first who ever accomplished this feat. On this voyage he made large collections of curiosities, and found out many things never known before.

NORFOLK (*nor'fok*), a city of S. E. Virginia, on the Elizabeth River, 8 miles from its mouth in Hampton Roads; pop. 35,000, or about as large as Binghamton, N. Y. It has a fine harbor, which, with the railroads and canals that meet there, has given the city a large trade. Great quantities of oysters are got in the neighborhood, and many of the early spring fruits sold in Northern markets are brought from Norfolk. Near the city, at Gosport, is a United States navy-yard, noted for its great granite dry dock, which cost nearly a million dollars. When the Civil War began there were twelve United States vessels in the navy-yard. When Southern soldiers took the city, the ships were burned or sunk to prevent them from being captured. The navy-yard afterward became one of the chief naval stations of the Confederates. One of the sunken ships, called the Merrimack, was raised, and the Confederates put iron armor on it, named it the Virginia, and sent it to destroy the Union fleet in Hampton Roads, but it was driven off by the Monitor built by ERICSSON. The Union army recaptured Norfolk May 10, 1862.

NOR'MAN-DY. See FRANCE.

NOR'MANS. See NORTHMEN.

NOR'RIS-TOWN, a town of E. Pennsylvania, on the Schuylkill River, 16 miles N.W. of Philadelphia; pop. 20,000, or about as large as Nashua, N. H. It contains large blast-furnaces and rolling-mills, woollen and cotton mills, and manufactories of machinery, glass, tacks, and many other things. A large trade is carried on, both by the river and by railroads. Near by are large marble quarries, lime-kilns, and iron-mines.

NORTH-AMP'TON, a town of England on the River Nen, 60 miles N.W. of London; pop. 52,000, or nearly as large as Hartford, Conn. It is most noted for its great manufactories of boots and shoes, but there are also iron and brass foundries, flour-mills, breweries, and coach factories.

NORTHAMPTON, a town of Massachusetts on the Connecticut River; pop. 15,000, or about as large as Galesburg, Ill. It is a very beautiful place, with wide, shady streets. The State lunatic asylum, a deaf-mute institute, and a large water-cure establishment are located there. There are manufactories of skates, machinery, silk, cotton, cutlery, and rubber goods, and at Florence, near by, is a large sewing-machine factory. The town was first settled in 1654.

NORTH CAROLINA (*kar-o-li'-nah*), one of the Southern States of the United States, on the Atlantic Ocean, between Virginia and South Carolina; area, 50,700 square miles, or nearly as large as New York and Connecticut put together; pop. 1,618,000, or nearly two and one sixth times that of Connecticut; capital, Raleigh. The western part is mountainous, some peaks being more than a mile high; but near the coast the land is low and often swampy, with great pine forests, where bears and other wild animals are common. Along the sea-coast are large bays or sounds separated from the ocean by long sandy islands. There are several gold mines in North Carolina, and more zinc is found there than in all the rest of the United States. Most of the farms are in the western and middle parts. Quantities of corn, tobacco, sweet potatoes, and peanuts are raised. The pine region is not good for farms, but the trees make excellent masts, and large numbers are sent to other States and to Europe. Many people are employed in splitting shingles and making turpentine and resin. The exports of turpentine are very large. The turpentine and shingle makers, who live in the woods, are mostly negroes, who make up about one third of the population.

Sir Walter RALEIGH tried to found a colony in what is now North Carolina, in 1585, but failed. In 1663 CHARLES II. gave the country south of Virginia to some noblemen, who named it after him, Carolina. In 1729 this was made into two colonies, called North Carolina and South Carolina. North Carolina was one of the thirteen original States. In 1861 it seceded and joined the Confederate States, but in 1868 it again became a State of the Union.

NORTH DAKOTA, a State of the United States, between Minnesota and Montana, and adjoining the Canadian border; area, 70,795 square miles, or not quite as large as Nebraska; pop. 183,000, or not quite one sixth that of Nebraska; capital, Bismarck. The Missouri River flows southeasterly through the State. The soil is very fertile, and large crops of wheat are raised, the Dakota wheat farms being the largest in the world. The climate is healthy, though the weather is very severe in winter, blizzards being frequent.

The first white settlement was made at Pembina about 1780. In 1861 the Territory of Dakota was formed, and in 1889 it was split into two States named NORTH

DAKOTA and SOUTH DAKOTA, both being admitted into the Union on the 3d of November in that year.

NORTH'MEN, the name commonly given to the ancient people of SCANDINAVIA. They were a strong, bold race, fond of the sea and a roving life, and they often made piratical expeditions against the more southern parts of Europe.

A Viking's Ship.

They called themselves vikings (bay men), because they found shelter for their ships in bays. In their sharp, swift vessels they visited the coasts of England, France, and Germany, plundering cities and killing all who resisted them. They ravaged the coasts of Spain, and plundered Italy, Greece, and Asia Minor, and even went into Russia. In 860 they discovered and settled Iceland, and a few years later Greenland, and about the year 1000 some of them sailed down the coast of North America as far as Rhode Island.

Among the famous leaders of the Northmen was HASTINGS, and another was Rolf, Rou, or Rollo, who invaded France and made a settlement on the River Seine at Rouen. King Charles the Simple, not able to drive him off, gave Rollo his daughter in marriage, and a part of his territory, which has ever since been called Normandy, while the Northmen who settled there have been known as Normans. Rollo became the first Duke of Normandy, and was the ancestor of WILLIAM the Conqueror.

NORTH SEA, or German Ocean, a sea between Great Britain and the mainland of Europe; length, 700 miles; greatest breadth, 400 miles. In most places the depth is not very great. There are many bays and harbors along the coasts, and some of the most important seaport towns in Europe are situated on them. The North Sea is noted for its fisheries.

NORWALK (*nor'wok*), a town of Connecticut, on Long Island Sound, at the mouth of the Norwalk River; pop. 18,000, or about as large as Sandusky, Ohio. It has a good port for small vessels, and the trade by sea is important. The city is noted for its manufactures, especially of felt-cloth, cassimeres, hats, shirts, and locks. Norwalk was settled about 1640. During the Revolution it was burned by the British (1779).

NOR'WAY, a N. country of Europe, between Sweden and the Atlantic and Arctic Oceans; area, 122,000 square miles, or about three times as large as Ohio; pop. 1,807,000, or not quite half that of Ohio; capital, CHRISTIANIA. It is a very mountainous country. Some of the peaks are a mile and a half high, and others are noted for their strange forms. One, called the Kilhorn, is shaped like a church steeple, and has a large hole through it near the top. Another, the Hornellen mountain, has a high, pointed peak, which is bent over so that it seems ready to topple over. There are many beautiful waterfalls, some of which are five times as high as Niagara. The country abounds in small lakes. The shores, which are rocky and high, are cut into by many long narrow bays, or fiords ; some

of these have rocky walls, nearly a mile high, and their scenery is among the grandest in the world. Great numbers of islands are scattered along the coast, and it is said that more than 1200 have people living on them. On Magerö island, in the Arctic Ocean, is the North Cape, the most northern point in Europe. On the north-west coast are the Lofoden Islands, near the southern end of which is the famous Maelstrom, a whirlpool in the ocean. During storms it is very dangerous, even to large ships, which it destroys by dashing them against the rocks, but in calm weather it may be crossed even by small boats. Old stories of the Maelstrom say that ships have been carried down in the whirlpool to the bottom of the sea, but this is not true. Norway has mines of iron, copper, silver, and other minerals. There are large forests of pine and other timbers, great quantities of which are cut and sent to other countries. Most of the soil is poor and the people are unskilful farmers, so that there are few good farms. The principal crop is barley. During some seasons hardly any grain will grow, and to keep the people from starving, great government storehouses have been made, in which the farmers store their grain in good years for use in bad years. The people have many cattle, sheep, goats, and ponies, and in the northern part they keep large droves of reindeer. The climate is much like that of New England.

Most of the people of Norway are Scandinavians, much like those of Sweden and Denmark. They are excellent sailors, and have more ships than any other nation of the same size in the world. Many are engaged in fishing for cod-fish and mackerel, near the coasts. In the northern part of the country are many Laplanders and Finns (see Finland). Norway is a kingdom governed by the king of Sweden, but it is considered a separate country, and has a congress of its own. The king lives half the year in Norway and the other half in Sweden.

Norway is called by the Norwegians Norge. It gets its name from its old name Nordrike, which means "northern kingdom." In early times it was cut up into many small kingdoms, but these were all united by a chief named Harold Harfager, about the end of the 9th century. Many of the chiefs whom he conquered went away in their ships to seek new homes, and became bold pirates called NORTHMEN, who settled ICELAND and founded Normandy in France.

In modern times Norway belonged to Denmark (1387 to 1814), until it was joined to SWEDEN.

NORWICH (*nor'rich*), a city of S. E. Connecticut on the Yantic and Shetucket Rivers, where they unite to form the Thames; pop. 16,000, or about as large as Sheboygan, Wis. It is built mostly on a side hill, and looks very beautiful from the river. It is noted for its manufactures, especially of iron, machinery, printing-presses, type, locks, fire-arms, paper, organs, cotton, and worsted. The port is good, though not deep enough for very large vessels, and Norwich has an important trade. It was settled in 1659, when the Indian chief UNCAS sold the site to the whites for about $350.

NORWICH (*nor'rij*), a city of E. England, 98 miles N. E. of London; pop. 88,000, or about as large as Syracuse, N. Y. It has been noted for eight centuries for its woollen manufactures, which were begun there in the reign of King Henry I. by people from Flanders. Their cloths were called worsted, because they got their yarn from the village of Worstead, nine miles from Norwich. Many shawls, bombazines, muslin de laines, and other woollen goods are made there. Norwich has a fine old castle, and a cathedral, begun in 1094, which has a very tall steeple.

Three miles south of Norwich is a small place which the Romans used to call Vena Icenorum. When the Danes began to invade England, the inhabitants of this little place built a castle where Norwich now is, and called it the North Wic ("northern station"), and from this Norwich got its name.

NOTTINGHAM (*not'ting-am*), a city of Central England, on the River Leen, near its mouth in the Trent; pop. 187,000, or about twice as large as Albany, N. Y. It is noted for its manufactures; more stockings and socks and more lace are made there than in any other English city, and it was the first place where lace was made by machinery. The country around Nottingham is noted for its beautiful hills and valleys, and the city itself is built on a steep hillside. Nottingham gets its name from the Saxon Snotingaham, which means a retreat among the rocks. It was so called from the many caves which were once used there for houses, some of which still remain. The city was founded before the time of King Alfred, and in later times it was a very important fortress. Richard III. marched from Nottingham to the battle of Bosworth Field, and Richard Cœur de Lion held two parliaments there. When the English civil war began in 1642, King Charles I. set up his royal standard in the city, and the spot where it stood is still shown, but the city was taken by the Parliamentarians the next year. Near Nottingham was Sherwood Forest, famous for the exploits of Robin Hood. Nearly all of it is now cultivated.

NOUREDDIN (*noor-ed-deen'*), a famous sultan of Syria and Egypt, born in Damascus about 1116. His whole name was Malek al-Adel Nur ed-Din Mahmoud, but he is commonly called Noureddin (Light of the Faith). His father, Zenghi, ruler of Syria, died in 1145, and Noureddin succeeded him, and made his capital at ALEPPO. He made war on the Crusaders, drove them from Edessa, conquered the greater part f Syria, and changed his capital to Damascus. He afterward conquered Egypt and ruled it through his general Shirkuh, whom he left there. The Caliph of Bagdad gave him the title of sultan, and it is said that he ruled wisely and well. He died in Damascus when about fifty-eight years old (1173 or 1174).

NOVA SCOTIA (*no'vah sko-she'ah*), a province of the Dominion of Canada, on the Atlantic Ocean, S.E. of New Brunswick ; area, 21,730 square miles, or about twice as large as Maryland; pop. 491,000, or not quite half that of Maryland; capital, HALIFAX. It is made up of a peninsula, connected with the mainland by an isthmus fourteen miles wide; and of the island of Cape Breton, E. of the peninsula and separated from it by a strait a mile across. The surface is rolling or hilly, and the coasts are very rocky, but there are many good harbors. The climate is much like that of New York.

Nova Scotia has fine beds of coal and gypsum, and several gold mines. Much lumber is cut in the forests, and there are many fine farms, especially in the northern part. The fisheries near the coast are very important. Many ships are built, and there is a large trade with other countries, especially in coal, timber, and fish.

The French, who were the first to settle Nova Scotia (1604), called it Acadia, or New France. England claimed the country, and called it Nova Scotia, or New Scotland, and there were many bitter quarrels about its possession. In 1713 it was finally given up to the English, and the French settled on the island of Cape Breton and built LOUISBURG. The French who remained in Nova Scotia were afterward accused by the English of stirring up the Indians to fight them, and in 1755 their houses and lands were seized, and

they were all carried away and scattered among the other English settlements. They were sent off in such haste that, in some cases, members of the same family were forced to go on board different ships, which sailed to different ports and separated them forever. Longfellow's poem of "Evangeline" is a story of one of the French families who were thus driven from their homes.

NOVA ZEMBLA (*no'vah zem'-blah*), a group of two or three islands in the Arctic Ocean, N. of Russia ; area, 30,000 square miles. They are mountainous and very cold, so that the ground is almost always covered with snow and ice. The only plants are mosses and lichens (C. C. T.,352, I., u.), and a few small shrubs. Reindeer, white bears, and other animals of cold climates are found. Nobody lives on the islands, but they are visited every year by hunters and fishermen from Russia, to which country they belong. The name Nova Zembla, or, in Russian, Novaya Zemlya, means New Land. The islands were first found in 1556. It was on Nova Zembla that Willem BARENTZ passed a winter (1596-7).

NOV-GO-ROD', a town of N. W. Russia, on the River Volkhov, which flows through the city ; pop. 20,000, or about as large as Jackson, Mich. Novgorod was founded by the Slavs in A.D. 500, and in 862, when Prince RURIK founded the Russian Empire, Novgorod was the first capital. In 1862 the 1000th anniversary of the empire was celebrated there, and a magnificent monument, called the Millennial Monument, was built to commemorate it. In the 15th century Novgorod was one of the most important cities of Europe.

NUBIA (*nu'be-ah*), a country of N. E. Africa, between the Red Sea and the Desert of Sahara. The River Nile flows through it from south to north. Nearly all the northern part is covered with hot, sandy deserts, where rain never falls, and there are no springs nor streams. Southern Nubia is much more pleasant, a large part of the land being fertile. The people are an Arab-like race, who live in huts, and are very poor and ignorant. Since 1821 Nubia has belonged to Egypt, Kordofan and Sennaar now form a part of Southern Nubia.

NUMA (*nu'mah*) **POM·PIL'I-US,** second king of Rome. He was chosen by the people to succeed Romulus. He made wise laws, divided the people into classes according to their trades and pursuits, built temples, and made rules for religious matters. He pretended that a nymph, named Egeria, advised him in all important matters, and he used to go to a sacred grove near Rome to consult her. When he died she is said to have melted away in tears, and to have become a fountain. During his reign the temple of JANUS was shut, for there were no wars. He died after reigning thirty-nine years (about 670 B.C.).

NUMANTIA (*nu-man'she-ah*), an ancient city of Spain, on the River Douro, famous for its defence against the Romans. Publius Cornelius Scipio the Younger laid siege to it (A.D. 134) with 60,000 men, and surrounded it so that no one could escape. The people fought for fifteen months, refusing to surrender. At last there was no more resistance, and Scipio marched into the city. The houses were all closed, and no one was to be seen. The few whom the plague and famine had spared had killed themselves. Scipio was enraged, and utterly destroyed the city.

NUMIDIA (*nu-mid'e-ah*), the ancient name of that part of the N. coast of Africa between MAURITANIA and Carthage, or nearly the same as modern Algeria. It was divided among many tribes, some of which were ruled by MASSINISSA, JUGURTHA, and JUBA. Numidia was made a Roman province in 46 B.C.

NUÑEZ (*noon'yeth*), **Alvar,** a noted Spanish explorer, born about 1490. He was chief officer of an expedition which went to Florida under the command of Pamfilo de Narvaez, who had been appointed governor. Being attacked by the Indians, the company were obliged to retreat to the coast, where they built boats and started for Mexico. One of the vessels was blown out to sea, and Narvaez was drowned. Nuñez, with a few comrades, escaped to the land of Texas or Mexico, where he made friends with the Indians by giving them medicines. After a while he travelled westward, probably through what is now New Mexico. He suffered many hardships, and finally, at the end of eight years, reached the Spanish settlements on the Pacific coast. Afterward he went to South America, explored Paraguay, and conquered many warlike tribes ; but being accused of crime by one of his officers, he was sent to Spain, and banished to Africa. The king afterward recalled him and made him a judge in the city of Seville, where he died when about seventy-four years old (1564).

NUREMBERG (*noo'rem-ba-erg*), a city of Germany, in Bavaria, 92 miles N. of Munich ; pop. 115,000, or about twice as large as Trenton, N. J. It is a very quaint old town, most of the houses having steep, pointed roofs and arched windows, as it was the custom to build them hundreds of years ago. The Town Hall, which is one of the most famous buildings in Europe, contains many paintings by Albert DÜRER and other great artists, and under it are shown the cells where prisoners were kept in old times, and the torture chamber where they were tortured to make them confess their crimes. Another curious place is the Gänsemarkt, or Goose Market, where thousands of geese are sold. The city was formerly surrounded by a wall and a wide ditch or moat, defended by many towers, but these have mostly been made into parks and promenades. Nuremberg has a large trade in looking-glasses, lead pencils, carvings in wood, bone, and metals, toys, dolls, and paints. So many toys are made there that it has been called the toy-shop of Europe. Watches were first made there, and for a long time were called Nuremberg eggs (C. C. T., 639, I., l.).

Nuremberg is called by the Germans Nürnberg. It gets its name from its old name, Norimburga, which means the " fort of the Noricii," a German tribe who lived there.

N'YANZA, the name of two large lakes in Central Africa, which form the sources of the River Nile. The one farthest east is called the Victoria N'yanza, and its waters flow through the Somerset or Victoria River to Lake Albert N'yanza, from which the White Nile flows. The Victoria N'yanza was discovered by Capt. J. H. Speke in 1858, and the Albert N'yanza in 1863 by Sir Samuel W. Baker, who named it after Prince Albert of England. The country around these lakes is fertile and beautiful, but is inhabited by savage negro tribes, who often attack travellers. On this account neither of the lakes has been fully explored ; but in 1875 STANLEY sailed nearly around Victoria N'yanza, and visited most of its coasts.

N'yanza is a negro word, meaning a lake or sea.

NYMPHS (*nimfs*), in ancient fable, a kind of being between gods and men, but loved and honored by both. Everything in nature had its own special nymph. They were not immortal, but died when the object of their care died, and the object was said to languish if the nymph deserted it. All the most important nymphs had names of their own. They are represented as young and lovely maidens. The DRYADS, NEREIDS, and NAIADS were nymphs.

O

OAKLAND, a city of California on San Francisco Bay, opposite San Francisco ; pop. 49,000, or about the same as Bridgeport, Conn. It is the end of the Central Pacific Railroad, which runs out on a long pier to connect with ferry-boats for San Francisco. Oakland is noted for its fine drives and beautiful scenery, and many rich San Francisco merchants live there. The University of California is situated at Berkeley, four miles north of Oakland.

OATES (*otes*), **Titus,** the contriver of the Popish Plot, born in England about 1620. He was the son of a clergyman, and himself took orders in the Church of England, and became a chaplain in the navy, but was dismissed for bad conduct. He then became a Roman Catholic, and lived for some months in the Jesuit college at St. Omer in France, from which he was also expelled for bad conduct. He then went back to England, and made up a story of a great plot in which he said the pope and the king of France were going to massacre the Protestants, including the king, to burn London, and to put on the throne the Duke of York, the king's brother. Several distinguished Roman Catholic noblemen were named by him as concerned in the plot. His foolish story was believed, and several Roman Catholics were executed ; but after a while people came to their senses, and saw how unlikely the story was. The bad character of Oates was then shown up, the Duke of York had him fined $100,000 for libel, and, as he could not pay the fine, imprisoned for debt. When the Duke of York became King James II., he had him sentenced to stand in the pillory five times a year, to be whipped, and to be imprisoned for life. Oates was pardoned in the reign of William and Mary, and lived seventeen years afterward, dying in London when eighty-five years old (July 23, 1705).

O'CON'NELL, Daniel, an Irish statesman, born in County Kerry, Ireland, Aug. 6, 1775. He became a lawyer in 1798, and soon began to take part in politics on the side of the Roman Catholics, claiming that they should have equal rights with the Protestants, and that Ireland should have a government of its own. In 1828 he was elected to Parliament, but refused to take the oath against the Catholic Church, and this and his speeches had such an effect that the Catholics were at length given the rights they sought. O'Connell then entered Parliament (1829), and was afterward re-elected many times. To reward him for his services, the Irish people made a yearly subscription for him, and gave him the name of " Liberator."

In 1842 and 1843 immense meetings were held in Ireland by those who favored a separate government, and O'Connell made many exciting speeches. It is said that half a million people attended some of these meetings, and at length they became so warlike that the government suppressed them, and arrested O'Connell and some others (1843). They were tried and found guilty of sedition, but they appealed to the English Parliament and were finally acquitted. Being opposed by many of his old friends, O'Connell at length fell ill, and died on his way to Rome, at Genoa, when seventy-one years old (May 15, 1847).

OCTAVIA (*ok-ta've-ah*), sister of the Emperor AUGUSTUS, born about 70 B.C. She married Marcellus, and, after his death, Mark ANTONY. Antony loved her for a time, but afterward gave her up for CLEOPATRA, Queen of Egypt, and this did much to bring about the quarrel between him and Octavius (Augustus). From her two daughters, children of Antony, were descended the emperors Caligula, Claudius, and Nero. She died when about fifty-nine years old (11 B.C.).

OC-TA'VI-US. See AUGUSTUS.

ODESSA (*o-des'sah*), a city of S. W. Russia, on a bay of the Black Sea ; pop. 304,000, or about a fifth larger than Buffalo, N. Y. It is built on a table-land, with high bluffs rising up directly from the shore, which is reached by a broad stairway of 200 steps. The harbor is very good, but during two months of the winter it is generally closed by ice. More grain is sent out of Odessa than from any other port in Europe, and there is also a large trade in tallow, wool, and timber. The city has a fine cathedral, and a university with about two hundred students. Odessa was founded in 1794.

O'DIN, or **WODIN,** the chief god

Odin, Thor, and Frigga.

of the Scandinavians. He was the creator and preserver of the world, and the god of war. His wife was Frigga, who was next to him in power, and their most famous children were Thor and Balder. The fourth day of the week was named after him, Wodensday, or Wednesday, as we call it now.

O-DO-A'CER, or **O-DO-VA'KER,** a barbarian general of the WESTERN EMPIRE, who became a king in Italy. He was the son of an officer of ATTILA, joined the Roman army, and rose to high rank. When ROMULUS (Augustulus) became emperor, the barbarian soldiers, not satisfied with their pay, chose Odoacer for their leader, and drove Romulus from his throne. This was the end of the Western Empire, for Odoacer would not take the title of emperor. He called himself king only, and ruled subject to the Emperor ZENO at Constantinople. He made RAVENNA his capital, and governed well for eighteen years, but was at last defeated and killed by THEODORIC the Ostrogoth, who became king in his stead.

ŒD'IPUS (*ed'e-pus*), in Greek fable, a king of Thebes. An oracle having told Laius that he should be killed by his own son, he had his first-born son cast on Mt. Cithæron in hope that he would perish. A shepherd found the child and took him to King Polybus of Corinth, who named him Œdipus, and brought him up as his own son. When Œdipus was grown up an oracle told him that he was destined to kill his father and marry his mother. To avoid this fate he fled from Corinth to Thebes. On the road he met Laius, whom he killed in a quarrel, not knowing that he was his father. Arriving at Thebes he solved the riddle of the SPHINX, and as a reward was made king. He married Jocasta, the queen, not knowing that she was his mother. They had four children, and then Œdipus found out that he had really killed his father and married his mother. He was so shocked that he put out his own eyes. Jocasta hung herself.

OG'DENS-BURG, a city of N. New York, on the St. Lawrence River; pop. 12,000, or about as large as Shreveport, La. It is often called the Maple City, from the many fine maple trees which shade the streets. Ogdensburg has a large trade, especially in grain and lumber, and it contains many flour-mills, saw-mills, and shingle and stave works. It was founded in 1749, and became a city in 1868.

O-HI'O, one of the Western States of the United States, between Pennsylvania and Indiana; area, 40,000 square miles, or a little less than that of Louisiana; pop. 3,672,000, or not quite three and a half times that of Louisiana; capital, COLUMBUS. Most of the land is level or rolling, and there are no very high hills, though many of the rivers flow in deep valleys with steep bluffs along the sides. Although an inland State, Ohio has Lake Erie on the north and the Ohio River on the south; and these have helped to make it one of the most important States in the Union.

There are many mines of coal and iron, and quarries of fine limestone and sandstone, used for building. The land is very rich, and nearly all of it has been made into fine farms. Taken altogether Ohio is the most important farming State in the Union, excepting New York and Illinois. Great quantities of corn and wheat are raised, and twice as much flax is grown as in all the other States put together. Ohio is noted for fine cattle and horses and more sheep are raised than in any other State. The manufactures are no less important, only two or three States being ahead of Ohio in this respect. It has also more miles of railroad than any other State except Pennsylvania and New York; so that Ohio is very rich.

The French were the first to visit Ohio, and they did not give up their claims to it until they lost all their power in America (1763). After the war of the Revolution, Connecticut, Massachusetts, New York, and Virginia claimed parts of Ohio; but they gave up their rights to the United States, and Ohio was made a Territory in 1787, and a State of the Union in 1802.

O'KEN, Lorenz, a German writer on natural history, born at Bohlsbach, in Würtemberg, Aug. 1, 1779, and afterward professor in the universities of Jena, Munich, and finally of Zurich. He published several works on natural history, some of which were translated into English. He died in Zurich when seventy-two years old (Aug. 11, 1851). Oken was not very rich, but he had very fine collections. One day, after he had been showing these to Professor Agassiz, he invited him to dinner. "But," he added, "my collections cost me so much that I have to dine every other day on potatoes and salt. I am sorry that you have come on the potatoes-and-salt day." So these two great naturalists sat down to a dinner of potatoes.

OKLAHOMA, a Territory of the United States, between Kansas and Texas; area 35,000 square miles, or about as large as Indiana; pop. 62,000, or about one thirty-sixth that of Indiana; capital, Guthrie. The surface is mostly prairie, but the soil and climate are not very favorable for farming. The territory consists of two detached sections, between which lies the tract known as the Cherokee Outlet. One of these sections was formerly the strip of public land, called "No Man's Land," which by an oversight had never been included in any of the surrounding States or territories. The other section was formerly a part of the Indian Territory, but the white people

kept constantly encroaching on it, and many armed attempts were made to open it for settlement. The settlers were constantly removed by United States troops; but at last by treaty with the Indians, the country was permanently opened. At noon on April 22, 1889, the "boomers," as the prospective settlers were called, were allowed to cross the boundary, and by night the new Territory had an increase of population of 50,000.

OLDHAM (*old'am*), a town of England, 6 miles N.E. of Manchester; pop. 147,000, or nearly twice that of Fall River, Mass. It has more than one hundred and fifty cotton-spinning mills, besides

Foot Race in Armor.

manufactories of fustian, velveteen, corduroy, hats, and many other things. Near the town are rich coal mines.

OL'MUTZ, a town of N. Austria, on an island in the March River; pop. 20,000, or about as large as Racine, Wis. It is surrounded by strong walls and forts, and is one of the principal military stations of Austria. Many prisoners of state have been kept there, among others Gen. Lafayette. Olmütz is nearly two thousand years old.

OLYMPIA (*o-lim'pe-ah*), a plain of ancient Greece, on the banks of the River Alpheus, in Elis in the Peloponnesus, where the Olympic games were held. It was famous for its sacred grove, in which was the temple of the Olympian Zeus, or Jupiter Olympius, containing the great gold and ivory statue of the god by PHIDIAS. The grove was surrounded by a wall, which also inclosed the gymnasium, the race-course, and many other temples and public buildings, shown in the picture at the beginning of this book, in which Olympia is represented as it was when in its glory before fire, earthquake, and flood destroyed it. The statue of Zeus was carried to Constantinople.

The **Olympic Games,** held once in four years, were the oldest and most noted of all the great festivals of Greece. They were begun nearly a thousand years before Christ, and were kept up until Christianity became the religion of the Roman Empire, when the Emperor Theodosius put an end to them. The games were at first attended only by the people of Elis, but in time they became so famous that people went to them from all the Greek colonies in Europe, Asia, and Africa, and even kings thought it an honor to strive in

was set up in the sacred grove at Olympia.

The games were at first simply foot races between men, but in time wrestling, boxing, and leaping matches were added, and then races

Wrestling Match.

in armor, trials in throwing the javelin and the discus or quoit, races on horseback, and two and four-horse chariot races. There were also contests for boys, in which they ran races, boxed, and wrestled. Those who took part in the most of the games were entirely naked. No women were allowed to be present,

Boxing Match.

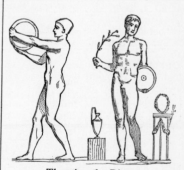

Throwing the Discus.

them, though the only prize given was a simple crown of olive-leaves. But the victor in the games was a great man in the state, and was considered to give much glory to his family; his praises were sung by famous poets, and often his statue

but women were permitted to enter chariots in the races. The exercises usually lasted four or five days, and besides the regular games there were literary contests, in which poets, historians, and other writers read their works. Artists and sculptors also exhibited their pictures and statues there. The festival usually ended with sacrifices, grand processions, and banquets to the victors.

The **Olympiads** were the periods of four years between any two celebrations of the Olympic games. They were marked by numbers, the first Olymp'ad being reckoned from the victory of Corœbus in the foot race (776 B.C.), which was the first one recorded. In time the Greeks always dated every event by the Olympiad in which it took place, just as the Romans dated from the foundation of Rome. Thus they would say that a certain event took place in the 3d year of the 170th Olympiad. The last Olympiad was the 293d (A.D. 394).

OLYMPIAS (*o-lim'pe-as*), wife of Philip, King of Macedon, and mother of Alexander the Great. She was not happy with her husband, and left him and fled to her brother, the king of Epirus, whom she persuaded to make war on Philip. Not long after, Philip was killed, and then she returned to Macedonia, where she remained until the death of her son Alexander (323 B.C.), when she again fled to Epirus and took an active part in the war between the two countries. She was defeated and slain at Pydna (316 B.C.).

OLYM'PUS, the ancient name of a high range of mountains in Greece between Thessaly and Macedonia. Their tops are covered with snow nine months in the year. In Greek fable, the summit of the highest peak was supposed to be the home of Zeus or Jupiter, and the other gods of heaven, and the clouds which hang about it were thought to hide the entrance to heaven.

OMAHA (*o'ma-haw*), a city of E. Nebraska, on the Missouri River, opposite Council Bluffs, Ia.; pop.140,-000, or about twice as large as Cambridge, Mass. It is the largest city in the State, and, being the eastern end of the Union Pacific Railroad, is very important. Several other railroads meet there, and by means of these and of steamboats on the river a large trade is carried on. The city has several smelting works, for preparing gold, silver, lead, and zinc from ores, brought from mines farther west, and very large railroad machine-shops. Omaha was settled in 1854, and was the capital until Nebraska became a State.

O'MAR I., the second of the CALIPHS, born about 581. He came to the caliphate on the death of ABUBEKR. Through his conquests the Saracen empire grew in all directions, Syria, Persia, and Egypt being rapidly added to its territory. The mosque of Omar, built on the site of Solomon's Temple, was erected by him. Through his talents, both as a general and as a lawgiver, was laid the foundation of the vast Arabian empire. While he was engaged at his devotions in the mosque at Medina he was stabbed three times by a Persian slave, who had vainly applied to him to be excused from paying tribute to his master. In his time the Arabians first began to reckon their dates from the Hegira, 622, the year of the flight of the Prophet from Mecca to Medina. He died when sixty-three years old (A.D. 644), and was succeeded by Othman.

ON-TA'RI-O, LAKE, a great lake of North America, between New York and Canada ; area, 6300 square miles, or one and a half times as large as Connecticut. By the Niagara River, which flows into it near the western end, it receives the waters of four other great lakes, and it has its outlet by the St. Lawrence River, at the north - eastern end. The lake is about 800 feet deep, and it is hardly ever frozen.

O-POR'TO, a city of N. W. Portugal, on the River Douro, 3 miles from the sea ; pop. 106,000, or nearly as large as Indianapolis, Ind. It is the most important seaport of Portugal, and has a large trade, especially in port wine, which gets its name from Oporto. The city is built partly on level ground near the river, and partly on two hills. Most of the streets are narrow and crooked, and some are mere steps cut in the hillsides, but there are many fine public buildings. The name Oporto is made from the Latin Portus, meaning a port. It is one of the oldest towns in Portugal.

OP'TIC, Oliver, an American writer of books for young folks, born in Medway, Mass., July 30, 1822. His real name is William T. Adams, and he was for several years a public school teacher in Boston. He has written a large number of books which are published in several series, called "Army and Navy Stories," "Boat Club Series," "Great Western Series," "Lake Shore Series," "Onward and Upward Series," "Riverdale Story Books," "Sailor Boy Series," "Soldier Boy Series," "Starry Flag Series," "Woodville Stories," "Yacht Club Series," and "Young America Abroad Series." Each of these is composed of several books, making more than eighty volumes in all. "Oliver Optic's Magazine for Boys and Girls" was edited by him for many years, but it was discontinued in 1875.

OR'E-GON, a Pacific State of the United States, N. of California; area, 95,270 square miles, or more than twice as large as New York State; pop. 314,000, or about one nineteenth that of New York State; capital, SALEM. It is divided into two parts by the Cascade Mountains, some of the peaks of which are more than two miles high, and always covered with snow. West of these are lower mountain-chains, covered with forests, and with beautiful valleys between them. One of these valleys—that of the Willamette River —is the finest part of the State, and most of the people live there. East of the Cascade range the country is a high table-land, with hardly any forest. Very few people except Indians

live in this region. Many of the rivers run in deep ravines or cañons, nearly half a mile deep, and with rocky sides like walls. Oregon has fine mines of gold, iron, and coal, fine salmon fisheries, and plenty of excellent timber.

Salmon-Fishing in the Columbia River.

Oregon was named from the Oregon (or COLUMBIA) River, which got its name from an Indian word meaning "good" or "fine" river. It was a part of Louisiana, bought from France in 1803, but much of it was claimed by Great Britain, and the dispute about it was not settled until 1846. It became a Territory in 1848, and a State of the Union in 1859.

ORESTES (*o-res'teez*), in Greek fable, a son of AGAMEMNON and Clytemnestra. He avenged the death of his father by killing his mother and her lover Ægisthus, and afterward became insane and was tormented by the FURIES. The oracle at DELPHI told him that he would get relief if he would go to Tauris and bring away the image of Diana. He and his friend Pylades went there, but were captured, and would have been sacrificed but for IPHIGENIA, Orestes's sister and priestess of Diana, who saved them and fled with them and the image.

Orestes became king of Mycenæ, and afterward of Argos. Æschylus, Sophocles, and Euripides wrote tragedies from this story.

OR'I-GEN, one of the fathers of the Church, born in Alexandria, Egypt, about 185. At the age of seventeen he lost his father, who suffered martyrdom for the Christian religion. Origen supported his bereaved family by teaching school, finally receiving a good position at the head of the great Christian school of Alexandria. During the persecutions of the Christians by Maximinus he was obliged to flee to Cappadocia, where he lived for two years. He died at Tyre, when sixty-nine years old (254). He was one of the most learned writers of his time, but few of his writings have come down to us.

ORINOCO (*o-re-no'ko*), a river of VENEZUELA, which flows into the Atlantic by seventeen mouths after a course of about 1500 miles. It is one of the largest rivers in South America, being only surpassed by the AMAZONS and the PLATA. Its mouth is sixty miles wide. Steamers go up it seven hundred miles, but above that the channel is stopped by rapids. Above these rapids the Orinoco is connected with the Rio Negro, by the wonderful River Cassiquiare, a stream half a mile wide, which flows sometimes into the Rio Negro and sometimes into the Orinoco. By this channel boats can pass from the Orinoco to the Amazons. The Orinoco is bordered in most places by great grassy plains, or llanos, on which cattle are pastured in the dry season; but in the rainy months the whole country is flooded like a lake; then the herds seek the higher land, and canoes can pass across the country from one side to the other. In other places along the river there are great forests, with rubber and cinchona trees, and many beautiful palms. The climate is hot and unwholesome, and mosquitoes are so numerous

that few people will live near the river. The Orinoco was discovered about the year 1500.

O·RI'ON, in Greek fable, a mighty giant and hunter. He fell in love with Merope, and to please her killed all the wild beasts on the island of Chios, where she lived. But her father kept putting off the marriage, and at last had Orion's eyes put out because he had insulted Merope. Orion recovered his sight by turning his eyeballs to the rays of the rising sun, and then he went to Crete and lived with Diana as a hunter. Some say he was shot by Diana; others, that he was killed by a scorpion. Jupiter placed him among the stars after his death.

ORK'NEY ISLANDS, a group of sixty-seven islands, near the N. end of Scotland, to which they belong; area, 500 square miles, or about two fifths as large as Rhode Island; pop. 32,000, or a little less than one eleventh that of Rhode Island; capital, Kirkwall. Most of the islands are small and rocky, with few trees, and only twenty-nine are inhabited. Most of the people are engaged in raising cattle, sheep, and ponies, and in fishing for cod and herrings. Many of them collect seaweed and burn it for the ashes, called kelp, used in making glass. About 2000 women are employed in making straw braid for bonnets. Though the islands are so far north, they are not very cold, even in winter. The name Orkney is made from the old Gaelic name, Orc-inis, which means the "islands of whales."

ORLEANS (*or'le-unz*, French *or-la-ong'*), a city of France on the River Loire; pop. 61,000, or about as large as Troy, N. Y. The older part has narrow and crooked streets, and most of the houses are made of wood, but some of them are very interesting. In one of them Joan of Arc was born, and in another King Francis I. lived. The cathedral is very beautiful, and there are some fine modern streets and buildings. In the square of Martroy is a bronze statue of Joan of Arc on horseback and four bronze bas-reliefs of scenes in her life. The walls which once surrounded the city have been turned into promenades.

Orleans was once a town of the Carnutes, a half-savage nation of ancient Gaul, and was called Genabum. It was taken and burned by Cæsar (52 B.C.), and rebuilt by the Emperor AURELIAN, and called after him Aurelianum ; and this name has become changed in time to Orleans. In 1429, when the city was besieged by the English, it was relieved by JOAN OF ARC, who was therefore called the "Maid of Orleans." She entered the town with soldiers and provisions, and then went out with the garrison, and forced the English to raise the siege.

OR·LOFF', Gregory, Count, a favorite of the Empress CATHERINE II. of Russia, born in 1734. He was an officer in the army, and came under the notice of Catherine when she was Grand Duchess. Having aided her in getting the throne (1762), he was given high honors, and was ennobled, together with his four brothers. It is said that the empress offered to marry him privately, but he refused, as he wanted her to do it publicly and to make him emperor. She was offended at this, and exiled him from court. He died in Moscow in 1783. It was he who bought for the empress the famous Orloff diamond (C. C. T., 172, II,u.).

ORPHEUS (*or'fe-us* or *or'fuse*), in Greek fable, a poet and musician, son of Apollo and Calliope, one of the MUSES. Apollo gave him a lyre, and the Muses taught him how to use it. By his wonderful music and song he could tame wild beasts, move rocks and trees, and do other remarkable things. His wife, Eurydice, having died, he went down to the lower world to beg that she might return. PLUTO agreed to his request, on condition that he should not look back at Eurydice until they had reached the upper world. But when they had nearly come to the opening above, Orpheus looked back to see if she were really following. She was there ; but instantly she fell back, the entrance closed, and he never saw her again. From that time his lyre was silent. In his grief he treated the Thracian women who were celebrating the feast of BACCHUS with contempt, and they fell upon him and tore him in pieces.

OSAKA. See OZAKA.

OSCEOLA (*os-se-o'lah*), a chief of the Seminole Indians, born in Georgia in 1804. His father was an English trader among the Indians, and his mother was the daughter of a chief. When he was four years old his mother took him to Florida, where he lived among the Seminoles, and finally married an Indian woman. One day some white men carried off his wife, claiming that she was their slave. Osceola became so enraged that he threatened to kill his persecutors, and on this account an Indian agent, Gen. Thompson, put him in prison. After his release, finding Thompson outside the fort one day, he killed him with his companions, and so began a war on the whites, which was called the second Seminole war. Osceola fought bravely and skilfully against larger forces than his own, but was finally defeated. In 1837 he was captured, imprisoned in Fort Moultrie, Charleston, where he died at the age of thirty-four (Jan. 30, 1838).

O·SI'RIS, one of the chief gods of the ancient Egyptians. According to the legends, with him civilization began, and

Osiris.

from him all that was good and moral came. He was killed in a fight with Typhon, or Evil, and his body was thrown into the Nile, and thence carried to the sea. But his wife ISIS found it, and his soul was believed to have entered into the bull APIS. After his descent into the lower regions he had another life, and was worshipped under the name of SERAPIS.

OSH-KOSH′, a city of Wisconsin on the W. Shore of Lake Winnebago; pop. 23,000, or about as large as Petersburg, Va. The country near it is a fine farming region, and by means of the rivers it is connected with the great forests of Wisconsin. These give Oshkosh a large trade in farm products and lumber. The city has many sawmills, sash and door factories, and machine-shops. Oshkosh was settled in 1836. It has been nearly destroyed by fire four times.

OSSIAN (*osh′e-an*), a Celtic bard, supposed to have lived in Scotland or Ireland about fifteen hundred years ago. According to tradition he was the son of Fingal, King of Morven, a famous hero, and he was blind. Probably his poems were spoken at feasts and public gatherings of the half-savage people, who then lived in Scotland and Ireland. For hundreds of years they were recited among the peasants, but other people knew nothing about them until 1760, when a young Scotchman, named James Macpherson, published what he called an English translation of a few of the poems. They excited so much interest that he soon published other and larger ones, called "Fingal" and "Temora." These translations were in a peculiar kind of prose, and it is probable that Macpherson added a good deal to the fragments which he had heard among the Scotch peasants. Indeed many persons thought that he wrote them altogether, but it is now known that he did not. Ossian's poems are remarkable for their grandeur and wild beauty, and are very different from all other poetry. They have been published in nearly all European languages and in the original

Gaelic form. They were favorites with Goethe, Napoleon, and other distinguished men.

OS-TEND′, a seaport town of Belgium, on the North Sea; pop. 24,000, or about as large as Pueblo, Col. Next to Antwerp, it is the principal port of Belgium; and a very large trade is carried on, especially with England. Among the things sold are butter, eggs, meat, and delicious oysters, for which Ostend is famous. The young oysters are brought from England, and kept in great salt-water reservoirs until they become very fat, when they are sent back to England.

Ostend is a very old town. It was destroyed by the sea in 1333, and for a long time after it was a mere village. The Prince of Orange had strong walls and forts made there, and when, soon afterward, the Spaniards attacked the city (July, 1601), it stood a siege of more than three years before it was taken, in which more than 100,000 lives were lost. In 1854 the American ministers to England, France, and Spain met at Ostend, and drew up a paper saying that there was no safety for the United States except in getting Cuba. This paper is commonly called the "Ostend Manifesto."

OS-WE′GO, a city of N. Y. on Lake Ontario, at the mouth of the Oswego River; pop. 22,000, or about as large as Springfield, Mo. The port is one of the best on the lake, and a very large trade is carried on, especially in grain, coal, and lumber. Among the manufactories are flouring mills, a woollen factory, iron works, steam-engine works, and the largest starch factory in the world. The harbor and city are defended by Fort Ontario. Oswego was founded by the English about 1721. In 1756 it was captured by the French and Indians, and in 1812 by the British. It became a city in 1848.

OTH′MAN, or **OS′MAN,** called the Conqueror, the founder of the Ottoman Empire, and of the family now reigning in Turkey, born in Bithynia in 1259. He was the son of Ortho-grul, a Turkish soldier. According to the Ottomans, their empire had a very humble beginning. It is said by them that Othman himself drove the plough with his servants, and that he used to raise a banner on a pole to call them home when he wished to stop work at noon. These servants were his first follow-ers in war, and they used the same banner that they were accustomed to in the field. The twenty-seven years of Othman's reign were spent in wars with the Greek Empire, from which he conquered several prov-inces. Othman died when sixty-seven years old (1326), and was suc-ceeded by his son Orkhan, who was the first to take the title of sultan. The Ottoman Empire gets its name from Othman, and the Turks are sometimes called from him Osmanlis.

O'THO, Marcus Salvius, a Roman emperor, born A.D. 32. He had been the companion of Nero, and after the death of Nero he stood by Galba until he became offended be-cause Galba adopted Piso instead of him as his successor. He then got up a revolt among the soldiers, who killed Galba and made Otho em-peror (69). But the army in Ger-many proclaimed as emperor their general Vitellius, who started for Rome to take the throne. He de-feated the army of Otho, and when Otho heard the news he arranged his affairs with great coolness, and then killed himself, after a reign of ninety-five days (April 15, 69).

OTHO I., called the Great, Em-peror of Germany, born in 912. He was the son of Henry I., and suc-ceeded him, being crowned at Aachen in 936. Lothaire, the last king of Italy, having been poisoned by Berenger, one of his lords, Ade-laide, his queen, sought the protec-tion of Otho against the murderer, who tried to compel her to marry his son. Otho defeated Berenger, married Adelaide, and was crowned

King of Italy. Entreated by Pope John XII., who needed aid against this same Berenger, Otho went a second time to Italy, and on this occasion received from the Pope the imperial crown. Ever afterward the German kings claimed the right to be crowned in Milan and in Rome. Thus grew up the Holy Roman Empire, that strange state which claimed to be the old empire of the Cæsars continued through Charle-magne, and which lasted, until its overthrow by Napoleon, nearly nine hundred years. Otho also gave a severe defeat to the Huns at Lech-feld. He died at Memleben, Thu-ringia, when sixty-one years old (May 7, 973), and was succeeded by his son Otho II.

OTHO II., Emperor of Germany, born in 955. He was the son of Otho I., and succeeded him in 973, having been crowned King of Italy during the lifetime of his father. The custom of crowning the emper-or's son, and giving him the title of King of Rome, continued as long as the empire lasted. Otho had many wars, that in which he was most in-terested being one in lower Italy to recover from the Saracens the pos-sessions of his wife Theophania, daughter of the Byzantine emperor. Being overcome near Basantello, he fell into the hands of the enemy, from whom he escaped only by swim-ming. While planning another ex-pedition, he died at Rome, when twenty-eight years old (Dec. 7, 983). He was succeeded by his son Otho III.

OTHO III., Emperor of Germany, born in 980. He was the son, of Otho II., and succeeded him when only three years old, under the guar-dianship of his mother Theophania and his grandmother Adelaide. When he was fifteen years old he was declared of age to reign. He had been so carefully trained in all the learning of the age that he was called the " wonder of the world." He had a plan for once more uniting the Eastern and Western Empires, thus bringing the entire known world under his rule, Rome being the centre of the empire. His people were much troubled by the barbarous tribes around them, and they used to wish that their king would do something to relieve them ; but Otho was too much bent on his vaster schemes. When at AACHEN he opened the tomb of Charlemagne, and beside his gorgeously arrayed body, which he found seated on its throne clothed in royal robes, we may fancy that he dreamed of forming an empire which should far outshine that of the renowned Charles. Otho did not live to carry out his favorite idea, but died at Paterno when twenty-two years old (Jan. 23, 1002), and was succeeded by Henry II.

OTHO IV., Emperor of Germany, born in 1174. He was the son of Henry the Lion, Duke of Saxony and Bavaria, and was elected emperor by the party of the GUELPHS, being crowned in 1209 to succeed Henry VI. The Ghibellines had elected Philip, the late emperor's brother. In consequence of this double election a war took place which lasted ten years. Philip would probably have won the day, but he was murdered, and Otho was crowned. A second civil war soon began, Otho having made enemies of the German princes, and they having chosen for Emperor Frederick, the young son of Henry VI. Being unable to carry on the war, he was forced to retire to his paternal estates, dying shortly afterward, when forty-four years old (May 19, 1218). He was succeeded by Frederick II.

OTTAWA (*ot'ta-waw*), a city, capital of the Dominion of Canada, on the Ottawa River, 97 miles above its mouth in the St. Lawrence ; pop. 40,000, or about as large as Harrisburg, Penn. It is a handsome city, with wide, pleasant streets, and many fine buildings. The government buildings, begun in 1860, and the corner-stone of which was laid

by the Prince of Wales, are among the finest buildings in America. The house of the Governor-General is at New Edinburgh, near the city. Ottawa has many manufactures and a large trade, especially in lumber.

Ottawa was founded in 1827 by a Colonel By, and at first it was called Bytown. It became a city in 1854, and was made the capital of Canada in 1858.

OV'ID (Publius Ovidius Naso), a Roman poet, born at Sulmo, about 90 miles east of Rome, March 20, 43 B.C. He came of a noble family, and studied to be a lawyer, but his love of poetry interfered so much that he gave it up. After travelling in Asia and Sicily he settled in Rome, and for many years lived in an idle way, surrounded by a large circle of friends, among whom were the Emperor Augustus, Horace, and other noted men. When fifty years old he was banished by the emperor for some unknown offence to Tomi, a small town on the shore of the Euxine or Black Sea. The people were barbarous, and the climate was severe, and he found it very lonesome living there. So he sent many humble entreaties to the emperor to let him go back to Rome, but the emperor refused, and he died of grief in the tenth year of his exile (A.D. 18). He was one of the finest of the Latin poets. His chief work, called "Metamorphoses," is in fifteen books. Among his others are his "Heroides," or twenty-one letters from heroines to their lovers ; his "Amores," or love elegies ; his "Tristia," or mournful poems, describing the sorrows of his exile, and a number of others.

O'WEN, Richard, a British scientist, born in Lancaster in 1804. He has made a particular study of comparative anatomy, a science which treats of the way in which animals and plants are made, and has also carefully examined the laws which regulate health. By his close study of beasts, birds, reptiles, and fishes he has enabled naturalists to classify them more exactly than was ever done before. He belongs to a great many learned societies, and has received medals from several European colleges.

OXFORD (*ox'furd*), a city of England, at the junction of the Cherwell and the Isis, or Upper Thames ; pop. 53,000, or a little larger than Manchester, N. H. It is famous for its university, which is one of the two greatest seats of learning in England, the other being the University of Cambridge. Oxford University is divided into twenty colleges and five halls, each with a different name. Each college has a building in which the students board and room, arid those who wish to study at the university can only do so by being admitted to one of the colleges after an examination. The colleges have no separate professors, but students who belong to them attend the lectures of the university professors, and sometimes have private tutors. Students are graduated from the university, not from the colleges. If they choose they can be examined for " honors." Those who graduate in this way are divided into four classes, according to the merit of their examinations, and the names of those in each class are published. It is very difficult to get a place in the first class. Those who do are often made " fellows" of their colleges ; they then receive a yearly salary, and can live in the college buildings as long as they choose.

Many of the college buildings are very old and interesting. Beside them the university has museums, laboratories, chapels, a printing-house, called the Clarendon Press, and one of the largest and finest libraries in England. Generally Oxford has about 3500 students.

It is said that Oxford University sprang from a school which was founded at Oxford by King ALFRED. The colleges were founded at different times, from 1249 to 1870.

OX'US, the ancient name of the Amoo or Amoo Daria, a river of W. Asia. It rises in Turkistan, about 15,000 feet or nearly three miles above the sea, and flows through several mouths into the Sea of Aral. This river is interesting, because the ARYANS, or principal races of man, are supposed to have first lived near its head waters.

OZAKA (*o-zah'kah*), a city of Japan on the main island, 25 miles S. W. of Kioto ; pop. 443,000, or not quite as large as Boston, Mass. It is built on a fertile plain, in which are many streams and canals. Several canals pass through the city, and they are crossed by more than a thousand bridges. The city is defended by a castle and two forts, in which several thousand soldiers are kept. Ozaka has an important trade, and many ships visit the harbor. Much of the Japanese money is coined there, and the government has there a foundry where large cannon are cast.

P

PA-CIF'IC O'CEAN, that part of the ocean which lies between America and Asia and Australia. It is the largest of all the oceans, being twice as large as the Atlantic, and containing more than one half of all the salt water on the globe. It is noted for the great number of its islands, which are mostly either volcanic or coral islands. Its tides are lower and its waters are more calm and tranquil than those of the Atlantic.

The Pacific Ocean was first seen by BALBOA (1513). It was first sailed on by Magalhaens, who gave it its name on account of the constant fair weather which he had on his voyage. In some old books it is sometimes called the South Sea, but this name has now gone out of use.

PACK'ARD, Alpheus Spring, Jr., an American writer on natural history, born in Brunswick, Me., Feb. 19, 1839. He became a physician in 1864, but most of his time is given to natural history, especially entomology, or the science of insects. He is an officer of the Peabody Academy of Sciences at Salem, Mass., is professor of zoology and geology at Brown University. Dr. Packard has written a "Guide to the Study of Insects," "Our Common Insects," several "Zoologies," and other books.

PADUA (*pad'u-ah*), a city of N. Italy, 20 miles W. of Venice; pop. 47,000, or a little larger than Saginaw, Mich. It is surrounded by a wall with seven gates, but much of it has fallen to ruin. The university of Padua is one of the oldest and most celebrated in Europe. It has about 1100 students, seventy-two professors, and a large library. The botanical garden of Padua is the oldest in Europe.

Padua is a very old city, but nothing is known of its beginning. The Romans called it Patavium, and from this has come its modern Italian name of Padova, which we call Padua. LIVY was born there.

PÆSTUM (*pes'tum*), an ancient city of S. Italy, on the Gulf of Salerno, about 40 miles S.E. of Naples. It was founded by Greeks from SYBARIS (524 B.C.), and grew to be very rich and powerful. Some say it was destroyed by the Saracens in the 11th century, but according to Strabo its ruin was caused by the unhealthfulness of its site. Though it is now so unhealthful that no one can live near it, it is much visited by travelers to see its splendid ruins, especially the temples of Neptune and Ceres, which are among the best specimens of Doric architecture in existence.

PAGANINI (*pah-gah-ne'ne*), **Nicolo,** a famous Italian violin-player, born in Genoa, Feb. 18, 1784. He played the violin when only six years old; when eight he wrote a piece of music, and when nine he played in a public concert and won great applause. In his fifteenth year he ran away from his father and gave concerts for himself, and made so much money that he was led to gambling and other vices. But he soon began to practise his music again and traveled all over Europe, giving concerts in all the great cities, and winning money and fame everywhere. Among his pieces was one called "Napoleon," which was played on only one string. At last he got so famous that poems were written about him, medals were struck in his honor, and people wore Paganini hats and Paganini coats. He left a very large fortune at his death, which took place at Nice when he was fifty-six years old (May 27, 1840).

PAGE, William, an American

painter, born in Albany, N. Y., Jan. 23, 1811. He began to draw and paint when a child. He is chiefly known by his portraits, which have great merit, but he has also painted some very fine ideal pictures, among which are a "Venus," a "Holy Family," and a "Head of Christ." He lived in Rome for many years, and died in Tottenville, S. I., when seventy-four years old (Oct. 1, 1885).

PAINE (*pane*), **Thomas,** a famous writer, born in Thetford, England, Jan. 29, 1737. He was the son of a Quaker, and was brought up to the trade of a ship-stay maker. When thirty-seven years old (1774) he came to America by the advice of FRANKLIN. In the beginning of the Revolution he took the side of the Americans and wrote a pamphlet called "Common Cense" (1776), in which he advised them to separate from England and to set up a government of their own. This did much to stir up the people, and helped greatly to bring about the independence of the colonies. When the war broke out he joined the army, and in the winter of 1776-77 he published a paper called the "Crisis," in which was first used the phrase : "These are the times that try men's souls."

Paine performed many other services, and was rewarded by Congress and given a farm in New Rochelle by the State of New York. In 1787 he went back to Europe and wrote the "Rights of Man," which was very popular. In 1795 he published a book against the Christian religion, called "The Age of Reason," which gave much offense to many of his friends. He came back to the United States in 1802, and spent the rest of his life in obscurity. He died in New York when seventy-two years old (June 8, 1809).

PAISLEY (*paze'le*), a town of Scotland, 8 miles W. by S. of Glasgow ; pop. 56,000, or nearly as large as Trenton, N. J. It is noted for its manufactures, especially of fine shawls, silk gauze, muslins, plaids, handkerchiefs, carpets, and threads.

A priory was built on the site of Paisley in 1160, and the town gradually grew up around it.

PAIXHANS (*pake-son'*), **Henri Joseph,** a French inventor, born in Metz, Jan. 22, 1783. He was a general in the army, and was the first in France to make cannons to shoot hollow shot, which were named after him Paixhan guns ; but they were nearly the same as our Columbiads, invented by Col. Bomford, and used in the war of 1812-1814. Gen. Paixhans wrote several works on military and naval subjects. He died near Metz when seventy-one years old (Aug. 19, 1854).

PALENQUE (*pah-lenk'a*), the name given by the Spaniards to the ruins of an ancient town in S. Mexico, on the river Chacamas, about 8 miles from the village of Santo Domingo de Palenque. The ruins, which are surrounded by a thick forest, are made up of terraces built like pyramids cut off at the top, with stone buildings on them. The principal building, commonly called the palace, which is very large, is built of cut stone cemented with mortar and covered with figures of men and animals, and with hieroglyphics in an unknown language.

It is not known who built these wonderful structures, but the city was not known to the Spaniards, who conquered Mexico, and the ruins were not discovered until 1750.

PA-LER'MO, a city of Italy, capital of the Island of Sicily, on a bay on the N. side of the island ; pop. 267,000, or somewhat larger than Cleveland, Ohio. The bay and mountains near by are celebrated for their beautiful scenery, and the city itself is very handsome, having a royal palace and many splendid churches. The university has fine museums and a library. Palermo has a large trade in oranges, lemons, and other fruits, and many boats from there are engaged in the tunny fishery.

Palermo was first built by the Phœnicians in very early times. The Greeks called it Panormus, which means "spacious harbor" and its modern name has grown out of that. The city has suffered much from earthquakes.

The Palace, Palenque. (See page 616.)

PALES (*pa'leez*), in Roman fable, the guardian of shepherds and of their flocks and pastures. Pales is sometimes described as a man, and sometimes as a woman.

PAL'ES-TINE, a country in the S.W. part of Turkey in Asia, on the Mediterranean Sea; area 12,000 square miles, or one and a fourth times as large as New Hampshire; pop. over 1,000,000, or about three times that of New Hampshire. It is divided into two nearly equal parts by the Jordan, a small river which flows south through the waters of Merom and the Lake of Genesseret, or Sea of Galilee, and finally into the Dead Sea. The Jordan, except near its source, is below the level of the ocean, and the Dead Sea is a quarter of a mile below the Mediterranean. The waters of the Dead Sea are very salt and contain no fish. On each side of the Jordan are mountains and hills, beyond which, on the eastern side, the country is a desert, while on the western side are narrow plains between the mountains and the sea. The plains are very fertile, but the mountains are now sterile, though in former times they were well cultivated. Most of the cities and villages of Palestine are on the western side of the Jordan. The only seaport is Joppa or Jaffa. The people are of various races, including many Arabs, Syrians, Turks, and Jews. Most of them are Mohammedans, but some of the Syrians are Christians. Nearly all are very poor and ignorant.

Palestine is not now a very important country, but it is very interesting on account of being the scene of most of the events told about in the Bible. The Hebrews, Israelites, or Jews conquered it from a dark race who were divided into many tribes and kingdoms. One of the kingdoms was called Philistia, or in Hebrew *Palesheth*, from which the word Palestine has been made. In the Bible the region west of the Jordan is sometimes called the land of Canaan, and that east of it the land of Gilead. The Hebrews reached the height of their power under their kings David and Solomon. After Solomon died the country was divided into two kingdoms, called Judah and Israel or Samaria. The Hebrews were at different times subject to the Babylonians, Greeks, Egyptians, and Syrians. Finally they were conquered by the Romans, and in the time of Christ Palestine was divided into three Roman provinces, called Judea, Samaria, and Galilee. Judea was farthest south, and contained Jerusalem and Bethlehem, Samaria was in the middle, and Galilee was farthest north. Soon after Christ died the Jews rebelled against the Romans, and in the war which followed great numbers of them were killed. Jerusalem was taken by Titus after a terrible siege (A.D. 70), the temple was burned, and thousands of Jews were carried captive to Rome. They rebelled many times after that, but were always conquered, and at length they were dispersed to all parts of the world. Palestine was conquered by the Persians in 614, and by the Arabs in 637. In the middle ages immense armies were sent from Europe to conquer Palestine, and deliver Jerusalem and other sacred places from the Arabs. These expeditions are called the CRUSADES. In 1507 the Turks took Palestine, and since then it has been a part of the Turkish Empire.

PALFREY (*pawl'fry*), **John Gor-**

ham, a noted American writer of history, born in Boston, May 2, 1796. He was graduated at Harvard College when nineteen years old, and became a clergyman and a professor in the Harvard theological school. From 1835 to 1842 he edited the " North American Review," and was elected to Congress in 1846. His " History of New England " is his best known work. He died in Cambridge, Mass., when eighty-five years old (April 26,1881).

PALGRAVE (*pawl'grave*), Sir **Francis,** a noted English writer, born in London in July, 1788. He was of a Jewish family named Cohen, but changed that name for Palgrave, the maiden name of his wife's mother. He was educated a lawyer, and was made a knight in 1832 for his services in writing about the laws. But he is best known for his " History of Normandy and England," and other learned historical works. He died at Hampstead when seventy-three years old (July 6, 1861).

PAL'IS-SY, Bernard, a noted French potter, born near Agen about 1510. When a boy he was apprenticed to a potter. At that time the Italians were famous for making very fine pottery, and Palissy, who had become much interested in the art, determined to find out how they did it. He spent sixteen years and all his property in trying to discover the secret of the enamel or glaze which they used (C. C. T., 487, I., u.), and at last succeeded in making even better ware than they did. In time he became very famous, and the pottery made by him is still highly prized.

Having become a Protestant, he was thrown into prison in Bordeaux, but was finally set free and made potter to the king. He removed to Paris and set up his works in a place called the Tuileries (tile-kilns) from the tile-works there. Shortly afterward a palace was built there, and it has ever since borne the name of the Tuileries. Palissy was employed to adorn the gardens of the palace, and this saved him from the massacre of Saint Bartholomew; but at last he got into trouble on account of his religion, and was imprisoned in the Bastile, where he died when about eighty years old (1590).

PAL'LAS. See MINERVA.

PALMER (*pah'mer*), **Erastus Dow,** an American sculptor, born in Pompey, N. Y., April 2, 1817. In early life he was a carpenter, and did not begin to be a sculptor until nearly thirty years old. Since then he has been very successful in his art. Among his works is a fine marble group of sixteen figures, representing the "Landing of the Pilgrims." His studio is in Albany, N. Y.

PALMERSTON (*pah'mer-stun*), **Henry John Temple,** Viscount, a British statesman, born in London, Oct. 20, 1784. He was the son of an Irish peer, and a descendant of Sir William Temple. Many high offices in the government were held by him during the reigns of William IV. and Victoria. When minister of foreign affairs, he had to settle many difficult questions, and twice he filled the office of Prime Minister. He was much liked, and to the last society was glad to welcome him to its circles. He died at Brockett Hall, Herts, when eighty-one years old (Oct. 18, 1865), and was buried in Westminster Abbey.

Ruins of Palmyra.

PALMYRA (*pal-mi'rah*), an ancient city of Syria, in an oasis of the desert, 120 miles N.E. of Damascus. It is supposed to be the same as Tadmor, said to have been built by Solomon nearly 3000 years ago. The city gained its greatest prosperity under Queen ZENOBIA. Palmyra then became one of the most famous cities in the world, and its merchants carried on an immense trade with Asia and Europe. After Zenobia was captured by the Romans, the people of Palmyra rebelled and killed the Roman garrison; and to punish them the Emperor AURELIAN destroyed the city. It was rebuilt by Justinian (A.D. 527), but was afterward captured by the Saracens, who pillaged it in 744. At present there is only a small village on its site, but remains of the magnificent palace built by Zenobia and others can still be seen there. Rows of beautiful marble columns are still standing, and there are many towers which were once used for tombs.

Palmyra means City of Palms, and Tadmor is a Hebrew translation of the same name.

PALO ALTO (*pah'lo ahl'to*), a wood in S. Texas, 8 miles N.N.E. of Matamoras, Mexico, noted for a battle fought there during the Mexican war between a United States army under General Taylor and the Mexicans under General Arista, May 8, 1846. Taylor was marching to Fort Brown, near Matamoras, when he found the Mexican army in front of him. Though they had twice as many men, he defeated them after a battle of five hours. The Mexicans retreated to Resaca de la Palma, where, on the next day, another victory was won by the Americans, the Mexicans being driven back into Mexico.

Palo Alto is Spanish for "High Woods." Resaca de la Palma means "Ravine of the Palms," the battle-field taking its name from a ravine overgrown with palm-trees.

PAMPHYLIA (*pam-fil'e-ah*). See ASIA MINOR.

PAN, in Greek fable, the god of flocks and shepherds, fishermen and bee-keepers. He also watched over hunters, but was dreaded by travel-ers. He was a favorite with all the gods, especially with Bacchus. He lived in grottoes and played on the shepherd's pipes, which he was the first to make. His voice was so loud and frightful that he scared away the TITANS in their war with the gods. He is represented with the head and body of a man and the beard, horns, feet, and tail of a goat.

PANAMA (*pan-a-mah'*), **Isthmus of,** a narrow neck of land connect-ing North and South America. In its narrowest part it is only 30 miles wide. Through it runs a range of mountains, which form a part of the Andes, but in some places there are passes only 300 feet above the sea. The mountains and plains are co-vered with thick forests, and the climate is hot and unhealthy.

The Isthmus of Panama was dis-covered by BALBOA in 1513. When Americans began to settle in Cali-fornia and Oregon the journey across the continent was very dan-gerous, and that by ships around Cape Horn was long and tedious. To avoid these routes a railroad was built across the isthmus, from Aspinwall to Panama, which is one of the most important railroads in the world. M. de LESSEPS at-tempted to make a ship canal across the isthmus, but after considerable progress the work was abandoned on account of the great expense.

PANAMA, a city of Colombia, on the S. side of the Isthmus of Pana-ma, on a bay of the Pacific Ocean; pop. 25,000, or about as large as Taunton, Mass. Nearly all its im-portance is due to the Panama Rail-road, which gives it a large trade. The bay is so shallow that steamers are obliged to land their cargoes on islands several miles from the town to which they are taken by small boats.

Panama was founded by the Span-iards in 1518. It was destroyed by the Buccaneers in 1670, and the present town was afterward built, six miles from the site of the old one.

PAN-DO'RA, in Greek fable, the first woman, made by Vulcan at Jupiter's command, and endowed with gifts by all the gods and god-desses. Hence her name, which means "every gift." Jupiter gave her a box containing all the evils that can come to men, and sent her to Prometheus, hoping that he would take her as his wife; but PROMETHEUS refused to have her. His brother, Epimetheus, however, was charmed by her and opened the box, letting loose all the evils, for which act he was turned into an ape. Pandora shut the box quickly; but it was too late; only Hope re-mained, with which Jupiter had meant to console men at last for all troubles.

PAOLI (*pa-o'le*), **Pasquale,** a Cor-sican general, born in 1726. He became commander of the Corsican army in 1755, and gained many victories over the Genoese, who then claimed Corsica. The Genoese at length sold their rights to the French, who invaded Corsica with a large army. Paoli at first beat them back, but in 1769 they conquered the island and Paoli fled to England. When France became a republic, Paoli was made governor of Corsica, but he soon became dissatisfied with the French Government and revolted against it. He was assisted by the English, who drove the French from the island, making themselves rulers there, but doing little for Paoli. He went to London, where he died at the age of eighty-one years (Feb. 5, 1807).

PAPHLAGONIA (*paf-la-go'ne-ah*). See ASIA MINOR.

PAPUA (*pap'poo-ah*), or **New Guinea**, an island in the Pacific Ocean, N. of Australia; area 275,-000 square miles, or about as large as Texas; pop. unknown. This is the largest island in the world, except Australia and perhaps Borneo. Only a small part of it has been explored, but it is known that there are many mountains in the interior, some of the peaks being more than two miles high. The country is covered with thick forests, and some of the trees are as large as any in the world. The principal animals are wild hogs, opossums, and tree-kangaroos. Among the many handsome birds, the most beautiful and curious are the birds of Paradise, which are found only in Papua and a few islands near it. The largest and the smallest kinds of parrots known are found there, and more than forty kinds of pigeons, of which one kind has a beautiful crown of feathers. Immense serpents called pythons are sometimes seen, and crocodiles are found in the rivers. The climate is warm and damp.

The people are a black race, much like negroes. They have ugly faces and thick, bushy hair, which they stain red. They are divided into many tribes, all of which are savages, and so treacherous and cruel that it is almost impossible to travel in their country. Their arms are bows and arrows, lances, and clubs, and they build huts of bamboo. The Dutch have settlements in the north-western part of Papua, and they claim nearly half of the island. Their principal settlement is Dorey, on the northern coast.

Papua was discovered in the 16th century by the Portuguese, who called it New Guinea because the people looked like those of Guinea in Africa. The name Papua is made from the Malay wood *papu-vah*, which means "crisp-haired."

PAR-A-CEL'SUS, the fictitious name of Philippus Aureolus Theophrastus Bombastus von Hohenheim, a Swiss alchemist, born in 1493. He was the son of a physician, and himself studied medicine a little while, but he claimed to be so wise in the healing art that he was supposed to be aided by the evil one. Other doctors looked on him as a quack, but in spite of this he had many patients, and among them some very distinguished men. Besides medicine he learned the arts of the sorcerer and juggler, and pretended to have found out the elixir of life, by the use of which one could live forever. But at last he was found out, and he died in poverty in Salzburg when forty-eight years old (Sept. 23, 1541).

PARAGUAY (*pah-rah-gwi'*), a country of South America, S.W. of Brazil; area about 90,000 square miles, or nearly the same as that of Oregon; pop. about 330,000, or a little more than that of Oregon; capital, ASUNCION. It lies mostly between the two great rivers, Paraguay and Paraná, and from this it gets its name, which means the "place of waters." At the southern end, where these rivers meet, the land is low and generally swampy, but farther north it is covered with forest, where jaguars and other wild beasts are still found.

Paraguay was first settled by the Spaniards in 1537; it became independent by a revolution begun in

1811. Involved in a war with Brazil, the Argentine Republic, and Uruguay, which lasted until 1870, more than half the people died in battle, or of disease brought on in the swamps and woods to which they had fled; in the end, those who survived were obliged to submit to the armies brought against them. The people are mostly Indians, there being only a few whites and negroes. Spanish is spoken in the towns, but the Indian language is still used in the interior. The country is a republic, but it is badly governed.

PAR′IS, son of Priam King of TROY, and of Hecuba. His mother having dreamed of him as a blazing torch which set fire to the city, he was left on Mt. Ida as soon as he was born. A shepherd found him and brought him up as his own son. He grew up very handsome, and when Juno, Minerva, and Venus quarreled about a golden apple,

Porte Saint Denis.   (See page 623.)

inscribed "To the Fairest," which Eris, the god of strife, had thrown among them, he was chosen by Jupiter to decide which of them was most worthy of it. He gave the apple to Venus, and she promised him the most beautiful woman in the world for his wife.

CASSANDRA, his sister, declared that he was the child of Priam, and the king acknowledged him as his son and a prince of Troy. Paris, having heard that HELEN, wife of King MENELAUS of Sparta, was the most beautiful woman in the world, deserted his wife Œnone, went to Greece and, with the aid of Venus, carried her off to Troy. This led to the siege of Troy, for the Greeks sided with Menelaus, who was determined to get his wife back. Paris twice met Menelaus in battle; once he fled, and the second time he was defeated, but was saved by Venus. Paris was finally wounded in one of the fights and went to Œnone to heal him, but she refused and he went back to Troy. She repented and followed him, but too late to save him, and she killed herself.

PAR'IS (French *par-e'*), the capital of France and the largest city in Europe, except London, on the river Seine, 111 miles from its mouth; pop. 2,345,000, or about half as large again as New York City. It lies on both sides of the river, and on two islands in it, many fine bridges connecting the different parts. The city covers more than 28¼ square miles within the walls, which are 34 feet high and fronted by a deep ditch. Outside of the walls are large suburbs and many strong forts. The old walls, destroyed in the 17th century, formed a much smaller circle, which has been turned into fine streets called the *boulevards intérieurs*, or inner rampart-streets. Other wide streets are also called

Arc de l'Étoile.

boulevards. They are lined with stores and gayly decorated restaurants and on pleasant days are thronged with people. On the Boulevard Saint Denis is a triumphal arch called the Porte Saint Denis, built in 1672 in memory of the rapid conquests of Louis XIV. in Germany.

Paris is famous for its squares or places, gardens, and promenades. Among the finest squares are the Place de la Concorde, the Place du Carrousel, the Place de l'Hôtel de Ville, the Place de la Bastile, and the Place du Palais Royal. The Place de la Concorde (Concord Square) is beautified with many statues and fountains. When the French revolution broke out, the statue of Louis XV. stood in its centre, but it was melted up to make cannons, and near it was set up the guillotine, where hundreds of persons were beheaded. The obelisk of Luxor now standing there is an Egyptian column, which for more than 3000 years stood in front of the temple at Thebes. Leading from the Place de la Concorde is the avenue called the Champs Elysées (Elysian Fields), a wide, shady promenade like a long park. At the farther end is a splendid triumphal arch, begun by Napoleon and finished by Louis Philippe. It is called the Arc de l'Étoile (Arch of the Star), because it stands where many streets meet forming a star. The Place de la Bastile, on the site of the old Bas-tile prison, is now beautified by the Column of July, a bronze pillar in memory of the people who fell in the revolution of 1830. The Champ de Mars (Field of Mars) is a great parade-ground, where grand parades and ceremonies take place. The buildings of the great Exposition of 1867 were placed there.

The Place Vendôme is an eight-sided square, so named because the palace of the Duke of Vendôme stood there. A large statue of Louis XIV. on horseback used to

Place Vendôme.

stand in the middle of it, but it was destroyed in the Reign of Terror. In its place is now the Column of Vendôme, built by Napoleon in memory of his German victories in 1805. It is in imitation of the Column of Trajan at Rome, but is larger. The shaft is of stone, but is covered with bronze plates, cast out of 1200 Austrian and Russian cannons, and covered with bas-reliefs with more than 2000 figures illustrating the battles. On the top is a statue of Napoleon. In 1871 the Communists threw down the column, but it was set up again in 1874. The Jardin des Plantes (Garden of Plants) is a park containing a very fine menagerie, a botanical garden, and a museum of natural history. The Bois de Boulogne (Boulogne Wood) and the Versailles Parks are outside the walls.

Among the many palaces of Paris, the most beautiful is the Louvre, which has a magnificent museum and one of the finest art-galleries in the world. The Tuileries Palace, which was formerly connected with the Louvre, was burned in the Commune rebellion of 1871. The Elysée Palace is the residence of the French President. In the Invalides Palace is the Church of St. Louis, which contains the tomb of Napoleon. Nôtre Dame, or Our Lady's Cathedral, on an island in the Seine, is one of the finest Gothic churches in the world. It was begun in 1163, on the site of a much older church, and took several hundred years to build. The National Library of Paris is the largest in the world, and there are many other fine libraries and museums. The University Acade-my, formerly the University of Paris, is attended by nearly 11,000 students. The Polytechnic School, College of France, and College of St. Barbe are other famous schools. Paris has thousands of manufactories, those of jewelry, gloves, boots and shoes, artificial flowers, perfumery, bronzes, and surgical and philosophical instruments being most celebrated. It has a larger trade than any other city in Europe except London, commerce being carried on by railroads and by small vessels on the river.

Tomb of Napoleon.

Paris was named after the Parisii, who had a town on an island in the Seine before Christ. They were attacked by Julius Cæsar, but burned their town rather than yield (52 B.C.). Paris became the residence of the Roman governors of Gaul, but most of the earlier French kings did not live there. Since the 10th century it has been the capital of France, though the kings have sometimes been obliged to hold their courts in other places. The French revolution began there, and Louis XVI. and Marie Antoinette were beheaded (1793) in the Place de la Concorde, then called the Square of the Revolution. Napoleon did much to beautify the city, which was captured by the allies in 1814, and again after the battle of Waterloo in 1815. In 1830 and in 1848 there were other revolutions in Paris, and it may be said that every great movement of the French people has commenced there. In 1871 Paris was taken by the Germans, after a siege of five months in which the people suffered much from famine, and could only send letters out of the city by balloons and carrier-pigeons. Hardly had the Germans left, when many of the people rebelled against the French Government and drove it out of the city, setting up a separate city government, which they called the Commune (March 18, 1871). A new siege followed, and after several bloody battles, some of them in the city streets, the Commune was finally defeated (May 28). When the Communists saw that they would be beaten, they set the Tuileries and many other palaces on fire, and committed terrible deeds. Since that time Paris has had no more revolutions, and some of the burned palaces have been rebuilt.

PARK'MAN, Francis, a noted American writer of history, born in Boston, Sept. 16, 1823. He was graduated at Harvard College when twenty-one years old, and two years afterward went to the far West and lived for several months among the wild Indians among the Rocky Mountains. While there he suffered so much that his health was seriously injured, and he got a disease of the eyes which often makes him unable to read. But notwithstanding this he has written some very able historical works, among which are "The Conspiracy of PONTIAC," "Pioneers of France in the New World," and "Count Frontenac and New France under Louis XIV."

PARMA (*par'mah*), a city of N. Italy, on the river Parma, a branch of the Po; pop. 44,000, or about as large as Lawrence, Mass. It has many splendid palaces and churches, and beautiful parks and gardens. The most celebrated building is the Farnese Palace, which contains a large theatre, museum, and library. The University of Parma has two hundred students. The principal trade is in silk. Parma is a very ancient city, and was important under the Romans. In modern times it was the capital of the Duchy of Parma, but

in 1861 it was united to the kingdom of Italy.

PAR-ME'NI-O, a Macedonian general, born about 400 B.C. He was a favorite general of King Philip of Macedon, and afterward of Alexander the Great. The latter made him second in command, and he led part of the Macedonian army in the battles of Granicus, Issus, and Arbela. Parmenio's son, Philotas, was accused of plotting against Alexander, and when he was tortured to confess, he said that his father also was guilty. For this Alexander ordered Parmenio to be assassinated (330 B.C.).

PAR-NAS'SUS, a mountain of Greece, in Phocis, famous in fable as a favorite meeting place of Apollo and the Muses. Its caverns and springs were also frequented by some of the other gods and goddesses. Delphi, famous for its oracle, was on its southern slope, the fountain of Castalia sprang from its sides, and the Corcyrean cave, the home of Pan and the Muses, was on its western slope. Parnassus rises about a mile and a half above the sea, and its sides are covered with beautiful forests and abound in crags and caverns, while its top is covered with snow most of the year.

PA'ROS, an island of Greece, one of the CYCLADES; area about 80 square miles; pop. 7000. In ancient times it was famous for its marble quarries, which furnished stone for many of the finest statues, but they are not worked now. The island produces olives, wine, and cotton.

PARR, Thomas, an Englishman, born in Wimmington, a town of W. England, in 1483. He was called Old Parr, because he lived to a greater age than any other man known in modern times. It is said that he first married when eighty years old, and was married again when one hundred and twenty. When one hundred and fifty-two years old he was brought to London, where he soon after died (Nov. 15, 1635). Many persons doubt if he really did live so long.

PARRHASIUS (*par-ra'she-us*), a Greek painter who lived about 400 B.C. In a trial of skill between him and Zeuxis, another painter, Zeuxis painted such natural-looking grapes that the birds picked at them. Parrhasius painted a curtain which Zeuxis, thinking it a real curtain, asked Parrhasius to pull aside in order that he might see his picture. When he saw that he had been deceived, Zeuxis gave the prize to Parrhasius, saying it re- quired greater skill to deceive men than to deceive birds.

PAR'RY, Sir **William Edward,** an English arctic explorer, born in Bath, Dec. 19, 1790. He entered the navy when only thirteen years old, and after making two voyages to the polar seas, was put in com- mand of an arctic expedition of two vessels, to find a north-west passage; that is, a way around the north part of America to Asia. He went through Wellington Channel and into Melville Sound, and on Sept. 4th reached a point further west than any one had sailed be-

View of Mount Parnassus.   (Page **626.**)

fore, thus earning £5000 ($25,000), which Parliament had offered to the first ship's company which should go so far west in that region. The explorers spent the winter on Mel- ville Island and were frozen in for ten months. When the ice melted they went back to England.

Parry afterward made three more arctic voyages, and on the last one tried to reach the North Pole, in boats fitted with runners, which could be used either as boats or sledges. With these he went farther north than any other person had gone up to that time, but was at length stopped by a half-frozen sea, in which his vessels were useless either as sledges or boats (1827). On his return to England he was made a knight, and during the rest of his life was employed in many important public offices. He pub- lished accounts of his voyages and also several other books. He died at Ems, Germany, when sixty-four years old (July 8, 1855).

PARTHIA (*par'the-ah*), an an- cient country of W. Asia, S.E. of the Caspian Sea, in what is now a part of Persia. The people were rough and warlike, and famed for their horsemanship and skill with the bow. The Parthians at different times were ruled by the Assyrians, Persians, Macedonians, and Syrians, but about 250 B.C. they set up a kingdom of their own under Arsaces, whose family ruled for nearly 500 years and formed a vast empire, which at one time almost rivaled Rome. The Romans did not conquer them, but they were finally subdued by the Persians.

PAR'TON, James, an American author, born in Canterbury, England, Feb. 9, 1822. He was brought to New York when but five years old. For three years, he was one of the editors of the Home Journal, but he now occupies himself in writing books at Newburyport, Mass. He has written many works, among them lives of "Horace Greeley," "Aaron Burr," and "Thomas Jefferson." He is now at work on a life of "Voltaire."

PASCAL (*pas'kal*), **Blaise,** a noted French writer, born in Clermont, June 19, 1623. When very young he showed great genius, especially in mathematics, and without being taught found out the most of geometry. When only sixteen years old he wrote a book on mathematics, and when twenty-six he ranked with the great scholars of his time. In 1654 he suddenly stopped his studies and went to Port Royal and spent most of the rest of his life writing religious works. He died in Paris when nearly thirty-nine years old (Aug. 19, 1662).

PATAGONIA (*pat-a-go'ne-ah*), a southern country of South America, between the ANDES and the Atlantic Ocean ; area about 350,000 square miles, or nearly the same as Texas and the Indian Territory put together. The southern end, about the Strait of Magellan, is partly covered with forest, but all the eastern and northern portion is made up of treeless plains, where the only plants are grass, herbs, and low shrubs. It is a very wild

and dismal region, roamed over by pumas, deer, and the rhea, or American ostrich, The climate is hot in our winter and cold in our summer. The few people are roving Indians, who in the northern parts have horses and cattle. Patagonia is claimed by both Chili and the Argentine Republic.

Patagonia was first visited in 1520 by the Portuguese, who gave it this name (which means the "country of the large feet") because they found some large footprints on the shore.

PAT'ERSON, a city of N. E. New Jersey, 17 miles from New York ; pop. 78,000, or about the same as Lowell, Mass. It is on the Passaic River, at the beautiful Passaic Falls, which are about fifty feet high. They furnish the water-power for many large manufactories, the most important of which are locomotive-works and silk-factories. The river is crossed by fourteen bridges.

Paterson was founded in 1792 and was named after William Paterson, then governor of New Jersey.

PA·TRO'CLUS. See ACHILLES.

PAUL I., Czar of Russia, born Oct. 12, 1754. He was the son of Peter III. and CATHARINE II., and succeeded his mother Nov. 17, 1776. Hated by his mother, who banished him from court and had him brought up in ignorance of public affairs, he, in his turn, had conceived a violent dislike to her, and when he became emperor his chief aim seems to have been to undo all that she had done. His very first acts made people think him crazy, as indeed he was. Before Catherine's burial he had his murdered father's coffin taken from the grave and laid beside his mother, who was supposed to have been a party to his murder. A true love-knot was made to unite the two coffins with the motto "Divided in life, united in death," and two of the murderers were forced to stand beside their victim for three hours as chief mourners. At first he joined in the wars against Napoleon, but he afterward took his side and challenged to single combat any sovereign who would not join him in an alliance against England. He did so many strange things that at last some of his ministers murdered him, when he was forty-six years old (March 23, 1801). He was succeeded by his son Alexander I.

PAULDING, James Kirke, an American author, born in Dutchess Co., N. Y. Aug. 27, 1779. He was a brother-in-law of Washington Irving, and wrote part of the "Salmagundi" papers, now forming part of Irving's works. Afterward he wrote many tales, sketches, and poems, among them the poem of "The Backwoodsman" and "The Dutchman's Fireside," a romance which became very popular. From 1837 to 1841 Mr. Paulding was Secretary of the Navy. He died at Hyde Park, near his birthplace, when eighty years old (Apr. 6, 1860).

PAULUS, Lucius Æmilius, a famous Roman general, born in Rome about 230 B.C. When thirty-nine years old he was sent to govern Further Spain, and fought successfully there and afterward in Liguria. In 168 he conquered Perseus, king of Macedon, at the battle of Pydna, and returned with great quantities of treasure to Rome, where he was given a triumph. He was the father of SCIPIO Africanus the Younger.

PAUSANIAS (*pau-sa'ne-as*), a noted Spartan general, nephew of LEONIDAS. He led the Greek army against the Persians at PLATÆA (479 B.C.), where he won such fame that he became proud and boastful, and, despising Spartan simplicity, he tried to give his country to XERXES. Being found out in this he was imprisoned, but on account of his great services was finally released. He then

tried to make the Helots, or Greek slaves, revolt, but a slave betrayed him, and when about to be arrested in Athens, he fled for refuge to the temple of Minerva. The people built up the doors with stones and he starved to death, (468 B.C.). It is said that his mother placed the first stone.

PAVIA (*pah-ve'ah*), a city of N. Italy, on the river Ticino, near the place where it joins the Po; pop. 30,000, or about as large as Terre Haute, Ind. It is surrounded by an old wall, and contains many ancient palaces and churches. It was once noted for its curious square towers, which were used as prisons or as fortresses, from which it was called the "city of a hundred towers." Some of these are still standing, and are as high as a common church-steeple. The university of Pavia, the oldest in Italy, is said to have been founded by CHARLES THE GREAT. The river at Pavia is crossed by a curious covered bridge, more than five hundred years old.

In the time of the Roman Empire, Pavia was called Ticonum.

PAW-TUCK'ET, a town of Rhode Island, on the Pawtucket River, 4 miles N. of Providence; pop. 28,000, or about as large as Bay City, Mich. The first cotton factory in the United States was built there (1790), and for a long time Pawtucket was the greatest manufacturing town in the country. It is still one of the most important, having many large manufactories of cotton and woolen cloth, yarn, thread, hair-cloth, card-board machinery, steam fire-engines, leather, and many other things. Just above the town are falls, which furnish water-power for the factories. Pawtucket was in Massachusetts until 1861, when it was joined to Rhode Island.

PEABODY, George, an American merchant, born in Danvers, Mass., Feb. 18, 1795. He was a merchant first In Georgetown, D. C., and afterward in Baltimore. In 1837 he went to London, and in 1843 set up a banking house there, and in time became very rich. He was very generous, and gave away large sums both in England and America. Among his gifts were nearly $2,500,000 for lodging houses for the poor of London, $3,500,000 for helping education in the Southern States, $1,000,000 for the Peabody Institute, founded by him in Baltimore, $150,000 for the Peabody Museum at Salem, Mass., and an equal sum for each of the museums at Harvard and Yale colleges. Queen Victoria offered to make him a baronet, but he declined. He died in London when seventy-four years old (Nov. 4, 1869). His funeral was celebrated in Westminster Abbey, and his body was afterward sent to America on an English ship-of-war. Notwithstanding his many gifts he left about $5,000,000 to his relatives.

PEALE, Charles Wilson, an American painter, born in Chesterton, Md., April 16, 1741. He was by turns a saddler, a watchmaker, a silversmith, a carver, a dentist, and a painter. He studied art under COPLEY and Benjamin WEST, and became noted as a portrait-painter. Among his works were several portraits of Washington, and portraits of many other noted Americans. He was the founder of Peale's Museum in Philadelphia. He died in Philadelphia when nearly eighty-six years old (Feb. 22, 1827).

Rembrandt Peale, his son, born in Bucks Co., Pa., Feb. 22, 1778, became also a noted painter both of historical pictures and of portraits. He also painted a portrait of Washington when he was President. Among his best-known works are the "Court of Death" and the "Roman Daughter." He died in Philadelphia when eighty-two years old (Oct. 3, 1860),

PEDRO (*pa'dro*), **II., Dom,** second Emperor of Brazil, born in Rio de Janeiro, Dec. 2, 1825. When only six years old he became emperor, by the abdication of his father, but was not crowned until he was fifteen years old (July 18, 1841). Until 1842 there were many civil wars in his empire. In 1852 he was engaged in a war with the Argentine Republic, and from 1867 to 1869 in one with Paraguay. During the latter years of his reign he has made two voyages to Europe and one to the United States. In 1889 Brazil became a republic and Dom Pedro was quietly deposed, and sailed for Lisbon, Portugal. He died in Paris when sixty-six years old (December 5, 1891).

PE'DRO THE CRUEL, King of Castile and Leon, born in Burgos, Aug. 30, 1334. He was the son of Alphonso XI., and succeeded him in 1350. This monster crowded into his life of thirty-four years a fearful number of murders; and his cruelties at last so disgusted his subjects that they rose in rebellion and gave the crown to his half-brother, Henry of Trastamare. Pedro fled to France, where the English were at that time engaged in war, and entreated the aid of the Black Prince, which was readily given. The French took the side of Henry, and the English soon left Pedro in disgust. Pedro was defeated and slain by his rival when thirty-four years old (March 14, 1369). He was succeeded by the victorious Henry, under the title of Henry II.

PEEL, Sir Robert, an English statesman, born near Bury, Lancashire, Feb. 5, 1788. He was the son of Sir Robert Peel, a rich cotton manufacturer and member of Parliament. Robert was educated at Oxford, where he took very high honors; entered Parliament the next year (1809), and for more than forty years took a leading part in English politics. The two public acts by which he is best known were his advocacy of the Catholic Emancipation Act and the repeal of the corn laws. Up to his time Roman Catholics had been shut out from many positions in the government, and the Catholic Emancipation Act was a bill putting them on the same footing with others. At first Peel was opposed to setting aside the old laws against the Roman Catholics, for which reason he was hated in Ireland and nicknamed "Orange Peel," "Orangeman" being a name among the Irish for Protestants. Although English landholders disliked him for doing away with the corn laws, or duties on breadstuffs, the laboring man blessed his name for enabling him to buy bread for his starving family. The queen valued his services so highly that she wanted to raise him to the peerage— that is, make a lord of him—but he counted it a greater honor to go down to posterity by the name he had so long and so honorably worn than to be known by a new title, and, in his will, he solemnly warned his children never to depart from his example. He was thrown from his horse June 29, 1850, and died of his injuries when sixty-two years old (July 2, 1850).

PEG'A-SUS, in Greek fable, a winged horse, said to have sprung from the blood of Medusa when PERSEUS cut her head off. Pegasus is sometimes described as carrying the thunderbolts of Jupiter, and sometimes as belonging to Apollo and the Muses. He carried BELLEROPHON in his fight with Chimæra, and with a stroke of his hoof made the fountain called Hippocrene on Mount Helicon. Finally he became a constellation in the heavens.

PE-KING', a city, capital of the Chinese Empire, on a sandy plain, near the river Tunghui, about 100 miles from the sea; pop. 1,500,-000, or a little less than New

York. It consists of four separate cities, lying one within the other, and separated by walls. In the middle is the Kinching (Prohibited City), containing the emperor's palace and the houses of his principal officers. The emperor's palace is called the Tranquil Palace of Heaven, and the empress lives in the Palace of Earth's Repose. The imperial garden is a beautiful place, full of groves and bowers, artificial lakes, temples, and flowerbeds. The Huangchin (Imperial City), which surrounds the Kinching, contains the houses of many court officers, a beautiful park, and numerous temples, one of which is dedicated to Yuen-fi, the supposed discoverer of the silk-worm. The Nuiching (Tartar City) comes next, and beyond all is the Waiching (Chinese City), surrounded by a wall thirty feet high. Peking has many wide streets and good brick houses, generally one story high and roofed with tiles. The shops are open in front, and customers stand in the street. There are hardly any manufactures, and but little trade. Everything is very dear, and many of the people are miserably poor.

Peking or Pekin, in Chinese, means Northern Capital. The city is one of the most ancient in China, and became the capital about 1290.

PE-LOP'I-DAS, a noted Theban general. He was the friend of EPAMINONDAS, who saved his life in battle. Pelopidas was very rich and wished to share his money with Epaminondas, who was poor; but his friends would not let him do this. When Thebes was taken by the Spartans (382 B.C.), Pelopidas raised an army and went to its rescue. He and six others in the disguise of peasants, entered the city, where he killed the Spartan general Leontiades with his own hand, and with the help of the army outside expelled the Spartan soldiers. He afterward defeated the Spartans at Tegyra, and shared with Epaminondas the honor of the great victory of LEUCTRA (371). Pelopidas was sent as an ambassador to Alexander the tyrant of Pheræ, who treacherously imprisoned him; but he was soon after released by Epaminondas. He led an army to the rescue of Thessaly from Alexander, and in rashly trying to capture him lost his life (364 B.C.).

PE-LO-PON-NE'SUS, the ancient name of the southern part of Greece, the peninsula called in modern times the Morea. It is joined to northern Greece by the Isthmus of Corinth. In ancient times it was divided into five states, Achaia, Argolis, Laconia, Messenia, and Elis, and had many famous cities, among which were Sparta, Mycenæ, and Mantinea. Peloponnesus means the Island of Pelops. It was so called by the Greeks because PELOPS was supposed to have settled a colony there.

PE'LOPS, in Greek fable, the son of TANTALUS and grandson of Jupiter. His father killed him and served up his limbs at a banquet of the gods. They all refused to touch the meat except Ceres, who ate one shoulder. Jupiter had him restored to life, and in the place of that shoulder gave him one of ivory which had wonderful power and could heal diseases by its touch. Pelops afterward asked Œnomaus, king of Pisa in Elis, for his daughter Hippodamia in marriage. An oracle had told the king that his son-in-law should kill him, so he refused Pelops unless he would run a chariot-race with him, telling him he should die if he failed. Pelops bribed Myrtilus, the king's charioteer, who let the king's chariot break down in the race and the king was killed. Pelops then married Hippodamia and became so powerful that all Greece was called Peloponnesus after him. Instead of keeping his word to Myrtilus, he threw him into the sea, after which

many misfortunes befell him and his family.

PEM'BER-TON, John C., an American general, born in Philadelphia in 1817. He was a graduate of West Point, and was promoted for gallant conduct in the Mexican war. He entered the Confederate army in 1861 as a colonel, but soon became a general, and in 1862 was made commander in Mississippi. Gen. Grant defeated him at the battles of Champion Hills and Big Black River (May 16 and 17, 1863), and besieged him in Vicksburg, where he was finally obliged to surrender, July 4, 1863. He died at Penllyn, Pa., when sixty-four years old (July 13, 1881).

PE-NEL'O-PE, in Greek fable, the wife of Ulysses. While Ulysses was away at the siege of TROY, she was sought by several lovers. But she said that she could not decide between them until she had finished weaving a robe which she had begun. Every night she secretly unraveled all that she had woven during the day, and thus kept them waiting for twenty years, when her husband returned and killed all his rivals. She was the mother of Telemachus.

PENN, William, the founder of Pennsylvania, born in London, Oct. 14, 1644. He was educated at the university of Oxford, and while there became a member of the Society of Friends, which displeased his father very much. Because he would not take off his hat when in the presence of the king, his father turned him out of doors, and he was sent to prison several times for preaching in the streets and going to Quaker meetings. The English Government owed his father a large sum of money, and after he died they gave his son the whole region called PENNSYLVANIA, in payment of the debt. In 1682 he went to see his new lands, and soon after reaching the Delaware River he made a treaty with many Indian tribes, whom he met under a great elm-tree at Shakamaxon, or the "place of kings." Penn carried no fire-arms, because he did not think it right to use them. He told the Indians that he wanted always to live in love and friendship with them, and that he would not take their land by force, but would buy it of them. The Indians loved

William Penn.

him so for his kindness and justice that they kept the treaty for sixty years. Penn laid out his city of PHILADELPHIA soon afterward, and after a stay of two years went back to England, leaving a colony of 7000 persons. He induced the king to pardon many Quakers, who had been shut up in prisons, and after ten years returned to govern Pennsylvania. He died at Ruscombe, Berkshire, at the age of nearly seventy-four (July 30, 1718).

PENNSYLVANIA (*pen-sil-vay'-ne-ah*), a State of the United States, between New York and Maryland; area 46,000 square miles, or nearly the same as that of New York; pop. about 5,258,000, or an eighth less than that of New York; capital, HARRISBURG. The Alleghany and other mountain ranges cross the State from north-east to south-west, and are noted for their wild and beautiful scenery. West of the mountains, the land is hilly

or rolling, and the south-eastern part is level.

Pennsylvania is noted for its coal-mines, about twice as much coal being dug there as in all the rest of the United States. West of the Alleghenies the coal is soft, or bituminous, but east of them it is anthracite, or hard coal, the best in the world. In both regions there are also rich iron-mines, often near the coal-mines, so that it is very convenient to use the coal for smelting the iron ore. In the north-western part of the State are many wonderful petroleum-wells, which produce three times as much petroleum as all the rest of the world. In some places the oil is carried from the wells through tubes many miles long, and thousands of railroad-cars are loaded with it.

The farms of Pennsylvania are almost as important as the mines, and the forests are very rich in pine and other fine lumber, which is brought down the rivers in great rafts. In manufactures, especially of iron and steel, it is ahead of every other State. Nearly half the railroad iron sold in the United States, and a fifth of the steam-engines and machinery, come from Pennsylvania, and four times as much steel is made there as in all the other States put together.

King CHARLES II. gave the country west of the Delaware River to William Penn, who wanted to name it Sylvania (Forest-land), but the King added Penn to it in honor, as he said, of Admiral Penn, William Penn's father. Pennsylvania was one of the thirteen original States of the Union.

PEORIA (*pe-o're-ah*), a city of Illinois, on the Illinois River; pop. 41,000, or about as large as New Bedford, Mass. Steamboats go up the river from the Mississippi to this place, and by means of them and of several railroads which meet there a large trade is carried on. The city contains large rolling-mills, foundries, saw-mills, breweries, and manufactories of farmers' tools, machinery and carriages. The Frenchman La Salle established a trading-post on the site of Peoria about 1680, but the first permanent settlement was made there in 1819.

PEP'IN (French *peh-pan'*), called the Short, first Carlovingian king of France, born about 715. He was the son of CHARLES MARTEL, Mayor of the Palace under Dagobert III. Pepin put Childeric, the last of the Merovingians, into a convent, and was himself crowned at Soissons in 752. Notwithstanding his short stature, he was noted for his great strength, and was always successful in his many wars against the Saracens, Lombards, and Saxons. He gave to Pope Stephen the part of Italy extending south from Ravenna, which he had taken from the Lombards. In this way the popes became temporal princes, this land continuing under their rule until very lately, when it was taken from them and joined to the rest of Italy. Pepin died when fifty-three years old (741), and was succeeded by his son CHARLES THE GREAT.

PEP'PER-ELL, Sir **William,** a noted American general, born at Kittery Point, Maine, June 27, 1696. For thirty-two years he was a member of King George's council for the province of Massachusetts. In 1745 the English, being at war with France, wished to take LOUISBURG, a very strong French fortress on the island of Cape Breton, Nova Scotia. An American army was placed under the command of Pepperell and sailed for Louisburg in one hundred vessels. After a siege of nearly fifty days, the fort surrendered. The British Government made Pepperell a baronet for his services, and afterward he went to England and became a lieutenant-general in the British army. For two years he acted as

governor of Massachusetts. He died at Kittery Point, at the age of sixty-three (July 6, 1759).

PEPYS (*peps*), **Samuel,** an English gentleman, celebrated as the writer of a diary called "Pepys' Diary," born Feb. 23, 1633. He was educated at Cambridge University, and in 1660 became clerk of the acts of the navy. In this position he was brought into contact with many persons of rank, and he kept a diary of his daily life and of the doings and sayings of those whom he met. It was written in short-hand and lay unread for more than a century, but was finally deciphered and printed. It is a very amusing book, and gives a good picture of life and manners in the time of Charles II. Pepys died when seventy years old (May 26, 1703).

PER'CI-VAL, James Gates, a noted American poet and scholar, born in Berlin, Conn., Sept. 15, 1795. He was graduated at Yale College when twenty years old and studied medicine, but gave most of his time to writing. In 1822 he published a poem called "Prometheus," and afterward published "A Dream of a Day," and other poems. He aided Noah WEBSTER in making his dictionary, made a geological survey of Connecticut, and was appointed (1854) State geologist of Wisconsin. While engaged in this last work he died at Hazel Green, Wisconsin, when sixty years old (May 2, 1856).

PER-DIC'CAS, a favorite general of ALEXANDER THE GREAT, who led a division of the Macedonian army in the invasion of Asia. It is said that Alexander, on his death-bed, gave him his signet-ring, and Perdiccas was then looked upon as regent. He was suspected by the generals of having designs to seize upon the throne, so they formed a league against him. Perdiccas marched against Ptolemy in Egypt, but in trying to cross the Nile lost so many soldiers that his army mutinied and some of his officers went to his tent and killed him (321 B.C.).

PE-RI-AN'DER, a ruler or tyrant of Corinth, Greece, born about 665 B.C. He was a learned man, but very despotic and cruel. It is said that he sent to Thrasybulus, tyrant of Miletus, asking the best way to govern. Thrasybulus took the messenger to a corn-field and broke off all the highest ears of corn. Periander understood from this that he should kill or banish all the important men of Corinth, which he accordingly did. Once he invited all the Corinthian ladies to a festival, and when they had come he ordered them to take off all their rich ornaments, that he might keep them. At length, in a fit of jealousy, he killed his wife, Melissa. His son, Lycophron, discovered the crime and refused to live longer with his father. He was, therefore, banished to Corcyra, but Periander afterward repented, and invited his son to return and rule the kingdom, promising to give up the throne and go himself to live in Corcyra. Lycophron would have done this, but the people of Corcyra hated Periander, and to prevent his coming they put Lycophron to death. When the king heard of this, he died of grief, at the age of eighty years (about 585 B.C.).

PER'I-CLES, a famous Athenian statesman, born in Athens, about 495 B.C. He was of an ancient and noble family, and had such great talents that he became in time the ruler of ATHENS, and so famous were the years of his rule that they are always spoken of as "The age of Pericles." Under him Athens was adorned with magnificent temples and buildings, among them the Parthenon, and even the lowest classes of the people were made to love art, literature, and poetry. By his means, too, Athens won the greatest fame abroad and reached

the height of her power. She became the leader of Greece, and most of the smaller states paid tribute to her. Sparta became jealous of her,

Pericles.

and the war called the Peloponnesian War broke out between the two (431). In the second year of this war a plague in Athens swept away thousands of the people, among others two of Pericles' sons and finally Pericles himself. After his death Athens began to go down in importance. He died when sixty-five years old (429 B.C.). Pericles was the husband of the famous ASPASIA.

PERNAMBUCO (*per-nahm-boo'-ko*), a city on the eastern coast of Brazil; pop. about 130,000, or nearly as large as Providence, R. I. The older part of the town, often called Recife, is on a narrow sand-bar, which is separated from the mainland by an inlet of the sea, crossed by a fine iron bridge. In Recife the streets are so narrow and crooked that carts cannot be used; goods are carried on the backs of horses, and hundreds of negro porters may be seen carrying sacks of sugar on their heads. The modern part of the city is well laid out, with broad, straight streets, and has many fine public buildings. The harbor is formed by a narrow reef against which the surf breaks with great violence; as very large ships cannot pass behind this reef, they are obliged to anchor without, in the open roadstead. Pernambuco is nearer to Europe than any other city in South America, and is connected with LISBON by a telegraphic cable. It has a large trade in sugar, molasses, rum, cotton, and hides.

The name Pernambuco is made from two Indian words meaning "open sea." The city was founded by the Portuguese about the year 1530.

PERPIGNAN (*per-pene-yon'*), a city of S. France, on the border of Spain, 6 miles from the Mediterranean Sea; pop. 34,000, or about as large as Norfolk, Va. It is a strong fortress, and commands the road from Spain into France. It has a considerable trade in wine, liqueurs, brandy, olive oil, and cork.

PER'RY, Matthew Calbraith, an American naval commander, brother of Oliver Hazard Perry, born in South Kingston, R. I., in 1795. In 1819, while cruising on the coast of Africa, he chose the place for the first settlement in LIBERIA. During the Mexican War he commanded the United States fleet in the Gulf of Mexico, and aided in the siege of Vera-Cruz. In 1852 he was sent to Japan with a fleet, and succeeded in opening that country to foreign trade (1854). He died in New York when sixty-three years old (March 4, 1858). A bronze statue has been erected to his memory in the public square at Newport.

PER'RY, Oliver Hazard, a famous American naval commander, born

in Newport, Rhode Island, Aug. 23, 1785. During the war of 1812 he was chosen to fit out a fleet at Presque Isle (now Erie) on Lake Erie. After equipping nine vessels, he sailed against the British fleet, which had only six ships, but larger and stronger ones than those of the Americans. The English attacked the Lawrence, Perry's flag ship, so hotly that out of 101 men on it only 18 were uninjured. In this strait Perry left the Lawrence in a

Oliver Hazard Perry.

small boat and was rowed to the Niagara, escaping unharmed from the cannon-balls that splashed around him. After that the Americans gained a splendid victory, taking all the English ships. For this service Congress gave Perry a gold medal and promoted him to be a captain. In 1819 he commanded a fleet which sailed to Colombia and ascended the Orinoco River. While returning he died of yellow fever at Port of Spain, Trinidad, when thirty-four years old (Aug. 23, 1819). In 1860 a marble statue of him was erected at Cleveland, Ohio.

PER·SEP'O·LIS. See SHIRAZ.

PER'SE·US (or *per'soos*), in Greek fable, the son of Jupiter and DANAE, daughter of King Acrisius of Argos. Acrisius, having been told by an oracle that he should be killed by his grandson, had Danae and her son shut up in a chest and thrown into the sea. The chest floated to Seriphus, one of the Cyclades Islands, where Perseus was brought up by King Polydectes. Polydectes sought to win the love of Danae, but she did not like him, and he shut her up in prison and said she should never come out until Perseus brought him the head of the Gorgon MEDUSA. Perseus did this by the aid of the gods. Minerva gave him a mirror in which he might see the face of Medusa, for upon Medusa herself he could not look and live; Mercury gave him a sword which would slay all mortal things on which it fell; and the Nymphs gave him the helmet of Pluto, which made the wearer invisible, a bag in which to put the head of Medusa, and the golden sandals of Mercury, which would carry him swifter than a dream. Thus armed he went to the dwelling of Medusa, and cut off her head.

On his way back, Perseus turned ATLAS into a mountain, and saved ANDROMEDA and married her. He then hastened to Seriphus, delivered his mother from prison, and with Medusa's head turned the tyrant Polydectes into stone. Perseus gave back to Mercury the sword, the sandals, and the helmet of Pluto, and Minerva took Medusa's head and placed it on her shield. He then returned with Danae to Argos, and his grandfather Acrisius fled in fear to Larissa. Perseus went there to take part in the games, and while throwing quoits accidentally killed Acrisius; and thus the prophecy was fulfilled.

PERSIA (*per'she-ah*), a country of W. Asia, between Turkey and Afghanistan; area, 600,000 square miles, or three times as large as France; pop. 7,000,000, or about two elevenths that of France; capital, TEHERAN. It is a table-land, crossed by many mountain ranges, which in the north-eastern part are very high. Most of the plains between them are barren, sandy deserts, often covered with salt, but wherever there is water the deserts give place to beautiful farms and gardens. The climate is generally dry and warm, and sometimes there are terrible droughts, one of which, a few years ago, caused the death of 2,000,000 people.

Iron, copper, lead, coal, and bitumen are found in Persia, and there are mines of turquoise. In the fertile regions wheat, barley, and maize are grown, and oranges, apples, and other fruits. Flowers, especially roses, are abundant, and the date-palm is seen about every village. Silk-worms are reared in many places. The Persians are mnch like the Turks, but there are also many Arabs, who live in villages or wander in the desert, sleeping in tents and pasturing their sheep and cattle wherever they can find grass. In the cities are many rich merchants, who carry on a large trade in silk, and beautiful shawls and carpets which are made there. The king of Persia, called the Shah, is often very despotic and cruel. It is said that he has more jewels and precious stones than any other ruler in the world, and he also has fine palaces and many hundred wives, but most of his subjects are miserably poor and ignorant.

Persia is a very old country, and it was once much larger and more powerful than it now is. Among its famous kings were CYRUS, DARIUS, and XERXES. The ancient Persians were worshipers of fire, but in the year 636 their country was conquered by the Arabs, who forced them to become Mohammedans.

PERTH, a city of Scotland, on the river Tay, 33 miles N. by W. of Edinburgh; pop. 29,000, or nearly as large as Chattanooga, Tenn. It is a handsome city, ornamented with parks and terraces, and with fine stone houses. The penitentiary there is the principal prison of Scotland. There are important manufactures of cotton cloth, and many ships are built there. The salmon-fisheries near Perth are among the best in Scotland.

Perth got its name from its ancient name Barr-Tatha, which means the "height on the river Tay." The town was probably founded by the Romans, and it was the capital of Scotland for many years. Many important events of Scottish history occurred there.

PER'TI-NAX, Helvius, a Roman Emperor, born in A.D. 126. He was the son of a charcoal-burner, but was well educated and won high rank in the army by his bravery and skill. On the death of Commodus, he was proclaimed emperor amid the rejoicings of the people. In attempting to correct abuses and to make reforms in the army, he made enemies, and he was murdered in his palace after a reign of but three months (A.D. 193).

PE-RU', a W. country of South America, on the Pacific Ocean; area 500,000 square miles, or about twice as large as Italy; pop. 2,630,-000, or about one twelfth that of Italy; capital, LIMA. The Andes Mountains pass through the western part of the country, about 100 miles from the sea, and they abound in grand and beautiful scenery. The region between the mountains and the sea is very dry, and hardly any trees grow there, but the great plain on the eastern side of the Andes is the most rainy country in the world, and it is covered with thick forests, in which the Amazons and many of its branches take their rise.

Silver is the most important mineral of Peru, and gold, quicksilver, borax, and salt are found there. But the richest mines are those of guano and nitrate of soda, immense quantities of which are sent to other countries, to be used as fertilizers to enrich the soil. Cinchona, or Peruvian bark, is obtained in the great eastern forests. Only a small portion of the Peruvian people are whites, the rest being Indians or mixed races. Spanish is the common language. Peru is a republic, but it has had so many civil wars and quarrels with other nations that it is not very prosperous.

When America was discovered, Peru had great cities and was rich in gold and silver. To get this wealth PIZARRO invaded the country in 1531, and soon conquered it. After that Peru was ruled by Spain until 1821, when it became free by a revolution. Since 1879 it has been at war with Chili, which ended disastrously and in loss of territory.

PESARO (*pa-sah'ro*), a city of Italy, on the Adriatic Sea, at the mouth of the river Toglio; pop. 19,000, or about as large as Nashua, N. H. It is more than two thousand years old, and was a flourishing place under the Roman emperors. Many beautiful churches and palaces, built in the middle ages, can still be seen there. Formerly Pesaro was famous for its manufactories of pottery, but they are not now very important.

PESTH. See BUDA-PESTH.

PE'TER I., called the Great, Emperor of Russia, fifth of the House of Romanoff, born near Moscow, June 10, 1672. He was the son of the Czar Alexis, and succeeded his brother Feodor when ten years old, in 1682. His brother, the idiotic Ivan, had been crowned as joint ruler with him, but on account of their youth the whole power was in the hands of their sister Sophia and her minister Galitzin. Sophia had no mind ever to give up this power. Ivan was too weak to give her any uneasiness, and, that Peter might not know how to rule, she had him brought up in complete ignorance. He had at this time a great dislike to the sight of a body of water, and could never pass even a brook without trembling. Sophia once said to her minister Galitzin, "It would be a pity indeed if we could not keep the power in our own hands, when we have to deal with only a poor half-blind epileptic and a little fellow who trembles if his foot is wet up to his ankle." "Madam," said the far-seeing minister, "say what you will of Ivan, of him we need fear nothing; but Peter! Peter! he is the one that alarms me. He has a thirst for knowledge that cannot be quenched. In the ignorance we have left him he wants to know everything. You say he fears the sight of water. One day he will conquer this feeling; all tells me that one day he will become the best sailor of the North." And this prophecy of Galitzin was verified. When Peter was seventeen years old he thrust the ambitious Sophia into a convent, and afterward reigned alone, the weak Ivan giving up his share in the government.

At this time Russia was more Asiatic in its customs than European. Peter at once set to work to introduce the habits of the nations about him. He made his subjects lay aside their flowing eastern robes, and had hung up at the gates of every town coats to serve as models for their new costume. A tax of a hundred roubles a year was laid on beards, so that a beard was a luxury none but the wealthy could afford. That he might study the civilized arts of other countries he left his dominions and spent some time abroad, traveling, not as the ruler of Russia, but as a private individual. To learn ship-building he entered as a workman in the dockyard at Amsterdam, and worked hard as a ship-carpenter, living on the wages he earned, cooking his own food, and living in all respects like the other workmen, who little suspected that Peterbas (Master Peter) was other than the hard worker and jolly companion he seemed.

Once he had a fisticuff with an English workman, who soon made the "Emperor of all the Russias" measure his length on the ground. "I must learn to box," said he, getting up. As Galitzin had said, Peter wanted to know everything. From Amsterdam he extended his travels to the Hague, to Utrecht, to England, to Vienna, everywhere

Peter the Great.

observing carefully what he saw for the benefit of his own kingdom. Surgery, natural philosophy, engineering, manufacturing, law making, in fact every department of knowledge received the most careful attention. He could scarcely wait to return home to put into practice what he had learned. Soon a war broke out with Charles XII. of Sweden. The undisciplined troops of Peter were no match for the trained soldiers of Charles, and at first the Russians were beaten

"No matter," said Peter, "they will teach us to beat them some day," and so it proved. After the victory of PULTOWA, which sent Charles a fugitive to Turkey, Peter treated his Swedish prisoners most graciously. The generals were invited to supper with him in his tent. When the glasses were filled, he raised his to his lips, and bowing to his prisoners drank "To the health of my masters in the art of war."

Peter knew that Russia never could be weaned from its old Asiatic customs as long as Moscow remained its capital, so he built the city of St. Petersburg and made it the seat of his empire. To tell all that this great man did for his country would be a heard task. It is a pity that he did not learn better to control his own passions, especially his love of brandy, in which he too often indulged. His son Alexis did not like his father's reforms, and often showed a rebellious spirit. He was tried and condemned to death for treason, but died a few days after his sentence, and people have always had suspicions about the manner of his death. Peter died in St. Petersburg when nearly fifty-three years old (Feb. 8, 1725), and was succeeded by his wife, Catherine I.

PETER II., Emperor of Russia, born Oct. 23, 1715. He was the son of Alexis and grandson of Peter the Great, and succeeded the Empress Catharine I. in 1727, when only twelve years old. His reign was short and uninteresting. He died when fourteen years old (Feb. 9, 1730), and was succeeded by Anna, the niece of Peter the Great. Peter II. was the last of the male line of Romanoff.

PETER III., Emperor of Russia, born in Kiel, Feb. 21, 1728. He was the son of the Duke Charles Frederick of Holstein, and of Anna, daughter of Peter the Great, and succeeded his aunt the Empress Elizabeth, Jan. 5, 1762. He was an ignorant buffoon, low in his tastes and delighting above all things in coarse wit. His wife, Catharine, was a woman of great talent. The people were soon disgusted with his conduct, and a party was formed to make over the government to his wife. He was strangled in bed by two of her friends, dying when thirty-four years old (July 17, 1762), and was succeeded by his wife, Catharine II.

PETER THE HERMIT, a famous monk who preached the first CRUSADE, born in Amiens, France, in the 11th century. He was at first a soldier, but on the death of his wife became a monk, and about 1093 went on a pilgrimage to Jerusalem. He saw the Christians so oppressed there that when he came back he went around preaching and trying to stir up the people to go to rescue the Holy Land from the Infidels. Peter led the first army there, which was defeated by the Saracens. He also went with GODFREY de Bouillon on the second Crusade, and when Jerusalem was taken, preached to the Crusaders on the Mount of Olives. He died in a monastery in Belgium in 1115. There is a bronze statue of him at Amiens.

PETERMANN (*pa'ter-mahn*), **August,** a German geographer, born in Prussian Saxony, April 18, 1822. He assisted in preparing many great atlases, among them Keith Johnston's and Stieler's. In 1854 he became superintendent of the geographical institute of Justus Perthes at Gotha, and the next year became editor of the geographical magazine called the "Mittheilungen," one of the best geographical journals in the world. Petermann died in Gotha when fifty-six years old (Sept. 27, 1878).

PE'TERS-BURG, a city of Virginia, on the Appomattox River, 23 miles S. of Richmond; pop. 23,-000, or about as large as Oshkosh, Wis. It has manufactories of cotton and tobacco, and carries on a considerable trade both by the river and by railroads which meet there. During the last ten months of the Civil War Petersburg was one of the principal defences of Richmond, and the Confederates were besieged there by the Union army under General Grant. The first attack was made on June 15, 1864. After a bloody battle the Unionists were driven back, and though they repeated the attack on succeeding days, they had no better success. Meanwhile, General Lee, who commanded the Confederates, was strengthening the forts around the city. The Unionists secretly dug a mine under one of these forts, and one day blew it up with gunpowder, destroying the garrison. The moment this was done several thousand Union soldiers rushed into the gap that had been made, intending thus to break through and take the city, but the explosion had left a deep pit with steep sides, which the soldiers could not climb, and there they were caught as in a trap. The Confederates, as soon as they had recovered from their surprise, began to fire into the pit, and a terrible slaughter ensued. At length the Unionists were driven back, after they had lost several thousand men in killed, wounded, and prisoners (July 30, 1864).

General Grant then tried to capture the railroads by which the Confederates brought provisions into Petersburg and Richmond, but failed. On March 25, 1865, the Confederates made a sortie from Petersburg and captured Fort Steadman, one of the Union forts, but they were soon driven back with great loss. Grant now sent General Sheridan, with a large army, to make another attempt to capture the railroads. General Lee, leaving a small part of his army to guard the forts, went with the rest to meet Sheridan at Five Forks, a place where five roads meet, about 10 miles S.W. of Petersburg. There a great battle was fought and the Confederates were completely defeated; many thousands of them being captured (April 1, 1865). At the same time an attack was made on the forts of Petersburg, and, as only a small army was left to defend them, they were soon captured. On April 3 the Confederates abandoned Petersburg and Richmond, and soon after the war was closed by the capture of General Lee's army at Appomattox.

PE-TER-WAR'DEIN, a town and fortress of Austro-Hungary, on the river Danube, 42 miles N.W. of Belgrade; pop. 5000, besides the garrison, which is sometimes 10,-000 soldiers. The fortress is so strong that it is called "the Hungarian Gibraltar." It consists of two parts, one on a high rock, and the other at its base, surrounding the town. The fortress is very important, because by it an enemy's fleet could be stopped from going up the Danube.

Peterwardein was a Roman fort, called Acumincum, nearly two thousand years ago. Its present name, which means the "fortress of Peter," was given it because Peter the Hermit collected there the soldiers for the first CRUSADE. Prince Eugene won there a great victory over the Turks (Aug. 5, 1716).

PETRA (*pe'trah*), a city of ancient Edom, about 50 miles S. of the Dead Sea. It was built amongst rugged mountains, and the principal entrance to it was by a winding street through a deep ravine, the cliffs on each side of which were lined with tombs cut out of the solid rock. Its site was long unknown, but it was discovered in 1812 by BURCKHARDT. Among the ruins are a beautiful temple and a large theatre with seats enough for 3,000 spectators, all hewn out of rock. The name Petra means rock.

PETRARCH (*pe'trark*), **Francesco,** a famous Italian poet, born in Arezzo, July 20, 1304. His early

Ruins of Petra.   (See page 641.)

love for poetry displeased his parents, who wished him to study law, but they could not make him give it up. He wrote much in Latin prose and verse, as well as in his own tongue, but his fame rests chiefly on his sonnets in praise of Laura de Sade, a beautiful married woman whom he first saw in a church in Avignon. He fell so violently in love with her that it affected his whole life; and Petrarch and Laura are often spoken of together. Petrarch was a great collector of ancient manuscripts of Greek and Latin writers, many of which, but for him, would have been lost. In 1340 the Roman senate and the University of Paris offered him the laurel crown for poetry on

the same day. He accepted that of Rome, and was crowned with great state at the Capitol in 1341. Few of his works have been translated into English. He was found dead in his library at Arqua near Padua, when seventy years old (July 18, 1374).

PHÆ'DRUS, a Latin writer of fables, born twenty or thirty years B.C. He was brought to Rome as a slave, but set free by the Emperor Augustus. Ninety-seven of his fables in verse have come down to us, the subjects and thoughts of which were for the most part taken from Æsop.

PHA'E-THON, or **Phaeton,** in Greek fable, the son of Helios, the sun-god. He persuaded his father to let him drive the chariot of the sun through the heavens for one day. The horses would not obey him, rushed madly out of their path, and so near the earth that the chariot was about setting the earth on fire, when Jupiter killed Phaethon with a thunderbolt, and he fell into the river Po.

PHAL'A-RIS, a ruler or tyrant of Agrigentum in Sicily, who reigned in the 5th century before Christ. At first he ruled his people kindly, but afterward he became very cruel. It is said that he hired a Greek artist to make him a hollow brass bull in which he could punish people by roasting them to death; and the first one burned was the artist himself. Phalaris made his people hate him so that finally they stoned him to death (about 555 B.C.).

PHA'RA-OH. See EGYPT.

PHARSALUS (*far-sa'lus*), an ancient city of Thessaly, famous for the battle of Pharsalia which was fought near it between two Roman armies commanded by Cæsar and Pompey, Aug. 9, 48 B.C. Pompey had more than twice as many soldiers as Cæsar, but Cæsar moved his army with so much skill that Pompey was completely defeated. This was one of the most important battles in the history of the world, for from it began the Roman Empire.

PHID'I-AS, or **Pheidias,** a famous sculptor of ancient Greece, born in Athens about 490 B.C. As almost all his statues were of gods and goddesses, he was called "the sculptor of the gods." His two greatest statues were the Athena or Minerva of the Parthenon, which was more than fifty feet high, and the Jupiter Olympus at OLYMPIA, which was about sixty feet high. Phidias and his assistants were busy on this statue nearly five years, and the Greeks thought it a misfortune to die without having seen it. It was made of ivory and gold, and the god was represented seated on a throne, holding in his right hand a statue of Victory. This great statue sat in the temple for 800 years,

Independence Hall, as it was in 1776. (See page 644.)

and was finally taken by the Emperor Theodosius I. to Constantinople, where it perished by fire (A.D. 475). Besides these, Phidias made a great many other statues for Athens and other Greek cities. He was thrown into prison on false accusations, and died there (about 432 B.C.).

PHILADELPHIA (*fil-a-del'fe-ah*), a city of E. Pennsylvania, on the Delaware River, at the mouth of the Schuylkill; pop. 1,047,000, or not quite five sevenths as large as New York. It is the principal city of the State, and the third largest city in the United States. The streets are regularly laid out, and there are many handsome buildings. The new City Hall is one of the most magnificent buildings in the United States. The principal building of GIRARD College is said to be the finest specimen of Greek architecture built in modern times. The University of Pennsylvania has 1600 students, and the Medical School connected with it is one of the best in the country. The Academy of Natural Sciences has a very fine natural history museum, its collection of stuffed birds being the most complete in the world. There are other museums in the city, and several large libraries. The United States Mint in Philadelphia is the largest and oldest in the country. Independence Hall, formerly the old State House of Pennsylvania, in which the Declaration of Independence was signed, contains portraits of famous Americans and many historical relics, among them the old liberty bell, which was rung when independence was declared. It is now cracked so as to be of no use, and stands on a pedestal in the hall. In Carpenter's Hall the first Continental Congress met in 1774. Fairmount Park is one of the largest parks in the world, extending nearly

Carpenter's Hall.

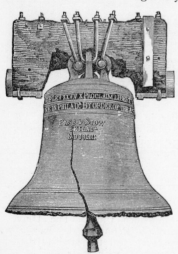

The Liberty Bell.

fourteen miles along the banks of the Schuylkill River and Wissahickon Creek. It contains the finest menagerie in America, with many other attractions.

Next to New York, Philadelphia is the greatest manufacturing city in America, it being especially noted for its large iron-works, cotton and woolen mills, sugar refineries, printing-houses, and manufactories of clothing, boots and shoes, carpets, drugs and medicines, and machinery. A very large trade is carried on, especially in coal and petroleum. The largest vessels can ascend the Delaware to its wharves, and many railways meet in the city.

The name Philadelphia, which means brotherly love, was given to the city by William PENN, who founded the city in 1681. A small monument still marks the place where Penn made a treaty with the Indians. Until the present century Philadelphia was the largest and most important city of the United States. During the Revolution the Continental Congress met there until the city was taken by the British (Sept., 1777), and again after they evacuated it (June, 1778). The battle of GERMANTOWN was fought within the present limits of the city (Oct. 4, 1777). In 1876 the centennial, or one hundreth year of American independence, was celebrated in Philadelphia by a great Exhibition, in which all nations took part. Magnificent buildings were erected in Fairmount Park, and they were filled with specimens of the products, arts, and manufactures of the whole world, but especially of the United States. On the one hundredth anniversary of the Declaration of Independence (July 4, 1876) the Exhibition was opened by President Grant, who was accompanied by the Emperor Dom Pedro II. of Brazil, then on a visit to this country, and it was closed on November 10.

PHILIP I., fourth Capetian king of France, born in 1053. He was the son of Henry I., and succeeded him (1060) when but seven years old. During the half century in which this king reigned great things were going on in Europe. His neighbor Duke William of Normandy was taking England, Gregory VII. was reforming the Church and raising the papacy to its highest point, and Crusaders were fighting in the Holy Land and establishing in Jerusalem a Christian kingdom. But in all these things Philip took little interest. He was always jealous of the Duke of Normandy, and he showed his spite by taking the part of William's rebellious sons against him. He died, when fifty-five years old, in 1108, and was succeeded by his son Louis VI.

PHILIP II., called Augustus, the seventh Capetian king of France, born in 1165. He was the son of Louis VII., and succeeded him, when fifteen years old, in 1180. He was considered by those who lived in his time the ablest king that had

sat on the French throne since Charles the Great. Philip went on the third Crusade at the same time with Richard of England and Frederick Barbarossa of Germany, but these princes could not agree when they reached the Holy Land, and their quarrels kept them from acting to any advantage. When King John of England seized the crown belonging to his nephew Arthur of Brittany, Philip took up Arthur's cause and made war on John, taking from him all his French lands but Guienne. The pope at that time was Innocent III., a very able man. Philip fell under his censure because he had shut up his wife in a convent and married another. Innocent told him that this was a sin, but Philip paid no attention to him until the pope laid France under an interdict. This was considered a terrible thing in those days. For a whole year the churches were closed, the dead were not allowed burial in holy ground, and the whole nation were treated as heathens. Philip could not stand his people's reproaches, so he submitted to the pope and brought back his wife, sending away the one who had taken her place. Philip Augustus was a successful ruler and made many improvements in France. He died in Mantes when sixty-eigth years old (July 14, 1223), and was succeeded by his son Louis VIII.

PHILIP III., called the Bold, tenth Capetian king of France, born in 1245. He was the son of LOUIS IX., and succeeded him (1270) when twenty-five years old. He was with his father when he died at the siege of Tunis, and was at once proclaimed king in the English camp. Having made a peace with the Saracens, he returned to France, taking with him the remains of his wife, his father, and his brother. The chief event of Philip's reign was a war with Pedro of Aragon, whose crown the pope had offered to the French king for his son Charles of Valois. He crossed the Pyrenees with an army, but was compelled to retreat, and died at Perpignan when forty-one years old (1285). He was succeeded by his son Philip IV.

PHILIP IV., called the Fair, eleventh Capetian king of France, born at Fontainebleau in 1268. He was the son of Philip III., and succeeded him (1285) when seventeen years old. This monarch was one of the worst kings that ever reigned, and he well merits the name given him by Dante, "the Pest of France." He was cunning and greedy of money, and did not care how he got it. To make the most of his money he debased the coinage—that is, mixed in with the gold and silver a great amount of poor metal—persecuted the Lombards and Jews, who were his richest subjects, and laid on his people all sorts of heavy taxes. Pope Boniface VIII. complained of some of the taxes that were laid on the clergy, and thus began between Philip and the pope a bitter quarrel, during which Boniface died, worn out with the struggle. His successor, Clement V., was but the tool of Philip, and at his request moved from Rome to Avignon, France. The seventy years during which the popes lived at Avignon are called "the Babylonish Captivity," after the captivity of the Jews in Babylon. To please Philip, Clement agreed to put down the order of the Knights TEMPLARS, whom Philip charged with fearful crimes. Their real crime in his eyes was that they were rich, and he wanted their money. Jacques de Molay, the Grand Master of the order, and three other knights were burnt alive. It is said that as the smoke curled around their aged forms, a voice was heard saying, "I call thee, Clement, Pope of Rome, and on thee, Philip, King of France, to appear, the one within forty days, the other in less than a year, before the judgment seat of God, to answer for your crimes done upon me and my brethren." Whether this story be true or not, both sovereigns died within the periods of time stated, Philip from an accident received while hunting. He was forty-six years old at his death (Nov. 29, 1314). He was succeeded by his son Louis X.

PHILIP V., thirteenth Capetian king of France, born in 1294. He was the son of Philip IV., and succeeded his brother Louis X. in 1316. His reign of six miserable years was without credit to himself or to his country. It was a time marked by fearful persecutions of the Jews. Philip died at Long Champs when twenty-eight years old (Jan. 3, 1322), and was succeeded by his brother Charles IV.

PHILIP VI., first Valois king of France, born in 1293. He was the son of Charles of Valois, brother of Philip IV., and succeeded his cousin Charles IV. in 1328, that monarch leaving only a daughter, who could not rule because the Salic law shut out women from the throne. Edward III. of England, whose mother was a daughter of Philip IV., thought he had a better right to the crown than Philip, and came into France with a great army. Thus began the hundred years' war between England and France. Philip suffered a severe defeat at CRÉCY. CALAIS, too, was taken by Edward, and came very near being destroyed by the angry conqueror.

Philip laid a tax on salt. The Latin word for salt being "sal," Edward was able to make a pun, saying that Philip was "the inventor of the Salic law." Philip paid him back by calling him a wool-merchant, because it was from England that Flanders got the wool which she used in her manufactories of woolen cloths. The eldest son of the king of France was first called dauphin during this reign. The name came from Dauphiny, a province which was ceded to the French king on the death of the last count without heirs. These counts were called dauphins from the dolphin (French *dauphin*) on their coat of arms. Philip died near Chartres when fifty-seven years old (Aug. 22, 1350), and was succeeded by his son John the Good.

PHILIP II., King of Macedon, born at Pella in 382 B.C. He was the son of Amyntas II., and succeeded his brother Perdiccas, 359 B.C. When quite a young man, Philip had spent three years as a hostage at Thebes in the family of EPAMINONDAS. There he became familiar not only with the politics of the Greeks, but also with their mode of warfare, knowledge which was afterward of the greatest service to him. When he came to the throne, Macedon was attacked by enemies from without and rent by contending parties within, but in less than two years Philip overcame these troubles and seated himself firmly on the throne. At once he set to work on his favorite design of subjugating the disunited Greek states. This project his energy and shrewdness enabled him to carry out in spite of the opposition of DEMOSTHENES. Athens headed a league against him, but he defeated the allied armies at Chæronea, and was henceforth master of Greece. Philip was about forming an expedition against Persia when he was stabbed by a young Macedonian of his body-guard, while at the wedding festival of his daughter. He died at Ægæ when forty-six years old (336 B.C.), and was succeeded by his son ALEXANDER THE GREAT.

PHILIP V., king of Macedon, born 237 B.C. He was the son of Demetrius II., and succeeded his uncle Antigonus Doson in 220. Rome was at that time fast making herself mistress of the world, but Philip lacked the wisdom to see that from that quarter came the real danger to his empire, and turned his attention entirely to the East. He had the imprudence to offend some states of the Achæan League, who were allies of Rome, and this led to war. He was defeated at Cynoscephalæ (197), and Macedon became the submissive ally of her conqueror. Phillip died when fifty-eight years old (179 B.C.), and was succeded by his son Perseus, the last of the Macedonian kings.

PHILIP I., King of Castile, born in Bruges, July 22, 1478. He was the son of the Emperor Maximilian I., and became king of Castile in right of his wife Joanna, daughter of Ferdinand and Isabella. The claims of Philip and Joanna were acknowledged by the Castilian Cortes, but Ferdinand did not wish to give up that kingdom. Just as war between Philip and Ferdinand seemed about to break out, Philip died of a fever brought on by his bad habits. He was the father of the great Charles I. of Spain, who was also Charles V. of Germany, and of the Emperor Ferdinand I. He died at Burgos when twenty-eight years old (1506), and was succeeded by his son Charles I.

PHILIP II., King of Spain, born in Valladolid, May 21, 1527. He was the son of Charles V., Emperor of Germany and King of Spain, and succeeded him in 1556. On giving up the Spanish crown, Charles had said to his son, "I leave you a heavy burthen; since I wore it I have never spent a day without uneasiness." If the great Charles found the crown a burthen, what must it have been to Philip! His rule extended over not only Spain but vast dominions in America, the East Indies and Africa, the Two Sicilies, Milan, Burgundy, and the Netherlands. Philip had neither the character nor the abilities fitting him to manage this vast empire. His main object in life was to support the Roman Catholic religion and to root out heresy from his dominions, " Better not reign at all than reign over heretics," he was in the habit of saying. The Court of the Inquisition now began to try heretics, as all were called who in any way disagreed with what was taught by the Roman Catholic Church, and many of the noblest and best of the Spaniards were dragged from their homes on the least suspicion, examined in secret, put to torture, and if found guilty were led forth to a public square and burned, the king and crowds of his nobles looking on and calling this an *auto da fe* (act of faith).

Philip undertook various wars, first one with France, in which was fought the battle of St. Quentin. During the engagement he made a vow that if he were preserved he would build a church and monastery in honor of St. Lawrence, on whose day it was fought. To keep this vow he built the palace of the Escurial, in the mountains about twenty miles from Madrid. It is planned with three ranges of buildings in the form of a gridiron, the saint, according to tradition, having been roasted to death on a gridiron. These three lines of buildings form a palace, a convent, and a church. When Philip tried to force the Inquisition on his subjects in the Netherlands, they rebelled under the leadership of Prince William of Orange, and a war went on which, in the reign of his grandson, resulted in their shaking off the Spanish yoke. Then Philip fitted out the Armada, a great fleet which was to conquer England and bring that country back to the Church of Rome ; but it was overthrown partly by storms and partly by English valor. The last of Philip's wars was in the cause of the League, a party formed in France against Henry of Navarre, afterward HENRY IV. Almost all these

wars were unsuccessful, and he was glad to make peace. Philip was jealous, gloomy, and suspicious, trusting none, and he cannot be said to have loved any one but himself. His eldest son, Don Carlos, died in prison (1568), and many writers believe that he was put to death by order of Philip. Philip was the husband of Queen Mary I. of England. With him passed away the greatness of Spain. He died in the palace of the Escurial when seventy-one years old (Sept. 13, 1598), and was succeeded by his son Philip III.

PHILIP III., King of Spain, born in 1578. He was the son of Philip II., and succeeded him in 1598. Under his rule Spain declined very fast. The chief event of his reign was the driving of the Moors from Spain. This cruel act drove into exile 600,000 of Spain's best people, and deprived her of a great deal of wealth. Philip was so great a slave to form that his last illness was owing to his too great exposure to the heat of a strong fire, the servant whose duty it was to move the king's chair being absent, and etiquette forbidding the king to do so himself. He died when forty-three years old (March, 1621), and was succeeded by his son Philip IV.

PHILIP IV., King of Spain, born in 1639. He was the son of Philip III., and succeeded him, when he was sixteen years old, in 1655. His reign is one of the most disastrous in the annals of Spain. The people of Catalonia, one of his provinces, revolted, and they were helped by France, which led to war with that power. At the same time Portugal, which had belonged to Spain since the days of Philip II., set up a king of her own, the Duke of Braganza. In Naples a revolt of the people took place headed by a young fisherman named MASANIELLO, and most disgraceful of all was the end of the long war in the Netherlands, which forced him to consent to the independence of the seven United Provinces. Philip died when twenty-six years old (.665), and was succeeded by his son Charles II.

PHILIP V., the first Bourbon king of Spain, born in Versailles, Dec. 19, 1683. He was the son of Louis the Dauphin and grandson of Louis XIV. of France, and before becoming king of Spain had been called Duke of Anjou. He succeeded his grand-uncle Charles II., who died Nov. 1, 1700, leaving a will making him his heir. This will led to a war of thirteen years, the war of the Spanish Succession, some of the European nations being unwilling that the Bourbons should rule in both France and Spain, and preferring the Archduke Charles of Austria. The Treaty of Utrecht, which put an end to the war, declared that Philip should have the crown of Spain, but that he should give up the Sicilies, the Netherlands, and Gibraltar. He also had to give up all claims to the crown of France in behalf of himself and his successors. This king was indolent and weak-minded, but his prime minister, Cardinal Alberoni, a man of great force of mind, did a great deal for the country. He tried to get back the Spanish possessions given up by the Treaty of Utrecht, but this led to an alliance against Spain which she could not withstand. Philip resigned his crown to his son Louis, but he was obliged to take it back again, as Louis died shortly after. Philip died in Madrid when sixty-three years old (July 9, 1746), and was succeeded by another son, Ferdinand VI.

PHILIP, King, or Pometacom, a sachem or chief of the Pokanoket Indians of Massachusetts, son of MASSASOIT. His English name was given to him by the colonists, with whom his father was friendly. Philip became sachem in 1662, and promised to remain a friend of the whites, but in 1675 he made an alliance with the Narragansett Indians, and began a war on the colonists, burning their villages and killing all who fell into his hands. In December, 1675, a thousand colonists, commanded by Josiah Winslow, attacked and destroyed a fort and village of the Narragansetts, killing so many of them that they were obliged to give up the war. Philip was hunted from place to place, and finally killed at Mt. Hope, Rhode Island (Aug. 12, 1676). His body was cut into four quarters, and his head was kept on a gibbet at Plymouth for twenty years.

PHILIP THE BOLD, Duke of Burgundy, born Jan. 15, 1342. He was the son of John the Good, king of France, who gave him the duchy of Burgundy as a reward for the courage shown by him at the battle of POICTIERS. When his nephew, Charles VI. of France, became insane, Philip took the place of regent; that is, ruler for the king. This often led to disputes between him and his relatives, but he succeeded in keeping his place as long as he lived. He died, when sixty-two years old, in Hainault (April 27, 1404), and was succeeded in the dukedom by his son John, called the Fearless.

PHILIP THE GOOD, Duke of Burgundy, born in Dijon, June 13, 1396. He was the son of John the Fearless, and became Duke of Burgundy in 1419, after his father was slain at the bridge of Montereau. In order to avenge his father's death, which Charles, the young Dauphin of France, had caused, he put himself at the head of a party of French, and made with Henry V. of England a treaty giving him the crown of France on the death of Charles VI. But afterward he was sorry for having done this, and helped to drive the English out of France. He was a wise ruler, and was much loved by his subjects. He died in Bruges when seventy-one years old (1467), and was succeeded by his son the famous Charles the Bold.

PHI-LIP'PI, an ancient city of Macedonia, near the Ægean Sea. It was originally called Crenides, or the " Place of Fountains," but King Philip of Macedon conquered it (357 B.C.), and it received its new name in honor of him. Two great battles were fought at Philippi, between the armies of BRUTUS and CASSIUS on one side and those of ANTONY and Octavius (AUGUSTUS) on the other. In the first battle Brutus defeated Octavius, but Antony and his army gained the advantage over Cassius. In the second battle, twenty days afterward, the army of Brutus was completely beaten (42 B.C.). Philippi was the first place in Europe where St. Paul preached, and his Epistle to the Philippians was written to the church which he founded there. Nothing is now left of Philippi but ruins.

P H I L I P P I N E (*fil'ip-pin*) **ISLANDS,** a group of islands in the East Indian Archipelago, S.E. of China; area, 112,000 square miles, or three times as large as New York State; pop.5,559,000,or about twelve thirteenths that of New York; capital, MANILA. There are nine large islands, of which the largest is Luzon, and about 1200 small ones, most of which are mere rocks. All the large islands are high and often mountainous, and many of them are covered with forests. The climate is very warm. The principal things grown are rice, sugar-cane, indigo, tobacco, and coffee. Rice is the principal grain, and the food of all the poorer classes. Most of the people are Malays, but there are also many Chinese and several thousand Spaniards and descendants of Spaniards. In the interior of the large islands live a savage people called Negritos, much like the people of PAPUA.

The Philippine Islands were first found by Magalhaens in 1521. They were named after King Philip II. of Spain, who sent a fleet of ships there and conquered some of the islands; and they have belonged to Spain ever since.

PHILOPŒMEN (*fil-o-pe'men*), a Greek general, born about 252 B.C. He was the son of Crangis, a prominent citizen of Megalopolis, a town in Arcadia. During the troubled state of Greece, after the death of Alexander the Great, several small states of Achaia formed a league for mutual protection. Philopœmen was, after the death of Aratus, their leader. When the Messsenians revolted against the league, Philopœmen, although an old man of seventy, and sick in bed at the time, put himself at the head of his army and went to meet the rebels. During the battle he was taken prisoner by his enemies, and condemned to drink poison. When the cup was handed to him, he asked the bearer if he knew what had become of the Achæan cavalry and especially of his friend Lycortas. The answer was, " They have retired in safety." "Then we are not altogether unhappy," said the aged general, taking the cup and drinking off the contents. He died in Messene when in his seventieth year (183 B.C.). Statues were erected to his memory in most of the Greek cities. He has been called "the last of the Greeks."

PHIPS or **Phipps,** Sir **William,** a governor of Massachusetts Colony, born in Woolwich, Me., Feb. 2, 1651. When young he was a shepherd and afterward a ship-carpenter, and he only learned to read when twenty-three years old. Ten years afterward he recovered an immense treasure from a Spanish ship that had been wrecked on the Bahama Islands. For this service he received nearly $80,000, and was made a knight and high sheriff of New England. In 1690 he had command of the fleet which captured Port

Royal, and in 1692 he was chosen captain-general, and governor of Massachusetts. He had much to do with having the supposed witches executed in SALEM. After two years, Phips was called to England to answer charges which had been made against him, and died soon after reaching London, when forty-four years old (Feb. 18, 1695).

PHOCION (*fo'she-on*), an Athenian general, born about 402 B.C. During the contest which ended in the subjugation of Greece by Philip of Macedon, he was the head of the aristocratic party, who were in favor of Philip, while Demosthenes led the opposite party. Some years after the death of Demosthenes the democratic party gained the upper hand, and having taken Phocion, they made him drink poison. He was not so great an orator as Demosthenes, but his short, cutting speeches were so telling that Demosthenes, seeing him rise, once said, "Here comes the cleaver of my harangues." A year after his death, the Athenians raised a statue to his memory. He died when eighty-five years old (317 B.C.).

PHŒNICIA (*fe-nish'e-ah*), the name given by the Greeks to an ancient country on the Mediterranian Sea, north of Palestine. The name means either a palm-country or a red country, but the people who lived there called it Canaan, or low land. Its principal cities were TYRE and SIDON; and these and other cities had each its own king, but one was generally greater than the rest, who paid tribute to him. Many of the people were slaves. The Phœnicians were famous for their skill as sailors, and they founded many colonies on the Mediterranean, and even beyond the Strait of Gibraltar. Among these colonies were CARTHAGE, Panormus (PALERMO), and CADIZ. Among the manufactures of Phœnicia were glass, jewels, and the famous Tyrian purple (C. C. T., 403, I., u.). The

Phœnicians were also celebrated workers in metals, and had great skill in mining. They worked mines of many different metals in Spain, and even went to Britain for tin. They were, too, noted for their learning, and from them came most of the letters of the alphabet (C. C. T., 659, I.).

Phœnicia was so ancient a country that it is not even known when it was founded, but the people were SEMITES. Their greatest prosperity was during the 9th and 8th centuries B.C., when their merchants traded with all parts of the then known world. Hiram, one of their kings, sent workmen to help Solomon in building the Temple of Jerusalem. At different times Phœnicia was subject to Assyria, Egypt, Babylon, Persia, and Macedonia, and it was finally conquered by the Romans in 64 B.C. It is now a part of Turkey in Asia.

PHRYGIA (*frij'e-ah*). See ASIA MINOR.

PHRYXUS (*frix'us*). See ARGONAUTS.

PICHEGRU(*peesh-groo'*),**Charles,** a French general, born at Arbois, Feb. 16, 1761. He became a teacher of mathematics at the military school of Brienne, where Napoleon was one of his students. When the French Revolution broke out, he joined the republican army, and soon became a general, commanding an army on the Rhine in 1793. In 1795 he captured Amsterdam, and set up a republic in the Netherlands. Soon after, he commanded against the Austrians on the Rhine, but being bribed by the Bourbons, allowed the Austrians to drive him back. For this he was deprived of his command, and banished to Cayenne. He escaped in 1798, went to London, and made there with Georges Cadoudal and others a plan to kill Napoleon. The conspirators went secretly to Paris (1803), but were discovered and arrested, and before his trial was finished Pichegru was found strangled in his cell, when forty-three years old (April 5, 1804).

PIED'MONT, a N.W. part of Italy, lying next to Switzerland and France; area, 11,301 square miles, or about as large as Maryland; pop. 3,297,000, or three and one sixth times that of Maryland.

The name means "Foot of the Mountain," the country being surrounded on three sides by high mountains. In the 14th and 15th centuries Piedmont was governed by independent princes, but it was afterward united to Savoy, and finally to Sardinia and Italy.

PIERCE (*perss*), **Franklin,** fourteenth President of the United States, born in Hillsborough, N. H.,

Franklin Pierce.

Nov. 23, 1804. He was the son of a general in the Revolutionary War who became afterward governor of New Hampshire. Franklin was graduated at Bowdoin College in 1824, studied law for several years, was sent to the legislature in 1829, and in 1833 went to Congress, where he kept his place first in the House and then in the Senate for eight years. He was in favor of having Texas come into the Union; and going as a volunteer to the Mexican war, be became first a colonel and

then a brigadier-general, and fought bravely until the war was ended. He was elected President in 1853, and died in Concord when sixty-five years old (Oct. 8, 1869).

PIG'MIES. See PYGMIES.

PIN'DAR, a noted Greek poet, born in Thebes, about 520 B.C. In Pindar's day, the composer of lyric poetry—that is, songs—composed also the music and dances which generally accompanied them. The music to which Pindar's verses were set having been lost, the metre seems to us very strange. For centuries, the iron chair on which he sat while writing hymns to the gods was shown at Delphi. When Thebes was taken and leveled to the ground by command of Alexander the Great, he gave strict orders that no harm should be done to the house where Pindar had lived. He died when eighty years old (440 B.C.).

PIN'ZON (Spanish *pene-thone'*), **Martin Alonzo,** a navigator of Palos, Spain, who helped Columbus in fitting out his ships. He also went with Columbus as commander of one of the ships, the Pinta; but he was envious of Columbus, and tried to get some of the fame of the voyage for himself. Francisco Martin Pinzon, a younger brother, was pilot of the Pinta on the same voyage.

PINZON, Vincente Yañez, a navigator of Palos, brother of Martin Alonzo Pinzon. He commanded the ship Niña in the fleet of Columbus. In 1499 Vincente, having fitted out four ships, sailed for the New World. In January, 1500, he discovered BRAZIL and took possession of the country for Spain, but as the natives were hostile he went to sea again, and sailing north-west, discovered the mouths of the AMAZONS. While returning to Spain a terrible hurricane struck his ships, and two of them were lost with all on board. The king of Spain gave Vincente Pinzon a grant of some of the lands that he had discovered, but he never settled them. In 1506 he discovered the peninsula of Yucatan.

PISA (*pe'sah*), a city of W. Italy, on the river Arno, near its mouth; pop. 38,000, or nearly as large as San Antonio, Tex. It is famous for its beautiful marble palaces and churches. Four of the most noted of its buildings, the Cathedral, Baptistery, Campo Santo, and Leaning Tower, are about seven hundred years old. They are placed near each other, and are built in the same style, so that they look like parts of one building. The Leaning Tower, which is very high (179 feet), is divided into eight stories, each surrounded by a gallery open to the outside. Instead of standing straight, the tower leans about thirteen feet to one side, so that it appears to be falling over. In the top are seven large bells. The University of Pisa has about 600 students and a large library. The city is surrounded by a wall, and defended by a citadel.

Pisa is a very old city. In the 9th century it became independent, and for a long time it was one of the richest and most powerful cities in Italy.

PISIDIA (*pi-sid'e-ah*). See ASIA MINOR.

PI-SIS'TRA-TUS, a tyrant or ruler of Athens, born about 612 B.C. He was the son of Hippocrates, who left him a large fortune, and he was brave, ambitious, and eloquent, and by his kindness and generosity won the love of the poorer classes. He usurped the throne, and although he was twice driven away, he regained it and ruled with mildness and justice. He kept all the wise laws of Solon, who was his friend and relative. The first public library at Athens was formed by him, and he collected and arranged the poems of Homer. He died when about thirty-nine years old (527 B.C.).

PITCAIRN (*pit'kairn*) **ISLAND,** an island in the South Pacific ocean, E.S.E. of the Society Islands; area less than 2 square miles. It is high and rocky, but the soil is very fertile and covered with forests and meadows. There are a few small streams which sometimes dry up; then the people use water which they keep in tanks. There are no native animals, but domestic ones have been carried there, and many goats have run wild.

Pitcairn Island was first found in 1767, and was named after a naval officer who first saw it. In 1789 the crew of a ship called the Bounty mutinied, not far from Tahiti. They put the captain and those who would not join them in an open boat and set them adrift on the ocean, where they sailed for forty-six days before reaching inhabited land. The mutineers returned to Tahiti, and some of them remained there; but the rest, taking some native men and women, went in the ship to Pitcairn Island, which was then uninhabited. There they destroyed the ship and made houses and farms on the shore. The sailors married the Tahitan women and had many children. At first they quarreled much with each other, and killed the Tahitan men, but afterward they became very peaceable and religious, and one of their number, named John Adams, wrote out some laws by which they were governed. People supposed that the Bounty had sunk with its crew, and they were forgotten until 1808, when a ship which visited Pitcairn Island found their descendants living there. John Adams was the only one of the mutineers then alive. The families still increased, and in 1856 they were removed to the larger island of Norfolk, but some of them afterward went back to Pitcairn Island.

PITT, William, first Earl of Chatham, an English statesman, born

Nov. 15, 1708. He was the grandson of Thomas Pitt, Governor of Madras, who brought from India the famous Pitt diamond (C. C. T., 172, II., l). Pitt began life in the army as an officer of dragoons, but entered Parliament when twenty-seven years old and soon became noted. In 1757, on the breaking out of the Seven Years' War, he became prime minister, and his brief rule of four years was a glorious one in the history of Great Britain. The French were driven back across the Rhine, Canada was taken, and India won. When the Stamp Act, which was one of the principal causes of the Revolutionary War, was proposed in Parliament, he opposed it and said that England had no right to tax the colonies. But after the war had begun, he was in favor of carrying it on vigorously, and was bitter against those who wanted to let the colonies go. In the same year (1766) he was made a peer or lord, and received the titles of Viscount Pitt and Earl of Chatham. The people did not like him to take these titles, for they had been very proud of him as the "great commoner" (private citizen), as he was called. After making a speech in the House of Lords, opposing the acknowledging of the independence of the United States, he fell fainting to the floor, and died four days afterward, at Hayes, Kent, when seventy years old (May 11, 1778).

PITT, William, generally called the Younger, an English statesman, born at Hayes, Kent, May 28, 1759. He was the son of William Pitt, the first Earl of Chatham. He was very bright as a boy, astonishing every one by his knowledge and judgment. His tutor at Cambridge writes of him that at fourteen it was no uncommon thing for him to read at sight six or seven pages of THUCYDIDES, without more than two or three mistakes, and sometimes without one. He became

Prime Minister of England when he was but twenty-four years old, and held that office, with an interruption of three years, till his death in 1806. During these years, his life is his country's history. He was the life and soul of the resistance to Napoleon, and in keeping up the struggle he showed great talents, energy, and perseverance. The news of Napoleon's success at Austerlitz filled him with such sorrow that he actually died. His death took place at Putney, when he was forty-seven years old (Jan. 23, 1806).

PIT'TA-CUS, one of the seven wise men of Greece, born at Mytilene, Lesbos, about 652 B.C. When forty years old he commanded the army of Mytilene in a war against Athens, and though the Athenians were victorious, he slew their leader, Phrynon, who was renowned for his strength. When the people wished to reward him, he would only take as much land as he could throw his spear over; this land was used for religious purposes, and was long called the Pittacean land. Pittacus was elected ruler of Mytilene in 589 B.C., and he governed it wisely for ten years. Among his laws was one that crimes committed by drunken persons should have a double punishment. He died at Mytilene when about eighty-three years old (569 B.C.). Pittacus was celebrated as a poet, but none of his works have been preserved.

PITTSBURGH (*pits'burg*), a city of W. Pennsylvania, on the Allegheny and Monongahela rivers, where they unite to form the Ohio; pop. 239,000, or nearly as large as New Orleans, La. Opposite it, on the other side of the Allegheny River, is the city of Allegheny (pop. 105,000), which is really a part of Pittsburgh, though it has a separate government. The two are connected by six bridges. Pittsburgh is the largest city in Pennsylvania except Philadelphia, and is very important for its manufactures and trade. The country around abounds in coal and iron mines, and there are many iron furnaces in the city, in which about one fourth of all the iron mined in the United States is smelted, and great quantities of rails and other things are made. There are also large steel and copper works, glass-works, and petroleum refineries. Clouds of smoke from the furnaces hang over the city, and the finest buildings are soon covered with grime, and people have to wash their hands and faces a dozen times a day to keep them clean. Besides its manufactories, Pittsburgh has a large trade in coal, petroleum, and lumber. Steamboats can go up the Ohio to this place during six or eight months of the year.

Pittsburgh was settled in 1754 by the French, who built a fort there, which they called Fort Duquesne in honor of Governor Duquesne of Canada. The next year, the English General BRADDOCK marched against them, but was driven back and killed. In 1758, however, the English took Fort Duquesne, and built on its site a large fort, called Fort Pitt, after William PITT, then the Prime Minister of England. From this fort the town took its name of Pittsburgh.

PITTSFIELD, a town of W. Massachusetts, in a valley among the Berkshire hills, and surrounded by beautiful scenery ; pop. 17,000, or about as large as Jacksonville, Fla. It is noted for its manufactories of cotton, woolen, and silk goods, paper, and machinery. Pittsfield was named (1761) after the English statesman William Pitt.

PI'US, the name of nine popes.

Pius II., born near Siena, Oct. 18, 1405, became pope in 1458. He was famous before as a writer under the name of Æneas Silvius. He tried to get the Christian princes to go on a crusade against the Turks, but failing, died of a broken heart (Aug. 14, 1464).

Pius VII., born Aug. 14, 1742, became pope in 1800. In 1804 he went to Paris and crowned Napoleon, but soon after quarreled with him, and Napoleon added Rome and all the states of the Church to his own empire. The pope then excommunicated Napoleon—that is, turned him out of the Church—and Napoleon kept him a prisoner in France for five years. After the fall of Napoleon he got back his states and power again. He died in Rome, Aug. 20, 1823.

Pius IX., born May 13, 1792, became pope in 1846. At first he made reforms, lowered the taxes, aud helped manufactures and agriculture, but the people were not satisfied with the liberty he gave them, and a revolution broke out (1848), and he had to flee to the fortress of Gaeta for safety. The pope asked aid, and Austria sent an army into the north of Italy, and France sent troops to Rome, to which the pope returned in 1850. In 1859, when the Austrian troops left, northern Italy joined the kingdom of Italy, and Rome and the pope's states did the same when the French troops left Rome. After that the pope had no temporal power—that is, he lost all power as a sovereign, and was left only head of the Church. Pius IX. died in Rome when eighty-six years old (Feb. 7, 1878), after having been pope thirty-two years, or longer than any other pope.

PIZARRO (*pe-zah'ro*), **Francisco,** a famous Spanish soldier, conqueror of Peru, born about 1471. In his youth he was a swineherd, but he afterward joined a Spanish expedition to America, and in time came to be a leader in many adventures. In 1524 Pizarro and AL-MAGRO, having heard of the rich country called Peru, fitted out an expedition to conquer it, but could get so few soldiers that they were unsuccessful Pizarro, however, captured some of the Peruvian Indians and many gold ornaments, and carrying them to Spain, showed them to King Charles V. The king was so pleased that he made Pizarro governor of Peru, giving him the right to conqueror it, and money to pay an army (1529). Pizarro reached the coast of Peru in 1531, with less than 200 soldiers. He was well received by the Inca ATAHUALLPA, but he made him captive and, after taking an immense sum for his ransom, finally put him to death (1533). Soon after he conquered the whole country, and in 1535 founded Lima. Almagro, who had all along been one of Pizarro's generals, rebelled in 1538, but was defeated and killed. Almagro's son formed another rebellion, and several of his men attacked Pizarro in his palace at Lima. He fought bravely, killing three of his assailants, but was finally overpowered and killed, when seventy years old (June 26, 1541).

PLAN-TAG′E-NET, House of, a family of kings of England, who ruled from 1154 to 1485. Henry II., the first of this race, was the son of Geoffrey, Count of Anjou, and was king of England in right of his mother, Matilda, daughter of Henry I. The name is made up of the two Latin words *planta* (plant), and *genista* (broom), and it was taken by the counts of Anjou from the sprigs of broom which they wore in their helmets. Fourteen of England's rulers have been of this line, which is sometimes called the House of Anjou. The last was Richard III., who was slain at Bosworth Field, the crown then passing to the TUDORS.

PLATA, Rio de la (*re′o da lah plah′tah*), a great river of South America, formed by the union of the Paraguay and the Paraná. Including the Paraguay, it is, next to

the Amazon, the longest river in South America. It is 20 to 50 miles wide, and at its mouth widens into a bay 130 miles across. Small islands of floating grass are often seen on the Plata, and sometimes jaguars or other wild animals are found on them. The river was discovered about 1508 by the Spaniards, who called it Rio de la Plata, or River of Silver, because the Indians there gave them some pieces of silver brought from Peru.

PLATÆA (*pla-te′ah*), a city of ancient Greece, 7 miles S. by W. of Thebes. It was one of the oldest cities in Greece, and famous in history. Near it was fought the great battle of Platæa, between the Greeks and Persians. The Greeks had a larger army than they had ever before brought together, but it was much smaller than that of the Persians; yet the Persians were completely defeated, their camp being taken and their leader, MARDONIUS, killed (479 B.C.). At the same time the Persian fleet was defeated by the Greeks at Mycale, near Miletus. These defeats ended the Persian invasion of Greece.

PLA′TO, a famous Greek philosopher, born at Athens, about 429 B.C. His real name was Aristocles, but he was called Plato, which means broad, on account of the width of his forehead and his breast. When he was a baby he was taken to Mount Hymettus by his parents, who wished to offer gifts there to the gods, and while lying asleep the bees filled his mouth with honey. As a boy he was taught grammar, music, painting, and wrestling. At twenty he began to study under Socrates, who then taught philosophy in a grove near Athens, called the Academy. The night before he came, Socrates dreamed that a young swan settled on his knees, which, while he watched it, put forth feathers and flew, singing, into the air. When he saw Plato the next day, he said, "This is the bird." Just before his death, Plato had a like dream, in which he saw himself, in the form of a swan, flying from tree to tree, and giving much trouble to the bird-catchers. All these signs and dreams were believed to mean that he was to be a very great writer and thinker. He was also a soldier and a great traveler. His works are chiefly written in the form of dialogues, in all of which, except "The Laws," Socrates is the chief speaker. He died at Athens (348 B.C.), and was buried in the Academy.

PLAU'TUS, Titus Maccius, the greatest comic-play-writer of Rome, born about 254 B.C. He spent the greater part of his life at Rome, where it is said that at one time he made his living by grinding corn with a hand-mill for a baker. It is said that he was of low birth, and so deformed in body that nature would seem to have designed that his countrymen should laugh at his person no less than his wit. He was very popular in his own time, and his plays have been imitated by modern play-writers. He died when about seventy years old (184 B.C.).

PLINY (*plin'ny*), (**Caius Plinius Secundus**), called Pliny the Elder, a famous ancient writer on natural history, born A.D. 23. He served as a soldier in Germany, and was for a time ruler of Spain. He wrote many books, but the only one which has come down to us is the "Natural History," in which he treats of astronomy, natural philosophy, geography, agriculture, commerce, medicine, and the arts, as well as natural history. It is a very interesting book and contains a great deal of information, though it is not always trustworthy. At the time of the great eruption of Mount Vesuvius, by which Pompeii and Herculaneum were destroyed (79), Pliny was in command of a fleet which lay in the Bay of Naples.

His attention being called to a curious cloud rising over the mountains, he at once set sail for the coast, landed, and began the ascent of the volcano, although the people were flying for safety in all directions. Having satisfied his curiosity he returned to his friends, who were in great terror, told them there was no danger, and lay down and went to sleep in the midst of the noise and confusion. By morning the eruption had grown so violent that he followed the example of his friends, put a pillow over his head to keep the hot stones from hurting him, and made his way to the vessel. But the sea was too rough to embark, and he lay down on the sand. A strong smell of sulphur made his friends run away, and when his slaves tried to raise him he was found to be dead (August 25, 79).

PLINY (**Caius Plinius Cæcilius Secundus**), called Pliny the Younger, nephew and adopted son of Pliny the Elder, born at Como in the year 61 or 62. He was a very bright boy; when only fourteen years old he wrote a tragedy in Greek, and when eighteen he made speeches in the forum. Among his writings are a work in praise of the Emperor Trajan, whose friend he was, and ten books of letters, which some rank next to those of Cicero in interest and value. One of them is very interesting because it tells much about the early Christians. Pliny died about 116.

PLUTARCH (*plu'tark*), a famous Greek writer of biographies, born at Chæronea. He studied at Delphi and lived in Rome for some years, but passed the last part of his life in his native city. He wrote many books, but is best known by his "Parallel Lives" of noted Greeks and Romans. In this he writes the life of a Greek and then of a Roman, and after draws a parallel or comparison between the two. Forty-six of these lives have been preserved, and they are most interesting and valuable reading. Plutarch is said to have been Napoleon's favorite author when a boy. Though little is known of his life, his character is fairly well shown in the biographies he has written of others. From these one concludes that he thought most of those virtues which go to make men great soldiers, great statesmen, or good citizens, and that he held poets and artists in no high esteem. The date of his death is unknown, but some think it took place when he was seventy years old, in the reign of the Emperor Hadrian.

PLU'TO, in ancient fable, the god of the lower world. He was the brother of Jupiter and Neptune. His home was so gloomy that none

Pluto.

of the goddesses would marry him, so he determined to seize a wife by force. After an earthquake, he appeared in Sicily, and seeing PROS-ERPINE, the daughter of CERES, gathering flowers, he carried her away in his chariot and made her his wife. He is called Hades by Homer and other early Greek writers; but later that name is used only for his dwelling-place.

PLU'TUS, the god of riches. Jupiter caused him to become blind, so that he should bestow his favors on good and bad equally. He comes to men slowly and as if lame; but when he goes away he is provided with swift wings. In pictures he is a boy with a cornu-copia.

PLYMOUTH (*plim'uth*), a city of S.W. England, on Plymouth Sound, at the mouth of the river Plym; pop. 74,000, or nearly as large as Fall River, Mass. The river mouth forms a very fine harbor called Catwater, which is always crowded with merchant ships, steamers, and fishing vessels. At Devonport (pop. 49,000), situated on another harbor opening on Plymouth Sound, are great government dockyards, in which thousands of men are employed. The city and harbor of Devonport are very strongly fortified, and this is one of the principal stations for war ships, the harbor being large enough for the whole English navy. Between Devonport and Plymouth is the city of Stonehouse, and the three really form parts of the same city, together having a population of about 150,000.

Plymouth (that is, Plym mouth) is several hundred years old. In 1588 the English ships gathered there to fight the Spanish Armada.

PLYMOUTH, a town of E. Massachusetts, on Cape Cod Bay; pop. about 7000. It is the oldest town in New England, the Pilgrim Fathers having landed there on Dec. 22, 1620. They named it after Plymouth, England, the port from which they had sailed. During the following winter nearly half of them died of the cold and poor food, but others arrived, and in time the settlement became a thriving village. The rock on which the Pilgrims stepped when they landed has been covered with a handsome granite canopy. In the town is a fine monument in memory of the first settlers, surmounted by a large statue of "Faith." Pilgrim Hall, also built in memory of them, contains a library, a public hall, and many relics of the Pilgrims. At present Plymouth is chiefly noted for its manufactures, especially of cotton

Monument over Plymouth Rock.

and woolen cloth, cordage, twine, shoes, rivets and tacks, and sheet zinc.

PLYMOUTH, a town of E. North Carolina, on a creek which flows into Roanoke River; pop. about 2000. During the Civil War it was captured by the Union army in 1862, and recaptured, with the Union garrison, by the Confederates in April, 1864. The Confederates had an iron-clad vessel, called the Albemarle, which was the principal defense of the city. One day a party of thirteen men, under command of Lieutenant W. B. Cushing, stole out from the Union fleet in a boat, and blew up the Albemarle with a torpedo (Oct. 27, 1864). The waves caused by the explosion filled Cushing's boat, and the men were obliged to swim for their lives. All of them were killed or captured except Cushing and one other. Cushing reached the shore and hid himself in the thickets until night, when he found a skiff and paddled

off to the Union fleet. A few days afterward Plymouth was easily captured.

PO-CA-HON′TAS, an Indian woman of Virginia, daughter of the chief POWHATAN, born about 1595. She showed great liking for the white settlers, especially for Captain John SMITH. At one time when he had been taken prisoner and condemned to die, she rushed forward and begged her father to spare him. Her request was granted, and Smith returned safely to his people. At another time she went through a wood at night to warn Smith of a plot to destroy him. In April, 1613, she married John Rolfe, an Englishman, and in 1616 she went with him to England, where she was well received. But the climate was too severe for her, and she died in Gravesend (March, 1617). She left one son, Thomas

Pocahontas.

Rolfe, who went back to Virginia, and became a person of note in the

colony. From him are descended several of the principal Virginia families,

POE (*po*), **Edgar Allan,** an American poet and story writer, born in Boston, Mass., Feb. 19, 1809. He was left an orphan, and adopted by John Allan of Baltimore, who had him carefully trained. He entered the University of Virginia, but did not complete his course, and then went to the Military Academy at West Point, from which he is said to have been ex-

Edgar A. Poe.

pelled. When twenty years old he published a volume of poems of no great merit. He was for some years a writer for "Graham's Magazine," and published in it most of his tales and poems. Some of these show great ability, and have been translated into French and German. The best known of the poems are "The Raven," "The Bells," "Ulalume," and "Annabel Lee." His most remarkable tales are "The Fall of the House of Usher," "The Gold Bug," and "The Murders in the Rue Morgue." After a hard struggle with poverty, he died in Baltimore when forty years old (Oct. 7, 1849).

POITIERS (*poy-teerz'*), a town of W. France, on the river Clain ; pop. 37,000, or about as large at Portland, Me. It is surrounded by walls with five gates, all but one of which are reached by bridges over the river. The city has important manufactories of woolen goods, stockings, and lace.

In ancient times Poitiers was called Lemonum, and afterward Pictavi from the Celtic tribe of the Pictones, who lived there. Pictavi was gradually changed to Poictiers or Poitiers. King Clovis won a great victory there over ALARIC and the Visigoths (A.D. 507), and near the city the Saracens were defeated by CHARLES MARTEL (732). From 1152 to 1204 Poitiers was held by the English. But Poitiers is most celebrated in history for a great victory which Edward the Black Prince won there over King John the Good, Sept. 19, 1356. The French had ten times as many men as the English, but they had to advance to the attack along a narrow lane, with hedges on each side. The English archers plied their bows so well that the French soldiers began to retreat and an English charge utterly routed them, King John himself being captured. Poitiers again belonged to the English for some time, but it surrendered to the French in 1372, and when nearly all the rest of France had been conquered by the English, the French king Charles VII. held his court at Poitiers for fourteen years.

PO'LAND, a country forming the W. part of Russia ; area 49,100 square miles, or somewhat larger than New York State; pop. 8,308,000, or about two fifths more than that of New York. Most of it is a plain, covered in some parts with forests, and in others well cultivated. The climate is hot in summer and very cold in winter. The people, called Poles, have a language of their own. For nearly a thousand years Poland was an independent kingdom, and it became very powerful. It was weakened by wars and bad kings, and in 1772 it was conquered and divided between Russia, Prussia, and Austria. The Polish people had nothing to do with this division, and they made brave attempts to regain their liberty, but Russian, Prussian, and Austrian armies conquered them again (1792). Led by KOSCIUSZKO, the Poles revolted again, but were again defeated, Kosciuszko being captured (1794). A third division of the country followed, and this time its very name was changed. Many of the Poles went to fight under Napoleon, who conquered Prussian Poland (1807) and made it independent, calling it the Duchy of Warsaw. The Poles were very grateful and fought bravely for him, but when he was conquered they again lost their independence, the larger part of their country being given to Russia. It was formed into a kingdom, the Russian emperor being king, so that it was not really independent. The Poles rebelled in 1831, in 1846, and in 1863, but they were defeated each time after bloody battles, and hundreds were sent as exiles to Siberia. The Russian Government is doing all it can to turn the Poles into Russians, by changing their language and customs, but with little success.

POLK (*poke*), **James Knox,** eleventh President of the United States, born in Mecklenberg County, N.C., Nov. 2, 1795. He was of Irish descent, and his father was a farmer. The son graduated at the University of North Carolina in 1818, and became a lawyer in 1820. In 1823 he was elected to Congress, where he served for fourteen years, and then became governor of Tennessee. He was made President in 1845; and during his term of office the war with Mexico took place, and Wisconsin was admitted to the

Union. He died in Nashville when fifty-three years old (June 15, 1849).

James Knox Polk.

POLK, Leonidas, an American general, born in Raleigh, N. C., in 1806. He was graduated at West Point in 1827, but soon after became a clergyman, and finally a bishop in the Episcopal Church. When the Civil War broke out he was made a general in the Confederate army, and fought at the battles of Shiloh, Murfreesborough, and Chickamauga. In the spring of 1864 he commanded the Confederate army on the Mississippi. He was killed by a cannon-ball at the battle of Pine Mountain, near Marietta, Ga., when fifty-eight years old (June 14, 1864).

POL'LOK, Robert, a Scottish poet, born in 1799. He became a minister in 1827, and before that time had written several tales, but he is chiefly known for his long poem in blank verse, entitled "The Course of Time," of which more than a hundred thousand copies have been printed. While on his way to Italy for his health, Pollok died at Southampton, England, when twenty-eight years old (Sept. 15, 1827).

PO'LO, Marco, a Venetian traveler, born in Venice about 1254. In 1271 he went with his father and uncle to Asia, passing through Palestine, Persia, Tartary, the desert of Gobi, and finally reaching China, which Europeans then called Cathay (1275). The emperor of China gave them important offices in his government, and Polo was sent as ambassador to Thibet and other countries, being thus enabled o see many places which were generally closed to foreigners. For three years he was governor of a large city in China. The three men were so useful to the emperor that he would not allow them to return for sixteen years. They finally came back in a fleet which carried the Emperor's daughter to Persia, there to become the king's wife. On the voyage they touched at Borneo, Sumatra, Ceylon, and other places, and on reaching Persia were splendidly entertained for nine months. They then went to the Black Sea, and returned to Venice in a ship (1295).

They had almost forgotten their language, and their friends would hardly believe them, even when they showed the magnificent presents which they had received from the emperor of China. Polo was made commander of a ship in a war with Genoa, but was captured and kept prisoner for five years, during which he prepared an account of his travels. In his own time this was not believed, and even on his death-bed he was urged to retract his falsehoods. He died when about seventy years old (1324). Marco Polo was long remembered in China, and a bust of him is still to be seen in one of the temples of Canton.

PO-LYB'I-US, a Greek historian, born about 204 B.C. In the year 167 he was carried a prisoner to Rome with many others of his countrymen, and lived there seventeen years in the house of Lucius Æmilius PAULUS as teacher to his son Scipio. When he went back to Greece, he found a large party trying to stir up a war with Rome. Polybius knew the folly of this, but his countrymen paid no attention to his advice. After his death a monument was put up to his memory, with the inscription "Hellas would have been saved if the advice of Polybius had been followed." His great work is the History of Rome, from the capture of the city by the Gauls, 220 B.C., to the breaking out of the second Punic war, 146 B.C. He died when eighty-two years old (about 122 B.C.).

POLYCARP (*pol'e-karp*), one of the early Christian Fathers, born probably in Smyrna, in the first century. He was one of the Apostolic Fathers; that is, he lived at the same time with some of the apostles, and he was made bishop of Smyrna by St. John the Evangelist, whose disciple he was. During a persecution of the Christians, he was brought before the Roman proconsul and told that he could save his life by cursing Christ. But he replied, "Eighty and six years have I served him, and he has done me no ill, and how can I blaspheme my King who has saved me?" These words made the people angry, and they cried out that Polycarp must die at the stake. He was accordingly burned (168) on a spot now said to be marked by a tall cypress-tree on Mt. Pagus, overlooking the city of Smyrna.

POLYCLETUS (*pol-e-kle'tus*), a Greek sculptor, born probably at Sicyon, on the Gulf of Corinth, in the fifth century B.C. He was a fellow student of PHIDIAS, and some of his statues are said to have excelled in beauty those that Phidias made. One of his most celebrated works was a statue of the goddess Juno, partly made of ivory and with a robe of gold. Another, called the Spear Bearer, was so perfect in form that artists came from all parts of Greece to study it. Polycletus was also the greatest architect of his time and built the theatre at Epidaurus, said to have been the finest one in Greece or Italy.

POLYCRATES (*po-lik'ra-teez*), a ruler of Samos, who lived in the 6th century B.C. His two brothers helped him to get his throne, but instead of rewarding them he killed one and banished the other. He was very successful in his wars and undertakings, but his friend Amasis, king of Egypt, thought that some misfortune would surely follow such great success. He therefore advised Polycrates to sacrifice his most valuable possession to the god NEMESIS. It is said that Polycrates took this advice, and threw into the sea a very valuable ring, but the next day the ring was found in the stomach of a fish which the king was eating. After that Amasis was more fearful than ever, and the alliance between him and Polycrates was broken off. Polycrates was finally captured by Orœtes, the Persian satrap of Sardis, who crucified him in Magnesia (522 B.C.).

PO-LY-HYM'NI-A. See MUSES.

POLYNESIA (*pol-e-ne'she-ah*), a name given to all the small islands of the Pacific Ocean E. of the Philippines, Papua, and New Zealand. It includes the Hawaiian, Marquesas, Paumotou, Society, Samoan, Feejee, Friendly, Caroline, Ladrone, and many other groups. Polynesia is made from two Greek words meaning "many islands."

POLYPHEMUS (*pol-e-fe'mus*), the fabled chief of the CYCLOPS, who, according to Homer, were cannibals, and had only one eye in the middle of the forehead. He lived in a cave in Sicily, and kept a flock of giant sheep. One day Ulysses and his companions landed on the island and entered the cave while Polyphemus was away. When he

came back he found them asleep in the cave, so he shut them in by rolling a great stone before the mouth. He ate six of them, but Ulysses finally made him drunk with wine and burnt out his one eye. Then Ulysses fastened himself and his companions under the bodies of the giant sheep, and as Polyphemus could not see them when he drove the sheep to pasture, they were taken along and so escaped.

POLYXENA (*po-liks'e-nah*), daughter of Priam, King of Troy, and Hecuba. ACHILLES loved her, and when that hero was slain she was sacrificed to his ghost on his tomb. Some writers say she killed herself on his tomb.

PO-MO'NA, in Roman fable, the goddess of gardens and fruit trees. She was the wife of VERTUMNUS. In pictures she is generally a young woman with a cornucopia of flowers and fruit.

Pomona.

POMPEII (*pom-pe'yi*) and **HERCU-LA'-NE-UM,** two ancient cities of S. Italy, at the foot of Mount Vesuvius, and not far from Naples. They were favorite summer resorts of the rich Romans, many of whom had beautiful villas there. There were also many temples and palaces. On Aug. 24, A.D. 79, an eruption of Mt. Vesuvius buried both cities in mud, lava, and ashes, killing many of the people. For many centuries even their sites were forgotten, and a village was built on the lava, fifteen feet above the streets of Pompeii. In 1748 several statues and other objects were found in sinking a well, and since then more than a third of Pompeii and a large part of Herculaneum have been uncovered, so that many of the old Roman villas can now be seen almost as they were eighteen hundred years ago. In the streets, too, can be seen the ruts made by wheels, and the stepping-stones for people on foot, placed so wide apart that chariot wheels could pass between them. In one place was found the skeleton of a soldier who had

B.C. He was the son of Cneius Pompeius Strabo, under whom he served in the Italian campaigns. The most important of his military successes were his campaign against Mithridates, which made Pontus a Roman province, and his capture of Jerusalem which added Syria to the empire. After these exploits he entered Rome in triumph, at the end of a procession which lasted two days. It was opened with pictures and tablets telling how he had taken one thousand fortresses, nine hundred towns, and eight hundred ships; how he had founded thirty-nine cities, and raised the revenue of Rome to eighty-five millions of sesterces. Then came wagons loaded with treasure, then three hundred and twenty-four kings as prisoners, and last of all himself, the victorious general. Shortly after this he joined the party of Cæsar, and formed with him and Cassius a government called the first triumvirate. But he wanted to be the first man in Rome, and could not bear to be second to Cæsar, so he determined on war. The great struggle took place at PHARSALUS, B.C. 48, when Pompey

Street Scene in Ancient Pompeii.

died rather than desert his post, and a baker's oven contained loaves of bread which he was baking when the city was buried. In Naples there is a wonderful museum, filled with curiosities from these buried cities.

POMPEY (Cneius Pompeius Magnus), called the Great, a famous Roman general, born Sept. 29, 106

was defeated and fled to Egypt for protection. Ptolemy, the king of Egypt, had ordered that he should be murdered immediately on his arrival. His body was left on the sands and his head taken to Cæsar, who wept at the sight of it. He died when fifty-eight years old (Sept. 28, A.D. 48).

PONCE DE LEON (Spanish *pon'-*

tha da laon'), **Juan,** the discoverer of Florida, born in Leon, Spain, about 1460. He accompanied Columbus on his second expedition, and conquered PORTO RICO. Hearing from the natives that somewhere among the Bahama Islands there was a fountain whose waters could bring back youth and beauty, he started in search of it (1512). He came to what he took for a large island which he called Florida, that being the Spanish for Easter, the day on which he landed there. He found plenty of flowers, but no such stream as he was looking for. He was made governor of Florida, and tried to settle there; but the natives drove him away severely wounded, and he went to Cuba and died (1521).

PONDICHERRY (*pon-de-sher're*),

Discovery of Loaves of Bread in a Baker's Shop in Pompeii (page 664).

a city of S. India, on the Bay of Bengal, 85 miles S. of Madras; pop. 156,000, or nearly as large as Louisville, Ky. Pondicherry is the capital of the French possessions in India, which consist of about 112 square miles, a tract of country nearly twice as large as the District of Columbia. The French bought it of an Indian prince in 1672, and though it has been taken many times by the English, it has always been given up again.

PONTIAC (*pon'te-ak*), a North American Indian, chief of the Ottawa tribe, born about 1712. He was a friend of the French, but hated the English, and formed a conspiracy to drive the English out of the country. It was agreed to fall suddenly upon their forts and settlements in the west, killing the soldiers and people (May, 1763). Pontiac and his warriors were to attack the fort at Detroit, but though most of the other attacks were successful, this one was discovered in time and defeated. After that he besieged the fort for several months, but was at length driven away. He kept up the war for some

Pompey (page 664).

time longer, only submitting to the English in 1666. Three years afterward he was killed, while intoxicated, by an Illinois Indian, when fifty-seven years old (1769).

PON'TUS. See ASIA MINOR.

POPE, Alexander, a famous English poet, born in London, May 22, 1688. When only twelve years old some verses about his teacher gained him so severe a whipping that his parents took him home and he never after went to school. Being sickly and crooked in body, books formed his chief pleasure, and he went on with his studies by himself. His knowledge of Greek and Latin was never good, and the translations of the Iliad and Odyssey of Homer, on which his fame chiefly rests, were in great

part merely rhymed by him from literal prose versions made by other hands. Among his original works are his "Pastorals," written at the age of sixteen, "The Rape of the

Alexander Pope.

Lock," "The Dunciad," and the "Essay on Man." He died at Twickenham when fifty-six years old (May 30, 1744).

PORSENNA (*por-sen'nah* or *por'se-nah*), **Lars,** a king of the Etruscans, who lived about 500 B.C. It is said that the TARQUINS asked him for aid after they had been driven from Rome. He came with an army and took his stand on a hill on the right bank of the Tiber. The Romans tried in vain to drive him away, and were themselves saved only by the valor of Horatius Cocles, who defended the wooden bridge that crossed the river. After the Romans were saved, they destroyed the bridge, and Cocles, heavily armed as he was, had to swim to the opposite shore. Macaulay has told this story in his ballad of "Horatius." When Mutius Scævola, a Roman, told Porsenna that 300 noble Romans had sworn to kill him, he left Rome, and went home with his army.

PORT-AU-PRINCE (*port-o-prinss'*), a city, capital of HAYTI, West Indies, on the Bay of Gonaives, on the W. coast; pop. 61,000, or about the same as that of Dayton, Ohio. Though the harbor is not very good, the city has a large trade in coffee, cocoa, cotton, mahogany, logwood, tobacco, molasses, and rum. Most of the people are negroes and mulattoes.

Port-au-Prince is French for "harbor of the prince." The city was founded in 1749. It has been nearly destroyed several times by earthquakes.

PORTER, David, an American naval commander, born in Boston, Feb. 1, 1780. He entered the navy when eighteen years old, and soon became a commander. In the war with Tripoli he distinguished himself in several battles, but was taken prisoner in 1803, and not freed until peace was made. In the war of 1812 he commanded the frigate Essex, with which he captured many British vessels, but finally lost his own frigate in a battle with two British ships near Valparaiso, Chili (March 28, 1814). From 1825 to 1829 he was commander in chief of the navy of Mexico, and afterward was appointed United States Minister to Constantinople, where he died when sixty-three years old (March 28, 1843). Captain Porter published an account of his cruise in the Essex, and a description of Constantinople.

PORTER, David Dixon, son of David Porter, an American naval commander, born in Philadelphia, June 18, 1813. He entered the navy in 1829, served in the Mexican War and on the coast survey, and when the Civil War broke out was made a captain. He commanded a fleet on the Mississippi, and took part in the capture of Vicksburg, for which he was made a rear-admiral. In January, 1865, he commanded a fleet and army which captured Wilmington, N. C. Porter succeeded Farragut, in 1870, as full admiral of the U. S. navy. He died when seventy-eight years old (February 13, 1891).

POR'TER, Jane, an English novel writer, born at Durham in 1776. In 1803 she published her first novel, "Thaddeus of Warsaw," which was translated into several languages. She wrote also the "Scottish Chiefs," with Wallace and Bruce as heroes. Her most successful work was "Sir Edward Seaward's Diary," which was by many mistaken for an account of actual facts. She died in Bristol when seventy-four years old (May 24, 1850).

PORTER, NOAH, an American writer and scholar, ex-president of Yale College, born in Farmington, Conn., Dec. 14, 1811. He was graduated at Yale College in 1831, and while tutor there studied theology and became a Congregational minister. In 1846 he was chosen professor of moral and mental philosophy in Yale College. In 1871 he was elected president to succeed Dr. Woolsey. Dr. Porter was chief editor of the "Webster International Dictionary," and was the author of several very able books on the human mind and other subjects. He died when eighty-one years old (March 4, 1892).

PORT'LAND, the principal city of Maine, in the S.W. part of the State, on Casco Bay; pop. 36,000, or a little larger than Tacoma, Wash. The harbor is very fine, and the city is a handsome one with wide, shady streets. There is a large trade, especially in lumber, fish, and ice. The lumber comes mostly from Canada, and is sent to South America. Great quantities of lobsters are canned there, and there are many factories. Many ships are built near the city. Portland was first a part of the town of Falmouth, but was made a town by itself in 1786. It became a city in 1832. In 1866 about a third of the city was destroyed by a great fire.

PORTO RICO or **Puerto Rico** (*por'to* or *pwer'to re'ko*), one of the West India Islands, E. of Hayti;

area 3500 square miles, or nearly three times as large as the State of Rhode Island ; pop. 745,000, or nearly two and a sixth times that of Rhode Island ; capital, San Juan de Puerto Rico. It is high and rocky, but the soil is very fertile, and there are many fine plantations of sugar-cane, coffee, and tobacco. About one half of the people are whites, the rest being negroes and mulattoes. The chief trade is in sugar and coffee.

Puerto Rico in Spanish means rich port. The island was discovered in 1493 by Columbus, and it still belongs to Spain.

PORTS'MOUTH, a city of S. England, on the island of Portsea, near the coast; pop. 141,000, or a little larger than Omaha, Neb. It consists of two parts, Portsmouth and Portsea, separated by a narrow arm of the sea. Opposite the island, on the mainland, is the town of Gosport, and the channel between Gosport and Portsmouth forms the harbor. Portsmouth is one of the most strongly fortified places in England, 13,000 men being required to garrison it. A very large dockyard for ships of war has been made there.

Portsmouth was probably founded in the 4th or 5th century, and the English began to fortify it in the 14th century.

PORTSMOUTH, a city of New Hampshire, on the Piscataqua River, 3½ miles from the sea; pop. 10,000, or about as large as Anniston, Ala. What is commonly called the Portsmouth navy-yard is about half a mile from the city, on two islands in the river, in the town of Kittery, Maine. Portsmouth is the only seaport of New Hampshire, and has a very fine harbor. Many ships are built there.

PORTSMOUTH, a town of S. Ohio, on the Ohio River; pop. 12,000, or about as large as Dover, N. H. The country around it,

on both sides of the river, contains many rich iron-mines, and Portsmouth has a large trade in iron, iron-ore, and coal. It contains large rolling-mills, foundries, and many other manufactories.

PORTSMOUTH, a city of Virginia, opposite Norfolk ; pop. 13,-000, or about as large as Vicksburg, Miss. It has a very fine harbor, and is the seat of the Gosport navy - yard, sometimes called the Norfolk navy-yard, where the famous iron-clad, the Merrimac or Virginia, was fitted out by the Confederates in the Civil War.

POR'TU-GAL, a country of W. Europe, on the Atlantic ocean, W. of Spain ; area 36,500 square miles, or a little larger than the State of Maine; pop. 4,708,000, or a little more than seven times that of Maine; capital, LISBON. Most of the surface is mountainous, and some of the most beautiful scenery in Europe is found among its hills and valleys. The climate is warm and pleasant, so that it is a favorite country for travelers. Portugal is noted for its vineyards, where some of the finest wines in the world are made. The most celebrated kind is port wine, which gets its name from OPORTO, where much of it is shipped to foreign countries. There are also large olive orchards, and a great deal of olive oil is made. The cork tree grows in many places. The people of Portugal are much like Spaniards, and their language is similar to the Spanish. They are governed by a king and by a parliament called the Cortes.

The name Portugal was made from Portus Cale (Latin for harbor), the old name of the town of Oporto. In the time of the Romans Portugal was inhabited by a brave tribe called the Lusitani, and from them it was called Lusitania. From the 8th to the 11th century the country belonged to the Moors, but they were finally conquered (1139). King John I, and his son

Prince Henry the Navigator (1385–1460) made Portugal one of the greatest countries in Europe. They sent fleets to explore the coast of Africa, and finally, in the reign of King Emanuel the Fortunate (1495–1521), the Portuguese discovered Brazil, and sailed around the southern end of Africa to India. The Spaniards were making discoveries at the same time, and the two peoples quarreled so much that, to keep the peace, the pope divided all the world, except Europe, between them. As the world did not belong to him the division did not help matters much, and they went on quarreling. Portugal has since lost most of her great possessions, but she still has many colonies, of which the most important are Benguela and Mozambique in Africa, aud Goa, Timor, and MACAO in Asia and the Malay Archipelago.

PO'RUS, the Greek name of a king of India who lived in the time of Alexander the Great. He ruled a country east of the river Hydaspes, and when Alexander tried to cross the river, Porus met him with a large army and more than two hundred trained war elephants. He was defeated after a bloody battle, in which two of his sons were killed and he himself was captured. Alexander treated him well and made him his ally, enlarging his kingdom by giving him others which were conquered by the Greeks. When Alexander went away from India, he left his army in charge of Eudemus, who put Porus to death.

POTOSI (*po-to-se'*), a city of Bolivia, on the side of a mountain of the same name, 13,500 feet above the sea; pop. 12,000, or about as large as Appleton, Wis. The mountain has in it more than 5000 silver-mines, and the top is so honeycombed with the passages, that the miners now have to work below. During two hundred and fifty years these silver-mines have yielded $1,000,000,000. Potosi once had 150,000 inhabitants, but the greater part of the city is now in ruins. The principal building is the mint where the silver is coined. The plaza or square of Ayacucho was made to commemorate the battle of Ayacucho (1824), which made South America independent of Spain.

POTSDAM (*pots'dahm*), a city of Germany in Prussia, 17 miles S. W. of Berlin; pop. 51,000, or a little larger than Los Angeles, Cal. It is a beautiful place, with fine scenery around it, and it has been a favorite place of residence of many of the Prussian kings. In the royal palace, which is about two hundred years old, are shown the rooms where FREDERICK THE GREAT worked; and in the palace of Sans Souci, near the town, are the rooms in which he lived and died. They are kept just as he left them and even his clock was stopped at the moment of his death. There are other fine palaces near Potsdam.

Potsdam gets its name from an old word meaning "under the oaks." Before 1660, when the first palace was built there, it was only a fishing village.

POTTS'VILLE, a town of Pennsylvania, on the Schuylkill River; pop. 14,000, or about as large as Keokuk, Iowa. The country around it contains many rich coal-mines, and most of the people of Pottsville are engaged in mining or selling coal. The city has several iron furnaces, rolling-mills, and foundries, besides machine-shops and a carpet factory.

POW'ERS, Hiram, an American sculptor, born in Woodstock, Vermont, July 29, 1805. The best known of his works is a statue called "The Greek Slave," which has been often exhibited and several times copied. He went to Florence when he was thirty-two, and spent the rest of his life there. He died in Florence when sixty-eight years old (June 27, 1873).

POW-HAT-AN', a powerful Indian chief of Virginia, born about 1550. He ruled over thirty tribes when the English first settled at James River. He was opposed to them, although when Captain Smith first visited him he treated him kindly. Afterward when Smith was taken prisoner and the Indians were about to kill him, Powhatan spared his life at the prayer of his daughter POCAHONTAS. There were a great many troubles between the English and Powhatan until Pocahontas married John Rolfe, an Englishman. After that Powhatan was a true friend to them. He died when about sixty-eight years old (1618).

PRAXITELES (*prax-it'e-leez*), a Greek sculptor, who lived in Athens in the 4th century B.C. His statues were noted for their grace and beauty. His most famous one was the Cnidian Venus, so called because it was owned by the people of Cnidos. The Cnidians thought so highly of this statue that they refused to part with it when King Nicomedes offered to pay the whole of their public debt as its price. It was afterward taken to Constantinople, where it was destroyed by fire (about 475 A.D.).

PREBLE (*preb'l*), **Edward,** an American naval officer, born in Falmouth (now Portland), Me., Aug. 15, 1761. In 1803 he sailed in the Constitution in command of the fleet against Tripoli, and in August and September of the next year attacked the batteries and gunboats defending the city several times. For his services there he received the thanks of Congress and a gold medal. He died in Portland, Me., when forty-six years old (Aug. 25, 1807).

George Henry Preble, nephew of Edward Preble, and rear-admiral in the United States navy, was

born in Portland, Me., Feb. 25, 1816. He is the author of "History of the American Flag." He died in Brookline, Mass., when sixty-nine years old (March 1, 1885).

PRES'BURG, a city of Austro-Hungary, in Hungary, on the Danube, 35 miles below Vienna ; pop. 48,000, or a little smaller than Oakland, Cal. For more than two hundred years (1529 to 1784) it was the capital of Hungary, and among its principal buildings is the cathedral in which the kings of Hungary were crowned. Outside the town is a high mound of earth called the "King's Hill." Up this the king used to ride, after his coronation, holding in his hand the sword of Saint Stephen, which he brandished towards the four quarters of the heavens, meaning by this act that he would defend Hungary against all the world.

PRES'COTT, William Hickling, a famous American historian, born at Salem, Mass., May 4, 1796. He entered Harvard College when only fifteen years old, and the next year met with an accident which nearly made him blind for life. One of the students in fun threw a crust of bread at him in the college dining hall, which struck his left eye, and hurt it so that he entirely lost its sight. By and by the right eye grew inflamed by overuse, and he was quite blind for several weeks. He never after this was able to read for any length of time, but had to employ some one to read to him ; and in writing, he used a contrivance prepared for blind persons, and had his papers copied by a secretary. After ten years' labor he published a history of "The Reign of Ferdinand and Isabella," which at once made him famous. He afterward wrote "The Conquest of Mexico," and "The Conquest of Peru;" and his last work was an uncompleted "Life of Philip the Second." He died in Boston, in the sixty-third year of his age (Jan. 28, 1859).

PRES'TER JOHN, the name given by Europeans in the middle ages, to a person who was supposed to be the king and priest of a Christian country somewhere in the heart of Asia. Many wonderful stories were told of him, and a great many companies of people went in search of his kingdom ; but it has never been certainly known whether any such person ever really lived or not.

PRES'TON, a town of N. England, on the river Ribble, 190 miles N. W. of London ; pop. 97,000, or a little larger than Albany, N. Y. It is principally noted for its manufactures of cotton, but linen, worsted and machinery are also made there. Small vessels ascend the river to this place, and there is a considerable coasting trade. Formerly the city was noted for its many churches and convents, from which it was called Priests' Town, which has been changed in time to Preston.

PRES'TON-PANS, a village of Scotland, on the Frith of Forth, 8½ miles E. of Edinburgh, so called from the pans used there to make salt out of sea-water. It is famous as the scene of a battle in which the Pretender Charles Edward STUART defeated a royal army, Sept. 21, 1745. The Pretender's soldiers, most of whom were Highlanders, uttered a short prayer and then charged with a loud yell, and in five minutes the battle was won. On the next day the Pretender entered Edinburgh.

PRIEST'LEY, Joseph, a noted English philosopher, born near Leeds, England, March 13, 1733. He was brought up among very religious people and became a minister; but as he had doubts about many of the things that Christians believe, and denied many of the truths of the New Testament, he did not do well as a preacher. By teaching school he earned money to buy an air-pump and an electrical machine ; and then began to study natural philosophy, and to write books on scientific subjects. These were well received, and he became a member of the Royal Society, and was made a Doctor of Laws by the University of Edinburgh. He afterwards studied chemistry, and got a medal from the Royal Society for his discoveries. Among other things, he was the first to find out oxygen (C. C. T., 437, I., u.). He wrote a great many religious as well as scientific books, and in spite of his disbelief in Christianity, was a truly good and pious man. Being persecuted in England for his religious opinions, which he was too honest to hide, he came to America in 1794, and lived here for ten years. He died in Northumberland, Penn., when seventy-one years old (Feb. 6, 1804).

PRINCE EDWARD ISLAND, an island in the Gulf of St. Lawrence, forming a province of the Dominion of Canada ; area 2173 square miles, or a little larger than Delaware; pop. 109,000, or about two thirds that of Delaware. It is mostly flat and has a very fertile soil. The people are principally farmers. The island is separated from New Brunswick and Nova Scotia by Northumberland Sound, which is often frozen in winter, so that the mails have to be carried over in ice-boats.

Prince Edward Island formerly belonged to the French, who called it Isle St. Jean, or St. John Island. It came into the possession of Great Britain in 1763, and in 1800 its name was changed in honor of Edward, Duke of Kent, father of Queen Victoria.

PRINCE'TON, a town of New Jersey, 11 miles N.E. of Trenton ; pop. about 4000. It is noted as the seat of the College of New Jersey, commonly called Princeton College, one of the best in the United States, which was begun in 1746. It suffered much during the war of the Revolution, when its buildings were used as barracks and hospitals by both the Americans and the British. During the battle of Princeton a cannon-ball went through one of the buildings and destroyed a portrait of King GEORGE II. The frame was unhurt, and it now has in it a portrait of Washington, painted by PEALE. The college is rich, and has a fine library and museum and an observatory.

The battle of Princeton was won by Gen. Washington over the British (Jan. 3, 1777). Lord CORNWALLIS went with most of his troops from Princeton to TRENTON to attack the Americans, who had defeated the Hessians there about a week before. Washing-

ton, finding that Cornwallis had more men than himself, went by night to Princeton, and defeated the part of the British army left there. This greatly helped the Americans, who had suffered much before that, and they finally drove the British out of New Jersey.

PRI'OR, Matthew, an English poet, born in Dorsetshire, July 21, 1664. He was the son of a joiner, but was educated at Cambridge. The first poem which brought him into notice was "The City Mouse and Country Mouse," written in ridicule of Dryden's "Hind and Panther." Prior held several court offices under William and Mary.

Carrying the mails to Prince Edward Island (page 671).

His poems are light and sparkling, but are little read now. He died when fifty-seven years old (Sept. 18, 1721).

PRO'BUS, Marcus Aurelius, a Roman emperor, born at Sirmium, Pannonia, about A.D. 230. He joined the army when very young, and, getting the favor of the Emperor VALERIAN, was given a high command before he was of legal age; but he showed that he was worthy of it, and finally the Emperor TACITUS made him commander of all the Roman possessions in Asia. He was a great favorite with the soldiers, and after

the death of Tacitus they forced him to become emperor. He gained many victories over the Germans, and when peace was made returned to Rome and busied himself in framing better laws for the empire. When his soldiers had no more fighting to do he employed them in draining swamps and in planting vineyards, but they considered such work beneath them, and finally became so angry that they mutinied and killed him (A.D. 282).

PRO-ME'THE-US (or *pro-me'-thuse*), in Greek fable, one of the sons of Japetus, and brother of AT-

LAS and Epimetheus. He made a man of clay in the image of the gods, and then wanted some fire from heaven to warm it and give it life; but Jupiter refused to give him any. He then stole a little, which made Jupiter very angry, and in revenge he sent PANDORA with a box full of evils to him. But Prometheus would have nothing to do with her. Jupiter then chained him to a rock on Mount Caucasus, where a vulture gnawed all day at his liver, which grew again every night. Hercules at length killed the vulture and rescued Prometheus from his torments. ÆSCHYLUS wrote one of his finest plays about the story of Prometheus.

PROVENCE. See GAUL.

PROV'I-DENCE, a city, one of the capitals of Rhode Island, on an arm of Narragansett Bay, called Providence River; pop. 132,000, or nearly as large as St. Paul, Minn. Next to Boston, it is the largest and richest city in New England, and is noted for its manufactures. There are more than one hundred and thirty jewelry manufactories, and the Gorham silver works are the largest in the world. Among other things made are tools, screws, rifles, stoves, locomotives, steam-engines, and fire-engines. There are also many large woolen and cotton factories. Providence has a larger trade in print calicoes than any other city in the United States. The city has a fine harbor and is the principal port of Rhode Island.

Providence is the seat of Brown University, a college founded in 1764. It was named (1804) in honor of Nicholas Brown, who gave it much money. It has a fine library, a museum, and a portrait gallery.

Providence was first settled in 1636 by Roger WILLIAMS, who named it on account of his gratitude to Providence in giving him there a place to live where he was free from his enemies. It became a city in 1832.

PRUSSIA (*prush'e-ah*), a country of Europe, forming part of Germany; area 134,000 square miles, or about half as large as Texas; pop. 28,318,000, or a little more than four ninths that of the United States. It is the largest and most powerful of the German States, and its king is emperor of Germany. In shape it is very irregular, and small tracts lying within its boundaries belong to other states. Before 1866 these tracts were much more numerous, and Prussia itself was completely cut in two by German states which are now united with it. The people speak the German language, and most of them are Protestants.

The name Prussia came from the Porussi, a German tribe whose country now forms a part of the kingdom. In 1415 it was united to Brandenburg, whose rulers inherited or conquered other German states. The first king of Prussia was Frederick I., who was crowned on Jan. 18, 1701. His grandson Frederick the Great conquered Silesia and other countries, and made Prussia very powerful. In 1806 it was conquered by Napoleon, who took away many of the provinces, but they were afterward restored, and parts of Saxony and Pomerania were added to it. William I., the present king, began to reign in 1861, and aided by the great statesman Bismarck, has been very successful. In 1866 Austria and many of the German states made war on Prussia, but they were defeated, and Hanover and other states were added to Prussia. In 1870 the French declared war against Prussia, but the Prussians invaded France and compelled the French to sue for peace, and King William was crowned emperor of all Germany at Versailles (Jan. 18, 1871).

PSYCHE (*si'ke*), in Greek fable, a person meant to represent the human soul. She was said to be the youngest of three sisters, daughters of a king. She was so lovely that Venus got angry at the homage paid to her, and sent her son CU-PID to make her fall in love with some ugly mortal; but Cupid fell in love with her himself, and carried her to a safe place. He used to visit her only at night, and told her that he did so because he did not wish her to look upon him. Her sisters told her that he must be some horrid monster, who was afraid to be seen, and persuaded her to kill him while he slept. At night she took a lamp and a dagger and went to the couch where he was sleeping. Finding how beautiful he was, she turned to go away when a drop of oil from the lamp fell on his shoulder, and he awoke. With a look of reproach, he left her. Psyche in her grief tried to kill herself; but nothing in nature would kill her; then she applied to Venus, who made her her slave and gave her all sorts of hard labors. She was at last set free by Cupid, and they were married with the consent of Jupiter. In pictures she is generally represented as a maiden with the wings of a butterfly.

PTOLEMY (*tol'e-me*) **I.,** called Soter, first of the line of Greek kings in Egypt, born in 367 B.C. He was one of the ablest of the generals of ALEXANDER THE GREAT, and in the division of countries on the death of that monarch, he was given Egypt, which he soon made an independent kingdom. The title of king was taken by him in 306, and the name Soter ("Saviour") was given him by the inhabitants of Rhodes whom he saved from a powerful enemy. Ptolemy was a Greek, but his subjects were Egyptians. He tried hard to change them to Greek ideas and customs, and he succeeded in doing this in a very great degree owing to his tact and wisdom. He made Alexandria

the first commercial city in the world, and he also began the school and library for which it became so celebrated. A noble saying of his has been handed down, "It is better to make rich than to be rich." Ptolemy died at Alexandria when eighty-four years old (283 B.C.), and was succeeded by his son Ptolemy II.

PTOLEMY II., called Philadelphus, second of the Greek kings of Egypt, born in the island of Cos, 309 B.C. He was the son of Ptolemy I., and succeeded him 283 B.C. His marriage with his sister Arsinoe, which was not against the laws of Egypt, caused him to give himself the name Philadelphus (brother-lover). This ruler carried out his father's ideas and made Egypt a great kingdom. The museum at Alexandria was improved by the addition of botanical and zoological gardens, and the library enlarged. Great scholars were invited from all parts of the world to live in Alexandria, which thus became the centre of refinement and civilization. For the benefit of the Jews in his dominion, he had the Old Testament, which was all of the Bible that had then been written, translated into the Greek language. This is the translation known as the Septuagint (Greek *septuaginta*, seventy), so called because it was made by seventy men. Ptolemy built the light-house on the island of Pharos, at ALEXANDRIA. He died in Alexandria when sixty-two years old (247 B.C.), and was succeeded by his son Ptolemy III.

PTOLEMY III., called Euergetes, the third of the Greek kings of Egypt. The date of his birth is not known, but he came to the throne (247 B.C.) on the death of his father, Ptolemy II. He was not only a lover of science and learning, as the other Ptolemys had been, but a great warrior, and he greatly extended the bounds of his empire by his conquests. His name Euergetes ("Benefactor") was given him by his grateful subjects on his restoring to their temples the gods which Cambyses, the king of Persia, had carried away nearly three hundred years before. He died after a reign of twenty-five years (222 B.C.), and was succeeded by his son Ptolemy IV.

PTOLEMY CLAUDIUS (*tol'e-me klau'de-us*), an Egyptian mathematician, astronomer, and geographer, born in Pelusium in the second century. His work on astronomy is important because his views were those that were held by astronomers until their falsity was proved by COPERNICUS. According to the Ptolemaic system, or plan of Ptolemy, the earth is at rest in the centre of the universe, and the sun and stars move around it. Ptolemy's book was long lost, but an Arabic translation of it was found, which the Emperor Frederick II. had translated into Latin in 1250. The Arabs called it the Almagest (the greatest). Scarcely anything is known of Ptolemy's life.

PULASKI (*pu-las'ke*), **Casimir,** Count, a Polish patriot who fought in the war of the American Revolution, born March 4, 1747. With his father and his two brothers he fought bravely for the freedom of Poland. In 1771, he made an attempt to seize the king Stanislaus Augustus, but he failed and was sentenced to death. After many adventures he reached Turkey, where he remained until the cause of Poland became hopeless. Then, his father and brothers being dead, he came to help the Americans, arriving in Philadelphia in 1777. At first he entered the army as a volunteer; but he did such great service in the battle of the BRANDYWINE that he was put in command of the cavalry with the rank of brigadier-general. In 1778 Congress gave him leave to raise a body of men to be under his own command. It was called Pulaski's Legion, and was of much assistance to our armies. He was mortally wounded in the attack on Savannah, and was carried to the brig Wasp, which lay in the Savannah River, where he died two days later (Oct. 11, 1779). He was buried in the river. There is a monument to his memory in Savannah.

PULTOWA (*pul-to'vah*) or **Poltava,** a city of S. Russia, on the Vorskla, a branch of the river Dnieper; pop. 42,000, or about as large as Seattle, Wash. It is surrounded by walls and contains a strong citadel. Four miles S.W. of the city is the battle-field of Pultowa, where Peter the Great won a great victory over King Charles XII. of Sweden. Charles was marching to take Pultowa, but was met by a Russian army larger than his own. As he had been wounded before the battle he could not lead his men, and they were so severely beaten that Charles was obliged to fly for his life (July 8, 1709). A mound and cross mark the battle-field, and in the city there is a column erected in memory of the victory.

PU'RI-TANS, a religious party in England, which came into notice in the reign of Queen Elizabeth. They were first called Puritans (1564) in jest, because they were always calling for a *purer* form of worship and the leading of a *purer* life. They thought Queen Elizabeth did not make changes enough, and they gave her much trouble; but they were loyal and did not leave the English Church, though they did all they could to reform it. The Independents were another sect, sometimes wrongly called Puritans. They were so called because they separated themselves from the English Church and set up an independent church. The Pilgrims who settled at Plymouth were Independents, but those who settled on Massachusetts Bay and built Boston were Puritans.

PUSHKIN (*poosh'kin*), **Alexander Sergeyevitch,** a Russian poet, born June 6, 1799. He was the son of a nobleman, and when quite young became a government clerk, but, having written an "Ode to Liberty" which offended the emperor, lost the office. In 1825 the Emperor Nicholas made him clerk again, and appointed him to write a history of Peter the Great. His greatest work, "Eugene Onegin," is a romance in verse. Among his other writings are the poems "The Gypsies" and "Poltava," and "The Captive's Daughter," a novel. Pushkin was killed in a duel at St. Petersburg when thirty-seven years old (Feb. 10, 1837).

PUT'NAM, Israel, an American general, born at Salem, Mass., Jan. 7, 1718. When twenty-one years old he lived on a farm at Pomfret, Conn., and became quite famous for killing a she-wolf in her den

Israel Putnam.

(C. C. T., 653, II., 1.). During the French and Indian War he served as a captain, and afterward as a major. Once, when the barracks of Fort Edward were on fire, he saved the powder magazine, fighting the fire until he was severely burned.

Another time, when pursued by Indians, he escaped with his men by steering down the rapids of the Hudson, which had never before been passed by a boat. In 1758 he was captured by the Indians and bound to a tree while the fight went on around him. The Indians were driven away, but they took Putnam with them and decided to roast him alive. The savages bound him to a stake and lit a fire around it, but before he was much burned he was saved by a French officer.

Putnam afterward served in an expedition against Havana (1762), in the Pontiac war at Detroit (1764), and in an expedition to explore the Mississippi (1773). At the breaking out of the Revolution, when the news of the battle of Lexington came, he was ploughing in a field with a yoke of oxen. He turned the oxen loose, jumped on his horse, and rode in one day sixty-eight miles to Boston. He was made a brigadier-general by the State of Connecticut, and soon afterward Congress made him the first major-general in the Continental army. He was one of the commanders at the battle of Bunker Hill, where he distinguished himself by his coolness and bravery. In 1776 he fought in the battle at Long Island. Afterward he commanded the American armies in the Highlands of the Hudson, but two of his forts being taken he was obliged to retreat, and soon after his place was given to another general. Being stationed with a few soldiers in Connecticut, Putnam was attacked by the British under Tryon. He ordered his men to retreat to a swamp, where the British cavalry could not follow them, and he himself rode down a steep bank, getting a bullet through his hat as he went. In 1779 Putnam was again placed in command of the Highlands, where he and his cousin finished the fort at West Point. Not long after he was attacked with paralysis, and retired to his farm at Brooklyn, Conn., where he died at the age of seventy-two (May 19, 1790).

PYG·MA'LI·ON, in Greek fable, a king of Cyprus, who, having made a very beautiful ivory statue of the nymph of Galatea, fell in love with it. He prayed to Venus to give her life, and the goddess having done so, he married her.

PYG'MIES, a nation of dwarfs, believed by the ancients to live in the interior of Africa. They were so called from a Greek word (*pugme*) meaning a measure from the elbow to the fist, which was said to be about their height. According to Homer, they were always at war with their enemies the cranes. The story of the pygmies has commonly been thought to be a fable, but late travelers have found a race of negro dwarfs on the upper Nile, none of whom are five feet high.

The Great Pyramids.

PYR'A·MIDS, great stone monuments built by the ancients, especially in Egypt, but also in Persia, India and Mexico. The most celebrated are the three Pyramids of Memphis, Egypt, a few miles from the modern city of Cairo. They are built of blocks of stone so large that it is supposed the builders had powerful machinery for lifting them. The outside was covered with small stones and cement, so as to form a smooth surface, but in most places this has been broken away, leaving the stones like stairs by which one can climb to the top. The largest, called the Pyramid of Cheops, is 450 feet high and was formerly nearly thirty feet higher. In each of the pyramids are long passages leading to chambers near the middle, where the embalmed bodies of kings were placed in sarcophagi or stone coffins. The bodies have been taken away, but some of the coffins can still be seen,

It is supposed that the pyramids were built and used only as tombs of kings, though some persons believe that they had other uses. Near the Great Pyramids is the famous Sphinx.

PYR'A-MUS and **THISBE** (*thiz'be*), two fond lovers of Babylon who agreed to meet each other at the tomb of Ninus. Thisbe got there first and found a lioness which had just killed an ox. She fled, and in her fright dropped her mantle, which the lion tore. When Pyramus came and saw it all torn and bloody, he thought Thisbe was dead, and killed himself with his own sword. After a while Thisbe came back, and, finding him dead, killed herself with the same weapon. All this happened under a mulberry-tree, the berries of which had been white; but the poets say that they were changed to a blood-red from this time.

PYRENEES (*pir'en-neez*), a high chain of mountains forming the boundary between France and Spain, and stretching from the Mediterranean to the Bay of Biscay on the Atlantic. They are very rugged and picturesque, and inclose many beautiful valleys. There are seven passes, all more than a mile high, with carriage-roads through them.

PYRRHUS (*pir'rus*), King of Epirus, born about 318 B.C. He was a son of Æacides, who claimed descent from Achilles, and who was a brother of Olympias, mother of Alexander the Great. After the death of Alexander, Pyrrhus fought in the battle of Ipsus on the side of his brother-in-law DEMETRIUS POLIORCETES. The battle was won by the other side, but Pyrrhus fought so bravely that his fame spread over the world. Some time afterward he engaged in a war with Rome at the request of the people of Tarentum, who lived in southern Italy, and who begged his aid against that state. He

went with his elephants, but, although he gained several battles, he could not conquer the Romans. He found out this after his defeat at Beneventum, and went back to Epirus, invaded Macedonia, and became its king. He was killed while attacking Argos, by a heavy tile thrown by a woman from a housetop. He died when forty-six years old (272 B.C.).

PY·THAG'O·RAS, a famous Greek philosopher, born in Samos, about 580 B.C. He was the son of a rich merchant, and he is said to have spent thirty years in travel for the purpose of getting all the knowledge of every country. When he returned from his travels he settled down at Crotona and there opened a school, where he taught many strange things. He took great part in politics, and was opposed to the democratic party. Owing to this there was an uprising against his disciples, which ended in their banishment. Among the things taught by him were that numbers are the principle of all things, that the heavenly bodies in their motions make music, and that the soul after leaving the body goes into some other body, such as that of a bird, beast, or other animal. A story is told of him that he once begged that a certain dog should not be beaten, because he said he recognized in its cries the voice of one of his friends who had died. This last belief is called the doctrine of metempsychosis, or transmigration of souls. He was nearer right in his ideas of astronomy than those who came after him, for he taught that the sun is the centre around which the planets move. Two thousand years after his death wise men came to believe that he was right in this. He died when eighty years old (about 500 B.C.).

PYTH'E-AS, a Greek navigator, who lived about 300 B.C. He was a native of the colony of Massilia, now Marseilles, in France, and he made several voyages to countries which were then almost unknown. On one voyage he is said to have visited Britain and a country called Thule, which was probably Iceland.

Pytheas wrote two books describing his voyages, but they are now lost with the exception of a few fragments. He was the first to tell latitude by the sun.

Q

QUART'LEY, ARTHUR, an American painter, born in Paris, France, of English parents, May 24, 1839. He came to America when a boy of thirteen. He never had a teacher in painting, but his landscapes and marine views possess great merit. He died in New York when forty-seven years old (May 19, 1886).

QUEBEC (*kwe'bek*), a city of E. Canada, on the St. Lawrence River; pop. 62,000, or a little larger than Wilmington, Del. It is divided into two parts—the lower town, on a plain by the river shore; and the upper town, on a steep promontory about three hundred feet above the river. Many of the streets, especially of the lower town, are narrow and crooked, and the old buildings are very quaint and curious. The upper town is surrounded by a wall, and there is a great citadel overlooking the city; this and other forts below the city are so strong, that Quebec has been called the Gibraltar of America. The harbor is very fine and the largest vessels can lie at the wharves, but from November to April the river is frozen. The scenery around the city is very picturesque. Quebec has a greater commerce than any other city in Canada except MONT-REAL, the principal trade being in lumber, grain, and ships. There are large lumber-yards, and immense rafts of logs are always moored along the river shore below the city. The ships made at Quebec are noted for their beauty and strength. The city contains sev-

eral schools and colleges, and the Laval University, founded in 1663. About two thirds of the people of Quebec are French Canadians, and French is the language commonly spoken.

Quebec was founded by the French under CHAMPLAIN in 1608, and named after Quebec in Brittany. It was taken by the English in 1629 and again in 1759, when the English army was commanded by General WOLFE, who was killed in the battle. A monument erected where he fell bears this inscription: "Here Wolfe died victorious, Sept. 13, 1759." During the Revolutionary War, a small American army under Gen. MONTGOMERY attacked the city, but they were driven away and Montgomery was killed.

QUEENS'TOWN. See CORK.

QUINCY (*kwin'se*), a city of W. Illinois, on the Mississippi River; pop. 31,000, or nearly as large as Lancaster, Pa. Excepting Chicago and Peoria, it is the largest city in the State, and its manufactures and trade are very important. Among the things made there are wagons, plows, paper, flour, beer, and bricks, and many thousand hogs are killed and packed there every year.

Quincy was first settled in 1822, and became a city in 1839.

QUITO (*ke'to*), a city of S. America, capital of ECUADOR; pop. about 80,000, or about the same as New Haven, Conn. It is situated at the foot of the volcano of Pichincha, almost two miles above the sea; all around are snow-capped mountains of the Andes. Two deep ravines run through the city, and down them rush torrents of water from snow melted on these mountains. The streets are narrow, and generally unpaved; and owing to the frequent earthquakes, most of the houses are only one story high.

Fine gold lace is made there, and beautiful embroidery and needlework.

Quito was an ancient city of the Peruvian Indians, and its name in their language means the "deep ravine." It was conquered by the Spaniards under Pizarro.

R

RABELAIS (*rahb-la'*), **François,** a famous French author, born about 1490. He was of humble parents, and was first a monk, but becoming discontented, left his monastery and went to Montpellier, where he studied medicine. For a time he practiced medicine, but he is best known as an author. One of his books is very celebrated, "The Lives, Heroic Deeds, and Sayings of Gargantua and Pantagruel." It ridicules monks, priests, popes, kings, and statesmen, and is full of wit which is sometimes coarse. Rabelais was very kind to the poor and very fond of little children. He died when sixty-three years old (about 1553).

RACHEL (*rah-shel'*), or **Elizabeth Rachel Felix,** a famous French actress, born in Switzerland, Feb. 28, 1820. Her father was a Jewish peddler, and she traveled with him, singing and playing on the guitar to earn her living. One day while singing in a restaurant at Paris she attracted the attention of a theatrical manager, and through his influence she was educated in music and acting. She first had but little success, but finally her splendid acting in Corneille's play of "Les Horaces" (The HORATII) made her famous, and from that time her success was very great, and she gained a large fortune. During the French revolution of 1848 she often sang the "Marseillaise" hymn to immense audiences. In 1855 she came to the United States, and acted in "Joan of Arc," "Mary Stuart," and many other plays. She died near Toulon, France, when about thirty-eight years old (Jan. 3, 1858).

RACINE (*ras-seen'*), a city of S. E. Wisconsin, on Lake Michigan; pop. 21,000, or nearly as large as Meriden, Conn. It has one of the best harbors on the lake, and a large trade, especially in lumber. But Racine is principally noted for its manufactures. Among the things made there are wagons and carriages, fanning mills, leather trunks, woolen cloths, and wire. Racine College, which belongs to the Episcopal Church, has nearly two hundred students.

Racine was first settled in 1834, and it became a city in 1848.

RACINE (*rah-seen'*), **Jean,** a famous French writer of plays, born Dec. 21, 1639. He was the son of a customhouse officer, but his parents dying when he was but four years old, was brought up by his grandmother and aunt in the monastery of Port Royal. When twenty years old he went to Paris to see the world, and while there wrote a poem on the marriage of Louis XIV. At first he studied theology, but he soon gave it up, and becoming a friend of MOLIÈRE and Boileau, turned his attention to writing plays. In this he was so successful that he is considered the first tragic poet of France. His friend Madame de Maintenon induced him to write the plays of "Esther" and "Athalie" for the pupils of St. Cyr, a young ladies' school in which she was interested. Afterwards he wrote to the king a memoir on the state of France. Racine was no flatterer of royalty, and he told some truths which were not pleasant to Louis, whose favor from that time he lost.

Jean Racine.

He died in Paris, when sixty years old (April 22, 1699).

RALEIGH (*raw'ley*), Sir **Walter,** a famous English courtier and navigator, born at Hayes, Devonshire, in 1552. He was one of the most gallant soldiers, most fearless sailors, most able authors, and most accomplished courtiers of the reigns of Elizabeth and James I. A story is told of his first introduction to Elizabeth. One day the queen, in walking, came to a muddy place; she stopped, and Raleigh, seeing her pause, flung down his rich plush cloak for her to step on. That graceful act, which was just

the kind of attention that Elizabeth liked, gained the favor of a queen who knew how to honor those she loved. Elizabeth invited him to court, and gave him several honorable and profitable offices.

Having obtained permission to colonize North America, Raleigh sent out two expeditions, both unsuccessful, on account of the hostility of the Indians. The only results of these enterprises were the introduction of tobacco and potatoes into Europe. The name of

Sir Walter Raleigh.

Virginia, given to the colony in honor of the maiden queen, and Raleigh, that of the capital of North Carolina, still exist to remind Americans of the mother land.

There is another story of a wager won by Sir Walter of the queen, which was that he would tell the exact weight of the smoke of his tobacco. The queen attentively watched the curling wreaths, wondering by what process they were to be weighed in the balance. Having finished smoking, Sir Walter carefully collected the ashes, weighed them, deducted their weight from that of the tobacco, and gave the difference between the amounts as that of the smoke which had passed away.

With the death of Elizabeth, the scene changed for Raleigh. Enemies poisoned the mind of the new king, James, against him and he was shorn of nearly all his honors and rewards. But worse than this was in store for him. He was charged with having joined in a plot to place Lady Arabella STUART on the throne, and brought to trial. At that time Coke was lawyer for the Crown. "I want words," stormed the great prosecutor, "to express thy viperous treasons." "True," said Raleigh, "for you have spoken the same thing half a dozen times over already." But Raleigh's wit did not save him. For thirteen years, he languished in the gloomy Tower of London. This time was spent by him in making chemical experiments, and in writing his " History of the World."

He was greatly admired by Prince Henry, the king's son, who once said that no one but his father would keep such a bird (as Raleigh) in a cage. At length he was liberated by James, and sent with a fleet to the Orinoco River in search of a gold mine, which was said to be on its banks. During this cruise he captured a Spanish settlement, which so enraged the King of Spain that he directed his ambassador in London to demand vengeance. James at that time was anxious to please the Spanish king, as he was hoping to get his daughter as a bride for his son Charles, so he arrested Raleigh on his landing in England, and after a few months had him executed on the same old charge for which he had already suffered so much. Almost his last words, as he lifted the axe and passed his finger along the keen edge were: " This is a sharp medicine, but it will cure all diseases." He died when sixty-six years old (Oct. 29, 1618).

RAMILLIES (*ram'e-leez*), French *rah-meel-ye'*), a village of Belgium, 16 miles S. by E. of Louvain, noted for a victory won there by the Duke of MARLBOROUGH over a French and Bavarian army, commanded by Marshal Villeroi, May 23, 1706. Soon after this defeat the French surrendered all their cities and fortresses in the Netherlands.

RANDOLPH (*ran'dolf*), **John,** of Roanoke, an American orator, born in Chesterfield County, Va., June 2, 1773. At the age of twenty-six he entered upon public life as a member of Congress, and at once took a leading position in politics. He was conspicuous for his biting speeches, his many odd ways, and for a wit so sharp as to make him the terror of all who opposed him in Congress. Randolph prided himself on his descent from POCAHONTAS, and his marked Indian features bore witness to his origin. Many stories of him are still current in Charlotte County, Virginia, his old home. One relates to the peculiar way in which in his dealings with his slaves he applied the Scripture text, " To him that hath shall be given." He was a good master, and gave to each of his servants a patch of ground, encouraging him to cultivate it, and to sell its produce, and at Christmas he who had made the most money got the largest gift. Randolph died in Philadelphia when sixty years old (June 24, 1833).

RAPHAEL (*raf'a-el*), or **Raffaelle Sanzio,** the greatest of Italian painters, born at Urbino, April 6, 1483. He was the only son of Giovanni Sanzio, also a painter, who gave him his first lessons in art. Raphael's mother died when he was eight years old, and when he was thirteen his father sent him to Perugia to study art under Perugino. Timoteo Viti, another of his teachers, painted the boy's portrait when he was twelve years of age, and this picture is in the Borghese palace or gallery at Rome. It is a beautiful face and very thoughtful. At the age of sixteen Raphael went with an artist named Pinturicchio to Siena to assist him in painting the history of Pope Pius II. for the library of a cathedral ; and soon afterward he visited Florence, and studied the work of two great masters,—LEONARDO DA VINCI and MICHAEL ANGELO. Julius II. employed Raphael to paint pictures on the walls of the Vatican palace in Rome, and was so much pleased with his fine work that he ordered all the other pictures painted there to be rubbed

Raphael.

out and the walls to be prepared for Raphael alone. During five years Raphael painted many grand works for Julius II., among which are the " Deliverance of Peter from Prison," "God appearing to Noah," "Abraham's Sacrifice," "Jacob's Dream," and " Moses at the Burning Bush." After the death of Julius II. Raphael painted several years for Leo X., and made some important works for the Vatican from sacred subjects, seven of which are in the museum at South Kensington, England. One beautiful painting, made for a church in Palermo, was put on board of a ship that was wrecked. All the

people perished, but the case containing this picture floated and was saved before the water had had time to injure it. It is now in the Museum of Madrid, Spain. Raphael painted a great number of Madonnas (Italian for My Lady, a name given in art to the Mother of Christ), and also Holy Families which represent Mary and Joseph with the infant Saviour. The Sistine Madonna, or Madonna di San Sista (Italian for My Lady of St. Sixtus, so called because St. Sixtus, a pope, is one of the figures in the lower part of the canvas), is perhaps the best known and most admired of all of Raphael's paintings. It is one of the treasures of the DRESDEN gallery. Raphael's last work, the "Transfiguration of Christ," now in the Vatican, was not finished at the time of his death. A great many engravings have been made of the works of Raphael, which are highly prized.

Raphael was beloved by all who knew him, and there was great sorrow when he died, at the early age of thirty-seven (April 6, 1520). He had a magnificent funeral, and was buried where he had said he wished to be—in the Pantheon. More than a hundred years after his death (1633) Pope Gregory XVI. had his grave opened. The body was found to be in a pretty good state of preservation ; a second funeral was held, which was attended by eminent artists and men of rank, who moved about the church in a procession, bearing torches, while beautiful music was chanted, and his body then returned to its resting-place.

RAPP' (rahp), Jean, a French general, born in Colmar in 1772. He enlisted as a private when only sixteen years old, and rose to be a general under Napoleon. He was wounded more than twenty times. At Austerlitz a charge of his soldiers decided the battle, and after Napoleon's retreat from Russia he defended Dantzic against the Russians for a year, but was finally obliged to surrender. When Napoleon returned from Elba, he sent Gen. Rapp to fight the Austrians near the Rhine, but he was obliged to retreat, and after Napoleon's downfall he went to Switzerland, but returned to France in 1818 and was made a peer. He died in Paris when forty-nine years old (Nov. 8, 1821).

RAT'IS-BON, a city of Germany, in Bavaria, on the river Danube, opposite where the river Regen enters it; pop. 36,000, or about as large as Portland, Me. It is a very old city, with crooked streets and odd-shaped houses, and is celebrated for its beautiful Gothic cathedral, begun in 1275 and finished in 1875. Near Ratisbon, at Donaustauf, is the famous Walhalla, a fine marble building after the model of the Parthenon at Athens, in which is a great collection of the statues and busts of all the German heroes and other great men.

Ratisbon was called by the Romans Regina Castra (the fortress on the Regen), and it is still called by the Germans Regensburg.

RAVENNA (*rah-ven'nah*), a city of N.E. Italy, on the river Montone,

The Walhalla.

near the Adriatic Sea; pop. 19,000, or nearly as large as Waltham, Mass. It contains many ancient buildings, among them a cathedral founded in the 4th century, the ruined palace of Theodosius, and the tomb of Theoderic. Still more interesting is the tomb of DANTE, who died in Ravenna. It is small and plain, but thousands of travelers visit it every year. In 1865, when the 600th birthday of Dante was celebrated there, some bones said to be his were found concealed outside of the tomb, and they were reburied with great pomp. It is supposed that they had been taken out to keep them from being stolen by the Florentines, who, though they had treated Dante badly during his life, wanted his body brought home after his death.

Ravenna is a very ancient city. When the Roman Empire was overrun by barbarians, the emperors went to live there, because it could be more easily defended than Rome (A.D. 404). Afterwards it was the capital of the Gothic kings of Italy, and still later of the exarchs who ruled the country for the Eastern Empire. After many changes it was taken by Pepin the Short, who gave it to the pope (775). GASTON DE FOIX was killed under its walls. In 1860 Ravenna was united to the kingdom of Italy.

RAW'LINSON, George, brother of Sir Henry, an English writer of history, born in 1815. He was educated at Oxford, and was for many years professor of ancient

Tomb of Theodoric at Ravenna.

history there. He has published a work on the history of Chaldæa, Assyria, Babylonia, Media, and Persia, a "Manual of Ancient History," a translation of Herodotus, and other works. He is now canon of Canterbury Cathedral.

RAWLINSON, Sir Henry Cres-wicke, an English antiquary, born at Chadlington, Oxfordshire, in 1810. When but sixteen years old he entered the army in India. Owing to his great knowledge of the languages of the East, he has been appointed by the government to many important offices. In these he has had the chance to make interesting discoveries. Many of the things that we know about those Eastern lands have been found out by the inscriptions on tombs and ruins which he has deciphered, and about which he has written many books.

READE, Charles, a famous English novelist, born at Ipsden in 1814. His first novel, "Peg Woffington," written in 1852, at once gave him a high place as an author. This story was rapidly followed by others, some of them being "Never too Late to Mend," "The Cloister and the Hearth," and "Very Hard Cash." Reade nearly always has some good object in view in his writings. His "Hard Cash" was written to call attention to the treatment of lunatics in the public asylums, and much good was done by its means to that unfortunate class. He died at the age of seventy years (April 11, 1884).

READING (*red'ing*), a city of Pennsylvania, on the Schuylkill River; pop. 59,000, or nearly as large as Grand Rapids, Mich. Near the city are rich iron-mines, and the iron is used in many large furnaces, rolling-mills, foundries, and machine-shops. Besides these there are manufactories of iron-ware, nails, steam-boilers, and iron pipe, large brickyards and distilleries, a cotton-mill, hat-factories, and hundreds of workshops. In the machine-shops of the Philadelphia and Reading Railroad Company nearly 3000 men are employed. A large part of the farmers in the surrounding country are Germans. Reading was first laid out in 1748 and became a city in 1847.

REAUMUR (*ra-o-mure'*), René Antoine Ferchault de, a noted French writer and philosopher, born in La Rochelle, Feb. 28, 1683. He went to Paris in 1703, and soon became famous as a writer and inventor. He was the first to show in France how steel can be made from iron, and he found out a way of tinning iron. A kind of white porcelain first made by him is still called "Reaumur's porcelain," and the Reaumur thermometer (C. C. T., 615, I., l.) made by him (1730) is still used in Spain and some parts of Germany. He studied much about mollusks, or shellfish, and wrote some interesting books about insects. He died when seventy-four years old (Oct. 18, 1757).

RÉCAMIER (*ra-kah-me-a'*), Jeanne Françoise Julie Adelaide, a beautiful and famous French lady, born in Lyons, Dec. 4, 1777. She was the daughter of Jean Bernard, a notary of Lyons, and when fifteen years old became the wife of the banker M. Récamier, a man more than twice her age. Owing to her beauty, grace, and sweet manners, she became the most celebrated French woman of her day. Among her friends was Madame de Staël, who was exiled from Paris by Bonaparte on account of some books she had written that he did not like. After a while he grew jealous of Madame Récamier's friendship with Madame de Staël, and, fearing that she would use her power over people to turn them from his cause,

he banished her also. It was not till after Napoleon's fall that she returned to Paris.

The next year, after the battle of Waterloo, she was visited by the Duke of Wellington. He, knowing that his hostess had no reason to like Bonaparte, said, while speaking of him, "I have given him a good beating." This was enough; she could not bear that her guest should boast of his victory over her people, and she forbade him her house. Through her whole life this remarkable woman was loved and admired, no less when she was old and blind than when she was young. Every one of note who came to Paris asked to be introduced to her and left her house delighted. She died in Paris when seventy-two years old (May 11, 1849).

RED JACK'ET, or Sa-go-ye-wat'-ha ("He keeps them awake"), a noted chief of the Seneca tribe of Indians, born at Old Castle, on Seneca Lake, New York, in 1752. In early life he was noted for his swift running, and during the Revolution the British officers used to employ him as a messenger. One of them gave him a bright red coat, and after that he was called Red Jacket. He was a friend of the whites, though he wished to have the Indians keep their own lands; and when the Six Nations made a treaty to sell theirs, he opposed the treaty in an eloquent speech (1784). Some years after this he visited Gen. Washington, who gave him a silver medal. During the war of 1812 he was of great service to the American army, giving them important information and advice before the battle of Chippewa. In later life he visited New York and Washington, and the speeches that he made there are among the finest specimens of Indian eloquence. He died at Seneca Village, near Buffalo, N. Y., at the age of seventy-eight (Jan. 20, 1830).

RED RIVER, a river of North America, rising in N.W. Texas and flowing into the Mississippi 340 miles above its mouth; length about 1550 miles. It gets its name from the color of its waters, which are filled with earthy matter washed from its banks at all times excepting when it is very low. The great raft of Red River is an immense collection of trees and driftwood, (near Shreveport,) which once filled the river so as to make it impassable, but a channel wide enough for steamboats has been cut through it.

RED RIVER OF THE NORTH, a river of North America, rising in W. Minnesota and flowing N. through Manitoba into Lake Winnipeg; length about 750 miles. Small steamers ply on it, and much freight, principally furs, is floated down it in flat-boats.

RED SEA, a sea between Africa and Arabia, joined to the Indian Ocean by the strait of Babel-Mandeb, and to the Mediterranean by the Suez Canal; area 185,000 square miles, or about as large as the Black Sea. It gets its name from a kind of red seaweed which floats in its waters. The Red Sea is one of the warmest regions in the world, the thermometer sometimes rising to 132° F. As there are hardly any rains, its water is much more salt than that of the ocean.

The Israelites, when they were going from Egypt to Canaan, passed over a narrow place at the north end of the Red Sea. In ancient times the trade between India and Europe was carried on by ships on this sea, and caravans across the Isthmus of Suez. When a new route to India was found around the Cape of Good Hope the old one fell into disuse; but since the Suez Canal has been opened the Red Sea has once more become the great route between India and Europe.

REGILLUS (*re-jil'lus*), **Lake,** a small lake of ancient Latium in Italy, about 10 miles S.E. of Rome, where TARQUIN the Proud was defeated by the Romans. According to the story, the Romans were aided by CASTOR and Pollux, as told so well by Macaulay in his poem about the battle.

REGGIO (*red'jo*), a city of N. Italy, 16 miles W.N.W. of Modena; pop. 56,000, or about as large as Lynn, Mass. It has a fine cathedral and other interesting buildings, and a large trade is carried on in wine, silk, cheese, and hemp. The ancient Reggio or Regium Lepidi, was destroyed by the Goths, but rebuilt by Charlemagne in 409. It was the birthplace of ARIOSTO.

REG'U-LUS, Marcus Atilius, a noted Roman patriot and soldier. In the first Punic war he was sent to Africa with a large army, and though at first successful, was at last defeated and taken prisoner by the Carthaginians (255 B.C.). He was kept for five years, but in 250 he was sent with messengers to Rome with proposals of peace, the Carthaginians having made him promise that he would return if peace was not agreed upon. Every one expected that he would advise his countrymen to make peace; but, on the contrary, he persuaded them not to do so. Then, although he knew he was going back to imprisonment and perhaps to death, he kept his promise and returned to Carthage, where, according to some writers, he was put to a cruel and shameful death; but this story is not now believed.

REID (*reed*), **Mayne,** a writer of books for young folks, born in Ireland in 1818. He was the son of a Presbyterian minister, who educated him to become a minister also; but being fond of new places and new sights, he came in 1838 to America, and travelled in nearly all the States. He afterward fought in the Mexican war, and was wounded at

Chapultepec. Since 1850 he mostly lived in London, and wrote numerous stories of travel and adventure. He died at the age of sixty-five years (October 21, 1883).

REMBRANDT (*rem'brahnt*) **VAN RYN, Paul Harmens,** a famous Dutch painter, born in Leyden, July 15, 1607. His father was a miller named Rembrandt, and the son was called Van Ryn (of the Rhine) because the mill where he was born was on the banks of the old Rhine. He began to study painting when very young, and his first studio was in the mill, where

Rembrandt.

the only light was from a ventilator in the ceiling. Such a light would illuminate one side of every object, while the other side would be left in deep shade, and it is supposed that Rembrandt there learned to make the strong lights and shades for which his pictures are noted. Many of these are scenes from the Bible, among the most celebrated of which are "The Descent from the Cross," and "The Adoration of the Magi." Rembrandt also made many etchings which are as celebrated as his paintings. He received high prices for his works, and at one time he was rich, but

being involved in lawsuits for his wife, he became very poor. After 1630 he lived in Amsterdam, where he died at the age of sixty-two years (Oct. 8, 1669).

RE'MUS. See ROMULUS.

RENAN (*reh-non'*), **Joseph Ernest,** a famous French writer, born at Tréguier, Feb. 27, 1823. He was educated for a priest, but changed his mind and gave himself up to the study of the Hebrew, Arabic, and other Eastern languages, and wrote a very able book about them. In 1862 he was appointed professor of Hebrew in the college of France, but his ideas about religion were not liked, and he was dismissed. In 1863 he published a "Life of Jesus," in which he treated the New Testament account of him as a kind of romance. The work has been translated into many languages. He has since published "Saint Paul," "The Apostles," and other works. He died when sixty-nine years old (October 1, 1892).

RENNES (*ren*), a town of W. France, at the junction of the rivers Ille and Vilaine; pop. 66,000, or about as large as Atlanta, Ga. It is strongly fortified, and has several important colleges and seminaries. Linen and woolen cloth, leather, and pottery are made there. Rennes is a very ancient town. During the middle ages it was the capital of Brittany, and a very important military post. The English, under the Duke of Lancaster, besieged it for six months, but did not capture it (1356).

RESACA DE LA PALMA (*rasah'kah da lah pal'mah*). See PALO ALTO.

RE-VERE', **Paul,** an American patriot, born in Boston, Mass., Jan. 1, 1735. He was a goldsmith, but learned how to engrave on copper, and in 1775 engraved and printed the bills of paper money ordered by Congress. He was one of those who helped to throw the tea overboard in Boston harbor. When

Gen. Gage was getting ready to march from Boston to destroy the stores of the Americans at Concord, Revere rode, on the night of April 18, 1775, to Lexington, rousing each house on his way, and warning the people of Gage's plan. Longfellow has written a stirring poem about this, called "Paul Revere's Ride." Revere died in Boston when eighty-three years old (May 10, 1818).

REYKIAVIK (*ri'ke-a-vik*). See ICELAND.

REYNOLDS (*ren'olz*), Sir **Joshua,** a noted English portrait painter, born at Plympton, Devonshire, July 16, 1723. He began to study painting when very young, and after spending three years in Italy settled in London, where he became the greatest of all English portrait painters. He was especially celebrated for his pictures of ladies and children, but he also made portraits of many distinguished men. His historical pictures are less noted, and many of them are now almost ruined, owing to the poor quality of the paints used. In 1768 Reynolds became the first president of the Royal Academy, and was made a knight. He was also one of the founders of the "Literary Club," of which Johnson, Goldsmith, and other distinguished men were members. He died in London when sixty-eight years old (Feb. 23, 1792).

RHEA (*re'ah*). See CYBELE.

RHEIMS (*reemz*), a city of N.E. France, 82 miles N.E. of Paris; pop. 98,000, or a little larger than Albany, N. Y. It has a large trade in champagne wine, and cotton and woolen cloth. It is also celebrated for its beautiful cathedral, in which many of the kings of France were crowned. At their coronation they were anointed with oil from a glass flask, said to have been brought down from heaven by a dove when king CLOVIS was crowned at Rheims (496). During the French Revolution the flask was broken, and the pieces thrown away. Some person saved a piece with a little of the oil in it, and it was used at the coronation of Charles X. (1824).

RHINE (*rine*), a noted river of Europe, rising in the Alps of Switzerland and flowing through Germany and the Netherlands into the North Sea; length about 950 miles. It is commonly divided into three parts: the part above Basel is called the Upper Rhine, that between Basel and Cologne the Middle Rhine, and that from Cologne to the North Sea the Lower Rhine.

The Upper Rhine is navigable by rafts and small boats, but its course is much broken by rapids and falls. At Schaffhausen the river leaps down a rock seventy feet high. The Middle Rhine winds at first through a broad fertile valley, and then between two mountain regions, flowing now among beautiful vineclad hills and then between steep towering rocks crowned by old castles and other ruins. The famous Rhine wines come from this part of the Rhine, which is navigated by many steamboats. The Lower Rhine is a sluggish stream, deep enough for large ships, which runs through a low flat country, and finally loses itself among the sandbanks of the North Sea. The trade of the Rhine is very important, and more than a million travelers visit its beautiful scenery every year.

RHODE ISLAND, one of the New England States of the United States, on the Atlantic Ocean, between Connecticut and Massachusetts; area 1306 square miles, or more than four ninths that of Connecticut; pop. 346,000, or more than two fifths as much as that of Connecticut; capitals, PROVIDENCE and NEWPORT, the legislature meeting one year in Newport and the next in Providence. Most of the surface is hilly. In the south-eastern part is Narraganset Bay, which is one of the best harbors in the world. It contains several islands, on one of which, named Rhode Island, is the city of Newport.

Though Rhode Island is the smallest State in the Union, it is the most thickly populated of all, and is important in many ways. It has mines of iron and coal, quarries of marble, freestone, and granite, and many factories and workshops. For its size, it is the most important manufacturing State in the Union, and its people are very rich. The principal things made are cotton and woolen goods, iron-ware, leather and jewelry. More cotton prints and more screws are made there than in any other State.

The name Rhode Island was first given to the island on which Newport is built, some think because it was thought to look like the island of Rhodes in the Mediterranean, others because its shores looked red, from which the Dutch called it Rood Eylandt (Red Island). The first settlement was made by Roger Williams at Providence (1636), and a second one two years afterward on Rhode Island, which the Indians called Aquidnet. In 1663 the two settlements were made into a colony, called the colony of " Rhode Island and Providence Plantations." Rhode Island was one of the thirteen original States of the Union.

RHODES (*rodes*), an island of the Grecian Archipelago, 10 miles from the coast of Turkey in Asia; area 452 square miles, or a third as large as the State of Rhode Island; pop. 27,000, or about one thirteenth that of Rhode Island; capital, Rhodes (pop. 20,000). A mountain range runs through the island. The valleys are fertile, but only a part of the land is cultivated, the principal crops being cotton, oranges, citrons, olives, and grapes. There are fine quarries of marble, and sponges and red coral are obtained on the coast.

The island belongs to Turkey, but less than one fifth of the people are Turks, most of the rest being Greeks.

Rhodes, or in Greek Rhodos, means a rose, and the island was so named because roses were very plenty there. In ancient times this was one of the most powerful of the Greek islands. The city of Rhodes was celebrated for its many statues, among them the great brazen statue of Apollo, called the Colossus of Rhodes, which was one of the wonders of the world. It was 105 feet high, and hollow, with a staircase inside by which people could ascend to the head. This statue was erected to commemorate a victory over the Macedonians, and it was completed about 280 B.C. After standing fifty-six years it was thrown down by an earthquake, and it lay on the ground for nine centuries. Finally, it was broken up and sold for old metal, and it is said that the man who bought it loaded 900 camels with it. Rhodes was captured by the knights of St. John, or HOSPITALLERS, in 1309, and it belonged to them for more than 200 years. In 1522 they were attacked by an immense army of Turks, and after a long and heroic defence, were compelled to surrender.

RHÔNE (*rone*), a river of Europe, rising in the Alps of S. Switzerland, and flowing through Switzerland, and France to the Mediterranean Sea; length about 600 miles. Its sources are on Mt. Saint Gothard, partly from the lower end of the great Rhône glacier, more than a mile above the sea, and not far from the sources of the Rhine. In France it passes through a very rich and beautiful country, with many vineyards and several large cities on the banks. Before entering the Mediterranean it divides into two branches called the great and small Rhône.

RICHARD I., called Cœur de Lion (Lion Heart), second Plantagenet king of England, born in Oxford, Sept. 13, 1157. He was the son of Henry II., whom he succeeded in 1189. He was a very brave man, and had great strength, and delighted in nothing so much as in battle and slaughter. Before he came to the throne, he had joined his brothers in a rebellion against their father, but on his father's death he grieved bitterly for his undutiful conduct. Little of his ten years' reign was spent in England. Almost the first thing that he did was to join Philip II. of France in the third CRUSADE to the Holy Land. Richard did so many mighty deeds there that all Europe rang with his fame. He was the terror of the Saracens—so much so, that for years they would say to their horses, if they seemed afraid of any thing, "What, dost think that King Richard is in the bush?"

But the Crusaders did very little good, for the different princes quarreled so that they could not act together. Richard offended Leopold Duke of Austria, by tearing down a banner which he had planted on the walls of Acre, one of the Saracen towns that the Christians had taken, and putting up his own in its place. As Richard was on his way home he was shipwrecked near Trieste. He could not get home without going through the lands of his enemy, the Duke of Austria, so he put on a pilgrim's dress and hoped that no one would know him. But he forgot to take from his finger a costly ring that he wore, and that betrayed him. He fell into the hands of Leopold, who sold him to Henry VI., the German emperor. And so this great king, who had filled the world with his fame, was thrown into a dungeon and loaded with irons. It was a long time before his subjects in England knew what had become of him, for the place of his imprisonment was carefully hidden. At length a faithful squire, the minstrel Blondel,

who had wandered all through Germany looking for him, stopped beside a castle and began to play on his harp a tune which he knew that Richard was fond of. At once there came from an upper window, accompanying him, a voice which he knew to be the king's; and thus his prison was discovered. The faithful English gave freely of their silver to pay the heavy ransom required by Henry. The latter part of Richard's life was spent in France, warring against Philip Augustus. He died while besieging a castle in Normandy when forty-one years old (April 6, 1199), and was succeeded by his brother John, who had governed England during his absence.

RICHARD II., eighth Plantagenet king of England, born in Bordeaux in 1366. He was the son of Edward the Black Prince, and succeeded his grandfather Edward III. when he was eleven years old (1377). To support the wars which Edward III. had been carrying on in France, the people were burdened with heavy taxes, and from this arose a rebellion known as "Wat Tyler's Rebellion" from the rebel leader's name. In a battle between the rebels and the royal forces Wat Tyler was killed. The king, seeing the rebels in dismay, rode into their ranks, saying, "Be not distressed for the loss of your leader: I myself will lead you." This speech at once disarmed the rebels, and they returned to their homes, the king having promised to look into their complaints. Had Richard always acted with such prudence he might have been saved some of the troubles of his reign. Having banished his cousin, Henry Bolingbroke, and seized his estates, he went on a visit to Ireland. The exiled duke came to England, where he found a large party opposed to Richard, put himself at their head and made himself king. Richard, on his return, was seized and imprisoned in Pontefract Castle, where it is supposed he was murdered. He died, when thirty-four years old (February, 1400), and was succeeded by Henry IV.

RICHARD III., fourteenth and last of the Plantagenet kings of England, born at Fotheringay Castle, Oct. 2, 1452. He was the son of Richard Duke of York, and succeeded to the throne (1483) on the death of his nephew Edward V. He was Duke of Gloucester before becoming king of England, and was sometimes called "Crook-back," because one of his shoulders was higher than the other. During the wars of the Roses he fought bravely in the cause of his brother Edward IV., who rewarded him by many high offices, and on his death made him guardian of his young sons, one of whom was Edward, heir to the throne. Richard thought he would rather be king than uncle to a king; so having got Edward and his brother away from their mother, he put them in the Tower, where they are supposed to have been smothered, and had himself proclaimed king. The people did not like Richard, and Henry Duke of Richmond, heir to the Lancastrian claims, came to England to drive out the usurper. The battle of BOSWORTH was fought, and there Richard lost throne and life, his rival being crowned on the battlefield. He died when thirty-two years old (Aug. 22, 1485), and was succeeded by his rival Henry Tudor, as Henry VII.

RICH'ARDS, William T., an American painter, born in Philadelphia in 1833. His landscapes and sea views are noted for the care and truth to nature with which the foregrounds are painted. His studio is at Germantown, Pa.

RICH'ARDSON, Samuel, an English writer of novels, born in Derbyshire in 1689. During most of his life he was a printer, his first novel ("Pamela") having been written when he was more than fifty years old. He wrote also "Clarissa Har-lowe," and "Sir Charles Grandison," books which were much liked in their time, though now thought very tedious. Richardson's novels taught a pure morality, which was refreshing after the corrupt books that had been in fashion up to his time. He died in London when seventy-two years old (July 4, 1761).

RICHELIEU (*reesh-le-uh'*), **Armand Jean Duplessis,** Cardinal and Duke de, a French statesman, born in Paris, Sept. 5, 1585. He was educated for the army, but his elder

Richelieu.

brother having resigned the bishopric of Luçon, he took orders so that he might get that place. In 1616 he became Secretary of State to Louis XIII., in which office he soon became the most powerful man in Europe. The king did not like him, but he let him have his way because he had not the energy to oppose him. Three objects directed all his actions: to make the crown independent of the nobles, to put down the Huguenots, and to humble the power of the House of Austria; all of which he brought about in a way that proved him a master mind not only in his own but in any age. It was through his means that foreign powers took part in the THIRTY YEARS' WAR, which ended so badly for Austria and made France the first nation in Europe. When Peter the Great visited France, years after his death, he said, while standing beside his tomb, "How gladly would I give this great man half of my dominions if I could learn from him how to rule the other half." During the French Revolution the remains of Richelieu were dug up and scattered in every direction by the angry crowd. Richelieu was fond of splendor. He founded the Jardin des Plantes (Garden of Plants), and the College of the Sorbonne and built the Palais Royal. Many scholars, poets, and artists were aided by him. He died in Paris when fifty-seven years old (Dec. 4, 1642). Bulwer wrote a fine tragedy about Richelieu.

RICH'MOND, the capital and principal city of Virginia, on the James River; pop. 81,000, or a little larger than New Haven, Conn. The river there forms a fall, which furnishes the water-power for many great flouring-mills and machine-shops. Much of the flour made there is sent to Brazil, and it is said to be especially good for this purpose, because it does not spoil in a hot climate. Richmond also has a very large trade in tobacco, more being sent from there than from any other city in the United States. Vessels ascend the James almost to the city, and a canal has been made around the falls, beyond which the river can be navigated for 200 miles farther. About half the people of Richmond are negroes.

Richmond was founded in 1737 and became the State capital in 1779. In May, 1861, it was made the capital of the Southern Confederacy. The first Union army which marched to take it advanced from the northern side and was defeated at BULL RUN (1861). In the next spring, General McClellan collected a great army at Fortress Monroe and marched toward Richmond from the southeastern side, on the peninsula between the James and York rivers. He reached a point within four or five miles of the city, but after fighting many bloody battles near the CHICKAHOMINY River, he gave up the attempt to capture it. For the next two years no large army was sent against Richmond, and only a few thousand Confederate soldiers were kept there; but very strong forts were made around the city. Several times parties of Union cavalry attempted to pass them and free the Union prisoners in Richmond. One of these parties under General Kilpatrick reached a place within four miles of the city. At length (1864) General Grant and his army drove General Lee back from Northern Virginia, and the Unionists again approached Richmond. But the forts around the city were then too strong to be taken; so General Grant besieged PETERSBURG, hoping to take the railroads which meet there, by which the Confederates brought provisions into Richmond. Petersburg was taken after a siege of ten months, and General Lee being defeated at Five Forks, the Confederates abandoned Richmond (April 2, 1865). As they left they set fire to several large tobacco warehouses, and the flames spread until a third of the city was burned. The Union army entered on April 3.

RICHTER (*rikh'ter*), **Johann Paul Friedrich,** a famous German author, commonly called Jean Paul, born at Wunsiedel, Bavaria, March 21, 1763. He studied at Leipsic for four years, but being very poor had to leave and teach in private families. In the mean time he wrote much, and he soon became noted as an author and known everywhere. In 1804 he went to Bai-reuth, where he spent the rest of his life. The King of Bavaria gave him a pension of a thousand florins, and his writings became the fashion in Germany. All the women petted him and many fell in love with him; and it is said that the most distinguished ladies in Berlin used to send their footmen when he had his poodle trimmed to get a lock of its hair. His works best known to English readers are " Titan," " Flower, Fruit, and Thorn Pieces," and " Hesperus." He wrote in all sixty-four volumes. In the later part of his life he became blind. He died in Baireuth when sixty-two years old (Nov. 14, 1825).

RIENZI (*re-en'ze*), **Nicola Gabrini**, commonly called " the last of the Roman tribunes," born in Rome about 1312. He was well educated, and was a fine orator. At that time the pope lived in Avignon, and Rome was almost without any government, the citizens being robbed and ill-treated by nobles who lived in fortified houses. But at last the people made an attempt to free themselves, and chose Rienzi to be their tribune (1347). He did well for a while, but soon became elated by success, causing himself to be crowned with seven crowns, and living in great splendor and extravagance. In a few months his people became tired of him, and he was obliged to escape from the city in the dress of a monk. He was afterward recalled to Rome, and was assassinated when forty-two years old (Oct. 8, 1354), while making a speech to the people. His body was stabbed in more than a hundred places, and his head cut off.

RIGA (*re'gah*), a city of Russia, on the River Düna, 8 miles from the Gulf of Riga; pop. 175,000, or not quite as large as Newark, N. J. It has many large woolen and cotton mills, and carries on the largest trade of any city in Russia next

after SAINT PETERSBURG and ODESSA. Flax, grain, timber, hemp, and tobacco are sent to other countries. Many ships are built there.

Riga was first called Ria-lin, which means " fortress of the Rugii," a people who used to live there. The present city was begun in 1201.

RIMINI (*re'me-ne*), a city of Italy, on the Adriatic Sea, W. of Florence; pop. 37,000, or nearly as large as San Antonio, Tex. It is a very old town and contains many celebrated antiquities, especially a bridge of fine white marble, built by AUGUSTUS and TIBERIUS. The famous river Rubicon, which CÆSAR crossed when he marched against Rome, flows into the Adriatic a little north of Rimini.

Rimini was called Ariminum in ancient times, and this has become changed in time to its present name.

RIO DE JANEIRO (*re'o da zhah-na'ro*), in English commonly called Rio simply, the capital of Brazil and the largest city in South America; pop. about 500,000, or about twice as large as Buffalo, N. Y. It is built on a plain along the Bay of Rio de Janeiro, which is one of the safest and most beautiful harbors in the world. The entrance, which is less than a mile wide, is between high steep hills, defended by strong forts. From the sea the city looks very handsome, with its houses painted with bright colors peeping out from among the green trees; but when one goes ashore it is not quite so fine. Many of the streets are so narrow that wagons and carts cannot be used, their places being taken by negro porters who carry things on their heads. Still, as the emperor lives there, much is being done to improve the city, and some of the new parts are quite handsome. The climate of Rio is not healthful, but the place is so important that it is growing fast. It has a very large trade, especially in coffee, much of which is sent to the United States.

Rio de Janeiro means "River of January." The name was first given to the bay by a Spanish captain, who, sailing into it on January 1, 1515, thought it was the mouth of a river.

RIO GRANDE DEL NORTE (*re'o grahn'da dale nor'ta*), a river of North America, rising in Colorado and flowing S.E. through New Mexico and between Mexico and Texas, to the Gulf of Mexico; length 1800 miles. Small steamboats can ascend it about 450 miles, but the upper part has many rapids and falls. Most of the country through which the Rio Grande flows is dry and unfit for cultivation.

Rio Grande Del Norte means Great River of the North, a name given by the Mexicans because it lies to the north of their country. It is also called Rio Bravo del Norte (Wild River of the North), or simply Rio Grande (Great River).

RISTORI (*ris-to're*), **Adelaide**, a famous Italian actress, born in 1821. Her parents were poor actors and she was trained for the stage, playing first in comedy. In 1847 she married the Marquis del Grillo, and afterward became celebrated for her splendid acting in tragedies, her most famous characters being Medea, Lady Macbeth, Deborah, Judith, Mary Stuart, and Queen Elizabeth. In 1867, 1875, and 1885 she came to the United States and acted with great success.

RIT'TER, Carl, a noted German geographer, born at Quedlinburg, Aug. 7, 1779. He studied at Halle University, and afterward became a teacher and finally professor of geography in the University of Berlin. He was the first writer on what is called comparative geography, and his books became famous, most of them being translated from German into other languages. Among them are "Com-

parative Geography," "Comparative Geography of Palestine and the Sinaitic Peninsula," and "Universal Geography." Ritter died in Berlin when eighty years old (Sept. 28, 1859).

ROB'ERT-SON, William, a Scottish historian, born near Edinburgh, Sept. 19, 1721. He was a distinguished minister, and at one time principal of the University of Edinburgh. In 1764 he was chosen official historian of Scotland. His chief works are a "History of Scotland during the reigns of Mary and James VI.," "History of the Reign of the Emperor Charles V.," and "History of America." All of these are still read with interest. Mr. Robertson died near Edinburgh when nearly seventy-one years old (June 11, 1793).

ROBESPIERRE (*ro-bes-pe-air'*), **Maximilien Joseph François Isidore,**

Robespierre.

a French revolutionist, born at Arras, May 6, 1758. He was brought up in great poverty by his grandfather, as his father deserted him and his mother died early. At school he showed so much talent that his bishop sent him to college in Paris. He afterwards studied law, and practiced it at Arras. When the troubles began which led to the French Revolution, he soon became known as a speaker and writer on the side of the people, and rose rapidly to almost the highest power. He, with DANTON and MARAT, ruled France during the "Reign of Terror."

Robespierre seems not to have been a cruel man by nature, but only cold and narrow-minded, and unable to see any way of putting down what he thought wrong but that of killing all who did not agree with him. Thus, the next year (1794) after the execution of LOUIS XVI., he caused his friend Danton to be put to death. The killing went on for several months more, but at last the people got tired of it, and there was a general cry of "Down with the tyrant!" Robespierre raged and tried to speak, but there was such a noise that he could not be heard, and he was arrested and guillotined the next day when thirty-six years old (July 28, 1794).

ROB'IN HOOD. See HOOD, ROBIN.

ROB ROY, a noted Scottish outlaw, born about 1660. His real name was Robert Macgregor, but he is best known as Rob Roy (Red Robert). He was deprived of his lands because he had joined the Pretender, James STUART, and in revenge he annoyed his enemies for many years by sudden attacks on them and by bold robberies. His adventures have been made famous by Sir Walter Scott in his novel "Rob Roy." He died about 1738.

ROCHAMBEAU (*ro-sham-bo'*), **Jean Baptiste Donatien de Vimeur,** Count de, a French soldier, born in Vendôme, July 1, 1725. He entered the army in 1742, and became a general in 1756. In 1780 he was sent to command the French troops in America, where he remained helping Washington until peace was declared (1783), when he returned to France. In 1793, while Robespierre was in power, he was arrested, tried, and sentenced to death; but his execution was put off because there was not room for him on the cart in which prisoners rode

to the place of execution, and the death of Robespierre set him free before his turn came again. He died when nearly eighty-two years old (May 10, 1807).

ROCH'DALE, a city of England, on the river Roch, 10 miles N.N.E. of Manchester; pop. 69,000, or about as large as Cambridge, Mass. It is noted for its great manufactures of woolen and cotton goods, and for its brass and iron foundries and machine-shops. Coal and iron are mined, and slate and flag stones are quarried near it. John BRIGHT was a large manufacturer there.

ROCHEFOUCAULD (*rosh-foo-ko'*). See LA ROCHEFOUCAULD.

ROCHELLE, LA (*lah ro-shel'*), a town of W. France on the Bay of Biscay; pop. 22,000, or about as large as Cohoes, N. Y. It is surrounded by walls, and contains a cathedral and many other fine buildings, with some of the most beautiful squares and promenades in France. The town contains manufactories of cotton cloth, glass, and pottery, and many ships are built there.

La Rochelle ("The Little Rock") is many hundred years old. In 1557 the Huguenots or French Protestants got possession of it and kept it for seventy-two years. They were twice besieged, and the last time a wall was built by RICHELIEU across the mouth of the harbor to close it. Parts of this can still be seen at low tide.

ROCH'ES-TER, a city of W. New York, on the Genesee River, seven miles from its mouth in Lake Ontario; pop. 134,000, or about as large as St. Paul, Minn. The river has four high falls within the city, which furnish water-power for many large mills and manufactories. Among the most important things made there are flour, clothing, boots and shoes, beer, locomotives, steam-engines and tools. The city is also noted for its many large nurseries and gardens, from which plants and garden seeds are sent to all parts of the United States. Rochester University, which has its seat there, has one of the finest geological cabinets in the United States. The streets of Rochester are wide and handsome, with many fine buildings. Nearly all the houses are surrounded by yards and gardens. Rochester was first settled in 1810, and was laid out in 1812 by Nathaniel Rochester, after whom it was named.

ROCK'FORD, a city of N.W. Illinois, on the Rockford River; pop. 24,000, or a little larger than Newburg, N. Y. It has a large watch factory, several flour and paper mills, and manufactories of mowers and reapers, plows, tacks, sacks, cotton and woolen cloths, and many other things. The surrounding region is a rich farming country, and Rockford carries on a large trade in farm produce. Rockford was founded in 1836 and became a city in 1852.

ROCK ISLAND, a city of W. Illinois, on the Mississippi River; pop. 14,000, or about as large as Pottsville, Pa. The city gets its name from an island in the river, belonging to the United States, on which there is a United States arsenal and armory, with many work-shops and magazines. The arsenal is the largest in the country. During the Civil War many Confederate prisoners were kept on this island. Rock Island is connected with Davenport, Iowa, on the other side of the Mississippi, by a great two-story iron bridge with a road for carriages below and for railway trains above.

ROCKY MOUNTAINS. See AMERICA.

ROD'ER-IC, the last king of the Visigoths in Spain, reigned from 709 to 711. He became king by driving Witiza from the throne; but Witiza's sons and brother se-cretly asked the Arabs to come over from Africa and help them to regain their rights. The Arabs first captured Ceuta and then marched against Roderic. He had collected a much larger army than theirs, but part of his army was commanded by Witiza's sons, and at the great battle of Jeres de la Frontera they betrayed Roderic and he was killed (711).

ROD'NEY, George Brydges, Baron, an English admiral, born Feb. 19, 1718. He entered the navy when twenty years old, and became rear-admiral in 1759 and vice-admiral in 1762. In 1764 he was made a baronet, and in 1768 was chosen a member of Parliament. In 1779 he was appointed commander-in-chief in the West Indies. He sailed for Barbadoes with a large fleet, met a Spanish fleet off Cape St. Vincent, and defeated it after a bloody battle, capturing or destroying seven vessels (Jan. 1780). Not long after he met a large French fleet near Martinique, and though his captains refused to fight it at close quarters, he escaped with his ships when the French tried to capture him. In the war between England and Holland, Admiral Rodney captured several Dutch islands in the West Indies. In 1781 he was again sent to the West Indies, where he gained a great victory over a French fleet commanded by De Grasse. The battle lasted all day and many French ships were captured (April 12, 1782). For this victory Rodney was made a baron, and was given a large pension. He died in London when seventy-four years old (May 21, 1792).

ROGER (*roj'er*) **I.,** Count of Sicily, born in Normandy in 1031. He was the son of Tancred de Hauteville, lord of a small village in Normandy. He fought under his brother Robert, who conquered Lower Italy and afterwards passed over into Sicily, which was at that time held partly by Greeks and partly by Saracens. With the help of Robert, Roger took Palermo, the principal city on the island, driving the Saracens among the hills. In this way he became the founder of the kingdom of Naples. Roger died in Calabria when seventy years old (1101), and was succeeded by his son Roger II.

ROGER II., first king of Sicily, born in Calabria about 1095. He was the son of Roger I., and succeeded him in 1101, under the guardianship of his mother. On the death of his cousin, the son of Robert Guiscard, he seized all the Norman possessions in Southern Italy. After taking Naples he made it the capital of his provinces, to which he gave the name of Kingdom of the Two Sicilies. He died when fifty-nine years old (Feb. 26, 1154).

ROGERS (*roj'erz*) **John,** an English clergyman, born about 1500. He was educated at Cambridge University, and becoming a minister was made chaplain of the English colony at Antwerp in Holland. When King Edward VI. came to the throne Rogers went back to England and became a minister in London. After Queen Mary ascended the throne, he preached a sermon in which he told the people to stand by the doctrines taught in King Edward's time, and to resist the forms of the Catholic Church. For this and some books which he had written he was tried and condemned for heresy, and burned at Smithfield when about fifty-five years old (Feb. 4, 1555).

ROGERS, John, an American sculptor, born in Salem, Mass., Oct. 30, 1829. He was first a merchant's clerk, and then a machinist; but he afterward studied art, and he has become famous for his groups of small figures of scenes in the Civil War and in common life. Among his best known works are those illustrating the story of Rip Van Winkle.

ROGERS, Samuel, an English author, born at Newington Green, near London, July 30, 1763. He was a rich banker with a taste for poetry, but with no real genius. He published several volumes of poems, the best known of which is "The Pleasures of Memory," and was widely known, himself, as a warm-hearted and generous man, very agreeable in society, and very kind to young authors and those who were poor and unfortunate. He had a beautiful house in London filled with fine pictures and books, and many other works of art, and it became a gathering-place for all the famous English authors. He died there when ninety-two years old (Dec. 18, 1855).

RO'LAND, called by the Italians Orlando, a knight of the court of Charlemagne, and a famous hero of romance. It is not certain whether this was a real or an imaginary person. The story is that he was a nephew of Charlemagne, and that he fell at the pass of RONCESVAL-LES (778). Many poems and novels have been written in his praise.

ROLAND DE LA PLATIÈRE (*ro-lon' deh lah plah-te-air'*), **Jean Marie,** and **Manon,** a husband and wife, noted French revolutionists. M. Roland was born Feb. 18, 1734. His beautiful and gifted wife was twenty years younger, having been born March 17, 1754. He was appointed to represent the city of Lyons in the famous National Convention in the beginning of the French Revolution. His wife went with him to Paris, where she soon became the centre of a circle comprising among its members those most noted for wit or culture. The Rolands were Girondists, that is, they were republicans; but they looked with horror upon the bloody deeds of the worst members of that party, and they tried to lull the storm which they had helped to arouse. This caused them to be hated by the violent republicans, and among those who fell by the guillotine, Madame Roland was one of the most illustrious. She refused to leave Paris with her husband, although she was warned of her danger, and she was arrested and sentenced to execution. Her last act as she stood on the scaffold was to bow before the statue of Liberty and to say, "O Liberty! what crimes are committed in thy name." She died when thirty-seven years old, Nov. 9, 1793. A week after her execution (Nov. 15), M. Roland's body was found pierced through with a sword cane. A paper taken from his pocket concluded, "When I heard that my wife had been massacred, I would not stay any longer in a world stained with crimes."

ROL′LIN (French *ro-lan′*), **Charles,** a French historian, born in Paris, Jan. 30, 1661. He was a college professor, and afterward rector of the Paris University. He wrote several historical works, some of which have been translated into English. His "Ancient History" was very popular in its day, especially among young folks. Rollin died in Paris when eighty years old (Sept. 14, 1741).

ROL′LO. See NORTHMEN.

RO′MAN-OFF, House of, the name of the imperial family of Russia. Michael, the first and best czar of the family, was raised to the throne in 1612, and died in 1645. He was the grandfather of PETER THE GREAT. The male line died out in 1740, the present family being descended from Anna, a daughter of Peter the Great.

ROME, a city, capital of the kingdom of Italy and formerly of the Roman Empire, on the river Tiber; pop. 415,000, or about twice as large as Detroit, Mich. Its exact age is not known, though the ancient Romans believed that it was founded by ROMULUS (about 753 B.C.), said to have been descended from ÆNEAS. The first town was built on the Palatine Hill. Soon after the SABINES built another town on the Capitoline Hill, which in time was united with the first so that the two became one city; and finally the city grew until it covered five other hills, called the Aventine, the Cœlian, the Esquiline, the Viminal, and the Quirinal hills. Rome was at first ruled by kings, who had hardly any possessions outside of the city, but they gradually conquered neighboring cities until they governed a large state. The kings became very tyrannical, and TARQUIN the Proud, the last of them, was driven from his throne (about 510 B.C.).

The Romans then formed a republic, ruled by a senate and by two magistrates called prætors or consuls, who were chosen for one year. The people were divided into two classes or parties, called patricians or nobles, made up of the original Roman people, and plebeians or common people. As each of these wanted to rule, the division led to many quarrels. On this account the republic was not at first very powerful, and its enemies often defeated it. About 390 B.C. Rome was taken by the Gauls under BRENNUS, but they soon abandoned it.

The Romans, becoming more powerful, soon conquered the whole of Italy (about 282 B.C.), and as the conquered nations were well treated, they made them their friends and their allies in war. At length the Romans began to have wars with nations outside of Italy. Among the first were three wars with CARTHAGE, called the three Punic Wars. In the second of these HANNIBAL invaded Italy (218 B.C.), and in the third Carthage itself was taken and destroyed. Part of Northern Africa and Spain were thus added to the Roman dominions. The Romans were equally successful in other wars in Macedonia, Greece, Syria, Mesopotamia, Gaul, Britain, and Egypt, so that they finally conquered nearly all

Circus Maximus, as it was in the Time of the Emperors ; Palace of the Cæsars on the Palatine Hill on the left ; the Aventine Hill on the right.

countries then known.   About A.D. 115 their dominions attained their greatest extent, embracing all the countries that border on the Mediterranean Sea, as well as Britain and part of Western Asia, and having 120,000,000 inhabitants.   Rome was then the richest and most refined city in the world.

Meanwhile the government had been changed to an empire by Julius CÆSAR and his nephew AUGUSTUS, the latter being the first emperor (27 B.C.).   Most of the emperors were selfish tyrants, though a few were good rulers.   In A.D. 284 Diocletian divided the power with Maximian, each taking the title of Augustus, and the two ruling together.   Rome was given up as the capital, Diocletian living at Nicomedia and Maximian at Milan. Under them were two vice-emperors, called Cæsars, one of whom commonly lived in Gaul or Britain, and the other in the eastern provinces.   At last, after some civil wars the whole empire was joined together again under CONSTANTINE THE GREAT (323), who made his capital at Byzantium, afterward named Constantinople.   The last

The Capitol as it was in the time of the Emperors (page 702).

emperor who ruled the whole empire was THEODOSIUS, who on his death divided it among his two sons, giving the west to Honorius and the east to Arcadius; and thus the Roman Empire was split into two parts, the WESTERN EMPIRE and the EASTERN EMPIRE.

The Romans meanwhile had become luxurious and effeminate, and instead of fighting their own battles they hired armies from the nations they had conquered.   In time the soldiers, being more powerful than the people, became the real rulers, choosing emperors to suit themselves.   This led to many civil wars, by which the empire was weakened. At length the Goths, a brave but barbarous people of Northern Europe, invaded Italy and under their leader ALARIC took and sacked the city of Rome (A.D. 410), and soon after the Western Empire was broken up into many countries, most of which were ruled by Gothic kings. From these kingdoms the modern nations of Europe have grown.   In France, Spain, Portugal, and Italy, the languages now spoken resemble the Latin or Roman; while in Germany and Austria, where the Romans had few settlements, the German or modern Gothic is still used.

In the early times and under the first emperors the Romans were pagans, but when the apostles began to preach many became Christians. At first the Christians were persecuted, but the new belief continued to spread until it was made the religion of the empire by Constantine (A.D. 323). In time most of the bishops acknowledged the bishop of Rome as their chief, and he received the title of pope. Thus was founded the Roman Catholic Church. The popes were the chief rulers of Rome and the country around it until 1870, when the city was taken by Victor Emanuel, and became the capital of Italy.

In the time of the emperors Rome was adorned with beautiful buildings, and the Capitoline Hill was

Ruins of the Colosseum.

almost covered with temples and palaces. Among these was the splendid temple of Jupiter Capitolinus, called the Capitol, shown in the picture as it was when in its glory. The emperors themselves lived in a magnificent palace which covered many acres of ground. The Colosseum, an immense oval building, was used for games and gladiatorial shows, and many Christian martyrs were put to death there. It would hold 80,000 spectators, but the great Circus Maximus was still larger, having seats for 500,000 people. The walls of the Colosseum are still standing, but the Circus Maximus has been long destroyed. The Forum was a great open square where courts of justice were held, and where the people gathered on great occasions. It was adorned with

THE GREAT ARENA OF ROME—A Scene in the Time of the Emperors.

splendid triumphal arches and tall columns commemorating Roman victories, and with magnificent temples and other buildings. The arches of Titus and Constantine and the columns of Trajan and Antoninus can still be seen, each of the latter being more than 120 feet high. Most of the temples and palaces of Rome have disappeared or only remain as ruins. The best preserved of all is the Pantheon or Temple of all the Gods, which is now a church, and one of the most beautiful buildings in the world. The splendid mausoleum of Hadrian, built by that emperor for his tomb, is now the castle of Sant' Angelo. Rome has many fine modern buildings, including about 360 churches, and many palaces. St. Peter's, completed in 1626, is the finest and largest church in the world, its great dome being 148 feet wide, and the cross on its top 430 feet above the ground, or a third higher than the steeple of Trinity Church in New York. This and the other churches are adorned with hundreds of paintings and statues by the old masters. The Vatican Palace contains a magnificent museum and art galleries, and a fine library. Rome is visited every year by thousands of travelers, and many artists go there to study in the art galleries. It became the capital of Italy in 1870.

ROME, a city of New York, on the Mohawk River; pop. 15,000, or about as large as Ogden, Utah. It has large locomotive and car works, two rolling mills, a knitting mill, and other manufactories. The streets are wide and shady, and there are several beautiful parks adorned with fountains.

During the war of the Revolution, Fort Stanwix stood on the site of Rome. Rome became a city in 1870.

ROM'U-LUS, in Roman legend, the founder of Rome. According to the story, Romulus and Remus were the twin sons of the god Mars and of Rhea Silvia, a daughter of Numitor, king of Alba Longa. Amulius, a younger brother of Numitor, seized upon his throne, and ordered the children to be thrown into the Tiber; but the river had overflowed its banks, and the basket in which they were was left on dry land, at the foot of the Palatine Hill. A she-wolf found them, carried them to her den, and suckled them, and a woodpecker brought them food. At last they were found by a herdsman of the king, named Faustulus, who brought them up with his own children. When they grew up and found out the secret of their birth, they killed Amulius and restored Numitor to his throne.

Romulus and Remus did not like to live at Alba, but loved the banks of the Tiber where they had been brought up; so they said they would build a city there. They left it to the gods to decide which should name it, and watched the heavens for a sign. At sunrise Remus saw six vultures, but soon after Romulus saw twelve; therefore most people gave their voices for Romulus, and he built his city on the Palatine Hill and named it after himself Rome (753 B.C.) Remus was made angry by this, and when he saw the ramparts which had been built around the place marked out for the city, he scornfully leaped over them, saying, "Shall such defences as this keep your city?" For this Celer, who had charge of the building, struck Remus with a spade and killed him, and Romulus then became sole ruler of Rome.

Romulus made his city a place of refuge, where all who committed any crime might flee for safety, and soon gathered many people around him. They got wives from the SABINES, and the Romans and Sabines became one people. The Sabines, with their king Tatius, settled on the Saturnian Hill, called also Capitoline, and on the Quirinal Hill, and the Romans dwelt on the Palatine Hill. After a while Tatius was killed in war, and Romulus then ruled both nations; and his own people were called Romans, from their city, and the Sabines were called Quirites, from Quirium, the name of their city.

After reigning for a long time, Romulus one day called all the people together in the Field of Mars; and when they had assembled a great storm arose and all became as dark as night. The people, frightened, ran to their homes, but after the storm Romulus was nowhere to be found. The people did not know at first what had become of him, but at night Romulus appeared in more than mortal beauty to one Proculus Julius, who was on the way from Alba to Rome, and said to him: "Go and tell my people that they weep not for me any more; but bid them be brave and warlike, and so shall they make my city the greatest in the earth." Then the people knew that Romulus had been taken to heaven by his father Mars, and become a god; so they built a temple to him and worshiped him under the name of Quirinus. Romulus was succeeded by NUMA POMPILIUS.

RONCESVALLES (*ron-sa-vahl'-les*), or **Roncesvaux,** a hamlet in N. Spain, at the entrance of a pass across the Pyrenees mountains, between France and Spain. When CHARLES THE GREAT was returning from an invasion of Spain, his army was attacked there by the mountaineers and his whole rearguard was destroyed (778). ROLAND, Bernardo del Carpio, and other heroes were killed in this battle. The Black Prince led his army through this same pass (1367), and the French under Marshal Soult were forced to retreat there by Wellington (1813). In 1833 Don Carlos was declared to be King of Spain at Roncesvalles.

RON'DOUT. See KINGSTON.

RON-SARD', Pierre de, a French poet, born near Vendôme, Sept. 11, 1524. He was brought up at the French court as a page. When he gave to the public his first poems, they were warmly received, and he became the poet laureate, or court poet, of Charles IX. His reputation was great in his own time, kings rejoicing to do him honor. The great Italian poet Tasso came to Paris to show him the first part of his celebrated poem, "Jerusalem Delivered." Ronsard died near Tours when sixty-one years old (Dec. 27, 1585).

ROSA (*ro'sah*), **Salvator,** an Italian painter, born near Naples, June 20, 1615. When a young man he often spent weeks among the mountains and forests of Southern Italy, even living with robbers to obtain novel subjects for his sketches. Afterward he went to Rome and Florence, where he painted many fine pictures. The best known are landscapes, but he also made some celebrated historical paintings. He died in Rome when nearly fifty-eight years old (March 15, 1673).

ROSCIUS (*rosh'e-us*), **Quintus,** a famous Roman comic actor, born at Salonium. He taught Cicero the art of speaking, and in later life that great orator used to make trials of skill with his teacher. Once when Roscius was sued Cicero made in his favor an eloquent speech, which is still preserved. Roscius got such perfection in acting that in his time when any one excelled in anything he was called a Roscius. He made a large fortune on the stage, and was very rich when he died (62 B.C.).

ROSCOE, William, an English historian, born near Liverpool, March 8, 1753. In 1774 he became a lawyer in Liverpool, and was noted for his opposition to slavery, about which he wrote several books and pamphlets. His principal histories are "The Life of Lorenzo de' Medici" and "Life of Pope Leo X." Mr. Roscoe died in Liverpool when seventy-eight years old (June 27, 1831). Three of his sons, Robert, Thomas, and Henry Roscoe, were well-known authors, and his grandson Henry Enfield Roscoe is a distinguished chemist, and the author of several books on chemistry.

ROSE'CRANS, William Starke, an American general, born at Kingston, Ohio, Sept. 6, 1819. He was educated at West Point, and was an assistant professor there from 1844 to 1847. Afterward he became a civil engineer and architect at Cincinnati, but when the Civil War broke out he again entered the army, and in March, 1862, became a major-general. He commanded in Western Virginia, and afterward near the Mississippi, where he won the battle of Iuka (Sept. 19, 1862). Being made commander of the army of the Cumberland in Tennessee, he fought the battle of Murfreesborough or Stone River, which was one of the bloodiest of the war. It lasted from Dec. 26, 1862, to Jan. 2, 1863, but the severest fighting was on Dec. 31 and Jan. 2. Gen. Bragg, who commanded the Confederates, was at length obliged to retreat, and Gen. Rosecrans captured Murfreesborough on Jan. 5. Later in the year he took Chattanooga, but was defeated by Bragg at the battle of Chickamauga (Sept. 19 and 20, 1863), and soon after his command was taken from him. He was minister to Mexico in 1868 and 1869, and later registrar of the Treasury.

ROSETTA (*ro-zet'tah*), a town of Lower Egypt, on the west branch or outlet of the river Nile; 36 miles from Alexandria; pop. 17,000, or about as large as Danbury, Conn. It is one of the finest towns in Egypt. In 1799, while a French engineer was making an earthwork fort at Rosetta, he dug up a slab containing an inscription in two kinds of Egyptian hieroglyphics and the same translated into Greek. This slab was soon after captured by the English and sent to the British Museum. By carefully comparing the Greek inscriptions with the hieroglyphics, Champollion found out how to read the hieroglyphic writing, over which learned men had before vainly puzzled.

ROSS, Sir John, a British Arctic explorer, born in Scotland, June 24, 1777. He entered the navy when only eleven years old, and in 1812 became a captain. In 1818 he went with PARRY, each having command of a ship, to try to find a northwest passage around North America. In 1829 he was again sent to the Arctic regions in a steamer, and discovered the magnetic pole, to which the needle of the mariner's compass points. His ship was frozen up in the ice for four years, and he and his crew were at last rescued by a whaling ship after they had suffered terrible hardships and had been given up for dead. On his return (1834) Captain Ross was made a knight. In 1850 he went to the Arctic regions in a small vessel to search for the lost ships of Sir John Franklin, but he returned the next year without finding them. He published accounts of his voyages, and for his services he was made rear-admiral in 1851. He died in London, when eighty years old (Aug. 30, 1856).

Sir James Clark Ross, his nephew, born in London, April 15, 1800, went with his uncle on his first two Arctic voyages. In 1839 he commanded the Erebus, sent with another vessel to explore the Antarctic Ocean, and discovered the Antarctic Continent, already found in another place by WILKES. He called it Victoria Land, and a high volcano which he saw, was named Mt. Erebus after his ship. He wrote an account of this voyage, and for his services was knighted in 1844. He died at Aylesbury, England, when nearly sixty-two years old (April 3, 1862).

ROSSE, William Parsons, Earl of, an English astronomer, born in York, June 17, 1800. In 1826 he built near his castle at Parsonstown, in Ireland, a very large and fine observatory, and had made for it the largest reflecting telescope in the world. It was more than fifty feet long, and six feet across. This magnificent instrument was finished about 1844, and many new discoveries have been made with it. Lord Rosse was president of the British Association and of the Royal Society, and for six years he was chancellor of Trinity College, Dublin. He died at his castle when sixty-seven years old (Oct. 31, 1867).

ROSSETTI (*ros-set'te*), the name of an Italian family of two brothers, Dante Gabriel and William Michael, and two sisters, Christina Gabriella and Maria Francisca. Their father, Gabriel Rossetti, came from Naples to England in 1824. They are all celebrated in art and literature, but the most famous was the artist and poet Dante Gabriel, born in London in 1828. As an artist, he belonged to what is called the Pre-Raphaelite school, a way of painting which tries to represent nature just as it is, neither adding, omitting, nor changing anything. He is well known by his designs illustrating Tennyson's poems and other works. He published "The Early Italian Poets," and a volume of poems of his own. He died when fifty-four years old (April 9, 1882).

Christina Gabriella, born in 1830, has written "Goblin Market and other Poems," "Commonplace and other Short Stories in Prose," "Sing-Song, a Nursery Rhyme book," and other books.

ROSSINI (*ros-se'ne*), **Gioacchino,** an Italian writer of music, born in Pesaro, Feb. 29, 1792. His first opera was performed in Venice, when he was only eighteen years old, with some success, and three years afterwards he brought out his "Tancredi," which made him famous. His most celebrated work, "The Barber of Seville," a most charming comic opera, was first played in 1816, and his "William Tell" in 1828. When Rossini was thirty-one years old he went to Paris, where he was made director of the Italian opera, and afterward first composer to the grand opera. The "Stabat Mater," and the mass which was performed at his burial, were his only compositions during the last forty years of his life. He died in Paris, when seventy-six years old (Nov. 13, 1868).

ROS'TOCK, a town of N. Germany, on the river Warnow, 9 miles above its mouth in the Baltic Sea ; pop. 39,000, or about as large as Harrisburg, Pa. It contains a university founded in 1419, besides a school of navigation, and several other institutions. The town has a large trade, and is well fortified. It a very old place.

ROTHSCHILD (*ros'child*, German *rote'sheelt*), **Mayer Anselm,** a German banker, born in Frankfort in 1743. He was a Jew, and at first a poor clerk in Hanover. In time he became a banker in Frankfort, and was so honest and wise in his investments, that he gained the confidence of everybody. When Napoleon invaded Germany in 1806, the Elector William of Hesse Cassel was obliged to fly from the country, and he left $5,000,000 with Rothschild for safe keeping. The banker was allowed to use this money and gain what he could with it, and the Elector charged him no interest until he came back to his dominions in 1814. After that, he allowed Rothschild's sons to keep the money at a low rate of interest. It was repaid to the Elector's son in 1823, but meanwhile, Rothschild and his sons had gained an immense fortune by its use. Mayer Anselm died in Frankfort when sixty-nine years old (1812), but the sons continued the business, and became bankers in five cities—Anselm Rothschild in Frankfort, Solomon in Vienna, Nathan in London, Charles in Naples, and James in Paris. They always helped each other, and so increased their fortunes, and the firm is still kept up by members of their families in all these cities excepting Naples. All of them were made barons by the Emperor Francis of Austria. Lionel Nathan Rothschild, son of Nathan, was the first Jew who ever sat in the English Parliament.

ROT'TER-DAM, a city of the Netherlands, on the river Maas, 36 miles S.W. of Amsterdam; pop. 203,000, or nearly the size of Milwaukee, Wis. The city is famous for its canals, which are so deep that the largest ships can be loaded and unloaded in the middle of the town. Rotterdam has important cotton factories, sugar refineries, and brandy distilleries, and carries on a large trade with the East Indies, Europe, and America. Along the river is a fine quay which is bordered with elms planted nearly three hundred years ago.

Rotterdam gets its name from the little river Rotte which flows through the city and across which there is a large dam. The city is about 600 years old.

ROUBAIX (*roo-ba'*), a city of France, 6 miles N.E. of Lille; pop. 100,000, or not quite as large as Allegheny, Pa. It is famous for its manufactures, especially of silk, woolen, and cotton goods, called in trade "Roubaix articles." In 1800 Roubaix was only a small town, but it has grown very fast since 1850.

ROUEN (*roo-en'*, French *rwon*), a city of N. France on the river Seine; pop. 107,000, or a little larger than Denver, Col. Next to Lyons it is the greatest French manufacturing city, and it is especially noted for

its cotton factories, which are the most important in France. There are also manufactories of woolen cloth, lace, stockings, paper, and several ship-yards. Rouen has a fine library and museum and some of the most splendid Gothic churches in Europe. The cathedral of Notre Dame, which has a spire more than one and a half times as high as Trinity Church steeple, New York, has many beautiful painted windows and contains a statue of King RICHARD Cœur de Lion, whose heart was buried there. In one of the city squares, called the Square of La Pucelle (The Maid), is a statue of Joan of Arc, erected on the place where she was burned in 1431.

Under the Romans Rouen was called Rotomagus, and they made it the capital of a part of Gaul. Later it became the capital of Normandy, and was the scene of many important events in the wars between France and England.

ROUMANIA or **Rumania** (*roo-ma'-ne-ah*), a country of Europe, between Hungary and the Black Sea; area, 48,000 square miles, or about as large as New York State; pop. 5,376,-000, or about thirteen fourteenths that of New York; capital, BUCHAREST. The soil is rich, and most of the people are farmers or cattle breeders. The principal things raised are grain, tobacco, and wine. Roumania was formerly a part of Turkey in Asia, being divided into two principalities called Wallachia and Moldavia, but in 1861 these were united under the present name by the Sultan. In 1877, Roumania proclaimed its independence, and it was confirmed by the treaty of Berlin (July 13, 1878). It is ruled by a king, and a parliament of two houses like our congress.

ROUMELIA or **Rumelia** (*ru-me'le-ah*), the former name of the principal European province of Turkey, consisting of part of ancient Thrace and Macedonia. By the treaty of

Berlin (1878), a new half-independent state was formed out of it, called Eastern Roumelia; area 13,-500 square miles, or about as large as Maryland and Delaware together; pop. 750,000, or about seven-eighths that of Maryland. In 1885 Eastern Roumelia was annexed to Bulgaria, which is practically independent of Turkey. Its capital is Philippopolis (pop. 33,000). About one half the people are Mohammedans and the rest Christians of the Greek Church.

ROUSSEAU (*roos-so'*), **Jean Jacques,** a French author, born in Geneva, Switzerland, June 28, 1712. His family were Protestants who had taken refuge in Switzerland. His mother died in his infancy and he grew up neglected and fed his mind on wretched novels, that he found in the workshop of his father, a watchmaker. When he grew up he became tired of his native town, and, after wandering for some years, he at last went to Paris. Hearing that the academy at Dijon had offered a prize for the best answer to the question, "Has civilization tended to improve the morals?" he wrote an essay, which won the prize, in which he tried to prove that all the misery and crimes of mankind had been caused by civilization. After this he went on writing books which were eagerly read and admired by the young for the beauty of their style, but which did a great deal of harm by the ideas he put forth. Some of these were that all men are born equal; that to own property is a crime; that the soil belongs to no one; that monarchy means tyranny, and religion, superstition. These notions unsettled men's minds and helped to bring on the French Revolution. At last Rousseau was obliged to leave France. He went to England, where his behavior was so strange that people thought him crazy. Returning to Paris, he died there when sixty-six years old (July 2, 1778).

ROUSSEAU (*roos-so'*), **Philippe,** a French painter, born in Paris about 1808. He painted principally pictures in which animals are introduced in such a way as to recall the old fables in which these creatures play a part. He died when seventy-nine years old (December 4, 1887).

ROUSSEAU, Théodore, a French painter, born in Paris in 1812. He was a landscape painter of great merit. He died in 1867.

RUBENS (*roo'benz*), **Peter Paul,** a famous Flemish painter, born at Siegen, Germany, June 29, 1577.

Peter Paul Rubens.

He was so named because his birthday was the feast of Saints Peter and Paul. His father, who had been banished from Antwerp, died when his son was but eleven years old. His mother soon after returned there, where he first became page to a noble lady and afterward studied painting. When Rubens was about twenty-three years old he went to Italy, and the Duke of Mantua made him his court painter. He painted many fine pictures during his stay of eight years, and often made visits to Rome and Naples, to study the masters in art. When his mother died in 1608, he went back to his own country, and was made court painter there. Within a few years after this his master-pieces, "The Descent from the Cross" and "The Elevation of the Cross," were painted. In 1620 he was invited to France by Marie de' Medici, for whom he executed many great works. He was fond of having some one read history or poetry to him while he painted, and in this way he got a great deal of knowledge. It is said that he could read and speak seven lan-guages, and that the ancient and modern writers were alike familiar to him.

Rubens had many pupils, and also did a great deal of work. He painted history, Bible subjects, portraits, landscapes, animals, and almost everything that a painter can do. His pictures of children

Count Rudolph and the Priest (page 711).

are very charming. It is said that he finished about eighteen hundred works, but that his pupils did much of the actual labor on many of them. His gorgeous coloring has always been greatly admired and praised. There are twelve hundred engravings of his works.

Rubens was also a collector of beautiful things, and after his death a part of his collection was sold for more than one hundred thousand dollars. He died at the age of sixty-three (May 30, 1640) at Antwerp, and was buried under the altar in his private chapel, the Church of St. James, which is decorated with a magnificent work of his, and where he has a monu-ment.

RU'BI-CON. See CÆSAR, JULIUS.

RUDOLPH (*ru'dolf*) **I.,** called Rudolph of Hapsburg, Emperor of Germany, born May 1, 1218. He was the son of Count Albert IV. of Hapsburg, and the founder of the imperial house of Hapsburg, having been elected Emperor of Germany after the Hohenstaufen family died out. This was a time of great confusion and lawlessness, and Rudolph was chosen Emperor not because he was a great lord, but because he was a brave and upright man.

When there was talk of electing a new emperor, the Archbishop of Mayence recommended Rudolph. Once on a time Rudolph, while hunting in the mountains of Switzerland, found a priest, who was carrying the sacrament to a dying person, stopped by a mountain brook, the bridge over which had been swept away. Rudolph at once dismounted, made the priest get upon his horse, and so carried him safely over. The next day the priest sent back the horse, but Rudolph would not take it, saying that the horse which had carried his Lord was too good for him to ride on any more. This priest afterward became chaplain to the Archbishop of Mayence, and it is said that this story caused the Archbishop to recommend Rudolph as one worthy to be emperor.

For five hundred years, with but little interruption, his descendants were emperors of Germany, and one of them is now the emperor of Austria. Ottocar of Bohemia, who had hoped to be emperor of Germany, made war upon him, but was killed at the battle of Marchfeld and his lands of Austria, Styria and Carniola were taken by Rudolph for his sons. Rudolph knew a great deal about law, so much that his people called him "the living law." He died in Germersheim, when seventy-three years old (July 15, 1291), and was succeeded by Adolphus of Nassau.

RUDOLPH II., Emperor of Germany, born in Vienna, July 18, 1552.

He was the son of Maximilian II., and succeeded him Oct. 12, 1576. Under Maximilian the Protestants had had much liberty, but Rudolph was more severe with them, and they formed a Union against him. There would have been a war had not Matthias, Rudolph's brother, put himself at the head of the Hungarian nobles and forced Rudolph to give up the crown of Hungary to him. Soon after this, Bohemia, too, went over to Matthias, so Rudolph had nothing left but the title of emperor. He retired to Prague, where he spent his time in making collections of plants and animals, of which he was very fond. He died when fifty years old (Jan. 20, 1612), and was succeeded by his brother Matthias.

RUGBY, a town of England, on the river Avon, 83 miles N. W. of London; pop. 10,000, or about as large as La Salle, Ill. It is noted for its grammar school, which was founded in 1567, and is now one of the largest in England. It has fourteen teachers and about 1000 pupils. Dr. Thomas Arnold was head master from 1828 to 1842. The school is best known in America from Mr. Hughes's charming book, "Tom Brown's School Days." Mr. Hughes himself was a pupil at Rugby, and he has told some of his own experiences in the book.

RUMFORD, Benjamin Thompson, Count, an American natural philosopher, born in Woburn, Mass., March 26, 1753. On the breaking out of the Revolutionary War, he made enemies among the patriots, and went over to the British side, being Lord Howe's bearer of dispatches to England, after the fall of Boston. During the rest of the war, he took active part with the British. At its close in 1783, he went to England, and afterward entered the service of the Elector of Bavaria, who from that time took his advice in everything. He was made a knight in 1784, and in

1790 a Count of the Holy Roman Empire, the title "Rumford" being chosen by him from the town of Rumford (now Concord) in New Hampshire, where he had married his wife. He held many high offices, and the Bavarians owe a great deal to him for many improvements which he helped the Elector to make.

After the death of the Elector he went to Paris, and spent his time making experiments in natural philosophy. He found out a great deal about heat, and also about light and magnetism. He died near Paris when sixty-one years old (Aug. 21, 1814).

RUN'NY-MEDE, a meadow on the bank of the Thames, 20 miles W.S.W. of London; famous as the place where King John met his nobles and signed the celebrated agreement called Magna Charta or the Great Charter, June 15, 1215. By this the nobles gained many rights which the king had kept from them, and the charter has been called the "Keystone of English Liberty."

Copies of the charter, which were written on parchment at that time, are still preserved in the British Museum. The meadow is now used for a race-course.

RU'PERT, Prince, a Royalist general in the English civil war, born in Prague, Dec. 17, 1619. He was a cousin of Charles I., his father, Frederick V., Elector Palatine of Bavaria, having married Elizabeth, daughter of James I. of England. When the civil war broke out in England, he offered his services to Charles I., who put him in command of a regiment of horse. He was noted for his bravery, and the king knighted him and made him Duke of Cumberland in reward for his services. He won renown by his brilliant victories, but his rashness sometimes caused him to fail. In 1648 he was put in command of the fleet; but he

was defeated by BLAKE and went to the West Indies for a time, and then to France. After the restoration he returned to England, where he held several important positions under Charles II. During the latter part of his life, he was governor of Windsor Castle. He died in London when sixty-three years old (Nov. 29, 1682),

RU'RIK, the founder of the Russian Empire, lived in the 9th century. He was chief of the Varangian tribe of NORTHMEN, and was invited by the Finns to come and reign over them at Novgorod. He began his reign about 862, and was so successful that his descendants reigned for nearly 200 years. Rurik died in 879.

RUS'KIN, John, an English author, born in London, in February, 1819. Nearly all his works relate to the arts of painting, sculpture, and architecture, in all three of which branches he is a critic. His "Seven Lamps of Architecture" and "The Stones of Venice" are full of his love for the Gothic style of building. Of late he has written some books on political economy, or the best way to better the condition of the people, but he does not know so much about that as he does about art. He is now (1891) seventy-one years old.

RUS'SELL, John, Earl, an English statesman, born in London, Aug. 18, 1792. When twenty-one years old, he was elected to Parliament, and was re-elected many times. He was often employed in the most important government offices. During many years he was a member of the British ministry or cabinet, and from 1846 to 1852, and again from 1865 to 1866, he was Prime Minister. In 1861 he was made an earl. During the American Civil War, Lord Russell was unfriendly to the United States, and at one time it was feared that he would induce England to aid the Confederates. He wrote many historical and biographical works, among them the "Life of William, Lord Russell," and "Life and Times of Charles James Fox." Lord Russell died when eighty-five years old (May 28, 1878).

RUSSELL, John Scott, a famous civil engineer, born in Scotland in 1808. He was graduated at the University of Glasgow in 1824, and in 1832 became lecturer on natural philosophy in the University of Edinburgh. Soon after he became manager of the largest ship-building works in Scotland, and built some very large steamships. He found out the "wave system" of building vessels, by which the bows of vessels are so made that they go through waves much easier than vessels built in the old way, and this system was used by BRUNEL in building the Great Western and the Great Eastern steamships. He was the author of the plan of carrying railway cars on vessels, so that trains can be carried over rivers and lakes without disturbing passengers or goods. One of his latest works was the great dome in Vienna, which is nearly large enough to cover the whole of St. Paul's Cathedral in London. It is 360 feet in diameter, or nearly two and three fourths times as wide as the dome of the Capitol in Washington. He died when seventy-four years old (June 8, 1882).

RUSSELL, William, Lord, an English statesman, born Sept. 29, 1639. When twenty-one years old he was elected to Parliament, but for many years he took little part in its debates. About 1673 he became a leader of the Protestant party in England, and did so much to oppose the Catholics and King Charles II. that the king finally resolved to put him to death. Lord Russell, Algernon Sidney, and others were arrested and charged with a plot against the king's life, and though nothing could be proved against them, they were condemned to death. A plan was formed to procure Russell's escape, but he refused to enter into it, and was finally beheaded in London, when forty-three years old (July 21, 1683).

RUSSIA (*rush'e-ah*), a country of E. Europe, next to Asia; area, including FINLAND and Russian POLAND, 2,262,000 square miles, or about three fifths of all Europe; pop. 78,000,000, or one fourth that of Europe; capital, St. Petersburg. In addition to this, Russia rules all of SIBERIA and a vast territory in Central Asia, amounting to about 6,170,000 square miles more, or more than one third of all Asia. It is thus the largest country in the world, having in all an area of 8,432,000 square miles, or a sixth of all the land on the earth, and about one twenty-sixth part of all the surface, both land and sea. In this article only Russia proper will be told about, the other parts having titles of their own.

Russia is an immense plain, the northern part being covered in many places with forests or swamps while in the southern part there are great treeless regions called steppes. There are hardly any mountains in the country itself, but the rugged Caucasus range, on the southern boundary, has peaks more than three miles high. The Ural mountains on the eastern boundary are less than a mile high, and rise so gradually from the plain, that they do not seem like mountains at all.

Russia has many large rivers, and seaports on the Black Sea and the Baltic. In the northwestern part are many lakes. The climate of central and southern Russia is generally very cold in winter, and the summers are short and warm. In the most northern part it is so cold that the ground is frozen all through the year, and hardly any plants will grow.

Russia has rich mines of coal, iron, copper, silver, and gold, and many fine salt springs. Thousands of logs of timber are cut in the forest. In general the people are not very good farmers, yet in the southern part so much grain, hemp, and flax are grown, that great quantities are sent to other countries. Horses, cattle, sheep, and swine are very numerous, and there is a large trade in horses, wool, and hides. Tame reindeer are kept in the cold northern region, and in the southern part camels are used to carry burdens. Among the wild animals are bears, wolves, deer, elks, and the European bison, and many smaller animals are hunted for their furs, in which Russia has a large trade. There are fine fisheries along the coasts. The manufactures are not so important as those of other European countries, though of late years they have been increasing very fast.

The most important things made are woolen, cotton, linen, and silk goods, leather, soap and candles, iron-ware, and beet sugar. The principal manufacturing town is Moscow.

There are many different nations in Russia, but the largest and most important is that of the Russians proper, who have given their name and language to the country. Most of them are poor peasants, who, until 1861, were serfs or slaves of the rich people and nobles, and were often treated very cruelly. They are brave and good natured, but very ignorant and superstitious. The people who live in towns are more intelligent and cultured and they have certain rights of voting which are not given to the peasants. The nobles are very powerful and rich, and often live in great splendor. The Cossacks are a branch of the Russians who live in the southern part. They are very brave and warlike, and are always ready to take the field. These soldiers are always cavalry, and the principal riches of the Cossacks are their horses and cattle. Among other natives of Russia are the Finns of the northern part, the Poles of the west, the Tartars—a wandering people of the southern steppes, and many Germans and Scandinavians near the Baltic Sea. Most of the Russians belong to the Russian Church, a branch of the Greek Church, but there are also many Catholics, Protestants, and Jews, and most of the Tartars are Mohammedans. Russia is an empire, and its ruler, formerly called the Czar, has had since Peter the Great's time the title of emperor. He can do what he pleases with his subjects, even banishing them or putting them in prison at any time. There is no congress or parliament.

In ancient times the Russians were called Scythians and Sarmatians, and in later times Slavs. The Slavs had two governments, with capitals at Novgorod and Kiev. They quarreled among themselves, and in 862 the people of Novgorod invited Rurik, chief of the Varangian tribe of Northmen, called by the Slavs Rus, to come and be their ruler. Rurik thus laid the foundation of the Russian empire, and in 1862 the 1000th anniversary of his coming was celebrated at Novgorod. In 988 Vladimir the Great married the sister of the Greek emperor of the East, became a Christian, and set up churches and schools in the empire. Russia thus got its religion from the Eastern Church instead of from Rome, and it has ever since belonged to the Greek Church.

In the 13th century Russia was overrun by the Mongols or Moguls from Asia, and was subject to them until 1477, when it was freed. Russia then began to grow, and in the 16th century Ivan the Terrible extended it to the Caspian Sea. He was the first to take the title of

Czar, a Slav word meaning king; but in later times the Russian sovereigns, who have always wished to be looked on as the successors of the Greek emperors, have claimed that it is the Russian form of Cæsar. In 1589 the old line of Rurik came to an end, and after a time of confusion, the Russians chose (1613) Michael ROMANOFF to be their ruler. Russia conquered Siberia, and finally in the time of Peter the Great became very great and powerful. Peter took the title of emperor of all the Russias. During most of the eighteenth century Russia was ruled by women, among whom Catharine I. and Catharine II. were the most noted. Catharine II. added the Crimea to the empire, and joined with Prussia and Austria in dividing POLAND, which had long been the enemy of Russia. This brought Russia into the middle of Europe, where she could take part in affairs from which she had before been cut off. Russia has had several wars with the Turks for the possession of Constantinople, which she very much needs, because it guards the entrance of the Black Sea; but it is not probable that the other nations of Europe will ever permit her to take it, because with it she might become too powerful.

RUST'CHUK, a town of Bulgaria, on the river Danube; pop. 27,000, or about as large as Pawtucket, R. I. It has manufactories of silk, wool, cotton, and leather, and a considerable trade. Rustchuk is strongly fortified, and several battles have been fought there between the Turks and Russians. The Russians captured it after a long siege in 1810, and burned it when they left it in 1812. The forts were destroyed in 1829, but have since been rebuilt.

RUYTER (*ry'ter*), **Michael Adriaenszoon de,** a Dutch naval commander, born in Flushing in 1607. His parents apprenticed him to a shoemaker, but he ran away when eleven years old, went to sea as a cabin boy, and became in time an admiral. In 1647 he defeated an Algerine fleet four times as large as his own, and in 1655 he captured and hung a Spaniard named Armand de Diaz who had commanded a famous pirate fleet among the Algerines. In 1666 he fought the English fleet for three days in the Irish Sea, but had finally to retreat. The next year he sailed up the Thames and Medway and burned or captured the English vessels at Sheerness, though they were lying close to a fort, and forced the English to make peace. In 1671 De Ruyter had a bloody fight with a fleet of French and English ships, but neither side gained a victory. In 1675 he was sent to the Mediterranean, and near Sicily he fought a French fleet much larger than his own. Both his legs were shot off in the battle, and his fleet finally retreated to Syracuse, Sicily, where he died of his wounds, when sixty-nine years old (April 29, 1676).

RYS'WICK, a village of the Netherlands 2 miles S.E. of the Hague. It is noted for a treaty of peace, called the peace of Ryswick, which was concluded there, between France on one side, and Germany, Holland, England, and Spain on the other (1697). By this treaty a long war was ended, and many important results followed it.

S

SA'BINES, an ancient people of Italy, noted in the early legends of Rome. Though they were neighbors of the Romans, they would not give them their daughters in marriage. So Romulus gave out that he was going to keep a great festival with sports and games, and invited everybody to come. The Sabines and others came with their wives and their daughters; and while they were looking on at the games, the Romans rushed upon them and carried off the women to be their wives. The Sabines marched with a great army against Rome, and through the treachery of TARPEIA got possession of the fort on one of the hills. They then fought the Romans in the valley and drove them to the

Rome saved by the Sabine Women.

gate of the city; and they were getting the better of them, when on a sudden the Sabine women who had been carried off came running from the city, with their children in their arms, and threw themselves between their husbands and their fathers, and prayed them to cease their quarrel. So they made peace with one another, and the two people became as one.

SACHS (*sahks*), **Hans,** a German poet, born in Nuremberg, Nov. 5, 1494. He was a cobbler, but learned to sing and make verses from one of the meistersingers, or minstrels. It is said that he wrote 6,000 poems, only a quarter of which were ever printed. Some are plays, and others are rhymed fables, songs, or hymns. They often ridicule the Catholic priests, and during the Reformation they were favorite songs with the Protestants. Sachs died at his home in Nüremberg, when eighty-one years old (Jan. 20, 1576).

SAC·RA·MEN'TO, a city, capital of California, in the central part of the State, on a river of the same name; pop. 26,000, or about as large as Canton, Ohio. It is built on very low ground, but the streets have been built up beyond reach of the freshets which used to flood them. Sacramento is a handsome city, with wide shady streets. The State Capitol is one of the finest buildings in the United States, and its grounds occupy eighteen squares, which are beautifully laid out like a garden. The city has important manufactories, and carries on a large trade in marble and granite, from quarries in the neighborhood. The machine and car works of the Pacific Railroad are there.

Sacramento is a Spanish word, meaning sacrament, and was first given to the river. In 1841 a fort was built where the city now is, and called New Helvetia; but in 1848, when the town was begun, the name was changed to Sacramento.

SADOWA (*sah-do'vah*), a small village of N. W. Austria, in Bohemia, eight miles N. W. of Königgrätz, where the Prussians under King William I. gained a great victory over the Austrians commanded by General Benedek, July 3, 1866. More than 400,000 men fought in this battle, and 50,000 were killed and wounded. The Prussian soldiers were armed with the needle gun (C. C. T., 514, I., u.), with which they could fire faster and farther than their enemies. The Austrians were so badly defeated that they were obliged to give up the war. This is often called the battle of Königgrätz.

SAGHALIEN (*sag-hal'e-en*), or **Saghalin**, an island of East Asia, north of Japan; area, 25,000 square miles, or a little larger than West Virginia; pop., about 16,000, or one forty-sixth that of West Virginia. It is not yet well explored, but it is known that a high mountain-range runs through it, with hills and plains on each side. The people are Russians, Japanese, and half savages called Ainos. They live by fishing, and by hunting animals for their furs. Fish and furs are sent to Russia and Japan. Many Russian convicts are sent to Saghalien to work in the coal-mines.

The southern part of Saghalien was settled by Japanese, about the same time that the Russians invaded the northern part. As they were unable to arrange a boundary, the Japanese part was given up to the Russians in 1875.

SAGUENAY (*sahg-e-na'*), a river of Canada flowing into the St. Lawrence from the north 120 miles below Quebec; length, about 100 miles. It rises in a lake called Lake St. John, and flows for a long distance between high, rocky cliffs, forming some of the most magnificent scenery in the world. In one place the river is a mile and a half deep. Steamers ascend the Saguenay for seventy-five miles, and in the summer it is visited by hundreds of travellers.

SAG'I·NAW, a city of Michigan, on the W. side of Saginaw River; pop. 46,000, or about as large as Portland, Ore. On the opposite bank of the river is the former city of East Saginaw, which in 1890 was consolidated with Saginaw. The city has a large trade in lumber; and contains many saw-mills and manufactories of shingles, staves, barrels, and other articles of wood. It is also noted for its great salt-works, the salt being got from wells in the vicinity. Saginaw was founded in 1822, and East Saginaw in 1850.

SAHARA (*sah-hah'rah*), a great desert of N. Africa, the largest in the world, having an area of probably 2,000,000 square miles, or more than half as large as the United States. It extends 3,000 miles, from the Atlantic to the Nile, and beyond that there is a similar desert region to the E. coast of Africa. In some places it is 1,000 miles wide. There are many mountains in the desert, especially south of Algiers and Tripoli, and along the southern border, but the western and eastern parts are generally flat. The east part is often called the Libyan Desert. In some places the desert is covered with stones and gravel,

The Mirage of the Desert.

and in others there are great expanses of sand, which is blown about by the winds, forming drifts and little hills, as snow does. No plants grow, except in a few spots, called oases, where there are springs, surrounded by palms and other trees. Lions, antelopes, and other wild animals are found in these oases, and some of them are inhabited by Arabs; one or two even have towns in them. They are very fertile, yielding good crops of dates, barley, wheat, and millet. The Sahara is the hottest region in the world, and the sand is sometimes almost as hot as boiling water. Hot winds, called simooms, blow over the surface, often bearing clouds of dust and sand, which strike against the skin like hot needles. Yet large caravans cross the desert every year, passing from one oasis to another. Often the camels get no water for two or three days; and sometimes, when suffering with thirst, they and their drivers are tormented with what looks like a beautiful lake or a shining river in the distance. But when they try to get to it, it fades away, and they find out that it is only a sham. This appearance is called the mirage of the desert, but the Arabs call it the Lake of the Gazelles. Some parts of the Sahara are lower than the level of the ocean, and it is supposed that a great portion of it was once a sea, like the Mediterranean. It has been proposed to let the sea water in again by cutting a canal, thus making a channel for ships to the centre of Africa.

SAIGON (*si-gon'*), or **Saigun**, the capital of French Cochin China, on the River Saigon, 35 miles from its mouth in the China Sea; pop., 65,000, or a little larger than Memphis, Tenn. It consists of two towns, about 2 miles apart, and defended by a citadel in which the governor and garrison live. There is also a navy-yard and an arsenal. The city has a large trade in cinnamon, rice, and various fine woods. Saigon, which formerly belonged to Anam, was captured by the French in 1859.

SAINT AUGUSTINE (*aw-gus-teen'*), a city of N. E. Florida, on the Atlantic Ocean, between the mouths of the rivers Matanzas and St. Sebastian; pop., about 5,000. It has a good harbor, formed by an island in front of it. Many of the people are engaged in preparing palmetto straw, used for making hats. The climate is very mild and pleasant, and it is visited in the winter by many thousand Northerners. St. Augustine is the oldest town in the United States,

having been begun by the Spaniards in 1565. The Castle of San Marco, built by them, is still standing, but is now called Fort Marion. It is built of coquina, a kind of rock made of small sea-shells.

SAINT BER'NARD. See BERNARD, SAINT.

SAINT CATHARINES (*kath'ar-ins*), a town of Canada, on the Welland Canal, S. of Lake Ontario; pop., 10,000, or about as large as Alton, Ill. It has important manufactures, and ships are built there. Near the town are some celebrated mineral springs, often visited by invalids and travellers. The Welland Canal was made to let ships pass from Lake Erie to Lake Ontario, and to get around Niagara Falls.

SAINT CLOUD (*sent klowd*, French *son kloo'*), a town of France on the River Seine, forming a W. suburb of Paris; pop., about 6,000. Clodoald, a grandson of Clovis, built a convent there, called it after him, Saint Clodoald, and that name was changed in time to St. Cloud. The Palace of St. Cloud, built in 1572, was a favorite residence of Marie Antoinette, Napoleon, and other sovereigns. During the siege of Paris, 1870, it was nearly all burned.

SAINT CYR (*sent* or *son seer*), a village of France, in the great park of Versailles, 9 miles S. W. of Paris. It is famous for its military school, in which officers are trained for the French army and navy.

SAINT DENIS (*sent den'is*, French *son den-e'*), a town of France, 2 miles N. of Paris; pop. 48,000, or about as large as Oakland, Cal. It is famous for an old convent, founded there in the 7th century, over the tomb of Saint Denis. It had a very fine church, in which many of the early French kings were buried. During the French Revolution their tombs were destroyed; but the church was afterward repaired, and it is now one of the finest in France. The convent itself is used as an asylum and school for orphan children of members of the French Legion of Honor.

SAINT ETIENNE (*sent* or *sont et-e-en'*), a town of S. E. France, on a branch of the river Loire; pop., 118,000, or twice as large as Grand Rapids, Mich. It is one of the most important manufacturing towns in Europe; 40,000 weavers are employed there in the ribbon-factories, and more ribbons are made than in any other place in the world. There are also very large manufactories of fire-arms, and many steel and cutlery works. The town has a large trade in coal, which is mined near it.

SAINT GALL (*sent gawl*), a town of N.E. Switzerland; pop. 27,000, or nearly as large as Houston, Tex. It was named after the apostle of Switzerland, Gall, who founded a convent there in the 7th century. St. Gall is the principal trading city of N. E. Switzerland, and it is noted for its large manufactories of muslins and calicoes.

SAINT GERMAIN (*sent jer-mane'*), a town of France, 8 miles W. of Paris; pop., 22,000, or about as large as Springfield, Mo. It contains an old palace where many French kings lived, and in which King James II. of England died. During the French Revolution, the palace was used for barracks, and Napoleon changed it into a prison. It is now used as a museum of antiquities. Near Saint Germain is a large forest or park, and the town itself is a famous summer resort.

SAINT HELENA (*hel-le'nah*), an island in the S. Pacific Ocean, 1,200 miles W. of Africa; area, 47 square miles; pop., 6,500. It is very mountainous, and all around the shore are rocky cliffs, so that it is impossible to land, except in a few places. Only a small part of the land is cultivated, and nearly all the food and clothing is brought from other countries.

The island was first found by the Spanish in 1502 and named after Saint Helena, on whose anniversary (May 21) the discovery was made.

It now belongs to England. When Napoleon was finally defeated at Waterloo, he was exiled to Saint Helena, and lived there in a farmhouse called Longwood, from Oct. 16, 1815, until his death (May 5, 1821). During that time the English had strong forts on the island and kept many war ships there. In 1840, Napoleon's body was removed to France, and in 1858 the French government bought Longwood and the place where Napoleon had been buried, and decreed that a guard of honor should always be kept there.

SAINT HELIER (*sent hel'e-er*, French *sont a-le-a'*), the capital of the island of Jersey in the English Channel, on St. Aubin's Bay; pop., 27,000, or nearly as large as Sacramento, Cal. It has a fine harbor defended by two forts, and a good trade. Many ships go from Saint Hélier to fish on the Newfoundland banks. Saint Hélier is noted for its fine climate and beautiful scenery.

SAINTINE (*san-teen'*), the fictitious name of Joseph Xavier Boniface, a French writer, born in Paris, July 10, 1798. He wrote many plays and novels, but his best known work is "Picciola," a story which has been translated into all the European languages. He also wrote "The Solitary of Juan Fernandez, or the Real Robinson Crusoe." He died in Paris when sixty-seven years old (Jan. 21, 1865).

SAINT JOHN, the largest city of New Brunswick, on the River St. John, at its mouth in the Bay of Fundy; pop. 28,000, or about as large as Chelsea, Mass. It has one of the finest harbors in America, and a large trade is carried on, especially in lumber. Many ships are built there, and there are manufactories of iron, edge-tools, boots and shoes, leather, paper, cotton cloth, and many other things. The tide at St. John rises more than twenty feet, running into the river; at the ebb it rushes out again with great violence, forming a fall about seventeen feet high.

St. John was founded by Americans who sympathized with England during the Revolution, and after the war went from the United States to live in New Brunswick. It was made a city in 1785.

SAINT JOHN OF JERUSALEM. See HOSPITALLERS.

SAINT JOHN'S, a city, capital of Newfoundland, in the S. E. part of the island, in a bay of the Atlantic Ocean; pop. 29,000, or about as large as Chattanooga, Tenn. The harbor is a very fine one, and shelters hundreds of fishing-vessels, besides many larger ships which go to England and the United States. Nearly all the people of St. John's are engaged in fishing, or in trading with the fishermen. Along the shores of the harbor are great stages and frames for drying codfish, and there are large factories where seal and cod-liver oil are made. Great quantities of codfish, seal-skins and oil are sent to other countries. St. John's was probably first settled by the French, in the early part of the 16th century.

SAINT JO'SEPH, a city of N. W. Missouri, on the Missouri River; pop. 52,000, or about as large as Hartford, Conn. It has more manufactories than any other city west of the Mississippi, except San Francisco. Among them are large flouring-mills, a starch-factory, wagon-factories, boot and shoe factories, and a woolen-mill. Many thousand hogs are killed and packed there every year. A very large trade is carried on by steamboats and by several railroads which meet in the city. Saint Joseph was laid out in 1846, and became a city in 1857.

SAINT LAW'RENCE, a river of N.

America, flowing from Lake Ontario into the Gulf of St. Lawrence; length, about 750 miles. In most places it is more than two miles wide, and below Quebec it widens to thirty miles. There are several lakes through which the river flows. One of these, just below Lake Ontario, is called the Lake of the Thousand Islands, from the many little islands scattered over it. Between Lake Ontario and Montreal are several rapids, the most important being

Entrance to St. John's.

Lachine and Cedar Rapids. Steamboats can go down these, but they go up through canals cut along the banks. By aid of the canals, large vessels can pass from Chicago and Lake Michigan to the Atlantic Ocean, and so to any port in the world. Immense rafts of logs also descend these rapids.

The **Gulf of St. Lawrence,** which may be considered a part of the river, is 100 miles wide, and its water reaches the ocean by three channels. The waters of Lakes Ontario, Erie, St. Clair, Huron, Superior, Michigan, and many smaller lakes pass through the St. Lawrence, and all these may be looked upon as parts of it. Counting them with it, the St. Lawrence is more than 2,000 miles long, and has more water than any other river in the world.

SAINT LOUIS (*loo'e* or *loo'is*), a city of E. Missouri on the Mississippi River, 20 miles below the mouth of the Missouri; pop. 452,000, or a little larger than Boston, Mass. It is the principal city in the State, and one of the largest in the United States. Being near the junction of the Mississippi and Missouri, St. Louis is naturally the port for steamboats from both rivers. Besides this, it has an immense trade by many railroads which meet there. The city is still more important for its manufactures, in which it surpasses every other place in the Union, except New York and Philadelphia. More flour is made there than in any other city, and there are very large manufactories of iron and steel, machinery, saddles and harnesses, and clothing. Another important business is the killing and packing of hogs, in which St. Louis stands next to Chicago and Cincinnati. The city contains many colleges, seminaries, and medical schools. St. Louis was founded in 1764 by the French, who named it in honor of Louis XV. of France.

SAINT MALO (*sent mah-lo'*), a town of France, on a rocky peninsula in the English Channel; pop., 11,000, or about as large as Auburn, Me. It is strongly fortified, and is connected with the mainland by a long narrow causeway. The tides rise there very high. At low tide the harbor is dry, and at high tide it has forty to fifty feet of water in it. Chateaubriand was born at St. Malo, and is buried on a rock in the harbor.

SAINT PAUL, a city, capital of the State of Minnesota, on the Mississippi River; pop. 133,000, or nearly as large as Rochester, N. Y. Steamboats ascend the river as far as this city, which is almost at the head of navigation. By these and by many railroad lines which meet there, St. Paul carries on a very

large trade, especially in grain, flour, and various kinds of merchandise from the Eastern States. There are manufactures of farmers' tools, wagons, beer, and many other things. The city has a fine park and many beautiful residences. The first house was built on the site of St. Paul in 1838, and in 1841 a Jesuit missionary built a log chapel there. This was dedicated to St. Paul, and from it the city got its name.

SAINT PE'TERS-BURG, a city, capital of Russia, on the riva Neva, near its mouth; pop. 861,000, or nearly twice as large as Baltimore, Md. It is built partly on the mainland and partly on islands in the river. It has so many splendid buildings, that it is called the City of Palaces. The Winter Palace, one of the residences of the emperor, is one of the largest palaces in the world, and is inhabited by about 6000 persons when the emperor lives there; it is adorned with magnificent paintings, statues, and malachite tables and vases. The Hermitage, a palace connected with it, has forty rooms full of paintings, and a splendid museum and library. In the Taurida Palace there is a ball-room as large as ten ordinary houses. Among the churches is that of St. Peter and St. Paul, in which all the Russian emperors, from the time of Peter the Great, have been buried. The Isaac Church is one of the finest in Europe. The Imperial Library of St. Petersburg is one of the three largest in the world, and there are fine museums, and a university with 2200 students.

St. Petersburg is noted for its manufactures of tapestry, glass, porcelain, malachite ornaments, cotton, silk, and many other things. A very large trade is carried on. The river being too shallow for large vessels, the port of St. Petersburg is at Cronstadt, on the Gulf of Finland. In winter the city is very cold, and the people dress in furs. The summers are warm, and there is much sickness, owing to many of the poorer class living in cellars. At that time, the emperor and his nobles generally leave the city. The islands on which the city is built, being low and flat, are subject to inundations, which have often caused great damage.

St. Petersburg was founded in 1703 by Peter the Great, who made it his capital in 1712, in the place of Moscow.

SAINT PIERRE (*sent peer*, French, *son pe-air¹*) a town of the island of Martinique, West Indies ; pop. 20,° 000, or nearly as large as Chester, Pa. It is the largest town in the French West India Islands, and has a considerable trade. It was settled by the French in 1635.

SAINT PIERRE, Jacques Henri Bernardin de, a French writer, born in Havre, Jan. 19, 1737. He was educated to be a priest, but gave up his studies, and for many years led an adventurous life in different countries of Europe. In 1766 he went to Madagascar, and afterward to Mauritius, where he spent many years. On his return to France (1771) he published an account of his voyage, and several other works. But he is best known for his beautiful story of " Paul and Virginia," which has been translated into many languages. The scene is laid in Mauritius. Saint Pierre's two children, like the hero and heroine of the story, were named Paul and Virginia. He died at Éragny-sur-Oise, when seventy-seven years old (Jan. 21. 1814).

SAINT THOM'AS, an island of the West Indies, 30 miles E. of Porto Rico ; area, 35 square miles ; pop., 15,000. It is high, rocky, and so barren that little is raised on it. Nearly all of the people live in the town of Charlotte Amalie, which, being nearer to Europe than any other port in the West Indies, has a large trade. Earthquakes are common, and one which occurred in 1867 was followed by a huge wave,

which rolled in from the sea and sunk nearly every ship in the harbor.

St. Thomas has belonged to several different nations, and it is now a colony of Denmark.

SA'LA, George Augustus Henry, an English writer, born in London in 1828. His father was an Italian, and his mother a West Indian, who went to England as a singer. Sala was educated to be an artist, but he became a writer for magazines, and afterward a writer for newspapers. The magazine called " Temple Bar," was begun and edited by him. He has published several novels and books of travel.

SAL'A-DIN, Sultan of Egypt and Syria, born in 1137. His real name was Salah-ed-Din (Arabic for integrity or holiness of the faith), but the English shortened it to Saladin. In 1168 Saladin became ruler of Egypt under NOUREDDIN, and when Noureddin died Saladin became sultan of Egypt and Syria. In 1186 he attacked the Christians in Palestine, and defeated them in a great battle at Tiberias (1187), in which 30,000 Christians were killed or captured. He took Jerusalem (Oct. 2, 1187), and besieged Acre, but was at length obliged to retreat before the Christian garrison. In 1189 the third Crusade began, the Christian army being led against Saladin by King RICHARD Cœur de Lion of England and King Philip Augustus of France. They besieged Acre for two years, and when they finally took it, Richard led his army to Ascalon, his march of eleven days being a continual battle with Saladin's soldiers. The Crusaders took Ascalon, and in 1192 came within three days' march of Jerusalem, but they quarrelled among themselves and finally gave up the conquest, signing a truce for three years. Saladin died at Damascus when fifty-six years old (March 4, 1193). There is much about this famous man in Sir Walter Scott's novel " The Talisman."

SALAMANCA (*sah-lah-mang'-kah*), a city of W. Spain, on the River Tormes; pop. 22,000, or about as large as Cohoes, N. Y. It is sometimes called Roma la Chica, or little Rome, on account of its many beautiful buildings. The finest of these is the cathedral, begun in 1513. The University of Salamanca was formerly one of the most celebrated in Europe, having 10,000 students, but it is now almost deserted. Salamanca is one of the oldest cities in Spain, and was called Salmantica by the Romans. The battle of Salamanca, in which an English and Spanish army under the Duke of Wellington defeated the French (July 22, 1812), was fought four miles from the city.

SAL'A·MIS, an island of Greece, 10 miles W. of Athens; area, 30 square miles. It is separated from the mainland by a narrow channel in which was fought the great naval battle of Salamis, between the Greek and Persian fleets. The Greeks, commanded by THEMISTOCLES, had sailed into the channel, and the Persians closed it at both ends with their ships, while the land side was guarded by the Persian army under XERXES. The Greeks, obliged to fight or surrender, attacked the Persians so bravely, that they gained a great victory, sinking two hundred ships and capturing many others. Xerxes, who had witnessed the battle from a throne on shore, immediately fled to Persia, leaving his army under the command of Mardonius.

SALEM, a city of E. Massachusetts, on a peninsula of Massachusetts Bay, 14 miles N. by E. of Boston; pop., 31,000, or about as large as Quincy, Ill. It is noted for its manufactures, especially of leather, cotton cloth, machinery, and railroad cars. Formerly it was one of the greatest trading ports in the country, sending ships to all parts of the world, and having a larger East Indian trade than all the other ports put together. The captains who had been around Cape Horn or the Cape of Good Hope formed a society, and a museum of curiosities which they had brought home. This museum now forms part of the museum of the Peabody Academy of Sciences, founded by George Peabody, who was a native of Salem. The Essex Institute has a fine library and a collection of natural history specimens, which are also in the Peabody Academy. There are several other important societies.

Salem is the oldest town in Massachusetts except Plymouth, having been founded in 1628. In 1692 it was the scene of a strong excitement called Salem witchcraft. Several young girls had been in the habit of meeting an old Indian woman, who pretended to teach them tricks in magic. After a while, they showed, or pretended to show, many strange symptoms, such as dropping down insensible, writhing as if in agony, or going into spasms. A physician declared that they were bewitched, and on being questioned, the children accused three women of bewitching them. They afterwards accused others, who were brought to trial and condemned on the children's testimony, and twenty persons, including a clergyman, were hung on what is now called Gallows Hill. More than a hundred were imprisoned, and the people were terribly excited, for in those days everybody believed in witchcraft, and thought it the greatest of all crimes. But after a while they saw how hasty they had been, and the prisoners were released. During the Revolution one hundred and fifty-eight privateers or private ships of war were sent out of Salem, and they captured nearly four hundred and fifty English vessels.

SA'LEM, a city, capital of the State of Oregon, on the Willamette River; pop. 8000, or about as large as Cranston, R. I. It is surrounded by beautiful prairie land, on which are many fine farms. The city has several mills and manufactories, a State penitentiary, and other public buildings. It is the seat of Willamette University. Salem was founded in 1834, and became the capital of Oregon in 1860.

SALISBURY (*sawlz'ber-re*), a city of England, on the River Avon; pop. 15,000, or about as large as Lebanon, Pa. It is noted for its splendid cathedral, built in the 13th century. In later times it became partly ruined, but a few years ago it was repaired. Salisbury has important manufactories of cutlery.

SAL'LUST (**Caius Sallustius Crispus**), a Roman historian, born 86 B.C. When forty years old he went with Julius Cæsar to Africa, was made governor of Numidia, and got great wealth by plundering the inhabitants. After his return to Rome, he spent his days in writing the history of his time, and in forming the splendid gardens on the Quirinal Hill, which became famous as the Gardens of Sallust. His works, "The Conspiracy of Catiline," and "Jugurthine War," are celebrated. Sallust died in Rome when fifty-two years old (34 B.C.).

SALONICA (*sah-lo-ne'kah*), a town in the S. part of Turkey in Europe, on the Gulf of Salonica; pop. 150,000, or a little larger than Omaha, Neb. It is celebrated for its many beautiful churches and mosques, some of which are very ancient. Salonica is surrounded by walls, and defended by a castle. It has manufactories of woollen, silk, and hardware, and a considerable trade is carried on. More than a quarter of the people are Jews, and many are Greeks. In ancient times Salonica was a much larger city. It was called Therma, or warm springs, from some springs near it, and afterward Thessalonica. St. Paul preached there, and one of his epistles is addressed to the Thessalonians.

SALT LAKE, GREAT. See UTAH.

SALT LAKE CITY, the capital of Utah, in the N. part of the Territory, near the Wasatch Mountains, and 12 miles from Great Salt Lake; pop., 49,000, or about as large as Lawrence, Mass. It is very handsomely laid out with wide, regular streets, all of which are lined with shade-trees, and there are many public squares. Among the larger buildings is the Mormon Tabernacle, which is covered with a dome-shaped roof, and is large enough to seat 15,000 people. Its great organ is only a little smaller than the one in the Boston Music Hall, which is the largest in the United States.

Salt Lake City was settled in 1847 by the Mormons, led by Brigham YOUNG. For a long time nearly all the people were Mormons, and even now about two-thirds of them belong to that sect.

SALZBURG (*saltz'burg*), a city of N. Austria, on the River Salzach; pop. 28,000, or about as large as Houston, Tex. The river passes there between two high mountains, at the foot of which is the city, forming one of the grandest landscapes in the world. In one of the squares there is a monument to Mozart, who was born in the city. There are many mineral springs and noted salt-mines near the city, which gets its name from them, Salzburg meaning Salt City.

SAMARCAND (*sah-mar-kahnd'*), a city of Asia, in Turkistan, in the valley of the River Zerafshan; pop., 33,000, or about as large as Duluth, Minn. It is surrounded by walls, and has a citadel where many soldiers are kept. The country around is very fertile and beautiful, and from a distance the city presents a fine appearance; but when one enters it the streets are seen to be narrow and dirty, and many of the houses are mere huts. The only fine buildings are the ancient palaces and mosques. In the citadel is the palace of TIMOUR, or Tamerlane, containing many beautiful rooms, where he lived, and a great green stone on which his throne was placed. The stone is 4½ feet high; and it is said that, when Timour ascended it, he always made some noble prisoner get on his hands and knees to serve for a step.

The tomb of Timour is in a beautiful chapel, surrounded by a walled garden. There is also a palace in which Timour lived in the summer, and a mosque built during his reign. The city abounds in ruins of ancient houses and temples.

Samarcand is one of the oldest cities in the world. Ancient books call it Maracanda, the capital of a kingdom called Sogdiana, which was conquered by Alexander the Great in 328 B.C. In the 14th century Timour made it his capital; and under him and his successors it was a very large and rich city, with many manufactures and an immense trade. Since 1868 it has belonged to the Russians.

SAMOAN (*sah-mo'an*), or **Navigator's Islands,** an archipelago of 13 islands, in the S. Pacific Ocean, about 400 miles N. E. of the Fiji Islands; area, 1,125 square miles, or nearly as large as Rhode Island; pop., 35,000, or nearly the same as that of Norfolk, Va.; capital, Apia. They are high and rocky, some of the peaks being nearly a mile above the sea. There are several fine harbors. In one of the islands are many wonderful caves, which have been explored for more than two miles without finding the end. Most of the people are of a brown race, much like those of the Sandwich Islands. Formerly they were savages and idolaters, but most of them are now Christians.

The Samoan Islands were named by Bougainville, a Frenchman, who first found them in 1768, the Navigator's Islands, on account of the skill which the natives showed in navigating their canoes.

SA'MOS, an island of the Grecian Archipelago, close to Asia Minor;

area, 213 square miles; pop., about 45,000. Two mountain-chains pass through it, and they abound in beautiful scenery. Grain, olives, grapes, and cotton, are the principal crops. Most of the people are Greeks, but the island belongs to Turkey. In ancient times Samos was inhabited by Greeks, and the capital, also called Samos, was one of the finest Grecian cities.

SAN ANTONIO (*sahn ahn-to'ne-o*), a city of S. W. Texas, on the San Antonio River, 75 miles S. W. of Austin; pop. 38,000, or nearly as large as Sioux City, Iowa. The river and a branch called the San Pedro divide the town into three parts. One, called the old town, is now the business part, and has many handsome stores. In the second, called Chihuahua, most of the people are Mexicans, who live in one-story houses built of stone and logs, and with thatched roofs. Alamo, the third part, is mostly inhabited by Germans. In a large square in Alamo is the celebrated ALAMO fortress. San Antonio is the principal city of W. Texas, and has a large trade. San Antonio was founded in 1714 by the Spaniards, who built a fort there. The name came from a convent which was built in Alamo in 1718, and dedicated to Saint Anthony (in Spanish, San Antonio).

SAND, George. See DUDEVANT.

SAN-DUS'KY, a city of N. Ohio, on an inlet of Lake Erie; pop., 18,000, or nearly as large as Orange, N. J. It has a large, safe harbor, and carries on an important trade in fresh and salted fish, and lumber. Sandusky is celebrated for its manufactures of handles, spokes, hubs, and other wood-work, and carpenters' tools. Large quantities of limestone are quarried there, and a great deal of lime is made. The city is in the midst of the best vine-growing district of the United States, and has a large trade in wine.

SAND'WICH ISLANDS. See HAWAIIAN ISLANDS.

SAN FRAN CIS'CO, the chief city of California, in the western part of the State, on a peninsula between San Francisco Bay and the Pacific Ocean; pop. 299,000, or a little larger than Cincinnati, O. The peninsula is a barren waste, covered with rocky hills and sand-dunes, and with hardly any cultivated land. But many million dollars have been spent in grading the city streets, some of the hills having been entirely cut away, while part of the bay has been filled up to give more room for houses. In one place a beautiful park has been made. Among the fine buildings are the City Hall and the Palace Hotel, which is said to be the largest hotel in the world.

A part of San Francisco is called China-town, because it is almost entirely inhabited by Chinamen. They have built many temples, or "joss-houses," where they worship the gods of their religion. The climate of San Francisco is very even, very hot and cold days being alike unknown there. Flowers bloom all the year round, and even tropical fruits grow well. Earthquakes are common, but are hardly ever severe.

San Francisco owes its importance to its harbor, which is one of the finest and largest in the world. It is visited by hundreds of ships, and the city has an immense trade with Europe, New York, and countries in the Pacific Ocean. The principal things sent out are grain, flour, wool, wines, and quicksilver. Among those brought in are tea from China, lumber from Oregon, coal from Australia, Vancouver's Island, and England, and sugar, rice, and coffee from various countries. There is also a very great trade by the Pacific Railroad, which has its western end near San Francisco. Many of the great mines of California and Nevada are owned by San Francisco merchants, some of whom are among the richest men in the world.

The site of San Francisco was first settled by Spanish missionaries to the Indians, in 1776. Later, a village called Yerba Buena was formed there, which in 1847 was named San Francisco, or St. Francis. It then had only 800 inhabitants; but after gold was found in California the city grew rapidly.

SAN MARINO (*sahn mah-rē'no*), a country of N. E. Italy, about 10 miles from the Adriatic Sea; area, 22 square miles; pop., about 8,000; capital, San Marino (pop., 6,000). The surface is mountainous, but there are many little farms; and wine, silk, and fruits are raised. San Marino is a republic, being governed by a council or congress of sixty persons, and two presidents, who are chosen every six months. San Marino is the smallest state in Europe, except Monaco, but it is the oldest of all. It was named after San Marino, or Saint Marinus, a hermit, who is said to have made a settlement there in the 4th century. Ever since, it has been independent.

SAN SALVADOR (*sahn sahl-vah-dore'*), the smallest country of Central America, on the Pacific Ocean, W. of Honduras; area, 7,500 square miles, or nearly the same as that of Massachusetts; pop., 664,000, or less than a third that of Massachusetts; capital, San Salvador (pop., 16,000). Most of the surface is mountainous, and there are many active volcanoes, some of which are more than a mile and a half high. The soil is rich, and most of the people are farmers. The principal thing raised is indigo. Fine timber, especially cedar, is got in the forests. The people are mostly Indians or mixed races. There are only nine thousand whites. San Salvador is a republic much like the United States, but it is often disturbed by civil wars, and the people are generally ignorant and poor.

San Salvador was conquered by the Spaniards from the Indians in 1524, and became independent of Spain in 1821.

SANTA ANNA (*sahn'tah ah'nah*),

Antonio Lopez de, a Mexican general, born in Jalapa, Feb. 21, 1798. After taking the lead in several insurrections, he became president of Mexico in 1833. In 1836 Texas, which then belonged to Mexico, revolted, and Santa Anna marched against it, and took the ALAMO fortress at San Antonio. Not long after, he was defeated and taken prisoner by Houston (April 21). In 1837 he lost a leg at the bombardment of Vera Cruz by the French. In 1841 he was again made president, but in 1845 was deposed and banished. When the Americans invaded Mexico (1846), Santa Anna was called back, and made president and general, to resist them, but was defeated in every battle. In 1853 Santa Anna was again chosen president for one year, and afterward president for life. But he was so despotic that the people rebelled, and after two years, he was obliged to leave the country.

When Maximilian was emperor, he made Santa Anna grand-marshal of the empire, but he plotted against the emperor's life, and was again obliged to leave Mexico (1865). He died when seventy-eight years old (June 20, 1876).

SANTA CRUZ (*sahn'tah krooz*), or **Saint Croix,** an island of the West Indies, S. E. of Porto Rico; area, 84 square miles; pop., 18,000; capital, Christiansted. It is covered with fine plantations, the principal crop being sugar-cane, from which sugar and rum are made. More than half of the people are negroes.

Santa Cruz was discovered by Columbus on his second voyage; and it has belonged to the Dutch, British, Spanish, and French, but is now a colony of Denmark.

SANTA FÉ (*sahn'tah fa'*), the capital and principal city of New Mexico, on the Santa Fé creek, 14 miles from the Rio Grande; pop., 8000, or about as large as Cranston, R. I. Most of the people are of Spanish or Mexican descent, and still speak the Spanish language. The houses, generally only one story high, are built of adobes, or sun-dried bricks. The farmers for a hundred miles around do their trading in Santa Fé, and their great covered wagons, drawn by oxen, are seen in long lines in the streets. The nearest railroad station is 190 miles away, and all the travelling is done by stages.

Santa Fé was an Indian village, first visited by the Spaniards about the year 1542. In 1640 it was made the capital of New Mexico.

SANTIAGO (*sahn-te-ah'go*), a city, capital of Chili, on the River Mapocho, 70 miles S.E. of its port, Valparaiso, on the Pacific; pop. 189,000, or about twice as large as Albany, N.Y. It is built in a valley among high mountains, about eight miles from the Andes. The city streets are wider and better paved than in most South American cities, and there are many fine houses and public buildings. The University of Santiago has 1,200 students. Earthquakes are very frequent, and the city has been several times partly destroyed by them.

Santiago was founded by the Spaniard, Pedro de Valdivia, in 1541. One of the old churches, called the Church of the Jesuits, caught fire in 1863 and 1600 people were burned to death.

SANTO DOMINGO (*sahn'to doming'go*). See HAYTI.

SANTO DOMINGO, a city, capital of the republic of Dominica, on the River Ozama, on the S. side of the Island of HAYTI; pop. 20,000. This is the oldest European settlement in the New World, having been founded by Bartholomew Columbus, brother of Christopher Columbus, in 1494. The body of Christopher Columbus was buried in the Cathedral there, but afterward removed to Havana, though some think that the wrong body was taken, and that one found in the Cathedral in 1877 is the true body of Columbus.

SA'POR I., King of Persia, who reigned from the death of his father, Artaxerxes, A.D. 240 to A.D. 309. He carried on important wars against the Romans, and took prisoner the emperor Valerian.

SAPOR II., King of Persia, began to reign when he was born, A.D. 309 or 310. He fought bloody battles against the Roman emperors Constantius and Julian. Julian entered Persia with an army, and was slain in 363. Sapor II. died about 380.

SAPPHO (*saf'fo*), a famous Greek poet, born at Mytilene, in the island of Lesbos, lived about 600 B.C. Little is known of her life, but she is said to have spent part of it in exile in Sicily. She wrote beautiful poems, of which one complete ode

Sappho.

to Aphrodite (Venus), the goddess of love and beauty, and several fragments remain. There is a story that she fell in love with a beautiful youth named Phaon, and because he did not love her threw herself from the Leucadian rock into the sea, but it is only a fable.

SAR'A-CENS, a name, at first of an Arab tribe, but afterward given to all the followers of Mohammed. The Saracen Empire was that founded by the CALIPHS, which, beginning in Arabia, extended itself over northern Africa, Syria, Persia, and a great part of Asia Minor, and even into the southern part of Spain. They tried at various times to spread themselves over the rest of Europe, but they were checked by CHARLES MARTEL at the battle of Tours, and thus South Western Europe was saved from their ravages.

Twenty years afterward there was a split in the empire, and a rival caliph was set up at Cordova in Spain. Thus there were two caliphates, the Eastern, whose capital was Damascus, and the Western whose chief seat was Cordova. The Eastern Caliphate was overthrown by the Moguls in the 13th century, and the Western was conquered in 1492 by Ferdinand and Isabella. Although these people ceased to be called Saracens, after their conquest by the Turks and Moguls, the conquerors soon adopted the religion of the conquered, and, being joined with them, became much the same people under the name of Turks. During the Crusades, the Christian nations of Europe fought with the Saracens for nearly two hundred years. As they were much more learned than the Europeans, they had a great influence over Western civilization, and all the arts and sciences were much advanced by contact with them. In Spain there are many beautiful ruins showing their skill in architecture, especially the Alhambra in GRANADA.

SARAGOSSA (*sah-rah-gos'sah*), a city of N. E. Spain, on the River Ebro; pop. 92,000, or nearly as large as Albany, N. Y. It has narrow and crooked streets, with many curious old buildings. The city is one of the most important in Spain, and carries on a large trade. The University of Saragossa is one of the oldest in the country.

Saragossa was founded by the Roman emperor Augustus (27 B.C.), and named Cæsarea Augusta, from which its present name has come. It was besieged by the French from June 16, to Aug. 14, 1808, and again from Dec. 20, 1808, to Feb. 21, 1809. The soldiers and people defended themselves with wonderful bravery; but a pestilence broke out in the city, killing nearly fifty thousand persons, and those who remained were at length compelled to surrender. A woman named Agustina, who had been a seller of lemonade in the city streets, became famous at this siege by her bravery. Once, when a cannoneer was killed, she snatched the match from his hand and fired off his cannon at the enemy. Agustina, who is commonly called the " Maid of Saragossa," was afterwards made a sublieutenant in the Spanish army, and was otherwise rewarded for her bravery. She died at Ceuta, Spain, when very old (1857).

SAR·A·TO'GA SPRINGS, a village of E. New York, 32 miles N. by W. of Albany; pop., 12,000, or about as large as Appleton, Wis. It is celebrated for its numerous mineral springs, which differ much in the kind and taste of their waters. The water is much used for drinking, and large quantities of it are bottled, and sent to all parts of the country. Saratoga has become one of the most fashionable watering places in the United States, and is visited every year by thousands of people, and many large hotels have been built there. Saratoga lake, three and a half miles from the village, is a beautiful sheet of water, seven miles long, and flowing into the Hudson through Fish Creek.

The name Saratoga is made from the Indian word Saraghoga, meaning the " Place of Herrings." It was first given to the lake, because herrings used to come into it from the Hudson. The first white man who visited the springs was Sir William JOHNSON, who was carried there by the Indians in 1767. The first house was built at Saratoga in 1773. In 1693 a battle was fought near the site of Saratoga, between the English, led by Major Peter Schuyler, and the French, in which the English were victorious.

During the Revolution, an English army, under General John BURGOYNE, came from Canada to the Hudson, by way of Lake George and Lake Champlain. They expected to meet another English army, which Sir Henry Clinton promised to bring up the Hudson from New York. Burgoyne crossed the Hudson not far from Saratoga Lake, and attacked the Americans near their fortified camp at Bemus's Heights. After a severe battle he was driven back (Sept. 19, 1777). He made another attack on Oct. 7, but the Americans led by Arnold and Morgan defeated him again. The first fight is generally called the battle of Stillwater or Bemus's Heights, and the second the battle of Saratoga. Soon after, Gen. Gates arrived with large re-enforcements for the Americans. Burgoyne was cut off from Canada, the Americans having taken the forts at Ticonderoga and Crown Point, near the mouth of Lake George ; a fleet of boats, which was coming to bring him provisions, was captured, and Sir Henry Clinton did not arrive ; so Burgoyne was compelled to surrender to Gen. Gates (Oct. 17, 1777). The Americans took nearly 6,000 prisoners, and forty-two cannon : these and the muskets and ammunition were of great use to them. This battle is generally looked upon as the turning point of the war of the Revolution, for it became clear after it that America would gain its independence.

SAR·DA·NA·PA'LUS, the last king of the Assyrian empire of Nineveh. He spent his life in his palace, living in great splendor, surrounded by women, and often dressed in women's clothes. He took no interest in the welfare of his people, who at last made war upon him. Finding he should be defeated, he collected all his women and treasures and caused a funeral pyre to be erected, and perished with them in the flames. Some writers think that no such person as Sardanapalus ever lived.

SARDINIA (*sar-din'e-ah*), an island in the Mediterranean Sea, W. of Italy and N.W. of Sicily; area, including several small islands near it, 9,400 square miles, or nearly as large as Vermont; pop. 736,000, or about two and a fourth times that of Vermont. It is mountainous, but has many fertile plains and valleys, abounding in beautiful scenery. The principal crops are barley, wheat, and maize, but there are also many vineyards, and very fine wine is made. Forests of pine, chestnut, and cork-trees cover the mountain sides, and in one place there is a forest of orange-trees. The farmers keep many sheep and goats, and make cheese from their milk. The people are much like those of Italy, to which country the island belongs.

Sardinia gets its name from the Sardi, an ancient people who lived there. The island was settled by Greeks in the 6th century B.C., and afterward belonged to the Carthaginians and the Romans. It belonged to Spain from 1326 to 1713, when it was given up to the Emperor Charles VI. of Germany. He gave it to Duke Victor Amadeus of Savoy, in exchange for Sicily, and Amadeus united the island with a part of northern Italy to make the kingdom of Sardinia. The last king of Sardinia was Victor Emanuel II., who, in 1861 became the first king of Italy.

SAR'DIS, or **Sardes,** an ancient city of Asia Minor, on the River Pactolus, about 45 miles E. of Smyrna. It was the capital of the kingdom of Lydia, and is said to have been named after the Lydian god of

the sun. At one time it was very populous and rich. Its greatest prosperity was during the reign of King CRŒSUS, who built a magnificent palace there, and otherwise adorned the city. The Persian King Cyrus captured Sardis from Crœsus (about 554 B.C.), and from that time its power declined. In the time of Christ it was destroyed by a terrible earthquake. It was afterwards rebuilt by the Romans. In 1402 Sardis was almost entirely destroyed by TIMOUR. Remains of the palace of Crœsus and of other rich buildings can still be seen there.

SARDOU (*sar-doo'*), **Victorien,** a French play-writer, born in Paris Sept. 7, 1831. In early life he was very poor, and his first play, written in 1854, was not liked. In 1858 he married an actress, and thus made acquaintances, chief among them Sarah Bernhardt, who helped him to bring out his plays. He became very successful and made a large fortune. Among his plays are "A Scrap of Paper," "Diplomacy," and "Fedora."

SAT'URN, in ancient Roman fable, a god or a king who brought agriculture and civilization into Italy, and at his death was taken up among the gods. His home was on the Capitoline Hill, which was sometimes called after him, the Saturnian Hill, and his reign was called the Golden Age. He is the same as the Cronos of Greek fable, the son of Heaven and Earth, and father of Jupiter, Juno, Neptune, and Pluto. He is often represented as Time, holding in his hand a scythe, and devouring his own children.

SA-VAN'NAH, the second largest city of Georgia, on the Savannah River, 18 miles from its mouth; pop., 43,000, or about as large as Hoboken, N. J. It is a handsome city, with broad shaded streets, and many beautiful squares. The houses are surrounded with flower gardens, which are in bloom all the year. The harbor is one of the best in the

Southern States, and Savannah has a large trade, more cotton being shipped there than in any other port in the United States except New Orleans. The harbor is defended by strong forts, called Fort Pulaski and Fort Jackson.

Savannah was founded by the English General Oglethorpe, in 1733. During the war of the Revolution it was taken by the British (Dec. 29, 1778), and in trying to recover it, Count Pulaski of the American army was killed (1779). During the Civil War, Savannah was held by the Confederates until it was taken by Gen. Sherman (Dec. 21, 1864), who had marched across Georgia from Atlanta.

SAVONAROLA (*sah-vo-nah-ro' lah*), **Girolamo,** an Italian monk, born in Ferrara, Sept. 21, 1452. He became a Dominican monk at Bologna in 1475, and in 1482, having been made a priest, he was sent to preach in the convent of San Marco in Florence. He was so small a man, and had such a harsh voice, that the people did not like him, and after a while he was sent to another convent at Brescia. There he became so renowned as a preacher that he was called back to Florence, where he soon became the most powerful man in the city. In 1493, the Pope appointed him vicar-general of the Dominican monks, and he labored to make the order better and purer. Savonarola was opposed to the Medici family, who ruled Florence, and he encouraged the French king, Charles VIII., to take the city. The French remained only a short time, and when they went away Savonarola set up a kind of republic, which had very severe laws to govern morals. He preached against amusements of all kinds, and against the corruptions of the priests and monks in the Catholic Church, even demanding that the pope should be deposed. The pope excommunicated him, that is, put him out of the church, but this only

made him more popular in Florence. At length, however, his enemies succeeded in having him banished. He shut himself up in the convent of San Marco, but was obliged to surrender after a severe struggle. Savonarola was tried, condemned to death, and strangled when forty-five years old (May 23, 1498).

SAVOY (*sah-voy'*), a part of S. E. France, lying between the Alps and the River Rhone; area, 3,888 square miles, or about three-fourths as large as Connecticut; pop. 524,000, or five sevenths that of Connecticut. From 1048 to 1860, it was governed by independent counts and dukes, who, at one time, were very powerful. They conquered parts of northern Italy, and in 1720 Duke Amadeus II. became king of Sardinia. From him descended Victor Emanuel, king of Italy, who, in 1860, ceded his old territory of Savoy to France. The people of Savoy, called Savoyards, are an honest, industrious race, who go to other countries to make money, but generally go home again to live.

SAXE, John Godfrey, an American writer, born in Highgate, Vt., June 2, 1816. He became a lawyer, and editor of the "Burlington Sentinel" newspaper, and in 1856 was made State Attorney. He has published several books, principally of poems, including "The Times," "Clever Stories of Many Nations," and "Fables and Legends in Rhyme." Many of his poems are humorous, and they are much read and liked. He died when seventy-one years old (March 31, 1887).

SAXONS. See ANGLO SAXONS.

SAXONY, a kingdom of the German Empire, S. of Prussia; area, 5788 square miles, or about as large as Connecticut and Rhode Island together; pop. 3,182,000, or nearly three times their population; capital, DRESDEN. In the southern part are many mountains noted for beautiful scenery, but the northern part is flat or rolling, and very fertile. Farming and mining are the principal pursuits of the people, but there are also large manufactures. Saxony was named after the Saxons, who conquered it in the 9th or 10th century. Its rulers became very powerful, and during the Reformation they were noted as defenders of the Protestant religion. They were called electors until 1806, when Napoleon changed the country into a kingdom. The first king, Frederick Augustus I., was an ally of Napoleon, and when Napoleon was conquered, part of the Saxon kingdom was given to Prussia. This is now called Prussian Saxony.

SCÆVOLA (*sev'o-lah*), **Caius Mucius,** a hero of Roman story, said to have lived about the end of the 6th century B.C. When Lars Porsena, king of Clusium, was besieging Rome, Mucius went into his camp to slay him, but by mistake killed his secretary. Mucius then said that 300 young Romans had sworn to kill Porsena; and when Porsena threatened to burn him alive unless he would tell their names, Mucius, to show he was not afraid, thrust his right hand into a fire until it was burned off. Porsena, struck by such courage, set him free, and made peace with Rome. Mucius received the surname Scævola (left-handed) in honor of this deed.

SCANDINAVIA (*skan-di-na've-ah*), the ancient name of that part of northern Europe now included in Denmark, Norway, Sweden, and Iceland. The people originally spoke the same language, and were sometimes united into one nation.

SCHENECTADY (*sken-ek'ta-de*), a city of E. New York, on the Mohawk River, 17 miles N. W. of Albany; pop., 20,000, or about as large as Woonsocket, R.I. It has large locomotive and engine works, and manufactures of stoves, fire-engines, agricultural tools, shawls, and brooms. Schenectady is the seat of Union University, one of the best colleges in the country, and now nearly a hundred years old, having been begun in 1795.

Schenectady was settled in 1661. In 1690, and again in 1748, it was taken by French and Indians from Canada, and nearly all the people were killed. It became a city in 1798.

SCHIEDAM (*ske-dahm'*), a town of the Netherlands, on the River Schie, 4 miles W. of Rotterdam; pop., 25,000, or about as large as Taunton, Mass. It has more than three hundred distilleries, and carries on a larger trade in liquors than any other town in the Netherlands. The gin made there, called Hollands, or Schiedam Schnapps, is sent to all parts of the world.

Schiedam means the dam on the River Schie.

SCHILLER (*shil'ler*), **Johann Christoph Friedrich von,** a famous German poet, born at Marbach, Würtemberg, Nov. 10, 1759. His name is the greatest in German literature, after that of GOETHE. He was of humble parentage, and received his

Schiller.

education at the ducal military school in Stuttgart, studied medicine, and became (1780) a surgeon in the army. But poetry filled his soul; and before he left the university he had written a play called

"The Robbers," which at once gave him a high place among play-writers. In the little town of Weimar he first met the poet Goethe. At first the two poets did not like each other; but they afterward became dear friends, Goethe's stronger nature strengthening and upholding the sensitive Schiller. His best works are the tragedies "Wallenstein," "Marie Stuart," "William Tell," and "Joan of Arc." "The Song of the Bell," "The Diver," and his ballads, made him a favorite with the people. On the hundredth anniversary of his birth (1859) a sum of money was raised, called the Schiller Fund, the interest of which is used to support poor authors. The remains of Schiller now rest beside those of Goethe, in the vault of the ducal palace of WEIMAR, where he died when forty-five years old (May 9, 1805).

SCHLIEMANN (*shle'mahn*), **Heinrich,** a noted German traveller, born at Kalkhorst, Mechlenburg-Schwerin, in 1822. He was the son of a poor man, and had to make his own way in the world, beginning when fourteen years old as clerk in a grocer's store. All his leisure hours were spent in learning languages, for which he had a great love. His learning Russian was the means of his making a fortune in the business which he set up in St. Petersburg. He then gave up business, and began a series of travels in the East. In 1870 he made excavations on the site of ancient TROY, and discovered what he claims to be the ruins of the city. He found many curious things there, among them what he calls the treasure-chest of King Priam. But the best scholars do not think that the ruins found are those of Troy.

Schliemann has since made excavations at MYCENÆ, and has found there what he claims to be the tomb of Agamemnon, with many curious articles of gold and bronze. He died in Naples when sixty-eight years old (December 26, 1890).

SCHOFIELD (*sko'field*), **John Mc Allister,** an American general, born in Chautauqua Co., New York, Sept. 29, 1831. He was graduated at West Point, and in the second year of the Civil War became a major-general, fighting under Gen. Sherman at Atlanta. While Sherman marched from Atlanta through Georgia, Schofield was sent against Gen. Hood, in Tennessee, and defeated him at the battle of Franklin (Nov. 30, 1864). In 1865 he commanded in North Carolina, taking Wilmington (Feb. 22), and gaining other victories. In 1868, he was secretary of war for a short time.

SCHREYER (*shri'er*), **Adolphe,** a German painter, born at Frankfort-on-the-Main in 1828. He is an artist of great merit, whose pictures of battle-scenes, Eastern life, or Russian wintry landscapes, all receive high praise. Most of his pictures have horses in them.

SCHUBERT (*shu'bert*), **Franz,** a German musician, born near Vienna Jan. 31, 1797. He is best known by his songs, which have a sad melody peculiar to themselves. His music was not much liked during his life, but it became more popular when he had passed away. His finest work is thought to be the "Erl King." After a life of disappointment, he died, when thirty-one years old (Nov. 19, 1828).

SCHUMANN (*shu'mahn*), **Robert,** a German writer of music, born in Zwickau, Saxony, Jan. 8, 1810. When only eleven years old, he composed little pieces for the piano. He was self-taught till he was eighteen years old, when he went to Munich to study. To save himself the long hours of practising necessary to learn to play on the piano, he made a machine for his fingers, which so injured them that he had to give up all idea of ever being a pianist. His chief work is "Paradise and the Peri," a cantata. Toward the end of his life, he lost his reason and tried to drown himself in the

Rhine; but he was saved and taken to a lunatic asylum near Bonn, where he died when forty-six years old (July 29, 1856).

SCIO (*si'o*), an island belonging to Turkey, in the E. part of the Mediterranean Sea, 4 miles from the coast of Asiatic Turkey; area, 400 square miles, or about a third as large as the State of Rhode Island; pop., 70,000, or a fifth that of Rhode Island; capital, Scio. It is very hilly, and the soil is rocky and dry, but the people water their land from wells or small streams, and keep the fields so bright and green that they have made it one of the most beautiful islands in the world. The most important product is gum-mastic, in which Scio has a larger trade than any other region. Silk, cotton, and grapes are raised, and a great deal of wine is made. In ancient times, the wine of this island was famous. Most of the people are Turks, though there are many Greek families there.

The ancients called Scio Chios (modern Greek, *Che'os*), and the early inhabitants were much like Greeks. After belonging to several different countries, the island was conquered by the Turks in the 14th century. It afterwards fell into the hands of the Genoese, who kept it for more than two hundred years (1346-1566), after which it was again taken by the Turks. When the Greeks rebelled against Turkey (1822), the people of Scio joined them, but they were soon conquered, and after the Turks had murdered many thousands of them, they sold nearly all the rest into slavery.

SCIPIO (*sip'e-o*), **Publius Cornelius,** called Africanus Major (the Greater), a famous Roman general, born about 234 B.C. When very young he fought with great bravery in the battles of the Ticinus (218), and CANNÆ (216), and when but twenty-four years old he was given command of the army in Spain (210). By a quick march he captured New

Carthage (Cartagena), the capital and treasure city of the Carthaginians, where all their military stores and hostages were, and in the next three years he drove them out and made himself master of Spain. This ended the second Punic War. Scipio went back to Rome (206) and was made consul for the next year. HANNIBAL was then in Italy; and Scipio advised that instead of fighting him there any longer, the Ro-

Scipio Africanus Major.

mans should attack Carthage; but the senate feared that this was too daring, and would not give him an army. Scipio's fame, however, soon got him an army of volunteers, and in the year 204 he crossed into Africa, and began the siege of Utica. Hannibal then had to leave Italy and go back to defend Carthage. After destroying two Carthaginian armies, Scipio met Hannibal at Zama in Numidia (Oct. 19, 202), and totally defeated him.

He then went back to Rome (201),

and was given the surname of Africanus (African), the first Roman who
got a title from the country he had
conquered. He is commonly called
Major (Greater), to distinguish him
from the younger Scipio, who is
called Minor (Lesser). He was also
made consul the second time, but
refused all other honors, though the
people were ready to make him
consul for life. He was reckoned
the ablest general the Romans ever
had, and was so popular that when
his brother Lucius was attacked for
bribery and arrested, Africanus
released him by force, and the
senate thought it best not to notice
his violence; and when his enemies
charged him with the same crime,
he disdained making any defence,
but addressed the people with great
eloquence, reminding them that the
day was the anniversary of the
victory of Zama, and commanded
them to go to the Capitol with him
and thank the gods for giving them
so great a general. He spent the
rest of his life on his estate at
Liternum, where he died about 183
B.C. His daughter Cornelia was the
mother of the Gracchi.

**SCIPIO, Publius Cornelius Æmili-
anus,** called Africanus Minor (the
Lesser), a famous Roman general,
born about 185 B.C. He was the
son of Lucius Æmilius Paulus, the
conqueror of Macedonia, and was
adopted by Publius Scipio, the son
of Africanus Major. He won great
fame for his courage and ability in
his first campaign in Spain. In the
beginning of the third Punic war
(149), he was sent to Africa under
Manilius, a poor general, and more
than once Scipio saved the Roman
army by his skill and bravery. In
147 he was made consul and given
command of the army in Africa,
and in 146 he took CARTHAGE after
a stubborn defence, and ended the
third Punic war. For this he was
given a triumph and the title of
Africanus. In 134 he was again
made consul, and was sent to carry

on the war against Spain, which had
revolted, where he made a brilliant
campaign, ending with the capture
of Numantia, which he destroyed,
and was given the title of Numan-
tinus. Shortly after Scipio's return
to Rome (129), he was found dead in
his room, and it was generally
believed that he had been murdered.
Scipio was a fine scholar as well as
a brave general.

**SCIPIO, Quintus Cæcilius Metel-
lus Pius,** a noted Roman general.
He was the adopted son of Metellus
Pius, who was noted in the struggle
between CÆSAR and POMPEY. It is
thought that Scipio was the one who
warned Cicero of the Catiline conspiracy. When Pompey was made
sole consul Scipio was chosen by
him as joint consul (52), and did all
he could to destroy the power of
Cæsar. After the battle of Pharsalia
(48), Scipio fled to Africa where he
took command of the army there,
but was defeated by Cæsar at the
battle of Thapsus, and to escape
capture stabbed himself and sprang
into the sea (46 B.C.).

SCOT'LAND, a country of N.W.
Europe, forming the N. part of the
island of Great Britain; area, with
the islands belonging to it, 30,463
square miles, or not quite as large
as Indiana; pop. 3,736,000, or more
than that of Indiana and Alabama
together; capital, EDINBURGH. All
the northern part, called the Highlands, is covered with mountains,
none very high, but famed for their
wildness and grandeur, and for their
beautiful lakes and glens. In the
southern part, called the Lowlands,
are also many mountains and hills,
with fine valleys and plains between
them. The coasts of Scotland have
so many bays and peninsulas that
their entire length is about 3,000
miles, or one-fourth more than the
whole Atlantic seacoast of the
United States. In several places
the country is nearly cut in two by
deep bays, called friths or firths.
The northern part is indeed cut off

from the rest by bays and lakes which have been joined together by a deep channel called the Caledonian Canal, through which ships can pass from the North Sea to the Irish Sea. The climate of Scotland is much like that of New England, and even in the most northern part the winters are never very cold.

Scotland has rich mines of coal and iron, and quarries of sandstone, granite, and other building stones. Much of the soil is poor, but the people are skilful farmers, and by industry and patience have made some of the finest farms in the world. They raise large quantities of oats, wheat, barley, potatoes, and turnips, and keep a great many cattle and sheep. Along the coasts are rich fisheries of herring and cod, and thousands of salmon are caught in the rivers. Scotland has factories of cotton, linen, and woollen cloths, which are among the largest in Europe, and the iron ships made there are the best in the world. Among other important manufactures are paper, glass, hardware, machinery, beer, and whiskey.

The Scottish people are divided into Highlanders and Lowlanders. The Highlanders speak a language called Gaelic or Erse, which is something like the Irish. Many of them still wear the old national costume, which consists of a coat, vest, and kilt or skirt of plaid cloth, the knees being left bare, and the feet and ankles covered with short stockings. They wear also a kind of cap called a bonnet, and a scarf or shawl called the plaid. The Lowland language is much like the English. Of late years both Lowlanders and Highlanders have generally adopted the English language and costume. Scotland forms a part of England, but the Scottish people have their own laws and law-courts, and church government. A large part of the people are Presbyterians.

When southern Britain was conquered by the Romans, Scotland, called by them Caledonia, was inhabited by savage tribes. They were so brave and warlike that the Romans could not entirely conquer them, and to keep them from invading England, two great walls were built across the island, the first between the Firths of Clyde and Forth, and the second near the northern boundary of England. At that time the principal tribe of Caledonia was that of the Picts, but in about 503, the Scots, a people from Ireland, invaded the country, and settled in the western part. In 836 their king, Kenneth MacAlpin, conquered nearly the whole of Caledonia, which after that was called Scotland. The Scots had many wars with the English (told about under the names of sovereigns), and at times their kingdom was subject to England. In 1603 King James VI. of Scotland became James I. of England, and the two countries then became one, though it was not until 1707 that the full union was brought about.

SCOTT, Sir Walter, a famous Scottish writer of novels, born in

Sir Walter Scott.

Edinburgh, Aug. 15, 1771. When only eighteen months old he had a fever, which gave his right leg the lameness which he never got over. He not did win many honors at school, for he was not a hard student, and when he grew up he was very sorry for this. In the life which he wrote of himself he says, "It is with the deepest regret that I recollect in my manhood the opportunities which I neglected in my youth." Though he did not shine in the class-room, he was very popular with his companions, on account of the stories which he knew so well how to tell. When he became a man he studied law and began to practise; but he never liked it, and he soon gave it up for literature. His first works were the beautiful poems, "The Lay of the Last Minstrel," "Marmion," and "The Lady of the Lake." These brought him fame, and a fortune sufficient to buy a small farm on the River Tweed, to which he gave the name of ABBOTSFORD.

Scott had been writing poetry for about ten years, when, one day, as he was hunting for some fishing-tackle, he came upon some loose sheets of a story which he had begun several years before, but which had been lying all that time forgotten in his cabinet. At once he set to work to finish it. This was "Waverley," the first of the novels called from it the "Waverley Novels," which came out one after another and without the author's name. Among the best of these are "Ivanhoe," "Kenilworth," "The Talisman," "The Antiquary," and "Rob Roy." Many years went by before he was known to be the author of these delightful books. The money that came from them was spent in beautifying his home, and collecting the curiosities which made it almost a museum.

In 1825 many people failed in Scotland, and among them a publishing house in which Scott had become a partner. Not only was his fortune gone, but the firm owed many debts, his share of which amounted to

nearly £140,000 ($700,000). His friends offered to help him pay this money; but he was too independent to accept their kindness, so he went on writing harder than ever to free himself from debt. During these sad years he wrote for children "The Tales of a Grandfather." At last, in the midst of his toil, he had a stroke of paralysis, and was never quite himself again. He went to Italy to build up his health; but his great labors had worn him out, and he came home only to die. His death took place at Abbotsford, when he was sixty-one years old (Sept. 21, 1832).

SCOTT, Winfield, an American general, born at Petersburg, Va., June 13, 1786. He became a lawyer,

Winfield Scott.

but in 1808 entered the army as a captain. When the war of 1812 broke out, Scott was made a lieutenant-colonel. At the battle of Queenstown, on the Niagara River, the Americans under him were at first victorious; but in the end, not receiving re-enforcements, he and his whole army were captured. He was exchanged soon after, became a brigadier-general, captured Fort Erie on the Niagara River, and soon after won the battles of Chippewa and Lundy's Lane. At the close of the war Scott was made a major-general, and Congress gave him a gold medal for his services.

During the next thirty years he was constantly employed in important posts. In 1841 he became commander-in-chief of the United States army. When the Mexican war began he sailed with an army to Vera Cruz, which he captured (March 29, 1847). He then marched toward the city of Mexico, won the victories of Cerro Gordo (April 18, 1847), Contreras and Churubusco (Aug. 20), and Chapultepec (Sept. 13), and finally captured the city of Mexico (Sept. 14, 1847). In 1852 he was a candidate for president, but was defeated by Franklin Pierce. When the Civil War broke out he was still in command of the army; but, being old and infirm, retired from service, and went to live at West Point, where he died at the age of nearly eighty years (May 29, 1866).

SCRAN'TON, a city of Pennsylvania, on the Lackawanna River; pop. 75,000, or a little larger than Fall River, Mass. The valley of the Lackawanna is one of the richest anthracite-coal regions in the world, and hundreds of mines are worked there. It is bordered by hills and mountains, over which the coal is taken by railroad, sometimes sixty or eighty cars in a train. Scranton also has many large blast furnaces, rolling-mills, foundries, and machine shops. Nearly half the people are foreigners, principally Irish, German, and Welsh miners, who pass nearly half their lives under ground. The coal mines extend under the streets, and at one time, some of the houses sank down many feet, the ground having given way beneath them.

Scranton was named after the Scranton family, who went there from Connecticut about 1840, and engaged in the iron and coal business. The first rolling-mill was built there in 1844, before there were any houses. Scranton became a city in 1866.

SCRIBE (*skreeb*), **Augustin Eugène,** a French play-writer, born in Paris,

Dec. 24, 1791. He studied law, but began to write plays when only twenty years old. At first they were unsuccessful; but afterward they were so well received that he gained a large fortune. It is said that he wrote more than 350 plays, in some of which he was assisted by other writers. He also wrote the words for many celebrated operas; among others, "Fra Diavalo" and "The Circassian," for Auber, "Sicilian Vespers," for Verdi, and "Robert the Devil" and "The Huguenots," for Meyerbeer. He died in Paris when sixty-nine years old (Feb. 20, 1861).

SCYTHIA (*sith'e-ah*), a name given, in ancient times, to a great region in Europe and Asia, north of the River Danube and the Black and Caspian Seas, and extending eastward nearly to China. The people, called Scythians, were very warlike and savage, and were divided into many tribes. One of these tribes, called the Sarmatians, conquered many of the others, and in time the western part of Scythia took the name of Sarmatia, while the eastern part kept its old title until after the time of Christ.

SEBASTOPOL, or **Sevastopol** (*sev-as-to'pol*), a city of S. Russia, in the CRIMEA, on an arm of the Black Sea; pop. 34,000, or about as large as Augusta, Ga. It was a small village until 1780, when the Russians made it a station for their armies and ships. They built many forts and improved the bay, until it became one of the best and strongest harbors in the world for ships of war. In 1854 the city was attacked by the English, French, Sardinians, and Turks. The Russians had sunk ships in the mouth of the harbor, so that the fleets of their enemies could not come in and bombard the town. The attack was, therefore, made from the land side, and many bloody battles were fought. Finally, after the siege had lasted a year, the allies got their batteries into position, and began a furious bombardment, which lasted for three days. At the end of that time, two of the forts were taken by storm (Sept. 8, 1855), and the Russians, after blowing up their other forts, retreated across the harbor. All their costly docks and arsenals were destroyed by the allies, who remained in Sevastopol for a year. Since then, many of the works have been rebuilt.

SEDAN (*seh-dong'*), a city of N. E. France, on the River Meuse; pop., 20,000, or about as large as Lynchburg, Va. It is strongly fortified, and has been a very important place in the wars between the French and Germans. It was captured by the Germans in 1815, and held by them for more than a year. Soon after the Franco-Prussian war began, the French under the Emperor Napoleon III. and Marshal MacMahon were defeated at Sedan in a terrible battle (Sept. 1, 1870). The Germans then surrounded them and shut them up in the city, and as they had no provisions, they were obliged to surrender. The emperor himself surrendered to King William on Sept. 2.

SEINE (*sane*), a river of France, rising in the E. part of the country, and flowing N. W. to the English Channel; length nearly 500 miles. It can be navigated by large vessels as far as Rouen, 44 miles from its mouth, and by small vessels 300 miles farther. At Paris it is less than a tenth of a mile wide, but at its mouth it is seven miles. Besides Paris there are many other important cities and towns on its banks.

SELEUCUS (*se-lu'kus*) **I., Nicator,** founder of the line of kings of Syria, called after him the Seleucidæ, born about 358 B.C. He was the son of Antiochus, a general of Philip of Macedon, and became one of the best officers of Alexander the Great, in whose army he held very high rank. After the death of Alexander, he became ruler of Babylonia, and in time got possession of other parts of Asia and formed the Syrian monarchy, which included a large part of Asia Minor, Media, Persia, Assyria, Babylonia, and other countries. He built the city of Seleucia on the Tigris, and made it his capital, but afterward changed it to ANTIOCH. In trying to add Macedonia to his dominions he was assassinated at Lysimachia in 280, and was succeeded by his son, ANTIOCHUS I.

SE-MIR'A-MIS, a famous queen of Assyria, said to have reigned about 2,000 years B.C. She married Ninus, king of Assyria, and after his death became sole ruler. She built many cities, and made improvements all over her kingdom; and was also very warlike, and conquered several nations. Some say she was put to death by her son Ninyas, others that she was changed into a dove and flew away; but there is so much fable mixed with her history that we hardly know whether she really lived or not.

SEM'ITES, or **Shem'ites,** the name commonly given to a family of peoples separate from the ARYANS, who lived mostly in south-west Asia. They got their name from Shem, son of Noah, from whom, according to the Bible, they are descended. Though as important in the world's history as the Aryan nations, they have kept closer together than the Aryans have, and not scattered so much over the world, at least not until late times. Their languages have also changed much less than have those of the Aryans, and they have therefore kept more like one family. They generally worshipped only one God, and the three one-God religions — the Jewish, the Christian, and the Mohammedan — all came from them. Among the Semitic nations or Semites are the Syrians and Chaldears, Hebrews, Phœnicians, Arabs, and the people of Abyssinia and Ethiopia.

SEMMES (*sems*), **Raphael,** an American naval officer, born in Charles Co., Maryland, Sept. 27, 1809. He entered the United States navy and served in the Mexican War. When the Civil War broke out he resigned and was made commander of the Confederate steamer "Sumter." With this he captured several Union merchant ships, but having entered the harbor of Tangier, Morocco, he was so closely watched there by a United States war vessel that he sold his ship, to prevent its capture. In 1862 he took command of the steamer "Alabama," which had been built for him in England, and with it captured many American vessels, causing a loss of millions of dollars. Finally, the United States steamer "Kearsarge" met the "Alabama," nine miles from CHERBOURG, France, and sank her after a short battle. Semmes and many of his crew were saved by the English yacht "Deerhound," and taken to England. He has written several books about his adventures during the Mexican War and Civil War. He died in Mobile, Ala., when sixty-eight years old (Aug. 30, 1877).

SENNACHERIB (*sen-nak'er-ib*), a famous king of Assyria, who succeeded his father, Sargon, in 704 B.C. He twice subdued great revolts in Babylonia, and carried on successful wars against Egypt, Ethiopia, Phœnicia, Armenia, and Media. He invaded Judah, carried 200,000 Jews into captivity, and forced King Hezekiah to pay him tribute-money. The next year Hezekiah revolted, and Sennacherib made a second expedition into Palestine, where, according to the Bible, his whole army was cut off in a single night. He made Nineveh his capital, and adorned it with magnificent buildings. Sennacherib reigned 22 years, and was murdered by his two sons (682 B.C.).

SER'A-PIS, a god of the ancient Egyptians, worshipped with great honors in the reigns of the Ptolemies. Serapis is made from Osiris-Apis, and is said to have been the name given to the bull APIS after death, when it had become a god. He is generally represented as a man with a bull's head. Splendid temples were erected to Serapis, the grandest of which were the Serapeum at Alexandria, and that at Memphis. The Serapeum at Alexandria was destroyed by order of the emperor Theodosius in 389, and the colossal statue of Serapis, made of wood plated with metal, was burned.

SER-TO'RI-US, Quintus, a Roman general, born about 121 B.C. In the civil wars between MARIUS and SULLA, Sertorius fought on the side of Marius, after whose death he became ruler of Spain. When Sulla returned to Rome, he sent an army to Spain against Sertorius; but the latter held out for a long time against the Roman armies. At length Pompey was sent against him, but he too failed. Finally an offer was made of a large sum of money and several acres of land to any one who would slay Sertorius; and he was killed at a banquet by one of his own generals. He died when about forty-nine years old (72 B.C.).

SER-VE'TUS, Michael (the Latin name of Miguel Servedo), a Spanish writer, born near Saragossa in 1509. He was a very learned man; but he seems to have been an uneasy spirit, roaming about, now practising law at one place, and now medicine at another. He wrote books on medicine, and some on theology, in which he put his own views about religion. His books were condemned by the Church, and he was arrested and imprisoned by the Inquisition on a charge of heresy. He would have been acquitted for lack of evidence had not CALVIN, when he heard of his arrest, sent to the court letters written by Servetus to him as proof of his guilt. It is said that the cardinal who was conducting the trial laughed heartily at the idea of one heretic's accusing another. Servetus escaped from the inquisitors, and foolishly went to Geneva, where Calvin lived. Calvin had Servetus brought to trial on charges of heresy; and he was condemned, and burned on a hill near Geneva, when forty-four years old (Oct. 27, 1553).

SERVIA (*ser've-ah*), a country of S. Europe, between Turkey, Austria, and Roumania; area, 20,850 square miles, or half as large as Louisiana; pop., 2,096,000, or nearly twice that of Louisiana; capital, BELGRADE. Most of the surface is mountainous and rocky, but in the central and northern parts are large fertile plains. Grain and hemp are raised, but cattle, horses, and sheep form the principal riches of the country. The people, called Serbs, or Slavs, resemble Russians, and most of them are Christians, belonging to the Greek Church. They are brave and hospitable, but generally ignorant and superstitious. The country is ruled by a prince, and a congress chosen by the people.

From 1093 to 1459 Servia was an independent kingdom, and at one time it was very powerful. Afterward it was conquered by the Turks, and it remained subject to them until 1878, when it again became independent.

SER'VI-US TUL'LI-US, the sixth king of Rome, began to reign 578 B.C. He was a good and wise king, and made just laws to protect the poor from the injustice of the rich. He had two daughters, the younger of whom, Tullia, plotted with her husband, Lucius Tarquin, to kill her father and seize the throne. Some of the nobles joined them, and Servius was slain, after reigning forty-four years, and TARQUIN became king (534 B.C.).

SE-SOS'TRIS, or **Rameses II.,** a famous king of Egypt who reigned about 1350 B.C. His reign lasted for sixty-six years, and was marked by great victories in war, and the building of many magnificent palaces

and temples. Ethiopia and Arabia were conquered by him. He also built more than a hundred temples in Egypt, a great wall of sun-dried bricks along the edge of the desert more than 187 miles long, and also a great many obelisks or columns on which were engraved pictured histories of his conquests. These great works were done by prisoners taken in war, and he used to celebrate his triumphs by making captive kings drag his chariot. He got to be very old and blind; and life being a great burden to him, he killed himself. Remains of many of his palaces can still be seen in Egypt.

SEVEN PINES. See CHICKAHOMINY.

SEVEN YEARS' WAR, a contest in which the principal European powers were engaged from 1756 to 1763. The Empress MARIA THERESA, wishing to re-conquer Silesia, which she had been forced to give up to Frederick the Great of Prussia, induced France, Russia, and most of the German states to join her against Frederick, whose only allies were England and four of the smaller German states. This war was not confined to Europe, but extended wherever the English and French had colonies, all over the world, and during these seven years, it was waged with varying successes, Frederick holding out bravely against the immense army brought against him, although often defeated. He seemed to be nearly exhausted, when the death of Elizabeth, empress of Russia, and the coming to the throne of Peter III., a great admirer of Frederick, withdrew Russia from the alliance against him. The peace of Hubertsburg, in 1763, left him in possession of Silesia, and made Prussia one of the five great powers of Europe. The colonial contests between the French and English all ended in favor of the English, who got all the French colonies in America.

SE·VE'RUS, Lucius Septimius, a Roman emperor, born near Leptis, Africa (April 11, A.D. 146). He was chosen by his soldiers to succeed the Emperor PERTINAX, and marched at once to Rome, where he was made emperor (A.D. 193). He had two rivals to the throne, but he defeated them after several bloody battles and put them to death. He then marched into Asia, conquered the Parthians, and plundered Ctesiphon, their capital. In 208, he set out with a large army to quell a rebellion in Britain. While there, he began building a great wall across the island, to protect the people of south Britain from those of the north; but he died before it was finished, at York (Feb. 4, 211).

SEVILLE (*se-vil*, Spanish Sevilla, *sa-veel'yah*), a city of S. W. Spain, on the Guadalquivir River; pop., 143,000, or a little larger than Omaha, Neb. It stands in a beautiful plain, and is surrounded by an

Soldiers of Frederick the Great in the Seven Years' War.

ancient wall, with sixty-six towers and fourteen gates. Most of the streets are narrow and crooked, but there are many very beautiful houses. The cathedral, formerly a Moorish mosque, is one of the largest and finest in Spain. It is remarkable for its beautiful square tower, called the Giralda, which is very high (350 feet), and so covered with filigree work that it looks like lace. The cathedral contains many beautiful paintings, and has one of the largest organs in the world. Other interesting buildings are the Alcazar, an old Moorish castle noted for the beauty of its rooms; and the Tower of Gold, said to have been built by the Romans, and long used to keep the gold and silver brought by the Spaniards from America. The bull-ring of Seville, where bullfights take place, is large enough to hold 11,000 people.

Seville was built by the Phœnicians, who called it Sephala ("marshy plain "), a name which has been changed in time into Seville. The city was taken by Julius Cæsar, who made it a Roman colony (45 B.C.). The Goths made it the capital of Spain. From 711 until 1248 it belonged to the Moors, and it became a very large and splendid city with 300,000 inhabitants. It was re-taken by the Spaniards in 1248 and again made the capital of Spain. For a long time it had nearly all the Spanish trade with America, but in the early part of the 18th century the river bed became so filled with sand that the large ships could not go up

it: the port was, therefore, changed to CADIZ.

SÈVRES (*saiv'r*), a town of France, on the River Seine, 6 miles S.W. of Paris; pop. 7000. It is famous for its great porcelain factory, which was removed from Vincennes to Sèvres in 1756. At one time it belonged to the king of France, Louis XV. Many distinguished artists are employed there, in designing and painting vases, and other objects of porcelain. Some of the vases made are among the finest in the world, and are worth thousands of dollars. During the

Sèvres Porcelain Factory.

Franco-Prussian war, Sèvres was taken by the Germans (Sept. 19, 1870), and was afterwards bombarded by the French.

SEW'ARD, William Henry, an American statesman, born in Florida, Orange Co., New York, May 16, 1801. He became a lawyer in Auburn, N.Y., in 1822, and in 1830 he was elected to the Senate of New-York State. From 1838 to 1843 he was governor of New York, and afterwards became one of the most distinguished lawyers in the country. In 1849 he was chosen to the United-

States Senate, of which he became one of the leading members, distinguishing himself for his opposition to slavery. When Mr. Lincoln became President, in 1861, he made Mr. Seward his Secretary of State, and during the Civil War he rendered many important services. Shortly before Mr. Lincoln was killed, Mr. Seward had been thrown from his carriage, and badly hurt. While lying in his bed an assassin entered his room and stabbed him several times, but failed to kill him. Mr. Seward was also Secretary of

State under President Johnson. Among other things brought about by him, was the purchase of Alaska from Russia. In 1869 Mr. Seward retired from public life, and made a journey to California, Oregon, and Alaska; and in 1870 he made a voyage round the world, being everywhere received with great honor. He died at his home in Auburn, when seventy-one years old (Oct. 10, 1872).

SEYCHELLES (*sa-shel'*). See MAURITIUS.

SEYMOUR (*se'more*), **Horatio,** an American statesman, born in Pompey, Onondago Co., New York, May 31, 1810. He became a lawyer in Utica, N.Y., and a noted man in public affairs. He served several times as a member of the Assembly, of which he was speaker in 1845; and in 1852, and again in 1862, he was governor of New York State. In 1868 he presided over the National Democratic Convention and was made a candidate for President of the United States, but was defeated by Gen. Grant. He died when seventy-six years old (February 12, 1886).

SHAFTS'BUR·Y, Anthony Ashley Cooper, Earl of, an English politician, born in Dorsetshire, July 22, 1621. In the English civil war he at first upheld King Charles, but afterwards joined the Parliamentary army, and became a member of Parliament under Cromwell. He opposed many of Cromwell's measures, and was active in restoring Charles II. to the throne. For this Charles gave him many important offices, and in 1672 made him Earl of Shaftsbury, and Lord Chancellor He was ignorant of his duties, and, being vain and arrogant, soon began to oppose the king, who dismissed him from office and imprisoned him, releasing him only when he begged pardon on his knees. Again opposing the king in Parliament, he was forced to fly to Amsterdam, where he soon after died, at the age of sixty-one years (Jan. 22, 1683).

SHAKE'SPEARE, William, the greatest English play-writer and poet, born in Stratford-upon-Avon, Warwickshire, in April, 1564. A writer of a hundred years ago has said, "All that is known with certainty about Shakespeare is, that he was born at Stratford-upon-Avon, married, and had children there, went to London as an actor, and wrote poems and plays; returned to Stratford, made his will, died, and was buried." Although a century has passed since this was written, and people have all this time been trying very hard to find out something more about this great man, we still know little more than this. The house is still standing in which he was born, and is yearly visited by persons from every part of the world, who admire his genius. It has been bought by the English Government, so that it may be well preserved, and may stand forever in remembrance of the wonderful being who first saw light beneath its roof. Not far from this house stands Stratford church, beneath the chancel of which Shakespeare lies buried. Many thought that his remains ought to be moved to Westminster Abbey, but the four lines carved on the flat stone over his grave have kept them in their quiet resting-place in his native town : —

"Good friend for Jesus sake forbeare
To digg the dust enclosed heare.
Blest be ye man yt spares these stones
And curst be he yt moves my bones."

Though our certain knowledge of Shakespeare is so little, there are some stories about his life that may or may not be true. His father, John Shakespeare, was, according to some, a wool-comber, to others a glover, and to others again a butcher; and his mother was Mary Arden, who seems to have belonged to a better family than her husband. Their son William was sent to the Stratford grammar school, and there learned the "little Latin and the less Greek" which he is said to have known. When he was eighteen years old, the poet married Anne Hathaway, who was eight years older than himself. There is a story that the wild youths of Stratford were often guilty of hunting deer in the park of Sir Thomas Lucy, a knight who lived at Charlecote, three miles from Stratford, and that Shakespeare was caught one night with the rest and locked up until morning. He is said to have been so angry at this that he stuck on the park gate some verses making fun of Sir Thomas. This made

William Shakespeare.

the old knight his enemy, and on this account he had to leave Stratford. He then went to London, where he soon became a prosperous actor, play-writer, and part owner of the Blackfriars and Globe Theatres. His thirty-seven plays were first put together and published in 1623, seven years after his death. The most famous are the tragedies of "Hamlet," "Othello," "Macbeth," and "King Lear;" the comedies, "Midsummer Night's Dream" and "Merchant of Venice;" and the historical plays, "Richard III.," "Coriolanus," and "Julius Cæsar." In 1612, when he was forty-eight years old, he went back to Stratford, and died there when fifty-two years old (April 23, 1616). He is thought

by many to be the greatest poet that ever lived.

SHA'MYL (that is, Samuel), a chieftain of the Caucasus, born about 1797. In 1834 he became leader of a sect of Mohammedans, which became very large and powerful, and Shamyl began a war on Russia, defeating a Russian army in 1837. In 1839 the Russians took Akulgo, one of his fortresses, and it was supposed that he had been killed there, but he soon afterward re-appeared, and kept up the war successfully for many years; but at length his people quarrelled with him, and so many soldiers left his army that he was at last taken prisoner (Sept. 6, 1859). He was treated kindly, and allowed to live in a palace near St. Petersburg. In 1870 he made a pilgrimage to Mecca, and died on his journey at Medina, Arabia, when seventy-four years old (March, 1871).

SHANGHAI (*shang-hī'*), or **Shanghae,** a seaport city of E. China, on the Wu-sung River, near where it empties into the mouth of the Yangtse-Kiang; pop. 355,000, or nearly twice as large as Newark, N. J. The older part is surrounded by a wall, and has very narrow and dirty streets, but contains some handsome temples and other buildings. The foreign merchants have a fine town of their own outside the walls, and divided into three parts for the English, French, and Americans. Shanghai has a very large trade in tea, silk, cotton, porcelain, and many other things, and the harbor is always crowded with ships and junks.

The name Shanghai means "approaching the sea." The city was taken by the English in 1842, and when they gave it up in 1843, it was made one of the ports opened to foreign trade.

SHAW'NEES. See AMERICAN INDIANS.

SHEER'NESS, a town of S. E. England, on the island of Sheppey, at the junction of the River Medway with the Thames, 37 miles below London; pop., 14,000, or about as large as Newburyport, Mass. It is noted for its great navy-yard, which contains large ship-yards and buildings, and is defended by strong fortifications. The town is visited in summer by many people from London.

SHEF'FIELD, a city of Central England, at the junction of the rivers Sheaf and Don, 141 miles N. N. W. of London; pop. 333,000, or about twice as large as Minneapolis, Minn. The Don and several other rivers furnish a fine water-power, and coal and iron mines near the city give fuel for furnaces, and material for making iron and steel ware. With these to help it, Sheffield has become one of the greatest manufacturing cities in the world. More knives, scissors, saws, and tools of all kinds are made there than anywhere else, and there are also immense factories of wire, fish-hooks, springs, needles, and other articles of steel; German silver, britannia and white metal, brass, machinery, spectacles, snuff, and many other things. The Rodgers pocket-knives made there are considered the best in the world. The hundreds of furnaces and foundries make the town so smoky that it always seems covered with a cloud.

Sheffield means the "field on the Sheaf," the name of the river on which it stands. It was an old Saxon town, and was noted for its cutlery at an early date.

SHEL'LEY, Percy Bysshe, an English poet, born at Field Place, near Horsham, Sussex, Aug. 4, 1792. He was the son of a baronet. When a schoolboy he wrote two novels, and he continued to write after entering college at Oxford. A pamphlet written by him, called the "Necessity of Atheism," led to his being sent away from college; after which he wrote a beautiful poem called "Queen Mab." Among his other poems are "Alastor, or the Spirit of Solitude," "The Revolt of Islam," "Prometheus Un-

bound," and "The Cenci," a tragedy. Boating was a favorite amusement of his; and one day (July 8, 1822) a squall upset his little craft in the Gulf of Spezia, and he was drowned at the early age of thirty.

SHER'I-DAN, Philip Henry, an American general, born at Somerset, O., March 6, 1831. He was graduated at West Point in 1853. When the Civil War broke out, he was made a captain, and rose rapidly in rank until he became a major-general in 1863. At first he served in the Mississippi Valley, taking part in many battles; but in 1864 he was made commander of cavalry in the army of the Potomac, and in the battles of the Wilderness, North Anna, Spottsylvania, and Cold Harbor, he was one of the most important leaders. In August he was placed in command of the Union army in the Shenandoah Valley, where he defeated Gen. Early at WINCHESTER and in other battles. On April 1, 1865, he gained the battle of Five Forks; and, when Lee retreated from Richmond, he led the pursuit. Since the war he has commanded in several military departments. In 1869 he was made lieutenant-general. On the retirement of Gen. Sherman, Nov. 1, 1883, he became commander of all the United States armies, and on June 1, 1888, was made a full General. He died when fifty-seven years old (Aug. 5, 1888).

SHERIDAN, Richard Brinsley, a British writer and statesman, born in Dublin, Ireland, September, 1751. He wrote several comedies, including "The Rivals," and "The School for Scandal;" was elected to Parliament, and held several important government offices. Some of his speeches are among the finest in the English language. As he grew older he lost his popularity, and, living extravagantly, he got into debt, for which at one time he was imprisoned. Even during his last illness in London, an officer came to arrest him, and would have carried him to prison but for his physician. He died friendless and broken-hearted, when nearly sixty-five years old (July 7, 1816).

SHER'MAN, William Tecumseh, an American general, born at Lancaster, O., Feb. 8, 1820. He was graduated at West Point and served in various places until 1853, when he resigned. When the Civil War broke out he re-entered the army, soon became a general, and fought in the battles of Bull Run and Shiloh. He was under Gen. Grant at the siege of Vicksburg and in the battle of Chattanooga, and in March, 1864, he was made commander of the United States armies in Ohio, Kentucky, Tennessee, and Arkansas. He soon invaded Georgia, defeated the Confederate generals, Johnston and Hood, in several battles, and besieged Atlanta. The

William T. Sherman.

Confederates retreated from Atlanta (Sept. 1, 1864), and in November Gen. Sherman and his army began a march eastward, through the heart of the Confederate States. Nothing was heard of his army until he captured Savannah, and wrote to President Lincoln : " I have the honor to present you with the city of Savannah as a Christmas present." From Savannah, Sherman marched northward through Georgia and South Carolina into North Carolina, where

he captured Raleigh (April 13, 1865). He was opposed by Gen. Johnston, who commanded the last large Confederate army, and who finally surrendered with all his men (April 26, 1865). In 1866 Sherman was made lieutenant-general, and when Gen. Grant became President, Sherman succeeded him as full general (March 4, 1869). In 1871 he travelled in Europe and the East, and in 1884 was retired from active service. He died in New York when seventy-one years old (February 14, 1891).

SHET'LAND ISLANDS, a group of about 100 islands, 100 miles N.E. of Scotland, to which they belong; area, 450 square miles, or one-third as large as Rhode Island; pop., 29,000, or about the same as that of Waterbury, Conn. Capital, Lerwick. The islands are high and rocky, with rugged and picturesque coasts. Many of them are very small, and only about twenty-five are inhabited. There are no trees, but very good pastures, on which the farmers feed their sheep, cattle, and ponies, all of which are very small. Shetland ponies, or "shelties" as they are often called, have round, thick bodies, and short legs, but their strength is very great for their size. One, only about half as high as a common horse, has been known to carry a heavy man forty miles in a day. They are very handsome and docile, and are easily taken care of. Many of them are sent from the islands to different parts of Europe for young folks to ride upon, and some even to the United States.

On the coasts there are fine fisheries, which employ many people. The climate is not very cold, but it is often very foggy and stormy. In the winter the days are only a few hours long, but in the summer the sun does not set until late at night, and twilight lasts until morning.

The name Shetland is changed from the old Scandinavian name Hjaltiland, which means "Viking's Island."

SHIELDS (*sheelds*), **South,** a town of N. England, on the S. bank of the River Tyne, near its mouth; pop. 57,000, or nearly as large as Trenton, N. J. Opposite it is the town of North Shields, with a pop. of 12,000. Both are noted for their manufacture of articles used on ships, and of glass, pottery, and alum. There are large docks for repairing ships. In old times the fishermen along the Tyne lived in huts, called sheels, and this name has been changed to Shields.

SHILOH (*shi'lo*), the name of a church near Pittsburg Landing, on the Tennessee River, in Tennessee, near which a battle was fought during the Civil War, between a Union army under Gen. Grant, and the Confederates commanded by Generals A. S. Johnston and Beauregard, April 6 and 7, 1862. Gen. Grant had reached Pittsburg Landing with part of his army, and was waiting for the arrival of Gen. Buell with the rest, when he was attacked by the Confederates (April 6). At first the Unionists were driven back, and some of their soldiers were captured, but in the afternoon Gen. Buell and his soldiers arrived, and on the next day the Confederates were attacked in turn, and finally forced to retreat. Among their killed was Gen. Johnston. This is sometimes called the battle of Pittsburg Landing.

SHIRAZ (*she-rahz'*), a city of S. Persia, on a plain nearly a mile above the sea; pop. 30,000, or nearly as large as Salem, Mass. It is one of the handsomest of the Persian cities, and the plain around it is one of the most beautiful in the world, being planted with hundreds of fine orchards and gardens. Near the city are many plantations of roses, from which great quantities of rose-water are made, and the city has a large trade.

Shiraz was founded in the 7th century. From 1760 to 1796 it was the capital of Persia. The Persian people revere the city, because it was the birthplace and home of their great poets Saadi and Hafiz, both of whom were buried there. Thirty-five miles north-east of Shiraz are the ruins of the ancient city of Persepolis, which was the capital of Persia under Xerxes and Darius. Remains of their palaces can still be seen there. Persepolis was destroyed by Alexander the Great (331 B.C.).

SHIR'LAW, Walter, an American painter, born in Paisley, Scotland, Aug. 6, 1837. He was brought to America when three years old. He paints ideal heads, and landscapes with figures. He has a studio in New York.

SHOSH'O·NES. See AMERICAN INDIANS.

SIAM (*se-ahm'*), a country of S. E. Asia, S. of Burmah; area, 260,000 square miles, or nearly as large as Texas; pop. 10,000,000, or about four times that of Texas; capital, BANGKOK. It is generally hilly or mountainous, but near the rivers are large plains which are overflowed every year. The whole country is very rich and beautiful. The climate is warm, and instead of winter there is a rainy season, lasting from June to October.

Gold, copper, iron, tin, and lead abound, and among the precious stones are rubies, sapphires, and topazes. In the forests are obtained gutta-percha, lac, gamboge, and many valuable woods. Among the wild animals are elephants, rhinoceroses, tigers, monkeys, peacocks, and fowls like our tame ones. The elephants of Siam are larger and stronger than those of other countries, and are much prized in India. Sometimes albinos (C. C. T., 7, I, l.) are caught. They are called white, but they are really a dark cream color. All such elephants belong to the king, and are looked upon by the people as sacred; and the money and the flag of Siam have a white elephant on them. The people, most of whom are like the Chinese, are mostly Buddhists. The poor live in huts, often built on rafts in the rivers, but the rich have fine palaces, with European furniture. One third of the common people are slaves, and men often sell their children or their wives, or become slaves themselves for debts. Siam has two kings, but one is more powerful than the other. They are treated as though they were gods, and even the princes kneel when they approach them. The queen has a separate court, and a guard of female soldiers.

The name Siam, or Siyam, means "dark" in the Malay language, and perhaps comes from the color of the people. Siam was a kingdom before Christ. In the 15th century it was first visited by the Portuguese and Spanish. Of late years, some of the kings have shown a desire to introduce more civilized customs.

SIBERIA (*si-be're-ah*), a part of Russia, occupying the whole of northern Asia; area, 4,800,000 square miles, or a fifth larger than all Europe; pop. 4,314,000, or about three fourths that of New York State. It is separated from the Chinese Empire by the ALTAI Mountains, and from European Russia by the URAL Mountains. The rest of the country is a great plain, covered in the southern part with forests or prairie. Northern Siberia is a cold, dreary region, with vast barren plains and frozen swamps. Bones of mammoths, a kind of elephant which lived thousands of years ago, are found in large numbers in these swamps, and the people dig out the ivory tusks to sell. The bodies of these mammoths sometimes have the frozen flesh so well preserved that it is eaten by dogs. Siberia has many large rivers, most of which flow into the Arctic sea. In the winter, they are often frozen solid near their mouths, where the climate is coldest; the waters above then overflow into the valleys, freezing

and covering them with ice many feet thick.

Siberia is rich in mines of gold, silver, copper, lead, zinc, antimony, iron, and arsenic. Topazes and emeralds are also found, and there are quarries of jasper, porphyry, and malachite, from which beautiful ornaments are made. Salt is so abundant in some of the lakes that in summer it hardens on the surface like ice, and men and even horses can cross on it. Only a small part of the soil is good for farms, but the prairies give excellent pasturage, and the people have immense flocks of sheep, and droves of horses and cattle. Reindeer are kept in the northern part.

More than half of the inhabitants are Russians, most of whom were convicts exiled from Russia for crimes. There are also many native tribes, among them the Calmucks, Yakuts, Tunguses, and Koricks. Many of these are wandering tribes who live in tents or huts, and keep sheep or reindeer. There is a large trade in furs, cattle, fish, and many other things, and nearly all the trade between Russia and China is carried on across Siberia. At certain seasons large fairs are held in the cities.

Genghis Khan and his successors conquered part of Siberia. The Russians first went there in 1580, and conquered the whole country in about eighty years.

SIB'YLS, the name given by the Greeks and Romans to old women who were believed to have the gift of prophecy. The most famous one was the Cumæan sibyl, who lived at Cumæ, in Italy. She is said to have offered to King Tarquinius Priscus nine books of prophecies, but she asked so large a sum for them that he refused to buy them. She went away and burned three of the books, and then asked the same price for the six left. When the king again refused, she burned three more, and still asked the same price for the three remaining. The king, thinking that they must be very valuable, then bought them, and they were long kept in the temple of Jupiter Capitolinus in Rome, and consulted on great occasions. They were finally destroyed when the temple was burned (83 B.C.).

SICILY (*sis'il-e*), the largest island in the Mediterranean Sea, separated from the S. end of Italy by the Strait of Messina; area, 11,300 square miles, or about as large as Maryland; pop. 3,226,000, or about three times that of Maryland. The northern part is very mountainous, with peaks over a mile high; but some portions of the southern part are flat. Near the eastern coast is the volcano of Mount Ætna, which is more than two miles high, and has a crater seven hundred feet deep. It is noted for its terrible eruptions. In one which occurred in 1669, a stream of lava destroyed fourteen villages, and poured into the city of Catania at the foot of the mountain, though walls sixty feet high had been built to keep it out.

Rich mines of sulphur are found near Mount Ætna, and the island has many quarries of marble and other valuable stones. On most of the plains the soil is very fertile; and though the people are not good farmers, they obtain large crops of grain, olives, and grapes. Many silk-worms are reared. Large forests are on the mountains, and there is an important trade in timber. The climate is mild and pleasant. Sicily belongs to Italy; and most of the people are much like the Italians, but in their language the Italian is mixed with many Arabic words.

Sicily was first called by the Greek sailors Trinacria ("three-cornered"), because it is shaped like a triangle; it was next called Sicania, from the Sicani, a people living in it; and finally Sicilia, from the Siculi, a people who removed there from the mainland of Italy.

The Italians now call it Sicilia (se-che'le-ah).

The ancient Phœnicians had colonies in Sicily; and it afterward belonged to the Greeks, Carthaginians, Syracusans, and Romans. In the 5th century it was conquered by the Ostrogoths, and in 830 by the Saracens, or Arabs. In the 11th century the Saracens were driven out by the Normans, who founded the kingdom of the two Sicilies, by uniting the island to Naples. At one time this was a powerful kingdom, but it was finally united to Italy in 1860.

SID'DONS, Sarah, an English actress, born in Wales, July 5, 1755. She was the oldest child of Roger KEMBLE, an actor, and when thirteen years old took the principal parts in English operas. At the age of eighteen she married Mr. Siddons, a young actor. All the time she was on the stage, which was until she retired, at the age of fifty-seven, she was regarded as the first living actress, and a woman of wonderful genius. Her great part was that of Lady Macbeth; but she was also very successful as Ophelia, Desdemona, Portia, and Queen Catherine. Much of her success was owing to her beautiful form and expressive face. As a woman, she led a blameless life, and died in London when she was seventy-six years old (June 8, 1831).

SI'DON, an ancient city of Phœnicia, on the Mediterranean Sea, 23 miles N. of Tyre. The Phœnicians often called themselves Sidonians, and probably Sidon was their oldest city. The time of its greatest prosperity was about three thousand years ago. The Sidonians founded Tyre, which in time became a much larger city. The Persians, having conquered Phœnicia, Sidon rebelled against them, but was captured and destroyed (351 B.C.). It was rebuilt; but though it is often mentioned in history after that time, it never became very powerful. A town called Saida now stands near its site.

SID'NEY, Algernon, an English statesman, born about 1622. He was the son of the second Earl of Leicester, and the grand-nephew of Sir Philip Sidney. He took sides against King Charles I., in the Civil War, and he was one of the judges at his trial. Although he did not sign the warrant for the execution, he afterwards spoke of it as the "justest and bravest action that ever was done in England or anywhere else." So ardent a Republican was he that he opposed even Cromwell's government, because it was not liberal enough. During the reign of Charles II., he always acted with the party against the Crown, and when, in 1663, the Rye House Plot, a scheme for murdering the king, was found out, he was arrested as one of those concerned in it. There was little proof against him, but he was, nevertheless, executed. He died when sixty-one years old (Dec. 7, 1683).

SIDNEY, Sir Philip, a famous English author, soldier, and courtier, born at Penshurst, Kent, Nov. 29, 1554. His father was Sir Henry Sidney, a favorite of Edward VI., and his mother was a daughter of the Duke of Northumberland. Sir Philip Sidney has always been held up as the best English model of knightly virtues, and his character has been a favorite theme with poets. Queen Elizabeth valued him so highly, that, when he wished to go on one of Sir Walter Raleigh's expeditions, she forbade it, "lest she should lose the jewel of her court." His two most celebrated literary works are the "Defense of Poesie," and the romance of "Arcadia." He came to his death on the field of Zutphen, in the Netherlands, whither he had been sent by the queen in command of some troops to aid those provinces in their struggle with Philip II. While being carried from the field, wounded, and faint

from the loss of blood, he called for drink; but, as he was putting the bottle to his lips, he saw a poor soldier, who also was being carried off, looking longingly at the bottle. Sir Philip, before he had tasted a drop, at once handed it to the man, with the words, "Thy necessity is yet greater than mine." He died when thirty-two years old (Oct. 7, 1586), and was publicly mourned in England.

SIENA (*se-a'nah*), a city of central Italy, 31 miles S. by E. of Florence; pop. 25,000, or about the same as Taunton, Mass. It is built on two hills, in the midst of a large plain. The streets are mostly narrow, and often so steep that wagons cannot go up them. There are several fine churches, and a once famous university. Around the city are seen remains of a very ancient wall, which was built by the Etruscans more than two thousand years ago. Siena was once the capital of a rich and powerful republic, which was often at war with Florence and other cities.

SIERRA LEONE (*se-er'rah le-o'ne*), a country of W. Africa, on the Atlantic Ocean, N.W. of Liberia; area, 468 square miles, or about a third as large as Rhode Island; pop., 60,000, or about a sixth that of Rhode Island; capital, Free Town. The country is partly a mountainous peninsula, and partly low and flat. The climate, especially on the low ground, is so unhealthy that few white men care to live there, and most of the people are negroes.

The name Sierra Leone, which means Lion Mountain, was first given to the peninsula by the Spanish. The colony was founded in 1787, by some Englishmen, who sent to Sierra Leone some poor negroes from London. In 1807 the colony was ceded to England, to which country it still belongs. The English war-vessels, having orders to seize slave-ships, thousands of negroes were freed by them and taken to Sierra Leone, and the colony was increased by liberated slaves from the West Indies and other places.

SIGISMUND (*sij'is-mund*), Emperor of Germany, born in 1368. He was the son of the Emperor Charles IV., and succeeded Rupert, who had been chosen in 1433. The great event of Sigismund's reign was the calling of the Council of Constance, to decide which was the true pope of three men, each claiming to have been elected, and to reform some of the evils that had grown up in the Church. Sigismund opened the council with a speech in which he made a mistake in his Latin. When it was pointed out, he answered, " I am King of the Romans, and above the rules of grammar." Among those who came to this council were a priest from Bohemia, named John Huss, and his friend Jerome of Prague. Sigismund died when sixty-nine years old (Dec. 9, 1437), and was succeeded by his son-in-law, Albert II.

SIGOURNEY (*sig'ur-ny*), **Lydia Huntley,** an American writer, born at Norwich, Conn., Sept. 1, 1791. Her name was Lydia Huntley until she married Charles Sigourney, a merchant of Hartford, in 1819. Four years before her marriage she had published a book called "Moral Pieces in Prose and Verse," and during the rest of her life she wrote nearly sixty volumes of poetry and prose. She died at Hartford when seventy-three years old (June 10, 1865).

SI-LE'NUS, in Greek and Roman fable, a satyr, the constant companion of Bacchus. He is represented as a fat, bald-headed old man, with a gay face, always drunk, and riding upon an ass. Sometimes he has small horns on his head, and lower limbs like a goat. He is also represented as having the gift of prophecy.

SILISTRIA (*se-lis'tre-ah*), a town of Bulgaria, on the River Danube;

pop. 11,000, or about as large as Weymouth, Mass. It is a very ancient place, and being strongly fortified, it has often been an important military post in the wars between Turkey and Russia. It was taken by the Russians in 1829, and in 1854 it was bombarded and nearly destroyed by them, but they were finally compelled to retreat without taking the city.

SIL'LI-MAN, Benjamin, an American scholar and writer, born in Trumbull, Conn., Aug. 8, 1779. He was graduated at Yale College in 1796, and was first a tutor and afterward became professor of chemistry in that college. He also lectured on geology, and was one of the first in this country to give popular lectures on scientific subjects. In 1818 he started the "American Journal of Science and Arts," commonly known as "Silliman's Journal," and edited it for twenty-eight years. Professor Silliman travelled in Europe, and published an interesting account of it, called "A Visit to Europe." He also published a chemistry and other works. He died in New Haven when eighty-five years old (Nov. 24, 1864).

Benjamin Silliman, his son, born in New Haven, Dec. 4, 1816, is also noted as a lecturer in Yale College on chemistry, mineralogy, and geology. He has published a chemistry and other works.

SIMLA (*sim'lah*), a town of N. India, near the Himalaya Mountains; pop., 15,000, or about as large as Galesburg, Ill. It is built on a hill, more than a mile above the sea, and surrounded by very grand and beautiful mountain scenery. The climate is cool and healthful, and during the hot summer months many thousand people, both natives and Englishmen, go there to live. Among them are the viceroy and chief officials, who go there from Calcutta early in the hot season, so that Simla is really the summer capital of India.

SIMMS, William Gilmore, an American poet and writer of novels, born in Charleston, S. C., April 17, 1806. He began life as clerk in a drug store, then studied law, and afterward edited a newspaper for four years. After that he turned to novel-writing, and had great success. Many of his stories are tales of the American Revolution. He also wrote poems, dramas, histories, and biographies. He died in Charleston when sixty-four years old (June 11, 1870).

SIMONIDES (*si-mon'i-deez*), a Greek poet, born in the island of Ceos about 556 B.C. Although living at the same time with ANACREON and PINDAR, Simonides was the most noted lyric poet of the age. He competed with Æschylus for the prize for the best poem on those who fell in the battle of Marathon, and won it. Because, however, he took pay for what he wrote, he was accused of avarice. During the Persian war, he was often employed by the different states of Greece to write inscriptions for the tombs of those who fell. Some of these have come down to us. One of the best known is that written upon the Spartans who fell at Thermopylæ. "Stranger, tell the Lacedæmonians that we are lying here in obedience to their laws." There is also another upon the Athenians who fell at Marathon, "Fighting in the van of the Greeks, the Athenians at Marathon destroyed the power of the glittering Medians." Simonides died in Syracuse when eighty-nine years old (467 B.C.).

SINGAPORE (*sing-gah-pore'*), a city on an island near the S. end of the Malay Peninsula ; pop. 139,000, or about as large as Omaha, Neb. It is the capital of the English colonies, called the Straits Settlements, which include Singapore, Malacca, and Wellesley, and the island of Penang. The harbor is very fine, and a large trade is carried on, especially in tin, pepper, nutmegs, rattans, coffee, gutta-percha, caoutchouc, and sago. More than half the people are Chinese, and most of the others are Malays or other natives, only a few being Europeans. About 2,000 convicts from India are kept there.

The name Singapore, or Singapura, is Malayan, and means "lion's town." It was formerly the capital of a Malay kingdom. In 1819 the English began a settlement there, and it soon became one of their most important colonies.

SING SING, a village of New York, on the Hudson River, 30 miles N. of New-York City ; pop., about 9500, or about the same as Wausau, Wis. It has several manufactories, but is principally noted for its State prison, in which more than 1300 convicts can be kept. There are two buildings, a large one for men and a smaller one for women. Attached to these are many workshops where the prisoners work during the day ; but at night each one is locked up in a separate cell.

Sing Sing prison was begun in 1825, the first workmen being convicts from Auburn State Prison.

SIN'O·PE, a town of Asiatic Turkey, on the S. shore of the Black Sea ; pop., 10,000, or about as large as Portsmouth, N.H. It is defended by an ancient castle, and by strong modern forts. The harbor is the best in that part of the Black Sea, and it has the only shipyard in Turkey, except that of Constantinople. Many Turkish war vessels are built there.

Sinope is a very ancient place, having been a city more than 600 B.C. During the Crimean War the Turkish fleet was destroyed at Sinope by the Russians, only one steamer escaping (Nov. 30, 1853). The town was afterward bombarded.

SIOUX (*sooz*). See AMERICAN INDIANS.

SIRENS, in Greek fable, two or three sea nymphs, who enticed sailors by their sweet songs, and then devoured them. When Orpheus surpassed them in singing, the sirens sprang into the sea, and were changed into rocks.

SIS'Y-PHUS, in Greek fable, the founder and king of Corinth. For his wickedness to men and gods, he was punished after death by having to roll a huge rock up a steep hill. As soon as he got it to the top it would roll back to the bottom, and he had to begin his labor again, so that his work was never ended.

SIT'KA. See ALASKA.

SIX NATIONS. See AMERICAN INDIANS.

SIVA, one of the Hindoo gods, forming, with BRAHMA and VISHNU, the Hindoo Trinity. Siva is called the destroyer of all things, but he is also a reproducer; to destroy, according to the Hindoo belief, being only to reproduce in another form. Siva is sometimes called Mahadeva (the great god).

SIX'TUS, the name of five popes.

Sixtus V., the most noted one, was born Dec. 15, 1521, and became pope in 1585. He made many reforms, and tried hard to raise the papacy to its former power. He founded the Vatican Library, built the great dome of St. Peter's, and set up the obelisk before the church. The Society of Jesus, or Order of the Jesuits, was begun under his reign. Sixtus V. died in Rome when seventy years old (Aug. 24, 1590).

SKYE. See HEBRIDES.

SMITH, John, the founder of Virginia, born in Lincolnshire, England, in January, 1579. He became a noted soldier, and at one time was taken prisoner by the Turks and made a slave. A Turkish lady fell in love with him, and her brother in revenge treated Smith so badly that the latter killed him; he then disguised himself in the dead man's clothes, and escaped from the country. In 1606 Smith sailed with Newport and many others to America, and founded Jamestown, in Virginia (1607), where Smith be-

came the real head of the colony, though he had not been elected leader. He made many excursions to explore the country and obtain corn from the Indians, and the Indians once kept him a prisoner for seven weeks. It is said that they

John Smith.

were about to kill him and that his life was saved by POCAHONTAS, daughter of the chief, who begged her father to spare the captive. Smith afterward became president of the colony, and through his efforts it finally succeeded. He returned to England in 1609, and in 1614 explored the New England coast. In his later life, he wrote several books about his travels. He died in London when fifty-two years old (June 21, 1631).

SMOLLETT, Tobias George, a British author, born in Scotland in 1721. He began life as an apothecary boy; but he did not like the business, and, having written a tragedy called the "Regicide," he carried it to London, hoping it would bring him fame and fortune. But he could not sell his poem, and took a place as surgeon's mate in the navy. In this way he gained the knowledge of sailors and of sailor life which appears in many of his books. In 1748 he published a novel called "The Adventures of Roderick Random," and soon afterward another, "The Adventures of Peregrine Pickle," which, though powerful works, are rather coarse. Smollett also wrote a history of England in sixteen volumes, but only the last five volumes, which continue Hume's history, are much read now. He died in Leghorn, Italy, when fifty years old (Oct. 21, 1771).

SMYRNA (*smir'nah*), a town in the W. part of Asiatic Turkey, on the Gulf of Smyrna; pop. 187,000, or a little larger than Newark, N. J. It has one of the finest harbors in the world, and a very large trade is carried on, especially in cotton, figs, raisins, licorice, opium, and sponges. The streets are generally narrow and dirty, and many of the people are very poor. A large part of the inhabitants are Christians.

Smyrna was an ancient Greek city, and is noted in history. It was one of the seven cities claimed as the birth-place of Homer.

SO·BI·ES'KI. See JOHN III. SO-BIESKI.

SOCI'ETY ISLANDS, a group of islands in the Pacific Ocean, S. of the equator, and about midway between Australia and South America; area, 666 square miles, or about half as large as Rhode Island;

A Tahitian Canoe.

pop., about 18,000. There are two groups, one of which, the smaller, is generally called the Society Islands, while the other, 70 miles S. E., is often called the Tahiti Islands, from its largest island. Nearly all are mountainous; and they are surrounded by a ring of coral-reefs, within which are excellent harbors. The climate is warm all the year round, and the islands abound in fruits. The natives are a dark-skinned race, good-natured and pleasant, but very lazy. They have curious canoes, fitted with out-riggers, like the one shown in the picture. There are also many white people and Chinese on the islands, which are often visited by ships. The chief trade is in cocoanut-oil, arrowroot, sugar, and pearl.

It is said that these islands were

first found by the Spaniards in 1606. Since 1843, the Tahiti group has belonged to France, though the native kings and queens are allowed to govern it. The other group is independent.

SOCRATES (*sok'ra-teez*), a famous Greek philosopher, born near Athens about 470 B.C. He was the son of the sculptor Sophroniscus, and was trained in his father's art, but soon gave it up for the study of philosophy. He is said to have been ugly, with a flat nose, thick lips, squat figure, and bad gait; but he had great strength, and trained himself to live on coarse food, to wear few clothes, and to bear heat and cold. He used to wander about the streets, talking with the people, and charming every one with his conversation. In his time, the morals of the Athenians had become corrupted, virtue and honesty being less valued than wit and intelligence. This state of things had been brought about by the sophists, false teachers, who, by their crooked reasonings, put lies in the place of truth, and made truth into error. Socrates showed up the tricks of these people, and aroused in the bosoms of his pupils a love of justice and virtue. He wrote no book, and had no school; but he almost lived in the streets, and mixed with men wherever he could find listeners, and talked and taught, not for pay, but from a love of truth. The sophists could not answer his arguments, and they were angry because he won so many talented young men from their teachings: so they brought against him the charge of corrupting the Athenian youth, and teaching about false gods. Socrates showed that there was no truth in these charges; but nevertheless his judges condemned him to die by poison. His friends urged him to fly: he refused their advice, and, while uttering sublime thoughts on the undying nature of the soul, he drank off the poison. Xantippe, the wife of Soc-rates, has come down to us as a great scold. It is said that her husband married her expressly on that account, as a means of self-discipline. The praises that have been lavished on this great man are unequalled.

Socrates.

Xenophon says, "He was so wise as never to err in judging of good and evil, nor did he need the aid of others to help him to judge between them. I cannot but regard him as the most excellent and happy of mankind." He died in Athens when about seventy-one years old (399 B.C.).

SOISSONS (*swahs-song'*), a town of N. France, on the River Aisne; pop., 11,000, or about as large as Medford, Mass. It is surrounded by walls, and has a castle, a cathedral, and other interesting buildings. Tapestry, linen, stockings, leather, earthen-ware, and other things, are made there.

Soissons was named after the Suessiones, who lived there in the time of Cæsar. King Clovis held his court there. During the Franco-German War it was taken by the Germans (Oct. 16, 1870).

SOLFERINO (*sol-fa-rē'no*), a village of N. Italy, 20 miles S.E. of Brescia, noted for a great victory won there by the French and Sardinian armies over the Austrians, June 24, 1859. The Emperor Napoleon III. and King Victor Emanuel led the allied armies, and the Austrians were commanded by the Emperor Francis Joseph. The battle lasted sixteen hours, and nearly 40,000 men were killed and wounded. After this defeat the Austrians were obliged to sue for peace. For many years the bones of the fallen soldiers were scattered thickly over the battle-field; but in 1870 they were collected, and put into three tombs.

SO'LON, an Athenian lawgiver, born about 638 B.C. He was a descendant of the royal house of Codrus, and one of the seven wise men of Greece. In his youth he travelled as a merchant in the East, and brought back with him to Athens the wisdom of that part of the world.

Solon.

In 594 he was made archon, or chief ruler, and he caused to be made a code of laws, which were so wise and just that they have served as a model to other nations. By these laws the mass of the people were first given a share in the government, and this led to making Athens a democracy. Solon died when about seventy-nine years old (559 B.C.).

SOL'Y-MAN II., called the Magnificent, an Ottoman sultan, born about 1495. He was the son of Selim I., and succeeded him in 1520. Under his rule the Turkish Empire reached its greatest limits, and began immediately to decline under his successors. He was one of the greatest rulers produced by the Turkish nation, having many fine qualities, such as energy, honesty, love of justice, and temperance. He was both a statesman and a soldier; but his temper led him to commit horrible cruelties. Most of his reign was spent in trying to penetrate into Western Europe. The Hungarians were routed by him at Mohacz; but he repeatedly failed in his attempts to take Vienna, which all nations united to defend, regarding it as the bulwark of Christendom. Solyman died when seventy-one years old, while besieging the fortress of Sziget in Hungary (Sept. 5, 1566).

SOM'ER-VILLE, a city of Massachusetts, on the Mystic River, close to Boston; pop. 40,000, or nearly as large as Erie, Pa. It is connected with Boston, where most of the people have their business, by horse and steam cars. The city contains large brick yards, and manufactories of glass-ware, earthenware, and many other things. It is also noted for its very large insane-asylum. Somerville was separated from Charlestown in 1842, and became a city in 1872.

SOODAN, or **SOUDAN** (*soodahn'*), a part of Central Africa lying south of the Desert of Sahara. It is inhabited by many negro tribes, who are generally savage and treacherous. Traders from Morocco, Tunis, and Tripoli, cross the desert to Soodan, trading with the negroes for ivory, gold-dust, and slaves. The eastern part commonly called *the* Soodan, is a province of Egypt.

SOPHOCLES (*Sof'o-kleez*), a Greek tragic poet, born at Colonus, 496 B.C. When sixteen years old, he led the chorus which danced to the choral song celebrating the Greek victory over the Persians at Salamis. He lived in Athens in the time of Pericles, the age of so many great men. When twenty-seven years old, he won a poetical prize over ÆSCHYLUS, who till this time had been the first of Greek poets, and Æschylus left Athens. Ancient and modern judges give to Sophocles the place at the head of the Greek drama. Of the one hundred and thirty plays which he is said to have written, but seven have come down to us. They are "King Œdipus," "Œdipus at Colonus," "Antigone," "Electra," "Trachinian Women," "Ajax," and "Philoctetes." Sophocles died when ninety years old (406 B.C.).

SOR-REN'TO, a city of S. Italy, on the sea-coast, 16 miles S. E. of Naples; pop., 6,000. It was a Greek settlement and a beautiful place under the Romans. It is noted for several curious grottos, and is visited by many travellers.

SOULT (*soolt*), **Nicolas Jean de Dieu,** Duke of Dalmatia, a famous French soldier, born March 29, 1769. He joined the army when only sixteen years old, and became a general at twenty-five. In 1804 Napoleon made him a marshal, and three years afterward Duke of Dalmatia; and in 1808 he was sent to Spain, where he showed great skill in fighting against Sir John MOORE and Wellington, but was finally obliged to surrender at TOULOUSE (1814). After the fall of Napoleon Soult was made minister of war by Louis XVIII.; but as he joined Napoleon again and fought at Waterloo he was banished from 1816 to 1819. But he afterward got back his honors and became a peer of France, and in 1847, when he left public life, the title of marshal general was given him. He died

when eighty-two years old (Nov. 26, 1851).

SOUTH AMERICA. See AMERICA.

SOUTHAMPTON (*suth-hamp'ton*), a city on the S. coast of England, opposite the Isle of Wight, 70 miles S.W. of London; pop, 60,000, or about as large as Grand Rapids, Mich. The mouth of the River Test, called Southampton Water, forms its harbor, and very fine docks and piers have been made, so that Southampton has become one of the principal ports of England. Many large ships are built there.

Southampton is an old Saxon town, and its name means the "south home-dwelling."

SOUTH AUSTRALIA. See AUSTRALIA.

SOUTH CAROLINA (*kar-o-li'nah*), a Southern State of the United States, on the Atlantic Ocean, between North Carolina and Georgia; area, 34,000 square miles, or a little less than that of Maine; pop. 1,151,000, or nearly one and three fourth times that of Maine; capital, Columbia (pop. 15,000). The N. W. part is covered with mountains, and in the central part is a lower region covered with pine forests, and very thinly settled. Near the coast the land is flat and often swampy.

In the mountain region gold is found. Near the coast are beds of mineral manure, called phosphate, said to be the remains of animals which lived in the early ages of the world. Great quantities are sent to Europe and the Northern States. Very fine porcelain clay, or kaolin, is also found in this State. The principal crop in South Carolina is cotton; but more rice is raised than in any other State, and wheat, corn, and tobacco are grown in many places. Near the coast are many low islands, where sea-island cotton (C. C. T., 154, II.) is grown. The palmetto palm grows in many places; and from this, South Carolina is sometimes called the "Palmetto

State." More than half the people are negroes who were once slaves. The principal city is CHARLESTON.

South Carolina once formed, with NORTH CAROLINA, a colony called Carolina, after King CHARLES II. South Carolina was one of the thirteen original States of the Union. In 1861 it seceded, and joined the Confederate States, and in 1868 again became a State of the Union.

SOUTH DAKOTA, a Western State of the United States, between North Dakota and Nebraska; area, 77,650 square miles, or about the same as Nebraska; pop. 328,000, or not quite one third that of Nebraska; capital, Pierre. The surface is largely undulating plain; but there are some mountainous parts. Near the centre of the State are the "Bad Lands," a rough and desert region. Gold and silver are mined in the Black Hills, and there are rich tin mines. The agricultural products are large, grain of all kinds being very abundant. The State formed the southern part of the former Territory of Dakota, and was admitted to the Union Nov. 3, 1889.

SOUTHEY (*sow'the*), **Robert,** an English author, born in Bristol, Aug. 12, 1774. He was sent away from Westminster school when eighteen years old, because he had written a piece against flogging, in a magazine gotten up by the older boys. The same year (1792) he went to Oxford, where he became great friends with Samuel Taylor COLERIDGE. He made his home near Keswick, in a beautiful neighborhood called the Lake District, where he had his friend Coleridge and the poet WORDSWORTH as neighbors. The three are sometimes called the "lake poets." In 1813 he was made poet laureate, and as such he had to write poetry for the court whenever there was occasion for any. His chief poetical works are "Thalaba the Destroyer," a story of an Arabian hero, "The Curse of Kehama," founded on Hindoo fables, and

"Roderick, the Last of the Goths," a story of the overthrow of the Gothic kingdom in Spain by the Moors. He also translated the "Chronicles of the CID" from the Spanish, and wrote a "History of Brazil," lives of Nelson and Bunyan, and other prose works. Hard work caused his mind to give way, and he died when sixty-nine years old (March 21, 1843).

SPAIN, a S.W. country of Europe, forming, with Portugal, a peninsula between the Mediterranean Sea and the Atlantic Ocean; area (including the Balearic Islands), 193,000 square miles, or rather more than two thirds as much as that of Texas; pop. 16,-945,000, or not quite two sevenths that of the United States; capital, MADRID. Spain is separated from France by the PYRENEES Mountains, which in some places are nearly two miles high, and are so rugged that they are crossed by large roads in only two places. The northern and central parts form a table-land, crossed by many mountain chains. In the southern part is the beautiful valley of Andalusia, separated from the table-lands by the Sierra Morena, or Brown Mountains, and bordered on the southern side by the Sierra Nevada, or Snowy Range. The high rock of GIBRALTAR, on the southern coast, belongs to England. The town of Ceuta, on the northern coast of Africa, the CANARY ISLANDS, and the Balearic Islands in the Mediterranean, form a part of Spain; and CUBA, PORTO RICO, and the PHILIPPINE ISLANDS are her colonies. In old times Spain was divided into different parts, called Andalusia, Estremadura, Murcia, Valencia, Catalonia, Aragon, Navarre, Old Castile, New Castile, Leon, Galicia, and Asturias; and these names are still commonly used for these parts. Several of them were once independent kingdoms.

Spain has mines of silver, copper, lead, quicksilver, tin, iron, salt, and coal. The soil is very fertile, and gives fine crops of wheat, corn, and flax. There are many vineyards, and wine and raisins are sent to other countries. More cork is got there than in any other country. There is a large trade in silk, wool, olives, and fruits. The principal manufactures are cotton cloth, silk, linen, glass-ware, and iron-ware. Compared with other large European countries, Spain has very few railroads, and not many good roads; and, though the people are very proud of their country, they do very little to make it better. Most of the poor people are ignorant and lazy, and very fond of music and dancing and of bull-fights; but the upper classes are intelligent and well educated. Besides the true Spaniards, there are in N. Spain about 650,000 people called Basques, who speak a language very different from the Spanish. In S. Spain live about 60,000 Modejars, or descendants of the ancient Moors, who still have many of their customs. Besides these, there are about 50,000 gypsies, who wander in bands through the country, and have a language of their own. The people of Spain are governed by a king and by a cortes, or parliament, much like the congress of the United States. The principal religion is the Roman Catholic.

Spain was settled early by the Phœnicians and the Greeks, who built many fine cities there. The Greeks called it Iberia, after the River Iberus, or EBRO. The Carthaginians, who next settled there, were driven out by the Romans (206 B.C.), who in time conquered all the country. They called it Hispania, and from this comes the modern name Spain. The Visigoths, a German tribe, took it from the Romans (about A.D. 471), and in the 8th century nearly the whole country was captured by the Arabs, or Moors, who ruled a large part of it until 1492, when they were driven out. In the 16th century Spain was the greatest power in the world. Its king, Charles I., was also emperor of Germany, and is commonly called in history Charles V. He ruled not only Spain and much of Germany, but also the NETHERLANDS, a large part of Italy, with Sicily and Sardinia, and had vast possessions in America. Under the reign of his son Philip II., this great empire began to decay, and Spain is now only a second-class power.

SPANDAU (*spahn' dow*), a town of Germany, in Prussia, on the River Spree, seven miles W. of Berlin; pop. 32,000, or about as large as Springfield, Ohio. It is strongly fortified, and contains a large prison, barracks, a royal foundry where cannon are made, and an artillery school, besides many manufactories. But the most important thing in Spandau is, that the treasury of the German Empire is kept in the citadel. It can only be unlocked by two keys used together: one of these keys is kept by the chancellor of the empire, and the other by the president of a committee of the German Congress, who have charge of the government debts.

SPARKS, Jared, an American historian, born at Wellington, Conn., May 10, 1789. From 1819 to 1823 he was a minister of a Unitarian congregation in Baltimore; but, being obliged to give it up on account of his health, he moved to Boston, and devoted himself to writing books. His principal works are historical; among them being the "Writings of George Washington," "Library of American Biography," and "Works of Benjamin Franklin," with notes and a Life of the Author. He died in Cambridge when seventy-seven years old (March 14, 1866).

SPARTA (*spar' tah*), an ancient city of Greece, capital of Laconia, or Lacedæmon. By obeying the laws of LYCURGUS, Sparta became so warlike that she was able to conquer many of the other states, and she thus became, in the 6th century B.C., the chief power in Greece. Sparta took part, with

Athens and the other cities, against the Persians; and it was Leonidas, King of Sparta, who held the Persians at bay at Thermopylæ, until all his little band was slain. After this war ended, the great strength which Athens had shown at sea made some of the cities think that she would be a better head than Sparta; so she, for a while, had the chief place. But Sparta could not bear to hold the second place; and in the year 431 B.C. a war broke out between the two rivals, which lasted twenty-nine years, and which is called the Peloponnesian War. It ended in the fall of Athens. Sparta was now again uppermost, and greater than ever. Her king, Agesilaus, soon after went with an army to conquer Persia; but he had to go home very suddenly to defend Sparta in another war waged against her by Athens, Argos, Corinth, and Thebes. Though Sparta was victorious in this war, the Thebans showed themselves very strong. Some years after this, Thebes and Sparta had another war. This time, Thebes was the conqueror, and Sparta was no more the leading city of Greece. She never got back her old position; and, after passing through many changes, she fell, with the other Greek cities, into the hands of the Romans (146 B.C.).

SPAR'TA·CUS, a Roman gladiator, of Thracian birth, who lived in the 1st century B.C. Gladiators were men who fought with swords and other weapons, and wounded and killed one another in the circus for the entertainment of the Roman people. They were either slaves or prisoners, and did not fight of their own accord, but were made to do it. They were trained in establishments whose master or keeper was called the "lanista." When any one wanted to get up a gladiators' fight, he would bargain with the lanista to furnish him so many gladiators. Rome once came very near paying dearly for this pastime. Spartacus

was one of these gladiators; and in the year 76 B.C. he and several others escaped from their keeper, and fled for refuge to the crater of Mount Vesuvius, where they were joined by a great many runaway slaves, several thousand in number. Thus began the Servile War, which lasted from 73 to 71 B.C. Under the lead of Spartacus, the slaves, who at one time numbered more than 100,000, defeated the Roman generals sent against them, and even threatened Rome. At last POMPEY the Great was sent to put them down, and Spartacus was defeated and killed.

SPENCER, Herbert, an English philosopher, born in Derby, April 27, 1820. He was principally educated by his father. His discoveries, which some think the greatest any man has made, are many laws that hold true of both things and thoughts—especially that all complicated things, creatures, ideas, feelings, customs, and laws have grown gradually out of simpler ones, the process being called evolution. Many people believed this before in regard to some things that we can see, but Spencer was the first to show it in regard to all things, and thoughts, and feelings, and customs and laws. He also has discovered many of the particular ways of evolution, so that, by the help of his discoveries, we can sometimes tell how best to make rules in school and laws in the state and many other things, so that they will work best. This saves a great deal of trouble and makes happiness come easier. Spencer was appreciated in America earlier than in England. He visited the United States in the fall of 1882, and was received with great honor.

SPEN'SER, Edmund, the second great English poet, born in London, probably in 1553. The first was Chaucer. Between Chaucer and Spenser were a hundred and fifty years without a great English poet. Spenser was a friend of a SIR PHILIP SIDNEY, and was introduced by him to Sir Walter Raleigh, another courtier. These two friends brought him to the notice of Queen Elizabeth, who gave him an estate in Ireland, and a castle called Kilcolman. There his friend Raleigh visited him; and there Spenser showed him the first three books of a poem he had been writing, the "Faerie Queene," which Raleigh said was "a dish to set before a queen." In time Spenser became sheriff of Cork; and this office often brought him into trouble with the Irish people, who thought it hard that they should have to obey English rulers. Soon after this he married, and brought his bride to his Irish castle. Scarcely were the newly-married couple well settled in their home, when the Irish made a rebellion, and set fire to his castle, he and his wife having hardly time to get away. Their new-born child was left behind, and burned to death. Three months after this, Spenser died in Westminster, England. The "Faerie Queene" is his greatest work. He died when forty-six years old (Jan. 16, 1599).

SPEZIA, LA (*lah sped'ze-ah*), a town of N. Italy, on the Gulf of Spezia; pop., 31,000, or about as large as Salem, Mass. Its harbor, which is surrounded by high mountains, is one of the largest and best in the world, and the city is frequented by many ships. The most important trade is in olive-oil and wine. The Italians have their principal navy-yard there.

SPHINX, in Greek fable, a monster with a body like a lion, wings like a bird, and a head like a woman. It is said to have wandered near Thebes, in Bœotia, asking the riddle, "What animal is that which goes on four feet in the morning, on two at noon, and on three in the evening?" and devouring all who could not solve it. The people became so terrified, that they offered the throne of Thebes to any one who would find the answer. Œdipus at length

solved the riddle, saying, "It is man; for he creeps on hands and feet when a child, walks on two feet in middle life, and uses a staff in old age." The Sphinx then died, and Œdipus became king.

Probably the Greeks got this fable from the Egyptians, who often made statues of sphinxes, and worshipped them. One of these statues, which can still be seen near the Pyramid, is 146 feet long, and was carved from solid rock. The Egyptian sphinxes had no wings, and their head was like that of a man instead of a woman.

SPIELHAGEN (*speel'hah-gen*), **Friedrich,** a German writer of novels, born in Madgeburg, Feb. 24, 1829. He studied at a German university, and afterward devoted himself to writing novels, some of which have been translated into English. These are, "Problematic Characters," and its continuation, "Through Night to Light," "The Hohensteins," "Hammer and Anvil," and others.

SPINOZA (*spe-no'zah*), **Baruch,** a Dutch philosopher, born of Jewish parents, in Amsterdam, Nov. 24, 1632. He was a very bright boy, and was educated by the rabbis in Hebrew, the holy writings of the Old Testament, and the Talmud, a book of Jewish legends. But before he was fifteen years old he became an unbeliever in his own religion, and at last went so far as to deny that there is a God. To account for things, he got up a system of his own, which he wrote in his book, "The Ethics." When he left Judaism, he changed his name from Baruch to Benedict. He died at The Hague when forty-five years old (Feb. 21, 1677).

SPIRE, or **Spires** (German, Speyer), a city of Germany, in Bavaria, on the River Rhine; pop. 16,000, or about as large as New Brighton, N.Y. It was a military station of the Romans, and afterward became the residence of the German emperors. During the Reformation, a diet, or congress, was held there, at which the reformed princes drew up a protest against the Catholics. From this they were afterwards called Protestants. Spire was burned by the French in 1689. At that time the splendid cathedral was partly destroyed; but it has since been rebuilt, and the tombs of eight emperors are still shown in it.

SPITZ-BERG'EN, a group of islands, in the Arctic Ocean, N. of Norway; area, 30,000 square miles, or not quite as large as South Carolina. They are very rugged, with high mountains, of which hardly any thing is known. Winter lasts from September to June, and for four months the sun is not seen at all. In the summer it is always daylight, but so cold, that snow lies on the ground, and only a few shrubs and mosses can grow. The animals are the polar bear, polar foxes, and reindeer. No people live in Spitzbergen; but it is often visited by whaling-ships. The islands are claimed by Russia. They were first found by the English in 1596; but the Dutch gave them the name of Spitzbergen, which means "pointed mountains."

SPOF'FORD, Harriet Elizabeth, an American authoress, born in Calais, Me, April 3, 1835. Her name before marriage was Prescott. She has published "Sir Rohan's Ghost," "The Amber Gods and Other Stories," and "New England Legend," and has written stories for "St. Nicholas" and other magazines.

SPRING'FIELD, a city, capital of Illinois, in the central part of the State, near the Sangamon River; pop. 25,000, or nearly as large as Gloucester, Mass. It has so many beautiful grounds and gardens, that it is often called the "Flower City." The State Capitol is one of the finest buildings in the country. There are important manufactories and mills, and the city has a large trade with the fertile country around it.

Springfield was founded in 1822, and became the State capital in 1837. It was the home of Lincoln, whose body rests under a magnificent monument in the Oak Ridge Cemetery, near the city.

SPRING'FIELD, a city of Massachusetts, on the Connecticut River, 98 miles from Boston; pop. 44,000, or as large as Salt Lake City, Utah. It is noted for its manufactures, especially of railroad cars, steam-engines, stationery, jewelry, cotton cloth, cartridges, and fire-arms. The United States armory is one of the largest in the country, and has many large buildings, in which several hundred men are employed in making rifles and carbines. The breechloading guns used in the United States army are made there (C. C. T., 513, II., u.). During the Civil War about 3,000 workmen were employed there, and 1,000 rifles were made every day. Near the armory is an arsenal in which 275,000 muskets and rifles are stored.

Springfield was founded in 1635, and was first called Agawam; but in 1638 it was named after Springfield, England, where some of the first settlers had lived. In 1675, during King Philip's War, the settlement was burned by the Indians. It became a city in 1852.

SPRING'FIELD, a city of Ohio, on Mad River, 45 miles W. of Columbus; pop. 32,000, or a little larger than Mobile, Ala. It is in a rich farming-region and a large trade is carried on in wheat, flour, corn, cattle, and swine. The town is also noted for its manufactures, especially of mowing-machines, and for its many large flour-mills. It is the site of Wittenberg College and Springfield Seminary.

SQUI'ER, Ephraim George, an American writer, born in Bethlehem, N.Y., June 17, 1821. He was brought up on a farm, became a newspaper editor, and in 1848 was sent as *chargé d'affaires* (government agent) to the republics of Central America, and in 1863 to Peru. While in those countries, he visited many places, and examined the old buildings and monuments still remaining; and, after his return to the United States, wrote several interesting books about them. His last work was on Peru. He died when sixty-seven years old (April 17, 1888).

STAF'FORD, William Howard, viscount, and English statesman, born Nov. 30, 1612. He was the son of Thomas, Earl of Arundel, and, like all the Howard family, was brought up a strict Roman Catholic. He fought on the side of Charles I.; but after the Restoration he often voted against the court, because he thought his services in the royal cause had not been properly rewarded. He was accused by Titus OATES of having a share in the proposed Papist plot to overthrow the government, and on that charge, although there was little to strengthen it, he was executed. On the scaffold he so earnestly declared his innocence, that the spectators cried, "We believe you, my lord; God bless you, my lord." He died when sixty-eight years old (Dec. 29, 1680).

STAN'DISH, Miles, the first military leader of the Puritan settlers in New England, born in Lancashire, England, about 1584. He came with the Pilgrims in 1620, and by his boldness and bravery did much to protect the settlers against the Indians. His wife, Rose, died during the first winter. He is said to have fallen in love afterward with Priscilla Mullins, but, instead of courting her himself, sent his friend John Alden to ask her to marry him. The result was that John married Priscilla. The story is well told by Longfellow in his poem called "The Courtship of Miles Standish." Miles Standish died in Duxbury, Mass., Oct. 3, 1656. A fine monument, with a bronze statue on it, has been erected there to his memory on a hill called after him Captain's Hill.

STANIS·LAS I. LESZCZYNSKI, (*lesh-chin'skee*), King of Poland, born in Lemberg, Oct. 20, 1677. He was the son of the grand treasurer of Poland. After Charles XII. of Sweden had driven Augustus II. from the throne of Poland, he named Stanislas for the place, and he was elected by the Polish diet. The defeat of Charles at Pultowa in 1709 restored Augustus, and Stanislas was compelled to fly. The French let him live in Alsace; and soon after, his daughter Marie became the wife of Louis XV., who, on the death of Augustus, undertook a war to put Stanislas on the throne of Poland. But the Russians were in favor of Augustus III., son of the late king; and Stanislas had to give up his claim, taking in exchange the dukedom of Lorraine. Here he spent the rest of his life, holding a brilliant court at Nancy, gathering learned men about him, and erecting magnificent buildings. He died in Nancy when eighty-nine years old (Feb. 23, 1766).

STANHOPE (*stan'op*), Lady **Hester Lucy,** a noted Englishwoman who left her country to live among the Arabs, born in London, March 12, 1776. She was the daughter of Earl Stanhope, and grand-daughter of the great Earl of Chatham, and was very talented and handsome. When quite young, she went to live with her uncle, William PITT, and acted as his private secretary. After his death, not having money enough to support herself in the luxury to which she had become accustomed, she gave up all society, and in 1810 left England, and went to live at a deserted convent among the half-savage tribes about Mount Lebanon in Syria. There she led a strange life. She dressed like a Mohammedan chieftain, even wearing the weapons and pipe, and adopted the habits and manners of the people about her, giving up every thing European. She gained great influence over the Arab tribes and their chiefs, who thought her a prophetess, and consulted her in all important matters. She turned the old convent into a fortress, guarded by a band of Albanians, and ruled there like a queen, giving aid to all who needed it. Indeed, she was so generous to others, that she was often in great want herself during the latter part of her life. She died in the sixty-fourth year of her age (June 23, 1839). No European was near her, and her servants robbed her house as soon as she was dead. She was buried in her own garden by the British consul at Beyrout, and Dr. Thomson, an American missionary.

STAN'LEY, Henry M., a famous African explorer, born near Denbigh, Wales, in 1840. His real name was John Rowlands; and he was sent, when only three years old, to the poor-house at St. Asaph, where he remained until he was thirteen, when he went to New Orleans as a cabin-boy on a vessel. There he was adopted by a merchant, who gave him his own name. When the war began, Stanley enlisted in the Confederate army, but was taken prisoner, and afterward joined the United States navy. When the war was over, he began to travel as correspondent for newspapers; and in 1869 Mr. Bennett of " The New York Herald " sent him to Africa to look for Dr. Livingstone, whom he found at Ujiji, on Lake Tanganyika, May 10, 1871. Stanley returned to England in November of the same year, and published a book called " How I met Livingstone." He returned to Africa in 1874 to explore the lake region near the equator, sailed all around Lake Victoria N'yanza, and made several very important discoveries. He came back in 1877 down the River Congo, he being the first white man who had ever sailed down that river. The natives were very hostile; and he had many adventures and hair-breadth escapes, which he has told about in his book called " Through the Dark

Continent." Starting again in 1879, he explored the Congo basin, and on his return in 1884 published " The Congo, and the Founding of its Free State." Stanley was now implored to go to the rescue of Emin Pasha, who was governor at Wadelai, and was in great danger of being annihilated by the Mahdi. He started across Africa in 1887, and returned safely with Emin in 1889, after having travelled about five thousand miles. In 1890 he published " In Darkest Africa," in which he describes the country and its people.

STARK, John, an officer in the American Revolution, born at Londonderry, N.H., Aug. 28, 1728. He distinguished himself in the war against the French and Indians; and, on the breaking out of the Revolution (1775), he was made colonel of a volunteer regiment, and fought at the battle of Bunker Hill. On Aug. 16, 1777, he defeated the British at Bennington, for which he was thanked by Congress and made brigadier-general. He died when ninety-four years old (May 8, 1822).

STEELE, Sir Richard, a British author, born in Dublin in 1671. He went to the University of Oxford, but failed to graduate, and entered the army as a private. At the end of a few years he gave up the army, and devoted himself to writing plays, some of which were, " The Funeral, or, Grief à la Mode," " The Tender Husband," and " The Lying Lover." His chief fame rests upon his connection with the " Tatler " and the " Spectator," two magazines among the first that were published in England. Addison was the ablest editor of these papers; but many of the articles were written by Steele. He died in Wales when fifty-eight years old (Sept. 1, 1729).

STE'PHEN, fourth and last Norman King of England, born about 1100. He was the son of Stephen, Count of Blois, and Adela, daughter of William the Conqueror. With other English nobles he had taken an oath to support Matilda, daughter of Henry I., as Queen of England; but this did not prevent him, on the death of the king in 1135, from hastening to England, and seizing the throne. Matilda's claim was upheld by the Duke of Gloucester in a war which went on through Stephen's entire reign of nineteen years. This was a most miserable time. The "Saxon Chronicle" says, "Thou mightest go a whole day's journey, and not find a man sitting in a town, nor an acre of land tilled. The poor died of hunger, and those who had been men well to do begged for bread." At last a treaty was made, deciding that Stephen might be king during his life, if he would agree that Matilda's son Henry should reign after him. Stephen was very willing that this should be, as his eldest son Eustace had just died. Stephen himself died a year after this, when fifty-four years old (Oct. 25, 1154). He was succeeded by Henry II., the first of the Plantagenet line.

STE'PHEN, the name of ten popes. **Stephen III.,** the most noted one, ruled from 752 to 757. The Lombards having invaded Italy, he asked Pepin, King of the Franks, and son of Charles Martel, to help him. Pepin drove out the Lombards, and became the real King of Rome, and this made the Franks the greatest people of the West. He gave the territory thus won to Stephen, and this began the temporal power of the popes.

STEPHENS (*ste'vens*), **Alexander Hamilton,** an American statesman, born in Georgia, Feb. 11, 1812. He became a lawyer and a member of the Georgia Legislature, and from 1843 to 1859 was a member of Congress. He opposed the secession of the Southern States in 1860; but in 1861 he was made vice-president of the Confederacy, and afterward did all he could to aid it. In February, 1865, he met Mr. Lincoln on a steamer in Hampton Roads, and tried to make peace, but without success. After the war he was imprisoned five months in Fort Warren, Boston Harbor. He was a member of Congress from 1873 to 1882, when he became Governor of Georgia. He died, when seventy-one years old (March 4, 1883), in Atlanta, Georgia. He was the author of histories of the war and of the United States.

STEPHENSON (*ste'ven-son*), **George,** an English railway engineer, the inventor of the locomotive, born at Wylam, Northumberland, June 9, 1781. He was the son of a poor colliery laborer, and when fourteen years old became an assistant

George Stephenson.

fireman in the colliery. He always took great delight in all kinds of machines, and was always contriving something new. At the age of eighteen he married, and was taught to read by his wife. The science of mechanics had for him a very great attraction; and when he was placed in charge of an engine, he studied it so carefully, that he could take it to pieces and put it together again. The engines of those days were stationary, and locomotives were unknown. People had often said what a good thing it would be if somebody only would invent an engine to draw wagons; but the wise shook their heads, and said that that was impossible. Stephenson, however, soon showed them that it was quite possible to make an engine that would go. In 1829 he won a prize of £500 ($2,500) for his engine, called the "Rocket," which ran at the rate of 30 miles an hour. Stephenson then set up works for building locomotives, and in his latter years gave much time to the care of great coalmines which he owned. Wealth flowed in upon him, but in no way changed his simple manners. The queen offered to make him a knight, but he declined the honor. He died at his estate of Tapton Park when sixty-seven years old (Aug. 12, 1848).

Robert Stephenson, his son, born Oct. 16, 1803, also became a famous engineer, and was engaged in many great works. He helped his father design locomotives, built several important railways, and was the engineer of the Britannia tubular bridge across Menai Strait, and the Victoria tubular bridge across the St. Lawrence at Montreal. He died in London when fifty-six years old (Oct. 12, 1859).

STERNE, Laurence, an English writer, born in Ireland, Nov. 24, 1713. Sterne was educated for the Church, and on being ordained was appointed to a place connected with the Cathedral of York. For twenty years he lived there, doing any thing and every thing except the duties of his profession. His two best known works are "Tristram Shandy" and the "Sentimental Journey." The first of these was much thought of in its day; but people have since found out that a great deal of its wisdom was borrowed from other authors. In his writings Sterne seems to be a man of very tender feelings; but he was a bad husband, and it is said that he let his mother die in the almshouse. He died in London when fifty-five years old (March 18, 1768).

STETTIN (*stet-teen'*), a city of Germany, in Prussia, on the River Oder; pop. 100,000, or a little larger than Albany, N. Y. It is surrounded by strong walls, and has a citadel and several forts. Stettin has many handsome buildings and squares, and is noted for its manufactories of woollen, linen, cotton, and chemicals. Small vessels can ascend the river to the city; but large ones stop at Swinemünde, a port on the Baltic Sea, from which freight is sent to Stettin by railroad. Stettin is more than a thousand years old. From 1648 to 1720 it belonged to Sweden.

STEUBEN (*stu-ben'*, German *stu'-ben*), **Frederic William Augustus,** Baron, an officer in the American Revolution, born in Magdeburg, Prussia, Nov. 15, 1730. He entered the Prussian army when only fourteen years old, rose rapidly, and was one of the young officers whom Frederic the Great chose to be under his own guidance. In 1777 Steuben came to America, and offered his services to Gen. Washington. He was made inspector-general, and by his careful training and strict discipline he soon got the army in good order. He also took part in several important battles. In 1790 an annuity, and a large grant of land near Utica, N.Y., were voted him for his services, and he spent the rest of his life on his property. He died near Utica, N.Y., when sixty-four years old (Nov. 28, 1794).

STEWART, Charles, an American naval commander, born in Philadelphia, July 28, 1778. He went to sea as a cabin-boy, but rapidly rose in rank, and in 1798 became commander of a United States ship. During the War of 1812 he commanded the frigate "Constitution," with which he captured the British man-of-war "Pictou," and several other vessels. On the night of Feb. 20, 1815, he fought two British vessels, the "Cyane" and "Levant," and captured them both in less than an hour.

He became a rear-admiral, finally retiring from the service in 1862. He died at Bordentown, N.J., when ninety-one years old (Nov. 7, 1869).

STILICHO (*stil'e-ko*), **Flavius,** a noted Roman general. He was the son of a Vandal officer under the Emperor Valens, and he married the niece of the Emperor Theodosius, who gave him command of the armies of Italy, and the care of his son Honorius. After the death of the emperor (395), Honorius became emperor in the West, and Arcadius, his brother, in the East, and three years afterward, Honorius married the daughter of Stilicho.

In 402 ALARIC invaded Italy; but Stilicho defeated him at Pollentia (403), and again soon after at Verona, and drove him out of Italy. Stilicho now made friends with Alaric, with the purpose of overthrowing Arcadius, hoping thus to make himself master of both the Eastern and Western Empires. But his enemies at court stirred up Honorius against him, and he was assassinated (Aug. 23, 408).

STIR'LING, a town of Scotland, on the River Forth, 31 miles W.N.W. of Edinburgh; pop. 12,000, or about as large as Shreveport, La. It is noted for its many ancient buildings, and especially its palace and castle, which are famous in Scottish history. In the castle, James II. and James V. were born, and William, Earl of Douglas, was assassinated. The battles of Stirling and Bannockburn were fought near the town, which has been besieged several times.

STOCK'HOLM, the capital and principal city of Sweden, on an arm of the Baltic Sea; pop. 244,000, or about as large as New Orleans, La. It is built partly on the mainland, and partly on several islands. The harbor is very fine; and the city, with its palaces and parks, and the background of forest-covered hills, is one of the most picturesque places in the world. The Royal Palace is a very large and handsome building of granite, and is splendidly furnished. Near it are the National Museum and the Royal Library. In the Riddarholm Church are shown the shrine of GUSTAVUS ADOLPHUS, the tombs of CHARLES XII., BERNADOTTE, and other kings. Stockholm has several colleges and the best medical school in Sweden, and is celebrated for its fine parks, the largest of which, called the Djurgard, or Deergarden, is three miles around, and contains the Rosendal Palace. The city has many manufactories, and carries on a large trade with all parts of the world.

The name Stockholm means Stake Island, and was given because the islands on which it is built were enlarged by piles or stakes. The city was probably founded in the 13th century, and has ever since been the capital of Sweden. It was taken by the Danes in 1502, and again in 1520, when such a terrible massacre took place that it was called the "blood bath of Stockholm."

STOCK'PORT, a town of England, on the River Mersey, at the junction of the Tame; pop. 60,000, or nearly as large as Grand Rapids, Mich. It is noted for its many cotton-mills, bleaching and dyeing houses, and print-mills. The surrounding country is rich in coal, which is used at Stockport in large iron and brass foundries. A splendid railroad viaduct crosses the River Mersey, and part of the city itself, by twenty-six immense arches. Stockport has a Sunday school, which is attended by nearly 4,000 children.

STOCK'TON, a city of California, on an arm of the San Joaquin River; pop. 14,000, or nearly as large as Watertown, N. Y. Vessels ascend the river from San Francisco to Stockton, and several railroads meet there. Stockton has a large trade, especially in wheat, wool, and other farm products. It is the site of the State Lunatic Asylum. Stockton was founded in 1849.

STOCK'TON, Francis Richard, an American writer for young folks, born in Philadelphia, Penn., April 5, 1834. He has written much for "St. Nicholas," of which he was for a long time assistant editor, and has published several books, among them "Tinga-ling," "Roundabout Rambles," "Tales out of School," "What might have been Expected," "Rudder Grange," and "A Jolly Fellowship."

STOD'DARD, Richard Henry, an American poet, born in Hingham, Mass., in July, 1825. For several years in his youth he worked in an iron foundry in New York, but in 1852 he got a place in the New York custom-house, where he staid until 1870. He wrote constantly while in both those positions, and for the last ten years has given all his time to writing. Among his works are "Adventures in Fairy-Land," "The King's Bell," "Little Red Riding-Hood," "The Children in the Wood," and "Putnam the Brave."

STOKE-UPON-TRENT, a town of England, on the River Trent; pop., 152,000, or twice as large as Nashville, Tenn. It is noted for its great potteries, in which a large part of the people who live there are employed. Among the many things made are statuettes, tiles, and porcelain ornaments and dishes.

One mile N. of Stoke-upon-Trent is the town of Hanley (pop., 40,000), which is also engaged in the manufacture of pottery.

STONEHENGE (*stone'henj*), the name given to a collection of great stones on Salisbury Plain, about eight miles N. of Salisbury, Eng. There are about 140 of them in all, and some of them are so large that they would weigh more than 100,000 pounds. Only a part of them are standing in their original places; but it can be seen that they were arranged in four circles, one within the other, or rather two ovals within two circles. In the centre is a flat sandstone slab about fifteen feet long. Bones of oxen, deer, and other animals, were found under this slab, mixed with burnt wood and bits of ancient pottery. It is supposed that the slab was an altar on which the deer and oxen were burned, and that the stones formed a temple of the ancient DRUIDS.

Stonehenge, in the Saxon language, means hanging stones.

STO'NY POINT, a rocky point of land on the W. bank of the Hudson River, 42 miles N. of New York City, and opposite Verplanck's Point on the E. bank. Between these two points the river is very narrow; and during the Revolution the Americans built forts on them to keep English ships from passing. The forts were captured by the British in June, 1779, but soon afterwards Stony Point was surprised in the night, and recaptured by the Americans under Gen. WAYNE (July 16, 1779). More than 600 men, forming the garrison, were killed, or taken prisoners. An attack was made at the same time on the Verplanck Point fort; but, as this was not captured, the Americans destroyed the fort on Stony Point, and abandoned it.

STO'RY, Joseph, an American lawyer, born in Marblehead Mass., Sept. 18, 1779. He was graduated at Harvard College in 1798, and became a lawyer in Salem, where he soon had a fine practice. He became a member of Congress, and associate judge of the United States Supreme Court, and at last head of the law school of Harvard University, where his fame drew many students. He published many law books, which are still in great use. Judge Story died in Cambridge when sixty-six years old (Sept. 10, 1845).

William Wetmore Story, his son, born in Salem, Feb. 12, 1819, is famous as a sculptor and writer. He was graduated at Harvard College in 1838, became a lawyer, and wrote several law books. In 1848 he went to Rome to study sculpture, and he has since lived there,

Among his works are several statues of distinguished Americans, "Little Red Riding-Hood," "Sappho," "Cleopatra," "Jerusalem," and several other fancy pieces. Mr. Story has also published several poems and a play entitled "Nero." He died when seventy-six years old (October 7, 1895).

STOWE (*sto*), **Harriet Elizabeth Beecher,** an American writer, born at Litchfield, Conn., June 15, 1812. She was the daughter of Dr. Lyman Beecher, and sister of Rev. Henry Ward Beecher, and married (1836) Rev. Calvin Ellis Stowe. She wrote at first for magazines, and published some stories for children. In 1851 she began to publish, in a newspaper called "The National Era," her story of "Uncle Tom's Cabin," which at once made her famous.

Harriet Beecher Stowe.

No American author ever gained such a sudden and great success, and no other English novel has been so widely read. It was quickly translated into all the European and many Asiatic languages. It has also been widely dramatized. She afterwards published many other novels and stories, among them "The Minister's Wooing," "The Pearl of Orr's Island," "Oldtown Folks," and "My Wife and I." She died at her home in Hartford, Conn., when eighty-four years old (July 1, 1896).

STRA'BO, a Greek geographer, born in Pontus, Asia Minor, about 54 B.C. He was well educated, and spent almost all his life in travel and study. His "Geography" is a work of great value. It is divided into seventeen books, and in it he describes chiefly places he had visited. He died about A.D. 24.

STRAF'FORD, Thomas Wentworth, Earl of, an English statesman born in London, April 13, 1593. He was elected to Parliament when only twenty-one years old. At first he sided with the enemies of the crown; but afterwards he joined the court party, and very soon became the king's most trusted counsellor. He was sent as governor to Ireland; but his rule was so severe that he was hated by the Irish people. The English, too, were many of them his enemies, because they blamed him for most of the king's acts against their liberty. In the Parliament which met on Nov. 3 he was charged with an attempt to overthrow the liberties of his country. He made in his own defence a most masterly speech; but it did not save him. King Charles, to his shame be it said, signed his death-warrant. Although Strafford had written to him a letter urging him to do so, and saying that he would willingly give up his life for the sake of peace, he exclaimed, when he was told of this, "Put not your trust in princes." In his walk from the Tower to the place of execution, his step and manner are described as being those of "a general marching at the head of an army to breathe victory, rather than those of a condemned man under the sentence of death." He died when forty-eight years old (May 12, 1641).

STRAITS SETTLEMENTS, a colony of Great Britain, in Asia, including SINGAPORE, Malacca, and Wellesley, with the Island of Penang; area, 1,350 square miles, or about as large as the State of Rhode Island; pop., 506,000, or nearly a third more than that of Rhode Island. The governor of the colony lives at Singapore. The people are mostly Malays and Chinese.

STRALSUND (*strahl'soont*), a town of Germany, in Prussia, on a strait of the Baltic Sea, which separates the Island of Rügen from the mainland; pop. 29,000, or about as large as Waterbury, Conn. It has an excellent harbor; and, being strongly fortified, it is a very important military and naval post. A large trade is carried on in wheat, malt, timber, wool, and linen, and there are manufactures of linen and woollen goods.

STRASBURG (*strahs'boorg*), a city of W. Germany, on the River Ill,

Strasburg Clock.

about a mile from the Rhine; pop. 112,000, or about one fourth as large as Boston, Mass. It is surrounded by a wall, and has a strong citadel and forts. The Cathedral of Strasburg is one of the finest buildings in the world. It has a magnificent spire (468 feet high), and is noted for its wonderful clock, which is 300 years old, and one of the largest and most curious ever made (C.C.T., 136, II., l.). Strasburg has a fine library, and a university with 850 students. There are important manufactures of woolen, linen, and cotton cloths, jewelry and clocks, and the city is noted for its *pâtés de foie gras*, often called Strasburg pies (C.C.T., 280, II., u.).

Strasburg was a Roman fortress called Argentoratum (silver town); and this was made by the Germans into Stratiburg, which means the same thing, and which finally became changed to its present form. In 1681 it became a French city, and remained so until 1870, when it was taken by the Germans, after a month's siege. During the bombardment the beautiful cathedral tower was much injured, and the library was burned; but both have since been restored.

STRAT'FORD-UPON-A'VON, a town of England, on the River Avon; pop. about 8000, or about as large as Kearney, Neb. Here Shakespeare was born, lived, and died, and was buried in a church near the river. His tomb and a part of his house are still shown. The house was purchased by a subscription of the English people, and it is kept as nearly as possible in the condition in which Shakespeare left it. The 300th birthday of Shakespeare was celebrated at Stratford on April 23, 1864.

STRAUSS (*strowss*), the name of four German musicians, — a father, Johann, and his three sons, Johann, Joseph, and Edouard, all of whom have composed beautiful music for dancing. Johann Strauss, the father, was born in Vienna, March 14, 1804, and died there Sept. 24, 1849. Johann, the son, has for many years been musical director of the court balls in Vienna. He has a band which has delighted all who have heard it play in the different European cities. The waltzes of this composer, numbering nearly four hundred, are the best ever written.

STRICK'LAND, Agnes, an English writer, born at Reydon Hall, Suffolk, July 19, 1796. She began to write when only sixteen years old. Her works are chiefly novels, biographies, historical sketches, and books for children. She is best known by her "Lives of the Queens of England" and "Lives of the Queens of Scotland," in writing which she was helped by her sisters. Her latest book is "Lives of the Tudor Princesses." She died in London when seventy-eight years old (July 13, 1874).

STRUVE (*stroo'veh*), **Friedrich Georg Wilhelm von,** a Russian astronomer, born in Altona, April 15, 1793. The observatory of Pulkova, the best building in the world for observing the heavenly bodies, was put up by him, and for twenty-five years he was its director. He found

Church at Stratford-upon-Avon where Shakespeare is buried. (See page **772.**)

out much that we know about the fixed stars, particularly those situated in that part of the heavens called the Milky Way. He died in St. Petersburg when seventy-one years old (Nov. 23, 1864).

STUART, Arabella, the only child of Charles Stuart, Earl of Lennox, born about 1575. She, as well as James I., was descended from Margaret Tudor, daughter of Henry VII., and she was therefore in the direct line of descent to the English crown. On the death of Queen Elizabeth, an unsuccessful plot was made to place her on the throne, and as long as she lived she was an object of jealousy to her royal cousin James. In 1610 she married William Seymour, who was also descended from Henry VII., through another daughter. This marriage so angered James, that he had Seymour put into the Tower, and his wife under control of the Bishop of Durham. Both she and her husband escaped, and made their way to the coast, where a vessel was in waiting to take them to France. The husband, arriving too late, was obliged to take another vessel. The one in which Lady Arabella sailed was captured by the English, and she was committed to the Tower, where her treatment was such, that she became insane, and soon died, when forty years old (Sept. 27, 1615).

STUART Gilbert Charles, a noted American painter, born in Rhode Island in 1756. He had his first lessons from a Scotch artist, and after painting for a short time in Newport, Boston, and New York, went to London (1778), where he was aided by Benjamin WEST. He soon became famous as a portrait painter, rivalling the best English artists of the day, and having among his sitters King George III. and many other people of rank. In 1793 he came back to America, and painted his famous portrait of Washington. He painted also Jefferson, Madison, Monroe, John Adams, John Quincy Adams, and many other distinguished men and women. In 1806 he went to Boston to live, and died there when seventy-two years old (July, 1828).

STU'ART, House of, the name of a royal family of Scotland and England, which gave to Scotland thirteen sovereigns, the last six of whom were also rulers of England. They are said to have been so called because their ancestor Walter, who lived in the 11th century, was steward of the household of Malcolm III., King of Scotland. His descendant, Walter Stuart, married Marjory, the daughter of Robert BRUCE; and his son Robert inherited the throne (1371) as the first of the Stuart line. They were a very unfortunate family; for, with very few exceptions, these thirteen rulers came to violent deaths. Their claim to the English throne was through Margaret Tudor, who married James IV. of Scotland. The same thread of misfortune runs through the lives of the English sovereigns of that name that appears in those of their Scottish forefathers, from the unfortunate Mary Queen of Scots down. Almost all the Stuarts were gifted with intelligence and refinement; and they had amiable qualities in full measure;

but the perseverance and sagacity of the Tudors were lacking to them, The male line died out in 1807 in the person of Henry Stuart, Cardinal York; the present royal family of England being descended from Elizabeth, daughter of James I.

STU'ART, James Francis Edward, called the Old Pretender, son of King James II. of England, born in London, June 10, 1688. He was only a few months old when his father was driven from England; and his youth was spent in France. When his father died, James was acknowledged as King of England by the principal rulers of Europe; but the English refused to allow his claim because he was a Roman Catholic, and when Queen Anne died, the crown was given to George I. Two attempts to gain the throne for him were made in Scotland; but, both failing, James retired to France, and gave up his claims to his son, Charles Edward Stuart. He died in Rome when seventy-eight years old (Jan. 2, 1766).

Stuart, Charles Edward, his son, called the Young Pretender, born in Rome, Dec. 31, 1720. Many believed that he was the rightful king of England; and in 1744, aided by the French, he gathered a large fleet and army, with which he intended to gain the English throne; but his ships were scattered by a storm, and he was obliged to give up the invasion. In 1745 he went to Scotland almost alone; but many of the Scotch were his friends; and he soon gathered an army, took Edinburgh, and defeated the English at the battle of Preston Pans (Sept. 22, 1745). He then invaded England; but when he was less than a hundred miles from London his followers lost heart, and he was obliged to retreat again to Scotland. On April 16, 1746, the English defeated him at the battle of CULLODEN, and his soldiers deserting him he wandered for five months in the Highlands, pursued by his enemies, and only saved by the faithfulness of a few friends, among whom was Flora MACDONALD. He finally escaped to France. The rest of his life was imbittered by many troubles and by his own dissipation. He died in Rome when sixty-seven years old (Jan. 30, 1788).

The followers of the two Pretenders were called Jacobites, or followers of King James, Jacobus being the Latin for James.

STUTTGART (*stoot'gart*), a city of S. Germany, capital of the kingdom of Würtemberg, near the River Neckar; pop. 126,000, or a little less than that of Providence, R. I. It lies in a beautiful valley, and with its fine old churches and palaces is a very interesting place. There are many parks and public gardens, several museums, and a very fine library, besides colleges, a military academy, and schools of painting and music. Stuttgart has important manufactories of woollen, silk, linen, and cotton goods, and philosophical instruments. Some of the largest book publishing houses in Germany are there.

It is not known when Stuttgart was founded; but it is more than six hundred years old. It has been the capital of Würtemberg since 1482.

STUY'VESANT (*sti've-sant*), **Petrus**, the last of the Dutch governors of New Netherlands, born in Holland in 1602. He arrived in America in May, 1647, and was governor seventeen years. He found the colony at war with the Indians; but he soon restored order, and made peace with the Indians. He then had trouble with the Swedish settlers near the Delaware, and in 1655 captured their colony. While he was governor, there were constant disputes between the Dutch and the English settlers, the English refusing to recognize the right of the Dutch to the land; and in 1664 the English king, Charles II., gave the land to his brother, the Duke of York. An English fleet arrived in the bay of New Amsterdam, now called New York, and demanded possession of the city. Stuyvesant wished to fight, but was obliged to give the city up to them. He spent

Petrus Stuyvesant.

the rest of his life quietly on his farm near New York. He died there when eighty years old (August, 1682). There is much about Stuyvesant in Irving's humorous "History of New York, by Diedrich Knickerbocker."

STYX, in Greek fable a river of HADES, or the lower world, around which it flowed nine times. When any one once crossed this river, it was impossible to return. The souls of the dead were believed to be carried over it by an aged boatman named CHARON. At the entrance to Hades was a grotto, in which lived a nymph, also named Styx, by whom the most solemn oaths of the gods were sworn.

SUCK'LING, Sir John, an English poet, born at Whitton, Middlesex, in 1609. After serving with the Swedes in the THIRTY-YEARS' WAR, he returned to England to shine a while at the court of Charles I. Though he was more desirous to win fame as a courtier than as a poet, he wrote some beautiful songs. Having been found out in a plot to free Lord Stafford, a prisoner confined by Parliament in the Tower, he fled to France, where he died, as some thought by his own hand, when thirty-three years old (1642).

SUCRE (*soo'kra*), or **Chuquisaca** (*choo-ke-sah'kah*), a city, former capital of Bolivia, on a table-land E. of the Andes, nearly two miles above the sea; pop. 19,000. or about the same as Orange, N. J. It has wide regular streets; but few of the houses are more than two stories high. Most of the people are Indians, or mixed breeds. The city was named after Gen. Antonio José de Sucre, who was president of Bolivia in 1825.

SUE (*su*), **Marie Joseph Eugene,** a French novelist, born at Paris, Dec. 10, 1804. Until he received a large fortune, which enabled him to devote himself to book writing, he was a surgeon, first in the army and then in the navy. His most famous works are, "Mysteries of Paris," a work full of pictures of wickedness, and the "Wandering Jew." Few novelists have written more works than have come from his pen. Being a strong republican in politics, he left France on the beginning of the empire in 1851, and went to live in Savoy, where he died when fifty-three years old (Aug. 3, 1857).

SUETONIUS (*swe-to'ne-us*) **TRAN-QUIL'LUS, Caius,** a noted Roman historian, born A.D. 72. He is principally known for his "Lives of the Twelve Cæsars," or the twelve emperors from Julius Cæsar to Domitian, concerning whose lives he tells many anecdotes. He also wrote books on "Illustrious Grammarians," and on "Celebrated Orators." Suetonius died about A.D. 140.

SUEZ (*soo'ez*), an isthmus between the Red and Mediterranean Seas, connecting Asia with Africa; width, in the narrowest part, about 72 miles. The surface is sandy, and most of it is only a few feet above the sea. In ancient times there was a canal across part of it, from the Red Sea to the Nile; but it became choked with sand. As the trade between Southern Asia and Europe increased, it was seen that such a canal would be very important, because ships could pass by it from China and

Bird's-eye View of the Suez Canal.

India to Europe, without going around Africa. M. Ferdinand de LESSEPS planned a new canal, which was finished in 1869, after ten years' labor by thousands of workmen. It is about 100 miles long, and deep enough for the largest ships; and, though its cost was very great, it has more than repaid the outlay by its usefulness. More than a thousand vessels pass through it every year, paying large tolls to the Canal Company.

SUEZ, a town of N. E. Egypt, on the Isthmus of Suez, at the head of the Gulf of Suez, which forms the northern end of the Red Sea; pop. 11,000, or about as large as Alameda, Cal. Until the canal was made, Suez was a small Arab village; but it has now become very important for its trade. New harbors and docks have been built, and these, with the large storehouses and other buildings belonging to the canal and steamboat companies, have totally changed the appearance of the place.

SU'I-DAS, a Greek writer who lived in the 10th or 11th century A.D. He wrote a cyclopædia of persons and places, in alphabetical order, which is valuable on account of its many extracts from ancient Greek authors, most of whose writings have been lost.

SUL'LA or **Syl'la, Lucius Cornelius,** a famous Roman general, born in 138 B.C. His family was noble but poor, yet Sulla managed to get a good education; and after a time a fortune was left to him, and then he got office and rank in Rome. In the year 107 B.C. he was sent to Africa to assist Marius in the war against Jugurtha. Marius received him coldly; but he soon got his favor by his bravery and skill as a soldier. Sulla soon got Bocchus to betray Jugurtha into his hands, and then claimed that he had ended the war by his capture, and after this Marius and Sulla became enemies.

The quarrel between them was only kept from bursting out into open strife by the terrible Social War which began in 90 B.C. Both had commands in this war; but Sulla won more fame than Marius, and was elected consul, and given the command in the war against MITHRIDATES. This so enraged Marius, who wanted this for himself, that he led his friends into a civil war, forced the Senate to give him the place, and drove Sulla from Rome. Sulla fled to his army, marched to Rome, and drove Marius and his friends into exile. This was the first civil war in Roman history.

He then sailed for Greece, and was away more than three years, fighting Mithridates. Meanwhile CINNA and the friends of Marius got the power in Rome, and declared Sulla a public enemy, took his property, and killed his friends. Sulla returned to Italy in the spring of 83 B.C., and marched for Rome. Marius and Cinna were then both dead; but the son of Marius was consul, and, the Marian party was strong. The Samnites joined the Marian party and marched against Rome, saying that the city must be destroyed. Sulla shut up young Marius in Præneste, and leaving a part of his army to besiege that place, marched to Rome and fought a great battle before the Colline Gate, in which it is said more than 50,000 fell on each side. By this the Samnites and the Marian party were both crushed, and young Marius then killed himself. Sulla now took the supreme power in Rome, with the title of Perpetual Dictator (82 B.C.). He took a cruel and bloody revenge on his enemies, and then passed laws restoring the power of the Senate, and taking away power from the people, which did more to prepare Rome for the empire than all which even Cæsar himself did. He then laid down the dictatorship, and went to live at his villa in Puteoli. He was given the surname of Felix (Prosperous), for his unbroken successes. He died when sixty years old (78 B.C.).

SUL'LI-VAN, Sir Arthur, an English writer of music, born in London in 1844. He is the son of a music teacher, and was brought up to follow his father's profession, and he is now the well-known composer of many overtures, songs, and operettas. None of his works have given him greater popularity than "Pinafore," with whose strains there are few, old or young, who are not familiar. His later works have been operettas called "The Gondoliers" and "Ivanhoe."

SUMATRA (*soo-mah'trah*), the most westerly island of the Malay Archipelago, S. of Eastern Asia, and directly under the equator; area, 160,000 square miles, or about as large as California; pop. 3,000,000, or nearly two and a half times that of California. A range of volcanic mountains runs through it, some of the peaks of which are burning volcanoes, and on each side of it are low plains covered with thick forests. The climate is warm and moist. From November to January it rains nearly all the time, and there are about 200 rainy days every year. The soil is very rich, and yields fine crops of rice, coffee, pepper, and tobacco. The principal things sent from there are pepper, nutmegs, cloves, mace, camphor, gold-dust, copper, tin, and gutta-percha. The rafflesia, a plant which grows there, has the largest flower known, it being a yard across. Among the wild animals are the orang-outang, found only in Sumatra and in Borneo, the tiger, rhinoceros, elephant, tapir, and many kinds of monkeys. Most of the people are Malays. About two-thirds of the island, in the southern and western parts, is claimed by the Dutch; but a portion of this is ruled for them by native chiefs. The rest, called Acheen, still belong to the natives.

The name of Sumatra is thought by some to come from the Sanscrit word *samudra*, meaning the ocean. The Arabs made voyages to the island in the 9th century, and it was visited in 1292 by Marco Polo, who, in his writings, called it Java the Less. The first settlement was made by the Dutch in 1649.

SUM'NER, Charles, an American statesman, born in Boston, Mass., Jan. 6, 1811. He became a successful lawyer; and, being appointed reporter to the United States Circuit Courts, he published several volumes of reports, besides editing a law journal. In 1845 he opposed the war with Mexico in several speeches, claiming that differences between nations should be settled without war. From 1851 until his death, Mr. Sumner was a member of the United States Senate. He was noted for his opposition to slavery. In 1856 some of the Southern members took so much offence at his speeches, that one of them named Brooks beat him with a cane until he was insensible, and he did not recover from his injuries for several years. During the war he made many able speeches on various subjects, and afterward he prepared the "Civil Rights Bill," intended to give negroes the same civil rights as whites. He died in Washington, D.C., when sixty-three years old (March 11, 1874).

SUN'DERLAND a town of N. England, on the North Sea, at the mouth of the River Wear; pop. 117,-000, or twice as large as Worcester, Mass. The harbor is formed by the river mouth, which is crossed by a bridge so high that ships can go under it. Many ships are built at Sunderland, and there are large manufactories of window glass, bottles, and pottery. The people carry on an important trade, both with other English ports and with foreign countries.

SU·PE'RI·OR, Lake, a lake of North America, between the United States and Canada; area, 32,000 square miles, or about as large as the State of Indiana. Excepting the Victoria N'Yanza in Africa, it is the largest fresh water lake in the world, having 1,500 miles of coast. Its average depth is about 1,000 feet. The shores are generally high and picturesque, some of the cliffs being worn into strange shapes by the waves. Among these are rocks on the southern shore called the "Pictured Rocks," on account of their strange forms and colors. There are rich copper, iron, and silver mines near Lake Superior. Much of the country around it is still wilderness.

SUR'REY, Henry Howard, Earl of, an English soldier and poet, born about 1516. He was the eldest son of Thomas Howard, third Duke of Norfolk. He was a very learned man, a brave soldier, and a fine poet. In 1544 he commanded the English army in France. His love for poetry was strengthened by his travels in Italy, and when he returned to England his chief pleasure was to write sonnets in imitation of the Italian. But the Seymour family thought the Howards were in the way of their ambition. So Surrey was tried on the charge of treason, doomed to die, and beheaded when thirty-one years old (Jan. 21, 1547). Surrey was the first to write sonnets and blank verse in the English language.

SUSA (*soo'sah*), an ancient city of Persia, near the Karun River, which flows into the Persian Gulf. It was one of the largest cities in the Persian Empire, and most of the Persian treasures were kept there. Alexander the Great conquered it in 325 B.C., and obtained such an immense plunder that he was able to give rich presents to all his generals and soldiers. In aftertimes Susa was so completely destroyed that even its site was long unknown. A few years ago some ruins were found with inscriptions which showed that they belonged to the long lost city.

SVEABORG (*sva'ah-borg*), the chief fortress of Finland, Russia, on the Gulf of Finland, near Helsingfors. It is built on seven rocky islands, all fortified, and joined together by bridges of boats. The chief fort contains a strong castle, and storehouses cut out of the solid rock. There are barracks for soldiers, and in an inside harbor seventy ships of war can anchor. The fortress, which was built in 1750, is so strong that it is sometimes called the " Gibraltar of the North."

SWANSEA (*swon'se*), a town of S. Wales on the River Tawy, at its mouth in the Bay of Swansea; pop. 66,000, or about as large as Atlanta, Ga. It has a larger trade in copper than any other city of Great Britain, the ore being brought to the port from different parts of the world, and smelted with coal from mines near the city. Swansea also has iron, tin, and zinc works, and potteries, and many ships are made there. The harbor is nearly dry at ebb tide; but at the flood, large vessels can enter the docks. Swansea is much visited for sea bathing.

SWE'DEN, a N. country of Europe, between Norway and the Baltic Sea; area, nearly 172,000 square miles, or about as large as New England, New York, New Jersey, and Pennsylvania put together; pop. 4,774,000, or more than nine tenths that of Pennsylvania; capital, STOCKHOLM. Between Sweden and Norway is a chain of mountains, and the line of separation is marked by a wide road cut through the forest, with stone pillars set up at intervals. The northern part of Sweden is very wild and rugged, with forests of birch, fir, and small pines, and many dreary swamps where wolves and bears are common. The southern part, where most of the people live, is a plain. On the coast are many long, narrow bays, called fiords, which are very deep, and are noted for their grand scenery. Sweden has many fine lakes, one of which, called Lake Wener, is one of the largest in Europe; another, Lake Mælar, contains more than 1,200 beautiful islands.

Sweden has mines of coal, zinc, copper, nickel, manganese, and silver, and some of the finest iron mines in the world; and much marble and porphyry are quarried. The best soil is in the southern part, and even there it is not very rich; but by industry and perseverance many fine farms have been made. The principal crops are oats, rye, barley, wheat, and potatoes, some of which are sent to other countries. One of the most important trades is in pine and fir timbers. The climate in the southern part is much like that of New York State; but in the northern part it is very cold, and for seven weeks in the winter the sun does not rise at all. The people are tall and strong, with fair skins, and sandy or yellow hair. Their language is much like the German. They are hard-working and frugal, and very intelligent. About half of them are peasants, who wear wooden shoes, and often have fanciful dresses, different in the various villages. Sweden and Norway are governed by the same king, who lives sometimes in one country, and sometimes in the other; but they are regarded as two kingdoms, and Sweden has its own Parliament, something like that of England. Most of the people belong to the Lutheran Church.

Sweden is in the Swedish language Sverige, which comes from the ancient name Sviarike, meaning the kingdom of the Suiones or Swedes, who are said to have come with ODIN from near the Black Sea. The Swedes became Christians in the 12th century. About the end of the 14th century Sweden, Norway, and Denmark were joined together under one ruler; but in 1523 Sweden became a separate kingdom under GUSTAVUS VASA. GUSTAVUS ADOLPHUS won some territory; but CHARLES XII. made Sweden greater than ever before. After his death Sweden lost power, and finally had to give up FINLAND to Russia (1809). In 1810 BERNADOTTE was chosen crown prince of Sweden. He joined the allied nations of Europe against Napoleon, while Denmark took the side of France; and when Napoleon fell, Norway was taken from the King of Denmark, and joined to Sweden to make up for the loss of Finland.

SWE'DEN·BORG, Emanuel, a Swedish philosopher, born in Stock-holm, Jan. 29, 1688. The name of the family, which at first was Swedberg, was changed to Swedenborg when it was made noble by Queen Ulrica, in 1719. Until he was fifty-seven years old, his life was spent in the pursuit of science, and his knowledge on scientific subjects was very exact. He tells us in his diary, that in 1745 he was called to a new and holy office by the Lord himself, who came to him, and showed him the things of the spirit world, and permitted him to talk with spirits and angels. After this he gave up science, and turned all his thoughts to the setting forth of the new religion which he said been given him. He is the founder of the sect called by his name Swedenborgians, or, as they call themselves, the New Jerusalem Church. Swedenborg died in London when eighty-four years old (March 29, 1772).

SWIFT, Jonathan, a British writer, born in Dublin, Nov. 30, 1667, of English ancestry. His early years were spent in poverty, his father having died before his birth, leaving nothing for the support of his family. For some time he lived with a wealthy relative, Sir William Temple, acting as his secretary, that is, writer; but he at last entered the Church, and finally became Dean of St. Patrick's, Dublin. He wrote much on various subjects, some political and some religious, and became famous. Almost all young folks have read his "Travels of Lemuel Gulliver;" but few know that the characters are meant to ridicule some of the great public men of the day. Other noted works of his are "The Tale of a Tub," and "The Battle of the Books." Swift's last days were very sad. First he grew deaf, and then, his mind being thrown entirely on itself, he became a lunatic. For ten hours a day he would walk up and down his room as if it were a cage, and he a wild beast. He knew that he would die a maniac, and willed all his fortune to found a hospital for idiots and incurable madmen. He died when nearly seventy-eight years old (Oct. 19, 1745).

SWIN'BURNE, Algernon Charles, an English poet, born in London, April 5, 1837. He went to Oxford University, but left it without taking a degree. Some of his works are "Atalanta in Calydon," "The Queen Mother," "A Song of Italy," and "Bothwell," a tragedy. He has also written many small poems and essays.

SWIT'ZER·LAND, a country of Europe, between Germany and

Lake Dwellings.

Italy; area, 16,000 square miles, or about half as large as Indiana; pop., 2,934,000, or nearly a third more than that of Indiana; capital, BERN. It is the highest and most mountainous region in Europe, the southern part being crossed by the ALPS, while even in the northern part, which is almost level, there are mountains nearly half a mile high. Many peaks of the Swiss Alps are from two to two and a half miles high, and always covered with snow and ice. Between France and Switzerland is the Jura range, not so high as the Alps. Among the mountains are many beautiful lakes, and the whole country is full of grand scenery, unequalled in any other country in the world.

In many of the lakes have been found curious relics of a people who lived so long ago that history has no record of them. These people lived in houses built in the lakes on platforms held up by piles driven into the bottom. They used to keep their boats under the houses, and had trap doors in the floors, through which they could fish. Only the remains of these dwellings are found now in the lake mud, with many bone, flint, and wooden tools, and other things used by them. In the picture one of these lake dwellings is shown as it is supposed to have been.

About two-thirds of Switzerland consists of bare rocks, snowy mountain-tops, glaciers, and lakes, so that very little is left for farms. Some of the people have vineyards, and others grow flax and hemp; but many are engaged in breeding cattle, which thrive well on the rich pastures of the valleys and mountain sides. Among the principal manufactures are silk cloths and ribbons, cotton cloth, embroidery, musical boxes, and fine watches. The poor people make beautiful carvings of wood, which they sell to travellers. The people of Switzerland are very industrious and intelligent, and very proud of their beautiful country. In the eastern part they speak French, in the southern part Italian, and, in the northern and western parts, German. More than half the Swiss are Protestants; the rest are Roman Catholics. Switzerland is a republic, governed by a Congress, which meets at Bern; but instead of a president there is a council of seven persons. The country is divided into cantons, each of which makes its own laws, like a State of the United States.

In ancient times Switzerland was inhabited by tribes called Helvetii. They were a brave people; but they were conquered by the Romans, and their country was made a province of the empire. It afterward belonged to the German Empire. When Albert, son of RUDOLPH of HAPSBURG, became emperor, he tried to join Switzerland to Austria; but the people resisted, and, after defeating the Austrians at MORGARTEN (1315), they formed a league or union among themselves. One of the members or states of this union was the Canton of Schwyz, from which the whole country came to be called Switzerland, and the people Swiss. But the country still belonged to the German Empire, and it did not become wholly independent until 1648. Since then, with a few changes in Bonaparte's time, it has remained a free country.

SYB'A·RIS, an ancient city of S. Italy, near the W. shore of the Gulf of Taranto. It was founded by the Greeks about 720 B.C., and became famous for its wealth and power. The people were noted for their love of luxury, and it is said that no trade which made a noise was allowed in the city. From it has come the word Sybarite, meaning a luxurious, effeminate person. Sybaris was finally destroyed by the people of Crotona.

SYD'NEY, a city of S. E. AUSTRALIA, capital of the colony of New South Wales, on Port Jackson, a bay of the Indian Ocean; pop., 367,000, or about twice as large as Newark, N. J. The harbor is a very fine one, defended by strong forts. The city has a larger trade than any other place in Australia, except MELBOURNE. It contains many handsome buildings, a university, and several fine parks and gardens.

Sydney was founded in 1788, and was named in honor of the Viscount Sydney, an English statesman. It became a city in 1842.

SYLLA. See SULLA.

SYRACUSE (*sir-a-kuze'*), a city of Central New York, near Onondaga

Lake; pop. 88,000, or about the same as Columbus, O. Many railroads and canals meet there, and the surrounding country is very fertile and thickly populated, so that the city has a large trade. The most important manufacture is salt, made from the water of salt springs and deep wells near the lake shore. The works are the largest in the United States. The salt water, drawn from the wells by steam-pumps, is left to grow thick in large wooden tanks, which cover several square miles of ground, each one having a roof which can be rolled over it in rainy weather. When sufficiently thickened, the water is drawn out, and boiled in kettles until it all passes off in steam, leaving the salt.

Syracuse was first settled in 1787, and in 1824 was named after Syracuse in Sicily. It became a city in 1847.

SYRACUSE, a city on the E. coast of Sicily; pop., 22,000, or a little larger than Zanesville, Ohio. It is fortified with walls and a citadel, and has a fine harbor. There is a small trade in wine, oil, and fruits; but the city is chiefly interesting for its old buildings and the ruins that show its former glory. In ancient times it was the largest city of Sicily, and is said to have had a million inhabitants. It consisted of five towns. The one which still remains was called Ortygia, and was first built on an island, but was afterward united to the mainland by a causeway: the others were on the shores around it, and were separated by walls. Of the rich palaces and villas hardly any thing remains; but the amphitheatres and the prisons, cut out of solid rock, can still be seen. There are also remains of an aqueduct, several ancient baths, and a spring, called the Fountain of ARETHUSA. In the city there is a museum containing a fine collection of vases, coins, and other things found among the ruins.

Syracuse was first built by the Corinthians about 734 B.C. It grew rapidly, and soon ruled nearly the whole of Sicily. After being, at different times, the ally of Carthage and of Rome, it was taken and plundered by the Romans under MARCELLUS (212 B.C.), and from that time began to decay.

SYRIA (*sir'e-ah*), a country of Turkey in Asia, between the Mediterranean and the River Euphrates, and including PALESTINE; area, 60,000 square miles, or about as large as Florida. Much of the western part is mountainous; but the eastern and southern parts are mostly a level desert. Most of the people are Arabs; but there are also many Turks, Greeks, Armenians, and Jews.

Syria, including Phœnicia and Palestine, was conquered by Alexander the Great. After him it became a kingdom, with ANTIOCH for its capital. It became a Roman province about 63 B.C. In the 7th century it was conquered by the Saracens, and in the 16th century by the Turks, and since then it has formed a part of the Turkish Empire.

T

TABRIZ (*tah-breez'*), a city of N. W. Persia; pop. 180,000, or about as large as Newark, N. J. It stands on a wide plain almost shut in by mountains, and is surrounded by brick walls. The streets are narrow, and most of the houses are small, but there are many mosques and large bazaars lined with shops. The eldest son of the Shah of Persia lives there, and is governor of the surrounding country. Tabriz has manufactures of cotton and silk, and a very large trade, it being on the caravan route through Persia. The country around it is very fertile, and contains many beautiful vineyards and gardens. Tabriz was anciently called Tauris, or the "mountain town," and this name has become changed to its present form.

TACITUS (*tas'e-tus*), **Caius Corne-lius,** a famous Roman historian, born about A.D. 55. He was edu-cated a lawyer, and for his skill and eloquence as an orator he re-ceived public office and other marks of favor from the Emperors Ves-pasian and Titus. In A.D. 78 he married the daughter of Julius AGRICOLA, whose life, written by him, is very valuable, because it tells much about the early history of Britain. But his most famous book is his "Annals," which gives the his-tory of the Roman Empire from the death of AUGUSTUS to the death of NERO. The Emperor Tacitus so admired his writings that he claimed relationship with him as an honor, and ordered that his works be placed in all the public libraries of the em-pire. He is still held to be one of the greatest of historians. He died about A.D. 117.

TACITUS, Marcus Claudius, a Roman emperor, born about 200. He succeeded the Emperor Aurelian in 275, being elected emperor by the Senate, after the assassination of the latter. His short reign of six months was full of promise of use-ful reforms. Some say that he was put to death by the army, others that he died of a fever. The works of the historian Tacitus, from whom he claimed descent, were particu-larly admired by him, and were by his order put in all the public libra-ries. He died when about seventy-six years old (276).

TAHITI (*tah-he'te.*) See SOCI-ETY ISLANDS.

TAINE (*tane*), **Hippolyte Adolphe,** a French writer, born in Vouziers, April 21, 1828. He was professor in the School of Fine Arts in Paris, but he is best known for his "His-tory of English Literature," which is one of the best ever written. He was the author also of many other works. He died when sixty-five years old (March 5, 1893).

TALFOURD (*tawl'furd*), Sir **Thomas Noon,** an English writer, born near Stafford, Jan. 26, 1795. He was by turns sergeant at law, member of Parliament, and judge. In Parliament he made a great ef-fort in behalf of authors, and had an act passed by which they could be secured in the profits their work might bring. His writings are chiefly tragedies, "Ion" being the most suc-cessful. He died in Stafford, when fifty-nine years old (March 13, 1854).

TALLAHASSEE (*tal-lah-has'se*), a city, capital of Florida, in the N. part of the State, twenty-one miles from the Gulf of Mexico; pop. 7000. It is beautifully situated, with streets and public squares shaded with evergreens, and houses surrounded by fine gardens. The principal public buildings are the capital and the court-house, both built of brick. The site of Tallahassee was se-lected for the State capital while it was still a wilderness. The town was founded in 1824.

TAL'LEY-RAND - PÉRIGORD (French, *tah-la-rong' pa-re-gor'*), **Charles Maurice,** Prince de, a French statesman, born in Paris, Feb. 13, 1754. He was the eldest son of the Count de Talleyrand-Périgord, but having been lamed by accident, when about a year old, he was compelled to give up his birthright to a younger brother, and to enter the Church. His wit and other brilliant gifts soon attracted attention, and won for him the office of agent general of the clergy. He was one of the first of the clergy to aid in supporting every liberal measure, and he was the principal character at the great feast to celebrate the taking of the Bastile on its first anniversary, appearing at the head of two hundred priests clothed in white, and girded with tri-colored scarfs, to consecrate the banner of the revolution upon the great altar erected in the Champ de Mars. He had many changes in his life. At one time he was an exile from France, spending nearly two years in the city of Philadelphia, in the United States. When Napoleon arose, he was his most ardent admirer and supporter, but, as he saw him about to start in his Russian campaign, he prophesied that that expedition was the "beginning of the end," and he was quite ready to welcome the Bourbon. Talleyrand was not in favor with Louis XVIII. and Charles X., but Louis Philippe took him into confidence and appointed him ambassador to England, in which office he served with great credit. Talleyrand has left behind him the reputation of having been one of the greatest diplomatists that the world has ever known. His talent for keeping a secret was something extraordinary. He never allowed word or look to show that he knew anything that others did not. The saying that men speak only in order to hide their thoughts is due to him. He died in Paris, when eighty-four years old (May 17, 1838).

He left some memoirs to be published thirty years after his death, but Napoleon III. prevented their being made public till twenty-two years later.

TAL'MA (French, *tahl-mah'*), **François Joseph,** a famous French tragic actor, born in Paris, Jan. 15, 1763. He first appeared on the stage in 1787, and at once attracted attention by dressing in the costume worn by the characters represented, actors before him having commonly dressed in the costume of their own time. Among the characters which he played best were Sulla, Orestes, Leonidas, Hamlet, and Othello. Talma was a great favorite with Napoleon, who, when a poor officer, had often borrowed money of him. He died in Paris, when sixty-three years old (Oct. 19, 1826).

TAM'ER-LANE. See TIMOUR.

TANCRED (*tang'kred*), a Sicilian prince, one of the heroes of the first Crusade, born in 1078. He joined the Crusaders under his cousin, Bohemond, in 1096, and soon became famous for his bravery and daring. During the siege of Antioch he is said to have killed seven hundred infidels himself, and at the storming of Jerusalem he and his men were the first to mount the walls. He was the only one of the Christian knights who was merciful to his enemies, and he saved the lives of many of the captured. He was made prince of Galilee or Tiberias, and governed Antioch for twelve years in the absence of Bohemond. He died at Antioch, when thirty-four years old (1112). Tancred is one of the principal characters in Tasso's "Jerusalem Delivered."

TANEY (*taw'ne*), **Roger Brooke,** an American lawyer, born in Calvert County, Md., March 17, 1777. He became Attorney-General of the United States in 1831, and Chief Justice in 1837. Among the cases which he decided was that of Dred Scott, a negro slave who claimed to be free because his master had taken him into a territory where slavery was not allowed by the United States. Judge Taney, and a majority of the judges, in their decision declared that negroes could only be citizens of some particular State, but not of the Union, and so could not have any of the rights secured to whites under the Constitution; that Congress had no power to forbid slavery in any Territory; and that slaves, if bought in Slave States, could then be moved to Free States and still remain slaves. This decision was much criticised by many, but it was also upheld by many who thought the case to have been properly decided according to the law. Chief Justice Taney died in Washington, when eighty-seven years old (Oct. 12, 1864).

TANGANYIKA (*tahn-gahn-ye'ka*), a lake in Central Africa, S. of the Victoria and Albert N'yanza lakes. It is about 400 miles long and 10 to 60 miles wide. The town of Ujiji, where Stanley found Livingstone, is on its eastern shore. Tanganyika was first found in 1858.

TAN'TA-LUS, in Greek fable, a son of Jupiter, and father of PELOPS and NIOBE. The gods made him immortal, but he offended Jupiter either by telling the secrets of the gods or by serving up his son Pelops at a feast he gave them, and, as a punishment, was tormented with a cruel hunger and thirst. He was made to stand in a lake of clear water, which moved away from him whenever he tried to drink of it, while about him were clusters of fruit, which went just beyond his reach when he tried to grasp them. At the same time a large rock was suspended above him, which seemed always ready to fall and crush him.

TARIFA (*tah-re'fah*), a town of S. Spain, on the Strait of Gibraltar; pop. 12,000, or about as large as Brookline, Mass. It was named after Tarif ibn Malek, an Arab chief, who landed there in 710. While the Moors ruled this part of Spain, vessels passing through the Straits of Gibraltar were made to pay duties at Tarifa, and in time all duties came to be called Tarifas, or, in English, tariffs. Tarifa was captured by the Spaniards in 1292.

TARLETON (*tarl'ton*), **Bannastre,** a British officer in the American Revolution, born in Liverpool, Aug. 21, 1754. He came to America with Cornwallis, and raised a body of troops, which was one of the best corps the British had in the South during the war. Tarleton was very daring and brave; but he was also very cruel. When the war was ended he returned to England, where he was a great favorite. He was sent to Parliament in 1790, and in 1818 was made a baronet. He died, when seventy-nine years old (Jan. 23, 1833).

TARPEIA (*tar-pe'yah*), daughter of Tarpeius, governor of the citadel of Rome in the time of ROMULUS. During the Sabine war she promised to open the gates of the citadel to the SABINES if they would give her what they wore on their left arms—meaning the bracelets which all the Sabine soldiers wore. They agreed; but as they entered the gate, they threw upon her their heavy shields, which they also "wore on their left arms," and she was crushed to death. The part of the hill where she was buried was called the Tarpeian Rock; and from it the Romans used to throw criminals down a steep precipice.

TAR'QUIN, Lucius, called Priscus, or the Elder, fifth king of Rome. King ANCUS MARTIUS made him guardian of his children, and when he died Tarquin got himself made king instead of the rightful heir. His reign was glorious. He carried on successful wars, built the great sewers in Rome, laid out the Forum, and begun a stone wall around the city. He was assassinated by order of the sons of Ancus (about 578 B.C.).

TARQUIN, Lucius, called Superbus, or the Proud, son of the first Tarquin and seventh and last king of Rome. He murdered his father-in-law, SERVIUS TULLIUS, seized the throne, and put to death all who opposed him. He was a cruel tyrant, and oppressed the people; but he was bold and warlike, and under him Rome gained great power and magnificence, and finally stood at the head of the Latin confederacy. In 510, while Tarquin was besieging Ardea, a strongly fortified town of the Rutuli, the people of Rome, headed by Lucius Junius BRUTUS, rose in rebellion. Tarquin hurried back; but the gates of the city were closed against him, and he was forced to flee. He made several attempts to regain his power, in which he was helped by the neighboring cities, and by Lars Porsena, of Clusium; but he did not succeed. Finally the contest was decided by the famous battle at Lake REGILLUS, in which the Romans gained a great victory. Tarquin fled to Cumæ, where he died, when about ninety years old (495 B.C.).

TARRAGONA (*tar-rah-go'nah*), a city of N.E. Spain, on the Mediterranean Sea; pop. 27,000, or about as large as Williamsport, Pa. It is built partly on a hill and partly on the low sea-shore, and is surrounded by a wall. The harbor is formed by a wall nearly a mile long, built into the sea. Wine, nuts, and licorice are sent from there to the United States and other countries. Tarragona was called by the Romans Tarraco, and was the capital of their province of Hispania Tarraconensis. It is said that it then had 1,000,000 people. It was destroyed by the Moors, and for 400 years had no inhabitants.

TAR'TA-RUS, in Greek fable, a deep abyss, as far beneath Hades as heaven is above earth, into which Jupiter used to hurl those who offended him, and where the wicked were punished after death.

TAR'TA-RY, the namely former given to a great region in Central Asia extending from the Caspian

Sea to Japan, and embracing the southern part of Russia in Asia, Turkistan, and part of the Chinese Empire. Sometimes the southeastern part of Russia in Europe was also included. It was so called from the Tartars, a wandering race, who inhabited it, and who, in the time of Genghis Khan and Timour, were very powerful. The name Tartary is now limited to Turkistan and the countries near it.

TASMANIA (*taz-ma'ne-ah*) (formerly called Van Dieman's Land), a large island in the Pacific Ocean, 120 miles S. of Australia; area, 26,200 square miles, or a little larger than West Virginia; pop. 151,000, or about one fifth that of West Virginia; capital, Hobart Town. Much of the surface is mountainous and covered with forests, but there are also large grassy plains. The climate is very mild and pleasant.

Tasmania has mines of gold, tin, iron, and coal. The soil is very fertile, but most of the farmers are engaged in sheep raising, and the principal trade is in wool. Among the wild animals are kangaroos and opossums, which are so numerous that there is a large trade in their skins.

Tasmania belongs to England, and nearly all the people are English. The island was discovered in 1642 by the Dutch navigator, Tasman, after whom it was named.

TAS'SO, Torquato, a famous Italian poet, born in Sorrento, March 11, 1544. Tasso was brought up to be a lawyer, but he found poetry more suited to his nature, so he left the law and gave himself up to writing. When but eighteen years old he wrote a poem called "Rinaldo," and about the same time began his greatest work, "Jerusalem Delivered." Some years afterward he went to live at Ferrara, whose duke, Alfonso II., had given him a place at court. There he finished his "Jerusalem Delivered," which made his name one of the first of his age.

But Tasso was not fitted to be a courtier, and he could not bear the slander and hatred which will wait upon those who hang on a prince's favors. He grew afraid of every one, and at last his mind became so unsettled that he fled to Sorrento. Here he regained his reason, but returning to Ferrara, he again became a lunatic, and was put by Duke Alfonso into an asylum, where he remained seven years. Some think that the cause of his malady was that he loved the Princess Eleonora, the duke's sister, and that she did not love him in return. At last the duke released him, and poor, sick, and suffering, he went to Naples. Pope Clement VIII. invited him to come to Rome to receive the laurel crown of the poet at the Capitol, but he died before the ceremony took place, when fifty-one years old (April 25, 1595).

TAUNTON (*tan'tun*), a city of S. Massachusetts, on a river of the same name; pop. 25,000, or about as large as Little Rock, Ark. It is noted for its manufactures of iron and brick. Among the things made there are locomotives, nails and tacks, machines of many kinds, stove linings, fire bricks, and crucibles. Its copper works are the largest and oldest in the United States. Among other manufactures are britannia and silver-plated ware, cotton and flannel goods, and carriages. The Taunton River is noted for its herring and shad fisheries.

Taunton was once an Indian settlement, called Cohannet, and was the favorite hunting ground of King PHILIP. It was settled in 1638 by a colony from Taunton, England.

TAY'LOR, Bayard, an American author, born at Kennett Square, Chester County, Penn., Jan. 11, 1825. He wrote verses for the magazines when seventeen years old and a printer's apprentice, and published a volume of poems called "Ximena" when nineteen; and soon after, with a knapsack on his

back, and a stout stick in his hand, made a journey through Europe on foot Coming home, he published a history of his travels in a book called "Views Afoot;" then edited a paper in Pennsylvania, and a year later, became one of the editors of the New York "Tribune." He then began a series of journeys, first in California and Mexico, then in Egypt, Asia Minor, Syria, Central Africa, China, Japan, and many other countries; and wrote very interesting accounts of what he did and saw in these far-off places for the "Tribune." These were afterward published in book form. Besides his many books of travel, he wrote four novels and several volumes of poems, and made a translation of Goethe's "Faust." He also delivered a great many lectures, and was constantly writing for the papers and magazines. He was sent as American minister to Berlin in 1877, and died there, when fifty-three years old (Dec. 19, 1878).

TAYLOR, Tom, an English author, born in Sunderland, Durham, in 1817. He was educated at Glasgow and Cambridge Universities, and was professor of English literature for two years at University College, London. He wrote for "Punch" and other English magazines, and was the author of a great many successful plays, among which "Our American Cousin," "The Unequal Match," "Still Waters Run Deep," are well known in this country. He also did a great deal of other literary work. He died, when sixty-three years old (July 12, 1880.)

TAYLOR, Zachary, twelfth President of the United States, born in Orange County, Va., Nov. 24, 1784. He worked upon his father's plantation until his twenty-fourth year, and then became a lieutenant in the army in place of a brother who had died. In 1810 he was made a captain, and two years after won the rank of major for his brave defence of Fort Harrison against the Indian

chief TECUMSEH. He was a colonel in the Black Hawk War, and
then fought the Seminoles in Florida
so successfully that he was made
commander of the United States
army there. During the war with
Mexico, General Taylor won splendid victories at Palo Alto, Monterey, Buena Vista, and other places,
and "Old Rough and Ready," as he
was nicknamed, became the most
popular man in the country. When
he came home from Mexico. in November, 1847, the people made a
jubilee wherever he went. The
streets and houses were illuminated,
and processions were formed to

Zachary Taylor.

meet him, while flags were flying
and bonfires blazing in his honor.
Soon afterward he was nominated
for the Presidency, and he was elected in 1849 over Lewis Cass. But he
lived only sixteen months after his
inauguration, and died in Washington (July 9, 1850), in the sixty-sixth
year of his age. FILLMORE, the vice
President, then became President.

TE-CUM'SEH, a noted North
American Indian, chief of the Shaw-
nee tribe, born in Ohio about 1770.
It is said that he behaved like a
coward in his first battle, and even
ran away, but afterward became
noted for his bravery. In 1804 he
and his brother formed a plan to

join all the western Indians against
the whites; but his brother was
defeated at the battle of TIPPECA-
NOE, and the plan failed. Tecumseh
then joined the English, and was
made brigadier-general, given command of all their Indian allies in
the war of 1812-1814, and he took
part in every important battle. He
was killed in the battle of the
Thames (Oct. 5, 1813).

TEHERAN (*ta-her-ahn'*), a city,
capital of Persia, S. of the Caspian
Sea, on a plain among high mountains; pop. 210,000, or a little
larger than Detroit, Mich. It is
surrounded by a mud wall and a
deep ditch, and the city gates are
shut every night. The streets are
narrow and dirty, and most of the
houses are very poor; but the Shah's
palace is a fine building, and one of
the mosques has a roof of gold.
The climate of Teheran is very unhealthy in hot weather, and the
Shah and all the richer people leave
the city in summer.

TELL, William, a fabled hero of
Switzerland. There is much doubt
among historians whether such a
person ever lived, but he lives in the
fancy of the Swiss peasantry, and
many monuments have been erected
to his memory. He is said to have
lived in the early part of the fourteenth century, and to have been
a hunter very skilful with the bow.
Tell, as the story goes, killed Gessler,
the Austrian governor, because he
had compelled him to shoot an apple from the head of his son as a
punishment for refusing to bow to
Gessler's cap hanging upon a pole
in the market place of Altorf, the
capital of Uri. This was the signal for a general uprising of the
Swiss against their foreign rulers,
who were driven out and their castles destroyed. It is said that Tell
fought in the battle of MORGARTEN
(1315), and that he was drowned
some years afterward while trying
to save a boy's life. Whether true
or not, the legend of William Tell is

a pretty story, which was long believed by the wise as well as the simple, and Schiller wrote a fine play about it.

TEM'PE, a beautiful valley in the N.E. part of Thessaly, between Mounts Olympus and Ossa. Hercules is said to have opened it to make a way to the sea for the River Peneus, which flows through it. Its beauty was much praised by the ancient poets, and it was the haunt of Apollo. The victors in the Pythian Games, held at Delphi, were crowned with laurel from the vale of Tempe.

TEM'PLARS, or Knights of the Temple, the most celebrated of the military orders established in the Middle Ages for the defence of the Christians in Palestine. It was founded in 1117 by two French knights, who undertook to escort pilgrims, and who made constant journeys from Jerusalem and the River Jordan. In time they were joined by others, and they finally became a numerous body. Their dress was a white tunic with a red cross on the left breast, and their banner of white linen striped with black, bearing the device, " Not unto us. O Lord, not unto us, but to Thy Name give the Glory," was called *Beauséant*, the name commonly given in those days to a horse marked with white and black.

As long as the order remained in the Holy Land it was true to the principles of its founders, but after the loss of their home in the East, the greater number of their members returned to France, where they gave themselves up to a life of self-indulgence. Their pride and wealth drew upon them the hatred and envy of many, and especially of Philip IV., King of France, who persuaded the Pope to let him destroy the order. He had them thrown into dungeons, and they perished by the sword, by hunger, and by fire. Jacques de Molay, their last Grand-Master, died the death of a hero, and from the midst of the flames called on both his persecutors, the Pope and the

King of France, to appear before God within a year. Both died within that time. Philip took their wealth, and the order everywhere ceased to exist (1314), except in Portugal, where it took the name of Knights of Christ.

TEN-NES-SEE', a State of the United States, on the Mississippi River, S. of Kentucky; area, about 45,-600 square miles, or nearly the same as that of Pennsylvania; pop. 1,768,000, or something less than a third that of Pennsylvania ; capital, NASHVILLE. The eastern part is crossed by the forest-covered Appalachian Mountains, and the scenery there is very grand and beautiful. The centre of the State is broken and hilly, and the western part, between the Tennessee River and the Mississippi, is a plain.

There are many mines of coal, iron, and copper, and quarries of marble and granite. Pine, chestnut, black walnut, and other fine timbers are cut in large quantities, and more red cedar is found there than in any other State. The principal crops are tobacco, corn, and wheat. In the southern part are fine cotton plantations, and large fields are planted with peanuts. The climate is mild and pleasant. About one quarter of the people are negroes.

Tennessee gets its name from Tannassee, the Indian name of the Little Tennessee River. The country was once a part of North Carolina. It became a Territory in 1794, and a State of the Union in 1796. In 1861 it seceded and joined the Confederate States, but in 1866 it again became a State of the Union.

TEN'NY-SON, Alfred, Lord, a famous English poet, born in Lincolnshire in 1809. His first poems were published when he was eighteen years old, in a small volume containing also some verses of his brother Charles, called " Poems by Two Brothers." Although he began writing so early, it was not until he was thirty-three years old that he wrote the

"Morte d'Arthur," "Locksley Hall," and the "Two Voices," which caused him to be considered the first poet of the age. In 1850, on the death of

Alfred Tennyson.

Wordsworth, he became poet-laureate, or poet for the crown. Tennyson's "Idylls of the King," consisting of nine poems, taken from stories about King ARTHUR, make together the most beautiful epic which the English language has produced for two hundred years. Tennyson wrote his poems very carefully, and went over them a great many times, changing words and altering phrases, until they were as perfect as he could make them. Among his other works are "Maud," "Enoch Arden," and three plays, called "Queen Mary," "Harold," and "The Foresters." In 1883 he was made a peer. His home in the Isle of Wight is called "Farringford." He died when eighty-three years old (October 6, 1892).

TER'ENCE (Publius Terentius Afer), a Roman comic poet, born in Carthage, about 195 B.C. He became the slave of a Roman senator, who had him well educated, and at last freed him. His first play, "Andria" (The Woman of Andros), made him famous, and introduced him into the best Roman society. Later in life he went to Greece, and there translated into Latin some of the comedies of the

Farringford, Tennyson's Home.

Greek poet, Menander. These translations were lost, and it is said that Terence died of grief on account of it, when about thirty-six years old (159 B.C.).

TERPSICHORE (*terp-sik'ore*), See MUSES.
TERRA DEL FUEGO. See TIERRA DEL FUEGO.
TERRE HAUTE (*ter-reh hote'*), a

city of W. Indiana, on the Wabash River; pop. 30,000, or about as large as Altoona, Pa. It is in a rich farming country, which also has many fine coal mines. The city has therefore a large trade carried on by steamboats, and by many railroad lines which meet there. Glass, iron, nails, and machinery are made there, and a great deal of pork is packed.

Terre Haute is a French name, and means "highland." The town was founded in 1816, and became a city in 1853.

TER-TUL'LI-AN, Quintus Septimius Florens, one of the early Fathers of the Church, born in Carthage, about A.D. 150. He was the son of a Roman centurion. Until between thirty and forty years old he lived a wild life in the midst of heathenism, but he then joined the Christians, and became an earnest believer in their religion. He was a very able and learned man, and his writings are keen and witty, full of learning in law and philosophy. Tertullian died between A.D. 220 and 240.

TEU-TON'IC KNIGHTS, a military and religious order, founded in Palestine during the Crusades by Frederick, Duke of Swabia, in 1190. Their dress was black with a white mantle, upon which was a black cross edged with silver. The most famous of its grand-masters was Hermann of Salza, to whose wisdom and piety popes and emperors united in doing honor. This order is less celebrated for its deeds in Palestine than for its services in civilizing the wild tribes on the shores of the Baltic, whither they retired when they came from the Holy Land. Under their care churches were founded, woods cleared and converted into farms, and the whole face of the country changed. The Teutonic Knights had frequent wars with Poland, in which they lost a great part of their territory in Prussia. Finally their grand-master, Albert of Brandenburg, became Duke of Prussia. In 1805 the emperor of

Austria was made grand-master of the order, but Napoleon, a few years later, declared it abolished. In 1840 it was once more set up by the Austrian Empire, and for three years Maximilian, the unfortunate emperor of Mexico, was its grand-master. Its chief at present is the Archduke William of Austria.

TEU'TONS. See GERMANY.

TEX'AS, a Southern Gulf State of the United States, between Louisiana and Mexico; area, 274,000 square miles, or more than four times that of New England; pop. 2,236,000, or more than five elevenths that of New England; capital, Austin. It is the largest of all the States, and the most southerly one except Florida. Much of Texas is prairie or rolling land covered with forest, and a very large part of it is good for farming. The chief crops are cotton and Indian corn. In the west part of the State are fine pasture lands, and great numbers of cattle and sheep are raised. There are more cattle in Texas than in any other State, and large numbers are sent from there to be killed for market. Wild horses, called "mustangs," roam over the great plains, and in the northwest are found buffaloes, antelopes, and other wild animals. A large part of the northwest is covered by the Llano Estacado (Spanish for "Staked Plain"), a barren plain, so called from the stems of a plant called yucca, which stand up everywhere like stakes. Texas has mines of copper, iron, lead, silver, and coal, but they are not worked much. The climate is so mild that oranges and other fruits of hot countries grow there.

Texas is an Indian word, said to mean "hunting-ground." Texas was once a part of Mexico, but after a war the people won their independence in 1836. In 1845 it joined the United States, and became a State of the Union. It seceded in 1861 and joined the Confederate States, but came into the Union again in 1870.

THACK'ER-AY, William Make-peace, a famous English writer, born at Calcutta, in 1811, where his father was in the service of the East India Company. When seven years old he was sent to England to school ; studied at the University of Cambridge, and then travelled through Germany, France, and Italy, with the idea of becoming an artist. He made a great many clever drawings, but came to the conclusion that he could do something else better, and so decided, when about thirty years old, to write books instead of painting pictures. He wrote at first un-

William Makepeace Thackeray.

der assumed names, and published " The Great Hoggarty Diamond," "Barry Lyndon," "The Paris Sketch-book," and other volumes under the name of Michael Angelo Titmarsh, or George Fitz-Boodle, Esq. When "Punch" was started, he wrote " Jeames's Diary" and " The Snob Papers" for it. " Vanity Fair," his first great novel, was published in his own name, and illustrated with his own drawings. The best of his other books are " Pendennis," "The Newcomes," " Henry Esmond," and " The Virginians." He wrote also a series of lectures on " The English Humorists of the

Eighteenth Century," and another on the " Four Georges." He delivered these for the first time in America in 1855. In January, 1860, he became editor of the " Cornhill Magazine," and published in it some other stories. He began another book called " Denis Duval," but died before it was half finished, being found dead in his bed in the early morning of December 24, 1863. The sudden death brought sorrow to many hearts both in England and America, for he was loved as a man as much as he was admired as an author.

THALES (*tha'leez*), one of the seven wise men of Greece, born in Miletus, Ionia, about 636 B.C. He founded a school of philosophy known as the Ionic school, and made several important discoveries in geometry and astronomy. It was he who fixed the length of a year at three hundred and sixty-five days, and he is said to have been the first of the Greeks to predict eclipses. He died about 546 B.C.

THALIA (*tha'le-ah*). See MUSES.

THAMES (*temz*), or **Isis,** the largest river of England, rising in the Cotswold Hills, near the mouth of the River Severn, and flowing E. to the North Sea ; length, 220 miles. At London it is less than a quarter of a mile wide, but at its mouth it is eighteen miles wide. Large vessels ascend to Deptford, a suburb of London. Probably the Thames has a larger commerce than any other river in the world, and at London many fine docks have been built. It is crossed by many fine bridges, and a number of tunnels pass underneath the bed. Several canals connect the Thames with other English rivers.

THEBES, an ancient city of Egypt, capital of Upper Egypt, and for a long time of the whole country, on the Nile. It was one of the largest and most splendid cities that has ever been built. It is not known exactly when it was founded, but it began to decline about 800 B.C., and after being several times pillaged it was finally destroyed about 86 B.C. Its ruins, on both sides of the river, are among the most magnificent in the world. On the east side, where most of the people lived, are the remains of the Palace of Luxor and the Temple of Karnak. In front of Luxor is a beautiful obelisk of red granite. There were once two of these, but one is now in the Place de la Concorde, Paris. The great hall in the Temple of Karnak is larger than twenty ordinary houses. On the western side of the river are the remains of splendid temples and palaces, with long avenues of sphinxes and rock-hewn tombs; and all the hills behind are full of sepulchres cut in the rock, where thousands of mummies have been found. Among other monuments there are two great statues, which with their pedestals are about as high as ten men (60 feet). One of these, which was afterward called the statue of Memnon, is said to have given out at sunrise a sound like the twanging of a harpstring; but as a square hole has been found in the body behind, it is thought that the sound was made by some person hidden within. This statue is supposed to be that of the Egyptian King Amenophis III., whose name the Greeks made into Memnon.

THEBES, a city of ancient Greece, in Bœotia, 35 miles N.W. of Athens. It was built around a hill on which stood a strong citadel, and the city itself was surrounded by a wall, with seven gates. Thebes is celebrated in Greek history, and from 371 to 362 B.C. it was the ruling city of Greece. It was destroyed by Alexander the Great in 335 B.C., but was rebuilt, and in the middle ages was a flourishing town. It is now a small village.

THE'MIS, in Greek fable, the goddess of justice. She was the first to utter oracles, and to introduce sacrifices in Greece. She lived on Olympus, and it was she who called together the assemblies of the gods. She is represented with her eyes bandaged, and holding a pair of scales in one hand and a sword in the other.

THEMISTOCLES (*the-mis'to-kleez*), a great Athenian general and statesman, born about 514 B.C. He was always very ambitious, and when about thirty years old he had become the greatest political leader

Themistocles.

in Athens. He persuaded the Athenians to build a large fleet to oppose the invasion of the Persians, and in command of it he defeated the Persians at Salamis. This victory made him so famous that he was declared the wisest man in Greece. In 471 he was tried for treason and exiled. He went to Argos; but before long he was guilty of treason there too, and fled to the court of Artaxerxes, King of Persia. He spent a year in learning the language, and then became the chief adviser of the king, who raised him to the highest honors. After travelling through Asia he settled at Magnesia, Asia Minor, where he died, about 449 B.C.

THE-OC'RI-TUS, a Greek poet, born in Syracuse, about 270 B.C. He lived for a time in ALEXAN-DRIA, where he had the favor of Ptolemy Philadelphus, in whose praise he wrote three of his poems, but spent the last of his life in Sicily. His writings are chiefly descriptive of the every-day life of the Sicilian shepherds. He was probably the first to write this simple kind of poetry, which is commonly called pastoral poetry.

THEODORIC (*the-od'o-rik*), called the Great, King of the Ostrogoths, born in Pannonia, in 455. He succeeded his father, Theodemir, on the throne in 475. His reign is chiefly noted for the invasion of Italy, the throne of which had been usurped by Odoacer. After several defeats, Odoacer shut himself up in his capital, Ravenna; but was obliged to give up the city at the end of three years. Theodoric had him put to death, and then became sole ruler of Italy, where he reigned with great honor for thirty-five years, during which time Italy prospered and improved in every way. He died, when seventy-one years old (A.D. 526).

THEODOSIUS (*the-o-do'she-us*), called the Great, a Roman Emperor, born in Spain, about A.D. 346. He was chosen by the Emperor Gratian to succeed Valens as ruler of the eastern part of the Roman Empire, Jan. 19, 379. By his skill in war he conquered the Goths, and by his kindness won them to agree not to molest his territory again. About a year after he became emperor he became a Christian, and his reign is famous for the zeal with which he upheld that faith and put down the pagans. In 383 Gratian was murdered and his throne seized by Maximus; but in a few years Theodosius defeated Maximus, and made Valentinian II., brother of Gratian, Emperor of the West. In 392 Valentinian was killed by his general, Arbogastes, and Theodosius again marched to the West. Hav-ing conquered Arbogastes, he became master of the whole Roman Empire. Four months later he died, while on his way to Constantinople, at Milan, when forty-nine years old (Jan. 17, 395).

THERMOPYLÆ (*ther-mop'i-le*), a narrow pass in Greece, between Mount Œta and a swamp, which separated it from the sea. It was the only road from northern to central Greece, and as it was only a few feet wide in two places, it could be easily defended against an enemy. Near it were some warm springs, from which was derived its name, meaning Warm Gate. When Xerxes and his immense army invaded Greece (480 B.C.), a Greek army, under Leonidas, King of Sparta, was sent to guard the pass of Ther-mopylæ. On the first attack the Persians were beaten back, but after a while they found a hidden path over the mountain, and sent a party to attack the Greeks in the rear. When Leonidas heard this he sent most of the army away, but 300 Spartans and 700 Thespians remained and fought until every one was killed. The only one who escaped was Aristodemus, a Spartan, who was sick and could not fight. When he returned to Sparta he was received with scorn, and at the battle of Platæa he redeemed his name by throwing himself into the midst of the enemy and fighting bravely until he was killed.

THE'SE-US (or *the'soos*), a famous hero of Greek fable, son of Ægeus, King of Athens, and Æthra, daughter of Pittheus, King of Trœzen. He was educated in Trœzen, and then sought his father's court. On his road he had several wonderful adventures, and destroyed several robbers and monsters. In imitation of Hercules, he performed many dangerous exploits, the most famous of which was the destruction of the Minotaur, a terrible monster of Crete, to whom the Athenians had been obliged to send every year seven youths and seven young girls to be devoured by him. Theseus offered to go as one of the victims, and was sent to Crete, where he won the love of Ariadne, daughter of King MINOS. She gave him a sword and a ball of thread, bidding him fasten the thread to the entrance of the labyrinth in which the monster was kept, and unwind it as he went in. He did so, killed the Minotaur, and found his way out by means of the thread. The vessel which carried the victims every year to Crete had always carried black sails, but King Ægeus had told Theseus to hoist white ones on his

Theseus killing the Minotaur. Ancient painting.

return, if successful. But he forgot this, and Ægeus, thinking his son was dead, threw himself into the sea. Theseus then became king, and ruled Athens wisely and justly. He defeated the AMAZONS and married Antiope, their queen, and was one of the ARGONAUTS. Afterward he married Phædra, daughter of King Minos and sister of Ariadne. Phædra fell in love with Hippolytus, the son of Theseus and Antiope, and because he did not return her love, accused him wrongfully to his father. Theseus in anger asked Neptune to destroy him, but when the god did it, Phædra confessed her guilt and hanged herself. This

story of Phædra was made into a tragedy by both Sophocles and Euripides, and in modern times by Racine. The Athenians finally turned against Theseus, and he fled to the island of Scyros, where he is said to have been killed by King Lycomedes. In after times the Athenians were told by an oracle to bring his body back. It was pretended that the body was found, and it was brought to Athens (469 B.C.) and the great temple called the Theseum was built over it.

THES'PIS, a Greek poet, born in Attica, about 550 B.C. It is thought that he was the founder of the Greek historical plays or tragedy, but it is more probable that he made a change in them. These old plays were mere songs accompanied with dances which described by actions the events they celebrated. Thespis put spoken dialogues in the intervals between the choruses to give a rest to the singers, and took these parts himself with his face covered with a linen mask, to represent the different characters whose parts he spoke. It is said that he used to go through Attica during the festivals to Bacchus in a cart, on which a stage was built, and give his plays.

THES'SA-LY, a country of ancient Greece, S. of Macedonia. It is a great plain, shut in by mountains. The soil is rich, and in ancient times Thessaly was famous for its wheat and its fine horses. It was conquered by the Macedonians, and fell with their country into the hands of the Romans. Most of it now belongs to Turkey, but a small part is in Greece.

THE'TIS, in Greek fable, one of the Nereids. Several of the gods wished to marry her, but were afraid to do so, because Themis had foretold that she should have a son who would be greater than his father. She married Peleus, and was the mother of ACHILLES.

THIBET (*tib'bet*), a country of Asia, north of India; area, 600,000 to 800,000 square miles ; pop. about 6,000,000. It is an arid table-land, the highest large one in the world, most of it being two to three miles above the sea. The Himalaya Mountains on the south, and the Kuen-lun range on the north, almost surround it, and the country itself is divided by a mountain range into two parts. The northern portion is very barren, and has hardly any inhabitants. The southern part, called Great Thibet, contains the principal cities. The climate is cold, but there are hardly any snows. Gold, silver, and lapis lazuli are the most important minerals. Barley is largely raised, and is the principal food of the people. Cashmere goats are kept in many places. The people, who are something like the Chinese, have a considerable trade in woollen cloths, shawls, and idols. The religion is Lamaism, a kind of Buddhism.

Thibet is divided into two provinces, each of which is ruled by a grand lama, who is a kind of priest and king combined. The people believe that the lama never really dies. They say that when the spirit leaves his body it enters that of some little boy who must be found and educated to take his place. Thibet is said to have been made a kingdom in the year A.D. 313. Since 1650 it has been subject to China.

THIERS (*te-air'*), **Louis Adolphe,** a French statesman and historian, born in Marseilles, April 16, 1797. He was a lawyer, but moved to Paris in 1821, to devote himself to politics and literature, and in both had great success. As a historian he holds a high place, his chief works being "History of the French Revolution" and "History of the Consulate and Empire." In his youth he was in favor of a limited monarchy, and he looked to the reign of Louis Philippe to find his idea carried out, but he gave up all part in the government when he saw that he had been disappointed in the character of the king. Though he was no republican, when the republic was a fact he determined to support it. He did not approve of the empire of Napoleon III., and he prophesied its ruin when he saw the emperor bent on the Prussian war. After that war he did much good to France by getting from the conquerors the best terms possible, and the people in gratitude made him president of the new republic ; but he held it only three years, retiring into private life at the end of that time. His house was destroyed by the French Communists, but was restored at the expense of the republic. Thiers died, when nearly eighty years old, Sept. 3, 1877.

THIRTY YEARS' WAR, a famous war, which lasted from 1618 to 1648, between the Emperor and the Roman Catholic States of Germany on one side, and the Protestant States with their allies, Denmark, Sweden, and France on the other. In a general way, the cause of this war was the division of the Empire into three parties—Lutherans, Calvinists, and Roman Catholics—which hated each other, and were ready for any cause to take arms against each other. More particularly, the war was owing to the ground of quarrel furnished by the church lands which Protestants had seized, and which were claimed by the Roman Catholic princes or bishops, and the rebellion in Bohemia, the Bohemians refusing obedience to their sovereign, the Emperor Ferdinand II., and choosing for their king Frederick, the Elector Palatine.

At first it was entirely a religious war, but after a while France, Denmark, and Sweden interfered, because they wanted to curb the growing power of the House of Austria. The system of warfare on both sides was merciless, and the misery inflicted on Germany untold. Finally, in 1648, the emperor had to submit to the Peace of Westphalia, which gave to France and Sweden parts of the Empire. Foreign nations were loud in their joy when this Peace was signed, but it left Germany a crushed and mangled form, from which life seemed to have departed. Among the most noted leaders in

Wallenstein's Soldiers in Camp.

this war were Tilly, Wallenstein, and Gustavus Adolphus.

THOMAS, George Henry, an American general, born in Southampton County, Va., July 31, 1816. He was graduated at West Point in 1836, served in the Mexican War and various Indian wars, and for three years was an instructor at West Pcint. During the first part of the Civil War he fought under Rosecrans and Grant, and in 1862 he became a major-general. When the Unionists were defeated at Chickamauga, he saved the army from destruction by a bold stand, and at Chattanooga his soldiers decided the victory. After serving under Sherman at Atlanta he commanded an army in Tennessee, with which he defeated the Confederate General Hood, near Nashville (Dec. 15 and 16, 1864). For this he received the thanks of Congress, and the State of Tennessee gave him a gold medal. In 1868 he declined the office of lieutenant-general, saying that he had done nothing to deserve it. He died at San Francisco, when fifty-three years old (March 28, 1870).

THOMPSON, Launt, an American sculptor, born in Ireland in 1833. He came to this country when fourteen, and studied art in E. D. Palmer's studio in Albany. While there he made a beautiful bust of " Little Nell," which made him well known. Among his other works are the statue of General Sedgwick, at West Point, and that of the Rev. Abraham Pierson, first President of Yale College, in the College grounds at New Haven. Since 1875 he has lived in Florence.

THOR, in Scandinavian fable, son of ODIN and Frigga. He was the defender of gods and men, had the care of agriculture and the family, and took charge of the seasons and the winds. Thunder was thought to be the noise of his chariot wheels.

He was armed with a terrible hammer, which he hurled at his victims, and which always returned to his hand. The fifth day of the week is named for him, Thorsday, or Thursday.

THOREAU (*tho-ro'*), **Henry David,** an American writer, born in Concord, Mass., July 12, 1817. Although he was educated at Harvard, he tried to support himself by working as a carpenter. He worked, however, only enough to provide for his wants, which were few, and spent the rest of his time in studying and writing. Many strange stories are told of his way of living. He built with his own hands a house on the shore of the Walden pond, near Concord, and lived in it a hermit's life, eating no meat and faring so frugally that he said his entire expenses were $70 a year. His life has been described by himself in his "Walden; or, Life in the Woods." He died, when forty-four years old (May 6, 1862).

THORWALDSEN (*tor'wald-sen*), **Bertel,** a Danish sculptor, born at sea, Nov. 19, 1770. His father, Gottschalk Thorwaldsen, was an Icelander, by trade a carver in wood, and was on his way to Denmark in search of employment when his son was born. Young Thorwaldsen early began to practise his father's calling, but he made little progress till he went to the free school of the Academy of Art at Copenhagen. When he was seventeen he gained a prize for a bas-relief designed by him, called the "Sleeping Beauty." Five years later he won the grand prize of the Academy, which was a sum of money to be received yearly for five years. This put it in his power to go to Rome to study his art. The first years of his life there were disappointing, and the five years for which his allowance was granted were nearly over, when his model of Jason was seen by an English gentleman, who ordered a copy of it in marble. This was the beginning of his fame, which went on increasing

until his death. The king of Denmark was anxious that he should go home to live in Copenhagen, and he did intend doing so, but his health could not stand the cold winters of the north, so he took up his abode in Rome, visiting Denmark occasionally. The genius of Thorwaldsen was fully appreciated by those of his own age. When he went from place to place, he was honored by the great as though he were a prince. His exquisite bas-reliefs of "Night" and "Morning" are familiar to all. His other well-known works are "The Triumphal Entry of Alexander into Babylon," a bas-relief; "Christ and the Twelve Apostles," a group now in the Cathedral Church of Copenhagen; and the "Preaching of St. John." The largest single work done by him is the colossal lion near Lucerne, Switzerland, a monument erected in memory of the Swiss guards who fell (Aug. 10. 1792) in defending the palace of the Tuileries in Paris from the attack of the French mob. This great sculptor died suddenly of heart disease, just after he had taken his seat in the theatre to see the play. He left to the city of Copenhagen his whole fortune and all his works of art. They have been placed in the museum built round his grave. He died in Copenhagen, when seventy-three years old (March 24, 1844).

THRACE, an ancient country lying S. of the Danube, between Macedonia and the Euxine (Black) Sea. It was inhabited by a barbarous people, who lived chiefly by robbery and plunder. They were conquered by Philip of Macedon, and their country finally fell into the hands of the Romans. It is now occupied by Bulgaria, Eastern Roumelia, and the district of Constantinople.

THRAS·Y·ME'NUS, a lake of Italy, 9 miles W. of the city of Perugia, and about 85 miles N. of Rome. In a narrow pass near the lake a Roman army commanded by Flaminius was surrounded by the Carthaginian army of HANNIBAL. The Romans fought bravely, but after half of them had been killed the rest were obliged to surrender (217 B.C.). Thrasymenus is now called the Lake of Perugia.

THUCYDIDES (*thu-sid'e-deez*), a famous Greek historian, born in Athens about 471 B.C. He was born of a noble and rich family, and was well educated. When a boy he is said to have been so much affected at hearing Herodotus read his history at OLYMPIA that he shed tears; and when he wrote history himself he made Herodotus his model, but he was a much better writer than Herodotus. Having been unsuccessful in a military expedition, he was sent into exile for twenty years, and employed his time in writing a history of the Peloponnesian War, in which he took part, and which was carried on by Athens against Sparta and other cities of the PELOPONNESUS for twenty-nine years (431 to 402 B.C.). Thucydides did not finish his history, which reaches only to the year 411 B.C. He is supposed to have died about 400 B.C., but it is not known where. Some writers say he was assassinated.

TI'BER, a river of Italy, rising in the Apennine mountains and flowing S. to the Mediterranean Sea by two mouths; length, 230 miles. In the upper part are many rapids, and the river passes for several miles through a narrow gorge. Small vessels go up it to Rome, which is eighteen miles from the mouth. The lower part of the Tiber is stained yellow with clay.

The Tiber is famous in many scenes of Roman and Italian history. The Romans looked upon it as sacred, and offered prayers to it.

TI·BE'RI·US, Claudius Nero Cæsar, a Roman emperor, born Nov. 16, 42 B.C. He was the son of the wife of Augustus by her first marriage. He was well educated, and early won fame and rank in the army. About 12 B.C. he was forced to divorce his wife and to marry the emperor's daughter Julia, and Augustus finally adopted him as his son and successor. When Augustus died (14) Tiberius took the throne. He was mild and just in the beginning, but at last grew to be jealous and cruel, and put to death all of whom he was afraid, among others his nephew Germanicus.

He chose for his chief minister a bad man named Sejanus, and in the year 26 left the government in his hands and went to the island of Capri, where he gave himself up to pleasure and vice. In 31 Sejanus

Tiberius.

was put to death by his orders, and he chose for his favorite Macro, who ruled as Sejanus had done. The emperor was now afraid to be seen, for he was bent nearly double, and his face was marked by ugly blotches, caused by his vices. The people were ordered not to disturb him, and soldiers were posted wherever he went to keep them away. At last, while on a journey, he fell into a fainting fit and was thought to be dead. CALIGULA was hailed as emperor, and everybody rejoiced;

but Tiberius recovered and asked for something to eat. All around him were frightened, but Macro drew the bed clothes over him and suffocated him (March 16, 37).

TI·BUL'LUS, Albius, a noted Roman poet, who lived in the time of the Emperor AUGUSTUS. He accompanied his patron, Messala, a Roman general, in campaigns in GAUL and in the East; but his health failing, he returned to Rome and retired to his estate, where he spent his time in writing elegiac or mournful poetry. He gained great fame by his writings, and had many friends.

The poet HORACE honored him with an ode, and on his death OVID mourned him in a funeral poem of great beauty. He died, when quite young (about 18 B.C.).

TI·CON·DE·RO'GA. See LAKE GEORGE.

TIERRA DEL FUEGO (*ti-er'rah del foo-a'go*), a group of islands at the southern end of South America. The largest, Tierra del Fuego proper, is nearly three hundred miles long; the others are much smaller; one, at the southern end, forms Cape Horn. All are very steep and rocky, often forming precipices at the shore. One of the mountains, Mt. Sarmiento, is a mile and a quarter high, and is always covered with snow. The climate is stormy, and often cold. The only people are a few Indians, who dress in skins and live in miserable huts. Tierra del Fuego is separated from Patagonia by the narrow and crooked Strait of Magellan, a channel bordered almost everywhere by precipices of rocks like walls. The strait was named after Magellan, or MAGALHAENS, who discovered it in 1520, when he was making the first voyage around the world. Seeing many Indian fires on the islands, he called the country Tierra del Fuego, or the " Land of Fire."

TIF'LIS, a city of Asiatic Russia, in Georgia, on the River Kur; pop.

90,000, or about as large as Columbus, Ohio. The older part is much like a Turkish city, with narrow streets and small flat-roofed houses, but the newer part is more like a town of Europe or America. Tiflis has manufactures of shawls and carpets, and a considerable trade. It is noted for its warm mineral springs, used for bathing, which are said to cure rheumatism and skin diseases. The Russians keep a very large army at and near Tiflis.

Tiflis is so called from its warm baths, its name being made from a word meaning warm. The town was first built in the 5th century, and it was for a long time the capital of Georgia. The Russians have held it since 1801.

TIGRANES (*ti-gra'neez*) **THE GREAT,** King of Armenia, came to the throne in 96 B.C. In the beginning of his reign he was so successful in his conquests that four kings served at his table and four more ran beside his horse, and he called himself the King of Kings. Afterward he took the side of MITHRIDATES, his father-in-law, against Rome, and was defeated by LUCULLUS, who took and pillaged his capital, Tigranocerta. He was humbled in another battle by Pompey, who would have sacked his capital again had not Tigranes gone to the Roman camp and laid his crown at Pompey's feet. Pompey treated him kindly, replaced him on his throne, and made him a vassal of Rome.

TI'GRIS, a river of Turkey in Asia, rising in the N. part and flowing S.W. until it joins the Euphrates near the head of the Persian Gulf; length 1150 miles. The Tigris is a very swift river, and is deeper than the Euphrates. Steamboats ascend it to Mosul, and above there the river is navigated by rafts, which descend it when the waters are highest, in March. After the Tigris joins the Euphrates it is called the Shatel-Arab.

The name Tigris is supposed to

have been made from the old Persian word *tigra*, meaning an arrow, and given to it on account of the swiftness of the current. In the Bible it is called Hiddekel. In ancient times this was the principal river of Assyria, and Nineveh, Seleucia, Ctesiphon, and other great cities were built on its banks. The principal modern cities are MOSUL and BAGDAD.

TIL'LY, Johann Tserclaes, Count, a German soldier, born in Brabant, in 1559. He was the commander-in-chief of the imperial armies in the Thirty Years' War. Many victories were won for the empire by this great master in the art of war, who, after being conqueror in thirty-six battles, met his first defeat at Leipsic, at the hands of GUSTAVUS ADOLPHUS. After again meeting the "Snow King," as the Germans called the northern hero, on the banks of the Lech, Count Tilly fought no more battles for his emperor, for he died of a mortal wound the next day.

Tilly was a brave soldier, but he was sometimes cruel. When he took Magdeburg he let his soldiers burn most of the town, and kill 25,000 of the inhabitants. But he had one soft place in his heart—his love for children. Once his armies were encamped before a town, threatening it with destruction. The citizens had heard that he loved children, so they sent out a troop of little ones to beg for his mercy. The war-worn veteran could not withstand their innocent appeal, and silently his armies moved off, leaving the town untouched. Ever since the inhabitants have had an annual celebration called the Children's Festival in remembrance of that day. Tilly died in Ingolstadt, when seventy-three years old (April 20, 1632).

TIM·BUC'TOO, a town of W. Africa, 9 miles N. of the River Niger, and on the S. border of the Desert of Sahara; pop. about 20,000, or as large as Lincoln, R. I. Many of the houses are mere huts, but some are two stories high, and are well made of stone or clay. The people are negroes and Arabs of different savage tribes, with a few merchants from Morocco and Tunis. Timbuctoo is the chief trading station of this part of Africa, and every year from November to January it is visited by thousands of people. The principal thing sold is gold dust. The city has a port called Kabara, on the Niger, but most of the trade is carried on by caravans, which cross the desert to Morocco and other places near the Mediterranean.

Timbuctoo was founded in the 12th century. For a long time Europeans knew of it only by reports of the Arab traders, but of late years it has been visited by several travellers.

TI·MO'LE·ON, a Greek general, liberator of Syracuse, born about 395 B.C. Syracuse was a Corinthian colony of Sicily. In 344 she sent an embassy to Corinth, the mother city, entreating her aid against two evil men, Syracusans, who were ruining her by their strife. Timoleon went with an army, overcame the leaders of both parties, and made Syracuse a flourishing colony. The Carthaginians shortly afterward made an attack upon her, but Timoleon again came to the rescue and drove them off. Toward the end of his life he became blind. When he died the people of Syracuse voted to honor him in all future time in the usual way of commemorating their heroes—with races, gymnastics, and public games. He died, when fifty-eight years old (337 B.C.).

TI'MON, called the Misanthrope (Man-hater), an Athenian who lived in the latter part of the 5th century B.C. Because he had been disappointed in some of his friends, he took to hating the whole human race, and shut himself up so that no one could even see him. There was only one person that he would let visit him, and that was ALCIBIADES.

They say that Timon was buried by the coast, and that the sea worked its way around his grave, cutting it off from the mainland, so that he was as solitary in death as he had been in life. Shakespeare has written a play about him, called " Timon of Athens."

TIMOUR (*ti-moor'*), or **Tam·er-lane'**, a famous Asiatic conqueror, born near SAMARCAND, April 9, 1336. He was the son of a chief of a Mongol tribe, and was descended on his mother's side from GENGHIS KHAN. He was lame from a wound received in battle, and was therefore called by his people Timour Lenk (Timour the Lame), which some writers have made into Tamerlane. When twenty-four years old he became head of his tribe, and in ten years he had conquered all the other tribes around him. He then made up his mind to be ruler of the whole world, and he was often heard to say that " as there is but one God in heaven, so there ought to be one lord on earth."

Timour was a Mohammedan of the Shiah sect, who believed that ALI was the rightful successor of Mohammed, and he looked upon the Mohammedans of the Sunnite sect, or those who believed in ABU BEKR, to be as bad as Christians or heathens. So, after he conquered all Central Asia, he turned his arms against BAJAZET, the Sultan of the Ottoman Turks, and utterly defeated him in the battle of Angora (1402). He next started to conquer China, but died on the way, on the Jaxartes River, when sixty-nine years old (Feb. 18, 1405). Timour was one of the greatest soldiers that ever lived, for no other man ever won by the sword so large a part of the world, nor ruled over so many conquered peoples. He ruled all the countries between the Mediterranean and Nile to the sources of the Ganges, but his great empire fell to pieces at his death. The MOGUL sovereigns of India were his descendants.

TIN·TO·RET'TO, a famous Italian artist, born in Venice in 1512. His real name was Giacomo Robusti, but as his father was a dyer (Italian *tintore*), he was commonly called Tintoretto. TITIAN, who was his first master, is said to have sent him home in less than two weeks because he painted so well that he became jealous of him. Tintoretto soon became very famous in Venice, and was noted for his portraits and his landscapes. The palaces of Venice are full of his brilliant works, and there is something of his in almost every collection in Europe. Among his most remarkable pictures are the " Miracle of St. Mark," in the Academy of Venice, and the " Crucifixion." His great picture of " Paradise," fixed to the ceiling of the library in the Ducal palace in Venice, is the largest oil painting in the world. The Venetians used to say that Tintoretto had three pencils— one of gold, one of silver, and a third of iron, because his work was not always the best he could do. It is said that he was call *Il Furioso* (Italian for " The Furious"), on account of his rapid painting, which was also sometimes rather careless. Tintoretto died in Venice, when eighty-two years old (1594).

TISSAPHERNES (*tis-sa-fer'neez*), a noted Persian general. He was one of the commanders of the army of Artaxerxes II. in the battle of Cunaxa, where CYRUS THE YOUNGER was defeated and killed, and he afterward followed and harassed XENOPHON in his famous retreat. For his services he was made ruler of the provinces which Cyrus had governed in Asia Minor, and was given the daughter of Artaxerxes in marriage. But after a while he lost his favor with the king, who sent a man to kill him (395 B.C.)

TI'TANS, in Greek fable, sons of Uranus or Heaven, and Gæa, Earth. There were six sons—Oceanus, Cœus, Crius, Hyperion, Japetus, and Cronus or Saturn ; and six daughters—Theia, Rhea, Themis, Mnemosyne, Phœbe, and Tethys. Having rebelled against their father, he shut them up in Tartarus. Cronus at last overpowered his father and set his brothers free. They afterward aided Cronus in a contest with his son Zeus, or JUPITER. Zeus was successful, and confined the Titans forever in a dungeon underground.

TI-THO'NUS, in Greek fable, son of Laomedon, brother of King PRIAM. He was married to Eos or Aurora, the Goddess of the Dawn, who asked the gods to make him immortal. But she forgot to ask the gift of eternal youth for him also, and in time he became infirm and old, and his immortality was a trial rather than a blessing.

TITIAN (*tish'e-an*), a famous Italian painter, born near Pieve di Cadore, in 1477. His whole name in Italian was Tiziano Vecellio, but in English he is commonly called Titian. When a child he showed his love for art by painting pictures with colors which he made by pressing out the juice of flowers. As he grew up he studied with several good artists, and in time became very famous. GIORGIONE was Titian's fellow-student and friend, and Titian's style of painting became much like his, so that on the death of Giorgione, in 1511, Titian finished some of his pictures. When thirty-seven he was invited to Ferrara by the Duke Alfonso, for whom he painted several celebrated pictures. At Ferrara he also made the acquaintance of the poet ARIOSTO and painted his portrait. From that time Titian received all the honor that could be bestowed upon an artist. He not only painted the potraits of popes, princes, and celebrated men, but he was with them as a friend. When the Emperor CHARLES V. went into Italy to be crowned he sent for Titian to Bologna, and was so much delighted with the portrait he painted of him

that he sent to him several times, made him a knight, and settled upon him a pension, which was afterward increased by PHILIP II.

Titian passed five years in Germany, and visited Spain, but his proper home was Venice, where he lived splendidly and kept up the rank due to his great merits. He was very busy with his work until the very last of his life. " The Martyrdom of St. Lawrence," one of his greatest pictures, was painted when he was eighty-one years old, and several others of his most re-

Titian.

markable pieces are of a still later date. As a master in color this artist has never been equalled. Titian also engraved upon copper and wood. He died in Venice, when ninety-nine years old (Aug. 27, 1576).

TITICACA (*te-te-kah'kah*), a lake of W. South America in a valley E. of the Andes, and more than 12,000 feet above the sea ; area, about 4,000 square miles, or about two thirds as large as Lake Ontario. It lies partly in Peru and partly in Bolivia. Scattered over it are many small islands remarkable for their wonderful ruined buildings, which were in nearly the same condition as now when the Spaniards conquered Peru. Nothing is certainly known of the people who built them, but the remains show that they were much better architects and builders than the Peruvians whom the Spaniards found in possession of the country.

TITUS, Flavius Sabinus Vespasianus, a Roman emperor, born December 30, A.D. 40. He was the oldest son of the Emperor Vespasian, and became early noted as a soldier and a scholar. When his father was made emperor Titus was left in Judea to carry on the Jewish war, which he ended by the capture of Jerusalem after a long siege, in which many thousands of the Jews

Titus.

perished (70). The news of this victory was received at Rome with great joy, and Vespasian and his son shared a triumph together. The Arch of Titus, still standing in Rome, was built in honor of this conquest of Judea. Titus now became joint ruler with his father, and did many cruel acts for the emperor ; he also gave himself up to a gay life, so that when he became emperor on the death of his father (79) people said he was a second Nero. But he proved to be a mild and good ruler ; he corrected many abuses, reformed the laws, pardoned his brother Do-

mitian, who conspired to kill him, and added many splendid buildings to the city. In the year he came to the throne took place the great eruption of Vesuvius, which destroyed Herculaneum, Pompeii, and many other towns. In the next year a great fire ravaged the city for three days, destroying the Capitol, Pompey's theatre, and a large number of houses, and also killing a great many people. Soon after a dreadful pestilence broke out. Titus used all the money in his treasury, and even stripped his palaces of treasures to get money for the people's relief. He was now beloved by all classes, and was called the " Delight of Mankind." After a reign of two years his health failed, and he went to his villa at Reate, in the country of the Sabines, where he died, when forty-one years old (Sept. 13, 81). He was succeeded by Domitian.

TIVOLI (*tiv'o-le*), a town of Italy, 16 miles E.N.E. of Rome ; pop. 10,000, or nearly as large as Hyde Park, Mass. It is built on the slope of a mountain, down which the River Teverone, the ancient Anio, tumbles in falls and cascades on its way to the Tiber. The great beauty of its scenery made it a famous summer resort in old times, and all around it are still to be seen the ruins of ancient Roman villas and temples. Many of the finest statues in the Vatican and other museums were found there. The poets Horace, Virgil, Catullus, and Propertius praise it in their verses. Syphax, King of Numidia, and Zenobia, Queen of Palmyra, spent their last days there.

TOBOLSK', a city of W. Siberia, on the River Tobol, where it joins the Irtish ; pop. 20,000, or about as large as McKeesport, Pa. It has a pretty site, but almost all its buildings are of wood. In its citadel is a large prison, and almost all the prisoners exiled to Siberia are collected there before they are sent to the different parts of the country. Tobolsk means the " town on the

Tobol." The place was first built by the Russians, in 1587, and it was once the capital of Siberia.

TOCQUEVILLE (*tok'vil*), **Alexis Charles Henri Clérel de,** a French writer, born in Paris, July 29, 1805. He studied law and became a judge, and in 1831 was sent to the United States to make observations on American penitentiaries. A report of this journey was published, but De Tocqueville is better known by his book on "Democracy in America," which describes American society and customs. Americans like this work very much, because, though it is often severe, it is truthful and fair. De Tocqueville held several important offices in France, and published other works, all of which have been translated into English. He died at Cannes, when nearly fifty-four years old (April 16, 1859).

TODLEBEN (*tot'la-ben*), **Franz Eduard,** a Russian engineer and general, born May 20, 1818. He studied at the School of Engineers in St. Petersburg, and afterward fought with the Russian army in several campaigns. During the Crimean War he became famous for his defence of SEBASTOPOL, where he showed great skill in making fortifications. In 1860 Gen. Todleben became chief of engineering for the Russian army. He published a history of the defence of Sebastopol. He died at Soden, in Germany, when sixty-six years old (July 1, 1884).

TOKIO (*to'ke-o*), a city, capital of Japan, in the E. part of the principal island, on the Bay of Yedo; pop. 1,313,000, or more than five sixths as large as New York. It contains many wide and handsome streets, and the houses are often built like those of America and Europe. As many of the people dress in the European style, Tokio appears much more civilized than the other Japanese cities. Interspersed with the houses are many fine parks and gardens, and canals run through some of the streets. In the centre of the city is a citadel, surrounded by three stone walls, one within the other; the two outer walls inclose large spaces, in which are many government buildings, arsenals, and factories. The Imperial University, which is situated there, has more than a hundred foreign professors. The city contains hundreds of shrines and Buddhist temples. Among the curious sights to be seen in the streets are carriages called *jinrikishas* (man-power carriages) drawn by men; and groups of jugglers, wrestlers, minstrels, and story-tellers. The bay of Tokio is shallow, and the port for large vessels is at YOKOHAMA, 18 miles distant.

Tokio means "Eastern Capital." It was formerly called Yedo, but the name was changed in 1868, when the emperor went there to live. It was founded in 1591. In 1656 and 1854 the city was partly destroyed by earthquakes and many persons were killed.

TO-LE'DO, a city of Spain, on the River Tagus, 42 miles S.S.W. of Madrid; pop. 21,000, or nearly as large as McKeesport, Pa. It is built on a high rocky hill, surrounded on three sides by the deep river; on the other side are two walls, which were first built by the Romans, but were repaired by the Goths, Moors, and Spaniards, to whom the city belonged at different times. The streets are narrow, crooked, and steep, and the town has a very ancient appearance. Toledo has several schools and colleges, and one of the finest cathedrals in Spain. There are manufactories of woollen, silk, and leather, and of the celebrated sword blades called Toledo blades.

Toledo gets its name from Toletum, its ancient name. It was taken by the Romans in 192 B.C., and by the Goths in A.D. 467. It belonged to the Moors from 714 to 1085, when it was captured by the Spaniards and made the capital of the Kingdom of Castile.

At one time it had 200,000 inhabitants.

TOLEDO, a city of N. Ohio, on the Maumee River, 8 miles from its mouth on the W. end of Lake Erie; pop. 81,000, or about as large as Richmond. Va. It has an excellent harbor, and many railroads meet in the city, which give it a large trade, especially in grain, flour, cattle, iron, and lumber. There are large lumber mills and iron-works, and manufactories of railroad cars, tools, and many other things.

Toledo was first settled in 1832.

TOOKE (*took*), **John Horne,** an English politician, born in Westminster, June 25, 1736. His real name was John Horne, the name Tooke being added when he was forty-six years old, out of regard to a Mr. Tooke, who made him his heir. Much against his will he entered the Church in his youth, but he found it did not suit him, and he then practised law. When the American Revolution broke out he felt much sympathy for the American colonies, and after the battle of Lexington he proposed a subscription " for the widows and orphans of the Americans murdered by the king's troops." For this he was imprisoned for a year, and fined £200. As an author he is known by his " Diversions of Purley," a curious book on grammar. He died when nearly seventy-six years old (March 18, 1812).

TOPEKA (*to-pe'kah*), a city, capital of Kansas, in the E. part of the State, on the Kansas River; pop. 31,000, or about as large as Salem, Mass. Besides the State House, a very fine building, it contains the State Insane Asylum and several colleges and schools. The country around is very fertile. Topeka was founded in 1854, and became the State capital in 1861.

TO-RON'TO, a city of Canada, capital of the Province of Ontario, on the N. shore of Lake Ontario; pop. 167,000, or a little larger than Minneapolis, Minn. It has a good harbor, formed by an island near the shore, and an important trade with other lake ports. The city has large manufactories of railroad cars, furniture, boots and shoes, and whiskey. Toronto University has the finest building in the province, and there are several important colleges, schools, and asylums.

Toronto was founded in 1794, and until 1834 was called York. It was the capital of Upper Canada until 1841, and when that formed a union with Lower Canada the legislatures met alternately in Toronto and Quebec from 1849 until 1858. Since 1867 it has been the capital of Ontario. During the war of 1812 Toronto was taken by the Americans and the public buildings were burned.

TORQUEMADA (*tor-ka-mah'dah*), **Tomas,** the first Spanish inquisitor-general, born at Torquemada about 1420. He belonged to the Dominicans, an order set up by the Roman Catholic Church to put down false belief in religion, and was selected by Ferdinand and Isabella as inquisitor. He worked so zealously in this office that the pope thought it necessary to appoint others to work with him and to check his zeal. The inquisition was a terrible court, whose business it was to examine into people's belief, to see whether it was correct or not. If the inquisitor-general thought his prisoner's views false he tried to change them, and if he could not, then the unfortunate one was put to death. Torquemada was very active against Jews and Moors. He died in Avila, when about seventy-eight years old (Sept. 16, 1498).

TOR-TU'GAS. See Dry Tortugas.

TOTILA (*tot'e-lah*), (properly Baduila), a Gothic king of Italy. Fifteen years after the fall of the emperors of Rome Italy was ruled by Theodoric, the brave King of the Goths, who founded an empire which lasted sixty-four years. Totila was the last of his successors. The Greek emperor Justinian, thinking it would be a good thing to unite Italy to his empire, sent BELISARIUS and NARSES, two of his generals, to put an end to the Gothic dominion. Totila, the Gothic king, was defeated by Narses, and slain in the battle of Tagina (A.D. 552). Italy was then ruled by the Byzantine Empire.

TOULMOUCHE (*tool-moosh'*), **Auguste,** a French painter, born at Nantes. His pictures most often represent the interior of rooms, with ladies reading, chatting, or amusing themselves in other ways. Some of his paintings have been brought to the United States.

TOULON (*too-long'*), a city of S.E. France, on a bay of the Mediterranean Sea; pop. 70,000, or about as large as Cambridge, Mass. It is noted for its great military post and navy yard, which are the largest on the Mediterranean and among the finest in the world. Ten thousand men are constantly employed there, and there are immense arsenals of arms and military stores. The bay is very strongly fortified. The city contains military and naval schools and a fine cathedral, and is ornamented with many fountains and shady promenades.

Toulon gets its name from Telo Martius, the name of its Roman founder, nearly two thousand years ago. The fortifications were first built to protect it from pirates. In 1793 the English got the city, and it was in driving them out that Napoleon first became noted as a commander.

TOULOUSE (*too-looz'*), a city of S. France, on the Garonne River; pop. 148,000, or nearly twice as large as Fall River, Mass. It has important manufactories of woollen and cotton cloth, machinery, cutlery, paper, and many other things, and a large trade in grain, wine, marble, and wood. Toulouse is not a handsome city, but it contains many curious old churches and public buildings. The church of St. Sernin, which is the finest of all, contains among its ornaments a caricature of CALVIN as a hog in a pulpit, with the inscription, "Calvin the hog preaching." Every year there is a festival of flowers in the principal public square, and formerly people went from all parts of France to see it.

Toulouse is a very ancient city, having been taken 106 B.C. by the Romans, who found immense treasures of gold and silver in it. In 1814 there was a great battle there, in which the French under Marshal SOULT were defeated by the English under the Duke of WELLINGTON.

TOURNAY (*toor-nay'*), a town of Belgium, on the River Scheldt, 45 miles S.W. of Brussels; pop. 35,000, or about as large as Binghamton, N.Y. Tournay used to be the capital of the Merovingian kings of the Franks, and in the church of St. Brice is still shown the tomb of Childeric I. The golden bees, which are supposed to have been a part of the ornaments of his robes, are also preserved there. It was from these that Napoleon got the idea of putting bees instead of the Bourbon *fleur de lis* on his imperial robes.

The Romans first built Tournay and called it Turris Nerviorum, the fort of the Nervii, an ancient tribe who lived near there, and from this has come its present name.

TOURS (*toor*), a city of France, at the junction of the Rivers Loire and Cher; pop. 60,000, or nearly as large as Grand Rapids, Mich. It has many fine buildings, and the ruins of the Cathedral of St. Martin of Tours, which was destroyed in 1793, are still admired for their beauty. The bridge over the Loire at Tours is one of the finest in France. The city has important manufactures of carpets, silks, and other cloths. It was the first French city where silk was woven, and for a long time it had the largest silk trade in France. Tours took its name from the ancient tribe of the Turones, who lived there before the Romans conquered Gaul.

TOUSSAINT (*too-san'*), **François Dominique,** called l'Ouverture, a Haytian general, born in 1743. He was a negro slave, and in 1791 joined an insurrection by which the slaves were made free, and masters of the island. In time he became the leader of the negroes, and when the English invaded Hayti, in 1793, he declared in favor of the French Republic, rescued a French army which the English had surrounded, and finally forced the whole English army to surrender (1797). The Spanish, who had had possession of the eastern part of the island, were also forced to submit, and Toussaint was made president of Hayti for life, subject to the government of France. But Bonaparte, who had become First Consul, did not favor Toussaint, and a large army was sent against him. He and his negro army resisted successfully, and the French were obliged to make peace with him ; but he was afterward treacherously seized and carried to France, where he was refused a trial, and finally died of cold and starvation in the dungeons of the Castle of Joux, near Besançon, when sixty years old (April 27, 1803).

TRAF-AL'GAR. See NELSON.

TRA'JAN, Marcus Ulpius, a Roman emperor, born of a Roman family, near Seville, Spain, Sept. 18, A.D. 52. He very early became a soldier, and was so successful in 'the Parthian and German wars that the Emperor Nerva adopted him, and on his death (98) Trajan became emperor, being the first Roman emperor born out of Italy. In 101 he made war against the Dacians, and in 106 their country was made a Roman province. The splendid column of Trajan, still standing in the Forum at Rome, was built in memory of this war. The emperor also exhibited shows

which lasted four months, in which 10,000 gladiators fought and 11,000 wild beasts were killed. Afterward he conquered the Parthians and Armenians, and extended his empire to the Caspian Sea. On his return he spent several years in adorning Rome and other cities with splendid buildings, in founding new cities, and in building roads, canals, bridges, and other public works. After eight years of peace he set out against the Parthians, who had revolted , and after conquering them

Trajan.

started again for Rome, but fell sick, and died at Selinus, in Cilicia (Aug., 117). His ashes were taken to Rome in a golden urn and buried under his column. His reign was thought to be the most brilliant of all the Roman emperors. A writer three centuries later says that "Trajan built the world over." His armies were never defeated, and in his time the empire reached its greatest extent.

TREB'I-ZOND, a city in the N.E. part of Asiatic Turkey, on the Black Sea ; pop. 45,000, or about as large as Lawrence, Mass. It is surrounded by walls, and has a very fine harbor. The houses, though only one story high, are generally well built, and often have fine gardens. There are many Greek churches and Mohammedan mosques, and a beautiful marble bath-house, one of the finest buildings in the city. Trebizond has a very large and important trade, both by ships and by caravans, from Turkey and Persia. It is said that the trade with Persia employs 60,000 pack-horses and 2000 camels, besides oxen and donkeys. Trebizond is more than 2000 years old. It was first built by the Greeks, who named it from its form Trapezus, which means table; and from this has grown its present name. XENO-

School, penitentiary, and lunatic asylum. It is celebrated for its potteries, where more crockery is made than in any other city in America. It has also large iron and woollen mills.

Trenton was first settled about 1680, and was named in 1720 in honor of Colonel Trent, a statesman of the time. During the Revolutionary War a British army of 1300 Hessians were encamped there. Washington secretly crossed the Delaware at night, surprised and defeated them, and captured more than 1000 of them, while the Americans did not lose a single man (Dec. 26, 1776). Trenton became the capital of New Jersey in 1790.

TREVES (*treevz*), a town of W. Germany, in Prussia, on the Moselle River; pop. 26,000, or about as large as Sacramento, Cal. It has many old buildings, among them a cathedral noted for its relics. Among these is the "holy coat," said to have been the seamless garment worn by Christ before he was crucified. In 1844 more than a million Catholics went to Treves to see this coat; but other Catholics claimed that this was idolatry, and on that account seceded and formed a church of their own called the

Porta Nigra, Treves.

PHON and his army stopped there to rest after their march through Persia.

TRENTON, a city, capital of New Jersey, in the N. part of the State, on the Delaware River; pop. 57,000, or nearly as large as Reading, Pa. Besides the Capitol building it contains the State arsenal, Normal

German Catholic Church. Treves was named after the Treviri, a German tribe who lived there nearly two thousand years ago. It was a colony of the Romans, and it still contains more remains of their buildings and public works than any other city in Germany. Among the best preserved of the Roman buildings is a very large structure called the Porta Nigra (Black Gate). Many of the later Roman emperors lived there.

TRIESTE (*tre-est*), a city, the chief seaport of Austria, on the coast of the Adriatic Sea, 70 miles E. N. E. of Venice; pop. 149,000, or somewhat larger than Omaha, Neb. Trieste has a large trade, especially with the East, and many steamers sail from there. It was called Tergeste before the time of Christ, but Trieste was of little consequence before the present century.

TRIN·I·DAD', the southernmost of the West India Islands, opposite the mouth of the Orinoco River; area, 1755 square miles, or one and a third times as large as the State of Rhode Island; pop. 183,000, or more than half that of Rhode Island; capital, Port of Spain. The northern part is high and rocky, and covered in many places with forests in which rosewood, mahogany, and other fine timbers are obtained. The southern part is low and flat, and most of it has been cleared to make plantations of sugar-cane, coffee, and cacao. In one place there is a lake of pitch, large quantities of which are sent to Paris to be used for pavements and roofing. Trinidad is a Spanish word meaning Trinity. The island was discovered by Columbus in 1498, and was taken from the Spanish by the British in 1797.

TRIPOLI (*trip'o-le*), a country of N. Africa, on the Mediterranean Sea, between Egypt and Algeria; area thought to be about 125,000 square miles, or about three times as large as Louisiana; pop. about 1,000,000, or about ten elevenths that of Louisiana; capital, Tripoli (pop. 30,000). Most of the interior is a sandy desert, where wild animals live. The sea-coast is more than 600 miles long, but the only good port is Tripoli, and around it is the most fertile part of the country. The people are mostly Moors, Jews, and negro slaves from Central Africa. They

are governed by a Bey or governor, appointed by the Sultan of Turkey. The states of Barca and Fezzan are governed by separate rulers, but pay a yearly tribute to Tripoli.

At one time pirates from Tripoli used to prey on the commerce of all Christian nations, and the ruler of that country used to seize ships in the Mediterranean and make slaves of their crews unless he was paid a certain amount of money every year. At last the United States got tired of this and made war against Tripoli (1801), this being our first foreign war. Gen. EATON took Derne, a town of Tripoli, and hoisted over it the flag of the United States, and this was the first and only time that our flag has ever been hoisted over any captured town in the Old World.

TRIP·TOL'E·MUS. See CERES.

TROL'LOPE, Frances Milton, an English writer, born in Hampshire about 1780. She visited the United States in 1829 and spent three years here, and when she returned to England published " Domestic Manners of the Americans," a book holding up the Americans to ridicule, but which met with much favor in England. After this she wrote a large number of books, mostly books of travel and novels. She died in Florence, Italy, when eighty-three years old (Oct. 6, 1863).

TROLLOPE, Anthony, a noted English writer of novels, son of Frances Trollope, born April 24, 1815. He was for many years in the British postal service, and travelled much in foreign countries on business of the post-office; but he is best known for his novels, of which he has published a great many. Among the best of them are " Framley Parsonage," " Orley Farm," and " Barchester Towers." He died when sixty-seven years old (Dec. 6, 1882).

TROLLOPE, Thomas Adolphus, an English writer, son of Frances Trollope, born April 29, 1810. In 1841 he went to Florence to live, and he has published many books on

Italy, and several novels. He died November 11, 1892.

TROMP, Martin Harpertzoon van, a famous Dutch admiral, born at Briel in 1597. His father, a commander in the Dutch navy, took him to sea when he was a mere boy. In a battle with an English vessel off the coast of Guinea, the father was killed and the son taken prisoner, and for more than two years he was made to work as a cabin-boy. When he became a man he entered the Dutch navy, and in 1639 became Admiral of Holland. He fought against the Spaniards, but is chiefly famous for his naval battles with the English under Admiral BLAKE. In the first battle (May 19, 1652) the Dutch were defeated ; but soon after (Nov. 29) Tromp gained a great victory, after which he sailed up the English Channel with a broom fastened to his masthead to show that he had swept his enemies from the seas. But Blake finally got the better of him, and at last, in a battle off the coast of Holland, Tromp was defeated and killed, when fifty-six years old (July 31, 1653).

Cornelis, his son, born in Rotterdam, Sept. 9, 1629, also became famous as an admiral. In 1666 he and De RUYTER defeated the English after a battle of four days. He died in Amsterdam, when sixty-two years old (May 29, 1691).

TROW'BRIDGE, John Townsend, an American writer, born in Ogden, N. Y., Sept. 18, 1827. He began to write for newspapers in Boston when twenty years old, and soon after became known as a story writer. He has published many novels, and some stories for young folks. Among his works are " Laurence's Adventures," " Jack Hazard and his Fortunes," " Doing his Best," " The Young Surveyor," " His Own Master," and " Young Joe, and Other Boys." Mr. Trowbridge was for a time editor of " Our Young Folks" magazine.

TROY, an ancient city in the N. W. part of Asia Minor. Our principal knowledge of it is got from Homer's poem, the "Iliad," so called from Ilium or Ilion, another name for the city. According to the " Iliad," Troy stood at the foot of Mount Ida, with a great plain between it and the sea. Priam, who ruled the city and the country around it, had many children, one of whom, PARIS, carried off HELEN, wife of MENELAUS. After spending ten years in collecting an army, the Greeks sailed against Troy, to revenge this outrage, with more than 1100 ships and 100,000 men, under the command of AGAMEMNON. Ten years more were spent in the siege, but finally the Greeks took the city and utterly destroyed it, only ÆNEAS and Antenor escaping with their families. Among the noble Greeks who fought in the war, besides Agamemnon and Menelaus, were ACHILLES, Patroclus, ULYSSES, Ajax, Diomedes, and Palamedes ; and among the bravest of the Trojans were Hector, Æneas, and Sarpedon.

The " Iliad" ends with the funeral of Hector ; but in the Æneid of Virgil is told how the Greeks, failing to take Troy by force, resorted to stratagem. They built a very large wooden horse, and inside of it hid some of the bravest of their warriors, among them Menelaus and Ulysses. They made believe that this was a peace-offering to Minerva, in order that she might give them a safe return to their homes. Leaving it in the plain before the city, they set sail in their ships, but went no farther than Tenedos, an island near the coast. There was great joy in Troy when the Greeks departed, and some proposed that the horse should be taken into the city. But others opposed this, and LAOCOÖN said, " Touch it not, for as for these men of Greece, I fear them, even though they bring gifts in their hands." And as he spoke he cast his great spear at the horse. Soon after this Laocoön and his sons were devoured by serpents, and the people said the gods had slain him because he had cast his spear against Minerva's horse. So all cried out that the horse must be taken into the city, and putting rollers under it they drew it in with ropes. When night was come the Greeks left Tenedos and sailed back to Troy ; and the warriors in the horse came out through a secret door, and opening the gates of the city let in their friends, who quickly got possession. Thus Troy was taken and destroyed. A few years ago Dr. SCHLIEMANN dug where he supposed the ancient city stood, and found many remains which he called the ruins of Troy.

TROY, a city of E. New York, on the Hudson River, at the head of steamboat navigation ; pop. 61,000, or not quite as large as Dayton, Ohio. A great dam has been made across the Hudson opposite the city ; this and the falls of some smaller streams furnish water power for many large mills and factories. Troy has more and larger iron-works than any other city of America east of the Alleghany Mountains. The stove works and bell foundries are the largest in the United States, and there are great manufactories of railroad cars, machines, tools, and many other things. Troy also has the most important shirt and collar factories, and the largest manufactory of mathematical instruments in the country. There are great steam laundries which receive clothes to be washed from Boston, New York, and many other cities. Among the public buildings is the Rensselaer Polytechnic Institute, one of the best scientific schools in the country.

Troy was founded about 1789, and was named after the ancient city of Troy in Asia Minor. It became a city in 1816.

TRUM'BULL, John, an American poet, born in Watertown, Conn., April 24, 1750. He was graduated at Yale College in 1767, studied law and became a judge. His best-known poem is "McFingal," a satire on the Tories of the Revolution. It was very popular in its day, and was reprinted many times. Trumbull died in Detroit, Mich., when eighty years old (May 12, 1831).

TRUMBULL, John, an American painter, son of Jonathan Trumbull, born in Lebanon, Conn., June 6, 1756. He was graduated at Harvard College in 1773. When the Revolution broke out he joined the army, became aide-de-camp to Washington, and afterward had the rank of colonel. After the war he studied painting under Benjamin West in London, and painted many historical pictures, among them the "Battle of Bunker Hill" and the "Death of Montgomery before Quebec." Four of his pictures—the "Declaration of Independence," the "Surrender of Burgoyne," the "Surrender of Cornwallis," and the "Resignation of Washington at Annapolis"—are in the rotunda of the Capitol at Washington. Trumbull painted copies of many of his pictures, and when he died left a collection of them to Yale College, where they are preserved in the art gallery. He died in New York, when eighty-seven years old (Nov. 10, 1843).

TRUM'BULL, Jonathan, an American statesman, born in Lebanon, Conn., Oct. 12, 1710. He studied to be a minister, but became a merchant. In 1733 he was elected a member of the Assembly of Connecticut, and became speaker, judge, deputy-governor, and finally (1769) governor of the colony. He was one of the first to resist the harsh laws of Great Britain which led to the Revolution, and when the war broke out he did much to make it successful. Washington often asked his advice, and sometimes when he had a question to decide he would say in fun, "Let us hear what Brother Jonathan has to say about it." In time "Brother Jonathan" became a kind of nickname for the United States. He died when nearly seventy-five years old (Aug. 17, 1785).

TUCSON (*tus-son'*), the capital and principal city of Arizona, in the S. part of the territory, near the Santa Cruz River ; pop. about 7000. Three quarters of the people are descend-ants of Mexicans, and still speak the Spanish language. The town, with its narrow streets and great open squares, looks much like a Mexican city, and most of the houses are built of adobe, or sun-dried bricks. Tucson was a Mexican military post before Arizona became a part of the United States.

TU'DOR, House of, the name of a line of English sovereigns, who ruled from 1485 to 1603, the first being Henry VII. The Tudors who have sat on the throne of England are five : Henry VII., Henry VIII., Edward VI., Mary I., and Elizabeth. The family descended from a Welsh gentleman, Owen ap Tudor, whose son Edmund, Earl of Richmond, married Margaret Beaufort, heiress of the Lancastrian claims, and was the father of Henry VII. The family traits were pride, reserve, perseverance, and political wisdom, all of which were possessed in a great degree by Elizabeth, the last Tudor, on whose death the crown passed to the Scotch Stuarts, descendants of Henry VII. in the female line.

TU·IS'CO, in Scandinavian fable, the god of war and fame, son of Odin. The ancient Germans honored him as the founder of their nation. He made wise laws, and the third day of the week, on which the judges among the early Germans held their meetings, was named for him, Tuesday.

TUL'LUS HOS·TIL'I·US, third king of Rome. He began to reign in 673 B.C., and was soon engaged in a war with Alba, during which the famous combat between the HORATII and the Curiatii took place. Having conquered the Albans, he destroyed their city and brought the people to Rome as

slaves. His house was struck by lightning, and he and all his family were killed (641 B.C.).

TU'NIS, a country of N. Africa, on the Mediterranean Sea, between Algeria and Tripoli ; area, 45,000 square miles, or nearly as large as New York State ; pop. 2,000,000, or about one third that of New York State; capital, TUNIS In the northwestern part are high forest-covered mountains, and south of them is a grassy table-land with desert beyond. The climate is mild and healthful.

Tunis has mines of silver, lead, and copper, and raises wheat, barley, maize, olives, and dates. Most of the people in the interior are Arabs, who dwell in tents and wander from place to place, and Kabyles, who live in villages. Near the coast are many Turks and Moors. The principal religion is the Mohammedan. Tunis is governed by a ruler called the Bey, who does what he pleases with his subjects, and is often very despotic and cruel. He used to pay a sum of money as tribute every year to Turkey, but since 1871 this has been stopped, and now Tunis is really independent, although the Bey promises to help Turkey with troops in case of war.

TUNIS, a city, capital of Tunis, on a salt lake opening into the Gulf of Tunis; pop. 130,000, or about as large as Providence, R. I. It is surrounded by two walls, and is defended by strong forts and a castle. From a distance the city with its white houses and palaces has a very fine appearance ; but a nearer view shows that the streets are narrow and dirty, and most of the houses are small, with no windows on the street side. The Bey, however, has a fine palace, and there are many handsome mosques and barracks for soldiers. The harbor is not very good, and large ships have to anchor in the Gulf of Tunis. The city has manufactures of woollen and silk, leather, and perfumeries, and a large trade is carried on. Gold dust and ivory are brought from the interior of Africa and sent from Tunis to other countries. Near the city are important sponge fisheries. Tunis is a very old city. Not far from it is the site of CARTHAGE.

TUP'PER, Martin Farquhar, an English writer, born in London, July 17, 1810. He was educated at Oxford, and studied law, but he has devoted himself chiefly to writing. His most famous work is "Proverbial Philosophy," which was first published in 1838. He has written a great deal both in prose and in verse. His works comprise novels, poems, essays on science and art, and other subjects. He died in London when seventy-nine years old (Nov. 29, 1889).

TU·RA'NI·ANS, the name given to most of the peoples of Asia who are neither ARYANS nor SEMITES. The word comes from the old name Turan (land of darkness), given by the Persians to the country around them inhabited by wandering races, while their own country was called Iran (land of light). The principal Turanian peoples are the Chinese, the Mongols, and the Turks or Tartars. The Turanians were in Europe in very early times, but they were all driven out by the Aryans, excepting a few in out-of-the-way places, like the Finns and Lapps in the north, and perhaps the Basques in Spain. The Turanian peoples are much more numerous than the Aryans or the Semites.

TURENNE (*tu-ren'*), **Henri de la Tour d'Auvergne,** Viscount de, a French soldier, born in Sedan, Sept. 11, 1611. He was the second son of Henri de Bouillon, Prince of Sedan, and Elizabeth of Nassau, the daughter of William the Silent, Stadtholder of Holland. When but fourteen years old he was sent to Holland to learn the art of war from his uncle, MAURICE of Nassau, the greatest soldier of his age. When he grew up, France had good use for her soldiers in the Thirty Years' War, in which Turenne won his first laurels. In after years his brilliant exploits gave glory to the military campaigns of Louis XIV. When on the eve of a battle near Sasbach, he was killed by a chance shot just as he was about leading his troops into action. The French soldiers in anguish cried, "Our father is dead," and the hostile general declared that a man had fallen "who did honor to human nature." Such was the respect in which this great man was held even by his foes that the French leaders were allowed to withdraw from the action in silence to mourn their illustrious dead. He died, when sixty-four years old (July 27, 1675). Next to Napoleon, Turenne is considered the greatest general of France.

TURGENIEFF (*toor-gane'yeff*) **Ivan,** a Russian novelist, born in Orel, Nov. 9, 1818. He was at one time a clerk in the service of the government, but was banished for writing some poems in which his ideas about freedom were displeasing to the emperor. After several years he was allowed to go back, but afterward lived most of the time in Paris. Among his novels are "Fathers and Sons," "Smoke," and "Virgin Soil." The last is a story of the present political troubles in Russia, in which the Nihilists take so large a part. He died at Bougival, France, in his sixty-sixth year (Sept. 3, 1883).

TURIN (*too'rin*), a city of N.W. Italy, on the river Po, 77 miles S. W. of Milan; pop. 312,000, or three times as large as Allegheny, Pa. The city is famed for its beautiful palaces, churches, promenades, and bridges. The royal palace is very large, and contains a library and a museum of ancient armor and weapons. There are several other museums and picture galleries. The University of Turin has a fine building, with a large library. The city has an extensive trade in silk, and there are manufactories of silk-cloth, jewellery, furniture, and carriages.

Turin gets its name from an ancient people called the Taurini ("dwellers on hills"), who once lived there. The city was conquered by Hannibal, and afterward by the Romans. It was the capital of the Kingdom of Sardinia from 1814 to 1860, and of the Kingdom of Italy from 1860 to 1865.

TUR'KEY, or the **Ottoman Empire,** a country of W. Asia and S.E. Europe, N. and E. of the Mediterranean Sea; area of the whole Turkish Empire, in Europe, Asia, and Africa, 1,117,000 square miles, or less than a third that of the United States; pop. 34,322,000, or more than seven thir-teenths that of the United States; capital, CONSTANTINOPLE. Turkey in Europe is separated from Turkey in Asia by the Black Sea and Sea of Marmora, and the Straits of the Dardanelles and Bosporus. The eastern part of Asiatic Turkey, called Mesopotamia, consists of plains and table-lands, many of which are sandy deserts ; but in the western and northern parts, and in European Turkey are many mountain chains. The valleys between these are generally fertile, but the people are poor farmers, and the land is not well cultivated. The principal crops are maize, rice, barley, wheat,

Turkish Galley.

rye, millet, and cotton. There are many large flocks of sheep and goats, herds of oxen, asses, and camels, and some of the finest horses in the world. Among the minerals are iron, lead, copper, silver, and emery.

Only about 2,500,000 of the people are Turks, the rest being Greeks, Armenians, Arabs, Syrians, and several other nations who are subject to the Turks. The principal religion is the Mohammedan, and the Koran, or Mohammedan Bible, is the highest authority in all law mat-ters ; but there are also many Christians belonging to the Greek and Armenian churches. The ruler of Turkey is called the Sultan. He is often very despotic, and, even when he is not, his officers oppress the people terribly, laying such heavy taxes that most of them are kept miserably poor. As they have no good schools, they are also very ignorant. Owing to these causes, Turkey is not at all prosperous ; it has few manufactures, and the government itself is so deeply in debt that it is doubtful if it ever will pay what it owes.

The Turks first lived in Turkistan. but the Ottoman Empire was founded by OTHMAN, who, in 1299, conquered the city of Nicæa, 54 miles S.E. of Constantinople. His successors gradually overran the EASTERN EMPIRE, and under Mohammed II. finally destroyed it by taking Constantinople (May 29, 1453). The Turks also conquered Greece, Egypt, Assyria, Syria, Mesopotamia, and part of Austria; Tunis and Tripoli were subject to them, and they became one of the most powerful nations in the world. The Mediterranean was covered with their war ships, called galleys, and they became the terror of all Christian nations. But they soon became indolent and weak, and lost their military skill. In the sixteenth and seventeenth centuries they were worsted in wars with Austria and Russia; the Greeks rebelled and became independent (1829), and there were several bloody civil wars. The Russians ever since the time of Peter the Great have been trying to take Constantinople, but the other nations of Europe think that would make Russia too powerful for their own safety, and to prevent it they have helped Turkey with fleets and armies. By this means the Russians were conquered in the war in the Crimea (1855); but in 1877, when the people of Northern European Turkey rebelled, the Russians helped them, and their armies marched across Turkey and besieged Constantinople. The city would have fallen if the other nations had not interfered again. The Russians finally made peace, but by the treaty of Berlin (1878) Turkey lost a good deal of territory in Asia, while the half-independent states of BULGARIA and Eastern ROUMELIA was made out of part of the rest of Turkey in Europe; Bosnia and Herzegovina were given to Austria, and Roumania, Servia, and Montenegro

each got some more territory. So that Turkey in Europe is now only about 62,000 square miles, or smaller than the State of Missouri, while Turkey in Asia contains about 710,-000 square miles, or about eleven times as large as Turkey in Europe.

TUR-KIS'TAN, a country of W. Asia, E. of the Caspian Sea, and N. of Persia and Afghanistan. The eastern part is mountainous, but the western part consists of plains or steppes. Many of the people belong to wandering tribes, called Kirghiz; those who live in town are called Sarts. They are all Mohammedans, and their language resembles the Persian. Most of the country itself is unproductive, but a large trade is carried on by caravans with India, Russia, Persia, and China. Turkistan was so called from the Turks, who formerly lived there, as some of their descendants do now. It was also called Independent Tartary. It was gradually conquered by the Russians, who in 1876 made it into a separate government.

TUR'NER, Joseph Mallord William, a famous English painter, born in London, April 23, 1775. He was the son of a hairdresser, and when a youth was employed by an engraver to color prints. Afterward he became famous, especially for his paintings of rivers, the sea, and ships, and many persons considered him the greatest of English landscape painters. Among his best-known pictures are " The Fighting Temeraire Towed to her Last Moorings," "The Bay of Baiæ," " The Sun Rising through a Mist," and " The Slave Ship." The last is owned in America. Some of his books of engravings, such as the "Rivers of England" and the " Rivers of France," are as famous as his paintings. Turner never married, and he was very eccentric, often disappearing for months together, so that no one knew where he was. He died in Chelsea, when seventy-six years old (Dec. 19, 1851).

TUS·CA·RO'RAS. See AMERI-
CAN INDIANS.

TUS'CU·LUM, an ancient city of
Italy, on a mountain about nine
miles E. of Rome. Many of the
Roman emperors, nobles, and rich
people had villas there, and their
ruins can still be seen. The modern town of Frascati is on the
mountain side about two miles from
the site of Tusculum.

TY'LER, John, tenth President of
the United States, born in Charles
City County, Va., March 29, 1790.
He was educated at William and
Mary College, and became a success-

John Tyler.

ful lawyer. When only twenty-one
years old he was sent to the State
Legislature, and served five times,
and in 1816 went to Congress. He
served in the Legislature again in
1823, then became governor of Virginia, and in 1827 was elected to
the Senate of the United States. In
1840 he was chosen Vice-President
when General Harrison was elected
President ; and one month later, by
the death of Harrison, he became
President himself. During his ad-
ministration Texas was brought into
the Union. After leaving the
White House he did not hold any
public office again until 1861 when

he was president of a convention
that met at Washington to make
some arrangements for preventing
the war between the North and
South. As no agreement for peace
could be made, he took sides with
the South, and became a member of
the Confederate Congress at Rich
mond, where he died, when nearly
seventy-two years old (Jan. 17,1862).

TYN'DALE, William, an English
reformer and translator of the Bible,
born about 1484. He was educated
at Oxford, and then became a priest
at Cambridge. He embraced the
doctrines of Luther, and spoke so
boldly in their favor that he was
turned out of the priesthood and
obliged at last to flee from England.
He went to Germany, where he met
Luther and other reformers, and
translated the New Testament,
which was printed, at first without a
name, at Worms in 1535. This was
the first printed edition of any part
of the Scriptures in English. I was
sent to England, and was gladly
welcomed by the people ; but the
priests caused all the copies they
could get hold of to be publicly
burned, and forbade the sale or use
of them. Tyndale next began to
translate the Old Testament ; but
while at work on it he was seized
and thrown into prison through the
influence of Henry VIII. of England. According to a law for the
punishment of heretics, he was
strangled and then burned, at Vil-
voorden, in Brabant (Oct. 6, 1536).

TYN'DALL, John, a noted British
natural philosopher, born in Ireland, Aug. 21, 1820. When a young
man he was first a surveyor, and
afterward a railway engineer ; then
became a teacher in Queenwood
College, and in 1847 went to Germany to attend lectures on science.
While there he made discoveries
in magnetism (C.C.T., 373, II., l.)
which made him well known. In
1856 he went to Switzerland with
Professor Huxley and made studies
of the glaciers, or ice-rivers of the

Alps, about which he published several books. He has also studied heat and light, and settled some important questions that have been disputed by others. He visited the United States in 1872 and lectured in different cities, giving all the money which he made ($15,000) to form a fund for the aid of American students of science. He has written many valuable books, and was an authority in all scientific matters. He died when seventy-four years old (December 4, 1893).

TY'PHON, in Greek fable, a horrible monster with a head reaching to the stars, eyes which shot forth fire, and hands extending from the east to the west, on which were a hundred snakes instead of fingers. Huge snakes were also twisted about his body. He fought against the gods, and Jupiter at last conquered him and buried him under Mount Ætna, where he was thought to be constantly striving to lift himself, and sending forth flames from his mouth. He was the father of Chimæra, Cerberus, and the Sphinx.

TYRE, the largest city of ancient PHŒNICIA, on the Mediterranean Sea. In the Bible it is sometimes called the "daughter of Sidon," because it was founded by the Sidonians, whose city lay 23 miles north of it. It was built at first on the mainland, but afterward it extended to an island near the shore, and this finally became the most important part of the city. Tyre was defended by strong walls and castles, and it had many rich temples and palaces. Its ships sailed to all parts of the Mediterranean, and even to Britain.

Carthage and many other cities were founded by its people. Tyre was besieged by the Assyrians under Sargon for five years, and afterward by Nebuchednezzar for thirteen years, but neither of them could take the island part. Alexander the Great finally captured it by building an embankment or mole from the mainland to the island. Alexander burned the city, but he afterward rebuilt it, though it never became as important as it had been. Tyre was finally destroyed by an earthquake in the 13th century. At present there is only a little village called Sur on the site, and hardly anything remains of the magnificent city. The mole built by Alexander has been increased by ruins and rubbish until it has changed the island into a peninsula.

TYROL (*tir'rol*), the most westerly part of Austria, lying next to Switzerland and Italy; area, 11,325 square miles, or about as large as Maryland; pop. 810,000, or not quite four fifths that of Maryland. The Alps lie partly in Tyrol, and the scenery there is as grand and picturesque as in Switzerland. About two thirds of the people speak the German language, and the rest are Italians. Tyrol has belonged sometimes to Austria and sometimes to Bavaria, but the people always look upon themselves as Austrians, and they are very patriotic. In 1809, when their country had been given to Bavaria, they rebelled under Andreas HOFER, women and men fighting together until hundreds were killed. Since 1814 Tyrol has been a part of Austria.

U

UHLAND (*oo'lahnt*), **Johann Ludwig,** a German poet, born in Tübingen, April 26, 1787. His two plays "Duke Ernest of Swabia" and "Louis the Bavarian" are interesting, but his chief fame comes from his patriotic songs and ballads. He died in Tübingen when seventy-five years old (Nov. 13, 1862).

ULM, a city of Germany, in Würtemberg, on the river Danube, 45 miles S.E. of Stuttgart ; pop. 34,000, or about as large as Youngstown, Ohio. It is a quaint old city with many curious buildings, among which are several fine palaces and the Ulm Cathedral, one of the most magnificent churches in Germany. The city library is one of the oldest in Germany and has in it many rare manuscripts. Ulm is defended by strong walls and forts and is an important military post. The Austrian Gen. Mack, with 23,000 men, surrendered there to Napoleon (Oct. 20, 1805).

ULYSSES (*u-lis'seez*), or **Odysseus** (*o-dis'soos*), King of Ithaca, one of the Greek leaders in the war against TROY. His wife was Penelope, and they had a son named Telemachus. Ulysses did not want to go to the war, and to avoid it made believe that he was crazy and plowed the sand on the beach. Palamedes found out the trick by putting Telemachus, then a baby, in the furrow, for Ulysses turned aside his plow so as not to hurt his son. So Ulysses went with twelve ships to Troy, where he greatly aided the Greeks by his valor, skill, and wisdom. After the death of Achilles, Ulysses and Ajax became rivals for his armor, which was offered as a prize to the greatest soldier, and Ulysses won it. He helped Diomedes to carry off from Troy the Palladium, or wooden statue of Minerva which

Jupiter threw down from heaven, and he is said to have invented the wooden horse by which Troy was taken, and was one of the warriors hidden inside of it. After the destruction of Troy he sailed for home with his twelve ships, but met with many wonderful adventures before reaching it. His voyage, which took ten years, is the subject of the Odyssey of Homer. His ships were first driven to the land of the Lotophagi (Lotus-eaters), where the people gave some of his sailors lotus fruit, of which whoever eats cares not to see wife or children or country again. The sailors, when they had eaten it, said they would not sail any more ; but Ulysses bade his companions bind them and carry them to the ships, and so they all escaped. They next visited the land of the Cyclops, where they entered the Cave of POLYPHEMUS, a giant twenty feet high, who ate six of them. Ulysses made him drunk with wine, put out his one eye, and escaped with the rest of his companions and again set sail. Polyphemus, who was the son of Neptune, prayed his father to stir up the sea, and so they had a very stormy voyage afterward. When they reached the island of Æolus, that god gave Ulysses a bag filled with the right wind to take him home, but some of his men opened it without his knowledge and the ships were driven back again. A visit to the country of the cannibal Læstrygones ended in the loss of all his ships but one. After that he visited CIRCE, went by the island of the SIRENS in safety, and passed between Scylla and Charybdis with the loss of six of his companions. Soon after his vessel was struck by lightning and all on board drowned excepting Ulysses, who was carried to the island of Ogygia, where the nymph Calypso lived. Calypso promised him immortality if he would marry her, but after a stay of several years he escaped on a raft, and finally, after an absence of twenty years, reached Ithaca alone and disguised as a beggar. He found his palace filled with suitors who were seeking the hand of his wife, but he slew them all with the aid of Minerva and Telemachus, and thus released PENELOPE from her troubles.

UNCAS (*ung'kas*), a North American Indian, chief of the Mohegan tribe, in Connecticut. He was first a chief of the Pequot tribe; but he rebelled against Sassacus, the sachem (1634), left the Pequots, and became chief of the Mohegans. In 1637 he helped the English in a war against the Pequots, and received part of their lands as a reward. The Indians made war upon him several times, but with the help of the English he always defeated them. In 1643 he defeated and took prisoner the Narragansett sachem Miantonomoh, and killed him. Many complaints were made of his cruelty and injustice, and he is said to have been a very wicked man. He was very old when he died (about 1680).

UNITED STATES OF AMERICA, a country of North America; area, with ALASKA, 3,603,884 square miles, or about seven eighths as large as the Chinese Empire and nearly half as large as the British Empire; pop. about 62,622,000, or less than one sixth that of China; capital, WASHINGTON. The western part is crossed from N.N.W. to S.S.E. by two great mountain chains, the Rocky Mountains and the Sierra Nevada (Snowy Range). Each of these ranges has peaks more than two miles and a half high, and between them lies a great table-land, crossed by many lesser mountain chains. The Alleghany Mountains, in the Eastern United States, run from N.E. to S.W., and are divided into many minor chains, the highest peaks being about a mile and a quarter above the sea. Between the Rocky Mountains and the Alleghanies is a great plain, crossed by many rivers, most of which flow into the Mississippi. The mountain regions abound in wild and beautiful scenery, the Yellowstone National Park and the Yosemite Valley being among the grandest regions in the world. Among other great natural curiosities are Niagara Falls, the Mammoth, Wyandotte, and Weyer's Caves, and the deep cañons, or ravines, through which the Colorado and other western rivers flow. The climate of the Northern United States is very variable, the winters being cold and stormy, while some of the summer weather is even warmer than that of the tropics. In the Southern States the climate is much more equable, and in Florida and Texas it is very mild.

The United States excels all other countries in the extent of its beds of coal, in its petroleum wells and salt springs, and in the richness of its mines of gold, silver, copper, lead, mercury, iron, and many other metals. Most of the gold, silver, and mercury is found among the western mountains, while coal, iron, and petroleum abound most in the central and eastern parts, copper near Lake Superior, and lead near the Mississippi River. Granite, marble, and other fine building stones are quarried in many places. Almost the only sterile parts of the country are between the Rocky Mountains and the Sierra Nevada, where are large tracts which cannot be cultivated, and others which have to be artificially watered.

The great central plain is one of the most fertile regions in the world, and more corn and wheat are raised there than in any other country, so that great quantities are sold to other nations. Cotton and sugar-cane are cultivated in the Southern States, more cotton being sold there than in any other part of the world. The forests abound in oak, pine, cedar, maple, walnut, and many other valuable timbers, and hundreds of ship-loads of them are sent to other nations every year. Great droves of cattle are pastured in Texas and other south-western States, and cows, horses, and sheep are plentiful almost everywhere. Among wild animals are black and grizzly bears, the puma or American panther, and several kinds of deer. Buffaloes, formerly found in immense numbers, are nearly extinct.

In manufactures the United States excels all other nations, except England, France, and Germany. The principal manufacturing cities are in the north-eastern part, where are hundreds of rolling-mills and other iron-works, cotton and woolen factories, flour and saw mills, petroleum and sugar refineries, and manufactories of clothing, boots and shoes, hardware, cutlery, machinery, locomotives, railroad-cars, and many other things. This part of the United States is also the most thickly inhabited, and it has the largest trade.

The United States consists of forty-four States, six Territories, and the district of Columbia. Each of the States chooses its own governor and other officers, and a legislature which makes its laws. On this account the laws are often different in the various States. The territories are thinly settled regions, each of which has a governor and secretary appointed by the President of the United States, and a legislature chosen by the people. When they become populous enough, Congress generally admits them as States into the Union. The Congress of the United States consists of a Senate and House of Representatives. The Senate is composed of two members from each State, who are chosen by the State legislatures, and serve for six years. The House of Representatives has 332 members, divided among the States according to their population, and chosen by the votes of the people for two years. Congress can make laws about the army and navy, the national debt, or any other thing which affects the whole nation, but it cannot change the State laws. The President and Vice President of the United States are chosen for four years, by what is called the Electoral College, to which each State sends as many members as it has senators and representatives in Congress. These electors are chosen by the votes of the people in the different States. Generally there are two great political parties, each of which tries to get the more electors, and thus choose the President. The President is commander-in-chief of the army and navy, and he has the power to appoint, with the consent of the Senate, all ambassadors, ministers, and consuls, judges of the Supreme Court, and most other officers of the United States. The President also appoints, with the consent of the Senate, a cabinet of seven officers, as follows: 1. A Secretary of State, who arranges the business of the United States with foreign nations; 2. A Secretary of the Treasury, who attends to the finances and the coining of money; 3. A Secretary of the Interior, who oversees the public lands and mines, and has charge of patents, government publications, asylums and hospitals, and the Indian tribes; 4. A Secretary of War, who has charge of the army; 5. A Secretary of the Navy, who has charge of government ships; 6. An Attorney-general, who is the principal government lawyer; 7. A Postmaster-general, who has charge of post-offices and mails. If Congress votes for a law, the President can veto it —that is, he can send it back to Congress within ten days, without signing it, at the same time stating his objections to it. If Congress votes for it again, it still becomes a law, notwithstanding the veto. In case the President dies, resigns, or is unable to fulfill the duties of his office, the Vice President takes his place.

The land now included in the United States was settled at different times by several European nations. The southern part, including Florida, New Mexico and California, was colonized by the Spaniards; the French settled in Louisiana, along the Mississippi River, and in Illinois and Michigan; the Swedes had colonies in Delaware; the Dutch in New York and New Jersey; and the English took possession of other parts of the Atlantic coast. The Dutch and Swedish colonies were afterwards driven out by the English, who also had several wars with the French colonists. In 1754 a bloody war broke out between the English and French, which was called the French and Indian war, because the French employed Indian tribes to help them. This war lasted until 1769, and ended in the surrender of the French settlements in Canada and north of the Ohio River to the English. Thus, the English gained possession of all of Eastern North America north of Florida and Louisiana. The portion now included in the United States was divided into thirteen colonies, called New Hampshire, Massachusetts, Rhode Island, Connecticut, New York, New Jersey, Delaware, Pennsylvania, Maryland, Virginia, North Carolina, South Carolina, and Georgia. These colonies were like States, except that the governors and principal officers were appointed by the King of England. The English government oppressed the colonies with heavy taxes and severe laws, and finally the colonists rebelled. The war of the Revolution, which followed, lasted for seven years (1775 to 1782), the Americans being commanded by Gen. Washington. Soon after it commenced, a congress of the colonies, which had met in Philadelphia, signed the Declaration of Independence, in which they declared that the colonies were no longer subject to the King of England (July 4, 1776). The American armies were badly armed and equipped, and were often beaten, but they kept up their courage to the end. During the last years of the war, France became an ally of the Americans, helping them with armies and fleets, and finally the English gave up the struggle.

In 1787 the Constitution of the United States was prepared, and the thirteen colonies (now called States) soon agreed to it, and Washington was chosen the first President (1789). Gradually other States were admitted to the Union, as they became settled, and in 1803 Louisiana, which then included all the country not belonging to Spain west of the Mississippi River and south of the British possessions, was purchased of France. In 1812 a second war broke out between England and the United States, but it was ended by a treaty of peace in 1815. In 1819 Spain ceded Florida to the United States, and in 1845 Texas, which had separated from Mexico, was admitted to the Union. This led to a war with Mexico (1846–47), in which the United States were successful, and the Mexicans compelled to give up New Mexico and California to their conquerors.

Until the present century slaves were kept in some of the Northern States, but slavery was soon abolished everywhere except in the Southern States. The southern people wished to take their slaves into the territories, and most of the northern people were opposed to their doing so. This and other questions about slavery led to a quarrel between the North and the South, and the Southern States separated from the Union, forming a republic which they called the Confederate States of America. A bloody Civil War followed which lasted for four years (1861 to 1865), in which thousands of soldiers were killed on both sides. On Jan. 1, 1863, President Lincoln declared all slaves to be free, and the Confederates being finally conquered, slavery ceased to exist in the United States. The Southern States were soon re-admitted to the Union, and in 1870 the right to vote was given to the negroes. In 1867 Alaska was purchased of Russia. In 1876 the people of the United States celebrated the one hundredth year of their independence with great rejoicings.

UP'SAL or **Upsala** (*up-sah'lah*), a city of Sweden. on the river Sala, 40 miles N.N.W. of Stockholm; pop. 22,000, or about as large as Fitchburg, Mass. It contains the principal Swedish university, which was founded in 1477 and was enriched by Gustavus Adolphus. It has 100 professors and teachers, and nearly 3000 students, with very fine museums and a library. Upsal has fine parks and buildings and the most celebrated cathedral in Sweden.

Upsala (Upsalr) means the high halls. It is said that ODIN had his capital near Upsala. In ancient times the kings were elected there, the warriors lifting them on great stones and afterwards engraving their names and the date of their election on other stones, which were set up in a field called the Mora Meadow. These stones can still be seen there.

URAL (*yoo'ral*) **MOUNTAINS,** a chain of mountains between Europe and Asia, separating European Russia and Siberia. Only a few of them are as much as a mile above the sea, and only the most northern part of the range is covered with snow in summer. The land slopes so gently that the Urals would hardly be called mountains except for the great

plains on each side of them. The mountains are clothed with pine forests, and on the eastern side are many rich mines of gold, platinum, copper, and iron. Diamonds, emeralds, and other precious stones are also found in the Urals.

URANIA (*u-ra'ne-ah*). See MUSES.

U'RA-NUS, the ancient Greek god of heaven. He was the husband of Gæa or Terra (Earth) and the father of Oceanus, Cronus or Saturn, the Cyclops, and the Titans. The Romans called him Cœlus (Heaven).

URUGUAY (*oo'roo-gwi*), a country of South America, on the Atlantic coast, S. of Brazil; area 65,000 square miles, or about as large as Missouri; pop 648,000, or less than a fourth that of Missouri; capital MONTEVIDEO. It is covered with grassy plains or pampas, crossed here and there by ranges of wooded hills. Immense herds of cattle are raised on the plains, and their hides and tallow are the principal things sent to other countries. Half of the people are white foreigners, and the rest are mixed races, with a few negroes; the Indians are entirely gone. The government is a republic much like that of the United States. Uruguay was first settled by Jesuit missionaries in 1622. The country was held sometimes by Spain and sometimes by Portugal, but in 1821 it was united to Brazil. It became independent in 1828.

UTAH (*yoo'taw*), a territory of the United States, between Colorado and Nevada; area 84,000 square miles, or about as large as Minnesota; pop. 208,000, or less than a sixth that of Minnesota; capital, SALT LAKE CITY. The Wahsatch Mountains cross the country from north to south. East of them is a dry plain, through which the rivers flow in ravines or cañons, which, in some places, are more than a mile deep, and have rocky sides like walls. West of the mountains most of the rivers flow into the Great Salt Lake and other lakes near it, which have no outlet to the sea. The water of these lakes is so salt that fish cannot live in it, and so dense that a man can float on the surface with his head and feet above water.

Utah has mines of gold, silver, and a kind of soft coal. It is richer in iron than any other part of the United States, but as yet only a few iron mines have been worked. Salt is got from the Great Salt Lake, and also from mines of rock salt. The waters of other lakes contain borax, alum, and soda, and there are large beds of sulphur. In eastern Utah most of the land is too dry for planting, and in the western part many of the farms are watered from the rivers.

Most of the people of Utah are Mormons, or believers in the Book of Mormon, said to have been found by Joseph Smith. They allow a man to have many wives, and have other strange doctrines, taught by Joseph Smith and by Brigham Young, who, until lately, was their leader. Formerly the Mormons were settled at Nauvoo, Illinois, but in 1845 they were driven away from there and went to Utah. In 1849 they wanted to have their country made a State of the Union, but Congress would not allow this, so it was made into a Territory, and named after the Utah or Ute Indians who lived there.

UTICA (*u'te-kah*), an ancient city of the Phœnicians, in Northern Africa, not far from the present city of Tunis. It is said to have been founded 287 years before CARTHAGE, which was near it. After the fall of Carthage the Roman governors of Northern Africa lived in Utica. It was destroyed by the Arabs in the 7th century. Among the ruins, which can still be seen, are great reservoirs where water was stored during sieges, and an immense amphitheatre with an artificial lake on which mimic naval battles were shown.

UTICA (*u'te-kah*), a city of central New York, on the Mohawk River, 83 miles W.N.W. of Albany; pop. 44,000, or nearly as large as Hoboken, N. J. It has a large trade, and contains engine and machinery works, iron and brass foundries, and many other important manufactories. In the country around Utica more cheese is made than in any other part of the United States. One of the New York State Lunatic Asylums is there. In 1758 a fort called Fort Schuyler was built on the site of Utica, which was then a wilderness. A village sprung up around it, and in 1798 this was named Utica, after ancient Utica. It became a city in 1832.

UTRECHT (*yoo'trekt*), a city of the Netherlands, on the old Rhine, 20 miles S.E. of Amsterdam; pop. 85,000, or a little larger than Worcester, Mass. It is defended by strong forts, but the city walls have been turned into a carriage drive and promenade. The building used for government offices is called the "Pope's House," because it was built by Pope Adrian VI., who was born in Utrecht in 1459. Utrecht contains a celebrated university which is attended by 500 students and has a botanical garden, fine museums, and a library. It has large manufactures of plush (called Utrecht velvet), carpets, cotton, silk, linen, and woolen cloths, and cigars, and many books are printed there.

Utrecht is the oldest city in the Netherlands. The Romans called it Ultrajectum, which means beyond the ford, and this name has changed to Utrecht. The republic called the United Netherlands was formed at Utrecht in 1579, and in 1713 a great treaty of peace was signed there by ambassadors from nearly all the countries of Europe. This was called the Peace of Utrecht.

V

VALENCIA (*vah-len'she-ah*), a city of E. Spain, on the river Guadalquivir, near its mouth in the Mediterranean; pop. 171,000, or twice as large as Worcester, Mass. The older part is surrounded by a high wall and the streets within it are narrow and dark, but the new city outside of the walls is very fine. Along the river shore is a broad quay planted with shade trees, and a beautiful avenue called the Alameda leads to the port on the sea. Among the buildings is a fine cathedral, some portions of which are 600 years old. Valencia has a university, large museums and picture galleries, and the finest botanical garden in Spain. The port is a very fine one, protected from the sea by two great walls or moles, one of which is more than a mile long. Probably more oranges are sent from Valencia than from any other place in the world, and there is also a large trade in silk, wine, nuts, and raisins. The city has manufactures of silk, linen, and woolen goods, hats, gloves, and fans. Valencia was a town 2000 years ago. It became a colony of the Romans (138 B.C.) and was called by them Valentia (the powerful), and has ever since kept the name.

VALENCIENNES, (*vah-long-se-en'*), a town of N. France, on the river Scheldt; pop. 28,000, or nearly as large as Pawtucket, R. I. It is defended by a fortress on an island in the river. One fourth of all the coal mined in France is dug near the city, and there are important manufactures of linen, muslins, beet sugar, and gold and silver tissue. It was once famous for the manufacture of a kind of lace called Valenciennes, but not much is made now.

Valenciennes is a very old place, and is said to have been named after the Emperor Valentinian.

VA'LENS, a Roman emperor of the East, born about A.D. 328. He was made emperor of the East by his brother VALENTINIAN I., in March, 364. His reign was disturbed by revolts which the Goths aided. They were for a time put down; but before long trouble arose again between the Goths and the Romans in Greece, and in a battle near Adrianople the Romans were defeated. Valens escaped by night to a hut, which was set on fire, and he was burned to death (Aug. 9, 378).

VAL'EN-TINE, Saint, a bishop living in the third century. He was beheaded at Rome in the reign of the Emperor Claudius, A.D. 270, and was soon declared a saint, the 14th of February being devoted to him. He was so noted for his love and charity that the custom of sending valentines on that day is supposed by some persons to have begun from that.

VAL-EN-TIN'I-AN I., Flavius, a Roman emperor, born in Pannonia (now Hungary), A.D. 321. He was of a good family and a Christian, and when forty-two years old became a captain in the guards of the Emperor JOVIAN. When Jovian died (364), the leaders of the army gave the throne to Valentinian. He made his brother VA-LENS emperor with him, giving him the East to rule, while he himself ruled the West. Valentinian proved to be one of the ablest of the emperors; he defended his country against the barbarians, and did much good to his people, but he was cruel and had a bad temper. While talking one day to some German ambassadors, he gave way to a fit of rage, broke a blood vessel, and died when fifty-four years old (Nov. 17, 375).

VALENTINIAN II., Flavius, a Roman emperor, son of the first Emperor Valentinian, born about 371. When his father died, he was only four years old, but the soldiers made his elder brother GRATIAN give him a part of his empire. When Gratian was killed, Valentinian became sole emperor, but he had much trouble, and was finally strangled in Gaul by one of his generals when twenty-one years old (392).

VALENTINIAN III., Placidius, a Roman emperor, born about 419. He was a grandson of THEODOSIUS THE GREAT, and came to the throne when only six years old (425). During the early part of his reign his mother ruled for him; and when he grew up he disgraced himself by every vice. In 454 he killed with his own hand the great general AËTIUS, the conqueror of ATTILA, of whom he had become jealous; and he was finally slain himself (455), when thirty-five years old, by a man whom he had injured.

VA-LE'RI-AN, Publius Licinius, a Roman emperor. He was descended from a noble Roman family, and by his talents and virtues rose to high honors. On the death of the Emperor Gallus, A.D. 253, Valerian was chosen by the soldiers to succeed him. He associated his son Gallienus with himself in the government. His reign was troubled by frequent invasions of the barbarian tribes in the west and the Persians in the east. In 260, as he was marching against the Persians, he was surrounded near Edusa, and taken prisoner. The Persians treated him with great cruelty: it is said that their king, Sapor, used him as a foot-stool whenever he mounted his horse. Valerian died in captivity, and after his death his skin was stuffed and kept in one of the Persian temples, as a trophy of their victory over the Romans.

VA-LE'RI-US COR'VUS, Marcus, a noted Roman general, born about 371 B.C. He is said to have got the name of Corvus (Latin for "crow") because he once killed a Gaul, who had challenged him to fight, with the aid of a crow, which perched upon his helmet and flapped its wings and pecked at the Gaul's face so that he could not see well. Valerius gained many victories over the enemies of Rome, and was chosen consul six times. He died when a hundred years old (271 B.C.).

VALETTA (*va-let'tah*). See MALTA.

VALHALLA (*vahl-hahl'lah*), in Scandinavian fable, the future home of the heroes who fell in battle. They were brought there by the warrior angels, the Valkyrs, who were daughters of Odin, and welcomed with great honors to a beautiful palace, where they spent their time in mock battles and feasting. A hero received greater honor if he brought many followers with him; therefore, when a leader fell, his comrades would often kill themselves, that they might be laid in the same grave with him. His horse, weapons, and treasures were also buried with him.

VAL-LA-DO-LID' (Spanish, *vahl-yah-do-leed'*), a city of N.W. Spain, on the Pisuerga River; pop. 62,000, or about as large as Wilmington, Del. It was once an important city, and was the capital of Spain in the time of CHARLES V. and PHILIP II., who adorned it with many fine buildings; but after Madrid was made the capital it fell into decay. The University of Valladolid, where law and medicine are studied, is more than 500 years old. There are manufactories of silks, laces, and paper, and the city has a large trade in grain.

VALOIS (*vahl-wah'*), **House of,** See CAPET.

VALPARAISO (*vahl-pah-ri'so*), a city of CHILI, on the bay of Valparaiso, 70 miles N.W. of SANTIAGO; pop. about 105,000, or not quite as large as Allegheny, Pa. Excepting Santiago, it is the largest city in Chili. It is built at the foot and on the sides of beautiful hills which surround the bay, and looks very fine from the sea. The bay, which is defended by fifteen forts, is one of the best harbors in the South Pacific, and many foreign merchant ships and men-of-war are always to be seen there. Valparaiso is one of the most enterprising places in South America, and has water and gas works, and lines of horse-cars, which are not found in all South American cities. It has been nearly destroyed several times by earthquakes.

Valparaiso means the "Valley of Paradise," a name given to it on account of the beauty of its site. It was founded in 1544.

VAN BU'REN, Martin, eighth President of the United States, born

Martin Van Buren.

at Kinderhook, New York, Dec. 5, 1782. He began to study law when only fourteen years old, and soon got into public life. He was surrogate of Columbia county in 1808, a member of the state senate in 1812, and for several years attorney-general of the State. He became known as a leader in political matters, was in the United States Senate in 1821, Governor of New York (1828), Secretary of State under President Jackson (1829), Minister to England (1831), and finally President of the United States in 1837. He served only one term, but was nominated again in 1848, and defeated by Gen. Taylor. He died at Kinderhook, when seventy-nine years old (July 24, 1862).

VANCOUVER (*van-koo'ver*) **ISLAND,** an island of the Dominion of Canada, on the Pacific coast of North America; area 18,000 square miles, or about half as large as the State of Maine; pop. about 25,000. The surface is mountainous, and the principal mineral is coal, much of which is sent to San Francisco. The chief city, Victoria, is the capital of British Columbia. Vancouver was first settled by the Spaniards, but in 1792 it was given up to the English navigator George Vancouver, after whom it was named.

VAN'DALS, an ancient branch of the Germans, generally considered the same as the Goths. They first appeared on the northern coasts of Germany, and in the 5th century A.D. passed through Germany and Gaul and over the Pyrenees into Spain, where they founded a kingdom called Vandalusia (now Andalusia). In 429 they crossed from Spain into Africa, under their leader Genseric, conquered the whole northern coast, and founded a kingdom with CARTHAGE for its capital. They conquered also Sicily, Sardinia, and Corsica, and in 455 took and plundered Rome. They were finally conquered by BELISARIUS (534) and their kingdom destroyed.

VANDAMME (*von-dam'*), **Dominique,** Count, a French soldier, born in Cassel, Flanders, Nov. 5,

1770. He fought in most of the campaigns of the French republic, the consulate, and the empire, and won great fame in Napoleon's victories, being present at Austerlitz, Eckmühl, and Waterloo. When Louis XVIII. was restored in 1815, Vandamme was banished, and he lived for four years in the United States. On his return to France, he was restored to his rank in the army. He died at Cassel when sixty-years old (July 15, 1830).

VAN-DYKE' or **Van Dyck'**, Sir **Anthony,** a famous Flemish painter, born in Antwerp, March 22,

Anthony Vandyke.

1599. He began to study art when eleven years old, was the best pupil of RUBENS, and finally became a better portrait painter than his teacher. When twenty-one years old he went to Italy and painted portraits in many cities, and finally won such fame that he was invited to England (1632) by King CHARLES I., who made him a knight and gave him a pension. He lived like a prince, and always went magnificently dressed and surrounded by many followers; but he worked very hard and painted a very large number of portraits, among them several

of the king and many others of the great men of the time. He died in London when only forty-two years old (Dec. 9, 1641), and was buried in St. Paul's Cathedral.

VANE, Sir **Henry,** an English statesman, Governor of Massachusetts, born in 1612. He was opposed to the English Church, and in 1635 came to America to join the Puritans in Massachusetts. The next year he was chosen governor; but religious troubles arose in the colony, and in 1637 he returned to England. In 1640 he was elected to Parliament and was knighted, although he was not a royalist. He was always opposed to Cromwell, who hated him and at one time imprisoned him, in the hope of frightening him into submission; but he was soon set free, and Cromwell tried in other ways to win him to his side; but Vane remained firm and true to his party. After the death of Cromwell, he was again elected to Parliament, and was the leader of the republican party. On the restoration of the king, Charles II., Vane was arrested and imprisoned; but the king promised to spare his life. Charles, however, broke his word, and Vane was tried on a charge of high treason and condemned to die. At the scaffold he tried to address the people; but his voice was drowned by the noise of drums and trumpets. He was beheaded on Tower Hill, London, when fifty years old (June 14, 1662).

VARNA (*var'nah*), a city and seaport of BULGARIA, on the Black Sea; pop. 25,000, or about as large as Auburn, N. Y. It is surrounded by walls, and has a fine harbor which is visited by many ships. A large trade is carried on in grain, wool, and tallow. About half the people are Christians, and the rest Mohammedans. Varna in Turkish means the fortress. It was an ancient Greek city called Odessus. It has been besieged many times.

King Ladislas of Poland was killed there in a battle against the Turks (1444).

VAR′RO, Marcus Terentius, a famous Roman poet and historian, born in Rome in 116 B.C. In the civil war between Cæsar and Pompey, he took the side of Pompey, until Pompey was finally defeated at Pharsalus, when he went to Rome and made his submission to Cæsar. After the death of Cæsar he went to one of his villas near Tusculum to spend the rest of his life in writing. His great wealth tempted Antony to put him on the list of those who were to be killed as enemies of his government; but Varro fled and hid himself for some time in a house which Antony is said to have often visited while he was concealed there. Octavius at last befriended him, and he went back to his villa, which with five or six more of his houses had been sacked and his large library burned. He wrote most of his works, nearly all of which are lost, after he was eighty years old. He died when about eighty-eight years old (28 B.C.)

VASA (*vah′sah*), **Gustavus.** See GUSTAVUS I.

VAS′CO DA GAMA (*gah′mah*). See GAMA.

VAUBAN (*vo-bon′*), **Sebastien Leprestre,** Marquis de, a famous French military engineer, born in Burgundy, May 15, 1633. He early won fame by his skill in conducting sieges during the wars of Louis XIV., and he made many improvements in the art of fortification. In 1703 he was made a marshal of France for his services. He wrote books on the art of attacking and of defending places. Vauban died in Paris when nearly seventy-four years old (March 30, 1707).

VED′DER, Elihu, an American painter, born in New York in February, 1836. His taste for art showed itself in early childhood. Among his works are "The Lair of the Sea-Serpent," an "Arab

listening to the Sphinx," and a "Crucifixion." He lives in Rome.

VEGA (*va′gah*), **Lope de,** a famous Spanish play-writer, born in Madrid, Nov. 25, 1562. The family name of this writer was Carpio, the name Vega being taken from that of his father's estate. After finishing his studies he became secretary of a Spanish nobleman, for whom he wrote his first poem, "Arcadia." In 1588 he went as a soldier on the great fleet called the Armada against England. After he had twice been a widower, he became a monk of the order of St. Francis. But whatever place he held, he always wrote, and the number of his works is wonderful, including eighteen hundred plays and other poems. Great honors were paid him, and the whole nation loved him. When he died he had a splendid funeral, the services lasting nine days. He died in Madrid when nearly seventy-three years old (Aug. 26, 1635).

VELASQUEZ (*ve-las′kez*, Spanish *va-lahs′keth*), **Diego Rodriguez de Silva y,** a famous Spanish painter, born in Seville in 1599. His parents, who were of high birth but poor, gave their son a good education. He had much fondness for drawing, and though he had some instruction, he was really self-taught. He used to paint pictures of poor peasants; and we are told that he kept one lad for a study and painted him in a great many different ways. In this way he gained great skill in taking likenesses. When about twenty-four years old he was invited to Madrid, and made painter to Philip IV., of whom he painted many portraits, and was ever afterward the king's favorite. Charles I. of England, then Prince of Wales, happened to be in Madrid when Velasquez was there, and had his portrait painted by the great artist. Velasquez spent a year and a half in Italy, studying and painting. When he returned to Madrid, a painting-room was given him in the palace, of which Philip kept a key, that he might at pleasure see the artist at work. He went a second time to Italy, as the agent of the king, to collect works of art, and was received everywhere with attention and kindness. At Rome he painted portraits of many distinguished persons. He died in Madrid when sixty-one years old (Aug. 7, 1660), and was buried with magnificent ceremonies.

VENDÉE, La (*lah von-da'*), a department of France, originally a part of the old province of Poitou, its western coast bordering on the bay of Biscay. This department has always been famous for its loyalty to the ancient kings, which it signally displayed during the times of the French Revolution. The population of la Vendée was a simple race that clung with reverence to their king and their clergy, and to the church usages which had been dear to them from their youth. When their children were forced into the armies of the republic, to fight against all that they held sacred, an insurrection broke out which was not put down till the land had become a desert, and thousands of the inhabitants had wet the soil with their blood.

VENDOME (*von-dome'*), **Louis Joseph,** Duke de, a French general, born in Paris, July 1, 1654. He entered the army when eighteen years old, and having distinguished himself in many battles, was soon placed in command of large armies. In 1697 he captured Barcelona in Spain, and afterward defeated Prince Eugene in Italy at the battle of Cassano (1705). In 1708, he was defeated at the battle of Oudenarde, in Belgium, by Prince Eugene and MARLBOROUGH. He afterward fought for King Philip I. of Spain. He died in Spain when nearly fifty-eight years old (June 11, 1712).

VENEZUELA (*ven-e-zwe'lah*), **United States of,** a northern country of South America; area about 400,000 square miles, or twice as large as France; pop. about 2,234,-000, or about a seventeenth that of France; capital, CARÁCAS. The north-western part is mountainous, some of the peaks being nearly three miles high; in the south-eastern part are lower mountains, and the whole central portion is occupied by the great plains of the ORINOCO Valley.

The country contains mines of gold, silver, and copper, but these are little worked. Among the many wonderful trees is a kind of mimosa, which spreads its branches like an umbrella over a space of several hundred feet, and the cow tree, from which milk is obtained. Wild animals, such as jaguars and deer, are numerous. The climate is hot and unwholesome on the plains and by the sea shore, but cool and pleasant among the mountains. The people, who are mostly Indians and mixed races, are chiefly employed in farming and in cattle raising.

Venezuela is a republic, much like the United States, but it is badly governed, and there have been many civil wars.

The name Venezuela means "Little Venice," and the country was so called by the early voyagers from an Indian village built on piles in the water, which made them think of Venice. The country was discovered by Columbus in 1498. It belonged to Spain until 1819, when it was declared independent.

VENICE (*ven'iss*), a city of Italy, at the head of the Adriatic Sea; pop. 152,000, or twice as large as Nashville, Tenn. It is built on seventy-two small islands, connected by four hundred bridges. Between the islands are canals, which take the place of streets, and instead of using carriages and horse cars, the people sail about in black boats called gondolas. At night, when

The Rialto, Venice.

the city is lighted by lamps, the dark waters and moving gondolas are wonderfully beautiful. The principal canal, called the Canal-azzo, is crossed by the Rialto, a wide bridge with three passages, which are lined with shops. The most beautiful part of Venice is St. Mark's Place, which contains a splendid cathedral, the Palace of the Doges, or ancient rulers of the city, and many other fine buildings. The bronze horses of St. Mark, which stand over the cathedral door, were brought from Constantinople in the time of the Crusades, and they are so natural that they seem to be alive. Back of the Doges' Palace is a canal, beyond which is a prison. People who were condemned by the Doges passed from the palace to the prison by a bridge, called the Bridge of Sighs. Venice is cele-brated for its beautiful glass ware, and it also has manufactories of iron and bronze work, machines, silver ware, and mosaics.

Venice was first settled about the year 475, by Italian fugitives, who fled from the invasion of ATTILA, and sought a retreat on these islands. For hundreds of years it was the most splendid city of Europe, and all the commerce of the East centered there. In 1797 the city lost its independence, and after changing rulers many times, it was annexed to Italy in 1866.

VE'NUS, the Roman goddess of love and beauty, known to the Greeks by the name of Aphrodite (from *aphros*, the scum of the sea). She was supposed to have sprung from the foam of the sea, and landed first at Cythera, whence she went to Cy-prus, and these two isl-ands were the chief places of her worship. Many of the gods wished to marry her; but Vulcan became her husband. She was more beautiful than any other goddess, and Paris awarded to her the golden apple, the prize of beauty. She was the mother of Æneas, the Trojan hero, and of Cupid, the god of love, who was her constant attendant.

Venus.

VERA CRUZ (*va'rah kroos*), a city of Mexico, on the Gulf of Mexico; pop. about 24,000, or nearly the same as that of Rockford, Ill. It is built on very low ground, and has a wall around it. About half a mile from the shore is an island on which is the famous Castle of San Juan de Ulloa, captured by Gen. Scott in 1847. The only harbor is the open space between the city and this island, and vessels lying in it are not very safe, yet Vera Cruz is the most important seaport of Mexico and has a large trade.

The whole name of the city is Villa Rica de Vera Cruz (Spanish for "Rich City of the True Cross"), which was given it by Cortez when he founded it in 1519.

VERDI (*ver'de*), **Giuseppe,** an Italian writer of music, born in the

Giuseppe Verdi.

Duchy of Parma, Italy, Oct. 9, 1814. His father was an innkeeper, too poor to have him properly instructed in music, but a rich man finally aided him, and he was enabled to study in Milan. His first opera was a failure, but in 1842 he brought out "Nabuco," which at once made him famous. Since then he has written many beautiful operas, among them

"Ernani," "Rigoletto," "Il Trovatore," "La Traviata," and "Aida." Once, when one of his operas was played in Venice, he was escorted to and from the theatre by a triumphal procession, and offered a golden crown. At present he is a senator of the kingdom of Italy.

VER-MONT', one of the New England States of the United States, between New York and New Hampshire; area 10,200 square miles, or about a tenth less than that of Maryland; pop. 332,000, or a little more than a third that of Maryland; capital, MONTPELIER. It is hilly, and is crossed from north to south by the Green Mountains, so called because covered with green fields and woods. Among the hills are many little lakes, and beautiful glens and waterfalls, which are often visited by travelers. In 1810 the people wanted to turn the water of one of the lakes, called Long Pond, which then flowed into the Lamoille River, into the Barton River, which empties into Lake Memphremagog. So they dug a new channel; but as soon as the water began to run through it, it dug a channel for itself faster than they could, and in a few minutes all the water rushed out together in a wave as high as a house, which never stopped until it reached Lake Memphremagog, twenty-seven miles distant. The place where the lake was is now called "Runaway Pond."

Vermont has very fine quarries of marble and slate. Most of the land is not very good for grain, but it is excellent for pastures. Maple trees are plentiful, and more maple sugar is made there than in any other State. The winters are very cold.

The name Vermont is made from *Verd Mont*, two French words meaning Green Mountain; and in English it is often called the "Green Mountain State." Vermont was first settled by whites in 1724. Before the war of the Revolution it was claimed by New York, but the people, led by Ethan ALLEN and Seth Warner, formed themselves into bands called "Green Mountain Boys" and drove off the New York officers. The quarrel was not settled until after the Revolution, and Vermont did not become a State of the Union until 1791.

VERNE, Jules, a noted French writer of romances, born at Nantes, Feb. 8, 1828. He studied law, and afterwards wrote several plays; but he is best known for his romances, which are stories of impossible adventures, written in such a plausible manner, that the reader almost

Jules Verne.

thinks they are true. All of these books have been translated into English and other languages, and they are much read in the United States. Among them are "Around the World in Eighty Days," "Five Weeks in a Balloon" (telling about a balloon voyage across Africa), "From the Earth to the Moon," "Twenty Thousand Leagues under the Sea," "The Mysterious Island,"

and "Captain Hatteras" (describing a voyage to the North Pole).

VERNET (*ver-na'*), **Jean Émile Horace,** commonly called Horace Vernet, a famous French painter, born in Paris, June 30, 1789. He was the son of Carle Vernet, also a distinguished painter, and from him he learned to paint battle scenes, for which he became famous. He also made many pictures of Arab life, which he had studied in Algiers. Vernet died in Paris, when seventy-three years old (Jan. 17, 1863).

VER'NON, Edward, a noted English admiral, born in Westminster, Nov. 12, 1684. He entered the navy when very young, and became a rear-admiral when only twenty-four years old (1708). In 1739 he was sent against the Spanish city of Porto Bello in New Granada, which he had declared could be captured with six ships. The English government did not believe that he could do this, and only let him make the attempt to satisfy the people, who liked Vernon very much, but he really did take the city with six men-of-war. In 1741 he was sent with a large fleet and army against Carthagena, but he was repulsed and thousands of his men died of wounds and sickness. Lawrence Washington, eldest brother of George Washington, was with Admiral Vernon on this expedition, and he liked him so much that he named his house on the Potomac Mount Vernon. Admiral Vernon died at his home in Suffolk, when nearly seventy-three years old (Oct. 29, 1757).

VERONA (*va-ro'nah*), a city of N.E. Italy, on the River Adige, 62 miles W. of Venice; pop, 61,000, or about as large as Troy, N. Y. It is very strongly fortified and is surrounded by walls, some parts of which are nearly 1500 years old. The city is celebrated for its fine palaces, churches, and remains of ancient Roman buildings. Among the Roman remains is a splendid marble amphitheatre, built about the same time with the Colosseum at Rome, which would hold 22,000 people. A tomb, said to be that of Juliet, the heroine of Shakespeare's play of "Romeo and Juliet," is also pointed out, but the real tomb was destroyed long ago.

Verona was a city two thousand years ago. In the 13th and 14th centuries it was ruled by the Scala family. It afterward belonged to Milan and to Venice, and then to France and to Austria; but finally became a part of the kingdom of Italy in 1866.

VERRAZZANO (*ver-rad-zah'no*), **Giovanni da,** an Italian navigator, born near Florence about 1485. He was employed by the French government to make explorations, and some suppose that a ship, commanded by him, was the first French vessel that visited the coast of North America. Verrazzano became a famous corsair, and captured many Spanish and Portuguese ships, among others a ship which Cortez sent to Spain with more

Ruins of Roman Amphitheatre at Verona.

than $1,500,000 worth of treasures from Mexico. He was finally captured and executed at Puerto del Pico, Spain, when about forty-two years old (1527).

VERRES (*ver'reez*), a Roman governor, noted for his greed and cruelty. In the year 73 B.C. he was made governor of the rich province of Sicily, which he plundered for three years and stripped of its paintings, statues, and every public and private ornament, impoverishing the people more than years of war had done. The Sicilians had him brought to trial at Rome, and employed Cicero against him. The able lawyer Hortensius defended

him, and though many powerful nobles were his friends, no threats nor bribes could save him. Before the end of the trial Verres fled to Massilia (Marseilles), where he lived twenty-seven years in exile. His ill-gotten wealth was the cause of his death, for to get it Antony put him to death (43 B.C.).

VERSAILLES (*ver-saylz'*), a city of France, a few miles S.W. of Paris; pop. 50,000, or nearly as large as Los Angeles, Cal. Louis XIII. had a villa there, in which he used to live while hunting in the neighborhood. His son Louis XIV. built there the largest and most magnificent palace in France, and adorned it with so many paintings and statues that the whole country was made poor by their cost. It is said that Louis was afraid to let people know how great the expense really was, so he burned all the papers that related to it. The palace forms three sides of a great square, within and around which are splendid gardens and orange groves, with many fountains and several smaller palaces. To get more water for the fountains, an army of 40,000 men was employed in an attempt to bring the river Eure ninety miles to Versailles. Louis finally had to give up this plan after many of the soldiers had died, but even without the River Eure the fountains are the largest and finest in the world, and every Sunday, when they are in full play, thousands of people go from Paris to see them. Versailles was the residence of the French kings until the Revolution, and it is celebrated for many scenes of French history. During the Franco-German war, King William of Prussia lived in the palace, and it was there that he was declared Emperor of Germany (Jan. 18, 1871). Since 1875 Versailles has been the legal capital of France, and the French Congress meets there, but most of the government business is done in Paris.

VER·TUM'NUS, in Roman fable, the god who guarded the growth of plants in spring, the crops in summer, and the fruits in autumn. In order to gain the love of Pomona, the guardian of fruit trees, he disguised himself at one time as a fisherman, at another as a peasant, and in several other ways; but he did not succeed until he took the form of a handsome young man, when she married him.

VESPASIAN (*ves-pa'zhe-an*), Titus Flavius, a Roman Emperor, born Nov. 17, A.D. 9. He did not come from any of the great and ancient families of Rome, but was of common birth, and the first plebeian who ruled the Roman Em-

pire. He went into the army and served with distinction in Thrace, Britain, and Africa, and won rank and fame. In A.D. 66 he sent by Nero to conduct the war against the Jews in Palestine who had revolted from Roman authority. He marched into Judea with an army of 60,000 soldiers, and speedily conquered the entire province with the exception of Jerusalem. While finishing his plans for its conquest, Nero died and was quickly succeeded by the emperors Galba, Otho, and Vitellius. On the revolt of the Romans against

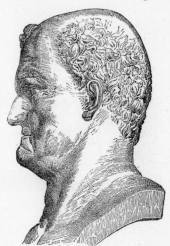

Vespasian.

Vitellius, Vespasian was proclaimed emperor by the armies of the East, and leaving his son Titus to conduct the siege of Jerusalem, he went to Rome. Vitellius had been driven out and killed by the soldiers, and in A.D. 70 Vespasian was recognized as emperor by the Senate and hailed by the people. He corrected the abuses and extravagance of the former emperors, framed just laws, lightened the burdens of the people, and a long time of peace and good government was given to Rome. He adorned the city with magnificent buildings, statues, fountains, and paintings, and firmly established his family on the throne. He died at Reate when nearly seventy years old (June 24, A.D. 79).

VESPUCCI (*ves-poot'che*), **Amer. igo,** an Italian navigator after whom America was named, born in Florence, March 9, 1451. Being sent to Seville, Spain, on business, he there met Columbus, and was so pleased with his accounts of new countries that he determined to fit out an expedition of discovery. He sailed from Spain in 1499, and reached the northern

Amerigo Vespucci.

coast of South America, which he explored for several hundred miles. In 1501 the King of Portugal sent him to explore the coast of Brazil, and in 1503 he commanded a ship in a Portuguese fleet which sailed for Malacca; his ship became separated from the rest and reached Brazil, where he discovered the Bay of All Saints, and built a fort on the coast. Returning from this voyage, he entered the service of Spain and was made Chief Pilot, with a large salary and the care of all maps and charts of new discoveries. He died at Seville, Spain, when nearly sixty-one years old (Feb. 22, 1512). In

a letter written in 1504, Vespucci claimed to have made a voyage to South America in 1497, which would make him the first discoverer of the mainland of America; but it appears that this letter was false. Vespucci probably had no intention of giving his name to America, that honor really belonging to his friend Columbus. The name Americi Terra (Land of Amerigo) was first used for America in a book published in 1507.

VESTA (*ves'tah*), the Roman goddess of the home or hearth, daughter of Saturn and Rhea. Her brother, Jupiter, gave her permission not to marry, and she was allowed to receive the first share of all sacrifices. She was the special

Vesta.

guardian of houses, and hearths were held sacred to her. In her temples a fire was kept constantly burning before the altar, and was tended by virgins, who were called vestals. At first there were four of these vestals; but afterwards their number was increased to six. Their chief duty was to watch the fire by turns, day and night, for if it was allowed to go out, it was thought an omen of terrible evil. If by any chance it went out, it was rekindled either by rubbing pieces of wood together or by means of a burning-glass. The vestals were selected between the ages of six and ten years, and were made to take a vow to remain unmarried for thirty years. If one of them broke this vow, she was either stoned to death or buried alive. After the thirty years had passed, they were free to marry if they wanted to do so. In Greek fable Vesta is known under the name of Hestia, and her priestesses were widows instead of virgins.

VE-SU'VI-US. See NAPLES.

VE-VAY', a town of W. Switzerland, on the Lake of Geneva; pop. 8000. It is famous for its beautiful scenery, and is visited every summer by many travelers. Jean Jacques ROUSSEAU and other celebrated persons have lived at Vevay.

VIBERT (*ve-bair'*), Georges Jean, a French painter and author, born at Paris in 1840. His pictures belong to the class called *genre*, in which human beings, who may or may not be historical characters, are painted in such groups and attitudes as to tell a story. The background of such paintings is usually a landscape, but may be an interior of a room.

VICHY (*ve'che*), a town of central France, on the river Allier, or about the same as Millville, N. J.; pop. 10,000. It is famous for its mineral springs, which are visited every year by thousands of invalids and pleasure-seekers. The water is used both for bathing and drinking, and a great deal of it is bottled and sent to the United States and other countries. Vichy was noted in the times of the Romans, and the remains of their marble baths have been found there.

VICKS'BURG, a city of Mississippi, on the Mississippi River; pop. 13,000, or about as large as Woburn, Mass. Most of the houses are built on a hill which forms terraces above the river. The country around has many large cotton plantations, and a great deal of cotton is shipped at Vicksburg on steamboats. Vicksburg was founded

in 1836. During the Civil War the Confederates built strong forts and batteries there to keep vessels from going up and down the river. In 1862 these were bombarded by a Union fleet under Admiral Farragut, and in 1863 Gen. Grant besieged the city, which was defended by a Confederate army under Gen. Pemberton. The Union army surrounded the city, and the Confederates, being out of provisions and ammunition, were obliged to surrender (July 4, 1863), with many prisoners, cannon, and stores. On the same day was won the battle of GETTYSBURG, and it is thought that these two battles decided the fate of the war.

VIC'TOR EM·AN'U·EL, King of Sardinia and afterward King of Italy, born in Turin, March 14, 1820. He was the son of Charles Albert, of Sardinia, and he became king of that country in 1849, when his father gave up the throne. The young king found himself in much trouble, for his country was at war with Austria, and the Italians had just been defeated in the battle of Novara. Peace had first to be made, and, that being done, order restored. But he had a very wise counselor in Count CAVOUR, and Sardinia was soon so well ruled that other Italian States, under the leadership of Gen. Garibaldi, rose against their kings and joined themselves to her. A successful war with Austria, in which Sardinia was aided by France, added Lombardy to the dominions of Victor Emanuel, and at last, after the Franco-Prussian war, when the French could no longer spare their soldiers to keep Pope Pius IX. on his throne, the States of the Church became a part of the Kingdom of Italy. On July 2, 1871, Victor Emanuel entered Rome, and he soon made it the capital of Italy. Most of the Italians were very glad to see Italy one nation, instead of a great many little kingdoms, as it had been. Victor Emanuel died when nearly fifty-eight years old (Jan. 9, 1878), and was succeeded by his son Humbert.

VICTORIA (*vik-to're-ah*). See AUSTRALIA.

VICTORIA ALEXANDRINA, Queen of Great Britain and Ireland and Empress of India, born in Kensington Palace, May 24, 1819. She is the sixth ruler of the House of Hanover, and the only child of Edward, Duke of Kent, the fourth son of George III., and she succeeded her uncle William IV. when she

Queen Victoria.

was but eighteen years old (1837). She has enjoyed a reign of peace and prosperity unexampled in the history of England, and her life has been happier than usually falls to the lot of those whose fate it is to wear a crown. Three years after she came to the throne she married her cousin Prince ALBERT, of Saxe Coburg Gotha. The only reproach that her people have cast upon her is that she spent too much time in mourning when the loss of her husband left her a widow. Some of the chief events of her reign have been the repeal of the duties on corn, thus making bread cheaper for the poor; the Crimean War, in which England fought Russia to keep her from swallowing up Turkey; and the Indian mutiny, when the Indian soldiers in the army rose and killed so many English officers and their families in India. Queen Victoria has a large family of sons and daughters. The daughters are, like their mother, sensible women, who know how to do a great many things and are not helpless ladies like so many in lower stations. Queen Victoria was proclaimed Empress of India, Jan. 1, 1877. She is now (1891) seventy-two years old. At her death she will be succeeded by her son ALBERT EDWARD, Prince of Wales.

VIENNA (*ve-en'nah;* German Wien, *veen*), the capital of the Austro-Hungarian monarchy, on the river Danube, which is joined there by a small stream, called the Wien; pop. 1,104,000, or less than three fourths that of New York City. It is one of the most beautiful cities in Europe, and is noted for its magnificent palaces, churches, and monuments. In the Imperial Palace is a chamber of treasures, which contains the crown and sceptre of the German Emperor, and many splendid jewels, including the largest emerald known. It also has a cabinet of antiquities, with a very large collection of coins, and many other curiosities. In the Belvidere Palace, built by Prince Eugene of Savoy, is a splendid gallery of paintings, and a fine museum. The Imperial Cabinet of Natural History is one of the largest in the world, and the Imperial Library is surpassed by only three or four in Europe. The University of Vienna has 6000 students, and is celebrated for its school of medicine. The finest church of Vienna is St. Stephen's Cathedral, which was begun in the

14th century. It has one of the highest steeples in Europe, and contains the tombs of many distinguished persons, including that of the Emperor Frederick III., which has 200 figures carved on it. The principal park is the Prater, on an island in the Danube, where the great Vienna Exposition was held in 1873. Vienna has a very large trade, especially with Turkey and Asia. It is noted for its manufactures of fancy leather, meerschaum pipes, jewelry, clocks, musical and optical instruments, and silks and velvets.

Vienna is a very old city, having been a Roman military post called Vindobona. In 1529, and again in 1683, it was heroically defended against the Turks, who had invaded Austria. It was twice taken by Napoleon, and after his downfall a meeting called the Congress of Vienna was held there by the sovereigns of Europe, where many important questions were decided, (1814 and 1815).

VILLARS (*ve-yar'*), **Claude Louis Hector,** Duke de, a famous French soldier, born in Moulins, May 8, 1653. He began life as a page at court, where he became a favorite with King Louis XIV. From his earliest years he loved a soldier's life, and the king once said, "A single shot can't be fired without this boy's starting from the ground to witness it." He entered the army when nineteen years old, fought under Turenne and other famous generals, and became a marshal of France in 1702. In 1709 he commanded the army against MARLBOROUGH and Prince EUGENE at MALPLAQUET, where he was badly wounded. He afterward defeated Prince Eugene. A year before his death, although he had reached the age of eighty years, he received the rank of Marshal General of the armies of France, an office previously given to no one but Turenne. He died in Turin, when eighty-one years old (June 17, 1734).

VINCENNES (*vin-senz'*), a town of France, forming an E. suburb of Paris; pop. 22,000, or about as large as Poughkeepsie, N. Y. It is very strongly fortified, and has an old castle where many celebrated persons have lived and died. The Duke D'ENGHIEN was shot there (1804). Connected with the castle is a stone tower, which was used as a dungeon for prisoners of state. Vincennes contains the principal arsenal and armory of Paris, and a school where sharpshooters, called the Chasseurs de Vincennes (Huntsmen of Vincennes), are trained. There is a fine park, part of which is used as a parade ground.

VINCI (*vin'che*), **Leonardo da,** an Italian painter, born near Florence in 1452. He was the son of a nobleman, and when very young showed great aptness not only for painting, but for music and poetry. He lived at different times in Florence, Milan, and Rome. In Milan he painted many of his greatest pictures, among them the "Last Supper," which has been called "the triumph of Christian art." In later life he visited France, where he died near Amboise, when sixty-seven years old (May 2, 1519). Beside his paintings, da Vinci planned many fine buildings and engineering works, and he was one of the most learned men of his times.

VIR'GIL (**Publius Virgilius**), a famous Roman poet, born near Mantua, Oct. 15, 70 B.C. He lived in the time of Augustus, the first emperor of Rome, and was much helped by his chief adviser Mæcenas. The poet was of delicate health, and so retiring in manners that he could hardly have pushed his way without Mæcenas. His principal writings are the "Bucolics," also called "Eclogues," the "Georgics," and the "Æneid." In the "Georgics" we learn all that the Romans knew of farming and such matters. The "Æneid" tells us of the adventures of ÆNEAS. Virgil's works have always been much used as school books. They are read for their correct Latin by all who wish to learn that language. He must have been much thought of in the Middle Ages, the time between the fifth and the fifteenth centuries, for the Italian poet Dante, who wrote then, calls him his master, and speaks of himself as going under his lead on a visit to the spirit world. Virgil died in Brundusium, on his way home from Greece, when fifty-one years old (Sept. 22, 19 B.C.). His grave is near Naples.

VIRGINIA (*vir-jin'e-ah*), a Southern Atlantic State of the United States, N. of North Carolina; area 40,000 square miles, or about the same as that of Ohio; pop. 1,656,000, or more than four ninths that of Ohio; capital, RICHMOND. The western part is crossed by the Kittatinny Mountains and the Blue Ridge, between which is the fertile "Valley of Virginia" or Shenandoah Valley, sometimes called the "Garden of America." This region is noted for its grand scenery and its many natural curiosities, such as caves, sulphur and mineral springs, and the celebrated Natural Bridge. The eastern part of the State is a low plain, and along the coast are many excellent harbors. Most of these open into Chesapeake Bay, for Virginia has only a short coast on the ocean. In the south-eastern corner, and lying partly in North Carolina, is the great Dismal Swamp, covered with thick forest, in which bears and other wild animals are common. In the centre is a lake. Before the negroes were freed, many of them who escaped from their masters used to live in this swamp.

Virginia is rich in mines, especially of coal, iron, rock salt, and gold. The forests are full of fine timbers, and along the coast are excellent fisheries and oyster beds, many million bushels of oysters being sent from there every year. There are many fine farms, especially in the Valley of Virginia, the principal crops being corn, wheat, and tobacco. More tobacco and snuff are made in Virginia than in any other State. There are also important iron-works and cotton factories. More than two fifths of the people are negroes. Virginia was named after Queen Elizabeth, the "virgin queen." The name was first given to what is now NORTH CAROLINA, but when the settlements there failed it was kept by the people who settled in what is now Virginia. Virginia was first settled at JAMESTOWN in 1607, and is therefore the oldest of the English colonies in America. It was one of the thirteen original States. It seceded in 1861 and joined the Confederate States, but became a State of the Union again in 1870.

VIRGINIA CITY, a city of W. Nevada, among the Washoe Mountains; pop. about 2000. In 1858 a Virginian miner found silver there, and a mining town sprung up which was named in honor of the discoverer. In time the silver vein called the Comstock Lode was found to be the richest in the world, and many mines were made in it, among them those called the "Gould and Curry," "Ophir," "Best and Belcher," "Consolidated Virginia," and "California." To drain the mines and reach a part of the silver vein that has not been worked, a long tunnel called the Sutro Tunnel was dug. In 1875 more than half of Virginia City was burned.

VISH'NU, a god of the Hindoos, one of their Trimurti, or Trinity. Their Trinity comprises Brahma the creator, Vishnu the preserver, and Siva the destroyer. Vishnu is the only one who is mentioned in their hymns alone without the other members of the Trimurti.

VIS'I·GOTHS. See GOTHS.

VISTULA (*vis'tu-lah*), a river of Europe, rising in N. Austria and flowing through Russian Poland and Germany into the Baltic Sea; length, 650 miles. It can be navigated to Cracow, about 550 miles. Above that are falls, one near Vistula being two hundred feet high.

VI-TEL'LI-US, Aulus, a Roman emperor, born about A.D. 15. He was a great favorite with CALIGULA, CLAUDIUS, and NERO. GALBA sent him to command the army in lower Germany, and he became so much liked by the soldiers that in a month they made him emperor (69). Galba was killed shortly after by the friends of Otho, and Vitellius went to Rome, defeating Otho's army by the way. He did not reign long, for Vespasian was proclaimed emperor by the army of the East, and his generals marched to Rome, and Vitellius was killed (69).

VITORIA (*ve-to're-ah*), a town of N. Spain, 29 miles S.S.E. of Bilbao; pop. 28,000, or nearly as large as Bay City, Mich. The town is noted for a great victory won there by Wellington over a French army under Joseph BONAPARTE and Gen. JOURDAN (June 21, 1813). Many prisoners and cannon and an immense booty were taken, and the French were soon after driven out of Spain. Vitoria in Spanish means victory, and the town got its name from a victory won there by King Sancho of Navarre over the Moors (about 1180).

VLADIMIR (*vlah'de-meer*), called the Great, a ruler of Russia who lived in the last part of the tenth century and the first part of the eleventh. Many benefits were conferred upon Russia under his rule. At first he was a heathen, but he finally joined the Greek Church. It is said that he had made up his mind to give up his idols, but was much puzzled as to what

form of religion should take their place. Mohammedanism had many attractions for him, but he gave up all thought of that when he learned that it forbade the use of wine. At last Vladimir consulted his nobles on the subject, and their answer was, "If the Greek religion was not good, thy grandmother Olga would not have adopted it." So he became a Greek Christian and insisted on all his subjects being Greeks. He died in 1014.

VOLGA (*vol'gah*), a river of Russia and the largest one in Europe, rising 200 miles S. of St. Petersburg, and flowing into the Caspian Sea, into which it empties by many mouths; length 2300 miles. There are many important cities on the banks, and a very large trade is carried on by the river and by canals which connect it with the White and Baltic seas. But during part of the year the Volga is closed by ice. The river has large fisheries of salmon and sturgeon.

VOLTA (*vol'tah*), **Alessandro,** an Italian scientist, born in Como, Feb. 18, 1745. For thirty years he studied and taught in the University of Pavia. He is famous for his great invention of the voltaic pile, an instrument for making electricity. Bonaparte treated him with great honor, and invited him to Paris to show him his experiments. In 1802 Volta was chosen a member of the French institute. He died when eighty-two years of age (April 5, 1827).

VOLTAIRE (*vol-tair'*), François Marie Arouet de, a famous French writer, born in Paris, Nov. 21, 1694. Arouet was the name of his family, and Voltaire is said to have been that of his mother's estate. This celebrated author had many talents: he was a poet, a historian, and a philosopher. In all his writings, we see his ready wit and his great power of making fun of whatever he did not like, also his hatred of all religion, which he did his best to overturn. He was in a great part the cause of a widespread unbelief which ended in the French Revolution. Yet Voltaire was not the very bad man that he is generally represented to be. Among his last words were, " I die worshiping God, loving my friends, not hating my enemies, but detesting superstition."

Voltaire's talents made him admired by Frederick the Great, King of Prussia, who invited him to spend some time at his court. He lived three years with the king at Potsdam, but at the end of that time they parted not very good friends. The last twenty years of his life were spent at a little town called Ferney, near Geneva, in Switzerland; and on account of this, he is sometimes called the "Sage of Ferney." His chief works are the "Life of Charles XII.," "Age of Louis XIV.," a poem called "Henriade," the plays of "Zaire" and "Mérope," and "Essay on the Manners and Spirit of Nations." He died in Paris, when eighty-four years old (May 30, 1778).

VUL'CAN, the Roman god of fire and of metals, son of Jupiter and Juno. His mother was said to have driven him from Olympus, because he was deformed; but another story is that his father threw him out because·he tried to help his mother, who had been fastened by Jupiter with a golden chain. He fell upon the island of Lemnos, and was lamed by his fall. He then set up a forge and taught men how to soften and work metals by means of fire. He also lived in the Lipari Isles and in Sicily, where he had his workshop in Mount Ætna. There, aided by the CYCLOPS, he made Jupiter's thunderbolts and the armor for the gods. He tried to win Minerva for his wife; but not succeeding, he married Venus.

Vulcan.

W

WAGNER (*wahg'ner*), **Richard,** a famous German writer of music, born in Leipsic, May 22, 1813. His father died when Richard was a baby, and the boy received only a slight education; but he was very bright, and wrote plays when twelve years old. At fifteen he heard some of Beethoven's music played, and he then made up his mind to be a musician. For many years his attempts to write music which would please the public were failures, and he was often in want. But in 1858 he found a friend and patron in the King of Bavaria, who became his great admirer, and gave him the means to bring out his works. Wagner tried very hard to break down the French and Italian opera, and to build up one that was more suited to the Germans. Up to this time the music

Richard Wagner.

had been the chief thing in an opera, and the play of little value, and sometimes very silly. Wagner thought that the play should be the chief thing, and that the music should be suited to it, not it to the music. This was a new idea, so Wagner's music is called the "music of the future." The "Nibelungen Ring," and his last opera, "Parsifal," were performed in the town of Baireuth, in a theatre planned by himself on purpose for them. His other operas are "Rienzi," "The Flying Dutchman," "Tannhäuser," "Lohengrin," "The Mastersingers," and "Tristan and Isolde." He wrote the grand march for the American Centennial in 1876. He died at Venice, when seventy years old (Feb. 13, 1883).

WAGRAM (*wah'gram*), a village of Austria, on the river Rossbach, 11 miles N.E. of Vienna. It is celebrated for a victory which Napoleon won there over the Austrians commanded by the Archduke Charles. Napoleon had captured Vienna, but had been defeated at the battles of Aspern and Essling (May 21 and 22, 1809). He retreated, but soon became strong enough to march again against his enemies, After a desperate and bloody battle at Wagram (July 5 and 6, 1809), the Austrians fled to the Heights of Znaym, and soon after they were forced to sue for peace.

WAHLBERG (*vahl'ba-erg*), **Alfred,** a Swedish painter, born in Stockholm. He paints beautiful moonlight scenes, which have been exhibited in Paris and London, and gained high praise. He is called the best living painter of moonlight.

WALES, a country of the British Empire, forming a peninsula on the W. side of Great Britain; area 7377 square miles, or nearly as large as Massachusetts; pop. 1,361,000, or more than four sevenths that of Massachusetts. It is a very rugged country, with mountains and valleys abounding in beautiful scenery, and is visited by thousands of travelers every year. Wales is rich in minerals, having many mines of coal, iron, lead, zinc, copper, and tin; and fine quarries of limestone, paving stones, and roofing slates. Most of the surface is rocky and rather barren, yet by hard work the Welsh have made many good farms. Much grain is raised in the southern part, and in other places many cattle and sheep are pastured. There is a large trade in butter, cheese, wool, mutton, and grain, and the manufactures, especially of flannel and of iron-ware, are very important.

The people of Wales are noted for their generosity and bravery, and also for their hot temper. They have a language much like that of the ancient Britons, from whom they are descended, but most of them speak English also. The country is a principality, the eldest son of the English king or queen being called Prince of Wales. Really he has little to do with the government, and the Welsh people elect members of Parliament just as the English do.

The Welsh people were CELTS, who called themselves Cymry or Kymry, a word meaning countrymen, or those not foreigners. The Romans made this into Cambria, and called the country by that name. They were never wholly conquered by the Romans, though CARACTACUS, one of their chiefs, was taken and sent to Rome. When the ANGLO-SAXONS came to Britain they called the Kymry Wealh or Wälsch (foreigners), and the part of the island where they lived got from them the name of Wales. The Welsh kept up a brave fight against the Saxons, and for a long time kept them out of their country. They were at first divided into several small tribes, but in the 9th century the country united under King Roderick the Great. The English gained power over the country little by little, until they forced the Welsh kings to pay tribute to them.

The Welsh having refused to pay this to William the Conqueror, William invaded Wales and conquered it. After that the English kings always claimed Wales, but the people constantly rebelled. Llewellyn ap Gryffyth, their Prince, fought against King Edward I., but was defeated and killed (1282). The next year, his brother David, who had succeeded him, was captured and executed as a traitor, and Wales was declared to be a part of England. The son of King Edward, born in CAERNARVON Castle, was the first English Prince of Wales.

WALLACE (*wol'lis*), **William,** a famous Scottish patriot and soldier, born about 1270. He was noted for his great strength and courage, and for his devotion to his country, which he determined to free from the rule of Edward I., King of England. At the head of a small band of followers he made several successful attacks on the English, and many of the Scotch barons, encouraged by these successes, joined him, and soon a large force was collected. The English governor of Scotland, the Earl of Surrey, with an army of more than 50,000 men, marched against them. The two armies met at Stirling Bridge, on the banks of the Forth, where the English were defeated with great loss (Sept. 10, 1297). Wallace then ravaged the northern counties of England, and on his return he was elected guardian of Scotland. King Edward then collected an army of more than 87,000 men, and marched into Scotland. A battle was fought at Falkirk (July 22, 1298), in which the Scotch were defeated with terrible loss, and Wallace with a few followers fled to the mountains. Here he lived for several years, worrying the English whenever he got a chance. Large rewards were offered for his arrest, and at last he was betrayed into the hands of the English. He was taken to London,

tried for treason, and executed (Aug. 23, 1305). His head was set up on London Bridge, and the four parts of his body were sent to Newcastle, Berwick, Stirling, and Perth, by way of frightening people against rebelling any more.

WALLACHIA (*waw-la'ke-ah*). See ROUMANIA.

WALLENSTEIN (*wol'len-stine*), **Albrecht Wenzel Eusebius von,** Count, and Duke of Friedland, a famous German soldier, born in Bohemia, Sept. 14, 1583. His parents were Protestants, but he became a Ro-

Albrecht Wallenstein.

man Catholic and spent most of his life in religious wars, fighting the Protestants in what is commonly called the THIRTY YEARS' WAR. When war broke out between the Austrian Emperor with Denmark, Saxony and the Free Towns, Wallenstein offered to raise forty thousand men for his sovereign. With these he did good service, and as his reward got great riches, and was made a sovereign prince. But the robberies and cruelties of his soldiers, who are said to have plundered four hundred millions of dollars in seven years, made him unpopular. The German princes insisted on his dismissal, and in 1630 forced Ferdinand II. to give him up, and take away his duchy. Wallenstein retired for a year to Prague, where he lived in royal splendor, surrounded by guards, and waited on by sixty young gentlemen as pages. Meantime GUSTAVUS Adolphus, King of Sweden, declared war against the Emperor. In great terror at the approach of the Swedes, Ferdinand recalled Wallenstein, and made him general-in-chief of his armies, but he was defeated by Gustavus at Lützen (Nov. 6, 1632), though Gustavus himself was killed.

After this Wallenstein did very little against the Swedes, who still carried on the war, and the emperor was led to suspect him of being unfaithful to him. There were even rumors that he wanted to make himself king of Bohemia, and at last the command was taken away from him. Shortly afterward he was murdered at Eger, when fifty years old (Feb. 25, 1634). SCHILLER wrote two great plays, "The Piccolomini" and the "Death of Wallenstein," on this subject. Wallenstein had no children; his daughter Thekla in the play is the invention of the poet.

WAL'LER, Edmund, an English poet, born March 3, 1605. He lived in the time of Charles I., Oliver Cromwell, and Charles II. At the age of eighteen he was a member of Parliament, and at first was on the side of the people against King Charles I. Afterward he went over to the other party, and even engaged in a plot to seize some of the chief men in Parliament. For this he came near losing his life. He wrote verses in praise of Cromwell, and also made a poem to welcome Charles II. when he was restored to the throne. He was a favorite at court, and was noted for his wit. He died when eighty-two years old (Oct. 21, 1687).

WAL'POLE, Sir Robert, Earl of Orford, an English statesman, born at Houghton, in Norfolk, Aug. 26,

1676. Walpole began public life as a member of Parliament, and an ardent supporter of the House of HANOVER. Many offices under the government were held by him, and for twenty-one years he was Prime Minister of England. His public acts made him many enemies, but he was always sure of the hearty support of his king, George II., who burst into tears when he resigned his office. Time has proved that he was right in some of his most unpopular acts. He died in London, when sixty-eight years old, (March 18, 1745). His son, Horace Walpole, born in London, Oct. 5, 1717, is famed for a strange irregular house which he built and named Strawberry Hill, and for the curiosities of all sorts which he collected there. He wrote a novel called "The Castle of Otranto," and other books. Horace Walpole died when seventy-nine years old (1797).

WAL'SALL, a city of England, 7 miles N.W. of Birmingham; pop. 59,000, or about as large as Reading, Pa. It is noted for its manufactories of saddlery and hardware. Near the town are many coal and iron mines and lime-kilns.

WALSINGHAM (*wol'sing-am*), Sir Francis, an English statesman, born at Chiselhurst, Kent, about 1536. He was the agent employed by Queen Elizabeth in many of her difficult enterprises, and was twice sent by her on missions to France. In 1573 he became one of her secretaries of state. Fifty-three agents and eighteen spies are said to have been kept by him at foreign courts, to inform him as to what was going on there. By means of his shrewdness he was of great use to his royal mistress, in enabling her to foil the plans of the artful sovereigns who were her enemies. He was one of the chief persons to track out the famous Babington conspiracy to murder Elizabeth, in which Mary Queen of Scots was said to be concerned, and to bring her to execution. He died very poor, near London, when fifty-four years old (April 6, 1590).

WAL'THAM, a town of Massachusetts, on the Charles river, ten miles W. by N. of Boston; pop. 19,000, or about as large as Bayonne, N. J. The factory of the American Watch Company there is the largest of its kind in the world, and it was the first one where watches were made by machinery. There are also manufactories of cotton cloth, stockings and machinery.

WALTON (*wol'tun*), **Isaak,** a noted English author, born at Stafford, Aug. 9, 1593. In early life he was a linen-draper in London, but when he had made money enough he gave most of his time to writing and to a quiet life in the country. He wrote several biographies and other works, but he is best known for his book, called "The Complete Angler." It was greatly admired, and it is still read and enjoyed for its quaint, charming thoughts. Walton died in Winchester when ninety years old (Dec. 15, 1683).

WAR'BECK, Perkin, a pretender to the throne of England, in the reign of Henry VII. He called himself Richard Plantagenet, Duke of York, and said that he was the younger of the two princes, children of King Edward IV., who were thought to have been murdered in the Tower of London, by their uncle Richard. But most people believed that he was the son of a Jew of Tournay, and that he had been trained to represent the young Duke of York, whom he resembled. The people of England and many of the nobles believed in him, and several of them openly declared themselves on his side. In 1495, with the aid of the Duchess of Burgundy, who treated him as her nephew, he attempted to invade England, but he was not successful. He then went to Scotland, where he was received as the Duke of York by James IV., and was married to Lady Catharine Gordon, a member of the royal family. The Scottish king, however, was soon persuaded to give up his cause, and Warbeck went to Ireland, and from there landed in Cornwall, where he was joined by about 3000 followers, and where he, for the first time, called himself Richard IV. of England. He laid siege to Exeter; but finding it impossible to resist the English forces, he fled to Beaulieu. He was taken prisoner, but was promised pardon if he would publicly confess himself an impostor. This he did, but he was still kept in prison. He made two or three attempts to escape, but was always caught again. At last he was tried, condemned, and hanged at Tyburn (Nov. 23, 1499).

WARD, John Quincy Adams, an American sculptor, born in Urbana, Ohio, June 29, 1830. His statue of the "Indian Hunter" in the New York Central Park, and his "Freedman," which is on the steps of the Capitol at Washington, are among the best examples of American sculpture. The Seventh Regiment statue and the Shakespeare of the Central Park are also by him. His studio is in New York.

WAR'NER, Charles Dudley, an American writer, born in Plainfield, Mass., Sept. 12, 1829. He was graduated at Hamilton College in 1851, and became a lawyer, but since 1860 has been editor of a newspaper in Hartford, Conn. He is the author of "My Summer in a Garden," "Back Log Studies," and several books of travel. He and Mr. Clemens (Mark Twain) wrote together a novel called "The Gilded Age."

WAR'NER, Olin L., an American sculptor, born in Suffield, Conn., in 1844. He is one of the most promising of the younger artists. Among his works are a fine statuette called "Twilight" and some excellent portrait busts. His studio is in New York.

WAR'NER, Susan, an American writer, born in New York in 1818. She has for many years lived on an island in the Hudson River, opposite West Point. Miss Warner has written several novels, and, in connection with her sister, Miss Anna B. Warner, some stories for children; but she is best known as the author of "The Wide, Wide World," "Queechy," "The Hills of the Shatemuc," and "Wych Hazel," which have been much read both in America and in Europe.

WAR'REN, Joseph, a noted American patriot, born in Roxbury, Mass., June 11, 1741. He was graduated at Harvard College, and soon became one of the best physicians in Boston. In the troubles with Great Britain, he was a firm supporter of the cause of the colonists. In 1774 he was president of the Massachusetts Congress, and the next year he was made a major-general, three days before the battle of Bunker Hill. On the day of the battle, he joined the men as a volunteer and fought bravely, being one of the last to leave the field. As he was going, a ball struck him in the head and killed him (June 17, 1775). He was buried on the spot where he fell; but his remains were afterward removed to his family vault in Boston. He was only thirty-four years old when he fell. A statue of Gen. Warren was placed on Bunker Hill in 1857.

WAR'SAW, a city of W. Russia, capital of Poland, on the Vistula River; pop. 454,000, or a little larger than St. Louis, Mo. It is surrounded by walls and ditches, and has a very strong citadel. The finest building is the Royal Palace, which contains splendid rooms, formerly used by the Congress of Poland. There are other palaces belonging to nobles in and near the city, with many fine museums, parks, and gardens, and a university

with nearly a thousand students. The city has a large trade and manufactories of cloth, carpets, pianos, and many other things.

Warsaw, or Warszawa, as the Poles call it, means the "fortified place." It became the capital of Poland in 1609. The Russians took it in 1764, and it was afterward held by the Prussians and by the French. In 1813 the Russians got it again, and though the people have rebelled several times, they still hold it.

WARWICK (*wor'rik*), a town of England, on the river Avon, 85 miles N.W. of London; pop. 12,000, or about as large as Superior, Wis. It is noted for its ancient castle, one of the oldest and best preserved in England. One of the towers was built before the year 1400, and another is still older. A few years ago, part of the castle was burned, and some of the paintings and old relics were destroyed; but the burned portion has since been rebuilt. Warwick contains many other old buildings.

WARWICK, a town on Narragansett Bay, Rhode Island, 10 miles S. by W. of Providence; pop. 18,000, or about as large as Hamilton, Ohio. It is formed by the union of several villages, among them Natick, Phœnix, and Crompton. The town is noted for its large cotton mills and other manufactories, and the shores of the bay are much visited during the summer. In one place there is a large rock, called Drum Rock, balanced on another so nicely that a child can move it, making a noise like a drum, which can be heard at a great distance. Warwick was settled about 1640.

WARWICK (*wor'rik*), **Guy,** Earl of, a fabulous English champion, supposed to have lived in the time of the early Saxon kings. Many people think that there never was really such a person, but that he was a character invented by romancers; others say that he was a real person. The peasants who live in Warwickshire, near Warwick Castle, could not be convinced that their hero, Guy, did not have something to do with building this castle, in the porter's lodge of which are shown his porridge pot (a huge iron vessel) and part of his armor. In the neighborhood of the castle is Guy's Cliff, the fabled hermit's cell of the hero.

WARWICK, Richard Neville, Earl of, called the King Maker, born soon after 1420. He was the eldest son of Richard Neville, Earl of Salisbury, but married the daughter of the Earl of Warwick, got the great estates of that family, and became the mightiest noble in England and the favorite of the people. In the Wars of the Roses, he fought at first on the side of the Yorkists and gained many battles against the forces of Henry VI., but when Edward IV., after reaching the throne through his means, refused to choose a wife to suit him, the Earl married his own daughter to young Edward, son of the imprisoned King Henry. He then drove Edward out of the kingdom and restored Henry to his throne. But Edward came back, defeated the Lancastrians in the battle of Bar-

Capitol at Washington.

net, in which the King Maker was slain, and got his throne again. Warwick has been called "the last of the barons." He died when fifty-one years old (April 14, 1471).

WASH'ING-TON, a city, capital of the United States, in the District of Columbia, on the Potomac River; pop. 230,000, or a little larger than Pittsburg, Pa. All the smaller streets are laid out to form squares, but there are twenty-one wide avenues, named after States of the Union, which radiate from the Capitol and President's house. Of these, Massachusetts Avenue is the finest, and Pennsylvania Avenue contains the principal stores. The Capitol, which is built of white marble, stands on a hill, and its great dome and columns can be seen from all parts of the city. It is more than a seventh of a mile long (751 feet), and covers 3½ acres of ground. The dome is 135½ feet across, and 287½ feet above the basement floor. From its top, which is surrounded by a bronze statue of Liberty more than three times as high as a man (19½ feet), a splendid view is obtained of all the country around. The Capitol contains the Senate Chamber, Chamber of Representatives, and many other rooms, nearly all of which are ornamented with statues and paintings. The Library of Congress, which is also in the Capitol, is the largest in the United States. It receives a copy of every book published in the country.

The President's house, called the White House, is a large but not handsome building surrounded with fine grounds. The Treasury Department, a very large and grand building, contains the offices of the Secretary of the Treasury and his under officers. Beneath it are vaults where immense sums of money are kept. The Departments of State, War, and the Navy have their offices in another large building. The Department of the Interior contains the Patent Office and a museum of models of many thousand inventions which have been patented there. The Department of Agriculture contains a museum of plants, seeds, and all sorts of farm implements and produce, and connected with it are fine greenhouses. The General Post Office is a large marble building, containing the rooms of the Postmaster-General and his officers, the Dead Letter Office, and the Washington city post-office.

The Smithsonian Institution has one of the largest natural history museums in the world, including all the collections made by United States surveys. The Corcoran Art Gallery, founded by W. W. Corcoran, a Washington banker, contains a fine collection of paintings. At the south end of the city is a large Arsenal, and not far from it is the Navy-yard. The United States Naval Observatory, from which longitude is often reckoned, is in the western part of the city. Washington has many fine statues and monuments, including the great Washington Monument, which is the largest in the country, being 550 feet high.

The site of the city was selected by Washington, and it was named after him (1791). He himself laid the corner stone of the Capitol (Sept. 18, 1793), but he did not live to see the government established there in 1800. The foundation of the main building of the new Capitol was laid in 1818, and the whole was finished in 1827. In 1851 the wings were begun, and the building as it now is was finished in 1867. In 1814 Washington was taken by the British (Aug. 24), and the public buildings were burned. During the Civil War, the city was strongly fortified.

WASH'ING-TON, a Pacific State of the United States, between Oregon and Canada; area 70,000 square miles, or twice that of the State of Maine; pop. 349,000, or a little more than that of Rhode Island; capital, Olympia. The western part is mountainous, and covered in most places with forest; the eastern part is a table-land, almost without trees, and generally too dry for farms, though it is good for pastures. Between these two regions are the Cascade Mountains, rising in high peaks, some of which are more than two miles above the sea, and covered always with snow.

Washington has mines of gold and lead; but the chief trade is in pine, fir, and cedar lumber. Most of the people live in the western part, the greatest eastern plains being almost deserted, except by Indians.

Washington was once a part of Oregon, but was made into a separate territory in 1853, and became a State of the Union in 1889.

WASH'ING-TON, George, first President of the United States, born in Westmoreland Co., Va., Feb. 22, 1732. The house in which George was born was burned down when he was a boy, and the place where it stood is marked by a stone slab, with an inscription, put there in 1815. His father removed to a house near Fredericksburg, where he died when George was eleven years old. George had only a common school education, but studied also bookkeeping and surveying. His copy-books, written in a very neat hand, are still preserved. From his youth he was noted for honor and truthfulness, and he excelled in athletic sports and horsemanship. His father had left a large estate, and when his elder brother Lawrence died (1752), George in-

George Washington.

herited from him the estate of Mt Vernon. When he grew up he became a surveyor, and was employed by Lord FAIRFAX in surveying his estates in the Shenandoah Valley, then a wilderness. In the winter of 1753 and 1754 he carried a letter from the Governor of Virginia, 500 miles through the wilderness, to a French fort near Lake Erie. On his return he was in great danger from the Indians, and was nearly drowned in crossing the Alleghany River. In 1754 he was made a lieutenant colonel, and sent with a regiment to build forts near the Ohio River, and to drive away the French. He built a fort called Fort Necessity, and killed or captured a small party of French soldiers, but being attacked by a French army much larger than his own, he was obliged to surrender, though he and his soldiers were allowed to return to Virginia.

Washington served with ability during the rest of the French and Indian war, and after the defeat of Gen. BRADDOCK he saved the army by his skill and courage. In this fight he had two horses shot under him, and five bullets passed through his coat. On his return he was made commander of an army of 2000 men raised in Virginia, and during the rest of the French and Indian war he performed many important services. In 1759 he resigned, and in the same year he married Mrs. Martha Custis, and went to live on his estate at Mt. Vernon. In the Virginia Legislature, of which he was a member, he took the part of the colonists, against the oppressions of the English. Soon after the Revolutionary War broke out, he was appointed Commander-in-Chief of the American armies (June 15, 1775). He immediately went to Massachusetts, and after a siege of eight months compelled the British to leave Boston (March 17, 1776). He then went with his army to New York. The Americans were badly armed and equipped, and they were soon attacked by a British army much larger than theirs, commanded by Sir Henry Clinton. At the battle of Long Island, near Brooklyn, Washington was defeated (Aug. 27, 1776), and soon after he was obliged to give up New York. Being again defeated at White Plains, he retreated through New Jersey, reaching Pennsylvania with only 3000 half-starved soldiers. Yet with this little army he won the battles of Trenton (Dec. 26, 1776) and Princeton (Jan. 3, 1777). By

ЗДЕ

the end of the winter, the American army was increased to 7500 men. On Sept. 11, 1777, Washington was defeated at the battle of the Brandywine, and the British took Philadelphia. Washington attacked them at Germantown, seven miles from Philadelphia, but was again defeated, and soon after he and his army went into winter quarters at Valley Forge, where they suffered many privations. In June, 1778, the British retreated from Philadelphia to New York, and Washington followed and fought a battle with them at Monmouth. In 1779 and 1780 he himself did not fight any great battles, but in 1781 his army besieged Cornwallis, at Yorktown, Virginia, and compelled him to surrender, with his whole army (Oct. 19). The British finally gave up the war in 1783. Washington had lost more battles than he had gained, but by his self-sacrifice and perseverance he had won the love and respect of all Americans. After great defeats, when other men would have given up, he always remained hopeful, and success never caused him to become heedless of danger. Thus the Americans owe their liberty to him. As soon as the war closed, he went back to Mt. Vernon and became a farmer again, but in 1787 he was president of a convention which met in Philadelphia to form a constitution for the United States. The constitution having been adopted, Washington was made President of the United States in 1788, and inaugurated in New York (April 30, 1789).

When Washington became President the country was in a bad condition, but by his wisdom and that of his Cabinet and Congress, prosperity soon returned. In 1792 he was re-elected, but in 1796 he refused another re-election, and sent a farewell address to Congress. In 1797 he returned to Mt. Vernon, but soon after he was called to be general of the army, as a war with France was expected. Before the question was settled, Washington was attacked with a severe cold, produced by a ride in the rain. He grew worse, and after two days' illness died at Mt. Vernon, when sixty-seven years old (Dec. 14, 1799). The picture of Washington is from the portrait by Gilbert Stuart.

WATERBURY (*waw'ter-ber-ry*), a city of Connecticut, on the Naugatuck River; pop. 29,000, or about as large as Galveston, Tex. It is noted for its manufactures, especially of brass-ware, in which it surpasses every other city of the United States. Among the things made there are buttons, pins, hooks and eyes, the metal parts of kerosene lamps, brass kettles, brass wire, clocks, and almost every kind of article made out of metal. Nearly half the people in the city are employed in the manufactories. Waterbury was settled in 1667 and became a city in 1853.

WATERLOO (*waw-ter-loo'*), a village of Belgium, 8 miles S. by E. from Brussels; pop. about 3000. Near it was fought the battle of Waterloo, in which Napoleon was finally defeated by the Duke of Wellington, June 18, 1815. Wellington had an army of English, Dutch, and German soldiers near Brussels, and a Prussian army under General BLÜCHER was marching to reinforce him. Napoleon moved his army so as to get between them, and sent General Ney to attack the English at Quatre Bras, while he himself attacked the Prussians at Ligny. The Prussians were defeated, but Ney was driven back from Quatre Bras (June 16). Napoleon then sent part of his soldiers under Marshal Grouchy to pursue the Prussians, while he marched to meet Wellington at Waterloo. He arrived there late on the afternoon of June 17, and the battle began on the next morning. It was a very long and bloody one. The English were at length driven back and almost defeated. But meanwhile the Prussians had escaped from Grouchy, and now began to arrive. Napoleon sent messengers to Grouchy ordering him to come with his part of the army and aid him; but the messengers were killed or lost, and Grouchy did not get the orders until too late. His generals, hearing the cannonade at Waterloo, urged him to go without orders, and if he had done this Napoleon would probably have been saved. The English were continually receiving reinforcements of Prussians, and the French soon began to give way. At seven o'clock in the evening Napoleon sent his guard under General Ney for a last charge. Ney led them on foot, for five horses had been shot under him; his clothes were torn, and he was covered with blood and dust. Just at this moment Blücher arrived with his whole army, and Ney and the guards were driven back, leaving hundreds of dead on the field. Napoleon collected one regiment of the guards around him, and said that he would die with them; but his generals forced him away. The regiment, surrounded by the English, was ordered to surrender. "The guard dies, but never surrenders," replied their commander, and the soldiers, crying "Long Live the Emperor!" charged upon the English, until nearly every one had fallen. The French lost 30,000 men and nearly all their cannon. Napoleon escaped to Paris.

WA'TER-TOWN, a city of N. New York, on the Black River, 10 miles above its mouth in Lake Ontario; pop. 15,000, or about as large as Stockton, Cal. The river has several falls within the city, which furnish water-power for large flouring and paper-mills. There are also manufactories of steam-engines, sewing-machines, knitting-machines, wagons, and boots and shoes. The country around Watertown has many fine farms, and abounds in limestone and iron, in which a large trade is carried on. Watertown was settled in 1800, and became a city in 1869.

WA'TER-VILLE, a town of Maine, on the Kennebec River; pop. about 4500. The Kennebec here forms a fine fall called Ticonic Falls, and the water-power is used in several mills and manufactories. Waterville is the seat of Colby Univer-

Statue of James Watt at Birmingham.

sity, which belongs to the Baptist Church, and has about 200 students.

WATT, James, the inventor or rather improver of the steam-engine, born at Greenock, Scotland, Jan. 19, 1736. When only fourteen years old he made an electrical machine. In 1755 he became a maker of mathematical instruments in London, and in 1756 was appointed instrument-maker for the University of Glasgow. In 1758 he began to experiment with steam. A very clumsy steam-engine had already been invented, but Watt changed and improved it very much, and finally made an engine very like those now used. This was patented in 1784. Watt afterward became a surveyor and engineer, and was employed on many important works. In 1774 he became a partner of Matthew Boulton and founded the Soho steam-engine works near Birmingham, where they manufactured the improved steam-engines, and in time became very rich. Watt invented the letter-copying press and many other useful things, and he was the first to use steam for warming houses. He died at Heathfield, near · Birmingham, when eighty-three years old (Aug. 25, 1819).

WATTS (*wots*), **Isaac,** an English clergyman, born July 17, 1674. In 1702 he became pastor of an Independent congregation in London, which position he held until his death, thirty-six years later. He wrote many works on religion and other subjects; but he is chiefly known for his hymns and psalms, which are still sung in churches, and for his " Divine Songs attempted in Easy Language for the Use of Children." He died in London when seventy-four years old (Nov. 25, 1748).

WAYNE, Anthony, an American general in the Revolution, born at Waynesborough, Penn., Jan. 1, 1745. He was educated in Philadelphia, and at the age of eighteen became a land surveyor, and was sent by Franklin to form a settlement in Nova Scotia. When the war began he raised a regiment, of which he was made colonel, and in 1776 he was sent to Canada. His first battle was at Three Rivers, and when the Americans withdrew from Canada, he was left in command of the fortresses of Ti-

conderoga and Independence. In 1777 he was made a brigadier-general, and joined Washington in New Jersey. He distinguished himself at the battles of the Brandywine and of Germantown, and captured supplies for the Americans when they were suffering for want of provisions at Valley Forge. He surprised and took the strong fortification at Stony Point on the Hudson, July 15, 1779. This was the most brilliant victory of the whole war, and gained for him the thanks and praise of all his countrymen. He fought in many other

Anthony Wayne.

battles, and was called "Mad Anthony" on account of his daring and bravery. After the war he retired to his farm at Waynesborough; but in 1792 he was sent to take command in the war against the western Indians, whom he kept in check until his death. He died at Presque Isle, now called Erie, Penn., when fifty-one years old (Dec. 14, 1796).

WEBER (*wa'ber*), **Karl Maria Friedrich Ernst von,** Baron, a German writer of music, born near Lübeck, Dec. 18, 1786. His father, who also was a musician, gave him a good education, particularly in music and painting, and he began to publish music when twelve years old. His first operas were failures, but when thirty-six years old he wrote "Der Freischütz," which made him famous. This and "Oberon" are his best works. The latter was written for the London stage, and Weber himself was its manager. He stands at the head of the kind of music called the romantic. He died in London, when forty years old (June 5, 1826).

WEB'STER, Daniel, a famous American statesman, born in Salisbury (now Franklin), N. H., Jan.

Daniel Webster.

18, 1782. He had but little schooling when young, but studied so hard at home that he was able to enter Dartmouth College when he was fifteen. While there he helped to pay his own expenses by teaching school in the long winter vacations; and after he was graduated in 1801, he taught in a Maine academy for a year, getting a salary of $350, the greater part of which he saved to help a younger brother through college, earning his money to pay his board meanwhile by copying law papers in the winter evenings. After leaving the academy he studied law in Boston, where he was admitted to the bar, in 1805,

and became at once successful in his profession.

In the autumn of 1812 he was elected a member of Congress, and made himself famous by his first speech. He was elected a second time in 1814, and after that busied himself chiefly with his profession for the next seven years. In 1823 he was again in the House of Representatives; and the next year was elected to the United States Senate, where he kept his seat until he was made Secretary of State under President Harrison (1841). He was in the Senate again in 1845, and in 1850 was Secretary of State under President Fillmore. His health was injured by a fall from his carriage two years afterward, and he died at his farm in Marshfield, Mass., when seventy years old (Oct. 24, 1852). Mr. Webster was one of the most distinguished of American statesmen and orators; and his death is said to have called forth more funeral orations than that of any other great man since Washington.

WEBSTER, Noah, an American author, born in Hartford, Conn., Oct. 16, 1758. He was graduated at Yale College in 1778 and studied law; but he devoted himself principally to teaching and literary work for some years. He wrote a great deal on scientific subjects, and edited several papers and magazines. He is chiefly noted for his "Dictionary of the English Language." In order to do his work thoroughly he spent ten years in the study of those languages from which our words are formed before he began the dictionary, on which he then worked eleven years. It was published in 1828, but since then it has been revised and added to several times. As it stands now it is considered one of the best ever published. Webster also published the "Elementary Spelling Book," which is much used in schools. Webster was a judge, a member of the State legislature, and one of the founders of Amherst College. He died in New Haven, Conn., when in his eighty-fifth year (May 28, 1843).

WEDG'WOOD, Josiah, an English potter, born in Burslem, Staffordshire, July 12, 1730. When he was ten years old, he was put to work in his brother's pottery in Burslem, and in 1759 he started a pottery of his own in the same place. He did much to improve the art of pottery, and soon produced a beautiful cream-colored porcelain, which is known as "Queen's Ware," because Queen Charlotte admired it so much that she made him her potter. His ware is famous for the beauty and gracefulness of its form and designs. He became very rich, and built a village which he called Etruria, to which he moved his factories in 1771. He also built there a fine mansion for himself, where he died, when nearly sixty-five years old (Jan. 3, 1795).

WEIMAR (*wi'mar*), a city of Germany 53 miles S. W. of Leipsic;

Ducal Palace, Weimar.

pop. 22,000, or about as large as Council Bluffs, Iowa. It was the residence of GOETHE and SCHIL-LER, who made the city so celebrated for learning and art that it was called the Northern Athens. Both of them are buried in the Weimar cemetery, and statues and busts in their honor adorn the museums and the ducal palace. Weimar contains an art school and is a favorite resort of artists. Weimar means "abounding in the vine."

WEL'LING-TON, Arthur Welles-ley, Duke of, a famous British general and statesman, born near Dublin, Ireland, May 1, 1769. He was the third son of Garret Wellesley, Earl of Mornington. He went into the army before he was eighteen years old, and first became famous in India, whither he was sent against the Sultan Tippoo Sahib, who was trying to drive the English out of that country. Tippoo's power was put down by the battle of Seringapatam (1799), and the

English then had to contend with the Mahrattas, a Mohammedan nation in India. Their power was forever broken by the great battle of Assaye (1803), and Wellington, as a reward for his valor, was made a knight. But he won greater glory in Spain, where he was sent in 1808 to aid the Spaniards against Napoleon, who had driven their king from the throne, and set up in his place his own brother Joseph Bonaparte. The war that this led to, called the Peninsular War, lasted four years, during which Wellington won many victories

Duke of Wellington.

over the French and at last drove them out of Spain. The first of these victories was at Talavera (July 27 and 28, 1809), and after it the conqueror was made Baron Douro of Wellesley and Viscount Wellington of Talavera. After each success new honors and new titles were showered upon him by the Spanish and English nations, and after the battle of Vitoria (June 21, 1813), which drove the French across the Pyrenees, he was made Duke of Wellington.

When Napoleon escaped from Elba, the island to which he had been banished, and once more put himself at the head of the French, the allies, Prussia, Russia, Austria, and England, made Wellington commander-in-chief of their armies. At Waterloo he once more gained a splendid victory (June 18, 1815), which hurled Napoleon from his throne to a prison on the island of St. Helena. For this victory, England gave him a splendid estate worth more than $1,000,000. On his return to England, he took part in politics, but he had little talent as a statesman. He always voted with the Tories, the party who were not in favor of making changes in the government. For this reason, he was sometimes disliked by those who thought that reforms were needed. For nearly three years, from Jan., 1828, to Nov., 1830, he was Prime Minister, and he held many other important offices. He was called the "Iron Duke," on account of his firmness and his great powers of endurance. He lived to be very old, and kept nearly all his powers to the last. He died near Deal, England, when eighty-three years old (Sept. 14, 1852). He had a splendid funeral, and was buried in St. Paul's Cathedral. The Queen loved him very much, and one of her sons, Arthur, Duke of Connaught, was his namesake and godson.

WEL'LING-TON, the capital of New Zealand, on North Island; pop. 33,000, or about at large as Duluth, Minn. Its harbor, called Port Nicholson, is very fine, and there is a considerable trade in wool, tallow, timbers, and gum. Wellington is the oldest white town in New Zealand, having been settled in 1839.

WES'LEY, John, a famous English clergyman, founder of the Methodists, born at Epworth, Lincolnshire, June 17, 1703. He was the son of an English clergyman, was educated at Oxford, and became a minister of the Church of England. He came to America in 1735 and preached in Georgia, but was too strict in his views to suit the colonists, and soon went back to England, where, finding the churches closed against him on account of his having changed his views in religion, he began to preach to great congregations in the open air. He held prayer-meetings in a building that had been a foundry, and there the society of Methodists was first begun. It was afterwards turned to a chapel. Wesley was a very good man, whose one object in life was to convert sinners; and to do this he spared neither money, nor time, nor labor. He gave away great sums of money in charity, and spent his life in traveling and preaching, making long journeys on horseback in all weathers, in order to preach every day in different places. He wrote, besides, a great many religious books, and a number of hymns. He died in London, when eighty-eight years old (March 2, 1791).

WEST, Benjamin, a noted American painter, born in Springfield, Pa., Oct. 10, 1738. His parents were Friends or Quakers. He began to paint when only seven years old, and it is said that once, when he wanted to paint a picture of his baby sister, he made brushes of hairs which he pulled from his cat's tail. Afterward he became a portrait painter in New York, and in 1760 went to Europe, finally settling in London, where he painted many famous historical pictures and scenes from the Bible. Among the most noted of these were "Death on the Pale Horse" and "The Death of Gen. Wolfe." In 1792 West was made President of the Royal Academy. He died in London, when eighty-one years old (March 11, 1820).

WEST INDIES (*in'diz*), an archipelago of about one thousand islands, forming a great curve between the Caribbean Sea and the Atlantic Ocean; total area 96,000 square miles, or about as large as Oregon; pop. 4,600,000, or less than four fifths that of New York State. They are divided into several groups: 1. the Bahamas, the most northerly portion; 2. the Greater Antilles, consisting of Cuba, Hayti, Porto Rico, and Jamaica, with some smaller islands near them; 3. the Lesser Antilles, or Windward Islands; 4. a small group, near the coast of Venezuela. The Bahamas are low and flat, but all the other islands are high and rocky, and many rise in precipices from the sea. They are really a chain of mountains in the ocean, the tops only being above the water. In many parts, especially of the Lesser Antilles, are volcanoes, and earthquakes are common. The climate is very warm on the coasts, but cool and pleasant on the mountains. Terrible hurricanes blow over the islands almost every year.

The forests of the West Indies abound in mahogany and other fine woods, and cotton, sugar-cane, coffee, and other tropical plants are grown on nearly all the islands. Beautiful birds are seen everywhere, but there are no large wild animals. A large part of the people are negroes or mulattoes, but the better class are white. The only independent island is HAYTI, which is divided into two republics. The rest belong to Spain, England, France, Holland, Denmark, Sweden, and Venezuela.

The West Indies were the first part of the western continent discovered by Columbus, and he named them so because he supposed he had reached India by sailing westward. The Carib and Arrawak Indians, who lived on the islands, were enslaved and ill treated by the Spaniards until nearly all were killed. In the 17th century, the sailors of many nations united against the Spaniards, in great piratical bands, called BUCCA-NEERS. They captured and sunk Spanish ships, sacked their cities, and did an immense amount of harm to them. Some of the English and French colonies have sprung from the Buccaneers' settlements, but many islands have been bought or conquered by the different nations to whom they now belong.

WEST POINT, a village of E. New York, on the Hudson River; pop. 1000. It lies at the foot of the Highlands, and the scenery around is very grand and beautiful. The village is famous as the seat of the United States Military Academy, where young men are educated to be officers in the army. Each member of the House of Representatives can recommend one student to the Secretary of War, by whom the appointments are made, and ten others are chosen by the President. If the young men chosen pass the examinations they enter the academy, and are then called cadets. They receive $500 a year and their rations, but are obliged to pay for their uniforms, books, and other expenses. The course of instruction is four years long. Besides their other studies the cadets have lessons in military drill, riding, fencing, artillery practice, and military engineering. During the Summer they live in tents and perform military duties. The discipline is very strict, and the course of study is so difficult that less than half the students graduate. Those who do become officers in the army.

West Point gets its name from the long rocky point on which it is built. This point and another on the eastern side make one of the narrowest places on the lower Hudson. During the Revolutionary War, the English wished to use the Hudson as a ship channel between their armies in Canada and New York City, but they were kept from this by forts which the Americans built at this narrow place.

WEST VIRGINIA (*vir-jin'e-ah*), a Southern State of the United States, between Virginia and Ohio; area 23,000 square miles, or just half as much as that of Pennsylvania; pop. 763,000, or more than one seventh that of Pennsylvania; capital, WHEELING. The eastern part is a mountainous region covered almost everywhere with forests, where wild animals are still common, and almost the only people are lumbermen and hunters. The western part is hilly, but very good for farms, and most of the people live there.

West Virginia is rich in mines of coal and iron. There are many petroleum wells, and some of the finest salt beds in the United States are found near Charleston. Much oak, hemlock, and other woods are cut in the forests.

West Virginia was a part of Virginia until 1863, when it was made into a separate State.

WEST'ERN EMPIRE, the name given to the western of the two parts into which the Roman empire was divided on the death of Theodosius the Great, A.D. 395. By the will of that emperor, this part fell to Honorius, his youngest son, a boy of eleven, who was put under the guardianship of STILICHO. As long as the latter lived, the empire was able to hold its own against the hosts of barbarous tribes that were trying to overrun it, but on his death a flood of Goths and Vandals at two different times plundered Rome. The Roman power was fast nearing the end. Valentinian succeeded Honorius. At last, after the imperial crown had been passed from hand to hand as a plaything, scarce worth the having, it fell into the grasp of Orestes, an ambitious general, who placed it on the brow of his son Romulus Augustulus. Upon this, the German troops in the Roman army mutinied, demanding a third part of the lands of Italy, which not being granted, Odoacer, prince of the Heruli, commanded Orestes to be put to death, and he himself took the title of King of Italy. The inoffensive Romulus Augustulus retired upon a pension. Thus fell the Western Empire (A.D. 476), eighty-one years after its separation from the East. It is a curious circumstance that its last emperor should have combined the names Romulus, that of Rome's founder, and Augustus (Augustulus, meaning little Augustus), that of its first emperor.

WHATE′LY, Richard, an English bishop and writer, born in London, Feb. 1, 1787. He was graduated at Oxford, and in 1831 became Archbishop of Dublin. In this office he took great pains to be of use to the Irish, in their missions, schools, and charities. He published " Historic Doubts relative to Napoleon Bonaparte," "Elements of Rhetoric," "Elements of Logic," and many other works. He died in Dublin, when seventy-six years old (Oct. 8, 1863).

WHEAT′STONE, Sir **Charles,** a noted English inventor, born in Gloucester, in 1802. He was a musical instrument maker, and in order to improve his work, made many experiments in sound and electricity. In 1834 he became a professor in Kings College, London. He invented many optical and electrical instruments, among them the stereoscope (C.C.T., 592, I.) and the electric alarm. Before he knew of Morse's discovery, Wheatstone had contrived a kind of telegraph, and he was one of the first to patent the telegraph in England, but it was not put into practical use until after Morse's. In 1868 he was made a knight. He died in Paris, when seventy-three years old (Oct. 19, 1875).

WHEE′LING, the capital of West Virginia, on the Ohio River ; pop. 35,000, or about as large as Holyoke, Mass. Part of it is built on an island in the river. It contains large foundries, nail and spikeworks, rolling mills, glass works, and other manufactories, and an important trade is carried on. Coal is found near the city. Wheeling was founded in 1774. It was the State capital from 1863 to 1870, and was again made the capital in 1875.

WHITE, Peregrine, the first child of English parents born in New England, born on board the Mayflower, in Cape Cod harbor, about Dec. 10, 1620. On account of his being the first born he was given 200 acres of land by the general court. He died when nearly eighty-four years old (July 20, 1704).

WHITE, Richard Grant, an American writer, born in New York, May 22, 1822. He was graduated at the University of New York in 1839, and became a lawyer, but gave up his profession for writing. He has published "Shakespeare's Scholar," a "Life of Shakespeare," and an edition of Shakespeare's works ; also a book of essays on the English language called "Words and their Uses." He died when sixty-three years old (April 8, 1885).

WHITE′FIELD, George, a famous Methodist preacher, born in Gloucester, England, Dec. 16, 1714. He was the son of an inn-keeper, and after his father's death had to leave school, and helped his mother in the coarse work about the inn. But while he was doing this with his hands, his mind was busy composing sermons. He contrived to go to college at Oxford when eighteen years old, and when twenty-two became a minister. After preaching a while in England, he came to America; but went back within a year, and like WESLEY began to preach out of doors. Crowds of people came to hear him, and a great many were made better by his sermons, though he was sometimes badly treated by mobs. He traveled a great deal in Scotland and Ireland, and make seven journeys to America, where he finally died at Newburyport, Mass., when fifty-five years old (Sept. 30, 1770). He was the founder of what are called the Calvinistic Methodists.

WHITE MOUNTAINS. See NEW HAMPSHIRE.

WHITE SEA, a large gulf of the Arctic Ocean in northern Russia; area 44,000 square miles, or a fourth larger than Lake Superior. It is very crooked, and has high rocky shores, and many small islands. White whales, seals, cod, salmon, and herrings are caught there in great numbers. The surface is frozen during half of the year. The White Sea was discovered by Captain Richard Chancellor, an Englishman, in 1553.

WHIT'NEY, Eli, an American inventor, born in Westborough, Mass., Dec. 8, 1765. He is chiefly famous for the invention of the cotton-gin, a machine for separating the cotton from the seed. His model was stolen before he could get it patented, and although, with the aid of a Mr. Miller, who furnished him money, he started factories in Connecticut for making cotton-gins, he was constantly engaged in lawsuits with people who had stolen his invention. He also had large factories at Whitneyville, Conn., for the manufacture of fire-arms, in which he made several improvements. He died in New Haven, Conn., when fifty-nine years old (Jan. 8, 1825).

WHIT'TI-ER, John Greenleaf, an American writer, born in Haverhill, Mass., Dec. 17, 1807. He worked on a farm and at shoemaking until he was eighteen years old, when he spent two years studying at the town academy. In 1829 he became editor of a paper in Boston, and from that time on devoted himself to literary pursuits.

He has written in prose and poetry, and is one of the most popular poets of America. His first volume of poems was published in 1849. Among his poems are "Moll Pitcher," "Home Ballads," "Snow Bound," "Ballads of New England," "Child Life," and a "Centennial Hymn" (1876). He died when eighty-five years old (Sept. 7, 1892).

WHITT'REDGE, Worthington, an American painter, born in Ohio, in 1820. He has painted portraits, but is chiefly known by his landscapes of Western scenery and his forest views. He has a studio in New York.

WHIT'WORTH, Sir Joseph, an English inventor, born in Stockport, in 1803. He founded a large manufactory in Birmingham, where he invented and manufactured useful machines. In 1854 he invented an improved rifle, and afterward a breech-loading cannon, called the Whitworth cannon. Mr. Whitworth was made a baronet in 1869. He died at Monte Carlo when eighty-four years old (January 22, 1887).

WHYM'PER, Edward, an English traveler, born in London, April 27, 1840. He is a member of the English Alpine or Mountain Club, and has climbed many mountains which no one had been able to ascend before him. In 1865 he was one of the first party which climbed the Matterhorn, in the Alps. In descending, three of his companions, and a guide fell over a precipice and were killed. In 1867 and 1872 Mr. Whymper visited Greenland, where he met with many strange adventures. In 1880 he twice ascended the peak of Chimborazo in Ecuador, one of the highest of the Andes. He has written "Scrambles among the Alps," which describes some of his adventures.

WID'IN, a city and fortress of BULGARIA, on the river Danube; pop. 15,000, or about as large as

Lebanon, Pa. Its walls and citadel are so strong that it has never been taken, though it has often been attacked. At high tide ships from the Black Sea go up to it, and it has a large trade in grain, wine, and salt.

WIELAND (*we'land*, German *we'lahnt*), **Christoph Martin,** a German writer, born in Würtemberg, Sept. 5, 1733. He was the son of a Protestant minister. When very young he showed great taste for poetry, and under his father's care received a fine literary education. After finishing his studies, he went to Switzerland, and lived by turns in Zürich and Berne, writing all the time, but making his living by teaching. In 1767 he was chosen professor in the University of Erfurt, and at the end of six years went to Weimar to be the tutor of the young duke Charles Augustus. There he staid till his death, living in a very friendly way with the poets Goethe and Schiller and the other learned men of the court. His greatest work is the poem "Oberon." His verses are natural and full of grace. He admired Shakespeare, and taught the German people to admire him too. He died in Weimar, when eighty years old (Jan. 20, 1813).

WIESBADEN (*wees'bah-den*), a city of Germany, in Prussia, 20 miles W. by S. of Frankfort; pop. 55,000, or about as large as Lynn, Mass. It is noted for its springs of warm and mineral water, which are used for drinking and bathing and are visited every year by thousands of sick people and pleasure-seekers. The principal spring, called the Kochbrunnen, is almost hot enough to scald the skin. Formerly Wiesbaden was notorious for its fashionable gambling houses, but they were closed in 1872.

The Wiesbaden springs were known to the Romans, who had a military station there; remains of a castle and baths, which they built, have been lately found.

WIGHT (*wite*), **Isle of,** an island in the English Channel, 2 miles from the S. coast of England; area 160 square miles; pop. 74,000. It has many hills and plains, and is famous for its picturesque scenery. In the summer many travellers go there, and Queen Victoria has a villa, called Osborne House, near East Cowes, on the northern shore. The soil is very fertile, and some of the finest farms in England have been made on the island; and besides raising large quantities of grain, the farmers keep many sheep which are noted for their fine wool. There are several coal mines, and an important trade is carried on in sand and flints used for making glass. Very large barracks for soldiers have been made on the island.

WIL'BER-FORCE, William, an English philanthropist (lover of mankind), born in Hull, Aug. 24, 1759. He was the son of Robert Wilberforce, who died, leaving his son when nine years old under the care of his uncle and mother. As a boy, he was very delicate, but he lived to grow up and spend a long life working for the good of his fellow-men. From the time he entered Parliament, at the age of twenty-one, till he died, an old man of seventy-four, he spent all his powers in works of humanity. Among the first things to attract his notice was the African slave trade. At that time, it was quite a common thing for people to send vessels to Africa to seize the natives and sell them as slaves. Men made large fortunes in this way, but Wilberforce thought it a wicked way to make money, and he proposed to Parliament that a law should be made against this. They were not ready to do so at once, but Wilberforce kept trying, and at last after twenty years he succeeded in having the law passed. Then he set his heart on freeing all the slaves owned by the English in the West India Islands. This was a hard thing to do, as it would take a great deal of money to pay their masters for them. Three days before his death, he was rejoiced by the news that Parliament had passed a bill giving £20,000,000 for this purpose. He was a sincere Christian, and did a kind act whenever it came in his way. He tried to prevail on his country not to lay such heavy taxes on her American colonies, and raised his voice in every good cause. He was a fine speaker and very eloquent. He died in London when seventy-four years old (July 29, 1833).

WIL'DER-NESS, The, a wild region in E. Virginia, on the S. side of the Rapidan River. The forests which covered it have been cut away, and low trees, bushes, and brambles have sprung up, making the country difficult to cross. Several roads pass through it in different directions. During the Civil War, when Gen. Grant and his army began to march toward Richmond, their route lay first through the Wilderness, by one of these roads. Gen. Grant's plan was to march around the Confederates, and get between them and Richmond, but as soon as Gen. Lee heard that the Unionists were moving he attacked them in the Wilderness with his whole army, and a terrible battle ensued, which lasted for three days (May 5 to 7, 1864). This was called the Battle of the Wilderness. Neither side gained much advantage, though their loss in killed and wounded was terrible. On May 8, Gen. Grant continued his march toward Richmond, but at the same time Gen. Lee marched by a parallel road, and on reaching Spottsylvania Court-house the Unionists found the Confederates again in front of them. The battle of Spottsylvania, which followed, also lasted for three days (May 10 to 12), and it was one of the most terrible

of the war. In some places the forest was entirely destroyed by cannon balls and bullets, and one large tree was cut down by rifle balls. Gen. Grant still tried to march around the Confederates, but as before they kept in front of him, and another battle was fought on the North Anna River (May 23 and 24). By precisely the same movements, the two armies finally met at Cold Harbor. See (CHICKAHOMINY.)

WILKES (*wilks*), **Charles,** an American naval officer, born in New York in 1801. In 1838 he commanded a fleet of five ships sent by the United States to explore the Southern and Pacific oceans. He made important discoveries in the Antarctic regions, explored many islands and coasts, and after sailing around the world, returned in 1842. An account of the expedition was afterward published, most of which was written by him. In 1861, while in command of the San Jacinto in the West Indies, he stopped the British steamer Trent and took from her Messrs. Mason and Slidell, who were going to England and France as agents for the Confederate States. England demanded that they should be given up, and, though Congress thanked Wilkes for his act, the President did not approve of it, and gave them up. Wilkes became rear-admiral in 1866, and died when seventy-six years old (Feb. 8, 1877).

WILKESBARRE (*wilks'bar-re*), a city of Pennsylvania, on the N. branch of the Susquehanna River; pop. 38,000, or about as large as Sioux City, Iowa. It is in the beautiful Wyoming Valley, and all around it are rich mines of anthracite coal, in which the city has a very large trade. It also contains large locomotive and car works, and manufactories of machinery, mining-engines, carriages, and many other things.

Wilkesbarre was named after John Wilkes and Col. Isaac Barré, two members of the British Parliament who were friendly to the Americans. It became a city in 1871.

WILKIE (*wil'ke*), Sir **David,** a noted Scottish painter, born at Cults, Fifeshire, Nov. 18, 1785. His father, a Scotch clergyman, was much disappointed because his boy would be a painter, but sent him when fourteen years old to study painting in Edinburgh, where he remained five years. When twenty years old he went to London, and studied at the Royal Academy; and the next year he exhibited a picture called the "Village Politicians." This was soon followed by other pictures, chiefly of home scenes, for which he became famous. Among the best of these are "Blindman's Buff," "The Rabbit on the Wall," "Chelsea Pensioners Reading News of the Battle of Waterloo," and "Sir Walter Scott and his Family." When thirty-five years old he became painter to the King, and in 1836 he was made a knight. A year before his death, Wilkie went to Eastern countries for materials to paint a Scripture scene, and made many sketches for it, but died on his homeward voyage near Gibraltar, in his fifty-sixth year (June 1, 1841), and was buried at sea. Many engravings of his best works have been made.

WIL'KINSON, Sir **John Gardner,** a distinguished English scholar in the antiquities of Egypt, born Oct. 5, 1797. He lived in Egypt twelve years, and found out so many things not before known about the history, geography, and architecture of that country that he became famous, and the Queen made him a knight. When he came home, he brought with him many curious things, which he gave to his old school at Harrow for a museum. He wrote several books about his discoveries, among them, " Popular Account of the Ancient Egyptians" and "The Egyptians under the Pharaohs," which are the best accounts of the life and manners of that people we have. He died when seventy-eight years old (Oct. 29, 1875).

WIL'LARD, Emma, an American writer and teacher, born in Berlin, Conn., Feb. 23, 1787. She began teaching when only seventeen years old. She was especially interested in the education of girls, and in 1818 established at Waterford a young ladies' seminary, which she afterwards removed to Troy, N. Y. Mrs. Willard wrote some excellent school books, and did much to improve female education in America. She died in Troy, N. Y. (April 15, 1870).

WILLIAM (*wil'yam*), **I.,** called the Conqueror, first Norman king of England, born at Falaise, Normandy, in 1027. He was the son of Robert I., Duke of Normandy, and was crowned King of England, Dec. 25, 1066. On the death of EDWARD THE CONFESSOR, William claimed the throne, saying that Edward had made a will naming him to succeed him. But the English would not agree to this, and they chose HAROLD, a Saxon, for their king, so William had no other way of getting the throne than to take it by force. He came over from Normandy with a large army, while Harold was fighting the Norwegians in the north, and encamped near Hastings. Harold hurried down to meet him, and the battle of Hastings, or Senlac, as it is often called, was fought Oct. 14, 1066. The Saxon king was slain, and William became master of England. At first his rule was mild, but the Saxons could not bear to obey a king who was a stranger to them, and William soon began treating them very harshly. Foreign habits and laws were brought in, the lands of the Saxons were given to Norman nobles, and great suffering was caused,

As William had gotten the land only by the sword, it was very natural for him to be afraid that the Saxons would plot to kill him. A bell called the "Curfew Bell" was rung every night at eight o'clock, as a notice that all lights and fires should be put out. The Saxons objected very much to being put to bed in that way. There is a curious book called the Doomsday Book, which William had made. It tells who owned all the land at that time, and how much every estate was worth, and many other interesting things. William wanted to do away with the old Saxon tongue, and made laws requiring that everything important should be written in Norman French. But although he conquered the Saxons, to destroy their language was more than he could do. In course of time the two languages became one, and the English of to-day is the tongue of the old Saxons with a mixture of that of their Norman rulers. It took a long time for the two races that fought at Hastings to be friends, but at length their hatred died out, and it is the union of the Norman and Saxon spirit that has made England the great nation she is. William, at the close of his life, had a war with the King of France. Having burned the French town of Mantes, he was riding over the smoking ruins, when his horse stepped on some embers, and plunged so that William was badly hurt. He died from this, when sixty years old (Sept. 9, 1087), and was buried at CAEN. He was succeeded by his son William II.

WILLIAM II., second Norman king of England, born in Normandy about 1056. He was the son of William I., the Conqueror, and succeeded him Sept. 26, 1087. He was called Rufus ("red") from the color of his hair. While his father was dying in Normandy, he hurried to England and had himself crowned

king in place of his older brother Robert. In 1096 he also got Normandy from Robert, for a sum of money which Robert wanted to enable him to join the first crusade. William built London Bridge and finished the Tower and Westminster Hall. He was slain while hunting in the New Forest, by an arrow shot, some say accidentally, by Sir Walter Tyrrel. He died when forty-four years old (Aug. 2, 1100), and was succeeded by his brother Henry I.

WILLIAM III., King of England and Stadtholder of Holland, born at the Hague, Nov. 4, 1650. He was the son of William II., Prince of Orange, and the Princess Mary of England, daughter of Charles I. At a very early age he became stadtholder (chief ruler) of his native state, at a time when she was threatened by Louis XIV. When it seemed as if all was lost, he cut the dikes, the great walls built by the Hollanders to keep the sea from flooding their lowlands. The rushing waters ruined the fields, but drove out the invaders, and peace was soon made. William was married to his cousin Mary, daughter of King James II., of England. Three years of the rule of that sovereign were as much as the liberty-loving English could stand; so they sent to Holland and asked the Prince of Orange and his wife to come and be their rulers. They had little opposition in England, James having fled with his family to France; but in Ireland most of the people were unwilling to have the new rulers, and William was obliged to fight the battle of the BOYNE and defeat them before they would be quiet. The few Irish who were on his side were Protestants, and were called Orangemen. To this day the Protestant Irish bear that name, and even now there is very apt to be fighting between Roman Catholic Irish and Orangemen on the 12th of

July, the day of the battle of the Boyne. The change from the rule of James II. to that of William and Mary is call the Revolution of 1688. The English knew that William was a great soldier and ruler, and so they were glad to have him fight their battles against the French, but he had not pleasant manners, and they never liked him as a man. William and Mary were equal in power, and ruled together as William III. and Mary II. After Mary's death (Dec. 28, 1694), William ruled alone. He died from a fall from his horse in Kensington, when fifty-two years old (March 8, 1702), and was succeeded by his wife's sister Anne.

WILLIAM IV., fifth Hanoverian king of Great Britain, born in London, Aug. 21, 1765. He was the son of George III., and succeeded his brother George IV. June 26, 1830. He was brought up in the navy, in which he served with credit. The celebrated Reform Bill was passed in his reign, which gave the middle classes of the large towns more to say about the way the laws should be made. Up to this time the chief power had been in the hands of the landholding nobility. The first act of the reformed Parliament was to set free all the slaves in the English colonies by paying the owners for them. This is the last reign in which we hear anything of Whigs or Tories, the names of two political parties. The Tories changed their name to Conservatives, and the Whigs became known as Liberals. The Conservatives are those who wish to make few changes in the government, whereas the Liberals are often wanting to bring in new ways. Those who are very liberal indeed, and who want to make everything over new, are called Radicals. William died at Windsor, when seventy-two years old (June 20, 1837), and was succeeded by his niece, the present queen, Victoria, his

brother, the Duke of Cumberland, becoming King of Hanover.

WILLIAM I., seventh King of Prussia and Emperor of Germany, born March 22, 1797. He was the son of Frederick William III., and succeeded his brother Frederick William IV. Jan. 2, 1861. At first he was not liked by his people, they thought he was in favor of ruling very strictly, but he won their hearts by his successes in war, which made Germany the first power in Europe. His war with Denmark in 1864 gave Prussia the two duchies of Schleswig and Holstein; the Austrian campaign of

William I.

1866 saw Austria, her old rival, humbled, but it was the Franco-Prussian war, which put an end to the empire of the third Napoleon, that raised the enthusiasm of his people to the highest bounds. The German princes offered him the imperial crown, and in the palace of Versailles (Jan. 18, 1871) he was proclaimed Emperor of Germany.

William was noted for his calm judgment, his wisdom in choosing his statesmen and generals, and his firmness in supporting them. BISMARCK, his prime minister, is still considered the greatest statesman in Europe, and Von MOLTKE, the commander of his armies, the greatest soldier. He retained wonderful vigor to a great age, and was loved almost as a father by his subjects. He died in his ninety-first year (March 9, 1888), and was succeeded by his son FREDERICK III.

WILLIAM II., ninth King of Prussia and Emperor of Germany, son of Frederick III. Born January 29, 1859; ascended the throne June 15, 1888.

WILLIAM OF NASSAU, called the Silent, Prince of Orange, and Count of Nassau, born in Nassau, April 16, 1533. This prince is the great hero of Holland, and well deserves the high place he holds in history, for his heroic efforts which freed his country from the rule of Spain. At the age of fifteen, he was page to CHARLES V., who saw his talents and foretold his future greatness. When Charles made his last public appearance in the Netherlands, when he gave up the throne of those states to his son PHILIP II., it was on the shoulder of William of Orange that he leaned. The love of Charles for William seems to have been of itself enough to make Philip dislike him; and when that monarch set about putting down the rebellious Netherlanders, he found himself everywhere crossed by William. One after another of the ablest generals and statesmen of Spain were sent against him, but he was more than a match for them all. The best known incident of the terrible struggle in the Netherlands is the siege of LEYDEN, during which the citizens, closely blockaded by Spanish troops, suffered terribly for food; still their spirit kept up, and they took an oath never to surrender. When they could hold out no longer, William broke down the dykes and let the sea in. On came the swelling floods, washing away the fortifications of the Spanish, and drowning many of their troops, thus saving the city. In the town hall of Leyden may to-day be seen the stuffed skins of the carrier pigeons which, during the siege, flew above the heads of the enemy, carrying dispatches under their wings. William gave Philip II. so much trouble that he offered a large sum of money to any one that would kill him, and a Frenchman shot him through the body as he was leaving his dining room. He was called " The Silent" on account of his wonderful command over his tongue, and in fact over every feature of his countenance, which enabled him to hide his inmost thoughts. He died in Delft, when fifty-one years old (July 10, 1584).

WILLIAMS, (wil'yams), **Roger,** the founder of Rhode Island, born in Wales, in 1599. He was educated at Cambridge University, and became a clergyman in the English Church before he was twenty-four years old. Afterwards he joined the Puritans, and came to America (1631) to look for religious liberty; but was persecuted by the Massachusetts Puritans because he denied the right of the magistrates to punish people for religious offenses. Being banished from the Plymouth colony (1635), he and a few friends made a settlement on Narragansett Bay which they called PROVIDENCE. He founded the first Baptist church there in March, 1639; but in his government of the colony every one was allowed to act according to his own conscience in matters of religion. He died when eighty-four years old (1683).

WILLIAMSBURG (wil'yamsburg), a city of Virginia, between the York and James rivers, 50 miles E.S.E. of Richmond; pop. about 2000. The college of William and Mary, near the city, is the oldest college in the United States, except Harvard, having been founded in 1693. It was named after the king and queen who then reigned in England. Before the Revolution it was the richest college in America, but it lost nearly all its estates during the war. Among the distinguished men who studied there were Jefferson, Monroe, Tyler, Chief Justice Marshall, John Randolph of Roanoke, and Winfield Scott. Williamsburg also contains the oldest lunatic asylum in the United States, it having been opened in 1773.

Williamsburg was the capital of Virginia from 1700 to 1780. During the Civil War a battle was fought there. (See Chickahominy).

WILLIAMSPORT (*wil'yams-port*), a city of Pennsylvania, on the W. branch of the Susquehanna; pop. 27,000, or about as large as Pawtucket, R. I. It is noted for its trade in lumber, principally pine and hemlock, which is brought down the Susquehanna in great rafts. In the spring the river for three or four miles above the town is filled with floating rafts. There are many large saw-mills and planing-mills, and manufactories of saws, files, and carriages. Williamsport was settled in 1797, and became a city in 1866.

WILLIAMSTOWN (*wil'yams-town*), a town in the N.W. corner of Massachusetts; pop. about 3800. It was named after Colonel Ephraim Williams, who, dying in 1755, left his property to found a free school at some place in western Massachusetts, which should be called Williamstown. The school was not opened until 1791, and in 1795 it was changed to a college. Williams College has since become one of the best in Massachusetts, and many distinguished men have been graduated there. Generally about 200 students attend it. Williamstown also has a preparatory school for the college, and it contains two factories of print cloths.

WIL'LIS, Nathaniel Parker, an American writer, born in Portland, Maine, Jan. 20, 1806. He was the son of Nathaniel Willis, a newspaper editor, and began his literary life before he left Yale College,

where he was graduated in 1827, by taking a prize of $50 offered by a magazine for the best poem. He afterward wrote much for magazines and newspapers both in this country and in Europe, where he traveled much. Up to the time of his death, he wrote for the *Home Journal*, a weekly paper in New York started by himself. Many poems written by him on sacred subjects have been put into readers made for children. Some of his works are "People I have Met," "Famous Persons and Places," and "Paul Fane." He died at his place, called "Idlewild," near Newburg, N. Y., when sixty-one years old (Jan. 21, 1867).

WIL'MING-TON, the principal city of Delaware, in the N. part of the State, on Brandywine Creek; pop. 61,000, or about as large as Dayton, Ohio. It is noted for its great factories and mills. More railroad-cars are made there than in any other city in the United States, and there are very large paper-mills, powder-mills, machine-shops, cotton-mills, and manufactories of carriages and morocco. Many ships are built there, and it is the first place in the country where iron ships were made. Among the other manufactures are sulphuric acid and chemicals, tobacco, snuff, parlor matches, bricks, and fertilizers. The city carries on a large trade by ships and by the numerous railroads which meet there.

Near Wilmington was made the first Swedish settlement in America (1638), and a Swedish church built there in 1698 is still standing. The present town was first built in 1732, and it became a city in 1832.

WILNA (*vil'nah*), or **Vilna,** a city of W. Russia, 400 miles S.W. of St. Petersburg; pop. 103,000, or nearly as large as Allegheny, Pa. It is built among hills overlooking the river Viliya, and contains many beautiful churches. Among them is a marble chapel in which is the silver coffin of the Polish saint Casimir, and the large and magnificent churches of St. Peter's and St. John's. The people carry on a large trade with ports on the Baltic Sea.

Wilna was founded in the 13th century, and was the capital of Lithuania. In the 16th century it had 1,000,000 inhabitants.

WIL'SON, Alexander, an American writer on natural history, born in Paisley, Scotland, July 6, 1766. He came to America in 1794, and being very poor was obliged to work very hard for a living. At one time he was a peddler, and afterward he taught school in various places. Wherever he went he observed the habits and forms of birds, and in 1804 he began to form a collection of them, making long journeys alone through the wilderness to obtain the finest kinds. He also learned to make drawings, and finally, aided by Mr. Bradford, a Philadelphia publisher, he began a magnificent work on the birds of North America, with colored drawings of the different species. It consisted of nine large volumes, to which four volumes were afterward added by Prince Charles Lucien Bonaparte. Before the whole work was published Mr. Wilson died in Philadelphia, when forty-seven years old (Aug. 23, 1813).

WIN'CHES-TER, a city of S. England, on the river Itchen, 62 miles S.W. of London; pop. 18,000, or about as large as San José, Cal. It contains a large and beautiful cathedral, a college founded nearly 500 years ago, and a fine palace of King Charles II., now used as barracks for soldiers. On one side of the city an old Norman gateway can still be seen, and there are several other ancient buildings, but the most interesting thing is an old castle, which has in it a curious round table, said to be the one used by King Arthur and his Knights of the Round Table.

Winchester was an important place in the time of the old Britons, who called it Caer Gwent, or the White City. When the Danes ruled England it became their capital, and remained so until after the death of Henry II.

WIN'CHES-TER, a city of N. Virginia; pop. about 5500. It lies in the fertile valley of the Shenandoah River, which, during the Civil War, was the scene of much fighting. Winchester was captured several times by the Confederates and Unionists, and many battles were fought near it. The first was at Kernstown, where the Confederates under General Jackson attacked the Union General Shields and his army, but were defeated and obliged to retreat (March 23, 1862). When the Confederates under General Lee were marching to invade Pennsylvania, they drove a Union army out of Winchester and captured 4000 soldiers (June 14 and 15, 1863). On July 24, 1864, the Unionists under General Crook were defeated near Winchester by the Confederates under General Early. Soon after, General Sheridan defeated Early after a bloody battle at Opequan Creek, four miles from Winchester (Sept. 19, 1864). This is sometimes called the battle of Winchester, and sometimes the battle of the Opequan. Early retreated to Fisher's Hill, eight miles from Winchester, where he was again attacked and defeated (Sept. 22, 1864). The Union army then moved back to Cedar Creek, near Winchester, where a camp was formed. While Sheridan was absent in Washington, General Early led his army at night over a lonely mountain-path and surprised the Union camp, and by nine o'clock in the morning many of the Unionists were flying in dismay to Winchester. But meanwhile General Sheridan arrived in time to stop the flight, and, bringing up fresh troops from Winchester, changed the defeat into a complete victory, capturing all the Confederate cannon and stores and many prisoners (Oct. 19, 1864).

WINDSOR (*win'zer*), a town of England, on the river Thames, 23 miles W. of London; pop. 12,000, or about as large as Saratoga Springs, N. Y. It is noted for its great palace, called Windsor Castle, where many of the kings and queens of England have lived. The palace is in the middle of a park, called the "Little Park," and the buildings, which lie around a great courtyard, cover twelve acres of ground. In St. George's Chapel are buried many kings and queens, among them the unfortunate CHARLES I. The keep, or round tower, on a hill in the centre, was formerly used for state prisoners, and is the place where King James I. of Scotland was imprisoned. The palace rooms are adorned with hundreds of fine paintings and statues, and there is a splendid museum of curiosities and a fine library. The "Great Park," near the castle, is eighteen miles around, and Windsor Forest is a still larger park.

Windsor was called by the Saxons Windlesora, which means the winding shore. Some of the Saxon kings lived there, but the castle was not built until the time of William the Conqueror. The present building was begun in the reigns of Henry I., II., and III., and additions have been made to it by many of the later sovereigns. George IV. made the most changes in it. Queen Victoria seldom lives there.

WINKELRIED (*wink'el-reed*), Arnold Von, a Swiss patriot, whose valor in 1386 enabled fourteen hundred poorly armed Swiss peasants to win the battle of Sempach against four thousand Austrian veterans. The Austrian commander, Leopold, had arranged his men close together, so as to form a wall of armor

bristling with the points of lances. The Swiss peasants rushed upon the enemy, but were driven back with great slaughter. They would have been lost had not Arnold Von Winkelried, crying out, "I will make a way for you, comrades; take care of my wife and children," rushed on the line of spears, catching as many as he could grasp, and pressing them all against his breast. Through the opening thus made rushed the Swiss mountaineers, and defeated their enemies with great slaughter. This happened nearly five hundred years ago. A monument was raised to his memory in Unterwalden, his native canton, in 1865.

WINONA (*wi-no'nah*), a city of S.E. Minnesota, on the Mississippi River, 96 miles S.E. of St. Paul; pop. 18,000, or about as large as Key West, Fla. It is noted for its very large trade in lumber and grain, in which it surpasses nearly all the cities of the north-western States. There are also several large saw-mills and manufactories of carriages and farmers' tools. The first State normal school of Minnesota is in the city, and has a very fine building.

Winona was settled in 1851, and became a city in 1857.

WINS'LOW, Edward, Governor of Plymouth Colony, born in Worcestershire, England, Oct. 19, 1595. He was one of the Pilgrims of the Mayflower, and won the friendship of the Indian chief Massasoit by curing him of an illness. He was chosen governor three times. He wrote several works, chiefly about affairs in New England. In 1655 he, with two others, was sent by Cromwell to take charge of an expedition against the Spaniards in the West Indies, and died at sea (May 8, 1655).

WIN'THROP, John, Governor of the colony of Massachusetts, born in Groton, England, Jan. 11, 1588. He came to America in 1630 with a company of 900 persons, and was for many years governor and deputy governor, and was a very popular and good ruler. He died in Boston at the age of sixty-one (March 26, 1649). For nineteen years Winthrop kept a journal of everything

John Winthrop.

that happened in the colony, and in 1790 a part of this journal was published. In 1816 the rest of the manuscript, which had been lost, was found in the tower of the Old South Church in Boston, and published.

WIN'THROP, John, Governor of Connecticut, son of John Winthrop, born in Groton, England, Feb. 12, 1606. In 1627 he took part in an expedition which was sent to aid the French Protestants at Rochelle. In 1635 he was sent to America by an English company. He built a fort at the mouth of the Connecticut River, and in 1645 founded the city of New London. After that he was governor of Connecticut for seventeen years, and in 1661 he got from Charles II. the charter which made Connecticut and New Haven into one colony. He died in Boston at the age of seventy (April 5, 1676).

WIN'THROP, Theodore, a noted American story-writer, born in New Haven, Conn., Sept. 22, 1828. He was graduated at Yale College in 1848, and afterward traveled for his health in many countries in Europe. On his return home he spent two years in Panama, and then visited California and Oregon. In 1856 he became a lawyer in New York. When the Civil War broke out, he joined the army and became a major and military secretary of General Butler. He went with an expedition sent from Fortress Monroe to attack the Confederates at Great Bethel, and was shot dead while leading a charge (June 10, 1861). His books were published after his death. Among them are "Cecil Dreeme," "John Brent," "Canoe and Saddle," and "Life in the Open Air."

WIRT, William, an American author and lawyer, born in Bladensburg, Md., Nov. 8, 1772. He was left an orphan when eight years old, and when fifteen began to support himself by teaching; but he found time to study law, and became one of the best lawyers in the United States. He was the author of a book called "Letters of a British Spy," which was very popular in their time. He also wrote "Sketches of the Life and Character of Patrick Henry," another very successful book. From 1817 to 1829 he was Attorney-General of the United States. He died in Washington, D. C., when sixty-one years old (Feb. 18, 1834).

WIS-CON'SIN, a State of the United States, W. of Lake Michigan; area about 54,000 square miles, or nearly the same as that of New York and Massachusetts together; pop. 1,687,000, or about two sevenths that of New York; capital, MADISON. The whole of this State is a plain. In the southern part are prairies, but much of the northern part is covered with forest, where wild animals are still common. Wisconsin has long coasts on Lake Michigan and Lake Superior, and there are many smaller lakes within the State itself. Some of these are very beautiful, and they abound in fine fish.

The most important minerals are lead and zinc. Immense quantities of pine and other lumber are cut in the forests and brought down in great rafts to the lake-shore towns, where they are sawn into boards. As fast as the trees are cut away the land is turned into farms, and already Wisconsin is one of the most important farming States in the Union. The principal crops are wheat, corn, and oats.

Wisconsin is the Indian name of the Wisconsin River, and is said to mean "wild rushing river." Wisconsin was once a part of Michigan. It became a Territory in 1838, and a State of the Union in 1848.

WIT'TEN-BERG, a town of Germany, in Prussia, on the river Elbe, 53 miles S.W. of Berlin; pop. 14,-000, or about as large as Keokuk, Iowa. It is famous as the place where the Reformation began. Its university, founded in 1502 and famed for the teachings of LUTHER and MELANCHTHON, was united in 1815 to that of Halle, but the convent in which Luther lived is still standing, and is used for a theological seminary. It was at Wittenberg that Luther nailed his theses, or declarations, to the church door. The church was burned in a bombardment, but was rebuilt in 1817, and on the bronze doors the theses are engraved in Latin just as Luther wrote them. In the same church are the tombs of Luther and Melanchthon, and in the great square, or market-place, there is a large bronze statue of Luther, and near it one of Melanchthon.

WOLCOTT (*wool'kot*), **Oliver,** a signer of the Declaration of Independence, son of Roger Wolcott, governor of Connecticut, born in Windsor, Conn., Nov. 26, 1726. He served as a captain in the French and Indian war, and afterward became a major-general of militia and a judge. During the Revolution he sometimes fought with the army, and at other times was a member of Congress, signing the declaration with the other members in 1776. He was lieutenant-governor of Connecticut from 1786 to 1796, when he was elected governor. Before his term of office expired, he died in Litchfield, when seventy-one years old (Dec. 1, 1797). His son Oliver was Secretary of the Treasury of the United States from 1795 to 1800, and governor of Connecticut from 1818 to 1827.

WOLFE, James, a noted English general, born at Westerham, Kent,

James Wolfe.

Jan. 2, 1726. He entered the army at an early age, and when thirty-three years old (1759) was made major-general and put in command of the expedition against Quebec. He landed with his army near the city and tried, vainly, for two months to capture the French forts by bombarding them. On one side of the city there was a hill called the "Heights of Abraham," which was poorly defended because the French thought it was too steep to climb. One night, however, Wolfe climbed this height with 3600 soldiers, and, before morning, appeared behind the city. A terrible battle ensued and the French were defeated, but Wolfe was shot and died just as the victory was gained (Sept. 13, 1759). The French general, MONTCALM, was also killed, and five days afterward Quebec surrendered to the English. A monument to General Wolfe was erected in Westminster Abbey, and in Quebec there is a monument in memory of both Wolfe and Montcalm.

WOLSELEY (*wools'ly*), **Sir Garnet Joseph,** a British soldier, born near Dublin, Ireland, June 4, 1833. He entered the army when nineteen years old, and served with honor in India, in the Crimean War, and in China. In 1873 he was chosen to command the expedition against Ashantee, and captured Coomassie, the capital (Feb. 5, 1874). For this he received the thanks of Parliament, a grant of £25,000 ($125,000), and other honors. In 1878 he was made commander-in-chief of the island of Cyprus, and in 1879 was sent to South Africa, where he closed the Zulu war. Since then he has seen much service in Egypt, and is now commander-in-chief of the forces in Ireland.

WOLSEY (*wool'se*), **Thomas,** an English bishop and cardinal, born in Ipswich in 1471. His father was a poor man, but was able to give his son a good education. Thomas became a priest, then chaplain to Henry VII., and finally became Lord Chancellor of King Henry VIII. His rise was owing to his pleasing manners, shrewdness, talent, and learning. He was very fond of show. His palace of York-place (now Whitehall) was royally furnished, and his household consisted of 500 persons, many of them men of rank. But Wolsey was not yet satisfied: he wanted to be pope; and this led to his fall. He was employed by the king to help bring about his divorce from Queen Catherine. But Charles V., Emperor of Germany, was nephew of the queen,

and his favor was necessary to Wolsey to secure his election as pope; so he did not try very hard for the divorce. Finally Henry grew angry at what he thought his bad management of the business, and Wolsey was deprived of all his estates and ordered to retire to a country house. Not satisfied with his disgrace, his enemies at last had him arrested for treason. As they were bringing him to London, he became ill on the road, and stopped at the monastery at Leicester. Entering the gate, he said, " Father Abbot, I am come to lay my bones among you." So it was; the monks carried him to his bed, and in three days the great cardinal died, when fifty-nine years old (Nov. 29, 1530). He said on his death-bed, " If I had served God as diligently as I have done the king, he would not have given me over in my gray hairs."

WOLVERHAMPTON (*wool-ver-hamp'tun*), a town of England, 12 miles N.W. of Birmingham; pop. 76,000, or about as large as Nashville, Tenn. Around it are many rich mines of coal and iron, which are used in Wolverhampton in great iron and steel works. The city also has large brass foundries and manufactories of tin and Japanned ware and papier maché.

This town was first called Hampton. In 996 Wulfrune, a sister of Ethelred II., founded a church and college there, and after that it was called Wulfrune's Hampton. This became changed in time to Wolverhampton.

WOOD'WORTH, Samuel, an American writer, born in Scituate, Mass., Jan. 13, 1785. He was a printer, and wrote several plays and poems, but is best known as the author of the song, " The Old Oaken Bucket." He died in New York, when nearly fifty-seven years old (Dec. 9, 1842).

WOOL'SEY, Theodore Dwight, a noted American scholar and writer, born in New York, Oct. 31, 1801.

He was graduated at Yale College in 1820, and became a Congregational minister. For many years he was professor of Greek in Yale College, and for twenty-five years (1846 to 1871) president of the college. He has edited many of the plays of Euripides, Sophocles, and Æschylus for the use of students, and has published an "Introduction to the Study of International Law," and other works. He died in New Haven when eighty-eight years old (July 1, 1889).

WOOLWICH (*wool'ich*), a city of England, on the Thames, now forming a suburb of London; pop. 37,000, or nearly as large as Portland, Me. It is noted for its great arsenal and military workshops, which are the largest in England, and employ nearly all the Woolwich people. The arsenal covers 100 acres of ground, and contains immense quantities of cannons, guns, and ammunition. All the cannons of the English army, navy, and forts are tried at Woolwich before they are used. There is a model-room containing patterns of every kind of cannon and other articles used by the English artillery soldiers. The principal military school of England is at Woolwich, and many soldiers are kept there. On the opposite side of the Thames is North Woolwich, where ocean-telegraph cables and many other things are made. Woolwich was anciently Hylvich, which means hill town.

WOON-SOCK'ET, a town of Rhode Island, on the Blackstone River, 16 miles from Providence; pop. 21,000, or about as large as Jackson, Mich. It is noted for its many cotton and woolen mills, in which thousands of people are employed. There are also large machine shops and manufactories of rubber goods, washing-machines, and musical instruments. Woonsocket Hill, near the city, is the highest point in Rhode Island, it being 580 feet above the sea. On its top is a pond.

Woonsocket was separated from the neighboring towns of Smithfield and Cumberland in 1867.

WORCESTER (*woos'ter*), a city of England, on the river Severn; pop. 34,000, or about as large as Norfolk, Va. It has important manufactures of porcelain, iron, leather, gloves, and lace. Its cathedral is one of the finest churches in England. Worcester was a city of the Britons, and the Romans had a fort there. It was twice burned by the Danes. The last battle between the armies of Cromwell and King Charles II. was fought there, and the king's soldiers were badly beaten (Sept. 3, 1651). Cromwell called the battle a "crowning mercy."

WORCESTER, a city of Massachusetts, 40 miles W.S.W. of Boston; pop. 85,000, or somewhat larger than Toledo, Ohio. It is noted for its manufactures. More than 1500 people are employed there in making boots and shoes, and there are large manufactories of machinery and tools, thread yarn, carpets, blankets, jewelry, and many other things. The schools of Worcester are among the best in the United States, and its Institute of Science gives instruction in science and mechanics; connected with it is a machine-shop, in which the students can work for practice. The American Antiquarian Society of Worcester is one of the most important societies in the United States, and has fine buildings with a large library and cabinets.

Worcester was begun in 1713, became a town in 1722, and a city in 1848.

WORCESTER, Joseph Emerson, an American author, born in Bedford, N.H., Aug. 24, 1784. He was graduated at Yale College in 1811, and went to Salem, Mass., where he taught school for several years.

In 1819 he removed to Cambridge, Mass. He published several works on geography and history; but he is chiefly famous for his dictionaries, the first of which was published in 1850. After this he prepared several new ones, and in 1860 published his chief work, "A Dictionary of the English Language," which is one of the largest and most complete ever published. He died, when eighty-one years old, in Cambridge, Mass. (Oct. 27, 1865).

WORDS'WORTH, William, a famous English poet, born at Cockermouth, Cumberlandshire, April 7, 1770. His mother died when he was eight years old, and soon after he was sent to school until he was seventeen. He then entered St. John's College, Cambridge, where he was graduated in 1791. While at school and college he wrote several poems, and two years after leaving college published some of them, but they were not successful. He was very poor at this time, but after a while he had some money left to him, and he and his sister Dorothy went to live at Alfoxden, near the home of the poet COLERIDGE, his warm friend. The two poets used to ramble together about the country so much that they were suspected of plotting treason, and a spy was employed to watch them and find out their secrets.

During this time Wordsworth was writing constantly, and in 1798 he published a book of poems, called "Lyrical Ballads," some of which are among the sweetest poetry of England. In 1802 he married and settled among the lakes in the north of England, first at Grassmere, and later at Rydal Mount. The poet Southey lived in the neighborhood, and Coleridge made them frequent visits; and the three poets are sometimes called together the "Lake Poets." Wordsworth wrote a great deal, and his poems were not at first liked by many people; but they have since gained many admirers. On the death of Southey, in 1843, he was made poet-laureate. He died at Rydal Mount when seventy years old (April 23, 1850).

WORMS (*wurmz*), a city of W. Germany, on the river Rhine; pop. 22,000, or about as large as Meriden, Conn. It is a curious old town with crooked streets and many quaint buildings, among them an ancient cathedral which was begun in the 8th century. There is also a Jewish synagogue which is eight hundred years old. The city has a large trade, and cigars, leather-work, and other things are made there.

Worms is one of the oldest cities in Germany. An old German poem, the Niebelungenlied tells how King Günther of Worms had a sister Chriemhild, the most beautiful woman in the world. Siegfried, who was in love with her, had taken an immense treasure of gold and precious stones from the Niebelungen kings, a fabled race of that time. But Chriemhild had resolved not to marry, and though Siegfried was braver and stronger than any of his rivals, he could not gain her hand. King Günther also fell in love with a queen named Brunehild, but she was a very brave and warlike woman, and told him that she would not marry him unless he would conquer her in three combats; if Günther was beaten he was to lose his life. Siegfried promised to help King Günther if, in case he was successful, the king would give him Chriemhild for his wife, and to this Günther consented. Siegfried had a cap which made him invisible, and when Queen Brunehild came out with her spear and golden shield to fight the king, Siegfried stood behind him in his invisible cap. So, though Brunehild thought she was fighting with one man, she was really fighting two, and she was finally vanquished. Günther married her, and Siegfried married Chriemhild, but Chriemhild, who hated Brunehild, told her one day how she had been cheated in the combat. This made Brunehild very angry, and she vowed to be revenged, so she hired a man named Hagen to kill Siegfried. The latter had a charmed life and could only be wounded between his shoulders, but Hagen discovered this secret and soon after killed him. He also took away the Niebelungen treasure and threw it into the Rhine. After living at Worms for thirteen years longer, Chriemhild married Etzel or ATTILA, King of Hungary. She did this only that she might have a means of revenging herself on Hagen. After a while she persuaded her husband to invite Günther and Hagen with an army of 10,000 soldiers to Hungary. When they arrived there they were treacherously assaulted by an army of Huns, and after a terrible battle only Günther and Hagen were left alive. They were bound and taken to Chriemhild. She ordered Hagen to tell where he had put the Niebelungen treasure, but he refused to tell so long as the king was alive. The king was then killed, but Hagen still refused to tell his secret, and Chriemhild, seizing the sword of Siegfried, cut off his head at a single blow. The Hunnish warrior Hildebrand, disdaining to see so brave a man killed by a woman's hand, immediately killed Chriemhild. So after all the Niebelungen treasure was never found, and the German peasants say that it lies at the bottom of the Rhine near Worms.

Though most of this Niebelungenlied is a fable, Worms has many real histories connected with it. Charlemagne sometimes lived there, and in 1521 the Emperor Charles V. held his first Diet or Congress at Worms. It was then that Luther appeared before the Diet and declared that he would not give up the Protestant religion.

WRANGELL (*vrahng'gel*), **Ferdinand,** Baron, a Russian naval officer and explorer, born in Esthonia about 1795. In 1820 he took charge of an expedition sent to explore the frozen polar sea with sledges. Afterward he made a voyage around the world. From 1829 to 1834 he was governor of Russian America, and he also held other important offices. He died at Dorpat (June 6, 1870). An account of his arctic expedition has been published in German and Russian, and translated into English. A large tract of land in the Polar Sea north of Siberia, which Wrangell tried in vain to reach, is called in memory of him Wrangell Land.

WREN, Sir **Christopher,** a noted English architect, born at East Knoyle, Wiltshire, Oct. 20, 1632. While young he found out how to make several useful instruments, among which was the wheel barometer, and he wrote many papers on science. He was graduated at Oxford in 1650, and ten years afterward became professor of astronomy there. In 1663 he was chosen to make designs for restoring Saint Paul's Cathedral in London, which was very much out of repair, and he went to France to study for the work; but the cathedral was burned in the great London fire (1666), and Wren was asked to make a new one. The first stone was laid June 21, 1675, and Wren's son Christopher laid the last stone thirty-five years later. Besides St. Paul's, he designed many other of the principal churches, palaces, and other public buildings in England. He also held many positions of honor and trust, and was made a knight by Charles II. (1673). The last years of his life were spent at Hampton Court. He died when in his ninety-first year (Feb. 25, 1732).

He was buried in Saint Paul's, and a marble slab over his tomb bears this inscription in Latin: *Si monumentum requiris, circumspice* (If you seek his monument, look around).

WÜRTEMBERG, or **Wirtemberg,** a country in the S.W. part of the German Empire, W. of Bavaria; area, 7531 square miles, or nearly as large as Massachusetts; pop. 1,995,-000, or more than six sevenths that of Massachusetts; capital, STUTT-GART. It is crossed by a range of mountains called the Swabian Alps, and on either side of them the country is hilly. About two thirds of the people are Protestants and the rest Catholics. They are governed by a king and parliament, and send several members to the German congress. Würtemberg was founded by Count Alric, who ruled part of the territory in the 13th century. After 1495 the rulers were called Dukes until 1806, when they received the title of King.

WÜRZ'BURG, a city of Germany, in Bavaria, on the river Main; pop. 55,000, or about as large as Lynn, Mass. It contains many fine buildings, among them a cathedral nine hundred years old, and one of the most beautiful palaces in Europe, where the bishop of Würzburg lives. The river is crossed by a curious stone bridge with many statues of saints along the sides. The university of Würzburg, founded in 1403, has nearly 1000 students, most of whom study medicine. Connected with it are a fine library, museums, a botanical garden, and three hospitals where the students can see sick people treated. The city has manufactures of wine, leather, tobacco, and railway carriages. Würzburg was first built in the 6th century. On the opposite side of the Main there is a strong fortress called Marienberg, which was bombarded and captured by the Prussians in 1866 and was afterward used for a prison, in which during the Franco-German war of 1870 more than 7000 French prisoners were kept.

WYCLIFFE (*wik'lif*), **John de,** a noted English reformer, born in Yorkshire about 1324. He belonged to a noble family, was educated at Oxford, and soon became known for his religious writings and for his writings against the monks. He resisted the payment of the annual tribute to the pope, and preached against the doctrines of the Romish church. He also translated the Bible from Latin into English, so that the people could read it for themselves. He was several times tried for heresy, but through the aid of his friends escaped punishment. He died Dec. 31, 1384, and many years after his bones were taken up and burned as those of a heretic. Wycliffe has been called the "morning star of the Reformation." His followers were nicknamed Lollards (idle wanderers) because they wandered around preaching.

WY-O'MING, a State of the United States, S. of Montana; area nearly 98,000 square miles, or more than twice as large as Pennsylvania; pop. 61,000, or about one eighty-seventh that of Pennsylvania; capital, Cheyenne. The surface is mountainous, many of the peaks rising more than two miles above the sea. These mountains are noted for their grand scenery and many natural curiosities. One part of Wyoming in the N.W. corner is so strange and beautiful that it has been made into a National Park. Bears, wolves, and antelopes are very common. There are also some tribes of wild Indians, and the United States has several forts in the Territory to protect settlers. In 1876 Gen. Custer and many troops were killed in a fight with the Indians in the north-east part of Wyoming. Wyoming has mines of gold, iron, and other metals, and much soft coal. Much of the land is too dry for farming, or can only be used when watered by ditches dug from the rivers, but a great deal can be used for pasture. The climate is cool in summer and very cold in winter. Wyoming gets its name from an Indian word meaning "large plains." The Territory was made in 1868 out of parts of Dakota, Idaho, and Utah, and in 1890 became a State of the Union.

X

XAV'I-ER, Francis, Saint, a Spanish missionary called the Apostle of the Indies, born at the castle of Xavier in Navarre, April 7, 1506. His father was councilor of state to the king of Navarre. He belonged to the order of the Jesuits, and was for ten years a missionary in the East, and during this time it is said that he baptized more than one million persons and planted the Christian faith in fifty-two kingdoms. On landing in Goa, the capital of the Portuguese Indies, he took up his abode in the hospital, and every day went with a bell in his hand through the streets, calling upon the inhabitants to send their children and slaves to be instructed. The people of those Eastern countries thought that he could work miracles. He died near Macao, China, when forty-six years old (Dec. 2, 1552).

XENOPHON (*zen'o-fon*), an Athenian author, supposed to have been born about 444 B.C. He was the pupil of Socrates, about whom he wrote a book. But he is best known by his historical work called the "Anabasis," an account of the campaign of CYRUS THE YOUNGER in Persia against his brother King Artaxerxes to deprive him of his crown. In his army were many Spartan and other Greek troops who fought for pay and went with him to Persia. After the battle of Cunaxa, where Cyrus fell, the Greeks were summoned to surrender, and when they refused their leaders were invited to an interview with the Persians and murdered. Xenophon then placed himself at the head of this helpless host and led them under the most dreadful hardships through Asia Minor to the Black Sea, and thence to Byzantium. When they caught the first glimpse of the sea-coast from a hill, Xenophon tells us that they fell on their knees and greeted it with a shout of joy. This is the famous "Retreat of the Ten Thousand." The book in which Xenophon defends Socrates, his master, from the charges against him is called the "Memorabilia." Xenophon also wrote a book called the "Cyropædia," a kind of romance about Cyrus the Elder, and other works.

XERES (*ha-res'*). See JEREZ.

XERXES (*zerks'eez*), a famous king of Persia, who reigned in the 5th century B.C. He was the son of DARIUS Histaspis, and he continued the war against Greece which his father had begun. In the year 481 he assembled at Sardis the largest army ever seen, numbering, according to Herodotus, 1,700,000 foot soldiers and 80,000 horsemen, with a great number of war chariots and camels. He had also a fleet of more than 1200 ships of war and 3000 other vessels. This great force crossed from Asia into Europe at ABYDOS, marched through Macedonia and Thrace, and entered Greece over the Olympus mountains. The Greeks first checked the Persians at THERMOPYLÆ. After that a storm destroyed many of the ships of the great fleet. The Greeks defeated the rest at Artemisium and Salamis, and Xerxes returned disheartened to Persia, leaving MARDONIUS to carry on the war. The Persians were soon defeated at Platæa and Mycale, and that ended the attempt to conquer Greece. Xerxes was murdered by one of his officers in 465, and was succeeded by his son Artaxerxes.

XIMENES (*ze-me'neez*) **DE CISNEROS, Francisco,** a Spanish statesman, born in 1436. He was a Franciscan monk who became confessor to Queen Isabella, and was made by her archbishop of Toledo. Thinking this too great an honor for a lowly monk, he declined it, but the pope commanded him to take the place. In this high position he was still the poor Franciscan, wearing the garb of his order under his splendid archbishop's robes. He was made a cardinal in 1507. When Isabella died, Ximenes was named regent in the absence of Ferdinand, and ruled with the greatest wisdom. Ferdinand before his death again appointed him regent for the young Charles, his grandson. But the Spanish lords worked upon the mind of Charles so that he dismissed his faithful servant. Ximenes died a few days after his dismissal, in the eighty-first year of his age (Nov. 8, 1517). Cardinal Ximenes was the founder of the university of Alcalá de Henares, and had printed there the famous Complutensian Bible, so called from Complutum, the Latin name of Alcalá. This Bible is a polyglot—that is, it is in several languages (Hebrew, Latin, and Greek)—and is the first one of that kind ever printed.

Y

YAKUTSK (*yah-kootsk'*), a city of E. Siberia, on the river Lena; pop. 8000, or about as large as Cumberland, R. I. It is the principal city of that part of Siberia, and carries on a large trade, especially in furs and provisions. Great fairs are held there every year in July. Goods from Europe and China are brought down the river to Yakutsk, whence some of them are sent by caravans to Okhotsk.

Yakutsk is named from the Yakuts, a Tartar tribe.

YANK'TON, the former capital of Dakota Territory, on the Missouri River; pop. about 6000. It has a good trade, especially in grains, lumber, and stores for the United States soldiers on the upper Missouri. There are several railroad machine-shops, foundries, and other manufactories. Yankton was named after a band of Indians who once lived there. The first white settlement was made in 1859.

YARKAND (*yar-kahnd'*), a city of E. Turkistan, on the river Yarkand; pop. 60,000, or about the same as Troy, N.Y. It is defended by an earthen wall and two stone citadels, and several canals run through the streets. There are many mosques, Mohammedan colleges, and two large bazaars, with hundreds of shops. The city has manufactures of silk, cotton, linen, and woolen cloths. There is also a large trade in horses, and horseflesh is sold in the markets for eating.

Yarkand was the capital of a Mohammedan kingdom called Kashgar, which was conquered by the Chinese in 1757. In 1863 the Chinese were driven out.

YAR'MOUTH, a city on the E. coast of England, at the mouth of the river Yare; pop. 46,000, or a fourth larger than Saginaw, Mich. It is noted for its great herring-fisheries, in which it surpasses all other ports in England. An excellent harbor has been made for the fishing vessels, though it is not deep enough for large ships. The city has important manufactories of crape and silk goods, and many boats and ships are built there. Yarmouth (that is, Yare-Mouth) is built over an old bed of the river, which in the 11th century was filled up with mud and sand by the river, which formed a new channel. The principal part of Yarmouth is called Great Yarmouth. Little Yarmouth is a village on the opposite side of the river.

YED'O. See TOKIO.

YEKATERINBURG (*ya-kah-ter-een-boorg'*), a city of Russia, on the E. side of the Ural Mountains; pop. 32,000, or about as large as Quincy, Ill. The country around is an important mining region, and the city contains mining schools, a mint where copper is coined, and government iron-works and machine-shops. Precious stones brought from Siberia are cut and polished there, and jasper vases are decorated with delicate carvings. In the government iron-works many beautiful monuments are made.

Yekaterinburg was founded in 1722, and was named in honor of the Russian Empress CATHERINE II.

YEL'LOW SEA, a sea E. of China, between Corea and the mainland. The Gulf of Pecheli, which forms its north-western part, receives the Hoang-Ho and other large rivers. The sea is very shallow, and the yellow clay of the bottom becomes mixed with the water, giving it a yellow tinge.

YEL'LOW-STONE, a river of the United States, rising in N.W. Wyoming, and flowing through Montana to the Missouri River; length

600 miles. It rises in Yellowstone Lake, among high mountains, nearly a mile and a half above the sea. Around this lake, a region in Wyoming, with a small strip of Montana, has been set aside as a National Park, in which no settlements will ever be allowed. This park is 65 miles long from N. to S. and 55 miles wide, and it contains

The Giant.

some of the most wonderful natural curiosities in the world. Among them are many thousand springs, some of which are geysers, or spouting springs, throwing water or mud from 50 to 200 feet into the air. The geysers have been given different names, such as the Giant, the Giantess, Old Faithful, the Beehive, and the Grand Geyser. Others have hot, or mineral waters, and form colored incrustations of lime or silica about their edges, in hundreds of beautiful forms. The Yellowstone and its tributaries within the park flow through deep ravines, or cañons, the sides of which rise nearly a quarter of a mile straight up from the water. In one of the cañons the Yellowstone has two falls, the first 140 and the second 360 feet high. On Tower Creek, which flows into the Yellowstone, there is a high fall, surrounded by tower-shaped masses of rock. Several other rivers rise in the National Park, two of which flow into the Columbia and Colorado rivers,

and so reach the Pacific. All of them are noted for their wild scenery. The head-waters of the Yellowstone were discovered by a party of surveyors in 1869. They were explored in 1871 by Prof. Hayden, and on his recommendation Congress made the region into a National Park.

YEM'EN. See ARABIA.

YEZO. See JAPAN.

YOKOHAMA (*yo-ko-hah'mah*), the principal seaport of Japan, on the eastern side of the island of Niphon, at the head of the Bay of Yedo, and not far from TOKIO; pop. 120,000, or twice as large as Grand

Hot Springs of the Yellowstone.

Rapids, Mich. The streets are wide, well paved, and lighted with gas, and there are many fine shops and warehouses. Carts are generally drawn by men, and people ride in a carriage like a large baby-wagon, pulled by a man in front. The Japanese call such a wagon a *jinrikisha*, but some wag has called it a "pull-man car." A picture of one is given in the article JAPAN. The scenery around Yokohama is very beautiful. About 1200 of the inhabitants are Europeans and Americans, and there are 1000 Chinese; the rest are Japanese. Yokohama

has a very large trade, especially in tea, silk, and lacquered ware.

The name Yokohama means "across the strand." Until 1854 the place was a small fishing village; but when the trade of Japan was opened to the world, this was chosen as the foreign port. In 1866 a large part of the town was destroyed by fire.

YONGE (*yung*), **Charlotte Mary,** an English writer, born in Hampshire in 1823. She is the daughter of an army officer. The profits from the sale of her most popular novel, the "Heir of Redcliffe," were used by her to fit out a missionary schooner, the "Southern Cross," for her friend Bishop Selwyn of New Zealand, and the $10,000 received for the "Daisy Chain," another of her books, went to build a mission college at Auckland. Miss Yonge has written several histories for young people, the "Kings of England," "History of France," "Landmarks of History," etc. The "Chaplet of Pearls" written by her is a beautiful story of France in the times of the massacre of St. Bartholomew.

YON'KERS, a city of New York, on the Hudson River, opposite the Palisades and close to New York City; pop. 32,000, or about as large as Springfield, Ohio. Many new York merchants live there, and have built fine houses along the river shore and on the highlands near it. It is a very pleasant place to live in, for the streets are wide and shady and the surrounding scenery is very fine. Yonkers has manufactories of felt hats, sewing-silk, ribbons, carpets, and lead-pencils.

Yonkers was settled in 1650, and became a city in 1872. For a long time the site belonged to a family named Philipse, and their old stone mansion is now used for a city hall.

YORK, a city of N. England, on the river Ouse, 38 miles N.E. of Manchester; pop. 50,000, or about as large as Des Moines, Iowa. It is partly surrounded by ancient walls, and contains many interesting buildings. The finest of all is the cathedral, called York Minster, which is thought by many to be the most beautiful church in England. It was begun in the 12th century, on the site of a still older church, and is built in the form of a cross, with three richly ornamented towers. One of the windows is higher than a common four-story house (78 feet), and has pictures in stained glass of more than two hundred events in history. The cathe-

dral has twelve bells, one of which is the largest in England. The Archbishop of York is, next to the Archbishop of Canterbury, the most important officer in the English Church.

York was the Roman capitol of Britain, or England, and Septimius Severus and Constantine Chlorus, two Roman emperors, died there. Constantine the Great was proclaimed emperor in York. William the Conqueror destroyed the city, and it was again destroyed by fire in 1137.

YORK, a city of E. Pennsylvania, 28 miles S.S.E. of Harrisburg; pop. 21,000, or about as large as Jackson, Mich. The surrounding country is very beautiful and fertile and York has a large trade in grain and other farm products. It contains some of the largest manufactories of farmers' tools in the United States, besides several railroad-car shops, a shoe-factory, a match-factory, and large paper-mills.

York was settled in 1741. During the Revolution the Continental Congress met there from Sept. 30, 1777, to July, 1778.

YORK, House of, a family of English kings, a branch of the PLANTAGENET family, who sat on the throne from 1461 to 1485. The famous Wars of the Roses, between the two royal lines of York and Lancaster, having ended in favor of the Yorkists, Edward IV. was proclaimed king in the place of Henry VI. of Lancaster. The Yorkists were descended from a third son of Edward III., and the Lancastrians from the fourth son of that ruler. That is why so many persons thought the Yorkists had the best right to the throne. The Yorkist kings were Edward IV., Edward V., and Richard III., who was killed at BOSWORTH. The race of Tudor then came in.

YORK'TOWN, a village of Virginia, on the York River, 10 miles from its mouth; pop. about 1000,

It is noted for two sieges, one during the Revolution and the other during the Civil War. In 1781 an English army was stationed there under Lord CORNWALLIS, and strong forts and intrenchments were made around the village. General Washington, in command of the American army and the French allies, began the siege of Yorktown on Sept. 28. Washington had twice as many men as Cornwallis, and the English could not escape in ships because there was a French fleet at the mouth of the river. The Americans destroyed some of the English ships, and finally, after making an unsuccessful attempt to escape, Cornwallis was obliged to surrender with 8000 men (Oct. 19, 1781). Soon afterward the war was brought to a close.

The second siege of Yorktown was in 1862. When General McClellan began his march from Fortress Monroe toward Richmond, he found the Confederates intrenched at Yorktown. At first they were commanded by General Magruder, but afterward they received large reinforcements, and the command was given to General Joseph E. JOHNSTON. The Unionists began the siege on April 5, but just as General McClellan had his batteries ready for a bombardment, the Confederates quietly marched out of the town and escaped (May 4, 1862).

YOSEMITE (*yo-sem'e-te*) **VALLEY,** a famous valley in Mariposa County, California, noted for the splendor of its scenery. It is in the Sierra Nevada mountains, about 150 miles E. by S. of San Francisco, and nearly in the center of the State. It is much like a deep gorge cut directly across the mountain chain, not straight, but winding; and is about six miles long and a half mile to a mile wide, while the mountains rise on each side about a mile high. These walls are near-

ly straight up and down, and have many singular and grand forms, which have been given different names, such as the Cathedral Rocks, the Spires, the Domes, the Sentinels, the Three Brothers, and El Capitan (Spanish for The Captain). The river Merced runs through with many graceful windings, and forms several of the most beautiful waterfalls in the world. Among these is the Bridal Veil Fall (900 feet high), the Yosemite Fall (2600 feet), the Vernal Fall (400 feet), and the Nevada Fall (600 feet). The Yosemite Fall is said to be higher than any other fall in the world having as much water.

Yosemite means a "full-grown grizzly bear," and was the name of a chief of the Indians who used to live in the valley. The Indians call the valley Ah-wah-nee. White men first went into the valley in 1851, and the Indians were soon after driven out. In 1864 Congress gave it to California, to be kept forever as a park for the use of the publis. Many visitors go there every year.

YOUMANS (*yoo'mans*), **Edward Livingston,** an American writer, born in Coeymans, N. Y., June 3, 1821. When only thirteen years old he was afflicted with a disease of the eyes, which made him blind for several years, but with the aid of his sister he was enabled to study chemistry and other studies, and he made a machine by which he was able to write. Although he can now see, he has always had much trouble with his eyes, yet he has been able to do a great deal of writing on scientific subjects, and he is now well known both in this country and in Europe. Since 1872 he has been the principal editor of the " Popular Science Monthly," which has done much for the cause of science in the United States. He died January 18, 1887.

Eliza Anne Youmans, his sister, became interested in science from helping him in his studies, and she has published several books for children intended to give them a taste for science. Among her works are the "First Book of Botany" and the "Second Book of Botany."

YOUNG, Brigham, a ruler of the Mormons, born in Whitingham, Vt., June 1, 1801. He was poorly educated, and worked as a painter and glazier until 1831, when he joined the Mormons, and soon became one of their leaders. When Joseph Smith died (1844), Young was made president in his place, and he led the Mormons from Illinois to Utah, where they founded SALT LAKE CITY. He was governor of Utah Territory from 1850 to 1854, but after that a governor was appointed who was not a Mormon, and Young refused to obey him until the United States sent an army there to enforce the laws (1857). Young taught that the Mormons could have many wives, and he himself had a large number. By using his office for his own advantage he became very rich, and he also encouraged many crimes which were committed by a secret society called the "Danites." He died when seventy-six years old (Aug. 29, 1877).

YOUNG, Edward, an English poet, born near Winchester in 1684. He was educated at Oxford, and 1727 he entered the church and became rector of Welwyn in Hertfordshire. Many successful plays were written by him before he became a clergyman, and some essays, but he wrote nothing so celebrated as his "Night Thoughts," a religious poem composed after the death of his wife. He died when eighty-one years old (April 12, 1765).

Z

ZAMACOIS (*zah-mah-ko-ese'*), **Eduardo,** a Spanish painter, born in Bilbao about 1837. He studied in Paris under Meissonier, and became famous for his small figure pictures, which were finished with great care. Several of his works are owned in the United States. He painted part of the time in Paris and part of the time in Madrid, where he died when about thirty-four years old (January, 1871).

ZAMBESI (*zahm-ba'ze*), a river of S. Africa, flowing S. and then E. through a wild region, and emptying into the Mozambique Channel; length about 1800 miles. It was partly explored by Livingston, who discovered the great cataract called the Victoria Falls, about 800 miles from the mouth. The river there falls into a deep, narrow chasm, from which it sends up clouds of spray. The negroes call the falls Mosioatunya, or "Smoke sounds there." The chasm is 100 miles long and very crooked. Below it the river can be navigated.

ZANES'VILLE, a city of Ohio, on the Muskingum River; pop. 21,-000, or about as large as York, Pa. It is noted for its manufactures. The surrounding country is rich in coal and iron, which furnish fuel and material for great blast-furnaces, foundries, and rolling-mills in the city. There are also large machine-shops, glass-works, paper-mills, and many other manufactories.

Zanesville was first settled in 1799. From 1810 to 1812 it was the capital of Ohio.

ZAN'TE. See IONIAN ISLANDS.

ZANZIBAR (*zahn-ze-bar'*), the name given by Europeans to a city on a coral island of the same name near the E. coast of Africa; pop. 100,-000, or nearly as large as Allegheny,

Pa. It is important on account of its excellent harbor, which is visited by many ships. Ivory, gum-copal, and cloves are brought there from the neighboring coasts, and Zanzibar has a larger trade in these than any other place in Africa. Most of the people are Arabs, but there are also many negroes, Madagascans, and Hindoos. Zanzibar city and island are governed by a sultan or king, who also rules the neighboring islands of Pemba and Mafia, and several towns on the coast of Africa. He claims the whole coast for several hundred miles, but his rule is hardly recognized outside of his walled cities. Zanzibar formerly belonged to Oman in Arabia, but it became independent in 1862.

ZE'NO, Emperor of the East, born in Isauria, Asia Minor. He married Ariadne, daughter of the Emperor Leo I., who, having no children, named Zeno as his successor; but, being a foreigner, the people of

Victoria Falls, Zambesi River.

Constantinople would not have him; so Leo I. chose Zeno's son as Leo II. But Leo II. died the same year as Leo I., and Zeno took the empire. His reign was continually disturbed by wars with the Goths and by revolts at home. Zeno was weak and cowardly and gave himself up to pleasure. It is said that his wife buried him alive while he was drunk, and married Anastasius, his successor (491).

ZENO, a famous Greek philosopher, born at Elea, in Southern Italy, about 490 B.C. He taught philosophy all his life, and PERICLES and other noted men were his scholars. Zeno took part in a revolt against Nearchus, the tyrant of Elea, and, being found out, was brought before him and commanded to tell the names of his associates. After naming all the tyrant's friends as his aiders in the conspiracy, he bit off his own tongue and threw it in the tyrant's face.

Nearchus then put him to death by torture.

ZENOBIA (*ze-no'be-ah*), **Septimia,** Queen of Palmyra. She was the daughter of an Arab chief and the wife of Odenathus, King of Palmyra, and was remarkable for her great beauty and learning. She spoke the Latin, Greek, Syriac, and Egyptian languages besides her own, and was the friend and protector of learned men. She accompanied her husband in his wars, and it said that the success of some of his greatest battles with the Persians was owing to her prudence and bravery. On the death of her husband (A.D. 266) she took the title of Queen of the East, and for five years ruled with firmness and success, though the Romans tried to take away her power. At last the Emperor AURELIAN defeated her in two battles (270) and besieged her in Palmyra. She defended herself with great bravery, until she found that the city could not hold out any longer, when she tried to escape, but was pursued and captured. To save her own life, she laid all the blame of the war upon her advisers, especially the noted LONGINUS, who had been her chief counselor and instructor. She was made to grace the triumph of Aurelian, and was carried through the streets of Rome, adorned with jewels and almost fainting beneath the weight of golden chains. Aurelian gave her a handsome residence near TIVOLI, where she passed the rest of her life in comfort and luxury.

ZEU'XIS, a famous Greek painter, born at Heraclea about 450 B.C. He was noted for his skill in imitating natural objects, and for his effects of light and shade. He once painted a boy holding some grapes, which were so natural that the birds pecked at them; but he was not satisfied, for, he said, if the boy had been as perfect as the grapes the birds would have been afraid

to come near him. Pliny tells about a trial of skill which he had with PARRHASIUS, in which the latter surpassed him. His most celebrated work was a picture of Helen, which he painted for the city of Crotona. Zeuxis died in the early part of the 5th century B.C.

ZIEM (*zeem*), **Felix,** a French painter, born at Beaune, about 1822. His pictures represent landscapes, and fruits and flowers chiefly, but he has also painted historical scenes. Some of his paintings are owned in the United States.

ZIN'ZEN-DORF, Nikolaus Ludwig, Count, founder of the Moravians, or United Brethren, born in Dresden, May 26, 1700. He belonged to a noble family, was educated at the University of Wittenberg, and afterward studied theology. In 1722 he allowed some emigrant Moravians to make a settlement on one of his estates, and became their ruler and teacher. In 1734 he became a minister, and then traveled into different countries to make converts; and being forbidden on account of his doctrines to return to his native country, he went to Berlin, where he was consecrated bishop of the Moravian congregation. He afterward came to America, and preached for two years; then returned to Europe, and preached in England and Holland for some years. He established missions in the East Indies and other far-off places, founded a Moravian academy, and wrote more than a hundred books about their history and labors, and other religious subjects. He died at the settlement on his own estate, called Herrnhut (protection of the Lord), when sixty years old (May 9, 1760).

ZISKA (*zis'kah*), **John,** the military leader of the Hussites, or followers of John HUSS, born at Trocznow, Bavaria, in 1360. He was of a noble family, and when twelve years old became a page at the court of King Wenceslas of Bohemia. Not liking court life, he turned soldier and fought against the Turks in Hungary, and afterward joined the English army in France and fought at AGINCOURT. He had early joined the Hussites, and when the great civil war broke out in Bohemia, after the burning of Huss, he became their leader. Soon after the war began King Wenceslas died and the Emperor Sigismund of Germany claimed the throne of Bohemia; but the Hussites would not own him, and Ziska often defeated his armies. He made a fortified camp on a steep mountain which was given the name of Mount Tabor, and from which his followers were called Taborites. Ziska had lost one eye when a boy, and the other was put out by an arrow, but he knew the country so well that he still commanded his army in all their battles. He is said to have been the victor in more than a hundred engagements, and to have won thirteen great battles. At last the emperor, seeing that he could not conquer him, offered to give the Bohemians freedom of religion and to make Ziska governor of Bohemia. Ziska consented, but before the treaty was made he died, when six-four years old (Oct. 12, 1424), and the war went on for many years more.

ZO'I-LUS, a noted Greek critic and grammarian, who lived about 350 B.C. He is chiefly noted for his severe criticisms of Homer. He also attacked the works of Demosthenes, Plato, Aristotle, and other authors of his time very harshly.

ZOR-O-AS'TER, the founder of the Magian religion, or the religion of the ancient Persians. It is not known when he lived, and some think that he never lived at all. His doctrines are those taught in the Zend-Avesta, a religious book in the language of ancient Persia, which pretends to give the revelations made by Ormuzd to Zoroaster. Zoroaster taught that the world is the scene of a conflict between Or-muzd, or the good spirit, and Ahriman, or the evil spirit, and that Ahriman will be finally overcome and will sink with his followers into darkness. The religion of Zoroaster finally sunk into a worship of the sun and of fire, and is still believed in by the Parsees of Persia and of India.

ZÜRICH (*zoo'rik*), a city of N. Switzerland, on Lake Zürich; pop. 90,000, or about as large as Columbus, Ohio. The river Linimat, which is the outlet of the lake, divides Zürich into two parts, called the great and small city. There are many interesting old buildings which, with the fine streets and promenades and beautiful scenery around it, make Zürich a favorite place with travelers. The university of Zürich has nearly 550 students, and the city has long been noted for its learning. There are important manufactories of silk and cotton cloth, paper, and machinery, and a large trade is carried on, especially in books.

Zürich is a very old town; it became a free city in 1219. The old cathedral is still celebrated as the place where Zwingli, the Swiss reformer, preached. The first English Bible ever printed was translated and published at Zürich by Miles Coverdale (1535).

Lake Zürich is twenty-five miles long, from one to two miles wide, and very deep. It is surrounded by beautiful hills covered with fine vineyards, farms, and orchards, with many pretty villages along the shores.

ZUYDER ZEE (*zi'der ze*). See NETHERLANDS.

ZWINGLI (*zwing'glee*), **Ulric,** a Swiss reformer, born in Wildhaus, Jan. 1, 1484. His father was a shepherd, and Ulric helped him to tend sheep. In the winter evenings his mother told him Bible stories, and his father talked to the children about the wrongs their country had suffered and the brave deeds that had been done by Swiss heroes. He studied at the universities of Vienna and Basel, and became pastor of a large parish when only twenty-two years old. He soon began to doubt many things taught in the church, and after a while to preach against them. By his efforts a reform was brought about in religion in Switzerland, entirely separate from Luther's reform in Germany. In 1518 Zwingli was elected to the cathedral church in Zürich, and preached the Gospel to great crowds, teaching patriotism as well as piety, and shar..ing the people for hiring themselves as soldiers to fight for foreign countries. He changed many of the ceremonies of the church, and got the law abolished which prevented priests from marrying. There was, of course, much opposition to these reforms, and in 1531 war was begun between the Catholic and the Protestant cantons. Zwingli went into battle as chaplain, and while taking care of a dying soldier was killed at Kappel, when forty-six years old (Oct. 11, 1531).

INDEX.

Five Weeks in a Balloon, 834
Flaccus, Valerius, 168
Flag, First American, 434
Flagging Stones, 449
Flaminius, 799
Flanders, 300, 484
Flavius Arrianus, 67
Flax, 412, 604, 714
Flaxman, John, 300
Fletcher, John, 96
Flemings, 300
Flemish, 98
Flodden, 301
Flodden Field, Battle of, 260, 301
Flood, 252
Flora, 301
Florence, Italy, 237, 301, 355, 539, 732
Florence, Mass., 596
Florence Sewing Machines, 596
Florida, 252, 301, 374, 601, 665
Florida Keys, 302
Florida Reef, 302
Flotow, Friedrich von, 302
Flour, 693, 722
Flower City, 764
Flower, largest known, 778
Floyd, Gen., 304
Foe, Daniel, 244
Fond du Lac, 303
Fontaine. See La Fontaine.
Fontainebleau, 302
Fontenoy, Battle of, 303, 483
Foix, Count of, 318
Foochow, 303
Foote, Commodore, 304, 347
Forest City, 201
Forest, General, 534
Forests in Germany, 332
Formosa, 303
Fornoro, Battle of, 94
Forrest, Edward, 503
Fort Adams, 584
Fort Brown, 620
Fort Carillon, 553
Fort Cataraqui, 448
Fort Donelson, 303
Fort Duquesne, 655
Fort Edward, N. Y., 255, 676
Fort Erie, 738
Fort Frontenac, 448
Fort Gaines, 548
Fort Griswold, 465, 582
Fort Harrison, 788
Fort Henry, 303
Fort Jackson, 732
Fort Jefferson, 264
Fort Leavenworth, 465
Fort Marion, 719
Fort McHenry, 90, 447
Fort Morgan, 548
Fort Moultrie, 183, 425
Fort Necessity, 851
Fort Ontario, 611
Fort Pitt, 655
Fort Pulaski, 732
Fort Schuyler, 825
Fort Stanwix, 704
Fort Steadman, 641
Fort Sumter, 96, 183, 242
Fort Trumbull, 582
Fort Washington, Battle of, 398
Fort Wayne, 252, 304

Fort William, 148
Fort William Henry, 331
Forth, Frith of, 469
Fortress of Gibraltar, 337
Fortress of Konigstein, 452
Fortress Monroe, 242, 693
Forum Alieni, 297
Forum at Rome, 230, 702, 786
Fossil Animals, 231, 234, 506, 521, 573, 750
Foster, Stephen Collins, 304
Fotheringay, 304
Fotheringay Castle, 524
Founder of Cities, 382
Fountain at Cincinnati, 196
Fountain of Arethusa, 783
Fountain of Youth, 665
Fountains of Versailles, 836
Fouqué, Friedrich, 304
Four Georges, 366
Fowler, The, 382
Fowls, 749
Fox, Charles James, 304
Fox, George, 305
Foxes, 40
France, 202, 234, 249, 305, 312, 328, 330, 345, 378, 379, 489, 504
France, Capital of, 836
France, Isle of, 527
Francis II., Austria, 82
Francis Joseph, Austria, 309, 758
Francis I., France, 94, 179, 260, 307
Francis II., France, 168, 308
Francis I., Germany, 308, 515, 516
Francis II., Germany, 308
Francis II., Naples, 121
Francis of Assisi, Saint, 309
Francis, Sir Philip, 309
Franciscans, 309
François de Lorraine, 356
Franconenford, 310
Franconia, 312, 328
Franconian Emperors of Germany, 334, 355
Frankenburg, 2
Frankfort, 2, 310
Franklin, Battle of, 393, 734
Franklin, Benjamin, 310
Franklin, James, 310, 584
Franklin, Lady, 311
Franklin, Sir John, 311
Frankfort-on-the-Main, 310
Frankfort-on-the-Oder, 310
Frankreich, 328
Franks, 306, 312, 328, 333, 345, 571, 767
Frascati, 818
Frauenburg, 217
Frazier's Farm, Battle of, 190
Frederick Augustus I., Saxony, 733
Frederick Barbarossa, 2, 23, 312, 384
Frederick V., Bavaria, 712
Frederick I., Germany. See Frederick Barbarossa.
Frederick II., Germany, 2, 313
Frederick III., Germany, 313
Frederick III., Germany, 316
Frederick, Grand Duke, 86
Frederick III., Hungary, 526
Frederick II., Prussia. See Frederick the Great.

Frederick, Duke of Suabia, 211, 792
Frederick II., Suabia, 312
Frederick the Fair, 491
Frederick the Great, 182, 314, 390, 436, 515, 742
Frederick the Great, History of, 160
Frederick William I., Prussia, 314
Frederick William II., Prussia, 315
Frederick William III., Prussia, 315
Frederick William IV., Prussia, 316
Frederick William, Crown Prince of Prussia, 867
Frederick William, Elector of Brandenburg, 313
Fredericksburg, Va., 316
Fredericksburg, Battle of, 141, 316
Frederickshald, 182
Fredericton, 579
Freehold, N. J., 552
Freeman, Edward Augustus, 316
Freiberg, 316
Freiburg, 316
Fremont, John Charles, 161, 317
Fremont's Peak, 317
French, First Visit of, to North America, 835
French Guiana, 355
French Opera, 843
French Possessions in India, 665
French Republic, 181
French Revolution, 237
French Revolution, History of, 160
French Settlements in the United States, 823
Frère, Pierre Edouard, 317
Freyberg, 316
Friar Tuck, 393
Fribourg, 317
Friedenstein, Palace of, 345
Friedland, 315
Friedland, Battle of, 317
Friendly Islands, 663
Friends, Society of, 305, 632
Frigga, 603
Frisians, 333, 377
Friths, 736
Friuli, Duke of, 268
Frobisher, Sir Martin, 280, 317, 353
Froissart, Jehan or Jean, 318
Frondeurs, 530
Frontenac, Fort, 448
Froude, James Anthony, 318
Fruits, 582
Funchal, 504
Fundy, Bay of, 579
Funeral of Raphael, 683
Fugger Family, 78
Fugues, 85
Fujinoyama, 320
Fulbert, 4
Fulda River, 165
Fulton, Robert, 318
Fünen, 249
Furies, 320, 608

Ninyas, 740
Niobe, 355, 786
Nippon, 423
Nismes, 594
Nizhni Novgorod, 595
Nizza, 592
Noah, 252, 740
Noah's Ark, 65
No Man's Land, 605
Nordenskjöld, Niis Adolf, 595
Nordrike, 599
Norfolk, Island of, 653
Norfolk, Va., 596
Norfolk Navy Yard, 668
Norge, 599
Noricii, 602
Normandy, 177, 249, 307, 484, 598
Normans, 307, 598
Norristown, 596
North, Christopher, 422
North America, 37
North America, Discovery of, 143
North American Review, 236, 618
Northampton, England, 596
Northampton, Mass., 596
North Anna, Battle of the, 347, 863
North Atlantic, 75
North Cape, 598
North Carolina, 596
North Dakota, 597
Northern Ocean, 60
Northern States, 823
North Island, 590
Northmen, 31, 176, 177, 179, 247, 307, 353, 525, 584, 597, 599
North Pole, 60
North River, 400
North Sea, 598
North Shields, 749
Northumberland Sound, 671
North Virginia, 580
North-west Passage, 317, 627
North-west Passage, Voyage in search of, 311
North Wic, 599
North Woolwich, 874
Norwalk, Conn., 598
Norway, 249, 598, 780
Norway, Union with Sweden, 102
Norwich, Conn., 599
Norwich, England, 599
Nôtre Dame Cathedral, 625
Notium, Battle of, 499
Notte, Picture, 221
Nottingham Castle, 561
Nouaillé, 462
Noureddin, 88, 599, 723
Novara, Battle of, 180, 838
Nova Scotia, 51, 600
Novaya Zemlya, 600
Nova Zembla, 92, 600
Novgorod, 417, 600, 714
Novum Organum, 85
Nubia, 600
Nuestra Señora de la Asuncion, 72
Nuiching, 631
Nullification, 149
Numantia, 601, 736
Numa Pompilius, 601

Numea, 579
Numerian, 255
Numidia, 31, 601
Numitor, 12, 704
Nun, Cape, 384
Nuñez, Alvar, 601
Nuremberg, 601
Nurnberg, 602
Nutmegs, 551, 754, 778
N'yanza, 14, 602
Nymphs, 568, 602, 637
Nymphs of the Sea, 321, 575

Oahu, 392
Oak, Royal, 176
Oak Bluffs, 521
Oakland, 602
Oak of St. Louis, 485
Oases, 718
Oates, Titus, 602, 765
Oats, 406
Obelisk, 29, 377
Obelisk, Paris, 205
Obelisk, Rome, 205
Obelisk, Luxor, 623
Oberhausen, Battle at, 463
O Boys, Carry Me 'Long, Song, 304
Observatory, Greenwich, 353
Observatory, Pulkova, 772
Observatory of Tycho Brahe, 123
Observatory, United States Naval, 850
Ocean Drive, Newport, 584
Oceanus, 575, 803
Ocmulgee River, 503
O'Connell, Daniel, 603
Octavia, 603
Octavia, wife of Nero, 576
Octavius. See Augustus.
Odenathus, 886
Odenwald, 86
Oder River, 125, 768, 332
Odessa, 603
Odessus, 829
Odin, 603, 780, 814, 824, 827
Odoacer, 346, 604, 795, 860
Odovaker, 604
Odysseus, 820
Odyssey, 391, 820
Œdipus, 53, 604, 763
Œneus, 533
Œnone, 622
Œta, Mount, 795
Ogdensburg, 604
Oglethorpe, Gen. James, 332, 732
Ogygia, 821
Ohio, 604
Ohio, Falls of the, 492
Ohio River, 268, 604, 655
Oh Susanna, Song, 304
Oil, Anointing, 689
Ojibwas, 40
Okeechobee Swamp, 301
Okefinokee Swamp, 332
Oken, Lorenz, 605
Okhotsk Sea, 43
Oklahoma, 409, 605
Old Castile, 165, 760
Old Castle, 686
Oldest Man, 626
Old Folks at Home, Song, 304
Old Guard, 853
Oldham, 605

Old Kentucky Home, Song, 304
Old Manse, 373
Old Mill, Newport, 584
Old Pan, 626
Old Probabilities, 567
Old Style, 354
Old Uncle Ned, Song, 304
Olga, 842
Olive Oil, 416
Olive Orchards, 668
Oliver Optic, 608
Olives, 306, 416
Olive Wood, 428
Olmütz, 605
Olympia, 605, 643
Olympiads, 607
Olympias, 24, 607, 678
Olympia, Washington Territory, 850
Olympic Games, 605, 606
Olympus, 131, 172, 440, 607, 795
Omaha, 607
Omahas, 41
Oman, 58, 566
Omar I., 28, 607
Omar, Mosque of, 428
Ommiyades, Caliphs, 150
Omphale, 386
On, 377
Oneidas, 41
Onondaga Lake, 782, 783
Onondagas, 41
Ontario, Lake, 607
Opera, French, 843
Opera, German, 843
Opera, Italian, 508, 843
Operas:
Abencerrages, 5
Aida, 833
Barber of Seville, 707
Black Domino, The, 77
Bohemian Girl, 89
Circassian, 739
Crown Diamonds, 77
Der Freischutz, 855
Domino Noir, 77
Don Giovanni, 564
Don Juan, 564
Don Pasquale, 259
Don Sebastian, 259
Elixir of Love, 77
Enchantress, 89
Ernani, 833
Faust, 346, 445
Flying Dutchman, 844
Fra Diavolo, 77, 739
Huguenots, 538, 739
I Puritani, 99
Jephthah, 538
Joan of Arc, 89
La Favorita, 259
La Fille du Regiment, 259
La Sonnambula, 99
La Traviata, 833
L'Elixir d'Amour, 77
Les Diamants de la Couronne, 77
Lohengrin, 844
Lucia di Lammermoor, 259
Lucrezia Borgia, 259
Magic Flute, 564
Marriage of Figaro, 564
Martha, 302
Masaniello, 77, 524